INTERPRETATION OF THE MEANINGS OF

THE
NOBLE
QUR'ÂN

A Summarised Version of At-Tabarî,
Al-Qurtubî and Ibn Kathîr
with Comments from Sahîh Al-Bukhârî

Dr. Muhammad Taqî-ud-Dîn Al-Hilâlî
Ph.D. (Berlin)
&
Dr. Muhammad Muhsin Khan
Formerly at Madinah Al-Munawwarah

تفسير معاني
القرآن الكريم

INTERPRETATION OF THE MEANINGS OF

THE NOBLE
QUR'ÂN

IN THE ENGLISH LANGUAGE

Summarized Version of At-Tabarî, Al-Qurtubî, and
Ibn Kathîr with Comments from Sahîh Al-Bukhârî

Summarized in One Volume

**Dr. Muhammad Taqi-ud-din al-Hilâlî,
Dr. Muhammad Muhsin Khân**
Islamic University, Al Madinah Al-Munawwarah

www.idaraimpex.com

INTERPRETATION OF THE MEANINGS OF

THE NOBLE QUR'ÂN

A Summarized Version of At-Tabarî, Al-Qurtubî, and
Ibn Kathîr with Comments from Sahîh Al-Bukhârî

**Dr. Muhammad Taqi-ud-din al-Hilâlî,
Dr. Muhammad Muhsin Khân**
Islamic University, Al Madinah Al-Munawwarah

9 788171 016457   00000

ISBN : 81-7101-645-6
Edition : 2016
TP-531-16

Published by Mohammad Yunus for

IDARA IMPEX

D-80, Abul Fazal Enclave-I, Jamia Nagar
New Delhi-110 025 (India)
Tel.: +91-11-2695 6832 & 085888 33786
Fax: +91-11-6617 3545 Email: **info@idara.in**
Online Store: **www.idarastore.com**

Retail Shop: **IDARA IMPEX**
Shop 6, Nizamia Complex, Gali Gadrian, Near Karim's Hotel
Hazrat Nizamuddin, New Delhi-13 (India) Tel.: 085888 44786

3

بسم الله الرحمن الرحيم

المملكة العربية السعودية

الرقم ٧/١٣٣٥

رئاسة إدارات البحوث العلمية والإفتاء والدعوة والإرشاد

التاريخ ٢١/١١/١٤٠٤

المرفقات

مكتب الرئيس

الموضوع

إلى من يهمه الأمر

السلام عليكم ورحمة الله وبركاته أما بعد:

فإن الرئاسة العامة لإدارات البحوث العلمية والإفتاء والدعوة والإرشاد بالمملكة العربية السعودية تقرر أن الدكتور محمد تقي الدين الهلالي والدكتور محمد محسن خان قد قاما بترجمة معاني القرآن الكريم وصحيح الإمام البخاري وكتاب اللؤلؤ والمرجان فيما اتفق عليه البخاري ومسلم إلى اللغة الانجليزية ترجمة صحيحة. وذلك أثناء عملهما في الجامعة الإسلامية بالمدينة المنورة، فلا مانع من الفسح لهذه الكتب بالدخول إلى المملكة وتداولها لعدم المحذور فيها. والله ولي التوفيق. وصلى الله وسلم على نبينا محمد وآله وصحبه.

الرئيس العام
لإدارات البحوث العلمية والإفتاء والدعوة والإرشاد

عبدالعزيز بن عبدالله بن باز

بسم الله الرحمن الرحيم

المملكة العربية السعودية
الجامعة الإسلامية
بالمدينة المنورة

الرقم
التاريخ ١٤١٠/١٤٩٨
التوابع

لمن يهمه الأمر

الدكتور محمد تقي الدين الهلالي :
الدكتور محمد محسن خان :

نقرر الأمانة العامة للجامعة الإسلامية بالمدينة المنورة أن المذكورين
بعاليه كانا من ضمن العاملين بالجامعة . وإنهما قد قاما أثناء ذلك بترجمة
معاني القرآن الكريم باللغة الانجليزية ، وترجمة صحيح البخاري بها
أيضاً .

ولقد سدت بحمد الله فراغاً كبيراً يحتاج العالم الإسلامي لملئه . كما أن
المذكورين يمتازان بحسن العقيدة السليمة من الشوائب ، وبالصفات
الحميدة .

وبناء على الرغبة أعطيا هذه الشهادة . والله ولي التوفيق .
وصلى الله وسلم وبارك على نبينا محمد وعلى آله وصحبه .

الأمين العام بالجامعة

عمر محمد فلاتة

مقدمة الطبعة الجديدة

عام ١٩٩٦م

الحمد لله رب العالمين، والصَّلاة والسَّلام على سيد المرسلين محمد ﷺ وبعد:

فهذه هي الطبعة الجديدة لكتاب تفسير معاني القرآن الكريم باللغة الإنجليزية بعد مراجعتها وتعديلها وقد راعينا فيها الآتي:

١ ـ أوردنا لكل آية من المتن العربي تحتها تفسيرها باللغة الإنجليزية.

٢ ـ اخترنا النص العربي للقرآن الكريم من مصحف المدينة المنورة الذي تمَّ طبعه في مجمع الملك فهد لطباعة المصحف الشريف عام ١٤٠٥هـ. بناءً على أمر فضيلة رئيس الجامعة الإسلامية بالمدينة المنورة بدلاً من نسخة المصحف الذي سبق أن طبع في هذا الكتاب في أمريكا وتركيا بخط الشيخ حامد الآمدي التركي.

٣ ـ أدخلنا الأحاديث التي كانت في الهامش في الطبعة السابقة ضمن التفسير وأضفنا أحاديث عديدة من صحيح البخاري مع أبوابها.

٤ ـ أجرينا بعض التعديلات في الحذف والزيادة والتغيير في بعض الألفاظ باللغة الإنجليزية مراعاة لدقة المعاني.

٥ ـ لا يسمح بعد صدور هذه الطبعة الجديدة لكتاب معاني القرآن الكريم باللغة الإنجليزية بإعادة طبع غيرها من الطبعات السابقة.

٦ ـ الطبعة الجديدة لهذا الكتاب تنقسم على نوعين:

(أ) النوع المختصر وهو مجلد واحد.

(ب) النوع الثاني بالتفصيل في تسع مجلدات.

المترجم

الدكتور/ محمد محسن خان

تحريراً في ٢٨/ ٢/ ١٤١٧هـ

١٤/ ٧/ ١٩٩٦م

PREFACE TO THE EDITION

All the praises and thanks are to Allâh, the Lord of 'Âlamîn (mankind, jinn and all that exists) and peace be upon the Master of the Messengers, Muhammad ﷺ .

This interpretation of the meanings of the Noble Qur'ân has been revised and the following changes have been made:

1. Each Verse has been put separately with its English interpretation.

2. The Arabic text of the Noble Qur'ân has been taken from *Mushaf Al-Madînah An-Nabawîyyah*, which has been printed by the *Mujamma' of King Fahd of Saudi Arabia for the printing of Al-Mushaf Ash-Sharîf*, in the year 1405 A.H. according to the instructions of the Chancellor of the Islâmic University, instead of the old Arabic text of the previous print of this book which was printed in the United States and Turkey by the Turkish Calligrapher Sheikh Hamid Al-Amadî.

3. There are some additions and subtractions of Chapters and *Ahâdîth* from *Sahîh Al-Bukhârî* and other *Ahâdîth* collections.

4. Some additions, corrections, and alterations have been made to improve the English translation and to bring the English interpretation very close to the correct and exact meanings of the Arabic text.

5. As regards the old edition of this Book, nobody is allowed to reprint or to reproduce it after this new edition has been published.

6. This new edition is in two forms — one in a detailed form (in 9 volumes), and the other in a summarized form (in 1 volume).

3 Rajab, 1405 A.H. — March 23, 1985.

Translators:
Dr. Muhammad Taqî-ud-Dîn Al-Hilâlî
Dr. Muhammad Muhsin Khân

CONTENTS

1. Certificates

   A: Sheikh 'Abdul-'Aziz bin 'Abdullâh bin Bâz, Dar-ul-Iftâ, (Presidency of Islamic Research, Ifta, Call and Propagation), Riyâdh...3

   B: Sheikh Umar Fullata, General Secretary of Islamic University, Al-Madinah Al-Munawwarah............................4

2. Preface for   New Edition A: (Arabic)......................................5

                                          B: (English)......................................6

4. **The Noble Qur'ân**...9

5. Index of *Sûrah* — Chapters..1132

6. List of Prostration places in the Noble Qur'ân....................1134

7. List of Prophets mentioned in the Noble Qur'ân.................1135

8. The Noble Qur'ân, a Miracle from Allâh (to Prophet Muhammad ﷺ)...1136

9. *Appendix I* — Glossary..1138

10. *Appendix II* —

   a. *Tauhîd* (Islamic Monotheism)..1169

   b. *Shahâdah* - Confession of a Muslim...............................1171

   c. Polytheism and Disbelief...1177

   d. Polytheism and its various manifestations 1178

   e. Jesus and Muhammad (peace be upon them) in Bible and Qur'ân...1181

11. *Appendix III* — Brief Index 1194

Sûrat Al-Fâtihah (The Opening) I

1. In the Name of Allâh, the Most Gracious, the Most Merciful.

2. All the praises and thanks are to Allâh, the Lord[1] of the 'Âlamîn (mankind, jinn and all that exists).[2]

3. The Most Gracious, the Most Merciful.

---

[1] (V.1:2) Lord: The actual word used in the Qur'ân is *Rabb*. There is no proper equivalent for *Rabb* in English language. It means the One and the Only Lord for all the universe, its Creator, Owner, Organizer, Provider, Master, Planner, Sustainer, Cherisher, and Giver of security. *Rabb* is also one of the Names of Allâh.

We have used the word "Lord" as the nearest to *Rabb*. All occurrences of "Lord" in the interpretation of the meanings of the Noble Qur'ân actually mean *Rabb* and should be understood as such.

[2] (V.1:2). Narrated Abu Sa'îd bin Al-Mu'alla: While I was praying in the mosque, Allâh's Messenger ﷺ called me but I did not respond to him. Later I said, "O Allâh's Messenger, I was praying." He said, "Didn't Allâh say, 'Answer Allâh (by obeying Him) and His Messenger when he (ﷺ) calls you.' " (V.8:24).

He then said to me, "I will teach you a *Sûrah* which is the greatest *Sûrah* in the Qur'ân, before you leave the mosque." Then he got hold of my hand, and when he intended to leave the mosque, I said to him, "Didn't you say to me, 'I will teach you a *Sûrah* which is the greatest *Sûrah* in the Qur'ân?' " He said, "*Al-Hamdu lillâhi Rabbil-'âlamîn* [i.e. all the praises and thanks are to Allâh, the Lord of the 'Âlamîn (mankind, jinn and all that exists)], *Sûrat Al-Fâtihah* which is *As-Sab' Al-Mathânî* (i.e. the seven repeatedly recited Verses) and the Grand Qur'ân which has been given to me." (*Sahih Al-Bukhâri*, Vol.6, *Hadîth* No.1).

4. The Only Owner (and the Only Ruling Judge) of the Day of Recompense (i.e. the Day of Resurrection)

5. You (Alone) we worship, and You (Alone) we ask for help (for everything).

6. Guide us to the Straight Way.[1]

7. The Way of those on whom You have bestowed Your Grace[2], not (the way) of those who earned Your Anger[3] (such as the Jews), nor of those

---

[1] (V.1:6) Guidance is of two kinds:

a) Guidance of *Taufîq* and it is totally from Allâh, i.e. Allâh opens one's heart to receive the truth (from disbelief to Belief in Islâmic Monotheism).

b) Guidance of *Irshâd* through preaching by Allâh's Messengers and pious preachers who preach the truth i.e. Islâmic Monotheism.

[2] (V.1:7) i.e. the way of the Prophets, the *Siddîqûn* (i.e. those followers of the Prophet, who were first and foremost to believe in him, like Abu Bakr As-Siddîq), the martyrs and the righteous, [as Allâh عزّ وجلّ said: "And whoso obeys Allâh and the Messenger (Muhammad صلى الله عليه وسلم), then they will be in the company of those on whom Allâh has bestowed His Grace, of the Prophets, the *Siddîqûn*, the martyrs, and the righteous. And how excellent these companions are!" (V.4:69)].

[3] (V.1:7) Narrated Adi bin Hâtim رضى الله عنه: I asked Allâh's Messenger صلى الله عليه وسلم about the Statement of Allâh: 1. " غير المغضوب *Gharil maghdubi 'alaihim* [not (the way) of those who earned عليهم Your Anger]," hê صلى الله عليه وسلم replied: "They are the Jews". And 2. "والالضالين *Walad dâllîn* (nor of those who went astray)," he صلى الله عليه وسلم replied: "The Christians, and they are the ones who went astray". [This *Hadith* is quoted by At-Tirmidhi and Musnad Abu Dâwûd].

who went astray (such as the Christians).[1], [2], [3]

---

[1] (V.1:7) Narration about Zaid bin 'Amr bin Nufail.

Narrated 'Abdullah bin 'Umar رضى الله عنهما: The Prophet صلى الله عليه وسلم met Zaid bin 'Amr bin Nufail in the bottom of (the valley of) Baldah before the descent of any Divine revelation to the Prophet صلى الله عليه وسلم. A meal was presented to the Prophet صلى الله عليه وسلم but he refused to eat from it. (Then it was presented to Zaid) who said, "I do not eat anything which you slaughter on your *Nusub** in the name of your idols. I eat only those (animals meat) on which Allâh's Name has been mentioned at the time of (their) slaughtering." Zaid bin 'Amr used to criticise the way Quraish used to slaughter their animals and used to say,"Allâh has created the sheep and He has sent the water for it from the sky, and He has grown the grass for it from the earth; yet you slaughter it in others than the Name of Allâh." He used to say so, for he rejected that practice and considered it as something abominable.

* *Nusub:* See the glossary.

Narrated Ibn 'Umar رضى الله عنهما: Zaid bin 'Amr bin Nufail went to Shâm (the region comprising Syria, Lebanon, Palestine and Jordan), enquiring about a true religion to follow. He met a Jewish religious scholar and asked him about their religion. He said, "I intend to embrace your religion, so tell me something about it." The Jew said, "You will not embrace our religion unless you receive your share of Allâh's Anger." Zaid said, "I do not run except from Allâh's Anger, and I will never bear a bit of it if I have the power to avoid it. Can you tell me of some other religion?" He said, "I do not know any other religion except *Hanîf* (Islâmic Monotheism)." Zaid enquired, "What is *Hanîf*?" He said, "*Hanîf* is the religion of (the Prophet) Abraham (عليه السلام), he was neither a Jew nor a Christian, and he used to worship none but Allâh [(Alone) — Islâmic Monotheism]." Then Zaid went out and met a Christian religious scholar and told him the same (as before). The Christian said, "You will not embrace our religion unless you get a share of Allâh's Curse." Zaid replied, "I do not run except from Allâh's Curse, and I will never bear any of Allâh's Curse and His Anger if I have the power to avoid them. Will you tell me of some other religion?" He replied, "I do not know any other religion except *Hanîf* (Islâmic Monotheism)." Zaid enquired, "What is *Hanîf?*" He replied "*Hanîf* is the religion of (the Prophet) Abraham (عليه السلام) he was neither a Jew nor a Christian, (and he used to worship none but Allâh [(Alone) — Islâmic Monotheism]." When Zaid heard their statement about (the religion of) Abraham, he left that place, and when he came out, he raised both his hands and said, "O Allâh! I make You my Witness that I am on the religion of Abraham".

Narrated Asmâ' bint Abî Bakr رضي الله عنهما: I saw Zaid bin 'Amr bin Nufail standing with his back against the *Ka'bah* and saying, "O people of Quraish! By Allâh, none amongst you is on the religion of Abraham except me." She added: He (Zaid) used to preserve the lives of little girls; if somebody wanted to kill his daughter he would say to him, "Do not kill her for I will feed her on your behalf." So he would take her, and when she grew up nicely, he would say to her father, 'Now if you will (wish), I will give her to you, and if you will (wish), I will feed her on your behalf." (*Sahih Al-Bukhâri*, Vol.5, *Hadîth* No.169).

[2] (V.1:7): Narrated 'Ubâdah bin As-Sâmit رضي الله عنه: Allâh's Messenger صلى الله عليه وسلم said, "Whoever does not recite *Sûrat Al-Fâtihah* in his prayer, his prayer is invalid." (*Sahih Al-Bukhâri*, Vol.1, *Hadîth* No.723).

[3] (V.1:7): Narrated Abu Hurairah رضي الله عنه: Allâh's Messenger صلى الله عليه وسلم said, "When the *Imâm* says: *Ghairil-maghdubi 'alaihim walad-dâllîn*. [i.e. not the way of those who earned Your Anger, nor the way of those who went astray (1:7)], then you must say, *Âmîn*, for if one's utterance of *Âmîn* coincides with that of the angels, then his past sins will be forgiven." (*Sahih Al-Bukhâri*, Vol.6, *Hadîth* No.2).

Sûrat Al-Baqarah (The Cow) II

*In the Name of Allâh,
the Most Gracious, the Most Merciful*

1. *Alif-Lâm-Mîm.* [These letters are one of the miracles of the Qur'ân and none but Allâh (Alone) knows their meanings.]

2. This is the Book (the Qur'ân), whereof there is no doubt, a guidance to those who are *Al-Muttaqûn* [the pious and righteous persons who fear Allâh much (abstain from all kinds of sins and evil deeds which He has forbidden) and love Allâh much (perform all kinds of good deeds which He has ordained)].

3. Who believe in the *Ghaib*[1] and perform *As-Salât (Iqâmat-as-Salât)*,[2]

---

[1] (V.2:3): *Al-Ghaib*: literally means a thing not seen. But this word includes vast meanings: Belief in Allâh, Angels, Holy Books, Allâh's Messengers, Day of Resurrection and *Al-Qadar* (Divine Preordainments). It also includes what Allâh and His Messenger صلى الله عليه وسلم informed about the knowledge of the matters of past, present, and future e.g., news about the creation of the heavens and earth, botanical and zoological life, the news about the nations of the past, and about Paradise and Hell.

[2] (V.2:3): *Iqâmat-as-Salât* إقامة الصلاة : The performance of *Salât* (prayers). It means that:

a) Every Muslim, male or female, is obliged to offer his *Salât* (prayers) regularly five times a day at the specified times; the male in a mosque in congregation and the female at home. As the Prophet صلى الله عليه وسلم has said: "Order your children for *Salât* (prayers) at the age of seven and beat them (about it) at the age of ten." The chief (of a family, town, tribe) and the Muslim rulers of a country are held responsible before Allâh in case of non-fulfillment of this obligation by the Muslims under their authority.

and spend out of what we have provided for them [i.e. give Zakât,[1] spend on themselves, their parents, their children, their wives, and also give charity to the poor and also in Allâh's Cause — Jihâd].

4. And who believe in (the Qur'ân and the Sunnah)[2] which has been sent down (revealed) to you (Muhammad صلى الله عليه وسلم) and in that which were sent down before you [the Taurât (Torah)

---

b) One must offer the Salât (prayers) as the Prophet صلى الله عليه وسلم used to offer them with all their rules and regulations, i.e., standing, bowing, prostrating, sitting, as he صلى الله عليه وسلم has said: "Offer your Salât (prayers) the way you see me offering them (see Sahih Al-Bukhâri, Vol. 1, H.No. 604 and Vol. 9, H.No. 352)." [For the characteristics of the Salât (prayer) of the Prophet صلى الله عليه وسلم see Sahih Al-Bukhâri, Vol.1, H.No. 702, 703, 704, 723, 786, 787].

[1] (V.2:3) Zakât زكاة: A certain fixed proportion of the wealth and of every kind of the property liable to Zakât of a Muslim to be paid yearly for the benefit of the poor in the Muslim community. The payment of Zakât is obligatory as it is one of the five pillars of Islâm. Zakât is the major economic means for establishing social justice and leading the Muslim society to prosperity and security. [See Sahih Al-Bukhâri, Vol. 2, Book of Zakât, No. 24]

[2] (V.2:4) Narrated Ibn 'Umar رضي الله عنهما; Allâh's Messenger صلى الله عليه وسلم said: Islâm is based on (the following) five (principles):
1. To testify that "Lâ ilâha illallâh wa anna Muhammad-ur-Rasûl Allâh" (none has the right to be worshipped but Allâh and that Muhammad صلى الله عليه وسلم is the Messenger of Allâh).
2. Iqâmat-as-Salât: to perform the five (compulsory congregational) Salât (prayers).
3. To pay Zakât.
4. To perform Hajj (i.e. pilgrimage to Makkah).
5. To observe Saum (fasting) during the month of Ramadan.
(Sahih Al-Bukhâri, Vol. 1, Hadith No. 7).

and the Injeel (Gospel)] and they believe with certainty in the Hereafter. (Resurrection, recompense of their good and bad deeds, Paradise and Hell).

5. They are on (true) guidance from their Lord, and they are the successful.

6. Verily, those who disbelieve, it is the same to them whether you (O Muhammad صلى الله عليه وسلم) warn them or do not warn them, they will not believe.

7. Allâh has set a seal on their hearts and on their hearing, (i.e. they are closed from accepting Allâh's Guidance), and on their eyes there is a covering. Theirs will be a great torment.

8. And of mankind, there are some (hypocrites) who say: "We believe in Allâh and the Last Day" while in fact they believe not.

9. They (think to) deceive Allâh and those who believe, while they only deceive themselves, and perceive (it) not!

10. In their hearts is a disease (of doubt and hypocrisy) and Allâh has increased their disease. A painful torment is theirs because they used to tell lies.

11. And when it is said to them: "Make not mischief on the earth," they say: "We are only peace-makers."

12. Verily, they are the ones who make mischief, but they perceive not.

13. And when it is said to them (hypocrites): "Believe as the people (followers of Muhammad صلى الله عليه وسلم *Al-Ansâr* and *Al-Muhâjirûn*) have believed," they say: "Shall we believe as the fools have believed?" Verily, they are the fools, but they know not.

14. And when they meet those who believe, they say: "We believe," but when they are alone with their *Shayâtîn* (devils — polytheists, hypocrites), they say: "Truly, we are with you; verily, we were but mocking."

15. Allâh mocks at them and gives them increase in their wrong-doing to wander blindly.

16. These are they who have purchased error for guidance, so their commerce was profitless. And they were not guided.

17. Their likeness is as the likeness of one who kindled a fire; then, when it lighted all around him, Allâh took away their light and left them in darkness. (So) they could not see.

18. They are deaf, dumb, and blind, so they return not (to the Right Path).

19. Or like a rainstorm from the sky, wherein is darkness, thunder, and lightning. They thrust their fingers in their ears to keep out the stunning thunderclap for fear of death. But Allâh ever encompasses the disbelievers (i.e. Allâh will gather them all together).

20. The lightning almost snatches away their sight, whenever it flashes for them, they walk therein, and when darkness covers them, they stand still. And if Allâh willed, He could have taken away their hearing and their sight. Certainly, Allâh has power over all things.

21. O mankind! Worship your Lord (Allâh), Who created you and those who were before you so that you may become *Al-Muttaqûn* (the pious. See V.2:2).

22. Who has made the earth a resting place for you, and the sky as a canopy, and sent down water (rain) from the sky and brought forth therewith fruits as a provision for you. Then do not set up rivals unto Allâh (in worship) while you know (that He Alone has the right to be worshipped).[1]

23. And if you (Arab pagans, Jews, and Christians) are in doubt concerning that which We have sent down (i.e. the Qur'ân) to Our slave (Muhammad صلى الله عليه وسلم), then produce a *Sûrah* (chapter) of the like thereof and call your witnesses (supporters and helpers) besides Allâh, if you are truthful.

24. But if you do it not, and you can never do it, then fear the Fire (Hell) whose fuel is men and stones, prepared for the disbelievers.

---

[1] (V.2:22) Narrated 'Abdullâh رضي الله عنه: I asked the Prophet صلى الله عليه وسلم, "What is the greatest sin in consideration with Allâh?" He said, "That you set up a rival unto Allâh though He Alone created you." I said, "That is indeed a great sin." Then I asked, "What is next?" He said, "To kill your son lest he should share your food with you." I asked, "What is next?" He said, "To commit illegal sexual intercourse with the wife of your neighbour." (*Sahih Al-Bukhâri*, Vol.6, *Hadîth* No.4).

25. And give glad tidings to those who believe and do righteous good deeds, that for them will be Gardens under which rivers flow (Paradise). Every time they will be provided with a fruit therefrom, they will say: "This is what we were provided with before," and they will be given things in resemblance (i.e. in the same form but different in taste) and they shall have therein *Azwâjun Mutahharatun*[1] (purified mates or wives), and they will abide therein forever.

26. Verily, Allâh is not ashamed to set forth a parable even of a mosquito or so much more when it is bigger (or less when it is smaller) than it. And as for those who believe, they know that it is the Truth from their Lord, but as for those who disbelieve, they say: "What did Allâh intend by this parable?" By it He misleads many, and many He guides thereby. And He misleads thereby only those who are *Al-Fâsiqûn* (the rebellious, disobedient to Allâh)[2].

27. Those who break Allâh's Covenant after ratifying it, and sever what Allâh has ordered to be joined (as regards Allâh's religion of Islâmic Monotheism, and to practise its laws on the earth and also as regards keeping

---

[1] (V.2:25) Having no menses, stools, urine. See *Tafsir Ibn Kathir*, Vol. 1, page 63 and also see the footnote of (V.29:64)

[2] (V.2:26) We have retained this peculiar English construction in order to capture the Arabic idiom here.

good relations with kith and kin[1], and do mischief on earth, it is they who are the losers.

28. How can you disbelieve in Allâh? Seeing that you were dead and He gave you life. Then He will give you death, then again will bring you to life (on the Day of Resurrection) and then unto Him you will return. (See V.40:11)

29. He it is Who created for you all that is on earth. Then He rose over (*Istawâ*) towards the heaven and made them seven heavens and He is the All-Knower of everything.

30. And (remember) when your Lord said to the angels: "Verily, I am going to place (mankind) generations after generations on earth." They said: "Will You place therein those who will make mischief therein and shed blood, — while we glorify You with praises and thanks and sanctify You." He (Allâh) said: "I know that which you do not know."

31. And He taught Adam all the names (of everything),[2] then He

---

[1] (V.2:27) Narrated Jubâir bin Mut'im ‎رضي الله عنه that he heard the Prophet ‎صلى الله عليه وسلم saying, "[‎القاطع] *Al-Qâti'* (the person who severs the bond of kinship) will not enter Paradise." (*Sahih Al-Bukhâri*, Vol.8, *Hadith* No.13).

[2] (V.2:31) The Statement of Allâh ‎تعالى: 'And He taught Adam all the names (of everything).'

Narrated Anas ‎رضي الله عنه: The Prophet ‎صلى الله عليه وسلم said, "On the Day of Resurrection the believers will assemble and say, 'Let us ask somebody to intercede for us with our Lord.' So they will go to Adam and say, 'You are the father of all the people, and Allâh created you with His Own Hands, and ordered the angels to prostrate themselves to you, and taught you the names of all things; so please intercede for us with your Lord, so that He may relieve us from this place of ours.' Adam will say, 'I am not fit for this (i.e. intercession for you).' Then Adam will remember his sin and feel ashamed thereof. He will say, 'Go to Nûh (Noah), for he was the first Messenger, Allâh sent to the inhabitants of the earth.' They will go to him and Nûh (Noah) will say, 'I am not fit for this undertaking.' He will remember his appeal to his Lord to do something of which he had no knowledge, then he will feel ashamed thereof and will say, 'Go to Khalil-ur-Rahmân* [i.e. Ibrâhîm (Abraham)]. They will go to him and he will say, 'I am not fit for this undertaking. Go to Mûsâ (Moses), the slave to whom Allâh spoke (directly) and gave him the Taurât (Torah).' So they will go to him and he will say, 'I am not fit for this undertaking,' and he will mention (his) killing a person who was not a killer, and so he will feel ashamed thereof before his Lord, and he will say, 'Go to 'Îsâ (Jesus), Allâh's slave, His Messenger and Allâh's Word and a spirit coming from Him.** 'Îsâ (Jesus) will say, 'I am not fit for this undertaking, go to Muhammad (صلى الله عليه وسلم) the slave of. Allâh whose past and future sins were forgiven by Allâh.' So they will come to me and I will proceed till I ask my Lord's Permission and I will be given permission. When I see my Lord, I will fall down in prostration and He will let me remain in that state as long He wishes and then I will be addressed: '(Muhammad!) Raise your head. Ask, and your request will be granted; say, and your saying will be listened to; intercede, and your intercession will be accepted.' I will raise my head and praise Allâh with a saying (i.e. invocation) He will teach me, and then I will intercede. He will fix a limit for me (to intercede) whom I will admit into Paradise. Then I will come back again to Allâh, and when I see my Lord, the same thing will happen to me. And then I will intercede and Allâh will fix a limit for me (to intercede) whom I will admit into Paradise, then I will come back for the third time; and then I will come back for the fourth time, and will say, 'None remains in Hell but those whom the Qur'ân has imprisoned (in Hell) and who have been destined to an eternal stay in Hell.'" (The compiler) Abu 'Abdullâh said: 'But those whom the Qur'ân has imprisoned in Hell' refers to the Statement of Allâh: خَالِدِينَ فِيهَا: "To abide therein forever." (Sahih Al-Bukhâri, Vol.6, Hadîth No.3).

showed them to the angels and said, "Tell Me the names of these if you are truthful."

32. They (angels) said: "Glory is to You, we have no knowledge except what you have taught us. Verily, it is You, the All-Knower, the All-Wise."

33. He said: "O Adam! Inform them of their names," and when he had informed them of their names, He said: "Did I not tell you that I know the *Ghaib* (Unseen) in the heavens and the earth, and I know what you reveal and what you have been concealing?"

34. And (remember) when We said to the angels: "Prostrate yourselves before Adam." And they prostrated except *Iblîs* (Satan), he refused and was proud and was one of the disbelievers (disobedient to Allâh).

35. And We said: "O Adam! Dwell you and your wife in the Paradise and eat both of you freely with pleasure and delight, of things therein as wherever you will, but come not near this tree or you both will be of the *Zâlimûn* (wrong-doers)."

36. Then the *Shaitân* (Satan) made them slip therefrom (the Paradise), and got them out from that in which they

---

*The intimate friend of the Most Gracious (Allâh).

**This may wrongly be understood as the spirit or soul of Allâh, in fact, it is a soul created by Allâh, i.e. 'Isâ (Jesus). It was His Word: "Be!" — and he was (created like the creation of Adam). Please see the word *Rûh-ullâh* in the glossary for further details.

were. We said: "Get you down, all, with enmity between yourselves. On earth will be a dwelling place for you and an enjoyment for a time."

37. Then Adam received from his Lord Words.[1] And his Lord pardoned him (accepted his repentance). Verily, He is the One Who forgives (accepts repentance), the Most Merciful.

38. We said: "Get down all of you from this place (the Paradise), then whenever there comes to you Guidance from Me, and whoever follows My Guidance, there shall be no fear on them, nor shall they grieve.

39. But those who disbelieve and belie Our *Ayât* (proofs, evidences, verses, lessons, signs, revelations, etc.) — such are the dwellers of the Fire. They shall abide therein forever.

40. O Children of Israel! Remember My Favour which I bestowed upon you, and fulfil (your obligations to) My Covenant (with you) so that I fulfil (My Obligations to) your covenant (with Me), and fear none but Me.

41. And believe in what I have sent down (this Qur'ân), confirming that which is with you, [the Taurât (Torah) and the Injeel (Gospel)], and be not the first to disbelieve therein, and buy [get

---

[1] (V.2:37): These words are mentioned in the Qur'ân; (Verse 7:23): They are: "Our Lord! We have wronged ourselves. If You forgive us not, and bestow not upon us Your Mercy, we shall certainly be of the losers."

(أخذ اجرا)] not with My Verses [the Taurât (Torah) and the Injeel (Gospel)] a small price (i.e. getting a small gain by selling My Verses), and fear Me and Me Alone. (*Tafsir At-Tabarî*).

فَنَنَا قَلِيلًا وَإِنَّنَ فَأَتَّقُونِ ﴿

42. And mix not truth with falsehood, nor conceal the truth [i.e. Muhammad صلى الله عليه وسلم is Allâh's Messenger and his qualities are written in your Scriptures, the Taurât (Torah) and the Injeel (Gospel)] while you know (the truth).[1]

وَلَا تَلْبِسُوا ٱلْحَقَّ بِٱلْبَـٰطِلِ وَتَكْتُمُوا ٱلْحَقَّ وَأَنتُمْ تَعْلَمُونَ ﴿

43. And perform As-Salât (Iqâmat-as-Salât), and give Zakât, and bow down (or submit yourselves with obedience to Allâh) along with Ar-Râki'ûn.[2]

وَأَقِيمُوا ٱلصَّلَوٰةَ وَءَاتُوا ٱلزَّكَوٰةَ وَٱرْكَعُوا مَعَ ٱلرَّٰكِعِينَ ﴿

---

[1] (V.2:42): Narrated 'Atâ bin Yasâr: I met 'Abdullâh bin 'Amr bin Al-'Aas and asked him, "Tell me about the description of Allâh's Messenger صلى الله عليه وسلم which is mentioned in the Taurât (Torah)." He replied, "Yes. By Allâh, he is described in the Taurât (Torah) with some of the qualities attributed to him in the Qur'ân as follows: 'O Prophet! We have sent you as a witness (for Allâh's true religion). And a giver of glad tidings (to the faithful believers). And a warner (to the disbelievers), and a guardian of the illiterates. You are My slave and My Messenger I have named you Al-Mûtawakkil (who depends upon Allâh). You are neither discourteous, harsh nor a noise-maker in the markets, and you do not do evil to those who do evil to you, but you deal with them with forgiveness and kindness. Allâh will not let him (the Prophet صلى الله عليه وسلم) die till he makes straight the crooked people by making them say: '*Lâ ilâha illallâh,*' (none has the right to be worshipped but Allâh), by which 'blind eyes, deaf ears and closed hearts' will be opened." (*Sahih Al-Bukhari*, Vol.3, *Hadîth* No.335).

[2] (V.2:43) Ar-Râki'ûn: Those who bow down or submit themselves with obedience to Allâh with Muhammad صلى الله عليه وسلم as the

44. Enjoin you *Al-Birr* (piety and righteousness and every act of obedience to Allâh) on the people and you forget (to practise it) yourselves,[1] while you recite the Scripture [the Taurât (Torah)]! Have you then no sense?

﴿ أَتَأْمُرُونَ ٱلنَّاسَ بِٱلْبِرِّ وَتَنسَوْنَ أَنفُسَكُمْ وَأَنتُمْ تَتْلُونَ ٱلْكِتَٰبَ أَفَلَا تَعْقِلُونَ ﴾

45. And seek help in patience and *As-Salât* (the prayer) and truly, it is extremely heavy and hard except for *Al-Khâshi'ûn* [i.e. the true believers in Allâh — those who obey Allâh with full submission, fear much from His punishment, and believe in His Promise (Paradise) and in His Warnings (Hell)].

﴿ وَٱسْتَعِينُوا بِٱلصَّبْرِ وَٱلصَّلَوٰةِ وَإِنَّهَا لَكَبِيرَةٌ إِلَّا عَلَى ٱلْخَٰشِعِينَ ﴾

46. (They are those) who are certain that they are going to meet their Lord, and that unto Him they are going to return.

﴿ ٱلَّذِينَ يَظُنُّونَ أَنَّهُم مُّلَٰقُوا رَبِّهِمْ وَأَنَّهُمْ إِلَيْهِ رَٰجِعُونَ ﴾

Muslims have done, i.e., embrace Islâm (worshipping none but Allâh Alone and doing good with the only intention of seeking Allâh's Pleasure).

[1] (V.2:44) Narrated Abu Wâ'il رضي الله عنه: Someone said to Usâmah, "Will you not talk to this ('Uthmân)?" Usâmah said, "I talked to him (secretly) without being the first man to open an evil door. I will never tell a ruler who rules over two men or more that he is good after I heard Allâh's Messenger صلى الله عليه وسلم saying: "A man will be brought and put in Hell (Fire) and will circumambulate (go round and round) in Hell (Fire) like a donkey of a (flour) grinding mill, and all the people of Hell (Fire) will gather around him and will say to him, 'O so-and-so! Didn't you use to order others for *Al-Ma'rûf* (Islâmic Monotheism and all that is good) and forbid them from *Al-Munkar* (polytheism, disbelief, and all that is evil)?' That man will say, 'I used to order others to do *Al-Mar'ûf* (Islâmic Monotheism and all that good) but I myself never used to do it, and I used to forbid others from *Al-Munkar* (polytheism, disbelief, and all that is evil) while I myself used to do *Al-Munkar* (polytheism, disbelief and all that is evil)'". (*Ṣaḥīḥ Al-Bukhârī*, Vol.9, *Ḥadîth* No.218).

47. O Children of Israel! Remember My Favour which I bestowed upon you and that I preferred you to the *'Âlamîn* [mankind and jinn (of your time period, in the past)].

48. And fear a Day (of Judgement) when a person shall not avail another, nor will intercession be accepted from him nor will compensation be taken from him nor will they be helped.

49. And (remember) when We delivered you from Fir'aun's (Pharaoh) people, who were afflicting you with a horrible torment, killing your sons and sparing your women, and therein was a mighty trial from your Lord.

50. And (remember) when We separated the sea for you and saved you and drowned Fir'aun's (Pharaoh) people while you were looking (at them, when the sea-water covered them).

51. And (remember) when We appointed for Mûsâ (Moses) forty nights, and (in his absence) you took the calf (for worship), and you were *Zâlimûn* (polytheists and wrong-doers).

52. Then after that We forgave you so that you might be grateful.

53. And (remember) when We gave Mûsâ (Moses) the Scripture [the Taurât (Torah)] and the criterion (of right and wrong) so that you may be guided aright.

54. And (remember) when Mûsâ (Moses) said to his people: "O my people! Verily, you have wronged yourselves by worshipping the calf. So turn in repentance to your Creator and kill yourselves (the innocent kill the wrongdoers among you), that will be better for you with your Creator." Then He accepted your repentance. Truly, He is the One Who accepts repentance, the Most Merciful.

بِأَتِّخَاذِكُمُ الْعِجْلَ فَتُوبُوٓا إِلَىٰ بَارِئِكُمْ فَاقْتُلُوٓا أَنفُسَكُمْ ذَٰلِكُمْ خَيْرٌ لَّكُمْ عِندَ بَارِئِكُمْ فَتَابَ عَلَيْكُمْ إِنَّهُ هُوَ التَّوَّابُ الرَّحِيمُ ۝

55. And (remember) when you said: "O Mûsâ (Moses)! We shall never believe in you until we see Allâh plainly." But you were seized with a thunderbolt (lightning) while you were looking.

وَإِذْ قُلْتُمْ يَٰمُوسَىٰ لَن نُّؤْمِنَ لَكَ حَتَّىٰ نَرَى اللَّهَ جَهْرَةً فَأَخَذَتْكُمُ الصَّٰعِقَةُ وَأَنتُمْ تَنظُرُونَ ۝

56. Then We raised you up after your death, so that you might be grateful.

ثُمَّ بَعَثْنَٰكُم مِّنۢ بَعْدِ مَوْتِكُمْ لَعَلَّكُمْ تَشْكُرُونَ ۝

57. And We shaded you with clouds and sent down on you Al-Manna[1] and the quails, (saying): "Eat of the good lawful things We have provided for you," (but they rebelled). And they did not wrong Us but they wronged themselves.

وَظَلَّلْنَا عَلَيْكُمُ الْغَمَامَ وَأَنزَلْنَا عَلَيْكُمُ الْمَنَّ وَالسَّلْوَىٰ كُلُوا۟ مِن طَيِّبَٰتِ مَا رَزَقْنَٰكُمْ وَمَا ظَلَمُونَا وَلَٰكِن كَانُوٓا۟ أَنفُسَهُمْ يَظْلِمُونَ ۝

58. And (remember) when We said: "Enter this town (Jerusalem) and eat bountifully therein with pleasure and delight wherever you wish, and enter the gate in prostration (or bowing with humility) and say: 'Forgive us,' and We

وَإِذْ قُلْنَا ادْخُلُوا۟ هَٰذِهِ الْقَرْيَةَ فَكُلُوا۟ مِنْهَا حَيْثُ شِئْتُمْ رَغَدًا وَادْخُلُوا۟ الْبَابَ سُجَّدًا وَقُولُوا۟ حِطَّةٌ نَّغْفِرْ لَكُمْ خَطَٰيَٰكُمْ وَسَنَزِيدُ الْمُحْسِنِينَ ۝

---

[1] (V.2:57) Mujâhid said, "Al-Manna is a kind of sweet gum, and As-Salwâ, a kind of bird (i.e. quails)"… Narrated Said bin Zaid رضى الله عنه Allâh's Messenger صلى الله عليه وسلم said, "The Kam'a (truffle — i.e. a kind of edible fungus) is like the Manna (as it is obtained without any effort) and its water is a (medicine) cure for eye trouble." (Sahih Al-Bukhâri, Vol. 6, Hadîth No. 5).

shall forgive you your sins and shall increase (reward) for the good-doers."

59. But those who did wrong changed the word from that which had been told to them for another, so We sent upon the wrong-doers *Rijzan* (a punishment)[1] from the heaven because of their rebelling against Allâh's obedience. (*Tafsîr At-Tabarî*).

فَبَدَّلَ ٱلَّذِينَ ظَلَمُواْ قَوْلًا غَيْرَ ٱلَّذِى قِيلَ لَهُمْ فَأَنزَلْنَا عَلَى ٱلَّذِينَ ظَلَمُواْ رِجْزًا مِّنَ ٱلسَّمَآءِ بِمَا كَانُواْ يَفْسُقُونَ

60. And (remember) when Mûsâ (Moses) asked for water for his people, We said: "Strike the stone with your stick." Then gushed forth therefrom twelve springs. Each (group of) people knew its own place for water. "Eat and drink of that which Allâh has provided and do not act corruptly, making mischief on the earth."

۞ وَإِذِ ٱسْتَسْقَىٰ مُوسَىٰ لِقَوْمِهِۦ فَقُلْنَا ٱضْرِب بِّعَصَاكَ ٱلْحَجَرَ فَٱنفَجَرَتْ مِنْهُ ٱثْنَتَا عَشْرَةَ عَيْنًا قَدْ عَلِمَ كُلُّ أُنَاسٍ مَّشْرَبَهُمْ كُلُواْ وَٱشْرَبُواْ مِن رِّزْقِ ٱللَّهِ وَلَا تَعْثَوْا۟ فِى ٱلْأَرْضِ مُفْسِدِينَ

61. And (remember) when you said, "O Mûsâ (Moses)! We cannot endure one kind of food. So invoke your Lord for us to bring forth for us of what the earth grows, its herbs, its cucumbers, its *Fûm* (wheat or garlic), its lentils and its onions." He said, "Would you exchange that which is better for that which is lower? Go you down to any town and you shall find what you want!" And they were covered with humiliation and

وَإِذْ قُلْتُمْ يَٰمُوسَىٰ لَن نَّصْبِرَ عَلَىٰ طَعَامٍ وَٰحِدٍ فَٱدْعُ لَنَا رَبَّكَ يُخْرِجْ لَنَا مِمَّا تُنۢبِتُ ٱلْأَرْضُ مِنۢ بَقْلِهَا وَقِثَّآئِهَا وَفُومِهَا وَعَدَسِهَا وَبَصَلِهَا قَالَ أَتَسْتَبْدِلُونَ ٱلَّذِى هُوَ أَدْنَىٰ بِٱلَّذِى هُوَ خَيْرٌ ٱهْبِطُواْ مِصْرًا فَإِنَّ لَكُم مَّا سَأَلْتُمْ وَضُرِبَتْ عَلَيْهِمُ ٱلذِّلَّةُ

---

[1] (V.2:59) Narrated Usâmah bin Zaid رضي الله عنه: Allâh's Messenger صلى الله عليه وسلم said, "Plague was a means of torture sent on a group of Israelis (or on some people before you). So if you hear of its spread in a land, don't approach it, and if plague should appear in a land where you are present, then don't leave that land in order to run away from it (i.e. plague)." (*Sahih Al-Bukhâri*, Vol.4, *Hadîth* No.679).

misery, and they drew on themselves the Wrath of Allâh. That was because they used to disbelieve the *Ayât* (proofs, evidences, verses, lessons, signs, revelations etc.) of Allâh and killed the Prophets wrongfully. That was because they disobeyed and used to transgress the bounds (in their disobedience to Allâh, i.e. commit crimes and sins).

62. Verily, those who believe and those who are Jews and Christians, and Sabians,[1] whoever believes in Allâh and the Last Day and does righteous good deeds shall have their reward with their Lord, on them shall be no fear, nor shall they grieve.[2]

63. And (O Children of Israel, remember) when We took your covenant and We raised above you the Mount (saying): "Hold fast to that which We have given you, and remember that which is therein so that you may become *Al-Muttaqûn* (the pious. See V.2:2).

---

[1] (V.2:62) A past nation used to live in Musal (Iraq) and say *Lâ ilâha illallâh* (none has the right to be worshipped but Allâh) and used to read *Az-Zabur* (the Psalms of the Sabians) and they were neither Jews nor Christians.

[2] (V.2:62) This Verse (and Verse 5:69), mentioned in the Qur'ân should not be misinterpreted by the reader as mentioned by Ibn Abbâs رضي الله عنهما (*Tafsîr At-Tabari*, Vol. I, Page 323) that the provision of this Verse was abrogated by the Verse 3:85: "And whosoever seeks a religion other than Islâm, it will never be accepted of him, and in the Hereafter, he will be one of the losers." [i.e. after the coming of Prophet Muhammad صلى الله عليه وسلم on the earth, no other religion except Islâm, will be accepted from anyone].

64. Then after that you turned you. Had it not been for the Grace and Mercy of Allâh upon you, indeed you would have been among the losers.

65. And indeed you knew those amongst you who transgressed in the matter of the Sabbath (i.e. Saturday). We said to them: "Be you monkeys, despised and rejected."

66. So We made this punishment an example to their own and to succeeding generations and a lesson to those who are Al-Muttaqûn (the pious. See V.2:2).

67. And (remember) when Mûsâ (Moses) said to his people: "Verily, Allâh commands you that you slaughter a cow." They said, "Do you make fun of us?" He said, "I take Allâh's Refuge from being among Al-Jâhilûn (the ignorant or the foolish)."

68. They said, "Call upon your Lord for us that He may make plain to us what it is!" He said, "He says, 'Verily, it is a cow neither too old nor too young, but (it is) between the two conditions', so do what you are commanded."

69. They said, "Call upon your Lord for us to make plain to us its colour." He said, "He says, 'It is a yellow cow, bright in its colour, pleasing the beholders.' "

70. They said, "Call upon your Lord for us to make plain to us what it is. Verily, to us all cows are alike. And surely, if Allâh wills, we will be guided."

71. He [Mûsâ (Moses)] said, "He says, 'It is a cow neither trained to till the soil nor water the fields, sound, having no other colour except bright yellow.' " They said, "Now you have brought the truth." So they slaughtered it though they were near to not doing it.

قَالَ إِنَّهُ يَقُولُ إِنَّهَا بَقَرَةٌ لَّا ذَلُولٌ تُثِيرُ الْأَرْضَ وَلَا تَسْقِي الْحَرْثَ مُسَلَّمَةٌ لَّا شِيَةَ فِيهَا قَالُوا الْـَٰٔنَ جِئْتَ بِالْحَقِّ فَذَبَحُوهَا وَمَا كَادُوا يَفْعَلُونَ ۝

72. And (remember) when you killed a man and fell into dispute among yourselves as to the crime. But Allâh brought forth that which you were hiding.

وَإِذْ قَتَلْتُمْ نَفْسًا فَادَّارَأْتُمْ فِيهَا وَاللَّهُ مُخْرِجٌ مَّا كُنتُمْ تَكْتُمُونَ ۝

73. So We said: "Strike him (the dead man) with a piece of it (the cow)." Thus Allâh brings the dead to life and shows you His *Ayât* (proofs, evidences, verses, lessons, signs, revelations, etc.) so that you may understand.

فَقُلْنَا اضْرِبُوهُ بِبَعْضِهَا كَذَٰلِكَ يُحْيِ اللَّهُ الْمَوْتَىٰ وَيُرِيكُمْ ءَايَٰتِهِ لَعَلَّكُمْ تَعْقِلُونَ ۝

74. Then, after that, your hearts were hardened and became as stones or even worse in hardness. And indeed, there are stones out of which rivers gush forth, and indeed, there are of them (stones) which split asunder so that water flows from them, and indeed, there are of them (stones) which fall down for fear of Allâh. And Allâh is not unaware of what you do.

ثُمَّ قَسَتْ قُلُوبُكُم مِّنۢ بَعْدِ ذَٰلِكَ فَهِيَ كَالْحِجَارَةِ أَوْ أَشَدُّ قَسْوَةً وَإِنَّ مِنَ الْحِجَارَةِ لَمَا يَتَفَجَّرُ مِنْهُ الْأَنْهَٰرُ وَإِنَّ مِنْهَا لَمَا يَشَّقَّقُ فَيَخْرُجُ مِنْهُ الْمَاءُ وَإِنَّ مِنْهَا لَمَا يَهْبِطُ مِنْ خَشْيَةِ اللَّهِ وَمَا اللَّهُ بِغَٰفِلٍ عَمَّا تَعْمَلُونَ ۝

75. Do you (faithful believers) covet that they will believe in your religion inspite of the fact that a party of them (Jewish rabbis) used to hear the Word of Allâh [the Taurât (Torah)], then they used to change it knowingly after they understood it?

۞ أَفَتَطْمَعُونَ أَن يُؤْمِنُوا لَكُمْ وَقَدْ كَانَ فَرِيقٌ مِّنْهُمْ يَسْمَعُونَ كَلَٰمَ اللَّهِ ثُمَّ يُحَرِّفُونَهُ مِنۢ بَعْدِ مَا عَقَلُوهُ وَهُمْ يَعْلَمُونَ ۝

76. And when they (Jews) meet those who believe (Muslims), they say, "We believe", but when they meet one another in private, they say, "Shall you (Jews) tell them (Muslims) what Allâh has revealed to you [Jews, about the description and the qualities of Prophet Muhammad صلى الله عليه وسلم, that which are written in the Taurât (Torah)],[1] that they (Muslims) may argue with you (Jews) about it before your Lord?" Have you (Jews) then no understanding?

77. Know they (Jews) not that Allâh knows what they conceal and what they reveal?

78. And there are among them (Jews) unlettered people, who know not the Book, but they trust upon false desires and they but guess.

79. Then woe to those who write the Book with their own hands and then say, "This is from Allâh," to purchase with it a little price! Woe to them for what their hands have written and woe to them for that they earn thereby.

80. And they (Jews) say, "The Fire (i.e. Hell-fire on the Day of Resurrection) shall not touch us but for a few numbered days." Say (O Muhammad صلى الله عليه وسلم to them): "Have you taken a covenant from Allâh, so that Allâh will not break His Covenant? Or is it that you say of Allâh what you know not?"

---

[1] (V.2:76) See the footnote of (V.2:42)

81. Yes! Whosoever earns evil and his sin has surrounded him, they are dwellers of the Fire (i.e. Hell); they will dwell therein forever.

82. And those who believe (in the Oneness of Allâh تعالى - Islâmic Monotheism) and do righteous good deeds, they are dwellers of Paradise, they will dwell therein forever. (See V.2:257)

83. And (remember) when We took a covenant from the Children of Israel, (saying): Worship none but Allâh (Alone) and be dutiful and good to parents, and to kindred, and to orphans and Al-Masâkîn[1] (the poor), and speak good to people [i.e. enjoin righteousness and forbid evil, and say the truth about Muhammad صلى الله عليه وسلم], and perform As-Salât (Iqâmat-as-Salât), and give Zakât. Then you slid back, except a few of you, while you are backsliders. (Tafsir Al-Qurtubî).

84. And (remember) when We took your covenant (saying): Shed not the blood of your (people), nor turn out your own people from their dwellings.

---

[1] (V.2:83) Narrated Abu Hurairah رضى الله عنه Allâh's Messenger صلى الله عليه وسلم said, "Al-Miskîn (the poor) is not the one who goes round the people and asks them for a mouthful or two (of meals) or a date or two, but Al-Miskîn (the poor) is that who has not enough (money) to satisfy his needs and whose condition is not known to others, that others may give him something in charity, and who does not beg of people." (Sahih Al-Bukhâri, Vol. 2, Hadith No. 557). [Please also see Tafsir At-Tabarî, Vol. 10, Page 158 (Verse 9:60)]

Then, (this) you ratified and (to this) you bear witness.

85. After this, it is you who kill one another and drive out a party of you from their homes, assist (their enemies) against them, in sin and transgression. And if they come to you as captives, you ransom them, although their expulsion was forbidden to you. Then do you believe in a part of the Scripture and reject the rest? Then what is the recompense of those who do so among you, except disgrace in the life of this world, and on the Day of Resurrection they shall be consigned to the most grievous torment. And Allâh is not unaware of what you do.

86. Those are they who have bought the life of this world at the price of the Hereafter. Their torment shall not be lightened nor shall they be helped.

87. And indeed, We gave Mûsâ (Moses) the Book and followed him up with a succession of Messengers. And We gave 'Îsâ (Jesus), the son of Maryam (Mary), clear signs and supported him with Rûh-ul-Qudus [Jibraîl (Gabriel) عليه السلام]. Is it that whenever there came to you a Messenger with what you yourselves desired not, you grew arrogant? Some you disbelieved and some you killed.

88. And they say, "Our hearts are wrapped (i.e. do not hear or understand Allâh's Word)." Nay, Allâh has cursed them for their disbelief, so little is that which they believe.

89. And when there came to them (the Jews), a Book (this Qur'ân) from Allâh confirming what is with them [the Taurât (Torah) and the Injeel (Gospel)], although aforetime they had invoked Allâh (for coming of Muhammad صلى الله عليه وسلم) in order to gain victory over those who disbelieved, then when there came to them that which they had recognised, they disbelieved in it. So let the Curse of Allâh be on the disbelievers.

90. How bad is that for which they have sold their ownselves, that they should disbelieve in that which Allâh has revealed (the Qur'ân), grudging that Allâh should reveal of His Grace unto whom He wills of His slaves. So they have drawn on themselves wrath upon wrath. And for the disbelievers, there is disgracing torment.

91. And when it is said to them (the Jews), "Believe in what Allâh has sent down," they say, "We believe in what was sent down to us." And they disbelieve in that which came after it, while it is the truth confirming what is with them. Say (O Muhammad صلى الله عليه وسلم to them): "Why then have you killed the Prophets of Allâh aforetime, if you indeed have been believers?"

92. And indeed Mûsâ (Moses) came to you with clear proofs, yet you worshipped the calf after he left, and you were Zâlimûn (polytheists and wrong-doers).

93. And (remember) when We took your covenant and We raised above you the Mount (saying), "Hold firmly to what We have given you and hear (Our Word)." They said, "We have heard and disobeyed." And their hearts absorbed (the worship of) the calf because of their disbelief. Say: "Worst indeed is that which your faith enjoins on you if you are believers."

وَإِذْ أَخَذْنَا مِيثَٰقَكُمْ وَرَفَعْنَا فَوْقَكُمُ ٱلطُّورَ خُذُواْ مَآ ءَاتَيْنَٰكُم بِقُوَّةٍ وَٱسْمَعُواْ قَالُواْ سَمِعْنَا وَعَصَيْنَا وَأُشْرِبُواْ فِى قُلُوبِهِمُ ٱلْعِجْلَ بِكُفْرِهِمْ قُلْ بِئْسَمَا يَأْمُرُكُم بِهِۦٓ إِيمَٰنُكُمْ إِن كُنتُم مُّؤْمِنِينَ ۝

94. Say to (them): "If the home of the Hereafter with Allâh is indeed for you specially and not for others, of mankind, then long for death if you are truthful."

قُلْ إِن كَانَتْ لَكُمُ ٱلدَّارُ ٱلْءَاخِرَةُ عِندَ ٱللَّهِ خَالِصَةً مِّن دُونِ ٱلنَّاسِ فَتَمَنَّوُاْ ٱلْمَوْتَ إِن كُنتُمْ صَٰدِقِينَ ۝

95. But they will never long for it because of what their hands have sent before them (i.e. what they have done). And Allâh is All-Aware of the Zâlimûn (polytheists and wrong-doers).

وَلَن يَتَمَنَّوْهُ أَبَدًۢا بِمَا قَدَّمَتْ أَيْدِيهِمْ وَٱللَّهُ عَلِيمٌۢ بِٱلظَّٰلِمِينَ ۝

96. And verily, you will find them (the Jews) the greediest of mankind for life and (even greedier) than those who ascribe partners to Allâh (and do not believe in Resurrection — Majûs, pagans, and idolaters). Everyone of them wishes that he could be given a life of a thousand years. But the grant of such life will not save him even a little from (due) punishment. And Allâh is All-Seer of what they do.

وَلَتَجِدَنَّهُمْ أَحْرَصَ ٱلنَّاسِ عَلَىٰ حَيَوٰةٍ وَمِنَ ٱلَّذِينَ أَشْرَكُواْ يَوَدُّ أَحَدُهُمْ لَوْ يُعَمَّرُ أَلْفَ سَنَةٍ وَمَا هُوَ بِمُزَحْزِحِهِۦ مِنَ ٱلْعَذَابِ أَن يُعَمَّرَ وَٱللَّهُ بَصِيرٌۢ بِمَا يَعْمَلُونَ ۝

97. Say (O Muhammad صلى الله عليه وسلم): "Whoever is an enemy to Jibraîl (Gabriel) (let him die in his fury), for indeed he has brought it (this Qur'ân) down to your heart by Allâh's

قُلْ مَن كَانَ عَدُوًّا لِّجِبْرِيلَ فَإِنَّهُۥ نَزَّلَهُۥ عَلَىٰ قَلْبِكَ بِإِذْنِ ٱللَّهِ مُصَدِّقًا لِّمَا بَيْنَ يَدَيْهِ

Permission, confirming what came before it [i.e. the Taurât (Torah) and the Injeel (Gospel)] and guidance and glad tidings for the believers.

98. "Whoever is an enemy to Allâh, His Angels, His Messengers, Jibraîl (Gabriel) and Mikael (Michael), then verily, Allâh is an enemy to the disbelievers."

99. And indeed We have sent down to you manifest Ayât (these Verses of the Qur'ân which inform in detail about the news of the Jews and their secret intentions), and none disbelieve in them but Fâsiqûn (those who rebel against Allâh's Command).

100. Is it not (the case) that every time they make a covenant, some party among them throw it aside? Nay! (the truth is:) most of them believe not.

101. And when there came to them a Messenger from Allâh (i.e. Muhammad صلى الله عليه وسلم) confirming what was with them, a party of those who were given the Scripture threw away the Book of Allâh behind their backs as if they did not know!

102. They followed what the Shayâtîn (devils) gave out (falsely of the magic) in the lifetime of Sulaimân (Solomon). Sulaimân did not disbelieve, but the Shayâtîn (devils) disbelieved, teaching men magic and such things that came down at Babylon to the two angels, Hârût and Mârût, but neither of these two (angels) taught anyone (such things) till they had said, "We are only for trial, so disbelieve not (by learning this magic from us)." And from these (angels) people learn that by which they cause separation between man and his wife, but they could not thus harm anyone except by Allâh's Leave. And they learn that which harms them and profits them not. And indeed they knew that the buyers of it (magic) would have no share in the Hereafter. And how bad indeed was that for which they sold their ownselves, if they but knew.

103. And if they had believed and guarded themselves from evil and kept their duty to Allâh, far better would have been the reward from their Lord, if they but knew!

104. O you who believe! Say not (to the Messenger صلى الله عليه وسلم) *Râ'ina*[1] but say *Unzurna* (make us understand) and hear. And for the disbelievers there is a painful torment. (See Verse 4:46)

105. Neither those who disbelieve among the people of the Scripture (Jews and Christians) nor *Al-Mushrikûn* (the idolaters, polytheists, disbelievers in the Oneness of Allâh, pagans) like that there should be sent down unto you any good from your Lord. But Allâh chooses for

---

[1] (V.2:104) *Râ'ina*: In Arabic means "Be careful; Listen to us, and we listen to you", whereas in Hebrew it means "an insult", and the Jews used to say it to the Prophet صلى الله عليه وسلم with bad intentions. (See V.4:46)

His Mercy whom He wills. And Allâh is the Owner of Great Bounty.

106. Whatever a Verse (revelation) do We abrogate or cause to be forgotten, We bring a better one or similar to it. Know you not that Allâh is able to do all things?

107. Know you not that it is Allâh to Whom belongs the dominion of the heavens and the earth? And besides Allâh you have neither any *Walî* (protector or guardian) nor any helper.

108. Or do you want to ask your Messenger (Muhammad صلى الله عليه وسلم) as Mûsâ (Moses) was asked before (i.e. show us openly our Lord)? And he who changes Faith for disbelief, verily, he has gone astray from the Right Way.

109. Many of the people of the Scripture (Jews and Christians) wish that if they could turn you away as disbelievers after you have believed, out of envy from their ownselves, even after the truth (that Muhammad صلى الله عليه وسلم is Allâh's Messenger) has become manifest unto them. But forgive and overlook, till Allâh brings His Command.[1] Verily, Allâh is Able to do all things.

110. And perform *As-Salât (Iqâmat-as-Salât)*, and give *Zakât*, and whatever of good (deeds that Allâh loves) you send forth for yourselves before you,

---

[1] (V.2:109) The provision of this verse has been abrogated by the (V.9:29). (*Tafsir At-Tabari*)

you shall find it with Allâh. Certainly, Allâh is All-Seer of what you do.

111. And they say, "None shall enter Paradise unless he is a Jew or a Christian." These are their own desires. Say (O Muhammad صلى الله عليه وسلم), "Produce your proof if you are truthful."

112. Yes, but whoever submits his face (himself) to Allâh (i.e. follows Allâh's religion of Islâmic Monotheism) and he is a *Muhsin* [1] then his reward is with his Lord (Allâh), on such shall be no fear, nor shall they grieve. [See *Tafsîr Ibn Kathîr*].

113. The Jews said that the Christians follow nothing (i.e. are not on the right religion); and the Christians said that the Jews follow nothing (i.e. are not on the right religion); though they both recite the Scripture. Like unto their word, said (the pagans) who know not. Allâh will judge between them on the Day of Resurrection about that wherein they have been differing.

114. And who are more unjust than those who forbid that Allâh's Name be glorified and mentioned much (i.e. prayers and invocations) in Allâh's mosques and strive for their ruin? It was not fitting that such should themselves

---

[1] (V.2:112) *Muhsin*: A good-doer who performs good deeds totally for Allâh's sake only without any show off or to gain praise or fame, and in accordance with the *Sunnah* of Allâh's Messenger Muhammad صلى الله عليه وسلم.

enter them (Allâh's mosques) except in fear. For them there is disgrace in this world, and they will have a great torment in the Hereafter.

أَن يَدْخُلُوهَا إِلَّا خَآئِفِينَ لَهُمْ فِى الدُّنْيَا خِزْىٌ وَلَهُمْ فِى الْآخِرَةِ عَذَابٌ عَظِيمٌ ﴿١١٤﴾

115. And to Allâh belong the east and the west, so wherever you turn (yourselves or your faces) there is the Face of Allâh (and He is High above, over His Throne). Surely, Allâh is All-Sufficient for His creatures' needs, All-Knowing.

وَلِلَّهِ الْمَشْرِقُ وَالْمَغْرِبُ فَأَيْنَمَا تُوَلُّوا فَثَمَّ وَجْهُ اللَّهِ إِنَّ اللَّهَ وَاسِعٌ عَلِيمٌ ﴿١١٥﴾

116. And they (Jews, Christians and pagans) say: Allâh has begotten a son (children or offspring).[1] Glory is to Him (Exalted is He above all that they associate with Him). Nay, to Him belongs all that is in the heavens and on earth, and all surrender with obedience (in worship) to Him.

وَقَالُوا اتَّخَذَ اللَّهُ وَلَدًا سُبْحَانَهُ بَل لَّهُ مَا فِى السَّمَاوَاتِ وَالْأَرْضِ كُلٌّ لَّهُ قَانِتُونَ ﴿١١٦﴾

117. The Originator of the heavens and the earth. When He decrees a matter, He only says to it : "Be!" — and it is.

بَدِيعُ السَّمَاوَاتِ وَالْأَرْضِ وَإِذَا قَضَى أَمْرًا فَإِنَّمَا يَقُولُ لَهُ كُن فَيَكُونُ ﴿١١٧﴾

118. And those who have no knowledge say: "Why does not Allâh

وَقَالَ الَّذِينَ لَا يَعْلَمُونَ لَوْلَا يُكَلِّمُنَا اللَّهُ أَوْ تَأْتِينَا آيَةٌ

---

[1] (V.2:116) "They (Jews, Christians and pagans) say: Allâh has begotten a son (children, offspring). Glory is to Him…Nay…."
Narrated Ibn 'Abbâs رضي الله عنهما: The Prophet صلى الله عليه وسلم said, "Allâh said, 'The son of Adam tells lies against Me though he has no right to do so, and he abuses Me though he has no right to do so. As for his telling lies against Me, he claims that I cannot re-create him as I created him before; and for his abusing Me: it is his statement that I have a son (or offspring) No! Glorified be Me! I am far from taking a wife or a son (or offspring).' " (Sahih Al-Bukhâri, Vol. 6, Hadîth No. 9).

speak to us (face to face) or why does not a sign come to us?" So said the people before them words of similar import. Their hearts are alike, We have indeed made plain the signs for people who believe with certainty.

كَذَٰلِكَ قَالَ الَّذِينَ مِن قَبْلِهِم مِّثْلَ قَوْلِهِمْ تَشَٰبَهَتْ قُلُوبُهُمْ قَدْ بَيَّنَّا الْآيَٰتِ لِقَوْمٍ يُوقِنُونَ ﴿١١٨﴾

119. Verily, We have sent you (O Muhammad صلى الله عليه وسلم) with the truth (Islâm), a bringer of glad tidings (for those who believe in what you brought, that they will enter Paradise) and a warner (for those who disbelieve in what you brought, that they will enter the Hell-fire).[1] And you will not be asked about the dwellers of the blazing Fire.

إِنَّا أَرْسَلْنَٰكَ بِالْحَقِّ بَشِيرًا وَنَذِيرًا وَلَا تُسْـَٔلُ عَنْ أَصْحَٰبِ الْجَحِيمِ ﴿١١٩﴾

120. Never will the Jews nor the Christians be pleased with you (O Muhammad صلى الله عليه وسلم) till you follow their religion. Say: "Verily, the Guidance of Allâh (i.e. Islâmic Monotheism) that is the (only) Guidance. And if you (O Muhammad صلى الله عليه وسلم) were to follow their (Jews and Christians) desires after what you have received of Knowledge (i.e. the Qur'ân), then you would have against Allâh neither any *Walî* (protector or guardian) nor any helper.

وَلَن تَرْضَىٰ عَنكَ الْيَهُودُ وَلَا النَّصَٰرَىٰ حَتَّىٰ تَتَّبِعَ مِلَّتَهُمْ قُلْ إِنَّ هُدَى اللَّهِ هُوَ الْهُدَىٰ وَلَئِنِ اتَّبَعْتَ أَهْوَاءَهُم بَعْدَ الَّذِي جَاءَكَ مِنَ الْعِلْمِ مَا لَكَ مِنَ اللَّهِ مِن وَلِيٍّ وَلَا نَصِيرٍ ﴿١٢٠﴾

121. Those (who embraced Islâm from Banî Israel) to whom We gave the Book [the Taurât (Torah)] [or those (Muhammad's companions) to whom We have given the Book (the Qur'ân)]

الَّذِينَ آتَيْنَٰهُمُ الْكِتَٰبَ يَتْلُونَهُ حَقَّ تِلَاوَتِهِ أُولَٰئِكَ يُؤْمِنُونَ بِهِ وَمَن يَكْفُرْ بِهِ فَأُولَٰئِكَ هُمُ الْخَٰسِرُونَ ﴿١٢١﴾

[1] (V.2:119) See the footnote of (V.3:85).

recite it (i.e. obey its orders and follow its teachings) as it should be recited (i.e. followed), they are the ones who believe therein. And whoso disbelieve in it (the Qur'ân), those are they who are the losers. (*Tafsir Al-Qurtubî*).

122. O Children of Israel! Remember My Favour which I bestowed upon you and that I preferred you to the '*Âlamîn* [mankind and jinn (of your time period, in the past)].

123. And fear the Day (of Judgement) when no person shall avail another, nor shall compensation be accepted from him, nor shall intercession be of use to him, nor shall they be helped.

124. And (remember) when the Lord of Ibrâhîm (Abraham) [i.e., Allâh] tried him with (certain) Commands,[1] which

---

[1] (V.2:124) It is said that those commands are many. Some of them are as follows:

(A) To invite mankind to the *Tauhîd* (Islamic Monotheism).

(B) To show mankind the *Manâsik* (See V.2:128).

(C) To practise the characteristics of *Al-Fitrah*:

Narrated Abu Hurairah رضي الله عنه : I heard the Prophet صلى الله عليه وسلم saying: "Five practices are characteristic of *Al-Fitrah*:

(1) Circumcision.

(2) Shaving the pubic hair.

(3) Cutting the moustaches short.

(4) Clipping the nails.

(5) and depilating the hair of the armpits.

(*Sahih Al-Bukhari*, Hadith No. 779, Vol.7)

Narrated Ibn Umar رضي الله عنهما : Allâh's Messenger صلى الله عليه وسلم said: "Cut the moustaches short and leave the beard (as it is)." (*Sahih Al-Bukhari*, Hadith No. 781, Vol.7)

he fulfilled. He (Allâh) said (to him), "Verily, I am going to make you an *Imâm* (a leader) for mankind (to follow you)." [Ibrâhîm (Abraham)] said, "And of my offspring (to make leaders)." (Allâh) said, "My Covenant (Prophethood) includes not *Zâlimûn* (polytheists and wrong-doers)."

125. And (remember) when We made the House (the *Ka'bah* at Makkah) a place of resort for mankind and a place of safety. And take you (people) the *Maqâm* (place) of Ibrâhîm (Abraham) [or the stone on which Ibrâhîm (Abraham) عليه السلام stood while he was building the *Ka'bah*] as a place of prayer (for some of your prayers, e.g. two *Rak'at* after the *Tawâf* of the *Ka'bah* at Makkah), and We commanded Ibrâhîm (Abraham) and Ismâ'îl (Ishmael) that they should purify My House (the *Ka'bah* at Makkah) for those who are circumambulating it, or staying (*I'tikâf*), or bowing or prostrating themselves (there, in prayer).

126. And (remember) when Ibrâhîm (Abraham) said, "My Lord, make this city (Makkah) a place of security and provide its people with fruits, such of them as believe in Allâh and the Last Day." He (Allâh) answered: "As for

---

(D) It is also mentioned that Ibrâhîm عليه السلام was put to test: (1) When he عليه السلام was thrown in the Fire. (2) When he عليه السلام was ordered to slaughter his son.

[*Tafsir Ibn Kathir*, Vol.I, pages 164-166]

him who disbelieves, I shall leave him in contentment for a while, then I shall compel him to the torment of the Fire, and worst indeed is that destination!"

127. And (remember) when Ibrâhîm (Abraham) and (his son) Ismâ'îl (Ishmael) were raising the foundations of the House (the Ka'bah at Makkah), (saying), "Our Lord! Accept (this service) from us. Verily, You are the All-Hearer, the All-Knower."[1]

128. "Our Lord! And make us submissive unto You and of our offspring a nation submissive unto You, and show us our *Manâsik*[2] (all the ceremonies of pilgrimage — Hajj and 'Umrah), and accept our repentance. Truly, You are the One Who accepts repentance, the Most Merciful.

129. "Our Lord! Send amongst them a Messenger of their own (and indeed Allâh answered their invocation by sending Muhammad صلى الله عليه وسلم), who shall recite unto them Your Verses and instruct them in the Book (this Qur'ân) and *Al-Hikmah* (full knowledge of the Islâmic laws and jurisprudence or wisdom or Prophethood), and purify them. Verily, You are the All-Mighty, the All-Wise."

---

[1] (V.2:127) See the footnote of (V.14:37).

[2] (V.2:128) *Manâsik*: i.e. *Ihrâm; Tawâf* of the *Ka'bah; Sa'y* of *As-Safâ* and *Al-Marwah*, stay at *'Arafât, Muzdalifah* and *Mîna; Ramy* of *Jamarât;* slaughtering of *Hady* (animal). For details see "The Book of *Hajj* and *'Umrah"*, *Sahih Al-Bukhâri,* Vol.2,3.

130. And who turns away from the religion of Ibrâhîm (Abraham) (i.e. Islâmic Monotheism) except him who befools himself? Truly, We chose him in this world and verily, in the Hereafter he will be among the righteous.

وَمَن يَرْغَبُ عَن مِّلَّةِ إِبْرَٰهِـۧمَ إِلَّا مَن سَفِهَ نَفْسَهُۥ وَلَقَدِ ٱصْطَفَيْنَٰهُ فِى ٱلدُّنْيَا وَإِنَّهُۥ فِى ٱلْءَاخِرَةِ لَمِنَ ٱلصَّٰلِحِينَ ۝

131. When his Lord said to him, "Submit (i.e. be a Muslim)!" He said, "I have submitted myself (as a Muslim) to the Lord of the 'Âlamîn (mankind, jinn and all that exists)."

إِذْ قَالَ لَهُۥ رَبُّهُۥٓ أَسْلِمْ قَالَ أَسْلَمْتُ لِرَبِّ ٱلْعَٰلَمِينَ ۝

132. And this (submission to Allâh, Islâm) was enjoined by Ibrâhîm (Abraham) upon his sons and by Ya'qûb (Jacob) (saying), "O my sons! Allâh has chosen for you the (true) religion, then die not except in the Faith of Islâm (as Muslims — Islâmic Monotheism)."

وَوَصَّىٰ بِهَآ إِبْرَٰهِـۧمُ بَنِيهِ وَيَعْقُوبُ يَٰبَنِىَّ إِنَّ ٱللَّهَ ٱصْطَفَىٰ لَكُمُ ٱلدِّينَ فَلَا تَمُوتُنَّ إِلَّا وَأَنتُم مُّسْلِمُونَ ۝

133. Or were you witnesses when death approached Ya'qûb (Jacob)? When he said unto his sons, "What will you worship after me?" They said, "We shall worship your Ilâh (God — Allâh) the Ilâh (God) of your fathers, Ibrâhîm (Abraham), Ismâ'îl (Ishmael), Ishâq (Isaac), One Ilâh (God), and to Him we submit (in Islâm)."

أَمْ كُنتُمْ شُهَدَآءَ إِذْ حَضَرَ يَعْقُوبَ ٱلْمَوْتُ إِذْ قَالَ لِبَنِيهِ مَا تَعْبُدُونَ مِنۢ بَعْدِى قَالُوا۟ نَعْبُدُ إِلَٰهَكَ وَإِلَٰهَ ءَابَآئِكَ إِبْرَٰهِـۧمَ وَإِسْمَٰعِيلَ وَإِسْحَٰقَ إِلَٰهًا وَٰحِدًا وَنَحْنُ لَهُۥ مُسْلِمُونَ ۝

134. That was a nation who has passed away. They shall receive the reward of what they earned and you of what you earn. And you will not be asked of what they used to do.

تِلْكَ أُمَّةٌ قَدْ خَلَتْ لَهَا مَا كَسَبَتْ وَلَكُم مَّا كَسَبْتُمْ وَلَا تُسْـَٔلُونَ عَمَّا كَانُوا۟ يَعْمَلُونَ ۝

135. And they say, "Be Jews or Christians, then you will be guided."

وَقَالُوا۟ كُونُوا۟ هُودًا

Say (to them O Muhammad صلى الله عليه
وسلم), "Nay, (we follow) only the religion
of Ibrâhîm (Abraham), *Hanîf* [Islâmic
Monotheism, i.e. to worship none but
Allâh (Alone)], and he was not of *Al-
Mushrikûn* (those who worshipped
others along with Allâh — see
V.2:105)."[1]

أَوَنَصَرَىٰ تَهۡتَدُواْ قُلۡ بَلۡ مِلَّةَ
إِبۡرَٰهِـۧمَ حَنِيفًا وَمَا كَانَ مِنَ
ٱلۡمُشۡرِكِينَ ١٣٥

---

[1] (V.2:135) Narration about Zaid bin 'Amr bin Nufail.

Narrated 'Abdullah bin 'Umar رضي الله عنهما: The Prophet صلى الله عليه وسلم
met Zaid bin 'Amr bin Nufail in the bottom of (the valley of)
Baldah before the descent of any Divine revelation to the Prophet
صلى الله عليه وسلم. A meal was presented to the Prophet صلى الله عليه وسلم but
he refused to eat from it. (Then it was presented to Zaid) who said,
"I do not eat anything which you slaughter on your *Nusub** in the
name of your idols. I eat only those (animals meat) on which
Allâh's Name has been mentioned at the time of (their)
slaughtering." Zaid bin 'Amr used to criticise the way Quraish used
to slaughter their animals and used to say, "Allâh has created the
sheep and He has sent the water for it from the sky, and He has
grown the grass for it from the earth; yet you slaughter it in others
than the Name of Allâh." He used to say so, for he rejected that
practice and considered it as something abominable.

Narrated Ibn 'Umar رضي الله عنهما: Zaid bin 'Amr bin Nufail went to
Shâm (the region comprising Syria, Lebanon, Palestine and Jordan),
enquiring about a true religion to follow. He met a Jewish religious
scholar and asked him about their religion. He said, "I intend to
embrace your religion, so tell me something about it." The Jew said,
"You will not embrace our religion unless you receive your share of
Allâh's Anger." Zaid said, "I do not run except from Allâh's Anger,
and I will never bear a bit of it if I have the power to avoid it. Can
you tell me of some other religion?" He said, "I do not know any
other religion except *Hanîf* (Islâmic Monotheism)." Zaid enquired,
"What is *Hanîf*?" He said, "*Hanîf* is the religion of (the Prophet)
Ibrâhîm [Abraham عليه السلام)], he was neither a Jew nor a Christian,
and he used to worship none but Allâh [(Alone) — Islâmic
Monotheism]." Then Zaid went out and met a Christian religious
scholar and told him the same (as before). The Christian said, "You

136. Say (O Muslims), "We believe in Allâh and that which has been sent down to us and that which has been sent down to Ibrâhîm (Abraham), Ismâ'îl (Ishmael), Ishâq (Isaac), Ya'qûb (Jacob), and to Al-Asbât [the offspring of the twelve sons of Ya'qûb (Jacob)], and that which has been given to Mûsâ (Moses) and 'Îsâ (Jesus), and that which has been given to the Prophets from their Lord. We make no distinction between any of them, and to Him we have submitted (in Islâm)."

قُولُوٓا۟ءَامَنَّا بِٱللَّهِ وَمَآ أُنزِلَ إِلَيْنَا وَمَآ أُنزِلَ إِلَىٰٓ إِبْرَٰهِـۧمَ وَإِسْمَٰعِيلَ وَإِسْحَٰقَ وَيَعْقُوبَ وَٱلْأَسْبَاطِ وَمَآ أُوتِىَ مُوسَىٰ وَعِيسَىٰ وَمَآ أُوتِىَ ٱلنَّبِيُّونَ مِن رَّبِّهِمْ لَا نُفَرِّقُ بَيْنَ أَحَدٍ مِّنْهُمْ وَنَحْنُ لَهُۥ مُسْلِمُونَ ۝

will not embrace our religion unless you get a share of Allâh's Curse." Zaid replied, "I do not run except from Allâh's Curse, and I will never bear any of Allâh's Curse and His Anger if I have the power to avoid them. Will you tell me of some other religion?" He replied, "I do not know any other religion except *Hanîf* (Islâmic Monotheism)." Zaid enquired, "What is *Hanîf?*" He replied "*Hanîf* is the religion of (the Prophet) Ibrâhîm [Abraham (عليه السلام)], he was neither a Jew nor a Christian, and he used to worship none but Allâh [(Alone) — Islâmic Monotheism]." When Zaid heard this statement about the religion(of) Ibrâhîm (Abraham), he left that place, and when he came out, he raised both his hands and said, "O Allâh! I make You my Witness that I am on the religion of Ibrâhîm (Abraham)".

Narrated Asmâ bint Abu Bakr رضي الله عنهما: I saw Zaid bin 'Amr bin Nufail standing with his back against the *Ka'bah* and saying, "O people of Quraish! By Allâh, none amongst you is on the religion of Ibrâhîm (Abraham) except me." She added: He (Zaid) used to preserve the lives of little girls; if somebody wanted to kill his daughter he would say to him, "Do not kill her for I will feed her on your behalf." So he would take her, and when she grew up nicely, he would say to her father, "Now if you will (wish), I will give her to you, and if you will (wish), I will feed her on your behalf." *(Sahih Al-Bukhâri,* Vol.5, *Hadîth* No.169).

* *Nusub:* See the glossary.

137. So if they believe in the like of that which you believe then they are rightly guided; but if they turn away, then they are only in opposition. So Allâh will suffice for you against them. And He is the All-Hearer, the All-Knower.

فَإِنْ ءَامَنُوا بِمِثْلِ مَا ءَامَنتُم بِهِ فَقَدِ اهْتَدَوا وَإِن تَوَلَّوْا فَإِنَّمَا هُمْ فِي شِقَاقٍ فَسَيَكْفِيكَهُمُ اللَّهُ وَهُوَ السَّمِيعُ الْعَلِيمُ ۝

138. [Our *Sibghah* (religion) is the *Sibghah* (religion) of Allâh (Islâm) and which *Sibghah* (religion) can be better than Allâh's? And we are His worshippers. [*Tafsir Ibn Kathîr.*]

صِبْغَةَ اللَّهِ وَمَنْ أَحْسَنُ مِنَ اللَّهِ صِبْغَةً وَنَحْنُ لَهُ عَبِدُونَ ۝

139. Say (O Muhammad صلى الله عليه وسلم to the Jews and Christians), "Dispute you with us about Allâh while He is our Lord and your Lord? And we are to be rewarded for our deeds and you for your deeds.[1] And we are sincere to

قُلْ أَتُحَآجُّونَنَا فِي اللَّهِ وَهُوَ رَبُّنَا وَرَبُّكُمْ وَلَنَا أَعْمَلُنَا وَلَكُمْ أَعْمَلُكُمْ وَنَحْنُ لَهُ مُخْلِصُونَ ۝

---

[1] (V.2:139):

a) Narrated Al-Mughîrah bin Shu'bah: The Prophet صلى الله عليه وسلم used to pray so much that his feet used to become edematous or swollen, and when he was asked as to why he prays so much, he would say: "Shall I not be a thankful slave (to Allâh)?" (*Sahih Al-Bukhâri*, Vol. 8, *Hadith* No. 478).

b) Narrated 'Aishah رضى الله عنها: The Prophet صلى الله عليه وسلم said, "Do good deeds properly, sincerely and moderately, and receive good news because one's good deeds will not make him enter Paradise." They asked, "Even you, O Allâh's Messenger?" He said, "Even I, unless and until Allâh protects or covers me with His pardon and His Mercy." (*Sahih Al-Bukhâri*, Vol. 8, *Hadith* No. 474).

c) Narrated Abu Hurairah رضى الله عنه: Allâh's Messenger صلى الله عليه وسلم said, "If I had gold equal to the mountain of Uhud, it would not please me that anything of it should remain with me after three nights (i.e., I would spend all of it in Allâh's Cause) except what I would keep for repaying debts." (*Sahih Al-Bukhâri*, Vol. 8, *Hadith* No. 452.

Him [in worship and obedience (i.e. we worship Him Alone and none else, and we obey His Orders)]."

140. Or say you that Ibrâhîm (Abraham), Ismâ'îl (Ishmael), Ishâq (Isaac), Ya'qûb (Jacob) and *Al-Asbât* [the offspring of the twelve sons of Ya'qûb (Jacob)] were Jews or Christians? Say, "Do you know better or does Allâh (know better... that they all were Muslims)? And who is more unjust than he who conceals the testimony [i.e. to believe in Prophet Muhammad صلى الله عليه وسلم when he comes, as is written in their Books. (See Verse 7:157)] he has from Allâh? And Allâh is not unaware of what you do."

141. That was a nation who has passed away. They shall receive the reward of what they earned, and you of what you earn. And you will not be asked of what they used to do.

---

d) Narrated 'Abdullâh رضي الله عنه: The Prophet صلى الله عليه وسلم said, "Who among you considers the wealth of his heirs dearer to him than his own wealth?" They replied, "O Allâh's Messenger! There is none among us but loves his own wealth more." The Prophet صلى الله عليه وسلم said, "So his wealth is whatever he spends (in Allâh's Cause) during his life (on good deeds) while the wealth of his heirs is whatever he leaves after his death." (*Sahih Al-Bukhâri*, Vol. 8, *Hadith* No. 449).

e) Narrated Abu Hurairah رضي الله عنه: The Prophet صلى الله عليه وسلم said, "While a dog was going round a well and was about to die of thirst, an Israeli prostitute saw it and took off her shoes and watered it. So Allâh forgave her because of that good deed." (*Sahih Al-Bukhâri*, Vol. 4, *Hadith* No. 673).

142. The fools (pagans, hypocrites, and Jews) among the people will say, "What has turned them (Muslims) from their *Qiblah* [prayer direction (towards Jerusalem)] to which they used to face in prayer." Say, (O Muhammad صلى الله عليه وسلم) "To Allâh belong both, east and the west. He guides whom He wills to the Straight Way."

143. Thus We have made you [true Muslims — real believers of Islâmic Monotheism, true followers of Prophet Muhammad صلى الله عليه وسلم and his *Sunnah* (legal ways)], a just (and the best) nation, that you be witnesses over mankind[1] and the Messenger (Muhammad صلى الله عليه وسلم) be a witness over you. And We made the *Qiblah* (prayer direction towards Jerusalem)

---

[1] (V.2:143) Narrated Abu Sa'îd Al-Khudrî رضي الله عنه: Allâh's Messenger صلى الله عليه وسلم said "Nûh (Noah) will be called on the Day of Resurrection and he will say, '*Labbaik* and *Sa'daik*, (I respond to Your Call and I am obedient to Your Orders) O my Lord! Allâh will say, 'Did you convey Our Message of Islâmic Monotheism?' Nûh (Noah) will say, 'Yes'. His nation will then be asked, 'Did he convey Our Message of Islâmic Monotheism to you?'They will say, 'No warner came to us.' Then Allâh will say [to Nûh (Noah)], 'Who will bear witness in your favour?' He will say, 'Muhammad (صلى الله عليه وسلم) and his followers.' So they (i.e., Muslims) will testify that he conveyed the Message — and the Messenger (Muhammad صلى الله عليه وسلم) will be a witness over you, and that is what is meant by the Statement of Allâh عز وجل: We made you [true Muslims — real believers of Islâmic Monotheism, true followers of Prophet Muhammad صلى الله عليه وسلم and his *Sunnah* (legal ways)] a just (and the best) nation that you be witnesses over mankind and the Messenger (Muhammad صلى الله عليه وسلم) will be a witness over you." (*Sahih Al-Bukhâri*, Vol.6, *Hadîth* No.14).

which you used to face, only to test those who followed the Messenger (Muhammad صلى الله عليه وسلم) from those who would turn on their heels (i.e. disobey the Messenger). Indeed it was great (heavy) except for those whom Allâh guided. And Allâh would never make your faith (prayers) to be lost (i.e. your prayers offered towards Jerusalem). Truly, Allâh is full of kindness, the Most Merciful towards mankind.

144. Verily, We have seen the turning of your (Muhammad's صلى الله عليه وسلم) face towards the heaven. Surely, We shall turn you to a *Qiblah* (prayer direction) that shall please you, so turn your face in the direction of *Al-Masjid-Al-Harâm* (at Makkah). And wheresoever you people are, turn your faces (in prayer) in that direction. Certainly, the people who were given the Scripture (i.e. Jews and the Christians) know well that, that (your turning towards the direction of the *Ka'bah* at Makkah in prayers) is the truth from their Lord. And Allâh is not unaware of what they do.

145. And even if you were to bring to the people of the Scripture (Jews and Christians) all the *Ayât* (proofs, evidences, verses, lessons, signs, revelations, etc.), they would not follow your *Qiblah* (prayer direction), nor are you going to follow their *Qiblah* (prayer direction). And they will not follow each other's *Qiblah* (prayer direction). Verily, if you follow their desires after that which you have received of knowledge (from Allâh), then indeed you will be one of the *Zâlimûn* (polytheists, wrong-doers).

146. Those to whom We gave the Scripture (Jews and Christians) recognise him (Muhammad صلى الله عليه وسلم or the *Ka'bah* at Makkah) as they recognise their sons. But verily, a party of them conceal the truth while they know it — [i.e. the qualities of Muhammad صلى الله عليه وسلم which are written in the Taurât (Torah) and the Injeel (Gospel)].[1]

147. (This is) the truth from your Lord. So be you not one of those who doubt.

148. For every nation there is a direction to which they face (in their prayers). So hasten towards all that is good. Wheresoever you may be, Allâh will bring you together (on the Day of Resurrection). Truly, Allâh is Able to do all things.

149. And from wheresoever you start forth (for prayers), turn your face in the direction of *Al-Masjid-Al-Harâm* (at Makkah), that is indeed the truth from your Lord. And Allâh is not unaware of what you do.

---

[1] (V.2:146) See the footnote of (V.2:76) (Qualities of Muhammad صلى الله عليه وسلم).

150. And from whithersoever you start forth (for prayers), turn your face in the direction of *Al-Masjid-Al-Harâm* (at Makkah), and wheresoever you are, turn your faces towards it (when you pray) so that men may have no argument against you except those of them that are wrong-doers, so fear them not, but fear Me! — And so that I may complete My Blessings on you and that you may be guided.

151. Similarly (to complete My Blessings on you), We have sent among you a Messenger (Muhammad صلى الله عليه وسلم) of your own, reciting to you Our Verses (the Qur'ân) and purifying you, and teaching you the Book (the Qur'ân) and the *Hikmah* (i.e. Sunnah, Islâmic laws and *Fiqh* — jurisprudence), and teaching you that which you used not to know.

152. Therefore remember Me (by praying, glorifying).[1] I will remember you, and be grateful to Me (for My countless Favours on you) and never be ungrateful to Me.

---

[1] (V.2:152)

a) See the footnote of (V.13:28).

b) Narrated Abu Hurairah رضي الله عنه The Prophet صلى الله عليه وسلم said, "Allâh عز وجل says, I am just as My slave thinks I am, (i.e. I am Able to do for him what he thinks I can do for him) and I am with him if he remembers Me. If he remembers Me in himself, I too, remember him in Myself; and if he remembers Me in a group of people, I remember him in a group that is better than them; and if he comes one span nearer to Me, I go one cubit nearer to him; and if he comes one cubit nearer to Me, I go a distance of two outstretched arms nearer to him; and if he comes to Me walking, I go to him running." (*Sahih Al-Bukhâri*, Vol.9, *Hadîth* No.502).

153. O you who believe! Seek help in patience and *As-Salât* (the prayer). Truly, Allâh is with *As-Sâbirûn* (the patient).

154. And say not of those who are killed in the way of Allâh, "They are dead." Nay, they are living, but you perceive (it) not.

155. And certainly, We shall test you with something of fear, hunger, loss of wealth, lives and fruits, but give glad tidings to *As-Sâbirîn* (the patient).

156. Who, when afflicted with calamity, say: "Truly, to Allâh we belong and truly, to Him we shall return."

157. They are those on whom are the *Salawât* (i.e. who are blessed and will be forgiven) from their Lord, and (they are those who) receive His Mercy, and it is they who are the guided ones.

158. Verily, *As-Safâ* and *Al-Marwah* (two mountains in Makkah) are of the Symbols of Allâh. So it is not a sin on him who performs *Hajj* or *'Umrah* (pilgrimage) of the House (the *Ka'bah* at Makkah) to perform the going (*Tawâf*) between them (*As-Safâ* and *Al-Marwah*)[1]. And whoever does good voluntarily, then verily, Allâh is All-Recogniser, All-Knower.

159. Verily, those who conceal the clear proofs, evidences and the

---

[1] (V.2:158) See the footnote of (V.14:37).

guidance, which We have sent down, after We have made it clear for the people in the Book, they are the ones cursed by Allâh and cursed by the cursers.

160. Except those who repent and do righteous deeds, and openly declare (the truth which they concealed). These, I will accept their repentance. And I am the One Who accepts repentance, the Most Merciful.

161. Verily, those who disbelieve, and die while they are disbelievers, it is they on whom is the Curse of Allâh and of the angels and of mankind, combined.

162. They will abide therein (under the curse in Hell), their punishment will neither be lightened, nor will they be reprieved.

163. And your *Ilâh* (God) is One *Ilâh* (God — Allâh), *Lâ ilâha illa Huwa* (there is none who has the right to be worshipped but He), the Most Gracious, the Most Merciful.

164. Verily, in the creation of the heavens and the earth, and in the alternation of night and day, and the ships which sail through the sea with that which is of use to mankind, and the water (rain) which Allâh sends down from the sky and makes the earth alive therewith after its death, and the moving (living) creatures of all kinds that He has scattered therein, and in the veering of winds and clouds which are held between the sky and the earth, are indeed *Ayât* (proofs, evidences, signs, etc.) for people of understanding.

165. And of mankind are some who take (for worship) others besides Allâh as rivals[1] (to Allâh). They love them as they love Allâh. But those who believe, love Allâh more (than anything else). If only, those who do wrong could see, when they will see the torment, that all power belongs to Allâh and that Allâh is Severe in punishment.

166. When those who were followed disown (declare themselves innocent of) those who followed (them), and they see the torment, then all their relations will be cut off from them.

167. And those who followed will say: "If only we had one more chance to return (to the worldly life), we would disown (declare ourselves as innocent from) them as they have disowned (declared themselves as innocent from) us." Thus Allâh will show them their deeds as regrets for them. And they will never get out of the Fire.

168. O mankind! Eat of that which is lawful and good on the earth, and

---

[1] (V.2:165) Narrated 'Abdullâh رضي الله عنه The Prophet صلى الله عليه وسلم said one statement and I said another. The Prophet صلى الله عليه وسلم said: "Whoever dies while still invoking anything other than Allâh as a rival to Allâh, will enter Hell (Fire)." And I said, "Whoever dies without invoking anything as a rival to Allâh, will enter Paradise." (*Sahîh Al-Bukhâri*, Vol.6, *Hadîth* NO.24).

follow not the footsteps of *Shaitân* (Satan). Verily, he is to you an open enemy.

169. He [*Shaitân* (Satan)] commands you only what is evil and *Fahshâ* (sinful), and that you should say against Allâh what you know not.

170. When it is said to them: "Follow what Allâh has sent down." They say: "Nay! We shall follow what we found our fathers following." (Would they do that!) even though their fathers did not understand anything nor were they guided?

171. And the example of those who disbelieve is as that of him who shouts to (flock of sheep) that hears nothing but calls and cries. (They are) deaf, dumb and blind. So they do not understand. (*Tafsîr Al-Qurtubi*).

172. O you who believe (in the Oneness of Allâh — Islâmic Monotheism)! Eat of the lawful things that We have provided you[1] with, and

---

[1] (V.2:172) Narrated An-Nu'mân bin Bashîr رضي الله عنه I heard Allâh's Messenger صلى الله عليه وسلم saying, "Both legal and illegal things are evident but in between them there are doubtful (unclear) things, and most of the people have no knowledge about them. So whoever saves himself from these unclear things, he saves his religion and his honour. And whoever indulges in these unclear things is like a shepherd who grazes (his animals) near the *Himâ* (private pasture) of someone else, and at any moment he is liable to get in it. (O people!) Beware! Every king has a *Himâ* and the *Himâ* of Allâh عز on the earth is His illegal (forbidden) things. Beware! There is a piece of flesh in the body if it becomes good (reformed), the whole

be grateful to Allâh, if it is indeed He Whom you worship.

173. He has forbidden you only the *Maitah* (dead animals), and blood, and the flesh of swine, and that which is slaughtered as a sacrifice for others than Allâh (or has been slaughtered for idols, on which Allâh's Name has not been mentioned while slaughtering). But if one is forced by necessity without willful disobedience nor transgressing due limits, then there is no sin on him. Truly, Allâh is Oft-Forgiving, Most Merciful.

174. Verily, those who conceal what Allâh has sent down of the Book, and purchase a small gain therewith (of worldly things), they eat into their bellies nothing but fire. Allâh will not speak to them on the Day of Resurrection, nor purify them, and theirs will be a painful torment.

175. Those are they who have purchased error at the price of Guidance, and torment at the price of Forgiveness. So how bold they are (for evil deeds which will push them) to the Fire.

176. That is because Allâh has sent down the Book (the Qur'ân) in truth. And verily, those who disputed as regards the Book are far away in opposition.

body becomes good, but if it gets spoilt, the whole body gets spoilt and that is the heart." (*Sahih Al-Bukhâri*, Vol.1, *Hadîth* No.49).

177. It is not *Al-Birr* (piety, righteousness, and every act of obedience to Allâh) that you turn your faces towards east and (or) west (in prayers); but *Al-Birr* is (the quality of) the one who believes in Allâh, the Last Day, the Angels, the Book, the Prophets[1] and gives his wealth, in spite of love for it, to the kinsfolk, to the orphans, and to *Al-Masâkîn* (the poor), and to the wayfarer, and to those who ask, and to set slaves free, performs *As-Salât* (*Iqâmat-as-Salât*), and gives the *Zakât*, and who fulfil their covenant when they make it, and who are patient in extreme poverty and ailment (disease) and at the time of fighting (during the battles). Such are the people of the truth and they are *Al-Muttaqûn* (the pious. See V.2:2).

178. O you who believe! *Al-Qisâs* (the Law of Equality in punishment) is prescribed for you in case of murder: the free for the free, the slave for the slave, and the female for the female. But if the killer is forgiven by the brother (or the relatives) of the killed against blood-money, then adhering to it with fairness and payment of the blood-money to the heir should be made in fairness. This is an alleviation and a mercy from your Lord. So after this whoever transgresses the limits (i.e. kills the killer after taking the blood-money), he shall have a painful torment.

---

[1] (V.2:177) See the footnote of (V.3:85).

179. And there is (a saving of) life for you in *Al-Qisâs* (the Law of Equality in punishment), O men of understanding, that you may become *Al-Muttaqûn* (the pious. See V.2:2).

وَلَكُمْ فِى ٱلْقِصَاصِ حَيَوٰةٌ يَٰٓأُوْلِى ٱلْأَلْبَٰبِ لَعَلَّكُمْ تَتَّقُونَ ۝

180. It is prescribed for you, when death approaches any of you, if he leaves wealth, that he makes a bequest to parents and next of kin, according to reasonable manners. (This is) a duty upon *Al-Muttaqûn* (the pious. See V.2:2).

كُتِبَ عَلَيْكُمْ إِذَا حَضَرَ أَحَدَكُمُ ٱلْمَوْتُ إِن تَرَكَ خَيْرًا ٱلْوَصِيَّةُ لِلْوَٰلِدَيْنِ وَٱلْأَقْرَبِينَ بِٱلْمَعْرُوفِ حَقًّا عَلَى ٱلْمُتَّقِينَ ۝

181. Then whoever changes the bequest after hearing it, the sin shall be on those who make the change. Truly, Allâh is All-Hearer, All-Knower.

فَمَنۢ بَدَّلَهُۥ بَعْدَمَا سَمِعَهُۥ فَإِنَّمَآ إِثْمُهُۥ عَلَى ٱلَّذِينَ يُبَدِّلُونَهُۥٓ إِنَّ ٱللَّهَ سَمِيعٌ عَلِيمٌ ۝

182. But he who fears from a testator some unjust act or wrong-doing, and thereupon he makes peace between the parties concerned, there shall be no sin on him. Certainly, Allâh is Oft-Forgiving, Most Merciful.

فَمَنْ خَافَ مِن مُّوصٍ جَنَفًا أَوْ إِثْمًا فَأَصْلَحَ بَيْنَهُمْ فَلَآ إِثْمَ عَلَيْهِ إِنَّ ٱللَّهَ غَفُورٌ رَّحِيمٌ ۝

183. O you who believe! Observing *As-Saum* (the fasting)[1] is prescribed for you as it was prescribed for those before you, that you may become *Al-Muttaqûn* (the pious. See V.2:2).

يَٰٓأَيُّهَا ٱلَّذِينَ ءَامَنُوا۟ كُتِبَ عَلَيْكُمُ ٱلصِّيَامُ كَمَا كُتِبَ عَلَى ٱلَّذِينَ مِن قَبْلِكُمْ لَعَلَّكُمْ تَتَّقُونَ ۝

184. [Observing *Saum* (fasts) for a fixed number of days, but if any of you is ill or on a journey, the same number (should be made up) from other days.

أَيَّامًا مَّعْدُودَٰتٍ فَمَن كَانَ مِنكُم مَّرِيضًا أَوْ عَلَىٰ سَفَرٍ فَعِدَّةٌ

---

[1] (V.2:183) *As-Saum* means fasting i.e. not to eat or drink or have sexual relations from the *Adhân* of the *Fajr* (early morning) prayer till the sunset.

And as for those who can fast with difficulty, (e.g. an old man), they have (a choice either to fast or) to feed a *Miskîn* (poor person) for every day. But whoever does good of his own accord, it is better for him. And that you fast is better for you if only you know.[1]

185. The month of Ramadan in which was revealed the Qur'ân, a guidance for mankind and clear proofs for the guidance and the criterion (between right and wrong). So whoever of you sights (the crescent on the first night of) the month (of Ramadan i.e. is present at his home,) he must observe *Saum* (fasts) that month, and whoever is ill or on a journey, the same number [of days which one did not observe *Saum* (fasts) must be made up] from other days. Allâh intends for you ease, and He does not want to make things difficult for you. (He wants that you) must complete the same number (of days), and that you must magnify Allâh [i.e. to say *Takbîr* (*Allâhu Akbar*; Allâh is the Most Great)] for having guided you so that you may be grateful to Him.[2]

---

[1] (V.2:184) The provision of this Verse has been abrogated by the next Verse: 185, with few exceptions, i.e., very old person, or pregnancy.

[2] (V.2:185)

(A) Narrated Talhah bin 'Ubaidullâh: A bedouin with unkempt hair came to Allâh's Messenger صلى الله عليه وسلم and said, "O Allâh's Messenger! Inform me what Allâh has made compulsory for me as regards the *Salât* (prayers)." He replied: "You have to offer perfectly the five compulsory *Salât* (prayers) in a day and night (24 hours), unless you want to pray *Nawâfil*." The bedouin further asked, "Inform me what Allâh has made compulsory for me as regards *Saum* (fasting)." He replied, "You have to fast during the whole month of Ramadân, unless you want to fast more as *Nawâfil*." The bedouin further asked, "Tell me how much *Zakât* Allâh has enjoined on me." The narrator added: Then, Allâh's Messenger صلى الله عليه وسلم informed him all about the Laws (i.e. fundamentals) of Islâm. The bedouin then said, "By Him Who has honoured you, I will neither perform any *Nawâfil* nor will I decrease what Allâh has enjoined on me." Allâh's Messenger صلى الله عليه وسلم said, "If he is saying the truth, he will succeed (or he will be granted Paradise)." (*Sahih Al-Bukhâri, Hadîth* No. 115, Vol. 3).

(B) Narrated Abu Huraihah رضي الله عنه : Allâh's Messenger صلى الله عليه وسلم said, "*As-Siyâm* (the fasting) is *Junnah* (protection or shield or a screen or a shelter from the Hell-fire*). So, the person observing *Saum* (fasting) should avoid sexual relation with his wife and should not behave foolishly and impudently, and if somebody fights with him or abuses him, he should say to him twice, 'I am fasting.'" The Prophet صلى الله عليه وسلم added, "By Him in Whose Hand my soul is, the smell coming out from the mouth of a fasting person is better with Allâh تعالى than the smell of musk. (Allâh says about the fasting person), 'He has left his food, drink and desires for My sake. The *Saum* (fast) is for Me.** So I will reward (the fasting person) for it and the reward of good deeds is multiplied ten times.' " (*Sahih Al-Bukhâri, Hadîth* No. 118, Vol. 3).

* See *Fath Al-Bârî*.

** Although all practices of worshipping are for Allâh, here Allâh تعالى singles out *Saum* (fasting), because fasting cannot be practiced for the sake of showing off, as nobody except Allâh can know whether one is fasting or not. Therefore, fasting is a pure performance that cannot be blemished with hypocrisy. (*Fath Al-Bârî*)

(C) Narrated Abu Huraihah رضي الله عنه : The Prophet صلى الله عليه وسلم said, "Whoever does not give up lying speech — false statements (i.e. telling lies) and acting on those (lies); and evil actions, then Allâh is not in need of his leaving his food and drink (i.e. Allâh will not accept his fasting*)". (*Sahih Al-Bukhâri, Hadîth* No. 127, Vol. 3).

* See *Fath Al-Bârî*.

186. And when My slaves ask you (O Muhammad صلى الله عليه وسلم) concerning Me, then (answer them), I am indeed near (to them by My Knowledge). I respond to the invocations of the supplicant when he calls on Me (without any mediator or intercessor). So let them obey Me and believe in Me, so that they may be led aright[1].

187. It is made lawful for you to have sexual relations with your wives on the night of As-Saum (the fasts). They are Libâs [i.e. body cover, or screen, or Sakan, (i.e. you enjoy the pleasure of living with her — in Verse 7:189) Tafsîr At-Tabarî] for you and you are the same for them. Allâh knows that you used to deceive yourselves, so He turned to you (accepted your repentance) and forgave you. So now have sexual relations with them and seek that which Allâh has ordained for

---

[1] (V.2:186) Narrated Abu Hurairah رضى الله عنه: Allâh's Messenger صلى الله عليه وسلم said, "Allâh said, 'I will declare war against him who shows hostility to a pious worshipper of Mine. And the most beloved things with which My slave comes nearer to Me, is what I have enjoined upon him; and My slave keeps on coming closer to Me through performing Nawâfil (praying or doing extra deeds besides what is obligatory) till I love him. Then I become his sense of hearing with which he hears, and his sense of sight with which he sees, and his hand with which he grips, and his leg with which he walks; and if he asks Me, I will give him; and if he asks My Protection (Refuge), I will protect him; (i.e. give him My Refuge), and I do not hesitate to do anything as I hesitate to take the soul of the believer, for he hates death, and I hate to disappoint him.'" (Sahih Al-Bukhârî, Vol.8, Hadîth No. 509).

you (offspring), and eat and drink until the white thread (light) of dawn appears to you distinct from the black thread (darkness of night), then complete your *Saum* (fast) till the nightfall. And do not have sexual relations with them (your wives) while you are in *I'tikâf* (i.e. confining oneself in a mosque for prayers and invocations leaving the worldly activities) in the mosques. These are the limits (set) by Allâh, so approach them not. Thus does Allâh make clear His *Ayât* (proofs, evidences, lessons, signs, revelations, verses, laws, legal and illegal things, Allâh's set limits, orders, etc.) to mankind that they may become *Al-Muttaqûn* (the pious. See V.2:2).

إِلَى ٱلَّيْلِ وَلَا تُبَـٰشِرُوهُنَّ وَأَنتُمْ عَـٰكِفُونَ فِى ٱلْمَسَـٰجِدِ تِلْكَ حُدُودُ ٱللَّهِ فَلَا تَقْرَبُوهَا كَذَٰلِكَ يُبَيِّنُ ٱللَّهُ ءَايَـٰتِهِۦ لِلنَّاسِ لَعَلَّهُمْ يَتَّقُونَ ۝

188. And eat up not one another's property unjustly (in any illegal way e.g. stealing, robbing, deceiving), nor give bribery to the rulers (judges before presenting your cases) that you may knowingly eat up a part of the property of others sinfully.

وَلَا تَأْكُلُوٓاْ أَمْوَٰلَكُم بَيْنَكُم بِٱلْبَٰطِلِ وَتُدْلُواْ بِهَآ إِلَى ٱلْحُكَّامِ لِتَأْكُلُواْ فَرِيقًا مِّنْ أَمْوَٰلِ ٱلنَّاسِ بِٱلْإِثْمِ وَأَنتُمْ تَعْلَمُونَ ۝

189. They ask you (O Muhammad صلى الله عليه وسلم) about the new moons. Say: These are signs to mark fixed periods of time for mankind and for the pilgrimage. It is not *Al-Birr* (piety, righteousness) that you enter the houses from the back but *Al-Birr* (is the quality of the one) who fears Allâh. So enter houses through their proper doors, and fear Allâh that you may be successful.

۞ يَسْـَٔلُونَكَ عَنِ ٱلْأَهِلَّةِ قُلْ هِىَ مَوَٰقِيتُ لِلنَّاسِ وَٱلْحَجِّ وَلَيْسَ ٱلْبِرُّ بِأَن تَأْتُواْ ٱلْبُيُوتَ مِن ظُهُورِهَا وَلَٰكِنَّ ٱلْبِرَّ مَنِ ٱتَّقَىٰ وَأْتُواْ ٱلْبُيُوتَ مِنْ أَبْوَٰبِهَا وَٱتَّقُواْ ٱللَّهَ لَعَلَّكُمْ تُفْلِحُونَ ۝

190. And fight in the Way of Allâh[1] those who fight you, but transgress not the limits. Truly, Allâh likes not the transgressors. [This Verse is the first one that was revealed in connection with *Jihâd*, but it was supplemented by another (9:36)].

وَقَٰتِلُوا۟ فِى سَبِيلِ ٱللَّهِ ٱلَّذِينَ يُقَٰتِلُونَكُمْ وَلَا تَعْتَدُوٓا۟ إِنَّ ٱللَّهَ لَا يُحِبُّ ٱلْمُعْتَدِينَ ۝

191. And kill them wherever you find them, and turn them out from where they have turned you out. And *Al-Fitnah* [2] is worse than killing. And fight not with them at *Al-Masjid-Al-Harâm* (the sanctuary at

وَٱقْتُلُوهُمْ حَيْثُ ثَقِفْتُمُوهُمْ وَأَخْرِجُوهُم مِّنْ حَيْثُ أَخْرَجُوكُمْ وَٱلْفِتْنَةُ أَشَدُّ مِنَ ٱلْقَتْلِ وَلَا

---

[1] (V.2:190) *Al-Jihâd* (holy fighting) in Allâh's Cause (with full force of numbers and weaponry) is given the utmost importance in Islâm and is one of its pillars (on which it stands). By *Jihâd* Islâm is established, Allâh's Word is made superior, (His Word being *Lâ ilaha illallâh* which means none has the right to be worshipped but Allâh), and His religion (Islâm) is propagated. By abandoning *Jihâd* (may Allâh protect us from that) Islâm is destroyed and the Muslims fall into an inferior position; their honour is lost, their lands are stolen, their rule and authority vanish. *Jihâd* is an obligatory duty in Islâm on every Muslim, and he who tries to escape from this duty, or does not in his innermost heart wish to fulfil this duty, dies with one of the qualities of a hypocrite.

Narrated 'Abdullâh bin Mas'ûd رضى الله عنه: I asked Allâh's Messenger صلى الله عليه وسلم, "O Allâh's Messenger! What is the best deed?" He replied, "To offer the *Salât* (prayers) at their early fixed stated times." I asked, "What is next in goodness?" He replied, "To be good and dutiful to your parents." I further asked, "What is next in goodness?" He replied, "To participate in *Jihâd* in Allâh's Cause." I did not ask Allâh's Messenger صلى الله عليه وسلم anymore and if I had asked him more, he would have told me more. (*Sahih Al-Bukhâri*, Vol.4, *Hadîth* No.41).

[2] (V.2:191) *Al-Fitnah*: (polytheism, to disbelieve after one has believed in Allâh, or a calamity or an affliction).

Makkah),[1] unless they (first) fight you there. But if they attack you, then kill them. Such is the recompense of the disbelievers.

192. But if they cease, then Allâh is Oft-Forgiving, Most Merciful.

193. And fight them until there is no more *Fitnah* (disbelief and worshipping of others along with Allâh) and (all and every kind of) worship is for Allâh (Alone).[2] But if they cease, let there be

نُقَتِّلُوكُمْ عِندَ ٱلْمَسْجِدِ ٱلْحَرَامِ حَتَّىٰ يُقَٰتِلُوكُمْ فِيهِ فَإِن قَٰتَلُوكُمْ فَٱقْتُلُوهُمْ كَذَٰلِكَ جَزَآءُ ٱلْكَٰفِرِينَ ۝ فَإِنِ ٱنتَهَوْا فَإِنَّ ٱللَّهَ غَفُورٌ رَّحِيمٌ ۝ وَقَٰتِلُوهُمْ حَتَّىٰ لَا تَكُونَ فِتْنَةٌ وَيَكُونَ ٱلدِّينُ لِلَّهِ فَإِنِ ٱنتَهَوْا فَلَا عُدْوَٰنَ إِلَّا عَلَى ٱلظَّٰلِمِينَ ۝

---

[1] (V.2:191) Narrated Abu Bakrah رضي الله عنه: The Prophet صلى الله عليه وسلم delivered to us a *Khutbah* (religious talk) on the day of *Nahr* (10th of *Dhul Hijjah*). He said, "Do you know what is the day today?" We said, "Allâh and His Messenger know better." He remained silent till we thought that he might give that day another name. He said, "Isn't it the day of *Nahr*?" We said, "It is." He further asked, "Which month is this?" We said, "Allâh and His Messenger know better." He remained silent till we thought that he might give it another name. He then said, "Isn't it the month of *Dhul-Hijjah*?" We replied: "Yes, it is." He further asked, "What town is this?" We replied, "Allâh and His Messenger know it better." He remained silent till we thought that he might give it another name. He then said, "Isn't it the forbidden (sacred) town (of Makkah)?" We said, "Yes, it is." He said, "No doubt, your blood and your properties are sacred to one another like the sanctity of this day of yours, in this month of yours, in this town of yours, till the day you meet your Lord. No doubt! Haven't I conveyed Allâh's Message to you?" We said, "Yes." He said, "O Allâh! Be witness. So it is incumbent upon those who are present to convey it (this information) to those who are absent because the informed one might comprehend it (what I have said) better than the present audience, who will convey it to him. Beware! Do not renegate (as) disbelievers after me by striking the necks (cutting the throats) of one another." (*Sahih Al-Bukhâri*, Vol.2, *Hadîth* No.797).

[2] (V.2:193)

(A) Narrated Ibn 'Umar رضي الله عنهما: Allâh's Messenger صلى الله عليه وسلم said, "I have been ordered (by Allâh) to fight against the people till

no transgression except against *Az-Zâlimûn* (the polytheists, and wrong-doers)

194. The sacred month is for the sacred month, and for the prohibited things, there is the Law of Equality (*Qisâs*). Then whoever transgresses the prohibition against you, you transgress likewise against him. And fear Allâh, and know that Allâh is with *Al-Muttaqûn* (the pious. See V.2:2).

الشَّهْرُ الْحَرَامُ بِالشَّهْرِ الْحَرَامِ وَالْحُرُمَاتُ قِصَاصٌ فَمَنِ اعْتَدَى عَلَيْكُمْ فَاعْتَدُوا عَلَيْهِ بِمِثْلِ مَا اعْتَدَى عَلَيْكُمْ وَاتَّقُوا اللَّهَ وَاعْلَمُوا أَنَّ اللَّهَ مَعَ الْمُتَّقِينَ ۞

195. And spend in the Cause of Allâh (i.e. *Jihâd* of all kinds) and do not throw yourselves into destruction (by not spending your wealth in the Cause of Allâh), and do good. Truly, Allâh loves *Al-Muhsinûn* [1] (the good-doers).

وَأَنفِقُوا فِي سَبِيلِ اللَّهِ وَلَا تُلْقُوا بِأَيْدِيكُمْ إِلَى التَّهْلُكَةِ وَأَحْسِنُوا إِنَّ اللَّهَ يُحِبُّ الْمُحْسِنِينَ ۞

196. And perform properly (i.e. all the ceremonies according to the ways of Prophet Muhammad صلى الله عليه وسلم), the *Hajj* and 'Umrah (i.e. the pilgrimage to Makkah) for Allâh. But if you are prevented (from completing them), sacrifice a *Hady* (animal, i.e. a sheep, a cow, or a camel) such as you can afford, and do not shave your heads

وَأَتِمُّوا الْحَجَّ وَالْعُمْرَةَ لِلَّهِ فَإِنْ أُحْصِرْتُمْ فَمَا اسْتَيْسَرَ مِنَ الْهَدْيِ وَلَا تَحْلِقُوا رُءُوسَكُمْ حَتَّى يَبْلُغَ الْهَدْيُ مَحِلَّهُ فَمَن كَانَ مِنكُم مَّرِيضًا أَوْ بِهِ أَذًى مِّن رَّأْسِهِ فَفِدْيَةٌ

---

they testify that *Lâ ilâha illallâh wa Anna Muhammmad-ur-Rasûl Allâh* (none has the right to be worshipped but Allâh عز وجل and that Muhammad صلى الله عليه وسلم is the Messenger of Allâh), and perform *As-Salât* (*Iqâmat-as-Salât*) and give *Zakât*, so if they perform all that, then they save their lives, and properties from me except for Islâmic laws, and their reckoning (accounts) will be with (done by) Allâh." (*Sahîh Al-Bukhâri*, Vol.1, *Hadîth* No.24).

(B) See (V.8:39) and its footnote.

[1] (V.2:195) See (V.2:112).

until the *Hady* reaches the place of sacrifice. And whosoever of you is ill or has an ailment in his scalp (necessitating shaving), he must pay a *Fidyah* (ransom) of either observing *Saum* (fasts) (three days) or giving *Sadaqah* (charity — feeding six poor persons) or offering sacrifice (one sheep). Then if you are in safety and whosoever performs the *'Umrah* in the months of *Hajj*, before (performing) the *Hajj*, (i.e. *Hajj-at-Tamattu'* and *Al-Qirân*), he must slaughter a *Hady* such as he can afford, but if he cannot afford it, he should observe *Saum* (fasts) three days during the *Hajj* and seven days after his return (to his home), making ten days in all. This is for him whose family is not present at *Al-Masjid-Al-Harâm* (i.e. non-resident of Makkah). And fear Allâh much and know that Allâh is Severe in punishment.[1]

---

[1] (V.2:196) Islâm demolishes all the previous evil deeds and so does migration (for Allâh's sake) and *Hajj* (pilgrimage to Makkah). [*Al-Lu'lu' wal Marjân*, Vol. 1, Ch.52, P.205]. The obligation of performing *'Umrah* and its superiority. Ibn 'Umar رضي الله عنهما said, "*Hajj* and *'Umrah* are obligatory for everybody." And Ibn 'Abbâs رضي الله عنهما said, "*'Umrah* is mentioned in conjunction with *Hajj* in the Book of Allâh عزّ وجلّ : 'And perform properly *Hajj* and *'Umrah* for Allâh.' " (2:196).

Narrated Abu Hurairah رضي الله عنه : Allâh's Messenger صلى الله عليه وسلم said, "(The performance of) *'Umrah* is an expiation for the sins committed (between it and the previous one). And the reward of *Hajj Mabrûr* (the one accepted by Allâh) is nothing except Paradise." (*Sahih Al-Bukhâri*, Vol.3, *Hadîth* No.1).

197. The *Hajj* (pilgrimage) is (in) the well-known (lunar year) months (i.e. the 10th month, the 11th month and the first ten days of the 12th month of the Islâmic calendar, i.e. two months and en days). So whosoever intends to erform *Hajj*[1] (therein by assuming *Ihrâm*), then he should not have sexual relations (with his wife), nor commit sin, nor dispute unjustly during the *Hajj*. And whatever good you do, (be sure) Allâh knows it. And take a provision (with you) for the journey, but the best provision is *At-Taqwa* (piety, righteousness). So fear Me, O men of understanding!

أَلْحَجُّ أَشْهُرٌ مَّعْلُومَتٌ فَمَن فَرَضَ فِيهِنَّ ٱلْحَجَّ فَلَا رَفَثَ وَلَا فُسُوقَ وَلَا جِدَالَ فِى ٱلْحَجِّ وَمَا تَفْعَلُواْ مِنْ خَيْرٍ يَعْلَمْهُ ٱللَّهُ وَتَزَوَّدُواْ فَإِنَّ خَيْرَ ٱلزَّادِ ٱلتَّقْوَىٰ وَٱتَّقُونِ يَٰٓأُوْلِى ٱلْأَلْبَٰبِ ۝

198. There is no sin on you if you seek the Bounty of your Lord (during pilgrimage by trading). Then when you leave *'Arafât*,[2] remember Allâh (by

لَيْسَ عَلَيْكُمْ جُنَاحٌ أَن تَبْتَغُواْ فَضْلًا مِّن رَّبِّكُمْ

---

[1] (V.2:197) What is said regarding *Hajj At-Tamattu'*, *Hajj Al-Qirân*, and *Hajj Al-Ifrâd*. And whoever has not brought a *Hady* with him, he should finish the *Ihrâm* of *Hajj*, and make it as *'Umrah* (and then assume another *Ihrâm* for *Hajj* from Makkah). There are three ways of performing *Hajj* — as follows:

a) *Hajj At-Tamattu'*: It means that you have no *Hady* with you and you assume *Ihrâm* only for *'Umrah* first and after *'Umrah* you finish your *Ihrâm* and assume another *Ihrâm* for performing *Hajj*, from Makkah, but you have to slaughter a *Hady*.

b) *Hajj Al-Qirân*: It means that one should have a *Hady* with him and should perform *'Umrah* and then *Hajj* with the same state of *Ihrâm*.

c) *Hajj Al-Ifrâd*: It means that one assumes *Ihrâm* with the intention of performing *Hajj* only and does not perform *'Umrah*.

[2] (V.2:198) *'Arafât*: a well-known place near Makkah where pilgrims have to spend the 9th day of *Dhul-Hijjah*.

glorifying His Praises, i.e. prayers and invocations) at the *Mash'ar-il-Harâm.*[1] And remember Him (by invoking Allâh for all good) as He has guided you, and verily, you were, before, of those who were astray.

199. Then depart from the place whence all the people depart and ask Allâh for His Forgiveness. Truly, Allâh is Oft-Forgiving, Most-Merciful.

200. So when you have accomplished your *Manâsik,*[2] remember Allâh as you remember your forefathers or with a far more remembrance. But of mankind there are some who say: "Our Lord! Give us (Your Bounties) in this world!" and for such there will be no portion in the Hereafter.

201. And of them there are some who say: "Our Lord! Give us in this world that which is good and in the Hereafter that which is good, and save us from the torment of the Fire!"

202. For them there will be alloted a share for what they have earned. And Allâh is Swift at reckoning.

---

[1] (V.2:198) *Al-Mash'ar-ul-Harâm,* i.e. *Muzdalifah* a well-known place near Makkah, where pilgrims have to stop and stay for the whole night of the 10th of *Dhul-Hijjah,* or a great part of it.

[2] (V.2:200) *Manâsik:* i.e. *Ihrâm, Tawâf* of the *Ka'bah* and *As-Safâ* and *Al-Marwah,* stay at *'Arafât, Muzdalifah* and *Mina, Ramy* of *Jamarât,* (stoning of the specified pillars in *Mina*) slaughtering of *Hady* (animal).

203. And remember Allâh during the appointed Days.[1] But whosoever hastens to leave in two days, there is no sin on him and whosoever stays on, there is no sin on him, if his aim is to do good and obey Allâh (fear Him), and know that you will surely, be gathered unto Him.

204. And of mankind there is he whose speech may please you (O Muhammad صلى الله عليه وسلم), in this worldly life, and he calls Allâh to witness as to that which is in his heart, yet he is the most quarrelsome of the opponents.[2]

205. And when he turns away (from you O Muhammad صلى الله عليه وسلم), his effort in the land is to make mischief therein and to destroy the crops and the cattle, and Allâh likes not mischief.

---

[1] (V.2:203) These are the three days of staying at Mîna during the Hajj; 11th, 12th and 13th days of the month of Dhul-Hijjah, by saying Allâhu Akbar (Allâh is the Most Great) much, and while slaughtering Hady (animals) and during the Ramy of Jamarât.

[2] (V.2:204)

(A) Narrated 'Aishah رضي الله عنها : The Prophet صلى الله عليه وسلم said, "The most hated person to Allâh is the one who is most quarrelsome of the opponents." (Sahih Al-Bukhâri, Vol.3, Hadîth No.637).

(B) Narrated Abu Umamah رضي الله عنه : Allâh's Messenger صلى الله عليه وسلم said: "(a) I guarantee a home in Paradise for a person who gives up arguments and disputes even if he is on the truth. (b) And [I (also) guarantee] a home in the middle of Paradise for a person who gives up lying (false statements) even while joking. (c) And [I (also) guarantee] a home in the highest part of Paradise for a person who has a high standard of character."

(This Hadîth is quoted by Abu Dâwûd, At-Tirmidhi, Nasa'i and Ibn Majah).

206. And when it is said to him, "Fear Allâh", he is led by arrogance to (more) crime. So enough for him is Hell, and worst indeed is that place to rest!

وَإِذَا قِيلَ لَهُ ٱتَّقِ ٱللَّهَ أَخَذَتْهُ ٱلْعِزَّةُ بِٱلْإِثْمِ فَحَسْبُهُ جَهَنَّمُ وَلَبِئْسَ ٱلْمِهَادُ ۝

207. And of mankind is he who would sell himself, seeking the Pleasure of Allâh. And Allâh is full of kindness to (His) slaves.

وَمِنَ ٱلنَّاسِ مَن يَشْرِى نَفْسَهُ ٱبْتِغَآءَ مَرْضَاتِ ٱللَّهِ وَٱللَّهُ رَءُوفُ بِٱلْعِبَادِ ۝

208. O you who believe! Enter perfectly in Islâm (by obeying all the rules and regulations of the Islâmic religion) and follow not the footsteps of *Shaitân* (Satan). Verily, He is to you a plain enemy.

يَـٰٓأَيُّهَا ٱلَّذِينَ ءَامَنُوا ٱدْخُلُوا فِى ٱلسِّلْمِ كَآفَّةً وَلَا تَتَّبِعُوا خُطُوَٰتِ ٱلشَّيْطَـٰنِ إِنَّهُ لَكُمْ عَدُوٌّ مُّبِينٌ ۝

209. Then if you slide back after the clear signs (Prophet Muhammad صلى الله عليه وسلم and this Qur'ân, and Islâm) have come to you, then know that Allâh is All-Mighty, All-Wise.

فَإِن زَلَلْتُم مِّنۢ بَعْدِ مَا جَآءَتْكُمُ ٱلْبَيِّنَـٰتُ فَٱعْلَمُوٓا أَنَّ ٱللَّهَ عَزِيزٌ حَكِيمٌ ۝

210. Do they then wait for anything other than that Allâh should come to them in the shadows of the clouds and the angels? (Then) the case would be already judged. And to Allâh return all matters (for decision).

هَلْ يَنظُرُونَ إِلَّآ أَن يَأْتِيَهُمُ ٱللَّهُ فِى ظُلَلٍ مِّنَ ٱلْغَمَامِ وَٱلْمَلَـٰٓئِكَةُ وَقُضِىَ ٱلْأَمْرُ وَإِلَى ٱللَّهِ تُرْجَعُ ٱلْأُمُورُ ۝

211. Ask the Children of Israel how many clear *Ayât* (proofs, evidences, verses, lessons, signs, revelations, etc.) We gave them. And whoever changes Allâh's Favour after it had come to him, [e.g. renounces the religion of Allâh (Islâm) and accepts *Kufr* (disbelief)] then surely, Allâh is Severe in punishment.

سَلْ بَنِىٓ إِسْرَٰٓءِيلَ كَمْ ءَاتَيْنَـٰهُم مِّنْ ءَايَةٍ بَيِّنَةٍ وَمَن يُبَدِّلْ نِعْمَةَ ٱللَّهِ مِنۢ بَعْدِ مَا جَآءَتْهُ فَإِنَّ ٱللَّهَ شَدِيدُ ٱلْعِقَابِ ۝

212. Beautified is the life of this world for those who disbelieve, and

زُيِّنَ لِلَّذِينَ كَفَرُوا ٱلْحَيَوٰةُ ٱلدُّنْيَا

they mock at those who believe. But those who obey Allâh's Orders and keep away from what He has forbidden, will be above them on the Day of Resurrection. And Allâh gives (of His Bounty, Blessings, Favours, and Honours on the Day of Resurrection) to whom He wills without limit.

213. Mankind were one community and Allâh sent Prophets with glad tidings and warnings, and with them He sent down the Scripture in truth to judge between people in matters wherein they differed. And only those to whom (the Scripture) was given differed concerning it after clear proofs had come unto them through hatred, one to another. Then Allâh by His Leave guided those who believed to the truth of that wherein they differed. And Allâh guides whom He wills to the Straight Path.

214. Or think you that you will enter Paradise without such (trials) as came to those who passed away before you? They were afflicted with severe poverty and ailments and were so shaken that even the Messenger and those who believed along with him said, "When (will come) the Help of Allâh?" Yes! Certainly, the Help of Allâh is near!

215. They ask you (O Muhammad صلى الله عليه وسلم) what they should spend. Say: Whatever you spend of good must be for parents and kindred and orphans and *Al-Masâkîn* (the poor) and the wayfarers, and whatever you do of good deeds, truly, Allâh knows it well.

216. *Jihâd*[1] (holy fighting in Allâh's cause) is ordained for you (Muslims) though you dislike it, and it may be that you dislike a thing which is good for you and that you like a thing which is bad for you. Allâh knows but you do not know.

وَأَبْنِ السَّبِيلِ وَمَا تَفْعَلُوا مِنْ خَيْرٍ فَإِنَّ اللَّهَ بِهِ عَلِيمٌ ۝

كُتِبَ عَلَيْكُمُ الْقِتَالُ وَهُوَ كُرْهٌ لَّكُمْ وَعَسَىٰ أَن تَكْرَهُوا شَيْئًا وَهُوَ خَيْرٌ لَّكُمْ وَعَسَىٰ أَن تُحِبُّوا شَيْئًا وَهُوَ شَرٌّ لَّكُمْ وَاللَّهُ يَعْلَمُ وَأَنتُمْ لَا تَعْلَمُونَ ۝

217. They ask you concerning fighting in the Sacred Months (i.e. 1st, 7th, 11th and 12th months of the Islâmic calendar). Say, "Fighting therein is a great (transgression)[2] but a greater (transgression) with Allâh is to prevent mankind from following the Way of Allâh, to disbelieve in Him, to prevent access to *Al-Masjid-Al-Harâm* (at Makkah), and to drive out its inhabitants, and *Al-Fitnah*[3] is worse than killing. And they will never cease fighting you until they turn you back from your religion (Islâmic Monotheism) if they can. And whosoever of you turns back from his religion and dies as a disbeliever, then his deeds will be lost in this life and in the Hereafter, and they will be the

يَسْأَلُونَكَ عَنِ الشَّهْرِ الْحَرَامِ قِتَالٍ فِيهِ قُلْ قِتَالٌ فِيهِ كَبِيرٌ وَصَدٌّ عَن سَبِيلِ اللَّهِ وَكُفْرٌ بِهِ وَالْمَسْجِدِ الْحَرَامِ وَإِخْرَاجُ أَهْلِهِ مِنْهُ أَكْبَرُ عِندَ اللَّهِ وَالْفِتْنَةُ أَكْبَرُ مِنَ الْقَتْلِ وَلَا يَزَالُونَ يُقَاتِلُونَكُمْ حَتَّىٰ يَرُدُّوكُمْ عَن دِينِكُمْ إِنِ اسْتَطَاعُوا وَمَن يَرْتَدِدْ مِنكُمْ عَن دِينِهِ فَيَمُتْ وَهُوَ كَافِرٌ فَأُولَٰئِكَ حَبِطَتْ أَعْمَالُهُمْ فِي الدُّنْيَا وَالْآخِرَةِ وَأُولَٰئِكَ أَصْحَابُ النَّارِ هُمْ فِيهَا خَالِدُونَ ۝

---

[1] (V.2:216) See the footnote of (V.2:190).

[2] (V.2:217) The provision of this Verse has been abrogated by Verse 9:36. *Jihâd* cf., (V.2:216).

[3] (V.2:217) *Fitnah*: (polytheism and to disbelieve after one has believed in Allâh, or a trial or a calamity or an affliction or to set up rivals in worship with Allâh).

dwellers of the Fire. They will abide therein forever."

إِنَّ ٱلَّذِينَ ءَامَنُواْ وَٱلَّذِينَ

218. Verily, those who have believed, and those who have emigrated (for Allâh's religion) and have striven hard in the Way of Allâh, all these hope for Allâh's Mercy. And Allâh is Oft-Forgiving, Most-Merciful.

هَاجَرُواْ وَجَٰهَدُواْ فِى سَبِيلِ ٱللَّهِ أُوْلَٰٓئِكَ يَرْجُونَ رَحْمَتَ ٱللَّهِ وَٱللَّهُ غَفُورٌ رَّحِيمٌ ﴿٢١٨﴾

219. They ask you (O Muhammad صلى الله عليه وسلم) concerning alcoholic drink and gambling[1]. Say: "In them is a great sin,

۞ يَسْـَٔلُونَكَ عَنِ ٱلْخَمْرِ وَٱلْمَيْسِرِ قُلْ فِيهِمَآ إِثْمٌ كَبِيرٌ

---

[1] (V.2:219):

a) Narrated Abu Hurairah رضي الله عنه: Allâh's Messenger صلى الله عليه وسلم said, "Whoever takes an oath in which he (forgetfully) mentions *Lat* and *'Uzza* (i.e. two idols of Arab pagans) should say: *"La ilaha illallâh"* (none has the right to be worshipped but Allâh), and whoever says to his companion, 'Come along, let us gamble,' must give alms (as an expiation)." (*Sahih Al-Bukhâri*, Vol.6, *Hadîth* No.383).

b) Narrated Ibn 'Umar رضي الله عنهما: Allâh's Messenger صلى الله عليه وسلم said, "Whoever drinks alcoholic drinks in this world and does not repent (i.e. stops drinking alcoholic drinks, and begs Allâh to forgive him before his death) will be deprived of it in the Hereafter." (*Sahih Al-Bukhâri*, Vol.7, *Hadîth* No.481).

c) Narrated Anas رضي الله عنه: I heard from Allâh's Messenger صلى الله عليه وسلم a narration which none other than I will narrate to you. The Prophet صلى الله عليه وسلم said, "From among the portents of the Hour are the following: General ignorance (in religious affairs) will prevail, (religious) knowledge will decrease, illegal sexual intercourse will prevail, alcoholic drinks will be drunk (in abundance), men will decrease and women will increase so much so that for every fifty women there will be one man to look after them." (*Sahih Al-Bukhâri*, Vol. 7, *Hadîth* No. 483).

d) Narrated Abu Hurairah رضي الله عنه: The Prophet صلى الله عليه وسلم said, "An adulterer, at the time he is committing illegal sexual intercourse is not a believer; and a person, at the time of drinking an

and (some) benefits for men, but the sin of them is greater than their benefit." And they ask you what they ought to spend. Say: "That which is beyond your needs." Thus Allâh makes clear to you His Laws in order that you may give thought.[1]"

220. In (to) this worldly life and in the Hereafter. And they ask you concerning orphans. Say: "The best thing is to work honestly in their property, and if you mix your affairs with theirs, then they are your brothers. And Allâh knows him who means mischief (e.g. to swallow their property) from him who means good (e.g. to save their property). And if Allâh had wished, He could have put you into difficulties. Truly, Allâh is All-Mighty, All-Wise."

221. And do not marry Al-Mushrikât (idolatresses) till they believe (worship Allâh Alone). And indeed a slave woman who believes is better than a (free) Mushrikah (idolatress), even

وَمَنَٰفِعُ لِلنَّاسِ وَإِثْمُهُمَآ أَكْبَرُ مِن نَّفْعِهِمَا وَيَسْـَٔلُونَكَ مَاذَا يُنفِقُونَ قُلِ ٱلْعَفْوَ كَذَٰلِكَ يُبَيِّنُ ٱللَّهُ لَكُمُ ٱلْـَٔايَٰتِ لَعَلَّكُمْ تَتَفَكَّرُونَ ۝

فِى ٱلدُّنْيَا وَٱلْـَٔاخِرَةِ وَيَسْـَٔلُونَكَ عَنِ ٱلْيَتَٰمَىٰ قُلْ إِصْلَاحٌ لَّهُمْ خَيْرٌ وَإِن تُخَالِطُوهُمْ فَإِخْوَٰنُكُمْ وَٱللَّهُ يَعْلَمُ ٱلْمُفْسِدَ مِنَ ٱلْمُصْلِحِ وَلَوْ شَآءَ ٱللَّهُ لَأَعْنَتَكُمْ إِنَّ ٱللَّهَ عَزِيزٌ حَكِيمٌ ۝

وَلَا تَنكِحُوا۟ ٱلْمُشْرِكَٰتِ حَتَّىٰ يُؤْمِنَّ وَلَأَمَةٌ مُّؤْمِنَةٌ خَيْرٌ مِّن مُّشْرِكَةٍ وَلَوْ أَعْجَبَتْكُمْ وَ

---

alcoholic drink is not a believer; and a thief, at the time of stealing is not a believer."

Ibn Shihâb said: 'Abdul Mâlik bin Abî-Bakr bin 'Abdur-Rahmân bin Al-Hârith bin Hishâm told me that Abu Bakr used to narrate that narration to him on the authority of Abu Hurairah. He used to add that Abu Bakr used to mention, besides the above cases: "And he who robs (takes illegally something by force) while the people are looking at him, is not a believer at the time he is robbing (taking it)." (*Sahih Al-Bukhâri*, Vol.7, *Hadîth* No. 484).

[1] (V.2:219) The provision of this Verse concerning alcoholic drinks and gambling has been abrogated by the Verse 5:90.

though she pleases you. And give not (your daughters) in marriage to *Al-Mushrikûn*[1] till they believe (in Allâh Alone) and verily, a believing slave is better than a (free) *Mushrik* (idolater), even though he pleases you. Those (*Al-Mushrikûn*) invite you to the Fire, but Allâh invites (you) to Paradise and Forgiveness by His Leave, and makes His *Ayât* (proofs, evidences, verses, lessons, signs, revelations, etc.) clear to mankind that they may remember.

222. They ask you concerning menstruation. Say: that is an *Adha* (a harmful thing for a husband to have a sexual intercourse with his wife while she is having her menses), therefore keep away from women during menses and go not unto them till they are purified (from menses and have taken a bath). And when they have purified themselves, then go in unto them as Allâh has ordained for you (go in unto them in any manner as long as it is in their vagina). Truly, Allâh loves those who turn unto Him in repentance and loves those who purify themselves (by taking a bath and cleaning and washing thoroughly their private parts and bodies for their prayers).

---

[1] (V.2:221) *Al-Mushrikûn*: polytheists, pagans, idolaters, and disbelievers in the Oneness of Allâh and in His Messenger Muhammad صلى الله عليه وسلم.

223. Your wives are a tilth for you, so go to your tilth,[1] when or how you will, and send (good deeds, or ask Allâh to bestow upon you pious offspring) for your ownselves beforehand. And fear Allâh, and know that you are to meet Him (in the Hereafter), and give good tidings to the believers (O Muhammad صلى الله عليه وسلم).

نِسَآؤُكُمْ حَرْثٌ لَّكُمْ فَأْتُوا حَرْثَكُمْ أَنَّى شِئْتُمْ وَقَدِّمُوا لِأَنفُسِكُمْ وَاتَّقُوا اللَّهَ وَاعْلَمُوا أَنَّكُم مُّلَاقُوهُ وَبَشِّرِ الْمُؤْمِنِينَ ٢٢٣

224. And make not Allâh's (Name) an excuse in your oaths against your doing good and acting piously, and making peace among mankind. And Allâh is All-Hearer, All-Knower (i.e. do not swear much and if you have sworn against doing something good then give an expiation for the oath and do good).[2]

وَلَا تَجْعَلُوا اللَّهَ عُرْضَةً لِّأَيْمَانِكُمْ أَن تَبَرُّوا وَتَتَّقُوا وَتُصْلِحُوا بَيْنَ النَّاسِ وَاللَّهُ سَمِيعٌ عَلِيمٌ ٢٢٤

225. Allâh will not call you to account for that which is unintentional in your oaths, but He will call you to account for that which your hearts have earned. And Allâh is Oft-Forgiving, Most-Forbearing.

لَّا يُؤَاخِذُكُمُ اللَّهُ بِاللَّغْوِ فِي أَيْمَانِكُمْ وَلَٰكِن يُؤَاخِذُكُم بِمَا كَسَبَتْ قُلُوبُكُمْ وَاللَّهُ غَفُورٌ حَلِيمٌ ٢٢٥

226. Those who take an oath[3] not to have sexual relation with their wives

لِّلَّذِينَ يُؤْلُونَ مِن نِّسَآئِهِمْ تَرَبُّصُ

---

[1] (V.2:223) Have sexual relations with your wives in any manner as long as it is in the vagina and not in the anus.

[2] (V.2:224) See the footnote of (V.5:89).

[3] (V.2:226) Narrated Nâfi': Ibn 'Umar used to say about *Al-'Îlâ* (الإيلاء)* which Allâh defined (in the Holy Book), "If the period of *Al-'Îlâ* (الإيلاء) expires, then the husband has either to retain his wife in a handsome manner or to divorce her as Allâh [أمر وعلا] has ordered." Ibn 'Umar added, "When the period of four months has expired, the husband should divorce his wife, but the divorce does not occur

must wait for four months, then if they return (change their idea in this period), verily, Allâh is Oft-Forgiving, Most Merciful.

227. And if they decide upon divorce, then Allâh is All-Hearer, All-Knower.

228. And divorced women shall wait (as regards their marriage) for three menstrual periods, and it is not lawful for them to conceal what Allâh has created in their wombs, if they believe in Allâh and the Last Day. And their husbands have the better right to take them back in that period, if they wish for reconciliation. And they (women) have rights (over their husbands as regards living expenses) similar (to those of their husbands) over them (as regards obedience and respect) to what is reasonable, but men have a degree (of responsibility) over them. And Allâh is All-Mighty, All-Wise.

229. The divorce is twice, after that, either you retain her on reasonable terms or release her with kindness. And it is not lawful for you (men) to take back (from your wives) any of your *Mahr* (bridal-money given by the

---

unless the husband himself declares it. This has been mentioned by 'Uthmân, 'Alî, Abu Ad-Dardâ', 'Âishah and twelve other Companions of the Prophet صلى الله عليه وسلم." (*Sahih Al-Bukhâri*, Vol.7, *Hadîth* No. 213).

* *Al-'Îlâ'* (الإيلاء): means the oath taken by a husband that he would not approach his wife for a certain period.

husband to his wife at the time of marriage) which you have given them, except when both parties fear that they would be unable to keep the limits ordained by Allâh (e.g. to deal with each other on a fair basis). Then if you fear that they would not be able to keep the limits ordained by Allâh, then there is no sin on either of them if she gives back (the Mahr or a part of it) for her Al-Khul' (divorce).[1] These are the limits ordained by Allâh, so do not transgress them. And whoever transgresses the limits ordained by Allâh, then such are the Zâlimûn (wrong-doers).

أَلَّا يُقِيمَاحُدُودَ اللَّهِ فَإِنْ خِفْتُمْ أَلَّا يُقِيمَاحُدُودَ اللَّهِ فَلَاجُنَاحَ عَلَيْهِمَافِيمَاافْتَدَتْ بِهِ تِلْكَ حُدُودُ اللَّهِ فَلَا تَعْتَدُوهَا وَمَن يَتَعَدَّ حُدُودَ اللَّهِ فَأُوْلَٰٓئِكَ هُمُ الظَّٰلِمُونَ ۝

230. And if he has divorced her (the third time), then she is not lawful unto him thereafter until she has married another husband. Then, if the other husband divorces her, it is no sin on both of them that they reunite, provided they feel that they can keep the limits

فَإِن طَلَّقَهَا فَلَا تَحِلُّ لَهُ مِنۢ بَعْدُ حَتَّىٰ تَنكِحَ زَوْجًا غَيْرَهُۥ فَإِن طَلَّقَهَا فَلَاجُنَاحَ عَلَيْهِمَآ أَن يَتَرَاجَعَآ إِن ظَنَّآ أَن يُقِيمَا حُدُودَ اللَّهِ وَتِلْكَ حُدُودُ اللَّهِ يُبَيِّنُهَا

---

[1] (V.2:229): Al-Khul'* الخلع and how a divorce is given according to it.

Narrated Ibn 'Abbâs رضى الله عنهما: The wife of Thâbit bin Qais came to the Prophet صلى الله عليه وسلم and said, "O Allâh's Messenger! I do not blame Thâbit for defects in his character or his religion, but I, being a Muslim, dislike to behave in an un-Islâmic manner (if I remain with him)." On that Allâh's Messenger صلى الله عليه وسلم said (to her), "Will you give back the garden which your husband has given you (as Mahr)?" She said, "Yes." Then the Prophet صلى الله عليه وسلم said to Thâbit, "O Thâbit! Accept your garden, and divorce her once." (Sahih Al-Bukhâri, Vol.7, Hadîth No.197).

* 'Al-Khul' الخلع means the parting of a wife from her husband by giving him a certain compensation.

ordained by Allâh. These are the limits of Allâh, which He makes plain for the people who have knowledge.

لِقَوْمٍ يَعْلَمُونَ ۝

231. And when you have divorced women and they have fulfilled the term of their prescribed period, either take them back on reasonable basis or set them free on reasonable basis. But do not take them back to hurt them, and whoever does that, then he has wronged himself. And treat not the Verses (Laws) of Allâh as a jest, but remember Allâh's Favours on you (i.e. Islâm), and that which He has sent down to you of the Book (i.e. the Qur'ân) and *Al-Hikmah* (the Prophet's *Sunnah* — legal ways — Islâmic jurisprudence) whereby He instructs you. And fear Allâh, and know that Allâh is All-Aware of everything.

وَإِذَا طَلَّقْتُمُ النِّسَاءَ فَبَلَغْنَ أَجَلَهُنَّ فَأَمْسِكُوهُنَّ بِمَعْرُوفٍ أَوْ سَرِّحُوهُنَّ بِمَعْرُوفٍ وَلَا تُمْسِكُوهُنَّ ضِرَارًا لِّتَعْتَدُوا وَمَن يَفْعَلْ ذَٰلِكَ فَقَدْ ظَلَمَ نَفْسَهُ وَلَا تَتَّخِذُوا ءَايَاتِ اللَّهِ هُزُوًا وَاذْكُرُوا نِعْمَتَ اللَّهِ عَلَيْكُمْ وَمَا أَنزَلَ عَلَيْكُم مِّنَ الْكِتَابِ وَالْحِكْمَةِ يَعِظُكُم بِهِ وَاتَّقُوا اللَّهَ وَاعْلَمُوا أَنَّ اللَّهَ بِكُلِّ شَيْءٍ عَلِيمٌ ۝

232. And when you have divorced women and they have fulfilled the term of their prescribed period, do not prevent them from marrying their (former) husbands, if they mutually agree on reasonable basis. This (instruction) is an admonition for him among you who believes in Allâh and the Last Day. That is more virtuous and purer for you. Allâh knows and you know not.

وَإِذَا طَلَّقْتُمُ النِّسَاءَ فَبَلَغْنَ أَجَلَهُنَّ فَلَا تَعْضُلُوهُنَّ أَن يَنكِحْنَ أَزْوَاجَهُنَّ إِذَا تَرَاضَوْا بَيْنَهُم بِالْمَعْرُوفِ ذَٰلِكَ يُوعَظُ بِهِ مَن كَانَ مِنكُمْ يُؤْمِنُ بِاللَّهِ وَالْيَوْمِ الْآخِرِ ذَٰلِكُمْ أَزْكَىٰ لَكُمْ وَأَطْهَرُ وَاللَّهُ يَعْلَمُ وَأَنتُمْ لَا تَعْلَمُونَ ۝

233. The mothers shall give suck to their children for two whole years, (that is) for those (parents) who desire to complete the term of suckling, but the father of the child shall bear the cost of

وَالْوَالِدَاتُ يُرْضِعْنَ أَوْلَادَهُنَّ حَوْلَيْنِ كَامِلَيْنِ لِمَنْ أَرَادَ أَن يُتِمَّ الرَّضَاعَةَ وَعَلَى الْمَوْلُودِ لَهُ رِزْقُهُنَّ

the mother's food and clothing on a reasonable basis. No person shall have a burden laid on him greater than he can bear. No mother shall be treated unfairly on account of her child, nor father on account of his child. And on the (father's) heir is incumbent the like of that (which was incumbent on the father). If they both decide on weaning, by mutual consent, and after due consultation, there is no sin on them. And if you decide on a foster suckling-mother for your children, there is no sin on you, provided you pay (the mother) what you agreed (to give her) on reasonable basis. And fear Allâh and know that Allâh is All-Seer of what you do.

234. And those of you who die and leave wives behind them, they (the wives) shall wait (as regards their marriage) for four months and ten days, then when they have fulfilled their term, there is no sin on you if they (the wives) dispose of themselves in a just and honourable manner (i.e. they can marry). And Allâh is Well-Acquainted with what you do.

235. And there is no sin on you if you make a hint of betrothal or conceal it in yourself, Allâh knows that you will remember them, but do not make a promise of contract with them in secret except that you speak an honourable saying according to the Islâmic law.[1] And do not consummate the marriage until the term prescribed is fulfilled. And know that Allâh knows what is in your minds, so fear Him. And know that Allâh is Oft-Forgiving, Most Forbearing.

تَقُولُوا قَوْلًا مَّعْرُوفًا وَلَا تَعْزِمُوا عُقْدَةَ ٱلنِّكَاحِ حَتَّىٰ يَبْلُغَ ٱلْكِتَٰبُ أَجَلَهُۥ وَٱعْلَمُوٓا۟ أَنَّ ٱللَّهَ يَعْلَمُ مَا فِىٓ أَنفُسِكُمْ فَٱحْذَرُوهُ وَٱعْلَمُوٓا۟ أَنَّ ٱللَّهَ غَفُورٌ حَلِيمٌ ۝

236. There is no sin on you, if you divorce women while yet you have not touched (had sexual relation with) them, nor appointed unto them their *Mahr* (bridal-money given by the husband to his wife at the time of marriage). But bestow on them (a suitable gift), the rich according to his means, and the poor according to his means, a gift of reasonable amount is a duty on the doers of good.

لَّا جُنَاحَ عَلَيْكُمْ إِن طَلَّقْتُمُ ٱلنِّسَآءَ مَا لَمْ تَمَسُّوهُنَّ أَوْ تَفْرِضُوا۟ لَهُنَّ فَرِيضَةً ۚ وَمَتِّعُوهُنَّ عَلَى ٱلْمُوسِعِ قَدَرُهُۥ وَعَلَى ٱلْمُقْتِرِ قَدَرُهُۥ مَتَٰعًۢا بِٱلْمَعْرُوفِ ۖ حَقًّا عَلَى ٱلْمُحْسِنِينَ ۝

237. And if you divorce them before you have touched (had a sexual relation with) them, and you have appointed unto them the *Mahr* (bridal-money given by the husbands to his wife at the time of marriage), then pay half of that (*Mahr*), unless they (the women) agree to forego it, or he (the husband), in whose hands is the marriage tie, agrees to forego and give her full appointed *Mahr*. And to forego and give (her the full *Mahr*) is nearer to *At-Taqwa* (piety, righteousness). And do not forget liberality between yourselves. Truly, Allâh is All-Seer of what you do.

وَإِن طَلَّقْتُمُوهُنَّ مِن قَبْلِ أَن تَمَسُّوهُنَّ وَقَدْ فَرَضْتُمْ لَهُنَّ فَرِيضَةً فَنِصْفُ مَا فَرَضْتُمْ إِلَّآ أَن يَعْفُونَ أَوْ يَعْفُوَا۟ ٱلَّذِى بِيَدِهِۦ عُقْدَةُ ٱلنِّكَاحِ ۚ وَأَن تَعْفُوٓا۟ أَقْرَبُ لِلتَّقْوَىٰ ۚ وَلَا تَنسَوُا۟ ٱلْفَضْلَ بَيْنَكُمْ ۚ إِنَّ ٱللَّهَ بِمَا تَعْمَلُونَ بَصِيرٌ ۝

---

[1] (V.2:235) e.g., you can say to her, "If one finds a wife like you, he will be happy"

238. Guard strictly (five obligatory) As-Salawât (the prayers) especially the middle Salât (i.e. the best prayer - 'Asr).[1] And stand before Allâh with obedience [and do not speak to others during the Salât (prayers)].

حَٰفِظُواْ عَلَى ٱلصَّلَوَٰتِ وَٱلصَّلَوٰةِ ٱلۡوُسۡطَىٰ وَقُومُواْ لِلَّهِ قَٰنِتِينَ ﴿٢٣٨﴾

239. And if you fear (an enemy), perfrom Salât (pray) on foot or riding.[2] And when you are in safety, offer the

فَإِنۡ خِفۡتُمۡ فَرِجَالًا أَوۡ رُكۡبَانًا فَإِذَآ أَمِنتُمۡ فَٱذۡكُرُواْ ٱللَّهَ كَمَا

---

[1] (V.2:238).

a) The sin of one who misses the 'Asr prayer (intentionally):*

Narrated Ibn 'Umar رضى الله عنهما: Allâh's Messenger صلى الله عليه وسلم said, "Whoever misses the 'Asr prayers (intentionally), then it is as if he lost his family and property." (Sahih Al-Bukhâri, Vol.1, Hadîth No.527).

(b) One who omits (does not offer) the 'Asr prayer (intentionally):*

Narrated Abu Al-Malih: We were with Buraidah in a battle on a cloudy day and he said, "Offer the 'Asr prayer early as the Prophet صلى الله عليه وسلم said, "Whoever omits the 'Asr prayer, all his (good) deeds will be lost." (Sahih Al-Bukhâri, Vol.1, Hadîth No.528).

* i.e. the one who omits (does not offer) the 'Asr prayer intentionally until its stated time is over and if he prays after that time, then it is useless.

[2] (V.2:239) Narrated Sâlih Khawwat or Sahl bin Abî Hathmah concerning those who witnessed the Fear Prayer that was performed in the battle of Dhat-ur-Riqa' in the company of Allâh's Messenger صلى الله عليه وسلم: One batch lined up behind him while another batch (lined up) facing the enemy. The Prophet صلى الله عليه وسلم led the batch that was with him in one Rak'ah, and he stayed in the standing posture while that batch completed their (two Rak'at) prayer by themselves and went away, lining in the face of the enemy, while the other batch came and he (i.e. the Prophet صلى الله عليه وسلم) offered his remaining Rak'ah with them, and then, kept on sitting till they completed their prayer by themselves, and he then finished his prayer with Taslîm along with them. [Sahih Al-Bukhâri, Vol. 5, Hadîth No. 451].

Salât (prayer) in the manner He has taught you, which you knew not (before).

240. And those of you who die and leave behind wives should bequeath for their wives a year's maintenance and residence without turning them out, but if they (wives) leave, there is no sin on you for that which they do of themselves, provided it is honourable (e.g. lawful marriage). And Allâh is All-Mighty, All-Wise.[1]

241. And for divorced women, maintenance (should be provided) on reasonable (scale). This is a duty on *Al-Muttaqûn* (the pious. See V.2:2).

242. Thus Allâh makes clear His *Ayât* (Laws) to you, in order that you may understand.

243. Did you (O Muhammad صلى الله عليه وسلم) not think of those who went forth from their homes in thousands, fearing death? Allâh said to them, "Die". And then He restored them to life. Truly, Allâh is full of bounty to mankind, but most men thank not.

244. And fight in the Way of Allâh and know that Allâh is All-Hearer, All-Knower.

245. Who is he that will lend to Allâh a goodly loan so that He may multiply it to him many times? And it is Allâh

---

[1] (V.2:240) The provision of this Verse has been abrogated by Verse 4:12.

that decreases or increases (your provisions), and unto Him you shall return.

كَثِيرَةً وَٱللَّهُ يَقۡبِضُ وَيَبۡسُطُ وَإِلَيۡهِ تُرۡجَعُونَ ﴿٢٤٥﴾

246. Have you not thought about the group of the Children of Israel after (the time of) Mûsâ (Moses)? When they said to a Prophet of theirs, "Appoint for us a king and we will fight in Allâh's Way." He said, "Would you then refrain from fighting, if fighting was prescribed for you?" They said, "Why should we not fight in Allâh's Way while we have been driven out of our homes and our children (families have been taken as captives)?" But when fighting was ordered for them, they turned away, all except a few of them. And Allâh is All-Aware of the *Zâlimûn* (polytheists and wrong-doers).

أَلَمۡ تَرَ إِلَى ٱلۡمَلَإِ مِنۢ بَنِىٓ إِسۡرَٰٓءِيلَ مِنۢ بَعۡدِ مُوسَىٰٓ إِذۡ قَالُواْ لِنَبِىٍّ لَّهُمُ ٱبۡعَثۡ لَنَا مَلِكًا نُّقَٰتِلۡ فِى سَبِيلِ ٱللَّهِ قَالَ هَلۡ عَسَيۡتُمۡ إِن كُتِبَ عَلَيۡكُمُ ٱلۡقِتَالُ أَلَّا تُقَٰتِلُواْ قَالُواْ وَمَا لَنَآ أَلَّا نُقَٰتِلَ فِى سَبِيلِ ٱللَّهِ وَقَدۡ أُخۡرِجۡنَا مِن دِيَٰرِنَا وَأَبۡنَآئِنَا فَلَمَّا كُتِبَ عَلَيۡهِمُ ٱلۡقِتَالُ تَوَلَّوۡاْ إِلَّا قَلِيلًا مِّنۡهُمۡ وَٱللَّهُ عَلِيمٌۢ بِٱلظَّٰلِمِينَ ﴿٢٤٦﴾

247. And their Prophet (Samuel عليه السلام) said to them, "Indeed Allâh has appointed Talût (Saul) as a king over you." They said, "How can he be a king over us when we are fitter than him for the kingdom, and he has not been given enough wealth." He said: "Verily, Allâh has chosen him above you and has increased him abundantly in knowledge and stature. And Allâh grants His kingdom to whom He Wills. And Allâh is All-Sufficient for His creatures' needs, All-Knower."

وَقَالَ لَهُمۡ نَبِيُّهُمۡ إِنَّ ٱللَّهَ قَدۡ بَعَثَ لَكُمۡ طَالُوتَ مَلِكًا قَالُوٓاْ أَنَّىٰ يَكُونُ لَهُ ٱلۡمُلۡكُ عَلَيۡنَا وَنَحۡنُ أَحَقُّ بِٱلۡمُلۡكِ مِنۡهُ وَلَمۡ يُؤۡتَ سَعَةً مِّنَ ٱلۡمَالِ قَالَ إِنَّ ٱللَّهَ ٱصۡطَفَىٰهُ عَلَيۡكُمۡ وَزَادَهُۥ بَسۡطَةً فِى ٱلۡعِلۡمِ وَٱلۡجِسۡمِ وَٱللَّهُ يُؤۡتِى مُلۡكَهُۥ مَن يَشَآءُ وَٱللَّهُ وَٰسِعٌ عَلِيمٌ ﴿٢٤٧﴾

248. And their Prophet (Samuel عليه السلام) said to them: Verily! The sign of His kingdom is that there shall come to you *At-Tâbût* (a wooden box), wherein

وَقَالَ لَهُمۡ نَبِيُّهُمۡ إِنَّ ءَايَةَ مُلۡكِهِۦٓ أَن يَأۡتِيَكُمُ ٱلتَّابُوتُ فِيهِ سَكِينَةٌ مِّن رَّبِّكُمۡ وَبَقِيَّةٌ

is *Sakinah*[1] (peace and reassurance) from your Lord and a remnant of that which Mûsâ (Moses) and Hârûn (Aaron) left behind, carried by the angels. Verily, in this is a sign for you if you are indeed believers.

249. Then when Talût (Saul) set out with the army, he said: "Verily, Allâh will try you by a river. So whoever drinks thereof, he is not of me; and whoever tastes it not, he is of me, except him who takes (thereof) in the hollow of his hand." Yet, they drank thereof, all, except a few of them. So when he had crossed it (the river), he and those who believed with him, they said: "We have no power this day against Jâlût (Goliath) and his hosts." But those who knew with certainty that they were to meet their Lord, said: "How often a small group overcame a mighty host by Allâh's Leave?" And Allâh is with As-Sâbirûn (the patient).

250. And when they advanced to meet Jâlût (Goliath) and his forces, they invoked: "Our Lord! Pour forth on us patience, and set firm our feet

---

[1] (V.2:248) Narrated Al-Barâ': A man was reciting *Sûrat Al-Kahf* and his horse was tied with two ropes beside him. A cloud came down and spread over that man, and it kept on coming closer and closer to him till his horse started jumping (as if afraid of something). When it was morning, the man came to the Prophet صلى الله عليه وسلم and told him of that experience. The Prophet صلى الله عليه وسلم said, "That was *As-Sakînah* (tranquillity or peace and reassurance along with angels), which descended because of (the recitation of) the Qur'ân." (*Sahih Al-Bukhâri*, Vol.6, *Hadîth* No. 531).

and make us victorious over the disbelieving people."

251. So they routed them by Allâh's Leave and Dâwûd (David) killed Jâlût (Goliath), and Allâh gave him [Dâwûd (David)] the kingdom [after the death of Talût (Saul) and Samuel] and *Al-Hikmah* (Prophethood),[1] and taught him of that which He willed. And if Allâh did not check one set of people by means of another, the earth would indeed be full of mischief. But Allâh is full of bounty to the *'Âlamîn* (mankind, jinn and all that exists).

252. These are the Verses of Allâh, We recite them to you (O Muhammad صلى الله عليه وسلم) in truth, and surely, you are one of the Messengers (of Allâh).[2]

---

[1] (V.2:251) See *Tafsir At-Tabarî*.

[2] (V.2:252)

A. Narrated Jâbir bin 'Abdullâh رضى الله عنهما: The Prophet صلى الله عليه وسلم said, "I have been given five (things) which were not given to anyone else before me:

a) Allâh made me victorious by awe, (by His frightening my enemies) for a distance of one month's journey.

b) The earth has been made for me (and for my followers) a place for praying and a thing to purify (perform *Tayammum*), therefore anyone of my followers can pray wherever he is, at the time of a prayer.

c) The booty has been made *Halâl* (lawful) to me yet it was not lawful to anyone else before me.

d) I have been given the right of intercession (on the Day of Resurrection).

e) Every Prophet used to be sent to his nation only, but I have been sent to all mankind." (*Sahih Al-Bukhâri*, Vol.1, *Hadîth* No.331).

B. Narrated Abu Hurairah رضى الله عنه: Allâh's Messenger صلى الله عليه وسلم said, "My similitude in comparison with the other Prophets before me is that of a man who has built a house nicely and beautifully, except for a place of one brick in a corner. The people go round about it and wonder at its beauty, but say: 'Would that this brick be put in its place!' So I am that brick, and I am the last (end) of the Prophets." (*Sahih Al-Bukhâri*, Vol. 4, *Hadîth* No. 735).

C. Narrated Ibn Mas'ud رضى الله عنه: As if I saw the Prophet صلى الله عليه وسلم talking about one of the Prophets whose nation had beaten him and caused him to bleed, while he was cleaning the blood off his face and saying, "O Allâh! Forgive my nation, for they have no knowledge." (*Sahih Al-Bukhâri*, Vol. 4, *Hadith* No. 683).

D. Narrated 'Âishah رضى الله عنها and Ibn 'Abbâs رضى الله عنهما: On his deathbed Allâh's Messenger صلى الله عليه وسلم put a sheet over his face and when he felt hot, he would remove it from his face. When in that state (of putting and removing the sheet) he said, "May Allâh's Curse be on the Jews and the Christians for they built places of worship at the graves of their Prophets." (By that) he intended to warn (the Muslims) from what they (i.e., Jews and Christians) had done. (*Sahih Bukhâri*, Vol. 4, *Hadith* No. 660).

E. Narrated Abu Hurairah رضى الله عنه: The Prophet صلى الله عليه وسلم said, "The Isrâelis used to be ruled and guided by Prophets. Whenever a Prophet died, another would take over his place. There will be no Prophet after me, but there will be caliphs who will increase in number." The people asked, "O Allâh's Messenger! What do you order us (to do)?" He said, "Obey the one who will be given the *Bai'ah* — pledge first.* Fulfil their (i.e., the caliphs') rights, for Allâh will ask them about (any shortcomings) in ruling those whom Allâh has put under their guardianship." (*Sahih Al-Bukhâri*, Vol. 4, *Hadith* No. 661).

* If the *Bai'ah* (pledge) is given to a caliph and after a while another caliph is given the *Bai'ah* (pledge) by some members of the society, the common Muslims should abide by the *Bai'ah* (pledge) given to the first caliph, for the election of the second is invalid.

253. Those Messengers! We preferred some of them to others; to some of them Allâh spoke (directly); others He raised to degrees (of honour); and to 'Îsâ (Jesus), the son of Maryam (Mary), We gave clear proofs and evidences, and supported him with Rûh-ul-Qudus [Jibrael (Gabriel)]. If Allâh had willed, succeeding generations would not have fought against each other, after clear Verses of Allâh had come to them, but they differed — some of them believed and others disbelieved. If Allâh had willed, they would not have fought against one another, but Allâh does what He likes.

‏۞ تِلْكَ ٱلرُّسُلُ فَضَّلْنَا بَعْضَهُمْ عَلَىٰ بَعْضٍ مِّنْهُم مَّن كَلَّمَ ٱللَّهُ وَرَفَعَ بَعْضَهُمْ دَرَجَٰتٍ وَءَاتَيْنَا عِيسَى ٱبْنَ مَرْيَمَ ٱلْبَيِّنَٰتِ وَأَيَّدْنَٰهُ بِرُوحِ ٱلْقُدُسِ وَلَوْ شَآءَ ٱللَّهُ مَا ٱقْتَتَلَ ٱلَّذِينَ مِنۢ بَعْدِهِم مِّنۢ بَعْدِ مَا جَآءَتْهُمُ ٱلْبَيِّنَٰتُ وَلَٰكِنِ ٱخْتَلَفُوا۟ فَمِنْهُم مَّنْ ءَامَنَ وَمِنْهُم مَّن كَفَرَ وَلَوْ شَآءَ ٱللَّهُ مَا ٱقْتَتَلُوا۟ وَلَٰكِنَّ ٱللَّهَ يَفْعَلُ مَا يُرِيدُ ۝‏

254. O you who believe! Spend of that with which We have provided for you, before a Day comes when there will be no bargaining, nor friendship, nor intercession. And it is the disbelievers who are the Zâlimûn (wrong-doers).

‏يَٰٓأَيُّهَا ٱلَّذِينَ ءَامَنُوٓا۟ أَنفِقُوا۟ مِمَّا رَزَقْنَٰكُم مِّن قَبْلِ أَن يَأْتِىَ يَوْمٌ لَّا بَيْعٌ فِيهِ وَلَا خُلَّةٌ وَلَا شَفَٰعَةٌ وَٱلْكَٰفِرُونَ هُمُ ٱلظَّٰلِمُونَ ۝‏

255. Allâh! Lâ ilâha illa Huwa (none has the right to be worshipped but He), the Ever Living, the One Who sustains and protects all that exists. Neither slumber nor sleep overtakes Him. To Him belongs whatever is in the heavens and whatever is on the earth. Who is he that can intercede with Him except with His Permission? He knows what happens to them (His creatures) in this world, and what will happen to them in the Hereafter. And they will never compass anything of His Knowledge

‏ٱللَّهُ لَآ إِلَٰهَ إِلَّا هُوَ ٱلْحَىُّ ٱلْقَيُّومُ لَا تَأْخُذُهُۥ سِنَةٌ وَلَا نَوْمٌ لَّهُۥ مَا فِى ٱلسَّمَٰوَٰتِ وَمَا فِى ٱلْأَرْضِ مَن ذَا ٱلَّذِى يَشْفَعُ عِندَهُۥٓ إِلَّا بِإِذْنِهِۦ يَعْلَمُ مَا بَيْنَ أَيْدِيهِمْ وَمَا خَلْفَهُمْ وَلَا يُحِيطُونَ بِشَىْءٍ مِّنْ عِلْمِهِۦٓ إِلَّا بِمَا شَآءَ وَسِعَ كُرْسِيُّهُ ٱلسَّمَٰوَٰتِ وَٱلْأَرْضَ وَلَا يَـُٔودُهُۥ حِفْظُهُمَا وَهُوَ ٱلْعَلِىُّ‏

except that which He wills. His *Kursî* [1]
extends over the heavens and the earth,
and He feels no fatigue in guarding and
preserving them. And He is the Most
High, the Most Great. [This Verse
2:255 is called *Ayat-ul-Kursî*.]

256. There is no compulsion in
religion. Verily, the Right Path has
become distinct from the wrong path.

---

[1] (V.2:255). *Kursî*: literally a footstool or chair, and sometimes
wrongly translated as Throne. The *Kursî* mentioned in this Verse
should be distinguished from the *'Arsh* (Throne) mentioned in
V.7:58, 10:3, 85:15 and elsewhere. Prophet Muhammad صلى الله عليه وسلم
said: "The *Kursî* compared to the *'Arsh* is nothing but like a ring
thrown out upon open space of the desert." If the *Kursî* extends
over the entire universe, then how much greater is the *'Arsh*. Indeed
Allâh, the Creator of both the *Kursi* and the *'Arsh*, is the Most
Great. Ibn Taimiyah said:

a) To believe in the *Kursî*.

b) To believe in the *'Arsh* (Throne). It is narrated from Muhammad
bin 'Abdullâh and from other religious scholars that the *Kursî* is in
front of the *'Arsh* (Throne) and it is at the level of the Feet. [*Fatâwa
Ibn Taimiyah*]

Narrated Abu Hurairah رضى الله عنه: Allâh's Messenger صلى الله عليه وسلم
ordered me to guard the *Zakât* revenue of Ramadân. Then
somebody came to me and started stealing of the foodstuff. I caught
him and said, "I will take you to Allâh's Messenger صلى الله عليه وسلم
!" Then Abu Hurairah described the whole narration and said: That
person said (to me), "(Please don't take me to Allâh's Messenger صلى
الله عليه وسلم and I will tell you a few words by which Allâh will benefit
you). When you go to your bed, recite *Ayat-ul-Kursî*, (2:255) for
then there will be a guard from Allâh who will protect you all night
long, and Satan will not be able to come near you till dawn." (When
the Prophet وسلم صلى الله عليه heard the story) he said (to me), "He (who
came to you at night) told you the truth although he is a liar; and it
was Satan." (*Sahih Al-Bukhâri*, Vol.6, *Hadith* No.530).

Whoever disbelieves in *Tâghût*[1] and believes in Allâh, then he has grasped the most trustworthy handhold that will never break. And Allâh is All-Hearer, All-Knower.

257. Allâh is the *Walî* (Protector or Guardian) of those who believe. He brings them out from darkness into light. But as for those who disbelieve, their *Auliyâ* (supporters and helpers) are *Tâghût* [false deities and false leaders], they bring them out from light into darkness. Those are the dwellers of the Fire, and they will abide therein forever. (See V.2:81,82)

258. Have you not looked at him who disputed with Ibrâhîm (Abraham) about his Lord (Allâh), because Allâh had given him the kingdom? When Ibrâhîm (Abraham) said (to him): "My Lord (Allâh) is He Who gives life and causes death." He said, "I give life and cause death." Ibrâhîm (Abraham) said, "Verily, Allâh causes the sun to rise from the east; then cause it you to rise from the west." So the disbeliever was utterly defeated. And Allâh guides not the people, who are *Zâlimûn* (wrong-doers).

---

[1] (V.2:256) The word *Tâghût* covers a wide range of meanings: It means anything worshipped other than the Real God (Allâh), i.e. all the false deities. It may be satan, devils, idols, stones, sun, stars, angels, human beings e.g. Messengers of Allâh, who were falsely worshipped and taken as *Tâghût*. Likewise saints, graves, rulers and leaders are falsely worshipped and wrongly followed. Sometimes *Tâghût* means a false judge who gives a false judgement (See V.4:60). [See *Tafsir Ibn Kathir*].

259. Or like the one who passed by a town and it had tumbled over its roofs. He said: "Oh! How will Allâh ever bring it to life after its death?" So Allâh caused him to die for a hundred years, then raised him up (again). He said: "How long did you remain (dead)?" He (the man) said: "(Perhaps) I remained (dead) a day or part of a day." He said: "Nay, you have remained (dead) for a hundred years, look at your food and your drink, they show no change; and look at your donkey! And thus We have made of you a sign for the people. Look at the bones, how We bring them together and clothe them with flesh". When this was clearly shown to him, he said, "I know (now) that Allâh is Able to do all things."

260. And (remember) when Ibrâhîm (Abraham) said, "My Lord! Show me how You give life to the dead." He (Allâh) said: "Do you not believe?" He [Ibrâhîm (Abraham)] said: "Yes (I believe), but to be stronger in Faith." He said: "Take four birds, then cause them to incline towards you (then slaughter them, cut them into pieces), and then put a portion of them on every hill, and call them, they will come to you in haste. And know that Allâh is All-Mighty, All-Wise."

261. The likeness of those who spend their wealth in the way of Allâh, is as the likeness of a grain (of corn); it grows seven ears, and each ear has a hundred grains. Allâh gives manifold increase to whom He wills. And Allâh is All-Sufficient for His creatures' needs, All-Knower.

262. Those who spend their wealth in the Cause of Allâh, and do not follow up their gifts with reminders of their generosity or with injury, their reward is with their Lord. On them shall be no fear, nor shall they grieve.

263. Kind words and forgiving of faults are better than *Sadaqah* (charity) followed by injury. And Allâh is Rich (Free of all needs) and He is Most-Forbearing.

264. O you who believe! Do not render in vain your *Sadaqah* (charity) by reminders of your generosity or by injury, like him who spends his wealth to be seen of men, and he does not believe in Allâh, nor in the Last Day. His likeness is the likeness of a smooth rock on which is a little dust; on it falls heavy rain which leaves it bare. They are not able to do anything with what they have earned. And Allâh does not guide the disbelieving people.

265. And the likeness of those who spend their wealth seeking Allâh's Pleasure while they in their ownselves are sure and certain that Allâh will reward them (for their spending in His Cause), is the likeness of a garden on a height; heavy rain falls on it and it doubles its yield of harvest. And if it does not receive heavy rain, light rain suffices it. And Allâh is All-Seer (knows well) of what you do.

266. Would any of you wish to have a garden with date-palms and vines, with rivers flowing underneath, and all kinds of fruits for him therein, while he is stricken with old age, and his children are weak (not able to look after themselves), then it is struck with a fiery whirlwind, so that it is burnt? Thus does Allâh make clear His *Ayât* (proofs, evidences, verses) to you that you may give thought.[1]

267. O you who believe! Spend of the good things which you have (legally) earned, and of that which We have produced from the earth for you, and do not aim at that which is bad to spend from it, (though) you would not accept it save if you close your eyes and tolerate therein. And know that Allâh is Rich (Free of all needs), and Worthy of all praise.

268. *Shaitân* (Satan) threatens you with poverty and orders you to commit *Fahshâ* (evil deeds, illegal sexual intercourse, sins); whereas Allâh promises you Forgiveness from Himself and Bounty, and Allâh is All-Sufficient for His creatures' needs, All-Knower.

269. He grants *Hikmah*[2] to whom He wills, and he, to whom *Hikmah* is

---

[1] (V.2:266) 'Umar رضى الله عنه said, "This is an example for a rich man who does good deeds out of obedience to Allâh, and then Allâh sends him Satan whereupon he commits sins till all his good deeds are lost." (*Sahih Al-Bukhâri*, Vol.6, *Hadîth* No. 62).

[2] (V.2:269) *Hikmah*: literally means wisdom, but it means here the knowledge, and the understanding of the Qur'ân, and the *Sunnah* and one's ability to speak and act in the correct and right way.

granted, is indeed granted abundant good. But none remember (will receive admonition) except men of understanding.

270. And whatever you spend for spendings (e.g., in *Sadaqah* — charity for Allâh's Cause) or whatever vow you make, be sure Allâh knows it all. And for the *Zâlimûn* (wrong-doers) there are no helpers.

271. If you disclose your *Sadaqât* (alms-giving), it is well; but if you conceal them and give them to the poor, that is better for you. (Allâh) will expiate you some of your sins. And Allâh is Well-Acquainted with what you do.

272. Not upon you (Muhammad ﷺ) is their guidance, but Allâh guides whom He wills. And whatever you spend in good, it is for yourselves, when you spend not except seeking Allâh's Countenance. And whatever you spend in good, it will be repaid to you in full, and you shall not be wronged.

273. (Charity is) for *Fuqarâ* (the poor), who in Allâh's Cause are restricted (from travel), and cannot move about in the land (for trade or work). The one who knows them not, thinks that they are rich because of their modesty. You may know them by their mark, they do not beg of people at all.[1]

أُوتِىَ خَيْرًا كَثِيرًا ۗ وَمَا يَذَّكَّرُ إِلَّآ أُوْلُوا الْأَلْبَٰبِ ۝ وَمَآ أَنفَقْتُم مِّن نَّفَقَةٍ أَوْ نَذَرْتُم مِّن نَّذْرٍ فَإِنَّ اللَّهَ يَعْلَمُهُ ۗ وَمَا لِلظَّٰلِمِينَ مِنْ أَنصَارٍ ۝ إِن تُبْدُوا الصَّدَقَٰتِ فَنِعِمَّا هِىَ ۖ وَإِن تُخْفُوهَا وَتُؤْتُوهَا الْفُقَرَآءَ فَهُوَ خَيْرٌ لَّكُمْ ۚ وَيُكَفِّرُ عَنكُم مِّن سَيِّـَٔاتِكُمْ ۗ وَاللَّهُ بِمَا تَعْمَلُونَ خَبِيرٌ ۝ لَّيْسَ عَلَيْكَ هُدَىٰهُمْ وَلَٰكِنَّ اللَّهَ يَهْدِى مَن يَشَآءُ ۗ وَمَا تُنفِقُوا مِنْ خَيْرٍ فَلِأَنفُسِكُمْ ۚ وَمَا تُنفِقُونَ إِلَّا ابْتِغَآءَ وَجْهِ اللَّهِ ۚ وَمَا تُنفِقُوا مِنْ خَيْرٍ يُوَفَّ إِلَيْكُمْ وَأَنتُمْ لَا تُظْلَمُونَ ۝ لِلْفُقَرَآءِ الَّذِينَ أُحْصِرُوا فِى سَبِيلِ اللَّهِ لَا يَسْتَطِيعُونَ ضَرْبًا فِى الْأَرْضِ يَحْسَبُهُمُ الْجَاهِلُ أَغْنِيَآءَ مِنَ التَّعَفُّفِ تَعْرِفُهُم بِسِيمَٰهُمْ

---

[1] (V.2:273) The Arabic word *Ilhâfa* literally means: "to beg with importunity," but Imâm Tabari in his *Tafsir* and the majority of the religious scholars agree that the Verse means: "They do not beg of people at all."

And whatever you spend in good, surely, Allâh knows it well.

274. Those who spend their wealth (in Allâh's Cause) by night and day, in secret and in public, they shall have their reward with their Lord. On them shall be no fear, nor shall they grieve.[1]

275. Those who eat *Ribâ*[2] (usury) will not stand (on the Day of Resurrection) except like the standing of a person beaten by *Shaitân* (Satan)

لَا يَسْتَطِيعُونَ النَّاسَ إِلْحَافًا وَمَا تُنفِقُوا مِنْ خَيْرٍ فَإِنَّ اللَّهَ بِهِ عَلِيمٌ ۝ الَّذِينَ يُنفِقُونَ أَمْوَالَهُم بِالَّيْلِ وَالنَّهَارِ سِرًّا وَعَلَانِيَةً فَلَهُمْ أَجْرُهُمْ عِندَ رَبِّهِمْ وَلَا خَوْفٌ عَلَيْهِمْ وَلَا هُمْ يَحْزَنُونَ ۝ الَّذِينَ يَأْكُلُونَ الرِّبَا لَا

---

[1] (V.2:274) Narrated Abu Hurairah رضي الله عنه The Prophet صلى الله عليه وسلم said, "Seven people will be shaded by Allâh under His Shade on the Day (i.e. the Day of Resurrection) when there will be no shade except His. They are:

a) a just ruler;

b) a young man who has been brought up in the worship of Allâh, [i.e.worships Allâh (Alone) sincerely from his childhood];

c) a man whose heart is attached to the mosques (who offers the five compulsory congregational prayers in the mosques);

d) two persons who love each other only for Allâh's sake, and they meet and part in Allâh's Cause only;

e) a man who refuses the call of a charming woman of noble birth for illegal sexual intercourse with her and says: I fear Allâh;

f) a person who practises charity so secretly that his left hand does not know what his right hand has given (i.e., nobody knows how much he has given in charity).

g) a person who remembers Allâh in seclusion and his eyes become flooded with tears."

(*Sahih Al-Bukhâri*, Vol.2, *Hadîth* No.504).

[2] (V.2:275) *Riba':* Usury which is of two major kinds; (A) *Riba An-Nasî'a* i.e. interest on lent money; (B) *Riba Al-Fadl,* i.e. taking a superior thing of the same kind of goods by giving more of the same kind of goods of inferior quality, e.g., dates of superior quality for dates of inferior quality in great amounts.

leading him to insanity. That is because they say: "Trading is only like *Ribâ* (usury)," whereas Allâh has permitted trading and forbidden *Ribâ* (usury). So whosoever receives an admonition from his Lord and stops eating *Ribâ* (usury) shall not be punished for the past; his case is for Allâh (to judge); but whoever returns [to *Ribâ* (usury)], such are the dwellers of the Fire — they will abide therein.

276. Allâh will destroy *Ribâ* (usury) and will give increase for *Sadaqât* (deeds of charity, alms) And Allâh likes not the disbelievers, sinners.

277. Truly, those who believe, and do deeds of righteousness, and perform *As-Salât* (Iqâmat-as-Salât), and give *Zakât*, they will have their reward with their Lord. On them shall be no fear, nor shall they grieve.

278. O you who believe! Be afraid of Allâh and give up what remains (due to you) from *Ribâ* (usury) (from now onward), if you are (really) believers.[1]

---

[1] (V.2:278)

a) Narrated 'Aun bin Abu Juhaifah رضي الله عنه : My father bought a slave who practised the profession of cupping. (My father broke the slave's instruments of cupping, I asked my father why he had done so. He replied, "The Prophet صلى الله عليه وسلم forbade the acceptance of the price of dog or blood, and also forbade the profession of tattooing, or getting tattooed and receiving or giving *Ribâ* (usury), and cursed the picture-makers." (*Sahih Al-Bukhâri*, Vol.3, *Hadîth* No.299).

279. And if you do not do it, then take a notice of war from Allâh and His Messenger[1] but if you repent, you shall

وَإِن لَّمْ تَفْعَلُوا فَأْذَنُوا بِحَرْبٍ مِّنَ اللّٰهِ وَرَسُولِهِ ۖ وَإِن تُبْتُمْ فَلَكُمْ

---

b) Narrated Abu Juhaifah that he had bought a slave whose profession was cupping and then said: The Prophet صلى الله عليه وسلم forbade taking the price of blood and the price of a dog and the earnings of a prostitute, and cursed the one who took or gave *Ribâ* (usury), and the lady who tattooed others or got herself tattooed, and the picture-maker. (*Sahih Al-Bukhâri,* Vol.7, *Hadîth* No.845).

[1] (2:279)

a) Narrated Abu Sa'îd Al-Khudrî رضى الله عنه: Once Bilâl brought *Barni* (a kind of) dates to the Prophet صلى الله عليه وسلم and the Prophet صلى الله عليه وسلم asked him, "From where have you brought these?" Bilâl replied, "I had some inferior kind of dates and exchanged two *Sâ'* of it for one *Sâ* of *Barni* dates, in order to give it to the Prophet صلى الله عليه وسلم to eat." Thereupon the Prophet صلى الله عليه وسلم said, "Beware! Beware! This is definitely *Ribâ* (usury)! This is definitely *Ribâ* (usury)! Don't do so, but if you want to buy (a superior kind of dates) sell the inferior kind of dates for money and then, buy the superior kind of dates with that money." (*Sahih Al-Bukhâri,* Vol.3, *Hadîth* No.506).

b) Narrated Sumurah bin Jundub رضى الله عنه: Allâh's Messenger صلى الله عليه وسلم very often used to ask his companions, "Did anyone of you see a dream?" So, dreams would be narrated to him by those whom Allâh willed to relate. One morning the Prophet صلى الله عليه وسلم said. "Last night two persons (angels) came to me (in a dream) and woke me up and said to me, 'Proceed!' I set out with them and we came across a man lying down, and behold, another man was standing over his head, holding a big rock. Behold, he was throwing the rock at the man's head, smashing it. The rock rolled away and the thrower followed it and took it back. By the time he reached the man, his head returned to its normal state. The thrower then did the same as he had done before. I said to my two companions, 'Subhan Allâh! Who are these two persons?' They said, 'Proceed!' So we proceeded and came to a man lying in a prone position, and another man standing over his head with an iron hook, and behold, he would put the hook in one side of the man's mouth and tear off that side of his face to the back (of the neck), and similarly tear his nose from front to back, and his eye from front to back. Then he turned to the other (second) side of the man's face and did just as he had done with the first side. He hardly completed that (second) side when the first side returned to its normal state. Then he returned to it to repeat what he had done before. I said to my two companions, 'Subhan Allâh! Who are these two persons?' They said to me, 'Proceed!' So we proceeded and came across something like a Tannur (a kind of baking oven, a pit usually clay-lined for baking bread)." I think the Prophet صلى الله عليه وسلم said, "In that oven there was much noise and voices." The Prophet صلى الله عليه وسلم added, "We looked into it and found naked men and women, and behold, a flame of fire was reaching to them from underneath, and when it reached them, they cried loudly. I asked them, 'Who are these?' They said to me, 'Proceed!' And so we proceeded and came across a river." I think he said, " — red like blood." The Prophet صلى الله عليه وسلم added, "And behold, in the river there was a man swimming, and on the bank there was a man who had collected many stones. Behold, while the other man was swimming, he went near him. The former opened his mouth and the latter (on the bank) threw a stone into his mouth whereupon he went swimming again. Then again he (the former) returned to him (the latter), and every time the former returned, he opened his mouth, and the latter threw a stone into his mouth, (and so on) the performance was repeated. I asked my two companions, 'Who are these two persons?' They replied, 'Proceed! Proceed!' And we proceeded till we came to a man with a repulsive appearance, the most repulsive appearance you ever saw a man having! Beside him there was a fire, and he was kindling it and running around it. I asked my companions, 'Who is this (man)?' They said to me, 'Proceed! Proceed!' So we proceeded till we reached a garden of deep green dense vegetation, having all sorts of spring colours. In the midst of the garden there was a very tall man, and I could hardly see his head because of his great height, and around him there were children in such a large number as I have never seen. I said to my companions, 'Who is this?' They replied, 'Proceed! Proceed!' So we proceeded till we came to a majestic huge garden, greater and better than I have ever seen! My two companions said to me, 'Ascend up' and I ascended up." The Prophet صلى الله عليه وسلم added, "So we ascended till we reached a city built of gold and silver bricks, and we went to its gate and asked (the gatekeeper) to open the gate, and it was opened and we entered the city and found in it men with one side of their bodies as handsome as the most handsome person you have ever seen, and the other side as ugly as the ugliest person you have ever seen. My two companions ordered those men to throw themselves into the river. Behold, there was a river flowing across (the city), and its water was like milk in whiteness. Those men went and threw themselves in it and then returned to us after the ugliness (of their bodies) had disappeared, and they became in the best shape." The Prophet صلى الله عليه وسلم further added, "My two companions (angels) said to me, 'This place is the *'Adn* Paradise, and that is your place.' I raised up my sight, and behold, there I saw a palace like a white cloud! My two companions said to me, 'That (palace) is your place.' I said to them, 'May Allâh bless you both! Let me enter it.' They replied, 'As for now, you will not enter it, but you shall enter it (one day).' I said to them, 'I have seen many wonders tonight. What does all that mean which I have seen?' They replied, 'We will inform you: As for the first man you came upon whose head was being smashed with the rock, he is the symbol of the one who studies the Qur'ân, and then neither recites it, nor acts on its orders, and sleeps, neglecting the enjoined prayers. As for the man you came upon, whose sides of mouth, nostrils, and eyes were torn off from front to back, he is the symbol of the man who goes out of his house in the morning and tells lies that are spread all over the world. And those naked men and women whom you saw in a construction resembling an oven, they are the adulterers and the adulteresses, and the man whom you saw swimming in the river, and was given a stone to swallow, is the eater of *Ribâ* (usury), and the bad looking man whom you saw near the fire kindling it and going around it, is *Mâlik*; the gatekeeper of Hell, and the tall man whom you saw in the garden, is Ibrâhîm (Abraham), and the children around him are those who die on *Al-Fitrah* (the Islâmic Faith of Monotheism).' " The narrator added: Some Muslims asked the Prophet صلى الله عليه وسلم, "O Allâh's Messenger! What about the children of *Al-Mushrikûn*?*" The Prophet صلى الله عليه وسلم replied, "And also the children of *Al-Mushrikûn*." The Prophet صلى الله عليه وسلم added, "My two companions added, 'The men you saw half handsome and half ugly were those persons who had mixed an act that was good with another that was evil, but Allâh forgave them.' " (*Sahih Al-Bukhâri*, Vol. 9, *Hadîth* No. 171).

* *Al-Mushrikun*: polytheists, pagans, idolaters, and disbelievers in the Oneness of Allâh and in His Messenger Muhammad صلى الله عليه وسلم .

have your capital sums. Deal not unjustly (by asking more than your capital sums), and you shall not be dealt with unjustly (by receiving less than your capital sums).

280. And if the debtor is in a hard time (has no money), then grant him time till it is easy for him to repay; but if you remit it by way of charity, that is better for you if you did but know.[1]

281. And be afraid of the Day when you shall be brought back to Allâh. Then every person shall be paid what he earned, and they shall not be dealt with unjustly.

282. O you who believe! When you contract a debt for a fixed period, write it down. Let a scribe write it down in justice between you. Let not the scribe refuse to write as Allâh has taught him, so let him write. Let him (the debtor) who incurs the liability dictate, and he must fear Allâh, his Lord, and diminish not anything of what he owes. But if the debtor is of poor understanding, or weak, or is unable to dictate for himself, then let his guardian dictate in justice. And get two witnesses out of your own men. And if there are not two men (available), then a man and two women, such as you agree for

---

[1] (V.2:280) Narrated Abu Hurairah رضي الله عنه Allâh's Messenger صلى الله عليه وسلم said, "A man used to give loans to the people, and used to say to his servant, 'If the debtor is poor, forgive him, so that Allâh may forgive us.' So when he met Allâh (after his death), Allâh forgave him." (Sahih Al-Bukhâri, Vol.4, Hadîth No.687).

witnesses, so that if one of them (two women) errs, the other can remind her. And the witnesses should not refuse when they are called (for evidence). You should not become weary to write it (your contract), whether it be small or big, for its fixed term, that is more just with Allâh; more solid as evidence, and more convenient to prevent doubts among yourselves, save when it is a present trade which you carry out on the spot among yourselves, then there is no sin on you if you do not write it down. But take witnesses whenever you make a commercial contract. Let neither scribe nor witness suffer any harm, but if you do (such harm), it would be wickedness in you. So be afraid of Allâh; and Allâh teaches you. And Allâh is the All-Knower of everything.

283. And if you are on a journey and cannot find a scribe, then let there be a pledge taken (mortgaging),[1] then if one of you entrust the other, let the one who is entrusted discharge his trust (faithfully), and let him be afraid of Allâh, his Lord. And conceal not the evidence for he, who hides it, surely, his heart is sinful. And Allâh is All-Knower of what you do.

284. To Allâh belongs all that is in the heavens and all that is on the earth, and whether you disclose what is in

---

[1] (V.2:283) Narrated 'Âishah رضي الله عنها : The Prophet صلى الله عليه وسلم bought some foodstuff on credit for a limited period and mortgaged his armour for it. (*Sahih Al-Bukhâri*, Vol.3, *Hadîth* No.686)

your ownselves or conceal it, Allâh will call you to account for it. Then He forgives whom He wills and punishes whom He wills. And Allâh is Able to do all things.

285. The Messenger (Muhammad صلى الله عليه وسلم) believes in what has been sent down to him from his Lord, and (so do) the believers. Each one believes in Allâh, His Angels, His Books, and His Messengers. (They say,) "We make no distinction between one another of His Messengers" — and they say, "We hear, and we obey. (We seek) Your Forgiveness, our Lord, and to You is the return (of all)."

286. Allâh burdens not a person beyond his scope. He gets reward for that (good) which he has earned, and he is punished for that (evil) which he has earned. "Our Lord! Punish us not if we forget or fall into error, our Lord! Lay not on us a burden like that which You did lay on those before us (Jews and Christians), our Lord! Put not on us a burden greater than we have strength to bear. Pardon us and grant us Forgiveness. Have mercy on us. You are our *Maulâ* (Patron, Supporter and Protector) and give us victory over the disbelieving people.[1]"

---

[1] (V.2:286) Narrated Abu Mas'ûd Al-Badri رضي الله عنه: Allâh's Messenger صلى الله عليه وسلم said, "Whosoever recited the last two Verses of *Sûrat Al-Baqarah* at night, that will be sufficient for him." (*Sahih Al-Bukhâri*, Vol.5, *Hadîth* No.345).

Sûrat Âl-'Imrân
(The Family of Imran) III

بِسْمِ اللهِ الرَّحْمٰنِ الرَّحِيمِ

*In the Name of Allâh
the Most Gracious, the Most Merciful.*

1. *Alif—Lâm—Mîm.* [These letters are one of the miracles of the Qur'ân, and none but Allâh (Alone) knows their meanings].

2. Allâh! *Lâ ilâha illa Huwa* (none has the right to be worshipped but He), the Ever Living, the One Who sustains and protects all that exists.

3. It is He Who has sent down the Book (the Qur'ân) to you (Muhammad صلى الله عليه وسلم) with truth, confirming what came before it. And he sent down the Taurât (Torah) and the Injeel (Gospel),

4. Aforetime, as a guidance to mankind. And He sent down the criterion [of judgement between right and wrong (this Qur'ân)]. Truly, those who disbelieve in the *Ayât* (proofs, evidences, verses, lessons, signs, revelations, etc.) of Allâh, for them there is a severe torment; and Allâh is All-Mighty, All-Able of Retribution.

5. Truly, nothing is hidden from Allâh, in the earth or in the heaven.

6. He it is Who shapes you in the wombs as He wills. *Lâ ilâha illa Huwa* (none has the right to be worshipped but He), the All-Mighty, the All-Wise.

7. It is He Who has sent down to you (Muhammad صلى الله عليه وسلم) the Book (this Qur'ân). In it are Verses that are entirely clear, they are the foundations of the Book [and those are the Verses of *Al-Ahkâm* (commandments), *Al-Fara'id* (obligatory duties) and *Al-Hudud* (legal laws for the punishment of thieves, adulterers)]; and others not entirely clear. So as for those in whose hearts there is a deviation (from the truth) they follow that which is not entirely clear thereof, seeking *Al-Fitnah* (polytheism and trials), and seeking for its hidden meanings, but none knows its hidden meanings save Allâh. And those who are firmly grounded in knowledge say: "We believe in it; the whole of it (clear and unclear Verses) are from our Lord." And none receive admonition except men of understanding. (*Tafsir At-Tabarî*).

هُوَ ٱلَّذِىٓ أَنزَلَ عَلَيۡكَ ٱلۡكِتَٰبَ مِنۡهُ ءَايَٰتٌ مُّحۡكَمَٰتٌ هُنَّ أُمُّ ٱلۡكِتَٰبِ وَأُخَرُ مُتَشَٰبِهَٰتٌ فَأَمَّا ٱلَّذِينَ فِى قُلُوبِهِمۡ زَيۡغٌ فَيَتَّبِعُونَ مَا تَشَٰبَهَ مِنۡهُ ٱبۡتِغَآءَ ٱلۡفِتۡنَةِ وَٱبۡتِغَآءَ تَأۡوِيلِهِۦ وَمَا يَعۡلَمُ تَأۡوِيلَهُۥٓ إِلَّا ٱللَّهُ وَٱلرَّٰسِخُونَ فِى ٱلۡعِلۡمِ يَقُولُونَ ءَامَنَّا بِهِۦ كُلٌّ مِّنۡ عِندِ رَبِّنَا وَمَا يَذَّكَّرُ إِلَّآ أُوْلُواْ ٱلۡأَلۡبَٰبِ ٧

8. (They say): "Our Lord! Let not our hearts deviate (from the truth) after You have guided us, and grant us mercy from You. Truly, You are the Bestower."

رَبَّنَا لَا تُزِغۡ قُلُوبَنَا بَعۡدَ إِذۡ هَدَيۡتَنَا وَهَبۡ لَنَا مِن لَّدُنكَ رَحۡمَةً إِنَّكَ أَنتَ ٱلۡوَهَّابُ ٨

9. "Our Lord! Verily, it is You Who will gather mankind together on the Day about which there is no doubt. Verily, Allâh never breaks His Promise".

رَبَّنَآ إِنَّكَ جَامِعُ ٱلنَّاسِ لِيَوۡمٍ لَّا رَيۡبَ فِيهِ إِنَّ ٱللَّهَ لَا يُخۡلِفُ ٱلۡمِيعَادَ ٩

10. Verily, those who disbelieve, neither their properties nor their offspring will avail them whatsoever against Allâh; and it is they who will be fuel of the Fire.

إِنَّ ٱلَّذِينَ كَفَرُواْ لَن تُغۡنِيَ عَنۡهُمۡ أَمۡوَٰلُهُمۡ وَلَآ أَوۡلَٰدُهُم مِّنَ ٱللَّهِ شَيۡـًٔا وَأُوْلَٰٓئِكَ هُمۡ وَقُودُ ٱلنَّارِ ١٠

11. Like the behaviour of the people of Fir'aun (Pharaoh) and those before them; they belied Our *Ayât* (proofs, evidences, verses, lessons, signs, revelations, etc.). So Allâh seized (destroyed) them for their sins. And Allâh is Severe in punishment.

كَدَأْبِ ءَالِ فِرْعَوْنَ وَالَّذِينَ مِن قَبْلِهِمْ كَذَّبُوا بِـَٔايَٰتِنَا فَأَخَذَهُمُ ٱللَّهُ بِذُنُوبِهِمْ وَٱللَّهُ شَدِيدُ ٱلْعِقَابِ ﴿١١﴾

12. Say (O Muhammad صلى الله عليه وسلم) to those who disbelieve: "You will be defeated and gathered together to Hell, and worst indeed is that place of rest."

قُل لِّلَّذِينَ كَفَرُوا سَتُغْلَبُونَ وَتُحْشَرُونَ إِلَىٰ جَهَنَّمَ وَبِئْسَ ٱلْمِهَادُ ﴿١٢﴾

13. There has already been a sign for you (O Jews) in the two armies that met (in combat i.e. the battle of Badr). One was fighting in the Cause of Allâh, and as for the other, (they) were disbelievers. They (the believers) saw them (the disbelievers) with their own eyes twice their number (although they were thrice their number). And Allâh supports with His Victory whom He wills. Verily, in this is a lesson for those who understand. (See Verse 8:44). (*Tafsir At-Tabarî*).

قَدْ كَانَ لَكُمْ ءَايَةٌ فِي فِئَتَيْنِ ٱلْتَقَتَا فِئَةٌ تُقَٰتِلُ فِي سَبِيلِ ٱللَّهِ وَأُخْرَىٰ كَافِرَةٌ يَرَوْنَهُم مِّثْلَيْهِمْ رَأْيَ ٱلْعَيْنِ وَٱللَّهُ يُؤَيِّدُ بِنَصْرِهِۦ مَن يَشَآءُ إِنَّ فِي ذَٰلِكَ لَعِبْرَةً لِّأُو۟لِي ٱلْأَبْصَٰرِ ﴿١٣﴾

14. Beautified for men is the love of things they covet; women, children, much of gold and silver (wealth), branded beautiful horses, cattle and well-tilled land. This is the pleasure of the present world's life; but Allâh has the excellent return (Paradise with flowing rivers) with Him.

زُيِّنَ لِلنَّاسِ حُبُّ ٱلشَّهَوَٰتِ مِنَ ٱلنِّسَآءِ وَٱلْبَنِينَ وَٱلْقَنَٰطِيرِ ٱلْمُقَنطَرَةِ مِنَ ٱلذَّهَبِ وَٱلْفِضَّةِ وَٱلْخَيْلِ ٱلْمُسَوَّمَةِ وَٱلْأَنْعَٰمِ وَٱلْحَرْثِ ذَٰلِكَ مَتَٰعُ ٱلْحَيَوٰةِ ٱلدُّنْيَا وَٱللَّهُ عِندَهُۥ حُسْنُ ٱلْمَـَٔابِ ﴿١٤﴾

15. Say: "Shall I inform you of things far better than those? For *Al-Muttaqûn* (the pious. See V.2:2) there are Gardens (Paradise) with their Lord, underneath

۞ قُلْ أَؤُنَبِّئُكُم بِخَيْرٍ مِّن ذَٰلِكُمْ لِلَّذِينَ ٱتَّقَوْا عِندَ رَبِّهِمْ جَنَّٰتٌ

which rivers flow. Therein (is their) eternal (home) and *Azwâjun Mutahharatun*[1] (purified mates or wives). And Allâh will be pleased with them. And Allâh is All-Seer of the (His) slaves".

16. Those who say: "Our Lord! We have indeed believed, so forgive us our sins and save us from the punishment of the Fire."

17. (They are) those who are patient, those who are true (in Faith, words, and deeds), and obedient with sincere devotion in worship to Allâh. Those who spend [give the *Zakât* and alms in the Way of Allâh] and those who pray and beg Allâh's Pardon in the last hours of the night.

18. Allâh bears witness that *Lâ ilâha illa Huwa* (none has the right to be worshipped but He), and the angels, and those having knowledge (also give this witness); (He always) maintains His creation in Justice. *Lâ ilâha illa Huwa* (none has the right to be worshipped but He), the All-Mighty, the All-Wise.

19. Truly, the religion with Allâh is Islâm. Those who were given the Scripture (Jews and Christians) did not differ except, out of mutual jealousy, after knowledge had come to them. And whoever disbelieves in the *Ayât* (proofs, evidences, verses, signs,

---

[1] (V.3:15) i.e., they will have no menses, urine, or stool. See *Tafsir Ibn Kathir* and also see footnote of (V.29:64).

revelations, etc.) of Allâh, then surely, Allâh is Swift in calling to account.

20. So if they dispute with you (Muhammad صلى الله عليه وسلم) say: "I have submitted myself to Allâh (in Islâm), and (so have) those who follow me." And say to those who were given the Scripture (Jews and Christians) and to those who are illiterates (Arab pagans): "Do you (also) submit yourselves (to Allâh in Islâm)?" If they do, they are rightly guided; but if they turn away, your duty is only to convey the Message; and Allâh is All-Seer of (His) slaves.[1]

21. Verily, those who disbelieve in the *Ayât* (proofs, evidences, verses, lessons, signs, revelations, etc.) of Allâh and kill the Prophets without right, and kill those men who order just dealings, … then announce to them a painful torment.

22. They are those whose works will be lost in this world and in the Hereafter, and they will have no helpers.

23. Have you not seen those who have been given a portion of the Scripture? They are being invited to the Book of Allâh to settle their dispute, then a party of them turn away, and they are averse.

24. This is because they say: "The Fire shall not touch us but for a number

---

[1] (V.3:20): See footnote of (V.3:85).

of days." And that which they used to invent regarding their religion has deceived them.

وَغَرَّهُمْ فِي دِينِهِم مَّا كَانُوا يَفْتَرُونَ ۝

25. How (will it be) when We gather them together on the Day about which there is no doubt (i.e. the Day of Resurrection). And each person will be paid in full what he has earned? And they will not be dealt with unjustly.

فَكَيْفَ إِذَا جَمَعْنَاهُمْ لِيَوْمٍ لَّا رَيْبَ فِيهِ وَوُفِّيَتْ كُلُّ نَفْسٍ مَّا كَسَبَتْ وَهُمْ لَا يُظْلَمُونَ ۝

26. Say (O Muhammad صلى الله عليه وسلم): "O Allâh! Possessor of the kingdom, You give the kingdom to whom You will, and You take the kingdom from whom You will, and You endue with honour whom You will, and You humiliate whom You will. In Your Hand[1] is the good. Verily, You are Able to do all things.

قُلِ اللَّهُمَّ مَالِكَ الْمُلْكِ تُؤْتِي الْمُلْكَ مَن تَشَاءُ وَتَنزِعُ الْمُلْكَ مِمَّن تَشَاءُ وَتُعِزُّ مَن تَشَاءُ وَتُذِلُّ مَن تَشَاءُ بِيَدِكَ الْخَيْرُ إِنَّكَ عَلَىٰ كُلِّ شَيْءٍ قَدِيرٌ ۝

27. You make the night to enter into the day, and You make the day to enter into the night (i.e. increase and decrease in the hours of the night and the day during winter and summer), You bring the living out of the dead, and You bring the dead out of the living. And You give wealth and sustenance to whom You will, without limit (measure or account).

تُولِجُ الَّيْلَ فِي النَّهَارِ وَتُولِجُ النَّهَارَ فِي الَّيْلِ وَتُخْرِجُ الْحَيَّ مِنَ الْمَيِّتِ وَتُخْرِجُ الْمَيِّتَ مِنَ الْحَيِّ وَتَرْزُقُ مَن تَشَاءُ بِغَيْرِ حِسَابٍ ۝

28. Let not the believers take the disbelievers as *Auliyâ* (supporters, helpers) instead of the believers, and whoever does that will never be helped by Allâh in' any way, except if you indeed fear a danger from them. And

لَّا يَتَّخِذِ الْمُؤْمِنُونَ الْكَافِرِينَ أَوْلِيَاءَ مِن دُونِ الْمُؤْمِنِينَ وَمَن يَفْعَلْ ذَٰلِكَ فَلَيْسَ مِنَ اللَّهِ فِي شَيْءٍ إِلَّا أَن تَتَّقُوا مِنْهُمْ تُقَاةً

---

[1] (V.3:26): See the footnote of (V.3:73)

Allâh warns you against Himself (His punishment),[1] and to Allâh is the final return.

29. Say (O Muhammad صلى الله عليه وسلم): "Whether you hide what is in your breasts or reveal it, Allâh knows it, and He knows what is in the heavens and what is in the earth. And Allâh is Able to do all things."

30. On the Day when every person will be confronted with all the good he has done, and all the evil he has done, he will wish that there were a great distance between him and his evil. And Allâh warns you against Himself (His punishment) and Allâh is full of kindness to (His) slaves.

31. Say (O Muhammad صلى الله عليه وسلم to mankind): "If you (really) love Allâh then follow me (i.e. accept Islâmic Monotheism, follow the Qur'ân and the Sunnah), Allâh will love you and forgive you of your sins. And Allâh is Oft-Forgiving, Most Merciful."

---

[1] (V.3:28) The Statement of Allâh عزوجل "But Allâh warns you against Himself (i.e. His punishment)." (3:28).

Narrated 'Abdullâh رضي الله عنه: The Prophet صلى الله عليه وسلم said, "There is none who has a greater sense of *Ghairah** than Allâh, and for that reason He has forbidden *Al-Fawâhish*, (the shameful deeds and sins, e.g. illegal sexual intercourse). And there is none who likes to be praised more than Allâh does." (*Sahih Al-Bukhâri*, Vol. 9, *Hadîth* No. 500).

* *Ghairah:* a feeling of great fury and anger when one's honour and prestige are injured or challenged.

32. Say (O Muhammad صلى الله عليه وسلم): "Obey Allâh and the Messenger (Muhammad صلى الله عليه وسلم)." But if they turn away, then Allâh does not like the disbelievers.[1]

قُلْ أَطِيعُوا۟ ٱللَّهَ وَٱلرَّسُولَ فَإِن تَوَلَّوْا۟ فَإِنَّ ٱللَّهَ لَا يُحِبُّ ٱلْكَٰفِرِينَ ٣٢

33. Allâh chose Adam, Nûh (Noah), the family of Ibrâhîm (Abraham) and the family of 'Imrân above the 'Âlamîn (mankind and jinn) (of their times).

۞ إِنَّ ٱللَّهَ ٱصْطَفَىٰٓ ءَادَمَ وَنُوحًا وَءَالَ إِبْرَٰهِيمَ وَءَالَ عِمْرَٰنَ عَلَى ٱلْعَٰلَمِينَ ٣٣

34. Offspring, one of the other, and Allâh is the All-Hearer, All-Knower.

ذُرِّيَّةًۢ بَعْضُهَا مِنۢ بَعْضٍ وَٱللَّهُ سَمِيعٌ عَلِيمٌ ٣٤

35. (Remember) when the wife of 'Imrân said: "O my Lord! I have vowed to You what (the child that) is in my womb to be dedicated for Your services (free from all worldly work; to serve Your place of worship), so accept this, from me. Verily, You are the All-Hearer, the All-Knowing."

إِذْ قَالَتِ ٱمْرَأَتُ عِمْرَٰنَ رَبِّ إِنِّي نَذَرْتُ لَكَ مَا فِى بَطْنِى مُحَرَّرًا فَتَقَبَّلْ مِنِّىٓ إِنَّكَ أَنتَ ٱلسَّمِيعُ ٱلْعَلِيمُ ٣٥

36. Then when she gave birth to her [child Maryam (Mary)], she said: "O my Lord! I have given birth to a female child," — and Allâh knew better what she brought forth, — "And the male is not like the female, and I have named her Maryam[2] (Mary), and I seek refuge with You (Allâh) for her and for her offspring from Shaitân (Satan), the outcast."

فَلَمَّا وَضَعَتْهَا قَالَتْ رَبِّ إِنِّى وَضَعْتُهَآ أُنثَىٰ وَٱللَّهُ أَعْلَمُ بِمَا وَضَعَتْ وَلَيْسَ ٱلذَّكَرُ كَٱلْأُنثَىٰ وَإِنِّى سَمَّيْتُهَا مَرْيَمَ وَإِنِّىٓ أُعِيذُهَا بِكَ وَذُرِّيَّتَهَا مِنَ ٱلشَّيْطَٰنِ ٱلرَّجِيمِ ٣٦

37. So her Lord (Allâh) accepted her with goodly acceptance. He made her grow in a good manner and put her

فَتَقَبَّلَهَا رَبُّهَا بِقَبُولٍ حَسَنٍ وَأَنۢبَتَهَا نَبَاتًا حَسَنًا وَكَفَّلَهَا زَكَرِيَّا كُلَّمَا دَخَلَ عَلَيْهَا

---

[1] (V.3:32) See the footnote of (V.3:85).

[2] (V.3:36) Maryam (مريم) literally means: maidservant of Allâh.

under the care of Zakariyyâ (Zachariya). Every time he entered Al-Mihrâb[1] to (visit) her , he found her supplied with sustenance. He said: "O Maryam (Mary)! From where have you got this?" She said, "This is from Allâh." Verily, Allâh provides sustenance to whom He wills, without limit.

38. At that time Zakariyyâ (Zachariya) invoked his Lord, saying: "O my Lord! Grant me from You, a good offspring. You are indeed the All-Hearer of invocation."

39. Then the angels called him, while he was standing in prayer in Al-Mihrâb (a praying place or a private room), (saying): "Allâh gives you glad tidings of Yahyâ (John), confirming (believing in) the word from Allâh [i.e. the creation of 'Îsâ (Jesus) عليه السلام, the Word from Allâh ("Be!" — and he was!)], noble, keeping away from sexual relations with women, a Prophet, from among the righteous."

40. He said: "O my Lord! How can I have a son when I am very old, and my wife is barren?" (Allâh) said: "Thus Allâh does what He wills."

41. He said: "O my Lord! Make a sign for me." (Allâh) said: "Your sign is that you shall not speak to mankind for three days except with signals. And remember your Lord much (by praising Him again and again), and glorify

---

[1] (V.3:37):- *Al-Mihrâb*: a praying place or a private room.

(Him) in the afternoon and in the morning.[1]"

42. And (remember) when the angels said: "O Maryam (Mary)! Verily, Allâh has chosen you, purified you (from polytheism and disbelief), and chosen you above the women of the *'Âlamîn* (mankind and jinn) (of her lifetime)."

وَإِذْ قَالَتِ ٱلْمَلَٰٓئِكَةُ يَٰمَرْيَمُ إِنَّ ٱللَّهَ ٱصْطَفَىٰكِ وَطَهَّرَكِ وَٱصْطَفَىٰكِ عَلَىٰ نِسَآءِ ٱلْعَٰلَمِينَ ﴿٤٢﴾

43. O Mary! "Submit yourself with obedience to your Lord (Allâh, by worshipping none but Him Alone) and prostrate yourself, and bow down along with *Ar-Râki'ûn* (those who bow down)."

يَٰمَرْيَمُ ٱقْنُتِى لِرَبِّكِ وَٱسْجُدِى وَٱرْكَعِى مَعَ ٱلرَّٰكِعِينَ ﴿٤٣﴾

44. This is a part of the news of the *Ghaib* (Unseen, i.e. the news of the past nations of which you have no knowledge) which We reveal to you (O Muhammad صلى الله عليه وسلم). You were not with them, when they cast lots with their pens as to which of them should be charged with the care of Maryam (Mary); nor were you with them when they disputed.

ذَٰلِكَ مِنْ أَنۢبَآءِ ٱلْغَيْبِ نُوحِيهِ إِلَيْكَ وَمَا كُنتَ لَدَيْهِمْ إِذْ يُلْقُونَ أَقْلَٰمَهُمْ أَيُّهُمْ يَكْفُلُ مَرْيَمَ وَمَا كُنتَ لَدَيْهِمْ إِذْ يَخْتَصِمُونَ ﴿٤٤﴾

45. (Remember) when the angels said: "O Maryam (Mary)! Verily, Allâh gives you the glad tidings of a Word ["Be!" — and he was! i.e. 'Îsâ (Jesus) the son of Maryam (Mary)] from Him, his name will be the Messiah 'Îsâ (Jesus), the son of Maryam (Mary), held in honour in this world and in the Hereafter, and will be one of those who are near to Allâh."

إِذْ قَالَتِ ٱلْمَلَٰٓئِكَةُ يَٰمَرْيَمُ إِنَّ ٱللَّهَ يُبَشِّرُكِ بِكَلِمَةٍ مِّنْهُ ٱسْمُهُ ٱلْمَسِيحُ عِيسَى ٱبْنُ مَرْيَمَ وَجِيهًا فِى ٱلدُّنْيَا وَٱلْءَاخِرَةِ وَمِنَ ٱلْمُقَرَّبِينَ ﴿٤٥﴾

---

[1] (V.3:41) See·Tafsîr Al-Qurtubî.

46. "He will speak to the people, in the cradle[1] and in manhood, and he will be one of the righteous."

وَيُكَلِّمُ ٱلنَّاسَ فِي ٱلْمَهْدِ وَكَهْلًا وَمِنَ ٱلصَّـٰلِحِينَ ٤٦

47. She said: "O my Lord! How shall I have a son when no man has touched me." He said: "So (it will be) for Allâh creates what He wills. When He has decreed something, He says to it only: "Be!"—and it is.

قَالَتْ رَبِّ أَنَّىٰ يَكُونُ لِى وَلَدٌ وَلَمْ يَمْسَسْنِي بَشَرٌ قَالَ كَذَٰلِكِ ٱللَّهُ يَخْلُقُ مَا يَشَآءُ إِذَا قَضَىٰٓ أَمْرًا فَإِنَّمَا يَقُولُ لَهُ كُن فَيَكُونُ ٤٧

---

[1] (V.3:46) Narrated Abu Hurairah رضى الله عنه: The Prophet صلى الله عليه وسلم said, "None spoke in cradle but three:(The first was) Jesus, (the second child was): There was a man from *Banî Israel* called *Juraij*. While he was offering prayer, his mother came and called him. He said (to himself), "Shall I answer her or keep on praying?" (He went on praying and did not answer her). His mother said, "O Allâh! Do not let him die till he sees the faces of prostitutes." So while he was in his hermitage, a lady came and sought to seduce him, but he refused. So she went to a shepherd and presented herself to him to commit illegal sexual intercourse with her, and then later she gave birth to a child and claimed that it belonged to Juraij. The people, therefore, came to him and dismantled his hermitage and expelled him out of it and abused him. Juraij performed ablution and offered prayer, and then came to the child and said: "O child! Who is your father?" The child replied, "The shepherd" (after hearing this) the people said, "We shall rebuild your hermitage of gold," but he said: "No, of nothing but mud." (The third was the hero of the following story): A lady from *Banî Israel* was nursing her child at her breast when a handsome rider passed by her. She said, "O Allâh! Make my child like him." On that the child left her breast and facing the rider said: "O Allâh! Do not make me like him." The child then started to suck her breast again. [Abu Hurairah further said, "As if I were now looking at the Prophet صلى الله عليه وسلم sucking his finger (in way of demonstration)."]. After a while they (some people) passed by, with a lady slave and she (i.e. the child's mother) said,"O Allâh! Do not make my child like this (slave-girl)!" On that the child left her breast, and said, "O Allâh! Make me like her." When she asked why, the child replied, "The rider is one of the tyrants while this slave-girl is falsely accused of theft and illegal sexual intercourse." (*Sahih Al-Bukhâri*, Vol. 4, *Hadîth* No. 645).

48. And He (Allâh) will teach him ['Îsâ (Jesus)] the Book and Al-Hikmah (i.e. the Sunnah, the faultless speech of the Prophets, wisdom), (and) the Taurât (Torah) and the Injeel (Gospel).

49. And will make him ['Îsâ (Jesus)] a Messenger to the Children of Israel (saying): "I have come to you with a sign from your Lord, that I design for you out of clay, a figure like that of a bird, and breathe into it, and it becomes a bird by Allâh's Leave; and I heal him who was born blind, and the leper, and I bring the dead to life by Allâh's Leave. And I inform you of what you eat, and what you store in your houses. Surely, therein is a sign for you, if you believe.

50. And I have come confirming that which was before me of the Taurât (Torah), and to make lawful to you part of what was forbidden to you, and I have come to you with a proof from your Lord. So fear Allâh and obey me.

51. Truly, Allâh is my Lord and your Lord, so worship Him (Alone). This is the Straight Path.

52. Then when 'Îsâ (Jesus) came to know of their disbelief, he said: "Who will be my helpers in Allâh's Cause?" Al-Hawâriûn (the disciples) said: "We are the helpers of Allâh; we believe in Allâh, and bear witness that we are Muslims (i.e. we submit to Allâh)."

53. Our Lord! We believe in what You have sent down, and we follow the

Messenger ['Îsâ (Jesus)]; so write us down among those who bear witness (to the truth i.e. *Lâ ilâha illallâh* — none has the right to be worshipped but Allâh).

الرَّسُولَ فَٱكْتُبْنَا مَعَ ٱلشَّهِدِينَ ۝

54. And they (disbelievers) plotted [to kill 'Îsâ (Jesus)], [عليه السلام], and Allâh planned too. And Allâh is the Best of the planners.

وَمَكَرُوا۟ وَمَكَرَ ٱللَّهُ وَٱللَّهُ خَيْرُ ٱلْمَـٰكِرِينَ ۝

55. And (remember) when Allâh said: "O 'Îsâ (Jesus)! I will take you and raise you to Myself and clear you [of the forged statement that 'Îsâ (Jesus) is Allâh's son] of those who disbelieve, and I will make those who follow you (Monotheists, who worship none but Allâh) superior to those who disbelieve [in the Oneness of Allâh, or disbelieve in some of His Messengers, e.g. Muhammad صلى الله عليه وسلم, 'Îsâ (Jesus), Mûsâ (Moses), or in His Holy Books, e.g. the Taurât (Torah), the Injeel (Gospel), the Qur'ân] till the Day of Resurrection.[1] Then you will return to

إِذْ قَالَ ٱللَّهُ يَـٰعِيسَىٰٓ إِنِّى مُتَوَفِّيكَ وَرَافِعُكَ إِلَىَّ وَمُطَهِّرُكَ مِنَ ٱلَّذِينَ كَفَرُوا۟ وَجَاعِلُ ٱلَّذِينَ ٱتَّبَعُوكَ فَوْقَ ٱلَّذِينَ كَفَرُوٓا۟ إِلَىٰ يَوْمِ ٱلْقِيَـٰمَةِ ثُمَّ إِلَىَّ مَرْجِعُكُمْ فَأَحْكُمُ بَيْنَكُمْ فِيمَا كُنتُمْ فِيهِ تَخْتَلِفُونَ ۝

---

[1] (V.3:55) The advent (descent) of 'Îsâ (Jesus), [son of Maryam (Mary)] عليه السلام.

a) Narrated Abu Hurairah رضى الله عنه Allâh's Messenger صلى الله عليه وسلم said, "By Him in Whose Hand my soul is, surely ['Îsâ (Jesus)], the son of Maryam (Mary) عليه السلام will shortly descend amongst you (Muslims), and will judge mankind justly by the law of the Qur'ân (as a just ruler); he will break the cross and kill the pigs and there will be no *Jizyah** (i.e. taxation taken from non-Muslims). Money will be in abundance so that nobody will accept it, and a single prostration to Allâh (in prayer) will be better than the whole world and whatever is in it." Abu Hurairah added: "If you wish, you can recite (this Verse of the Qur'ân): "And there is none of the people

Me and I will judge between you in the matters in which you used to dispute."

56. "As to those who disbelieve, I will punish them with a severe torment in this world and in the Hereafter, and they will have no helpers.

فَأَمَّا الَّذِينَ كَفَرُوا فَأُعَذِّبُهُمْ عَذَابًا شَدِيدًا فِي الدُّنْيَا وَالْآخِرَةِ وَمَا لَهُم مِّن نَّاصِرِينَ ۝

57. And as for those who believe (in the Oneness of Allâh) and do righteous good deeds, Allâh will pay them their reward in full. And Allâh does not like the *Zalimûn* (polytheists and wrongdoers).

وَأَمَّا الَّذِينَ ءَامَنُوا وَعَمِلُوا الصَّالِحَاتِ فَيُوَفِّيهِمْ أُجُورَهُمْ وَاللَّهُ لَا يُحِبُّ الظَّالِمِينَ ۝

58. This is what We recite to you (O Muhammad صلى الله عليه وسلم) of the Verses and the Wise Reminder (i.e. the Qur'ân).

ذَٰلِكَ نَتْلُوهُ عَلَيْكَ مِنَ الْآيَاتِ وَالذِّكْرِ الْحَكِيمِ ۝

59. Verily, the likeness of 'Îsâ (Jesus) before Allâh is the likeness of Adam. He created him from dust, then (He) said to him: "Be!" — and he was.

إِنَّ مَثَلَ عِيسَىٰ عِندَ اللَّهِ كَمَثَلِ ءَادَمَ خَلَقَهُ مِن تُرَابٍ ثُمَّ قَالَ لَهُ كُن فَيَكُونُ ۝

---

of the Scriptures (Jews and Christians) but must believe in him [i.e. 'Îsâ (Jesus) عليه السلام as a Messenger of Allâh and a human being] before his ['Îsâ (Jesus) السلام عليه or a Jew's or Christian's] death, and on the Day of Resurrection, he ['Îsâ (Jesus) عليه السلام] will be a witness against them." (4:159).

(See *Fath Al-Bari*) According to the quotation of Kushmaihani there is the word *Al-Jizyah* instead of *Al-Harb*. (*Sahih Al-Bukhâri*, Vol.4, *Hadîth* No.657).

b) Narrated Abu Hurairah رضى الله عنه: Allâh's Messenger صلى الله عليه وسلم said: "How will you be when the son of Maryam (Mary) [i.e. 'Îsâ (Jesus) عليه السلام] descends amongst you, and he will judge people by the Law of the Qur'ân and not by the law of the Injeel (Gospel)." (*Fath Al-Bari*) (*Sahih Al-Bukhâri*, Vol.4, *Hadîth* No. 658).

* The *Jîzyah*: a tax imposed on non-Muslims (who would keep their own religion, rather than embrace Islâm) will not be accepted by 'Îsâ (Jesus) عليه السلام, but all people will be required to embrace Islâm and there will be no other alternative.

60. (This is) the truth from your Lord, so be not of those who doubt.

ٱلۡحَقُّ مِن رَّبِّكَ فَلَا تَكُن مِّنَ ٱلۡمُمۡتَرِينَ

61. Then whoever disputes with you concerning him ['Îsâ (Jesus)] after (all this) knowledge that has come to you [i.e. 'Îsâ (Jesus) being a slave of Allâh, and having no share in Divinity], say: (O Muhammad صلى الله عليه وسلم) "Come, let us call our sons and your sons, our women and your women, ourselves and yourselves — then we pray and invoke (sincerely) the Curse of Allâh upon those who lie."

فَمَنۡ حَآجَّكَ فِيهِ مِنۢ بَعۡدِ مَا جَآءَكَ مِنَ ٱلۡعِلۡمِ فَقُلۡ تَعَالَوۡاْ نَدۡعُ أَبۡنَآءَنَا وَأَبۡنَآءَكُمۡ وَنِسَآءَنَا وَنِسَآءَكُمۡ وَأَنفُسَنَا وَأَنفُسَكُمۡ ثُمَّ نَبۡتَهِلۡ فَنَجۡعَل لَّعۡنَتَ ٱللَّهِ عَلَى ٱلۡكَٰذِبِينَ

62. Verily, this is the true narrative [about the story of 'Îsâ (Jesus)], and, *Lâ ilâha illallâh* (none has the right to be worshipped but Allâh, the One and the Only True God, Who has neither a wife nor a son). And indeed, Allâh is the All-Mighty, the All-Wise.

إِنَّ هَٰذَا لَهُوَ ٱلۡقَصَصُ ٱلۡحَقُّ وَمَا مِنۡ إِلَٰهٍ إِلَّا ٱللَّهُ وَإِنَّ ٱللَّهَ لَهُوَ ٱلۡعَزِيزُ ٱلۡحَكِيمُ

63. And if they turn away (and do not accept these true proofs and evidences), then surely, Allâh is All-Aware of those who do mischief.

فَإِن تَوَلَّوۡاْ فَإِنَّ ٱللَّهَ عَلِيمٌۢ بِٱلۡمُفۡسِدِينَ

64. Say (O Muhammad صلى الله عليه وسلم): "O people of the Scripture (Jews and Christians): Come to a word that is just between us and you, that we worship none but Allâh (Alone), and that we associate no partners with Him, and that none of us shall take others as lords besides Allâh.[1] Then, if they turn

قُلۡ يَٰٓأَهۡلَ ٱلۡكِتَٰبِ تَعَالَوۡاْ إِلَىٰ كَلِمَةٍ سَوَآءٍۭ بَيۡنَنَا وَبَيۡنَكُمۡ أَلَّا نَعۡبُدَ إِلَّا ٱللَّهَ وَلَا نُشۡرِكَ بِهِۦ شَيۡـٔٗا وَلَا يَتَّخِذَ بَعۡضُنَا بَعۡضًا أَرۡبَابٗا مِّن دُونِ ٱللَّهِ فَإِن

---

[1] (V.3:64) Narrated Ibn 'Abbâs رضي الله عنهما: Abu Sufyân narrated to me personally, saying, "I set out during the truce that had been concluded between me and Allâh's Messenger صلى الله عليه وسلم. While I

was in Shâm, a letter sent by the Prophet صلى الله عليه وسلم was brought to Heraclius. Dihya Al-Kalbi had brought and given it to the governor of Busra, and the latter forwarded it to Heraclius. Heraclius said, 'Is there anyone from the people of this man who claims to be a Prophet?' The people replied, 'Yes,' so, along with some other Quraishi men, I was called and we entered upon Heraclius, and we were seated in front of him. Then he said, 'Who amongst you is the nearest relative to the man who claims to be a Prophet?' I (Abu Sufyân) replied: 'I am the nearest relative to him from amongst the group.' So they made me sit in front of him and made my companions sit behind me. Then he called upon his translator and said (to him). 'Tell them (i.e. Abu Sufyân's companions) that I am going to ask him (i.e. Abu Sufyân) regarding that man who claims to be a Prophet. So, if he tells me a lie, they should contradict him (instantly).' By Allâh, had I not been afraid of my companions would consider me a liar, I would have told lies. Heraclius then said to his translator, 'Ask him: What is his (i.e. the Prophet's) family status amongst you?' I said, 'He belongs to a noble family amongst us.' Heraclius said, 'Was any of his ancestors a king?' I said, 'No.' He said, 'Did you ever accuse him of telling lies before his saying what he has said?' I said, 'No'. He said, 'Do the nobles follow him or the poor people?' I said, 'It is the poor who follow him.' He said, 'Is the number of his followers increasing or decreasing?' I said, 'They are increasing.' He said, 'Does anyone renounce his religion (i.e. Islâm) after embracing it, being displeased with it?' I said, 'No.' He said, 'Did you fight with him?' I replied, 'Yes.' He said, 'How was your fighting with him?' I said, 'The fighting between us was undecided and victory was shared by him and us in turns. He inflicts casualties upon us and we inflict casualties upon him.' He said, 'Did he ever betray?' I said, 'No, but now we are away from him in this truce and we do not know what he will do in it.' " Abu Sufyân added, "By Allâh, I was not able to insert in my speech a word (against him) except that Heraclius said, 'Did anybody else (amongst you) ever claim the same (i.e. to be Allâh's Prophet) before him?' I said, 'No'. Then Heraclius told his translator to tell me (i.e. Abu Sufyân), 'I asked you about his family status amongst you, and you told me that he comes from a noble family amongst you. Verily, all Messengers come from the noblest family among their people. Then I asked you whether any of his ancestors was a king, and you denied that.Thereupon I thought that had one of his forefathers been a king, I would have said that he (i.e. Muhammad ﷺ) was seeking to rule the kingdom of his forefathers. Then I asked you regarding his followers, whether they were the noble or the poor among the people, and you said that they were only poor (who follow him). In fact, such are the followers of the Messengers. Then I asked you whether you have ever accused him of telling lies before he said what he said, and your reply was in the negative. Therefore, I took for granted that a man who did not tell a lie about others, could never tell a lie about Allâh. Then I asked you whether anyone of his followers had renounced his religion (i.e. Islâm) after embracing it, being displeased with it, and you denied that. And such is Faith when its delight enters the heart and mixes with it completely. Then I asked you whether his followers were increasing or decreasing. You claimed that they were increasing, that is the way of true Faith till it is complete. Then I asked you whether you had ever fought with him, and you claimed that you had fought with him and the battle between you and him was undecided and the victory was shared by you and him in turns; he inflicted casualties upon you and you inflicted casualties upon them. Such is the case with the Messengers, they are put to trials and the final victory is for them. Then I asked you whether he has ever betrayed anyone; you claimed that he had never betrayed. Indeed, Messengers never betray. Then I asked you whether anyone had said this statement before him; and you denied that. Thereupon I thought if somebody had said that statement before him, then I would have said that he was but a man copying some sayings said before him.' " Abu Sufyân said, "Heraclius then asked me, 'What does he order you to do?' I said, 'He orders us (to offer) prayers and (to pay) Zakât, and to keep good relationship with the kith and kin, and to be chaste.' Then Heraclius said, 'If whatever you have said is true, then he is really a Prophet. I knew that he (i.e. the Prophet ﷺ) was going to appear, but I never thought that he would be from amongst you. If I were certain that I can reach him, I would like to meet him and if I were with him, I would wash his feet; and his kingdom will expand (surely) to what is under my feet.' Then Heraclius asked for the letter of Allâh's Messenger ﷺ and read it, wherein was written:

In the Name of Allâh, the Most Gracious, the Most Merciful.

(This letter is) from Muhammad, Messenger of Allâh, to Heraclius, the sovereign of Byzantine ...

away, say: "Bear witness that we are Muslims."

تَوَلَّوْا فَقُولُوا۟ ٱشْهَدُوا۟ بِأَنَّا مُسْلِمُونَ ۝

65. O people of the Scripture (Jews and Christians)! Why do you dispute about Ibrâhîm (Abraham), while the Taurât (Torah) and the Injeel (Gospel) were not revealed till after him? Have you then no sense?

يَـٰٓأَهْلَ ٱلْكِتَـٰبِ لِمَ تُحَآجُّونَ فِىٓ إِبْرَٰهِيمَ وَمَآ أُنزِلَتِ ٱلتَّوْرَىٰةُ وَٱلْإِنجِيلُ إِلَّا مِنۢ بَعْدِهِۦٓ أَفَلَا تَعْقِلُونَ ۝

Peace be upon him who follows the Right Path. Now then, I call you to embrace Islâm. Embrace Islâm and you will be saved (from Allâh's punishment); embrace Islâm, and Allâh will give you a double reward, but if you reject this, you will be responsible for the sins of all the people of your kingdom: (Allâh's Statement):

"O people of the Scripture (Jews and Christians)! Come to a word that is just between us and you, that we worship none but Allâh (Alone) ... bear witness that we are Muslims." (3:64).

"When he finished reading the letter, voices grew louder near him and there was a great hue and cry, and we were ordered to go out." Abu Sufyân added, "While coming out, I said to my companions, 'The matter of Ibn Abu Kabshah* (i.e. Muhammad صلى الله عليه وسلم) has become so prominent that even the king of Banu Al-Asfar (i.e. the Romans) is afraid of him.' So I continued to believe that Allâh's Messenger صلى الله عليه وسلم would be victorious, till Allâh made me embrace Islâm." Az-Zuhri said, "Heraclius then invited all the chiefs of the Byzantine and had them assembled in his house and said, 'O group of Byzantine! Do you wish to have a permanent success and guidance and that your kingdom should remain with you?' (Immediately after hearing that), they rushed towards the gate like onagers, but they found them closed. Heraclius then said, 'Bring them back to me.' So he called them and said, 'I just wanted to test the strength of your adherence to your religion. Now I have observed of you that which I like.' Then the people fell in prostration before him and became pleased with him." (*Sahih Al-Bukhâri*, Vol.6, *Hadîth* No.75).

* Abu Kabshah was not the father of the Prophet صلى الله عليه وسلم but it was a mockery done by Abu Sufyân out of hostility against the Prophet صلى الله عليه وسلم.

66. Verily, you are those who have disputed about that of which you have knowledge. Why do you then dispute concerning that of which you have no knowledge? It is Allâh Who knows, and you know not.

هَٰٓأَنتُمۡ هَٰٓؤُلَآءِ حَٰجَجۡتُمۡ فِيمَا لَكُم بِهِۦ عِلۡمٌ فَلِمَ تُحَآجُّونَ فِيمَا لَيۡسَ لَكُم بِهِۦ عِلۡمٌ وَٱللَّهُ يَعۡلَمُ وَأَنتُمۡ لَا تَعۡلَمُونَ ٦٦

67. Ibrâhîm (Abraham) was neither a Jew nor a Christian, but he was a true Muslim *Hanîfa* (Islâmic Monotheism — to worship none but Allâh Alone) and he was not of *Al-Mushrikûn* (See V.2:105).[1]

مَا كَانَ إِبۡرَٰهِيمُ يَهُودِيًّا وَلَا نَصۡرَانِيًّا وَلَٰكِن كَانَ حَنِيفًا مُّسۡلِمًا وَمَا كَانَ مِنَ ٱلۡمُشۡرِكِينَ ٦٧

68. Verily, among mankind who have the best claim to Ibrâhîm (Abraham) are those who followed him, and this Prophet (Muhammad صلى الله عليه وسلم) and those who have believed (Muslims). And Allâh is the *Walî* (Protector and Helper) of the believers.

إِنَّ أَوۡلَى ٱلنَّاسِ بِإِبۡرَٰهِيمَ لَلَّذِينَ ٱتَّبَعُوهُ وَهَٰذَا ٱلنَّبِيُّ وَٱلَّذِينَ ءَامَنُوا۟ وَٱللَّهُ وَلِيُّ ٱلۡمُؤۡمِنِينَ ٦٨

69. A party of the people of the Scripture (Jews and Christians) wish to lead you astray. But they shall not lead astray anyone except themselves, and they perceive not.

وَدَّت طَّآئِفَةٌ مِّنۡ أَهۡلِ ٱلۡكِتَٰبِ لَوۡ يُضِلُّونَكُمۡ وَمَا يُضِلُّونَ إِلَّآ أَنفُسَهُمۡ وَمَا يَشۡعُرُونَ ٦٩

70. "O people of the Scripture! (Jews and Christians): Why do you disbelieve in the *Ayât* of Allâh, [the Verses about Prophet Muhammad صلى الله عليه وسلم present in the Taurât (Torah) and the Injeel (Gospel)] while you (yourselves) bear witness (to their truth)."

يَٰٓأَهۡلَ ٱلۡكِتَٰبِ لِمَ تَكۡفُرُونَ بِـَٔايَٰتِ ٱللَّهِ وَأَنتُمۡ تَشۡهَدُونَ ٧٠

71. "O people of the Scripture (Jews and Christians): Why do you mix truth

يَٰٓأَهۡلَ ٱلۡكِتَٰبِ لِمَ تَلۡبِسُونَ ٱلۡحَقَّ بِٱلۡبَٰطِلِ وَتَكۡتُمُونَ ٱلۡحَقَّ

---

[1] (V.3:67) See the footnote of (V.2:135).

with falsehood and conceal the truth while you know?"

72. And a party of the people of the Scripture say: "Believe in the morning in that which is revealed to the believers (Muslims), and reject it at the end of the day, so that they may turn back."

73. And believe no one except the one who follows your religion. Say (O Muhammad صلى الله عليه وسلم): "Verily, right guidance is the Guidance of Allâh" and do not believe that anyone can receive like that which you have received (of Revelation) except when he follows your religion, otherwise they would engage you in argument before your Lord. Say (O Muhammad صلى الله عليه وسلم): "All the bounty is in the Hand[1] of

وَأَنتُمْ تَعْلَمُونَ ۝

وَقَالَت طَّآئِفَةٌ مِّنْ أَهْلِ ٱلْكِتَبِ ءَامِنُوا۟ بِٱلَّذِىٓ أُنزِلَ عَلَى ٱلَّذِينَ ءَامَنُوا۟ وَجْهَ ٱلنَّهَارِ وَٱكْفُرُوٓا۟ ءَاخِرَهُۥ لَعَلَّهُمْ يَرْجِعُونَ ۝

وَلَا تُؤْمِنُوٓا۟ إِلَّا لِمَن تَبِعَ دِينَكُمْ قُلْ إِنَّ ٱلْهُدَىٰ هُدَى ٱللَّهِ أَن يُؤْتَىٰٓ أَحَدٌ مِّثْلَ مَآ أُوتِيتُمْ أَوْ يُحَآجُّوكُمْ عِندَ رَبِّكُمْ قُلْ إِنَّ ٱلْفَضْلَ بِيَدِ ٱللَّهِ يُؤْتِيهِ مَن يَشَآءُ وَٱللَّهُ وَٰسِعٌ عَلِيمٌ ۝

---

[1] (V.3:73) "The Qualities of Allâh" صفات الله عز وجل

إن جميع ما ورد في كتاب الله عز وجل من صفات الله تعالى كالوجه والعين واليد والساق والمجيء، والإستواء وغيرها من الصفات، أو مما وصفه الرسول صلى الله عليه وسلم وثبت في الأحاديث النبوية الصحيحة كالنزول، والضحك، وغيرها فإن العلماء بالكتاب والسنة يؤمنون بهذه الصفات، ويثبتونها لله تعالى من غير تأويل أو تشبيه أو تعطيل، وهي صفات تليق بالله تعالى لا تشبه صفات أحد من المخلوقات لقوله تعالى {ليس كمثله شيء} ١١/٤٢ وقوله تعالى {ولم يكن له كفواً أحد} ٤/١١٢.

Sifât-ullâh (Qualities of Allâh).

All that has been revealed in Allâh's Book [the Qur'ân] as regards the [Sifât] Qualities of Allâh عز وجل the Most High, like His Face, Eyes, Hands, Shins, (Legs), His Coming, His Istawa (rising over His Throne) and others, or all that Allâh's Messenger صلى الله عليه وسلم qualified Him in the true authentic Prophet's Ahâdîth (narrations) as regards His Qualities like [Nuzûl], His Descent or His laughing and others, the religious scholars of the Qur'ân and the Sunnah" believe in these Qualities of Allâh and they confirm that these are really His Qualities, without Ta'wîl (interpreting their meanings into different

Allâh; He grants [...] And Allâh is All-Sufficient He wills. creatures' needs, the All-Know[...] for His

74. He selects for His Mercy ([...] and the Qur'ân with Prophethood[...] whom He wills and Allâh is the Owner of Great Bounty.

75. Among the people of the Scripture (Jews and Christians) is he who, if entrusted with a *Qintâr* (a great amount of wealth), will readily pay it back; and among them there is he who, if entrusted with a single silver coin, will not repay it unless you constantly stand demanding, because they say: "There is no blame on us to betray and take the properties of the illiterates (Arabs)." But they tell a lie against Allâh while they know it.

76. Yes, whoever fulfils his pledge and fears Allâh much; verily, then Allâh loves those who are *Al-Muttaqûn* (the pious. See V.2:2).

77. Verily, those who purchase a small gain at the cost of Allâh's Covenant and their oaths, they shall have no portion in the Hereafter

---

things) or *Tashbîh* (giving resemblance or similarity to any of the creatures) or [*Ta'tîl*] (i.e. completely ignoring or denying them i.e., there is no Face, or Eyes or Hands, or Shins, for Allâh). These Qualities befit or suit only for Allâh Alone, and He does not resemble any of (His) creatures. As Allâh's Statement (in the Qur'ân): (1) "There is nothing like unto Him, and He is the All-Hearer, the All-Seer." (V.42:11) (2) "There is none comparable unto Him." (V.112:4)

يُكَلِّمُهُمُ اللّهُ وَلَا يَنظُرُ إِلَيْهِمْ
يَوْمَ الْقِيَامَةِ وَلَا يُزَكِّيهِمْ
وَلَهُمْ عَذَابٌ أَلِيمٌ ۝

...(Paradise). Neither will Allâh speak to them, nor look at them on the Day of Resurrection, nor will He purify them, and they shall have a painful torment.

78. And verily, among them is a party who distort the Book with their tongues (as they read), so that you may think it is from the Book, but it is not from the Book, and they say: "This is from Allâh," but it is not from Allâh; and they speak a lie against Allâh while they know it.

وَإِنَّ مِنْهُمْ لَفَرِيقًا يَلْوُونَ
أَلْسِنَتَهُم بِالْكِتَابِ لِتَحْسَبُوهُ
مِنَ الْكِتَابِ وَمَا هُوَ مِنَ
الْكِتَابِ وَيَقُولُونَ هُوَ مِنْ
عِندِ اللّهِ وَمَا هُوَ مِنْ عِندِ اللّهِ
وَيَقُولُونَ عَلَى اللّهِ الْكَذِبَ وَهُمْ
يَعْلَمُونَ ۝

79. It is not (possible) for any human being to whom Allâh has given the Book and Al-Hukm (the knowledge and understanding of the laws of religion) and Prophethood to say to the people: "Be my worshippers rather than Allâh's." On the contrary (he would say): "Be you Rabbâniyûn (learned men of religion who practise what they know and also preach others), because you are teaching the Book, and you are studying it."

مَا كَانَ لِبَشَرٍ أَن
يُؤْتِيَهُ اللّهُ الْكِتَابَ وَالْحُكْمَ
وَالنُّبُوَّةَ ثُمَّ يَقُولَ لِلنَّاسِ كُونُوا
عِبَادًا لِّي مِن دُونِ اللّهِ وَلَٰكِن
كُونُوا رَبَّانِيِّينَ بِمَا كُنتُمْ
تُعَلِّمُونَ الْكِتَابَ
وَبِمَا كُنتُمْ تَدْرُسُونَ ۝

80. Nor would he order you to take angels and Prophets for lords (gods).[1] Would he order you to disbelieve after

وَلَا يَأْمُرَكُمْ أَن تَتَّخِذُوا الْمَلَائِكَةَ
وَالنَّبِيِّينَ أَرْبَابًا أَيَأْمُرُكُم بِالْكُفْرِ

---

[1] (V.3:80) Narrated 'Umar رضي الله عنه: I heard the Prophet صلى الله عليه وسلم saying, "Do not exaggerate in praising me as the Christians praised the son of Maryam (Mary)*, for I am only a slave. So call me the slave of Allâh and His Messenger," (Sahih Al-Bukhâri, Vol.4, Hadîth No. 654).

* The Christians overpraised 'Îsâ (Jesus) عليه السلام till they took him as a god besides Allâh.

will come (Muhammad صلى الله عليه وسلم confirming what is with you; you must, then, believe in him and help him." Allâh said: "Do you agree (to it) and will you take up My Covenant (which I conclude with you)?" They said: "We agree." He said: "Then bear witness; and I am with you among the witnesses (for this)."

82. Then whoever turns away after this, they are the *Fâsiqûn* (rebellious: those who turn away from Allâh's Obedience).

83. Do they seek other than the religion of Allâh (the true Islâmic Monotheism —worshipping none but Allâh Alone), while to Him submitted all creatures in the heavens and the earth, willingly or unwillingly. And to Him shall they all be returned.

84. Say (O Muhammad صلى الله عليه وسلم): "We believe in Allâh and in what has been sent down to us, and what was sent down to Ibrâhîm (Abraham), Ismâ'îl (Ishmael), Ishâq (Isaac), Ya'qûb (Jacob) and Al-Asbât [the offspring of the twelve sons of Ya'qûb (Jacob)] and what was given to Mûsâ (Moses), 'Îsâ (Jesus) and the Prophets from their

مِنۡهُمۡ وَنَحۡنُ

وَمَن يَبۡتَغِ غَيۡرَ ٱلۡإِسۡلَٰمِ دِينٗا

فَلَن يُقۡبَلَ مِنۡهُ وَهُوَ فِي ٱلۡأٓخِرَةِ

مِنَ ٱلۡخَٰسِرِينَ ٨٥

make   ver be
Hereafter he
(Allâh) we
other
losers.[1]
another
ac

(V.3:85).

بر.. is obligatory to have Belief in the Messengership of the
Prophet (Muhammad صلى الله عليه وسلم). Narrated Abu Hurairah رضى الله عنه
Allâh's Messenger صلى الله عليه وسلم said: "By Him (Allâh) in Whose
Hand Muhammad's soul is, there is none from amongst the Jews
and the Christians (of these present nations) who hears about me
and then dies without believing in the Message with which I have
been sent (i.e. Islâmic Monotheism), but he will be from the
dwellers of the (Hell) Fire." (Sahih Muslim, the Book of Faith,
Vol.1, Hadith No. 240). [See also (V.3:116)].

b) The asking of (angel) Jibrael (Gabriel) from the Prophet صلى الله عليه
وسلم about Belief, Islâm, Ihsân (perfection) and the knowledge of
the Hour (Doomsday), and their explanation given to him by the
Prophet صلى الله عليه وسلم. Then the Prophet صلى الله عليه وسلم said (to his
Companions): "Jibrael (Gabriel) عليه السلام came to teach you your
religion." So the Prophet صلى الله عليه وسلم regarded all that as a religion.
And all that which the Prophet صلى الله عليه وسلم explained to the
delegation of 'Abdûl-Qais was a part of faith. (See Sahih Al-
Bukhâri, Vol. I, Hadîth No.50 and 87) And the Statement of Allâh
عز وجل: "And whoever seeks a religion other than Islâm, it will never
be accepted of him." (3:85).

Narrated Abu Hurairah رضى الله عنه: One day while the Prophet صلى الله عليه
وسلم was sitting in the company of some people, (the angel) Jibrael
(Gabriel) عليه السلام came and asked, "What is Faith?" Allâh's
Messenger صلى الله عليه وسلم replied, "Faith is to believe in Allâh, His
angels, (the) Meeting with Him, His Messengers, and to believe in
Resurrection."* Then he further asked, "What is Islâm?" Allâh's
Messenger صلى الله عليه وسلم replied, "To worship Allâh Alone and none
else, to perform As-Salât (Iqamât-as-Salât), to give the Zakât and to
observe Saum (fasts) during the month of Ramadân,"** then he further
asked, "What is Ihsân (perfection)?" Allâh's Messenger صلى الله عليه وسلم

124. (Remember) when you (Muhammad صلى الله عليه وسلم) said to the believers, "Is it not enough for you that your Lord (Allâh) should help you with three thousand angels sent down?"

125. "Yes, if you hold on to patience and piety, and the enemy comes rushing at you; your Lord will help you with five-thousand angels having marks (of distinction)."

126. Allâh made it not but as a message of good news for you and as an assurance to your hearts. And there is no victory except from Allâh, the All-Mighty, the All-Wise.

127. That He might cut off a part of those who disbelieve, or expose them to infamy, so that they retire frustrated.

128. Not for you (O Muhammad صلى الله عليه وسلم, but for Allâh) is the decision; whether He turns in mercy to (pardons) them or punishes them; verily, they are the *Zâlimûn* (polytheists, disobedients and wrongdoers).

129. And to Allâh belongs all that is in the heavens and all that is in the earth. He forgives whom He wills, and punishes whom He wills. And Allâh is Oft-Forgiving, Most Merciful.

130. O you who believe! Eat not *Ribâ* (usury)[1] doubled and multiplied,

---

[1] (V.3:130)
a) See (V.2:275) and its footnote.

but fear Allâh that you may be successful.

131. And fear the Fire, which is prepared for the disbelievers.

132. And obey Allâh and the Messenger (Muhammad صلى الله عليه وسلم) that you may obtain mercy.[1]

133. And march forth in the way (which leads to) forgiveness from your Lord, and for Paradise as wide as are the heavens and the earth, prepared for *Al-Muttaqûn* (the pious. See V.2:2).

134. Those who spend (in Allâh's Cause) in prosperity and in adversity,[2]

---

b) Narrated Abu Hurairah رضى الله عنه: The Prophet صلى الله عليه وسلم said, "Avoid the seven great destructive sins." The people enquired, "O Allâh's Messenger! What are they?" He said, "(1) To join others in worship along with Allâh, (2) to practise sorcery, (3) to kill a person which Allâh has forbidden except for a just cause (according to Islâmic law), (4) to eat up *Ribâ* (usury), (5) to eat up an orphan's wealth, (6) to show one's back to the enemy and fleeing from the battlefield at the time of fighting, (7) and to accuse chaste women, who never even think of anything touching their chastity and are true believers". (*Sahih Al-Bukhâri*, Vol. 4, *Hadîth* No. 28).

c) See the footnote (A) of the (V.2:278).

d) See the footnote (B) of the (V.2:278).

[1] (V.3:132) See the footnote of (V.3:85).

[2] (V.3:134) Narrated Abu Hurairah رضى الله عنه: The Prophet صلى الله عليه وسلم said, "Charity is obligatory everyday on every joint of a human being*. If one helps a person in matters concerning his riding animal by helping him to ride on it or by lifting his luggage on to it, all this will be regarded as charity. A good word, and every step one takes to offer the compulsory congregational prayer is regarded as charity; and guiding somebody on the road is regarded as charity." (*Sahih Al-Bukhâri*, Vol.4, *Hadîth* No.141).

who repress anger,[1] and who pardon men; verily, Allâh loves *Al-Muhsinûn*[2] (the good-doers).

135. And those who, when they have committed *Fâhishah* (illegal sexual intercourse) or wronged themselves with evil, remember Allâh and ask forgiveness for their sins; — and none can forgive sins but Allâh — and do not persist in what (wrong) they have done, while they know.[3]

136. For such, the reward is Forgiveness from their Lord, and Gardens with rivers flowing underneath (Paradise), wherein they shall abide forever. How excellent is this reward for the doers (who do righteous deeds according to Allâh's Orders).

137. Many similar ways (and mishaps of life) were faced by nations (believers and disbelievers) that have passed away before you (as you have faced in the battle of Uhud), so travel through the earth, and see what was the

---

* To show gratitude to Allâh for keeping your body safe and sound, you should give in charity or do charitable deeds.

[1] (V.3:134) Narrated Abu Hurairah رضي الله عنه: Allâh's Messenger صلى الله عليه وسلم said, "The strong is not the one who overcomes the people by his strength, but the strong is the one who controls himself while in anger." (*Sahih Al-Bukhâri*, Vol.8, *Hadîth* No.135).

[2] (V.3:134) *Al-Muhsinûn*: Doers of good, those who perform good deeds totally for Allâh's sake only without any show-off or to gain praise or fame, and they do them in accordance with the *Sunnah* (legal ways) of Allâh's Messenger, Muhammad صلى الله عليه وسلم.

[3] (V.3:135) See the footnote of (V.42:25).

end of those who disbelieved (in the Oneness of Allâh, and disobeyed Him and His Messengers).

138. This (the Qur'ân) is a plain statement for mankind, a guidance and instruction to those who are Al-Muttaqûn (the pious. See V.2:2).

139. So do not become weak (against your enemy), nor be sad, and you will be superior (in victory) if you are indeed (true) believers.

140. If a wound (and killing) has touched you, be sure a similar wound (and killing) has touched the others. And so are the days (good and not so good), We give to men by turns, that Allâh may test those who believe, and that He may take martyrs from among you. And Allâh likes not the Zâlimûn (polytheists and wrong-doers).

141. And that Allâh may test (or purify) the believers (from sins) and destroy the disbelievers.

142. Do you think that you will enter Paradise before Allâh tests those of you who fought (in His Cause) and (also) tests those who are As-Sâbirûn (the patient)?

143. You did indeed wish for death (Ash-Shahâdah — martyrdom) before you met it. Now you have seen it openly with your own eyes.

144. Muhammad (صلى الله عليه وسلم) is no more than a Messenger, and indeed (many) Messengers have passed away before him. If he dies or is killed, will you then turn back on your heels (as disbelievers)? And he who turns back on his heels, not the least harm will he do to Allâh; and Allâh will give reward to those who are grateful.

145. And no person can ever die except by Allâh's Leave and at an appointed term. And whoever desires a reward in (this) world, We shall give him of it; and whoever desires a reward in the Hereafter, We shall give him thereof. And We shall reward the grateful.

146. And many a Prophet (i.e. many from amongst the Prophets) fought in Allâh's Cause) and along with him (fought) large bands of religious learned men. But they never lost heart for that which did befall them in Allâh's Way, nor did they weaken nor degrade themselves. And Allâh loves *As-Sâbirûn* (the patient).

147. And they said nothing but: "Our Lord! Forgive us our sins and our transgressions (in keeping our duties to You), establish our feet firmly, and give us victory over the disbelieving folk."

148. So Allâh gave them the reward of this world, and the excellent reward of the Hereafter. And Allâh loves *Al-Muhsinûn* (the good-doers — See the footnote of V.3:134 and of V.9:120).

149. O you who believe! If you obey those who disbelieve, they will send you back on your heels, and you will turn back (from Faith) as losers.[1]

150. Nay, Allâh is your *Maulâ* (Patron, Lord, Helper, Protector), and He is the Best of helpers.

151. We shall cast terror into the hearts of those who disbelieve, because they joined others in worship with Allâh, for which He had sent no authority; their abode will be the Fire and how evil is the abode of the *Zâlimûn* (polytheists and wrong-doers).

152. And Allâh did indeed fulfil His Promise to you when you were killing them (your enemy) with His Permission; until (the moment) you lost your courage and fell to disputing about the order, and disobeyed after He showed you (of the booty) which you love. Among you are some that desire this world and some that desire the Hereafter. Then He made you flee from them (your enemy), that He might test you. But surely, He forgave you, and Allâh is Most Gracious to the believers.

---

[1] (V.3:149) What is said about residence (staying) in the land of *Ash-Shirk* (polytheism i.e. the land where polytheism is practised). Narrated Sumurah bin Jundûb رضى الله عنه Allâh's Messenger صلى الله عليه وسلم said:- "Anybody (from among the Muslims) who meets, gathers together, lives, and stays (permanently) with a *Mushrik* (polytheist or a disbeliever in the Oneness of Allâh) and agrees to his ways, opinions and (enjoys) his living with him (*Mushrik*) then he (that Muslim) is like him (*Mushrik*). (This *Hadîth* indicates that a Muslim should not stay in a non-Muslim country, he must emigrate to a Muslim country, where Islâm is practised.)" [The Book of *Jihâd, Abu Dâwûd*].

153. (And remember) when you ran away (dreadfully) without even casting a side glance at anyone, and the Messenger (Muhammad صلى الله عليه وسلم) was in your rear calling you back. There did Allâh give you one distress after another by way of requital to teach you not to grieve for that which had escaped you, nor for that which had befallen you. And Allâh is Well-Aware of all that you do.

154. Then after the distress, He sent down security for you. Slumber overtook a party of you, while another party was thinking about themselves (as how to save their ownselves, ignoring the others and the Prophet صلى الله عليه وسلم and thought wrongly of Allâh — the thought of ignorance. They said, "Have we any part in the affair?" Say (O Muhammad صلى الله عليه وسلم): "Indeed the affair belongs wholly to Allâh." They hide within themselves what they dare not reveal to you, saying: "If we had anything to do with the affair, none of us would have been killed here." Say: "Even if you had remained in your homes, those for whom death was decreed would certainly have gone forth to the place of their death," but that Allâh might test what is in your breasts; and to purify[1] that which was in your hearts (sins), and Allâh is All-Knower of what is in (your) breasts.

---

[1] (V.3:154) The Arabic word *Yumahhisu* has three meanings: (1) To test, (2) To purify, (3) To get rid of (*Tafsir Al-Qurtubi*).

155. Those of you who turned back on the day the two hosts met (i.e. the battle of Uhud), it was *Shaitân* (Satan) who caused them to backslide (run away from the battlefield) because of some (sins) they had earned. But Allâh, indeed, has forgiven them. Surely, Allâh is Oft-Forgiving, Most Forbearing.

156. O you who believe! Be not like those who disbelieve (hypocrites) and who say to their brethren when they travel through the earth or go out to fight: "If they had stayed with us, they would not have died or been killed," so that Allâh may make it a cause of regret in their hearts. It is Allâh that gives life and causes death. And Allâh is All-Seer of what you do.

157. And if you are killed or die in the Way of Allâh, forgiveness and mercy from Allâh are far better than all that they amass (of worldly wealths).

158. And whether you die, or are killed, verily, unto Allâh you shall be gathered.

159. And by the Mercy of Allâh, you dealt with them gently. And had you been severe and harsh-hearted, they would have broken away from about you; so pass over (their faults), and ask (Allâh's) Forgiveness for them; and consult them in the affairs. Then when you have taken a decision, put your trust in Allâh, certainly, Allâh loves those who put their trust (in Him).

160. If Allâh helps you, none can overcome you; and if He forsakes you, who is there after Him that can help you? And in Allâh (Alone) let believers put their trust.

إِن يَنصُرُكُمُ ٱللَّهُ فَلَا غَالِبَ لَكُمْ وَإِن يَخْذُلْكُمْ فَمَن ذَا ٱلَّذِى يَنصُرُكُم مِّنۢ بَعْدِهِۦ وَعَلَى ٱللَّهِ فَلْيَتَوَكَّلِ ٱلْمُؤْمِنُونَ ١٦٠

161. It is not for any Prophet to take illegally a part of the booty (Ghulul),[1] and whosoever deceives his companions as regards the booty, he shall bring forth on the Day of Resurrection that which he took (illegally). Then every person shall be paid in full what he has earned, and they shall not be dealt with unjustly.

وَمَا كَانَ لِنَبِىٍّ أَن يَغُلَّ وَمَن يَغْلُلْ يَأْتِ بِمَا غَلَّ يَوْمَ ٱلْقِيَٰمَةِ ثُمَّ تُوَفَّىٰ كُلُّ نَفْسٍ مَّا كَسَبَتْ وَهُمْ لَا يُظْلَمُونَ ١٦١

---

[1] (V.3:161) Al-Ghulul: (Stealing from the war booty before its distribution), and the Statement of Allâh تعالى: "And whosoever deceives his companions as regards booty, he shall bring forth on the Day of Resurrection that which he took (illegally)".

Narrated Abu Hurairah رضي الله عنه: The Prophet صلى الله عليه وسلم got up amongst us and mentioned Al-Ghulul, emphasized its magnitude and declared that it was a great sin saying, "Don't commit Ghulul for I should not like to see anyone amongst you on the Day of Resurrection, carrying over his neck a sheep that will be bleating, or carrying over his neck a horse that will be neighing. Such a man will be saying: 'O Allâh's Messenger! Intercede with Allâh for me,' and I will reply, 'I can't help you, for I have conveyed Allâh's Message to you.' Nor should I like to see a man carrying over his neck, a camel that will be grunting. Such a man will say, 'O Allâh's Messenger! Intercede with Allâh for me,' and I will say, 'I can't help you for I have conveyed Allâh's Message to you'; or one carrying over his neck gold and silver and saying, 'O Allâh's Messenger! Intercede with Allâh for me.' And I will say, 'I can't help you, for I have conveyed Allâh's Message to you, or one carrying clothes that will be fluttering, and the man will say, 'O Allâh's Messenger! Intercede with Allâh for me.' And I will say, 'I can't help you, for I have conveyed Allâh's Message to you.' "
(Sahih Al-Bukhâri, Vol. 4, Hadîth No. 307).

162. Is then one who follows (seeks) the good Pleasure of Allâh (by not taking illegally a part of the booty) like the one who draws on himself the Wrath of Allâh (by taking a part of the booty illegally — *Ghulul*)? — his abode is Hell, and worst, indeed is that destination!

أَفَمَنِ ٱتَّبَعَ رِضْوَٰنَ ٱللَّهِ كَمَنۢ بَآءَ بِسَخَطٍ مِّنَ ٱللَّهِ وَمَأْوَىٰهُ جَهَنَّمُ ۚ وَبِئْسَ ٱلْمَصِيرُ ۝

163. They are in varying grades with Allâh, and Allâh is All-Seer of what they do.

هُمْ دَرَجَٰتٌ عِندَ ٱللَّهِ ۗ وَٱللَّهُ بَصِيرٌۢ بِمَا يَعْمَلُونَ ۝

164. Indeed Allâh conferred a great favour on the believers when He sent among them a Messenger (Muhammad صلى الله عليه وسلم) from among themselves, reciting unto them His Verses (the Qur'ân). and purifying them (from sins by their following him), and instructing them (in) the Book (the Qur'ân) and *Al-Hikmah* [the wisdom and the *Sunnah* of the Prophet صلى الله عليه وسلم (i.e. his legal ways, statements and acts of worship)], while before that they had been in manifest error.[1]

لَقَدْ مَنَّ ٱللَّهُ عَلَى ٱلْمُؤْمِنِينَ إِذْ بَعَثَ فِيهِمْ رَسُولًا مِّنْ أَنفُسِهِمْ يَتْلُوا۟ عَلَيْهِمْ ءَايَٰتِهِۦ وَيُزَكِّيهِمْ وَيُعَلِّمُهُمُ ٱلْكِتَٰبَ وَٱلْحِكْمَةَ وَإِن كَانُوا۟ مِن قَبْلُ لَفِى ضَلَٰلٍ مُّبِينٍ ۝

---

[1] (V.3:164) Following the *Sunnah* (legal ways) of the Prophet صلى الله عليه وسلم. And the Statement of Allâh عز و جل - "And make us leaders for the righteous." (V.25:74).

Mujâhid said, "(Make us) a community that follows the *Muttaqûn* (righteous) people who preceded us, and whom those succeeding may follow." Ibn 'Aun said, "(There are) three things which I love for myself and for my brothers, i.e. this *Sunnah* (the legal ways of the Prophet صلى الله عليه وسلم) which they should learn and ask about; the Qur'ân which they should understand and ask the people about; and that they should leave the people except when intending to do good (for them)." (*Sahih Al-Bukhâri*, Vol. 9, Chap. 2, P. 282).

A) Narrated Hudhaifah: Allâh's Messenger صلى الله عليه وسلم said to us, "Certainly *Al-Amânah* (the trust or the moral responsibility or honesty, and all the duties which Allâh has ordained) descended from the heavens and settled in the roots of the hearts of men (faithful believers), and then the Qur'ân was revealed and the people read the Qur'ân, (and learnt *Al-Amânah* from it) and also learnt it from the *Sunnah*. [Both the Qur'ân and *As-Sunnah* strengthened their (the faithful believers') *Amânah*.]" (*Sahih Al-Bukhâri*, Vol.9, Hadîth No.381).

B) Narrated Abu Hurairah رضي الله عنه: Allâh's Messenger صلى الله عليه وسلم said, "All my followers will enter Paradise except those who refuse." They said, "O Allâh's Messenger! Who will refuse?" He said, "Whoever obeys me will enter Paradise, and whoever disobeys me is the one who refuses (to enter it)." (*Sahih Al-Bukhâri*, Vol.9, Hadîth No.384).

C) Narrated Jâbir bin 'Abdullâh رضي الله عنهما: Some angels came to Prophet Muhammad صلى الله عليه وسلم while he was sleeping. Some of them said, "He is sleeping." Others said, "His eyes are sleeping but his heart is awake." Then they said, "There is an example for this companion of yours." One of them said, "Then set forth an example for him." Some of them said, "He is sleeping." The others said, "His eyes are sleeping but his heart is awake." Then they said, "His example is that of a man who has built a house and then offered therein a banquet and sent an inviter (messenger) to invite the people. So whosoever accepted the invitation of the inviter, entered the house and ate of the banquet, and whoever did not accept the invitation of the inviter, did not enter the house, nor did he eat of the banquet." Then the angels said, "Interpret this parable to him so that he may understand it." Some of them said, "He is sleeping." The others said, "His eyes are sleeping but his heart is awake." And then they said, "The house stands for Paradise and the call-maker is Muhammad صلى الله عليه وسلم and whoever obeys Muhammad صلى الله عليه وسلم, obeys Allâh; and whoever disobeys Muhammad صلى الله عليه وسلم, disobeys Allâh. Muhammad صلى الله عليه وسلم separated the people (i.e., through his message; the good is distinguished from the bad, and the believers from the disbelievers)." (*Sahih Al-Bukhâri*, Vol. 9, Hadîth No.385).

165. (What is the matter with you?) When a single disaster smites you, although you smote (your enemies) with one twice as great, you say: "From where does this come to us?" Say (to them), "It is from yourselves (because of your evil deeds)." And Allâh has power over all things.

أَوَلَمَّا أَصَٰبَتْكُم مُّصِيبَةٌ قَدْ أَصَبْتُم مِّثْلَيْهَا قُلْتُمْ أَنَّىٰ هَٰذَا قُلْ هُوَ مِنْ عِندِ أَنفُسِكُمْ إِنَّ ٱللَّهَ عَلَىٰ كُلِّ شَىْءٍ قَدِيرٌ ۝

166. And what you suffered (of the disaster) on the day (of the battle of Uhud when) the two armies met, was by the leave of Allâh, in order that He might test the believers.

وَمَآ أَصَٰبَكُمْ يَوْمَ ٱلْتَقَى ٱلْجَمْعَانِ فَبِإِذْنِ ٱللَّهِ وَلِيَعْلَمَ ٱلْمُؤْمِنِينَ ۝

167. And that He might test the hypocrites, it was said to them: "Come, fight in the Way of Allâh or (at least) defend yourselves." They said: "Had we known that fighting will take place, we would certainly have followed you." They were that day, nearer to disbelief than to Faith, saying with their mouths what was not in their

وَلِيَعْلَمَ ٱلَّذِينَ نَافَقُواْ وَقِيلَ لَهُمْ تَعَالَوْاْ قَٰتِلُواْ فِى سَبِيلِ ٱللَّهِ أَوِ ٱدْفَعُواْ قَالُواْ لَوْ نَعْلَمُ قِتَالًا لَّٱتَّبَعْنَٰكُمْ هُمْ لِلْكُفْرِ يَوْمَئِذٍ أَقْرَبُ مِنْهُمْ لِلْإِيمَٰنِ يَقُولُونَ بِأَفْوَٰهِهِم مَّا لَيْسَ

D) Narrated Abu Mûsâ رضى الله عنه : The Prophet صلى الله عليه وسلم said, "My example, and the example of what I have been sent with, is that of a man who came to some people and said, 'O people I have seen the enemy's army with my own eyes, and I am the naked warner; so protect yourselves!' Then a group of his people obeyed him and fled at night proceeding stealthily till they were safe, while another group of them disbelieved him and stayed at their places till morning when the army came upon them, and killed and ruined them completely. So this is the example of that person who obeys me and follows that truth which I have brought (the Qur'ân and the *Sunnah*), and the example of the one who disobeys me and disbelieves the truth I have brought." (*Sahih Al-Bukhari*, Vol. 9, *Hadîth* No. 387).

hearts. And Allâh has full knowledge of what they conceal.

168. (They are) the ones who said about their killed brethren while they themselves sat (at home): "If only they had listened to us, they would not have been killed." Say: "Avert death from your ownselves, if you speak the truth."

169. Think not of those who are killed in the Way of Allâh as dead. Nay, they are alive, with their Lord, and they have provision.

170. They rejoice in what Allâh has bestowed upon them of His Bounty and rejoice for the sake of those who have not yet joined them, but are left behind (not yet martyred) that on them no fear shall come, nor shall they grieve.

171. They rejoice in a Grace and a Bounty from Allâh, and that Allâh will not waste the reward of the believers.

172. Those who answered (the Call of) Allâh and the Messenger (Muhammad صلى الله عليه وسلم) after being wounded; for those of them who did good deeds and feared Allâh, there is a great reward.

173. Those (i.e. believers) unto whom the people (hypocrites) said, "Verily, the people (pagans) have gathered against you (a great army), therefore, fear them." But it (only) increased them in Faith, and they said: "Allâh (Alone) is Sufficient for us,

في قُلُوبِهِمْ وَٱللَّهُ أَعْلَمُ بِمَا يَكْتُمُونَ ١ ٱلَّذِينَ قَالُوا لِإِخْوَٰنِهِمْ وَقَعَدُوا لَوْ أَطَاعُونَا مَا قُتِلُوا قُلْ فَٱدْرَءُوا عَنْ أَنفُسِكُمُ ٱلْمَوْتَ إِن كُنتُمْ صَٰدِقِينَ ١ وَلَا تَحْسَبَنَّ ٱلَّذِينَ قُتِلُوا فِي سَبِيلِ ٱللَّهِ أَمْوَٰتَۢا بَلْ أَحْيَآءٌ عِندَ رَبِّهِمْ يُرْزَقُونَ ١ فَرِحِينَ بِمَآ ءَاتَىٰهُمُ ٱللَّهُ مِن فَضْلِهِۦ وَيَسْتَبْشِرُونَ بِٱلَّذِينَ لَمْ يَلْحَقُوا بِهِم مِّنْ خَلْفِهِمْ أَلَّا خَوْفٌ عَلَيْهِمْ وَلَا هُمْ يَحْزَنُونَ ١ ۞ يَسْتَبْشِرُونَ بِنِعْمَةٍ مِّنَ ٱللَّهِ وَفَضْلٍ وَأَنَّ ٱللَّهَ لَا يُضِيعُ أَجْرَ ٱلْمُؤْمِنِينَ ١ ٱلَّذِينَ ٱسْتَجَابُوا لِلَّهِ وَٱلرَّسُولِ مِنۢ بَعْدِ مَآ أَصَابَهُمُ ٱلْقَرْحُ لِلَّذِينَ أَحْسَنُوا مِنْهُمْ وَٱتَّقَوْا أَجْرٌ عَظِيمٌ ١ ٱلَّذِينَ قَالَ لَهُمُ ٱلنَّاسُ إِنَّ ٱلنَّاسَ قَدْ جَمَعُوا لَكُمْ فَٱخْشَوْهُمْ فَزَادَهُمْ إِيمَٰنَا وَقَالُوا حَسْبُنَا ٱللَّهُ وَنِعْمَ ٱلْوَكِيلُ ١

and He is the Best Disposer of affairs (for us)."[1]"

174. So they returned with Grace and Bounty from Allâh. No harm touched them; and they followed the good Pleasure of Allâh. And Allâh is the Owner of Great Bounty.

فَٱنقَلَبُوا۟ بِنِعْمَةٍ مِّنَ ٱللَّهِ وَفَضْلٍ لَّمْ يَمْسَسْهُمْ سُوٓءٌ وَٱتَّبَعُوا۟ رِضْوَٰنَ ٱللَّهِ وَٱللَّهُ ذُو فَضْلٍ عَظِيمٍ ١٧٤

175. It is only *Shaitân* (Satan) that suggests to you the fear of his *Auliyâ'* [supporters and friends (polytheists, disbelievers in the Oneness of Allâh and in His Messenger, Muhammad صلى الله عليه وسلم)]; so fear them not, but fear Me, if you are (true) believers.

إِنَّمَا ذَٰلِكُمُ ٱلشَّيْطَٰنُ يُخَوِّفُ أَوْلِيَآءَهُۥ فَلَا تَخَافُوهُمْ وَخَافُونِ إِن كُنتُم مُّؤْمِنِينَ ١٧٥

176. And let not those grieve you (O Muhammad صلى الله عليه وسلم) who rush with haste to disbelieve; verily, not the least harm will they do to Allâh. It is Allâh's Will to give them no portion in the

وَلَا يَحْزُنكَ ٱلَّذِينَ يُسَٰرِعُونَ فِى ٱلْكُفْرِ إِنَّهُمْ لَن يَضُرُّوا۟ ٱللَّهَ شَيْـًٔا يُرِيدُ ٱللَّهُ أَلَّا يَجْعَلَ لَهُمْ حَظًّا فِى ٱلْءَاخِرَةِ

---

[1] (V.3:173) Allâh's Statement:- "Those (i.e. believers) unto whom the people (hypocrites) said, 'Verily, the people (pagans) have gathered against you (a great army), therefore, fear them.' "

a) Narrated Ibn 'Abbâs رضى الله عنهما (The saying:) "Allâh (Alone) is Sufficient for us, and He is the Best Disposer of affairs (for us)" was said by Ibrâhîm (Abraham) عليه السلام when he was thrown into the fire; and it was said by Muhammad صلى الله عليه وسلم when they (i.e. hypocrites) said, "Verily, the people (pagans) have gathered against you (a great army), therefore, fear them," but it (only) increased them in Faith and they said: "Allâh (Alone) is Sufficient for us, and He is the Best Disposer of affairs (for us)." (V.3:173) (*Sahih Al-Bukhâri*, Vol. 6, *Hadîth* No. 86).

b) Narrated Ibn 'Abbâs رضى الله عنهما The last statement of Ibrâhîm (Abraham) عليه السلام when he was thrown into the fire, was: "Allâh (Alone) is Sufficient for me and He is the Best Disposer of (of my affairs)." (*Sahih Al-Bukhâri*, Vol. 6, *Hadîth* No. 87).

Hereafter. For them there is a great torment.

177. Verily, those who purchase disbelief at the price of Faith, not the least harm will they do to Allâh. For them, there is a painful torment.

178. And let not the disbelievers think that Our postponing of their punishment is good for them. We postpone the punishment only so that they may increase in sinfulness. And for them is a disgracing torment.

179. Allâh will not leave the believers in the state in which you are now, until He distinguishes the wicked from the good. Nor will Allâh disclose to you the secrets of the *Ghaib* (Unseen), but Allâh chooses of His Messengers whom He wills. So believe in Allâh and His Messengers. And if you believe and fear Allâh, then for you there is a great reward.

180. And let not those who covetously withhold of that which Allâh has bestowed on them of His Bounty (wealth) think that it is good for them (and so they do not pay the obligatory *Zakât*). Nay, it will be worse for them; the things which they covetously withheld shall be tied to their necks like a collar on the Day of Resurrection.[1] And to Allâh belongs

وَلَهُمْ عَذَابٌ عَظِيمٌ ﴿١٧٦﴾

إِنَّ ٱلَّذِينَ ٱشْتَرَوُاْ ٱلْكُفْرَ بِٱلْإِيمَـٰنِ لَن يَضُرُّواْ ٱللَّهَ شَيْـًٔا وَلَهُمْ عَذَابٌ أَلِيمٌ ﴿١٧٧﴾

وَلَا يَحْسَبَنَّ ٱلَّذِينَ كَفَرُوٓاْ أَنَّمَا نُمْلِي لَهُمْ خَيْرٌ لِّأَنفُسِهِمْ إِنَّمَا نُمْلِي لَهُمْ لِيَزْدَادُوٓاْ إِثْمًا وَلَهُمْ عَذَابٌ مُّهِينٌ ﴿١٧٨﴾

مَّا كَانَ ٱللَّهُ لِيَذَرَ ٱلْمُؤْمِنِينَ عَلَىٰ مَآ أَنتُمْ عَلَيْهِ حَتَّىٰ يَمِيزَ ٱلْخَبِيثَ مِنَ ٱلطَّيِّبِ وَمَا كَانَ ٱللَّهُ لِيُطْلِعَكُمْ عَلَى ٱلْغَيْبِ وَلَـٰكِنَّ ٱللَّهَ يَجْتَبِي مِن رُّسُلِهِۦ مَن يَشَآءُ فَـَٔامِنُواْ بِٱللَّهِ وَرُسُلِهِۦ وَإِن تُؤْمِنُواْ وَتَتَّقُواْ فَلَكُمْ أَجْرٌ عَظِيمٌ ﴿١٧٩﴾

وَلَا يَحْسَبَنَّ ٱلَّذِينَ يَبْخَلُونَ بِمَآ ءَاتَىٰهُمُ ٱللَّهُ مِن فَضْلِهِۦ هُوَ خَيْرًا لَّهُم بَلْ هُوَ شَرٌّ لَّهُمْ سَيُطَوَّقُونَ مَا بَخِلُواْ بِهِۦ يَوْمَ ٱلْقِيَـٰمَةِ وَلِلَّهِ مِيرَٰثُ

---

[1] (V.3:180) "Let not those who covetously withhold of that which Allâh has bestowed upon them of His Bounty ... shall be tied to their necks like a collar."

the heritage of the heavens and the earth; and Allâh is Well-Acquainted with all that you do.

السَّمَوَاتِ وَٱلأَرْضِ وَٱللَّهُ بِمَا تَعْمَلُونَ خَبِيرٌ ۝

181. Indeed, Allâh has heard the statement of those (Jews) who say: "Truly, Allâh is poor and we are rich!" We shall record what they have said and their killing of the Prophets unjustly, and We shall say: "Taste you the torment of the burning (Fire)."

لَّقَدْ سَمِعَ ٱللَّهُ قَوْلَ ٱلَّذِينَ قَالُوٓاْ إِنَّ ٱللَّهَ فَقِيرٌ وَنَحْنُ أَغْنِيَآءُ سَنَكْتُبُ مَا قَالُواْ وَقَتْلَهُمُ ٱلأَنبِيَآءَ بِغَيْرِ حَقٍّ وَنَقُولُ ذُوقُواْ عَذَابَ ٱلْحَرِيقِ ۝

182. This is because of that (evil) which your hands have sent before you. And certainly, Allâh is never unjust to (His) slaves.

ذَٰلِكَ بِمَا قَدَّمَتْ أَيْدِيكُمْ وَأَنَّ ٱللَّهَ لَيْسَ بِظَلَّامٍ لِّلْعَبِيدِ ۝

183. Those (Jews) who said: "Verily, Allâh has taken our promise not to believe in any Messenger unless he brings to us an offering which the fire (from heaven) shall devour." Say: "Verily, there came to you Messengers before me, with clear signs and even with what you speak of; why then did you kill them, if you are truthful?"

ٱلَّذِينَ قَالُوٓاْ إِنَّ ٱللَّهَ عَهِدَ إِلَيْنَآ أَلَّا نُؤْمِنَ لِرَسُولٍ حَتَّىٰ يَأْتِيَنَا بِقُرْبَانٍ تَأْكُلُهُ ٱلنَّارُ قُلْ قَدْ جَآءَكُمْ رُسُلٌ مِّن قَبْلِي بِٱلْبَيِّنَتِ وَبِٱلَّذِي قُلْتُمْ فَلِمَ قَتَلْتُمُوهُمْ إِن كُنتُمْ صَدِقِينَ ۝

Narrated Abu Hurairah رضي الله عنه : Allâh's Messenger صلى الله عليه وسلم said, "Anyone whom Allâh has given wealth but he does not pay its *Zakât;* then, on the Day of Resurrection, his wealth will be presented to him in the shape of a bald-headed poisonous male snake with two poisonous glands* in its mouth and it will encircle itself round his neck and bite him over his cheeks and say, 'I am your wealth, I am your treasure.'" Then the Prophet صلى الله عليه وسلم recited this Divine Verse: "And let not those who covetously withhold of that which Allâh has bestowed upon them of His Bounty." (V.3:180).

*Fath Al-Bâri (Sahih Al-Bukhâri, Vol. 6, Hadîth No. 88).

184. Then if they reject you (O Muhammad صلى الله عليه وسلم) so were Messengers rejected before you, who came with *Al-Bayyinât* (clear signs, proofs, evidences) and the Scripture and the Book of Enlightenment.

فَإِن كَذَّبُوكَ فَقَدْ كُذِّبَ رُسُلٌ مِّن قَبْلِكَ جَآءُو بِٱلْبَيِّنَٰتِ وَٱلزُّبُرِ وَٱلْكِتَٰبِ ٱلْمُنِيرِ ۝

185. Everyone shall taste death. And only on the Day of Resurrection shall you be paid your wages in full. And whoever is removed away from the Fire and admitted to Paradise, he indeed is successful. The life of this world is only the enjoyment of deception (a deceiving thing).

كُلُّ نَفْسٍ ذَآئِقَةُ ٱلْمَوْتِ وَإِنَّمَا تُوَفَّوْنَ أُجُورَكُمْ يَوْمَ ٱلْقِيَٰمَةِ فَمَن زُحْزِحَ عَنِ ٱلنَّارِ وَأُدْخِلَ ٱلْجَنَّةَ فَقَدْ فَازَ وَمَا ٱلْحَيَوٰةُ ٱلدُّنْيَآ إِلَّا مَتَٰعُ ٱلْغُرُورِ ۝

186. You shall certainly be tried and tested in your wealth and properties and in your personal selves, and you shall certainly hear much that will grieve you from those who received the Scripture before you (Jews and Christians) and from those who ascribe partners to Allâh; but if you persevere patiently, and become *Al-Muttaqûn* (the pious. See V.2:2) then verily, that will be a determining factor in all affairs (and that is from the great matters which you must hold on with all your efforts).

۞ لَتُبْلَوُنَّ فِىٓ أَمْوَٰلِكُمْ وَأَنفُسِكُمْ وَلَتَسْمَعُنَّ مِنَ ٱلَّذِينَ أُوتُوا۟ ٱلْكِتَٰبَ مِن قَبْلِكُمْ وَمِنَ ٱلَّذِينَ أَشْرَكُوٓا۟ أَذًى كَثِيرًا وَإِن تَصْبِرُوا۟ وَتَتَّقُوا۟ فَإِنَّ ذَٰلِكَ مِنْ عَزْمِ ٱلْأُمُورِ ۝

187. (And remember) when Allâh took a covenant from those who were given the Scripture (Jews and Christians) to make it (the news of the coming of Prophet Muhammad صلى الله عليه وسلم and the religious knowledge) known and clear to mankind, and not to hide it, but they threw it away behind their backs, and purchased with it some

وَإِذْ أَخَذَ ٱللَّهُ مِيثَٰقَ ٱلَّذِينَ أُوتُوا۟ ٱلْكِتَٰبَ لَتُبَيِّنُنَّهُۥ لِلنَّاسِ وَلَا تَكْتُمُونَهُۥ فَنَبَذُوهُ وَرَآءَ ظُهُورِهِمْ وَٱشْتَرَوْا۟ بِهِۦ ثَمَنًا قَلِيلًا فَبِئْسَ مَا يَشْتَرُونَ ۝

miserable gain! And indeed worst is that which they bought.

188. Think not that those who rejoice in what they have done (or brought about), and love to be praised for what they have not done,— think not you that they are rescued from the torment, and for them is a painful torment.

189. And to Allâh belongs the dominion of the heavens and the earth, and Allâh has power over all things.

190. Verily, in the creation of the heavens and the earth, and in the alternation of night and day, there are indeed signs for men of understanding.

191. Those who remember Allâh (always, and in prayers) standing, sitting, and lying down on their sides, and think deeply about the creation of the heavens and the earth, (saying): "Our Lord! You have not created (all) this without purpose, glory to You! (Exalted are You above all that they associate with You as partners). Give us salvation from the torment of the Fire.

192. "Our Lord! Verily, whom You admit to the Fire, indeed, You have disgraced him; and never will the Zâlimûn (polytheists and wrong-doers) find any helpers.

193. "Our Lord! Verily, we have heard the call of one (Muhammad صلى الله عليه وسلم) calling to Faith: 'Believe in your Lord,' and we have believed. Our Lord! Forgive us our sins and expiate from us our evil deeds, and make us die (in the state of righteousness) along with *Al-Abrâr* (the believers of Islamic Monotheism, the pious and righteous).

194. "Our Lord! Grant us what You promised unto us through Your Messengers and disgrace us not on the Day of Resurrection, for You never break (Your) Promise."

195. So their Lord accepted of them (their supplication and answered them), "Never will I allow to be lost the work of any of you, be he male or female. You are (members) one of another, so those who emigrated and were driven out from their homes, and suffered harm in My Cause, and who fought, and were killed (in My Cause), verily, I will expiate from them their evil deeds and admit them into Gardens under which rivers flow (in Paradise); a reward from Allâh, and with Allâh is the best of rewards."

196. Let not the free disposal (and affluence) of the disbelievers throughout the land deceive you.

197. A brief enjoyment; then, their ultimate abode is Hell; and worst indeed is that place for rest.

198. But, for those who fear their Lord, are Gardens under which rivers flow (in Paradise); therein are they to dwell (for ever), an entertainment from Allâh; and that which is with Allâh is the Best for *Al-Abrâr* (the believers of

ذُنُوبَنَا وَكَفِّرْ عَنَّا سَيِّئَاتِنَا وَتَوَفَّنَا مَعَ الْأَبْرَارِ ﴿١٩٣﴾

رَبَّنَا وَءَاتِنَا مَا وَعَدتَّنَا عَلَىٰ رُسُلِكَ وَلَا تُخْزِنَا يَوْمَ الْقِيَامَةِ إِنَّكَ لَا تُخْلِفُ الْمِيعَادَ ﴿١٩٤﴾

فَاسْتَجَابَ لَهُمْ رَبُّهُمْ أَنِّي لَا أُضِيعُ عَمَلَ عَامِلٍ مِّنكُم مِّن ذَكَرٍ أَوْ أُنثَىٰ بَعْضُكُم مِّنۢ بَعْضٍ فَالَّذِينَ هَاجَرُوا وَأُخْرِجُوا مِن دِيَٰرِهِمْ وَأُوذُوا فِي سَبِيلِي وَقَٰتَلُوا وَقُتِلُوا لَأُكَفِّرَنَّ عَنْهُمْ سَيِّئَاتِهِمْ وَلَأُدْخِلَنَّهُمْ جَنَّٰتٍ تَجْرِي مِن تَحْتِهَا الْأَنْهَٰرُ ثَوَابًا مِّنْ عِندِ اللَّهِ وَاللَّهُ عِندَهُ حُسْنُ الثَّوَابِ ﴿١٩٥﴾

لَا يَغُرَّنَّكَ تَقَلُّبُ الَّذِينَ كَفَرُوا فِي الْبِلَٰدِ ﴿١٩٦﴾

مَتَٰعٌ قَلِيلٌ ثُمَّ مَأْوَاهُمْ جَهَنَّمُ وَبِئْسَ الْمِهَادُ ﴿١٩٧﴾

لَٰكِنِ الَّذِينَ اتَّقَوْا رَبَّهُمْ لَهُمْ جَنَّٰتٌ تَجْرِي مِن تَحْتِهَا الْأَنْهَٰرُ خَٰلِدِينَ فِيهَا نُزُلًا مِّنْ عِندِ اللَّهِ وَمَا

Islamic Monotheism, the pious and righteous).

199. And there are, certainly, among the people of the Scripture (Jews and Christians), those who believe in Allâh and in that which has been revealed to you, and in that which has been revealed to them, humbling themselves before Allâh. They do not sell the Verses of Allâh for a little price, for them is a reward with their Lord. Surely, Allâh is Swift in account.

200. O you who believe! Endure and be more patient (than your enemy), and guard your territory by stationing army units permanently at the places from where the enemy can attack you, and fear Allâh, so that you may be successful.

Sûrat An-Nisâ' (The Women) IV

In the Name of Allâh,
the Most Gracious, the Most Merciful

1. O mankind! Be dutiful to your Lord, Who created you from a single person (Adam), and from him (Adam) He created his wife [Hawwâ (Eve)], and from them both He created many men and women; and fear Allâh through Whom you demand (your mutual rights), and (do not cut the relations of) the wombs (kinship).[1] Surely, Allâh is Ever an All-Watcher over you.

---

[1] (V.4:1) See the footnote of (V.2:27).

2. And give unto orphans their property and do not exchange (your) bad things for (their) good ones; and devour not their substance (by adding it) to your substance. Surely, this is a great sin.[1]

3. And if you fear that you shall not be able to deal justly with the orphan girls then marry (other) women of your choice, two or three, or four; but if you fear that you shall not be able to deal justly (with them), then only one or (slaves) that your right hands possess. That is nearer to prevent you from doing injustice.

4. And give to the women (whom you marry) their *Mahr* (obligatory bridal-money given by the husband to his wife at the time of marriage) with a good heart; but if they, of their own good pleasure, remit any part of it to you, take it, and enjoy it without fear of any harm (as Allâh has made it lawful).

5. And give not unto the foolish your property which Allâh has made a means of support for you,[2] but feed and

وَءَاتُوا۟ ٱلْيَتَـٰمَىٰٓ أَمْوَٰلَهُمْ وَلَا تَتَبَدَّلُوا۟ ٱلْخَبِيثَ بِٱلطَّيِّبِ وَلَا تَأْكُلُوٓا۟ أَمْوَٰلَهُمْ إِلَىٰٓ أَمْوَٰلِكُمْ إِنَّهُۥ كَانَ حُوبًا كَبِيرًا ۝

وَإِنْ خِفْتُمْ أَلَّا تُقْسِطُوا۟ فِى ٱلْيَتَـٰمَىٰ فَٱنكِحُوا۟ مَا طَابَ لَكُم مِّنَ ٱلنِّسَآءِ مَثْنَىٰ وَثُلَـٰثَ وَرُبَـٰعَ فَإِنْ خِفْتُمْ أَلَّا تَعْدِلُوا۟ فَوَٰحِدَةً أَوْ مَا مَلَكَتْ أَيْمَـٰنُكُمْ ذَٰلِكَ أَدْنَىٰٓ أَلَّا تَعُولُوا۟ ۝

وَءَاتُوا۟ ٱلنِّسَآءَ صَدُقَـٰتِهِنَّ نِحْلَةً فَإِن طِبْنَ لَكُمْ عَن شَىْءٍ مِّنْهُ نَفْسًا فَكُلُوهُ هَنِيٓـًٔا مَّرِيٓـًٔا ۝

وَلَا تُؤْتُوا۟ ٱلسُّفَهَآءَ أَمْوَٰلَكُمُ ٱلَّتِى جَعَلَ ٱللَّهُ لَكُمْ قِيَـٰمًا وَٱرْزُقُوهُمْ

---

[1] (V.4:2). See the footnote of (V.3:130).

[2] (V.4:5) Narrated Al-Mughîrah bin Shu'bah رضى الله عنه : The Prophet صلى الله عليه وسلم said, "Allâh has forbidden for you: (1) To be undutiful to your mothers, (2) to bury your daughters alive, (3) not to pay the rights of the others (e.g. *Zakât*, charity) and (4) to beg of men (i.e. begging). And Allâh has hated for you: (1) Sinful and useless talk like backbiting, or that you talk too much about others, (2) to ask too many questions, (in disputed religious matters) and (3) to waste the wealth (by extravagance with lack of wisdom and thinking)." (*Sahih Al-Bukhâri*, Vol. 3, *Hadîth* No. 591).

clothe them therewith, and speak to them words of kindness and justice.

6. And try orphans (as regards their intelligence) until they reach the age of marriage; if then you find sound judgement in them,* release their property to them, but consume it not wastefully, and hastily fearing that they should grow up, and whoever (amongst guardians) is rich, he should take no wages, but if he is poor, let him have for himself what is just and reasonable (according to his labour). And when you release their property to them, take witness in their presence; and Allâh is All-Sufficient in taking account.

7. There is a share for men and a share for women from what is left by parents and those nearest related, whether the property be small or large — a legal share.

8. And when the relatives and the orphans and Al-Masâkîn (the poor) are present at the time of division, give them out of the property, and speak to them words of kindness and justice.

9. And let those (executors and guardians) have the same fear in their minds as they would have for their own, if they had left weak offspring behind. So let them fear Allâh and speak right words.

10. Verily, those who unjustly eat up the property of orphans, they eat up

فِيهَا وَاكْسُوهُمْ وَقُولُوا لَهُمْ قَوْلًا مَّعْرُوفًا ﴿٥﴾

وَابْتَلُوا الْيَتَامَىٰ حَتَّىٰ إِذَا بَلَغُوا النِّكَاحَ فَإِنْ آنَسْتُم مِّنْهُمْ رُشْدًا فَادْفَعُوا إِلَيْهِمْ أَمْوَالَهُمْ ۖ وَلَا تَأْكُلُوهَا إِسْرَافًا وَبِدَارًا أَن يَكْبَرُوا ۚ وَمَن كَانَ غَنِيًّا فَلْيَسْتَعْفِفْ ۖ وَمَن كَانَ فَقِيرًا فَلْيَأْكُلْ بِالْمَعْرُوفِ ۚ فَإِذَا دَفَعْتُمْ إِلَيْهِمْ أَمْوَالَهُمْ فَأَشْهِدُوا عَلَيْهِمْ ۚ وَكَفَىٰ بِاللَّهِ حَسِيبًا ﴿٦﴾

لِّلرِّجَالِ نَصِيبٌ مِّمَّا تَرَكَ الْوَالِدَانِ وَالْأَقْرَبُونَ وَلِلنِّسَاءِ نَصِيبٌ مِّمَّا تَرَكَ الْوَالِدَانِ وَالْأَقْرَبُونَ مِمَّا قَلَّ مِنْهُ أَوْ كَثُرَ ۚ نَصِيبًا مَّفْرُوضًا ﴿٧﴾

وَإِذَا حَضَرَ الْقِسْمَةَ أُولُو الْقُرْبَىٰ وَالْيَتَامَىٰ وَالْمَسَاكِينُ فَارْزُقُوهُم مِّنْهُ وَقُولُوا لَهُمْ قَوْلًا مَّعْرُوفًا ﴿٨﴾

وَلْيَخْشَ الَّذِينَ لَوْ تَرَكُوا مِنْ خَلْفِهِمْ ذُرِّيَّةً ضِعَافًا خَافُوا عَلَيْهِمْ فَلْيَتَّقُوا اللَّهَ وَلْيَقُولُوا قَوْلًا سَدِيدًا ﴿٩﴾ إِنَّ الَّذِينَ يَأْكُلُونَ أَمْوَالَ الْيَتَامَىٰ ظُلْمًا إِنَّمَا يَأْكُلُونَ فِي بُطُونِهِمْ

only fire into their bellies, and they will be burnt in the blazing Fire!

11. Allâh commands you as regards your children's (inheritance): to the male, a portion equal to that of two females; if (there are) only daughters, two or more, their share is two-thirds of the inheritance; if only one, her share is half. For parents, a sixth share of inheritance to each if the deceased left children; if no children, and the parents are the (only) heirs, the mother has a third; if the deceased left brothers or (sisters), the mother has a sixth. (The distribution in all cases is) after the payment of legacies he may have bequeathed or debts. You know not which of them, whether your parents or your children, are nearest to you in benefit; (these fixed shares) are ordained by Allâh. And Allâh is Ever All-Knower, All-Wise.

12. In that which your wives leave, your share is a half if they have no child; but if they leave a child, you get a fourth of that which they leave after payment of legacies that they may have bequeathed or debts. In that which you leave, their (your wives') share is a fourth if you leave no child; but if you leave a child, they get an eighth of that which you leave after payment of legacies that you may have bequeathed or debts. If the man or woman whose **inheritance** is in question has left **neither** ascendants nor descendants, but has left a brother or a sister, each one of the two gets a sixth; but if more than two, they share in a third, after payment of lagacies he (or she) may have bequeathed or debts, so that no loss is caused (to anyone). This is a Commandment from Allâh; and Allâh is Ever All-Knowing, Most-Forbearing.

13. These are the limits (set by) Allâh (or ordainments as regards laws of inheritance), and whosoever obeys Allâh and His Messenger (Muhammad صلى الله عليه وسلم) will be admitted to Gardens under which rivers flow (in Paradise), to abide therein, and that will be the great success.

14. And whosoever disobeys Allâh and His Messenger (Muhammad صلى الله عليه وسلم), and transgresses His limits, He will cast him into the Fire, to abide therein; and he shall have a disgraceful torment.

15. And those of your women who commit illegal sexual intercourse, take the evidence of four witnesses from amongst you against them; and if they testify, confine them (i.e. women) to houses until death comes to them or Allâh ordains for them some (other) way.[1]

---

[1] (V.4:15) The provision of this Verse has been abrogated by the Verse of *Sûrat An-Nur* (V.24:2), ordaining lashing for the unmarried and stoning to death for the married, when four witnesses testify to the crime.

16. And the two persons (man and woman) among you who commit illegal sexual intercourse, hurt them both.[1] And if they repent (promise Allâh that they will never repeat, i.e. commit illegal sexual intercourse and other similar sins) and do righteous good deeds, leave them alone. Surely, Allâh is Ever All-Forgiving (the One Who forgives and accepts repentance), (and He is) Most Merciful.

17. Allâh accepts only the repentance of those who do evil in ignorance and foolishness and repent soon afterwards; it is they whom Allâh will forgive and Allâh is Ever All-Knower, All-Wise.

18. And of no effect is the repentance of those who continue to do evil deeds until death faces one of them and he says: "Now I repent;" nor of those who die while they are disbelievers. For them We have prepared a painful torment.

19. O you who believe! You are forbidden to inherit women against their will; and you should not treat them with harshness, that you may take away part of the *Mahr*[2] you have given them, unless they commit open illegal sexual intercourse; and live with them honourably. If you dislike them, it may

---

وَٱلَّذَانِ يَأْتِيَٰنِهَا مِنكُمْ فَـَٔاذُوهُمَا فَإِن تَابَا وَأَصْلَحَا فَأَعْرِضُوا عَنْهُمَآ إِنَّ ٱللَّهَ كَانَ تَوَّابًا رَّحِيمًا ﴿١٦﴾

إِنَّمَا ٱلتَّوْبَةُ عَلَى ٱللَّهِ لِلَّذِينَ يَعْمَلُونَ ٱلسُّوٓءَ بِجَهَٰلَةٍ ثُمَّ يَتُوبُونَ مِن قَرِيبٍ فَأُوْلَٰٓئِكَ يَتُوبُ ٱللَّهُ عَلَيْهِمْ وَكَانَ ٱللَّهُ عَلِيمًا حَكِيمًا ﴿١٧﴾

وَلَيْسَتِ ٱلتَّوْبَةُ لِلَّذِينَ يَعْمَلُونَ ٱلسَّيِّـَٔاتِ حَتَّىٰٓ إِذَا حَضَرَ أَحَدَهُمُ ٱلْمَوْتُ قَالَ إِنِّى تُبْتُ ٱلْـَٰٔنَ وَلَا ٱلَّذِينَ يَمُوتُونَ وَهُمْ كُفَّارٌ أُوْلَٰٓئِكَ أَعْتَدْنَا لَهُمْ عَذَابًا أَلِيمًا ﴿١٨﴾

يَٰٓأَيُّهَا ٱلَّذِينَ ءَامَنُوا لَا يَحِلُّ لَكُمْ أَن تَرِثُوا ٱلنِّسَآءَ كَرْهًا وَلَا تَعْضُلُوهُنَّ لِتَذْهَبُوا بِبَعْضِ مَآ ءَاتَيْتُمُوهُنَّ إِلَّآ أَن يَأْتِينَ بِفَٰحِشَةٍ مُّبَيِّنَةٍ وَعَاشِرُوهُنَّ بِٱلْمَعْرُوفِ فَإِن كَرِهْتُمُوهُنَّ

---

[1] (V.4:16) See (V.24:2).

[2] (V.4:19) *Mahr*: Bridal-money given by the husband to his wife at the time of marriage.

be that you dislike a thing and Allâh brings through it a great deal of good.

20. But if you intend to replace a wife by another and you have given one of them a *Qintâr* (of gold i.e. a great amount as *Mahr*), take not the least bit of it back; would you take it wrongfully without a right and (with) a manifest sin?

21. And how could you take it (back) while you have gone in unto each other, and they have taken from you a firm and strong covenant?

22. And marry not women whom your fathers married, except what has already passed; indeed it was shameful and most hateful, and an evil way.

23. Forbidden to you (for marriage) are: your mothers, your daughters, your sisters, your father's sisters, your mother's sisters, your brother's daughters, your sister's daughters, your foster mother who gave you suck, your foster milk suckling sisters, your wives' mothers, your step-daughters under your guardianship, born of your wives to whom you have gone in — but there is no sin on you if you have not gone in them (to marry their daughters), — the wives of your sons who (spring) from your own loins, and two sisters in wedlock at the same time, except for what has already passed; verily, Allâh is Oft-Forgiving, Most Merciful.

24. Also (forbidden are) women already married, except those (slaves) whom your right hands possess. Thus has Allâh ordained for you. All others are lawful, provided you seek (them in marriage) with *Mahr* (bridal-money given by the husband to his wife at the time of marriage) from your property, desiring chastity, not committing illegal sexual intercourse, so with those of whom you have enjoyed sexual relations, give them their *Mahr* as prescribed; but if after a *Mahr* is prescribed, you agree mutually (to give more), there is no sin on you. Surely, Allâh is Ever All-Knowing, All-Wise.

25. And whoever of you have not the means wherewith to wed free believing women, they may wed believing girls from among those (slaves) whom your right hands possess, and Allâh has full knowledge about your Faith; you are one from another. Wed them with the permission of their own folk (guardians, *Auliyâ'* or masters) and give them their *Mahr* according to what is reasonable; they (the above said slave-girls) should be chaste, not adulterous nor taking boy-friends. And after they have been taken in wedlock, if they commit illegal sexual intercourse, their punishment is half of that for free (unmarried) women.[1] This is for him

---

[1] (V.4:25) Female or male slaves (married or unmarried); if they commit adultery, their punishment is fifty (50) lashes (half of that which is for free unmarried women); neither stoning to death nor exile.

among you who is afraid of being harmed in his religion or in his body; but it is better for you that you practise self-restraint, and Allâh is Oft-Forgiving, Most Merciful.

ذَٰلِكَ لِمَنْ خَشِىَ ٱلْعَنَتَ مِنكُمْ وَأَن تَصْبِرُواْ خَيْرٌ لَّكُمْ وَٱللَّهُ غَفُورٌ رَّحِيمٌ ۝

26. Allâh wishes to make clear (what is lawful and what is unlawful) to you, and to show you the ways of those before you, and accept your repentance, and Allâh is All-Knower, All-Wise.

يُرِيدُ ٱللَّهُ لِيُبَيِّنَ لَكُمْ وَيَهْدِيَكُمْ سُنَنَ ٱلَّذِينَ مِن قَبْلِكُمْ وَيَتُوبَ عَلَيْكُمْ وَٱللَّهُ عَلِيمٌ حَكِيمٌ ۝

27. Allâh wishes to accept your repentance, but those who follow their lusts, wish that you (believers) should deviate tremendously away (from the Right Path).

وَٱللَّهُ يُرِيدُ أَن يَتُوبَ عَلَيْكُمْ وَيُرِيدُ ٱلَّذِينَ يَتَّبِعُونَ ٱلشَّهَوَٰتِ أَن تَمِيلُواْ مَيْلًا عَظِيمًا ۝

28. Allâh wishes to lighten (the burden) for you; and man was created weak (cannot be patient to leave sexual intercourse with woman).

يُرِيدُ ٱللَّهُ أَن يُخَفِّفَ عَنكُمْ وَخُلِقَ ٱلْإِنسَٰنُ ضَعِيفًا ۝

29. O you who believe! Eat not up your property among yourselves unjustly except it be a trade amongst you, by mutual consent. And do not kill yourselves (nor kill one another). Surely, Allâh is Most Merciful to you.[1]

يَٰٓأَيُّهَا ٱلَّذِينَ ءَامَنُواْ لَا تَأْكُلُوٓاْ أَمْوَٰلَكُم بَيْنَكُم بِٱلْبَٰطِلِ إِلَّآ أَن تَكُونَ تِجَٰرَةً عَن تَرَاضٍ مِّنكُمْ وَلَا تَقْتُلُوٓاْ أَنفُسَكُمْ إِنَّ ٱللَّهَ كَانَ بِكُمْ رَحِيمًا ۝

---

[1] (V.4:29) What is said about committing suicide.

Narrated Thâbit bin Ad-Dahhak رضي الله عنه The Prophet صلى الله عليه وسلم said, "Whoever intentionally swears falsely by a religion other than Islâm, then he is what he had said, (e.g. if he says, 'If such thing is not true then I am a Jew,' he is really a Jew if he is a liar). And whoever commits suicide with a piece of iron, will be punished with the same piece of iron in the Hell-fire."

Narrated Jundub: The Prophet صلى الله عليه وسلم said, "A man was inflicted with wounds and he commited suicide, and so Allâh said:

30. And whoever commits that through aggression and injustice, We shall cast him into the Fire, and that is easy for Allâh.

31. If you avoid the great sins[1] which you are forbidden to do, We shall expiate from you your (small) sins, and admit you to a Noble Entrance (i.e. Paradise).

32. And wish not for the things in which Allâh has made some of you to excel others. For men there is reward for what they have earned, (and likewise) for women there is reward for what they have earned, and ask Allâh of His Bounty. Surely, Allâh is Ever All-Knower of everything.

33. And to everyone, We have appointed heirs of that (property) left

---

My slave has caused death on himself hurriedly, so I forbid Paradise for him." (*Sahih Al-Bukhâri*, Vol. 2, *Hadîth* No. 445).

Narrated Abu Hurairah رضي الله عنه: The Prophet صلى الله عليه وسلم said, "He who commits suicide by throttling shall keep on throttling himself in the Hell-fire (forever), and he who commits suicide by stabbing himself shall keep on stabbing himself in the Hell-fire (forever)." (*Sahih Al-Bukhâri*, Vol.2, *Hadîth* No.446).

[1] (V.4:31) Narrated Abu Hurairah رضي الله عنه: The Prophet صلى الله عليه وسلم said: "Avoid the seven great destructive sins." They (the people) asked, "O Allâh's Messenger! What are they?" He said, "(1) To join partners in worship with Allâh, (2) to practise sorcery; (3) to kill a person which Allâh has forbidden except for a just cause (according to Islâmic law); (4) to eat up *Ribâ* (usury); (5) to eat up the property of an orphan; (6) to show one's back to the enemy and fleeing from the battlefield at the time of fighting and (7) to accuse chaste women who never even think of anything touching their chastity and are good believers." (*Sahih Al-Bukhâri*, Vol. 8, *Hadîth* No. 840).

by parents and relatives. To those also with whom you have made a pledge (brotherhood), give them their due portion (by *Wasiya* - wills).[1] Truly, Allâh is Ever a Witness over all things.

34. Men are the protectors and maintainers of women, because Allâh has made one of them to excel the other, and because they spend (to support them) from their means. Therefore the righteous women are devoutly obedient (to Allâh and to their husbands), and guard in the husband's absence what Allâh orders them to guard (e.g. their chastity and their husband's property). As to those women on whose part you see ill-conduct, admonish them (first), (next), refuse to share their beds, (and last) beat them (lightly, if it is useful); but if they return to obedience, seek not against them means (of annoyance). Surely, Allâh is Ever Most High, Most Great.

35. If you fear a breach between them twain (the man and his wife), appoint (two) arbitrators, one from his family and the other from her's; if they both wish for peace, Allâh will cause their reconciliation. Indeed Allâh is Ever All-Knower, Well-Acquainted with all things.

36. Worship Allâh and join none with Him (in worship); and do good to

---

[1] (V.4:33) See for details *Hadith* No. 489, Vol.3, *Sahih Al-Bukhari*.

parents, kinsfolk, orphans, *Al-Masâkîn* (the poor), the neighbour who is near of kin, the neighbour who is a stranger, the companion by your side, the wayfarer (you meet), and those (slaves) whom your right hands possess. Verily, Allâh does not like such as are proud and boastful.

37. Those who are miserly and enjoin miserliness on other men and hide what Allâh has bestowed upon them of His Bounties, and We have prepared for the disbelievers a disgraceful torment.[1]

38. And (also) those who spend of their substance to be seen of men, and believe not in Allâh and the Last Day [they are the friends of *Shaitân* (Satan)], and whoever takes *Shaitân* (Satan) as an intimate; then what a dreadful intimate he has!

39. And what loss have they if they had believed in Allâh and in the Last Day, and they spend out of what Allâh has given them for sustenance? And Allâh is Ever All-Knower of them.

40. Surely, Allâh wrongs not even of the weight of an atom (or a small ant),[2]

---

[1] (V.4:37) Narrated Abu Hurairah رضي الله عنه : The Prophet صلى الله عليه وسلم said, "Everyday two angels come down from heaven and one of them says, 'O Allâh! Compensate every person who spends in Your Cause,' and the other (angel) says, 'O Allâh! Destroy every miser.'" (*Sahih Al-Bukhâri*, Vol.2, *Hadîth* No.522).

[2] (V.4:40)

Narrated Abu Sa'îd Al-Khudrî رضي الله عنه : During the lifetime of the Prophet صلى الله عليه وسلم some people said, "O Allâh's Messenger! Shall we see our Lord on the Day of Resurrection?" The Prophet صلى الله عليه وسلم said: "Yes; do you have any difficulty in seeing the sun at midday when it is bright and there is no cloud in the sky?" They replied, "No." He said, "Do you have any difficulty in seeing the moon on a fullmoon night when it is bright and there is no cloud in the sky?" They replied, "No." The Prophet صلى الله عليه وسلم said, "(Similarly) you will have no difficulty in seeing Allâh (عز وجل) on the Day of Resurrection, as you have no difficulty in seeing either of them." On the Day of Resurrection, a call-maker will announce, "Let every nation follow that which they used to worship." Then none of those who used to worship anything other than Allâh like idols and other deities, but will fall in Hell (Fire), till there will remain none but those who used to worship Allâh, both those who were obedient (i.e. good) and those who were disobedient (i.e. bad) and the remaining party of the people of the Scripture. Then the Jews will be called upon and it will be said to them, "Who did you use to worship?" They will say, "We used to worship 'Uzair (Ezra), the son of Allâh." It will be said to them, "You are liars, for Allâh has never taken anyone as a wife or a son. What do you want now?" They will say, "O our Lord! We are thirsty, so give us something to drink." They will be directed and addressed thus, "Will you drink" whereupon they will be gathered unto Hell (Fire) which will look like a mirage whose different sides will be destroying each other. Then they will fall into the Fire. Afterwards the Christians will be called upon and it will be said to them, "Who did you use to worship?" They will say, "We used to worship 'Îsâ (Jesus), the son of Allâh." It will be said to them, "You are liars, for Allâh has never taken anyone as a wife or a son." Then it will be said to them, "What do you want now?" They will say what the former people have said (and will be thrown in the Hell-fire like the Jews). Then, when there remain (in the gathering) none but those who used to worship Allâh [Alone, the real Lord of the 'Âlamîn (mankind, jinn and all that exists)], whether they were obedient or disobedient. Then Allâh, [the Lord of the 'Âlamîn (mankind, jinn and all that exists)], will come to them in a shape nearest to the picture they had in their minds about Him. It will be said, "What are you waiting for? Every nation has followed what it used to worship." They will reply, "We left the people in the world when we were in great need of them and we did not take them as friends. Now we are waiting for our Lord Whom we used to worship." Allâh will say, "I am your Lord." They will say twice or thrice, "We do not worship anything besides Allâh." (*Sahih Al-Bukhâri*, Vol. 6, *Hadîth* No. 105).

but if there is any good (done), He doubles it, and gives from Him a great reward.

41. How (will it be) then, when We bring from each nation a witness and We bring you (O Muhammad صلى الله عليه وسلم) as a witness against these people?

42. On that day those who disbelieved and disobeyed the Messenger (Muhammad صلى الله عليه وسلم) will wish that they were buried in the earth, but they will never be able to hide a single fact from Allâh.[1]

43. O you who believe! Approach not *As-Salât* (the prayer) when you are in a drunken state until you know (the meaning) of what you utter, nor when you are in a state of *Janâba*, (i.e. in a state of sexual impurity and have not yet taken a bath) except when travelling on the road (without enough water, or just passing through a mosque), till you wash your whole body. And if you are ill, or on a journey, or one of you comes after answering the call of nature, or you have been in contact with women (by sexual relations) and you find no water, perform *Tayammum* with clean earth and rub therewith your faces and hands (*Tayammum*).[2] Truly, Allâh is Ever Oft-Pardoning, Oft-Forgiving.

---

[1] (V.4:42) See footnote of (V.3:85).

[2] (V.4:43) Strike your hands on the earth and then pass the palm of each one on the back of the other and then blow off the dust from them and then pass (rub) them on your face, this is called *Tayammum*.

44. Have you not seen those (the Jews) who were given a portion of the Book, purchasing the wrong path, and wish that you should go astray from the Right Path.

45. Allâh has full knowledge of your enemies, and Allâh is Sufficient as a *Walî* (Protector), and Allâh is Sufficient as a Helper.

46. Among those who are Jews, there are some who displace words from (their) right places and say: "We hear your word (O Muhammad ﷺ) and disobey," and "Hear and let you (O Muhammad ﷺ) hear nothing." And *Râ'ina*[1] with a twist of their tongues and as a mockery of the religion (Islâm). And if only they had said: "We hear and obey," and "Do make us understand," it would have been better for them, and more proper; but Allâh has cursed them for their disbelief, so they believe not except a few.

47. O you who have been given the Scripture (Jews and Christians)! Believe in what We have revealed (to Muhammad ﷺ) confirming what is (already) with you, before We efface faces (by making them like the back of necks; without nose, mouth and eyes) and turn them hindwards, or curse them as We cursed the Sabbath-

---

[1] (V.4:46) *Râ'ina*: means in Arabic "Be careful, listen to us, and we listen to you", whereas in Hebrew, it means "an insult".

breakers.[1] And the Commandment of Allâh is always executed.[2]

48. Verily, Allâh forgives not that partners should be set up with Him (in worship), but He forgives except that (anything else) to whom He wills; and whoever sets up partners with Allâh in worship, he has indeed invented a tremendous sin.[3]

49. Have you not seen those (Jews and Christians)[4] who claim sanctity for themselves. Nay, but Allâh sanctifies whom He Wills, and they will not be dealt with injustice even equal to the extent of a *Fatîlâ* (a scalish thread in the long slit of a date-stone).

50. Look, how they invent a lie against Allâh, and enough is that as a manifest sin.

51. Have you not seen those who were given a portion of the Scripture?

---

[1] (V.4:47) This Verse is a severe warning to the Jews and Christians, and an absolute obligation that they must believe in Allâh's Messenger Muhammad صلى الله عليه وسلم and in his Message of Islâmic Monotheism and in this Qur'ân.

[2] (V.4:47) See the footnote of the (V.3:85), and see (V.3:116), (V.8:39) and its footnote.

[3] (V.4:48) Narrated Anas رضي الله عنه : The Prophet صلى الله عليه وسلم said, "Allâh will say to that person of the (Hell) Fire who will receive the least punishment, 'If you had everything on the earth, would you give it as a ransom to free yourself from this Fire?' He will say, 'Yes.' Then Allâh will say, 'While you were in the backbone of Adam, I asked you much less than this, (i.e. not to worship others besides Me), but you insisted on worshipping others besides Me.'" (*Sahih Al-Bukhâri*, Vol. 4, *Hadîth* No. 551).

[4] (V.4:49) See *Tafseer Ibn Kathir*.

They believe in *Jibt* and *Tâghût*[1] and say to the disbelievers that they are better guided as regards the way than the believers (Muslims).

52. They are those whom Allâh has cursed, and he whom Allâh curses, you will not find for him (any) helper,

53. Or have they a share in the dominion? Then in that case they would not give mankind even a *Naqîra* (speck on the back of a date-stone).

54. Or do they envy men (Muhammad صلى الله عليه وسلم and his followers) for what Allâh has given them of His Bounty? Then We had already given the family of Ibrâhîm (Abraham) the Book and *Al-Hikmah* (*As-Sunnah* — Divine Revelation to those Prophets not written in the form of a book), and conferred upon them a great kingdom.

55. Of them were (some) who believed in him (Muhammad صلى الله عليه وسلم), and of them were (some) who averted their faces from him (Muhammad صلى الله عليه وسلم); and enough is Hell for burning (them).[2]

56. Surely, those who disbelieved in Our *Ayât* (proofs, evidences, verses,

---

[1] (V.4:51) The words "*Jibt* and *Tâghût*" cover wide meanings: It means anything worshipped other than the Real God (Allâh) i.e. all the false deities, it may be an idol, satan, graves, stone, sun, star, angel, human being, a Messenger or saints. [Please see *Tafsir Ibn Kathir*; and the footnote of (V.2:256)].

[2] (V.4:55). See the footnote of (V.3:85).

lessons, signs, revelations, etc.), We shall burn them in Fire. As often as their skins are roasted through, We shall change them for other skins that they may taste the punishment. Truly, Allâh is Ever Most Powerful, All-Wise.

57. But those who believe (in the Oneness of Allâh — Islâmic Monotheism) and do deeds of righteousness, We shall admit them to Gardens under which rivers flow (Paradise), abiding therein forever. Therein they shall have *Azwâjun Mutahharatun*[1] (purified mates or wives), and We shall admit them to shades wide and ever deepening (Paradise).[2]

58. Verily, Allâh commands that you should render back the trusts to those, to whom they are due; and that when you judge between men, you judge with justice. Verily, how excellent is the teaching which He (Allâh) gives you! Truly, Allâh is Ever All-Hearer, All-Seer.

59. O you who believe! Obey Allâh and obey the Messenger (Muhammad صلى الله عليه وسلم), and those of you (Muslims) who are in authority. (And)

---

[1] (V.4:57) Having no menses and stools, urine. See (V.2:25) and (V.3:15) and also see *Tafsir Ibn Kathir* and also see footnote of (V.29:64).

[2] (V.4:57) Narrated Anas bin Mâlik رضى الله عنه : The Prophet صلى الله عليه وسلم said, "There is a tree in Paradise (which is so big and huge that) if a rider travels in its shade for one hundred years, he will not be able to cross it." (*Sahih Al-Bukhâri*, Vol. 4, *Hadith* No.474).

if you differ in anything amongst yourselves, refer it to Allâh and His Messenger (صلى الله عليه وسلم), if you believe in Allâh and in the Last Day. That is better and more suitable for final determination.

60. Have you seen those (hypocrites) who claim that they believe in that which has been sent down to you, and that which was sent down before you, and they wish to go for judgement (in their disputes) to the *Tâghût* (false judges) while they have been ordered to reject them. But *Shaitân* (Satan) wishes to lead them far astray.[1]

61. And when it is said to them: "Come to what Allâh has sent down and to the Messenger (Muhammad صلى الله عليه وسلم)," you (Muhammad صلى الله عليه وسلم) see the hypocrites turn away from you (Muhammad صلى الله عليه وسلم) with aversion.

62. How then, when a catastrophe befalls them because of what their hands have sent forth, they come to you swearing by Allâh, "We meant no more than goodwill and conciliation!"

63. They (hypocrites) are those of whom Allâh knows what is in their hearts; so turn aside from them (do not punish them) but admonish them, and

إِلَى ٱللَّهِ وَٱلرَّسُولِ إِن كُنتُمْ تُؤْمِنُونَ بِٱللَّهِ وَٱلْيَوْمِ ٱلْأَخِرِ ذَٰلِكَ خَيْرٌ وَأَحْسَنُ تَأْوِيلًا ۝

أَلَمْ تَرَ إِلَى ٱلَّذِينَ يَزْعُمُونَ أَنَّهُمْ ءَامَنُواْ بِمَآ أُنزِلَ إِلَيْكَ وَمَآ أُنزِلَ مِن قَبْلِكَ يُرِيدُونَ أَن يَتَحَاكَمُوٓاْ إِلَى ٱلطَّٰغُوتِ وَقَدْ أُمِرُوٓاْ أَن يَكْفُرُواْ بِهِۦ وَيُرِيدُ ٱلشَّيْطَٰنُ أَن يُضِلَّهُمْ ضَلَٰلًۢا بَعِيدًا ۝

وَإِذَا قِيلَ لَهُمْ تَعَالَوْاْ إِلَىٰ مَآ أَنزَلَ ٱللَّهُ وَإِلَى ٱلرَّسُولِ رَأَيْتَ ٱلْمُنَٰفِقِينَ يَصُدُّونَ عَنكَ صُدُودًا ۝ فَكَيْفَ إِذَآ أَصَٰبَتْهُم مُّصِيبَةٌۢ بِمَا قَدَّمَتْ أَيْدِيهِمْ ثُمَّ جَآءُوكَ يَحْلِفُونَ بِٱللَّهِ إِنْ أَرَدْنَآ إِلَّآ إِحْسَٰنًا وَتَوْفِيقًا ۝

أُوْلَٰٓئِكَ ٱلَّذِينَ يَعْلَمُ ٱللَّهُ مَا فِى قُلُوبِهِمْ فَأَعْرِضْ عَنْهُمْ وَعِظْهُمْ وَقُل لَّهُمْ

---

[1] (V.4:60) This verse was revealed in connection with a hypocrite claiming to be a Muslim, who had a dispute with a Jew and he wanted to take his case to a soothsayer rather than to the Prophet (Muhammad صلى الله عليه وسلم) for judgement — For details, see *Tafsir At-Tabari.*

speak to them an effective word (i.e. to believe in Allâh, worship Him, obey Him, and be afraid of Him) to reach their innerselves.

64. We sent no Messenger, but to be obeyed by Allâh's Leave. If they (hypocrites), when they had been unjust to themselves, had come to you (Muhammad ﷺ) and begged Allâh's Forgiveness, and the Messenger had begged forgiveness for them: indeed, they would have found Allâh All-Forgiving (One Who forgives and accepts repentance), Most Merciful.

65. But no, by your Lord, they can have no Faith, until they make you (O Muhammad ﷺ) judge in all disputes between them, and find in themselves no resistance against your decisions, and accept (them) with full submission.

66. And if We had ordered them (saying), "Kill yourselves (i.e. the innocent ones kill the guilty ones) or leave your homes," very few of them would have done it; but if they had done what they were told, it would have been better for them, and would have strengthened their (Faith);

67. And indeed We should then have bestowed upon them a great reward from Ourselves.

68. And indeed We should have guided them to the Straight Way.

69. And whoso obey Allâh and the Messenger (Muhammad ﷺ),

then they will be in the company of those of whom Allâh has bestowed His Grace, of the Prophets, the *Siddiqûn* (those followers of the Prophets who were first and foremost to believe in them, like Abu Bakr As-Siddiq رضى الله عنه), the martyrs, and the righteous. And how excellent these companions are!

70. Such is the Bounty from Allâh, and Allâh is Sufficient as All-Knower.

71. O you who believe! Take your precautions, and either go forth (on an expedition) in parties, or go forth all together.

72. There is certainly among you he who would linger behind (from fighting in Allâh's Cause). If a misfortune befalls you, he says, "Indeed Allâh has favoured me in that I was not present among them."

73. But if a bounty (victory and booty) comes to you from Allâh, he would surely say — as if there had never been ties of affection between you and him — "Oh! I wish I had been with them; then I would have achieved a great success (a good share of booty)."

74. Let those (believers) who sell the life of this world for the Hereafter fight in the Cause of Allâh, and whoso fights in the Cause of Allâh, and is killed or gets victory, We shall bestow on him a great reward.

75. And what is wrong with you that you fight not in the Cause of Allâh, and for those weak, ill-treated and oppressed among men, women, and children, whose cry is: "Our Lord! Rescue us from this town whose people are oppressors; and raise for us from You one who will protect, and raise for us from You one who will help."

76. Those who believe, fight in the Cause of Allâh, and those who disbelieve, fight in the cause of *Tâghût* (Satan).[1] So fight you against the friends of *Shaitân* (Satan); ever feeble indeed is the plot of *Shaitân* (Satan).

77. Have you not seen those who were told to hold back their hands (from fighting) and perform *As-Salât* (*Iqâmat-as-Salât*), and give *Zakât*, but when the fighting was ordained for them, behold! a section of them fear men as they fear Allâh or even more. They say: "Our Lord! Why have you ordained for us fighting? Would that you had granted us respite for a short period?" Say: "Short is the enjoyment of this world. The Hereafter is (far) better for him who fears Allâh, and you shall not be dealt with unjustly even equal to the *Fatîlâ* (a scalish thread in the long slit of a date-stone)."

78. "Wheresoever you may be, death will overtake you even if you are in fortresses built up strong and high!" And if some good reaches them, they say, "This is from Allâh," but if some

[1] (V.4:76) *Tâghût*: See the footnote of (V.2:256).

evil befalls them, they say, "This is from you (O Muhammad صلى الله عليه وسلم)." Say: "All things are from Allâh," so what is wrong with these people that they fail to understand any word?

79. Whatever of good reaches you, is from Allâh, but whatever of evil befalls you, is from yourself. And We have sent you (O Muhammad صلى الله عليه وسلم) as a Messenger to mankind, and Allâh is Sufficient as a Witness.[1]

80. He who obeys the Messenger (Muhammad صلى الله عليه وسلم), has indeed obeyed Allâh, but he who turns away, then we have not sent you (O Muhammad صلى الله عليه وسلم) as a watcher over them.[2]

81. They say: "We are obedient," but when they leave you (Muhammad صلى الله عليه وسلم), a section of them spend all night in planning other than what you say. But Allâh records their nightly (plots).

---

[1] (V.4:79) See the footnote (A) of the (V.2:252).

[2] (V.4:80)

(A) Narrated Abu Hurairah رضي الله عنه Allâh's Messenger صلى الله عليه وسلم said, "Whoever obeys me, he obeys Allâh, and whoever disobeys me, he disobeys Allâh; and whoever obeys the ruler I appoint, he obeys me, and whoever disobeys him, he disobeys me." (*Sahih Al-Bukhâri,* Vol. 9, *Hadîth* No. 251).

(B) Narrated Abu Hurairah رضي الله عنه Allâh's Messenger صلى الله عليه وسلم said, "All my followers will enter Paradise except those who refuse." They said, "O Allâh's Messenger! Who will refuse?" He said, "Whoever obeys me will enter Paradise, and whoever disobeys me is the one who refuses (to enter it)." (*Sahih Al-Bukhâri,* Vol. 9, *Hadîth* No. 384).

So turn aside from them (do not punish them), and put your trust in Allâh. And Allâh is Ever All-Sufficient as a Disposer of affairs.

82. Do they not then consider the Qur'ân carefully? Had it been from other than Allâh, they would surely, have found therein many a contradiction.

83. When there comes to them some matter touching (public) safety or fear, they make it known (among the people); if only they had referred it to the Messenger or to those charged with authority among them, the proper investigators would have understood it from them (directly). Had it not been for the Grace and Mercy of Allâh upon you, you would have followed *Shaitân* (Satan), save a few of you.

84. Then fight (O Muhammad صلى الله عليه وسلم) in the Cause of Allâh, you are not tasked (held responsible) except for yourself, and incite the believers (to fight along with you), it may be that Allâh will restrain the evil might of the disbelievers. And Allâh is Stronger in Might and Stronger in punishing.

85. Whosoever intercedes for a good cause will have the reward thereof, and whosoever intercedes for an evil cause will have a share in its burden. And Allâh is Ever All-Able to do (and also an All-Witness to) everything.

86. When you are greeted with a greeting, greet in return with what is better than it, or (at least) return it equally. Certainly, Allâh is Ever a Careful Account Taker of all things.[1]

وَإِذَا حُيِّيتُم بِتَحِيَّةٍ فَحَيُّواْ بِأَحْسَنَ مِنْهَآ أَوْ رُدُّوهَآ إِنَّ ٱللَّهَ كَانَ عَلَىٰ كُلِّ شَيْءٍ حَسِيبًا ٨٦

87. Allâh! Lâ ilâha illa Huwa (none has the right to be worshipped but He). Surely, He will gather you together on the Day of Resurrection about which there is no doubt. And who is truer in statement than Allâh?

ٱللَّهُ لَآ إِلَـٰهَ إِلَّا هُوَ لَيَجْمَعَنَّكُمْ إِلَىٰ يَوْمِ ٱلْقِيَامَةِ لَا رَيْبَ فِيهِ وَمَنْ أَصْدَقُ مِنَ ٱللَّهِ حَدِيثًا ٨٧

88. Then what is the matter with you that you are divided into two parties

فَمَا لَكُمْ فِي ٱلْمُنَـٰفِقِينَ

---

[1] (V.4:86) How the Salâm (greeting) began.

Narrated Abu Hurairah رضي الله عنه : The Prophet صلى الله عليه وسلم said, "Allâh created Adam in His Image,* sixty cubits (about 30 metres) in height. When He created him, He said (to him), "Go and greet that group of angels sitting there, and listen what they will say in reply to you, for that will be your greeting and the greeting of your offspring. Adam (went and) said, "As-Salâmu 'Alaikum (peace be upon you)." They replied, "As-Salâmu 'Alaikum wa Rahmatullah (Peace and Allâh's Mercy be on you)." So they increased 'wa Rahmatullâh.' " The Prophet صلى الله عليه وسلم added, "So, whoever will enter Paradise, will be of the shape and picture of Adam. Since then the creation of Adam's (offspring) (i.e. stature of human beings) is being diminished continuously up to the present time." (Sahih Al-Bukhâri, Vol. 8, Hadîth No. 246).

* "His Image" means that Adam has been bestowed with life, knowledge, power of hearing, seeing and understanding, but the features of Adam are different from those of Allâh, only the names are the same, e.g., Allâh has life and knowledge and power of understanding, and Adam also has them, but there is no comparison between the Creator and the created thing. As Allâh says in the Qur'ân: "There is nothing like unto Him, and He is the All-Hearer, the All-Seer." (V.42:11). Allâh does not eat or sleep, while Adam used to eat and sleep. [For details See Fath Al-Bâri].

about the hypocrites? Allâh has cast them back (to disbelief) because of what they have earned. Do you want to guide him whom Allâh has made to go astray? And he whom Allâh has made to go astray, you will never find for him any way (of guidance).

89. They wish that you reject Faith, as they have rejected (Faith), and thus that you all become equal (like one another). So take not *Auliyâ'* (protectors or friends) from them, till they emigrate in the Way of Allâh (to Muhammad صلى الله عليه وسلم). But if they turn back (from Islâm), take (hold of) them and kill them wherever you find them, and take neither *Auliyâ'* (protectors or friends) nor helpers from them.

90. Except those who join a group, between you and whom there is a treaty (of peace), or those who approach you with their breasts restraining from fighting you as well as fighting their own people. Had Allâh willed, indeed He would have given them power over you, and they would have fought you. So if they withdraw from you, and fight not against you, and offer you peace, then Allâh has opened no way for you against them.

91. You will find others that wish to have security from you and security from their people. Every time they are sent back to temptation, they yield thereto. If they withdraw not from you,

فِئَتَيْنِ وَاللَّهُ أَرْكَسَهُم بِمَا كَسَبُوٓاْ أَتُرِيدُونَ أَن تَهْدُواْ مَنْ أَضَلَّ اللَّهُ وَمَن يُضْلِلِ اللَّهُ فَلَن تَجِدَ لَهُۥ سَبِيلًا ۝

وَدُّواْ لَوْ تَكْفُرُونَ كَمَا كَفَرُواْ فَتَكُونُونَ سَوَآءً فَلَا تَتَّخِذُواْ مِنْهُمْ أَوْلِيَآءَ حَتَّىٰ يُهَاجِرُواْ فِى سَبِيلِ اللَّهِ فَإِن تَوَلَّوْاْ فَخُذُوهُمْ وَاقْتُلُوهُمْ حَيْثُ وَجَدتُّمُوهُمْ وَلَا تَتَّخِذُواْ مِنْهُمْ وَلِيًّا وَلَا نَصِيرًا ۝

إِلَّا ٱلَّذِينَ يَصِلُونَ إِلَىٰ قَوْمٍ بَيْنَكُمْ وَبَيْنَهُم مِّيثَٰقٌ أَوْ جَآءُوكُمْ حَصِرَتْ صُدُورُهُمْ أَن يُقَٰتِلُوكُمْ أَوْ يُقَٰتِلُواْ قَوْمَهُمْ وَلَوْ شَآءَ اللَّهُ لَسَلَّطَهُمْ عَلَيْكُمْ فَلَقَٰتَلُوكُمْ فَإِنِ اعْتَزَلُوكُمْ فَلَمْ يُقَٰتِلُوكُمْ وَأَلْقَوْاْ إِلَيْكُمُ السَّلَمَ فَمَا جَعَلَ اللَّهُ لَكُمْ عَلَيْهِمْ سَبِيلًا ۝

سَتَجِدُونَ ءَاخَرِينَ يُرِيدُونَ أَن يَأْمَنُوكُمْ وَيَأْمَنُواْ قَوْمَهُمْ كُلَّ مَا رُدُّوٓاْ إِلَى ٱلْفِتْنَةِ أُرْكِسُواْ فِيهَا فَإِن لَّمْ

nor offer you peace, nor restrain their hands, take (hold of) them and kill them wherever you find them. In their case, We have provided you with a clear warrant against them.

92. It is not for a believer to kill a believer except (that it be) by mistake; and whosoever kills a believer by mistake, (it is ordained that) he must set free a believing slave and a compensation (blood-money, i.e. *Diya*) be given to the deceased's family unless they remit it. If the deceased belonged to a people at war with you and he was a believer, the freeing of a believing slave (is prescribed); and if he belonged to a people with whom you have a treaty of mutual alliance, compensation (blood-money — *Diya*) must be paid to his family, and a believing slave must be freed. And whoso finds this (the penance of freeing a slave) beyond his means, he must fast for two consecutive months in order to seek repentance from Allâh. And Allâh is Ever All-Knowing, All-Wise.

93. And whoever kills a believer intentionally, his recompense is Hell to abide therein; and the Wrath and the Curse of Allâh are upon him, and a great punishment is prepared for him.[1]

بَعْضُوكُمْ وَيُلْقُوا إِلَيْكُمُ ٱلسَّلَمَ وَيَكُفُّوٓا أَيْدِيَهُمْ فَخُذُوهُمْ وَٱقْتُلُوهُمْ حَيْثُ ثَقِفْتُمُوهُمْ وَأُوْلَٰٓئِكُمْ جَعَلْنَا لَكُمْ عَلَيْهِمْ سُلْطَٰنًا مُّبِينًا ٩١ وَمَا كَانَ لِمُؤْمِنٍ أَن يَقْتُلَ مُؤْمِنًا إِلَّا خَطَـًٔا وَمَن قَتَلَ مُؤْمِنًا خَطَـًٔا فَتَحْرِيرُ رَقَبَةٍ مُّؤْمِنَةٍ وَدِيَةٌ مُّسَلَّمَةٌ إِلَىٰٓ أَهْلِهِۦٓ إِلَّآ أَن يَصَّدَّقُوا۟ فَإِن كَانَ مِن قَوْمٍ عَدُوٍّ لَّكُمْ وَهُوَ مُؤْمِنٌ فَتَحْرِيرُ رَقَبَةٍ مُّؤْمِنَةٍ وَإِن كَانَ مِن قَوْمٍ بَيْنَكُمْ وَبَيْنَهُم مِّيثَٰقٌ فَدِيَةٌ مُّسَلَّمَةٌ إِلَىٰٓ أَهْلِهِۦ وَتَحْرِيرُ رَقَبَةٍ مُّؤْمِنَةٍ فَمَن لَّمْ يَجِدْ فَصِيَامُ شَهْرَيْنِ مُتَتَابِعَيْنِ تَوْبَةً مِّنَ ٱللَّهِ وَكَانَ ٱللَّهُ عَلِيمًا حَكِيمًا ٩٢ وَمَن يَقْتُلْ مُؤْمِنًا مُّتَعَمِّدًا فَجَزَآؤُهُۥ جَهَنَّمُ خَٰلِدًا فِيهَا وَغَضِبَ ٱللَّهُ عَلَيْهِ وَلَعَنَهُۥ وَأَعَدَّ لَهُۥ عَذَابًا عَظِيمًا ٩٣

---

[1] (V.4:93):

A) Narrated Ibn 'Umar رضي الله عنهما Allâh's Messenger صلى الله عليه وسلم said. "A faithful believer remains at liberty regarding his religion

94. O you who believe! When you go (to fight) in the Cause of Allâh, verify (the truth), and say not to anyone who greets you (by embracing Islâm): "You are not a believer"; seeking the perishable goods of the worldly life. There are much more profits and booties with Allâh. Even as he is now, so were you yourselves before till Allâh conferred on you His Favours (i.e. guided you to Islâm), therefore, be cautious in discrimination. Allâh is Ever Well-Aware of what you do.

95. Not equal are those of the believers who sit (at home), except those who are disabled (by injury or are blind or lame), and those who strive hard and fight in the Cause of Allâh with their wealth and their lives. Allâh has preferred in grades those who strive hard and fight with their wealth and their lives above those who sit (at home). Unto each, Allâh has promised good (Paradise), but Allâh has preferred those who strive hard and fight, above those who sit (at home) by a huge reward.

96. Degrees of (higher) grades from Him, and Forgiveness and Mercy. And Allâh is Ever Oft-Forgiving, Most Merciful.

97. Verily, as for those whom the angels take (in death) while they are

---

unless he kills somebody unlawfully." (*Sahih Al-Bukhâri*, Vol.9, *Hadith* No.2)

B) See the footnotes of (V.5:27, 32, 45 & 50).

wronging themselves (as they stayed among the disbelievers even though emigration was obligatory for them), they (angels) say (to them): "In what (condition) were you?" They reply: "We were weak and oppressed on the earth." They (angels) say: "Was not the earth of Allâh spacious enough for you to emigrate therein?" Such men will find their abode in Hell — what an evil destination![1]

98. Except the weak ones among men, women and children who cannot devise a plan, nor are they able to direct their way.

99. These are they whom Allâh is likely to forgive them, and Allâh is Ever Oft-Pardoning, Oft-Forgiving.

100. He who emigrates (from his home) in the Cause of Allâh, will find on earth many dwelling places and plenty to live by. And whosoever leaves his home as an emigrant unto Allâh and His Messenger, and death overtakes him, his reward is then surely, incumbent upon Allâh. And Allâh is Ever Oft-Forgiving, Most Merciful.

101. And when you (Muslims) travel in the land, there is no sin on you if you shorten As-Salât (the prayer) if you fear that the disbelievers may put you in trial (attack you), verily, the disbelievers are ever unto you open enemies.

---

[1] (V.4:97) See the footnote of the (V.3:149).

102. When you (O Messenger Muhammad ﷺ (صلى الله عليه وسلم) are among them, and lead them in *As-Salât* (the prayer), let one party of them stand up [in *Salât* (prayer)] with you taking their arms with them; when they finish their prostrations, let them take their positions in the rear and let the other party come up which have not yet prayed, and let them pray with you taking all the precautions and bearing arms. Those who disbelieve wish, if you were negligent of your arms and your baggage, to attack you in a single rush, but there is no sin on you if you put away your arms because of the inconvenience of rain or because you are ill, but take every precaution for yourselves. Verily, Allâh has prepared a humiliating torment for the disbelievers.[1]

103. When you have finished *As-Salât* (the congregational prayer), remember Allâh standing, sitting down, and (lying down) on your sides, but when you are free from danger, perform *As-Salât* (*Iqamat-as-Salât*). Verily, *As-Salât* (the prayer) is enjoined on the believers at fixed hours.

104. And don't be weak in the pursuit of the enemy; if you are suffering (hardships) then surely, they (too) are suffering (hardships) as you are suffering, but you have a hope from

وَإِذَا كُنتَ فِيهِمْ فَأَقَمْتَ لَهُمُ
الصَّلَوٰةَ فَلْتَقُمْ طَآئِفَةٌ مِّنْهُم
مَّعَكَ وَلْيَأْخُذُوٓا أَسْلِحَتَهُمْ
فَإِذَا سَجَدُوا فَلْيَكُونُوا مِن
وَرَآئِكُمْ وَلْتَأْتِ طَآئِفَةٌ
أُخْرَىٰ لَمْ يُصَلُّوا فَلْيُصَلُّوا
مَعَكَ وَلْيَأْخُذُوا حِذْرَهُمْ
وَأَسْلِحَتَهُمْ وَدَّ ٱلَّذِينَ كَفَرُوا لَوْ
تَغْفُلُونَ عَنْ أَسْلِحَتِكُمْ
وَأَمْتِعَتِكُمْ فَيَمِيلُونَ عَلَيْكُم مَّيْلَةً
وَٰحِدَةً وَلَا جُنَاحَ عَلَيْكُمْ
إِن كَانَ بِكُمْ أَذًى مِّن مَّطَرٍ أَوْ
كُنتُم مَّرْضَىٰ أَن تَضَعُوٓا
أَسْلِحَتَكُمْ وَخُذُوا حِذْرَكُمْ
إِنَّ ٱللَّهَ أَعَدَّ لِلْكَٰفِرِينَ عَذَابًا
مُّهِينًا ۝ فَإِذَا قَضَيْتُمُ
ٱلصَّلَوٰةَ فَٱذْكُرُوا ٱللَّهَ قِيَٰمًا
وَقُعُودًا وَعَلَىٰ جُنُوبِكُمْ فَإِذَا
ٱطْمَأْنَنتُمْ فَأَقِيمُوا ٱلصَّلَوٰةَ إِنَّ
ٱلصَّلَوٰةَ كَانَتْ عَلَى ٱلْمُؤْمِنِينَ
كِتَٰبًا مَّوْقُوتًا ۝
وَلَا تَهِنُوا
فِي ٱبْتِغَآءِ ٱلْقَوْمِ إِن تَكُونُوا
تَأْلَمُونَ فَإِنَّهُمْ يَأْلَمُونَ كَمَا
تَأْلَمُونَ وَتَرْجُونَ مِنَ ٱللَّهِ مَا لَا

---

[1] (V.4:102) See the footnote of (V.2:239).

Allâh (for the reward, i.e. Paradise) that for which they hope not; and Allâh is Ever All-Knowing, All-Wise.

105. Surely, We have sent down to you (O Muhammad صلى الله عليه وسلم) the Book (this Qur'ân) in truth that you might judge between men by that which Allâh has shown you (i.e. has taught you through Divine Revelation), so be not a pleader for the treacherous.

106. And seek the Forgiveness of Allâh,[1] certainly, Allâh is Ever Oft-Forgiving, Most Merciful.

107. And argue not on behalf of those who deceive themselves. Verily, Allâh does not like anyone who is a betrayer, sinner.

108. They may hide (their crimes) from men, but they cannot hide (them) from Allâh; for He is with them (by His Knowledge), when they plot by night in words that He does not approve. And Allâh ever encompasses what they do.

109. Lo! You are those who have argued for them in the life of this world, but who will argue for them on the Day of Resurrection against Allâh, or who will then be their defender?

---

[1] (V.4:106) The Prophet's seeking of Allâh's Forgiveness by daytime and at night.

Narrated Abu Hurairah رضى الله عنه: I heard Allâh's Messenger صلى الله عليه وسلم saying: "By Allâh! I seek Allâh's Forgiveness and turn to Him in repentance for more than seventy times a day." (*Sahîh Al-Bukhâri'*, Vol.8, *Hadîth* No.319).

110. And whoever does evil or wrongs himself but afterwards seeks Allâh's Forgiveness, he will find Allâh Oft-Forgiving, Most Merciful.

111. And whoever earns sin, he earns it only against himself. And Allâh is Ever All-Knowing, All-Wise.

112. And whoever earns a fault or a sin and then throws it on to someone innocent, he has indeed burdened himself with falsehood and a manifest sin.

113. Had not the Grace of Allâh and His Mercy been upon you (O Muhammad صلى الله عليه وسلم), a party of them would certainly have made a decision to mislead you, but (in fact) they mislead none except their own selves, and no harm can they do to you in the least. Allâh has sent down to you the book (the Qur'ân), and Al-Hikmah (Islâmic laws, knowledge of legal and illegal things i.e. the Prophet's Sunnah — legal ways), and taught you that which you knew not. And Ever Great is the Grace of Allâh unto you (O Muhammad صلى الله عليه وسلم).

114. There is no good in most of their secret talks save (in) him who orders Sadaqah (charity in Allâh's Cause), or Ma'rûf (Islâmic Monotheism and all the good and righteous deeds which Allâh has ordained), or conciliation between mankind; and he who does this, seeking the good Pleasure of Allâh, We shall give him a great reward.

وَمَن يَعْمَلْ سُوٓءًا أَوْ يَظْلِمْ نَفْسَهُۥ ثُمَّ يَسْتَغْفِرِ ٱللَّهَ يَجِدِ ٱللَّهَ غَفُورًا رَّحِيمًا ۝

وَمَن يَكْسِبْ إِثْمًا فَإِنَّمَا يَكْسِبُهُۥ عَلَىٰ نَفْسِهِۦ وَكَانَ ٱللَّهُ عَلِيمًا حَكِيمًا ۝

وَمَن يَكْسِبْ خَطِيٓئَةً أَوْ إِثْمًا ثُمَّ يَرْمِ بِهِۦ بَرِيٓئًا فَقَدِ ٱحْتَمَلَ بُهْتَٰنًا وَإِثْمًا مُّبِينًا ۝

وَلَوْلَا فَضْلُ ٱللَّهِ عَلَيْكَ وَرَحْمَتُهُۥ لَهَمَّت طَّآئِفَةٌ مِّنْهُمْ أَن يُضِلُّوكَ وَمَا يُضِلُّونَ إِلَّآ أَنفُسَهُمْ وَمَا يَضُرُّونَكَ مِن شَىْءٍ وَأَنزَلَ ٱللَّهُ عَلَيْكَ ٱلْكِتَٰبَ وَٱلْحِكْمَةَ وَعَلَّمَكَ مَا لَمْ تَكُن تَعْلَمُ وَكَانَ فَضْلُ ٱللَّهِ عَلَيْكَ عَظِيمًا ۝

۞ لَّا خَيْرَ فِى كَثِيرٍ مِّن نَّجْوَىٰهُمْ إِلَّا مَنْ أَمَرَ بِصَدَقَةٍ أَوْ مَعْرُوفٍ أَوْ إِصْلَٰحٍۢ بَيْنَ ٱلنَّاسِ وَمَن يَفْعَلْ ذَٰلِكَ ٱبْتِغَآءَ مَرْضَاتِ ٱللَّهِ فَسَوْفَ نُؤْتِيهِ أَجْرًا عَظِيمًا ۝

115. And whoever contradicts and opposes the Messenger (Muhammad صلى الله عليه وسلم) after the right path has been shown clearly to him, and follows other than the believers' way, We shall keep him in the path he has chosen, and burn him in Hell — what an evil destination![1]

116. Verily, Allâh forgives not (the sin of) setting up partners (in worship) with Him, but He forgives whom He wills sins other than that, and whoever sets up partners in worship with Allâh, has indeed strayed far away.

117. They (all those who worship others than Allâh) invoke nothing but female deities besides Him (Allâh), and they invoke nothing but *Shaitân* (Satan), a persistent rebel!

118. Allâh cursed him. And he [*Shaitân* (Satan)] said: "I will take an appointed portion of your slaves.

119. "Verily, I will mislead them, and surely, I will arouse in them false desires; and certainly, I will order them to slit the ears of cattle, and indeed I will order them to change the nature created by Allâh." And whoever takes *Shaitân* (Satan) as a *Walî* (protector or helper) instead of Allâh, has surely, suffered a manifest loss.[2]

120. He [*Shaitân* (Satan)] makes promises to them, and arouses in them

وَمَن يُشَاقِقِ ٱلرَّسُولَ مِنۢ بَعْدِ مَا تَبَيَّنَ لَهُ ٱلْهُدَىٰ وَيَتَّبِعْ غَيْرَ سَبِيلِ ٱلْمُؤْمِنِينَ نُوَلِّهِۦ مَا تَوَلَّىٰ وَنُصْلِهِۦ جَهَنَّمَ وَسَآءَتْ مَصِيرًا ﴿١١٥﴾

إِنَّ ٱللَّهَ لَا يَغْفِرُ أَن يُشْرَكَ بِهِۦ وَيَغْفِرُ مَا دُونَ ذَٰلِكَ لِمَن يَشَآءُ وَمَن يُشْرِكْ بِٱللَّهِ فَقَدْ ضَلَّ ضَلَٰلًۢا بَعِيدًا ﴿١١٦﴾

إِن يَدْعُونَ مِن دُونِهِۦٓ إِلَّآ إِنَٰثًا وَإِن يَدْعُونَ إِلَّا شَيْطَٰنًا مَّرِيدًا ﴿١١٧﴾

لَّعَنَهُ ٱللَّهُ وَقَالَ لَأَتَّخِذَنَّ مِنْ عِبَادِكَ نَصِيبًا مَّفْرُوضًا ﴿١١٨﴾

وَلَأُضِلَّنَّهُمْ وَلَأُمَنِّيَنَّهُمْ وَلَآمُرَنَّهُمْ فَلَيُبَتِّكُنَّ ءَاذَانَ ٱلْأَنْعَٰمِ وَلَآمُرَنَّهُمْ فَلَيُغَيِّرُنَّ خَلْقَ ٱللَّهِ وَمَن يَتَّخِذِ ٱلشَّيْطَٰنَ وَلِيًّا مِّن دُونِ ٱللَّهِ فَقَدْ خَسِرَ خُسْرَانًا مُّبِينًا ﴿١١٩﴾

يَعِدُهُمْ وَيُمَنِّيهِمْ وَمَا يَعِدُهُمُ

---

[1] (V.4:115) See the footnote of (V.3:85).

[2] (V.4:119) See the footnote of (V.59:7).

false desires; and *Shaitân*'s (Satân) promises are nothing but deceptions.

121. The dwelling of such (people) is Hell, and they will find no way of escape from it.

122. But those who believe (in the Oneness of Allâh — Islâmic Monotheism) and do deeds of righteousness, We shall admit them to the Gardens under which rivers flow (i.e. in Paradise) to dwell therein forever. Allâh's Promise is the Truth; and whose words can be truer than those of Allâh? (Of course, none).

123. It will not be in accordance with your desires (Muslims), nor those of the people of the Scripture (Jews and Christians), whosoever works evil, will have the recompense thereof, and he will not find any protector or helper besides Allâh.

124. And whoever does righteous good deeds, male or female, and is a (true) believer [in the Oneness of Allâh (Muslim)], such will enter Paradise and not the least injustice, even to the size of a *Naqîra* (speck on the back of a date-stone), will be done to them.

125. And who can be better in religion than one who submits his face (himself) to Allâh (i.e. follows Allâh's religion of Islâmic Monotheism); and he is a *Muhsin* (a good-doer — See V.2:112). And follows the religion of Ibrâhîm[1]

---

[1] (V.4:125) See the footnote of (V.2:135), the narration of Zaid bin 'Amr bin Nufail.

(Abraham) *Hanîf* (Islâmic Monotheism
— to worship none but Allâh Alone).
And Allâh did take Ibrâhîm (Abraham) as
a *Khalîl* (an intimate friend)!

126. And to Allâh belongs all that is
in the heavens and all that is in the
earth. And Allâh is Ever Encompassing
all things.

127. They ask your legal instruction
concerning women, say: Allâh instructs
you about them, and about what is
recited unto you in the Book
concerning the orphan girls whom you
give not the prescribed portions (as
regards *Mahr* and inheritance) and yet
whom you desire to marry, and
(concerning) the children who are weak
and oppressed, and that you stand firm for
justice to orphans. And whatever good
you do, Allâh is Ever All-Aware of it.

128. And if a woman fears cruelty or
desertion on her husband's part, there is
no sin on them both if they make terms
of peace between themselves; and
making peace is better. And human
inner-selves are swayed by greed. But if
you do good and keep away from evil,
verily, Allâh is Ever Well-Acquainted
with what you do.

129. You will never be able to do
perfect justice between wives even if it
is your ardent desire, so do not incline
too much to one of them (by giving her
more of your time and provision) so as
to leave the other hanging (i.e. neither
divorced nor married). And if you do

justice, and do all that is right and fear Allâh by keeping away from all that is wrong, then Allâh is Ever Oft-Forgiving, Most Merciful.

130. But if they separate (by divorce), Allâh will provide abundance for everyone of them from His Bounty. And Allâh is Ever All-Sufficient for His creatures' needs, All-Wise.

131. And to Allâh belongs all that is in the heavens and all that is in the earth. And verily, We have recommended to the people of the Scripture before you, and to you (O Muslims) that you (all) fear Allâh, and keep your duty to Him. But if you disbelieve, then unto Allâh belongs all that is in the heavens and all that is in the earth, and Allâh is Ever Rich (Free of all wants), Worthy of all praise.

132. And to Allâh belongs all that is in the heavens and all that is in the earth. And Allâh is Ever All-Sufficient as Disposer of affairs.

133. If He wills, He can take you away, O people, and bring others. And Allâh is Ever All-Potent over that.

134. Whoever desires a reward in this life of the world, then with Allâh (Alone and none else) is the reward of this worldly life and of the Hereafter. And Allâh is Ever All-Hearer, All-Seer.

135. O you who believe! Stand out firmly for justice, as witnesses to Allâh, even though it be against yourselves, or your parents, or your kin, be he rich or poor, Allâh is a Better Protector to both (than you). So follow not the lusts (of your hearts), lest you avoid justice; and if you distort your witness or refuse to give it, verily, Allâh is Ever Well-Acquainted with what you do.[1]

136. O you who believe! Believe in Allâh, and His Messenger (Muhammad صلى الله عليه وسلم), and the Book (the Qur'ân) which He has sent down to His Messenger, and the Scripture which He sent down to those before (him); and whosoever disbelieves in Allâh, His Angels, His Books, His Messengers, and the Last Day, then indeed he has strayed far away.

137. Verily, those who believe, then disbelieve, then believe (again), and (again) disbelieve, and go on increasing in disbelief; Allâh will not forgive them, nor guide them on the (Right) Way.

138. Give to the hypocrites the tidings that there is for them a painful torment.[2]

139. Those who take disbelievers for *Auliyâ'* (protectors or helpers or

---

[1] (V.4:135) Narrated Anas رضى الله عنه: The Prophet صلى الله عليه وسلم was asked about the great sins. He said, "They are:
a) To join others in worship with Allâh.
b) To be undutiful to one's parents.
c) To kill a person (which Allâh has forbidden to kill i.e., to commit the crime of murdering).
d) And to give a false witness."
(*Sahih Al-Bukhâri*, Vol. 3, *Hadîth* No. 821).

[2] (V.4:138) See "Hypocrisy" — Appendix 2.

friends) instead of believers, do they seek honour, power and glory with them? Verily, then to Allâh belongs all honour, power and glory.

140. And it has already been revealed to you in the Book (this Qur'ân) that when you hear the Verses of Allâh being denied and mocked at, then sit not with them, until they engage in a talk other than that; (but if you stayed with them) certainly in that case you would be like them. Surely, Allâh will collect the hypocrites and disbelievers all together in Hell.

141. Those (hyprocrites) who wait and watch about you; if you gain a victory from Allâh, they say: "Were we not with you?" But if the disbelievers gain a success, they say (to them): "Did we not gain mastery over you and did we not protect you from the believers?" Allâh will judge between you (all) on the Day of Resurrection. And never will Allâh grant to the disbelievers a way (to triumph) over the believers.

142. Verily, the hypocrites seek to deceive Allâh, but it is He Who deceives them.[1] And when they stand up for *As-Salât* (the prayer), they stand with laziness and to be seen of men, and they do not remember Allâh but little.

143. (They are) swaying between this and that, belonging neither to these nor to those; and he whom Allâh sends

---

[1] (V.4:142) See (V.57:12-15).

astray, you will not find for him a way (to the truth — Islâm).

144. O you who believe! Take not for *Auliyâ'* (protectors or helpers or friends) disbelievers instead of believers. Do you wish to offer Allâh a manifest proof against yourselves?

145. Verily, the hypocrites will be in the lowest depth (grade) of the Fire; no helper will you find for them.[1]

146. Except those who repent (from hypocrisy), do righteous good deeds, hold fast to Allâh, and purify their religion for Allâh (by worshipping none but Allâh, and do good for Allâh's sake only, not to show off), then they will be with the believers. And Allâh will grant the believers a great reward.

147. Why should Allâh punish you if you have thanked (Him) and have believed in Him. And Allâh is Ever All-Appreciative (of good), All-Knowing.

---

[1] (V.4:145):

a) Narrated 'Abdullâh bin 'Amr رضي الله عنه: The Prophet صلى الله عليه وسلم said: "Whoever has the following four (characteristics) will be a pure hypocrite and whoever has one of the following four characteristics will have one characteristic of hypocrisy unless and until he gives it up:

1. Whenever he is entrusted, he betrays (proves dishonest).
2. Whenever he speaks, he tells a lie.
3. Whenever he makes a covenant, he proves treacherous.
4. Whenever he quarrels, he behaves in a very imprudent, evil and insulting manner." (*Sahih Al-Bukhâri*, Vol. 1, *Hadith* No. 33).

b) See the footnote of (V.9:54).

c) Narrated Abu Hurairah رضي الله عنه: The Prophet صلى الله عليه وسلم said, "The worst people before Allâh on the Day of Resurrection will be the double-faced people who appear to some people with one face and to other people with another face." (*Sahih Al-Bukhâri*, Vol. 8, *Hadith* No. 84).

148. Allâh does not like that the evil should be uttered in public except by him who has been wronged. And Allâh is Ever All-Hearer, All-Knower.

149. Whether you (mankind) disclose (by good words of thanks) a good deed (done to you in the form of a favour by someone), or conceal it, or pardon an evil,…verily, Allâh is Ever Oft-Pardoning, All-Powerful.

150. Verily, those who disbelieve in Allâh and His Messengers and wish to make distinction between Allâh and His Messengers (by believing in Allâh and disbelieving in His Messengers) saying, "We believe in some but reject others," and wish to adopt a way in between.

151. They are in truth disbelievers. And We have prepared for the disbelievers a humiliating torment.

152. And those who believe in Allâh and His Messengers and make no distinction between any of them (Messengers), We shall give them their rewards; and Allâh is Ever Oft-Forgiving, Most Merciful.

153. The people of the Scripture (Jews) ask you to cause a book to descend upon them from heaven. Indeed they asked Mûsâ (Moses) for even greater than that, when they said: "Show us Allâh in public," but they were struck with thunderclap and lightning for their wickedness. Then they worshipped the calf even after clear proofs, evidences, and signs had come to them. (Even) so We forgave them. And We gave Mûsâ (Moses) a clear proof of authority.

154. And for their covenant, We raised over them the Mount and (on the other occasion) We said: "Enter the gate prostrating (or bowing) with humility;" and We commanded them: "Transgress not (by doing worldly works) on the Sabbath (Saturday)." And We took from them a firm covenant.[1]

155. Because of their breaking the covenant, and of their rejecting the *Ayât* (proofs, evidences, verses, lessons, signs, revelations, etc.) of Allâh, and of their killing the Prophets unjustly, and of their saying: "Our hearts are wrapped (with coverings, i.e. we do not understand what the Messengers say)" — nay, Allâh has set a seal upon their hearts because of their disbelief, so they believe not but a little.

156. And because of their (Jews) disbelief and uttering against Maryam (Mary) عليها السلام a grave false charge (that she has committed illegal sexual intercourse);

---

[1] (V.4:154) Narrated Abu Hurairah رضى الله عنه: Allâh's Messenger صلى الله عليه وسلم said, "It was said to Banî Israel, 'Enter the gate (of the town) bowing with humility (prostrating yourselves) and say: 'Repentance', but they changed the word and entered the town crawling on their buttocks and said: 'A wheat grain in the hair'*" (*Sahih Al-Bukhâri*, Vol. 4, *Hadîth* No. 615).

* They said so just to ridicule Allâh's Order as they were disobedient to Him. So Allâh punished them severely by sending on them punishment, most probably in the form of (an epidemic of) plague (See *Tafsir At-Tabari*).

157. And because of their saying (in boast), "We killed Messiah 'Îsâ (Jesus), son of Maryam (Mary), the Messenger of Allâh," — but they killed him not, nor crucified him, but the resemblance of 'Îsâ (Jesus) was put over another man (and they killed that man), and those who differ therein are full of doubts. They have no (certain) knowledge, they follow nothing but conjecture. For surely; they killed him not [i.e. 'Îsâ (Jesus), son of Maryam (Mary) [عليهما السلام]:

وَقَوْلِهِمْ إِنَّا قَتَلْنَا الْمَسِيحَ عِيسَى ابْنَ مَرْيَمَ رَسُولَ اللَّهِ وَمَا قَتَلُوهُ وَمَا صَلَبُوهُ وَلَٰكِن شُبِّهَ لَهُمْ وَإِنَّ الَّذِينَ اخْتَلَفُوا فِيهِ لَفِى شَكٍّ مِّنْهُ مَا لَهُم بِهِ مِنْ عِلْمٍ إِلَّا اتِّبَاعَ الظَّنِّ وَمَا قَتَلُوهُ يَقِينًا ﴿١٥٧﴾

158. But Allâh raised him ['Îsâ (Jesus)] up (with his body and soul) unto Himself (and he عليه السلام is in the heavens). And Allâh is Ever All-Powerful, All-Wise.

بَل رَّفَعَهُ اللَّهُ إِلَيْهِ وَكَانَ اللَّهُ عَزِيزًا حَكِيمًا ﴿١٥٨﴾

159. And there is none of the people of the Scripture (Jews and Christians) but must believe in him ['Îsâ (Jesus), son of Maryam (Mary), as only a Messenger of Allâh and a human being][1] before his ['Îsâ (Jesus) عليه السلام or a Jew's or a Christian's] death[2] (at the time of the appearance of the angel of death). And on the Day of Resurrection, he ['Îsâ (Jesus)] will be a witness against them.

وَإِن مِّنْ أَهْلِ الْكِتَابِ إِلَّا لَيُؤْمِنَنَّ بِهِ قَبْلَ مَوْتِهِ وَيَوْمَ الْقِيَامَةِ يَكُونُ عَلَيْهِمْ شَهِيدًا ﴿١٥٩﴾

---

[1] (V.4:159) See the footnote of (V.3:55).

[2] (V.4:159) — "Before his death," has two interpretations: before Jesus' death after his descent from the heavens, or a Jew's or a Christian's death, at the time of the appearance of the Angel of Death when he will realize that 'Îsâ (Jesus) was only a Messenger of Allâh, and had no share in Divinity.

160. For the wrong-doing of the Jews, We made unlawful for them certain good foods which had been lawful for them — and for their hindering many from Allâh's Way;

161. And their taking of *Ribâ* (usury) though they were forbidden from taking it and their devouring of men's substance wrongfully (bribery). And We have prepared for the disbelievers among them a painful torment.

162. But those among them who are well-grounded in knowledge, and the believers, believe in what has been sent down to you (Muhammad صلى الله عليه وسلم) and what was sent down before you; and those who perform *As-Salât* (Iqâmat-as-Salât), and give *Zakât* and believe in Allâh and in the Last Day, it is to whom We shall give a great reward.

163. Verily, We have sent the revelation to you (O Muhammad صلى الله عليه وسلم) [1] as We sent the revelation to

فَبِظُلْمٍ مِّنَ ٱلَّذِينَ هَادُواْ حَرَّمْنَا عَلَيْهِمْ طَيِّبَـٰتٍ أُحِلَّتْ لَهُمْ وَبِصَدِّهِمْ عَن سَبِيلِ ٱللَّهِ كَثِيرًا ۝

وَأَخْذِهِمُ ٱلرِّبَوٰاْ وَقَدْ نُهُواْ عَنْهُ وَأَكْلِهِمْ أَمْوَٰلَ ٱلنَّاسِ بِٱلْبَٰطِلِ وَأَعْتَدْنَا لِلْكَٰفِرِينَ مِنْهُمْ عَذَابًا أَلِيمًا ۝

لَّٰكِنِ ٱلرَّٰسِخُونَ فِي ٱلْعِلْمِ مِنْهُمْ وَٱلْمُؤْمِنُونَ يُؤْمِنُونَ بِمَآ أُنزِلَ إِلَيْكَ وَمَآ أُنزِلَ مِن قَبْلِكَ وَٱلْمُقِيمِينَ ٱلصَّلَوٰةَ وَٱلْمُؤْتُونَ ٱلزَّكَوٰةَ وَٱلْمُؤْمِنُونَ بِٱللَّهِ وَٱلْيَوْمِ ٱلْءَاخِرِ أُوْلَٰئِكَ سَنُؤْتِيهِمْ أَجْرًا عَظِيمًا ۝

﴿ إِنَّآ أَوْحَيْنَآ إِلَيْكَ كَمَآ أَوْحَيْنَآ إِلَىٰ نُوحٍ وَٱلنَّبِيِّـۧنَ مِنۢ

---

[1] (V.4:163) Ash-Shaikh Al-Imâm Al-Hâfiz Abu 'Abdullâh Muhammad bin Ismâ'îl bin Ibrâhîm bin Al-Mughîrah Al-Bukhâri (may Allâh مزوجل be Merciful to him) said: How the Divine Inspiration started to be revealed to Allâh's Messenger صلى الله عليه وسلم. And the Statement of Allâh تعالى : "Indeed, We have sent the revelation to you (O Muhammad صلى الله عليه وسلم as We sent the revelation to Nûh (Noah) and the Prophets after him." (V.4:163).

Narrated 'Umar bin Al-Khattâb رضى الله عنه : I heard Allâh's Messenger صلى الله عليه وسلم saying, "The reward of deeds depends upon the intentions and every person will get the reward according to what he has intended. So whoever emigrates for worldly benefits or for a woman to marry, his emigration will be for what he emigrated for." (Sahih Al-Bukhâri, Vol. 1, Hadîth No. 1).

Nûh (Noah) and the Prophets after him;
We (also) sent the revelation to Ibrâhîm
(Abraham), Ismâ'îl (Ishmael), Ishâq
(Isaac), Ya'qûb (Jacob), and Al-Asbât
[the offspring of the twelve sons of
Ya'qûb (Jacob)], 'Îsâ (Jesus), Ayûb
(Job), Yûnus (Jonah), Hârûn (Aaron),
and Sulaimân (Solomon); and to
Dâwûd (David) We gave the Zabûr
(Psalms).

164. And Messengers We have
mentioned to you before, and
Messengers We have not mentioned to
you, — and to Mûsâ (Moses) Allâh
spoke directly.

165. Messengers as bearers of good
news as well as of warning in order that
mankind should have no plea against
Allâh after the (coming of) Messengers.
And Allâh is Ever All-Powerful,
All-Wise.

166. But Allâh bears witness to that
which He has sent down (the Qur'ân)
unto you (O Muhammad صلى الله عليه وسلم); He
has sent it down with His Knowledge,

Narrated 'Âishah, the Mother of the faithful believers رضي الله عنها:
Al-Hârith bin Hishâm رضي الله عنه asked Allâh's Messenger صلى الله عليه وسلم:
"O Allâh's Messenger! How is the Divine Inspiration revealed to
you?" Allâh's Messenger صلى الله عليه وسلم replied, "Sometimes it is
(revealed) like the ringing of a bell, this form of revelation is the
hardest of all and then this state passes off after I have grasped what
is inspired. Sometimes the angel comes in the form of a man and
talks to me and I grasp whatever he says." 'Âishah رضي الله عنها added:
"Verily, I saw the Prophet صلى الله عليه وسلم being inspired divinely and
noticed the sweat dropping from his forehead on a very cold day as
the revelation was over." (*Sahih Al-Bukhâri*, Vol. 1, *Hadith* No. 2)

and the angels bear witness. And Allâh is All-Sufficient as a Witness.

وَكَفَىٰ بِٱللَّهِ شَهِيدًا ﴿١٦٦﴾

167. Verily, those who disbelieve [by concealing the truth about Prophet Muhammad صلى الله عليه وسلم and his message of true Islâmic Monotheism written in the Taurât (Torah) and the Injeel (Gospel) with them] and prevent (mankind) from the Path of Allâh (Islâmic Monotheism); they have certainly strayed far away. (Tafsir Al-Qurtubî).

إِنَّ ٱلَّذِينَ كَفَرُوا۟ وَصَدُّوا۟ عَن سَبِيلِ ٱللَّهِ قَدْ ضَلُّوا۟ ضَلَٰلًۢا بَعِيدًا ﴿١٦٧﴾

168. Verily, those who disbelieve and did wrong [by concealing the truth about Prophet Muhammad صلى الله عليه وسلم and his message of true Islâmic Monotheism written in the Taurât (Torah) and the Injeel (Gospel) with them]; Allâh will not forgive them, nor will He guide them to any way — (Tafsir Al-Qurtubî).

إِنَّ ٱلَّذِينَ كَفَرُوا۟ وَظَلَمُوا۟ لَمْ يَكُنِ ٱللَّهُ لِيَغْفِرَ لَهُمْ وَلَا لِيَهْدِيَهُمْ طَرِيقًا ﴿١٦٨﴾

169. Except the way of Hell, to dwell therein forever; and this is ever easy for Allâh.

إِلَّا طَرِيقَ جَهَنَّمَ خَٰلِدِينَ فِيهَآ أَبَدًا وَكَانَ ذَٰلِكَ عَلَى ٱللَّهِ يَسِيرًا ﴿١٦٩﴾

170. O mankind! Verily, there has come to you the Messenger (Muhammad صلى الله عليه وسلم) with the truth from your Lord. So believe in him, it is better for you. But if you disbelieve, then certainly to Allâh belongs all that is in the heavens and the earth. And Allâh is Ever All-Knowing, All-Wise.

يَٰٓأَيُّهَا ٱلنَّاسُ قَدْ جَآءَكُمُ ٱلرَّسُولُ بِٱلْحَقِّ مِن رَّبِّكُمْ فَـَٔامِنُوا۟ خَيْرًا لَّكُمْ وَإِن تَكْفُرُوا۟ فَإِنَّ لِلَّهِ مَا فِى ٱلسَّمَٰوَٰتِ وَٱلْأَرْضِ وَكَانَ ٱللَّهُ عَلِيمًا حَكِيمًا ﴿١٧٠﴾

171. O people of the Scripture! Do not exceed the limits in your religion, nor say of Allâh aught but the truth. The Messiah 'Îsâ (Jesus), son of Maryam (Mary), was (no more than) a

يَٰٓأَهْلَ ٱلْكِتَٰبِ لَا تَغْلُوا۟ فِى دِينِكُمْ وَلَا تَقُولُوا۟ عَلَى ٱللَّهِ إِلَّا ٱلْحَقَّ إِنَّمَا ٱلْمَسِيحُ عِيسَى ٱبْنُ مَرْيَمَ رَسُولُ

Messenger of Allâh and His Word, ("Be!" — and he was) which He bestowed on Maryam (Mary) and a spirit (Rûh)[1] created by Him; so believe in Allâh and His Messengers. Say not: "Three (trinity)!" Cease! (it is) better for you. For Allâh is the (only) One Ilâh (God), glory is to Him (Far Exalted is He) above having a son. To Him belongs all that is in the heavens and all that is in the earth. And Allâh is All-Sufficient as a Disposer of affairs.[2]

اللَّهِ وَكَلِمَتُهُ أَلْقَنَهَآ إِلَى مَرْيَمَ وَرُوحٌ مِّنْهُ فَـَامِنُواْ بِاللَّهِ وَرُسُلِهِۦ وَلَا تَقُولُواْ ثَلَنثَةٌ انتَهُواْ خَيْرًا لَّكُمْ إِنَّمَا ٱللَّهُ إِلَنهٌ وَحِدٌ سُبْحَننَهُۥٓ أَن يَكُونَ لَهُۥ وَلَدٌ لَّهُۥ مَا فِي ٱلسَّمَنوَتِ وَمَا فِي ٱلأَرْضِ وَكَفَى بِاللَّهِ وَكِيلًا ۝

---

[1] (V.4:171) Rûh-ullâh: According to the early religious scholars from among the Companions of the Prophet صلى الله عليه وسلم and their students and the Mujtahidûn, there is a rule to distinguish between the two nouns in the genitive construction:

a) When one of the two nouns is Allâh, and the other is a person or a thing, e.g. Allâh's House (Bait-ullâh); Allâh's Messenger (Rasûl-ullâh); and Allâh's slave ('Abdullâh); Allâh's spirit (Rûh-ullâh), the rule for the above words is that the second noun, i.e. house, messenger, slave or spirit is created by Allâh and is honourable in His Sight, and similarly, Allâh's spirit may be understood as the spirit of Allâh, in fact it is a soul created by Allâh, i.e. 'Isâ (Jesus). And it was His Word: "Be!" — and he was. [i.e. 'Isâ (Jesus) was created like Adam].

b) But when one of the two is Allâh and the second is neither a person nor a thing, then it is not a created thing but is a quality of Allâh e.g. Allâh's Knowledge ('Ilm-ullâh); Allâh's Life (Hayât-ullâh); Allâh's Statement (Kalâm-ullâh); Allâh's Self and (Dhat-ullâh).

[2] (V.4:171) Narrated 'Ubâdah رضى الله عنه The Prophet صلى الله عليه وسلم said, "If anyone testifies that Lâ ilâha illallâh (none has the right to be worshipped but Allâh Alone) Who has no partners, and that Muhammad صلى الله عليه وسلم is His slave and His Messenger, and that Jesus عليه السلام is Allâh's slave and His Messenger and His Word ("Be!" — and he was) which He bestowed on Mary and a spirit (Rûh) created by Him, and that Paradise is the truth, and Hell is the truth — Allâh will admit him into Paradise with the deeds which he had done even if those deeds were few." (Junâdah, the subnarrator said, "'Ubâdah added: 'Such a person can enter Paradise through any of its eight gates he likes.'") (Sahîh Al-Bukhârî, Vol. 4, Hadîth No. 644).

172. The Messiah will never be proud to reject to be a slave of Allâh, nor the angels who are the near (to Allâh). And whosoever rejects His worship and is proud, then He will gather them all together unto Himself.

173. So, as for those who believed (in the Oneness of Allâh — Islâmic Monotheism) and did deeds of righteousness, He will give them their (due) rewards — and more out of His Bounty. But as for those who refused His worship and were proud, He will punish them with a painful torment. And they will not find for themselves besides Allâh any protector or helper.

174. O mankind! Verily, there has come to you a convincing proof (Prophet Muhammad صلى الله عليه وسلم) from your Lord; and We sent down to you a manifest light (this Qur'ân).

175. So, as for those who believed in Allâh and held fast to Him, He will admit them to His Mercy and Grace (i.e. Paradise), and guide them to Himself by the Straight Path.

176. They ask you for a legal verdict. Say: "Allâh directs (thus) about Al-Kalâlah (those who leave neither descendants nor ascendants as heirs). If it is a man that dies leaving a sister, but no child, she shall have half the inheritance. If (such a deceased was) a woman, who left no child, her brother takes her inheritance. If there are two sisters, they shall have two-thirds of the inheritance; if there are brothers and sisters, the male will have twice the share of the female. (Thus) does Allâh make clear to you (His Law) lest you go astray. And Allâh is the All-Knower of everything."

رِجَالًا وَنِسَآءً فَلِلذَّكَرِ مِثْلُ حَظِّ الْأُنثَيَيْنِ يُبَيِّنُ اللَّهُ لَكُمْ أَن تَضِلُّوا وَاللَّهُ بِكُلِّ شَىْءٍ عَلِيمٌ ﴿﴾

Sûrat Al-Mâ'idah
(The Table spread with Food) V

سُورَةُ الْمَائِدَةِ

*In the Name of Allâh
the Most Gracious, the Most Merciful*

بِسْمِ اللَّهِ الرَّحْمَٰنِ الرَّحِيمِ

1. O you who believe! Fulfil (your) obligations. Lawful to you (for food) are all the beasts of cattle except that which will be announced to you (herein), game (also) being unlawful when you assume *Ihrâm* for *Hajj* or *'Umrah* (pilgrimage). Verily, Allâh commands that which He wills.

يَٰٓأَيُّهَا الَّذِينَ ءَامَنُوٓا أَوْفُوا بِالْعُقُودِ أُحِلَّتْ لَكُم بَهِيمَةُ الْأَنْعَٰمِ إِلَّا مَا يُتْلَىٰ عَلَيْكُمْ غَيْرَ مُحِلِّى الصَّيْدِ وَأَنتُمْ حُرُمٌ إِنَّ اللَّهَ يَحْكُمُ مَا يُرِيدُ ﴿١﴾

2. O you who believe! Violate not the sanctity of the Symbols of Allâh, nor of the Sacred Month, nor of the animals brought for sacrifice, nor the garlanded people or animals,[1] and others, nor the people coming to the Sacred House (Makkah), seeking the bounty and good pleasure of their Lord. But when you finish the *Ihrâm* (of *Hajj* or *'Umrah*), you may hunt, and let not the hatred of some people in (once) stopping you from *Al-Masjid Al-Harâm* (at Makkah) lead you to transgression (and hostility on your part). Help you one another in

يَٰٓأَيُّهَا الَّذِينَ ءَامَنُوا لَا تُحِلُّوا شَعَٰٓئِرَ اللَّهِ وَلَا الشَّهْرَ الْحَرَامَ وَلَا الْهَدْىَ وَلَا الْقَلَٰٓئِدَ وَلَآ ءَآمِّينَ الْبَيْتَ الْحَرَامَ يَبْتَغُونَ فَضْلًا مِّن رَّبِّهِمْ وَرِضْوَٰنًا وَإِذَا حَلَلْتُمْ فَاصْطَادُوا وَلَا يَجْرِمَنَّكُمْ شَنَـَٔانُ قَوْمٍ أَن صَدُّوكُمْ عَنِ الْمَسْجِدِ الْحَرَامِ أَن تَعْتَدُوا وَتَعَاوَنُوا عَلَى الْبِرِّ وَالتَّقْوَىٰ وَلَا تَعَاوَنُوا عَلَى الْإِثْمِ وَالْعُدْوَٰنِ وَاتَّقُوا اللَّهَ إِنَّ اللَّهَ

---

[1] (V.5:2) Marked by the garlands on their necks made from the outer part of the tree-stems (of Makkah) for their security.

Al-Birr and *At-Taqwa* (virtue, righteousness and piety); but do not help one another in sin and transgression. And fear Allâh. Verily, Allâh is Severe in punishment.

3. Forbidden to you (for food) are: *Al-Maitah* (the dead animals — cattle — beast not slaughtered), blood, the flesh of swine, and that on which Allâh's Name has not been mentioned while slaughtering (that which has been slaughtered as a sacrifice for others than Allâh, or has been slaughtered for idols) and that which has been killed by strangling, or by a violent blow, or by a headlong fall, or by the goring of horns — and that which has been (partly) eaten by a wild animal — unless you are able to slaughter it (before its death) and that which is sacrificed (slaughtered) on *An-Nusub*[1] (stone-altars). (Forbidden) also is to use arrows seeking luck or decision; (all) that is *Fisqun* (disobedience of Allâh and sin). This day, those who disbelieved have given up all hope of your religion; so fear them not, but fear Me. This day, I have perfected your religion for you, completed My Favour upon you, and have chosen for you Islâm as your religion. But as for him who is forced by severe hunger, with no inclination to sin (such can eat these above mentioned meats), then surely, Allâh is Oft-Forgiving, Most Merciful.

---

[1] (V.5:3) See the footnotes of (V.2:135) and (V.5:90).

4. They ask you (O Muhammad ﷺ وسلم عليه) what is lawful for them (as food). Say: "Lawful unto you are *At-Tayyibât* [all kinds of *Halâl* (lawful-good) foods which Allâh has made lawful (meat of slaughtered eatable animals, milk products, fats, vegetables and fruits)]. And those beasts and birds of prey which you have trained as hounds, training and teaching them (to catch) in the manner as directed to you by Allâh; so eat of what they catch for you, but pronounce the Name of Allâh over it, and fear Allâh. Verily, Allâh is Swift in reckoning."

يَسْتَلُونَكَ مَاذَآ أُحِلَّ لَهُمْ قُلْ
أُحِلَّ لَكُمُ ٱلطَّيِّبَـٰتُ وَمَا عَلَّمْتُم
مِّنَ ٱلْجَوَارِحِ مُكَلِّبِينَ تُعَلِّمُونَهُنَّ
مِمَّا عَلَّمَكُمُ ٱللَّهُ فَكُلُوا مِمَّآ أَمْسَكْنَ
عَلَيْكُمْ وَٱذْكُرُوا ٱسْمَ ٱللَّهِ عَلَيْهِ
وَٱتَّقُوا ٱللَّهَ إِنَّ ٱللَّهَ سَرِيعُ
ٱلْحِسَابِ ٤

5. Made lawful to you this day are *At-Tayyibât* [all kinds of *Halâl* (lawful) foods, which Allâh has made lawful (meat of slaughtered eatable animals, milk products, fats, vegetables and fruits). The food (slaughtered cattle, eatable animals) of the people of the Scripture (Jews and Christians) is lawful to you and yours is lawful to them. (Lawful to you in marriage) are chaste women from the believers and chaste women from those who were given the Scripture (Jews and Christians) before your time when you have given their due *Mahr* (bridal-money given by the husband to his wife at the time of marriage), desiring chastity (i.e. taking them in legal wedlock) not committing illegal sexual intercourse, nor taking them as girl-friends. And whosoever disbelieves in Faith [i.e. in the Oneness of Allâh and

ٱلْيَوْمَ أُحِلَّ لَكُمُ ٱلطَّيِّبَـٰتُ
وَطَعَامُ ٱلَّذِينَ أُوتُوا ٱلْكِتَـٰبَ حِلٌّ
لَّكُمْ وَطَعَامُكُمْ حِلٌّ لَّهُمْ
وَٱلْمُحْصَنَـٰتُ مِنَ ٱلْمُؤْمِنَـٰتِ
وَٱلْمُحْصَنَـٰتُ مِنَ ٱلَّذِينَ أُوتُوا
ٱلْكِتَـٰبَ مِن قَبْلِكُمْ
إِذَآ ءَاتَيْتُمُوهُنَّ أُجُورَهُنَّ
مُحْصِنِينَ غَيْرَ مُسَـٰفِحِينَ وَلَا
مُتَّخِذِىٓ أَخْدَانٍ وَمَن يَكْفُرْ
بِٱلْإِيمَـٰنِ فَقَدْ حَبِطَ عَمَلُهُ
وَهُوَ فِى ٱلْءَاخِرَةِ مِنَ ٱلْخَـٰسِرِينَ ٥

in all the other Articles of Faith i.e. His (Allâh's) Angels, His Holy Books, His Messengers, the Day of Resurrection and *Al-Qadar* (Divine Preordainments)], then fruitless is his work; and in the Hereafter he will be among the losers.

6. O you who believe! When you intend to offer *As-Salât* (the prayer), wash your faces and your hands (forearms) up to the elbows, rub (by passing wet hands over) your heads, and (wash) your feet up to the ankles.[1] If you are in a state of *Janâba* (i.e. after a sexual discharge), purify yourselves (bathe your whole body). But if you are ill or on a journey, or any of you comes after answering the call of nature, or you have been in contact with women (i.e. sexual intercourse), and you find no water, then perform *Tayammum* with clean earth and rub therewith your faces

---

[1] (V.5:6) The superiority of ablution. And *Al-Ghurr-ul-Muhajjalûn* (the parts of the body of the Muslims washed in ablution will shine on the Day of Resurrection and the angels will call them by that name) from the traces of ablution.

Narrated Nu'aim Al-Mujmir: Once I went up the roof of the mosque along with Abu Hurairah رضي الله عنه. He performed ablution and said, " I heard the Prophet صلى الله عليه وسلم saying, 'On the Day of Resurrection, my followers will be called *Al-Ghurr-ul-Muhajjalun* from the traces of ablution and whoever can increase the area of his radiance* should do so (by performing ablution in the most perfect manner).' " (*Sahih Al-Bukhâri*, Vol.1, *Hadith* No.138).

* The Prophet صلى الله عليه وسلم did not increase the area more than what is washed of the body parts while doing ablution as Allâh ordered to be washed in the Qur'ân. [For details about Wudu (ablution), see *Sahih Al-Bukhâri*, Vol.1, (The Book of Ablution)].

and hands.[1] Allâh does not want to place you in difficulty, but He wants to purify you, and to complete His Favour to you that you may be thankful.

7. And remember Allâh's Favour to you and His Covenant with which He bound you when you said: "We hear and we obey." And fear Allâh. Verily, Allâh is All-Knower of that which is in (the secrets of your) breasts.

8. O you who believe! Stand out firmly for Allâh as just witnesses; and let not the enmity and hatred of others make you avoid justice. Be just: that is nearer to piety; and fear Allâh. Verily, Allâh is Well-Acquainted with what you do.

9. Allâh has promised those who believe (in the Oneness of Allâh — Islâmic Monotheism) and do deeds of righteousness, that for them there is forgiveness and a great reward (i.e. Paradise).

10. And those who disbelieve and deny our *Ayât* (proofs, evidences, verses, lessons, signs, revelations, etc.) are those who will be the dwellers of the Hell-fire.

11. O you who believe! Remember the Favour of Allâh unto you when some people desired (made a plan) to

لِيَجْعَلَ عَلَيْكُم مِّنْ حَرَجٍ
وَلَكِن يُرِيدُ لِيُطَهِّرَكُمْ وَلِيُتِمَّ
نِعْمَتَهُ عَلَيْكُمْ لَعَلَّكُمْ
تَشْكُرُونَ ٦ وَاذْكُرُوا
نِعْمَةَ اللَّهِ عَلَيْكُمْ وَمِيثَـٰقَهُ
الَّذِى وَاثَقَكُم بِهِ إِذْ قُلْتُمْ
سَمِعْنَا وَأَطَعْنَا وَاتَّقُوا اللَّهَ
إِنَّ اللَّهَ عَلِيمٌ بِذَاتِ الصُّدُورِ
٧ يَـٰٓأَيُّهَا الَّذِينَ ءَامَنُوا
كُونُوا قَوَّٰمِينَ لِلَّهِ شُهَدَآءَ
بِالْقِسْطِ وَلَا يَجْرِمَنَّكُمْ
شَنَـَٔانُ قَوْمٍ عَلَىٰٓ أَلَّا تَعْدِلُوا
اعْدِلُوا هُوَ أَقْرَبُ لِلتَّقْوَىٰ
وَاتَّقُوا اللَّهَ إِنَّ اللَّهَ خَبِيرٌ
بِمَا تَعْمَلُونَ ٨ وَعَدَ اللَّهُ
الَّذِينَ ءَامَنُوا وَعَمِلُوا
الصَّـٰلِحَـٰتِ لَهُم مَّغْفِرَةٌ
وَأَجْرٌ عَظِيمٌ ٩
وَالَّذِينَ كَفَرُوا وَكَذَّبُوا
بِـَٔايَـٰتِنَآ أُوْلَـٰٓئِكَ أَصْحَـٰبُ
الْجَحِيمِ ٠
يَـٰٓأَيُّهَا الَّذِينَ ءَامَنُوا اذْكُرُوا
نِعْمَتَ اللَّهِ عَلَيْكُمْ إِذْ هَمَّ

---

[1] (V.5:6) Strike your hands on the earth and then pass the palm of each on the back of the other and then blow off the dust from them and then pass (rub) them on your face: this is called *Tayammum.*

stretch out their hands against you, but (Allâh) held back their hands from you. So fear Allâh. And in Allâh let the believers put their trust.

12. Indeed Allâh took the covenant from the Children of Israel (Jews), and We appointed twelve leaders among them. And Allâh said: "I am with you if you perform As-Salât (Iqâmat-as-Salât) and give Zakât and believe in My Messengers; honour and assist them, and lend a good loan to Allâh, verily, I will expiate your sins and admit you to Gardens under which rivers flow (in Paradise). But if any of you after this, disbelieved, he has indeed gone astray from the Straight Path."

13. So because of their breach of their covenant, We cursed them and made their hearts grow hard. They change the words from their (right) places and have abandoned a good part of the Message that was sent to them.[1] And you will not cease to discover deceit in them, except a few of them. But forgive them and overlook (their misdeeds). Verily, Allâh loves Al-Muhsinûn (good-doers — See V.2:112).

14. And from those who call themselves Christians, We took their covenant, but they have abandoned a

---

[1] (V.5:13) i.e. the Jews were ordered in the Taurât (Torah) to follow Prophet Muhammad صلى الله عليه وسلم when he would come as a Messenger of Allâh to all mankind. [See (V.7:157) and its footnote].

good part of the Message that was sent to them. [1] So We planted amongst them enmity and hatred till the Day of Resurrection (when they discarded Allâh's Book, disobeyed Allâh's Messengers and His Orders and transgressed beyond bounds in Allâh's disobedience); and Allâh will inform them of what they used to do.

15. O people of the Scripture (Jews and Christians)! Now has come to you Our Messenger (Muhammad صلى الله عليه وسلم) explaining to you much of that which you used to hide from the Scripture and pass over (i.e. leaving out without explaining) much. Indeed, there has come to you from Allâh a light (Prophet Muhammad صلى الله عليه وسلم) and a plain Book (this Qur'ân).

16. Wherewith Allâh guides all those who seek His Good Pleasure to ways of peace, and He brings them out of darkness by His Will unto light and guides them to the Straight Way (Islâmic Monotheism).

17. Surely, in disbelief are they who say that Allâh is the Messiah, son of Maryam (Mary). [2] Say (O Muhammad صلى الله عليه وسلم): "Who then has the least power against Allâh, if He were to destroy the Messiah, son of Maryam

---

[1] (V.5:14) The Christians were ordered in the Injeel (Gospel) to follow Prophet Muhammad صلى الله عليه وسلم when he would come as a Messenger of Allâh to all mankind. [See (V.7:157) and its footnote].

[2] (V.5:17) See the footnotes of (V.4:171).

(Mary), his mother, and all those who are on the earth together?" And to Allâh belongs the dominion of the heavens and the earth, and all that is between them. He creates what He wills. And Allâh is Able to do all things.

18. And (both) the Jews and the Christians say: "We are the children of Allâh and His loved ones." Say: "Why then does He punish you for your sins?" Nay, you are but human beings of those He has created, He forgives whom He wills and He punishes whom He wills. And to Allâh belongs the dominion of the heavens and the earth and all that is between them; and to Him is the return (of all).

19. O people of the Scripture (Jews and Christians)! Now has come to you Our Messenger (Muhammad صلى الله عليه وسلم) making (things) clear unto you, after a break in the (series) of Messengers, lest you say: "There came unto us no bringer of glad tidings and no warner.[1]" But now has come unto you a bringer of glad tidings and a warner. And Allâh is Able to do all things.

20. And (remember) when Mûsâ (Moses) said to his people: "O my people! Remember the Favour of Allâh to you: when He made Prophets among

يُهْلِكَ ٱلْمَسِيحَ ٱبْنَ مَرْيَمَ وَأُمَّهُۥ وَمَن فِي ٱلْأَرْضِ جَمِيعًا وَلِلَّهِ مُلْكُ ٱلسَّمَٰوَٰتِ وَٱلْأَرْضِ وَمَا بَيْنَهُمَا يَخْلُقُ مَا يَشَآءُ وَٱللَّهُ عَلَىٰ كُلِّ شَىْءٍ قَدِيرٌ ۝ وَقَالَتِ ٱلْيَهُودُ وَٱلنَّصَٰرَىٰ نَحْنُ أَبْنَٰٓؤُا۟ ٱللَّهِ وَأَحِبَّٰٓؤُهُۥ قُلْ فَلِمَ يُعَذِّبُكُم بِذُنُوبِكُم بَلْ أَنتُم بَشَرٌ مِّمَّنْ خَلَقَ يَغْفِرُ لِمَن يَشَآءُ وَيُعَذِّبُ مَن يَشَآءُ وَلِلَّهِ مُلْكُ ٱلسَّمَٰوَٰتِ وَٱلْأَرْضِ وَمَا بَيْنَهُمَا وَإِلَيْهِ ٱلْمَصِيرُ ۝ يَٰٓأَهْلَ ٱلْكِتَٰبِ قَدْ جَآءَكُمْ رَسُولُنَا يُبَيِّنُ لَكُمْ عَلَىٰ فَتْرَةٍ مِّنَ ٱلرُّسُلِ أَن تَقُولُوا۟ مَا جَآءَنَا مِنۢ بَشِيرٍ وَلَا نَذِيرٍ فَقَدْ جَآءَكُم بَشِيرٌ وَنَذِيرٌ وَٱللَّهُ عَلَىٰ كُلِّ شَىْءٍ قَدِيرٌ ۝ وَإِذْ قَالَ مُوسَىٰ لِقَوْمِهِۦ يَٰقَوْمِ ٱذْكُرُوا۟ نِعْمَةَ ٱللَّهِ عَلَيْكُمْ إِذْ جَعَلَ فِيكُمْ أَنۢبِيَآءَ وَجَعَلَكُم مُّلُوكًا وَءَاتَىٰكُم مَّا

---

[1] (V.5:19)

a) See the footnote of (V.3:85) and see (V.3:116).

b) See the footnote of (B) of (V.2:252).

you, made you kings and gave you what He had not given to anyother among the *'Âlamîn* (mankind and jinn, in the past)."

21. "O my people! Enter the holy land (Palestine) which Allâh has assigned to you and turn not back (in flight); for then you will be returned as losers."

22. They said: "O Mûsâ (Moses)! In it (this holy land) are a people of great strength, and we shall never enter it till they leave it; when they leave, then we will enter."

23. Two men of those who feared (Allâh and) on whom Allâh had bestowed His Grace (they were Yûsha' and Kâlab) said: "Assault them through the gate; for when you are in, victory will be yours; and put your trust in Allâh if you are believers indeed."

24. They said: "O Mûsâ (Moses)! We shall never enter it as long as they are there. So go you and your Lord and fight you two, we are sitting right here."

25. He [Mûsâ (Moses)] said: "O my Lord! I have power only over myself and my brother, so separate us from the people who are the *Fâsiqûn* (rebellious and disobedient to Allâh)!"

26. (Allâh) said: "Therefore it (this holy land) is forbidden to them for forty years; in distraction they will wander through the land. So be not sorrowful over the people who are the *Fâsiqûn* (rebellious and disobedient to Allâh)."

27. And (O Muhammad صلى الله عليه وسلم recite to them (the Jews) the story of the two sons of Adam (Hâbîl and Qâbîl) in truth; when each offered a sacrifice (to Allâh), it was accepted from the one but not from the other. The latter said to the former: "I will surely, kill you." [1] The former said: "Verily, Allâh accepts only from those who are Al-Muttaqûn (the pious. See V.2:2)."

28. "If you do stretch your hand against me to kill me, I shall never stretch my hand against you to kill you: for I fear Allâh, the Lord of the 'Âlamîn (mankind, jinn, and all that exists)."

29. "Verily, I intend to let you draw my sin on yourself as well as yours, then you will be one of the dwellers of the Fire; and that is the recompense of the Zâlimûn (polytheists and wrong-doers)."

30. So the Nafs (self) of the other (latter one) encouraged him and made fair-seeming to him the murder of his brother; he murdered him and became one of the losers.

31. Then Allâh sent a crow who scratched the ground to show him to

۞ وَٱتْلُ عَلَيْهِمْ نَبَأَ ٱبْنَىْ ءَادَمَ بِٱلْحَقِّ إِذْ قَرَّبَا قُرْبَانًا فَتُقُبِّلَ مِنْ أَحَدِهِمَا وَلَمْ يُتَقَبَّلْ مِنَ ٱلْآخَرِ قَالَ لَأَقْتُلَنَّكَ قَالَ إِنَّمَا يَتَقَبَّلُ ٱللَّهُ مِنَ ٱلْمُتَّقِينَ ٢٧

لَئِنۢ بَسَطتَ إِلَىَّ يَدَكَ لِتَقْتُلَنِي مَآ أَنَا۠ بِبَاسِطٍ يَدِىَ إِلَيْكَ لِأَقْتُلَكَ إِنِّىٓ أَخَافُ ٱللَّهَ رَبَّ ٱلْعَٰلَمِينَ ٢٨

إِنِّىٓ أُرِيدُ أَن تَبُوٓأَ بِإِثْمِى وَإِثْمِكَ فَتَكُونَ مِنْ أَصْحَٰبِ ٱلنَّارِ وَذَٰلِكَ جَزَٰٓؤُا۟ ٱلظَّٰلِمِينَ ٢٩

فَطَوَّعَتْ لَهُۥ نَفْسُهُۥ قَتْلَ أَخِيهِ فَقَتَلَهُۥ فَأَصْبَحَ مِنَ ٱلْخَٰسِرِينَ ٣٠

فَبَعَثَ ٱللَّهُ غُرَابًا يَبْحَثُ فِى ٱلْأَرْضِ لِيُرِيَهُۥ كَيْفَ يُوَٰرِى

---

[1] (V.5:27) Narrated 'Abdullâh رضى الله عنه: The Prophet صلى الله عليه وسلم said, "None (no human being) is killed or murdered (unjustly), but a part of responsibility for the crime is laid on the first son of Adam who invented the tradition of killing (murdering) on the earth. (It is said that he was Qâbîl)." (Sahih Al-Bukhâri, Vol.9, Hadith No.6)
Narrated 'Abdullâh bin 'Umar رضى الله عنهما: The Prophet صلى الله عليه وسلم said, "After me (i.e., after my death), do not become disbelievers, by striking (cutting) the necks of one another." (Sahih Al-Bukhâri, Vol.9, Hadith No.7).

hide the dead body of his brother. He (the murderer) said: "Woe to me! Am I not even able to be as this crow and to hide the dead body of my brother?" Then he became one of those who regretted.

32. Because of that We ordained for the Children of Israel that if anyone killed a person not in retaliation of murder, or (and) to spread mischief in the land — it would be as if he killed all mankind, and if anyone saved a life, it would be as if he saved the life of all mankind. And indeed, there came to them Our Messengers with clear proofs, evidences, and signs, even then after that many of them continued to exceed the limits (e.g. by doing oppression unjustly and exceeding beyond the limits set by Allâh by committing the major sins) in the land![1]

33. The recompense of those who wage war against Allâh and His Messenger and do mischief in the land is only that they shall be killed or crucified or their hands and their feet be cut off from opposite sides, or be exiled from the land. That is their disgrace in this world, and a great torment is theirs in the Hereafter.

---

[1] (V.5:32) Narrated Anas bin Mâlik رضي الله عنه: The Prophet صلى الله عليه وسلم said, "The biggest of *Al-Kabâ'ir* (the great sins) are: (1) To join others as partners in worship with Allâh, (2) to murder a human being, (3) to be undutiful to one's parents (4) and to make a false statement," or said, "to give a false witness."(*Sahih Al-Bukhâri*, Vol.9, *Hadith* No.10).

34. Except for those who (having fled away and then) came back (as Muslims) with repentance before they fall into your power; in that case, know that Allâh is Oft-Forgiving, Most Merciful.

إِلَّا ٱلَّذِينَ تَابُواْ مِن قَبْلِ أَن تَقْدِرُواْ عَلَيْهِمْ فَٱعْلَمُوٓاْ أَنَّ ٱللَّهَ غَفُورٌ رَّحِيمٌ ﴿٣٤﴾

35. O you who believe! Do your duty to Allâh and fear Him. And seek the means of approach to Him, and strive hard in His Cause (as much as you can), so that you may be successful.[1]

يَٰٓأَيُّهَا ٱلَّذِينَ ءَامَنُواْ ٱتَّقُواْ ٱللَّهَ وَٱبْتَغُوٓاْ إِلَيْهِ ٱلْوَسِيلَةَ وَجَٰهِدُواْ فِى سَبِيلِهِۦ لَعَلَّكُمْ تُفْلِحُونَ ﴿٣٥﴾

36. Verily, those who disbelieve, if they had all that is in the earth, and as much again therewith to ransom themselves thereby from the torment on the Day of Resurrection, it would never be accepted of them, and theirs would be a painful torment.[2]

إِنَّ ٱلَّذِينَ كَفَرُواْ لَوْ أَنَّ لَهُم مَّا فِى ٱلْأَرْضِ جَمِيعًا وَمِثْلَهُۥ مَعَهُۥ لِيَفْتَدُواْ بِهِۦ مِنْ عَذَابِ يَوْمِ ٱلْقِيَٰمَةِ مَا تُقُبِّلَ مِنْهُمْ وَلَهُمْ عَذَابٌ أَلِيمٌ ﴿٣٦﴾

37. They will long to get out of the Fire, but never will they get out therefrom; and theirs will be a lasting torment.

يُرِيدُونَ أَن يَخْرُجُواْ مِنَ ٱلنَّارِ وَمَا هُم بِخَٰرِجِينَ مِنْهَا وَلَهُمْ عَذَابٌ مُّقِيمٌ ﴿٣٧﴾

38. And (as for) the male thief and the female thief, cut off (from the wrist joint) their (right) hands as a recompense for that which they committed, a punishment by way of example from Allâh. And Allâh is All-Powerful, All-Wise.

وَٱلسَّارِقُ وَٱلسَّارِقَةُ فَٱقْطَعُوٓاْ أَيْدِيَهُمَا جَزَآءًۢ بِمَا كَسَبَا نَكَٰلًا مِّنَ ٱللَّهِ وَٱللَّهُ عَزِيزٌ حَكِيمٌ ﴿٣٨﴾

39. But whosoever repents after his crime and does righteous good deeds (by obeying Allâh), then verily, Allâh

فَمَن تَابَ مِنۢ بَعْدِ ظُلْمِهِۦ وَأَصْلَحَ فَإِنَّ ٱللَّهَ يَتُوبُ

---

[1] (V.5:35) See the footnote of (V.2:186).

[2] (V.5:36) See the footnote of (V.3:91).

will pardon him (accept his repentance). Verily, Allâh is Oft-Forgiving, Most Merciful.

40. Know you not that to Allâh (Alone) belongs the dominion of the heavens and the earth! He punishes whom He wills and He forgives whom He wills. And Allâh is Able to do all things.

41. O Messenger (Muhammad صلى الله عليه وسلم)! Let not those who hurry to fall into disbelief grieve you, of such who say: "We believe" with their mouths but their hearts have no faith. And of the Jews are men who listen much and eagerly to lies — listen to others who have not come to you. They change the words from their places; they say, "If you are given this, take it, but if you are not given this, then beware!" And whomsoever Allâh wants to put in *Al-Fitnah* [error, because of his rejecting of Faith], you can do nothing for him against Allâh. Those are the ones whose hearts Allâh does not want to purify (from disbelief and hypocrisy); for them there is a disgrace in this world, and in the Hereafter a great torment.

42. (They like to) listen to falsehood, to devour anything forbidden. So if they come to you (O Muhammad صلى الله عليه وسلم), either judge between them, or turn away from them. If you turn away from them, they cannot hurt you in the least. And if you judge, judge with justice between them. Verily, Allâh loves those who act justly.

43. But how do they come to you for decision while they have the Taurât (Torah), in which is the (plain) Decision of Allâh; yet even after that, they turn away. For they are not (really) believers.

44. Verily, We did send down the Taurât (Torah) [to Mûsâ (Moses)], therein was guidance and light, by which the Prophets, who submitted themselves to Allâh's Will, judged for the Jews. And the rabbis and the priests [too judged for the Jews by the Taurât (Torah) after those Prophets], for to them were entrusted the protection of Allâh's Book, and they were witnesses thereto. Therefore fear not men but fear Me (O Jews) and sell not My Verses for a miserable price. And whosoever does not judge by what Allâh has revealed, such are the *Kâfirûn* (i.e. disbelievers — of a lesser degree as they do not act on Allâh's Laws).[1]

45. And We ordained therein for them: "Life for life,[2] eye for eye, nose

إِنَّ ٱللَّهَ يُحِبُّ ٱلْمُقْسِطِينَ ﴿

وَكَيْفَ يُحَكِّمُونَكَ وَعِندَهُمُ ٱلتَّوْرَىٰةُ فِيهَا حُكْمُ ٱللَّهِ ثُمَّ يَتَوَلَّوْنَ مِنۢ بَعْدِ ذَٰلِكَ وَمَآ أُوْلَٰٓئِكَ بِٱلْمُؤْمِنِينَ ﴿

إِنَّآ أَنزَلْنَا ٱلتَّوْرَىٰةَ فِيهَا هُدًى وَنُورٌ يَحْكُمُ بِهَا ٱلنَّبِيُّونَ ٱلَّذِينَ أَسْلَمُوا۟ لِلَّذِينَ هَادُوا۟ وَٱلرَّبَّٰنِيُّونَ وَٱلْأَحْبَارُ بِمَا ٱسْتُحْفِظُوا۟ مِن كِتَٰبِ ٱللَّهِ وَكَانُوا۟ عَلَيْهِ شُهَدَآءَ فَلَا تَخْشَوُا۟ ٱلنَّاسَ وَٱخْشَوْنِ وَلَا تَشْتَرُوا۟ بِـَٔايَٰتِى ثَمَنًا قَلِيلًا وَمَن لَّمْ يَحْكُم بِمَآ أَنزَلَ ٱللَّهُ فَأُوْلَٰٓئِكَ هُمُ ٱلْكَٰفِرُونَ ﴿

وَكَتَبْنَا عَلَيْهِمْ فِيهَآ أَنَّ ٱلنَّفْسَ بِٱلنَّفْسِ وَٱلْعَيْنَ بِٱلْعَيْنِ وَٱلْأَنفَ بِٱلْأَنفِ وَٱلْأُذُنَ

---

[1] (V.5:44) For different degrees of *Kufr* (Disbelief) see Appendix 2, "Polytheism and Disbelief".

[2] (V.5:45) Narrated 'Abdullâh رضى الله عنه: Allâh's Messenger صلى الله عليه وسلم said, "The blood of a Muslim who confesses that *Lâ ilaha illallâh* (none has the right to be worshipped but Allâh) and that I am the Messenger of Allâh, cannot be shed except in three cases:

1) Life for life in case of intentional murder without right [i.e. in *Qisâs* (Law of Equality in punishment)].

2) A married person who commits illegal sexual intercourse, and

for nose, ear for ear, tooth for tooth, and wounds equal for equal." But if anyone remits the retaliation by way of charity, it shall be for him an expiation. And whosoever does not judge by that which Allâh has revealed, such are the Zâlimûn (polytheists and wrongdoers — of a lesser degree).

46. And in their footsteps, We sent 'Îsâ (Jesus), son of Maryam (Mary),[1] confirming the Taurât (Torah) that had come before him, and We gave him the Injeel (Gospel), in which was guidance and light and confirmation of the Taurât (Torah) that had come before it, a guidance and an admonition for Al-Muttaqûn (the pious. See V.2:2).

47. Let the people of the Injeel (Gospel) judge by what Allâh has revealed therein. And whosoever does not judge by what Allâh has revealed (then) such (people) are the Fâsiqûn [the rebellious i.e. disobedient (of a lesser degree)] to Allâh.

48. And We have sent down to you (O Muhammad ﷺ) the Book (this Qur'ân) in truth, confirming the

---

3) The one who reverts from Islâm (apostates) and leaves the group of Muslims (by innovating heresy, new ideas, new things, in the Islâmic Religion)." (See Fath Al-Bari for details). (Sahih Al-Bukhâri, Hadith No.17).

[1] (V.5:46) Narrated Abu Hurairah رضى الله عنه I heard Allâh's Messenger صلى الله عليه وسلم saying, "I am the nearest of all the people to the son of Maryam (Mary), and all the Prophets are paternal brothers, and there has been no Prophet between me and him [i.e., 'Îsâ (Jesus)]." (Sahih Al-Bukhari, Vol. 4, Hadith No. 651)

Scripture that came before it and *Mohayminan* (trustworthy in highness and a witness) over it (old Scriptures).[1] So judge among them by what Allâh has revealed, and follow not their vain desires, diverging away from the truth that has come to you. To each among you, We have prescribed a law and a clear way. If Allâh had willed, He would have made you one nation, but that (He) may test you in what He has given you; so compete in good deeds. The return of you (all) is to Allâh; then He will inform you about that in which you used to differ.

49. And so judge (you O Muhammad صلى الله عليه وسلم) among them by what Allâh has revealed and follow not their vain desires, but beware of them lest they turn you (O Muhammad صلى الله عليه وسلم) far away from some of that which Allâh has sent down to you. And if they turn away, then know that Allâh's Will is to punish them for some sins of theirs. And truly, most of men are *Fâsiqûn* (rebellious and disobedient to Allâh).

50. Do they then seek the judgement of (the days of) Ignorance?[2] And who

---

[1] (V.5:48) *Mohayminan*: that which testifies the truth that is therein and falsifies the falsehood that is added therein.

[2] (V.5:50): Narrated Ibn 'Abbâs رضي الله عنهما The Prophet صلى الله عليه وسلم said. "The most hated persons to Allâh are three: (1) A person who deviates from the right conduct, i.e., an evil doer, in the *Haram* (sanctuaries of Makkah and Al-Madinah); (2) a person who wants that the traditions of the pre-Islâmic period of Ignorance should remain in Islâm; and (3) a person who seeks to shed somebody's blood without any right." (*Sahih Al-Bukhâri*, Vol. 9. *Hadîth* No. 21).

لِقَوْمٍ يُوقِنُونَ ۝

is better in judgement than Allâh for a people who have firm Faith.

51. O you who believe! Take not the Jews and the Christians as *Auliyâ'* (friends, protectors, helpers), they are but *Auliyâ'* of each other. And if any amongst you takes them (as *Auliyâ'*), then surely, he is one of them. Verily, Allâh guides not those people who are the *Zâlimûn* (polytheists and wrong-doers and unjust).

52. And you see those in whose hearts there is a disease (of hypocrisy), they hurry to their friendship, saying: "We fear lest some misfortune of a disaster may befall us." Perhaps Allâh may bring a victory or a decision according to His Will. Then they will become regretful for what they have been keeping as a secret in themselves.

53. And those who believe will say: "Are these the (hypocrites) who swore their strongest oaths by Allâh that they were with you (Muslims)?" All that they did has been in vain (because of their hypocrisy), and they have become the losers.

54. O you who believe! Whoever from among you turns back from his religion (Islâm), Allâh will bring a people whom He will love and they will love Him; humble towards the believers, stern towards the disbelievers, fighting in the Way of Allâh, and never afraid of the blame of the blamers. That is the Grace of Allâh which He bestows on whom He wills. And Allâh is All-Sufficient for His creatures' needs, All-Knower.

عَلِيمٌ ٥٤

55. Verily, your *Walî* (Protector or Helper) is none other than Allâh, His Messenger, and the believers, — those who perform *As-Salât* (*Iqâmat-as-Salât*), and give *Zakât*, and they are *Râki'ûn*[1] (those who bow down or submit themselves with obedience to Allâh in prayer).

إِنَّمَا وَلِيُّكُمُ ٱللَّهُ وَرَسُولُهُۥ وَٱلَّذِينَ ءَامَنُواْ ٱلَّذِينَ يُقِيمُونَ ٱلصَّلَوٰةَ وَيُؤْتُونَ ٱلزَّكَوٰةَ وَهُمْ رَٰكِعُونَ ٥٥

56. And whosoever takes Allâh, His Messenger, and those who have believed, as Protectors, then the party of Allâh will be the victorious.[2]

وَمَن يَتَوَلَّ ٱللَّهَ وَرَسُولَهُۥ وَٱلَّذِينَ ءَامَنُواْ فَإِنَّ حِزْبَ ٱللَّهِ هُمُ ٱلْغَٰلِبُونَ ٥٦

57. O you who believe! Take not as *Auliyâ'* (protectors and helpers) those who take your religion as a mockery and fun from among those who received the Scripture (Jews and Christians) before you, and nor from among the disbelievers; and fear Allâh if you indeed are true believers.

يَٰٓأَيُّهَا ٱلَّذِينَ ءَامَنُواْ لَا تَتَّخِذُواْ ٱلَّذِينَ ٱتَّخَذُواْ دِينَكُمْ هُزُوًا وَلَعِبًا مِّنَ ٱلَّذِينَ أُوتُواْ ٱلْكِتَٰبَ مِن قَبْلِكُمْ وَٱلْكُفَّارَ أَوْلِيَآءَ وَٱتَّقُواْ ٱللَّهَ إِن كُنتُم مُّؤْمِنِينَ ٥٧

58. And when you proclaim the call for *As-Salât* [call for the prayer (*Adhân*)], they take it (but) as a mockery and fun; that is because they are a people who understand not.[3]

وَإِذَا نَادَيْتُمْ إِلَى ٱلصَّلَوٰةِ ٱتَّخَذُوهَا هُزُوًا وَلَعِبًا ذَٰلِكَ بِأَنَّهُمْ قَوْمٌ لَّا يَعْقِلُونَ ٥٨

---

[1] (V.5:55) See the footnote of (V.2:43).

[2] (V.5:56) See the footnotes (A) and (B) of (V.27:59).

[3] (V.5:58) How the *Adhân* (the call to prayer)* for the prayer was started. And the Statement of Allâh عز وجل:

"And when you proclaim the call to prayer (*Adhân*) they take it (but) as a mockery and fun that is because they are people who understand not." (V.5:58).

59. Say: "O people of the Scripture (Jews and Christians)! Do you criticize us for no other reason than that we believe in Allâh, and in (the revelation) which has been sent down to us and in that which has been sent down before (us), and that most of you are *Fâsiqûn* [rebellious and disobedient (to Allâh)]?"

قُلْ يَٰٓأَهْلَ ٱلْكِتَٰبِ هَلْ تَنقِمُونَ مِنَّآ إِلَّآ أَنْ ءَامَنَّا بِٱللَّهِ وَمَآ أُنزِلَ إِلَيْنَا وَمَآ أُنزِلَ مِن قَبْلُ وَأَنَّ أَكْثَرَكُمْ فَٰسِقُونَ ٥٩

60. Say (O Muhammad صلى الله عليه وسلم to the people of the Scripture): "Shall I inform you of something worse than that, regarding the recompense from Allâh: those (Jews) who incurred the Curse of Allâh and His Wrath, and those of whom (some) He transformed into monkeys and swines, and those who worshipped *Tâghût*[1] (false deities); such are worse in rank (on the Day of Resurrection in the Hell-fire),

قُلْ هَلْ أُنَبِّئُكُم بِشَرٍّ مِّن ذَٰلِكَ مَثُوبَةً عِندَ ٱللَّهِ مَن لَّعَنَهُ ٱللَّهُ وَغَضِبَ عَلَيْهِ وَجَعَلَ مِنْهُمُ ٱلْقِرَدَةَ وَٱلْخَنَازِيرَ وَعَبَدَ ٱلطَّٰغُوتَ أُوْلَٰٓئِكَ شَرٌّ مَّكَانًا وَأَضَلُّ عَن سَوَآءِ ٱلسَّبِيلِ ٦٠

And also the Statement of Allâh: عزوجل "When the call (*Adhân*) for the prayer is proclaimed on the day of Friday." (V.62:9).

Narrated Anas رضي الله عنه: The people mentioned the fire and the bell (they suggested those as signals to indicate the starting of prayers), and by that they mentioned the Jews and the Christians. Then Bilâl was ordered to pronounce *Adhân* for the prayer by saying its wordings twice (in doubles), and for the *Iqâmah* (the call for the actual standing of the prayers in rows) by saying its wordings once (in singles) (*Iqâmah* is pronounced when the people are ready for the prayer). (*Sahih Al-Bukhâri*, Vol. 1, *Hadith* No. 577).

*The wording of *Adhân*: *Allâhu-Akbar, Allâhu-Akbar, Allâhu-Akbar, Allâhu-Akbar; Ash-hadu an lâ ilah illallâh, Ash-hadu an lâ ilâha illallâh; Ash-hadu anna Muhammad-ar-Rasûl-Ullâh, Ash-hadu anna Muhammad-ar-Rasûl-Ullâh; Haiya-'alas-Salâh, Haiya 'alas-Salâh; Haiya 'alal-Falâh, Haiya 'alal-Falâh; Allâhu-Akbar, Allâhu-Akbar; Lâ ilâha illallâh.*

[1] (V.5:60) *Tâghût*: See the footnote of (V.2:256).

and far more astray from the Right Path (in the life of this world)."

61. When they come to you, they say: "We believe." But in fact they enter with (an intention of) disbelief and they go out with the same. And Allâh knows all what they were hiding.

62. And you see many of them (Jews) hurrying towards sin and transgression, and eating illegal things [as bribes and *Ribâ* (usury)]. Evil indeed is that which they have been doing.

63. Why do not the rabbis and the religious learned men forbid them from uttering sinful words and from eating illegal things. Evil indeed is that which they have been performing.

64. The Jews say: "Allâh's Hand is tied up (i.e. He does not give and spend of His Bounty)." Be their hands tied up and be they accursed for what they uttered. Nay, both His Hands[1] are widely outstretched. He spends (of His Bounty) as He wills. Verily, the Revelation that has come to you from your Lord (Allâh) increases in most of them (their) obstinate rebellion and

---

[1] (V.5:64) *Sifât-ullâh* صفات الله عز وجل (Qualities of Allâh): [See the footnote of (V.3:73)].

Narrated Ibn 'Umar: رضي الله عنهما Allâh's Messenger صلى الله عليه وسلم said, "On the Day of Resurrection, Allâh will grasp the whole (planet of) earth by His Hand, and all the heavens in His Right, and then He will say, 'I am the King.' "

Abu Hurairah said, "Allâh's Messenger صلى الله عليه وسلم said, 'Allâh will grasp the (planet of) earth.' " (*Sahih Al-Bukhâri*, Vol. 9, *Hadîth* No. 509).

disbelief. We have put enmity and hatred amongst them till the Day of Resurrection. Every time they kindled the fire of war, Allâh extinguished it; and they (ever) strive to make mischief on the earth. And Allâh does not like the *Mufsidûn* (mischief-makers).

إِلَىٰ يَوْمِ ٱلْقِيَٰمَةِ كُلَّمَآ أَوْقَدُوا نَارًا لِّلْحَرْبِ أَطْفَأَهَا ٱللَّهُ وَيَسْعَوْنَ فِي ٱلْأَرْضِ فَسَادًا وَٱللَّهُ لَا يُحِبُّ ٱلْمُفْسِدِينَ ۝

65. And if only the people of the Scripture (Jews and Christians) had believed (in Muhammad صلى الله عليه وسلم) and warded off evil (sin, ascribing partners to Allâh) and had become *Al-Muttaqûn* (the pious. See V.2:2) We would indeed have expiated from them their sins and admitted them to Gardens of pleasure (in Paradise).

وَلَوْ أَنَّ أَهْلَ ٱلْكِتَٰبِ ءَامَنُوا وَٱتَّقَوْا لَكَفَّرْنَا عَنْهُمْ سَيِّئَاتِهِمْ وَلَأَدْخَلْنَٰهُمْ جَنَّٰتِ ٱلنَّعِيمِ ۝

66. And if only they had acted according to the Taurât (Torah), the Injeel (Gospel), and what has (now) been sent down to them from their Lord (the Qur'ân), they would surely, have eaten provision from above them and from underneath their feet. There are from among them people who are on the right course (i.e. they act on the revelation and believe in Prophet Muhammad صلى الله عليه وسلم as 'Abdullâh bin Salâm[1] رضى الله عنه), but many of them do evil deeds.

وَلَوْ أَنَّهُمْ أَقَامُوا ٱلتَّوْرَىٰةَ وَٱلْإِنجِيلَ وَمَآ أُنزِلَ إِلَيْهِم مِّن رَّبِّهِمْ لَأَكَلُوا مِن فَوْقِهِمْ وَمِن تَحْتِ أَرْجُلِهِم مِّنْهُمْ أُمَّةٌ مُّقْتَصِدَةٌ وَكَثِيرٌ مِّنْهُمْ سَآءَ مَا يَعْمَلُونَ ۝

---

[1] (V.5:66) Narrated Anas رضى الله عنه: When the news of the arrival of the Prophet صلى الله عليه وسلم at Al-Madinah reached 'Abdullâh bin Salâm, he went to him (i.e. the Prophet صلى الله عليه وسلم) to ask him about certain things. He said, "I am going to ask you about three things which only a Prophet can answer: What is the first sign of the Hour? What is the first food which the people of Paradise will eat? Why does a child attract the similarity to his father or to his mother?" The Prophet صلى الله عليه وسلم replied, "Jibrael (Gabriel) has just

67. O Messenger (Muhammad صلى الله عليه وسلم)! Proclaim (the Message) which has been sent down to you from your Lord. And if you do not, then you have not conveyed His Message. Allâh will protect you from mankind. Verily, Allâh guides not the people who disbelieve.

68. Say (O Muhammad صلى الله عليه وسلم) "O people of the Scripture (Jews and Christians)! You have nothing (as regards guidance) till you act according

﴿ يَـٰٓأَيُّهَا ٱلرَّسُولُ بَلِّغْ مَآ أُنزِلَ إِلَيْكَ مِن رَّبِّكَ وَإِن لَّمْ تَفْعَلْ فَمَا بَلَّغْتَ رِسَالَتَهُ وَٱللَّهُ يَعْصِمُكَ مِنَ ٱلنَّاسِ إِنَّ ٱللَّهَ لَا يَهْدِى ٱلْقَوْمَ ٱلْكَـٰفِرِينَ ﴾

﴿ قُلْ يَـٰٓأَهْلَ ٱلْكِتَـٰبِ لَسْتُمْ عَلَىٰ شَىْءٍ حَتَّىٰ تُقِيمُوا۟ ٱلتَّوْرَىٰةَ وَٱلْإِنجِيلَ وَمَآ أُنزِلَ إِلَيْكُم ﴾

now informed me of that." Ibn Salâm said, "He [i.e. Jibrael (Gabriel)] is the enemy of the Jews from amongst the angels." The Prophet صلى الله عليه وسلم said, "As for the first sign of the Hour, it will be a fire that will collect (or gather) the people from the east to the west. As for the first meal which the people of Paradise will eat, it will be the caudate (extra) lobe of the fish-liver. As for the child; if the man's discharge precedes the woman's discharge, the child attracts the similarity to the man, and if the woman's discharge precedes the man's, then the child attracts the similarity to the woman." On this, 'Abdullâh bin Salâm said, "I testify that *Lâ ilâha illallâh* (none has the right to be worshipped but Allâh) and that you are the Messenger of Allâh", and added, "O Allâh's Messenger! Jews make such lies as make one astonished, so please ask them about me before they know about my conversion to Islâm." The Jews came and the Prophet صلى الله عليه وسلم said, "What kind of man is 'Abdullâh bin Salâm among you?" They replied, "The best of us and the son of the best of us and the most superior among us, and the son of the most superior among us." The Prophet صلى الله عليه وسلم said, "What would you think if 'Abdullâh bin Salâm should embrace Islâm?" They said, "May Allâh protect him from that." The Prophet صلى الله عليه وسلم repeated his question and they gave the same answer, then 'Abdullâh came out to them and said. "I testify that *Lâ ilâha illallâh* (none has the right to be worshipped by Allâh), and that Muhammad صلى الله عليه وسلم is the Messenger of Allâh!" On this, the Jews said, "He is the most wicked among us and the son of the most wicked among us." So they degraded him. On this, he (i.e.'Abdullâh bin Salâm) said, "It is this that I was afraid of, O Allâh's Messenger." (*Sahih Al-Bukhâri*, Vol.5, *Hadîth* No.275).

to the Taurât (Torah), the Injeel (Gospel), and what has (now) been sent down to you from your Lord (the Qur'ân)." Verily, that which has been sent down to you (Muhammad صلى الله عليه وسلم) from your Lord increases in most of them (their) obstinate rebellion and disbelief. So be not sorrowful over the people who disbelieve.

69. Surely, those who believe (in the Oneness of Allâh, in His Messenger Muhammad صلى الله عليه وسلم and all that was revealed to him from Allâh), and those who are the Jews and the Sabians and the Christians, — whosoever believed in Allâh and the Last Day, and worked righteousness, on them shall be no fear, nor shall they grieve.[1]

70. Verily, We took the covenant of the Children of Israel and sent Messengers to them. Whenever there came to them a Messenger with what they themselves desired not, — a group of them they called liars, and others among them they killed.

71. They thought there will be no *Fitnah* (trial or punishment), so they became blind and deaf; after that Allâh turned to them (with Forgiveness); yet again many of them became blind and deaf. And Allâh is the All-Seer of what they do.

---

[1] (V.5:69) This verse (V.5:69) and (Verse 2:62) should not be misinterpreted by the reader as mentioned by Ibn 'Abbâs (*Tafsir At-Tabarî*) that the provision of this Verse was abrogated by the (V.3:85). And after the coming of Prophet Muhammad صلى الله عليه وسلم no other religion except Islâm will be accepted from anyone.

72. Surely, they have disbelieved who say: "Allâh is the Messiah ['Îsâ (Jesus)], son of Maryam (Mary)." But the Messiah ['Îsâ (Jesus)] said: "O Children of Israel! Worship Allâh, my Lord and your Lord." Verily, whosoever sets up partners (in worship) with Allâh, then Allâh has forbidden Paradise to him, and the Fire will be his abode.[1] And for the Zâlimûn (polytheists and wrong-doers) there are no helpers.

73. Surely, disbelievers are those who said: "Allâh is the third of the three (in a Trinity)." But there is no Ilâh (god) (none who has the right to be worshipped) but One Ilâh (God — Allâh). And if they cease not from what they say, verily, a painful torment will befall on the disbelievers among them.

74. Will they not turn with repentance to Allâh and ask His Forgiveness? For Allâh is Oft-Forgiving, Most Merciful.[2]

75. The Messiah ['Îsâ (Jesus)], son of Maryam (Mary), was no more than a Messenger; many were the Messengers that passed away before him. His mother [Maryam (Mary)] was a Siddîqah [i.e. she believed in the Words of Allâh and His Books (See Verse 66:12)]. They both used to eat food (as

---

[1] (V.5:72): See the footnote of the (V.2:165).

[2] (V.5:74): Narrated Anas bin Mâlik رضى الله عنه Allâh's Messenger صلى الله عليه وسلم said, "Allâh is more pleased with the repentance of His slave than anyone of you is pleased with finding his camel which he had lost in a desert." (Sahih Al-Bukhâri, Vol. 8, Hadîth No. 321).

any other human being, while Allâh does not eat). Look how We make the *Ayât* (proofs, evidences, verses, lessons, signs, revelations, etc.) clear to them; yet look how they are deluded away (from the truth).

76. Say (O Muhammad صلى الله عليه وسلم to mankind): "How do you worship besides Allâh something which has no power either to harm or benefit you? But it is Allâh Who is the All-Hearer, All-Knower."

77. Say (O Muhammad صلى الله عليه وسلم): "O people of the Scripture (Jews and Christians)! Exceed not the limits in your religion (by believing in something) other than the truth, and do not follow the vain desires of people who went astray before and who misled many, and strayed (themselves) from the Right Path."

78. Those among the Children of Israel[1] who disbelieved were cursed by

اَلْآیَاتِ ثُمَّ ٱنظُرْ أَنَّى یُؤْفَكُونَ ۝

قُلْ أَتَعْبُدُونَ مِن دُونِ ٱللَّهِ مَا لَا یَمْلِكُ لَكُمْ ضَرًّا وَلَا نَفْعًا وَٱللَّهُ هُوَ ٱلسَّمِیعُ ٱلْعَلِیمُ ۝

قُلْ یَـٰٓأَهْلَ ٱلْكِتَـٰبِ لَا تَغْلُوا۟ فِی دِینِكُمْ غَیْرَ ٱلْحَقِّ وَلَا تَتَّبِعُوٓا۟ أَهْوَآءَ قَوْمٍ قَدْ ضَلُّوا۟ مِن قَبْلُ وَأَضَلُّوا۟ كَثِیرًا وَضَلُّوا۟ عَن سَوَآءِ ٱلسَّبِیلِ ۝

لُعِنَ ٱلَّذِینَ كَفَرُوا۟ مِنۢ

---

[1] (V.5:78). The tale of a leper, a bald man and a blind man:
Narrated Abu Hurairah رضي الله عنه that he heard Allâh's Messenger صلى الله عليه وسلم saying, "Allâh willed to test three Isrâelis who were a leper, a blind man and a bald headed man. So, He sent them an angel who came to the leper and said, 'What thing do you like most?' He replied, 'Good colour and good skin, for the people have a strong aversion to me.' The angel touched him and his illness was cured, and he was given a good colour and beautiful skin. The angel asked him, 'What kind of property do you like best?' He replied, 'Camels.' So he (i.e., the leper) was given a pregnant she-camel, and the angel said (to him), 'May Allâh bless you in it.' The angel then went to the bald-headed man and said, 'What thing do you like most?' He said, 'I like good hair and wish to be cured of this disease, for the people feel repulsion for me.' The angel touched him and his illness was cured, and he was given good hair. The

angel asked (him), 'What kind of property do you like best?' He replied 'Cows.' The angel gave him a pregnant cow and said, 'May Allâh bless in it.' The angel went to the blind man and asked, 'What thing do you like best?' He said, '(I like) that Allâh may restore my eyesight to me so that I may see the people.' The angel touched his eyes and Allâh gave him back his eyesight. The angel asked him, 'What kind of property do you like best?' He replied, 'Sheep.' The angel gave him a pregnant sheep. Afterwards, all the three pregnant animals gave birth to young ones, and multiplied and brought forth so much that one of the (three) men had a herd of camels filling a valley, and one had a herd of cows filling a valley, and one had a flock of sheep filling a valley. Then the angel, disguised in the shape and appearance of a leper, went to the leper and said, 'I am a poor man, who has lost all means of livelihood while on a journey. So none will satisfy my need except Allâh and then you. In the Name of Him Who has given you such nice colour and beautiful skin, and so much property, I ask you to give me a camel so that I may reach my destination.' The man replied, 'I have many obligations (so I cannot give you).' The angel said, 'I think I know you. Were you not a leper to whom the people had a strong aversion? Weren't you a poor man, and then Allâh gave you (all this property)?' He replied, '(This is all wrong,) I got this property through inheritance from my forefathers.' The angel said, 'If you are telling a lie then let Allâh make you as you were before.' Then the angel, disguised in the shape and appearance of a bald man, went to the bald man and said to him the same as he told the first one, and he too answered the same as the first one did. The angel said, 'If you are telling a lie, then let Allâh make you as you were before.' The angel, disguised in the shape of a blind man, went to the blind man and said, 'I am a poor man and a traveller, whose means of livelihood have been exhausted while on a journey. I have nobody to help me except Allâh, and after Him, you yourself. I ask you in the Name of Him Who has given you back your eyesight to give me a sheep, so that with its help, I may complete my journey.' The man said, 'No doubt, I was blind and Allâh gave me back my eyesight; I was poor and Allâh made me rich; so take anything you wish from my property. By Allâh, I will not stop you for taking anything (you need) of my property which you may take for Allâh's sake.' The angel replied, 'Keep your property with you. You (i.e., three men) have been tested and Allâh is pleased with you and is angry with your two companions.'" (*Sahih Al-Bukhâri*, Vol. 4, *Hadith* No. 670).

the tongue of Dawûd (David) and 'Îsâ (Jesus), son of Maryam (Mary). That was because they disobeyed (Allâh and the Messengers) and were ever transgressing beyond bounds.

79. They used not to forbid one another from the *Munkar* (wrong, evil-doing, sins, polytheism, disbelief) which they committed. Vile indeed was what they used to do.

80. You see many of them taking the disbelievers as their *Auliyâ'* (protectors and helpers). Evil indeed is that which their ownselves have sent forward before them; for that (reason) Allâh's Wrath fell upon them, and in torment they will abide.

81. And had they believed in Allâh, and in the Prophet (Muhammad صلى الله عليه وسلم) and in what has been revealed to him, never would they have taken them (the disbelievers) as *Auliyâ'* (protectors and helpers); but many of them are the *Fâsiqûn* (rebellious, disobedient to Allâh).

82. Verily, you will find the strongest among men in enmity to the believers (Muslims) the Jews and those who are *Al-Mushrikûn*,[1] and you will find the nearest in love to the believers (Muslims) those who say: "We are Christians." That is because amongst them are priests and monks, and they are not proud.

---

[1] (V.5:82) *Al-Mushrikûn*: idolaters, polytheists, pagans, disbelievers in the Oneness of Allâh.

83. And when they (who call themselves Christians) listen to what has been sent down to the Messenger (Muhammad صلى الله عليه وسلم), you see their eyes overflowing with tears because of the truth they have recognised. They say: "Our Lord! We believe; so write us down among the witnesses.

84. "And why should we not believe in Allâh and in that which has come to us of the truth (Islâmic Monotheism)? And we wish that our Lord will admit us (in Paradise on the Day of Resurrection) along with the righteous people (Prophet Muhammad صلى الله عليه وسلم and his Companions رضى الله عنهم)."

85. So because of what they said, Allâh rewarded them Gardens under which rivers flow (in Paradise), they will abide therein forever. Such is the reward of *Al-Muhsinûn* (the good-doers — see the footnote of V.9:120).

86. But those who disbelieved and belied Our *Ayât* (proofs, evidences, verses, lessons, signs, revelations, etc.), they shall be the dwellers of the (Hell) Fire.

87. O you who believe! Make not unlawful the *Tayyibât* (all that is good as regards foods, things, deeds, beliefs, persons) which Allâh has made lawful to you, and transgress not. Verily, Allâh does not like the transgressors.

88. And eat of the things which Allâh has provided for you, lawful and good, and fear Allâh in Whom you believe.

89. Allâh will not punish you for what is unintentional in your oaths, but He will punish you for your deliberate oaths; for its expiation (a deliberate oath) feed ten *Masâkîn* (poor persons), on a scale of the average of that with which you feed your own families, or clothe them or manumit a slave. But whosoever cannot afford (that), then he should fast for three days. That is the expiation for the oaths when you have sworn.[1] And protect your oaths (i.e. do not swear much).[2] Thus Allâh makes clear to you His *Ayât* (proofs, evidences, verses, lessons, signs, revelations, etc.) that you may be grateful.

90. O you who believe! Intoxicants (all kinds of alcoholic drinks), and gambling, and *Al-Ansâb*,[3] and

بِهِ مُؤْمِنُونَ ۞

لَا يُؤَاخِذُكُمُ ٱللَّهُ بِٱللَّغْوِ فِىٓ أَيْمَٰنِكُمْ وَلَٰكِن يُؤَاخِذُكُم بِمَا عَقَّدتُّمُ ٱلْأَيْمَٰنَ فَكَفَّٰرَتُهُۥٓ إِطْعَامُ عَشَرَةِ مَسَٰكِينَ مِنْ أَوْسَطِ مَا تُطْعِمُونَ أَهْلِيكُمْ أَوْ كِسْوَتُهُمْ أَوْ تَحْرِيرُ رَقَبَةٍ فَمَن لَّمْ يَجِدْ فَصِيَامُ ثَلَٰثَةِ أَيَّامٍ ذَٰلِكَ كَفَّٰرَةُ أَيْمَٰنِكُمْ إِذَا حَلَفْتُمْ وَٱحْفَظُوٓا أَيْمَٰنَكُمْ كَذَٰلِكَ يُبَيِّنُ ٱللَّهُ لَكُمْ ءَايَٰتِهِۦ لَعَلَّكُمْ تَشْكُرُونَ ۞ يَٰٓأَيُّهَا ٱلَّذِينَ ءَامَنُوٓا إِنَّمَا ٱلْخَمْرُ وَٱلْمَيْسِرُ وَٱلْأَنصَابُ وَٱلْأَزْلَٰمُ رِجْسٌ مِّنْ عَمَلِ

---

[1] (V.5:89) Narrated Abu Hurairah رضي الله عنه: The Prophet صلى الله عليه وسلم said, "We (Muslims) are the last (to come) in the world, but (will be) foremost on the Day of Resurrection." Allâh's Messenger صلى الله عليه وسلم also said, "By Allâh, if anyone of you insists on fulfilling an oath by which he may harm his family, he commits a greater sin in Allâh's consideration than that of dissolving his oath and making its expiation with that which Allâh has commanded." (*Sahih Al-Bukhâri*, Vol. 8, *Hadith* No. 621).

[2] (V.5:89) It is better not to take oaths, but if you have taken it, and later you find a better solution for the problem, then act according to the better one and give expiation for the oath.

[3] (V.5:90) Animals that are sacrificed (slaughtered) on *An-Nusub** and for the idols,

Narrated 'Abdullâh رضي الله عنه: Allâh's Messenger صلى الله عليه وسلم said that he met Zaid bin 'Amr bin Nufail at a place near Baldah and this had happened before Allâh's Messenger صلى الله عليه وسلم received the Divine Inspiration. Allâh's Messenger صلى الله عليه وسلم presented a dish of meat

Al-Azlâm (arrows for seeking luck or decision) are an abomination of Shaitân's (Satan) handiwork. So avoid (strictly all) that (abomination) in order that you may be successful[1]

91. Shaitân (Satan) wants only to excite enmity and hatred between you with intoxicants (alcoholic drinks) and gambling, and hinder you from the remembrance of Allâh and from As-Salât (the prayer). So, will you not then abstain?

الشَّيْطَنِ فَاجْتَنِبُوهُ لَعَلَّكُمْ تُفْلِحُونَ ۞

إِنَّمَا يُرِيدُ الشَّيْطَنُ أَن يُوقِعَ بَيْنَكُمُ الْعَدَوَةَ وَالْبَغْضَآءَ فِي الْخَمْرِ وَالْمَيْسِرِ وَيَصُدَّكُمْ عَن ذِكْرِ اللَّهِ وَعَنِ الصَّلَوةِ فَهَلْ أَنتُم مُّنتَهُونَ ۞

(that had been offered to him by the pagans) to Zaid bin 'Amr, but Zaid refused to eat of it and then said (to the pagans), "I do not eat of what you have sacrificed (slaughtered) on your stone-altars (Ansâb) nor do I eat except that on which Allâh's Name has been mentioned on slaughtering." (Sahih Al-Bukhâri, Vol.7, Hadîth No.407). [See also the footnote of (V.2:135)].

* An-Nusub were stone-altars at fixed places or graves, whereon sacrifices were slaughtered on certain occasions in the name of idols, jinn, angels, pious men, saints, in order to honour them, or to expect some benefit from them.

[1] (V.5:90) What is said regarding the one who regards an alcoholic drink lawful to drink, and calls it by another name.

Narrated Abu 'Aamir or Abu Mâlik Al-Ash'ari that he heard the Prophet صلى الله عليه وسلم saying, "From among my followers there will be some people who will consider illegal sexual intercourse, the wearing of silk, the drinking of alcoholic drinks, and the use of musical instruments as lawful. And (from them), there will be some who will stay near the side of a mountain, and in the evening their shepherd will come to them with their sheep and ask them for something, but they will say to him, 'Return to us tomorrow.' Allâh will destroy them during the night and will let the mountain fall on them, and He will transform the rest of them into monkeys and pigs and they will remain so till the Day of Resurrection." (Sahih Al-Bukhâri, Vol.7, Hadîth No.494B)

92. And obey Allâh and the Messenger (صلى الله عليه وسلم), and beware (of even coming near to drinking or gambling or Al-Ansâb, or Al-Azlâm) and fear Allâh. Then if you turn away, you should know that it is Our Messenger's duty to convey (the Message) in the clearest way.

93. Those who believe and do righteous good deeds, there is no sin on them for what they ate (in the past), if they fear Allâh (by keeping away from His forbidden things), and believe and do righteous good deeds, and again fear Allâh and believe, and once again fear Allâh and do good deeds with Ihsân (perfection). And Allâh loves the good-doers.

94. O you who believe! Allâh will certainly make a trial of you with something in (the matter of) the game that is well within the reach of your hands and your lances, that Allâh may test who fears Him unseen. Then whoever transgresses thereafter, for him there is a painful torment.

95. O you who believe! Kill not the game while you are in a state of Ihrâm [for Hajj or 'Umrah (pilgrimage)], and whosoever of you kills it intentionally, the penalty is an offering, brought to the Ka'bah, of an eatable animal (i.e. sheep, goat, cow) equivalent to the one he killed, as adjudged by two just men among you; or, for expiation, he should feed Masâkin (poor persons), or its equivalent in Saum (fasting), that he may taste the heaviness (punishment) of his deed. Allâh has forgiven what is past, but whosoever commits it again, Allâh will take retribution from him. And Allâh is All-Mighty, All-Able of Retribution.

عَفَا اللَّهُ عَمَّا سَلَفَ وَمَنْ عَادَ فَيَنْتَقِمُ اللَّهُ مِنْهُ وَاللَّهُ عَزِيزٌ ذُو انْتِقَامٍ ۝

96. Lawful to you is (the pursuit of) water-game and its use for food — for the benefit of yourselves and those who travel, but forbidden is (the pursuit of) land-game as long as you are in a state of *Ihrâm* (for *Hajj* or '*Umrah*). And fear Allâh to Whom you shall be gathered back.

أُحِلَّ لَكُمْ صَيْدُ الْبَحْرِ وَطَعَامُهُ مَتَاعًا لَّكُمْ وَلِلسَّيَّارَةِ وَحُرِّمَ عَلَيْكُمْ صَيْدُ الْبَرِّ مَا دُمْتُمْ حُرُمًا وَاتَّقُوا اللَّهَ الَّذِي إِلَيْهِ تُحْشَرُونَ ۝

97. Allâh has made the *Ka'bah*, the Sacred House, an asylum of security and benefits for mankind, and also the Sacred Month and the animals of offerings and the garlanded (people or animals, marked with the garlands on their necks made from the outer part of the stem of the Makkah trees for their security), that you may know that Allâh has knowledge of all that is in the heavens and all that is in the earth, and that Allâh is the All-Knower of everything.

۞ جَعَلَ اللَّهُ الْكَعْبَةَ الْبَيْتَ الْحَرَامَ قِيَامًا لِّلنَّاسِ وَالشَّهْرَ الْحَرَامَ وَالْهَدْيَ وَالْقَلَائِدَ ذَلِكَ لِتَعْلَمُوا أَنَّ اللَّهَ يَعْلَمُ مَا فِي السَّمَاوَاتِ وَمَا فِي الْأَرْضِ وَأَنَّ اللَّهَ بِكُلِّ شَيْءٍ عَلِيمٌ ۝

98. Know that Allâh is Severe in punishment and that Allâh is Oft-Forgiving, Most Merciful.

اعْلَمُوا أَنَّ اللَّهَ شَدِيدُ الْعِقَابِ وَأَنَّ اللَّهَ غَفُورٌ رَّحِيمٌ ۝

99. The duty of the Messenger [i.e. Our Messenger Muhammad صلى الله عليه وسلم whom We have sent to you, (O mankind)] is nothing but to convey (the Message). And Allâh knows all that you reveal and all that you conceal.

مَّا عَلَى الرَّسُولِ إِلَّا الْبَلَاغُ وَاللَّهُ يَعْلَمُ مَا تُبْدُونَ وَمَا تَكْتُمُونَ ۝

100. Say (O Muhammad صلى الله عليه وسلم):
"Not equal are *Al-Khabîth* (all that is evil and bad as regards things, deeds, beliefs, persons or foods) and *At-Tayyib* (all that is good as regards things, deeds, beliefs, persons or foods), even though the abundance of *Al-Khabîth* (evil) may please you." So fear Allâh,[1] O men of understanding in order that you may be successful.

قُل لَّا يَسْتَوِى ٱلْخَبِيثُ وَٱلطَّيِّبُ وَلَوْ أَعْجَبَكَ كَثْرَةُ ٱلْخَبِيثِ فَٱتَّقُوا۟ ٱللَّهَ يَـٰٓأُو۟لِى ٱلْأَلْبَـٰبِ لَعَلَّكُمْ تُفْلِحُونَ ﴿١٠٠﴾

101. O you who believe! Ask not about things which, if made plain to you, may cause you trouble. But if you ask about them while the Qur'ân is being revealed, they will be made plain to you. Allâh has forgiven that, and Allâh is Oft-Forgiving, Most Forbearing.

يَـٰٓأَيُّهَا ٱلَّذِينَ ءَامَنُوا۟ لَا تَسْـَٔلُوا۟ عَنْ أَشْيَآءَ إِن تُبْدَ لَكُمْ تَسُؤْكُمْ وَإِن تَسْـَٔلُوا۟ عَنْهَا حِينَ يُنَزَّلُ ٱلْقُرْءَانُ تُبْدَ لَكُمْ عَفَا ٱللَّهُ عَنْهَا وَٱللَّهُ غَفُورٌ حَلِيمٌ ﴿١٠١﴾

102. Before you, a community asked such questions, then on that account they became disbelievers.

قَدْ سَأَلَهَا قَوْمٌ مِّن قَبْلِكُمْ ثُمَّ أَصْبَحُوا۟ بِهَا كَـٰفِرِينَ ﴿١٠٢﴾

103. Allâh has not instituted things like *Bahîrah*[2] or a *Sâ'ibah*[3] or a *Wasîlah*[4] or a *Hâm*[5] (all these animals

مَا جَعَلَ ٱللَّهُ مِنۢ بَحِيرَةٍ وَلَا سَآئِبَةٍ وَلَا وَصِيلَةٍ وَلَا حَامٍ

---

[1] (V.5:100) Fear Allâh: i.e. abstain from all kinds of sins and evil deeds which He has forbidden and love Allâh much perform all kinds of good deeds which He has ordained.

[2] (V.5:103) *Bahîrah*: A she-camel whose milk was spared for the idols and nobody was allowed to milk it.

[3] (V.5:103) *Sâ'ibah*: A she-camel let loose for free pasture for their false gods, e.g. idols, and nothing was allowed to be carried on it.

[4] (V.5:103) *Wasîlah*: A she-camel set free for idols because it had given birth to a she-camel at its first delivery and then again gave birth to a she-camel at its second delivery.

[5] (V.5:103) *Hâm*: A stallion-camel freed from work for their idols, after it had finished a number of copulations assigned for it.

were liberated in honour of idols as practised by pagan Arabs in the pre-Islâmic period). But those who disbelieve invent lies against Allâh, and most of them have no understanding.

104. And when it is said to them: "Come to what Allâh has revealed and unto the Messenger (Muhammad صلى الله عليه وسلم for the verdict of that which you have made unlawful)." They say: "Enough for us is that which we found our fathers following," even though their fathers had no knowledge whatsoever and nor guidance.

105. O you who believe! Take care of your ownselves.[1] If you follow the (right) guidance [and enjoin what is right (Islâmic Monotheism and all that Islâm orders one to do) and forbid what is wrong (polytheism, disbelief and all that Islâm has forbidden)] no hurt can come to you from those who are in error. The return of you all is to Allâh, then He will inform you about (all) that which you used to do.

106. O you who believe! When death approaches any of you, and you make a bequest, (then take) the testimony of two just men of your own folk or two others from outside, while you are travelling through the land and death

ولَكِنَّ الَّذِينَ كَفَرُوا يَفْتَرُونَ عَلَى اللَّهِ الْكَذِبَ وَأَكْثَرُهُمْ لَا يَعْقِلُونَ ۝

وَإِذَا قِيلَ لَهُمْ تَعَالَوْا إِلَىٰ مَآ أَنزَلَ اللَّهُ وَإِلَى الرَّسُولِ قَالُوا حَسْبُنَا مَا وَجَدْنَا عَلَيْهِ ءَابَآءَنَآ أَوَلَوْ كَانَ ءَابَآؤُهُمْ لَا يَعْلَمُونَ شَيْئًا وَلَا يَهْتَدُونَ ۝

يَٰٓأَيُّهَا الَّذِينَ ءَامَنُوا عَلَيْكُمْ أَنفُسَكُمْ لَا يَضُرُّكُم مَّن ضَلَّ إِذَا اهْتَدَيْتُمْ إِلَى اللَّهِ مَرْجِعُكُمْ جَمِيعًا فَيُنَبِّئُكُم بِمَا كُنتُمْ تَعْمَلُونَ ۝

يَٰٓأَيُّهَا الَّذِينَ ءَامَنُوا شَهَٰدَةُ بَيْنِكُمْ إِذَا حَضَرَ أَحَدَكُمُ الْمَوْتُ حِينَ الْوَصِيَّةِ اثْنَانِ ذَوَا عَدْلٍ مِّنكُمْ أَوْ

---

[1] (V.5:105) Take care of your ownselves: i.e., do righteous deeds, fear Allâh much (abstain from all kinds of sins and evil deeds which He has forbidden) and love Allâh much (perform all kinds of good deeds which He has ordained).

befalls on you. Detain them both after *As-Salât* (the prayer), (then) if you are in doubt (about their truthfulness), let them both swear by Allâh (saying): "We wish not for any worldly gain in this, even though he (the beneficiary) be our near relative. We shall not hide Testimony of Allâh, for then indeed we should be of the sinful."

107. If then it gets known that these two had been guilty of sin, let two others stand forth in their places, nearest in kin from among those who claim a lawful right. Let them swear by Allâh (saying): "We affirm that our testimony is truer than that of both of them, and we have not trespassed (the truth), for then indeed we should be of the wrong-doers."

108. That should make it closer (to the fact) that their testimony would be in its true shape (and thus accepted), or else they would fear that (other) oaths would be admitted after their oaths. And fear Allâh and listen (with obedience to Him). And Allâh guides not the people who are *Al-Fâsiqûn* (the rebellious and disobedient).

109. On the Day when Allâh will gather the Messengers together and say to them: "What was the response you received (from men to your teaching)?" They will say: "We have no knowledge, verily, only You are the All-Knower of all that is hidden (or unseen)."

110. (Remember) when Allâh will say (on the Day of Resurrection). "O 'Îsâ (Jesus), son of Maryam (Mary)! Remember My Favour to you and to your mother when I supported you with *Rûh-ul-Qudus* [Jibrael (Gabriel)] so that you spoke to the people in the cradle [1] and in maturity; and when I taught you writing, *Al-Hikmah* (the power of understanding), the Taurât (Torah) and the Injeel (Gospel); and when you made out of the clay, a figure like that of a bird, by My Permission, and you breathed into it, and it became a bird by My Permission, and you healed those born blind, and the lepers by My Permission, and when you brought forth the dead by My Permission; and when I restrained the Children of Israel from you (when they resolved to kill you) as you came unto them with clear proofs, and the disbelievers among them said: 'This is nothing but evident magic.'"

111. And when I (Allâh) inspired *Al-Hawâriûn* (the disciples) [of 'Îsâ (Jesus)] to believe in Me and My Messenger, they said: "We believe. And bear witness that we are Muslims."

112. (Remember) when *Al-Hawâriûn* (the disciples) said: "O 'Îsâ (Jesus), son of Maryam (Mary)! Can your Lord send down to us a table spread (with food) from heaven?" 'Îsâ (Jesus) said: "Fear Allâh, if you are indeed believers."

اذْكُرْ نِعْمَتِى عَلَيْكَ وَعَلَى وَالِدَتِكَ إِذْ أَيَّدتُّكَ بِرُوحِ الْقُدُسِ تُكَلِّمُ النَّاسَ فِى الْمَهْدِ وَكَهْلاً وَإِذْ عَلَّمْتُكَ الْكِتَابَ وَالْحِكْمَةَ وَالتَّوْرَاةَ وَالإِنجِيلَ وَإِذْ تَخْلُقُ مِنَ الطِّينِ كَهَيْئَةِ الطَّيْرِ بِإِذْنِى فَتَنفُخُ فِيهَا فَتَكُونُ طَيْراً بِإِذْنِى وَتُبْرِئُ الأَكْمَهَ وَالأَبْرَصَ بِإِذْنِى وَإِذْ تُخْرِجُ الْمَوْتَى بِإِذْنِى وَإِذْ كَفَفْتُ بَنِى إِسْرَاءِيلَ عَنكَ إِذْ جِئْتَهُم بِالْبَيِّنَاتِ فَقَالَ الَّذِينَ كَفَرُوا مِنْهُمْ إِنْ هَذَا إِلاَّ سِحْرٌ مُّبِينٌ ﴿١١٠﴾ وَإِذْ أَوْحَيْتُ إِلَى الْحَوَارِيِّينَ أَنْ ءَامِنُوا بِى وَبِرَسُولِى قَالُوا ءَامَنَّا وَاشْهَدْ بِأَنَّنَا مُسْلِمُونَ ﴿١١١﴾ إِذْ قَالَ الْحَوَارِيُّونَ يَعِيسَى ابْنَ مَرْيَمَ هَلْ يَسْتَطِيعُ رَبُّكَ أَن يُنَزِّلَ عَلَيْنَا مَائِدَةً مِّنَ السَّمَاءِ قَالَ اتَّقُوا اللَّهَ إِن كُنتُم مُّؤْمِنِينَ ﴿١١٢﴾

---

[1] (V.5:110) See the footnote (V.3:46).

113. They said: "We wish to eat thereof and to satisfy our hearts (to be stronger in Faith), and to know that you have indeed told us the truth and that we ourselves be its witnesses."

قَالُوا نُرِيدُ أَن نَّأْكُلَ مِنْهَا وَتَطْمَئِنَّ قُلُوبُنَا وَنَعْلَمَ أَن قَدْ صَدَقْتَنَا وَنَكُونَ عَلَيْهَا مِنَ ٱلشَّٰهِدِينَ ۝

114. 'Îsâ (Jesus), son of Maryam (Mary), said: "O Allâh, our Lord! Send us from the heaven a table spread (with food) that there may be for us — for the first and the last of us — a festival and a sign from You; and provide us with sustenance, for You are the Best of sustainers."

قَالَ عِيسَى ٱبْنُ مَرْيَمَ ٱللَّهُمَّ رَبَّنَا أَنزِلْ عَلَيْنَا مَآئِدَةً مِّنَ ٱلسَّمَآءِ تَكُونُ لَنَا عِيدًا لِّأَوَّلِنَا وَءَاخِرِنَا وَءَايَةً مِّنكَ وَٱرْزُقْنَا وَأَنتَ خَيْرُ ٱلرَّٰزِقِينَ ۝

115. Allâh said: "I am going to send it down unto you, but if any of you after that disbelieves, then I will punish him with a torment such as I have not inflicted on anyone among (all) the 'Âlamîn (mankind and jinn)."

قَالَ ٱللَّهُ إِنِّى مُنَزِّلُهَا عَلَيْكُمْ فَمَن يَكْفُرْ بَعْدُ مِنكُمْ فَإِنِّى أُعَذِّبُهُۥ عَذَابًا لَّآ أُعَذِّبُهُۥٓ أَحَدًا مِّنَ ٱلْعَٰلَمِينَ ۝

116. And (remember) when Allâh will say (on the Day of Resurrection): "O 'Îsâ (Jesus), son of Maryam (Mary)! Did you say unto men: 'Worship me and my mother as two gods besides Allâh?' " He will say: "Glory is to You! It was not for me to say what I had no right (to say). Had I said such a thing, You would surely, have known it. You know what is in my inner-self though I do not know what is in Yours; truly, You, only You, are the All-Knower of all that is hidden (and unseen).

وَإِذْ قَالَ ٱللَّهُ يَٰعِيسَى ٱبْنَ مَرْيَمَ ءَأَنتَ قُلْتَ لِلنَّاسِ ٱتَّخِذُونِى وَأُمِّىَ إِلَٰهَيْنِ مِن دُونِ ٱللَّهِ قَالَ سُبْحَٰنَكَ مَا يَكُونُ لِىٓ أَنْ أَقُولَ مَا لَيْسَ لِى بِحَقٍّ إِن كُنتُ قُلْتُهُۥ فَقَدْ عَلِمْتَهُۥ تَعْلَمُ مَا فِى نَفْسِى وَلَآ أَعْلَمُ مَا فِى نَفْسِكَ إِنَّكَ أَنتَ عَلَّٰمُ ٱلْغُيُوبِ ۝

117. "Never did I say to them aught except what You (Allâh) did command me to say: 'Worship Allâh, my Lord and your Lord.' And I was a witness over them while I dwelt amongst them, but when You took me up, You were the Watcher over them; and You are a Witness to all things. (This is a great admonition and warning to the Christians of the whole world).

‫مَا قُلْتُ لَهُمْ إِلَّا مَا أَمَرْتَنِي بِهِ أَنِ‬
‫اعْبُدُوا اللَّهَ رَبِّي وَرَبَّكُمْ وَكُنتُ‬
‫عَلَيْهِمْ شَهِيدًا مَّا دُمْتُ فِيهِمْ فَلَمَّا‬
‫تَوَفَّيْتَنِي كُنتَ أَنتَ الرَّقِيبَ‬
‫عَلَيْهِمْ وَأَنتَ عَلَىٰ كُلِّ شَيْءٍ‬
‫شَهِيدٌ ١١٧‬

118. "If You punish them, they are Your slaves, and if You forgive them, verily, You, only You, are the All-Mighty, the All-Wise.[1]"

‫إِن تُعَذِّبْهُمْ فَإِنَّهُمْ عِبَادُكَ وَإِن‬
‫تَغْفِرْ لَهُمْ فَإِنَّكَ أَنتَ الْعَزِيزُ‬
‫الْحَكِيمُ ١١٨‬

119. Allâh will say: "This is a Day on which the truthful will profit from their truth: theirs are Gardens under which rivers flow (in Paradise) — they shall abide therein forever. Allâh is pleased with them and they with Him. That is the great success (Paradise).

‫قَالَ اللَّهُ هَٰذَا يَوْمُ يَنفَعُ الصَّادِقِينَ‬
‫صِدْقُهُمْ لَهُمْ جَنَّاتٌ تَجْرِي مِن‬
‫تَحْتِهَا الْأَنْهَارُ خَالِدِينَ فِيهَا أَبَدًا‬
‫رَّضِيَ اللَّهُ عَنْهُمْ وَرَضُوا عَنْهُ ذَٰلِكَ‬
‫الْفَوْزُ الْعَظِيمُ ١١٩‬

120. To Allâh belongs the dominion of the heavens and the earth and all that is therein, and He is Able to do all things.

‫لِلَّهِ مُلْكُ السَّمَاوَاتِ وَالْأَرْضِ وَمَا‬
‫فِيهِنَّ وَهُوَ عَلَىٰ كُلِّ شَيْءٍ قَدِيرٌ ١٢٠‬

---

[1] (V.5:118) Narrated Ibn 'Abbâs ‫رضى الله عنهما‬: The Prophet ‫صلى الله عليه وسلم‬ said, "You will be gathered (on the Day of Resurrection) and some people will be driven (by the angels) to the left side (and taken to Hell) whereupon I will say as the pious slave ['Îsâ (Jesus)] said: And I was a witness over them while I dwelt amongst them. ... the All-Mighty, the All-Wise." (V.5:117,118) (Sahih Al-Bukhâri, Vol.6, Hadîth No. 150).

Sûrat Al-An'âm (The Cattle) VI

*In the Name of Allâh
the Most Gracious, the Most Merciful*

1. All praises and thanks are to Allâh, Who (Alone) created the heavens and the earth, and originated the darkness and the light; yet those who disbelieve hold others as equal with their Lord.

2. He it is Who has created you from clay, and then has decreed a (stated) term (for you to die). And there is with Him another determined term (for you to be resurrected), yet you doubt (in the Resurrection).

3. And He is Allâh (to be worshipped Alone) in the heavens and on the earth; He knows what you conceal and what you reveal, and He knows what you earn (good or bad). (See V.43:84)

4. And never an Ayah (sign) comes to them from the Ayât (proofs, evidences, verses, lessons, signs, revelations, etc.) of their Lord, but that they have been turning away from it.

5. Indeed, they rejected the truth (the Qur'ân and Muhammad صلى الله عليه وسلم[1]) when it came to them, but there will come to them the news of that (the torment) which they used to mock at.

6. Have they not seen how many a generation before them We have destroyed whom We had established on

---

[1] (V.6:5) See the footnote of (V.3:85) and also see (V.3:116).

the earth such as We have not established you? And We poured out on them rain from the sky in abundance, and made the rivers flow under them. Yet We destroyed them for their sins, and We created after them other generations.

نُمَكِّن لَّكُمْ وَأَرْسَلْنَا السَّمَاءَ عَلَيْهِم مِّدْرَارًا وَجَعَلْنَا الْأَنْهَارَ تَجْرِي مِن تَحْتِهِمْ فَأَهْلَكْنَاهُم بِذُنُوبِهِمْ وَأَنشَأْنَا مِنْ بَعْدِهِمْ قَرْنًا ءَاخَرِينَ ٦

7. And even if We had sent down unto you (O Muhammad صلى الله عليه وسلم) a Message written on paper so that they could touch it with their hands, the disbelievers would have said: "This is nothing but obvious magic!"

وَلَوْ نَزَّلْنَا عَلَيْكَ كِتَابًا فِي قِرْطَاسٍ فَلَمَسُوهُ بِأَيْدِيهِمْ لَقَالَ الَّذِينَ كَفَرُوا إِنْ هَٰذَا إِلَّا سِحْرٌ مُّبِينٌ ٧

8. And they say: "Why has not an angel been sent down to him?" Had We sent down an angel, the matter would have been judged at once, and no respite would be granted to them.

وَقَالُوا لَوْلَا أُنزِلَ عَلَيْهِ مَلَكٌ وَلَوْ أَنزَلْنَا مَلَكًا لَّقُضِيَ الْأَمْرُ ثُمَّ لَا يُنظَرُونَ ٨

9. And had We appointed him an angel, We indeed would have made him a man, and We would have certainly confused them in which they are already confused (i.e. the Message of Prophet Muhammad صلى الله عليه وسلم).

وَلَوْ جَعَلْنَاهُ مَلَكًا لَّجَعَلْنَاهُ رَجُلًا وَلَلَبَسْنَا عَلَيْهِم مَّا يَلْبِسُونَ ٩

10. And indeed (many) Messengers before you were mocked at, but their scoffers were surrounded by the very thing that they used to mock at.

وَلَقَدِ اسْتُهْزِئَ بِرُسُلٍ مِّن قَبْلِكَ فَحَاقَ بِالَّذِينَ سَخِرُوا مِنْهُم مَّا كَانُوا بِهِ يَسْتَهْزِئُونَ ١٠

11. Say (O Muhammad صلى الله عليه وسلم) "Travel in the land and see what was the end of those who rejected truth."

قُلْ سِيرُوا فِي الْأَرْضِ ثُمَّ انظُرُوا كَيْفَ كَانَ عَاقِبَةُ الْمُكَذِّبِينَ ١١

12. Say (O Muhammad صلى الله عليه وسلم) "To whom belongs all that is in the heavens and the earth?" Say: "To Allâh.

قُل لِّمَن مَّا فِي السَّمَاوَاتِ وَالْأَرْضِ قُل لِّلَّهِ كَتَبَ عَلَىٰ

He has prescribed Mercy for Himself.[1] Indeed He will gather you together on the Day of Resurrection, about which there is no doubt. Those who have lost themselves will not believe [in Allâh as being the only *Ilâh* (God), and Muhammad صلى الله عليه وسلم as being one of His Messengers, and in Resurrection].

كَتَبَ عَلَىٰ نَفْسِهِ ٱلرَّحْمَةَ لَيَجْمَعَنَّكُمْ إِلَىٰ يَوْمِ ٱلْقِيَٰمَةِ لَا رَيْبَ فِيهِ ٱلَّذِينَ خَسِرُوٓا۟ أَنفُسَهُمْ فَهُمْ لَا يُؤْمِنُونَ ۝

13. And to Him belongs whatsoever exists in the night and the day, and He is the All-Hearing, the All-Knowing."

۞ وَلَهُۥ مَا سَكَنَ فِى ٱلَّيْلِ وَٱلنَّهَارِ وَهُوَ ٱلسَّمِيعُ ٱلْعَلِيمُ ۝

14. Say (O Muhammad صلى الله عليه وسلم): "Shall I take as a *Walî* (Helper, Protector, Lord and God) any other than Allâh, the Creator of the heavens and the earth? And it is He Who feeds but is not fed." Say: "Verily, I am commanded to be the first of those who submit themselves to Allâh (as Muslims)." And be not you (O Muhammad صلى الله عليه وسلم) of the *Mushrikûn* [polytheists, pagans, idolaters and disbelievers in the Oneness of Allâh]. (*Tafsir Al-Qurtubi*)

قُلْ أَغَيْرَ ٱللَّهِ أَتَّخِذُ وَلِيًّا فَاطِرِ ٱلسَّمَٰوَٰتِ وَٱلْأَرْضِ وَهُوَ يُطْعِمُ وَلَا يُطْعَمُ قُلْ إِنِّىٓ أُمِرْتُ أَنْ أَكُونَ أَوَّلَ مَنْ أَسْلَمَ وَلَا تَكُونَنَّ مِنَ ٱلْمُشْرِكِينَ ۝

15. Say: "I fear, if I disobey my Lord, the torment of a Mighty Day."

قُلْ إِنِّىٓ أَخَافُ إِنْ عَصَيْتُ رَبِّى عَذَابَ يَوْمٍ عَظِيمٍ ۝

---

[1] (V.6:12)

A) Narrated Abu Hurairah رضي الله عنه: I heard Allâh's Messenger صلى الله عليه وسلم saying, "Allâh has divided Mercy into one hundred parts, and He kept ninety-nine parts with Him and sent down one part to the earth, and because of that one single part, His creatures are merciful to each other, so that even the mare lifts up its hoof away from its baby animal, lest it should trample on it." (*Sahih Al-Bukhâri*, Vol.8, *Hadîth* No.29).

B) Narrated Abu Hurairah رضي الله عنه: Allâh's Messenger صلى الله عليه وسلم said, "When Allâh completed the creation, He wrote in His Book which is with Him on His Throne: 'Verily, My Mercy has overcome My Anger.'" (*Sahih Al-Bukhâri*, Vol.4, *Hadîth* No.416).

16. Who is averted from (such a torment) on that Day, (Allâh) has surely, been Merciful to him. And that would be the obvious success.

مَّن يُصْرَفْ عَنْهُ يَوْمَئِذٍ فَقَدْ رَحِمَهُۥ وَذَلِكَ ٱلْفَوْزُ ٱلْمُبِينُ ﴿١٦﴾

17. And if Allâh touches you with harm, none can remove it but He, and if He touches you with good, then He is Able to do all things.

وَإِن يَمْسَسْكَ ٱللَّهُ بِضُرٍّ فَلَا كَاشِفَ لَهُۥٓ إِلَّا هُوَ وَإِن يَمْسَسْكَ بِخَيْرٍ فَهُوَ عَلَىٰ كُلِّ شَىْءٍ قَدِيرٌ ﴿٧﴾

18. And He is the Irresistible (Supreme), above His slaves, and He is the All-Wise, Well-Acquainted with all things.

وَهُوَ ٱلْقَاهِرُ فَوْقَ عِبَادِهِۦ وَهُوَ ٱلْحَكِيمُ ٱلْخَبِيرُ ﴿١٨﴾

19. Say (O Muhammad صلى الله عليه وسلم): "What thing is the most great in witness?" Say: "Allâh (the Most Great!) is Witness between me and you; this Qur'ân has been revealed to me that I may therewith warn you and whomsoever it may reach. Can you verily, bear witness that besides Allâh there are other *alihâ* (gods)?" Say: "I bear no (such) witness!" Say: "But in truth He (Allâh) is the only one *Ilâh* (God). And truly, I am innocent of what you join in worship with Him."

قُلْ أَىُّ شَىْءٍ أَكْبَرُ شَهَدَةً قُلِ ٱللَّهُ شَهِيدٌۢ بَيْنِى وَبَيْنَكُمْ وَأُوحِىَ إِلَىَّ هَٰذَا ٱلْقُرْءَانُ لِأُنذِرَكُم بِهِۦ وَمَنۢ بَلَغَ أَئِنَّكُمْ لَتَشْهَدُونَ أَنَّ مَعَ ٱللَّهِ ءَالِهَةً أُخْرَىٰ قُل لَّآ أَشْهَدُ قُلْ إِنَّمَا هُوَ إِلَٰهٌ وَٰحِدٌ وَإِنَّنِى بَرِىٓءٌ مِّمَّا تُشْرِكُونَ ﴿١٩﴾

20. Those to whom We have given the Scripture (Jews and Christians) recognize him (i.e. Muhammad صلى الله عليه وسلم as a Messenger of Allâh, and they also know that there is no *Ilâh* (God) but Allâh and Islâm is Allâh's religion), as they recognize their own sons. Those who have lost (destroyed) themselves will not believe.[1] (*Tafsir At-Tabari*)

ٱلَّذِينَ ءَاتَيْنَٰهُمُ ٱلْكِتَٰبَ يَعْرِفُونَهُۥ كَمَا يَعْرِفُونَ أَبْنَآءَهُمُ ٱلَّذِينَ خَسِرُوٓا۟ أَنفُسَهُمْ فَهُمْ لَا يُؤْمِنُونَ ﴿٢٠﴾

---

[1] (V.6:20) See the footnote of (V.3:85).

21. And who does more aggression and wrong than he who invents a lie against Allâh or rejects His Ayât (proofs, evidences, verses, lessons, revelations, etc.)? Verily, the Zâlimûn (polytheists and wrong-doers) shall never be successful.

ومَنْ أَظْلَمُ مِمَّنِ ٱفْتَرَىٰ عَلَى ٱللَّهِ كَذِبًا أَوْ كَذَّبَ بِـَايَٰتِهِۦٓ إِنَّهُۥ لَا يُفْلِحُ ٱلظَّٰلِمُونَ ٢١

22. And on the Day when We shall gather them all together, then We shall say to those who joined partners (in worship with Us): "Where are your partners (false deities) whom you used to assert (as partners in worship with Allâh)?"

وَيَوْمَ نَحْشُرُهُمْ جَمِيعًا ثُمَّ نَقُولُ لِلَّذِينَ أَشْرَكُوٓاْ أَيْنَ شُرَكَآؤُكُمُ ٱلَّذِينَ كُنتُمْ تَزْعُمُونَ ٢٢

23. There will then be (left) no Fitnah (excuses or statements or arguments) for them but to say: "By Allâh, our Lord, we were not those who joined others in worship with Allâh."

ثُمَّ لَمْ تَكُن فِتْنَتُهُمْ إِلَّآ أَن قَالُوٓاْ وَٱللَّهِ رَبِّنَا مَا كُنَّا مُشْرِكِينَ ٢٣

24. Look! How they lie against themselves! But the (lie) which they invented will disappear from them.

ٱنظُرْ كَيْفَ كَذَبُواْ عَلَىٰٓ أَنفُسِهِمْ وَضَلَّ عَنْهُم مَّا كَانُواْ يَفْتَرُونَ ٢٤

25. And of them there are some who listen to you; but We have set veils on their hearts, so they understand it not, and deafness in their ears; and even if they see every one of the Ayât (proofs, evidences, verses, lessons, signs, revelations, etc.) they will not believe therein; to the point that when they come to you to argue with you, the disbelievers say: "These are nothing but tales of the men of old."

وَمِنْهُم مَّن يَسْتَمِعُ إِلَيْكَ وَجَعَلْنَا عَلَىٰ قُلُوبِهِمْ أَكِنَّةً أَن يَفْقَهُوهُ وَفِىٓ ءَاذَانِهِمْ وَقْرًا وَإِن يَرَوْاْ كُلَّ ءَايَةٍ لَّا يُؤْمِنُواْ بِهَا حَتَّىٰٓ إِذَا جَآءُوكَ يُجَٰدِلُونَكَ يَقُولُ ٱلَّذِينَ كَفَرُوٓاْ إِنْ هَٰذَآ إِلَّآ أَسَٰطِيرُ ٱلْأَوَّلِينَ ٢٥

26. And they prevent others from him (from following Prophet Muhammad صلى الله عليه وسلم) and they themselves keep away

وَهُمْ يَنْهَوْنَ عَنْهُ وَيَنْـَٔوْنَ عَنْهُ وَإِن يُهْلِكُونَ إِلَّآ أَنفُسَهُمْ

from him, and (by doing so) they destroy not but their ownselves, yet they perceive (it) not.

27. If you could but see when they will be held over the (Hell) Fire! They will say: "Would that we were but sent back (to the world)! Then we would not deny the *Ayât* (proofs, evidences, verses, lessons, revelations, etc.) of our Lord, and we would be of the believers!"

28. Nay, it has become manifest to them what they had been concealing before. But if they were returned (to the world), they would certainly revert to that which they were forbidden. And indeed they are liars.

29. And they said: "There is no (other life) but our (present) life of this world, and never shall we be resurrected (on the Day of Resurrection)."

30. If you could but see when they will be held (brought and made to stand) in front of their Lord! He will say: "Is not this (Resurrection and the taking of the accounts) the truth?" They will say: "Yes, by our Lord!" He will then say: "So taste you the torment because you used not to believe."

31. They indeed are losers who denied their Meeting with Allâh,[1] until

---

[1] (V.6:31) Narrated Abu Mûsâ: رضي الله عنه The Prophet صلى الله عليه وسلم said, "Whoever loves the Meeting with Allâh, Allâh too loves the Meeting with him; and whoever hates the Meeting with Allâh, Allâh too hates the Meeting with him." (*Sahih Al-Bukhâri*, Vol.8, *Hadith* No. 515).

حَتَّى إِذَا جَاءَتْهُمُ السَّاعَةُ بَغْتَةً

all of a sudden, the Hour (signs of death) is on them, and they say: "Alas for us that we gave no thought to it," while they will bear their burdens on their backs; and evil indeed are the burdens that they will bear!

قَالُوا يَا حَسْرَتَنَا عَلَى مَا فَرَّطْنَا فِيهَا وَهُمْ يَحْمِلُونَ أَوْزَارَهُمْ عَلَى ظُهُورِهِمْ أَلَا سَاءَ مَا يَزِرُونَ ۝

32. And the life of this world is nothing but play and amusement. But far better is the house in the Hereafter for those who are *Al-Muttaqûn* (the pious. See V.2:2). Will you not then understand?

وَمَا الْحَيَاةُ الدُّنْيَا إِلَّا لَعِبٌ وَلَهْوٌ وَلَلدَّارُ الْآخِرَةُ خَيْرٌ لِلَّذِينَ يَتَّقُونَ أَفَلَا تَعْقِلُونَ ۝

33. We know indeed the grief which their words cause you (O Muhammad صلى الله عليه وسلم): it is not you that they deny, but it is the Verses (the Qur'ân) of Allâh that the *Zâlimûn* (polytheists and wrong-doers) deny.

قَدْ نَعْلَمُ إِنَّهُ لَيَحْزُنُكَ الَّذِي يَقُولُونَ فَإِنَّهُمْ لَا يُكَذِّبُونَكَ وَلَكِنَّ الظَّالِمِينَ بِآيَاتِ اللَّهِ يَجْحَدُونَ ۝

34. Verily, (many) Messengers were denied before you (O Muhammad صلى الله عليه وسلم), but with patience they bore the denial, and they were hurt; till Our Help reached them, and none can alter the Words (Decisions) of Allâh. Surely, there has reached you the information (news) about the Messengers (before you).

وَلَقَدْ كُذِّبَتْ رُسُلٌ مِنْ قَبْلِكَ فَصَبَرُوا عَلَى مَا كُذِّبُوا وَأُوذُوا حَتَّى أَتَاهُمْ نَصْرُنَا وَلَا مُبَدِّلَ لِكَلِمَاتِ اللَّهِ وَلَقَدْ جَاءَكَ مِنْ نَبَإِ الْمُرْسَلِينَ ۝

35. If their aversion (from you, O Muhammad صلى الله عليه وسلم and from that with which you have been sent) is hard on you, (and you cannot be patient of their harm to you), then if you were able to seek a tunnel in the earth or a ladder to the sky, so that you may bring them a sign (and you cannot do it, so be patient). And had Allâh willed, He could have gathered them together (all) on true guidance, so be not you one of those who are *Al-Jâhilûn* (the ignorant).

وَإِنْ كَانَ كَبُرَ عَلَيْكَ إِعْرَاضُهُمْ فَإِنِ اسْتَطَعْتَ أَنْ تَبْتَغِيَ نَفَقًا فِي الْأَرْضِ أَوْ سُلَّمًا فِي السَّمَاءِ فَتَأْتِيَهُمْ بِآيَةٍ وَلَوْ شَاءَ اللَّهُ لَجَمَعَهُمْ عَلَى الْهُدَى فَلَا تَكُونَنَّ مِنَ الْجَاهِلِينَ ۝

36. It is only those who listen (to the Message of Prophet Muhammad صلى الله عليه وسلم) will respond (benefit from it), but as for the dead (disbelievers), Allâh will raise them up, then to Him they will be returned (for their recompense).

37. And they said: "Why is not a sign sent down to him from his Lord?" Say: "Allâh is certainly Able to send down a sign, but most of them know not."

38. There is not a moving (living) creature on earth, nor a bird that flies with its two wings, but are communities like you. We have neglected nothing in the Book, then unto their Lord they (all) shall be gathered.

39. Those who reject Our *Ayât* (proofs, evidences, verses, lessons, signs, revelations, etc.) are deaf and dumb in the darkness. Allâh sends astray whom He wills and He guides on the Straight Path whom He wills.

40. Say (O Muhammad صلى الله عليه وسلم): "Tell me if Allâh's Torment comes upon you, or the Hour comes upon you, would you then call upon any one other than Allâh? (Reply) if you are truthful!"

41. Nay! To Him Alone you would call, and, if He wills, He would remove that (distress) for which you call upon Him, and you would forget at that time whatever partners you joined (with Him in worship)!

42. Verily, We sent (Messengers) to many nations before you (O Muhammad

(صلى الله عليه وسلم). And We seized them with extreme poverty (or loss in wealth) and loss in health (with calamities) so that they might humble themselves (believe with humility).

43. When Our Torment reached them, why then did they not humble themselves (believe with humility)? But their hearts became hardened, and *Shaitân* (Satan) made fair-seeming to them that which they used to do.

44. So, when they forgot (the warning) with which they had been reminded, We opened for them the gates of every (pleasant) thing, until in the midst of their enjoyment in that which they were given, all of a sudden, We took them (in punishment), and lo! They were plunged into destruction with deep regrets and sorrows.

45. So the root of the people who did wrong was cut off. And all the praises and thanks are to Allâh, the Lord of the *'Âlamîn* (mankind, jinn, and all that exists).

46. Say (to the disbelievers): "Tell me, if Allâh took away your hearing and your sight, and sealed up your hearts, who is there — an *ilâh* (a god) other than Allâh who could restore them to you?" See how variously We explain the *Ayât* (proofs, evidences, verses, lessons, signs, revelations, etc.), yet they turn aside.

47 Say: "Tell me, if the punishment of Allâh comes to you suddenly (during the night), or openly (during the day), will any be destroyed except the *Zâlimûn* (polytheists and wrongdoing people)?"

عَذَابُ ٱللَّهِ بَغْتَةً أَوْ جَهْرَةً هَلْ يُهْلَكُ إِلَّا ٱلْقَوْمُ ٱلظَّٰلِمُونَ ٤٧

48 And We send not the Messengers but as givers of glad tidings and as warners. So whosoever believes and does righteous good deeds, upon such shall come no fear, nor shall they grieve.

وَمَا نُرْسِلُ ٱلْمُرْسَلِينَ إِلَّا مُبَشِّرِينَ وَمُنذِرِينَ فَمَنْ ءَامَنَ وَأَصْلَحَ فَلَا خَوْفٌ عَلَيْهِمْ وَلَا هُمْ يَحْزَنُونَ ٤٨

49. But those who reject Our *Ayât* (proofs, evidences, verses, lessons, signs, revelations, etc.), the torment will touch them for their disbelief[1] (and for their belying the Message of Muhammad (صلى الله عليه وسلم) [*Tafsir Al-Qurtubî*].

وَٱلَّذِينَ كَذَّبُوا۟ بِـَٔايَٰتِنَا يَمَسُّهُمُ ٱلْعَذَابُ بِمَا كَانُوا۟ يَفْسُقُونَ ٤٩

50. Say (O Muhammad صلى الله عليه وسلم): "I don't tell you that with me are the treasures of Allâh, nor (that) I know the Unseen; nor I tell you that I am an angel. I but follow what is revealed to me." Say: "Are the blind and the one who sees equal? Will you not then take thought?"

قُل لَّا أَقُولُ لَكُمْ عِندِى خَزَآئِنُ ٱللَّهِ وَلَا أَعْلَمُ ٱلْغَيْبَ وَلَا أَقُولُ لَكُمْ إِنِّى مَلَكٌ إِنْ أَتَّبِعُ إِلَّا مَا يُوحَىٰ إِلَىَّ قُلْ هَلْ يَسْتَوِى ٱلْأَعْمَىٰ وَٱلْبَصِيرُ أَفَلَا تَتَفَكَّرُونَ ٥٠

51. And warn therewith (the Qur'ân) those who fear that they will be gathered before their Lord, when there will be neither a protector nor an intercessor for them besides Him, so that they may fear Allâh and keep their duty to Him (by abstaining from committing sins and by doing all kinds of good deeds which He has ordained).

وَأَنذِرْ بِهِ ٱلَّذِينَ يَخَافُونَ أَن يُحْشَرُوا۟ إِلَىٰ رَبِّهِمْ لَيْسَ لَهُم مِّن دُونِهِۦ وَلِىٌّ وَلَا شَفِيعٌ لَّعَلَّهُمْ يَتَّقُونَ ٥١

---

[1] (V.6:49) See the footnote of (V.3:85).

52. And turn not away those who invoke their Lord, morning and afternoon seeking His Face. You are accountable for them in nothing, and they are accountable for you in nothing, that you may turn them away, and thus become of the *Zâlimûn* (unjust).

53. Thus We have tried some of them with others, that they might say: "Is it these (poor believers) whom Allâh has favoured from amongst us?" Does not Allâh know best those who are grateful?

54. When those who believe in Our *Ayât* (proofs, evidences, verses, lessons, signs, revelations, etc.) come to you, say: *"Salâmun 'Alaikum"* (peace be on you); your Lord has written (prescribed) Mercy for Himself, so that if any of you does evil in ignorance, and thereafter repents and does righteous good deeds (by obeying Allâh), then surely, He is Oft-Forgiving, Most Merciful.

55. And thus do We explain the *Ayât* (proofs, evidences, verses, lessons, signs, revelations, etc.) in detail, that the way of the *Mujrimûn* (criminals, polytheists, sinners) may become manifest.

56. Say (O Muhammad صلى الله عليه وسلم): "I have been forbidden to worship those whom you invoke (worship) besides Allâh." Say: "I will not follow your vain desires. If I did, I would go astray, and I would not be one of the rightly guided."

وَلَا تَطْرُدِ ٱلَّذِينَ يَدْعُونَ رَبَّهُم بِٱلْغَدَوٰةِ وَٱلْعَشِيِّ يُرِيدُونَ وَجْهَهُۥ مَا عَلَيْكَ مِنْ حِسَابِهِم مِّن شَىْءٍ وَمَا مِنْ حِسَابِكَ عَلَيْهِم مِّن شَىْءٍ فَتَطْرُدَهُمْ فَتَكُونَ مِنَ ٱلظَّٰلِمِينَ ٥٢ وَكَذَٰلِكَ فَتَنَّا بَعْضَهُم بِبَعْضٍ لِّيَقُولُوٓا۟ أَهَٰٓؤُلَآءِ مَنَّ ٱللَّهُ عَلَيْهِم مِّنۢ بَيْنِنَآ أَلَيْسَ ٱللَّهُ بِأَعْلَمَ بِٱلشَّٰكِرِينَ ٥٣ وَإِذَا جَآءَكَ ٱلَّذِينَ يُؤْمِنُونَ بِـَٔايَٰتِنَا فَقُلْ سَلَٰمٌ عَلَيْكُمْ كَتَبَ رَبُّكُمْ عَلَىٰ نَفْسِهِ ٱلرَّحْمَةَ أَنَّهُۥ مَنْ عَمِلَ مِنكُمْ سُوٓءًۢا بِجَهَٰلَةٍ ثُمَّ تَابَ مِنۢ بَعْدِهِۦ وَأَصْلَحَ فَأَنَّهُۥ غَفُورٌ رَّحِيمٌ ٥٤ وَكَذَٰلِكَ نُفَصِّلُ ٱلْـَٔايَٰتِ وَلِتَسْتَبِينَ سَبِيلُ ٱلْمُجْرِمِينَ ٥٥ قُلْ إِنِّى نُهِيتُ أَنْ أَعْبُدَ ٱلَّذِينَ تَدْعُونَ مِن دُونِ ٱللَّهِ قُل لَّآ أَتَّبِعُ أَهْوَآءَكُمْ قَدْ ضَلَلْتُ إِذًا وَمَآ أَنَا۠ مِنَ ٱلْمُهْتَدِينَ ٥٦

57. Say (O Muhammad (صلى الله عليه وسلم): "I am on clear proof from my Lord (Islâmic Monotheism), but you deny it (the truth that has come to me from Allâh). I have not gotten what you are asking for impatiently (the torment). The decision is only for Allâh, He declares the truth, and He is the Best of judges."

قُلْ إِنِّي عَلَىٰ بَيِّنَةٍ مِّن رَّبِّي وَكَذَّبْتُم بِهِۦ مَا عِندِي مَا تَسْتَعْجِلُونَ بِهِۦٓ إِنِ ٱلْحُكْمُ إِلَّا لِلَّهِ يَقُصُّ ٱلْحَقَّ وَهُوَ خَيْرُ ٱلْفَٰصِلِينَ ٥٧

58. Say: "If I had that which you are asking for impatiently (the torment), the matter would have been settled at once between me and you, but Allâh knows best the Zâlimûn (polytheists and wrongdoers)."

قُل لَّوْ أَنَّ عِندِي مَا تَسْتَعْجِلُونَ بِهِۦ لَقُضِيَ ٱلْأَمْرُ بَيْنِي وَبَيْنَكُمْ وَٱللَّهُ أَعْلَمُ بِٱلظَّٰلِمِينَ ٥٨

59. And with Him are the keys of the Ghaib (all that is hidden), none knows them but He. And He knows whatever there is in the land and in the sea; not a leaf falls, but he knows it. There is not a grain in the darkness of the earth nor anything fresh or dry, but is written in a Clear Record.

وَعِندَهُۥ مَفَاتِحُ ٱلْغَيْبِ لَا يَعْلَمُهَآ إِلَّا هُوَ وَيَعْلَمُ مَا فِي ٱلْبَرِّ وَٱلْبَحْرِ وَمَا تَسْقُطُ مِن وَرَقَةٍ إِلَّا يَعْلَمُهَا وَلَا حَبَّةٍ فِي ظُلُمَٰتِ ٱلْأَرْضِ وَلَا رَطْبٍ وَلَا يَابِسٍ إِلَّا فِي كِتَٰبٍ مُّبِينٍ ٥٩

60. It is He, Who takes your souls by night (when you are asleep), and has knowledge of all that you have done by day, then he raises (wakes) you up again that a term appointed (your life period) be fulfilled, then (in the end) unto Him will be your return. Then He will inform you of that which you used to do.

وَهُوَ ٱلَّذِي يَتَوَفَّىٰكُم بِٱلَّيْلِ وَيَعْلَمُ مَا جَرَحْتُم بِٱلنَّهَارِ ثُمَّ يَبْعَثُكُمْ فِيهِ لِيُقْضَىٰٓ أَجَلٌ مُّسَمًّى ثُمَّ إِلَيْهِ مَرْجِعُكُمْ ثُمَّ يُنَبِّئُكُم بِمَا كُنتُمْ تَعْمَلُونَ ٦٠

61. He is the Irresistible (Supreme), over His slaves, and He sends guardians (angels guarding and writing all of one's good and bad deeds) over you,[1]

وَهُوَ ٱلْقَاهِرُ فَوْقَ عِبَادِهِۦ وَيُرْسِلُ عَلَيْكُمْ حَفَظَةً حَتَّىٰٓ إِذَا جَآءَ

---

[1] (V.6:61):

a) Whoever intended to do a good deed or a bad deed.

until when death approaches one of
you, Our Messengers (angel of death
and his assistants) take his soul, and
they never neglect their duty.

أَحَدَكُمُ الْمَوْتُ تَوَفَّتْهُ
رُسُلُنَا وَهُمْ لَا يُفَرِّطُونَ ٦١

62. Then they are returned to Allâh,
their True *Maulâ* [True Master (God),
the Just Lord (to reward them)]. Surely,
for Him is the judgement and He is the
Swiftest in taking account.

ثُمَّ رُدُّوا إِلَى اللَّهِ مَوْلَاهُمُ الْحَقِّ
أَلَا لَهُ الْحُكْمُ وَهُوَ أَسْرَعُ
الْحَاسِبِينَ ٦٢

63. Say (O Muhammad صلى الله عليه وسلم):
"Who rescues you from the darkness of
the land and the sea (dangers like
storms), (when) you call upon Him in

قُلْ مَن يُنَجِّيكُم مِّن ظُلُمَاتِ الْبَرِّ
وَالْبَحْرِ تَدْعُونَهُ تَضَرُّعًا وَخُفْيَةً

Narrated Ibn 'Abbâs رضى الله عنهما: The Prophet صلى الله عليه وسلم narrating
about his Lord عز وجل said, "Allâh ordered (the appointed angels over
you) that the good and the bad deeds be written, and He then
showed (the way) how (to write). If somebody intends to do a good
deed and he does not do it, then Allâh will write for him a full good
deed (in his account with Him); and if he intends to do a good deed
and actually did it, then Allâh will write for him (in his account)
with Him (its reward equal) from ten to seven hundred times, to
many more times: and if somebody intended to do a bad deed and
he does not do it, then Allâh will write a full good deed (in his
account) with Him, and if he intended to do it (a bad deed) and
actually did it, then Allâh will write one bad deed (in his account)."
(*Sahîh Al-Bukhâri*, Vol. 8, *Hadîth* No.498).

b) Narrated Abu Hurairah رضى الله عنه: The Prophet صلى الله عليه وسلم said,
"Angels come (to you) in succession by night and day, and all of
them get together at the time of *Fajr* and *'Asr* prayers. Then those
who have stayed with you overnight, ascend unto Allâh Who asks
them (and He knows the answer better than they): "How have you
left My slaves?" They reply, "We left them while they were praying
and we came to them while they were praying." The Prophet صلى الله عليه وسلم
added: "If anyone of you says *Amîn* (during the prayer at the
end of the recitation of *Sûrat Al-Fâtihah*), and the angels in heaven
say the same, and the two sayings coincide, all his past sins will be
forgiven." (*Sahîh Al-Bukhâri*, Vol. 4, *Hadith* No. 446)

humility and in secret (saying): If He (Allâh) only saves us from this (danger), we shall truly, be grateful."

64. Say (O Muhammad صلى الله عليه وسلم): "Allâh rescues you from this and from all (other) distresses, and yet you worship others besides Allâh."

65. Say: "He has power to send torment on you from above or from under your feet, or to cover you with confusion in party strife, and make you to taste the violence of one another." See how variously We explain the *Ayât* (proofs, evidences, lessons, signs, revelations, etc.), so that they may understand.

66. But your people (O Muhammad صلى الله عليه وسلم) have denied it (the Qur'ân) though it is the truth. Say: "I am not a *Wakîl* (guardian) over you."

67. For every news there is a reality[1] and you will come to know.

68. And when you (Muhammad صلى الله عليه وسلم) see those who engage in a false conversation about Our Verses (of the Qur'ân) by mocking at them, stay away from them till they turn to another topic. And if *Shaitân* (Satan) causes you to forget, then after the remembrance sit not you in the company of those people who are the *Zâlimûn* (polytheists and wrongdoers).

---

[1] (V.6:67) For every news there is a reality: i.e., for everything there is an appointed term and for every deed there is a recompense.

69. Those who fear Allâh, keep their duty to Him and avoid evil are not responsible for them (the disbelievers) in any case, but (their duty) is to remind them, that they may fear Allâh (and refrain from mocking at the Qur'ân). [The provision of this Verse was abrogated by the Verse 4:140].

70. And leave alone those who take their religion as play and amusement, and whom the life of this world has deceived. But remind (them) with it (the Qur'ân) lest a person be given up to destruction for that which he has earned, when he will find for himself no protector or intercessor besides Allâh, and even if he offers every ransom, it will not be accepted from him. Such are they who are given up to destruction because of that which they have earned. For them will be a drink of boiling water and a painful torment because they used to disbelieve.

71. Say (O Muhammad صلى الله عليه وسلم) "Shall we invoke others besides Allâh (false deities), that can do us neither good nor harm, and shall we turn back on our heels after Allâh has guided us (to true Monotheism)? — like one whom the *Shayâtîn* (devils) have made to go astray in the land in confusion, his companions calling him to guidance (saying): 'Come to us.' " Say: "Verily, Allâh's Guidance is the only guidance, and we have been commanded to submit (ourselves) to the Lord of the *'Alamîn* (mankind, jinn and all that exists);

72. And to perform *As-Salât (Iqâmat-as-Salât)*, and to be obedient to Allâh and fear Him, and it is He to Whom you shall be gathered.

وَأَنْ أَقِيمُوا الصَّلَوٰةَ وَاتَّقُوهُ وَهُوَ الَّذِىٓ إِلَيْهِ تُحْشَرُونَ ﴿٧٢﴾

73. It is He Who has created the heavens and the earth in truth, and on the Day (i.e. the Day of Resurrection) He will say: "Be!", — and it is! His Word is the Truth. His will be the dominion on the Day when the Trumpet will be blown. All-Knower of the unseen and the seen. He is the All-Wise, Well-Aware (of all things).

وَهُوَ الَّذِى خَلَقَ السَّمَٰوَٰتِ وَالْأَرْضَ بِالْحَقِّ وَيَوْمَ يَقُولُ كُن فَيَكُونُ قَوْلُهُ الْحَقُّ وَلَهُ الْمُلْكُ يَوْمَ يُنفَخُ فِى الصُّورِ عَٰلِمُ الْغَيْبِ وَالشَّهَٰدَةِ وَهُوَ الْحَكِيمُ الْخَبِيرُ ﴿٧٣﴾

74. And (remember) when Ibrâhîm (Abraham) said to his father Âzar: "Do you take idols as *âlihâ* (gods)? Verily, I see you and your people in manifest error.[1]"

۞ وَإِذْ قَالَ إِبْرَٰهِيمُ لِأَبِيهِ ءَازَرَ أَتَتَّخِذُ أَصْنَامًا ءَالِهَةً إِنِّىٓ أَرَىٰكَ ﴿٧٤﴾

75. Thus did we show Ibrâhîm (Abraham) the kingdom of the heavens and the earth that he be one of those who have Faith with certainty.

وَقَوْمَكَ فِى ضَلَٰلٍ مُّبِينٍ وَكَذَٰلِكَ نُرِىٓ إِبْرَٰهِيمَ مَلَكُوتَ السَّمَٰوَٰتِ وَالْأَرْضِ وَلِيَكُونَ مِنَ الْمُوقِنِينَ ﴿٧٥﴾

---

[1] (V.6:74) Narrated Abu Hurairah رضي الله عنه The Prophet صلى الله عليه وسلم said, "On the Day of Resurrection Ibrâhîm (Abraham) will meet his father Âzar whose face will be dark and covered with dust. (The Prophet) Ibrâhîm will say (to him): 'Didn't I tell you not to disobey me?' His father will reply: 'Today I will not disobey you.' Ibrâhîm will say: 'O Lord! You promised me not to disgrace me on the Day of Resurrection; and what will be more disgraceful to me than cursing and dishonouring my father?' Then Allâh تعالى will say (to him): 'I have forbidden Paradise for the disbelievers.' Then he will be addressed, 'O Ibrâhîm! Look! What is underneath your feet?' He will look and there he will see a *Dhikh* (an animal-male Hyena,) blood-stained, which will be caught by the legs and thrown in the (Hell) Fire." (*Sahih Al-Bukhâri*, Vol.4, *Hadith* No.569).

76. When the night covered him over with darkness he saw a star. He said: "This is my lord." But when it set, he said: "I like not those that set."

77. When he saw the moon rising up, he said: "This is my lord." But when it set, he said: "Unless my Lord guides me, I shall surely, be among the people who went astray."

78. When he saw the sun rising up, he said: "This is my lord. This is greater." But when it set, he said: "O my people! I am indeed free from all that you join as partners (in worship with Allâh)."

79. Verily, I have turned my face towards Him Who has created the heavens and the earth *Hanîfa* (Islâmic Monotheism, i.e. worshipping none but Allâh Alone), and I am not of *Al-Mushrikûn*." (See V.2:105).

80. His people disputed with him. He said: "Do you dispute with me concerning Allâh while He has guided me, and I fear not those whom you associate with Him (Allâh) in worship. (Nothing can happen to me) except when my Lord (Allâh) wills something. My Lord comprehends in His Knowledge all things. Will you not then remember?

81. "And how should I fear those whom you associate in worship with Allâh (though they can neither benefit nor harm), while you fear not that you

فَلَمَّا جَنَّ عَلَيْهِ ٱلَّيْلُ رَءَا كَوْكَبًا قَالَ هَٰذَا رَبِّى فَلَمَّآ أَفَلَ قَالَ لَآ أُحِبُّ ٱلْأَفِلِينَ ٧٦

فَلَمَّا رَءَا ٱلْقَمَرَ بَازِغًا قَالَ هَٰذَا رَبِّى فَلَمَّآ أَفَلَ قَالَ لَئِن لَّمْ يَهْدِنِى رَبِّى لَأَكُونَنَّ مِنَ ٱلْقَوْمِ ٱلضَّآلِّينَ ٧٧

فَلَمَّا رَءَا ٱلشَّمْسَ بَازِغَةً قَالَ هَٰذَا رَبِّى هَٰذَآ أَكْبَرُ فَلَمَّآ أَفَلَتْ قَالَ يَٰقَوْمِ إِنِّى بَرِىٓءٌ مِّمَّا تُشْرِكُونَ ٧٨

إِنِّى وَجَّهْتُ وَجْهِىَ لِلَّذِى فَطَرَ ٱلسَّمَٰوَٰتِ وَٱلْأَرْضَ حَنِيفًا وَمَآ أَنَا۠ مِنَ ٱلْمُشْرِكِينَ ٧٩

وَحَآجَّهُۥ قَوْمُهُۥ قَالَ أَتُحَٰٓجُّوٓنِّى فِى ٱللَّهِ وَقَدْ هَدَىٰنِ وَلَآ أَخَافُ مَا تُشْرِكُونَ بِهِۦٓ إِلَّآ أَن يَشَآءَ رَبِّى شَيْـًٔا وَسِعَ رَبِّى كُلَّ شَىْءٍ عِلْمًا أَفَلَا تَتَذَكَّرُونَ ٨٠

وَكَيْفَ أَخَافُ مَآ أَشْرَكْتُمْ وَلَا تَخَافُونَ أَنَّكُمْ أَشْرَكْتُم بِٱللَّهِ مَا لَمْ يُنَزِّلْ بِهِۦ

have joined in worship with Allâh things for which He has not sent down to you any authority. (So) which of the two parties has more right to be in security? If you but know."

82. It is those who believe (in the Oneness of Allâh and worship none but Him Alone) and confuse not their belief with *Zulm* (wrong i.e. by worshipping others besides Allâh), for them (only) there is security and they are the guided.[1]

83. And that was Our Proof which We gave Ibrâhîm (Abraham) against his people. We raise whom We will in degrees. Certainly your Lord is All-Wise, All-Knowing.

84. And We bestowed upon him Ishâq (Isaac) and Ya'qûb (Jacob), each of them We guided, and before him, We guided Nûh (Noah), and among his progeny Dâwûd (David), Sulaimân (Solomon), Ayyub (Job), Yûsuf (Joseph), Mûsâ (Moses), and Hârûn (Aaron). Thus do We reward *Al-Muhsinûn* (the good-doers — see the footnote of V.9:120).

85. And Zakariyyâ (Zacharia), and Yahyâ (John) and 'Îsâ (Jesus) and Iliyâs (Elias), each one of them was of the righteous.

86. And Ismâ'îl (Ishmael) and Al-Yas'a (Elisha), and Yûnus (Jonah) and

---

[1] (V.6:82): See the footnote of (C) of (V.27:59).

Lût (Lot), and each one of them We preferred above the *'Âlamîn* [mankind and jinn (of their times)].

87. And also some of their fathers and their progeny and their brethren, We chose them, and We guided them to the Straight Path.

88. This is the Guidance of Allâh with which He guides whomsoever He wills of His slaves. But if they had joined in worship others with Allâh, all that they used to do would have been of no benefit to them.

89. They are those whom We gave the Book, *Al-Hukm* (understanding of the religious laws), and Prophethood. But if these disbelieve therein (the Book, *Al-Hukm* and Prophethood), then, indeed We have entrusted it to a people (such as the Companions of Prophet Muhammad صلى الله عليه وسلم) who are not disbelievers therein.

90. They are those whom Allâh had guided. So follow their guidance. Say: "No reward I ask of you for this (the Qur'ân). It is only a reminder for the *'Âlamîn* (mankind and jinn)."

91. They (the Jews, Quraish pagans, idolaters) did not estimate Allâh with an estimation due to Him when they said: "Nothing did Allâh send down to any human being (by inspiration)." Say (O Muhammad صلى الله عليه وسلم): "Who then sent down the Book which Mûsâ (Moses) brought, a light and a guidance to mankind which you (the Jews) have made into (separate) papersheets, disclosing (some of it) and concealing (much). And you (believers in Allâh and His Messenger Muhammad صلى الله عليه وسلم) were taught (through the Qur'ân) that which neither you nor your fathers knew." Say: "Allâh (sent it down)." Then leave them to play in their vain discussions. (*Tafsir Al-Qurtubî*).

92. And this (the Qur'ân) is a blessed Book which We have sent down, confirming (the revelations) which came before it, so that you may warn the Mother of Towns (i.e. Makkah) and all those around it. Those who believe in the Hereafter believe in it (the Qur'ân), and they are constant in guarding their *Salât* (prayers).

93. And who can be more unjust than he who invents a lie against Allâh, or says: "A revelation has come to me" whereas no revelation has come to him in anything; and who says, "I will reveal the like of what Allâh has revealed." And if you could but see when the *Zâlimûn* (polytheists and wrong-doers) are in the agonies of death, while the angels are stretching forth their hands (saying): "Deliver your souls! This day you shall be recompensed with the torment of degradation because of what you used to utter against Allâh other than the truth. And you used to reject His *Ayât* (proofs, evidences, verses, lessons, signs, revelations, etc.) with disrespect![1]"

---

[1] (V.6:93) A. What is said regarding the punishment in the grave. And the Statement of Allâh عز وجل :

"If you could but see when the Zâlimûn (polytheists and wrongdoers) are in the agonies of death while the angels are stretching forth their hands (saying): "Deliver your souls! This day you shall be recompensed with the torment of degradation." (V.6:93)

And also the Statement of Allâh تعالى : "Twice shall We punish them and thereafter, they shall be brought back to a great (horrible) torment." (V.9:101).

And also the Statement of Allâh تعالى :

"While an evil torment encompassed Fir'aun (Pharaoh)'s people; the Fire, they are exposed to it morning and afternoon, and on the Day when the Hour will be established (it will be said to the angels): 'Cause Fir'aun's people to enter the severest torment.' " (V.40: 45,46).

Narrated Al-Barâ' bin 'Âzib: The Prophet صلى الله عليه وسلم said,"When a faithful believer is made to sit in his grave, then (the angels) come to him and he testifies that Lâ ilâha illallâh wa Anna Muhammad-ur-Rasûl-Allâh (none has the right to be worshipped but Allâh and Muhammad صلى الله عليه وسلم is the Messenger of Allâh). And that corresponds to Allâh's Statement:'Allâh will keep firm those who believe with the word that stands firm.' (V.14:27)." (Sahih Al-Bukhâri, Vol.2, Hadîth No.450).

B. Narrated Anas رضي الله عنه : The Prophet صلى الله عليه وسلم said, "When a human being is laid in his grave and his companions return and he even hears their footsteps, two angels come to him and make him sit and ask him: 'What did you use to say about this man, Muhammad (صلى الله عليه وسلم)?' He will say: 'I testify that he is Allâh's slave and His Messenger.' Then it will be said to him, 'Look at your place in the Hell-fire. Allâh has changed for you a place in Paradise instead of it.'" The Prophet صلى الله عليه وسلم added, "The dead person will see both his places. But a disbeliever or a hypocrite will say to the angels, 'I do not know, but I used to say what the people used to say!' It will be said to him, 'Neither did you know nor did you take the guidance (by following the Qur'ân).' Then he will be hit with an iron hammer

94. And truly, you have come unto Us alone (without wealth, companions or anything else) as We created you the first time. You have left behind you all that which We had bestowed on you. We see not with you your intercessors whom you claimed to be partners with Allâh. Now all relations between you and them have been cut off, and all that you used to claim has vanished from you.

95. Verily, it is Allâh Who causes the seed-grain and the fruit-stone (like date-stone) to split and sprout. He brings forth the living from the dead, and it is He Who brings forth the dead from the living. Such is Allâh, then how are you deluded away from the truth?

96. (He is the) Cleaver of the daybreak. He has appointed the night for resting, and the sun and the moon for reckoning. Such is the measuring of the All-Mighty, the All-Knowing.

97. It is He Who has set the stars[1] for you, so that you may guide your course with their help through the

between his two ears, and he will cry and that cry will be heard by whatsoever near to him except human beings and jinn." (*Sahih Al-Bukhâri*, Vol. 2, *Hadith* No. 422)

[1] (V.6:97) (About the) Stars. Abu Qatâdah mentioned Allâh's Statement: "And We have adorned the nearest heaven with lamps," (V.67:5) and said, "The creation of these stars is for three purposes, i.e. as decoration of the nearest heaven, as missiles to hit the devils, and as signs to guide travellers. So, if anybody tries to find a different interpretation, he is mistaken and just wastes his efforts, and troubles himself with what is beyond his limited knowledge." (*Sahih Al-Bukhâri*, Vol. 4, Chap. 3, P. 282).

darkness of the land and the sea. We have (indeed) explained in detail Our *Ayât* (proofs, evidences, verses, lessons, signs, Revelations, etc.) for people who know.

98. It is He Who has created you from a single person (Adam), and has given you a place of residing (on the earth or in your mother's wombs) and a place of storage [in the earth (in your graves) or in your father's loins]. Indeed, We have explained in detail Our revelations (this Qur'ân) for people who understand.

99. It is He Who sends down water (rain) from the sky, and with it We bring forth vegetation of all kinds, and out of it We bring forth green stalks, from which We bring forth thick clustered grain. And out of the date-palm and its spathe come forth clusters of dates hanging low and near, and gardens of grapes, olives and pomegranates, each similar (in kind) yet different (in variety and taste). Look at their fruits when they begin to bear, and the ripeness thereof. Verily, in these things there are signs for people who believe.

100. Yet, they join the jinn as partners in worship with Allâh, though He has created them (the jinn); and they attribute falsely without knowledge sons and daughters to Him. He is Glorified and Exalted above all that (evil) they attribute to Him.

101. He is the Originator of the heavens and the earth. How can He have children when He has no wife? He created all things and He is the All-Knower of everything.[1]

102. Such is Allâh, your Lord! *Lâ ilâha illa Huwa* (none has the right to be worshipped but He), the Creator of all things. So worship Him (Alone), and He is the *Wakîl* (Trustee, Disposer of affairs or Guardian) over all things.

103. No vision can grasp Him, but He grasps all vision. He is *Al-Latîf* (the Most Subtle and Courteous), Well-Acquainted with all things.

104. Verily, proofs have come to you from your Lord, so whosoever sees, will do so for (the good of) his ownself, and whosoever blinds himself, will do so to his own harm, and I (Muhammad صلى الله عليه وسلم) am not a watcher over you.

105. Thus We explain variously the Verses so that they (the disbelievers) may say: "You have studied (the Books of the people of the Scripture and brought this Qur'ân from that)" and that We may make the matter clear for the people who have knowledge.

106. Follow what has been revealed to you (O Muhammad صلى الله عليه وسلم) from your Lord, *Lâ ilâha illa Huwa* (none has the right to be worshipped but He) and turn aside from *Al-Mushrikûn*.[2]

---

[1] (V.6:101) See the footnote of (V.2:116)

[2] (V.6:106). *Al-Mushrikûn*: polytheists, pagans, idolaters and disbelievers in the Oneness of Allâh and His Messenger Muhammad صلى الله عليه وسلم.

107. Had Allâh willed, they would not have taken others besides Him in worship. And We have not made you a watcher over them nor are you a *Wakîl* (disposer of affairs, guardian or a trustee) over them.

وَلَوْ شَاءَ اللَّهُ مَا أَشْرَكُوا وَمَا جَعَلْنَاكَ عَلَيْهِمْ حَفِيظًا وَمَا أَنتَ عَلَيْهِم بِوَكِيلٍ

108. And insult not those whom they (disbelievers) worship besides Allâh, lest they insult Allâh wrongfully without knowledge. Thus We have made fair-seeming to each people its own doings; then to their Lord is their return and He shall then inform them of all that they used to do.[1]

وَلَا تَسُبُّوا الَّذِينَ يَدْعُونَ مِن دُونِ اللَّهِ فَيَسُبُّوا اللَّهَ عَدْوًا بِغَيْرِ عِلْمٍ كَذَٰلِكَ زَيَّنَّا لِكُلِّ أُمَّةٍ عَمَلَهُمْ ثُمَّ إِلَىٰ رَبِّهِم مَّرْجِعُهُمْ فَيُنَبِّئُهُم بِمَا كَانُوا يَعْمَلُونَ

---

[1] (6:108) The tale of the cave:

Narrated Ibn 'Umâr رضي الله عنهما: Allâh's Messenger صلى الله عليه وسلم said, "Once three persons (from the previous nations) were travelling, and suddenly it started raining and they took shelter in a cave. The entrance of the cave got closed (suddenly by the falling of a huge rock) while they were inside. They said to each other, 'O You! Nothing can save you except the truth, so each of you should ask Allâh's Help by referring to such a deed as he thinks he did sincerely (i.e., just for gaining Allâh's Pleasure).' So one of them said, 'O Allâh! You know that I had a labourer who worked for me for one *Faraq* (i.e. three *Sa'*) of rice, but he departed, leaving it (i.e. his wages). I sowed that *Faraq* of rice and with its yield I bought cows (for him). Later on when came to me asking for his wages, I said (to him), 'Go to those cows and drive them away.' He said to me, 'But you have to pay me only a *Faraq* of rice.' I said to him, 'Go to those cows and take them, for they are the product of that *Faraq* (of rice).' So he drove them. O Allâh! If you consider that I did that for fear of You, then please remove the rock.' The rock shifted a bit from the mouth of the cave. The second one said, 'O Allâh, You know that I had old parents whom I used to provide with the milk of my sheep every night. One night I was delayed and when I came, they had slept, while my wife and children were

109. And they swear their strongest oaths by Allâh, that if there came to them a sign, they would surely believe therein. Say: "Signs are but with Allâh and what will make you (Muslims) perceive that (even) if it (the sign) came, they will not believe?"

وَأَقْسَمُواْ بِٱللَّهِ جَهْدَ أَيْمَٰنِهِمْ لَئِن جَآءَتْهُمْ ءَايَةٌ لَّيُؤْمِنُنَّ بِهَا قُلْ إِنَّمَا ٱلْءَايَٰتُ عِندَ ٱللَّهِ وَمَا يُشْعِرُكُمْ أَنَّهَآ إِذَا جَآءَتْ لَا يُؤْمِنُونَ ۝

110. And We shall turn their hearts and their eyes away (from guidance), as they refused to believe therein for the first time, and We shall leave them in their trespass to wander blindly.

وَنُقَلِّبُ أَفْئِدَتَهُمْ وَأَبْصَٰرَهُمْ كَمَا لَمْ يُؤْمِنُواْ بِهِۦٓ أَوَّلَ مَرَّةٍ وَنَذَرُهُمْ فِى طُغْيَٰنِهِمْ يَعْمَهُونَ ۝

---

crying with hunger. I used not to let them (i.e. my family) drink unless my parents had drunk first. So I disliked to wake them up and also disliked that they should sleep without drinking it, I kept on waiting (for them to wake) till it dawned. O Allâh! If You consider that I did that for fear of You, then please remove the rock.' So the rock shifted and they could see the sky through it. The (third) one said, 'O Allâh! You know that I had a cousin (i.e. my paternal uncle's daughter) who was most beloved to me and I sought to seduce her, but she refused, unless I paid her one-hundred Dinârs (i.e. gold pieces). So I collected the amount and brought it to her, and she allowed me to sleep with her. But when I sat between her legs, she said, 'Be afraid of Allâh, and do not deflower me but legally.' 'I got up and left the hundred Dinârs (for her). O Allâh! If You consider that I did that for fear of You than please remove the rock.' So Allâh released them (removed the rock) and they came out (of the cave)." [This *Hadith* indicates that one can only ask Allâh for help directly or through his performed good deeds. But to ask Allâh through dead or absent (prophets, saints, spirits, holy men, angels) is absolutely forbidden in Islâm and it is a kind of polytheism]. (*Sahih Al-Bukhâri*, Vol. 4, *Hadith* No. 671).

111. And even if We had sent down unto them angels, and the dead had spoken unto them, and We had gathered together all things before their very eyes, they would not have believed, unless Allâh willed, but most of them behave ignorantly.

وَلَوْ أَنَّنَا نَزَّلْنَا إِلَيْهِمُ ٱلْمَلَٰٓئِكَةَ وَكَلَّمَهُمُ ٱلْمَوْتَىٰ وَحَشَرْنَا عَلَيْهِمْ كُلَّ شَىْءٍ قُبُلًا مَّا كَانُواْ لِيُؤْمِنُوٓاْ إِلَّآ أَن يَشَآءَ ٱللَّهُ وَلَٰكِنَّ أَكْثَرَهُمْ يَجْهَلُونَ ﴿١١١﴾

112. And so We have appointed for every Prophet enemies — *Shayâtîn* (devils) among mankind and jinn, inspiring one another with adorned speech as a delusion (or by way of deception). If your Lord had so willed, they would not have done it; so leave them alone with their fabrications. (*T. Qurtubi*, V.7, P.67)

وَكَذَٰلِكَ جَعَلْنَا لِكُلِّ نَبِىٍّ عَدُوًّا شَيَٰطِينَ ٱلْإِنسِ وَٱلْجِنِّ يُوحِى بَعْضُهُمْ إِلَىٰ بَعْضٍ زُخْرُفَ ٱلْقَوْلِ غُرُورًا وَلَوْ شَآءَ رَبُّكَ مَا فَعَلُوهُ فَذَرْهُمْ وَمَا يَفْتَرُونَ ﴿١١٢﴾

113. (And this is in order) that the hearts of those who disbelieve in the Hereafter may incline to such (deceit), and that they may remain pleased with it, and that they may commit what they are committing (all kinds of sins and evil deeds).

وَلِتَصْغَىٰٓ إِلَيْهِ أَفْـِٔدَةُ ٱلَّذِينَ لَا يُؤْمِنُونَ بِٱلْآخِرَةِ وَلِيَرْضَوْهُ وَلِيَقْتَرِفُواْ مَا هُم مُّقْتَرِفُونَ ﴿١١٣﴾

114. [Say (O Muhammad صلى الله عليه وسلم) "Shall I seek a judge other than Allâh while it is He Who has sent down unto you the Book (the Qur'ân), explained in detail." Those unto whom We gave the Scripture [the Taurât (Torah) and the Injeel (Gospel)] know that it is revealed from your Lord in truth. So be not you of those who doubt.

أَفَغَيْرَ ٱللَّهِ أَبْتَغِى حَكَمًا وَهُوَ ٱلَّذِىٓ أَنزَلَ إِلَيْكُمُ ٱلْكِتَٰبَ مُفَصَّلًا وَٱلَّذِينَ ءَاتَيْنَٰهُمُ ٱلْكِتَٰبَ يَعْلَمُونَ أَنَّهُۥ مُنَزَّلٌ مِّن رَّبِّكَ بِٱلْحَقِّ فَلَا تَكُونَنَّ مِنَ ٱلْمُمْتَرِينَ ﴿١١٤﴾

115. And the Word of your Lord has been fulfilled in truth and in justice. None can change His Words. And He is the All-Hearer, the All-Knower.

وَتَمَّتْ كَلِمَتُ رَبِّكَ صِدْقًا وَعَدْلًا لَّا مُبَدِّلَ لِكَلِمَٰتِهِۦ وَهُوَ ٱلسَّمِيعُ ٱلْعَلِيمُ ﴿١١٥﴾

116. And if you obey most of those on the earth, they will mislead you far away from Allâh's Path. They follow nothing but conjectures, and they do nothing but lie.

117. Verily, your Lord! It is He Who knows best who strays from His Way, and He knows best the rightly guided ones.

118. So eat of that (meat) on which Allâh's Name has been pronounced (while slaughtering the animal), if you are believers in His *Ayât* (proofs, evidences, verses, lessons, signs, revelations, etc.).

119. And why should you not eat of that (meat) on which Allâh's Name has been pronounced (at the time of slaughtering the animal), while He has explained to you in detail what is forbidden to you, except under compulsion of necessity? And surely, many do lead (mankind) astray by their own desires through lack of knowledge. Certainly your Lord knows best the transgressors.

120. Leave (O mankind, all kinds of) sin, open and secret. Verily, those who commit sin will get due recompense for that which they used to commit.

121. Eat not (O believers) of that (meat) on which Allâh's Name has not been pronounced (at the time of the slaughtering of the animal), for sure it is *Fisq* (a sin and disobedience of Allâh). And certainly, the *Shayâtîn* (devils) do **inspire** their friends (from mankind) to dispute with you, and if you obey them[1] [by making Al-Maitah (a dead animal) lawful by eating it], then you would indeed be *Mushrikûn* (polytheists); [because they (devils and their friends) made lawful to you to eat that which Allâh has made unlawful to eat and you obeyed them by considering it lawful to eat, and by doing so you worshipped them; and to worship others besides Allâh is polytheism].

122. Is he who was dead (without Faith by ignorance and disbelief) and We gave him life (by knowledge and Faith) and set for him a light (of Belief) whereby he can walk amongst men — like him who is in the darkness (of disbelief, polytheism and hypocrisy) from which he can never come out? Thus it is made fair-seeming to the disbelievers that which they used to do.

123. And thus We have set up in every town great ones of its wicked people to plot therein. But they plot not except against their ownselves, and they perceive (it) not.

---

[1] (V.6:121) Narrated by Ahmad, At-Tirmidhi, and Ibn Jarir: Once while Allâh's Messenger صلى الله عليه وسلم was reciting the Verse (9:31) 'Adî bin Hâtim said, "O Allâh's Messenger! They do not worship them (i.e., rabbis and monks)." Allâh's Messenger صلى الله عليه وسلم said: "They certainly do. (They i.e., rabbis and monks) made lawful things as unlawful, and unlawful things as lawful, and they (i.e. Jews and Christians) followed them; and by doing so, they **really** worshipped them." (*Tafsir At-Tabari*).

124. And when there comes to them a sign (from Allâh) they say: "We shall not believe until we receive the like of that which the Messengers of Allâh had received." Allâh knows best with whom to place His Message. Humiliation and disgrace from Allâh and a severe torment will overtake the criminals (polytheists and sinners) for that which they used to plot.

125. And whomsoever Allâh wills to guide, He opens his breast to Islâm; and whomsoever He wills to send astray, He makes his breast closed and constricted, as if he is climbing up to the sky. Thus Allâh puts the wrath on those who believe not.[1]

126. And this is the Path of your Lord (the Qur'ân and Islâm) leading Straight. We have detailed Our Revelations for a people who take heed.

---

[1] (V.6:125) If Allâh تعالى wants to do good to a person, He makes him comprehend the religion [the understanding of the Qur'ân and the Sunnah (legal ways) of the Prophet صلى الله عليه وسلم].

Narrated Mu'awiyyâh رضى الله عنه in a Khutbah (religious talk): I heard Allâh's Messenger صلى الله عليه وسلم saying, "If Allâh wants to do good to a person, He makes him comprehend the religion [the understanding of the Qur'ân and the Sunnah (legal ways) of the Prophet صلى الله عليه وسلم]. I am just a distributor, but the grant is from Allâh. (And remember) that this nation (true Muslims, real followers of Islâmic Monotheism) will remain obedient to Allâh's Orders [i.e., following strictly Allâh's Book (the Qur'ân and the Prophet's Sunnah (legal ways)] and they will not be harmed by anyone who will oppose them (going on a different path) till Allâh's Order (Day of Judgement) is established." (Sahih Al-Bukhâri, Vol. 1, Hadîth No. 71).

127. For them will be the home of peace (Paradise) with their Lord. And He will be their *Walî* (Helper and Protector) because of what they used to do.

128. And on the Day when He will gather them (all) together (and say): "O you assembly of jinn! Many did you mislead of men," and their *Auliyâ'* (friends and helpers) amongst men will say: "Our Lord! We benefited one from the other, but now we have reached our appointed term which You did appoint for us." He will say: "The Fire be your dwelling-place, you will dwell therein forever, except as Allâh may will. Certainly your Lord is All-Wise, All-Knowing."

129. And thus We do make the *Zâlimûn* (polytheists and wrongdoers) *Auliyâ'* (supporters and helpers) of one another (in committing crimes), because of that which they used to earn.

130. O you assembly of jinn and mankind! "Did not there come to you Messengers from amongst you, reciting unto you My Verses and warning you of the meeting of this Day of yours?" They will say: "We bear witness against ourselves." It was the life of this world that deceived them. And they will bear witness against themselves that they were disbelievers.

131. This is because your Lord would not destroy the (populations of) towns for their wrong-doing (i.e. associating others in worship along with Allâh) while their people were unaware (so the Messengers were sent).

132. For all there will be degrees (or ranks) according to what they did. And your Lord is not unaware of what they do.

133. And your Lord is Rich (Free of all needs), full of Mercy; if He wills, He can destroy you, and in your place make whom He wills as your successors, as He raised you from the seed of other people.

134. Surely, that which you are promised will verily, come to pass, and you cannot escape (from the punishment of Allâh).

135. Say (O Muhammad صلى الله عليه وسلم): "O my people! Work according to your way, surely, I too am working (in my way), and you will come to know for which of us will be the (happy) end in the Hereafter. Certainly the *Zâlimûn* (polytheists and wrongdoers) will not be successful."

136. And they assign to Allâh a share of the tilth and cattle which He has created, and they say: "This is for Allâh" according to their claim, "and this is for our (Allâh's so-called) partners." But the share of their (Allâh's so-called) "partners" reaches not Allâh, while the share of Allâh reaches their (Allâh's so-called) "partners"! Evil is the way they judge!

137. And so to many of the *Mushrikûn* (polytheists — see V.2:105) their (Allâh's so-called) "partners" have made fair-seeming the killing of their children, in order to lead them to their own destruction and cause confusion in their religion. And if Allâh had willed, they would not have done so. So leave them alone with their fabrications.

138. And according to their claim, they say that such and such cattle and crops are forbidden, and none should eat of them except those whom we allow. And (they say) there are cattle forbidden to be used for burden (or any other work), and cattle on which (at slaughtering) the Name of Allâh is not pronounced; lying against Him (Allâh). He will recompense them for what they used to fabricate.

139. And they say: "What is in the bellies of such and such cattle (milk or foetus) is for our males alone, and forbidden to our females (girls and women), but if it is born dead, then all have shares therein." He will punish them for their attribution (of such false orders to Allâh). Verily, He is All-Wise, All-Knower. (*Tafsir At-Tabarî*).

140. Indeed lost are they who have killed their children, foolishly, without knowledge, and have forbidden that which Allâh has provided for them, inventing a lie against Allâh. They have indeed gone astray and were not guided.

141. And it is He Who produces gardens trellised and untrellised, and date-palms, and crops of different shape and taste (its fruits and its seeds) and olives, and pomegranates, similar (in kind) and different (in taste). Eat of their fruit when they ripen, but pay the due thereof (its *Zakât*, according to Allâh's Orders 1/10th or 1/20th) on the day of its harvest, and waste not by extravagance.[1] Verily, He likes not *Al-Musrifûn* (those who waste by extravagance),

142. And of the cattle (are some) for burden (like camel) and (some are) small (unable to carry burden like sheep and goats for food, meat, milk and wool). Eat of what Allâh has provided for you, and follow not the footsteps of *Shaitân* (Satan). Surely, he is to you an open enemy.

143. Eight pairs: of the sheep two (male and female),[2] and of the goats

وَهُوَ ٱلَّذِىٓ أَنشَأَ جَنَّٰتٍ
مَّعۡرُوشَٰتٍ وَغَيۡرَ مَعۡرُوشَٰتٍ
وَٱلنَّخۡلَ وَٱلزَّرۡعَ مُخۡتَلِفًا أُكُلُهُۥ
وَٱلزَّيۡتُونَ وَٱلرُّمَّانَ
مُتَشَٰبِهًا وَغَيۡرَ مُتَشَٰبِهٍۚ كُلُواْ
مِن ثَمَرِهِۦٓ إِذَآ أَثۡمَرَ وَءَاتُواْ
حَقَّهُۥ يَوۡمَ حَصَادِهِۦۖ وَلَا تُسۡرِفُوٓاْۚ
إِنَّهُۥ لَا يُحِبُّ
ٱلۡمُسۡرِفِينَ ﴿١٤١﴾

وَمِنَ ٱلۡأَنۡعَٰمِ حَمُولَةً
وَفَرۡشًاۚ كُلُواْ مِمَّا رَزَقَكُمُ
ٱللَّهُ وَلَا تَتَّبِعُواْ خُطُوَٰتِ
ٱلشَّيۡطَٰنِۚ إِنَّهُۥ لَكُمۡ عَدُوٌّ
مُّبِينٌ ﴿١٤٢﴾

ثَمَٰنِيَةَ أَزۡوَٰجٍۖ مِّنَ ٱلضَّأۡنِ
ٱثۡنَيۡنِ وَمِنَ ٱلۡمَعۡزِ ٱثۡنَيۡنِۗ

---

[1] (V.6:141): See the footnote of (V.4:5).

[2] (V.6:143) Narrated Abu Hurairah رضي الله عنه: I heard Allâh's Messenger صلى الله عليه وسلم saying, "While a shepherd was amongst his sheep, a wolf attacked them and took away one sheep. When the shepherd chased the wolf, the wolf turned towards him and said, 'Who will be its guard on the day of wild animals when nobody except I will be its shepherd'*. And while a man was driving a cow with a load on it, it turned towards him and spoke to him saying, 'I have not been created for this purpose, but for ploughing.' "The people said, 'Glorified is Allâh.' The Prophet صلى الله عليه وسلم said, "But I believe in it and so does Abu Bakr and 'Umar رضي الله عنهم (*Sahih Al-Bukhâri*, Vol. 5, *Hadîth* No. 15).

* It has been written that a wolf also spoke to a shepherd during the Prophet's lifetime near Al-Madinah, as narrated in *Musnad Imam*

two (male and female). Say: "Has He forbidden the two males or the two females, or (the young) which the wombs of the two females enclose? Inform me with knowledge if you are truthful."

قُلْ آلذَّكَرَيْنِ حَرَّمَ أَمِ الْأُنثَيَيْنِ أَمَّا اشْتَمَلَتْ عَلَيْهِ أَرْحَامُ الْأُنثَيَيْنِ نَبِّئُونِي بِعِلْمٍ إِن كُنتُمْ صَـٰدِقِينَ ١٤٣

144. And of the camels two (male and female), and of oxen two (male and female). Say: "Has He forbidden the two males or the two females or (the young) which the wombs of the two females enclose? Or were you present when Allâh ordered you such a thing? Then who does more wrong than one who invents a lie

وَمِنَ الْإِبِلِ اثْنَيْنِ وَمِنَ الْبَقَرِ اثْنَيْنِ قُلْ آلذَّكَرَيْنِ حَرَّمَ أَمِ الْأُنثَيَيْنِ أَمَّا اشْتَمَلَتْ عَلَيْهِ أَرْحَامُ الْأُنثَيَيْنِ أَمْ كُنتُمْ شُهَدَاءَ إِذْ وَصَّاكُمُ اللَّهُ بِهَـٰذَا فَمَنْ أَظْلَمُ مِمَّنِ

Ahmad in the *Musnad of Abu Sa'îd Al-Khudri* (رضي الله عنه) (Vol. 3, Page 83): Narrated Abu Sa'îd Al-Khudri (رضي الله عنه): (While a shepherd was in his herd of sheep), suddenly a wolf attacked a sheep and took it away, the shepherd chased the wolf and took back the sheep, the wolf sat on its tail and addressed the shepherd saying: "Be afraid of Allâh, you have taken the provision from me which Allâh gave me." The shepherd said: "What an amazing thing! A wolf sitting on its tail speaks to me in the language of a human being." The wolf said: "Shall I tell you something more amazing than this? There is Muhammad (صلى الله عليه وسلم) the Messenger of Allâh in Yathrib (Al-Madinah) informing the people about the news of the past." Then the shepherd (after hearing that) proceeded (towards Al-Madinah) driving his sheep till he entered Al-Madinah, cornered his sheep in a place, and came to Allâh's Messenger (صلى الله عليه وسلم) and informed the whole story. Allâh's Messenger (صلى الله عليه وسلم) ordered for the proclamation of a congregational *Salât* (صلاة جامعة), then he (صلى الله عليه وسلم) came out and asked the shepherd to inform the people (about the story), and he informed them. Then Allâh's Messenger (صلى الله عليه وسلم) said: "He (the shepherd) has spoken the truth. By Him (Allâh) in Whose Hand my soul is, the Day of Resurrection will not be established till beasts of prey (سباع) speak to the human beings, and the stick-lash and the shoe-laces of a person speak to him and his thigh informs him about his family as to what happened to them after him.

against Allâh, to lead mankind astray without knowledge. Certainly Allâh guides not the people who are *Zâlimûn* (polytheists and wrongdoers)."

145. Say (O Muhammad صلى الله عليه وسلم): "I find not in that which has been revealed to me anything forbidden to be eaten by one who wishes to eat it, unless it be *Maitah* (a dead animal) or blood poured forth (by slaughtering or the like), or the flesh of swine (pork); for that surely, is impure or impious (unlawful) meat (of an animal) which is slaughtered as a sacrifice for others than Allâh (or has been slaughtered for idols, or on which Allâh's Name has not been mentioned while slaughtering). But whosoever is forced by necessity without wilful disobedience, nor transgressing due limits; (for him) certainly, your Lord is Oft-Forgiving, Most Merciful."

146. And unto those who are Jews, We forbade every (animal) with undivided hoof, and We forbade them the fat of the ox and the sheep except what adheres to their backs or their entrails, or is mixed up with a bone. Thus We recompensed them for their rebellion [committing crimes like murdering the Prophets, eating of *Ribâ* (usury)]. And verily, We are Truthful.

147. If they (Jews) belie you (Muhammad صلى الله عليه وسلم) say: "Your Lord is the Owner of Vast Mercy, and never will His Wrath be turned back from the people who are *Mujrimûn* (criminals, polytheists, sinners)."

148. Those who took partners (in worship) with Allâh will say: "If Allâh had willed, we would not have taken partners (in worship) with Him, nor would our fathers, and we would not have forbidden anything (against His Will)." Likewise belied those who were before them, (they argued falsely with Allâh's Messengers), till they tasted Our Wrath. Say: "Have you any knowledge (proof) that you can produce before us? Verily, you follow nothing but guess and you do nothing but lie."

سَيَقُولُ ٱلَّذِينَ أَشْرَكُواْ لَوْ شَآءَ ٱللَّهُ مَآ أَشْرَكْنَا وَلَآ ءَابَآؤُنَا وَلَا حَرَّمْنَا مِن شَىْءٍ كَذَٰلِكَ كَذَّبَ ٱلَّذِينَ مِن قَبْلِهِمْ حَتَّىٰ ذَاقُواْ بَأْسَنَا قُلْ هَلْ عِندَكُم مِّنْ عِلْمٍ فَتُخْرِجُوهُ لَنَآ إِن تَتَّبِعُونَ إِلَّا ٱلظَّنَّ وَإِنْ أَنتُمْ إِلَّا تَخْرُصُونَ ۝

149. Say: "With Allâh is the perfect proof and argument, (i.e. the Oneness of Allâh, the sending of His Messengers and His Holy Books, to mankind); had He so willed, He would indeed have guided you all."

قُلْ فَلِلَّهِ ٱلْحُجَّةُ ٱلْبَٰلِغَةُ فَلَوْ شَآءَ لَهَدَىٰكُمْ أَجْمَعِينَ ۝

150. Say: "Bring forward your witnesses, who can testify that Allâh has forbidden this. Then if they testify, testify not you (O Muhammad صلى الله عليه وسلم) with them. And you should not follow the vain desires of such as treat Our *Ayât* (proofs, evidences, verses, lessons, signs, revelations, etc.) as falsehoods, and such as believe not in the Hereafter, and they hold others as equal (in worship) with their Lord."

قُلْ هَلُمَّ شُهَدَآءَكُمُ ٱلَّذِينَ يَشْهَدُونَ أَنَّ ٱللَّهَ حَرَّمَ هَٰذَا فَإِن شَهِدُواْ فَلَا تَشْهَدْ مَعَهُمْ وَلَا تَتَّبِعْ أَهْوَآءَ ٱلَّذِينَ كَذَّبُواْ بِـَٔايَٰتِنَا وَٱلَّذِينَ لَا يُؤْمِنُونَ بِٱلْأَخِرَةِ وَهُم بِرَبِّهِمْ يَعْدِلُونَ ۝

151. Say (O Muhammad صلى الله عليه وسلم) "Come, I will recite what your Lord has prohibited you from: Join not anything in worship with Him; be good and dutiful to your parents; kill not your children because of poverty — We

۞ قُلْ تَعَالَوْاْ أَتْلُ مَا حَرَّمَ رَبُّكُمْ عَلَيْكُمْ أَلَّا تُشْرِكُواْ بِهِ شَيْـًٔا وَبِٱلْوَٰلِدَيْنِ إِحْسَٰنًا وَلَا تَقْتُلُوٓاْ أَوْلَٰدَكُم مِّنْ إِمْلَٰقٍ نَّحْنُ نَرْزُقُكُمْ وَإِيَّاهُمْ

provide sustenance for you and for them; come not near to *Al-Fawâhish* (shameful sins and illegal sexual intercourse) whether committed openly or secretly; and kill not anyone whom Allâh has forbidden, except for a just cause (according to Islâmic law). This He has commanded you that you may understand.

152. "And come not near to the orphan's property, except to improve it, until he (or she) attains the age of full strength; and give full measure and full weight with justice. We burden not any person, but that which he can bear. And whenever you give your word (i.e. judge between men or give evidence), say the truth even if a near relative is concerned, and fulfil the Covenant of Allâh. This He commands you, that you may remember.[1]

153. "And verily, this (i.e. Allâh's Commandments mentioned in the above two Verses 151 and 152) is My straight path, so follow it, and follow not (other) paths, for they will separate you away from His path. This He has ordained for you that you may become *Al-Muttaqûn* (the pious. See V.2:2)."

154. Then, We gave Mûsâ (Moses) the Book [the Taurât (Torah)], to complete (Our Favour) upon those who

---

[1] (V.6:152):

A) See the footnotes of (V.3:130).

B) See the footnote of (V.4:135).

would do right, and explaining all things in detail and a guidance and a mercy that they might believe in the meeting with their Lord.

155. And this is a blessed Book (the Qur'ân) which We have sent down, so follow it and fear Allâh (i.e. do not disobey His Orders), that you may receive mercy (i.e. saved from the torment of Hell).

156. Lest you (pagan Arabs) should say: "The Book was sent down only to two sects before us (the Jews and the Christians), and for our part, we were in fact unaware of what they studied."

157. Or lest you (pagan Arabs) should say: "If only the Book had been sent down to us, we would surely have been better guided than they (Jews and Christians)." So now has come unto you a clear proof (the Qur'ân) from your Lord, and a guidance and a mercy. Who then does more wrong than one who rejects the Ayât (proofs, evidences, verses, lessons, signs, revelations, etc.) of Allâh and turns away therefrom? We shall requite those who turn away from Our Ayât with an evil torment, because of their turning away (from them). [Tafsir At-Tabari]

158. Do they then wait for anything other than that the angels should come to them, or that your Lord (Allâh) should come, or that some of the Signs of your Lord should come (i.e. portents of the Hour e.g., rising of the sun from the west)! The day that some of the Signs of your Lord do come, no good will it do to a person to believe then, if he believed not before, nor earned good (by performing deeds of righteousness) through his Faith. Say: "Wait you! we (too) are waiting."[1]

لَوۡتَكُنۡ ءَامَنَتۡ مِن قَبۡلُ أَوۡ كَسَبَتۡ فِىٓ إِيمَٰنِهَا خَيۡرٗاۗ قُلِ ٱنتَظِرُوٓاْ إِنَّا مُنتَظِرُونَ ١٥٨

159. Verily, those who divide their religion and break up into sects (all kinds of religious sects),[2] you (O

إِنَّ ٱلَّذِينَ فَرَّقُواْ دِينَهُمۡ وَكَانُواْ شِيَعٗا لَّسۡتَ مِنۡهُمۡ فِى شَىۡءٍۚ إِنَّمَآ

[1] (V.6:158):

A) Narrated Abu Hurairah رضى الله عنه: Allâh's Messenger صلى الله عليه وسلم said, "The Hour will not be established until the sun rises from the west; and when the people see it, then whoever will be living on the surface of the earth, will have faith, and that is (the time) when no good will it do to a person to believe then, if he believed not before." (6:158) (Sahih Al-Bukhâri, Vol.6, Hadith No.159).

B) Narrated Abu Hurairah رضى الله عنه: Allâh's Messenger صلى الله عليه وسلم said; "When the following three signs appear, no good will it do to a person to believe then if he believed not before:

1) Rising of the sun from the west.

2) (The coming of Al-Masîh) Ad-Dajjâl.

3) (The coming out of the) Dâbbat-ul-Ard (i.e. a beast from the earth)."

[Sahih Muslim — The Book of Fitan — The Signs of the coming of the Hour].

C) Narrated Anas رضى الله عنه: The Prophet صلى الله عليه وسلم said, "No Prophet was sent but that he warned his followers against the one-eyed liar (Al-Masîh Ad-Dajjâl). Beware! He is blind in one eye, and your Lord is not so, and there will be written between his (Al-Masîh Ad-Dajjâl's) eyes (the word) Kâfir (i.e., disbeliever)." [This Hadîth is also quoted by Abu Hurairah and Ibn 'Abbâs. (Sahih Al-Bukhâri, Vol. 9, Hadîth No. 245)].

[2] (V.6:159) It is said that the Prophet صلى الله عليه وسلم recited this Verse and said: "These people are those who invent new things (Bid'ah) in religion and the followers of the vain desires of this Muslim nation, and their repentance will not be accepted by Allâh." (Tafsir Al-Qurtubi).

Muhammad (صلى الله عليه وسلم) have no concern in them in the least. Their affair is only with Allâh, Who then will tell them what they used to do.

أَمْ هُمْ إِلَى ٱللَّهِ ثُمَّ يُنَبِّئُهُم بِمَا كَانُوا۟ يَعْمَلُونَ ﴿٥٩﴾

160. Whoever brings a good deed (Islâmic Monotheism and deeds of obedience to Allâh and His Messenger (صلى الله عليه وسلم) shall have ten times the like thereof to his credit, and whoever brings an evil deed (polytheism, disbelief, hypocrisy, and deeds of disobedience to Allâh and His Messenger (صلى الله عليه وسلم) shall have only the recompense of the like thereof, and they will not be wronged.[1]

مَن جَآءَ بِٱلْحَسَنَةِ فَلَهُۥ عَشْرُ أَمْثَالِهَا وَمَن جَآءَ بِٱلسَّيِّئَةِ فَلَا يُجْزَىٰٓ إِلَّا مِثْلَهَا وَهُمْ لَا يُظْلَمُونَ ﴿١٦٠﴾

161. Say (O Muhammad صلى الله عليه وسلم): "Truly, my Lord has guided me to a Straight Path, a right religion, the religion of Ibrâhîm (Abraham), Hanîfa [i.e. the true Islâmic Monotheism — to believe in One God (Allâh i.e. to worship none but Allâh, Alone)] and he was not of Al-Mushrikûn (See V.2:105)."

قُلْ إِنَّنِي هَدَىٰنِي رَبِّي إِلَىٰ صِرَٰطٍ مُّسْتَقِيمٍ دِينًا قِيَمًا مِّلَّةَ إِبْرَٰهِيمَ حَنِيفًا وَمَا كَانَ مِنَ ٱلْمُشْرِكِينَ ﴿١٦١﴾

162. Say (O Muhammad صلى الله عليه وسلم): "Verily, my Salât (prayer), my sacrifice, my living, and my dying are for Allâh, the Lord of the 'Âlamîn (mankind, jinn and all that exists).

قُلْ إِنَّ صَلَاتِي وَنُسُكِي وَمَحْيَايَ وَمَمَاتِي لِلَّهِ رَبِّ ٱلْعَٰلَمِينَ ﴿١٦٢﴾

[It has been narrated in the *Hadîth* Books (*At-Tirmidhî, Ibn Mâjah* and *Abu Dâwûd*) that the Prophet صلى الله عليه وسلم said: "The Jews and the Christians will be divided into seventy-one or seventy-two religious sects and this nation will be divided into seventy-three religious sects, — all in Hell, except one, and that one is: on which I and my Companions are today, i.e. following the Qur'ân and the Prophet's *Sunnah* (legal ways, orders, acts of worship, statements)"].

[1] (V.6:160) See the footnote of (V.6:61).

163. "He has no partner. And of this I have been commanded, and I am the first of the Muslims."

لَا شَرِيكَ لَهُۥ وَبِذَٰلِكَ أُمِرۡتُ وَأَنَا۠ أَوَّلُ ٱلۡمُسۡلِمِينَ ۝

164. Say: "Shall I seek a lord other than Allâh, while He is the Lord of all things? No person earns any (sin) except against himself (only), and no bearer of burdens shall bear the burden of another. Then unto your Lord is your return, so He will tell you that wherein you have been differing."

قُلۡ أَغَيۡرَ ٱللَّهِ أَبۡغِي رَبًّا وَهُوَ رَبُّ كُلِّ شَيۡءٍ وَلَا تَكۡسِبُ كُلُّ نَفۡسٍ إِلَّا عَلَيۡهَا وَلَا تَزِرُ وَازِرَةٌ وِزۡرَ أُخۡرَىٰ ثُمَّ إِلَىٰ رَبِّكُم مَّرۡجِعُكُمۡ فَيُنَبِّئُكُم بِمَا كُنتُمۡ فِيهِ تَخۡتَلِفُونَ ۝

165. And it is He Who has made you generations coming after generations, replacing each other on the earth. And He has raised you in ranks, some above others that He may try you in that which He has bestowed on you. Surely, your Lord is Swift in retribution, and certainly He is Oft-Forgiving, Most Merciful.

وَهُوَ ٱلَّذِي جَعَلَكُمۡ خَلَٰٓئِفَ ٱلۡأَرۡضِ وَرَفَعَ بَعۡضَكُمۡ فَوۡقَ بَعۡضٍ دَرَجَٰتٍ لِّيَبۡلُوَكُمۡ فِي مَآ ءَاتَىٰكُمۡ إِنَّ رَبَّكَ سَرِيعُ ٱلۡعِقَابِ وَإِنَّهُۥ لَغَفُورٌ رَّحِيمٌۢ ۝

Sûrat Al-A'râf [The Heights (or The Wall with Elevations)] VII

سُورَةُ ٱلۡأَعۡرَافِ

In the Name of Allâh the Most Gracious, the Most Merciful

بِسۡمِ ٱللَّهِ ٱلرَّحۡمَٰنِ ٱلرَّحِيمِ

1. *Alif-Lâm-Mîm-Sâd.* [These letters are one of the miracles of the Qur'ân and none but Allâh (Alone) knows their meanings.]

المٓصٓ ۝

2. (This is the) Book (the Qur'ân) sent down unto you (O Muhammad صلى الله عليه وسلم), so let not your breast be narrow therefrom, that you warn thereby; and a reminder unto the believers.

كِتَٰبٌ أُنزِلَ إِلَيۡكَ فَلَا يَكُن فِي صَدۡرِكَ حَرَجٌ مِّنۡهُ لِتُنذِرَ بِهِۦ وَذِكۡرَىٰ لِلۡمُؤۡمِنِينَ ۝

3. [Say (O Muhammad صلى الله عليه وسلم) to these idolaters (pagan Arabs) of your

ٱتَّبِعُوا۟ مَآ أُنزِلَ إِلَيۡكُم مِّن رَّبِّكُمۡ

folk:] Follow what has been sent down unto you from your Lord (the Qur'ân and Prophet Muhammad's *Sunnah*), and follow not any *Auliyâ'* (protectors and helpers who order you to associate partners in worship with Allâh, besides Him (Allâh). Little do you remember!

وَلَا تَتَّبِعُوا مِن دُونِهِ أَوْلِيَآءَ قَلِيلًا مَّا تَذَكَّرُونَ ۝

4. And a great number of towns (their population) We destroyed (for their crimes). Our torment came upon them (suddenly) by night or while they were taking their midday nap.

وَكَم مِّن قَرْيَةٍ أَهْلَكْنَٰهَا فَجَآءَهَا بَأْسُنَا بَيَٰتًا أَوْ هُمْ قَآئِلُونَ ۝

5. No cry did they utter when Our Torment came upon them but this: "Verily, we were *Zâlimûn* (polytheists and wrongdoers)".

فَمَا كَانَ دَعْوَىٰهُمْ إِذْ جَآءَهُم بَأْسُنَآ إِلَّآ أَن قَالُوٓا۟ إِنَّا كُنَّا ظَٰلِمِينَ ۝

6. Then surely, We shall question those (people) to whom it (the Book) was sent and verily, We shall question the Messengers.

فَلَنَسْـَٔلَنَّ ٱلَّذِينَ أُرْسِلَ إِلَيْهِمْ وَلَنَسْـَٔلَنَّ ٱلْمُرْسَلِينَ ۝

7. Then surely, We shall narrate unto them (their whole story) with knowledge, and indeed We have not been absent.

فَلَنَقُصَّنَّ عَلَيْهِم بِعِلْمٍ وَمَا كُنَّا غَآئِبِينَ ۝

8. And the weighing on that day (Day of Resurrection) will be the true (weighing).[1] So as for those whose

وَٱلْوَزْنُ يَوْمَئِذٍ ٱلْحَقُّ فَمَن ثَقُلَتْ مَوَٰزِينُهُ فَأُو۟لَٰٓئِكَ

---

[1] (V.7:8) The Statement of Allâh عز وجل:

"And We shall set up Balances of justice on the Day of Resurrection." (V.21:47).

The deeds and the statement of Adam's offspring will be weighed.

Narrated Abu Hurairah رضي الله عنه: The Prophet صلى الله عليه وسلم said, "(There are) two words (expressions or sayings) which are dear to the Most Gracious (Allâh) and very easy for the tongue to say, but

Scale (of good deeds) will be heavy, they will be the successful (by entering Paradise).

9. And as for those whose scale will be light, they are those who will lose their ownselves (by entering Hell) because they denied and rejected Our *Ayât* (proofs, evidences, verses, lessons, signs, revelations, etc.).

10. And surely, We gave you authority on the earth and appointed for you therein provisions (for your life). Little thanks do you give.

11. And surely, We created you (your father Adam) and then gave you shape (the noble shape of a human being); then We told the angels, "Prostrate yourselves to Adam", and they prostrated themselves, except *Iblîs* (Satan), he refused to be of those who prostrated themselves.

12. (Allâh) said: "What prevented you (O *Iblîs*) that you did not prostrate yourself, when I commanded you?" *Iblîs* said: "I am better than him

---

very heavy in the Balance. They are:

سبحان الله و بحمده ── سبحان الله العظيم

‘Subhân Allâhi-wa bihamdihi — Subhân Allâhil-'Azîm.’ " * (*Sahih Al-Bukhâri*, Vol.9, *Hadîth* No.652).

* ‘Glorified is Allâh and praised is He’ — ‘Glorified is Allâh, the Most Great.’ (or I deem Allâh above all those unsuitable things ascribed to Him, and free Him from resembling anything whatsoever, and I glorify His Praises! I deem Allâh, the Most Great above all those unsuitable things ascribed to Him and free Him from resembling anything whatsoever.

(Adam), You created me from fire, and him You created from clay."

وَخَلَقْتَهُ مِن طِينٍ ۝

13. (Allâh) said: "(O *Iblîs*) get down from this (Paradise), it is not for you to be arrogant here. Get out, for you are of those humiliated and disgraced."

قَالَ فَٱهۡبِطۡ مِنۡهَا فَمَا يَكُونُ لَكَ أَن تَتَكَبَّرَ فِيهَا فَٱخۡرُجۡ إِنَّكَ مِنَ ٱلصَّٰغِرِينَ ۝

14. (Iblîs) said: "Allow me respite till the Day they are raised up (i.e. the Day of Resurrection)."

قَالَ أَنظِرۡنِىٓ إِلَىٰ يَوۡمِ يُبۡعَثُونَ ۝

15. (Allâh) said: "You are of those respited."

قَالَ إِنَّكَ مِنَ ٱلۡمُنظَرِينَ ۝

16. (Iblîs) said: "Because You have sent me astray, surely, I will sit in wait against them (human beings) on Your straight path.

قَالَ فَبِمَآ أَغۡوَيۡتَنِى لَأَقۡعُدَنَّ لَهُمۡ صِرَٰطَكَ ٱلۡمُسۡتَقِيمَ ۝

17. "Then I will come to them from before them and behind them, from their right and from their left, and You will not find most of them as thankful ones (i.e. they will not be dutiful to You)."

ثُمَّ لَأَتِيَنَّهُم مِّنۢ بَيۡنِ أَيۡدِيهِمۡ وَمِنۡ خَلۡفِهِمۡ وَعَنۡ أَيۡمَٰنِهِمۡ وَعَن شَمَآئِلِهِمۡ وَلَا تَجِدُ أَكۡثَرَهُمۡ شَٰكِرِينَ ۝

18. (Allâh) said (to Iblîs): "Get out from this (Paradise) disgraced and expelled. Whoever of them (mankind) will follow you, then surely, I will fill Hell with you all."

قَالَ ٱخۡرُجۡ مِنۡهَا مَذۡءُومٗا مَّدۡحُورٗا لَّمَن تَبِعَكَ مِنۡهُمۡ لَأَمۡلَأَنَّ جَهَنَّمَ مِنكُمۡ أَجۡمَعِينَ ۝

19. "And O Adam! Dwell you and your wife in Paradise, and eat thereof as you both wish, but approach not this tree otherwise you both will be of the *Zâlimûn* (unjust and wrongdoers)."

وَيَٰٓـَٔادَمُ ٱسۡكُنۡ أَنتَ وَزَوۡجُكَ ٱلۡجَنَّةَ فَكُلَا مِنۡ حَيۡثُ شِئۡتُمَا وَلَا تَقۡرَبَا هَٰذِهِ ٱلشَّجَرَةَ فَتَكُونَا مِنَ ٱلظَّٰلِمِينَ ۝

20. Then *Shaitân* (Satan) whispered suggestions to them both in order to uncover that which was hidden from them of their private parts (before); he

فَوَسۡوَسَ لَهُمَا ٱلشَّيۡطَٰنُ لِيُبۡدِيَ لَهُمَا مَا وُۥرِيَ عَنۡهُمَا مِن سَوۡءَٰتِهِمَا

said: "Your Lord did not forbid you this tree save you should become angels or become of the immortals."

21. And he [*Shaitân* (Satan)] swore by Allâh to them both (saying): "Verily, I am one of the sincere well-wishers for you both."

22. So he misled them with deception. Then when they tasted of the tree, that which was hidden from them of their shame (private parts) became manifest to them and they began to cover themselves with the leaves of Paradise (in order to cover their shame). And their Lord called out to them (saying): "Did I not forbid you that tree and tell you: Verily, *Shaitân* (Satan) is an open enemy unto you?"

23. They said: "Our Lord! We have wronged ourselves. If You forgive us not, and bestow not upon us Your Mercy, we shall certainly be of the losers."

24. (Allâh) said: "Get down, one of you an enemy to the other [i.e. Adam, Hawwâ (Eve), and *Shaitân* (Satan)]. On earth will be a dwelling-place for you and an enjoyment for a time."

25. He said: "Therein you shall live, and therein you shall die, and from it you shall be brought out (i.e. resurrected)."

26. O Children of Adam! We have bestowed raiment upon you to cover yourselves (screen your private parts) and as an adornment; and the raiment of righteousness, that is better. Such are among the *Ayât* (proofs, evidences, verses, lessons, signs, revelations, etc.) of Allâh, that they may remember (i.e. leave falsehood and follow truth[1]).

27. O Children of Adam! Let not *Shaitân* (Satan) deceive you, as he got your parents [Adam and Hawwâ (Eve)] out of Paradise, stripping them of their raiments, to show them their private parts. Verily, he and *Qabîluhu* (his soldiers from the jinn or his tribe) see you from where you cannot see them. Verily, We made the *Shayâtîn* (devils) *Auliyâ'* (protectors and helpers) for those who believe not.

28. And when they commit a *Fâhisha* (evil deed, going round the *Ka'bah* in naked state, every kind of unlawful sexual intercourse), they say: "We found our fathers doing it, and Allâh has commanded it on us." Say: "Nay, Allâh never commands *Fâhisha*. Do you say of Allâh what you know not?"

29. Say (O Muhammad صلى الله عليه وسلم): My Lord has commanded justice and (said) that you should face Him only (i.e. worship none but Allâh and face

---

[1] (V.7:26) It is said that the pagan Arabs in the Pre-Islâmic Period of Ignorance used to do *Tawâf* (going round) of the *Ka'bah* in a naked state. So when Islâm became victorious and Makkah was conquered, the pagans and the polytheists were forbidden to enter Makkah, and none was allowed to do *Tawâf* of the *Ka'bah* in a naked state.

the *Qiblah*, i.e. the *Ka'bah* at Makkah during prayers) in every place of worship, in prayers (and not to face other false deities and idols), and invoke Him only making your religion sincere to Him (by not joining in worship any partner with Him and with the intention that you are doing your deeds for Allâh's sake only). As He brought you (into being) in the beginning, so shall you be brought into being [on the Day of Resurrection in two groups, one as a blessed one (believers), and the other as a wretched one (disbelievers)].

وَادْعُوهُ مُخْلِصِينَ لَهُ ٱلدِّينَ كَمَا بَدَأَكُمْ تَعُودُونَ ٢٩

30. A group He has guided, and a group deserved to be in error; (because) surely, they took the *Shayâtîn* (devils) as *Auliyâ'* (protectors and helpers) instead of Allâh, and think that they are guided.

فَرِيقًا هَدَىٰ وَفَرِيقًا حَقَّ عَلَيْهِمُ ٱلضَّلَـٰلَةُ إِنَّهُمُ ٱتَّخَذُواْ ٱلشَّيَـٰطِينَ أَوْلِيَآءَ مِن دُونِ ٱللَّهِ وَيَحْسَبُونَ أَنَّهُم مُّهْتَدُونَ ٣٠

31. O Children of Adam! Take your adornment (by wearing your clean clothes), while praying[1] and going

۞ يَـٰبَنِىٓ ءَادَمَ خُذُواْ زِينَتَكُمْ عِندَ كُلِّ مَسْجِدٍ وَكُلُواْ وَٱشْرَبُواْ

---

[1] (V.7:31) It is obligatory to wear the clothes while praying. And the Statement of Allâh عزوجل: "Take your adornment [(by wearing your clean clothes) covering completely the *'Aurah* (covering of one's *'Aurah* means: while praying, a male must cover himself with clothes from umbilicus of his abdomen up to his knees, and it is better that his both shoulders should be covered. And a female must cover all her body and feet except face, and it is better that both her hands are also covered)], while praying and going round (the *Tawâf* of) the *Ka'bah*."

In how many (what sort of) clothes a woman should pray 'Ikrimah said, "If she can cover all her body with one garment, it is sufficient."*

* It is agreed by the majority of the religious scholars that a woman while praying should cover herself completely except her face, and

round (the *Tawâf* of) the *Ka'bah*, and eat and drink but waste not by extravagance, certainly He (Allâh) likes not *Al-Musrifûn* (those who waste by extravagance).

32. Say (O Muhammad صلى الله عليه وسلم): "Who has forbidden the adornment with clothes given by Allâh, which He has produced for His slaves, and *At-Tayyibât* [all kinds of *Halâl* (lawful) things] of food?" Say: "They are, in the life of this world, for those who believe, (and) exclusively for them (believers) on the Day of Resurrection (the disbelievers will not share them)." Thus We explain the *Ayât* (Islâmic laws) in detail for people who have knowledge.

33. Say (O Muhammad صلى الله عليه وسلم): "(But) the things that my Lord has indeed forbidden are *Al-Fawâhish* (great evil sins, every kind of unlawful sexual intercourse) whether committed openly or secretly, sins (of all kinds), unrighteous oppression, joining partners (in worship) with Allâh for which He has given no authority, and

---

it is better that she should cover her hands with gloves or cloth, but her feet must be covered either with a long dress or she must wear socks to cover her feet. This verdict is based on the Prophet's statement (*Abu Dâwûd*).

Narrated 'Âishah رضي الله عنها: Allâh's Messenger صلى الله عليه وسلم used to offer the *Fajr* prayer and some believing women covered with their veiling sheets used to attend the *Fajr* prayer with him, and then they would return to their homes unrecognized. (*Sahih Al-Bukhâri*, Vol.1, *Hadîth* No. 368).

saying things about Allâh of which you have no knowledge."

34. And every nation has its appointed term; when their term comes, neither can they delay it nor can they advance it an hour (or a moment).

35. O Children of Adam! If there come to you Messengers from amongst you, reciting to you My Verses, then whosoever becomes pious and righteous, on them shall be no fear nor shall they grieve.

36. But those who reject Our *Ayât* (proofs, evidences, verses, lessons, signs, revelations, etc.) and treat them with arrogance, they are the dwellers of the (Hell) Fire, they will abide therein forever.

37. Who is more unjust than one who invents a lie against Allâh or rejects His *Ayât* (proofs, evidences, verses, lessons, signs, revelations, etc.)? For such their appointed portion (good things of this worldly life and their period of stay therein) will reach them from the Book (of Decrees) until when Our Messengers (the angel of death and his assistants) come to them to take their souls, they (the angels) will say: "Where are those whom you used to invoke and worship besides Allâh," they will reply, "They have vanished and deserted us." And they will bear witness against themselves, that they were disbelievers.

38. (Allâh) will say: "Enter you in the company of nations who passed away before you, of men and jinn, into the Fire." Every time a new nation enters, it curses its sister nation (that went before) until they reach all together in the Fire. The last of them will say to the first of them: "Our Lord! These misled us, so give them a double torment of the Fire." He will say: "For each one there is double (torment), but you know not."

39. The first of them will say to the last of them: "You were not better than us, so taste the torment for what you used to earn."

40. Verily, those who belie Our *Ayât* (proofs, evidences, verses, lessons, signs, revelations, etc.) and treat them with arrogance, for them the gates of heaven will not be opened, and they will not enter Paradise until the camel goes through the eye of the needle (which is impossible). Thus do We recompense the *Mujrimûn* (criminals, polytheists, sinners).

41. Theirs will be a bed of Hell (Fire), and over them coverings (of Hell-fire). Thus do We recompense the *Zâlimûn* (polytheists and wrongdoers).

42. But those who believed (in the Oneness of Allâh — Islâmic Monotheism), and worked righteousness — We tax not any person beyond his scope — such are the dwellers of Paradise. They will abide therein.

قَالَ ادْخُلُوا فِىٓ أُمَمٍ قَدْ خَلَتْ مِن قَبْلِكُم مِّنَ ٱلْجِنِّ وَٱلْإِنسِ فِى ٱلنَّارِ كُلَّمَا دَخَلَتْ أُمَّةٌ لَّعَنَتْ أُخْتَهَا حَتَّىٰٓ إِذَا ٱدَّارَكُوا۟ فِيهَا جَمِيعًا قَالَتْ أُخْرَىٰهُمْ لِأُولَىٰهُمْ رَبَّنَا هَٰٓؤُلَآءِ أَضَلُّونَا فَـَٔاتِهِمْ عَذَابًا ضِعْفًا مِّنَ ٱلنَّارِ قَالَ لِكُلٍّ ضِعْفٌ وَلَٰكِن لَّا تَعْلَمُونَ ﴿٣٨﴾

وَقَالَتْ أُولَىٰهُمْ لِأُخْرَىٰهُمْ فَمَا كَانَ لَكُمْ عَلَيْنَا مِن فَضْلٍ فَذُوقُوا۟ ٱلْعَذَابَ بِمَا كُنتُمْ تَكْسِبُونَ ﴿٣٩﴾

إِنَّ ٱلَّذِينَ كَذَّبُوا۟ بِـَٔايَٰتِنَا وَٱسْتَكْبَرُوا۟ عَنْهَا لَا تُفَتَّحُ لَهُمْ أَبْوَٰبُ ٱلسَّمَآءِ وَلَا يَدْخُلُونَ ٱلْجَنَّةَ حَتَّىٰ يَلِجَ ٱلْجَمَلُ فِى سَمِّ ٱلْخِيَاطِ وَكَذَٰلِكَ نَجْزِى ٱلْمُجْرِمِينَ ﴿٤٠﴾

لَهُم مِّن جَهَنَّمَ مِهَادٌ وَمِن فَوْقِهِمْ غَوَاشٍ وَكَذَٰلِكَ نَجْزِى ٱلظَّٰلِمِينَ ﴿٤١﴾

وَٱلَّذِينَ ءَامَنُوا۟ وَعَمِلُوا۟ ٱلصَّٰلِحَٰتِ لَا نُكَلِّفُ نَفْسًا إِلَّا وُسْعَهَآ أُو۟لَٰٓئِكَ أَصْحَٰبُ ٱلْجَنَّةِ هُمْ فِيهَا خَٰلِدُونَ ﴿٤٢﴾

43. And We shall remove from their breasts any (mutual) hatred or sense of injury (which they had, if at all, in the life of this world); rivers flowing under them, and they will say: "All the praises and thanks be to Allâh, Who has guided us to this, and never could we have found guidance, were it not that Allâh had guided us! Indeed, the Messengers of our Lord did come with the truth." And it will be cried out to them: "This is the Paradise which you have inherited for what you used to do."

وَنَزَعْنَا مَا فِي صُدُورِهِم مِّنْ غِلٍّ تَجْرِي مِن تَحْتِهِمُ الْأَنْهَارُ وَقَالُوا الْحَمْدُ لِلَّهِ الَّذِي هَدَانَا لِهَٰذَا وَمَا كُنَّا لِنَهْتَدِيَ لَوْلَا أَنْ هَدَانَا اللَّهُ لَقَدْ جَاءَتْ رُسُلُ رَبِّنَا بِالْحَقِّ وَنُودُوا أَن تِلْكُمُ الْجَنَّةُ أُورِثْتُمُوهَا بِمَا كُنتُمْ تَعْمَلُونَ ۝

44. And the dwellers of Paradise will call out to the dwellers of the Fire (saying): "We have indeed found true what our Lord had promised us; have you also found true what your Lord promised (warned)?" They shall say: "Yes." Then a crier will proclaim between them: "The Curse of Allâh is on the *Zâlimûn* (polytheists and wrongdoers)."

وَنَادَىٰ أَصْحَٰبُ الْجَنَّةِ أَصْحَٰبَ النَّارِ أَن قَدْ وَجَدْنَا مَا وَعَدَنَا رَبُّنَا حَقًّا فَهَلْ وَجَدتُّم مَّا وَعَدَ رَبُّكُمْ حَقًّا قَالُوا نَعَمْ فَأَذَّنَ مُؤَذِّنٌ بَيْنَهُمْ أَن لَّعْنَةُ اللَّهِ عَلَى الظَّٰلِمِينَ ۝

45. Those who hindered (men) from the path of Allâh, and would seek to make it crooked, and they were disbelievers in the Hereafter.

الَّذِينَ يَصُدُّونَ عَن سَبِيلِ اللَّهِ وَيَبْغُونَهَا عِوَجًا وَهُم بِالْآخِرَةِ كَٰفِرُونَ ۝

46. And between them will be a (barrier) screen and on *Al-A'râf* (a wall with elevated places) will be men (whose good and evil deeds would be equal in scale), who would recognise all (of the Paradise and Hell people), by their marks (the dwellers of Paradise by their white faces and the dwellers of Hell by their black faces) they will call

وَبَيْنَهُمَا حِجَابٌ وَعَلَى الْأَعْرَافِ رِجَالٌ يَعْرِفُونَ كُلًّۢا بِسِيمَٰهُمْ وَنَادَوْا أَصْحَٰبَ الْجَنَّةِ أَن سَلَٰمٌ عَلَيْكُمْ لَمْ يَدْخُلُوهَا وَهُمْ يَطْمَعُونَ ۝

out to the dwellers of Paradise, "*Salâmun 'Alaikûm*" (peace be on you), and at that time they (men on Al-A'râf) will not yet have entered it (Paradise), but they will hope to enter (it) with certainty.

47. And when their eyes will be turned towards the dwellers of the Fire, they will say: "Our Lord! Place us not with the people who are *Zâlimûn* (polytheists and wrongdoers)."

وَإِذَا صُرِفَتْ أَبْصَـٰرُهُمْ تِلْقَآءَ أَصْحَـٰبِ ٱلنَّارِ قَالُواْ رَبَّنَا لَا تَجْعَلْنَا مَعَ ٱلْقَوْمِ ٱلظَّـٰلِمِينَ ٤٧

48. And the men on Al-A'râf[1] (the wall) will call unto the men whom they would recognise by their marks, saying: "Of what benefit to you were your great numbers (and hoards of wealth), and your arrogance (against Faith)?"

وَنَادَىٰٓ أَصْحَـٰبُ ٱلْأَعْرَافِ رِجَالًا يَعْرِفُونَهُم بِسِيمَـٰهُمْ قَالُواْ مَآ أَغْنَىٰ عَنكُمْ جَمْعُكُمْ وَمَا كُنتُمْ تَسْتَكْبِرُونَ ٤٨

49. Are they those, of whom you swore that Allâh would never show them mercy. (Behold! It has been said to them): "Enter Paradise, no fear shall be on you, nor shall you grieve."

أَهَـٰٓؤُلَآءِ ٱلَّذِينَ أَقْسَمْتُمْ لَا يَنَالُهُمُ ٱللَّهُ بِرَحْمَةٍ ٱدْخُلُواْ ٱلْجَنَّةَ لَا خَوْفٌ عَلَيْكُمْ وَلَآ أَنتُمْ تَحْزَنُونَ ٤٩

50. And the dwellers of the Fire will call to the dwellers of Paradise: "Pour on us some water or anything that Allâh has provided you with." They will say: "Both (water and provision) Allâh has forbidden to the disbelievers."

وَنَادَىٰٓ أَصْحَـٰبُ ٱلنَّارِ أَصْحَـٰبَ ٱلْجَنَّةِ أَنْ أَفِيضُواْ عَلَيْنَا مِنَ ٱلْمَآءِ أَوْ مِمَّا رَزَقَكُمُ ٱللَّهُ قَالُوٓاْ إِنَّ ٱللَّهَ حَرَّمَهُمَا عَلَى ٱلْكَـٰفِرِينَ ٥٠

51. "Who took their religion as an amusement and play, and the life of the world deceived them." So this Day We

ٱلَّذِينَ ٱتَّخَذُواْ دِينَهُمْ لَهْوًا

---

[1] (V.7:48)

Al-A'râf: It is said that it is a wall between Paradise and Hell and it has on it elevated places. [Please see *Tafsir Al-Qurtubi* (for details)].

shall forget them as they forgot their meeting of this Day, and as they used to reject Our *Ayât* (proofs, evidences, verses, lessons, signs, revelations, etc.).

52. Certainly, We have brought to them a Book (the Qur'ân) which We have explained in detail with knowledge, — a guidance and a mercy to a people who believe.

53. Await they just for the final fulfillment of the event? On the Day the event is finally fulfilled (i.e. the Day of Resurrection), those who neglected it before will say: "Verily, the Messengers of our Lord did come with the truth, now are there any intercessors for us that they might intercede on our behalf? Or could we be sent back (to the first life of the world) so that we might do (good) deeds other than those (evil) deeds which we used to do?" Verily, they have lost their ownselves (i.e. destroyed themselves) and that which they used to fabricate (invoking and worshipping others besides Allâh) has gone away from them.

54. Indeed your Lord is Allâh, Who created the heavens and the earth in Six Days, and then He rose over (*Istawâ*) the Throne (really in a manner that suits His Majesty). He brings the night as a cover over the day, seeking it rapidly, and (He created) the sun, the moon, the stars subjected to His Command. Surely, His is the Creation and Commandment. Blessed is Allâh, the

Lord of the *'Âlamîn* (mankind, jinn and all that exists)!

55. Invoke your Lord with humility and in secret. He likes not the aggressors.

56. And do not do mischief on the earth, after it has been set in order, and invoke Him with fear and hope, Surely, Allâh's Mercy is (ever) near unto the good-doers.

57. And it is He Who sends the winds as heralds of glad tidings, going before His Mercy (rain). Till when they have carried a heavy-laden cloud, We drive it to a land that is dead, then We cause water (rain) to descend thereon. Then We produce every kind of fruit therewith. Similarly, We shall raise up the dead, so that you may remember or take heed.

58. The vegetation of a good land comes forth (easily) by the Permission of its Lord; and that which is bad, brings forth nothing but (a little) with difficulty. Thus do We explain variously the *Ayât* (proofs, evidences, verses, lessons, signs, revelations, etc.) for a people who give thanks.

59. Indeed, We sent Nûh (Noah) to his people and he said: "O my people! Worship • Allâh! You have no other *Ilâh* (God) but Him. (*Lâ ilâha illallâh:* none has the right to be worshipped but Allâh). Certainly, I fear for you the torment of a Great Day!"

60. The leaders of his people said: "Verily, we see you in plain error."

قَالَ ٱلْمَلَأُ مِن قَوْمِهِۦ إِنَّا لَنَرَىٰكَ فِى ضَلَٰلٍ مُّبِينٍ ۝

61. [Nûh (Noah)] said: "O my people! There is no error in me, but I am a Messenger from the Lord of the 'Âlamîn (mankind, jinn and all that exists)!

قَالَ يَٰقَوْمِ لَيْسَ بِى ضَلَٰلَةٌ وَلَٰكِنِّى رَسُولٌ مِّن رَّبِّ ٱلْعَٰلَمِينَ ۝

62. "I convey unto you the Messages of my Lord and give sincere advice to you. And I know from Allâh what you know not.

أُبَلِّغُكُمْ رِسَٰلَٰتِ رَبِّى وَأَنصَحُ لَكُمْ وَأَعْلَمُ مِنَ ٱللَّهِ مَا لَا تَعْلَمُونَ ۝

63. "Do you wonder that there has come to you a Reminder from your Lord through a man from amongst you, that he may warn you, so that you may fear Allâh and that you may receive (His) Mercy?"

أَوَعَجِبْتُمْ أَن جَآءَكُمْ ذِكْرٌ مِّن رَّبِّكُمْ عَلَىٰ رَجُلٍ مِّنكُمْ لِيُنذِرَكُمْ وَلِتَتَّقُوا وَلَعَلَّكُمْ تُرْحَمُونَ ۝

64. But they belied him, so We saved him and those along with him in the ship, and We drowned those who belied Our Ayât (proofs, evidences, verses, lessons, signs, revelations, etc.). They were indeed a blind people.

فَكَذَّبُوهُ فَأَنجَيْنَٰهُ وَٱلَّذِينَ مَعَهُۥ فِى ٱلْفُلْكِ وَأَغْرَقْنَا ٱلَّذِينَ كَذَّبُوا بِـَٔايَٰتِنَا إِنَّهُمْ كَانُوا قَوْمًا عَمِينَ ۝

65. And to 'Âd (people, We sent) their brother Hûd. He said: "O my people! Worship Allâh! You have no other Ilâh (God) but Him. (Lâ ilâha illallâh: none has the right to be worshipped but Allâh). Will you not fear (Allâh)?"

۞ وَإِلَىٰ عَادٍ أَخَاهُمْ هُودًا قَالَ يَٰقَوْمِ ٱعْبُدُوا ٱللَّهَ مَا لَكُم مِّنْ إِلَٰهٍ غَيْرُهُۥ أَفَلَا تَتَّقُونَ ۝

66. The leaders of those who disbelieved among his people said: "Verily, we see you in foolishness, and verily, we think you are one of the liars."

قَالَ ٱلْمَلَأُ ٱلَّذِينَ كَفَرُوا مِن قَوْمِهِۦ إِنَّا لَنَرَىٰكَ فِى سَفَاهَةٍ وَإِنَّا لَنَظُنُّكَ مِنَ ٱلْكَٰذِبِينَ ۝

67. (Hûd) said: "O my people! There is no foolishness in me, but (I am) a Messenger from the Lord of the 'Âlamîn (mankind, jinn and all that exists)!

قَالَ يَـٰقَوْمِ لَيْسَ بِي سَفَاهَةٌ وَلَـٰكِنِّي رَسُولٌ مِّن رَّبِّ ٱلْعَـٰلَمِينَ ٦٧

68. "I convey unto you the Messages of my Lord, and I am a trustworthy adviser (or well-wisher) for you.

أُبَلِّغُكُمْ رِسَـٰلَـٰتِ رَبِّي وَأَنَا۠ لَكُمْ نَاصِحٌ أَمِينٌ ٦٨

69. "Do you wonder that there has come to you a Reminder (and an advice) from your Lord through a man from amongst you to warn you? And remember that He made you successors after the people of Nûh (Noah) and increased you amply in stature. So remember the graces (bestowed upon you) from Allâh so that you may be successful."

أَوَعَجِبْتُمْ أَن جَآءَكُمْ ذِكْرٌ مِّن رَّبِّكُمْ عَلَىٰ رَجُلٍ مِّنكُمْ لِيُنذِرَكُمْ وَٱذْكُرُوٓاْ إِذْ جَعَلَكُمْ خُلَفَآءَ مِنۢ بَعْدِ قَوْمِ نُوحٍ وَزَادَكُمْ فِي ٱلْخَلْقِ بَصۜطَةً فَٱذْكُرُوٓاْ ءَالَآءَ ٱللَّهِ لَعَلَّكُمْ تُفْلِحُونَ ٦٩

70. They said: "You have come to us that we should worship Allâh Alone and forsake that which our fathers used to worship. So bring us that wherewith you have threatened us if you are of the truthful."

قَالُوٓاْ أَجِئْتَنَا لِنَعْبُدَ ٱللَّهَ وَحْدَهُ وَنَذَرَ مَا كَانَ يَعْبُدُ ءَابَآؤُنَا فَأْتِنَا بِمَا تَعِدُنَآ إِن كُنتَ مِنَ ٱلصَّـٰدِقِينَ ٧٠

71. (Hûd) said: "Torment and wrath have already fallen on you from your Lord. Dispute you with me over names which you have named — you and your fathers — with no authority from Allâh? Then wait, I am with you among those who wait."

قَالَ قَدْ وَقَعَ عَلَيْكُم مِّن رَّبِّكُمْ رِجْسٌ وَغَضَبٌ أَتُجَـٰدِلُونَنِي فِيٓ أَسْمَآءٍ سَمَّيْتُمُوهَآ أَنتُمْ وَءَابَآؤُكُم مَّآ أَنزَلَ ٱللَّهُ بِهَا مِن سُلْطَـٰنٍ فَٱنتَظِرُوٓاْ إِنِّي مَعَكُم مِّنَ ٱلْمُنتَظِرِينَ ٧١

72. So We saved him and those who were with him by a mercy from Us, and We cut the roots of those who belied Our *Ayât* (proofs, evidences, verses, lessons, signs, revelations, etc.); and they were not believers.

فَأَنجَيْنَـٰهُ وَٱلَّذِينَ مَعَهُۥ بِرَحْمَةٍ مِّنَّا وَقَطَعْنَا دَابِرَ ٱلَّذِينَ كَذَّبُواْ بِـَٔايَـٰتِنَا وَمَا كَانُواْ مُؤْمِنِينَ ٧٢

73. And to Thamûd (people, We sent) their brother Sâlih. He said: "O my people! Worship Allâh! You have no other *Ilâh* (God) but Him. (*Lâ ilâha illallâh*: none has the right to be worshipped but Allâh). Indeed there has come to you a clear sign (the miracle of the coming out of a huge she-camel from the midst of a rock) from your Lord. This she-camel of Allâh is a sign unto you; so you leave her to graze in Allâh's earth, and touch her not with harm, lest a painful torment should seize you.

74. And remember when He made you successors after 'Âd (people) and gave you habitations in the land, you build for yourselves palaces in plains, and carve out homes in the mountains. So remember the graces (bestowed upon you) from Allâh, and do not go about making mischief on the earth."

75. The leaders of those who were arrogant among his people said to those who were counted weak — to such of them as believed: "Know you that Sâlih is one sent from his Lord." They said: "We indeed believe in that with which he has been sent."

76. Those who were arrogant said: "Verily, we disbelieve in that which you believe in."

77. So they killed the she-camel and insolently defied the Commandment of their Lord, and said: "O Sâlih! Bring about your threats if you are indeed one of the Messengers (of Allâh)."

وَإِلَىٰ ثَمُودَ أَخَاهُمْ صَٰلِحًا
قَالَ يَٰقَوْمِ ٱعْبُدُوا۟ ٱللَّهَ مَا
لَكُم مِّنْ إِلَٰهٍ غَيْرُهُۥ قَدْ
جَآءَتْكُم بَيِّنَةٌ مِّن
رَّبِّكُمْ هَٰذِهِۦ نَاقَةُ ٱللَّهِ
لَكُمْ ءَايَةً فَذَرُوهَا تَأْكُلْ
فِىٓ أَرْضِ ٱللَّهِ وَلَا تَمَسُّوهَا بِسُوٓءٍ
فَيَأْخُذَكُمْ عَذَابٌ أَلِيمٌ ٧٣

وَٱذْكُرُوٓا۟ إِذْ جَعَلَكُمْ خُلَفَآءَ
مِنۢ بَعْدِ عَادٍ وَبَوَّأَكُمْ فِى
ٱلْأَرْضِ تَتَّخِذُونَ مِن
سُهُولِهَا قُصُورًا وَتَنْحِتُونَ
ٱلْجِبَالَ بُيُوتًا فَٱذْكُرُوٓا۟
ءَالَآءَ ٱللَّهِ وَلَا تَعْثَوْا۟ فِى ٱلْأَرْضِ
مُفْسِدِينَ ٧٤

قَالَ ٱلْمَلَأُ ٱلَّذِينَ ٱسْتَكْبَرُوا۟
مِن قَوْمِهِۦ لِلَّذِينَ ٱسْتُضْعِفُوا۟
لِمَنْ ءَامَنَ مِنْهُمْ أَتَعْلَمُونَ
أَنَّ صَٰلِحًا مُّرْسَلٌ مِّن رَّبِّهِۦ
قَالُوٓا۟ إِنَّا بِمَآ أُرْسِلَ بِهِۦ
مُؤْمِنُونَ ٧٥

قَالَ ٱلَّذِينَ
ٱسْتَكْبَرُوٓا۟ إِنَّا بِٱلَّذِىٓ
ءَامَنتُم بِهِۦ كَٰفِرُونَ ٧٦

فَعَقَرُوا۟ ٱلنَّاقَةَ وَعَتَوْا۟ عَنْ
أَمْرِ رَبِّهِمْ وَقَالُوا۟ يَٰصَٰلِحُ
ٱئْتِنَا بِمَا تَعِدُنَآ إِن كُنتَ مِنَ

78. So the earthquake seized them, and they lay (dead), prostrate in their homes.

79. Then he (Sâlih) turned from them, and said: "O my people! I have indeed conveyed to you the Message of my Lord, and have given you good advice but you like not good advisers."

80. And (remember) Lût (Lot), when he said to his people: "Do you commit the worst sin such as none preceding you has committed in the *'Âlamîn* (mankind and jinn)?

81. "Verily, you practise your lusts on men instead of women. Nay, but you are a people transgressing beyond bounds (by committing great sins)."

82. And the answer of his people was only that they said: "Drive them out of your town, these are indeed men who want to be pure (from sins)!"

83. Then We saved him and his family, except his wife; she was of those who remained behind (in the torment).

84. And We rained down on them a rain (of stones). Then see what was the end of the *Mujrimûn* (criminals, polytheists, sinners).

85. And to (the people of) Madyan (Midian), (We sent) their brother Shu'aib. He said: "O my people! Worship Allâh! You have no other *Ilâh* (God) but Him. [*Lâ ilâha illallâh* (none has the right to be worshipped but Allâh)]." Verily, a clear proof (sign) from your Lord has come unto you; so give full measure and full weight and wrong not men in their things, and do not do mischief on the earth after it has been set in order, that will be better for you, if you are believers.

86. "And sit not on every road, threatening, and hindering from the Path of Allâh those who believe in Him, and seeking to make it crooked. And remember when you were but few, and He multiplied you. And see what was the end of the *Mufsidûn* (mischief-makers, corrupters, liars).

87. "And if there is a party of you who believes in that with which I have been sent and a party who do not believe, so be patient until Allâh judges between us, and He is the Best of judges."[1]

---

[1] (V.7:87):

A) Narrated 'Abdullâh bin 'Umar رضي الله عنهما Allâh's Messenger صلى الله عليه وسلم said, "Surely, everyone of you is a guardian and is responsible for his charges: The *Imâm* (ruler) of the people is a guardian and is responsible for his subjects; a man is the guardian of his family (household) and is responsible for his subjects; a woman is the guardian of her husband's home and of her children and is responsible for them; and the slave of a man is a guardian of his master's property and is responsible for it. Surely, everyone of you is a guardian and responsible for his charges." (*Sahih Al-Bukhâri*, Vol. 9, *Hadîth* No. 252).

B) Narrated Tarîf Abî Tamîmah: I saw Safwân and Jundub and Safwân's companions when Jundub was advising. They said, "Did you hear something from Allâh's Messenger صلى الله عليه وسلم ?" Jundub said, "I heard him saying, 'Whoever does a good deed in order to show-off, Allâh will expose his intentions on the Day of Resurrection (before the people), and whoever puts the people into difficulties, Allâh will put him into difficulties on the Day of Resurrection.' " The people said (to Jundub), "Advise us." He said, "The first thing of the human body to putrefy is the abdomen, so he who can eat nothing but good food (Halâl and earned lawfully) should do so, and he who does as much as he can that nothing intervene between him and Paradise by not shedding even a handful of blood, (i.e. murdering) should do so." [Sahih Al-Bukhâri, Vol. 9, Hadîth No. 266].

C) Narrated Anas bin Mâlik رضى الله عنه: While the Prophet صلى الله عليه وسلم and I were coming out of the mosque, a man met us outside the gate. The man said, "O Allâh's Messenger! When will be the Hour?" The Prophet صلى الله عليه وسلم asked him, "What have you prepared for it?" The man became afraid and ashamed and then said, "O Allâh's Messenger! I haven't prepared for it much of Saum (fasts), Salât (prayers) or charitable gifts but I love Allâh and His Messenger." The Prophet صلى الله عليه وسلم said, "You will be with the one whom you love." [Sahih Al-Bukhâri, Vol. 9, Hadîth No. 267].

D) Narrated Abû Dharr رضى الله عنه: Once I went to him (the Prophet صلى الله عليه وسلم) and he said, "By Allâh in Whose Hand my soul is (or probably said, "By Allâh, except whom none has the right to be worshipped)" whoever had camels or cows or sheep and did not pay their Zakât, those animals will be brought on the Day of Resurrection far bigger and fatter than before and they will tread him under their hooves, and will butt him with their horns, and (those animals will come in circle): When the last does its turn, the first will start again, and this punishment will go on till Allâh has finished the judgements amongst the people." [Sahih Al-Bukhâri, Vol. 2, Hadîth No. 539].

88. The chiefs of those who were arrogant among his people said: "We shall certainly drive you out, O Shu'aib, and those who have believed with you from our town, or else you (all) shall return to our religion." He said: "Even though we hate it!"

89. "We should have invented a lie against Allâh if we returned to your religion, after Allâh has rescued us from it. And it is not for us to return to it unless Allâh, our Lord, should will. Our Lord comprehends all things in His Knowledge. In Allâh (Alone) we put our trust. Our Lord! Judge between us and our people in truth, for You are the Best of those who give judgment."

90. The chiefs of those who disbelieved among his people said (to their people): "If you follow Shu'aib, be sure then you will be the losers!"

91. So the earthquake seized them and they lay (dead), prostrate in their homes.

92. Those who belied Shu'aib, became as if they had never dwelt there (in their homes). Those who belied Shu'aib, they were the losers.

93. Then he (Shu'aib) turned from them and said: "O my people! I have indeed conveyed my Lord's Messages unto you and I have given you good advice. Then how can I sorrow for the disbelieving people's (destruction)."

94. And We sent no Prophet unto any town (and they denied him), but We

قَالَ ٱلْمَلَأُ ٱلَّذِينَ ٱسْتَكْبَرُوا۟ مِن قَوْمِهِۦ لَنُخْرِجَنَّكَ يَٰشُعَيْبُ وَٱلَّذِينَ ءَامَنُوا۟ مَعَكَ مِن قَرْيَتِنَآ أَوْ لَتَعُودُنَّ فِى مِلَّتِنَا قَالَ أَوَلَوْ كُنَّا كَٰرِهِينَ ۝

قَدِ ٱفْتَرَيْنَا عَلَى ٱللَّهِ كَذِبًا إِنْ عُدْنَا فِى مِلَّتِكُم بَعْدَ إِذْ نَجَّىٰنَا ٱللَّهُ مِنْهَا وَمَا يَكُونُ لَنَآ أَن نَّعُودَ فِيهَآ إِلَّآ أَن يَشَآءَ ٱللَّهُ رَبُّنَا وَسِعَ رَبُّنَا كُلَّ شَىْءٍ عِلْمًا عَلَى ٱللَّهِ تَوَكَّلْنَا رَبَّنَا ٱفْتَحْ بَيْنَنَا وَبَيْنَ قَوْمِنَا بِٱلْحَقِّ وَأَنتَ خَيْرُ ٱلْفَٰتِحِينَ ۝

وَقَالَ ٱلْمَلَأُ ٱلَّذِينَ كَفَرُوا۟ مِن قَوْمِهِۦ لَئِنِ ٱتَّبَعْتُمْ شُعَيْبًا إِنَّكُمْ إِذًا لَّخَٰسِرُونَ ۝

فَأَخَذَتْهُمُ ٱلرَّجْفَةُ فَأَصْبَحُوا۟ فِى دَارِهِمْ جَٰثِمِينَ ۝

ٱلَّذِينَ كَذَّبُوا۟ شُعَيْبًا كَأَن لَّمْ يَغْنَوْا۟ فِيهَا ٱلَّذِينَ كَذَّبُوا۟ شُعَيْبًا كَانُوا۟ هُمُ ٱلْخَٰسِرِينَ ۝

فَتَوَلَّىٰ عَنْهُمْ وَقَالَ يَٰقَوْمِ لَقَدْ أَبْلَغْتُكُمْ رِسَٰلَٰتِ رَبِّى وَنَصَحْتُ لَكُمْ فَكَيْفَ ءَاسَىٰ عَلَىٰ قَوْمٍ كَٰفِرِينَ ۝

وَمَآ أَرْسَلْنَا فِى قَرْيَةٍ مِّن نَّبِىٍّ

seized its people with suffering from extreme poverty (or loss in wealth) and loss of health (and calamities), so that they might humiliate themselves (and repent to Allâh).

95. Then We changed the evil for the good, until they increased in number and in wealth, and said: "Our fathers were touched with evil (loss of health and calamities) and with good (prosperity)." So We seized them all of a sudden while they were unaware.

96. And if the people of the towns had believed and had the *Taqwâ* (piety), certainly, We should have opened for them blessings from the heaven and the earth, but they belied (the Messengers). So We took them (with punishment) for what they used to earn (polytheism and crimes).

97. Did the people of the towns then feel secure against the coming of Our punishment by night while they were asleep?

98. Or, did the people of the towns then feel secure against the coming of Our punishment in the forenoon while they were playing?

99. Did they then feel secure against the Plan of Allâh? None feels secure from the Plan of Allâh except the people who are the losers.

100. Is it not clear to those who inherit the earth in succession from its (previous) possessors, that had We willed, We would have punished them for their sins. And We seal up their hearts so that they hear not?

101. Those were the towns whose story We relate unto you (O Muhammad صلى الله عليه وسلم). And there came indeed to them their Messengers with clear proofs, but they were not such as to believe in that which they had rejected before. Thus Allâh does seal up the hearts of the disbelievers (from every kind of religious guidance).

102. And most of them We found not true to their covenant, but most of them We found indeed *Fâsiqûn* (rebellious, disobedient to Allâh).

103. Then after them We sent Mûsâ (Moses) with Our Signs to Fir'aun (Pharaoh) and his chiefs, but they wrongfully rejected them. So see how was the end of the *Mufsidûn* (mischief-makers, corrupters).

104. And Mûsâ (Moses) said: "O Fir'aun (Pharaoh)! Verily, I am a Messenger from the Lord of the '*Âlamîn* (mankind, jinn and all that exists).

105. "Proper it is for me that I say nothing concerning Allâh but the truth. Indeed I have come unto you from your Lord with a clear proof. So let the Children of Israel depart along with me."

106. [Fir'aun (Pharaoh)] said: "If you have come with a sign, show it forth, if you are one of those who tell the truth."

107. Then [Mûsâ (Moses)] threw his stick and behold! it was a serpent, manifest!

فَأَلْقَىٰ عَصَاهُ فَإِذَا هِىَ ثُعْبَانٌ مُّبِينٌ ۝

108. And he drew out his hand, and behold! it was white (with radiance) for the beholders.

وَنَزَعَ يَدَهُ فَإِذَا هِىَ بَيْضَآءُ لِلنَّاظِرِينَ ۝

109. The chiefs of the people of Fir'aun (Pharaoh) said: "This is indeed a well-versed sorcerer;"

قَالَ الْمَلَأُ مِن قَوْمِ فِرْعَوْنَ إِنَّ هَٰذَا لَسَاحِرٌ عَلِيمٌ ۝

110. "He wants to get you out of your land, so what do you advise?"

يُرِيدُ أَن يُخْرِجَكُم مِّنْ أَرْضِكُمْ فَمَاذَا تَأْمُرُونَ ۝

111. They said: "Put him and his brother off (for a time), and send callers (men) to the cities to collect (and) —

قَالُوٓا أَرْجِهْ وَأَخَاهُ وَأَرْسِلْ فِى الْمَدَآئِنِ حَاشِرِينَ ۝

112. "That they bring to you all well-versed sorcerers."

يَأْتُوكَ بِكُلِّ سَاحِرٍ عَلِيمٍ ۝

113. And so the sorcerers came to Fir'aun (Pharaoh). They said: "Indeed there will be a (good) reward for us if we are the victors."

وَجَآءَ السَّحَرَةُ فِرْعَوْنَ قَالُوٓا إِنَّ لَنَا لَأَجْرًا إِن كُنَّا نَحْنُ الْغَالِبِينَ ۝

114. He said: "Yes, and moreover you will (in that case) be of the nearest (to me)."

قَالَ نَعَمْ وَإِنَّكُمْ لَمِنَ الْمُقَرَّبِينَ ۝

115. They said: "O Mûsâ (Moses)! Either you throw (first), or shall we have the (first) throw?"

قَالُوا يَٰمُوسَىٰٓ إِمَّآ أَن تُلْقِىَ وَإِمَّآ أَن نَّكُونَ نَحْنُ الْمُلْقِينَ ۝

116. He [Mûsâ (Moses)] said: "Throw you (first)." So when they threw, they bewitched the eyes of the people, and struck terror into them, and they displayed a great magic.

قَالَ أَلْقُوا فَلَمَّآ أَلْقَوْا سَحَرُوٓا أَعْيُنَ النَّاسِ وَاسْتَرْهَبُوهُمْ وَجَآءُو بِسِحْرٍ عَظِيمٍ ۝

117. And We revealed to Mûsâ (Moses) (saying): "Throw your stick," and behold! It swallowed up straight away all the falsehood which they showed.

۞ وَأَوْحَيْنَآ إِلَىٰ مُوسَىٰٓ أَنْ أَلْقِ عَصَاكَ فَإِذَا هِىَ تَلْقَفُ مَا يَأْفِكُونَ ۝

118. Thus truth was confirmed, and all that they did was made of no effect.

فَوَقَعَ الْحَقُّ وَبَطَلَ مَاكَانُوا يَعْمَلُونَ ۝ فَغُلِبُوا

119. So they were defeated there and returned disgraced.

هُنَالِكَ وَانقَلَبُوا صَٰغِرِينَ ۝

120. And the sorcerers fell down prostrate.

وَأُلْقِيَ السَّحَرَةُ سَٰجِدِينَ ۝

121. They said: "We believe in the Lord of the 'Âlamîn (mankind, jinn and all that exists).

قَالُوٓا ءَامَنَّا بِرَبِّ الْعَٰلَمِينَ ۝

122. "The Lord of Mûsâ (Moses) and Hârûn (Aaron)."

رَبِّ مُوسَىٰ وَهَٰرُونَ ۝

123. Fir'aun (Pharaoh) said: "You have believed in him [Mûsâ (Moses)] before I give you permission. Surely, this is a plot which you have plotted in the city to drive out its people, but you shall come to know.

قَالَ فِرْعَوْنُ ءَامَنتُم بِهِۦ قَبْلَ أَنْ ءَاذَنَ لَكُمْ إِنَّ هَٰذَا لَمَكْرٌ مَّكَرْتُمُوهُ فِي الْمَدِينَةِ لِتُخْرِجُوا مِنْهَآ أَهْلَهَا فَسَوْفَ تَعْلَمُونَ ۝

124. "Surely, I will cut off your hands and your feet from opposite sides, then I will crucify you all."

لَأُقَطِّعَنَّ أَيْدِيَكُمْ وَأَرْجُلَكُم مِّنْ خِلَٰفٍ ثُمَّ لَأُصَلِّبَنَّكُمْ أَجْمَعِينَ ۝

125. They said: "Verily, we are returning to our Lord.

قَالُوٓا إِنَّآ إِلَىٰ رَبِّنَا مُنقَلِبُونَ ۝

126. "And you take vengeance on us only because we believed in the Ayât (proofs, evidences, lessons, signs, etc.) of our Lord when they reached us! Our Lord! pour out on us patience, and cause us to die as Muslims."

وَمَا تَنقِمُ مِنَّآ إِلَّآ أَنْ ءَامَنَّا بِـَٔايَٰتِ رَبِّنَا لَمَّا جَآءَتْنَا رَبَّنَآ أَفْرِغْ عَلَيْنَا صَبْرًا وَتَوَفَّنَا مُسْلِمِينَ ۝

127. The chiefs of Fir'aun's (Pharaoh) people said: "Will you leave Mûsâ (Moses) and his people to spread mischief in the land, and to abandon you and your gods?" He said: "We will kill their sons, and let live their women,

وَقَالَ الْمَلَأُ مِن قَوْمِ فِرْعَوْنَ أَتَذَرُ مُوسَىٰ وَقَوْمَهُۥ لِيُفْسِدُوا فِي الْأَرْضِ وَيَذَرَكَ وَءَالِهَتَكَ قَالَ سَنُقَتِّلُ أَبْنَآءَهُمْ وَنَسْتَحْيِۦ

and we have indeed irresistible power over them."

128. Mûsâ (Moses) said to his people: "Seek help in Allâh and be patient. Verily, the earth is Allâh's. He gives it as a heritage to whom He wills of His slaves; and the (blessed) end is for the *Muttaqûn* (the pious. See V.2:2)."

129 They said: "We (Children of Israel) had suffered troubles before you came to us, and since you have come to us." He said: "It may be that your Lord will destroy your enemy and make you successors on the earth, so that He may see how you act?"

130. And indeed We punished the people of Fir'aun (Pharaoh) with years of drought and shortness of fruits (crops), that they might remember (take heed).

131. But whenever good came to them, they said: "Ours is this." And if evil afflicted them, they ascribed it to evil omens connected with Mûsâ (Moses) and those with him. Be informed! Verily, their evil omens are with Allâh but most of them know not.

132. They said [to Mûsâ (Moses)]: "Whatever *Ayât* (proofs, evidences, verses, lessons, signs, revelations, etc.) you may bring to us, to work therewith your sorcery on us, we shall never believe in you."

133. So We sent on them: the flood, the locusts, the lice, the frogs, and the blood: (as a succession of) manifest signs, yet they remained arrogant, and they were of those people who were *Mujrimûn* (criminals, polytheists, sinners).

مُفَصَّلَتٍ فَٱسْتَكْبَرُواْ وَكَانُواْ قَوْمًا مُّجْرِمِينَ ۝

134. And when the punishment fell on them they said: "O Mûsâ (Moses)! Invoke your Lord for us because of His Promise to you. If you will remove the punishment from us, we indeed shall believe in you, and we shall let the Children of Israel go with you."

وَلَمَّا وَقَعَ عَلَيْهِمُ ٱلرِّجْزُ قَالُواْ يَمُوسَى ٱدْعُ لَنَا رَبَّكَ بِمَا عَهِدَ عِندَكَ لَئِن كَشَفْتَ عَنَّا ٱلرِّجْزَ لَنُؤْمِنَنَّ لَكَ وَلَنُرْسِلَنَّ مَعَكَ بَنِى إِسْرَٰٓءِيلَ ۝

135. But when We removed the punishment from them to a fixed term, which they had to reach, behold! They broke their word!

فَلَمَّا كَشَفْنَا عَنْهُمُ ٱلرِّجْزَ إِلَىٰٓ أَجَلٍ هُم بَٰلِغُوهُ إِذَا هُمْ يَنكُثُونَ ۝

136. So We took retribution from them. We drowned them in the sea, because they belied Our *Ayât* (proofs, evidences, verses, lessons, signs, revelations, etc.) and were heedless about them.

فَٱنتَقَمْنَا مِنْهُمْ فَأَغْرَقْنَٰهُمْ فِى ٱلْيَمِّ بِأَنَّهُمْ كَذَّبُواْ بِـَٔايَٰتِنَا وَكَانُواْ عَنْهَا غَٰفِلِينَ ۝

137. And We made the people who were considered weak to inherit the eastern parts of the land and the western parts thereof which We have blessed. And the fair Word of your Lord was fulfilled for the Children of Israel, because of their endurance. And We destroyed completely all the great works and buildings which Fir'aun (Pharaoh) and his people erected.

وَأَوْرَثْنَا ٱلْقَوْمَ ٱلَّذِينَ كَانُواْ يُسْتَضْعَفُونَ مَشَٰرِقَ ٱلْأَرْضِ وَمَغَٰرِبَهَا ٱلَّتِى بَٰرَكْنَا فِيهَا وَتَمَّتْ كَلِمَتُ رَبِّكَ ٱلْحُسْنَىٰ عَلَىٰ بَنِىٓ إِسْرَٰٓءِيلَ بِمَا صَبَرُواْ وَدَمَّرْنَا مَا كَانَ يَصْنَعُ فِرْعَوْنُ وَقَوْمُهُۥ وَمَا كَانُواْ يَعْرِشُونَ ۝

138. And We brought the Children of Israel (with safety) across the sea, and they came upon a people devoted to

وَجَٰوَزْنَا بِبَنِىٓ إِسْرَٰٓءِيلَ ٱلْبَحْرَ

some of their idols (in worship). They said: "O Mûsâ (Moses)! Make for us an *ilâhan*[1] (a god) as they have *âlihah* (gods)." He said: "Verily, you are a people who know not (the Majesty and Greatness of Allâh and what is obligatory upon you, i.e. to worship none but Allâh Alone, the One and the Only God of all that exists)."

139. [Mûsâ (Moses) added:] "Verily, these people will be destroyed for that which they are engaged in (idols-worship). And all that they are doing is in vain."

140. He said: "Shall I seek for you an *ilâhan* (a god) other than Allâh, while He has given you superiority over the *'Âlamîn* (mankind and jinn of your time)."

141. And (remember) when We rescued you from Fir'aun's (Pharaoh) people, who were afflicting you with the worst torment, killing your sons and letting your women live. And in that was a great trial from your Lord.

142. And We appointed for Mûsâ (Moses) thirty nights and added (to the period) ten (more), and he completed the term, appointed by his Lord, of forty nights. And Mûsâ (Moses) said to his brother Hârûn (Aaron): "Replace me among my people, act in the Right Way (by ordering the people to obey Allâh and to worship Him Alone) and follow not the way of the *Mufsidûn* (mischief-makers)."

---

[1] (V.7:138) *Ilâhan*: Who has all the right to be worshipped.

143. And when Mûsâ (Moses) came at the time and place appointed by Us, and his Lord (Allâh) spoke to him; he said: "O my Lord! Show me (Yourself), that I may look upon You." Allâh said: "You cannot see Me, but look upon the mountain if it stands still in its place then you shall see Me." So when his Lord appeared to the mountain,[1] He made it collapse to dust, and Mûsâ (Moses) fell down unconscious. Then when he recovered his senses he said: "Glory is to You, I turn to You in repentance and I am the first of the believers."

144. (Allâh) said: "O Mûsâ (Moses) I have chosen you above men by My Messages, and by My speaking (to you). So hold that which I have given you and be of the grateful."

145. And We wrote for him on the Tablets the lesson to be drawn from all things and the explanation for all things (and said): Hold unto these with firmness, and enjoin your people to take the better there. I shall show you the home of Al-Fâsiqûn (the rebellious, disobedient to Allâh).

146. I shall turn away from My Ayât (verses of the Qur'ân) those who behave arrogantly on the earth, without a right, and (even) if they see all the

وَلَمَّا جَآءَ مُوسَىٰ لِمِيقَٰتِنَا وَكَلَّمَهُۥ رَبُّهُۥ قَالَ رَبِّ أَرِنِىٓ أَنظُرْ إِلَيْكَ قَالَ لَن تَرَىٰنِى وَلَٰكِنِ ٱنظُرْ إِلَى ٱلْجَبَلِ فَإِنِ ٱسْتَقَرَّ مَكَانَهُۥ فَسَوْفَ تَرَىٰنِى فَلَمَّا تَجَلَّىٰ رَبُّهُۥ لِلْجَبَلِ جَعَلَهُۥ دَكًّا وَخَرَّ مُوسَىٰ صَعِقًا فَلَمَّآ أَفَاقَ قَالَ سُبْحَٰنَكَ تُبْتُ إِلَيْكَ وَأَنَا۠ أَوَّلُ ٱلْمُؤْمِنِينَ ﴿١٤٣﴾

قَالَ يَٰمُوسَىٰٓ إِنِّى ٱصْطَفَيْتُكَ عَلَى ٱلنَّاسِ بِرِسَٰلَٰتِى وَبِكَلَٰمِى فَخُذْ مَآ ءَاتَيْتُكَ وَكُن مِّنَ ٱلشَّٰكِرِينَ ﴿١٤٤﴾

وَكَتَبْنَا لَهُۥ فِى ٱلْأَلْوَاحِ مِن كُلِّ شَىْءٍ مَّوْعِظَةً وَتَفْصِيلًا لِّكُلِّ شَىْءٍ فَخُذْهَا بِقُوَّةٍ وَأْمُرْ قَوْمَكَ يَأْخُذُوا۟ بِأَحْسَنِهَا سَأُو۟رِيكُمْ دَارَ ٱلْفَٰسِقِينَ ﴿١٤٥﴾

سَأَصْرِفُ عَنْ ءَايَٰتِىَ ٱلَّذِينَ يَتَكَبَّرُونَ فِى ٱلْأَرْضِ بِغَيْرِ

---

[1] (V.7:143) The appearance of Allâh جل جلاله to the mountain was very little of Him. It was approximately equal to the tip of one's little finger as explained by the Prophet صلى الله عليه وسلم when he recited this Verse. (This *Hadith* is quoted by *Tirmidhi*).

Ayât (proofs, evidences, verses, lessons, signs, revelations, etc.), they will not believe in them. And if they see the way of righteousness (monotheism, piety, and good deeds), they will not adopt it as the Way, but if they see the way of error (polytheism, crimes and evil deeds), they will adopt that way, that is because they have rejected Our Ayât (proofs, evidences, verses, lessons, signs, revelations, etc.) and were heedless (to learn a lesson) from them.

ٱلْحَقَّ وَإِن يَرَوْاْ كُلَّ ءَايَةٍ لَّا يُؤْمِنُواْ بِهَا وَإِن يَرَوْاْ سَبِيلَ ٱلرُّشْدِ لَا يَتَّخِذُوهُ سَبِيلًا وَإِن يَرَوْاْ سَبِيلَ ٱلْغَيِّ يَتَّخِذُوهُ سَبِيلًا ذَٰلِكَ بِأَنَّهُمْ كَذَّبُواْ بِـَٔايَٰتِنَا وَكَانُواْ عَنْهَا غَٰفِلِينَ ١٤٦

147. Those who deny Our Ayât (proofs, evidences, verses, lessons, signs, revelations, etc.) and the Meeting in the Hereafter (Day of Resurrection), vain are their deeds. Are they requited with anything except what they used to do?

وَٱلَّذِينَ كَذَّبُواْ بِـَٔايَٰتِنَا وَلِقَآءِ ٱلْءَاخِرَةِ حَبِطَتْ أَعْمَٰلُهُمْ هَلْ يُجْزَوْنَ إِلَّا مَا كَانُواْ يَعْمَلُونَ ١٤٧

148. And the people of Mûsâ (Moses) made in his absence, out of their ornaments, the image of a calf (for worship). It had a sound (as if it was mooing). Did they not see that it could neither speak to them nor guide them to the way? They took it (for worship) and they were Zâlimûn (wrongdoers).

وَٱتَّخَذَ قَوْمُ مُوسَىٰ مِنۢ بَعْدِهِۦ مِنْ حُلِيِّهِمْ عِجْلًا جَسَدًا لَّهُۥ خُوَارٌ أَلَمْ يَرَوْاْ أَنَّهُۥ لَا يُكَلِّمُهُمْ وَلَا يَهْدِيهِمْ سَبِيلًا ٱتَّخَذُوهُ وَكَانُواْ ظَٰلِمِينَ ١٤٨

149. And when they regretted and saw that they had gone astray, they (repented and) said: "If our Lord have not mercy upon us and forgive us, we shall certainly be of the losers."

وَلَمَّا سُقِطَ فِىٓ أَيْدِيهِمْ وَرَأَوْاْ أَنَّهُمْ قَدْ ضَلُّواْ قَالُواْ لَئِن لَّمْ يَرْحَمْنَا رَبُّنَا وَيَغْفِرْ لَنَا لَنَكُونَنَّ مِنَ ٱلْخَٰسِرِينَ ١٤٩

150. And when Mûsâ (Moses) returned to his people, angry and grieved, he said: "What an evil thing is that which you have done (i.e.

وَلَمَّا رَجَعَ مُوسَىٰٓ إِلَىٰ قَوْمِهِۦ غَضْبَٰنَ أَسِفًا قَالَ بِئْسَمَا خَلَفْتُمُونِى

worshipping the calf) during my absence. Did you hasten and go ahead as regards the matter of your Lord (you left His worship)?" And he threw down the Tablets and seized his brother by (the hair of) his head and dragged him towards him. Hârûn (Aaron) said: "O son of my mother! Indeed the people judged me weak and were about to kill me, so make not the enemies rejoice over me, nor put me amongst the people who are Zâlimûn (wrongdoers)."

151. Mûsâ (Moses) said: "O my Lord! Forgive me and my brother, and make us enter Your Mercy, for you are the Most Merciful of those who show mercy."

152. Certainly, those who took the calf (for worship), wrath from their Lord and humiliation will come upon them in the life of this world. Thus do We recompense those who invent lies.

153. But those who committed evil deeds and then repented afterwards and believed, verily, your Lord after (all) that is indeed Oft-Forgiving, Most Merciful.

154. And when the anger of Mûsâ (Moses) was calmed down, he took up the Tablets; and in their inscription was guidance and mercy for those who fear their Lord.

155. And Mûsâ (Moses) chose out of his people seventy (of the best) men for Our appointed time and place of meeting, and when they were seized

مِنۢ بَعْدِى أَعَجِلْتُمْ أَمْرَ رَبِّكُمْ وَأَلْقَى الْأَلْوَاحَ وَأَخَذَ بِرَأْسِ أَخِيهِ يَجُرُّهُ إِلَيْهِ قَالَ ابْنَ أُمَّ إِنَّ الْقَوْمَ اسْتَضْعَفُونِى وَكَادُوا يَقْتُلُونَنِى فَلَا تُشْمِتْ بِىَ الْأَعْدَاءَ وَلَا تَجْعَلْنِى مَعَ الْقَوْمِ الظَّـٰلِمِينَ ۝

قَالَ رَبِّ اغْفِرْ لِى وَلِأَخِى وَأَدْخِلْنَا فِى رَحْمَتِكَ وَأَنْتَ أَرْحَمُ الرَّٰحِمِينَ ۝

إِنَّ الَّذِينَ اتَّخَذُوا الْعِجْلَ سَيَنَالُهُمْ غَضَبٌ مِّن رَّبِّهِمْ وَذِلَّةٌ فِى الْحَيَوٰةِ الدُّنْيَا وَكَذَٰلِكَ نَجْزِى الْمُفْتَرِينَ ۝

وَالَّذِينَ عَمِلُوا السَّيِّئَاتِ ثُمَّ تَابُوا مِنۢ بَعْدِهَا وَءَامَنُوا إِنَّ رَبَّكَ مِنۢ بَعْدِهَا لَغَفُورٌ رَّحِيمٌ ۝

وَلَمَّا سَكَتَ عَن مُّوسَى الْغَضَبُ أَخَذَ الْأَلْوَاحَ وَفِى نُسْخَتِهَا هُدًى وَرَحْمَةٌ لِّلَّذِينَ هُمْ لِرَبِّهِمْ يَرْهَبُونَ ۝

وَاخْتَارَ مُوسَىٰ قَوْمَهُ سَبْعِينَ رَجُلًا لِّمِيقَاتِنَا فَلَمَّا أَخَذَتْهُمُ الرَّجْفَةُ قَالَ رَبِّ لَوْ شِئْتَ

with a violent earthquake, he said: "O my Lord, if it had been Your Will, You could have destroyed them and me before; would You destroy us for the deeds of the foolish ones among us? It is only Your trial by which You lead astray whom You will, and keep guided whom You will. You are our *Walî* (Protector), so forgive us and have Mercy on us: for You are the Best of those who forgive.

156. "And ordain for us good in this world, and in the Hereafter. Certainly we have turned unto You." He said: (As to) My punishment I afflict therewith whom I will and My Mercy embraces all things. That (Mercy) I shall ordain for those who are the *Muttaqûn* (the pious. See V.2:2), and give *Zakât*; and those who believe in Our *Ayât* (proofs, evidences, verses, lessons, signs and revelations, etc.);

157. Those who follow the Messenger, the Prophet who can neither read nor write (i.e. Muhammad صلى الله عليه وسلم) whom they find written with them in the Taurât (Torah) (Deut, xviii, 15) and the Injeel (Gospel) (John xiv, 16),[1] — he commands them for *Al-Ma'rûf* (i.e. Islâmic Monotheism and all that Islâm has ordained); and forbids them

---

[1] (V.7:157) There exists in the Taurât (Torah) and the Injeel (Gospel), even after the original text has been distorted, clear prophecies indicating the coming of Prophet Muhammad صلى الله عليه وسلم e.g. Deut. 18: 18;21:21; Psl. 118: 22-23; Isa. 42: 1-13; Hab. 3: 3-4; Matt. 21:42-43; Jn.14: 12-17, 26-28, 16: 7-14.

from *Al-Munkar* (i.e. disbelief, polytheism of all kinds, and all that Islâm has forbidden); he allows them as lawful *At-Tayyibât* (i.e. all good and lawful as regards things, deeds, beliefs, persons and foods), and prohibits them as unlawful *Al-Khabâ'ith* (i.e. all evil and unlawful as regards things, deeds, beliefs, persons and foods), he releases them from their heavy burdens (of Allâh's Covenant), and from the fetters (bindings) that were upon them. So those who believe in him (Muhammad صلى الله عليه وسلم), honour him, help him, and follow the light (the Qur'ân) which has been sent down with him, it is they who will be successful.[1]

158. Say (O Muhammad صلى الله عليه وسلم): "O mankind! Verily, I am sent to you all as the Messenger of Allâh — to Whom belongs the dominion of the heavens and the earth. *Lâ ilâha illa Huwa* (none has the right to be worshipped but He). It is He Who gives life and causes death. So believe in Allâh and His Messenger (Muhammad صلى الله عليه وسلم), the Prophet who can

---

[1] (V.7:157):

A) "O you who have been given the Scripture (Jews and Christians)! Believe in what We have revealed (to Muhammad صلى الله عليه وسلم) confirming what is (already) with you, before We efface faces [by making them (faces) like the backs of the necks; without nose, mouth, eyes], and turn them hindwards, or curse them as We cursed the Sabbath-breakers. And the Commandment of Allâh is always executed." (V.4:47).

B). See (V.57:28) and its footnote.

neither read nor write (i.e. Muhammad صلى الله عليه وسلم), who believes in Allâh and His Words [(this Qur'ân), the Taurât (Torah) and the Injeel (Gospel) and also Allâh's Word: "Be!" — and he was, i.e. 'Îsâ (Jesus) son of Maryam (Mary), عليها السلام], and follow him so that you may be guided.[1]"

يُؤۡمِنُ بِٱللَّهِ وَكَلِمَٰتِهِۦ وَٱتَّبِعُوهُ لَعَلَّكُمۡ تَهۡتَدُونَ ١٥٨

159. And of the people of Mûsâ (Moses) there is a community who lead (the men) with truth and establish justice therewith (i.e. judge among men with truth and justice).

وَمِن قَوۡمِ مُوسَىٰٓ أُمَّةٌ يَهۡدُونَ بِٱلۡحَقِّ وَبِهِۦ يَعۡدِلُونَ ١٥٩

160. And We divided them into twelve tribes (as distinct) nations. We revealed to Mûsâ (Moses) when his people asked him for water (saying): "Strike the stone with your stick", and there gushed forth out of it twelve springs, each group knew its own place for water. We shaded them with the clouds and sent down upon them *Al-Manna*[2] and the quails (saying): "Eat of the good things with which We have provided you." They harmed Us not but they used to harm themselves.

وَقَطَّعۡنَٰهُمُ ٱثۡنَتَيۡ عَشۡرَةَ أَسۡبَاطًا أُمَمًا وَأَوۡحَيۡنَآ إِلَىٰ مُوسَىٰٓ إِذِ ٱسۡتَسۡقَىٰهُ قَوۡمُهُۥٓ أَنِ ٱضۡرِب بِّعَصَاكَ ٱلۡحَجَرَ فَٱنۢبَجَسَتۡ مِنۡهُ ٱثۡنَتَا عَشۡرَةَ عَيۡنًا قَدۡ عَلِمَ كُلُّ أُنَاسٍ مَّشۡرَبَهُمۡ وَظَلَّلۡنَا عَلَيۡهِمُ ٱلۡغَمَٰمَ وَأَنزَلۡنَا عَلَيۡهِمُ ٱلۡمَنَّ وَٱلسَّلۡوَىٰ كُلُواْ مِن طَيِّبَٰتِ مَا رَزَقۡنَٰكُمۡ وَمَا ظَلَمُونَا وَلَٰكِن كَانُوٓاْ أَنفُسَهُمۡ يَظۡلِمُونَ ١٦٠

161. And (remember) when it was said to them: "Dwell in this town (Jerusalem) and eat therefrom wherever you wish, and say, '(O Allâh) forgive our sins'; and enter the gate prostrate (bowing with humility). We shall forgive you your wrongdoings. We

وَإِذۡ قِيلَ لَهُمُ ٱسۡكُنُواْ هَٰذِهِ ٱلۡقَرۡيَةَ وَكُلُواْ مِنۡهَا حَيۡثُ

---

[1] (V.7:158) See the footnote of (A) the (V.2:252).

[2] (V.7:160) See the footnote of (V.2:57).

shall increase (the reward) for the good-doers."

162. But those among them who did wrong changed the word that had been told to them. So We sent on them a torment from the heaven in return for their wrong-doings.[1]

163. And ask them (O Muhammad ﷺ) about the town that was by the sea; when they transgressed in the matter of the Sabbath (i.e. Saturday): when their fish came to them openly on the Sabbath day, and did not come to them on the day they had no Sabbath. Thus We made a trial of them, for they used to rebel against Allâh's Command (disobey Allâh) [see the Qur'ân: V.4:154 and its footnote].

164. And when a community among them said: "Why do you preach to a people whom Allâh is about to destroy or to punish with a severe torment?" (The preachers) said: "In order to be free from guilt before your Lord (Allâh), and perhaps they may fear Allâh."

165. So when they forgot the reminders that had been given to them, We rescued those who forbade evil, but We seized those who did wrong with a severe torment because they used to rebel against Allâh's Command (disobey Allâh).

166. So when they exceeded the limits of what they were prohibited, We

---

[1] (V.7:162): See (V.2:59) and its footnote.

said to them: "Be you monkeys, despised and rejected." (It is a severe warning to the mankind that they should not disobey what Allâh commands them to do, and keep far away from what He prohibits them).[1]

فَلَمَّا عَتَوْاْ عَن مَّا نُهُواْ عَنْهُ قُلْنَا لَهُمْ كُونُواْ قِرَدَةً خَٰسِـِٔينَ ۝

167. And (remember) when your Lord declared that He would certainly keep on sending against them (i.e. the Jews), till the Day of Resurrection, those who would afflict them with a humiliating torment. Verily, your Lord is Quick in Retribution (for the disobedient, wicked) and certainly He is Oft-Forgiving, Most Merciful (for the obedient and those who beg Allâh's Forgiveness).

وَإِذْ تَأَذَّنَ رَبُّكَ لَيَبْعَثَنَّ عَلَيْهِمْ إِلَىٰ يَوْمِ ٱلْقِيَٰمَةِ مَن يَسُومُهُمْ سُوٓءَ ٱلْعَذَابِ إِنَّ رَبَّكَ لَسَرِيعُ ٱلْعِقَابِ وَإِنَّهُۥ لَغَفُورٌ رَّحِيمٌ ۝

168. And We have broken them (i.e. the Jews) up into various separate groups on the earth: some of them are righteous and some are away from that. And We tried them with good (blessings) and evil (calamities) in order that they might turn (to Allâh's Obedience).

وَقَطَّعْنَٰهُمْ فِى ٱلْأَرْضِ أُمَمًا مِّنْهُمُ ٱلصَّٰلِحُونَ وَمِنْهُمْ دُونَ ذَٰلِكَ وَبَلَوْنَٰهُم بِٱلْحَسَنَٰتِ وَٱلسَّيِّـَٔاتِ لَعَلَّهُمْ يَرْجِعُونَ ۝

169. Then after them succeeded an (evil) generation, which inherited the Book, but they chose (for themselves) the goods of this low life (evil pleasures of this world) saying (as an excuse): "(Everything) will be forgiven to us." And if (again) the offer of the like (evil pleasures of this world) came their way, they would (again) seize them (would

فَخَلَفَ مِنۢ بَعْدِهِمْ خَلْفٌ وَرِثُواْ ٱلْكِتَٰبَ يَأْخُذُونَ عَرَضَ هَٰذَا ٱلْأَدْنَىٰ وَيَقُولُونَ سَيُغْفَرُ لَنَا وَإِن يَأْتِهِمْ عَرَضٌ مِّثْلُهُۥ يَأْخُذُوهُ أَلَمْ يُؤْخَذْ عَلَيْهِم مِّيثَٰقُ ٱلْكِتَٰبِ أَن لَّا يَقُولُواْ عَلَى ٱللَّهِ إِلَّا ٱلْحَقَّ

---

[1] (V.7:166) See the footnote of (V.9:112).

commit those sins). Was not the covenant of the Book taken from them that they would not say about Allâh anything but the truth? And they have studied what is in it (the Book). And the home of the Hereafter is better for those who are Al-Muttaqûn (the pious. See V.2:2). Do not you then understand?

170. And as to those who hold fast to the Book (i.e. act on its teachings) and perform As-Salât (Iqâmat-as-Salât), certainly We shall never waste the reward of those who do righteous deeds.

171. And (remember) when We raised the mountain over them as if it had been a canopy, and they thought that it was going to fall on them. (We said): "Hold firmly to what We have given you [i.e. the Taurât (Torah)], and remember that which is therein (act on its commandments), so that you may fear Allâh and obey Him."

172. And (remember) when your Lord brought forth from the Children of Adam, from their loins, their seed (or from Adam's loin his offspring) and made them testify as to themselves (saying): "Am I not your Lord?" They said: "Yes! We testify," lest you should say on the Day of Resurrection: "Verily, we have been unaware of this."

173. Or lest you should say: "It was only our fathers aforetime who took others as partners in worship along with Allâh, and we were (merely their) descendants after them; will You then destroy us because of the deeds of men who practised *Al-Bâtil* (i.e. polytheism and committing crimes and sins, invoking and worshipping others besides Allâh)?" (*Tafsir At-Tabarî*).

174. Thus do We explain the *Ayât* (proofs, evidences, verses, lessons, signs, revelations, etc.) in detail, so that they may turn (unto the truth).

175. And recite (O Muhammad صلى الله عليه وسلم) to them the story of him to whom We gave Our *Ayât* (proofs, evidences, verses, lessons, signs, revelations, etc.), but he threw them away; so *Shaitân* (Satan) followed him up, and he became of those who went astray.

176. And had We willed, We would surely, have elevated him therewith, but he clung to the earth and followed his own vain desire. So his parable is the parable of a dog: if you drive him away, he lolls his tongue out, or if you leave him alone, he (still) lolls his tongue out. Such is the parable of the people who reject Our *Ayât* (proofs, evidences, verses, lessons, signs, revelations, etc.). So relate the stories, perhaps they may reflect.

177. Evil is the parable of the people who rejected Our *Ayât* (proofs, evidences, verses and signs, etc.), and used to wrong their ownselves.

178. Whomsoever Allâh guides, he is the guided one, and whomsoever He sends astray, — then those! they are the losers.

179. And surely, We have created many of the jinn and mankind for Hell. They have hearts wherewith they understand not, and they have eyes wherewith they see not, and they have ears wherewith they hear not (the truth). They are like cattle, nay even more astray; those! They are the heedless ones.

180. And (all) the Most Beautiful Names belong to Allâh,[1] so call on Him by them, and leave the company of those who belie or deny (or utter impious speech against) His Names. They will be requited for what they used to do.

181. And of those whom We have created, there is a community who guides (others) with the truth, and establishes justice therewith.

182. Those who reject Our *Ayât* (proofs, evidences, verses, lessons, signs, revelations, etc.), We shall gradually seize them with punishment in ways they perceive not.

183. And I respite them; certainly My Plan is strong.

184. Do they not reflect? There is no madness in their companion (Muhammad صلى الله عليه وسلم). He is but a plain warner.

---

[1] (V.7:180) Allâh has one hundred minus one Names. (i.e. 99).

Narrated Abu Hurairah رضي الله عنه : Allâh has ninety-nine Names, i.e. one-hundred minus one; and whoever believes in their meanings and acts accordingly, will enter Paradise; and Allâh is *Witr* (one) and loves 'the *Witr*'. (*Sahih Al-Bukhâri*, Vol. 8, *Hadith* No. 419).

185. Do they not look in the dominion of the heavens and the earth and all things that Allâh has created; and that it may be that the end of their lives may be near. In what message after this will they then believe?

186. Whomsoever Allâh sends astray, none can guide him; and He lets them wander blindly in their transgressions.

187. They ask you about the Hour (Day of Resurrection): "When will be its appointed time?" Say: "The knowledge thereof is with my Lord (Alone). None can reveal its time but He. Heavy is its burden through the heavens and the earth. It shall not come upon you except all of a sudden." They ask you as if you have a good knowledge of it. Say: "The knowledge thereof is with Allâh (Alone), but most of mankind know not."[1]

188. Say (O Muhammad صلى الله عليه وسلم): "I possess no power over benefit or hurt to myself except as Allâh wills. If I had the knowledge of the *Ghaib* (Unseen), I should have secured for myself an abundance of wealth, and no evil should have touched me. I am but a

---

[1] (V.7:187): Narrated 'Abdullâh رضي الله عنه: Allâh's Messenger صلى الله عليه وسلم said, "The keys of the Unseen are five: Verily, Allâh! With Him (Alone) is the knowledge of the Hour, He sends down the rain, and knows that which is in the wombs. No person knows what he will earn tomorrow, and no person knows in what land he will die. Verily, Allâh is All-Knower, All-Aware." (V.31:34). (*Sahih Al-Bukhâri*, Vol. 6, *Hadith* No. 151).

warner, and a bringer of glad tidings unto people who believe."

189. It is He Who has created you from a single person (Adam), and (then) He has created from him his wife [Hawwâ (Eve)], in order that he might enjoy the pleasure of living with her. When he had sexual relation with her, she became pregnant and she carried it about lightly. Then when it became heavy, they both invoked Allâh, their Lord (saying): "If You give us a *Sâlih* (good in every aspect) child, we shall indeed be among the grateful."

190. But when He gave them a *Sâlih* (good in every aspect) child, they ascribed partners to Him (Allâh) in that which He has given to them. High is Allâh, Exalted above all that they ascribe as partners to Him.[1]

191. Do they attribute as partners to Allâh those who created nothing but they themselves are created?

192. No help can they give them, nor can they help themselves.

193. And if you call them to guidance, they follow you not. It is the same for you whether you call them or you keep silent.

194. Verily, those whom you call upon besides Allâh are slaves like you. So call upon them and let them answer you if you are truthful.

---

[1] (V.7:190) See the footnote of (V.30:30). Also see *Tafsir At-Tabarî* and *Tafsir Al-Qurtubî*, (for details).

195. Have they feet wherewith they walk? Or have they hands wherewith they hold? Or have they eyes wherewith they see? Or have they ears wherewith they hear? Say (O Muhammad صلى الله عليه وسلم): "Call your (so-called) partners (of Allâh) and then plot against me, and give me no respite!

196. "Verily, my *Walî* (Protector, Supporter, and Helper) is Allâh Who has revealed the Book (the Qur'ân), and He protects (supports and helps) the righteous.

197. "And those whom you call upon besides Him (Allâh) cannot help you nor can they help themselves."

198. And if you call them to guidance, they hear not and you will see them looking at you, yet they see not.

199. Show forgiveness, enjoin what is good, and turn away from the foolish (i.e. don't punish them).

200. And if an evil whisper comes to you from *Shaitân* (Satan), then seek refuge with Allâh. Verily, He is All-Hearer, All-Knower.

201. Verily, those who are *Al-Muttaqûn* (the pious. See V.2:2), when an evil thought comes to them from *Shaitân* (Satan), they remember (Allâh), and (indeed) they then see (aright).

202. But (as for) their brothers (the devils) they (i.e. the devils) plunge them deeper into error, and they never stop short.

203. And if you do not bring them a miracle [according to their (i.e. Quraish-pagans') proposal], they say: "Why have you not brought it?"[1] Say: "I but follow what is revealed to me from my Lord. This (the Qur'ân) is nothing but evidences from your Lord, and a guidance and a mercy for a people who believe."

وَإِذَا لَمْ تَأْتِهِم بِآيَةٍ قَالُوا لَوْلَا اجْتَبَيْتَهَا قُلْ إِنَّمَا أَتَّبِعُ مَا يُوحَىٰٓ إِلَيَّ مِن رَّبِّي هَٰذَا بَصَآئِرُ مِن رَّبِّكُمْ وَهُدًى وَرَحْمَةٌ لِّقَوْمٍ يُؤْمِنُونَ ۝

204. So, when the Qur'ân is recited, listen to it, and be silent that you may receive mercy. [i.e. during the compulsory congregational prayers when the *Imâm* (of a mosque) is leading the prayer (except *Sûrat Al-Fâtihah*), and also when he is delivering the Friday-prayer *Khutbah*]. [*Tafsir At-Tabari*]

وَإِذَا قُرِئَ الْقُرْآنُ فَاسْتَمِعُوا لَهُ وَأَنصِتُوا لَعَلَّكُمْ تُرْحَمُونَ ۝

205. And remember your Lord by your tongue and within yourself, humbly and with fear and without loudness in words in the mornings, and in the afternoons and be not of those who are neglectful.[2]

وَاذْكُر رَّبَّكَ فِي نَفْسِكَ تَضَرُّعًا وَخِيفَةً وَدُونَ الْجَهْرِ مِنَ الْقَوْلِ بِالْغُدُوِّ وَالْآصَالِ وَلَا تَكُن مِّنَ الْغَافِلِينَ ۝

206. Surely, those who are with your Lord (angels) are never too proud to perform acts of worship to Him, but they glorify His Praise and prostrate themselves before Him.

إِنَّ الَّذِينَ عِندَ رَبِّكَ لَا يَسْتَكْبِرُونَ عَنْ عِبَادَتِهِ وَيُسَبِّحُونَهُ وَلَهُ يَسْجُدُونَ ۩

---

[1] (V.7:203): Narrated Anas رضي الله عنه that the Makkan people (Quraish-pagans) requested Allâh's Messenger صلى الله عليه وسلم to show them a miracle, and so he showed them the splitting of the moon. (*Sahih Al-Bukhâri*, Vol.4. *Hadith* No.831).

[2] (V.7:205): See the footnote of (V.13:28).

Sûrat Al-Anfâl
(The Spoils of War) VIII

سُورَةُ الْأَنْفَال

In the Name of Allâh
the Most Gracious, the Most Merciful

بِسْمِ اللَّهِ الرَّحْمَنِ الرَّحِيمِ

1. They ask you (O Muhammad صلى الله عليه وسلم) about the spoils of war. Say: "The spoils are for Allâh and the Messenger." So fear Allâh and adjust all matters of difference among you, and obey Allâh and His Messenger (Muhammad صلى الله عليه وسلم), if you are believers.

يَسْئَلُونَكَ عَنِ الْأَنْفَالِ قُلِ الْأَنْفَالُ لِلَّهِ وَالرَّسُولِ فَاتَّقُوا اللَّهَ وَأَصْلِحُوا ذَاتَ بَيْنِكُمْ وَأَطِيعُوا اللَّهَ وَرَسُولَهُ إِن كُنتُم مُّؤْمِنِينَ ۝

2. The believers are only those who, when Allâh is mentioned, feel a fear in their hearts and when His Verses (this Qur'ân) are recited unto them, they (i.e. the Verses) increase their Faith; and they put their trust in their Lord (Alone).

إِنَّمَا الْمُؤْمِنُونَ الَّذِينَ إِذَا ذُكِرَ اللَّهُ وَجِلَتْ قُلُوبُهُمْ وَإِذَا تُلِيَتْ عَلَيْهِمْ ءَايَٰتُهُ زَادَتْهُمْ إِيمَٰنًا وَعَلَىٰ رَبِّهِمْ يَتَوَكَّلُونَ ۝

3. Who perform *As-Salât (Iqâmat-as-Salât)* and spend out of that We have provided them.

الَّذِينَ يُقِيمُونَ الصَّلَوٰةَ وَمِمَّا رَزَقْنَٰهُمْ يُنفِقُونَ ۝

4. It is they who are the believers in truth. For them are grades of dignity with their Lord, and forgiveness and a generous provision (Paradise).

أُوْلَٰئِكَ هُمُ الْمُؤْمِنُونَ حَقًّا لَّهُمْ دَرَجَٰتٌ عِندَ رَبِّهِمْ وَمَغْفِرَةٌ وَرِزْقٌ كَرِيمٌ ۝

5. As your Lord caused you (O Muhammad صلى الله عليه وسلم) to go out from your home with the truth; and verily, a party among the believers disliked it,

كَمَا أَخْرَجَكَ رَبُّكَ مِن بَيْتِكَ بِالْحَقِّ وَإِنَّ فَرِيقًا مِّنَ الْمُؤْمِنِينَ لَكَٰرِهُونَ ۝

6. Disputing with you concerning the truth after it was made manifest, as if they were being driven to death, while they were looking (at it).

يُجَٰدِلُونَكَ فِي الْحَقِّ بَعْدَمَا تَبَيَّنَ كَأَنَّمَا يُسَاقُونَ إِلَى الْمَوْتِ وَهُمْ يَنظُرُونَ ۝

7. And (remember) when Allâh promised you (Muslims) one of the two parties (of the enemy i.e. either the army or the caravan) that it should be yours; you wished that the one not armed (the caravan) should be yours, but Allâh willed to justify the truth by His Words and to cut off the roots of the disbelievers (i.e. in the battle of Badr).

وَإِذْ يَعِدُكُمُ اللَّهُ إِحْدَى الطَّائِفَتَيْنِ أَنَّهَا لَكُمْ وَتَوَدُّونَ أَنَّ غَيْرَ ذَاتِ الشَّوْكَةِ تَكُونُ لَكُمْ وَيُرِيدُ اللَّهُ أَن يُحِقَّ الْحَقَّ بِكَلِمَـٰتِهِۦ وَيَقْطَعَ دَابِرَ الْكَـٰفِرِينَ ٧

8. That He might cause the truth to triumph and bring falsehood to nothing, even though the *Mujrimûn* (disbelievers, polytheists, sinners, criminals) hate it.

لِيُحِقَّ الْحَقَّ وَيُبْطِلَ الْبَـٰطِلَ وَلَوْ كَرِهَ الْمُجْرِمُونَ ٨

9. (Remember) when you sought help of your Lord and He answered you (saying): "I will help you with a thousand of the angels each behind the other (following one another) in succession."

إِذْ تَسْتَغِيثُونَ رَبَّكُمْ فَاسْتَجَابَ لَكُمْ أَنِّى مُمِدُّكُم بِأَلْفٍ مِّنَ الْمَلَـٰئِكَةِ مُرْدِفِينَ ٩

10. Allâh made it only as glad tidings, and that your hearts be at rest therewith. And there is no victory except from Allâh. Verily, Allâh is All-Mighty, All-Wise.

وَمَا جَعَلَهُ اللَّهُ إِلَّا بُشْرَىٰ وَلِتَطْمَئِنَّ بِهِۦ قُلُوبُكُمْ وَمَا النَّصْرُ إِلَّا مِنْ عِندِ اللَّهِ إِنَّ اللَّهَ عَزِيزٌ حَكِيمٌ ١٠

11. (Remember) when He covered you with a slumber as a security from Him, and He caused water (rain) to descend on you from the sky, to clean you thereby and to remove from you the *Rijz* (whispering, evil-suggestions) of *Shaitân* (Satan), and to strengthen your hearts, and make your feet firm thereby.

إِذْ يُغَشِّيكُمُ النُّعَاسَ أَمَنَةً مِّنْهُ وَيُنَزِّلُ عَلَيْكُم مِّنَ السَّمَاءِ مَاءً لِّيُطَهِّرَكُم بِهِۦ وَيُذْهِبَ عَنكُمْ رِجْزَ الشَّيْطَـٰنِ وَلِيَرْبِطَ عَلَىٰ قُلُوبِكُمْ وَيُثَبِّتَ بِهِ الْأَقْدَامَ ١١

12. (Remember) when your Lord revealed to the angels, "Verily, I am with you, so keep firm those who have believed. I will cast terror into the hearts of those who have disbelieved, so strike them over the necks, and smite over all their fingers and toes."

إِذْ يُوحِي رَبُّكَ إِلَى الْمَلَـٰٓئِكَةِ أَنِّي مَعَكُمْ فَثَبِّتُوا الَّذِينَ ءَامَنُوا سَأُلْقِي فِي قُلُوبِ الَّذِينَ كَفَرُوا الرُّعْبَ فَاضْرِبُوا فَوْقَ الْأَعْنَاقِ وَاضْرِبُوا مِنْهُمْ كُلَّ بَنَانٍ ﴿١٢﴾

13. This is because they defied and disobeyed Allâh and His Messenger. And whoever defies and disobeys Allâh and His Messenger, then verily, Allâh is Severe in punishment.

ذَٰلِكَ بِأَنَّهُمْ شَاقُّوا اللَّهَ وَرَسُولَهُ وَمَن يُشَاقِقِ اللَّهَ وَرَسُولَهُ فَإِنَّ اللَّهَ شَدِيدُ الْعِقَابِ ﴿١٣﴾

14. This is (the torment), so taste it; and surely, for the disbelievers is the torment of the Fire.

ذَٰلِكُمْ فَذُوقُوهُ وَأَنَّ لِلْكَافِرِينَ عَذَابَ النَّارِ ﴿١٤﴾

15. O you who believe! When you meet those who disbelieve, in a battlefield, never turn your backs to them.

يَـٰٓأَيُّهَا الَّذِينَ ءَامَنُوا إِذَا لَقِيتُمُ الَّذِينَ كَفَرُوا زَحْفًا فَلَا تُوَلُّوهُمُ الْأَدْبَارَ ﴿١٥﴾

16. And whoever turns his back to them on such a day — unless it be a stratagem of war, or to retreat to a troop (of his own), — he indeed has drawn upon himself wrath from Allâh. And his abode is Hell, and worst indeed is that destination!

وَمَن يُوَلِّهِمْ يَوْمَئِذٍ دُبُرَهُ إِلَّا مُتَحَرِّفًا لِّقِتَالٍ أَوْ مُتَحَيِّزًا إِلَى فِئَةٍ فَقَدْ بَاءَ بِغَضَبٍ مِّنَ اللَّهِ وَمَأْوَىٰهُ جَهَنَّمُ وَبِئْسَ الْمَصِيرُ ﴿١٦﴾

17. You killed them not, but Allâh killed them. And you (Muhammad صلى الله عليه وسلم) threw not when you did throw, but Allâh threw, that He might test the believers by a fair trial from Him. Verily, Allâh is All-Hearer, All-Knower.

فَلَمْ تَقْتُلُوهُمْ وَلَـٰكِنَّ اللَّهَ قَتَلَهُمْ وَمَا رَمَيْتَ إِذْ رَمَيْتَ وَلَـٰكِنَّ اللَّهَ رَمَىٰ وَلِيُبْلِيَ الْمُؤْمِنِينَ مِنْهُ بَلَاءً حَسَنًا إِنَّ اللَّهَ سَمِيعٌ عَلِيمٌ ﴿١٧﴾

18. This (is the fact) and surely, Allâh weakens the deceitful plots of the disbelievers.

19. (O disbelievers) if you ask for a judgement, now has the judgement come unto you; and if you cease (to do wrong), it will be better for you, and if you return (to the attack), so shall We return, and your forces will be of no avail to you, however numerous it be; and verily, Allâh is with the believers.

20. O you who believe! Obey Allâh and His Messenger, and turn not away from him (i.e. Messenger Muhammad صلى الله عليه وسلم) while you are hearing.

21. And be not like those who say: "We have heard," but they hear not.

22. Verily, the worst of (moving) living creatures with Allâh are the deaf and the dumb, who understand not (i.e. the disbelievers).

23. Had Allâh known of any good in them, He would indeed have made them listen; and even if He had made them listen, they would but have turned away with aversion (to the truth).

24. O you who believe! Answer Allâh (by obeying Him) and (His) Messenger when he (صلى الله عليه وسلم) calls you[1] to that which will give you

---

[1] (V.8:24): See the footnote of (V.1:2).

life,[1] and know that Allâh comes in between a person and his heart (i.e. He prevents an evil person to decide anything). And verily, to Him you shall (all) be gathered.

25. And fear the *Fitnah* (affliction and trial) which affects not in particular (only) those of you who do wrong (but it may afflict all the good and the bad people), and know that Allâh is Severe in punishment.

26. And remember when you were few and were reckoned weak in the land, and were afraid that men might kidnap you, but He provided a safe place for you, strengthened you with His Help, and provided you with good things so that you might be grateful.

27. O you who believe! Betray not Allâh and His Messenger, nor betray knowingly your *Amânât* (things entrusted to you, and all the duties which Allâh has ordained for you).[2]

28. And know that your possessions and your children are but a trial and that surely, with Allâh is a mighty reward.

---

[1] (V.8:24): i.e., one is alive, — a true believer (of Islâmic Monotheism) who is obedient to Allâh and His Messenger (Muhammad صلى الله عليه وسلم) and follows the Qur'ân and Prophet's *Sunnah* practically, and he goes out for *Jihâd* in Allâh's Cause; in case he is martyred, that is not a death but an eternal life (in Paradise) forever, unlike to a disbeliever who is dead (as regards faith), and will be punished in Hell forever (neither alive nor dead).

[2] (V.8:27) See the footnote (A) of (V.3:164).

29. O you who believe! If you obey and fear Allâh, He will grant you *Furqân* [(a criterion to judge between right and wrong), or (*Makhraj*, i.e. a way for you to get out from every difficulty)], and will expiate for you your sins, and forgive you; and Allâh is the Owner of the Great Bounty.

30. And (remember) when the disbelievers plotted against you (O Muhammad صلى الله عليه وسلم) to imprison you, or to kill you, or to get you out (from your home, i.e. Makkah); they were plotting and Allâh too was plotting; and Allâh is the Best of those who plot.

31. And when Our Verses (of the Qur'ân) are recited to them, they say: "We have heard (the Qur'ân); if we wish we can say the like of this. This is nothing but the tales of the ancients."

32. And (remember) when they said: "O Allâh! If this (the Qur'ân) is indeed the truth (revealed) from You, then rain down stones on us from the sky or bring on us a painful torment."

33. And Allâh would not punish them while you (Muhammad صلى الله عليه وسلم) are amongst them, nor will He punish them while they seek (Allâh's) Forgiveness.

34. And why should not Allâh punish them while they hinder (men) from

Al-Masjid Al-Harâm, and they are not its guardians? None can be its guardians except *Al-Muttaqûn* (the pious. See V.2:2), but most of them know not.

35. Their *Salât* (prayer) at the House (of Allâh, i.e. the *Ka'bah* at Makkah) was nothing but whistling and clapping of hands. Therefore taste the punishment because you used to disbelieve.

36. Verily, those who disbelieve spend their wealth to hinder (men) from the Path of Allâh, and so will they continue to spend it; but in the end it will become an anguish for them. Then they will be overcome. And those who disbelieve will be gathered unto Hell.

37. In order that Allâh may distinguish the wicked (disbelievers, polytheists and doers of evil deeds) from the good (believers of Islâmic Monotheism and doers of righteous deeds), and put the wicked (disbelievers, polytheists and doers of evil deeds) one over another, heap them together and cast them into Hell. Those! it is they who are the losers.

38. Say to those who have disbelieved, if they cease (from disbelief), their past will be forgiven. But if they return (thereto), then the examples of those (punished) before them have already preceded (as a warning).

سُنَّةُ ٱلۡأَوَّلِينَ ٣٨

39. And fight them until there is no more *Fitnah* (disbelief and polytheism, i.e. worshipping others besides Allâh) and the religion (worship) will all be for Allâh Alone [in the whole of the world.[1]] But if they cease (worshipping others besides Allâh), then certainly, Allâh is All-Seer of what they do.[2]

وَقَـٰتِلُوهُمۡ حَتَّىٰ لَا تَكُونَ فِتۡنَةٌ وَيَكُونَ ٱلدِّينُ كُلُّهُۥ لِلَّهِۚ فَإِنِ ٱنتَهَوۡاْ فَإِنَّ ٱللَّهَ بِمَا يَعۡمَلُونَ بَصِيرٌ ٣٩

40. And if they turn away, then know that Allâh is your *Maulâ* (Patron, Lord, Protector and Supporter) — (what) an Excellent *Maulâ*, and (what) an Excellent Helper!

وَإِن تَوَلَّوۡاْ فَٱعۡلَمُوٓاْ أَنَّ ٱللَّهَ مَوۡلَىٰكُمۡۚ نِعۡمَ ٱلۡمَوۡلَىٰ وَنِعۡمَ ٱلنَّصِيرُ ٤٠

---

[1] (V.8:39) It is mentioned by some of the Islâmic religious scholars that, that will be at the time when 'Îsâ (Jesus), son of Maryam (Mary), عليهما السلام, will descend on the earth, and he will not accept any other religion except Islâm — the True Religion of Allâh — Islâmic Monotheism.

[2] (V.8:39)

A) See the footnote of (V.2:193).

B) Narrated Abu Hurairah رضي الله عنه: Allâh's Messenger صلى الله عليه وسلم said, "By Him (Allâh) in whose Hand my soul is, surely, the son of Maryam (Mary) ['Îsâ (Jesus)] عليهما السلام will shortly descend amongst you people (Muslims), and will judge mankind justly by the Law of the Qur'ân (as a just ruler), and will break the cross and kill the pigs and abolish the *Jizyah* [a tax taken from the people of the Scripture (Jews and Christians) who are in the protection of the Muslim government. This *Jizyah* tax will not be accepted by 'Îsâ (Jesus) السلام and all mankind will be required to embrace Islâm with no other alternative]. Then there will be abundance of money and nobody will accept charitable gifts." (See *Fath Al-Bari* for details). (*Sahih Al-Bukhâri*, Vol.3, Hadith No.425)

41. And know that whatever of war-booty that you may gain, verily, one-fifth (1/5th) of it is assigned to Allâh, and to the Messenger, and to the near relatives [of the Messenger (Muhammad صلى الله عليه وسلم)], (and also) the orphans, *Al-Masâkin* (the poor) and the wayfarer, if you have believed in Allâh and in that which We sent down to Our slave (Muhammad صلى الله عليه وسلم) on the Day of Criterion (between right and wrong), the Day when the two forces met (the battle of Badr); and Allâh is Able to do all things.

42. (And remember) when you (the Muslim army) were on the near side of the valley, and they on the farther side, and the caravan on the ground lower than you. Even if you had made a mutual appointment to meet, you would certainly have failed in the appointment, but (you met) that Allâh might accomplish a matter already ordained (in His Knowledge), so that those who were to be destroyed (for their rejecting the Faith) might be destroyed after a clear evidence, and those who were to live (i.e. believers) might live after a clear evidence. And surely, Allâh is All-Hearer, All-Knower.

43. (And remember) when Allâh showed them to you as few in your (i.e. Muhammad's صلى الله عليه وسلم) dream; if He had shown them to you as many, you would surely, have been discouraged, and you would surely, have disputed in making a decision. But Allâh saved (you). Certainly, He is the All-Knower of what is in the breasts.

44. And (remember) when you met (the army of the disbelievers on the Day of the battle of Badr), He showed them to you as few in your eyes and He made you appear as few in their eyes, so that Allâh might accomplish a matter already ordained (in His Knowledge), and to Allâh return all matters (for decision).

45. O you who believe! When you meet (an enemy) force, take a firm stand against them and remember the Name of Allâh much (both with tongue and mind), so that you may be successful.

46. And obey Allâh and His Messenger, and do not dispute (with one another) lest you lose courage and your strength departs, and be patient. Surely, Allâh is with those who are *As-Sâbirûn* (the patient).

47. And be not like those who come out of their homes boastfully and to be seen of men, and hinder (men) from the path of Allâh; and Allâh is *Muhîtun* (encircling and thoroughly comprehending) all that they do.

48. And (remember) when *Shaitân* (Satan) made their (evil) deeds seem fair to them and said, "No one of mankind can overcome you this Day (of the battle of Badr) and verily, I am your neighbour (for every help)." But when the two forces came in sight of each other, he ran away and said "Verily, I have nothing to do with you. Verily, I see what you see not. Verily, I fear Allâh for Allâh is Severe in punishment."

49. When the hypocrites and those in whose hearts was a disease (of disbelief) said: "These people (Muslims) are deceived by their religion." But whoever puts his trust in Allâh, then surely, Allâh is All-Mighty, All-Wise.

50. And if you could see when the angels take away the souls of those who disbelieve (at death); they smite their faces and their backs, (saying): "Taste the punishment of the blazing Fire."

51. "This is because of that which your hands had forwarded. And verily, Allâh is not unjust to His slaves."

52. Similar to the behaviour of the people of Fir'aun (Pharaoh), and of those before them — they rejected the Ayât (proofs, verses, etc.) of Allâh, so Allâh punished them for their sins. Verily, Allâh is All-Strong, Severe in punishment.

53. That is so because Allâh will never change a grace which He has bestowed on a people until they change what is in their ownselves. And verily, Allâh is All-Hearer, All-Knower.

54. Similar to the behaviour of the people of Fir'aun (Pharaoh), and those before them. They belied the Ayât (proofs, evidences, verses, lessons, signs, revelations, etc.) of their Lord, so We destroyed them for their sins, and We drowned the people of Fir'aun (Pharaoh) for they were all *Zâlimûn* (polytheists and wrongdoers).

55. Verily, the worst of moving (living) creatures before Allâh are those who disbelieve,[1] — so they shall not believe.

56. They are those with whom you made a covenant, but they break their covenant every time and they do not fear Allâh.

57. So if you gain the mastery over them in war, punish them severely in order to disperse those who are behind them, so that they may learn a lesson.

58. If you (O Muhammad صلى الله عليه وسلم) fear treachery from any people throw back (their covenant) to them (so as to be) on equal terms (that there will be no more covenant between you and them). Certainly Allâh likes not the treacherous.

59. And let not those who disbelieve think that they can outstrip (escape from the punishment). Verily, they will never be able to save themselves (from Allâh's punishment).

60. And make ready against them all you can of power, including steeds of war (tanks, planes, missiles, artillery) to threaten the enemy of Allâh and your

---

[1] (V.8:55) i.e. disbelieve in their Lord (Allâh), deny His Oneness, worship others besides Him, deny His Messengers, and believe not in the Divine Revelation.

enemy, and others besides whom, you may not know but whom Allâh does know. And whatever you shall spend in the Cause of Allâh shall be repaid unto you, and you shall not be treated unjustly.

61. But if they incline to peace, you also incline to it, and (put your) trust in Allâh. Verily, He is the All-Hearer, the All-Knower.

62. And if they intend to deceive you, then verily, Allâh is All-Sufficient for you. He it is Who has supported you with His Help and with the believers.

63. And He has united their (i.e. believers') hearts. If you had spent all that is in the earth, you could not have united their hearts, but Allâh has united them. Certainly He is All-Mighty, All-Wise.

64. O Prophet (Muhammad صلى الله عليه وسلم)! Allâh is Sufficient for you and for the believers who follow you.

65. O Prophet (Muhammad صلى الله عليه وسلم)! Urge the believers to fight. If there are twenty steadfast persons amongst you, they will overcome two hundreds, and if there be a hundred steadfast persons they will overcome a thousand of those who disbelieve, because they (the disbelievers) are people who do not understand.

66. Now Allâh has lightened your (task), for He knows that there is weakness in you. So if there are of you a hundred steadfast persons, they shall overcome two hundreds, and if there are a thousands of you, they shall overcome two thousands with the Leave of Allâh. And Allâh is with *As-Sâbirûn* (the patient).

67. It is not for a Prophet that he should have prisoners of war (and free them with ransom) until he had made a great slaughter (among his enemies) in the land. You desire the good of this world (i.e. the money of ransom for freeing the captives), but Allâh desires (for you) the Hereafter. And Allâh is All-Mighty, All-Wise.

68. Were it not a previous ordainment from Allâh, a severe torment would have touched you for what you took.

69. So enjoy what you have gotten of booty in war, lawful and good, and be afraid of Allâh. Certainly, Allâh is Oft-Forgiving, Most Merciful.

70. O Prophet (Muhammad صلى الله عليه وسلم)! Say to the captives that are in your hands: "If Allâh knows any good in your hearts, He will give you something better than what has been taken from you, and He will forgive you, and Allâh is Oft-Forgiving, Most Merciful."

71. But if they intend to betray you (O Muhammad صلى الله عليه وسلم), they indeed betrayed Allâh before. So He gave (you) power over them. And Allâh is All-Knower, All-Wise.

72. Verily, those who believed, and emigrated and strove hard and fought with their property and their lives in the Cause of Allâh as well as those who gave (them) asylum and help, — these are (all) allies to one another. And as to those who believed but did not emigrate (to you O Muhammad وسلم عليه الله صلى), you owe no duty of protection to them until they emigrate,[1] but if they seek your help in religion, it is your duty to help them except against a people with whom you have a treaty of mutual alliance; and Allâh is the All-Seer of what you do.

إِنَّ ٱلَّذِينَ ءَامَنُواْ وَهَاجَرُواْ وَجَـٰهَدُواْ بِأَمْوَٰلِهِمْ وَأَنفُسِهِمْ فِى سَبِيلِ ٱللَّهِ وَٱلَّذِينَ ءَاوَواْ وَّنَصَرُوٓاْ أُوْلَـٰٓئِكَ بَعْضُهُمْ أَوْلِيَآءُ بَعْضٍ ۚ وَٱلَّذِينَ ءَامَنُواْ وَلَمْ يُهَاجِرُواْ مَا لَكُم مِّن وَلَـٰيَتِهِم مِّن شَىْءٍ حَتَّىٰ يُهَاجِرُواْ ۚ وَإِنِ ٱسْتَنصَرُوكُمْ فِى ٱلدِّينِ فَعَلَيْكُمُ ٱلنَّصْرُ إِلَّا عَلَىٰ قَوْمٍۭ بَيْنَكُمْ وَبَيْنَهُم مِّيثَـٰقٌ ۗ وَٱللَّهُ بِمَا تَعْمَلُونَ بَصِيرٌ ۝

73. And those who disbelieve are allies of one another, (and) if you (Muslims of the whole world collectively) do not do so [i.e. become allies, as one united block under one *Khalîfah* (a chief Muslim ruler for the whole Muslim world) to make victorious Allâh's religion of Islâmic Monotheism], there will be *Fitnah* (wars, battles, polytheism) and oppression on the earth, and a great mischief and corruption (appearance of polytheism).[2]

وَٱلَّذِينَ كَفَرُواْ بَعْضُهُمْ أَوْلِيَآءُ بَعْضٍ ۚ إِلَّا تَفْعَلُوهُ تَكُن فِتْنَةٌ فِى ٱلْأَرْضِ وَفَسَادٌ كَبِيرٌ ۝

---

[1] (V.8:72): See the footnote of (V.3:149).

[2] (V.8:73) It has been mentioned in *Tafsir At-Tabari*, that the best interpretation of this Verse: - ["And those who disbelieve are allies of one another, (and) if you (Muslims of the whole world collectively) do not do so (i.e. become allies, as one united block — V.8:73).] is "That if you do not do what We (Allâh) have ordered you to do, [i.e. all of you (Muslims of the whole world) do not become allies as one united block to make Allâh's religion (Islâm)

74. And those who believed, and emigrated and strove hard in the Cause of Allâh (*Al-Jihâd*), as well as those who gave (them) asylum and aid — these are the believers in truth, for them is forgiveness and *Rizqun Karîm* (a generous provision i.e. Paradise!)

75. And those who believed afterwards, and emigrated and strove hard along with you (in the Cause of Allâh), they are of you. But kindred by blood are nearer to one another (regarding inheritance) in the decree ordained by Allâh. Verily, Allâh is the All-Knower of everything.

وَالَّذِينَ ءَامَنُوا وَهَاجَرُوا وَجَهَدُوا فِى سَبِيلِ اللَّهِ وَالَّذِينَ ءَاوَوا وَّنَصَرُوٓا أُوْلَٰٓئِكَ هُمُ الْمُؤْمِنُونَ حَقًّا لَّهُم مَّغْفِرَةٌ وَرِزْقٌ كَرِيمٌ ٧٤ وَالَّذِينَ ءَامَنُوا مِنۢ بَعْدُ وَهَاجَرُوا وَجَهَدُوا مَعَكُمْ فَأُوْلَٰٓئِكَ مِنكُمْ وَأُوْلُوا الْأَرْحَامِ بَعْضُهُمْ أَوْلَىٰ بِبَعْضٍ فِى كِتَٰبِ اللَّهِ إِنَّ اللَّهَ بِكُلِّ شَىْءٍ عَلِيمٌ ٧٥

---

victorious, there will be a great *Fitnah* (polytheism, wars, battles, killing, robbing, a great mischief, corruption and oppression, etc.)"].
And it is *Fitnah* to have many *Khalîfah* (Muslim rulers), as it has been mentioned in *Sahîh Muslim* by 'Arfajah, who said: I heard Allâh's Messenger صلى الله عليه وسلم saying: "When you all (Muslims) are united (as one block) under a single *Khalîfah* (a chief Muslim ruler), and a man comes up to disintegrate you and separate you into different groups, then kill that man."

Also there is another narration in *Sahîh Muslim*: Narrated Abu Sa'îd Al-Khudrî رضي الله عنه Allâh's Messenger صلى الله عليه وسلم said: "If the Muslim world gave the *Bai'a* (pledge) to two *Khalîfah* (chief Muslim rulers), the first one who was given the *Bai'a* (pledge) first will remain as the *Khalîfah*, then kill the latter (the second) one."

So it is a legal obligation, from the above-mentioned evident proofs (from the Qur'ân and the Prophet's statement), that there shall not be more than one *Khalîfah* (a chief Muslim ruler) for the whole Muslim world or otherwise there will be a great *Fitnah* (mischief and evil) amongst the Muslims, the ultimate results of which will not be worthy of praise.

Sûrat At-Taubah
(The Repentance) IX

1. Freedom from (all) obligations (is declared) from Allâh and His Messenger (صلى الله عليه وسلم) to those of the *Mushrikûn* (polytheists, pagans, idolaters, disbelievers in the Oneness of Allâh), with whom you made a treaty.

2. So travel freely (O *Mushrikûn* — See V.2:105) for four months (as you will) throughout the land, but know that you cannot escape (from the punishment of) Allâh; and Allâh will disgrace the disbelievers.

3. And a declaration from Allâh and His Messenger to mankind on the greatest day (the 10th of Dhul-Hijjah — the 12th month of Islâmic calendar) that Allâh is free from (all) obligations to the *Mushrikûn* (See V.2:105) and so is His Messenger. So if you (*Mushrikûn*) repent, it is better for you, but if you turn away, then know that you cannot escape (from the punishment of) Allâh. And give tidings (O Muhammad صلى الله عليه وسلم) of a painful torment to those who disbelieve.

4. Except those of the *Mushrikûn* (see V.2:105) with whom you have a treaty, and who have not subsequently failed you in aught, nor have supported anyone against you. So fulfil their treaty to them for the end of their term. Surely, Allâh loves *Al-Mattaqûn* (the pious. See V.2:2).

5. Then when the Sacred Months (the 1st, 7th, 11th, and 12th month of the Islâmic calendar) have passed, then kill the *Mushrikûn* (See V.2:105) wherever you find them, and capture them and besiege them, and lie in wait for them in every ambush. But if they repent and perform *As-Salât* (Iqâmat-as-Salât), and give *Zakât*, then leave their way free. Verily, Allâh is Oft-Forgiving, Most Merciful.[1]

فَإِذَا ٱنسَلَخَ ٱلْأَشْهُرُ ٱلْحُرُمُ فَٱقْتُلُوا ٱلْمُشْرِكِينَ حَيْثُ وَجَدتُّمُوهُمْ وَخُذُوهُمْ وَٱحْصُرُوهُمْ وَٱقْعُدُوا لَهُمْ كُلَّ مَرْصَدٍ فَإِن تَابُوا وَأَقَامُوا ٱلصَّلَوٰةَ وَءَاتَوُا ٱلزَّكَوٰةَ فَخَلُّوا سَبِيلَهُمْ إِنَّ ٱللَّهَ غَفُورٌ رَّحِيمٌ ٥

6. And if anyone of the *Mushrikûn* (polytheists, idolaters, pagans, disbelievers in the Oneness of Allâh) seeks your protection then grant him protection — so that he may hear the Word of Allâh (the Qur'ân) — and then escort him to where he can be secure, that is because they are men who know not.

وَإِنْ أَحَدٌ مِّنَ ٱلْمُشْرِكِينَ ٱسْتَجَارَكَ فَأَجِرْهُ حَتَّىٰ يَسْمَعَ كَلَٰمَ ٱللَّهِ ثُمَّ أَبْلِغْهُ مَأْمَنَهُۥ ذَٰلِكَ بِأَنَّهُمْ قَوْمٌ لَّا يَعْلَمُونَ ٦

7. How can there be a covenant with Allâh and with His Messenger for the *Mushrikûn* (polytheists, idolaters, pagans, disbelievers in the Oneness of Allâh) except those with whom you made a covenant near *Al-Masjid Al-Harâm* (at Makkah)? So long as they are true to you, stand you true to them. Verily, Allâh loves *Al-Muttaqûn* (the pious. See V.2:2).

كَيْفَ يَكُونُ لِلْمُشْرِكِينَ عَهْدٌ عِندَ ٱللَّهِ وَعِندَ رَسُولِهِۦٓ إِلَّا ٱلَّذِينَ عَٰهَدتُّمْ عِندَ ٱلْمَسْجِدِ ٱلْحَرَامِ فَمَا ٱسْتَقَٰمُوا لَكُمْ فَٱسْتَقِيمُوا لَهُمْ إِنَّ ٱللَّهَ يُحِبُّ ٱلْمُتَّقِينَ ٧

8. How (can there be such a covenant with them) that when you are overpowered by them, they regard not the ties, either of kinship or of covenant with you? With (good words from) their mouths they please you, but their hearts

كَيْفَ وَإِن يَظْهَرُوا عَلَيْكُمْ لَا يَرْقُبُوا فِيكُمْ إِلًّا وَلَا ذِمَّةً يُرْضُونَكُم بِأَفْوَٰهِهِمْ وَتَأْبَىٰ قُلُوبُهُمْ وَأَكْثَرُهُمْ

---

[1] (V.9:5) See the footnote of (V.2:193).

are averse to you, and most of them are *Fâsiqûn* (rebellious, disobedient to Allâh).

9. They have purchased with the *Ayât* (proofs, evidences, verses, lessons, signs, revelations, etc.) of Allâh a little gain, and they hindered men from His way; evil indeed is that which they used to do.

10. With regard to a believer, they respect not the ties, either of kinship or of covenant! It is they who are the transgressors.

11. But if they repent, perform *As-Salât* (Iqâmat-as-Salât) and give *Zakât*, then they are your brethren in religion. (In this way) We explain the *Ayât* (proofs, evidences, verses, lessons, signs, revelations, etc.) in detail for a people who know.

12. But if they violate their oaths after their covenant, and attack your religion with disapproval and criticism then fight (you) the leaders of disbelief (chiefs of Quraish pagans of Makkah) — for surely, their oaths are nothing to them — so that they may stop (evil actions).

13. Will you not fight a people who have violated their oaths (pagans of Makkah) and intended to expel the Messenger while they did attack you first? Do you fear them? Allâh has more right that you should fear Him if you are believers.

14. Fight against them so that Allâh will punish them by your hands and disgrace them and give you victory over them and heal the breasts of a believing people,

15. And remove the anger of their (believers') hearts. Allâh accepts the repentance of whom He wills. Allâh is All-Knowing, All-Wise.

16. Do you think that you shall be left alone while Allâh has not yet tested those among you who have striven hard and fought and have not taken *Walîjah* [(*Bitânah* — helpers, advisors and consultants from disbelievers, pagans) giving openly to them their secrets] besides Allâh and His Messenger, and the believers. Allâh is Well-Acquainted with what you do.

17. It is not for the *Mushrikûn* (polytheists, idolaters, pagans, disbelievers in the Oneness of Allâh), to maintain the Mosques of Allâh (i.e. to pray and worship Allâh therein, to look after their cleanliness and their building), while they witness against their ownselves of disbelief. The works of such are in vain and in Fire shall they abide.

18. The Mosques of Allâh shall be maintained only by those who believe in Allâh and the Last Day; perform *As-Salât (Iqâmat-as-Salât)*, and give *Zakât* and fear none but Allâh. It is they who are on true guidance.

19. Do you consider the providing of drinking water to the pilgrims and the maintenance of *Al-Masjid Al-Harâm* (at Makkah) as equal to the worth of those who believe in Allâh and the Last Day, and strive hard and fight in the Cause of Allâh? They are not equal before Allâh.

And Allâh guides not those people who are the *Zâlimûn* (polytheists and wrongdoers).

20. Those who believed (in the Oneness of Allâh — Islâmic Monotheism) and emigrated and strove hard and fought in Allâh's Cause with their wealth and their lives are far higher in degree with Allâh. They are the successful.[1]

---

[1] (V.9:20).

a. Narrated Abu Hurairah رضى الله عنه: The Prophet صلى الله عليه وسلم said, "Whoever believes in Allâh and His Messenger, performs *Salât* (*Iqamât-as-Salât*) and observes *Saum* (fasts) during the month of Ramadan, then it will be a promise binding upon Allâh to admit him to Paradise, no matter whether he fights in Allâh's Cause or remains in the land where he is born." The people said, "O Allâh's Messenger! Shall we acquaint the people with this good news?" He said, "Paradise has one hundred grades which Allâh has reserved for the *Mujahidûn* who fight in His Cause, and the distance between each of two grades is like the distance between the heaven and the earth. So, when, you ask Allâh (for something), ask for *Al-Firdaus* which is the middle and highest part of Paradise." [The subnarrator added, "I think the Prophet صلى الله عليه وسلم also said, 'Above it (i.e. *Al-Firdaus*) is the Throne of the Most Gracious (i.e. Allâh), and from it gush forth the rivers of Paradise'." (*Sahih Al-Bukhâri*, Vol.4, *Hadith* No.48).

b. The wish for martyrdom.

Narrated Abu Hurairah رضى الله عنه: The Prophet صلى الله عليه وسلم said, "By Him in Whose Hand my soul is! Were it not for some men amongst the believers who dislike to be left behind me, and whom I cannot provide with means of conveyance, I would certainly never remain behind any *Sariya* (army unit) going out for *Jihâd* in Allâh's Cause. By Him in Whose Hand my soul is! I would love to be martyred in Allâh's Cause and then come back to life, and then get martyred and then come back to life again, and then get martyred and then come back to life again, and then get martyred." (*Sahih Al-Bukhâri*, Vol.4, *Hadith* No.54).

21. Their Lord gives them glad tidings of Mercy from Him, and His being pleased (with them), and of Gardens (Paradise) for them wherein are everlasting delights.

22. They will dwell therein forever. Verily, with Allâh is a great reward.

23. O you who believe! Take not as *Auliyâ'* (supporters and helpers) your fathers and your brothers if they prefer disbelief to Belief. And whoever of you does so, then he is one of the *Zâlimûn* (wrongdoers).

24. Say: If your fathers, your sons, your brothers, your wives, your kindred, the wealth that you have gained, the commerce in which you fear a decline, and the dwellings in which you delight ... are dearer to you than Allâh and His Messenger, and striving hard and fighting in His Cause,[1] then wait until Allâh brings about His Decision (torment). And Allâh guides not the people who are *Al-Fâsiqûn* (the rebellious, disobedient to Allâh).

25. Truly, Allâh has given you victory on many battlefields, and on the Day of Hunain (battle) when you rejoiced at your great number, but it availed you naught and the earth, vast as it is, was straitened for you, then you turned back in flight.

26. Then Allâh did send down His *Sakînah* (calmness, tranquillity and

---

[1] (V.9:24): See the footnote of (V.2:190).

reassurance) on the Messenger (Muhammad صلى الله عليه وسلم), and on the believers, and sent down forces (angels) which you saw not, and punished the disbelievers. Such is the recompense of disbelievers.

27. Then after that Allâh will accept the repentance of whom He wills. And Allâh is Oft-Forgiving, Most Merciful.

28. O you who believe (in Allâh's Oneness and in His Messenger Muhammad صلى الله عليه وسلم)! Verily, the *Mushrikûn* (polytheists, pagans, idolaters, disbelievers in the Oneness of Allâh, and in the Message of Muhammad صلى الله عليه وسلم) are *Najasun* (impure).[1] So let them not come near *Al-Masjid Al-Harâm* (at Makkah) after this year; and if you fear poverty, Allâh will enrich you if He wills, out of His Bounty. Surely, Allâh is All-Knowing, All-Wise.

29. Fight against those who (1) believe not in Allâh, (2) nor in the Last Day, (3) nor forbid that which has been forbidden by Allâh and His Messenger (Muhammad صلى الله عليه وسلم) (4) and those who acknowledge not the religion of truth (i.e. Islâm) among the people of the Scripture (Jews and Christians), until

---

[1] (V.9:28) Their impurity is spiritual and physical: spiritual, because they don't believe in Allâh's Oneness and in His Prophet Muhammad صلى الله عليه وسلم; and physical, because they lack personal hygiene (filthy as regards urine, stools and blood etc.). And the word *Najas* is used only for those persons who have spiritual impurity e.g. *Al-Mushrikûn*.

they pay the *Jizyah*[1] with willing submission, and feel themselves subdued.

30. And the Jews say: 'Uzair (Ezra) is the son of Allâh, and the Christians say: Messiah is the son of Allâh. That is their saying with their mouths, resembling the saying of those who disbelieved aforetime. Allâh's Curse be on them, how they are deluded away from the truth![2]

31. They (Jews and Christians) took their rabbis and their monks to be their lords besides Allâh (by obeying them in things which they made lawful or unlawful according to their own desires without being ordered by Allâh), and (they also took as their Lord) Messiah, son of Maryam (Mary), while they (Jews and Christians) were commanded [in the Taurât (Torah) and the Injeel (Gospel)] to worship none but One *Ilâh* (God — Allâh) *Lâ ilâha illa Huwa* (none has the right to be worshipped but He)[3]. Praise and glory is to Him

ﺣَﺘَّﻰٰ ﻳُﻌْﻄُﻮﺍ۟ ﭐﻟْﺠِﺰْﻳَﺔَ ﻋَﻦ ﻳَﺪٍ

ﻭَﻫُﻢْ ﺻَٰﻐِﺮُﻭﻥَ ۝

ﻭَﻗَﺎﻟَﺖِ ﭐﻟْﻴَﻬُﻮﺩُ ﻋُﺰَﻳْﺮٌ ﭐﺑْﻦُ ﭐﻟﻠَّﻪِ

ﻭَﻗَﺎﻟَﺖِ ﭐﻟﻨَّﺼَٰﺮَﻯ ﭐﻟْﻤَﺴِﻴﺢُ

ﭐﺑْﻦُ ﭐﻟﻠَّﻪِ ﺫَٰﻟِﻚَ ﻗَﻮْﻟُﻬُﻢ

ﺑِﺄَﻓْﻮَٰﻫِﻬِﻢْ ﻳُﻀَٰﻬِﺌُﻮﻥَ

ﻗَﻮْﻝَ ﭐﻟَّﺬِﻳﻦَ ﻛَﻔَﺮُﻭﺍ۟ ﻣِﻦ ﻗَﺒْﻞُ

ﻗَٰﺘَﻠَﻬُﻢُ ﭐﻟﻠَّﻪُ ﺃَﻧَّﻰٰ

ﻳُﺆْﻓَﻜُﻮﻥَ ۝

ﭐﺗَّﺨَﺬُﻭﺍ۟ ﺃَﺣْﺒَﺎﺭَﻫُﻢْ

ﻭَﺭُﻫْﺒَٰﻨَﻬُﻢْ ﺃَﺭْﺑَﺎﺑًﺎ ﻣِّﻦ

ﺩُﻭﻥِ ﭐﻟﻠَّﻪِ ﻭَﭐﻟْﻤَﺴِﻴﺢَ ﭐﺑْﻦَ

ﻣَﺮْﻳَﻢَ ﻭَﻣَﺎٓ ﺃُﻣِﺮُﻭﺍ۟ ﺇِﻟَّﺎ

ﻟِﻴَﻌْﺒُﺪُﻭﺍ۟ ﺇِﻟَٰﻬًﺎ ﻭَٰﺣِﺪًﺍ

ﻟَّﺎٓ ﺇِﻟَٰﻪَ ﺇِﻟَّﺎ ﻫُﻮَ ﺳُﺒْﺤَٰﻨَﻪُۥ

ﻋَﻤَّﺎ ﻳُﺸْﺮِﻛُﻮﻥَ ۝

---

[1] (V.9:29) *Jizyah*: a tax levied from the people of the Scriptures (Jews and Christians, etc.), who are under the protection of a Muslim government.

[2] (V.9:30)

*(A) See the footnote of (V.2:116).

(B) See the footnote of (V.4:40) and the footnote (C) of (V.68:42).

[3] (V.9:31) Once while Allâh's Messenger ﺻﻠﻰ ﺍﻟﻠﻪ ﻋﻠﻴﻪ ﻭﺳﻠﻢ was reciting this Verse, 'Adî bin Hâtim said, "O Allâh's Messenger! They do not worship them (i.e. the rabbis and monks)." Allâh's Messenger ﺻﻠﻰ ﺍﻟﻠﻪ ﻋﻠﻴﻪ ﻭ ﺳﻠﻢ said: "They certainly do. [They (i.e. the rabbis and monks) made lawful things as unlawful and unlawful things as lawful, and they (i.e. Jews and Christians) followed them; and by doing so, they really worshipped them]." (Narrated by *Ahmad*, *At-Tirmidhî*, and *Ibn Jarîr*).

(far above is He) from having the partners they associate (with Him)."

32. They (the disbelievers, the Jews and the Christians) want to extinguish Allâh's Light (with which Muhammad صلى الله عليه وسلم has been sent — Islâmic Monotheism) with their mouths, but Allâh will not allow except that His Light should be perfected even though the *Kâfirûn* (disbelievers) hate (it).

33. It is He Who has sent His Messenger (Muhammad صلى الله عليه وسلم) with guidance and the religion of truth (Islâm), to make it superior over all religions even though the *Mushrikûn* (polytheists, pagans, idolaters, disbelievers in the Oneness of Allâh) hate (it).

34. O you who believe! Verily, there are many of the (Jewish) rabbis and the (Christian) monks who devour the wealth of mankind in falsehood, and hinder (them) from the Way of Allâh (i.e. Allâh's religion of Islâmic Monotheism). And those who hoard up gold and silver [*Al-Kanz:* the money, the *Zakât* of which has not been paid] and spend them not in the Way of Allâh, announce unto them a painful torment.

35. On the Day when that (*Al-Kanz:* money, gold and silver, the *Zakât* of which has not been paid) will be heated in the Fire of Hell and with it will be branded their foreheads, their flanks, and their backs, (and it will be said unto them):-"This is the treasure which you hoarded for yourselves. Now taste of what you used to hoard."[1]

36. Verily, the number of months with Allâh is twelve months (in a year), so was it ordained by Allâh on the Day when He created the heavens and the earth; of them four are Sacred (i.e. the 1st, the 7th, the 11th and the 12th months of the Islâmic calendar). That is the right religion, so wrong not yourselves therein, and fight against the *Mushrikûn* (polytheists, pagans, idolaters, disbelievers in the Oneness of Allâh) collectively[2] as they fight against you collectively. But know that Allâh is with those who are *Al-Muttaqûn* (the pious. See V.2:2).

37. The postponing (of a Sacred Month) is indeed an addition to disbelief: thereby the disbelievers are led astray, for they make it lawful one year and forbid it another year in order to adjust the number of months forbidden by Allâh, and make such forbidden ones lawful. The evil of their deeds is made fair-seeming to them. And Allâh guides not the people who disbelieve.

38. O you who believe! What is the matter with you, that when you are asked to march forth in the Cause of Allâh (i.e. *Jihâd*) you cling heavily to the earth? Are

---

[1] (V.9:35) See the footnote of (V.3:180).

[2] (V.9:36) See the footnotes of (V.2:193) and (V.8:73).

you pleased with the life of this world rather than the Hereafter? But little is the enjoyment of the life of this world as compared to the Hereafter.[1]

39. If you march not forth, He will punish you with a painful torment and will replace you by another people; and you cannot harm Him at all, and Allâh is Able to do all things.

40. If you help him (Muhammad صلى الله عليه وسلم) not (it does not matter), for Allâh did indeed help him when the disbelievers drove him out, the second of the two; when they (Muhammad صلى الله عليه وسلم and Abu Bakr رضي الله عنه) were in the cave, he (صلى الله عليه وسلم) said to his companion (Abu Bakr: رضي الله عنه): "Be not sad (or afraid), surely, Allâh is with us." Then Allâh sent down His Sakînah (calmness, tranquillity, peace) upon him, and strengthened him with forces (angels) which you saw not, and made the word of those who disbelieved the lowermost, while the Word of Allâh that became the uppermost; and Allâh is All-Mighty, All-Wise.

41. March forth, whether you are light (being healthy, young and wealthy) or heavy (being ill, old and

---

[1] (V.9:38) Narrated Anas bin Mâlik رضي الله عنه: The Prophet صلى الله عليه said, "Nobody who dies and finds good from Allâh (in the Hereafter) would wish to come back to this world, even if he were given the whole world and whatever is in it except the martyr who, on seeing the superiority of martyrdom would like to come back to the world and get killed again (in Allâh's Cause)." (Sahih Al-Bukhâri, Vol.4, Hadîth No.53-A).

poor), and strive hard with your wealth and your lives in the Cause of Allâh. This is better for you, if you but knew.

42. Had it been a near gain (booty in front of them) and an easy journey, they would have followed you, but the distance (Tabuk expedition) was long for them; and they would swear by Allâh, "If we only could, we would certainly have come forth with you." They destroy their ownselves, and Allâh knows that they are liars.

43. May Allâh forgive you (O Muhammad (ﷺ) . Why did you grant them leave (for remaining behind; you should have persisted as regards your order to them to proceed on *Jihâd*), until those who told the truth were seen by you in a clear light, and you had known the liars?

44. Those who believe in Allâh and the Last Day would not ask your leave to be exempted from fighting with their properties and their lives; and Allâh is the All-Knower of *Al-Muttaqûn* (the pious. See V.2:2).

45. It is only those who believe not in Allâh and the Last Day and whose hearts are in doubt that ask your leave (to be exempted from *Jihâd*). So in their doubts they waver.

46. And if they had intended to march out, certainly, they would have made some preparation for it; but Allâh was averse to their being sent forth, so

He made them lag behind, and it was said (to them), "Sit you among those who sit (at home)."

47. Had they marched out with you, they would have added to you nothing except disorder, and they would have hurried about in your midst (spreading corruption) and sowing sedition among you — and there are some among you who would have listened to them. And Allâh is the All-Knower of the Zâlimûn (polytheists and wrongdoers).

48. Verily, they had plotted sedition before, and had upset matters for you, until the truth (victory) came and the Decree of Allâh (His religion, Islâm) became manifest though they hated it.

49. And among them is he who says:"Grant me leave (to be exempted from Jihâd) and put me not into trial." Surely, they have fallen into trial. And verily, Hell is surrounding the disbelievers.

50. If good befalls you (O Muhammad ﷺ), it grieves them, but if a calamity overtakes you, they say: "We took our precaution beforehand" and they turn away rejoicing.

51. Say: "Nothing shall ever happen to us except what Allâh has ordained for us.[1] He is our Maulâ (Lord, Helper and Protector)." And in Allâh let the believers put their trust.

---

[1] (V.9:51) See the footnote of (V.57:22).

52. Say: "Do you wait for us (anything) except one of the two best things (martyrdom or victory); while we await for you either that Allâh will afflict you with a punishment from Himself or at our hands. So wait, we too are waiting with you."

53. Say: "Spend (in Allâh's Cause) willingly or unwillingly, it will not be accepted from you. Verily, you are ever a people who are *Fâsiqûn* (rebellious, disobedient to Allâh)."

54. And nothing prevents their contributions from being accepted from them except that they disbelieved in Allâh and in His Messenger (Muhammad صلى الله عليه وسلم), and that they came not to *As-Salât* (the prayer) except in a lazy state,[1] and that they offer not contributions but unwillingly.

55. So let not their wealth or their children amaze you (O Muhammad صلى الله عليه وسلم); in reality Allâh's Plan is to punish them with these things in the life of the this world, and that their souls shall depart (die) while they are disbelievers.

---

[1] (V.9:54) Narrated Abu Hurairah رضي الله عنه The Prophet صلى الله عليه وسلم said, "No *Salât* (prayer) is more heavy (harder) for the hypocrites than the *Fajr* and the *'Ishâ* prayer; but if they knew the reward for these *Salât* (prayers) at their respective times, they would certainly present themselves (in the mosques) even if they had to crawl." The Prophet صلى الله عليه وسلم added, "Certainly, I intended (or was about) to order the *Mu'adhdhin* (call-maker) to pronounce *Iqâmah* and order a man to lead the *Salât* (prayer), and then take a fire flame to burn all those (men along with their houses) who had not yet left their houses for the *Salât* (prayer) (in the mosques)." (*Sahih Al-Bukhâri*, Vol.1, *Hadith* No. 626).

56. They swear by Allâh that they are truly, of you while they are of you, but they are a people (hypocrites) who are afraid (that you may kill them).

57. Should they find a refuge, or caves, or a place of concealment, they would turn straightway thereto with a swift rush.

58. And of them are some who accuse you (O Muhammad صلى الله عليه وسلم) in the matter of (the distribution of) the alms. If they are given part thereof, they are pleased, but if they are not given thereof, behold! They are enraged! [1]

59. Would that they were contented with what Allâh and His Messenger (صلى الله عليه وسلم) gave them and had said: "Allâh is Sufficient for us. Allâh will give us of His Bounty, and so will His Messenger (from alms). We implore Allâh (to enrich us)."

60. As-Sadaqât (here it means Zakât) are only for the Fuqarâ' (poor), and Al-Masâkîn [2] (the poor) and those employed to collect (the funds); and to attract the hearts of those who have been inclined (towards Islâm); and to free the captives; and for those in debt; and for Allâh's Cause (i.e. for Mujâhidûn — those fighting in a holy battle), and for the wayfarer (a traveller who is cut off from everything); a duty

---

[1] (V.9:58) See the footnote of (V.20:134).

[2] (V.9:60) See the footnote of (V.2:83) and also see (V.2:273).

imposed by Allâh. And Allâh is All-Knower, All-Wise.

61. And among them are men who annoy the Prophet (Muhammad صلى الله عليه وسلم) and say: "He is (lending his) ear (to every news)." Say: "He listens to what is best for you; he believes in Allâh; has faith in the believers; and is a mercy to those of you who believe." But those who annoy Allâh's Messenger (Muhammad صلى الله عليه وسلم) will have a painful torment. [See V.33:57]

62. They swear by Allâh to you (Muslims) in order to please you, but it is more fitting that they should please Allâh and His Messenger (Muhammad صلى الله عليه وسلم), if they are believers.

63. Know they not that whoever opposes and shows hostility to Allâh (عز وجل) and His Messenger (صلى الله عليه وسلم), certainly for him will be the Fire of Hell to abide therein. That is the extreme disgrace.

64. The hypocrites fear lest a *Sûrah* (chapter of the Qur'ân) should be revealed about them, showing them what is in their hearts. Say: "(Go ahead and) mock! But certainly Allâh will bring to light all that you fear."

65. If you ask them (about this), they declare: "We were only talking idly and joking." Say: "Was it at Allâh (عز وجل), and His *Ayât* (proofs, evidences, verses, lessons, signs, revelations, etc.) and His Messenger (صلى الله عليه وسلم) that you were mocking?"

66. Make no excuse; you have disbelieved after you had believed. If We pardon some of you, We will punish others amongst you because they were *Mujrimûn* (disbelievers, polytheists, sinners, criminals).

67. The hypocrites, men and women, are one from another; they enjoin (on the people) *Al-Munkar* (i.e. disbelief and polytheism of all kinds and all that Islâm has forbidden), and forbid (people) from *Al-Ma'rûf* (i.e. Islâmic Monotheism and all that Islâm orders one to do), and they close their hands [from giving (spending in Allâh's Cause) alms]. They have forgotten Allâh, so He has forgotten them. Verily, the hypocrites are the *Fâsiqûn* (rebellious, disobedient to Allâh).

68. Allâh has promised to the hypocrites — men and women — and the disbelievers, the Fire of Hell; therein shall they abide. It will suffice them. Allâh has cursed them and for them is the lasting torment.

69. Like those before you: they were mightier than you in power, and more abundant in wealth and children. They had enjoyed their portion (awhile), so enjoy your portion (awhile) as those before you enjoyed their portion (awhile); and you indulged in play and pastime (and in telling lies against Allâh and His Messenger Muhammad صلى الله عليه وسلم as they indulged in play and pastime. Such are they whose deeds are in vain in this world and in the Hereafter. Such are they who are the losers.

70. Has not the story reached them of those before them? — The people of Nûh (Noah), 'Âd, and Thamûd, the people of Ibrâhîm (Abraham), the dwellers of Madyan (Midian) and the cities overthrown [i.e. the people to whom Lût (Lot) preached]; to them came their Messengers with clear proofs. So it was not Allâh Who wronged them, but they used to wrong themselves.

71. The believers, men and women, are *Auliyâ'* (helpers, supporters, friends, protectors) of one another; they enjoin (on the people) *Al-Ma'rûf* (i.e. Islâmic Monotheism and all that Islâm orders one to do), and forbid (people) from *Al-Munkar* (i.e. polytheism and disbelief of all kinds, and all that Islâm has forbidden); they perform *As-Salât (Iqâmat-as-Salât)*, and give the *Zakât*, and obey Allâh and His Messenger. Allâh will have His Mercy on them. Surely, Allâh is All-Mighty, All-Wise.

72. Allâh has promised to the believers —men and women, — Gardens under which rivers flow to dwell therein forever, and beautiful mansions in Gardens of *'Adn* (Eden Paradise). But the greatest bliss is the Good Pleasure of Allâh. That is the supreme success.

73. O Prophet (Muhammad صلى الله عليه وسلم)! Strive hard against the disbelievers and the hypocrites, and be harsh against them, their abode is Hell, — and worst indeed is that destination.

يَـٰٓأَيُّهَا ٱلنَّبِيُّ جَـٰهِدِ ٱلۡكُفَّارَ وَٱلۡمُنَـٰفِقِينَ وَٱغۡلُظۡ عَلَيۡهِمۡۚ وَمَأۡوَىٰهُمۡ جَهَنَّمُۖ وَبِئۡسَ ٱلۡمَصِيرُ ۝

74. They swear by Allâh that they said nothing (bad), but really they said the word of disbelief, and they disbelieved after accepting Islâm, and they resolved that (plot to murder Prophet Muhammad صلى الله عليه وسلم) which they were unable to carry out, and they could not find any cause to do so except that Allâh and His Messenger had enriched them of His Bounty. If then they repent, it will be better for them, but if they turn away; Allâh will punish them with a painful torment in this worldly life and in the Hereafter. And there is none for them on earth as a *Walî* (supporter, protector) or a helper.

يَحۡلِفُونَ بِٱللَّهِ مَا قَالُواْ وَلَقَدۡ قَالُواْ كَلِمَةَ ٱلۡكُفۡرِ وَكَفَرُواْ بَعۡدَ إِسۡلَـٰمِهِمۡ وَهَمُّواْ بِمَا لَمۡ يَنَالُواْۚ وَمَا نَقَمُوٓاْ إِلَّآ أَنۡ أَغۡنَىٰهُمُ ٱللَّهُ وَرَسُولُهُۥ مِن فَضۡلِهِۦۚ فَإِن يَتُوبُواْ يَكُ خَيۡرًا لَّهُمۡۖ وَإِن يَتَوَلَّوۡاْ يُعَذِّبۡهُمُ ٱللَّهُ عَذَابًا أَلِيمًا فِى ٱلدُّنۡيَا وَٱلۡأَخِرَةِۚ وَمَا لَهُمۡ فِى ٱلۡأَرۡضِ مِن وَلِىٍّ وَلَا نَصِيرٍ ۝

75. And of them are some who made a covenant with Allâh (saying): "If He bestowed on us of His Bounty, we will verily, give *Sadaqâh* (Zakât and voluntary charity in Allâh's Cause) and will be certainly among those who are righteous."

وَمِنۡهُم مَّنۡ عَـٰهَدَ ٱللَّهَ لَئِنۡ ءَاتَىٰنَا مِن فَضۡلِهِۦ لَنَصَّدَّقَنَّ وَلَنَكُونَنَّ مِنَ ٱلصَّـٰلِحِينَ ۝

76. Then when He gave them of His Bounty, they became niggardly [refused to pay the *Sadaqâh* (Zakât or voluntary charity)], and turned away, averse.

فَلَمَّآ ءَاتَىٰهُم مِّن فَضۡلِهِۦ بَخِلُواْ بِهِۦ وَتَوَلَّواْ وَّهُم مُّعۡرِضُونَ ۝

77. So He punished them by putting hypocrisy into their hearts till the Day whereon they shall meet Him, because they broke that (covenant with Allâh)

فَأَعۡقَبَهُمۡ نِفَاقًا فِى قُلُوبِهِمۡ إِلَىٰ يَوۡمِ يَلۡقَوۡنَهُۥ بِمَآ أَخۡلَفُواْ ٱللَّهَ مَا وَعَدُوهُ وَبِمَا كَانُواْ

which they had promised to Him and because they used to tell lies.

78. Know they not that Allâh knows their secret ideas, and their *Najwa*[1] (secret counsels), and that Allâh is the All-Knower of the Unseen.

79. Those who defame such of the believers who give charity (in Allâh's Cause) voluntarily, and such who could not find to give charity (in Allâh's Cause) except what is available to them — so they mock at them (believers); Allâh will throw back their mockery on them, and they shall have a painful torment.

80. Whether you (O Muhammad الله صلى) ask forgiveness for them (hypocrites) or ask not forgiveness for them — (and even) if you ask seventy times for their forgiveness — Allâh will not forgive them because they have disbelieved in Allâh and His Messenger (Muhammad صلى الله عليه وسلم). And Allâh guides not those people who are *Fâsiqûn* (rebellious, disobedient to Allâh).

81. Those who stayed away (from Tabûk expedition) rejoiced in their staying behind the Messenger of Allâh; they hated to strive and fight with their properties and their lives in the Cause of Allâh, and they said: "March not forth in the heat." Say: "The Fire of Hell is more intense in heat;" if only they could understand!

---

[1] (V.9:78) See the F.N. of (V.11:18).

82. So let them laugh a little and (they will) cry much as a recompense of what they used to earn (by committing sins).

فَلْيَضْحَكُوا قَلِيلًا وَلْيَبْكُوا كَثِيرًا جَزَاءً بِمَا كَانُوا يَكْسِبُونَ ۝

83. If Allâh brings you back to a party of them (the hypocrites), and they ask your permission to go out (to fight), say: "Never shall you go out with me nor fight an enemy with me; you were pleased to sit (inactive) on the first occasion, then you sit (now) with those who lag behind."

فَإِن رَّجَعَكَ اللَّهُ إِلَىٰ طَآئِفَةٍ مِّنْهُمْ فَاسْتَأْذَنُوكَ لِلْخُرُوجِ فَقُل لَّن تَخْرُجُوا مَعِيَ أَبَدًا وَلَن تُقَاتِلُوا مَعِيَ عَدُوًّا إِنَّكُمْ رَضِيتُم بِالْقُعُودِ أَوَّلَ مَرَّةٍ فَاقْعُدُوا مَعَ الْخَالِفِينَ ۝

84. And never (O Muhammad صلى الله عليه وسلم) pray (funeral prayer) for any of them (hypocrites) who dies, nor stand at his grave. Certainly they disbelieved in Allâh and His Messenger, and died while they were Fâsiqûn (rebellious, — disobedient to Allâh and His Messenger (صلى الله عليه وسلم).

وَلَا تُصَلِّ عَلَىٰ أَحَدٍ مِّنْهُم مَّاتَ أَبَدًا وَلَا تَقُمْ عَلَىٰ قَبْرِهِ إِنَّهُمْ كَفَرُوا بِاللَّهِ وَرَسُولِهِ وَمَاتُوا وَهُمْ فَاسِقُونَ ۝

85. And let not their wealth or their children amaze you. Allâh's Plan is to punish them with these things in this world, and that their souls shall depart (die) while they were disbelievers.

وَلَا تُعْجِبْكَ أَمْوَالُهُمْ وَأَوْلَادُهُمْ إِنَّمَا يُرِيدُ اللَّهُ أَن يُعَذِّبَهُم بِهَا فِي الدُّنْيَا وَتَزْهَقَ أَنفُسُهُمْ وَهُمْ كَافِرُونَ ۝

86. And when a Sûrah (chapter from the Qur'ân) is revealed, enjoining them to believe in Allâh and to strive hard and fight along with His Messenger, the wealthy among them ask your leave to exempt them (from Jihâd) and say, "Leave us (behind), we would be with those who sit (at home)."

وَإِذَا أُنزِلَتْ سُورَةٌ أَنْ آمِنُوا بِاللَّهِ وَجَاهِدُوا مَعَ رَسُولِهِ اسْتَأْذَنَكَ أُولُو الطَّوْلِ مِنْهُمْ وَقَالُوا ذَرْنَا نَكُن مَّعَ الْقَاعِدِينَ ۝

87. They are content to be with those (the women) who sit behind (at home).

رَضُوا بِأَن يَكُونُوا مَعَ الْخَوَالِفِ

Their hearts are sealed up (from all kinds of goodness and right guidance), so they understand not.

88. But the Messenger (Muhammad صلى الله عليه وسلم) and those who believed with him (in Islâmic Monotheism) strove hard and fought with their wealth and their lives (in Allâh's Cause). Such are they for whom are the good things, and it is they who will be successful.

89. For them Allâh has got ready Gardens (Paradise) under which rivers flow, to dwell therein forever. That is the supreme success.

90. And those who made excuses from the bedouins came (to you, O Prophet صلى الله عليه وسلم) asking your permission to exempt them (from the battle), and those who had lied to Allâh and His Messenger sat at home (without asking the permission for it); a painful torment will seize those of them who disbelieve.

91. There is no blame on those who are weak or ill or who find no resources to spend [in holy fighting (Jihâd)], if they are sincere and true (in duty) to Allâh and His Messenger.[1] No ground

---

[1] (V.9:91) CHAPTER. The Statement of the Prophet صلى الله عليه وسلم: "Religion is An-Nasîhah (to be sincere and true) to: 1. Allâh جل جلاله [i.e. obeying Him, by following His religion of Islamic Monotheism, attributing to Him what He deserves and doing Jihâd for His sake and to believe in Him, to fear Him much (abstain from all kinds of sins and evil deeds which He has forbidden) and love

(of complaint) can there be against the *Muhsinûn* (good-doers — See the footnote of V.9:120). And Allâh is Oft-Forgiving, Most Merciful.

92. Nor (is there blame) on those who came to you to be provided with mounts, when you said: "I can find no mounts for you," they turned back, while their eyes overflowing with tears of grief that they could not find anything to spend (for *Jihâd*).

Him much (perform all kinds of good deeds which He has ordained)], 2. to Allâh's Messenger [i.e., to respect him greatly and to believe that he (صلى الله عليه وسلم) is Allâh's Messenger, and to fight on his behalf both in his lifetime and after his death and to follow his *Sunnah* — (legal ways etc.)] 3. to the Muslim rulers [i.e. to help them in their job of leading Muslims to the right path and alarm them if they are heedless] and 4. to all the Muslims in common) [i.e. to order them for *Al-Ma'rûf* (i.e. Islâmic Monotheism, and all that Islâm orders one to do), and to forbid them from *Al-Munkar* (i.e. disbelief, polytheism of all kinds, and all that Islâm has forbidden), and to be merciful and kind to them].

And the Statement of Allâh تعالى : "If they are sincere and true (in duty) to Allâh (جل جلاله) and His Messenger (Muhammad صلى الله عليه وسلم)." (V.9:91).

Narrated Jarîr bin Abdullâh رضى الله عنه : I gave the *Bai'â* (pledge) to Allâh's Messenger صلى الله عليه وسلم for the following:

1. *Iqâmat-as-Salât* (to perform prayers).

2. To pay the *Zakât*.

3. And to be sincere and true to every Muslim [i.e. to order them for *Al-Ma'rûf* (i.e. Islâmic Monotheism, and all that Islâm orders one to do), and to forbid them from *Al-Munkar* (i.e. disbelief, polytheism of all kinds, and all that Islâm has forbidden), and to help them, and to be merciful and kind to them]. (*Sahih Al-Bukhâri*, Vol. 1, Hadith No. 54 and its Chapter No. 43).

93. The ground (of complaint) is only against those who are rich, and yet ask exemption.[1] They are content to be with (the women) who sit behind (at home) and Allâh has sealed up their hearts (from all kinds of goodness and right guidance) so that they know not (what they are losing).

إِنَّمَا السَّبِيلُ عَلَى الَّذِينَ
يَسْتَأْذِنُونَكَ وَهُمْ أَغْنِيَآءُ
رَضُوا بِأَن يَكُونُوا مَعَ الْخَوَالِفِ
وَطَبَعَ اللَّهُ عَلَىٰ قُلُوبِهِمْ فَهُمْ
لَا يَعْلَمُونَ ۝

---

[1] (V.9:93) Narrated Abu Hurairah رضى الله عنه The Prophet صلى الله عليه وسلم said, "A Prophet amongst the Prophets carried out a holy military expedition, so he said to his followers, 'Anyone who has married a woman and wants to consummate the marriage, and has not done so yet, should not accompany me; nor should a man who has built a house but has not completed its roof; nor a man who has sheep or she-camels and is waiting for the birth of their young ones.' So, the Prophet carried out the expedition and when he reached that town at the time or nearly at the time of the 'Asr prayer, he said to the sun, 'O sun! You are under Allâh's Order and I am under Allâh's Order. O Allâh! Stop it (i.e. the sun) from setting.' It was stopped till Allâh made him victorious. Then he collected the booty and the fire came to burn it, but it did not burn it*. He said (to his men), 'Some of you have stolen something from the booty. So one man from every tribe should give me a Bai'a (pledge) by shaking hands with me.' (They did so and) the hand of a man got stuck in the hand of their Prophet. Then that Prophet said (to the man), 'The theft has been committed by your people. So all the persons of your tribe should give me the Bai'a (pledge) by shaking hands with me.' The hands of two or three men got stuck in the hand of their Prophet and he said, 'You have committed the theft.' Then they brought a head of gold like the head of a cow and put it there, and the fire came and consumed the booty. The Prophet صلى الله عليه وسلم added: "Then Allâh saw our weakness and disability, so He made booty lawful for us." (Sahih Al-Bukhâri, Vol. 4, Hadith No. 353).

* Booty used to be burnt by a fire sent by Allâh.

94. They (the hypocrites) will present their excuses to you (Muslims), when you return to them. Say (O Muhammad ﷺ (صلى الله عليه وسلم) "Present no excuses, we shall not believe you. Allâh has already informed us of the news concerning you. Allâh and His Messenger will observe your deeds. In the end you will be brought back to the All-Knower of the unseen and the seen, then He (Allâh) will inform you of what you used to do." [Tafsir At-Tabari]

95. They will swear by Allâh to you (Muslims) when you return to them, that you may turn away from them. So turn away from them. Surely, they are *Rijsun* [i.e. *Najasun* (impure) because of their evil deeds], and Hell is their dwelling place — a recompense for that which they used to earn.

96. They (the hypocrites) swear to you (Muslims) that you may be pleased with them, but if you are pleased with them, certainly Allâh is not pleased with the people who are *Al-Fâsiqûn* (rebellious, disobedient to Allâh).

97. The bedouins are the worst in disbelief and hypocrisy, and more likely to be in ignorance of the limits (Allâh's Commandments and His Legal Laws) which Allâh has revealed to His Messenger. And Allâh is All-Knower, All-Wise.

98. And of the bedouins there are some who look upon what they spend (in Allâh's Cause) as a fine and watch for calamities for you, on them be the calamity of evil. And Allâh is All-Hearer, All-Knower.

99. And of the bedouins there are some who believe in Allâh and the Last Day, and look upon what they spend in Allâh's Cause as means of nearness to Allâh, and a cause of receiving the Messenger's invocations. Indeed these (spendings in Allâh's Cause) are a means of nearness for them. Allâh will admit them to His Mercy. Certainly Allâh is Oft-Forgiving, Most Merciful.

100. And the foremost to embrace Islâm of the *Muhâjirûn* (those who migrated from Makkah to Al-Madinah) and the *Ansâr* (the citizens of Al-Madinah who helped and gave aid to the *Muhâjirûn*) and also those who followed them exactly (in Faith). Allâh is well-pleased with them as they are well-pleased with Him. He has prepared for them Gardens under which rivers flow (Paradise), to dwell therein forever. That is the supreme success.

101. And among the bedouins around you, some are hypocrites, and so are some among the people of Al-Madinah who persist in hypocrisy; you (O Muhammad صلى الله عليه وسلم) know them not, We know them. We shall punish them twice, and thereafter they shall be brought back to a great (horrible) torment.

102. And (there are) others who have acknowledged their sins, they have mixed a deed that was righteous with another that was evil. Perhaps Allâh will turn unto them in forgiveness. Surely, Allâh is Oft-Forgiving, Most Merciful.[1]

103. Take *Sadaqah* (alms) from their wealth in order to purify them and sanctify them with it, and invoke Allâh for them. Verily, your invocations are a source of security for them; and Allâh is All-Hearer, All-Knower.

104. Know they not that Allâh accepts repentance from His slaves and takes the *Sadaqât* (alms, charity), and that Allâh Alone is the One Who forgives and accepts repentance, Most Merciful?

105. And say (O Muhammad صلى الله عليه وسلم) "Do deeds! Allâh will see your deeds, and (so will) His Messenger and

---

[1] (V.9:102) The Statement of Allâh عز وجل: "And (there are) others who have acknowledged their sins..." (V.9:102)

Narrated Samurah bin Jundub رضى الله عنه: Allâh's Messenger صلى الله عليه وسلم said, "Tonight two (visitors) came to me (in my dream) and took me to a town built with gold bricks and silver bricks. There, we met men who, (by) half of their bodies looked like the most handsome human beings you have ever seen, and (by) the other half, the ugliest human beings you have ever seen. Those two visitors said to those men: 'Go and dip yourselves in that river.' So they dipped themselves therein and then came to us, their ugliness having disappeared and they were in the most handsome shape. The visitors said, 'This is the *'Adn* Paradise, and that is your dwelling place.' Then they added, 'As for those people who were half ugly and half handsome, they were those who have mixed deeds that were good with deeds that were evil, but Allâh forgave them.'" (*Sahih Al-Bukhari*, Vol.6, *Hadith* No.196).

the believers. And you will be brought back to the All-Knower of the unseen and the seen. Then He will inform you of what you used to do."

106. And others are made to await for Allâh's Decree, whether He will punish them or will forgive them. And Allâh is All-Knowing, All-Wise.

107. And as for those who put up a mosque by way of harm and disbelief and to disunite the believers and as an outpost for those who warred against Allâh and His Messenger (Muhammad صلى الله عليه وسلم) aforetime, they will indeed swear that their intention is nothing but good. Allâh bears witness that they are certainly liars.

108. Never stand you therein. Verily, the mosque whose foundation was laid from the first day on piety is more worthy that you stand therein (to pray). In it are men who love to clean and to purify themselves. And Allâh loves those who make themselves clean and pure [i.e. who clean their private parts with dust (which has the properties of soap) and water from urine and stools, after answering the call of nature].

109. Is it then he who laid the foundation of his building on piety to Allâh and His Good Pleasure better, or he who laid the foundation of his building on the brink of an undetermined precipice ready to crumble down, so that it crumbled to pieces with him into the Fire of Hell.

And Allâh guides not the people who are the *Zâlimûn* (cruel, violent, proud, polytheist and wrongdoer).

110. The building which they built will never cease to be a cause of hypocrisy and doubt in their hearts unless their hearts are cut to pieces. (i.e. till they die). And Allâh is All-Knowing, All-Wise.

111. Verily, Allâh has purchased of the believers their lives and their properties for (the price) that theirs shall be the Paradise. They fight in Allâh's Cause, so they kill (others) and are killed. It is a promise in truth which is binding on Him in the Taurât (Torah) and the Injeel (Gospel) and the Qur'ân. And who is truer to his covenant than Allâh? Then rejoice in the bargain which you have concluded. That is the supreme success.[1]

---

[1] (V.9:111).

a) Narrated Abu Hurairah رضي الله عنه : Allâh's Messenger صلى الله عليه وسلم said, "Allâh guarantees him who strives in His Cause and whose motivation for going out is nothing but *Jihâd* in His Cause and belief in His Words (Islamic Monotheism), that He will admit him into Paradise (if martyred) or bring him back to his dwelling place whence he has come out with what he gains of reward or booty." (*Sahih Al-Bukhari*, Vol.4, *Hadith* No.352).

b) Narrated Jâbir bin 'Abdullâh رضي الله عنهما : On the day of the battle of Uhud, a man came to the Prophet صلى الله عليه وسلم and said, "Can you tell me where I will be if I should get martyred?" The Prophet صلى الله عليه وسلم replied, "In Paradise." The man threw away some dates he was carrying in his hand, and fought till he was martyred. (*Sahih Al-Bukhari*, Vol.5, *Hadith* No.377).

112. (The believers whose lives Allâh has purchased are) those who turn to Allâh in repentance (from polytheism and hypocrisy), who worship (Him), and praise (Him), who fast (or go out in Allâh's Cause), who bow down (in prayer), who prostrate themselves (in prayer), who enjoin (on people) Al-Ma'rûf (i.e. Islâmic Monotheism and all what Islâm has ordained) and forbid (people) from Al-Munkar (i.e. disbelief, polytheism of all kinds and all that Islâm has forbidden), and who observe the limits set by Allâh (do all that Allâh has ordained and abstain from all kinds of sins and evil deeds which Allâh has forbidden). And give glad tidings to the believers.[1]

التَّٰٓبُونَ ٱلۡعَٰبِدُونَ ٱلۡحَٰمِدُونَ ٱلسَّٰٓئِحُونَ ٱلرَّٰكِعُونَ ٱلسَّٰجِدُونَ ٱلۡأَمِرُونَ بِٱلۡمَعۡرُوفِ وَٱلنَّاهُونَ عَنِ ٱلۡمُنكَرِ وَٱلۡحَٰفِظُونَ لِحُدُودِ ٱللَّهِ وَبَشِّرِ ٱلۡمُؤۡمِنِينَ ١١٢

---

c) Narrated Ibn 'Umar رضى الله عنهما : I heard Allâh's Messenger صلى الله عليه وسلم saying: "If you (1) practised Bai' Al-'Inah (the 'Inah transaction i.e. selling goods to a person for a certain price and then buying them back from him for a far less price); (2) and followed the tails of the cows (i.e. indulged in agriculture and became content with it during the period of Jihâd); (3) and deserted the Jihâd (holy fighting) in Allâh's Cause, Allâh will cover you with humiliation, and it will not be removed till you return back to your religion." (Abu Dâwûd).

[1] (V.9:112) Narrated Sahl bin Sa'd: Allâh's Messenger صلى الله عليه وسلم said, "Whoever can guarantee (the chastity of) what is between his two jaw-bones and what is between his two legs (i.e., his mouth, tongue and his private parts)*, I guarantee Paradise for him." (Sahih Al-Bukhari, Vol. 8, Hadith No. 481)

* i.e. whoever protects his tongue from illegal talk e.g., to tell lies, or backbiting and his mouth from eating and drinking forbidden illegal things and his private parts from illegal sexual acts.

113. It is not (proper) for the Prophet and those who believe to ask Allâh's Forgiveness for the *Mushrikûn* (polytheists, idolaters, pagans, disbelievers in the Oneness of Allâh), even though they be of kin, after it has become clear to them that they are the dwellers of the Fire (because they died in a state of disbelief).

مَا كَانَ لِلنَّبِيِّ وَالَّذِينَ ءَامَنُوٓاْ أَن يَسْتَغْفِرُواْ لِلْمُشْرِكِينَ وَلَوْ كَانُوٓاْ أُوْلِي قُرْبَىٰ مِنۢ بَعْدِ مَا تَبَيَّنَ لَهُمْ أَنَّهُمْ أَصْحَٰبُ ٱلْجَحِيمِ ۝

114. And Ibrâhîm's (Abraham) invoking (of Allâh) for his father's forgiveness was only because of a promise he [Ibrâhîm (Abraham)] had made to him (his father). But when it became clear to him [Ibrâhîm (Abraham)] that his (father) is an enemy of Allâh, he dissociated himself from him. Verily, Ibrâhîm (Abraham) was *Awwah* (one who invokes Allâh with humility, glorifies Him and remembers Him much) and was forbearing. (*Tafsir Al-Qurtubî*).[1]

وَمَا كَانَ ٱسْتِغْفَارُ إِبْرَٰهِيمَ لِأَبِيهِ إِلَّا عَن مَّوْعِدَةٍ وَعَدَهَآ إِيَّاهُ فَلَمَّا تَبَيَّنَ لَهُۥٓ أَنَّهُۥ عَدُوٌّ لِّلَّهِ تَبَرَّأَ مِنْهُ إِنَّ إِبْرَٰهِيمَ لَأَوَّٰهٌ حَلِيمٌ ۝

115. And Allâh will never lead a people astray after He has guided them until He makes clear to them as to what they should avoid. Verily, Allâh is the All-Knower of everything.[2]

وَمَا كَانَ ٱللَّهُ لِيُضِلَّ قَوْمًۢا بَعْدَ إِذْ هَدَىٰهُمْ حَتَّىٰ يُبَيِّنَ لَهُم مَّا يَتَّقُونَ إِنَّ ٱللَّهَ بِكُلِّ شَيْءٍ عَلِيمٌ ۝

---

[1] (V.9:114) See the footnote of (V.6:74).

[2] (V.9:115) Killing the *Khawârij* (some people who dissented from the religion and disagreed with the rest of the Muslims), and the *Mulhidûn* (heretics) after the establishment of firm proof against them.

And the Statement of Allâh تعالى: 'And Allâh will never lead a people astray after He has guided them, until He makes clear to them as to what they should avoid...' (V.9:115) And Ibn 'Umar رضي الله عنهما used to consider them (the *Khawarij* and the *Mulhidûn*) the worst of

116. Verily, Allâh! Unto Him belongs the dominion of the heavens and the earth, He gives life and He causes death. And besides Allâh you have neither any *Walî* (protector or guardian) nor any helper.

إِنَّ ٱللَّهَ لَهُۥ مُلْكُ ٱلسَّمَٰوَٰتِ وَٱلْأَرْضِ يُحْيِۦ وَيُمِيتُ وَمَا لَكُم مِّن دُونِ ٱللَّهِ مِن وَلِيٍّ وَلَا نَصِيرٍ ۝

117. Allâh has forgiven the Prophet (صلى الله عليه وسلم), the *Muhâjirûn* (Muslim emigrants who left their homes and came to Al-Madinah) and the *Ansar* (Muslims of Al-Madinâh) who followed him (Muhammad صلى الله عليه وسلم in the time of distress (Tabûk expedition), after the hearts of a party of them had nearly deviated (from the Right Path), but He accepted their repentance. Certainly, He is unto them full of kindness, Most Merciful.

لَّقَد تَّابَ ٱللَّهُ عَلَى ٱلنَّبِيِّ وَٱلْمُهَٰجِرِينَ وَٱلْأَنصَارِ ٱلَّذِينَ ٱتَّبَعُوهُ فِي سَاعَةِ ٱلْعُسْرَةِ مِنۢ بَعْدِ مَا كَادَ يَزِيغُ قُلُوبُ فَرِيقٍ مِّنْهُمْ ثُمَّ تَابَ عَلَيْهِمْ إِنَّهُۥ بِهِمْ رَءُوفٌ رَّحِيمٌ ۝

118. And (He did forgive also) the three [who did not join the Tabûk expedition and whose case was deferred (by the Prophet صلى الله عليه وسلم) for Allâh's Decision] till for them the earth, vast as it is, was straitened and their ownselves were straitened to them, and they perceived that there is no fleeing from Allâh, and no refuge but with Him. Then, He forgave them (accepted their repentance), that they might beg for His pardon [repent (unto Him)]. Verily,

وَعَلَى ٱلثَّلَٰثَةِ ٱلَّذِينَ خُلِّفُوا۟ حَتَّىٰٓ إِذَا ضَاقَتْ عَلَيْهِمُ ٱلْأَرْضُ بِمَا رَحُبَتْ وَضَاقَتْ عَلَيْهِمْ أَنفُسُهُمْ وَظَنُّوٓا۟ أَن لَّا مَلْجَأَ مِنَ ٱللَّهِ إِلَّآ إِلَيْهِ ثُمَّ تَابَ

Allâh's creatures and said, "These people took some Verses that had been revealed concerning the disbelievers and interpreted them as describing the believers."

Narrated 'Abdullâh bin 'Umar رضي الله عنهما regarding *Al-Haruriyah*: The Prophet صلى الله عليه وسلم said, "They will go out of Islâm as an arrow darts out of the game's body." (*Sahih Al-Bukhari*, Vol.9, *Hadith* No.66).

Allâh is the One Who forgives and accepts repentance, Most Merciful.

119. O you who believe! Be afraid of Allâh, and be with those who are true (in words and deeds).[1]

120. It was not becoming of the people of Al-Madinah and the bedouins of the neighbourhood to remain behind Allâh's Messenger (Muhammad صلى الله عليه وسلم when fighting in Allâh's Cause) and (it was not becoming of them) to prefer their own lives to his life. That is

عَلَيْهِمْ إِنَّ تُوبُوٓاْ إِنَّ ٱللَّهَ هُوَ ٱلتَّوَّابُ ٱلرَّحِيمُ ۝

يَـٰٓأَيُّهَا ٱلَّذِينَ ءَامَنُواْ ٱتَّقُواْ ٱللَّهَ وَكُونُواْ مَعَ ٱلصَّـٰدِقِينَ ۝

مَا كَانَ لِأَهْلِ ٱلْمَدِينَةِ وَمَنْ حَوْلَهُم مِّنَ ٱلْأَعْرَابِ أَن يَتَخَلَّفُواْ عَن رَّسُولِ ٱللَّهِ وَلَا

---

[1] (V.9:119) The Statement of Allâh تعالى :

'O you who believe! Be afraid of Allâh, and be with those who are true (in words and deeds).' (V.9:119).

And what is forbidden as regards telling of lies.

a) Narrated 'Abdullâh رضى الله عنه : The Prophet صلى الله عليه وسلم said, "Truthfulness leads to Al-Birr (righteousness) and Al-Birr (righteousness) leads to Paradise. And a man keeps on telling the truth until he becomes a truthful person. Falsehood leads to Al-Fujûr (i.e. wickedness - evil-doing), and Al-Fujûr leads to the (Hell) Fire, and a man keeps on telling lies until he is written as a liar before Allâh." (Sahih Al-Bukhari, Vol.8, Hadith No.116).

b) Narrated Abu Hurairah رضى الله عنه : Allâh's Messenger صلى الله عليه وسلم said, "The signs of a hypocrite are three: Whenever he speaks, he tells a lie; and whenever he promises, he breaks his promise; and whenever he is entrusted, he betrays (proves to be dishonest)." (Sahih Al-Bukhari, Vol.8, Hadith No.117).

c) Narrated Samurah bin Jundub رضى الله عنه : The Prophet صلى الله عليه وسلم said, "I saw (in a dream), two men came to me." Then the Prophet صلى الله عليه وسلم narrated the story (saying): "They said: The person, the one whose cheek you saw being torn away (from the mouth to the ear) was a liar and used to tell lies and the people would report those lies on his authority till they spread all over the world. So he will be punished like that till the Day of Resurrection." (Sahih Al-Bukhari, Vol.8, Hadith No.118).

because they suffer neither thirst nor fatigue nor hunger in the Cause of Allâh, nor they take any step to raise the anger of disbelievers nor inflict any injury upon an enemy but is written to their credit as a deed of righteousness. Surely, Allâh wastes not the reward of the *Muhsinûn.*[1]

121. Nor do they spend anything (in Allâh's Cause) — small or great — nor cross a valley, but is written to their credit that Allâh may recompense them with the best of what they used to do (i.e. Allâh will reward their good deeds according to the reward of their best deeds which they did in the most perfect manner).[2]

---

[1] (V.9:120) *Muhsinûn:* Doers of good, i.e. those who perform good deeds totally for Allâh's sake only without any show-off or to gain praise or fame and they do them in accordance with the *Sunnah* (legal ways) of Allâh's Messenger, Muhammad صلى الله عليه وسلم.

[2] (V.9:121)

a) Islâm demolishes all the previous evil deeds and so do migration (for Allâh's sake) and Hajj (pilgrimage to Makkah). (*Sahih Muslim*)

b) What is said regarding the superiority of a person who embraces Islâm sincerely.

Narrated Abu Sa'îd Al-Khudrî رضي الله عنه: Allâh's Messenger صلى الله عليه وسلم said, "If a person embraces Islâm sincerely, then Allâh shall forgive all his past sins, and after that starts the settlement of accounts: the reward of his good deeds will be ten times to seven hundred times for each good deed, and an evil deed will be recorded as it is unless Allâh forgives it." (*Sahih Al-Bukhari*, Vol.1, Hadith No. 40A).

Narrated Abu Hurairah رضي الله عنه: Allâh's Messenger صلى الله عليه وسلم said, "If anyone of you improves (follow strictly) his Islâmic religion, then his good deeds will be rewarded ten times to seven hundred times for each good deed and a bad deed will be recorded as it is." (*Sahih Al-Bukhari*, Vol. 1, Hadith No. 40B).

122. And it is not (proper) for the believers to go out to fight (*Jihâd*) all together. Of every troop of them, a party only should go forth, that they (who are left behind) may get instructions in (Islâmic) religion, and that they may warn their people when they return to them, so that they may beware (of evil).

وَمَا كَانَ ٱلۡمُؤۡمِنُونَ لِيَنفِرُواْ كَآفَّةً فَلَوۡلَا نَفَرَ مِن كُلِّ فِرۡقَةٍ مِّنۡهُمۡ طَآئِفَةٌ لِّيَتَفَقَّهُواْ فِي ٱلدِّينِ وَلِيُنذِرُواْ قَوۡمَهُمۡ إِذَا رَجَعُوٓاْ إِلَيۡهِمۡ لَعَلَّهُمۡ يَحۡذَرُونَ ۝

123. O you who believe! Fight those of the disbelievers who are close to you, and let them find harshness in you; and know that Allâh is with those who are *Al-Muttaqûn* (the pious. See V.2:2).

يَٰٓأَيُّهَا ٱلَّذِينَ ءَامَنُواْ قَٰتِلُواْ ٱلَّذِينَ يَلُونَكُم مِّنَ ٱلۡكُفَّارِ وَلۡيَجِدُواْ فِيكُمۡ غِلۡظَةً وَٱعۡلَمُوٓاْ أَنَّ ٱللَّهَ مَعَ ٱلۡمُتَّقِينَ ۝

124. And whenever there comes down a *Sûrah* (chapter from the Qur'ân), some of them (hypocrites) say: "Which of you has had his Faith increased by it?" As for those who believe, it has increased their Faith, and they rejoice.

وَإِذَا مَآ أُنزِلَتۡ سُورَةٌ فَمِنۡهُم مَّن يَقُولُ أَيُّكُمۡ زَادَتۡهُ هَٰذِهِۦٓ إِيمَٰنًا فَأَمَّا ٱلَّذِينَ ءَامَنُواْ فَزَادَتۡهُمۡ إِيمَٰنًا وَهُمۡ يَسۡتَبۡشِرُونَ ۝

125. But as for those in whose hearts is a disease (of belief, disbelief and hypocrisy), it will add suspicion and doubt to their suspicion, disbelief and doubt; and they die while they are disbelievers.

وَأَمَّا ٱلَّذِينَ فِي قُلُوبِهِم مَّرَضٌ فَزَادَتۡهُمۡ رِجۡسًا إِلَىٰ رِجۡسِهِمۡ وَمَاتُواْ وَهُمۡ كَٰفِرُونَ ۝

126. See they not that they are put in trial once or twice every year (with different kinds of calamities, disease, famine)? Yet, they turn not in repentance, nor do they learn a lesson (from it).

أَوَلَا يَرَوۡنَ أَنَّهُمۡ يُفۡتَنُونَ فِي كُلِّ عَامٍ مَّرَّةً أَوۡ مَرَّتَيۡنِ ثُمَّ لَا يَتُوبُونَ وَلَا هُمۡ يَذَّكَّرُونَ ۝

127. And whenever there comes down a *Sûrah* (chapter from the Qur'ân), they look at one another (saying): "Does any one see you?" Then they turn away. Allâh has turned their hearts (from the light) because they are a people that understand not.

128. Verily, there has come unto you a Messenger (Muhammad صلى الله عليه وسلم) from amongst yourselves (i.e. whom you know well). It grieves him that you should receive any injury or difficulty. He (Muhammad صلى الله عليه وسلم) is anxious over you (to be rightly guided, to repent to Allâh, and beg Him to pardon and forgive your sins in order that you may enter Paradise and be saved from the punishment of the Hell-fire); for the believers (he صلى الله عليه وسلم is) full of pity, kind, and merciful.

129. But if they turn away, say (O Muhammad صلى الله عليه وسلم): "Allâh is sufficient for me. Lâ ilâha illa Huwa (none has the right to be worshipped but He) in Him I put my trust and He is the Lord of the Mighty Throne."[1]

Sûrat Yûnus (Jonah) X

*In the Name of Allâh
the Most Gracious, the Most Merciful*

1. Alif-Lâm-Râ. [These letters are one of the miracles of the Qur'ân, and none but Allâh (Alone) knows their meanings]. These are the Verses of the Book (the Qur'ân) Al-Hakîm.[2]

---

[1] (V.9:129) See the footnote of (V.3:173).

[2] (V.10:1) Al-Hakîm: Showing lawful and unlawful things, explaining Allâh's (Divine) Laws for mankind, leading them to eternal happiness by ordering them to follow the true Islâmic Monotheism, — worshipping none but Allâh Alone — that will guide them to Paradise and save them from Hell.

أَكَانَ لِلنَّاسِ عَجَبًا أَنْ أَوْحَيْنَا

2. Is it a wonder for mankind that We have sent Our Revelation[1] to a man from among themselves (i.e. Prophet Muhammad صلى الله عليه وسلم) (saying): "Warn mankind (of the coming torment in Hell), and give good news to those who believe (in the Oneness of Allâh and in His Prophet Muhammad صلى الله عليه وسلم) that they shall have with their Lord the rewards of their good deeds?" (But) the disbelievers say: "This is indeed an evident sorcerer (i.e. Prophet Muhammad صلى الله عليه وسلم and the Qur'ân)!

إِلَى رَجُلٍ مِّنْهُمْ أَنْ أَنذِرِ ٱلنَّاسَ وَبَشِّرِ ٱلَّذِينَ ءَامَنُوٓاْ أَنَّ لَهُمْ قَدَمَ صِدْقٍ عِندَ رَبِّهِمْ قَالَ ٱلْكَٰفِرُونَ إِنَّ هَٰذَا لَسَٰحِرٌ مُّبِينٌ ٢

3. Surely, your Lord is Allâh Who created the heavens and the earth in six Days and then rose over (*Istawâ*) the Throne (really in a manner that suits His Majesty), disposing the affair of all things. No intercessor (can plead with Him) except after His Leave. That is Allâh, your Lord; so worship Him (Alone). Then, will you not remember?

إِنَّ رَبَّكُمُ ٱللَّهُ ٱلَّذِي خَلَقَ ٱلسَّمَٰوَٰتِ وَٱلْأَرْضَ فِي سِتَّةِ أَيَّامٍ ثُمَّ ٱسْتَوَىٰ عَلَى ٱلْعَرْشِ يُدَبِّرُ ٱلْأَمْرَ مَا مِن شَفِيعٍ إِلَّا مِنۢ بَعْدِ إِذْنِهِ ذَٰلِكُمُ ٱللَّهُ رَبُّكُمْ فَٱعْبُدُوهُ أَفَلَا تَذَكَّرُونَ ٣

4. To Him will be the return of all of you. The Promise of Allâh is true. It is He Who begins the creation and then will repeat it, that He may reward with justice those who believed (in the Oneness of Allâh — Islâmic Monotheism) and did deeds of righteousness. But those who disbelieved will have a drink of boiling fluids and painful torment because they used to disbelieve.

إِلَيْهِ مَرْجِعُكُمْ جَمِيعًا وَعْدَ ٱللَّهِ حَقًّا إِنَّهُۥ يَبْدَؤُاْ ٱلْخَلْقَ ثُمَّ يُعِيدُهُۥ لِيَجْزِيَ ٱلَّذِينَ ءَامَنُوٱ وَعَمِلُوٱ ٱلصَّٰلِحَٰتِ بِٱلْقِسْطِ وَٱلَّذِينَ كَفَرُوٱ لَهُمْ شَرَابٌ مِّنْ حَمِيمٍ وَعَذَابٌ أَلِيمٌۢ بِمَا كَانُوٱ يَكْفُرُونَ ٤

5. It is He Who made the sun a shining thing and the moon as a light

هُوَ ٱلَّذِي جَعَلَ ٱلشَّمْسَ

---

[1] (V.10:2) See the footnote of (V.4:163).

and measured out for it stages that you might know the number of years and the reckoning. Allâh did not create this but in truth. He explains the *Ayât* (proofs, evidences, verses, lessons, signs, revelations, etc.) in detail for people who have knowledge.

6. Verily, in the alternation of the night and the day and in all that Allâh has created in the heavens and the earth are *Ayât* (proofs, evidences, verses, lessons, signs, revelations, etc.) for those who keep their duty to Allâh, and fear Him much.

7. Verily, those who hope not for their Meeting with Us, but are pleased and satisfied with the life of the present world, and those who are heedless of Our *Ayât* (proofs, evidences, verses, lessons, signs, revelations, etc.),

8. Those, their abode will be the Fire, because of what they used to earn.

9. Verily, those who believe[1] and do deeds of righteousness, their Lord will guide them through their Faith; under them will flow rivers in the Gardens of Delight (Paradise).

10. Their way of request therein will be *Subhânaka Allâhumma* (Glory to You, O Allâh!) and *Salâm* (peace, safety from evil) will be their greetings

---

[1] (V.10:9) Who believe in the Oneness of Allâh along with the six articles of Faith, i.e. to believe in Allâh, His Angels, His Books, His Messengers, Day of Resurrection, and *Al-Qadar* (Divine Preordainments) — Islâmic Monotheism.

therein (Paradise)! and the close of their request will be: *Al-Hamdu Lillâhi Rabbil-'Âlamîn* [All the praises and thanks are to Allâh, the Lord of *'Âlamîn* (mankind, jinn and all that exists)].

11. And were Allâh to hasten for mankind the evil (they invoke for themselves and for their children, while in a state of anger) as He hastens for them the good (they invoke) then they would have been ruined. So We leave those who expect not their Meeting with Us, in their trespasses, wandering blindly in distraction. (*Tafsir At-Tabarî*)

12. And when harm touches man, he invokes Us, lying on his side, or sitting or standing. But when We have removed his harm from him, he passes on as if he had never invoked Us for a harm that touched him! Thus it is made fair-seeming to the *Musrifûn*[1] that which they used to do.

13. And indeed, We destroyed generations before you when they did wrong, while their Messengers came to them with clear proofs, but they were not such as to believe! Thus do We requite the people who are *Mujrimûn* (disbelievers, polytheists, sinners and criminals).

14. Then We made you successors after them, generations after generations in the land, that We might see how you would work.

---

[1] (V.10:12) *Musrifûn*: Those who belied Allâh and His Prophets, and transgressed Allâh's limits by committing all kinds of crimes and sins.

15. And when Our clear Verses are recited unto them, those who hope not for their Meeting with Us, say: "Bring us a Qur'ân other than this, or change it." Say (O Muhammad صلى الله عليه وسلم): "It is not for me to change it on my own accord; I only follow that which is revealed unto me. Verily, I fear the torment of the Great Day (i.e. the Day of Resurrection) if I were to disobey my Lord."

16. Say (O Muhammad صلى الله عليه وسلم): "If Allâh had so willed, I should not have recited it to you nor would He have made it known to you. Verily, I have stayed amongst you a life time before this. Have you then no sense?"

17. So who does more wrong than he who forges a lie against Allâh or denies His *Ayât* (proofs, evidences, verses, lessons, signs, revelations, etc.)? Surely, the *Mujrimûn* (criminals, sinners, disbelievers and polytheists) will never be successful!

18. And they worship besides Allâh things that hurt them not, nor profit them, and they say: "These are our intercessors with Allâh." Say: "Do you inform Allâh of that which He knows not in the heavens and on the earth?" Glorified and Exalted is He above all that which they associate as partners (with Him)!

19. Mankind were but one community (i.e. on one religion — Islâmic Monotheism), then they differed (later); and had not it been for a Word that went forth before from your Lord, it would have been settled between them regarding what they differed.[1]

20. And they say: "How is it that not a sign is sent down on him from his Lord?" Say: "The Unseen belongs to Allâh Alone, so wait you, verily, I am with you among those who wait (for Allâh's Judgement)."

21. And when We let mankind taste mercy after some adversity has afflicted them, behold! They take to plotting against Our Ayât (proofs, evidences, verses, lessons, signs, revelations, etc.)! Say: "Allâh is more Swift in planning!" Certainly, Our Messengers (angels) record all of that which you plot.[2]

22. He it is Who enables you to travel through land and sea, till when you are in the ships, and they sail with them with a favourable wind, and they are glad therein, then comes a stormy wind and the waves come to them from all sides, and they think that they are encircled therein. Then they invoke

---

[1] (V.10:19) Narrated Abu Hurairah رضى الله عنه: The Prophet صلى الله عليه وسلم said, "Every child is born on Al-Fitrah [true faith of Islâmic Monotheism (i.e. to worship none but Allâh Alone)], his parents convert him to Judaism or Christianity or Magianism, as an animal gives birth to a perfect baby animal. Do you find it mutilated?" (Sahih Al-Bukhari, Vol.2, Hadith No.467). [See also the Qur'ân, Verse 30:30]

[2] (V.10:21) See the footnote (B) of (V.6:61).

Allâh, making their Faith pure for Him Alone, (saying): "If You (Allâh) deliver us from this, we shall truly, be of the grateful."[1]

23. But when He delivers them, behold! They rebel (disobey Allâh) in the earth wrongfully. O mankind! Your rebellion (disobedience to Allâh) is only against your ownselves, — a brief enjoyment of this worldly life, then (in the end) unto Us is your return, and We shall inform you of that which you used to do.

24. Verily, the likeness of (this) worldly life is as the water (rain) which We send down from the sky; so by it arises the intermingled produce of the earth of which men and cattle eat: until when the earth is clad in its adornments and is beautified, and its people think that they have all the powers of disposal over it, Our Command reaches it by night or by day and We make it like a clean-mown harvest, as if it had not flourished yesterday! Thus do We explain the *Ayât* (proofs, evidences, verses, lessons, signs, revelations, laws, etc.) in detail for the people who reflect.

25. Allâh calls to the Home of Peace (i.e. Paradise by accepting Allâh's religion of Islâmic Monotheism and by doing righteous good deeds and abstaining from polytheism and evil deeds) and guides whom He wills to the Straight Path.

---

[1] (V.10:22): See the footnote of (V.17:67).

26. For those who have done good is the best (reward, i.e. Paradise) and even more (i.e. having the honour of glancing at the Countenance of Allâh جل جلاله). Neither darkness nor dust nor any humiliating disgrace shall cover their faces. They are the dwellers of Paradise, they will abide therein forever.

۞ لِّلَّذِينَ أَحۡسَنُوا۟ ٱلۡحُسۡنَىٰ وَزِيَادَةٌۖ وَلَا يَرۡهَقُ وُجُوهَهُمۡ قَتَرٌ وَلَا ذِلَّةٌۚ أُو۟لَٰٓئِكَ أَصۡحَٰبُ ٱلۡجَنَّةِۖ هُمۡ فِيهَا خَٰلِدُونَ ۝

27. And those who have earned evil deeds, the recompense of an evil deed is the like thereof, and humiliating disgrace will cover them (their faces). No defender will they have from Allâh. Their faces will be covered as it were with pieces from the darkness of night. They are the dwellers of the Fire, they will abide therein forever.

وَٱلَّذِينَ كَسَبُوا۟ ٱلسَّيِّئَاتِ جَزَآءُ سَيِّئَةٍۭ بِمِثۡلِهَا وَتَرۡهَقُهُمۡ ذِلَّةٌۖ مَّا لَهُم مِّنَ ٱللَّهِ مِنۡ عَاصِمٍۖ كَأَنَّمَآ أُغۡشِيَتۡ وُجُوهُهُمۡ قِطَعٗا مِّنَ ٱلَّيۡلِ مُظۡلِمًاۚ أُو۟لَٰٓئِكَ أَصۡحَٰبُ ٱلنَّارِۖ هُمۡ فِيهَا خَٰلِدُونَ ۝

28. And the Day whereon We shall gather them all together, then We shall say to those who did set partners in worship with Us: "Stop at your place! You and your partners (whom you had worshipped in the worldly life)." Then We shall separate them, and their (Allâh's so-called) partners shall say: "It was not us that you used to worship."

وَيَوۡمَ نَحۡشُرُهُمۡ جَمِيعٗا ثُمَّ نَقُولُ لِلَّذِينَ أَشۡرَكُوا۟ مَكَانَكُمۡ أَنتُمۡ وَشُرَكَآؤُكُمۡۚ فَزَيَّلۡنَا بَيۡنَهُمۡۖ وَقَالَ شُرَكَآؤُهُم مَّا كُنتُمۡ إِيَّانَا تَعۡبُدُونَ ۝

29. "So sufficient is Allâh as a witness between us and you that we indeed knew nothing of your worship of us."

فَكَفَىٰ بِٱللَّهِ شَهِيدًۢا بَيۡنَنَا وَبَيۡنَكُمۡ إِن كُنَّا عَنۡ عِبَادَتِكُمۡ لَغَٰفِلِينَ ۝

30. There! Every person will know (exactly) what he had earned before and they will be brought back to Allâh, their rightful *Maulâ* (Lord), and their invented false deities will vanish from them.

هُنَالِكَ تَبۡلُوا۟ كُلُّ نَفۡسٍ مَّآ أَسۡلَفَتۡۚ وَرُدُّوٓا۟ إِلَى ٱللَّهِ مَوۡلَىٰهُمُ ٱلۡحَقِّۖ وَضَلَّ عَنۡهُم مَّا كَانُوا۟ يَفۡتَرُونَ ۝

31. Say (O Muhammad ﷺ) "Who provides for you from the sky and the earth? Or who owns hearing and sight? And who brings out the living from the dead and brings out the dead from the living? And who disposes the affairs?" They will say: "Allâh." Say: "Will you not then be afraid of Allâh's punishment (for setting up rivals in worship with Allâh)?"

32. Such is Allâh, your Lord in truth. So after the truth, what else can there be, save error? How then are you turned away?

33. Thus is the Word of your Lord justified against those who rebel (disobey Allâh) that they will not believe (in the Oneness of Allâh and in Muhammad ﷺ as the Messenger of Allâh).

34. Say: "Is there of your (Allâh's so-called) partners one that originates the creation and then repeats it?" Say: "Allâh originates the creation and then He repeats it. Then how are you deluded away (from the truth)?"

35. Say: "Is there of your (Allâh's so-called) partners one that guides to the truth?" Say: "It is Allâh Who guides to the truth. Is then He Who guides to the truth more worthy to be followed, or he who finds not guidance (himself) unless he is guided?" Then, what is the matter with you? How judge you?"

36. And most of them follow nothing but conjecture. Certainly, conjecture can be of no avail against the truth. Surely, Allâh is All-Aware of what they do.

لَا يُغْنِى مِنَ ٱلْحَقِّ شَيْئًا إِنَّ ٱللَّهَ عَلِيمٌۢ بِمَا يَفْعَلُونَ ۝

37. And this Qur'ân is not such as could ever be produced by other than Allâh (Lord of the heavens and the earth), but it is a confirmation of (the revelation)[1] which was before it [i.e. the Taurât (Torah), and the Injeel (Gospel)], and a full explanation of the Book (i.e. laws decreed for mankind) — wherein there is no doubt — from the the Lord of the 'Âlamîn (mankind, jinn, and all that exists).

وَمَا كَانَ هَٰذَا ٱلْقُرْآنُ أَن يُفْتَرَىٰ مِن دُونِ ٱللَّهِ وَلَٰكِن تَصْدِيقَ ٱلَّذِى بَيْنَ يَدَيْهِ وَتَفْصِيلَ ٱلْكِتَٰبِ لَا رَيْبَ فِيهِ مِن رَّبِّ ٱلْعَٰلَمِينَ ۝

38. Or do they say: "He (Muhammad صلى الله عليه وسلم) has forged it?' Say: "Bring then a Sûrah (chapter) like unto it, and call upon whomsoever you can besides Allâh, if you are truthful!"

أَمْ يَقُولُونَ ٱفْتَرَىٰهُ قُلْ فَأْتُوا۟ بِسُورَةٍ مِّثْلِهِ وَٱدْعُوا۟ مَنِ ٱسْتَطَعْتُم مِّن دُونِ ٱللَّهِ إِن كُنتُمْ صَٰدِقِينَ ۝

39. Nay, they have belied the knowledge whereof they could not comprehend and what has not yet been fulfilled (i.e. their punishment). Thus those before them did belie. Then see what was the end of the Zâlimûn (polytheists and wrongdoers)!

بَلْ كَذَّبُوا۟ بِمَا لَمْ يُحِيطُوا۟ بِعِلْمِهِۦ وَلَمَّا يَأْتِهِمْ تَأْوِيلُهُۥ كَذَٰلِكَ كَذَّبَ ٱلَّذِينَ مِن قَبْلِهِمْ فَٱنظُرْ كَيْفَ كَانَ عَٰقِبَةُ ٱلظَّٰلِمِينَ ۝

40. And of them there are some who believe therein; and of them there are

وَمِنْهُم مَّن يُؤْمِنُ بِهِۦ وَمِنْهُم

---

[1] (V.10:37) Narrated Abu Hurairah رضى الله عنه The Prophet صلى الله عليه وسلم said, "There was no Prophet among the Prophets but was given miracles because of which people had security or had belief, but what I have been given is the Divine Revelation which Allâh has revealed to me. So I hope that my followers will be more than those of any other Prophet on the Day of Resurrection." (Sahih Al-Bukhari, Vol.9, Hadith No.379).

some who believe not therein, and your Lord is All-Aware of the *Mufsidûn* (evil-doers and liars).

لَا يُؤْمِنُ بِهِ ۚ وَرَبُّكَ أَعْلَمُ بِالْمُفْسِدِينَ ۝

41. And if they belie you, say: "For me are my deeds and for you are your deeds! You are innocent of what I do, and I am innocent of what you do!"

وَإِن كَذَّبُوكَ فَقُل لِّى عَمَلِى وَلَكُمْ عَمَلُكُمْ ۖ أَنتُم بَرِيٓـُٔونَ مِمَّآ أَعْمَلُ وَأَنَا۠ بَرِىٓءٌ مِّمَّا تَعْمَلُونَ ۝

42. And among them are some who listen to you, but can you make the deaf to hear — even though they apprehend not?

وَمِنْهُم مَّن يَسْتَمِعُونَ إِلَيْكَ ۚ أَفَأَنتَ تُسْمِعُ ٱلصُّمَّ وَلَوْ كَانُوا۟ لَا يَعْقِلُونَ ۝

43. And among them are some who look at you, but can you guide the blind — even though they see not?

وَمِنْهُم مَّن يَنظُرُ إِلَيْكَ ۚ أَفَأَنتَ تَهْدِى ٱلْعُمْىَ وَلَوْ كَانُوا۟ لَا يُبْصِرُونَ ۝

44. Truly, Allâh wrongs not mankind in aught; but mankind wrong themselves.

إِنَّ ٱللَّهَ لَا يَظْلِمُ ٱلنَّاسَ شَيْـًٔا وَلَكِنَّ ٱلنَّاسَ أَنفُسَهُمْ يَظْلِمُونَ ۝

45. And on the Day when He shall gather (resurrect) them together, (it will be) as if they had not stayed (in the life of this world and graves) but an hour of a day. They will recognise each other. Ruined indeed will be those who denied the Meeting with Allâh and were not guided.

وَيَوْمَ يَحْشُرُهُمْ كَأَن لَّمْ يَلْبَثُوٓا۟ إِلَّا سَاعَةً مِّنَ ٱلنَّهَارِ يَتَعَارَفُونَ بَيْنَهُمْ ۚ قَدْ خَسِرَ ٱلَّذِينَ كَذَّبُوا۟ بِلِقَآءِ ٱللَّهِ وَمَا كَانُوا۟ مُهْتَدِينَ ۝

46. Whether We show you (in your lifetime, O Muhammad صلى الله عليه وسلم) some of what We promise them (the torment), or We cause you to die — still unto Us is their return, and moreover Allâh is Witness over what they used to do.

وَإِمَّا نُرِيَنَّكَ بَعْضَ ٱلَّذِى نَعِدُهُمْ أَوْ نَتَوَفَّيَنَّكَ فَإِلَيْنَا مَرْجِعُهُمْ ثُمَّ ٱللَّهُ شَهِيدٌ عَلَىٰ مَا يَفْعَلُونَ ۝

47. And for every *Ummah* (a community or a nation) there is a Messenger; when their Messenger comes, the matter will be judged

وَلِكُلِّ أُمَّةٍ رَّسُولٌ ۖ فَإِذَا جَآءَ رَسُولُهُمْ قُضِىَ بَيْنَهُم

between them with justice, and they will not be wronged.

48. And they say: "When will be this promise (the torment or the Day of Resurrection), if you speak the truth?"

49. Say (O Muhammad صلى الله عليه وسلم): "I have no power over any harm or profit to myself except what Allâh may will. For every *Ummah* (a community or a nation), there is a term appointed; when their term comes, neither can they delay it nor can they advance it an hour (or a moment)." (*Tafsir Al-Qurtubî*).

50. Say: "Tell me, if His torment should come to you by night or by day, which portion thereof would the *Mujrimûn* (disbelievers, polytheists, sinners, criminals) hasten on ?"

51. Is it then that when it has actually befallen, you will believe in it? What! Now (you believe)? And you used (aforetime) to hasten it on!"

52. Then it will be said to those who wronged themselves: "Taste you the everlasting torment! Are you recompensed (aught) save what you used to earn?"

53. And they ask you (O Muhammad صلى الله عليه وسلم) to inform them (saying): "Is it true (i.e. the torment and the establishment of the Hour — the Day of Resurrection)?" Say: "Yes! By my Lord! It is the very truth! and you cannot escape it!"

54. And if every person who had wronged (by disbelieving in Allâh and

by worshipping others besides Allâh)
possessed all that is on the earth and
sought to ransom himself therewith (it
will not be accepted), and they would
feel in their hearts regret when they see
the torment, and they will be judged
with justice, and no wrong will be done
unto them.[1]

55. No doubt, surely, all that is in the
heavens and the earth belongs to Allâh.
No doubt, surely, Allâh's Promise is
true. But most of them know not.

56. It is He Who gives life, and
causes death, and to Him you (all) shall
return.

57. O mankind! There has come to
you a good advice from your Lord (i.e.
the Qur'ân, enjoining all that is good
and forbidding all that is evil), and a
healing for that (disease of ignorance,
doubt, hypocrisy and differences)
which is in your breasts, — a guidance
and a mercy (explaining lawful and
unlawful things) for the believers.

58. Say: "In the Bounty of Allâh, and
in His Mercy (i.e. Islâm and the
Qur'ân); —therein let them rejoice."
That is better than what (the wealth)
they amass.

59. Say (O Muhammad صلى الله عليه وسلم to
these polytheists): "Tell me, what
provision Allâh has sent down to you!
And you have made of it lawful and

---

[1] (V.10:54) See the footnote of (V.3:91).

unlawful." Say (O Muhammad ﷺ): "Has Allâh permitted you (to do so), or do you invent a lie against Allâh?"

60. And what think those who invent a lie against Allâh, on the Day of Resurrection? [i.e. Do they think that they will be forgiven and excused! Nay, they will have an eternal punishment in the Fire of Hell). Truly, Allâh is full of Bounty to mankind, but most of them are ungrateful.

61. Neither you (O Muhammad ﷺ) do any deed nor recite any portion of the Qur'ân, nor you (O mankind) do any deed (good or evil), but We are Witness thereof, when you are doing it. And nothing is hidden from your Lord (so much as) the weight of an atom (or small ant) on the earth or in the heaven. Not what is less than that or what is greater than that but is (written) in a Clear Record. (Tafsîr At-Tabarî).

62. No doubt! Verily, the Auliyâ' of Allâh [i.e. those who believe in the Oneness of Allâh and fear Allâh much (abstain from all kinds of sins and evil deeds which he has forbidden), and love Allâh much (perform all kinds of good deeds which He has ordained)], no fear shall come upon them nor shall they grieve.[1]

---

[1] (V.10:62) Narrated Abu Sa'îd Al-Khudrî رضي الله عنه : Allâh's Messenger صلى الله عليه وسلم said, "When the funeral is ready and the men carry it on their shoulders, if the deceased was righteous, it will say: 'Present me (hurriedly).' and if he was not righteous, it will say:

63. Those who believed (in the Oneness of Allâh — Islâmic Monotheism), and used to fear Allâh much (by abstaining from evil deeds and sins and by doing righteous deeds).

الَّذِينَ ءَامَنُوا وَكَانُوا يَتَّقُونَ ٦٣

64. For them are glad tidings, in the life of the present world[1] (i.e. through a righteous dream seen by the person himself or shown to others), and in the Hereafter. No change can there be in the Words of Allâh. This is indeed the supreme success.

لَهُمُ الْبُشْرَىٰ فِي الْحَيَوٰةِ الدُّنْيَا وَفِي الْآخِرَةِ لَا تَبْدِيلَ لِكَلِمَتِ اللَّهِ ذَٰلِكَ هُوَ الْفَوْزُ الْعَظِيمُ ٦٤

65. And let not their speech grieve you (O Muhammad صلى الله عليه وسلم), for all power and honour belong to Allâh. He is the All-Hearer, the All-Knower.

وَلَا يَحْزُنكَ قَوْلُهُمْ إِنَّ الْعِزَّةَ لِلَّهِ جَمِيعًا هُوَ السَّمِيعُ الْعَلِيمُ ٦٥

66. No doubt! Verily, to Allâh belongs whosoever is in the heavens and whosoever is in the earth. And those who worship and invoke others besides Allâh, in fact they follow not the (Allâh's so-called) partners, they

أَلَا إِنَّ لِلَّهِ مَن فِي السَّمَٰوَٰتِ وَمَن فِي الْأَرْضِ وَمَا يَتَّبِعُ الَّذِينَ يَدْعُونَ مِن دُونِ اللَّهِ شُرَكَاءَ إِن يَتَّبِعُونَ

'Woe to it (me)! Where are they taking it (me)?' Its voice is heard by everything except man, and if he heard it, he would fall unconscious." (*Sahih Al-Bukhari*, Vol.2, *Hadith* No.400).

[1] (V.10:64).

a) Narrated Abu Hurairah رضي الله عنه I heard Allâh's Messenger صلى الله عليه وسلم saying: "Nothing is left of النبوة *An-Nubuwwah* (Prophethood) except *Al-Mubashshirât*." They asked, "What is *Al-Mubashshirât?*" He replied, "The true good dreams (that convey glad tidings)." (*Sahih Al-Bukhari*, Vol. 9, *Hadith* No. 119).

b) Narrated Abu Hurairah رضي الله عنه Allâh's Messenger صلى الله عليه وسلم said: "The (good) dream of a faithful believer is a part of the forty-six parts of the *An-Nubuwwah* (Prophethood)." (*Sahih Al-Bukhari*, Vol. 9, *Hadith* No. 117).

follow only a conjecture and they only invent lies.

إِلَّا ٱلظَّنَّ وَإِنْ هُمْ إِلَّا يَخْرُصُونَ ۝

67. He it is Who has appointed for you the night that you may rest therein, and the day to make things visible (to you). Verily, in this are Ayât (proofs, evidences, verses, lessons, signs, revelations, etc.) for a people who listen (i.e. those who think deeply).

هُوَ ٱلَّذِى جَعَلَ لَكُمُ ٱلَّيْلَ لِتَسْكُنُوا۟ فِيهِ وَٱلنَّهَارَ مُبْصِرًا ۚ إِنَّ فِى ذَٰلِكَ لَءَايَٰتٍ لِّقَوْمٍ يَسْمَعُونَ ۝

68. They (Jews, Christians and pagans) say: "Allâh has begotten a son (children)." Glory is to Him! He is Rich (Free of all needs). His is all that is in the heavens and all that is in the earth. No warrant you have for this. Do you say against Allâh what you know not.[1]

قَالُوا۟ ٱتَّخَذَ ٱللَّهُ وَلَدًا ۗ سُبْحَٰنَهُۥ ۖ هُوَ ٱلْغَنِىُّ ۖ لَهُۥ مَا فِى ٱلسَّمَٰوَٰتِ وَمَا فِى ٱلْأَرْضِ ۚ إِنْ عِندَكُم مِّن سُلْطَٰنٍۭ بِهَٰذَآ ۚ أَتَقُولُونَ عَلَى ٱللَّهِ مَا لَا تَعْلَمُونَ ۝

69. Say: "Verily, those who invent a lie against Allâh will never be successful" —

قُلْ إِنَّ ٱلَّذِينَ يَفْتَرُونَ عَلَى ٱللَّهِ ٱلْكَذِبَ لَا يُفْلِحُونَ ۝

70. (A brief) enjoyment in this world! and then unto Us will be their return, then We shall make them taste the severest torment because they used to disbelieve [in Allâh, belie His Messengers, deny and challenge His Ayât (proofs, signs, verses, etc.)].

مَتَٰعٌ فِى ٱلدُّنْيَا ثُمَّ إِلَيْنَا مَرْجِعُهُمْ ثُمَّ نُذِيقُهُمُ ٱلْعَذَابَ ٱلشَّدِيدَ بِمَا كَانُوا۟ يَكْفُرُونَ ۝

71. And recite to them the news of Nûh (Noah). When he said to his people: "O my people, if my stay (with you), and my reminding (you) of the Ayât (proofs, evidences, verses, lessons, signs, revelations, etc.) of Allâh is hard on you, then I put my trust in Allâh. So

۞ وَٱتْلُ عَلَيْهِمْ نَبَأَ نُوحٍ إِذْ قَالَ لِقَوْمِهِۦ يَٰقَوْمِ إِن كَانَ كَبُرَ عَلَيْكُم مَّقَامِى وَتَذْكِيرِى بِـَٔايَٰتِ ٱللَّهِ فَعَلَى ٱللَّهِ تَوَكَّلْتُ فَأَجْمِعُوٓا۟ أَمْرَكُمْ وَشُرَكَآءَكُمْ ثُمَّ لَا يَكُنْ

---

[1] (V.10:68) See the footnote of (V.6:101).

devise your plot, you and your partners, and let not your plot be in doubt for you. Then pass your sentence on me and give me no respite.

72. "But if you turn away [from accepting my doctrine of Islâmic Monotheism, i.e. to worship none but Allâh], then no reward have I asked of you, my reward is only from Allâh, and I have been commanded to be of the Muslims (i.e. those who submit to Allâh's Will)."

73. They denied him, but We delivered him, and those with him in the ship, and We made them generations replacing one after another, while We drowned those who belied Our *Ayât* (proofs, evidences, lessons, signs, revelations, etc.). Then see what was the end of those who were warned.

74. Then after him We sent Messengers to their people. They brought them clear proofs, but they would not believe what they had already rejected beforehand. Thus We seal the hearts of the transgressors (those who disbelieve in the Oneness of Allâh and disobey Him).

75. Then after them We sent Mûsâ (Moses) and Hârûn (Aaron) to Fir'aun (Pharaoh) and his chiefs with Our *Ayât* (proofs, evidences, verses, lessons, signs, revelations, etc.). But they behaved arrogantly and were *Mujrimûn* (disbelievers, sinners, polytheists and criminals) folk.

أَمْرَكُمْ عَلَيْكُمْ غُمَّةً ثُمَّ اقْضُوا إِلَيَّ وَلَا تُنظِرُونِ ٧١

فَإِن تَوَلَّيْتُمْ فَمَا سَأَلْتُكُم مِّنْ أَجْرٍ إِنْ أَجْرِيَ إِلَّا عَلَى اللَّهِ وَأُمِرْتُ أَنْ أَكُونَ مِنَ الْمُسْلِمِينَ ٧٢

فَكَذَّبُوهُ فَنَجَّيْنَاهُ وَمَن مَّعَهُ فِي الْفُلْكِ وَجَعَلْنَاهُمْ خَلَائِفَ وَأَغْرَقْنَا الَّذِينَ كَذَّبُوا بِـَٔايَاتِنَا فَانظُرْ كَيْفَ كَانَ عَاقِبَةُ الْمُنذَرِينَ ٧٣

ثُمَّ بَعَثْنَا مِنۢ بَعْدِهِ رُسُلًا إِلَىٰ قَوْمِهِمْ فَجَآءُوهُم بِالْبَيِّنَاتِ فَمَا كَانُوا لِيُؤْمِنُوا بِمَا كَذَّبُوا بِهِ مِن قَبْلُ كَذَٰلِكَ نَطْبَعُ عَلَىٰ قُلُوبِ الْمُعْتَدِينَ ٧٤

ثُمَّ بَعَثْنَا مِنۢ بَعْدِهِم مُّوسَىٰ وَهَارُونَ إِلَىٰ فِرْعَوْنَ وَمَلَإِيْهِ بِـَٔايَاتِنَا فَاسْتَكْبَرُوا وَكَانُوا قَوْمًا مُّجْرِمِينَ ٧٥

76. So when came to them the truth from Us, they said: "This is indeed clear magic."

فَلَمَّا جَاءَهُمُ الْحَقُّ مِنْ عِنْدِنَا قَالُوا إِنَّ هَٰذَا لَسِحْرٌ مُّبِينٌ ٧٦

77. Mûsâ (Moses) said: "Say you (this) about the truth when it has come to you? Is this magic? But the magicians will never be successful."

قَالَ مُوسَىٰ أَتَقُولُونَ لِلْحَقِّ لَمَّا جَاءَكُمْ أَسِحْرٌ هَٰذَا وَلَا يُفْلِحُ السَّاحِرُونَ ٧٧

78. They said: "Have you come to us to turn us away from that (Faith) we found our fathers following, and that you two may have greatness in the land? We are not going to believe you two!"

قَالُوٓا أَجِئْتَنَا لِتَلْفِتَنَا عَمَّا وَجَدْنَا عَلَيْهِ ءَابَآءَنَا وَتَكُونَ لَكُمَا الْكِبْرِيَآءُ فِي الْأَرْضِ وَمَا نَحْنُ لَكُمَا بِمُؤْمِنِينَ ٧٨

79. And Fir'aun (Pharaoh) said: "Bring me every well-versed sorcerer."

وَقَالَ فِرْعَوْنُ ائْتُونِي بِكُلِّ سَٰحِرٍ عَلِيمٍ ٧٩

80. And when the sorcerers came, Mûsâ (Moses) said to them: "Cast down what you want to cast!"

فَلَمَّا جَآءَ السَّحَرَةُ قَالَ لَهُم مُّوسَىٰٓ أَلْقُوا مَآ أَنتُم مُّلْقُونَ ٨٠

81. Then when they had cast down, Mûsâ (Moses) said: "What you have brought is sorcery, Allâh will surely, make it of no effect. Verily, Allâh does not set right the work of Al-Mufsidûn (the evil-doers and corrupters)."

فَلَمَّآ أَلْقَوْا قَالَ مُوسَىٰ مَا جِئْتُم بِهِ السِّحْرُ إِنَّ اللَّهَ سَيُبْطِلُهُۥٓ إِنَّ اللَّهَ لَا يُصْلِحُ عَمَلَ الْمُفْسِدِينَ ٨١

82. "And Allâh will establish and make apparent the truth by His Words, however much the *Mujrimûn* (criminals, disbelievers, polytheists and sinners) may hate (it)."

وَيُحِقُّ اللَّهُ الْحَقَّ بِكَلِمَٰتِهِۦ وَلَوْ كَرِهَ الْمُجْرِمُونَ ٨٢

83. But none believed in Mûsâ (Moses) except the offspring of his people, because of the fear of Fir'aun (Pharaoh) and his chiefs, lest they should persecute them; and verily, Fir'aun (Pharaoh) was an arrogant

فَمَآ ءَامَنَ لِمُوسَىٰٓ إِلَّا ذُرِّيَّةٌ مِّن قَوْمِهِۦ عَلَىٰ خَوْفٍ مِّن فِرْعَوْنَ وَمَلَإِيهِمْ أَن يَفْتِنَهُمْ وَإِنَّ فِرْعَوْنَ لَعَالٍ فِي الْأَرْضِ وَإِنَّهُۥ

tyrant on the earth, he was indeed one of the *Musrifûn* (polytheists, sinners and transgressors, those who give up the truth and follow the evil, and commit all kinds of great sins).

84. And Mûsâ (Moses) said: "O my people! If you have believed in Allâh, then put your trust in Him if you are Muslims (those who submit to Allâh's Will)."

85. They said: "In Allâh we put our trust. Our Lord! Make us not a trial for the folk who are *Zâlimûn* (polytheists and wrongdoers) (i.e. do not make them overpower us)."

86. "And save us by Your Mercy from the disbelieving folk."

87. And We revealed to Mûsâ (Moses) and his brother (saying): "Provide dwellings for your people in Egypt, and make your dwellings as places for your worship, and perform *As-Salât* (*Iqâmat-as-Salât*), and give glad tidings to the believers."

88. And Mûsâ (Moses) said: "Our Lord! You have indeed bestowed on Fir'aun (Pharaoh) and his chiefs splendour and wealth in the life of this world, our Lord! That they may lead men astray from Your Path. Our Lord! Destroy their wealth, and harden their hearts, so that they will not believe until they see the painful torment."

89. Allâh said: "Verily, the invocation of you both is accepted. So you both keep to the Straight Way (i.e. keep on doing good deeds and preaching Allâh's Message with patience), and follow not the path of those who know not (the truth i.e. to believe in the Oneness of Allâh, and also to believe in the Reward of Allâh: Paradise)."

90. And We took the Children of Israel across the sea, and Fir'aun (Pharaoh) with his hosts followed them in oppression and enmity, till when drowning overtook him, he said: "I believe that none has the right to be worshipped but He (Allâh) in Whom the Children of Israel believe, and I am one of the Muslims (those who submit to Allâh's Will)."

91. Now (you believe) while you refused to believe before and you were one of the *Mufsidûn* (evil-doers and the corrupters)?

92. So this day We shall deliver your (dead) body (out from the sea) that you may be a sign to those who come after you! And verily, many among mankind are heedless of Our *Ayât* (proofs, evidences, verses, lessons, signs, revelations, etc.).

93. And indeed We settled the Children of Israel in an honourable dwelling place (Shâm and Misr), and provided them with good things, and they differed not until the knowledge came to them. Verily, Allâh will judge between them on the Day of

Resurrection in that in which they used to differ.

فِيمَا كَانُوا فِيهِ يَخْتَلِفُونَ ۝

94. So if you (O Muhammad صلى الله عليه وسلم) are in doubt concerning that which We have revealed unto you, [i.e. that your name is written in the Taurât (Torah) and the Injeel (Gospel)], then ask those who are reading the Book [the Taurât (Torah) and the Injeel (Gospel)] before you. Verily, the truth has come to you from your Lord. So be not of those who doubt (it).[1]

فَإِن كُنتَ فِى شَكٍّ مِّمَّا أَنزَلْنَآ إِلَيْكَ فَسْـَٔلِ الَّذِينَ يَقْرَءُونَ الْكِتَٰبَ مِن قَبْلِكَ لَقَدْ جَآءَكَ الْحَقُّ مِن رَّبِّكَ فَلَا تَكُونَنَّ مِنَ الْمُمْتَرِينَ ۝

95. And be not one of those who belie the *Ayât* (proofs, evidences, verses, lessons, signs, revelations, etc.) of Allâh, for then you shall be one of the losers.

وَلَا تَكُونَنَّ مِنَ الَّذِينَ كَذَّبُوا بِـَٔايَٰتِ اللَّهِ فَتَكُونَ مِنَ الْخَٰسِرِينَ ۝

96. Truly, those, against whom the Word (Wrath) of your Lord has been justified, will not believe.

إِنَّ الَّذِينَ حَقَّتْ عَلَيْهِمْ كَلِمَتُ رَبِّكَ لَا يُؤْمِنُونَ ۝

97. Even if every sign should come to them, until they see the painful torment.

وَلَوْ جَآءَتْهُمْ كُلُّ ءَايَةٍ حَتَّىٰ يَرَوُا الْعَذَابَ الْأَلِيمَ ۝

98. Was there any town (community) that believed (after seeing the punishment), and its Faith (at that moment) saved it (from the punishment)? (The answer is none) — except the people of Yûnus (Jonah); when they believed, We removed from them the torment of disgrace in the life of the (present) world, and permitted them to enjoy for a while.

فَلَوْلَا كَانَتْ قَرْيَةٌ ءَامَنَتْ فَنَفَعَهَآ إِيمَٰنُهَآ إِلَّا قَوْمَ يُونُسَ لَمَّآ ءَامَنُوا كَشَفْنَا عَنْهُمْ عَذَابَ الْخِزْىِ فِى الْحَيَوٰةِ الدُّنْيَا وَمَتَّعْنَٰهُمْ إِلَىٰ حِينٍ ۝

---

[1] (V.10:94): See (V.2:76), (V.7:157) and their footnotes.

99. And had your Lord willed, those on earth would have believed, all of them together. So, will you (O Muhammad صلى الله عليه وسلم) then compel mankind, until they become believers.

وَلَوْ شَاءَ رَبُّكَ لَآمَنَ مَن فِى ٱلْأَرْضِ كُلُّهُمْ جَمِيعًا أَفَأَنتَ تُكْرِهُ ٱلنَّاسَ حَتَّىٰ يَكُونُوا۟ مُؤْمِنِينَ ۝

100. It is not for any person to believe, except by the Leave of Allâh, and He will put the wrath on those who are heedless.

وَمَا كَانَ لِنَفْسٍ أَن تُؤْمِنَ إِلَّا بِإِذْنِ ٱللَّهِ وَيَجْعَلُ ٱلرِّجْسَ عَلَى ٱلَّذِينَ لَا يَعْقِلُونَ ۝

101. Say: "Behold all that is in the heavens and the earth," but neither Ayât (proofs, evidences, verses, lessons, signs, revelations, etc.) nor warners benefit those who believe not.

قُلِ ٱنظُرُوا۟ مَاذَا فِى ٱلسَّمَٰوَٰتِ وَٱلْأَرْضِ وَمَا تُغْنِى ٱلْآيَٰتُ وَٱلنُّذُرُ عَن قَوْمٍ لَّا يُؤْمِنُونَ ۝

102. Then do they wait for (anything) save for (a destruction) like that of the days of the men who passed away before them? Say: "Wait then, I am (too) with you among those who wait."

فَهَلْ يَنتَظِرُونَ إِلَّا مِثْلَ أَيَّامِ ٱلَّذِينَ خَلَوْا۟ مِن قَبْلِهِمْ قُلْ فَٱنتَظِرُوٓا۟ إِنِّى مَعَكُم مِّنَ ٱلْمُنتَظِرِينَ ۝

103. Then (in the end) We save Our Messengers and those who believe! Thus it is incumbent upon Us to save the believers.

ثُمَّ نُنَجِّى رُسُلَنَا وَٱلَّذِينَ ءَامَنُوا۟ كَذَٰلِكَ حَقًّا عَلَيْنَا نُنجِ ٱلْمُؤْمِنِينَ ۝

104. Say (O Muhammad صلى الله عليه وسلم): "O you mankind! If you are in doubt as to my religion (Islâm), then (know that) I will never worship those whom you worship besides Allâh. But I worship Allâh Who causes you to die, and I am commanded to be one of the believers.

قُلْ يَٰٓأَيُّهَا ٱلنَّاسُ إِن كُنتُمْ فِى شَكٍّ مِّن دِينِى فَلَآ أَعْبُدُ ٱلَّذِينَ تَعْبُدُونَ مِن دُونِ ٱللَّهِ وَلَٰكِنْ أَعْبُدُ ٱللَّهَ ٱلَّذِى يَتَوَفَّىٰكُمْ وَأُمِرْتُ أَنْ أَكُونَ مِنَ ٱلْمُؤْمِنِينَ ۝

105. "And (it is revealed to me): Direct your face (O Muhammad صلى الله عليه وسلم) entirely towards the religion Hanîfan (Islâmic Monotheism, i.e. to worship none but Allâh Alone), and

وَأَنْ أَقِمْ وَجْهَكَ لِلدِّينِ حَنِيفًا وَلَا تَكُونَنَّ مِنَ

never be one of the *Mushrikûn* (those who ascribe partners to Allâh, polytheists, idolaters, disbelievers in the Oneness of Allâh, and those who worship others along with Allâh).

106. "And invoke not besides Allâh any such that will neither profit you nor hurt you, but if (in case) you did so, you shall certainly be one of the *Zâlimûn* (polytheists and wrongdoers).[1]"

107. And if Allâh touches you with hurt, there is none who can remove it but He; and if He intends any good for you, there is none who can repel His Favour which He causes 'it to reach whomsoever of His slaves He wills. And He is the Oft-Forgiving, the Most Merciful.

108. Say: "O you mankind! Now truth (i.e. the Qur'ân and Prophet Muhammad صلى الله عليه وسلم), has come to you from your Lord. So whosoever receives guidance, he does so for the good of his own self; and whosoever goes astray, he does so to his own loss; and I am not (set) over you as a *Wakîl* (disposer of affairs to oblige you for guidance)."

109. And (O Muhammad صلى الله عليه وسلم), follow the revelation sent unto you, and be patient till Allâh gives judgement. And He is the Best of judges.

---

[1] (V.10:106) See the footnote of (V.2:165).

Sûrat Hûd [(Prophet) Hûd] XI

In the Name of Allâh the Most Gracious, the Most Merciful

1. *Alif-Lâm-Râ.* [These letters are one of the miracles of the Qur'ân and none but Allâh (Alone) knows their meanings]. (This is) a Book, the Verses whereof are perfected (in every sphere of knowledge), and then explained in detail from One (Allâh), Who is All-Wise Well-Acquainted (with all things).

2. (Saying) worship none but Allâh. Verily, I [Muhammad صلى الله عليه وسلم] am unto you from Him a warner and a bringer of glad tidings.

3. And (commanding you): "Seek the forgiveness of your Lord, and turn to Him in repentance, that He may grant you good enjoyment, for a term appointed, and bestow His abounding Grace to every owner of grace (i.e. the one who helps and serves the needy and deserving, physically and with his wealth, and even with good words). But if you turn away, then I fear for you the torment of a Great Day (i.e. the Day of Resurrection).

4. To Allâh is your return, and He is Able to do all things."

5. No doubt! They did fold up their breasts, that they may hide from Him. Surely, even when they cover themselves with their garments, He knows what they conceal and what they reveal. Verily, He is the All-Knower of the (innermost secrets) of the breasts.

6. And no moving (living) creature is there on earth but its provision is due from Allâh. And He knows its dwelling place and its deposit (in the uterous or grave). All is in a Clear Book (*Al-Lauh Al-Mahfûz* — the Book of Decrees with Allâh).

7. And He it is Who has created the heavens and the earth in six Days and His Throne was on the water, that He might try you, which of you is the best in deeds. But if you were to say to them: "You shall indeed be raised up after death," those who disbelieve would be sure to say, "This is nothing but obvious magic.[1]"

8. And if We delay the torment for them till a determined term, they are sure to say, "What keeps it back?" Verily, on the day it reaches them, nothing will turn it away from them, and they will be surrounded by (or fall in) that at which they used to mock!

9. And if We give man a taste of Mercy from Us, and then withdraw it from him, verily, He is despairing, ungrateful.

---

[1] (V.11:7) Narrated Abu Hurairah رضي الله عنه : The Prophet صلى الله عليه وسلم said, "The Right (Hand) of Allâh is full, and (its fullness) is not affected by the continuous spending night and day. Do you see what He has spent since He created the heavens and the earth? Yet all that has not decreased what is in His Right Hand. His Throne is over the water, and in His other Hand is the Bounty or the Power to bring about death, and He raises some people and brings others down." (*Sahih Al-Bukhari*, Vol. 9, *Hadith* No. 515)

10. But if We let him taste good (favour) after evil (poverty and harm) has touched him, he is sure to say: "Ills have departed from me." Surely, he is exultant, and boastful (ungrateful to Allâh).

11. Except those who show patience and do righteous good deeds: those, theirs will be forgiveness and a great reward (Paradise).

12. So perchance you (Muhammad صلى الله عليه وسلم) may give up a part of what is revealed unto you, and that your breast feels straitened for it because they say, "Why has not a treasure been sent down unto him, or an angel has come with him?" But you are only a warner. And Allâh is a *Wakîl* (Disposer of affairs, Trustee, Guardian) over all things.

13. Or they say, "He (Prophet Muhammad صلى الله عليه وسلم) forged it (the Qur'ân)." Say: "Bring you then ten forged *Sûrah* (chapters) like unto it, and call whomsoever you can, other than Allâh (to your help), if you speak the truth!"

14. If then they answer you not, know then that it [the Revelation (this Qur'ân)] is sent down with the Knowledge of Allâh and that *Lâ ilâha illa Huwa*: (none has the right to be worshipped but He)! Will you then be Muslims (those who submit in Islâm)?

15. Whosoever desires the life of the world and its glitter, to them We shall pay in full (the wages of) their deeds therein, and they will have no diminution therein.

16. They are those for whom there is nothing in the Hereafter but Fire, and vain are the deeds they did therein. And of no effect is that which they used to do.

17. Can they (Muslims) who rely on a clear proof (the Qur'ân) from their Lord, and whom a witness [Jibrael (Gabriel (عليه السلام)] from Him follows it (can they be equal with the disbelievers); and before it, came the Book of Mûsâ (Moses), a guidance and a mercy, they believe therein, but those of the sects (Jews, Christians and all the other non-Muslim nations) that reject it (the Qur'ân), the Fire will be their promised meeting-place. So be not in doubt about it (i.e. those who denied Prophet Muhammad صلى الله عليه وسلم and also denied all that which he brought from Allâh. Surely, they will enter Hell. Verily, it is the truth from your Lord, but most of the mankind believe not.[1]

18. And who does more wrong than he who invents a lie against Allâh. Such will be brought before their Lord, and the witnesses will say, "These are the ones who lied against their Lord!" No doubt! the curse of Allâh is on the

---

[1] (V.11:17) See the footnote of (V.3:85) and the footnote (c) of (V.41:46).

Zâlimûn (polytheists, wrongdoers, oppressors).[1]

الظَّـٰلِمِينَ ۞

19. Those who hinder (others) from the Path of Allâh (Islâmic Monotheism), and seek a crookedness therein, while they are disbelievers in the Hereafter.

ٱلَّذِينَ يَصُدُّونَ عَن سَبِيلِ ٱللَّهِ وَيَبْغُونَهَا عِوَجًا وَهُم بِٱلْأَخِرَةِ هُمْ كَٰفِرُونَ ۞

20. By no means will they escape (from Allâh's Torment) on earth, nor have they protectors besides Allâh! Their torment will be doubled! They could not bear to hear (the preachers of the truth) and they used not to see (the truth because of their severe aversion, inspite of the fact that they had the sense of hearing and sight).

أُوْلَٰٓئِكَ لَمْ يَكُونُواْ مُعْجِزِينَ فِي ٱلْأَرْضِ وَمَا كَانَ لَهُم مِّن دُونِ ٱللَّهِ مِنْ أَوْلِيَآءَ يُضَٰعَفُ لَهُمُ ٱلْعَذَابُ مَا كَانُواْ يَسْتَطِيعُونَ ٱلسَّمْعَ وَمَا كَانُواْ يُبْصِرُونَ ۞

---

[1] (V.11:18) The Statement of Allâh عزوجل: "The witnesses will say: 'These are the ones who lied against their Lord...'"

Narrated Safwân bin Muhriz: While Ibn 'Umar was performing the *Tawâf* (around the *Ka'bah*), a man came up to him and said, "O Abu 'Abdur-Rahmân!" or said, "O Ibn 'Umar! Did you hear anything from the Prophet صلى الله عليه وسلم about *An-Najwa*?"* Ibn 'Umar said, "I heard the Prophet صلى الله عليه وسلم saying, 'The believer will be brought near his Lord.'" (Hishâm, a subnarrator said, reporting the Prophet's words), "The believer will come near (his Lord) till his Lord covers him with His Screen and makes him confess his sins. (Allâh will ask him). 'Do you know (that you did) such-and-such sin.' He will say twice, 'Yes, I know I did commit those sins.' Then Allâh will say, 'I did screen your sins in the world and I forgive them for you today.' Then the record of his good deeds will be folded up [i.e. the record (Book) of his good deeds will be given to him]. As for the others or the disbelievers, it will be announced publicly before the witnesses: 'These are ones who lied against their Lord.'" (Sahih Al-Bukhari, Vol.6, Hadith No.207).

*An-Najwa: the private talk between Allâh and His slave on the Day of Resurrection. It also means, a secret counsel or conference or consultation.

21. They are those who have lost their ownselves, and their invented false deities will vanish from them.

22. Certainly, they are those who will be the greatest losers in the Hereafter.

23. Verily, those who believe (in the Oneness of Allâh — Islâmic Monotheism) and do righteous good deeds, and humble themselves (in repentance and obedience) before their Lord, they will be the dwellers of Paradise to dwell therein forever.

24. The likeness of the two parties is as the blind and the deaf and the seer and the hearer. Are they equal when compared? Will you not then take heed?

25. And indeed We sent Nûh (Noah) to his people (and he said): "I have come to you as a plain warner."

26. "That you worship none but Allâh; surely, I fear for you the torment of a painful Day."

27. The chiefs who disbelieved among his people said: "We see you but a man like ourselves, nor do we see any follow you but the meanest among us and they (too) followed you without thinking. And we do not see in you any merit above us, in fact we think you are liars."

28. He said: "O my people! Tell me, if I have a clear proof from my Lord, and a Mercy (Prophethood) has come to me from Him, but that (Mercy) has

أُوْلَـٰئِكَ ٱلَّذِينَ خَسِرُوٓاْ أَنفُسَهُمْ وَضَلَّ عَنْهُم مَّا كَانُواْ يَفْتَرُونَ ٢١ لَا جَرَمَ أَنَّهُمْ فِي ٱلْأَخِرَةِ هُمُ ٱلْأَخْسَرُونَ ٢٢ إِنَّ ٱلَّذِينَ ءَامَنُواْ وَعَمِلُواْ ٱلصَّـٰلِحَـٰتِ وَأَخْبَتُوٓاْ إِلَىٰ رَبِّهِمْ أُوْلَـٰئِكَ أَصْحَـٰبُ ٱلْجَنَّةِ هُمْ فِيهَا خَـٰلِدُونَ ٢٣ ۞ مَثَلُ ٱلْفَرِيقَيْنِ كَٱلْأَعْمَىٰ وَٱلْأَصَمِّ وَٱلْبَصِيرِ وَٱلسَّمِيعِ هَلْ يَسْتَوِيَانِ مَثَلًا أَفَلَا تَذَكَّرُونَ ٢٤ وَلَقَدْ أَرْسَلْنَا نُوحًا إِلَىٰ قَوْمِهِۦٓ إِنِّي لَكُمْ نَذِيرٌ مُّبِينٌ ٢٥ أَن لَّا تَعْبُدُوٓاْ إِلَّا ٱللَّهَ إِنِّيٓ أَخَافُ عَلَيْكُمْ عَذَابَ يَوْمٍ أَلِيمٍ ٢٦ فَقَالَ ٱلْمَلَأُ ٱلَّذِينَ كَفَرُواْ مِن قَوْمِهِۦ مَا نَرَىٰكَ إِلَّا بَشَرًا مِّثْلَنَا وَمَا نَرَىٰكَ ٱتَّبَعَكَ إِلَّا ٱلَّذِينَ هُمْ أَرَاذِلُنَا بَادِيَ ٱلرَّأْيِ وَمَا نَرَىٰ لَكُمْ عَلَيْنَا مِن فَضْلٍۭ بَلْ نَظُنُّكُمْ كَـٰذِبِينَ ٢٧ قَالَ يَـٰقَوْمِ أَرَءَيْتُمْ إِن كُنتُ عَلَىٰ بَيِّنَةٍ مِّن رَّبِّي وَءَاتَىٰنِي رَحْمَةً مِّنْ عِندِهِۦ فَعُمِّيَتْ عَلَيْكُمْ أَنُلْزِمُكُمُوهَا

وَأَنتُمْ لَهَا كَـٰرِهُونَ ۝

been obscured from your sight. Shall we compel you to accept it (Islâmic Monotheism) when you have a strong hatred for it?

29. "And O my people! I ask of you no wealth for it, my reward is from none but Allâh. I am not going to drive away those who have believed. Surely, they are going to meet their Lord, but I see that you are a people that are ignorant.

وَيَـٰقَوْمِ لَآ أَسْـَٔلُكُمْ عَلَيْهِ مَالًا إِنْ أَجْرِىَ إِلَّا عَلَى ٱللَّهِ وَمَآ أَنَا۠ بِطَارِدِ ٱلَّذِينَ ءَامَنُوٓا۟ إِنَّهُم مُّلَـٰقُوا۟ رَبِّهِمْ وَلَـٰكِنِّىٓ أَرَىٰكُمْ قَوْمًا تَجْهَلُونَ ۝

30. "And O my people! Who will help me against Allâh, if I drove them away? Will you not then give a thought?

وَيَـٰقَوْمِ مَن يَنصُرُنِى مِنَ ٱللَّهِ إِن طَرَدتُّهُمْ أَفَلَا تَذَكَّرُونَ ۝

31. "And I do not say to you that with me are the Treasures of Allâh, "Nor that I know the *Ghaib* (Unseen); nor do I say I am an angel, and I do not say of those whom your eyes look upon that Allâh will not bestow any good on them. Allâh knows what is in their inner-selves (as regards belief). In that case, I should, indeed be one of the *Zâlimûn* (wrongdoers, oppressors)."

وَلَآ أَقُولُ لَكُمْ عِندِى خَزَآئِنُ ٱللَّهِ وَلَآ أَعْلَمُ ٱلْغَيْبَ وَلَآ أَقُولُ إِنِّى مَلَكٌ وَلَآ أَقُولُ لِلَّذِينَ تَزْدَرِىٓ أَعْيُنُكُمْ لَن يُؤْتِيَهُمُ ٱللَّهُ خَيْرًا ٱللَّهُ أَعْلَمُ بِمَا فِىٓ أَنفُسِهِمْ إِنِّىٓ إِذًا لَّمِنَ ٱلظَّـٰلِمِينَ ۝

32. They said: "O *Nûh* (Noah)! You have disputed with us and much have you prolonged the dispute with us, now bring upon us what you threaten us with, if you are of the truthful."

قَالُوا۟ يَـٰنُوحُ قَدْ جَـٰدَلْتَنَا فَأَكْثَرْتَ جِدَٰلَنَا فَأْتِنَا بِمَا تَعِدُنَآ إِن كُنتَ مِنَ ٱلصَّـٰدِقِينَ ۝

33. He said: "Only Allâh will bring it (the punishment) on you, if He wills, and then you will escape not.

قَالَ إِنَّمَا يَأْتِيكُم بِهِ ٱللَّهُ إِن شَآءَ وَمَآ أَنتُم بِمُعْجِزِينَ ۝

34. "And my advice will not profit you, even if I wish to give you good counsel, if Allâh's Will is to keep you

وَلَا يَنفَعُكُمْ نُصْحِىٓ إِنْ أَرَدتُّ أَنْ أَنصَحَ لَكُمْ إِن كَانَ ٱللَّهُ يُرِيدُ أَن يُغْوِيَكُمْ هُوَ رَبُّكُمْ

astray. He is your Lord! and to Him you shall return."

35. Or they (the pagans of Makkah) say: "He (Muhammad صلى الله عليه وسلم) has fabricated it (the Qur'ân)." Say: "If I have fabricated it, upon me be my crimes, but I am innocent of (all) those crimes which you commit."

36. And it was revealed to Nûh (Noah): "None of your people will believe except those who have believed already. So be not sad because of what they used to do.

37. "And construct the ship under Our Eyes and with Our Revelation, and call not upon Me on behalf of those who did wrong; they are surely, to be drowned."

38. And as he was constructing the ship, whenever the chiefs of his people passed by him, they mocked at him. He said: "If you mock at us, so do we mock at you likewise for your mocking.

39. "And you will know who it is on whom will come a torment that will cover him with disgrace and on whom will fall a lasting torment."

40. (So it was) till when Our Command came and the oven gushed forth (water like fountains from the earth). We said: "Embark therein, of each kind two (male and female), and your family — except him against whom the Word has already gone forth

— and those who believe. And none believed with him, except a few."

41. And he [Nûh (Noah) عليه السلام] said: "Embark therein: in the Name of Allâh will be its (moving) course and its (resting) anchorage. Surely, my Lord is Oft-Forgiving, Most Merciful." (*Tafsir At-Tabari*)

42. So it (the ship) sailed with them amidst waves like mountains, and Nûh (Noah) called out to his son, who had separated himself (apart): "O my son! Embark with us and be not with the disbelievers."

43. The son replied: "I will betake myself to some mountain, it will save me from the water." Nûh (Noah) said: "This day there is no saviour[1] from the Decree of Allâh except him on whom He has mercy." And waves came in between them, so he (the son) was among the drowned.

44. And it was said: "O earth! Swallow up your water, and O sky! Withhold (your rain)." And the water was made to subside and the Decree (of Allâh) was fulfilled (i.e. the destruction of the people of Nûh (Noah). And it (the ship) rested on (Mount) Judi, and it

---

[1] (V.11:43) Narrated Abu Sa'îd Al-Khudrî that the Prophet صلى الله عليه وسلم said, "No Caliph is appointed but has two groups of advisors: One group advises him to do good and urges him to adopt it, and the other group advises him to do bad and urges him to adopt it: and *Al-Ma'sûm* (the sinless or the saved or the protected) is the one whom Allâh protects." (*Sahih Al-Bukhari*, Vol.8, Hadith No.608).

was said: "Away with the people who are *Zalimûn* (polytheists and wrong-doing)!"

45. And Nûh (Noah) called upon his Lord and said, "O my Lord! Verily, my son is of my family! And certainly, Your Promise is true, and You are the Most Just of the judges."

46. He said: "O Nûh (Noah)! Surely, he is not of your family; verily, his work is unrighteous, so ask not of Me that of which you have no knowledge! I admonish you, lest you should be one of the ignorant."

47. Nûh (Noah) said: "O my Lord! I seek refuge with You from asking You that of which I have no knowledge. And unless You forgive me and have Mercy on me, I would indeed be one of the losers."

48. It was said: "O Nûh (Noah)! Come down (from the ship) with peace from Us and blessings on you and on the people who are with you (and on some of their off-spring), but (there will be other) people to whom We shall grant their pleasures (for a time), but in the end a painful torment will reach them from Us."

49. This is of the news of the Unseen which We reveal unto you (O Muhammad ﷺ); neither you nor your people knew it before this. So be patient. Surely, the (good) end is for the *Muttaqûn* (the pious. See V.2:2)

وَنَادَىٰ نُوحٌ رَّبَّهُۥ فَقَالَ رَبِّ إِنَّ ٱبْنِي مِنْ أَهْلِي وَإِنَّ وَعْدَكَ ٱلْحَقُّ وَأَنتَ أَحْكَمُ ٱلْحَٰكِمِينَ ٤٥

قَالَ يَٰنُوحُ إِنَّهُۥ لَيْسَ مِنْ أَهْلِكَ إِنَّهُۥ عَمَلٌ غَيْرُ صَٰلِحٍ فَلَا تَسْـَٔلْنِ مَا لَيْسَ لَكَ بِهِۦ عِلْمٌ إِنِّيٓ أَعِظُكَ أَن تَكُونَ مِنَ ٱلْجَٰهِلِينَ ٤٦

قَالَ رَبِّ إِنِّيٓ أَعُوذُ بِكَ أَنْ أَسْـَٔلَكَ مَا لَيْسَ لِي بِهِۦ عِلْمٌ وَإِلَّا تَغْفِرْ لِي وَتَرْحَمْنِيٓ أَكُن مِّنَ ٱلْخَٰسِرِينَ ٤٧

قِيلَ يَٰنُوحُ ٱهْبِطْ بِسَلَٰمٍ مِّنَّا وَبَرَكَٰتٍ عَلَيْكَ وَعَلَىٰٓ أُمَمٍ مِّمَّن مَّعَكَ وَأُمَمٌ سَنُمَتِّعُهُمْ ثُمَّ يَمَسُّهُم مِّنَّا عَذَابٌ أَلِيمٌ ٤٨

تِلْكَ مِنْ أَنۢبَآءِ ٱلْغَيْبِ نُوحِيهَآ إِلَيْكَ مَا كُنتَ تَعْلَمُهَآ أَنتَ وَلَا قَوْمُكَ مِن قَبْلِ هَٰذَا فَٱصْبِرْ إِنَّ ٱلْعَٰقِبَةَ لِلْمُتَّقِينَ ٤٩

50. And to the 'Âd (people We sent) their brother Hûd. He said, "O my people! Worship Allâh! You have no other *Ilâh* (god) but Him. Certainly, you do nothing but invent lies!

51. "O my people I ask of you no reward for it (the Message). My reward is only from Him Who created me. Will you not then understand?

52. "And O my people! Ask forgiveness of your Lord and then repent to Him, He will send you (from the sky) abundant rain, and add strength to your strength, so do not turn away as *Mujrimûn* (criminals, disbelievers in the Oneness of Allâh)."

53. They said: "O Hûd! No evidence have you brought us, and we shall not leave our gods for your (mere) saying! And we are not believers in you.

54. "All that we say is that some of our gods (false deities) have seized you with evil (madness)." He said: "I call Allâh to witness and bear you witness that I am free from that which you ascribe as partners in worship,

55. With Him (Allâh). So plot against me, all of you, and give me no respite.

56. "I put my trust in Allâh, my Lord and your Lord! There is not a moving (living) creature but He has the grasp of its forelock. Verily, my Lord is on the Straight Path (the truth).

57. "So if you turn away, still I have conveyed the Message with which I was sent to you. My Lord will make another people succeed you, and you will not harm Him in the least. Surely, my Lord is Guardian over all things."

58. And when Our Commandment came, We saved Hûd and those who believed with him by a Mercy from Us, and We saved them from a severe torment.

59. Such were 'Âd (people). They rejected the Ayât (proofs, evidences, verses, lessons, signs, revelations, etc.) of their Lord and disobeyed His Messengers, and followed the command of every proud, obstinate (oppressor of the truth from their leaders).

60. And they were pursued by a curse in this world and (so they will be) on the Day of Resurrection. No doubt! Verily, 'Âd disbelieved in their Lord. So away with 'Âd, the people of Hûd.

61. And to Thamûd (people We sent) their brother Sâlih. He said: "O my people! Worship Allâh: you have no other Ilâh (god) but Him. He brought you forth from the earth and settled you therein, then ask forgiveness of Him and turn to Him in repentance. Certainly, my Lord is Near (to all by His Knowledge), Responsive."

62. They said: "O Sâlih! You have been among us as a figure of good hope (and we wished for you to be our chief) till this [new thing which you have brought that we leave our gods and worship your God (Allâh) Alone]! Do you (now) forbid us the worship of what our fathers have worshipped? But we are really in grave doubt as to that to which you invite us (monotheism)."

63. He said: "O my people! Tell me, if I have a clear proof from my Lord, and there has come to me a Mercy (Prophethood) from Him, who then can help me against Allâh, if I were to disobey Him? Then you increase me not but in loss.

64. "And O my people! This she-camel of Allâh is a sign to you, so leave her to feed (graze) in Allâh's land, and touch her not with evil, lest a near torment should seize you."

65. But they killed her. So he said: "Enjoy yourselves in your homes for three days. This is a promise (i.e. a threat) that will not be belied."

66. So when Our Commandment came, We saved Sâlih and those who believed with him by a Mercy from Us, and from the disgrace of that Day. Verily, your Lord — He is the All-Strong, the All-Mighty.

67. And As-Saihah (torment — awful cry) overtook the wrongdoers, so they lay (dead), prostrate in their homes,

68. As if they had never lived there. No doubt! Verily, Thamûd disbelieved in their Lord. So away with Thamûd!

69. And verily, there came Our messengers to Ibrâhîm (Abraham) with glad tidings.They said: *Salâm* (greetings or peace!) He answered, *Salâm* (greetings or peace!) and he hastened to entertain them with a roasted calf.

سَلَمًا قَالَ سَلَمٌ فَمَا لَبِثَ أَن جَاءَ بِعِجْلٍ حَنِيذٍ ٦٩

70. But when he saw their hands went not towards it (the meal), he mistrusted them, and conceived a fear of them. They said: "Fear not, we have been sent against the people of Lût (Lot)."

فَلَمَّا رَءَآ أَيْدِيَهُمْ لَا تَصِلُ إِلَيْهِ نَكِرَهُمْ وَأَوْجَسَ مِنْهُمْ خِيفَةً قَالُوا لَا تَخَفْ إِنَّا أُرْسِلْنَا إِلَىٰ قَوْمِ لُوطٍ ٧٠

71. And his wife was standing (there), and she laughed [either, because the messengers did not eat their food or for being glad for the destruction of the people of Lût (Lot)]. But We gave her glad tidings of Ishâq (Isaac), and after Ishâq, of Ya'qûb (Jacob).

وَٱمْرَأَتُهُۥ قَآئِمَةٌ فَضَحِكَتْ فَبَشَّرْنَاهَا بِإِسْحَاقَ وَمِن وَرَآءِ إِسْحَاقَ يَعْقُوبَ ٧١

72. She said (in astonishment): "Woe unto me! Shall I bear a child while I am an old woman,[1] and here is my husband an old man? Verily, this is a strange thing!"

قَالَتْ يَـٰوَيْلَتَىٰٓ ءَأَلِدُ وَأَنَا۠ عَجُوزٌ وَهَـٰذَا بَعْلِى شَيْخًا إِنَّ هَـٰذَا لَشَىْءٌ عَجِيبٌ ٧٢

73. They said: "Do you wonder at the Decree of Allâh? The Mercy of Allâh and His Blessings be on you, O the family [of Ibrâhîm (Abraham)]. Surely, He (Allâh) is All-Praiseworthy, All-Glorious."

قَالُوٓا أَتَعْجَبِينَ مِنْ أَمْرِ ٱللَّهِ رَحْمَتُ ٱللَّهِ وَبَرَكَـٰتُهُۥ عَلَيْكُمْ أَهْلَ ٱلْبَيْتِ إِنَّهُۥ حَمِيدٌ مَّجِيدٌ ٧٣

74. Then when the fear had gone away from (the mind of) Ibrâhîm (Abraham), and the glad tidings had reached him, he began to plead with Us (Our messengers) for the people of Lût (Lot).

فَلَمَّا ذَهَبَ عَنْ إِبْرَٰهِيمَ ٱلرَّوْعُ وَجَآءَتْهُ ٱلْبُشْرَىٰ يُجَـٰدِلُنَا فِى قَوْمِ لُوطٍ ٧٤

---

[1] (V.11:72) See (V.51:29).

75. Verily, Ibrâhîm (Abraham) was, without doubt, forbearing, used to invoke Allâh with humility, and was repentant (to Allâh all the time, again and again).

إِنَّ إِبْرَٰهِيمَ لَحَلِيمٌ أَوَّٰهٌ مُّنِيبٌ ٧٥

76. "O Ibrâhîm (Abraham)! Forsake this. Indeed, the Commandment of your Lord has gone forth. Verily, there will come a torment for them which cannot be turned back."

يَٰٓإِبْرَٰهِيمُ أَعْرِضْ عَنْ هَٰذَآۖ إِنَّهُۥ قَدْ جَآءَ أَمْرُ رَبِّكَۖ وَإِنَّهُمْ ءَاتِيهِمْ عَذَابٌ غَيْرُ مَرْدُودٍ ٧٦

77. And when Our messengers came to Lût (Lot), he was grieved on account of them and felt himself straitened for them (lest the town people should approach them to commit sodomy with them). He said: "This is a distressful day."

وَلَمَّا جَآءَتْ رُسُلُنَا لُوطًا سِيٓءَ بِهِمْ وَضَاقَ بِهِمْ ذَرْعًا وَقَالَ هَٰذَا يَوْمٌ عَصِيبٌ ٧٧

78. And his people came rushing towards him, and since aforetime they used to commit crimes (sodomy), he said: "O my people! Here are my daughters (i.e. the women of the nation), they are purer for you (if you marry them lawfully). So fear Allâh and degrace me not with regard to my guests! Is there not among you a single right-minded man?"

وَجَآءَهُۥ قَوْمُهُۥ يُهْرَعُونَ إِلَيْهِ وَمِن قَبْلُ كَانُوا۟ يَعْمَلُونَ ٱلسَّيِّـَٔاتِۚ قَالَ يَٰقَوْمِ هَٰٓؤُلَآءِ بَنَاتِى هُنَّ أَطْهَرُ لَكُمْۖ فَٱتَّقُوا۟ ٱللَّهَ وَلَا تُخْزُونِ فِى ضَيْفِىٓۖ أَلَيْسَ مِنكُمْ رَجُلٌ رَّشِيدٌ ٧٨

79. They said: "Surely, you know that we have neither any desire nor need of your daughters, and indeed you know well what we want!"

قَالُوا۟ لَقَدْ عَلِمْتَ مَا لَنَا فِى بَنَاتِكَ مِنْ حَقٍّ وَإِنَّكَ لَتَعْلَمُ مَا نُرِيدُ ٧٩

80. He said: "Would that I had strength (men) to overpower you, or that I could betake myself to some powerful support (to resist you)."

قَالَ لَوْ أَنَّ لِى بِكُمْ قُوَّةً أَوْ ءَاوِىٓ إِلَىٰ رُكْنٍ شَدِيدٍ ٨٠

81. They (messengers) said: "O Lût (Lot)! Verily, we are the messengers

قَالُوا۟ يَٰلُوطُ إِنَّا رُسُلُ رَبِّكَ

from your Lord! They shall not reach you![1] So travel with your family in a part of the night, and let not any of you look back; but your wife (will remain behind), verily, the punishment which will afflict them, will afflict her. Indeed, morning is their appointed time. Is not the morning near?"

82. So when Our Commandment came, We turned (the towns of Sodom in Palestine) upside down, and rained on them stones of baked clay, in a well-arranged manner one after another;

83. Marked from your Lord; and they are not ever far from the *Zâlimûn* (polytheists, evil-doers).

84. And to the Madyan (Midian) people (We sent) their brother Shu'aib. He said: "O my people! Worship Allâh, you have no other *Ilâh* (god) but Him, and give not short measure or weight. I see you in prosperity and verily, I fear for you the torment of a Day encompassing.

85. "And O my people! Give full measure and weight in justice and reduce not the things that are due to the people, and do not commit mischief in the land, causing corruption.

86. "That which is left by Allâh for you (after giving the rights of the people) is better for you, if you are believers. And I am not a guardian over you."

---

[1] (V.11:81) See the Qur'ân (V.54:33-39).

87. They said: "O Shu'aib! Does your *Salât* (prayer) command that we give up what our fathers used to worship, or that we give up doing what we like with our property? Verily, you are the forbearer, right-minded!" (They said this sarcastically).

قَالُوا يَٰشُعَيْبُ أَصَلَوٰتُكَ تَأْمُرُكَ أَن نَّتْرُكَ مَا يَعْبُدُ ءَابَآؤُنَآ أَوْ أَن نَّفْعَلَ فِيٓ أَمْوَٰلِنَا مَا نَشَٰٓؤُا۟ إِنَّكَ لَأَنتَ ٱلْحَلِيمُ ٱلرَّشِيدُ ۝

88. He said: "O my people! Tell me if I have a clear evidence from my Lord and He has given me a good sustenance from Himself (shall I corrupt it by mixing it with the unlawfully earned money). I wish not, in contradiction to you, to do that which I forbid you. I only desire reform to the best of my power. And my guidance cannot come except from Allâh, in Him I trust and unto Him I repent.

قَالَ يَٰقَوْمِ أَرَءَيْتُمْ إِن كُنتُ عَلَىٰ بَيِّنَةٍ مِّن رَّبِّى وَرَزَقَنِى مِنْهُ رِزْقًا حَسَنًا وَمَآ أُرِيدُ أَنْ أُخَالِفَكُمْ إِلَىٰ مَآ أَنْهَىٰكُمْ عَنْهُ إِنْ أُرِيدُ إِلَّا ٱلْإِصْلَٰحَ مَا ٱسْتَطَعْتُ وَمَا تَوْفِيقِىٓ إِلَّا بِٱللَّهِ عَلَيْهِ تَوَكَّلْتُ وَإِلَيْهِ أُنِيبُ ۝

89. "And O my people! Let not my *Shiqâq*[1] cause you to suffer the fate similar to that of the people of Nûh (Noah) or of Hûd or of Sâlih, and the people of Lût (Lot) are not far off from you!

وَيَٰقَوْمِ لَا يَجْرِمَنَّكُمْ شِقَاقِىٓ أَن يُصِيبَكُم مِّثْلُ مَآ أَصَابَ قَوْمَ نُوحٍ أَوْ قَوْمَ هُودٍ أَوْ قَوْمَ صَٰلِحٍ وَمَا قَوْمُ لُوطٍ مِّنكُم بِبَعِيدٍ ۝

90. "And ask forgiveness of your Lord and turn unto Him in repentance. Verily, my Lord is Most Merciful, Most Loving."

وَٱسْتَغْفِرُوا۟ رَبَّكُمْ ثُمَّ تُوبُوٓا۟ إِلَيْهِ إِنَّ رَبِّى رَحِيمٌ وَدُودٌ ۝

91. They said: "O Shu'aib! We do not understand much of what you say, and we see you weak (it is said that he

قَالُوا۟ يَٰشُعَيْبُ مَا نَفْقَهُ كَثِيرًا مِّمَّا تَقُولُ وَإِنَّا لَنَرَىٰكَ فِينَا

---

[1] (V.11:89) i.e. separation, enmity, anger and opposition, because of your disbelief in the Oneness of Allâh (Monotheism), and your worship of the idols, and your defrauding of the people (in their things), and your giving of short measure and weights to the people.

was a blind man) among us. Were it not for your family, we should certainly have stoned you and you are not powerful against us."

92. He said: "O my people! Is then my family of more weight with you than Allâh? And you have cast Him away behind your backs. Verily, my Lord is surrounding all that you do.

93. "And O my people! Act according to your ability and way, and I am acting (on my way). You will come to know who it is on whom descends the torment that will cover him with ignomity, and who is a liar! And watch you! Verily, I too am watching with you."

94. And when Our Commandment came, We saved Shu'aib and those who believed with him by a Mercy from Us. And As-Saihah (torment — awful cry) seized the wrongdoers, and they lay (dead) prostrate in their homes.

95. As if they had never lived there! So away with Madyan (Midian) as away with Thamûd! (All nations were destroyed).

96. And indeed We sent Mûsâ (Moses) with Our Ayât (proofs, evidences, verses, lessons, signs, revelations, etc.) and a manifest authority.

97. To Fir'aun (Pharaoh) and his chiefs, but they followed the command of Fir'aun (Pharaoh), and the command

ضَعِيفًا وَلَوْلَا رَهْطُكَ لَرَجَمْنَاكَ وَمَا أَنتَ عَلَيْنَا بِعَزِيزٍ ۝ قَالَ يَٰقَوْمِ أَرَهْطِىٓ أَعَزُّ عَلَيْكُم مِّنَ ٱللَّهِ وَٱتَّخَذْتُمُوهُ وَرَآءَكُمْ ظِهْرِيًّا إِنَّ رَبِّى بِمَا تَعْمَلُونَ مُحِيطٌ ۝

وَيَٰقَوْمِ ٱعْمَلُواْ عَلَىٰ مَكَانَتِكُمْ إِنِّى عَٰمِلٌ سَوْفَ تَعْلَمُونَ مَن يَأْتِيهِ عَذَابٌ يُخْزِيهِ وَمَنْ هُوَ كَٰذِبٌ وَٱرْتَقِبُوٓاْ إِنِّى مَعَكُمْ رَقِيبٌ ۝ وَلَمَّا جَآءَ أَمْرُنَا نَجَّيْنَا شُعَيْبًا وَٱلَّذِينَ ءَامَنُواْ مَعَهُۥ بِرَحْمَةٍ مِّنَّا وَأَخَذَتِ ٱلَّذِينَ ظَلَمُواْ ٱلصَّيْحَةُ فَأَصْبَحُواْ فِى دِيَٰرِهِمْ جَٰثِمِينَ ۝ كَأَن لَّمْ يَغْنَوْاْ فِيهَآ أَلَا بُعْدًا لِّمَدْيَنَ كَمَا بَعِدَتْ ثَمُودُ ۝

وَلَقَدْ أَرْسَلْنَا مُوسَىٰ بِـَٔايَٰتِنَا وَسُلْطَٰنٍ مُّبِينٍ ۝

إِلَىٰ فِرْعَوْنَ وَمَلَإِيْهِۦ فَٱتَّبَعُوٓاْ أَمْرَ فِرْعَوْنَ وَمَآ أَمْرُ

of Fir'aun (Pharaoh) was no right guide.

فِرْعَوْنَ بِرَشِيدٍ ۝

98. He will go ahead of his people on the Day of Resurrection, and will lead them into the Fire, and evil indeed is the place to which they are led.

يَقْدُمُ قَوْمَهُ يَوْمَ الْقِيَامَةِ فَأَوْرَدَهُمُ النَّارَ وَبِئْسَ الْوِرْدُ الْمَوْرُودُ ۝

99. They were pursued by a curse in this (deceiving life of this world) and (so they will be pursued by a curse) on the Day of Resurrection. Evil indeed is the gift gifted [i.e., the curse (in this world) pursued by another curse (in the Hereafter)].

وَأُتْبِعُوا فِي هَذِهِ لَعْنَةً وَيَوْمَ الْقِيَامَةِ بِئْسَ الرِّفْدُ الْمَرْفُودُ ۝

100. That is some of the news of the (population of) towns which We relate unto you (O Muhammad صلى الله عليه وسلم); of them, some are (still) standing, and some have been (already) reaped.

ذَلِكَ مِنْ أَنْبَاءِ الْقُرَى نَقُصُّهُ عَلَيْكَ مِنْهَا قَائِمٌ وَحَصِيدٌ ۝

101. We wronged them not, but they wronged themselves. So their âlihah (gods), other than Allâh, whom they invoked, profited them naught when there came the Command of your Lord, nor did they add aught to them but destruction.

وَمَا ظَلَمْنَاهُمْ وَلَكِنْ ظَلَمُوا أَنْفُسَهُمْ فَمَا أَغْنَتْ عَنْهُمْ ءَالِهَتُهُمُ الَّتِي يَدْعُونَ مِنْ دُونِ اللهِ مِنْ شَيْءٍ لَمَّا جَاءَ أَمْرُ رَبِّكَ وَمَا زَادُوهُمْ غَيْرَ تَتْبِيبٍ ۝

102. Such is the Seizure of your Lord when He seizes the (population of) towns while they are doing wrong. Verily, His Seizure is painful, (and) severe.[1]

وَكَذَلِكَ أَخْذُ رَبِّكَ إِذَا أَخَذَ الْقُرَى وَهِيَ ظَالِمَةٌ إِنَّ أَخْذَهُ أَلِيمٌ شَدِيدٌ ۝

---

[1] (V.11:102) Narrated Abu Mûsâ رضي الله عنه: Allâh's Messenger صلى الله عليه وسلم said, "Allâh gives respite to a *Zâlim* (polytheist, wrongdoer, oppressor), but when He seizes (catches) him, He never releases him." Then he recited: "Such is the Seizure of your Lord when He

103. Indeed in that (there) is a sure lesson for those who fear the torment of the Hereafter. That is a Day whereon mankind will be gathered together, and that is a Day when all (the dwellers of the heavens and the earth) will be present.

104. And We delay it only for a term (already) fixed.

105. On the Day when it comes, no person shall speak except by His (Allâh's) Leave. Some among them will be wretched and (others) blessed.

106. As for those who are wretched, they will be in the Fire, sighing in a high and low tone.

107. They will dwell therein for all the time that the heavens and the earth endure, except as your Lord wills. Verily, your Lord is the Doer of whatsoever He intends (or wills).

108. And those who are blessed, they will be in Paradise, abiding therein for all the time that the heavens and the earth endure, except as your Lord wills: a gift without an end.

109. So be not in doubt (O Muhammad صلى الله عليه وسلم) as to what these people (pagans and polytheists) worship. They worship nothing but what their fathers worshipped before

---

seizes the (population of) towns while they are doing wrong: Verily, His Seizure is painful (and) severe." (*Sahih Al-Bukhari*, Vol.6, *Hadith* No.208).

(them). And verily, We shall repay them in full their portion without diminution.

110. Indeed, We gave the Book to Mûsâ (Moses), but differences arose therein, and had it not been for a Word that had gone forth before from your Lord, the case would have been judged between them, and indeed they are in grave doubt concerning it (this Qur'ân).

111. And verily, to each of them your Lord will repay their works in full. Surely, He is All-Aware of what they do.

112. So stand (ask Allâh to make) you (Muhammad صلى الله عليه وسلم) firm and straight (on the religion of Islâmic Monotheism) as you are commanded and those (your companions) who turn in repentance (unto Allâh) with you, and transgress not (Allâh's Legal Limits). Verily, He is All-Seer of what you do.

113. And incline not toward those who do wrong, lest the Fire should touch you, and you have no protectors other than Allâh, nor you would then be helped.[1]

لَمُوَفُّوهُمْ نَصِيبَهُمْ غَيْرَ مَنقُوصٍ ۝

وَلَقَدْ ءَاتَيْنَا مُوسَى ٱلْكِتَابَ فَٱخْتُلِفَ فِيهِ وَلَوْلَا كَلِمَةٌ سَبَقَتْ مِن رَّبِّكَ لَقُضِيَ بَيْنَهُمْ وَإِنَّهُمْ لَفِى شَكٍّ مِّنْهُ مُرِيبٍ ۝

وَإِنَّ كُلًّا لَّمَّا لَيُوَفِّيَنَّهُمْ رَبُّكَ أَعْمَالَهُمْ إِنَّهُۥ بِمَا يَعْمَلُونَ خَبِيرٌ ۝

فَٱسْتَقِمْ كَمَا أُمِرْتَ وَمَن تَابَ مَعَكَ وَلَا تَطْغَوْا۟ إِنَّهُۥ بِمَا تَعْمَلُونَ بَصِيرٌ ۝

وَلَا تَرْكَنُوٓا۟ إِلَى ٱلَّذِينَ ظَلَمُوا۟ فَتَمَسَّكُمُ ٱلنَّارُ وَمَا لَكُم مِّن دُونِ ٱللَّهِ مِنْ أَوْلِيَآءَ ثُمَّ لَا تُنصَرُونَ ۝

---

[1] (V.11:113) The sin of the person who gives refuge or helps a person who innovates an heresy (in the religion) or commits sins. This has been narrated by 'Ali رضي الله عنه on the authority of the Prophet صلى الله عليه وسلم.

Narrated 'Âsim: I said to Anas, "Did Allâh's Messenger صلى الله عليه وسلم make Al-Madinah a sanctuary?" He replied, "Yes, Al-Madinah is a sanctuary from such and such place to such and such place. It is forbidden to cut its trees, and whoever innovates a heresy in it or

وَأَقِمِ الصَّلَوٰةَ طَرَفَىِ النَّهَارِ وَزُلَفًا مِّنَ الَّيْلِ إِنَّ الْحَسَنَاتِ يُذْهِبْنَ السَّيِّئَاتِ ذَٰلِكَ ذِكْرَىٰ لِلذَّاكِرِينَ ١١٤

114. And perform *As-Salât* (*Iqâmat-as-Salât*), at the two ends of the day and some hours of the night [i.e. the five compulsory *Salât* (prayers)]. Verily, the good deeds remove the evil deeds (i.e. small sins). That is a reminder (an advice) for the mindful (those who accept advice).[1]

وَاصْبِرْ فَإِنَّ اللَّهَ لَا يُضِيعُ أَجْرَ الْمُحْسِنِينَ ١١٥

115. And be patient; verily, Allâh wastes not the reward of the good-doers.

فَلَوْلَا كَانَ مِنَ الْقُرُونِ مِن قَبْلِكُمْ أُولُوا بَقِيَّةٍ يَنْهَوْنَ عَنِ الْفَسَادِ فِي الْأَرْضِ إِلَّا قَلِيلًا

116. If only there had been among the generations before you persons having wisdom, prohibiting (others) from *Al-Fasâd* (disbelief, polytheism, and all kinds of crimes and sins) in the earth, —

---

commits a sin therein, will incur the Curse of Allâh, the angels, and all the people," Then Mûsâ bin Anas told me that Anas added, "… or gives refuge to such a heretic or a sinner …" (*Sahih Al-Bukhari*, Vol.9, *Hadith* No.409).

[1] (V.11:114):

(A) Narrated Ibn Mas'ûd رضي الله عنه: A man kissed a woman and then came to Allâh's Messenger صلى الله عليه وسلم and told him of that. So this Divine Revelation was revealed to the Prophet صلى الله عليه وسلم :- "And perform *As-Salât* (*Iqâmat-as-Salât*) at the two ends of the day, and in some hours of the night; [i.e. (five) compulsory *Salât* (prayers)]. Verily, the good deeds remove the evil deeds (small sins). That is a reminder for the mindful." (V.11:114). The man said, "Is this instruction for me only?" The Prophet صلى الله عليه وسلم said, "It is for all those of my followers who encounter a similar situation." (*Sahih Al-Bukhari*, Vol. 6, *Hadith* No: 209).

(B) Narrated Abû Dharr رضي الله عنه: Allâh's Messenger صلى الله عليه وسلم said to me: "(a) Be afraid of Allâh and keep your duty to him wherever you may be. (b) And follow up the evil deeds with the good deeds, (verily) the good deeds remove (blot out) the evil deeds. (c) And (treat) behave with the people in a high standard of character." (This *Hadith* is quoted by *At-Tirmidhi*).

except a few of those whom We saved from among them! Those who did wrong pursued the enjoyment of good things of (this worldly) life, and were *Mujrimûn* (criminals, disbelievers in Allâh, polytheists, sinners).

117. And your Lord would never destroy the towns wrongfully, while their people were right-doers.

118. And if your Lord had so willed, He could surely, have made mankind one *Ummah* [nation or community (following one religion i.e. Islâm)], but they will not cease to disagree.

119. Except him on whom your Lord has bestowed His Mercy (the follower of truth — Islâmic Monotheism) and for that[1] did He create them. And the Word of your Lord has been fulfilled (i.e. His Saying): "Surely, I shall fill Hell with jinn and men all together."

120. And all that We relate to you (O Muhammad صلى الله عليه وسلم) of the news of the Messengers is in order that We may make strong and firm your heart thereby. And in this (chapter of the Qur'ân) has come to you the truth, as well as an admonition and a reminder for the believers.

121. And say to those who do not believe: "Act according to your ability and way, We are acting (in our way).

---

[1] (V.11:119) i.e. to show mercy to the good-doers, the blessed ones who are destined to Paradise, and not to show mercy to the evil-doers, the wretched ones who are destined to Hell. [This is the statement of Ibn Abbas رضي الله عنهما as quoted in *Tafsir Qurtubi*].

122. And you wait ! We (too) are waiting."

123. And to Allâh belongs the *Ghaib* (Unseen) of the heavens and the earth, and to Him return all affairs (for decision). So worship Him (O Muhammad صلى الله عليه وسلم) and put your trust in Him. And your Lord is not unaware of what you (people) do."

Sûrat Yûsuf [(Prophet) Joseph] XII

In the Name of Allâh
the Most Gracious, the Most Merciful

1. *Alif-Lâm-Râ.* [These letters are one of the miracles of the Qur'ân, and none but Allâh (Alone) knows their meanings].

These are the Verses of the Clear Book (the Qur'ân that makes clear the legal and illegal things, legal laws, a guidance and a blessing).

2. Verily, We have sent it down as an Arabic Qur'ân in order that you may understand.

3. We relate unto you (Muhammad صلى الله عليه وسلم) the best of stories through Our Revelations unto you, of this Qur'ân. And before this (i.e. before the coming of Divine Revelation to you), you were among those who knew nothing about it (the Qur'ân).

4. (Remember) when Yûsuf (Joseph) said to his father: "O my father! Verily, I saw (in a dream) eleven stars and the sun and the moon — I saw them prostrating themselves to me."

5. He (the father) said: "O my son! Relate not your vision to your brothers, lest they should arrange a plot against you. Verily, *Shaitân* (Satan) is to man an open enemy."

6. "Thus will your Lord choose you and teach you the interpretation of dreams (and other things) and perfect His Favour on you and on the offspring of Ya'qûb (Jacob), as He perfected it on your fathers, Ibrâhîm (Abraham) and Ishâq (Isaac) aforetime! Verily, your Lord is All-Knowing, All-Wise."

7. Verily, in Yûsuf (Joseph) and his brethren, there were *Ayât* (proofs, evidences, verses, lessons, signs, revelations, etc.) for those who ask.

8. When they said: "Truly, Yûsuf (Joseph) and his brother (Benjamin) are dearer to our father than we, while we are '*Usbah* (a strong group). Really, our father is in a plain error."

9. "Kill Yûsuf (Joseph) or cast him out to some (other) land, so that the favour of your father may be given to you alone, and after that you will be righteous folk (by intending repentance before committing the sin)."

10. One from among them said: "Kill not Yûsuf (Joseph), but if you must do something, throw him down to the bottom of a well; he will be picked up by some caravan of travellers."

11. They said: "O our father! Why do you not trust us with Yûsuf (Joseph) though we are indeed his well-wishers?"

12. "Send him with us tomorrow to enjoy himself and play, and verily, we will take care of him."

أَرْسِلْهُ مَعَنَا غَدًا يَرْتَعْ وَيَلْعَبْ وَإِنَّا لَهُ لَحَٰفِظُونَ ١٢

13. He [Ya'qûb (Jacob)] said: "Truly, it saddens me that you should take him away. I fear lest a wolf should devour him, while you are careless of him."

قَالَ إِنِّي لَيَحْزُنُنِي أَن تَذْهَبُوا بِهِ وَأَخَافُ أَن يَأْكُلَهُ الذِّئْبُ وَأَنتُمْ عَنْهُ غَٰفِلُونَ ١٣

14. They said: "If a wolf devours him, while we are 'Usbah (a strong group to guard him), then surely, we are the losers."

قَالُوا لَئِنْ أَكَلَهُ الذِّئْبُ وَنَحْنُ عُصْبَةٌ إِنَّا إِذًا لَّخَٰسِرُونَ ١٤

15. So, when they took him away, they all agreed to throw him down to the bottom of the well, and We revealed to him: "Indeed, you shall (one day) inform them of this their affair, when they know (you) not."

فَلَمَّا ذَهَبُوا بِهِ وَأَجْمَعُوا أَن يَجْعَلُوهُ فِي غَيَٰبَتِ الْجُبِّ وَأَوْحَيْنَا إِلَيْهِ لَتُنَبِّئَنَّهُم بِأَمْرِهِمْ هَٰذَا وَهُمْ لَا يَشْعُرُونَ ١٥ وَجَاءُو

16. And they came to their father in the early part of the night weeping.

أَبَاهُمْ عِشَاءً يَبْكُونَ ١٦

17. They said: "O our father! We went racing with one another, and left Yûsuf (Joseph) by our belongings and a wolf devoured him; but you will never believe us even when we speak the truth."

قَالُوا يَٰأَبَانَا إِنَّا ذَهَبْنَا نَسْتَبِقُ وَتَرَكْنَا يُوسُفَ عِندَ مَتَٰعِنَا فَأَكَلَهُ الذِّئْبُ وَمَا أَنتَ بِمُؤْمِنٍ لَّنَا وَلَوْ كُنَّا صَٰدِقِينَ ١٧

18. And they brought his shirt stained with false blood. He said: "Nay, but your ownselves have made up a tale. So (for me) patience is most fitting. And it is Allâh (Alone) Whose help can be sought against that (lie) which you describe."

وَجَاءُو عَلَىٰ قَمِيصِهِ بِدَمٍ كَذِبٍ قَالَ بَلْ سَوَّلَتْ لَكُمْ أَنفُسُكُمْ أَمْرًا فَصَبْرٌ جَمِيلٌ وَاللَّهُ الْمُسْتَعَانُ عَلَىٰ مَا تَصِفُونَ ١٨

19. And there came a caravan of travellers and they sent their water-drawer, and he let down his bucket (into the well). He said: "What a good news! Here is a boy." So they hid

وَجَاءَتْ سَيَّارَةٌ فَأَرْسَلُوا وَارِدَهُمْ فَأَدْلَىٰ دَلْوَهُ قَالَ يَٰبُشْرَىٰ هَٰذَا غُلَٰمٌ وَأَسَرُّوهُ بِضَٰعَةً وَاللَّهُ

him as merchandise (a slave). And Allâh was the All-Knower of what they did.

20. And they sold him for a low price — for a few Dirhams (i.e. for a few silver coins). And they were of those who regarded him insignificant.

21. And he (the man) from Egypt who bought him, said to his wife: "Make his stay comfortable, may be he will profit us or we shall adopt him as a son." Thus did We establish Yûsuf (Joseph) in the land, that We might teach him the interpretation of events. And Allâh has full power and control over His Affairs, but most of men know not.

22. And when he [Yûsuf (Joseph)] attained his full manhood, We gave him wisdom and knowledge (the Prophethood), thus We reward the *Muhsinûn* (doers of good — see the footnote of V.9:120).

23. And she, in whose house he was, sought to seduce him (to do an evil act), and she closed the doors and said: "Come on, O you." He said: "I seek refuge in Allâh (or Allâh forbid)! Truly, he (your husband) is my master! He made my living in a great comfort! (So I will never betray him). Verily, the *Zâlimûn* (wrong and evil-doers) will never be successful."

24. And indeed she did desire him, and he would have inclined to her desire, had he not seen the evidence of his Lord. Thus it was, that We might turn away from him evil and illegal sexual intercourse. Surely, he was one of Our chosen, (guided) slaves.

25. So they raced with one another to the door, and she tore his shirt from the back. They both found her lord (i.e. her husband) at the door. She said: "What is the recompense (punishment) for him who intended an evil design against your wife, except that he be put in prison or a painful torment?"

26. He [Yûsuf (Joseph)] said: "It was she that sought to seduce me;" and a witness of her household bore witness (saying): "If it be that his shirt is torn from the front, then her tale is true and he is a liar!

27. "But if it be that his shirt is torn from the back, then she has told a lie and he is speaking the truth!"

28. So when he (her husband) saw his [(Yûsuf's (Joseph)] shirt torn at the back, he (her husband) said: "Surely, it is a plot of you women! Certainly mighty is your plot!

29. "O Yûsuf (Joseph)! Turn away from this! (O woman!) Ask forgiveness for your sin. Verily, you were of the sinful."

30. And women in the city said: "The wife of Al-'Azîz is seeking to seduce her (slave) young man, indeed she loves him violently; verily, we see her in plain error."

31. So when she heard of their accusation, she sent for them and prepared a banquet for them; she gave each one of them a knife (to cut the foodstuff with), and she said [(to Yûsuf (Joseph)]: "Come out before them." Then, when they saw him, they exalted him (at his beauty) and (in their astonishment) cut their hands. They

وَٱسۡتَبَقَا ٱلۡبَابَ وَقَدَّتۡ قَمِيصَهُۥ مِن دُبُرٍ وَأَلۡفَيَا سَيِّدَهَا لَدَا ٱلۡبَابِ قَالَتۡ مَا جَزَآءُ مَنۡ أَرَادَ بِأَهۡلِكَ سُوٓءًا إِلَّآ أَن يُسۡجَنَ أَوۡ عَذَابٌ أَلِيمٌ ﴿٢٥﴾

قَالَ هِىَ رَٰوَدَتۡنِى عَن نَّفۡسِى وَشَهِدَ شَاهِدٌ مِّنۡ أَهۡلِهَآ إِن كَانَ قَمِيصُهُۥ قُدَّ مِن قُبُلٍ فَصَدَقَتۡ وَهُوَ مِنَ ٱلۡكَٰذِبِينَ ﴿٢٦﴾ وَإِن كَانَ قَمِيصُهُۥ قُدَّ مِن دُبُرٍ فَكَذَبَتۡ وَهُوَ مِنَ ٱلصَّٰدِقِينَ ﴿٢٧﴾ فَلَمَّا رَءَا قَمِيصَهُۥ قُدَّ مِن دُبُرٍ قَالَ إِنَّهُۥ مِن كَيۡدِكُنَّ إِنَّ كَيۡدَكُنَّ عَظِيمٌ ﴿٢٨﴾ يُوسُفُ أَعۡرِضۡ عَنۡ هَٰذَا وَٱسۡتَغۡفِرِى لِذَنۢبِكِ إِنَّكِ كُنتِ مِنَ ٱلۡخَاطِئِينَ ﴿٢٩﴾ وَقَالَ نِسۡوَةٌ فِى ٱلۡمَدِينَةِ ٱمۡرَأَتُ ٱلۡعَزِيزِ تُرَٰوِدُ فَتَىٰهَا عَن نَّفۡسِهِۦ قَدۡ شَغَفَهَا حُبًّا إِنَّا لَنَرَىٰهَا فِى ضَلَٰلٍ مُّبِينٍ ﴿٣٠﴾ فَلَمَّا سَمِعَتۡ بِمَكۡرِهِنَّ أَرۡسَلَتۡ إِلَيۡهِنَّ وَأَعۡتَدَتۡ لَهُنَّ مُتَّكَـًٔا وَءَاتَتۡ كُلَّ وَٰحِدَةٍ مِّنۡهُنَّ سِكِّينًا وَقَالَتِ ٱخۡرُجۡ عَلَيۡهِنَّ فَلَمَّا رَأَيۡنَهُۥٓ أَكۡبَرۡنَهُۥ

said: "How perfect is Allâh (or Allâh forbid)! No man is this! This is none other than a noble angel!"

32. She said: "This is he (the young man) about whom you did blame me, and I did seek to seduce him, but he refused. And now if he refuses to obey my order, he shall certainly be cast into prison, and will be one of those who are disgraced."

33. He said: "O my Lord! Prison is dearer to me than that to which they invite me. Unless You turn away their plot from me, I will feel inclined towards them and be one (of those who commit sin and deserve blame or those who do deeds) of the ignorant."

34. So his Lord answered his invocation and turned away from him their plot. Verily, He is the All-Hearer, the All-Knower.

35. Then it occurred to them, after they had seen the proofs (of his innocence), to imprison him for a time.

36. And there entered with him two young men in the prison. One of them said: "Verily, I saw myself (in a dream) pressing wine." The other said: "Verily, I saw myself (in a dream) carrying bread on my head and birds were eating thereof." (They said): "Inform us of the interpretation of this. Verily, we think you are one of the *Muhsinûn* (doers of good)."

37. He said: "No food will come to you (in wakefulness or in dream) as your provision, but I will inform (in wakefulness) its interpretation before it (the food) comes. This is of that which my

Lord has taught me. Verily, I have abandoned the religion of a people that believe not in Allâh and are disbelievers in the Hereafter (i.e. the *Kan'âniûn* of Egypt who were polytheists and used to worship sun and other false deities).

38. "And I have followed the religion of my fathers,[1] — Ibrâhîm (Abraham), Ishâq (Isaac) and Ya'qûb (Jacob) [عليهم السلام], and never could we attribute any partners whatsoever to Allâh. This is from the Grace of Allâh to us and to mankind, but most men thank not (i.e. they neither believe in Allâh, nor worship Him).

39. "O two companions of the prison! Are many different lords (gods) better or Allâh, the One, the Irresistible?

40. "You do not worship besides Him but only names which you have named (forged) — you and your fathers — for which Allâh has sent down no authority. The command (or the judgement) is for none but Allâh. He has commanded that you worship none but Him (i.e. His Monotheism); that is the (true) straight religion, but most men know not.

41. "O two companions of the prison! As for one of you, he (as a servant) will pour out wine for his lord (king or master) to drink; and as for the other, he will be crucified and birds will eat from his head. Thus is the case judged concerning which you both did inquire."

---

[1] (V.12:38) See the footnote of (V.2:135).

42. And he said to the one whom he knew to be saved: "Mention me to your lord (i.e. your king, so as to get me out of the prison)." But *Shaitân* (Satan) made him forget to mention it to his lord [or Satan made {Yûsuf (Joseph)} to forget the remembrance of his Lord (Allâh) as to ask for His Help, instead of others]. So [Yûsuf (Joseph)] stayed in prison a few (more) years.

43. And the king (of Egypt) said: "Verily, I saw (in a dream) seven fat cows, whom seven lean ones were devouring, and seven green ears of corn, and (seven) others dry. O notables! Explain to me my dream, if it be that you can interpret dreams."

44. They said: "Mixed up false dreams and we are not skilled in the interpretation of dreams."

45. Then the man who was released (one of the two who were in prison), now at length remembered and said: "I will tell you its interpretation, so send me forth."

46. (He said): "O Yûsuf (Joseph), the man of truth! Explain to us (the dream) of seven fat cows whom seven lean ones were devouring, and of seven green ears of corn, and (seven) others dry, that I may return to the people, and that they may know."

47. [(Yûsuf (Joseph)] said: "For seven consecutive years, you shall sow as usual and that (the harvest) which you reap you shall leave it in the ears, (all) except a little of it which you may eat.

48. "Then will come after that, seven hard (years), which will devour what you have laid by in advance for them, (all) except a little of that which you have guarded (stored).

ثُمَّ يَأْتِى مِنۢ بَعْدِ ذَٰلِكَ سَبْعٌ شِدَادٌ يَأْكُلْنَ مَا قَدَّمْتُمْ لَهُنَّ إِلَّا قَلِيلًا مِّمَّا تُحْصِنُونَ ۝

49. "Then thereafter will come a year in which people will have abundant rain and in which they will press (wine and oil)."

ثُمَّ يَأْتِى مِنۢ بَعْدِ ذَٰلِكَ عَامٌ فِيهِ يُغَاثُ ٱلنَّاسُ وَفِيهِ يَعْصِرُونَ ۝

50. And the king said: "Bring him to me." But when the messenger came to him, [Yûsuf (Joseph)] said: "Return to your lord and ask him, 'What happened to the women who cut their hands? Surely, my Lord (Allâh) is Well-Aware of their plot.'"

وَقَالَ ٱلْمَلِكُ ٱئْتُونِى بِهِۦ فَلَمَّا جَآءَهُ ٱلرَّسُولُ قَالَ ٱرْجِعْ إِلَىٰ رَبِّكَ فَسْـَٔلْهُ مَا بَالُ ٱلنِّسْوَةِ ٱلَّـٰتِى قَطَّعْنَ أَيْدِيَهُنَّ إِنَّ رَبِّى بِكَيْدِهِنَّ عَلِيمٌ ۝

51. (The King) said (to the women): "What was your affair when you did seek to seduce Yûsuf (Joseph)?" The women said: "Allâh forbid! No evil know we against him." The wife of Al-'Azîz said: "Now the truth is manifest (to all); it was I who sought to seduce him, and he is surely, of the truthful."

قَالَ مَا خَطْبُكُنَّ إِذْ رَٰوَدتُّنَّ يُوسُفَ عَن نَّفْسِهِۦ قُلْنَ حَٰشَ لِلَّهِ مَا عَلِمْنَا عَلَيْهِ مِن سُوٓءٍ قَالَتِ ٱمْرَأَتُ ٱلْعَزِيزِ ٱلْـَٰٔنَ حَصْحَصَ ٱلْحَقُّ أَنَا۠ رَٰوَدتُّهُۥ عَن نَّفْسِهِۦ وَإِنَّهُۥ لَمِنَ ٱلصَّٰدِقِينَ ۝

52. [Then Yûsuf (Joseph) said: "I asked for this enquiry] in order that he (Al-'Azîz) may know that I betrayed him not in (his) absence." And, verily, Allâh guides not the plot of the betrayers.[1]

ذَٰلِكَ لِيَعْلَمَ أَنِّى لَمْ أَخُنْهُ بِٱلْغَيْبِ وَأَنَّ ٱللَّهَ لَا يَهْدِى كَيْدَ ٱلْخَآئِنِينَ ۝

---

[1] (V.12:52)

a) Narrated Ibn 'Umar رضى الله عنهما The Prophet صلى الله عليه وسلم said, "For every betrayer (perfidious person), a flag will be raised on the Day of Resurrection, and it will be announced (publicly): 'This is the betrayal (perfidy) of so-and-so, the son of so-and-so.'" (*Sahih Al-Bukhari*, Vol. 8, *Hadith* No. 196)

b) See the footnote of (V.4:145).

53. "And I free not myself (from the blame). Verily, the (human) self is inclined to evil, except when my Lord bestows His Mercy (upon whom He wills). Verily, my Lord is Oft-Forgiving, Most Merciful."

٥٣ وَمَا أُبَرِّئُ نَفْسِيٓ إِنَّ النَّفْسَ لَأَمَّارَةٌ بِالسُّوٓءِ إِلَّا مَا رَحِمَ رَبِّيٓ إِنَّ رَبِّي غَفُورٌ رَّحِيمٌ ٥٣

54. And the king said: "Bring him to me that I may attach him to my person." Then, when he spoke to him, he said: "Verily, this day, you are with us high in rank and fully trusted."

٥٤ وَقَالَ الْمَلِكُ ٱئْتُونِي بِهِۦٓ أَسْتَخْلِصْهُ لِنَفْسِي فَلَمَّا كَلَّمَهُۥ قَالَ إِنَّكَ الْيَوْمَ لَدَيْنَا مَكِينٌ أَمِينٌ ٥٤

55. [Yûsuf (Joseph)] said: "Set me over the store-houses of the land; I will indeed guard them with full knowledge" (as a minister of finance in Egypt).

٥٥ قَالَ اجْعَلْنِي عَلَىٰ خَزَآئِنِ الْأَرْضِ إِنِّي حَفِيظٌ عَلِيمٌ ٥٥

56. Thus did We give full authority to Yûsuf (Joseph) in the land, to take possession therein, when or where he likes. We bestow of Our Mercy on whom We will, and We make not to be lost the reward of Al-Muhsinûn (the good doers — See V.2:112).

٥٦ وَكَذَٰلِكَ مَكَّنَّا لِيُوسُفَ فِي الْأَرْضِ يَتَبَوَّأُ مِنْهَا حَيْثُ يَشَآءُ نُصِيبُ بِرَحْمَتِنَا مَن نَّشَآءُ وَلَا نُضِيعُ أَجْرَ الْمُحْسِنِينَ ٥٦

57. And verily, the reward of the Hereafter is better for those who believe and used to fear Allâh and keep their duty to Him (by abstaining from all kinds of sins and evil deeds and by performing all kinds of righteous good deeds).

٥٧ وَلَأَجْرُ الْآخِرَةِ خَيْرٌ لِّلَّذِينَ ءَامَنُوا۟ وَكَانُوا۟ يَتَّقُونَ ٥٧

58. And Yûsuf's (Joseph) brethren came and they entered unto him, and he recognized them, but they recognized him not.

٥٨ وَجَآءَ إِخْوَةُ يُوسُفَ فَدَخَلُوا۟ عَلَيْهِ فَعَرَفَهُمْ وَهُمْ لَهُۥ مُنكِرُونَ ٥٨

59. And when he had furnished them with their provisions (according to their

٥٩ وَلَمَّا جَهَّزَهُم بِجَهَازِهِمْ قَالَ

need), he said: "Bring me a brother of yours from your father (he meant Benjamin). See you not that I give full measure, and that I am the best of the hosts?

60. "But if you bring him not to me, there shall be no measure (of corn) for you with me, nor shall you come near me."

61. They said: "We shall try to get permission (for him) from his father, and verily, we shall do it."

62. And [Yûsuf (Joseph)] told his servants to put their money (with which they had bought the corn) into their bags, so that they might know it when they go back to their people; in order they might come again.

63. So, when they returned to their father, they said: "O our father! No more measure of grain shall we get (unless we take our brother). So send our brother with us, and we shall get our measure and truly, we will guard him."

64. He said: "Can I entrust him to you except as I entrusted his brother [Yûsuf (Joseph)] to you aforetime? But Allâh is the Best to guard, and He is the Most Merciful of those who show mercy."

65. And when they opened their bags, they found their money had been returned to them. They said: "O our father! What (more) can we desire?

This, our money has been returned to us; so we shall get (more) food for our family, and we shall guard our brother and add one more measure of a camel's load. This quantity is easy (for the king to give)."

66. He [Ya'qûb (Jacob)] said: "I will not send him with you until you swear a solemn oath to me in Allâh's Name, that you will bring him back to me unless you are yourselves surrounded (by enemies)," And when they had sworn their solemn oath, he said: "Allâh is the Witness to what we have said."

67. And he said: "O my sons! Do not enter by one gate, but enter by different gates, and I cannot avail you against Allâh at all. Verily, the decision rests only with Allâh. In Him, I put my trust and let all those that trust, put their trust in Him."[1]

---

[1] (V.12:67).

a) Narrated Ibn 'Abbâs رضي الله عنهما: Allâh's Messenger صلى الله عليه وسلم said, "Seventy thousand people of my followers will enter Paradise without account, and they are those who do not practise Ar-Ruqyyâ* and do not see an evil omen in things, and put their trust in their Lord." (Sahih Al-Bukhari, Vol. 8, Hadith No. 479)

* Ar-Ruqyyâ: See the glossary.

b) Narrated Abu Hurairah رضي الله عنه: The Prophet صلى الله عليه وسلم said, "An Israeli man asked another Israeli to lend him one thousand dinars. The second man required witnesses. The former replied, 'Allâh is Sufficient as a Witness.' The second said, 'I want a surety.' The former replied, 'Allâh is Sufficient as a Surety.' The second said, 'You are right' and lent him the money for a certain period. The debtor went across the sea. When he finished his job, he searched for a conveyance so that he might reach in time for the repayment of the debt, but he could not find any. So, he took a piece

68. And when they entered according to their father's advice, it did not avail them in the least against (the Will of) Allâh; it was but a need of Ya'qûb's (Jacob) inner-self which he discharged. And verily, he was endowed with knowledge because We had taught him, but most men know not.

وَلَمَّا دَخَلُوا مِنْ حَيْثُ أَمَرَهُمْ أَبُوهُم مَّا كَانَ يُغْنِي عَنْهُم مِّنَ اللَّهِ مِن شَيْءٍ إِلَّا حَاجَةً فِي نَفْسِ يَعْقُوبَ قَضَاهَا وَإِنَّهُ لَذُو عِلْمٍ لِّمَا عَلَّمْنَاهُ وَلَٰكِنَّ أَكْثَرَ النَّاسِ لَا يَعْلَمُونَ ٦٨

69. And when they went in before Yûsuf (Joseph), he took his brother (Benjamin) to himself and said: "Verily, I am your brother, so grieve not for what they used to do."

وَلَمَّا دَخَلُوا عَلَىٰ يُوسُفَ ءَاوَىٰ إِلَيْهِ أَخَاهُ قَالَ إِنِّي أَنَا۠

---

of wood and made a hole in it, inserted in it one thousand dinars and a letter to the lender and then closed (i.e. sealed) the hole tightly. He took the piece of wood to the sea and said. 'O Allâh! You know well that I took a loan of one thousand dinars from so-and-so. He demanded a surety from me but I told him that Allâh's Guarantee was sufficient and he accepted Your Guarantee. He then asked for a witness and I told him that Allâh was sufficient as a Witness, and he accepted You as a Witness. No doubt, I have tried hard to find a conveyance so that I could pay his money back but could not find, so I hand over this money to You.' Saying that, he threw the piece of wood into the sea till it went out far into it, and then he went away. Meanwhile he started searching for a conveyance in order to reach the creditor's country. One day the lender came out of his house to see whether a ship had arrived bringing his money, and all of a sudden he saw the piece of wood (in which his money had been deposited). He took it home to use for fire. When he sawed it, he found his money and the letter inside it. Shortly after that, the debtor came bringing one thousand dinars to him and said, 'By Allâh, I had been trying hard to get a boat so that I could bring you your money, but failed to get one before the one I have come by.' The lender asked, 'Have you sent something to me?' The debtor replied, 'I have told you I could not get a boat other than the one I have come by.' The lender said, 'Allâh has delivered on your behalf the money you sent in the piece of wood. So, you may keep your one thousand dinars and depart guided on the Right Path.'" (*Sahih Al-Bukhari*, Vol.3, *Hadith* No.488B).

70. So when he had furnished them forth with their provisions, he put the (golden) bowl in his brother's bag. Then a crier cried: "O you (in) the caravan! Surely, you are thieves!"

71. They, turning towards them, said: "What is it that you have lost?"

72. They said: "We have lost the (golden) bowl of the king and for him who produces it is (the reward of) a camel load; and I will be bound by it."

73. They said: "By Allâh! Indeed you know that we came not to make mischief in the land, and we are no thieves!"

74. They [Yûsuf's (Joseph) men] said: "What then shall be the penalty of him, if you are (proved to be) liars."

75. They [Yûsuf's (Joseph) brothers] said: "His penalty should be that he, in whose bag it is found, should be held for the punishment (of the crime). Thus we punish the Zâlimûn (wrongdoers)!"

76. So he [Yûsuf (Joseph)] began (the search) in their bags before the bag of his brother. Then he brought it out of his brother's bag. Thus did We plan for Yûsuf (Joseph). He could not take his brother by the law of the king (as a slave), except that Allâh willed it. (So Allâh made the brothers to bind themselves with their way of "punishment, i.e. enslaving of a thief.") We raise to degrees whom We will, but over all those endowed with knowledge is the All-Knowing (Allâh).

77. They [(Yûsuf's (Joseph) brothers'] said: "If he steals, there was a brother of his [Yûsuf (Joseph)] who did steal before (him)." But these things did Yûsuf (Joseph) keep in himself, revealing not the secrets to them. He said (within himself): "You are in worst case, and Allâh is the Best Knower of that which you describe!"

78. They said: "O ruler of the land! Verily, he has an old father (who will grieve for him); so take one of us in his place. Indeed we think that you are one of the *Muhsinûn* (good-doers — see the footnote of V.9:120)."

79. He said: "Allâh forbid, that we should take anyone but him with whom we found our property. Indeed (if we did so), we should be *Zâlimûn* (wrongdoers)."

80. So, when they despaired of him, they held a conference in private. The eldest among them said: "Know you not that your father took an oath from you in Allâh's Name, and before this you did fail in your duty with Yûsuf (Joseph)? Therefore I will not leave this land until my father permits me, or Allâh decides my case (by releasing Benjamin) and He is the Best of the judges.

81. "Return to your father and say, 'O our father! Verily, your son (Benjamin) has stolen, and we testify not except according to what we know, and we could not know the Unseen!

82. "And ask (the people of) the town where we have been, and the caravan in which we returned; and indeed we are telling the truth."

83. He [Ya'qûb (Jacob)] said: "Nay, but your ownselves have beguiled you into something. So patience is most fitting (for me). May be Allâh will bring them (back) all to me. Truly, He! Only He is All-Knowing, All-Wise."

84. And he turned away from them and said: "Alas, my grief for Yûsuf (Joseph)!" And he lost his sight because of the sorrow that he was suppressing.

85. They said: "By Allâh! You will never cease remembering Yûsuf (Joseph) until you become weak with old age, or until you be of the dead."

86. He said: "I only complain of my grief and sorrow to Allâh, and I know from Allâh that which you know not.

87. "O my sons! Go you and enquire about Yûsuf (Joseph) and his brother, and never give up hope of Allâh's Mercy. Certainly no one despairs of Allâh's Mercy, except the people who disbelieve."

88. Then, when they entered unto him [Yûsuf (Joseph)], they said: "O ruler of the land! A hard time has hit us and our family, and we have brought but poor capital, so pay us full measure and be charitable to us. Truly, Allâh does reward the charitable."

89. He said: "Do you know what you did with Yûsuf (Joseph) and his brother, when you were ignorant?"

أَقْلَفْنَا فِيهَا وَإِنَّا لَصَدِقُونَ ۞

قَالَ بَلْ سَوَّلَتْ لَكُمْ أَنفُسُكُمْ أَمْرًا فَصَبْرٌ جَمِيلٌ عَسَى اللَّهُ أَن يَأْتِيَنِي بِهِمْ جَمِيعًا إِنَّهُ هُوَ الْعَلِيمُ الْحَكِيمُ ۞

وَتَوَلَّىٰ عَنْهُمْ وَقَالَ يَٰأَسَفَىٰ عَلَىٰ يُوسُفَ وَابْيَضَّتْ عَيْنَاهُ مِنَ الْحُزْنِ فَهُوَ كَظِيمٌ ۞

قَالُواْ تَاللَّهِ تَفْتَؤُاْ تَذْكُرُ يُوسُفَ حَتَّىٰ تَكُونَ حَرَضًا أَوْ تَكُونَ مِنَ الْهَٰلِكِينَ ۞

قَالَ إِنَّمَآ أَشْكُواْ بَثِّي وَحُزْنِيٓ إِلَى اللَّهِ وَأَعْلَمُ مِنَ اللَّهِ مَا لَا تَعْلَمُونَ ۞

يَٰبَنِيَّ اذْهَبُواْ فَتَحَسَّسُواْ مِن يُوسُفَ وَأَخِيهِ وَلَا تَا۟يْـَٔسُواْ مِن رَّوْحِ اللَّهِ إِنَّهُۥ لَا يَا۟يْـَٔسُ مِن رَّوْحِ اللَّهِ إِلَّا الْقَوْمُ الْكَٰفِرُونَ ۞

فَلَمَّا دَخَلُواْ عَلَيْهِ قَالُواْ يَٰٓأَيُّهَا الْعَزِيزُ مَسَّنَا وَأَهْلَنَا الضُّرُّ وَجِئْنَا بِبِضَٰعَةٍ مُّزْجَىٰةٍ فَأَوْفِ لَنَا الْكَيْلَ وَتَصَدَّقْ عَلَيْنَآ إِنَّ اللَّهَ يَجْزِي الْمُتَصَدِّقِينَ ۞

قَالَ هَلْ عَلِمْتُم مَّا فَعَلْتُم بِيُوسُفَ وَأَخِيهِ إِذْ أَنتُمْ جَٰهِلُونَ ۞

90. They said: "Are you indeed Yûsuf (Joseph)?" He said: "I am Yûsuf (Joseph), and this is ˙my brother (Benjamin)ˌ. Allâh has indeed been gracious to us. Verily, he who fears Allâh with obedience to Him (by abstaining from sins and evil deeds, and by performing righteous good deeds), and is patient, then surely, Allâh makes not the reward of the *Muhsinûn* (good-doers — see V.2:112) to be lost."

قَالُوٓاْ أَءِنَّكَ لَأَنتَ يُوسُفُ قَالَ أَنَا۠ يُوسُفُ وَهَٰذَآ أَخِى قَدْ مَنَّ ٱللَّهُ عَلَيْنَآ إِنَّهُۥ مَن يَتَّقِ وَيَصْبِرْ فَإِنَّ ٱللَّهَ لَا يُضِيعُ أَجْرَ ٱلْمُحْسِنِينَ ٩٠

91. They said: "By Allâh! Indeed Allâh has preferred you above us, and we certainly have been sinners."

قَالُواْ تَٱللَّهِ لَقَدْ ءَاثَرَكَ ٱللَّهُ عَلَيْنَا وَإِن كُنَّا لَخَٰطِـِٔينَ ٩١

92. He said: "No reproach on you this day; may Allâh forgive you, and He is the Most Merciful of those who show mercy![1]

قَالَ لَا تَثْرِيبَ عَلَيْكُمُ ٱلْيَوْمَ يَغْفِرُ ٱللَّهُ لَكُمْ وَهُوَ أَرْحَمُ ٱلرَّٰحِمِينَ ٩٢

93. "Go with this shirt of mine, and cast it over the face of my father, he will become clear-sighted, and bring to me all your family."

ٱذْهَبُواْ بِقَمِيصِى هَٰذَا فَأَلْقُوهُ عَلَىٰ وَجْهِ أَبِى يَأْتِ بَصِيرًا وَأْتُونِى بِأَهْلِكُمْ أَجْمَعِينَ ٩٣

94. And when the caravan departed, their father said: "I do indeed feel the smell of Yûsuf (Joseph), if only you think me not a dotard (a person who has weakness of mind because of old age)."

وَلَمَّا فَصَلَتِ ٱلْعِيرُ قَالَ أَبُوهُمْ إِنِّى لَأَجِدُ رِيحَ يُوسُفَ لَوْلَآ أَن تُفَنِّدُونِ ٩٤

---

[1] (V.12:92) Narrated Abu Hurairah رضى الله عنه I heard Allâh's Messenger صلى الله عليه وسلم saying, "Verily, Allâh created mercy. The day He created it, He made it into one hundred parts. He withheld with Him ninety-nine parts, and sent its one part to all His creatures. Had a disbeliever known of all the mercy which is in the Hands of Allâh, he would not have lost hope of entering Paradise, and had a believer known of all the punishment which is present with Allâh, he would not have considered himself safe from the Hell-fire." (*Sahih Al-Bukhari*, Vol.8, Hadith No.476).

95. They said: "By Allâh! Certainly, you are in your old error."

قَالُوا تَاللَّهِ إِنَّكَ لَفِى ضَلَـٰلِكَ الْقَدِيمِ ﴿٩٥﴾

96. Then, when the bearer of the glad tidings arrived, he cast it (the shirt) over his face, and he became clear-sighted. He said: "Did I not say to you, 'I know from Allâh that which you know not.'"

فَلَمَّا أَن جَآءَ الْبَشِيرُ أَلْقَـٰهُ عَلَىٰ وَجْهِهِۦ فَارْتَدَّ بَصِيرًا قَالَ أَلَمْ أَقُل لَّكُمْ إِنِّىٓ أَعْلَمُ مِنَ اللَّهِ مَا لَا تَعْلَمُونَ ﴿٩٦﴾

97. They said: "O our father! Ask forgiveness (from Allâh) for our sins, indeed we have been sinners."

قَالُوا يَـٰٓأَبَانَا اسْتَغْفِرْ لَنَا ذُنُوبَنَآ إِنَّا كُنَّا خَـٰطِـِٔينَ ﴿٩٧﴾

98. He said: "I will ask my Lord for forgiveness for you, verily, He! Only He is the Oft-Forgiving, the Most Merciful."

قَالَ سَوْفَ أَسْتَغْفِرُ لَكُمْ رَبِّىٓ إِنَّهُۥ هُوَ الْغَفُورُ الرَّحِيمُ ﴿٩٨﴾

99. Then, when they came in before Yûsuf (Joseph), he took his parents to himself and said: "Enter Egypt, if Allâh wills, in security."

فَلَمَّا دَخَلُوا عَلَىٰ يُوسُفَ ءَاوَىٰٓ إِلَيْهِ أَبَوَيْهِ وَقَالَ ادْخُلُوا مِصْرَ إِن شَآءَ اللَّهُ ءَامِنِينَ ﴿٩٩﴾

100. And he raised his parents to the throne and they fell down before him prostrate. And he said: "O my father! This is the interpretation of my dream aforetime! My Lord has made it come true! He was indeed good to me, when He took me out of the prison, and brought you (all here) out of the bedouin-life, after *Shaitân* (Satan) had sown enmity between me and my brothers. Certainly, my Lord is the Most Courteous and Kind unto whom He wills. Truly, He! Only He is the All-Knowing, the All-Wise."

وَرَفَعَ أَبَوَيْهِ عَلَى الْعَرْشِ وَخَرُّوا لَهُۥ سُجَّدًا وَقَالَ يَـٰٓأَبَتِ هَـٰذَا تَأْوِيلُ رُءْيَـٰىَ مِن قَبْلُ قَدْ جَعَلَهَا رَبِّى حَقًّا وَقَدْ أَحْسَنَ بِىٓ إِذْ أَخْرَجَنِى مِنَ السِّجْنِ وَجَآءَ بِكُم مِّنَ الْبَدْوِ مِنۢ بَعْدِ أَن نَّزَغَ الشَّيْطَـٰنُ بَيْنِى وَبَيْنَ إِخْوَتِىٓ إِنَّ رَبِّى لَطِيفٌ لِّمَا يَشَآءُ إِنَّهُۥ هُوَ الْعَلِيمُ الْحَكِيمُ ﴿١٠٠﴾

101. "My Lord! You have indeed bestowed on me of the sovereignty, and taught me something of the

۞ رَبِّ قَدْ ءَاتَيْتَنِى مِنَ الْمُلْكِ

interpretation of dreams — the (Only) Creator of the heavens and the earth! You are my *Walî* (Protector, Helper, Supporter, Guardian, God, Lord) in this world and in the Hereafter. Cause me to die as a Muslim (the one submitting to Your Will), and join me with the righteous."

102. That is of the news of the *Ghaib* (Unseen) which We reveal to you (O Muhammad صلى الله عليه وسلم). You were not (present) with them when they arranged their plan together, and (while) they were plotting.

103. And most of mankind will not believe even if you desire it eagerly.

104. And no reward you (O Muhammad صلى الله عليه وسلم) ask of them (those who deny your Prophethood) for it; it (the Qur'ân) is no less than a Reminder and an advice unto the *'Âlamîn* (men and jinn).

105. And how many a sign in the heavens and the earth they pass by, while they are averse therefrom.

106. And most of them believe not in Allâh except that they attribute partners unto Him [i.e. they are *Mushrikûn* i.e. polytheists. See verse 6:121].

107. Do they then feel secure from the coming against them of the covering veil of the Torment of Allâh, or of the coming against them of the (Final) Hour, all of a sudden while they perceive not?

108. Say (O Muhammad ﷺ): "This is my way; I invite unto Allâh (i.e. to the Oneness of Allâh — Islâmic Monotheism) with sure knowledge, I and whosoever follows me (also must invite others to Allâh i.e. to the Oneness of Allâh — Islâmic Monotheism with sure knowledge). And Glorified and Exalted is Allâh (above all that they associate as partners with Him). And I am not of the *Mushrikûn* (polytheists, pagans, idolaters and disbelievers in the Oneness of Allâh; those who worship others along with Allâh or set up rivals or partners to Allâh)."

قُلْ هَٰذِهِۦ سَبِيلِىٓ أَدْعُوٓاْ إِلَى ٱللَّهِ عَلَىٰ بَصِيرَةٍ أَنَا۠ وَمَنِ ٱتَّبَعَنِى وَسُبْحَٰنَ ٱللَّهِ وَمَآ أَنَا۠ مِنَ ٱلْمُشْرِكِينَ ۝

109. And We sent not before you (as Messengers) any but men unto whom We revealed, from among the people of townships. Have they not travelled in the land and seen what was the end of those who were before them? And verily, the home of the Hereafter is best for those who fear Allâh and obey Him (by abstaining from sins and evil deeds, and by performing righteous good deeds). Do you not then understand?

وَمَآ أَرْسَلْنَا مِن قَبْلِكَ إِلَّا رِجَالًا نُّوحِىٓ إِلَيْهِم مِّنْ أَهْلِ ٱلْقُرَىٰٓ أَفَلَمْ يَسِيرُواْ فِى ٱلْأَرْضِ فَيَنظُرُواْ كَيْفَ كَانَ عَٰقِبَةُ ٱلَّذِينَ مِن قَبْلِهِمْ وَلَدَارُ ٱلْأَخِرَةِ خَيْرٌ لِّلَّذِينَ ٱتَّقَوْاْ أَفَلَا تَعْقِلُونَ ۝

110. (They were reprieved) until, when the Messengers gave up hope and thought that they were denied (by their people), then came to them Our Help, and who:nsoever We willed were rescued. And Our punishment cannot be warded off from the people who are *Mujrimûn* (criminals, sinners, disbelievers, polytheists).

حَتَّىٰٓ إِذَا ٱسْتَيْـَٔسَ ٱلرُّسُلُ وَظَنُّوٓاْ أَنَّهُمْ قَدْ كُذِبُواْ جَآءَهُمْ نَصْرُنَا فَنُجِّىَ مَن نَّشَآءُ وَلَا يُرَدُّ بَأْسُنَا عَنِ ٱلْقَوْمِ ٱلْمُجْرِمِينَ ۝

111. Indeed in their stories, there is a lesson for men of understanding. It (the Qur'ân) is not a forged statement but a confirmation of (Allâh's existing Books) which were before it [i.e. the Taurât (Torah), the Injeel (Gospel) and other Scriptures of Allâh] and a detailed explanation of everything and a guide and a Mercy for the people who believe.[1]

Sûrat Ar-Ra'd (The Thunder) XIII

*In the Name of Allâh
the Most Gracious, the Most Merciful*

1. *Alif-Lâm-Mîm-Râ.*

[These letters are one of the miracles of the Qur'ân; and none but Allâh (Alone) knows their meanings].

These are the Verses of the Book (the Qur'ân), and that which has been revealed unto you (Muhammad صلى الله عليه وسلم) from your Lord is the truth, but most men believe not.

2. Allâh is He Who raised the heavens without any pillars that you can see. Then, He rose above (*Istawâ*) the Throne (really in a manner that suits His Majesty). He has subjected the sun and the moon (to continue going round), each running (its course) for a term appointed. He manages and regulates all affairs; He explains the *Ayât* (proofs, evidences, verses, lessons, signs, revelations, etc.) in detail, that you may believe with certainty in the Meeting with your Lord.

---

[1] (V.12:111) See the footnote of V.6:125.

3. And it is He Who spread out the earth, and placed therein firm mountains and rivers and of every kind of fruits He made *Zawjain Ithnaîn* (two in pairs — may mean two kinds or it may mean: of two varieties, e.g. black and white, sweet and sour, small and big) He brings the night as a cover over the day. Verily, in these things, there are *Ayât* (proofs, evidences, lessons, signs, etc.) for people who reflect.

وَهُوَ ٱلَّذِى مَدَّ ٱلْأَرْضَ وَجَعَلَ فِيهَا رَوَٰسِىَ وَأَنْهَٰرًا وَمِن كُلِّ ٱلثَّمَرَٰتِ جَعَلَ فِيهَا زَوْجَيْنِ ٱثْنَيْنِ يُغْشِى ٱلَّيْلَ ٱلنَّهَارَ إِنَّ فِى ذَٰلِكَ لَءَايَٰتٍ لِّقَوْمٍ يَتَفَكَّرُونَ ٣

4. And in the earth are neighbouring tracts, and gardens of vines, and green crops (fields), and date-palms, growing into two or three from a single stem root, or otherwise (one stem root for every palm), watered with the same water; yet some of them We make more excellent than others to eat. Verily, in these things there are *Ayât* (proofs, evidences, lessons, signs) for the people who understand.

وَفِى ٱلْأَرْضِ قِطَعٌ مُّتَجَٰوِرَٰتٌ وَجَنَّٰتٌ مِّنْ أَعْنَٰبٍ وَزَرْعٌ وَنَخِيلٌ صِنْوَانٌ وَغَيْرُ صِنْوَانٍ يُسْقَىٰ بِمَآءٍ وَٰحِدٍ وَنُفَضِّلُ بَعْضَهَا عَلَىٰ بَعْضٍ فِى ٱلْأُكُلِ إِنَّ فِى ذَٰلِكَ لَءَايَٰتٍ لِّقَوْمٍ يَعْقِلُونَ ٤

5. And if you (O Muhammad صلى الله عليه وسلم) wonder (at these polytheists who deny your message of Islâmic Monotheism and have taken besides Allâh others for worship who can neither harm nor benefit), then wondrous is their saying: "When we are dust, shall we indeed then be (raised) in a new creation?" They are those who disbelieved in their Lord! They are those who will have iron chains tying their hands to their necks. They will be dwellers of the Fire to abide therein.

وَإِن تَعْجَبْ فَعَجَبٌ قَوْلُهُمْ أَءِذَا كُنَّا تُرَٰبًا أَءِنَّا لَفِى خَلْقٍ جَدِيدٍ أُوْلَٰٓئِكَ ٱلَّذِينَ كَفَرُواْ بِرَبِّهِمْ وَأُوْلَٰٓئِكَ ٱلْأَغْلَٰلُ فِىٓ أَعْنَاقِهِمْ وَأُوْلَٰٓئِكَ أَصْحَٰبُ ٱلنَّارِ هُمْ فِيهَا خَٰلِدُونَ ٥

6. They ask you to hasten the evil before the good, while (many)

وَيَسْتَعْجِلُونَكَ بِٱلسَّيِّئَةِ قَبْلَ

exemplary punishments have indeed occurred before them. But verily, your Lord is full of forgiveness for mankind inspite of their wrong-doing. And verily, your Lord is (also) Severe in punishment.

7. And the disbelievers say: "Why is not a sign sent down to him from his Lord?" You are only a warner, and to every people there is a guide.

8. Allâh knows what every female bears, and by how much the wombs fall short (of their time or number) or exceed. Everything with Him is in (due) proportion.

9. All-Knower of the Unseen and the seen, the Most Great, the Most High.

10. It is the same (to Him) whether any of you conceals his speech or declares it openly, whether he be hid by night or goes forth freely by day.

11. For him (each person), there are angels in succession, before and behind him.[1] They guard him by the Command of Allâh. Verily, Allâh will not change the (good) condition of a people as long as they do not change their state (of goodness) themselves (by committing sins and by being ungrateful and disobedient to Allâh). But when Allâh wills a people's punishment, there can be no turning back of it, and they will find besides Him no protector.

---

[1] (V.13:11) See the footnote (B) of (V.6:61).

12. It is He Who shows you the lightning, as a fear (for travellers) and as a hope (for those who wait for rain). And it is He Who brings up (or originates) the clouds, heavy (with water).

هُوَ ٱلَّذِى يُرِيكُمُ ٱلْبَرْقَ خَوْفًا وَطَمَعًا وَيُنشِئُ ٱلسَّحَابَ ٱلثِّقَالَ ﴿١٢﴾

13. And Ar-Ra'd[1] (thunder) glorifies and praises Him, and so do the angels because of His Awe. He sends the thunderbolts, and therewith He strikes whom He wills, yet they (disbelievers) dispute about Allâh. And He is Mighty in strength and Severe in punishment.

وَيُسَبِّحُ ٱلرَّعْدُ بِحَمْدِهِۦ وَٱلْمَلَـٰٓئِكَةُ مِنْ خِيفَتِهِۦ وَيُرْسِلُ ٱلصَّوَٰعِقَ فَيُصِيبُ بِهَا مَن يَشَآءُ وَهُمْ يُجَـٰدِلُونَ فِى ٱللَّهِ وَهُوَ شَدِيدُ ٱلْمِحَالِ ﴿١٣﴾

14. For Him (Allâh, Alone) is the Word of Truth (i.e. none has the right to be worshipped but Allâh). And those whom they (polytheists and disbelievers) invoke, answer them no more than one who stretches forth his hand (at the edge of a deep well) for water to reach his mouth, but it reaches him not; and the invocation of the disbelievers is nothing but an error (i.e. of no use).

لَهُۥ دَعْوَةُ ٱلْحَقِّ وَٱلَّذِينَ يَدْعُونَ مِن دُونِهِۦ لَا يَسْتَجِيبُونَ لَهُم بِشَىْءٍ إِلَّا كَبَـٰسِطِ كَفَّيْهِ إِلَى ٱلْمَآءِ لِيَبْلُغَ فَاهُ وَمَا هُوَ بِبَـٰلِغِهِۦ وَمَا دُعَآءُ ٱلْكَـٰفِرِينَ إِلَّا فِى ضَلَـٰلٍ ﴿١٤﴾

15. And unto Allâh (Alone) falls in prostration whoever is in the heavens and the earth, willingly or unwillingly, and so do their shadows in the mornings and in the afternoons.

وَلِلَّهِ يَسْجُدُ مَن فِى ٱلسَّمَـٰوَٰتِ وَٱلْأَرْضِ طَوْعًا وَكَرْهًا وَظِلَـٰلُهُم بِٱلْغُدُوِّ وَٱلْءَاصَالِ ۩ ﴿١٥﴾

16. Say (O Muhammad صلى الله عليه وسلم): "Who is the Lord of the heavens and the earth?" Say: "(It is) Allâh." Say:

قُل مَّن رَّبُّ ٱلسَّمَـٰوَٰتِ وَٱلْأَرْضِ قُلِ ٱللَّهُ قُلْ أَفَٱتَّخَذْتُم مِّن دُونِهِۦٓ

---

[1] (V.13:13) Ar-Ra'd: It is said that he is the angel in charge of clouds and he drives them as ordered by Allâh, and he glorifies His Praises. (Tafsîr Al-Qurtubî).

"Have you then taken (for worship) *Auliyâ'* (protectors) other than Him, such as have no power either for benefit or for harm to themselves?" Say: "Is the blind equal to the one who sees? Or darkness equal to light? Or do they assign to Allâh partners who created the like of His creation, so that the creation (which they made and His creation) seemed alike to them?" Say: "Allâh is the Creator of all things; and He is the One, the Irresistible."

أَوَلِيَآءَ لَا يَمْلِكُونَ لِأَنفُسِهِمْ نَفْعًا وَلَا ضَرًّا قُلْ هَلْ يَسْتَوِى الْأَعْمَىٰ وَالْبَصِيرُ أَمْ هَلْ تَسْتَوِى الظُّلُمَـٰتُ وَالنُّورُ أَمْ جَعَلُوا لِلَّهِ شُرَكَآءَ خَلَقُوا كَخَلْقِهِ فَتَشَـٰبَهَ الْخَلْقُ عَلَيْهِمْ قُلِ اللَّهُ خَـٰلِقُ كُلِّ شَىْءٍ وَهُوَ الْوَٰحِدُ الْقَهَّـٰرُ ۝

17. He sends down water (rain) from the sky, and the valleys flow according to their measure, but the flood bears away the foam that mounts up to the surface — and (also) from that (ore) which they heat in the fire in order to make ornaments or utensils, rises a foam like unto it, thus does Allâh (by parables) show forth truth and falsehood.[1] Then, as for the foam it passes away as scum upon the banks, while that which is for the good of mankind remains in the earth. Thus Allâh sets forth parables (for the truth and falsehood, i.e. Belief and disbelief).

أَنزَلَ مِنَ السَّمَآءِ مَآءً فَسَالَتْ أَوْدِيَةٌ بِقَدَرِهَا فَاحْتَمَلَ السَّيْلُ زَبَدًا رَّابِيًا وَمِمَّا يُوقِدُونَ عَلَيْهِ فِى النَّارِ ابْتِغَآءَ حِلْيَةٍ أَوْ مَتَـٰعٍ زَبَدٌ مِّثْلُهُ كَذَٰلِكَ يَضْرِبُ اللَّهُ الْحَقَّ وَالْبَـٰطِلَ فَأَمَّا الزَّبَدُ فَيَذْهَبُ جُفَآءً وَأَمَّا مَا يَنفَعُ النَّاسَ فَيَمْكُثُ فِى الْأَرْضِ كَذَٰلِكَ يَضْرِبُ اللَّهُ الْأَمْثَالَ ۝

18. For those who answered their Lord's Call [believed in the Oneness of Allâh and followed His Messenger Muhammad صلى الله عليه وسلم i.e. Islâmic Monotheism] is *Al-Husna* (i.e. Paradise). But those who answered not His Call (disbelieved in the Oneness of

لِلَّذِينَ اسْتَجَابُوا لِرَبِّهِمُ الْحُسْنَىٰ وَالَّذِينَ لَمْ يَسْتَجِيبُوا لَهُ لَوْ أَنَّ لَهُم مَّا فِى الْأَرْضِ جَمِيعًا وَمِثْلَهُ مَعَهُ لَافْتَدَوْا

---

[1] (V.13:17) See the footnote (A) of (V.9:119).

Allâh and followed not His Messenger Muhammad (صلى الله عليه وسلم), if they had all that is in the earth together with its like, they would offer it in order to save themselves (from the torment, it will be in vain). For them there will be the terrible reckoning. Their dwelling-place will be Hell; and worst indeed is that place for rest.[1]

بِهِۦ أُوْلَٰٓئِكَ لَهُمْ سُوٓءُ ٱلْحِسَابِ وَمَأْوَىٰهُمْ جَهَنَّمُ وَبِئْسَ ٱلْمِهَادُ ١٨

19. Shall he then who knows that what has been revealed unto you (O Muhammad صلى الله عليه وسلم) from your Lord is the truth like him who is blind? But it is only the men of understanding that pay heed.

۞ أَفَمَن يَعْلَمُ أَنَّمَآ أُنزِلَ إِلَيْكَ مِن رَّبِّكَ ٱلْحَقُّ كَمَنْ هُوَ أَعْمَىٰٓ إِنَّمَا يَتَذَكَّرُ أُوْلُوا۟ ٱلْأَلْبَٰبِ

20. Those who fulfil the Covenant of Allâh and break not the *Mîthâq* (bond, treaty, covenant).

ٱلَّذِينَ يُوفُونَ بِعَهْدِ ٱللَّهِ وَلَا يَنقُضُونَ ٱلْمِيثَٰقَ

21. And those who join that which Allâh has commanded to be joined (i.e. they are good to their relatives and do not sever the bond of kinship), and fear their Lord, and dread the terrible reckoning (i.e. abstain from all kinds of sins and evil deeds which Allâh has forbidden and perform all kinds of good deeds which Allâh has ordained).

وَٱلَّذِينَ يَصِلُونَ مَآ أَمَرَ ٱللَّهُ بِهِۦٓ أَن يُوصَلَ وَيَخْشَوْنَ رَبَّهُمْ وَيَخَافُونَ سُوٓءَ ٱلْحِسَابِ

22. And those who remain patient, seeking their Lord's Countenance, perform *As-Salât* (Iqâmat-as-Salât), and spend out of that which We have bestowed on them, secretly and openly, and defend evil with good, for such there is a good end.

وَٱلَّذِينَ صَبَرُوا۟ ٱبْتِغَآءَ وَجْهِ رَبِّهِمْ وَأَقَامُوا۟ ٱلصَّلَوٰةَ وَأَنفَقُوا۟ مِمَّا رَزَقْنَٰهُمْ سِرًّا وَعَلَانِيَةً وَيَدْرَءُونَ بِٱلْحَسَنَةِ ٱلسَّيِّئَةَ أُوْلَٰٓئِكَ لَهُمْ عُقْبَى ٱلدَّارِ

---

[1] (V.13:18) See the footnotes of (V.3:164), (V.3:85) and (V.3:91).

23. 'Adn (Eden) Paradise (everlasting Gardens), which they shall enter and (also) those who acted righteously from among their fathers, and their wives, and their offspring. And angels shall enter unto them from every gate (saying):

24. "Salâmun 'Alaikum (peace be upon you) for that you persevered in patience! Excellent indeed is the final home!"

25. And those who break the Covenant of Allâh, after its ratification, and sever that which Allâh has commanded to be joined (i.e. they sever the bond of kinship and are not good to their relatives), and work mischief in the land, on them is the curse (i.e. they will be far away from Allâh's Mercy), and for them is the unhappy (evil) home (i.e. Hell).[1]

26. Allâh increases the provision for whom He wills, and straitens (it for whom He wills), and they rejoice in the life of the world, whereas the life of this world as compared with the Hereafter is but a brief passing enjoyment.

27. And those who disbelieved say: "Why is not a sign sent down to him (Muhammad صلى الله عليه وسلم) from his Lord?" Say: "Verily, Allâh sends astray whom He wills and guides unto Himself those who turn to Him in repentance."

28. Those who believed (in the Oneness of Allâh — Islâmic

---

[1] (V.13:25) See the footnote of (V.2:27).

Monotheism), and whose hearts find rest in the remembrance of Allâh: verily, in the remembrance of Allâh do hearts find rest.[1]

أَلَا بِذِكْرِ ٱللَّهِ تَطْمَئِنُّ ٱلْقُلُوبُ ۝

29. Those who believed (in the Oneness of Allâh — Islâmic Monotheism), and work righteousness, *Tûbâ* (it means all kinds of happiness or name of a tree in Paradise) is for them and a beautiful place of (final) return.

ٱلَّذِينَ ءَامَنُوا وَعَمِلُوا ٱلصَّٰلِحَٰتِ طُوبَىٰ لَهُمْ وَحُسْنُ مَـَٔابٍ ۝

30. Thus have We sent you (O Muhammad صلى الله عليه وسلم) to a community before whom other communities have passed away, in order that you might

كَذَٰلِكَ أَرْسَلْنَٰكَ فِىٓ أُمَّةٍ قَدْ خَلَتْ مِن قَبْلِهَآ أُمَمٌ لِّتَتْلُوَا۟

---

[1] (V.13:28) The superiority of *Dhikr Allâh* ذكر الله [remembering Allâh (i.e. glorifying and praising Him)]

a) Narrated Abu Mûsâ رضى الله عنه: The Prophet صلى الله عليه وسلم said, "The example of the one who remembers (glorifies the Praises of) his Lord, (Allâh) in comparison to the one who does not remember (glorify the Praises) of his Lord, is that of a living creature compared to a dead one." (*Sahih Al-Bukhari*, Vol.8, *Hadith* No.416).

b) Narrated Abu Hurairah رضى الله عنه: Allâh's Messenger صلى الله عليه وسلم said, "Whoever says, *Subhân Allâhi wa bihamdihi*, one hundred times a day, will be forgiven all his sins even if they were as much as the foam of the sea." (*Sahih Al-Bukhari*, Vol.8, *Hadith* No.414).

c) Narrated Abu Hurairah رضى الله عنه: Allâh's Messenger صلى الله عليه وسلم said, "Whoever says: *Lâ ilâha illallâhu wahdahû lâ sharîka lahû, lahul-mulku wa lahul-hamdu wa Huwa 'alâ kulli shai'in Qadîr,** one hundred times will get the same reward as given for manumitting ten slaves; and one hundred good deeds will be written in his accounts, and one hundred sins will be deducted from his accounts, and it (his saying) will be a shield for him from Satan on that day till night, and nobody will be able to do a better deed except the one who does more than he." (*Sahih Al-Bukhari*, Vol.8, *Hadith* No.412).

* None has the right to be worshipped but Allâh (Alone) Who has no partner; to Him belongs the kingdom (of the universe), and for Him are all the praises, and He has the power to do everything.

recite unto them what We have revealed to you, while they disbelieve in the Most Gracious (Allâh) Say: "He is my Lord! *Lâ ilâha illâ Huwa* (none has the right to be worshipped but He)! In Him is my trust, and to Him will be my return with repentance."

31. And if there had been a Qur'ân with which mountains could be moved (from their places), or the earth could be cloven asunder, or the dead could be made to speak (it would not have been other than this Qur'ân). But the decision of all things is certainly with Allâh. Have not then those who believed yet known that had Allâh willed, He could have guided all mankind? And a disaster will not cease to strike those who disbelieved because of their (evil) deeds or it (i.e. the disaster) settles close to their homes, until the Promise of Allâh comes to pass. Certainly, Allâh does not break His Promise.

32. And indeed (many) Messengers were mocked at before you (O Muhammad صلى الله عليه وسلم), but I granted respite to those who disbelieved, and finally I punished them. Then how (terrible) was My punishment!

33. Is then He (Allâh) Who takes charge (guards, maintains, provides) of every person and knows all that he has earned (like any other deities who know nothing)? Yet, they ascribe partners to Allâh. Say: "Name them! Is it that you

will inform Him of something He knows not in the earth or is it (just) a show of false words." Nay! To those who disbelieved, their plotting is made fairseeming, and they have been hindered from the Right Path; and whom Allâh sends astray, for him there is no guide.

34. For them is a torment in the life of this world, and certainly, harder is the torment of the Hereafter. And they have no *Wâq* (defender or protector) against Allâh.

35. The description of the Paradise which the *Muttaqûn* (the pious. See V.2:2) have been promised: Underneath it rivers flow, its provision is eternal and so is its shade; this is the end (final destination) of the *Muttaqûn* (the pious), and the end (final destination) of the disbelievers is Fire. (See Verse 47:15)

36. Those to whom We have given the Book (such as 'Abdullâh bin Salâm and other Jews who embraced Islâm), rejoice at what has been revealed unto you (i.e. the Qur'ân),[1] but there are among the Confederates (from the Jews and pagans) those who reject a part thereof. Say (O Muhammad صلى الله عليه وسلم): "I am commanded only to worship Allâh (Alone) and not to join partners with Him. To Him (Alone) I call and to Him is my return."

---

[1] (V.13:36) See the footnote of (V.5:66).

37. And thus have We sent it (the Qur'ân) down to be a judgement of authority in Arabic. Were you (O Muhammad صلى الله عليه وسلم) to follow their (vain) desires after the knowledge which has come to you, then you will not have any *Walî* (protector) or *Wâq* (defender) against Allâh.

38. And indeed We sent Messengers before you (O Muhammad صلى الله عليه وسلم), and made for them wives and offspring. And it was not for a Messenger to bring a sign except by Allâh's Leave. (For) every matter there is a Decree (from Allâh). [*Tafsir At-Tabari*]

39. Allâh blots out what He wills and confirms (what He wills). And with Him is the Mother of the Book (*Al-Lauh Al-Mahfûz*)

40. Whether We show you (O Muhammad صلى الله عليه وسلم) part of what We have promised them or cause you to die, your duty is only to convey (the Message) and on Us is the reckoning.

41. See they not that We gradually reduce the land (of the disbelievers, by giving it to the believers, in war victories) from its outlying borders. And Allâh judges, there is none to put back His Judgement and He is Swift at reckoning.

42. And verily, those before them did devise plots, but all planning is Allâh's. He knows what every person earns, and

وَكَذَلِكَ أَنزَلْنَهُ حُكْمًا عَرَبِيًّا وَلَئِنِ ٱتَّبَعْتَ أَهْوَآءَهُم بَعْدَمَا جَآءَكَ مِنَ ٱلْعِلْمِ مَالَكَ مِنَ ٱللَّهِ مِن وَلِىٍّ وَلَا وَاقٍ ﴿٣٧﴾

وَلَقَدْ أَرْسَلْنَا رُسُلًا مِّن قَبْلِكَ وَجَعَلْنَا لَهُمْ أَزْوَٰجًا وَذُرِّيَّةً وَمَا كَانَ لِرَسُولٍ أَن يَأْتِىَ بِـَٔايَةٍ إِلَّا بِإِذْنِ ٱللَّهِ لِكُلِّ أَجَلٍ كِتَابٌ ﴿٣٨﴾

يَمْحُوا ٱللَّهُ مَا يَشَآءُ وَيُثْبِتُ وَعِندَهُۥٓ أُمُّ ٱلْكِتَبِ ﴿٣٩﴾

وَإِن مَّا نُرِيَنَّكَ بَعْضَ ٱلَّذِى نَعِدُهُمْ أَوْ نَتَوَفَّيَنَّكَ فَإِنَّمَا عَلَيْكَ ٱلْبَلَٰغُ وَعَلَيْنَا ٱلْحِسَابُ ﴿٤٠﴾

أَوَلَمْ يَرَوْا أَنَّا نَأْتِى ٱلْأَرْضَ نَنقُصُهَا مِنْ أَطْرَافِهَا وَٱللَّهُ يَحْكُمُ لَا مُعَقِّبَ لِحُكْمِهِۦ وَهُوَ سَرِيعُ ٱلْحِسَابِ ﴿٤١﴾

وَقَدْ مَكَرَ ٱلَّذِينَ مِن قَبْلِهِمْ فَلِلَّهِ ٱلْمَكْرُ جَمِيعًا يَعْلَمُ مَا تَكْسِبُ

the disbelievers will know who gets the good end (final destination).

43. And those who disbelieved, say: "You (O Muhammad صلى الله عليه وسلم) are not a Messenger." Say: "Sufficient as a witness between me and you is Allâh and those too who have knowledge of the Scripture (such as 'Abdullâh bin Salâm and other Jews and Christians who embraced Islâm)."

Sûrat Ibrâhîm (Abraham) XIV

In the Name of Allâh
the Most Gracious, the Most Merciful

1. *Alif-Lâm-Râ.*

[These letters are one of the miracles of the Qur'ân, and none but Allâh (Alone) knows their meanings].

(This is) a Book which We have revealed unto you (O Muhammad صلى الله عليه وسلم) in order that you might lead mankind out of darkness (of disbelief and polytheism) into light (of belief in the Oneness of Allâh and Islâmic Monotheism) by their Lord's Leave to the Path of the All-Mighty, the Owner of all Praise.

2. Allâh to Whom belongs all that is in the heavens and all that is in the earth! And woe unto the disbelievers from a severe torment.

3. Those who prefer the life of this world to the Hereafter, and hinder (men) from the Path of Allâh (i.e Islâm) and seek crookedness therein — they are far astray.

4. And We sent not a Messenger except with the language of his people, in order that he might make (the Message) clear for them. Then Allâh misleads whom He wills and guides whom He wills. And He is the All-Mighty, the All-Wise.

5. And indeed We sent Mûsâ (Moses) with Our *Ayât* (signs, proofs, and evidences) (saying): "Bring out your people from darkness into light, and remind them of the Annals of Allâh. Truly, therein are *Ayât* (evidences, proofs and signs) for every patient, thankful (person)."

6. And (remember) when Mûsâ (Moses) said to his people: "Call to mind Allâh's Favour to you, when He delivered you from Fir'aun's (Pharaoh) people who were afflicting you with horrible torment, and were slaughtering your sons and letting your women alive; and in it was a tremendous trial from your Lord."

7. And (remember) when your Lord proclaimed: "If you give thanks (by accepting Faith and worshipping none but Allâh), I will give you more (of My Blessings); but if you are thankless (i.e. disbelievers), verily, My punishment is indeed severe."

8. And Mûsâ (Moses) said: "If you disbelieve, you and all on earth together, then verily, Allâh is Rich

(Free of all needs), Owner of all praise."

9. Has not the news reached you, of those before you, the people of Nûh (Noah), and 'Âd, and Thamûd? And those after them? None knows them but Allâh. To them came their Messengers with clear proofs, but they put their hands in their mouths (biting them from anger) and said: "Verily, we disbelieve in that with which you have been sent, and we are really in grave doubt as to that to which you invite us (i.e. Islâmic Monotheism)."

10. Their Messengers said: "What! Can there be a doubt about Allâh, the Creator of the heavens and the earth? He calls you (to Monotheism and to be obedient to Allâh) that He may forgive you of your sins and give you respite for a term appointed." They said: "You are no more than human beings like us! You wish to turn us away from what our fathers used to worship. Then bring us a clear authority (i.e. a clear proof of what you say)."

11. Their Messengers said to them: "We are no more than human beings like you, but Allâh bestows His Grace to whom He wills of His slaves. It is not ours to bring you an authority (proof) except by the Permission of Allâh. And in Allâh (Alone) let the believers put their trust.

12. "And why should we not put our trust in Allâh while He indeed has guided us our ways? And we shall certainly bear with patience all the hurt you may cause us, and in Allâh (Alone) let those who trust, put their trust."

وَمَا لَنَا أَلَّا نَتَوَكَّلَ عَلَى اللَّهِ وَقَدْ هَدَىٰنَا سُبُلَنَا وَلَنَصْبِرَنَّ عَلَىٰ مَا آذَيْتُمُونَا وَعَلَى اللَّهِ فَلْيَتَوَكَّلِ الْمُتَوَكِّلُونَ ١٢

13. And those who disbelieved, said to their Messengers: "Surely, we shall drive you out of our land, or you shall return to our religion." So their Lord revealed to them: "Truly, we shall destroy the Zâlimûn (polytheists, disbelievers and wrongdoers.).

وَقَالَ الَّذِينَ كَفَرُوا لِرُسُلِهِمْ لَنُخْرِجَنَّكُم مِّنْ أَرْضِنَا أَوْ لَتَعُودُنَّ فِي مِلَّتِنَا فَأَوْحَىٰ إِلَيْهِمْ رَبُّهُمْ لَنُهْلِكَنَّ الظَّالِمِينَ ١٣

14. "And indeed, We shall make you dwell in the land after them. This is for him who fears standing before Me (on the Day of Resurrection or fears My punishment) and also fears My threat."

وَلَنُسْكِنَنَّكُمُ الْأَرْضَ مِنْ بَعْدِهِمْ ذَٰلِكَ لِمَنْ خَافَ مَقَامِي وَخَافَ وَعِيدِ ١٤

15. And they (the Messengers) sought victory and help [from their Lord (Allâh)], and every obstinate, arrogant dictator (who refuses to believe in the Oneness of Allâh) was brought to a complete loss and destruction.

وَاسْتَفْتَحُوا وَخَابَ كُلُّ جَبَّارٍ عَنِيدٍ ١٥

16. In front of him (every obstinate, arrogant dictator) is Hell, and he will be made to drink boiling, festering water.

مِّن وَرَائِهِ جَهَنَّمُ وَيُسْقَىٰ مِن مَّاءٍ صَدِيدٍ ١٦

17. He will sip it unwillingly, and he will find a great difficulty to swallow it down his throat,[1] and death will come

يَتَجَرَّعُهُ وَلَا يَكَادُ يُسِيغُهُ وَيَأْتِيهِ الْمَوْتُ مِن

---

[1] (V.14:17) Narrated Abu Hurairah رضى الله عنه The Prophet صلى الله عليه وسلم said, "The width between the two shoulders of a *Kâfir*

to him from every side, yet he will not die and in front of him, will be a great torment.

18. The parable of those who disbelieved in their Lord is that their works are as ashes, on which the wind blows furiously on a stormy day; they shall not be able to get aught of what they have earned. That is the straying, far away (from the Right Path).

19. Do you not see that Allâh has created the heavens and the earth with truth? If He wills, He can remove you and bring (in your place) a new creation!

20. And for Allâh that is not hard or difficult.

21. And they all shall appear before Allâh (on the Day of Resurrection); then the weak will say to those who were arrogant (chiefs): "Verily, we were following you; can you avail us anything against Allâh's Torment?" They will say: "Had Allâh guided us, we would have guided you. It makes no difference to us (now) whether we rage, or bear (these torments) with patience; there is no place of refuge for us."

22. And *Shaitân* (Satan) will say when the matter has been decided: "Verily, Allâh promised you a promise of truth. And I too promised you, but I

(disbeliever) will be equal to the distance covered by a fast rider in three days." (*Sahih Al-Bukhari*, Vol.8, *Hadith* No.559A).

betrayed you. I had no authority over you except that I called you, and you responded to me. So blame me not, but blame yourselves. I cannot help you, nor can you help me. I deny your former act in associating me (Satan) as a partner with Allâh (by obeying me in the life of the world). Verily, there is a painful torment for the Zâlimûn (polytheists and wrongdoers)."

كَانَ لِىَ عَلَيْكُم مِّن سُلْطَـٰنٍ إِلَّآ أَن دَعَوْتُكُمْ فَٱسْتَجَبْتُمْ لِى فَلَا تَلُومُونِى وَلُومُوٓاْ أَنفُسَكُم مَّآ أَنَا۠ بِمُصْرِخِكُمْ وَمَآ أَنتُم بِمُصْرِخِىَّ إِنِّى كَفَرْتُ بِمَآ أَشْرَكْتُمُونِ مِن قَبْلُ إِنَّ ٱلظَّـٰلِمِينَ لَهُمْ عَذَابٌ أَلِيمٌ ۝

23. And those who believed (in the Oneness of Allâh and His Messengers and whatever they brought) and did righteous deeds, will be made to enter Gardens under which rivers flow, — to dwell therein for ever (i.e. in Paradise), with the Permission of their Lord. Their greeting therein will be: Salâm (peace!).[1]

وَأُدْخِلَ ٱلَّذِينَ ءَامَنُواْ وَعَمِلُواْ ٱلصَّـٰلِحَـٰتِ جَنَّـٰتٍ تَجْرِى مِن تَحْتِهَا ٱلْأَنْهَـٰرُ خَـٰلِدِينَ فِيهَا بِإِذْنِ رَبِّهِمْ تَحِيَّتُهُمْ فِيهَا سَلَـٰمٌ ۝

24. See you not how Allâh sets forth a parable? A goodly word as a goodly tree, whose root is firmly fixed, and its branches (reach) to the sky (i.e. very high).

أَلَمْ تَرَ كَيْفَ ضَرَبَ ٱللَّهُ مَثَلًا كَلِمَةً طَيِّبَةً كَشَجَرَةٍ طَيِّبَةٍ أَصْلُهَا ثَابِتٌ وَفَرْعُهَا فِى ٱلسَّمَآءِ ۝

25. Giving its fruit at all times, by the Leave of its Lord, and Allâh sets forth parables for mankind in order that they may remember.

تُؤْتِىٓ أُكُلَهَا كُلَّ حِينٍ بِإِذْنِ رَبِّهَا وَيَضْرِبُ ٱللَّهُ ٱلْأَمْثَالَ لِلنَّاسِ لَعَلَّهُمْ يَتَذَكَّرُونَ ۝

26. And the parable of an evil word is that of an evil tree uprooted from the surface of earth, having no stability.

وَمَثَلُ كَلِمَةٍ خَبِيثَةٍ كَشَجَرَةٍ خَبِيثَةٍ ٱجْتُثَّتْ مِن فَوْقِ ٱلْأَرْضِ مَا لَهَا مِن قَرَارٍ ۝

---

[1] (V.14:23) See the footnote of (V.4:86).

27. Allâh will keep firm those who believe, with the word that stands firm in this world (i.e. they will keep on worshipping Allâh Alone and none else), and in the Hereafter.[1] And Allâh will cause to go astray those who are Zâlimûn (polytheists and wrongdoers), and Allâh does what He wills.[2]

بُثَبِّتُ اللَّهُ الَّذِينَ ءَامَنُوا بِالْقَوْلِ الثَّابِتِ فِي الْحَيَوٰةِ الدُّنْيَا وَفِي الْآخِرَةِ وَيُضِلُّ اللَّهُ الظَّـٰلِمِينَ وَيَفْعَلُ اللَّهُ مَا يَشَآءُ ۝

28. Have you not seen those who have changed the Blessings of Allâh into disbelief (by denying Prophet Muhammad صلى الله عليه وسلم and his Message of Islâm), and caused their people to dwell in the house of destruction?

۞ أَلَمْ تَرَ إِلَى الَّذِينَ بَدَّلُوا نِعْمَتَ اللَّهِ كُفْرًا وَأَحَلُّوا قَوْمَهُمْ دَارَ الْبَوَارِ ۝

29. Hell, in which they will burn, — and what an evil place to settle in!

جَهَنَّمَ يَصْلَوْنَهَا وَبِئْسَ الْقَرَارُ ۝

30. And they set up rivals to Allâh, to mislead (men) from His Path! Say: "Enjoy (your brief life)! But certainly, your destination is the (Hell) Fire!"

وَجَعَلُوا لِلَّهِ أَندَادًا لِّيُضِلُّوا عَن سَبِيلِهِ قُلْ تَمَتَّعُوا فَإِنَّ مَصِيرَكُمْ إِلَى النَّارِ ۝

31. Say (O Muhammad صلى الله عليه وسلم to 'Ibâdî (My slaves) who have

قُل لِّعِبَادِيَ الَّذِينَ ءَامَنُوا يُقِيمُوا الصَّلَوٰةَ وَيُنفِقُوا مِمَّا رَزَقْنَـٰهُمْ

---

[1] (V.14:27) i.e. immediately after their death (in their graves), when the angels (Munkar and Nakîr) will ask them three questions: As to: (1) Who is your Lord? (2) What is your religion? - and (3) What do you say about this man (Prophet Muhammad صلى الله عليه وسلم who was sent to you? The believers will give the correct answers, i.e. (1) My Lord is Allâh; (2) My religion is Islâm; and (3) This man Muhammad صلى الله عليه وسلم is Allâh's Messenger, and he came to us with clear signs and we believed in him, - while the wrongdoers who believed not in the message of Prophet Muhammad صلى الله عليه وسلم , will not be able to answer these questions. [See Tafsir Ibn Kathir].

[2] (V.14:27) See the footnotes of (V.3:85) and (V.6:93).

believed, that they should perform
As-Salât (Iqâmat-as-Salât), and spend
in charity out of the sustenance We
have given them, secretly and openly,
before the coming of a Day on which
there will be neither mutual bargaining
nor befriending.

32. Allâh is He Who has created the
heavens and the earth and sends down
water (rain) from the sky, and thereby
brought forth fruits as provision for
you; and He has made the ships to be of
service to you, that they may sail
through the sea by His Command; and
He has made rivers (also) to be of
service to you.

33. And He has made the sun and the
moon, both constantly pursuing their
courses, to be of service to you; and He
has made the night and the day, to be of
service to you.

34. And He gave you of all that you
asked for, and if you count the
Blessings of Allâh, never will you be
able to count them. Verily, man is
indeed an extreme wrongdoer, a
disbeliever (an extreme ingrate who
denies Allâh's Blessings by disbelief,
and by worshipping others besides
Allâh, and by disobeying Allâh and His
Prophet Muhammad صلى الله عليه وسلم).

35. And (remember) when Ibrâhîm
(Abraham) said: "O my Lord! Make
this city (Makkah) one of peace and

وَبَنِيَّ أَن نَّعْبُدَ ٱلْأَصْنَامَ ۝

security, and keep me and my sons away from worshipping idols.

36. "O my Lord! They have indeed led astray many among mankind. But whoso follows me, he verily, is of me. And whoso disobeys me, still You are indeed Oft-Forgiving, Most Merciful.

رَبِّ إِنَّهُنَّ أَضْلَلْنَ كَثِيرًا مِّنَ ٱلنَّاسِ فَمَن تَبِعَنِي فَإِنَّهُ مِنِّي وَمَنْ عَصَانِي فَإِنَّكَ غَفُورٌ رَّحِيمٌ ۝

37. "O our Lord! I have made some of my offspring to dwell in an uncultivable valley by Your Sacred House (the Ka'bah at Makkah) in order, O our Lord, that they may perform As-Salât (Iqâmat-as-Salât). So fill some hearts among men with love towards them, and (O Allâh) provide them with fruits so that they may give thanks.[1]

رَّبَّنَا إِنِّي أَسْكَنتُ مِن ذُرِّيَّتِي بِوَادٍ غَيْرِ ذِي زَرْعٍ عِندَ بَيْتِكَ ٱلْمُحَرَّمِ رَبَّنَا لِيُقِيمُواْ ٱلصَّلَوٰةَ فَٱجْعَلْ أَفْئِدَةً مِّنَ ٱلنَّاسِ تَهْوِيٓ إِلَيْهِمْ وَٱرْزُقْهُم مِّنَ ٱلثَّمَرَٰتِ لَعَلَّهُمْ يَشْكُرُونَ ۝

---

[1] (V.14:37). The Story of the building of the *Ka'bah* at Makkah: Narrated Ibn 'Abbâs رضي الله عنهما [On the authority of the Prophet صلى الله عليه وسلم (See *Fath Al-Bari*)]. The first lady to use a girdle was the mother of Ismâ'îl (Ishmael). She used a girdle so that she might hide her tracks from Sârah.* Ibrâhîm (Abraham) brought her and her son Ismâ'îl (Ishmael) while she used to nurse him at her breast, near the *Ka'bah* under a tree on the spot of *Zamzam*, at the highest place in the mosque. During those days there was nobody in Makkah, nor was there any water. So he made them sit over there and placed near them a leather bag containing some dates, and a small water-skin containing some water, and set out homeward. Ismâ'îl's (Ishmael) mother followed him saying, "O Ibrâhîm (Abraham)! Where are you going, leaving us in this valley where there is no person whose company we may enjoy, nor is there anything (to enjoy)?" She repeated that to him many times, but he did not look back at her. Then she asked him, "Has Allâh ordered you to do so?" He said, "Yes." She said, "Then He will not neglect us," and returned while Ibrâhîm (Abraham) proceeded onwards, and on reaching the Thaniyyah where they could not see him, he faced

the *Ka'bah*, and raising both hands invoked Allâh saying the following supplication:

'O our Lord! I have made some of my offspring to dwell in an uncultivable valley by Your Sacred House (the *Ka'bah* at Makkah); in order, O our Lord, that they may perform *As-Salât (Iqâmat-as-Salât)*. So fill some hearts among men with love towards them, and (O Allâh) provide them with fruits, so that they may give thanks.' (V.14:37)

Ismâ'îl's (Ishmael) mother went on suckling Ismâ'îl (Ishmael) and drinking from the water (she had). When the water in the water-skin had all been used up, she became thirsty and her child also became thirsty. She started looking at him [i.e. Ismâ'îl (Ishmael)] tossing in agony; she left him, for she could not endure looking at him, and found that the mountain of As-Safâ was the nearest mountain to her on that land. She stood on it and started looking at the valley keenly so that she might see somebody, but she could not see anybody. Then she descended from As-Safâ and when she reached the valley, she tucked up her robe and ran in the valley like a person in distress and trouble, till she crossed the valley and reached Al-Marwah mountain where she stood and started looking, expecting to see somebody, but she could not see anybody. She repeated that (running between As-Safâ and Al-Marwah) seven times." The Prophet صلى الله عليه وسلم said, "This is the source of the tradition of the *Sa'y* (the going) of people between them (i.e. As-Safâ and Al-Marwah). When she reached Al-Marwah (for the last time) she heard a voice and she asked herself to be quiet and listened attentively. She heard the voice again and said, 'O (whoever you may be)! You have made me hear your voice; have you got something to help me?' And behold! She saw an angel at the place of *Zamzam*, digging the earth with his heel (or his wing), till water flowed from that place. She started to make something like a basin around it, using her hands in this way and started filling her water-skin with water with her hands, and the water was flowing out after she had scooped some of it." The Prophet صلى الله عليه وسلم added, "May Allâh bestow mercy on Ismâ'îl's (Ishmael) mother! Had she let the *Zamzam* (flow without trying to control it) (or had she not scooped from that water) (to fill her water-skin), *Zamzam* would have been a stream flowing on the surface of the earth." The Prophet صلى الله عليه وسلم further added, "Then she drank (water) and suckled her child. The angel said to her, 'Don't be afraid of being neglected, for this is the House of Allâh which will be built by this boy and his father, and Allâh never neglects His people.' The House (i.e. *Ka'bah*) at that time was on a high place resembling a hillock, and when torrents came, they flowed to its right and left. She lived in that way till some people from the tribe of Jurhum or a family from Jurhum passed by her and her child, as they (i.e. the Jurhum people) were coming through the way of Kadâ'. They landed in the lower part of Makkah where they saw a bird that had the habit of flying around water and not leaving it. They said, 'This bird must be flying around water, though we know that there is no water in this valley.' They sent one or two messengers who discovered the source of water, and returned to inform them of the water. So, they all came (towards the water)." The Prophet ﷺ added, "Ismâ'îl's (Ishmael) mother was sitting near the water. They asked her, 'Do you allow us to stay with you?' She replied, 'Yes, but you will have no right to possess the water.' They agreed to that." The Prophet ﷺ further said, "Ismâ'îl's (Ishmael) mother was pleased with the whole situation as she used to love to enjoy the company of the people. So, they settled there, and later on they sent for their families who came and settled with them so that some families became permanent residents there. The child [i.e. Ismâ'îl (Ishmael)] grew up and learnt Arabic from them and (his virtues) caused them to love and admire him as he grew up, and when he reached the age of puberty they made him marry a woman from amongst them. After Ismâ'îl's (Ishmael) mother had died, Ibrâhîm (Abraham) came after Ismâ'îl's (Ishmael) marriage in order to see his family that he had left before, but he did not find Ismâ'îl (Ishmael) there. When he asked Ismâ'îl's (Ishmael) wife about him, she replied, 'He has gone in search of our livelihood.' Then he asked her about their way of living and their condition, and she replied, 'We are living in misery; we are living in hardship and destitution,' complaining to him. He said, 'When your husband returns, convey my salutation to him and tell him to change the threshold of the gate of his house).' When Ismâ'îl (Ishmael) came, he seemed to have felt something unusual, so he asked his wife, 'Has anyone visited you?' She replied, 'Yes, an old man of such and such description came and asked me about you and I informed him, and he asked about our state of living, and I told him that we were living in a hardship and poverty.' On that Ismâ'îl (Ishmael) said, 'Did he advise you anything?' She replied, 'Yes, he told me to convey his salutation to you and to tell you to change the threshold of your gate.' Ismâ'îl (Ishmael) said, 'It was my father, and he has ordered me to divorce you. Go back to your family.' So, Ismâ'îl (Ishmael) divorced her and married another woman from amongst them (i.e. Jurhum). Then Ibrâhîm (Abraham) stayed away from them for a period as long as Allâh wished and called on them again but did not find Ismâ'îl (Ishmael). So he came to Ismâ'îl's (Ishmael) wife and asked her about Ismâ'îl (Ishmael). She said, 'He has gone in search of our livelihood.' Ibrâhîm (Abraham) asked her, 'How are you getting on?' asking her about their sustenance and living. She replied, 'We are prosperous and well-off (i.e. we have everything in abundance).' Then she thanked Allâh عز وجل. Ibrâhîm (Abraham) said, 'What kind of food do you eat?' She said, 'Meat.' He said, 'What do you drink?' She said, 'Water.' He said, 'O Allâh! Bless their meat and water.' " The Prophet صلى الله عليه وسلم added, "At that time they did not have grain, and if they had grain, he would have also invoked Allâh to bless it." The Prophet صلى الله عليه وسلم added, "If somebody has only these two things as his sustenance, his health and disposition will be badly affected, unless he lives in Makkah." The Prophet صلى الله عليه وسلم added, "Then Ibrâhîm (Abraham) said to Ismâ'îl's (Ishmael) wife, 'When your husband comes, give my regards to him and tell him that he should keep firm the threshold of his gate.' When Ismâ'îl (Ishmael) came back, he asked his wife. 'Did anyone call on you?' She replied, 'Yes, a good-looking old man came to me,' so she praised him and added. 'He asked about you, and I informed him, and he asked about our livelihood and I told him that we were in a good condition.' Ismâ'îl (Ishmael) asked her, 'Did he give you any piece of advice?' She said, 'Yes, he told me to give his regards to you and ordered that you should keep firm the threshold of your gate.' On that Ismâ'îl (Ishmael) said, 'It was my father, and you are the threshold (of the gate). He has ordered me to keep you with me.' Then Ibrâhîm (Abraham) stayed away from them for a period as long as Allâh wished, and called on them afterwards. He saw Ismâ'îl (Ishmael) under a tree near Zamzam, sharpening his arrows. When he saw Ibrâhîm (Abraham), he rose up to welcome him (and they greeted each other as a father does with his son or a son does with his father). Ibrâhîm (Abraham) said, 'O Ismâ'îl (Ishmael)! Allâh has given me an order.' Ismâ'îl (Ishmael) said, 'Do what your Lord has ordered you to do.' Ibrâhîm

38. "O our Lord! Certainly, You know what we conceal and what we reveal. Nothing on the earth or in the heaven is hidden from Allâh.

رَبَّنَآ إِنَّكَ تَعۡلَمُ مَا نُخۡفِي وَمَا نُعۡلِنُ ۗ وَمَا يَخۡفَىٰ عَلَى ٱللَّهِ مِن شَيۡءٖ فِي ٱلۡأَرۡضِ وَلَا فِي ٱلسَّمَآءِ ﴿٣٨﴾

39. "All the praises and thanks are to Allâh, Who has given me in old age Ismâ'îl (Ishmael) and Ishâq (Isaac). Verily, My Lord is indeed the All-Hearer of invocations.

ٱلۡحَمۡدُ لِلَّهِ ٱلَّذِي وَهَبَ لِي عَلَى ٱلۡكِبَرِ إِسۡمَٰعِيلَ وَإِسۡحَٰقَ ۚ إِنَّ رَبِّي لَسَمِيعُ ٱلدُّعَآءِ ﴿٣٩﴾

40. "O my Lord! Make me one who performs *As-Salât (Iqâmat-as-Salât)*, and (also) from my offspring, our Lord! And accept my invocation.

رَبِّ ٱجۡعَلۡنِي مُقِيمَ ٱلصَّلَوٰةِ وَمِن ذُرِّيَّتِي ۚ رَبَّنَا وَتَقَبَّلۡ دُعَآءِ ﴿٤٠﴾

41. "Our Lord! Forgive me and my parents, and (all) the believers on the Day when the reckoning will be established."

رَبَّنَا ٱغۡفِرۡ لِي وَلِوَٰلِدَيَّ وَلِلۡمُؤۡمِنِينَ يَوۡمَ يَقُومُ ٱلۡحِسَابُ ﴿٤١﴾

(Abraham) asked, 'Will you help me?' Ismâ'îl (Ishmael) said, 'I will help you.' Ibrâhîm (Abraham) said, 'Allâh has ordered me to build a house here,' pointing to a hillock higher than the land surrounding it.' " The Prophet صلى الله عليه وسلم added, "Then they raised the foundations of the House (i.e. the Ka'bah). Ismâ'îl (Ishmael) brought the stones and Ibrâhîm (Abraham) was building; and when the walls became high, Ismâ'îl (Ishmael) brought this stone and put it for Ibrâhîm (Abraham) who stood over it and carried on building, while Ismâ'îl (Ishmael) was handing him the stones, and both of them were saying, 'O our Lord! Accept (this service) from us. Verily, You are the All-Hearer the All-Knower.' " (V.2:127).

The Prophet صلى الله عليه وسلم added, "Then both of them went on building and going round the Ka'bah saying 'O our Lord! Accept (this service) from us. Verily, You are the All-Hearer, the All-Knower.' " (V.2:127) [Sahih Al-Bukhari, Vol. 4, Hadith No. 583].

* When Ibrâhîm (Abraham) married Hâjar and she conceived Ismâ'îl (Ishmael), Sârah, Ibrâhîm (Abraham)'s first wife became jealous of her and swore that she would cut three parts from her body. So Hâjar tied a girdle round her waist and ran away, dragging her robe behind her so as to wipe out her tracks lest Sârah, should pursue her. "Allâh knows better."

42. Consider not that Allâh is unaware of that which the *Zâlimûn* (polytheists, wrongdoers) do, but He gives them respite up to a Day when the eyes will stare in horror.

43. (They will be) hastening forward with necks outstretched, their heads raised up (towards the sky), their gaze returning not towards them and their hearts empty (from thinking because of extreme fear).

44. And warn (O Muhammad صلى الله عليه وسلم) mankind of the Day when the torment will come unto them; then the wrongdoers will say: "Our Lord! Respite us for a little while, we will answer Your Call and follow the Messengers!" (It will be said): "Had you not sworn aforetime that you would not leave (the world for the Hereafter)."

45. "And you dwelt in the dwellings of men who wronged themselves, and it was clear to you how We had dealt with them. And We put forth (many) parables for you."

46. Indeed, they planned their plot, and their plot was with Allâh, though their plot was not such as to remove the mountains (real mountains or the Islâmic law) from their places (as it is of no importance) [*Tafsir Ibn Kathir*].[1]

---

[1] (V.14:46) It is said by some interpreters regarding this Verse that the Quraish pagans plotted against Prophet Muhammad صلى الله عليه وسلم

47. So think not that Allâh will fail to keep His Promise to His Messengers. Certainly, Allâh is All-Mighty, All-Able of Retribution.

فَلَا تَحْسَبَنَّ ٱللَّهَ مُخْلِفَ وَعْدِهِۦ رُسُلَهُۥٓ إِنَّ ٱللَّهَ عَزِيزٌ ذُو ٱنتِقَامٍ ٤٧

48. On the Day when the earth will be changed to another earth and so will be the heavens, and they (all creatures) will appear before Allâh, the One, the Irresistible.

يَوْمَ تُبَدَّلُ ٱلْأَرْضُ غَيْرَ ٱلْأَرْضِ وَٱلسَّمَٰوَٰتُ وَبَرَزُوا۟ لِلَّهِ ٱلْوَٰحِدِ ٱلْقَهَّارِ ٤٨

49. And you will see the *Mujrimûn* (criminals, disbelievers in the Oneness of Allâh — Islâmic Monotheism, polytheists) that Day *Muqarranûn*[1] (bound together in fetters).

وَتَرَى ٱلْمُجْرِمِينَ يَوْمَئِذٍ مُّقَرَّنِينَ فِى ٱلْأَصْفَادِ ٤٩

50. Their garments will be of pitch, and fire will cover their faces.

سَرَابِيلُهُم مِّن قَطِرَانٍ وَتَغْشَىٰ وُجُوهَهُمُ ٱلنَّارُ ٥٠

51. That Allâh may requite each person according to what he has earned. Truly, Allâh is Swift at reckoning.

لِيَجْزِىَ ٱللَّهُ كُلَّ نَفْسٍ مَّا كَسَبَتْ إِنَّ ٱللَّهَ سَرِيعُ ٱلْحِسَابِ ٥١

52. This (Qur'ân) is a Message for mankind (and a clear proof against them), in order that they may be warned thereby, and that they may know that He is the only One *Ilâh* (God — Allâh) — (none has the right to be worshipped but Allâh) — and that men of understanding may take heed.

هَٰذَا بَلَٰغٌ لِّلنَّاسِ وَلِيُنذَرُوا۟ بِهِۦ وَلِيَعْلَمُوٓا۟ أَنَّمَا هُوَ إِلَٰهٌ وَٰحِدٌ وَلِيَذَّكَّرَ أُو۟لُوا۟ ٱلْأَلْبَٰبِ ٥٢

---

to kill him but they failed and were unable to carry out their plot which they plotted.

[1] (V.14:49) *Muqarranûn* (bound in fetters mean): With their hands and feet tied to their necks with chains.

Sûrat Al-Hijr
(The Rocky Tract) XV

سُورَةُ الحِجْر

*In the Name of Allâh
the Most Gracious, the Most Merciful*

بِسْمِ اللهِ الرَّحْمَٰنِ الرَّحِيمِ

1. *Alif-Lâm-Râ.* [These letters are one of the miracles of the Qur'ân, and none but Allâh (Alone) knows their meanings].

الۤرۚ تِلۡكَ ءَايَٰتُ ٱلۡكِتَٰبِ وَقُرۡءَانٖ مُّبِينٖ ١

These are Verses of the Book and a plain Qur'ân.

2. How much will those who disbelieved desire that they were Muslims [those who have submitted themselves to Allâh's Will in Islâm i.e. Islâmic Monotheism — this will be on the Day of Resurrection when they will see the disbelievers going to Hell and the Muslims going to Paradise].[1]

رُّبَمَا يَوَدُّ ٱلَّذِينَ كَفَرُواْ لَوۡ كَانُواْ مُسۡلِمِينَ ٢

3. Leave them to eat and enjoy, and let them be preoccupied with (false) hope. They will come to know!

ذَرۡهُمۡ يَأۡكُلُواْ وَيَتَمَتَّعُواْ وَيُلۡهِهِمُ ٱلۡأَمَلُۖ فَسَوۡفَ يَعۡلَمُونَ ٣

4. And never did We destroy a township but there was a known decree for it.

وَمَآ أَهۡلَكۡنَا مِن قَرۡيَةٍ إِلَّا وَلَهَا كِتَابٌ مَّعۡلُومٌ ٤

5. No nation can advance its term, nor delay it.

مَّا تَسۡبِقُ مِنۡ أُمَّةٍ أَجَلَهَا وَمَا يَسۡتَـٔۡخِرُونَ ٥

6. And they say: "O you (Muhammad صلى الله عليه وسلم) to whom the *Dhikr* (the Qur'ân) has been sent down! Verily, you are a mad man!

وَقَالُواْ يَٰٓأَيُّهَا ٱلَّذِي نُزِّلَ عَلَيۡهِ ٱلذِّكۡرُ إِنَّكَ لَمَجۡنُونٌ ٦

7. "Why do you not bring angels to us if you are of the truthful?"

لَّوۡ مَا تَأۡتِينَا بِٱلۡمَلَٰٓئِكَةِ إِن كُنتَ مِنَ ٱلصَّٰدِقِينَ ٧

---

[1] (V.15:2): See the footnote of (V.3:85).

8. We send not the angels down except with the truth (i.e. for torment), and in that case, they (the disbelievers) would have no respite!

مَا نُنَزِّلُ الْمَلَٰٓئِكَةَ إِلَّا بِالْحَقِّ وَمَا كَانُوٓا۟ إِذًا مُّنظَرِينَ ٨

9. Verily, We, it is We Who have sent down the *Dhikr* (i.e. the Qur'ân) and surely, We will guard it (from corruption).[1]

إِنَّا نَحْنُ نَزَّلْنَا ٱلذِّكْرَ وَإِنَّا لَهُۥ لَحَٰفِظُونَ ٩

10. Indeed, We sent (Messengers) before you (O Muhammad صلى الله عليه وسلم) amongst the sects (communities) of old.

وَلَقَدْ أَرْسَلْنَا مِن قَبْلِكَ فِى شِيَعِ ٱلْأَوَّلِينَ ١٠

11. And never came a Messenger to them but they did mock at him.

وَمَا يَأْتِيهِم مِّن رَّسُولٍ إِلَّا كَانُوا۟ بِهِۦ يَسْتَهْزِءُونَ ١١

12. Thus do We let it (polytheism and disbelief) enter the hearts of the *Mujrimûn* [criminals, polytheists, pagans, (because of their mocking at the Messengers)].

كَذَٰلِكَ نَسْلُكُهُۥ فِى قُلُوبِ ٱلْمُجْرِمِينَ ١٢

13. They would not believe in it (the Qur'ân); and already the example of (Allâh's punishment of) the ancients (who disbelieved) has gone forth.

لَا يُؤْمِنُونَ بِهِۦ وَقَدْ خَلَتْ سُنَّةُ ٱلْأَوَّلِينَ ١٣

14. And even if We opened to them a gate from the heaven and they were to keep on ascending thereto (all the day long).

وَلَوْ فَتَحْنَا عَلَيْهِم بَابًا مِّنَ ٱلسَّمَآءِ فَظَلُّوا۟ فِيهِ يَعْرُجُونَ ١٤

---

[1] (V.15:9) This Verse is a challenge to mankind and everyone is obliged to believe in the miracles of this Qur'ân. It is a clear fact that more than 1400 years have elapsed and not a single word of this Qur'ân has been changed, although the disbelievers tried their utmost to change it in every way, but they failed miserably in their efforts. As it is mentioned in this holy Verse: "We will guard it." By Allâh! He has guarded it. On the contrary, all the other holy Books [the Taurât (Torah), the Injeel (Gospel)] have been corrupted in the form of additions or subtractions or alterations in the original text.

15. They would surely, say (in the evening): "Our eyes have been (as if) dazzled (we have not seen any angel or heaven). Nay, we are a people bewitched."

لَقَالُوٓا إِنَّمَا سُكِّرَتْ أَبْصَـٰرُنَا بَلْ نَحْنُ قَوْمٌ مَّسْحُورُونَ ١

16. And indeed, We have put the big stars in the heaven and We beautified it for the beholders.[1]

وَلَقَدْ جَعَلْنَا فِى ٱلسَّمَآءِ بُرُوجًا وَزَيَّنَّـٰهَا لِلنَّـٰظِرِينَ ١

17. And We have guarded it (near heaven) from every outcast *Shaitân* (devil).

وَحَفِظْنَـٰهَا مِن كُلِّ شَيْطَـٰنٍ رَّجِيمٍ ١

18. Except him (devil) who steals the hearing then he is pursued by a clear flaming fire.

إِلَّا مَنِ ٱسْتَرَقَ ٱلسَّمْعَ فَأَتْبَعَهُۥ شِهَابٌ مُّبِينٌ ١

19. And the earth We have spread out, and have placed therein firm mountains, and caused to grow therein all kinds of things in due proportion.

وَٱلْأَرْضَ مَدَدْنَـٰهَا وَأَلْقَيْنَا فِيهَا رَوَٰسِىَ وَأَنۢبَتْنَا فِيهَا مِن كُلِّ شَىْءٍ مَّوْزُونٍ ١

20. And We have provided therein means of living, for you and for those whom you provide not [moving (living) creatures, cattle, beasts, and other animals].

وَجَعَلْنَا لَكُمْ فِيهَا مَعَـٰيِشَ وَمَن لَّسْتُمْ لَهُۥ بِرَٰزِقِينَ ١

21. And there is not a thing, but with Us are the stores thereof. And We send it not down except in a known measure.

وَإِن مِّن شَىْءٍ إِلَّا عِندَنَا خَزَآئِنُهُۥ وَمَا نُنَزِّلُهُۥٓ إِلَّا بِقَدَرٍ مَّعْلُومٍ ١

22. And We send the winds fertilizing (to fill heavily the clouds with water), then cause the water (rain) to descend from the sky, and We give it to you to drink, and it is not you who are the owners of its stores [i.e. to give water to whom you like or to withhold it from whom you like].

وَأَرْسَلْنَا ٱلرِّيَـٰحَ لَوَٰقِحَ فَأَنزَلْنَا مِنَ ٱلسَّمَآءِ مَآءً فَأَسْقَيْنَـٰكُمُوهُ وَمَآ أَنتُمْ لَهُۥ بِخَـٰزِنِينَ ١

---

[1] (V.15:16) See the footnote of (V.6:97).

23. And certainly We! We it is Who give life, and cause death,[1] and We are the Inheritors.

وَإِنَّا لَنَحْنُ نُحْيِي وَنُمِيتُ وَنَحْنُ الْوَارِثُونَ ۝

24. And indeed, We know the first generations of you who had passed away, and indeed, We know the present generations of you (mankind), and also those who will come afterwards.

وَلَقَدْ عَلِمْنَا الْمُسْتَقْدِمِينَ مِنكُمْ وَلَقَدْ عَلِمْنَا الْمُسْتَأْخِرِينَ ۝

25. And verily, your Lord will gather them together. Truly, He is All-Wise, All-Knowing.

وَإِنَّ رَبَّكَ هُوَ يَحْشُرُهُمْ إِنَّهُ حَكِيمٌ عَلِيمٌ ۝

26. And indeed, We created man from dried (sounding) clay of altered mud.

وَلَقَدْ خَلَقْنَا الْإِنسَـٰنَ مِن صَلْصَـٰلٍ مِّنْ حَمَإٍ مَّسْنُونٍ ۝

27. And the jinn, We created aforetime from the smokeless flame of fire.

وَالْجَآنَّ خَلَقْنَـٰهُ مِن قَبْلُ مِن نَّارِ السَّمُومِ ۝

28. And (remember) when your Lord said to the angels: "I am going to create a man (Adam) from dried (sounding) clay of altered mud.

وَإِذْ قَالَ رَبُّكَ لِلْمَلَـٰٓئِكَةِ إِنِّي خَـٰلِقٌ بَشَرًا مِّن صَلْصَـٰلٍ مِّنْ حَمَإٍ مَّسْنُونٍ ۝

29. "So, when I have fashioned him completely and breathed into him (Adam) the soul which I created for him, then fall (you) down prostrating yourselves unto him."

فَإِذَا سَوَّيْتُهُ وَنَفَخْتُ فِيهِ مِن رُّوحِي فَقَعُوا لَهُ سَـٰجِدِينَ ۝

---

[1] (V.15:23) Narrated Abu Hurairah صلى الله عنه : Allâh's Messenger صلى الله عليه وسلم said: "When a person is dead, his deeds cease (are stopped) except three:

a) Deeds of continuous *Sadaqah* (act of charity), e.g. an orphan home or a well for giving water to drink.

b) (Written) knowledge with which mankind gets benefit.

c) A righteous, pious son (or daughter) who begs Allâh to forgive his (or her) parents." (*Sahih Muslim*, The Book of *Wasâyâ* (Wills and Testaments).

30. So the angels prostrated themselves, all of them together.

فَسَجَدَ ٱلْمَلَٰٓئِكَةُ كُلُّهُمْ أَجْمَعُونَ ۝

31. Except *Iblîs* (Satan) — he refused to be among the prostrators.

إِلَّآ إِبْلِيسَ أَبَىٰٓ أَن يَكُونَ مَعَ ٱلسَّٰجِدِينَ ۝

32. (Allâh) said: "O *Iblîs* (Satan)! What is your reason for not being among the prostrators?"

قَالَ يَٰٓإِبْلِيسُ مَا لَكَ أَلَّا تَكُونَ مَعَ ٱلسَّٰجِدِينَ ۝

33. [*Iblîs* (Satan)] said: "I am not the one to prostrate myself to a human being, whom You created from dried (sounding) clay of altered mud."

قَالَ لَمْ أَكُن لِّأَسْجُدَ لِبَشَرٍ خَلَقْتَهُۥ مِن صَلْصَٰلٍ مِّنْ حَمَإٍ مَّسْنُونٍ ۝

34. (Allâh) said: "Then, get out from here, for verily, you are *Rajîm* (an outcast or a cursed one)." [*Tafsîr At-Tabarî*]

قَالَ فَٱخْرُجْ مِنْهَا فَإِنَّكَ رَجِيمٌ ۝

35. "And verily, the curse shall be upon you till the Day of Recompense (i.e. the Day of Resurrection)."

وَإِنَّ عَلَيْكَ ٱللَّعْنَةَ إِلَىٰ يَوْمِ ٱلدِّينِ ۝

36. [*Iblîs* (Satan)] said: "O my Lord! Give me then respite till the Day they (the dead) will be resurrected."

قَالَ رَبِّ فَأَنظِرْنِىٓ إِلَىٰ يَوْمِ يُبْعَثُونَ ۝

37. Allâh said: "Then verily, you are of those reprieved,

قَالَ فَإِنَّكَ مِنَ ٱلْمُنظَرِينَ ۝

38. "Till the Day of the time appointed."

إِلَىٰ يَوْمِ ٱلْوَقْتِ ٱلْمَعْلُومِ ۝

39. [*Iblîs* (Satan)] said: "O my Lord! Because you misled me, I shall indeed adorn the path of error for them (mankind) on the earth, and I shall mislead them all.

قَالَ رَبِّ بِمَآ أَغْوَيْتَنِى لَأُزَيِّنَنَّ لَهُمْ فِى ٱلْأَرْضِ وَلَأُغْوِيَنَّهُمْ أَجْمَعِينَ ۝

40. "Except Your chosen, (guided) slaves among them."

إِلَّا عِبَادَكَ مِنْهُمُ ٱلْمُخْلَصِينَ ۝

41. (Allâh) said: "This is the Way which will lead straight to Me."

قَالَ هَٰذَا صِرَٰطٌ عَلَىَّ مُسْتَقِيمٌ ۝

42. "Certainly, you shall have no authority over My slaves, except those who follow you of the *Ghâwûn* (*Mushrikûn* and those who go astray, criminals, polytheists, and evil-doers).

إِنَّ عِبَادِى لَيْسَ لَكَ عَلَيْهِمْ سُلْطَانٌ إِلَّا مَنِ اتَّبَعَكَ مِنَ الْغَاوِينَ ۝

43. "And surely, Hell is the promised place for them all.

وَإِنَّ جَهَنَّمَ لَمَوْعِدُهُمْ أَجْمَعِينَ ۝

44. "It (Hell) has seven gates, for each of those gates is a (special) class (of sinners) assigned.

لَهَا سَبْعَةُ أَبْوَابٍ لِّكُلِّ بَابٍ مِّنْهُمْ جُزْءٌ مَّقْسُومٌ ۝

45. "Truly, the *Muttaqûn* (the pious. See V.2:2) will be amidst Gardens and water-springs (Paradise).

إِنَّ الْمُتَّقِينَ فِى جَنَّاتٍ وَعُيُونٍ ۝

46. "(It will be said to them): 'Enter therein (Paradise), in peace and security.'

ادْخُلُوهَا بِسَلَامٍ آمِنِينَ ۝

47. "And We shall remove from their breasts any deep feeling of bitterness (that they may have). (So they will be like) brothers facing each other on thrones.

وَنَزَعْنَا مَا فِى صُدُورِهِم مِّنْ غِلٍّ إِخْوَانًا عَلَى سُرُرٍ مُّتَقَابِلِينَ ۝

48. "No sense of fatigue shall touch them, nor shall they (ever) be asked to leave it."

لَا يَمَسُّهُمْ فِيهَا نَصَبٌ وَمَا هُم مِّنْهَا بِمُخْرَجِينَ ۝

49. Declare (O Muhammad ﷺ) unto My slaves, that truly, I am the Oft-Forgiving, the Most-Merciful.

نَبِّئْ عِبَادِى أَنِّى أَنَا الْغَفُورُ الرَّحِيمُ ۝

50. And that My Torment is indeed the most painful torment.

وَأَنَّ عَذَابِى هُوَ الْعَذَابُ الْأَلِيمُ ۝

51. And tell them about the guests (the angels) of Ibrâhîm (Abraham).

وَنَبِّئْهُمْ عَن ضَيْفِ إِبْرَاهِيمَ ۝

52. When they entered unto him, and said: *Salâman* (peace)! [Ibrâhîm

إِذْ دَخَلُوا عَلَيْهِ فَقَالُوا سَلَامًا قَالَ

(Abraham)] said: "Indeed! We are afraid of you."

53. They (the angels) said: "Do not be afraid! We give you glad tidings of a boy (son) possessing much knowledge and wisdom."

54. [Ibrâhîm (Abraham)] said: "Do you give me glad tidings (of a son) when old age has overtaken me? Of what then is your news?"

55. They (the angels) said: "We give you glad tidings in truth. So be not of the despairing."

56. [Ibrâhîm (Abraham)] said: "And who despairs of the Mercy of his Lord except those who are astray?"

57. [Ibrâhîm (Abraham) again] said: "What then is the business on which you have come, O messengers?"

58. They (the angels) said: "We have been sent to a people who are *Mujrimûn* (criminals, disbelievers, polytheists, sinners),

59. "(All) except the family of Lût (Lot). Them all we are surely, going to save (from destruction).

60. "Except his wife, of whom We have decreed that she shall be of those who remain behind (i.e. she will be destroyed)."

61. Then when the messengers (the angels) came unto the family of Lût (Lot).

62. He said: "Verily, you are people unknown to me."

63. They said: "Nay, we have come to you with that (torment) which they have been doubting.

قَالُوا بَلْ جِئْنَاكَ بِمَا كَانُوا فِيهِ يَمْتَرُونَ ٦٣

64. "And we have brought to you the truth (the news of the destruction of your nation) and certainly, we tell the truth.

وَأَتَيْنَاكَ بِالْحَقِّ وَإِنَّا لَصَادِقُونَ ٦٤

65. "Then travel in a part of the night with your family, and you go behind them in the rear, and let no one amongst you look back, but go on to where you are ordered."

فَأَسْرِ بِأَهْلِكَ بِقِطْعٍ مِنَ الَّيْلِ وَاتَّبِعْ أَدْبَارَهُمْ وَلَا يَلْتَفِتْ مِنْكُمْ أَحَدٌ وَامْضُوا حَيْثُ تُؤْمَرُونَ ٦٥

66. And We made known this decree to him, that the root of those (sinners) was to be cut off in the early morning.

وَقَضَيْنَا إِلَيْهِ ذَلِكَ الْأَمْرَ أَنَّ دَابِرَ هَؤُلَاءِ مَقْطُوعٌ مُصْبِحِينَ ٦٦

67. And the inhabitants of the city came rejoicing (at the news of the young men's arrival).

وَجَاءَ أَهْلُ الْمَدِينَةِ يَسْتَبْشِرُونَ ٦٧

68. [Lût (Lot)] said: "Verily, these are my guests, so shame me not.

قَالَ إِنَّ هَؤُلَاءِ ضَيْفِي فَلَا تَفْضَحُونِ ٦٨

69. "And fear Allâh and disgrace me not."

وَاتَّقُوا اللَّهَ وَلَا تُخْزُونِ ٦٩

70. They (people of the city) said: "Did we not forbid you from entertaining (or protecting) any of the 'Âlamîn (people, foreigners and strangers from us)?"

قَالُوا أَوَلَمْ نَنْهَكَ عَنِ الْعَالَمِينَ ٧٠

71. [Lût (Lot)] said: "These (the girls of the nation) are my daughters (to marry lawfully), if you must act (so)."

قَالَ هَؤُلَاءِ بَنَاتِي إِنْ كُنْتُمْ فَاعِلِينَ ٧١

72. Verily, by your life (O Muhammad صلى الله عليه وسلم), in their wild intoxication, they were wandering blindly.

لَعَمْرُكَ إِنَّهُمْ لَفِي سَكْرَتِهِمْ يَعْمَهُونَ ٧٢

73. So As-Saihah (torment — awful cry) overtook them at the time of sunrise.

فَأَخَذَتْهُمُ الصَّيْحَةُ مُشْرِقِينَ ٧٣

74. And We turned (the towns of Sodom in Palestine) upside down and rained down on them stones of baked clay.

فَجَعَلْنَا عَالِيَهَا سَافِلَهَا وَأَمْطَرْنَا عَلَيْهِمْ حِجَارَةً مِّن سِجِّيلٍ ۝

75. Surely, in this are signs for those who see (or understand or learn the lessons from the Signs of Allâh).

إِنَّ فِي ذَٰلِكَ لَآيَٰتٍ لِّلْمُتَوَسِّمِينَ ۝

76. And verily, they (the cities) were right on the highroad (from Makkah to Syria i.e. the place where the Dead Sea is now).[1]

وَإِنَّهَا لَبِسَبِيلٍ مُّقِيمٍ ۝

77. Surely, therein is indeed a sign for the believers.

إِنَّ فِي ذَٰلِكَ لَآيَةً لِّلْمُؤْمِنِينَ ۝

78. And the Dwellers of the Wood [i.e. the people of Madyan (Midian) to whom Prophet Shu'aib (عليه السلام) was sent by Allâh), were also *Zâlimûn* (polytheists and wrongdoers).

وَإِن كَانَ أَصْحَٰبُ الْأَيْكَةِ لَظَٰلِمِينَ ۝

79. So, We took vengeance on them. They are both on an open highway, plain to see.

فَانتَقَمْنَا مِنْهُمْ وَإِنَّهُمَا لَبِإِمَامٍ مُّبِينٍ ۝

80. And verily, the Dwellers of *Al-Hijr* (the rocky tract) denied the Messengers.

وَلَقَدْ كَذَّبَ أَصْحَٰبُ الْحِجْرِ الْمُرْسَلِينَ ۝

81. And We gave them Our Signs, but they were averse to them.

وَءَاتَيْنَٰهُمْ ءَايَٰتِنَا فَكَانُوا عَنْهَا مُعْرِضِينَ ۝

82. And they used to hew out dwellings from the mountains, (feeling themselves) secure.

وَكَانُوا يَنْحِتُونَ مِنَ الْجِبَالِ بُيُوتًا ءَامِنِينَ ۝

83. But *As-Saihah* (torment — awful cry) overtook them in the early morning (of the fourth day of their promised punishment days).

فَأَخَذَتْهُمُ الصَّيْحَةُ مُصْبِحِينَ ۝

---

[1] (V.15:76) Please see the Book of History by Ibn Kathir (كتاب التاريخ لابن كثير).

84. And all that they used to earn availed them not.

‏فَمَا أَغْنَىٰ عَنْهُم مَّا كَانُوا۟ يَكْسِبُونَ ٨٤‏

85. And We created not the heavens and the earth and all that is between them except with truth, and the Hour is surely, coming, so overlook (O Muhammad ﷺ), their faults with gracious forgiveness. [This was before the ordainment of *Jihâd* — holy fighting in Allâh's cause].

‏وَمَا خَلَقْنَا السَّمَوَٰتِ وَالْأَرْضَ وَمَا بَيْنَهُمَا إِلَّا بِالْحَقِّ وَإِنَّ السَّاعَةَ لَآتِيَةٌ فَاصْفَحِ الصَّفْحَ الْجَمِيلَ ٨٥‏

86. Verily, your Lord is the All-Knowing Creator.

‏إِنَّ رَبَّكَ هُوَ الْخَلَّٰقُ الْعَلِيمُ ٨٦‏

87. And indeed, We have bestowed upon you seven of *Al-Mathâni* (seven repeatedly recited Verses, (i.e. *Sûrat Al-Fâtihah*) and the Grand Qur'ân.[1]

‏وَلَقَدْ ءَاتَيْنَٰكَ سَبْعًا مِّنَ الْمَثَانِى وَالْقُرْءَانَ الْعَظِيمَ ٨٧‏

88. Look not with your eyes ambitiously at what We have bestowed on certain classes of them (the disbelievers), nor grieve over them. And lower your wings for the believers (be courteous to the fellow-believers).

‏لَا تَمُدَّنَّ عَيْنَيْكَ إِلَىٰ مَا مَتَّعْنَا بِهِ أَزْوَٰجًا مِّنْهُمْ وَلَا تَحْزَنْ عَلَيْهِمْ وَاخْفِضْ جَنَاحَكَ لِلْمُؤْمِنِينَ ٨٨‏

89. And say (O Muhammad ﷺ): "I am indeed a plain warner."

‏وَقُلْ إِنِّى أَنَا النَّذِيرُ الْمُبِينُ ٨٩‏

90. As We have sent down on the dividers, (Quraish pagans or Jews and Christians).

‏كَمَا أَنزَلْنَا عَلَى الْمُقْتَسِمِينَ ٩٠‏

91. Who have made the Qur'ân into parts (i.e. believed in one part and disbelieved in the other). [*Tafsir At-Tabari*]

‏الَّذِينَ جَعَلُوا الْقُرْءَانَ عِضِينَ ٩١‏

92. So, by your Lord, (O Muhammad ﷺ), We shall certainly call all of them to account.

‏فَوَرَبِّكَ لَنَسْأَلَنَّهُمْ أَجْمَعِينَ ٩٢‏

---

[1] (V.15:87) See the footnote of (V.1:2).

93. For all that they used to do.

عَمَّا كَانُوا يَعْمَلُونَ ۝

94. Therefore proclaim openly (Allâh's Message — Islâmic Monotheism) that which you are commanded, and turn away from Al-Mushrikûn (polytheists, idolaters, and disbelievers, — See V.2:105).

فَاصْدَعْ بِمَا تُؤْمَرُ وَأَعْرِضْ عَنِ الْمُشْرِكِينَ ۝

95. Truly, We will suffice you against the scoffers,

إِنَّا كَفَيْنَاكَ الْمُسْتَهْزِئِينَ ۝

96. Who set up along with Allâh another ilâh (god); but they will come to know.

الَّذِينَ يَجْعَلُونَ مَعَ اللَّهِ إِلَٰهًا ءَاخَرَ فَسَوْفَ يَعْلَمُونَ ۝

97. Indeed, We know that your breast is straitened at what they say.

وَلَقَدْ نَعْلَمُ أَنَّكَ يَضِيقُ صَدْرُكَ بِمَا يَقُولُونَ ۝

98. So glorify the praises of your Lord and be of those who prostrate themselves (to Him).[1]

فَسَبِّحْ بِحَمْدِ رَبِّكَ وَكُن مِّنَ السَّاجِدِينَ ۝

99. And worship your Lord until there comes unto you the certainty (i.e. death).[2]

وَاعْبُدْ رَبَّكَ حَتَّىٰ يَأْتِيَكَ الْيَقِينُ ۝

---

[1] (V.15:98).

a) Narrated Abu Ma'bad, the freed slave of Ibn 'Abbâs: Ibn 'Abbâs رضي الله عنهما told me, "In the lifetime of the Prophet صلى الله عليه وسلم, it was the custom to remember Allâh (Dhikr) by glorifying, praising and magnifying Allâh aloud after the compulsory congregational prayers." Ibn 'Abbâs further said, "When I heard the Dhikr, I would learn that the compulsory congregational prayer had ended." (Sahih Al-Bukhari, Vol.1, Hadith No.802).

b) Narrated Ibn 'Abbâs رضي الله عنهما: I used to recognize the completion of the prayer of the Prophet صلى الله عليه وسلم by hearing Takbîr. (Sahih Al-Bukhari, Vol.1, Hadith No.803).

[2] (V.15:99) Narrated Anas رضي الله عنه: Allâh's Messenger صلى الله عليه وسلم said, "None of you should long for death because of a calamity that had befallen him; and if he cannot, but long for death, then he

Sûrat An-Nahl (The Bee) XVI

سُورَةُ النَّحْلِ

*In the Name of Allâh
the Most Gracious, the Most Merciful*

بِسْمِ اللهِ الرَّحْمَنِ الرَّحِيمِ

1. The Event (the Hour or the punishment of disbelievers and polytheists or the Islâmic laws or commandments) ordained by Allâh will come to pass, so seek not to hasten it. Glorified and Exalted is He above all that they associate as partners with Him.

2. He sends down the angels with the *Rûh* (revelation) of His Command to whom of His slaves He wills (saying): "Warn mankind that *Lâ ilâha illa Ana* (none has the right to be worshipped but I), so fear Me (by abstaining from sins and evil deeds).

3. He has created the heavens and the earth with truth. High, is He Exalted above all that they associate as partners with Him.

4. He has created man from *Nutfah* (mixed drops of male and female sexual discharge), then behold, this same (man) becomes an open opponent.

5. And the cattle, He has created them for you; in them there is warmth (warm clothing), and numerous benefits, and of them you eat.

---

should say, 'O Allâh! Let me live as long as life is better for me, and take my life if death is better for me.'" (*Sahih Al-Bukhari*, Vol.8, *Hadith* No.362).

6. And wherein is beauty for you, when you bring them home in the evening, and as you lead them forth to pasture in the morning.

7. And they carry your loads to a land that you could not reach except with great trouble to yourselves. Truly, your Lord is full of kindness, Most Merciful.

8. And (He has created) horses, mules and donkeys, for you to ride and as an adornment. And He creates (other) things of which you have no knowledge.

9. And upon Allâh is the responsibility to explain the Straight Path.[1] But there are ways that turn aside (such as Paganism, Judaism, Christianity). And had He willed, He would have guided you all (mankind).

10. He it is Who sends down water (rain) from the sky; from it you drink and from it (grows) the vegetation on which you send your cattle to pasture.

11. With it He causes to grow for you the crops, the olives, the date-palms, the grapes, and every kind of fruit. Verily, in this is indeed an evident proof and a manifest sign for people who give thought.

---

[1] (V.16:9) Straight Path: i.e., Islâmic Monotheism for mankind i.e. to show them legal and illegal, good and evil things, so whosoever accepts the guidance, it will be for his own benefit and whosoever goes astray, it will be for his own destruction.

12. And He has subjected to you the night and the day, and the sun and the moon; and the stars are subjected by His Command. Surely, in this are proofs for people who understand.

وَسَخَّرَ لَكُمُ الَّيْلَ وَالنَّهَارَ وَالشَّمْسَ وَالْقَمَرَ وَالنُّجُومُ مُسَخَّرَاتٌ بِأَمْرِهِ إِنَّ فِي ذَٰلِكَ لَآيَاتٍ لِّقَوْمٍ يَعْقِلُونَ ﴿١٢﴾

13. And whatsoever He has created for you on the earth of varying colours [and qualities from vegetation and fruits (botanical life) and from animals (zoological life)]. Verily, in this is a sign for people who remember.

وَمَا ذَرَأَ لَكُمْ فِي الْأَرْضِ مُخْتَلِفًا أَلْوَانُهُ إِنَّ فِي ذَٰلِكَ لَآيَةً لِّقَوْمٍ يَذَّكَّرُونَ ﴿١٣﴾

14. And He it is Who has subjected the sea (to you), that you may eat thereof fresh tender meat (i.e. fish), and that you bring forth out of it ornaments to wear. And you see the ships ploughing through it, that you may seek (thus) of His Bounty (by transporting the goods from place to place) and that you may be grateful.

وَهُوَ الَّذِي سَخَّرَ الْبَحْرَ لِتَأْكُلُوا مِنْهُ لَحْمًا طَرِيًّا وَتَسْتَخْرِجُوا مِنْهُ حِلْيَةً تَلْبَسُونَهَا وَتَرَى الْفُلْكَ مَوَاخِرَ فِيهِ وَلِتَبْتَغُوا مِن فَضْلِهِ وَلَعَلَّكُمْ تَشْكُرُونَ ﴿١٤﴾

15. And He has affixed into the earth mountains standing firm, lest it should shake with you; and rivers and roads, that you may guide yourselves.

وَأَلْقَىٰ فِي الْأَرْضِ رَوَاسِيَ أَن تَمِيدَ بِكُمْ وَأَنْهَارًا وَسُبُلًا لَّعَلَّكُمْ تَهْتَدُونَ ﴿١٥﴾

16. And landmarks (signposts, during the day) and by the stars (during the night), they (mankind) guide themselves.

وَعَلَامَاتٍ وَبِالنَّجْمِ هُمْ يَهْتَدُونَ ﴿١٦﴾

17. Is then He, Who creates as one who creates not? Will you not then remember?

أَفَمَن يَخْلُقُ كَمَن لَّا يَخْلُقُ أَفَلَا تَذَكَّرُونَ ﴿١٧﴾

18. And if you would count the favours of Allâh, never could you be able to count them. Truly, Allâh is Oft-Forgiving, Most Merciful.

وَإِن تَعُدُّوا نِعْمَةَ اللَّهِ لَا تُحْصُوهَا إِنَّ اللَّهَ لَغَفُورٌ رَّحِيمٌ ﴿١٨﴾

19. And Allâh knows what you conceal and what you reveal.

وَاللَّهُ يَعْلَمُ مَا تُسِرُّونَ وَمَا تُعْلِنُونَ ۝

20. Those whom they (Al-Mushrikûn)[1] invoke besides Allâh have not created anything, but are themselves created.

وَالَّذِينَ يَدْعُونَ مِن دُونِ اللَّهِ لَا يَخْلُقُونَ شَيْئًا وَهُمْ يُخْلَقُونَ ۝

21. (They are) dead, not alive; and they know not when they will be raised up.

أَمْوَٰتٌ غَيْرُ أَحْيَآءٍ وَمَا يَشْعُرُونَ ۝ أَيَّانَ يُبْعَثُونَ ۝

22. Your Ilâh[2] (God) is One Ilâh (God — Allâh, none has the right to be worshipped but He). But for those who believe not in the Hereafter, their hearts deny (the faith in the Oneness of Allâh), and they are proud.[3]

إِلَٰهُكُمْ إِلَٰهٌ وَٰحِدٌ فَالَّذِينَ لَا يُؤْمِنُونَ بِالْآخِرَةِ قُلُوبُهُم مُّنكِرَةٌ وَهُم مُّسْتَكْبِرُونَ ۝

23. Certainly, Allâh knows what they conceal and what they reveal. Truly, He likes not the proud.

لَا جَرَمَ أَنَّ اللَّهَ يَعْلَمُ مَا يُسِرُّونَ وَمَا يُعْلِنُونَ إِنَّهُ لَا يُحِبُّ الْمُسْتَكْبِرِينَ ۝

24. And when it is said to them: "What is it that your Lord has sent down (unto Muhammad صلى الله عليه وسلم)?" They say: "Tales of the men of old!"

وَإِذَا قِيلَ لَهُم مَّاذَآ أَنزَلَ رَبُّكُمْ قَالُوٓا أَسَٰطِيرُ الْأَوَّلِينَ ۝

25. That they may bear their own burdens in full on the Day of Resurrection, and also of the burdens of those whom they misled without knowledge. Evil indeed is that which they shall bear!

لِيَحْمِلُوٓا أَوْزَارَهُمْ كَامِلَةً يَوْمَ الْقِيَٰمَةِ وَمِنْ أَوْزَارِ الَّذِينَ يُضِلُّونَهُم بِغَيْرِ عِلْمٍ أَلَا سَآءَ مَا يَزِرُونَ ۝

26. Those before them indeed plotted, but Allâh struck at the foundation of their building, and then

قَدْ مَكَرَ الَّذِينَ مِن قَبْلِهِمْ فَأَتَى اللَّهُ بُنْيَٰنَهُم مِّنَ الْقَوَاعِدِ فَخَرَّ عَلَيْهِمُ السَّقْفُ

---

[1] (V.16:20) Al-Mushrikûn: i.e. polytheists, pagans, idolaters, disbelievers in the Oneness of Allâh, those who worship others along with Allâh, and also those who set up rivals with (or partners to) Allâh.

[2] (V.16:22) Ilâh: He who has all the right to be worshipped.

[3] (V.16:22) See the footnote of (V.22:9).

the roof fell down upon them, from above them, and the torment overtook them from directions they did not perceive.

27. Then, on the Day of Resurrection, He will disgrace them and will say: "Where are My (so-called) partners concerning whom you used to disagree and dispute (with the believers, by defying and disobeying Allâh)?" Those who have been given the knowledge (about the Torment of Allâh for the disbelievers) will say: "Verily, disgrace and misery this Day are upon the disbelievers.

28. "Those whose lives the angels take while they are doing wrong to themselves (by disbelief and by associating partners in worship with Allâh and by committing all kinds of crimes and evil deeds)." Then, they will make (false) submission (saying): "We used not to do any evil." (The angels will reply): "Yes! Truly, Allâh is All-Knower of what you used to do.

29. "So enter the gates of Hell, to abide therein,[1] and indeed, what an evil abode will be for the arrogant."

30. And (when) it is said to those who are the *Muttaqûn* (the pious. See V.2:2) "What is it that your Lord has sent down?" They say: "That which is good." For those who do good in this world, there is good, and the home of the Hereafter will be better. And

---

[1] (V.16:29) See the footnote of (V.2:31)

excellent indeed will be the home (i.e. Paradise) of the *Muttaqûn* (the pious. See V.2:2).

31. *'Adn* (Eden) Paradise (Gardens of Eternity) which they will enter, under which rivers flow, they will have therein all that they wish. Thus Allâh rewards the *Muttaqûn* (the pious. See V.2:2).

32. Those whose lives the angels take while they are in a pious state (i.e. pure from all evil, and worshipping none but Allâh Alone) saying (to them): *Salâmun 'Alaikum* (peace be on you) enter you Paradise, because of that (the good) which you used to do (in the world)."

33. Do they (the disbelievers and polytheists) await but that the angels should come to them [to take away their souls (at death)], or there should come the command (i.e. the torment or the Day of Resurrection) of your Lord? Thus did those before them. And Allâh wronged them not, but they used to wrong themselves.

34. Then, the evil results of their deeds overtook them, and that at which they used to mock at surrounded them.

35. And those who joined others in worship with Allâh said: "If Allâh had so willed, neither we nor our fathers would have worshipped aught but Him, nor would we have forbidden anything without (Command from) Him." So did those before them. Then! Are the

الرُّسُلِ إِلَّا الْبَلَٰغُ الْمُبِينُ ۝

Messengers charged with anything but to convey clearly the Message?

36. And verily, We have sent among every *Ummah* (community, nation) a Messenger (proclaiming): "Worship Allâh (Alone), and avoid (or keep away from) *Tâghût*[1] (all false deities, i.e. do not worship *Tâghût* besides Allâh)." Then of them were some whom Allâh guided and of them were some upon whom the straying was justified. So travel through the land and see what was the end of those who denied (the truth).

وَلَقَدۡ بَعَثۡنَا فِى كُلِّ أُمَّةٍ رَّسُولًا أَنِ اعۡبُدُوا اللَّهَ وَاجۡتَنِبُوا الطَّٰغُوتَ فَمِنۡهُم مَّنۡ هَدَى اللَّهُ وَمِنۡهُم مَّنۡ حَقَّتۡ عَلَيۡهِ الضَّلَٰلَةُ فَسِيرُوا فِى الۡأَرۡضِ فَانظُرُوا كَيۡفَ كَانَ عَٰقِبَةُ الۡمُكَذِّبِينَ ۝

37. If you (O Muhammad صلى الله عليه وسلم) covet for their guidance,[2] then verily, Allâh guides not those whom He makes to go astray (or none can guide him whom Allâh sends astray). And they will have no helpers.

إِن تَحۡرِصۡ عَلَىٰ هُدَىٰهُمۡ فَإِنَّ اللَّهَ لَا يَهۡدِى مَن يُضِلُّ وَمَا لَهُم مِّن نَّٰصِرِينَ ۝

38. And they swear by Allâh their strongest oaths, that Allâh will not raise up him who dies. Yes, (He will raise them up), — a promise (binding) upon

وَأَقۡسَمُوا بِاللَّهِ جَهۡدَ أَيۡمَٰنِهِمۡ لَا يَبۡعَثُ اللَّهُ مَن يَمُوتُ بَلَىٰ وَعۡدًا عَلَيۡهِ حَقًّا وَلَٰكِنَّ أَكۡثَرَ النَّاسِ

---

[1] *Tâghut:* See the footnote of (V.2:256).

[2] (V.16:37) Narrated Abu Hurairah رضى الله عنه I heard Allâh's Messenger صلى الله عليه وسلم saying, "My example and the example of the people is that of a man who made a fire, and when it lighted what was around it, moths and other insects started falling into the fire. The man tried (his best) to prevent them, (from falling in the fire) but they overpowered him and rushed into the fire." The Prophet صلى الله عليه وسلم added; "Now, similarly, I take hold of the knots at your waist (belts) to prevent you from falling into the fire, but you insist on falling into it."* (*Sahih Al-Bukhari*, Vol.8, Hadith No.490).

*The fire symbolizes the unlawful deeds which the Prophet صلى الله عليه وسلم warned the people of.

Him in truth, but most of mankind know not.

39. In order that He may make manifest to them the truth of that wherein they differ, and that those who disbelieved (in Resurrection, and in the Oneness of Allâh) may know that they were liars.

40. Verily, Our Word unto a thing when We intend it, is only that We say unto it: "Be!" — and it is.

41. And as for those who emigrated for the Cause of Allâh, after they had been wronged, We will certainly give them goodly residence in this world, but indeed the reward of the Hereafter will be greater; if they but knew!

42. (They are) those who remained patient (in this world for Allâh's sake), and put their trust in their Lord (Allâh Alone).

43. And We sent not (as Our Messengers) before you (O Muhammad صلى الله عليه وسلم) any but men, whom We sent revelation, (to preach and invite mankind to believe in the Oneness of Allâh). So ask (you, O pagans of Makkah) of those who know the Scripture [learned men of the Taurât (Torah) and the Injeel (Gospel)], if you know not.

44. With clear signs and Books (We sent the Messengers). And We have also sent down unto you (O Muhammad صلى الله عليه وسلم) the *Dhikr* [reminder and the advice (i.e. the Qur'ân)], that you may explain clearly to men what is sent down to them, and that they may give thought.

45. Do then those who devise evil plots feel secure that Allâh will not sink them into the earth, or that the torment will not seize them from directions they perceive not?

أَفَأَمِنَ ٱلَّذِينَ مَكَرُواْ ٱلسَّيِّئَاتِ أَن يَخْسِفَ ٱللَّهُ بِهِمُ ٱلْأَرْضَ أَوْ يَأْتِيَهُمُ ٱلْعَذَابُ مِنْ حَيْثُ لَا يَشْعُرُونَ ۝

46. Or that He may catch them in the midst of their going to and fro (in their jobs), so that there be no escape for them (from Allâh's punishment)?

أَوْ يَأْخُذَهُمْ فِي تَقَلُّبِهِمْ فَمَا هُم بِمُعْجِزِينَ ۝

47. Or that He may catch them with gradual wasting (of their wealth and health). Truly, Your Lord is indeed full of kindness, Most Merciful?

أَوْ يَأْخُذَهُمْ عَلَىٰ تَخَوُّفٍ فَإِنَّ رَبَّكُمْ لَرَءُوفٌ رَّحِيمٌ ۝

48. Have they not observed things that Allâh has created: (how) their shadows incline to the right and to the left, making prostration unto Allâh, and they are lowly?

أَوَلَمْ يَرَوْاْ إِلَىٰ مَا خَلَقَ ٱللَّهُ مِن شَىْءٍ يَتَفَيَّؤُاْ ظِلَالُهُ عَنِ ٱلْيَمِينِ وَٱلشَّمَآئِلِ سُجَّدًا لِّلَّهِ وَهُمْ دَاخِرُونَ ۝

49. And to Allâh prostrate all that is in the heavens and all that is in the earth, of the moving (living) creatures and the angels, and they are not proud [i.e. they worship their Lord (Allâh) with humility].

وَلِلَّهِ يَسْجُدُ مَا فِي ٱلسَّمَٰوَٰتِ وَمَا فِي ٱلْأَرْضِ مِن دَآبَّةٍ وَٱلْمَلَٰٓئِكَةُ وَهُمْ لَا يَسْتَكْبِرُونَ ۝

50. They fear their Lord above them, and they do what they are commanded.

يَخَافُونَ رَبَّهُم مِّن فَوْقِهِمْ وَيَفْعَلُونَ مَا يُؤْمَرُونَ ۝

51. And Allâh said (O mankind!): "Take not *ilâhain* (two gods in worship). Verily, He (Allâh) is (the) only One *Ilâh*[1] (God). Then, fear Me (Allâh) much [and Me (Alone), i.e. be away from all kinds of sins and evil deeds that Allâh has forbidden and

وَقَالَ ٱللَّهُ لَا تَتَّخِذُوٓاْ إِلَٰهَيْنِ ٱثْنَيْنِ إِنَّمَا هُوَ إِلَٰهٌ وَٰحِدٌ فَإِيَّـٰىَ فَٱرْهَبُونِ ۝

---

[1] (V.16:51) *Ilâh*: Who has all the right to be worshipped.

do all that Allâh has ordained and worship none but Allâh].[1]

52. To Him belongs all that is in the heavens and (all that is in) the earth and *Ad-Dîn Wâsiba* is His [(i.e. perpetual sincere obedience to Allâh is obligatory). None has the right to be worshipped but Allâh)]. Will you then fear any other than Allâh?

وَلَهُ مَا فِى السَّمَوَاتِ وَالْأَرْضِ وَلَهُ الدِّينُ وَاصِبًا أَفَغَيْرَ اللَّهِ تَتَّقُونَ ٥٢

53. And whatever of blessings and good things you have, it is from Allâh. Then, when harm touches you, unto Him you cry aloud for help.

وَمَا بِكُم مِّن نِّعْمَةٍ فَمِنَ اللَّهِ ثُمَّ إِذَا مَسَّكُمُ الضُّرُّ فَإِلَيْهِ تَجْـَرُونَ ٥٣

54. Then, when He has removed the harm from you, behold! some of you associate others in worship with their Lord (Allâh).

ثُمَّ إِذَا كَشَفَ الضُّرَّ عَنكُمْ إِذَا فَرِيقٌ مِّنكُم بِرَبِّهِمْ يُشْرِكُونَ ٥٤

55. So (as a result of that) they deny (with ungratefulness) that (Allâh's Favours) which We have bestowed on them! Then enjoy yourselves (your short stay), but you will come to know (with regrets).

لِيَكْفُرُوا بِمَا آتَيْنَاهُمْ فَتَمَتَّعُوا فَسَوْفَ تَعْلَمُونَ ٥٥

56. And they assign a portion of that which We have provided them unto

وَيَجْعَلُونَ لِمَا لَا يَعْلَمُونَ نَصِيبًا مِّمَّا

---

[1] (V.16:51) Narrated 'Ubâdah ﺭﺿﻲ ﺍﷲ ﻋﻨﻪ The Prophet ﺻﻠﻰ ﺍﷲ ﻋﻠﻴﻪ ﻭﺳﻠﻢ said, "If anyone testifies that *Lâ ilâha illallâh* (none has the right to be worshipped but Allâh Alone) Who has no partners, and that Muhammad ﺻﻠﻰ ﺍﷲ ﻋﻠﻴﻪ ﻭﺳﻠﻢ is His slave and His Messenger, and that 'Îsâ (Jesus) ﻋﻠﻴﻪ ﺍﻟﺴﻼﻡ is Allâh's slave and His Messenger and His Word ("Be!" - and he was) which He bestowed on Maryam (Mary) and a spirit (*Rûh*) created by Him, and that Paradise is the truth, and Hell is the truth, Allâh will admit him into Paradise with the deeds which he had done even if those deeds were few." (Junadah, the subnarrator said, "'Ubâdah added, 'Such a person can enter Paradise through any of its eight gates he likes.'") (*Sahih Al-Bukhari*, Vol. 4, *Hadith* No. 644).

what they know not (false deities). By Allâh, you shall certainly be questioned about (all) that you used to fabricate.

57. And they assign daughters unto Allâh! — Glorified (and Exalted) is He above all that they associate with Him! And unto themselves what they desire;

58. And when the news of (the birth of) a female (child) is brought to any of them, his face becomes dark, and he is filled with inward grief!

59. He hides himself from the people because of the evil of that whereof he has been informed. Shall he keep her with dishonour or bury her in the earth?[1] Certainly, evil is their decision.

60. For those who believe not in the Hereafter is an evil description, and for Allâh is the highest description. And He is the All-Mighty, the All-Wise.

61. And if Allâh were to seize mankind for their wrong-doing, He would not leave on it (the earth) a single moving (living) creature, but He postpones them for an appointed term and when their term comes, neither can

---

[1] (V.16:59) Narrated Al-Mughirah: The Prophet ﷺ used to forbid (1) *Qîl* and *Qâl* (sinful and useless talk like backbiting, or that you talk too much about others); (2) asking too many questions (in disputed religious matters); (3) and wasting one's wealth (by extravagance) (4) and to be undutiful to one's mother (5) and to bury the daughters alive (6) and to prevent your favours (benevolence) to others (i.e. not to pay the rights of others: *Zakât*, charity). (7) and to beg of men or to ask others for something (except when it is unavoidable). (*Sahih Al-Bukhari*, Vol.9, Hadith No.395).

they delay nor can they advance it an hour (or a moment).

62. They assign to Allâh that which they dislike (for themselves), and their tongues assert the falsehood that the better things will be theirs. No doubt for them is the Fire, and they will be the first to be hastened on into it, and left there neglected. (*Tafsir Al-Qurtubî*)

63. By Allâh, We indeed sent (Messengers) to the nations before you (O Muhammad صلى الله عليه وسلم), but Shaitân (Satan) made their deeds fair-seeming to them. So he (Satan) is their *Wali* (helper) today (i.e. in this world), and theirs will be a painful torment.

64. And We have not sent down the Book (the Qur'ân) to you (O Muhammad صلى الله عليه وسلم), except that you may explain clearly unto them those things in which they differ, and (as) a guidance and a mercy for a folk who believe.

65. And Allâh sends down water (rain) from the sky, then He revives the earth therewith after its death. Verily, in this is a sign (clear proof) for people who listen (obey Allâh).

66. And verily, in the cattle, there is a lesson for you. We give you to drink of that which is in their bellies, from between excretions and blood, pure milk; palatable to the drinkers.

67. And from the fruits of date-palms and grapes, you derive strong drink and a goodly provision. Verily, therein is indeed a sign for people who have wisdom.

68. And your Lord inspired the bee, saying: "Take you habitations in the mountains and in the trees and in what they erect.

69. "Then, eat of all fruits, and follow the ways of your Lord made easy (for you)." There comes forth from their bellies, a drink of varying colour wherein is healing for men. Verily, in this is indeed a sign for people who think.

70. And Allâh has created you and then He will cause you to die; and of you there are some who are sent back to senility, so that they know nothing after having known (much). Truly, Allâh is All-Knowing, All-Powerful.

71. And Allâh has preferred some of you above others in wealth and properties. Then, those who are preferred will by no means hand over their wealth and properties to those (slaves) whom their right hands possess, so that they may be equal with them in respect thereof.[1] Do they then deny the Favour of Allâh?

حَسَنًا إِنَّ فِي ذَٰلِكَ لَآيَةً لِّقَوْمٍ يَعْقِلُونَ ۝

وَأَوْحَىٰ رَبُّكَ إِلَى ٱلنَّحْلِ أَنِ ٱتَّخِذِي مِنَ ٱلْجِبَالِ بُيُوتًا وَمِنَ ٱلشَّجَرِ وَمِمَّا يَعْرِشُونَ ۝

ثُمَّ كُلِي مِن كُلِّ ٱلثَّمَرَٰتِ فَٱسْلُكِي سُبُلَ رَبِّكِ ذُلُلًا يَخْرُجُ مِنۢ بُطُونِهَا شَرَابٌ مُّخْتَلِفٌ أَلْوَٰنُهُۥ فِيهِ شِفَآءٌ لِّلنَّاسِ إِنَّ فِي ذَٰلِكَ لَآيَةً لِّقَوْمٍ يَتَفَكَّرُونَ ۝

وَٱللَّهُ خَلَقَكُمْ ثُمَّ يَتَوَفَّىٰكُمْ وَمِنكُم مَّن يُرَدُّ إِلَىٰ أَرْذَلِ ٱلْعُمُرِ لِكَيْ لَا يَعْلَمَ بَعْدَ عِلْمٍ شَيْـًٔا إِنَّ ٱللَّهَ عَلِيمٌ قَدِيرٌ ۝

وَٱللَّهُ فَضَّلَ بَعْضَكُمْ عَلَىٰ بَعْضٍ فِي ٱلرِّزْقِ فَمَا ٱلَّذِينَ فُضِّلُوا۟ بِرَآدِّي رِزْقِهِمْ عَلَىٰ مَا مَلَكَتْ أَيْمَٰنُهُمْ فَهُمْ فِيهِ سَوَآءٌ أَفَبِنِعْمَةِ ٱللَّهِ يَجْحَدُونَ ۝

---

[1] (V.16:71):

a) This example Allâh has set forth for the polytheists (pagans) who associate false deities with Allâh, that they would not agree to share their wealth and properties with their slaves, then how do they agree to share false deities with Allâh in His worship?

72. And Allâh has made for you *Azwâj* (mates or wives) of your own kind, and has made for you, from your wives, sons and grandsons, and has

وَاللَّهُ جَعَلَ لَكُم مِّنْ أَنفُسِكُمْ
أَزْوَٰجًا وَجَعَلَ لَكُم مِّنْ
أَزْوَٰجِكُم بَنِينَ وَحَفَدَةً

---

b) Allâh's Statement: "And Allâh ..." (V.16:71). Narrated Abu Hurairah رضي الله عنه: The Prophet صلى الله عليه وسلم said, "Prophet Ibrâhîm (Abraham) emigrated with Sârah and entered a village where there was a king from amongst the kings or a tyrant from amongst the tyrants. (The king) was told that Ibrâhîm (Abraham) had entered (the village) accompanied by a woman who was one of the most charming women. So, the king sent for Ibrâhîm (Abraham) and asked, 'O Ibrâhîm (Abraham)! Who is this lady accompanying you?' Ibrâhîm (Abraham) replied, 'She is my sister (i.e., in religion).' Then Ibrâhîm (Abraham) returned to her and said, 'Do not contradict my statement, for I have informed them that you are my sister. By Allâh, there are not true believers on the earth except you and I.' Then Ibrâhîm (Abraham) sent her to the king. When the king got to her, she got up and performed ablution, offered *Salât* (prayer) and said, 'O Allâh! If I have believed in You and Your Messenger, and have saved my private parts from everybody except my husband, then please do not let this disbeliever overpower me.' On that the king fell in a state of unconsciousness (or had an epileptic fit) and started moving his legs. Seeing the condition of the king, Sârah said, 'O Allâh! If he should die, the people will say that I have killed him.' The king regained his power, and proceeded towards her but she got up again and performed ablution, offered *Salât* (prayer) and said, 'O Allâh! If I have believed in You and Your Messenger and have kept my private parts safe from all except my husband, then please do not let this disbeliever overpower me.' The king again fell in a state of unconsciousness (or had epileptic fit) and started moving his legs. On seeing that state of the king, Sârah said, 'O Allâh! If he should die, the people will say that I have killed him.' The king got either two or three attacks, and after recovering from the last attack he said, 'By Allâh! You have sent a Satan to me. Take her to Ibrâhîm (Abraham) and give her Agar (**Hagar**).' So she came back to Ibrâhîm (Abraham) and said, 'Allâh humiliated the disbeliever and gave us a slave-girl for service.'"
(*Sahih Al-Bukhari*, Vol. 3, Hadith No. 420)

bestowed on you good provision. Do they then believe in false deities and deny the Favour of Allâh (by not worshipping Allâh Alone)?

وَرَزَقَكُم مِّنَ الطَّيِّبَاتِ أَفَبِالْبَاطِلِ يُؤْمِنُونَ وَبِنِعْمَتِ اللَّهِ هُمْ يَكْفُرُونَ ٧٢

73. And they worship others besides Allâh — such as do not and cannot own any provision for them from the heavens or the earth?

وَيَعْبُدُونَ مِن دُونِ اللَّهِ مَا لَا يَمْلِكُ لَهُمْ رِزْقًا مِّنَ السَّمَاوَاتِ وَالْأَرْضِ شَيْئًا وَلَا يَسْتَطِيعُونَ ٧٣

74. So put not forward similitudes for Allâh (as there is nothing similar to Him, nor He resembles anything). Truly, Allâh knows and you know not.

فَلَا تَضْرِبُوا لِلَّهِ الْأَمْثَالَ إِنَّ اللَّهَ يَعْلَمُ وَأَنتُمْ لَا تَعْلَمُونَ ٧٤

75. Allâh puts forward the example of (two men — a believer and a disbeliever); a slave (disbeliever) under the possession of another, he has no power of any sort, and (the other), a man (believer) on whom We have bestowed a good provision from Us, and he spends thereof secretly and openly. Can they be equal? (By no means). All the praises and thanks are to Allâh. Nay! (But) most of them know not.

۞ ضَرَبَ اللَّهُ مَثَلًا عَبْدًا مَّمْلُوكًا لَّا يَقْدِرُ عَلَىٰ شَيْءٍ وَمَن رَّزَقْنَاهُ مِنَّا رِزْقًا حَسَنًا فَهُوَ يُنفِقُ مِنْهُ سِرًّا وَجَهْرًا هَلْ يَسْتَوُونَ الْحَمْدُ لِلَّهِ بَلْ أَكْثَرُهُمْ لَا يَعْلَمُونَ ٧٥

76. And Allâh puts forward (another) example of two men, one of them dumb, who has no power over anything (disbeliever), and he is a burden on his master; whichever way he directs him, he brings no good. Is such a man equal to one (believer in the Islâmic Monotheism) who commands justice, and is himself on the Straight Path?

وَضَرَبَ اللَّهُ مَثَلًا رَّجُلَيْنِ أَحَدُهُمَا أَبْكَمُ لَا يَقْدِرُ عَلَىٰ شَيْءٍ وَهُوَ كَلٌّ عَلَىٰ مَوْلَاهُ أَيْنَمَا يُوَجِّههُّ لَا يَأْتِ بِخَيْرٍ هَلْ يَسْتَوِي هُوَ وَمَن يَأْمُرُ بِالْعَدْلِ وَهُوَ عَلَىٰ صِرَاطٍ مُّسْتَقِيمٍ ٧٦

77. And to Allâh belongs the Unseen of the heavens and the earth. And the

وَلِلَّهِ غَيْبُ السَّمَاوَاتِ وَالْأَرْضِ وَمَا أَمْرُ

matter of the Hour is not but as a twinkling of the eye, or even nearer. Truly, Allâh is Able to do all things.

78. And Allâh has brought you out from the wombs of your mothers while you know nothing. And He gave you hearing, sight, and hearts that you might give thanks (to Allâh).

79. Do they not see the birds held (flying) in the midst of the sky? None holds them but Allâh [none gave them the ability to fly but Allâh]. Verily, in this are clear *Ayât* (proofs and signs) for people who believe (in the Oneness of Allâh).

80. And Allâh has made for you in your homes an abode, and made for you out of the hides of the cattle (tents for) dwelling, which you find so light (and handy) when you travel and when you stay (in your travels); and of their wool, fur, and hair (sheep wool, camel fur, and goat hair), furnishings and articles of convenience (e.g. carpets, blankets), comfort for a while.

81. And Allâh has made for you out of that which He has created shades, and has made for you places of refuge in the mountains, and has made for you garments to protect you from the heat (and cold), and coats of mail to protect you from your (mutual) violence. Thus does He perfect His favour unto you, that you may submit yourselves to His Will (in Islâm).

82. Then, if they turn away, your duty (O Muhammad صلى الله عليه وسلم) is only to convey (the Message) in a clear way.

فَإِن تَوَلَّوْا فَإِنَّمَا عَلَيْكَ ٱلْبَلَٰغُ ٱلْمُبِينُ ﴿٨٢﴾

83. They recognise the Grace of Allâh, yet they deny it (by worshipping others besides Allâh) and most of them are disbelievers (deny the Prophethood of Muhammad صلى الله عليه وسلم).

يَعْرِفُونَ نِعْمَتَ ٱللَّهِ ثُمَّ يُنكِرُونَهَا وَأَكْثَرُهُمُ ٱلْكَٰفِرُونَ ﴿٨٣﴾

84. And (remember) the Day when We shall raise up from each nation a witness (their Messenger), then, those who disbelieved will not be given leave (to put forward excuses), nor will they be allowed (to return to the world) to repent and ask for Allâh's Forgiveness (of their sins).

وَيَوْمَ نَبْعَثُ مِن كُلِّ أُمَّةٍ شَهِيدًا ثُمَّ لَا يُؤْذَنُ لِلَّذِينَ كَفَرُوا وَلَا هُمْ يُسْتَعْتَبُونَ ﴿٨٤﴾

85. And when those who did wrong (the disbelievers) will see the torment, then it will not be lightened unto them, nor will they be given respite.

وَإِذَا رَءَا ٱلَّذِينَ ظَلَمُوا ٱلْعَذَابَ فَلَا يُخَفَّفُ عَنْهُمْ وَلَا هُمْ يُنظَرُونَ ﴿٨٥﴾

86. And when those who associated partners with Allâh see their (Allâh's so-called) partners, they will say: "Our Lord! These are our partners whom we used to invoke besides you." But they will throw back their word at them (and say): "Surely, you indeed are liars!"

وَإِذَا رَءَا ٱلَّذِينَ أَشْرَكُوا شُرَكَآءَهُمْ قَالُوا رَبَّنَا هَٰٓؤُلَآءِ شُرَكَآؤُنَا ٱلَّذِينَ كُنَّا نَدْعُوا مِن دُونِكَ فَأَلْقَوْا إِلَيْهِمُ ٱلْقَوْلَ إِنَّكُمْ لَكَٰذِبُونَ ﴿٨٦﴾

87. And they will offer (their full) submission to Allâh (Alone) on that Day, and their invented false deities [all that they used to invoke besides Allâh, e.g. idols, saints, priests, monks, angels, jinn, Jibraîl (Gabriel), Messengers] will vanish from them.

وَأَلْقَوْا إِلَى ٱللَّهِ يَوْمَئِذٍ ٱلسَّلَمَ وَضَلَّ عَنْهُم مَّا كَانُوا يَفْتَرُونَ ﴿٨٧﴾

88. Those who disbelieved and hinder (men) from the Path of Allâh, for them We will add torment to the torment because they used to spread corruption [by disobeying Allâh themselves, as well as ordering others (mankind) to do so].

الَّذِينَ كَفَرُوا وَصَدُّوا عَن سَبِيلِ اللَّهِ زِدْنَاهُمْ عَذَابًا فَوْقَ الْعَذَابِ بِمَا كَانُوا يُفْسِدُونَ ٨٨

89. And (remember) the Day when We shall raise up from every nation a witness against them from amongst themselves. And We shall bring you (O Muhammad صلى الله عليه وسلم) as a witness against these. And We have sent down to you the Book (the Qur'ân) as an exposition of everything, a guidance, a mercy, and glad tidings for those who have submitted themselves (to Allâh as Muslims).

وَيَوْمَ نَبْعَثُ فِي كُلِّ أُمَّةٍ شَهِيدًا عَلَيْهِم مِّنْ أَنفُسِهِمْ وَجِئْنَا بِكَ شَهِيدًا عَلَى هَؤُلَاءِ وَنَزَّلْنَا عَلَيْكَ الْكِتَابَ تِبْيَانًا لِّكُلِّ شَيْءٍ وَهُدًى وَرَحْمَةً وَبُشْرَى لِلْمُسْلِمِينَ ٨٩

90. Verily, Allâh enjoins Al-'Adl (i.e. justice and worshipping none but Allâh Alone — Islâmic Monotheism) and Al-Ihsân [i.e. to be patient in performing your duties to Allâh, totally for Allâh's sake and in accordance with the Sunnah (legal ways) of the Prophet صلى الله عليه وسلم in a perfect manner], and giving (help) to kith and kin[1] (i.e. all that Allâh has ordered you to give them e.g., wealth, visiting, looking after them, or any other kind of help), and forbids Al-Fahshâ' (i.e. all evil deeds,

إِنَّ اللَّهَ يَأْمُرُ بِالْعَدْلِ وَالْإِحْسَانِ وَإِيتَاءِ ذِي الْقُرْبَى وَيَنْهَى عَنِ الْفَحْشَاءِ وَالْمُنكَرِ وَالْبَغْيِ يَعِظُكُمْ لَعَلَّكُمْ تَذَكَّرُونَ ٩٠

[1] (V.16:90) Degree of kinship: First of all, your parents, then your offspring, then your brothers and sisters, then your paternal uncles and aunts (from your father's side), then your maternal uncles and aunts (from your mother's side), and then other relatives.

e.g. illegal sexual acts, disobedience of parents, polytheism, to tell lies, to give false witness, to kill a life without right), and *Al-Munkar* (i.e. all that is prohibited by Islâmic law: polytheism of every kind, disbelief and every kind of evil deeds), and *Al-Baghy* (i.e. all kinds of oppression). He admonishes you, that you may take heed.

91. And fulfil the Covenant of Allâh (*Bai'ah*: pledge for Islâm) when you have covenanted, and break not the oaths after you have confirmed them — and indeed you have appointed Allâh your surety. Verily, Allâh knows what you do.

وَأَوْفُوا بِعَهْدِ اللَّهِ إِذَا عَهَدتُّمْ وَلَا تَنقُضُوا الْأَيْمَـٰنَ بَعْدَ تَوْكِيدِهَا وَقَدْ جَعَلْتُمُ اللَّهَ عَلَيْكُمْ كَفِيلًا إِنَّ اللَّهَ يَعْلَمُ مَا تَفْعَلُونَ ٩١

92. And be not like her who undoes the thread which she has spun, after it has become strong, by taking your oaths as a means of deception among yourselves, lest a nation should be more numerous than another nation. Allâh only tests you by this [i.e. who obeys Allâh and fulfils Allâh's Covenant and who disobeys Allâh and breaks Allâh's Covenant]. And on the Day of Resurrection, He will certainly make clear to you that wherein you used to differ [i.e. a believer confesses and believes in the Oneness of Allâh and in the Prophethood of Prophet Muhammad صلى الله عليه وسلم which the disbeliever denies and that is their difference amongst them in the life of this world].[1]

وَلَا تَكُونُوا كَالَّتِي نَقَضَتْ غَزْلَهَا مِنۢ بَعْدِ قُوَّةٍ أَنكَـٰثًا تَتَّخِذُونَ أَيْمَـٰنَكُمْ دَخَلًا بَيْنَكُمْ أَن تَكُونَ أُمَّةٌ هِيَ أَرْبَىٰ مِنْ أُمَّةٍ إِنَّمَا يَبْلُوكُمُ اللَّهُ بِهِ وَلَيُبَيِّنَنَّ لَكُمْ يَوْمَ الْقِيَـٰمَةِ مَا كُنتُمْ فِيهِ تَخْتَلِفُونَ ٩٢

---

[1] (V.16:92) See the footnote of (V.3:85).

93. And had Allâh willed, He could have made you (all) one nation, but He sends astray whom He wills and guides whom He wills. But you shall certainly be called to account for what you used to do.

وَلَوْ شَاءَ اللَّهُ لَجَعَلَكُمْ أُمَّةً وَاحِدَةً وَلَكِن يُضِلُّ مَن يَشَاءُ وَيَهْدِى مَن يَشَاءُ وَلَتُسْئَلُنَّ عَمَّا كُنتُمْ تَعْمَلُونَ ٩٣

94. And make not your oaths, a means of deception among yourselves, lest a foot should slip after being firmly planted, and you may have to taste the evil (punishment in this world) of having hindered (men) from the Path of Allâh (i.e. belief in the Oneness of Allâh and His Messenger, Muhammad (صلى الله عليه وسلم)), and yours will be a great torment (i.e. the Fire of Hell in the Hereafter).

وَلَا تَتَّخِذُوا أَيْمَٰنَكُمْ دَخَلًا بَيْنَكُمْ فَتَزِلَّ قَدَمٌ بَعْدَ ثُبُوتِهَا وَتَذُوقُوا السُّوءَ بِمَا صَدَدتُّمْ عَن سَبِيلِ اللَّهِ وَلَكُمْ عَذَابٌ عَظِيمٌ ٩٤

95. And purchase not a small gain at the cost of Allâh's Covenant. Verily, what is with Allâh is better for you if you did but know.

وَلَا تَشْتَرُوا بِعَهْدِ اللَّهِ ثَمَنًا قَلِيلًا إِنَّمَا عِندَ اللَّهِ هُوَ خَيْرٌ لَّكُمْ إِن كُنتُمْ تَعْلَمُونَ ٩٥

96. Whatever is with you, will be exhausted, and whatever is with Allâh (of good deeds) will remain. And those who are patient, We will certainly pay them a reward in proportion to the best of what they used to do.[1]

مَا عِندَكُمْ يَنفَدُ وَمَا عِندَ اللَّهِ بَاقٍ وَلَنَجْزِيَنَّ الَّذِينَ صَبَرُوا أَجْرَهُم بِأَحْسَنِ مَا كَانُوا يَعْمَلُونَ ٩٦

97. Whoever works righteousness — whether male or female — while he (or she) is a true believer (of Islâmic Monotheism) verily, to him We will give a good life (in this world with respect, contentment and lawful provision), and We shall pay them

مَنْ عَمِلَ صَٰلِحًا مِّن ذَكَرٍ أَوْ أُنثَىٰ وَهُوَ مُؤْمِنٌ فَلَنُحْيِيَنَّهُ حَيَوٰةً طَيِّبَةً وَلَنَجْزِيَنَّهُمْ أَجْرَهُم بِأَحْسَنِ مَا كَانُوا يَعْمَلُونَ ٩٧

---

[1] (V.16:96) See the footnote of (V.9:121).

certainly a reward in proportion to the best of what they used to do (i.e. Paradise in the Hereafter).

98. So when you want to recite the Qur'ân, seek refuge with Allâh from *Shaitân* (Satan), the outcast (the cursed one).

فَإِذَا قَرَأْتَ ٱلْقُرْءَانَ فَٱسْتَعِذْ بِٱللَّهِ مِنَ ٱلشَّيْطَٰنِ ٱلرَّجِيمِ ۞

99. Verily, he has no power over those who believe and put their trust only in their Lord (Allâh).

إِنَّهُ لَيْسَ لَهُۥ سُلْطَٰنٌ عَلَى ٱلَّذِينَ ءَامَنُوا وَعَلَىٰ رَبِّهِمْ يَتَوَكَّلُونَ ۞

100. His power is only over those who obey and follow him (Satan), and those who join partners with Him (Allâh i.e. those who are *Mushrikûn* i.e., polytheists. See Verse 6:121).

إِنَّمَا سُلْطَٰنُهُۥ عَلَى ٱلَّذِينَ يَتَوَلَّوْنَهُۥ وَٱلَّذِينَ هُم بِهِۦ مُشْرِكُونَ ۞

101. And when We change a Verse (of the Qur'ân), in place of another — and Allâh knows best what He sends down — they (the disbelievers) say: "You (O Muhammad صلى الله عليه وسلم) are but a *Muftari*! (forger, liar)." Nay, but most of them know not.

وَإِذَا بَدَّلْنَآ ءَايَةً مَّكَانَ ءَايَةٍ وَٱللَّهُ أَعْلَمُ بِمَا يُنَزِّلُ قَالُوٓا إِنَّمَآ أَنتَ مُفْتَرٍ بَلْ أَكْثَرُهُمْ لَا يَعْلَمُونَ ۞

102. Say (O Muhammad صلى الله عليه وسلم) *Ruh-ul-Qudus* [Jibrael (Gabriel)] has brought it (the Qur'ân) down from your Lord with truth, that it may make firm and strengthen (the Faith of) those who believe, and as a guidance and glad tidings to those who have submitted (to Allâh as Muslims).

قُلْ نَزَّلَهُۥ رُوحُ ٱلْقُدُسِ مِن رَّبِّكَ بِٱلْحَقِّ لِيُثَبِّتَ ٱلَّذِينَ ءَامَنُوا وَهُدًى وَبُشْرَىٰ لِلْمُسْلِمِينَ ۞

103. And indeed We know that they (polytheists and pagans) say: "It is only a human being who teaches him (Muhammad صلى الله عليه وسلم)." The tongue of the man they refer to is foreign,

وَلَقَدْ نَعْلَمُ أَنَّهُمْ يَقُولُونَ إِنَّمَا يُعَلِّمُهُۥ بَشَرٌ لِّسَانُ ٱلَّذِي يُلْحِدُونَ إِلَيْهِ

while this (the Qur'ân) is a clear Arabic tongue.

104. Verily, those who believe not in the *Ayât* (proofs, evidences, verses, lessons, signs, revelations, etc.) of Allâh, Allâh will not guide them and theirs will be a painful torment.

105. It is only those who believe not in the *Ayât* (proofs, evidences, verses, lessons, signs, revelations, etc.) of Allâh, who fabricate falsehood, and it is they who are liars.

106. Whoever disbelieved in Allâh after his belief, except him who is forced thereto and whose heart is at rest with Faith; but such as open their breasts to disbelief, on them is wrath from Allâh, and theirs will be a great torment.

107. That is because they loved and preferred the life of this world over that of the Hereafter. And Allâh guides not the people who disbelieve.

108. They are those upon whose hearts, hearing (ears) and sight (eyes) Allâh has set a seal. And they are the heedless!

109. No doubt, in the Hereafter, they will be the losers.

110. Then, verily, your Lord — for those who emigrated after they had been put to trials and thereafter strove hard and fought (for the Cause of Allâh) and were patient, verily, your

Lord afterward is, Oft-Forgiving, Most Merciful.

111. (Remember) the Day when every person will come up pleading for himself, and every one will be paid in full for what he did (good or evil, belief or disbelief in the life of this world) and they will not be dealt with unjustly.

112. And Allâh puts forward the example of a township (Makkah), that dwelt secure and well-content: its provision coming to it in abundance from every place, but it (its people) denied the Favours of Allâh (with ungratefulness). So Allâh made it taste extreme of hunger (famine) and fear, because of that (evil, i.e. denying Prophet Muhammad صلى الله عليه وسلم) which they (its people) used to do.[1]

113. And verily, there had come unto them a Messenger (Muhammad صلى الله عليه وسلم) from among themselves, but they denied him, so the torment overtook them while they were *Zâlimûn* (polytheists and wrongdoers).

---

[1] (V.16:112) Narrated Ibn ʿAbbâs رضي الله عنهما The Prophet صلى الله عليه وسلم said, "I was shown the Hell-fire and that the majority of its dwellers were women who were disbelievers or ungrateful." He was asked, "Do they disbelieve in Allâh?" (or are they ungrateful to Allâh?) He replied, "They are ungrateful to their husbands and are ungrateful for the favours and the good (charitable deeds) done to them. If you have always been good (benevolent) to one of them for a period of time and then she sees something in you (not of her liking), she will say, 'I have never seen any good from you.'" (Sahih Al-Bukhari, Vol.1, Hadith No.28).

114. So eat of the lawful and good food[1] which Allâh has provided for you. And be grateful for the Graces of Allâh, if it is He Whom you worship.

فَكُلُوا مِمَّا رَزَقَكُمُ اللّٰهُ حَلَالًا طَيِّبًا وَاشْكُرُوا نِعْمَتَ اللّٰهِ إِنْ كُنْتُمْ إِيَّاهُ تَعْبُدُونَ ۝

115. He has forbidden you only Al-Maitah (meat of a dead animal), blood, the flesh of swine, and any animal which is slaughtered as a sacrifice for others than Allâh (or has been slaughtered for idols or on which Allâh's Name has not been mentioned while slaughtering). But if one is forced by necessity, without wilful disobedience, and not transgressing, — then, Allâh is Oft-Forgiving, Most Merciful.

إِنَّمَا حَرَّمَ عَلَيْكُمُ الْمَيْتَةَ وَالدَّمَ وَلَحْمَ الْخِنزِيرِ وَمَا أُهِلَّ لِغَيْرِ اللّٰهِ بِهِ ۖ فَمَنِ اضْطُرَّ غَيْرَ بَاغٍ وَلَا عَادٍ فَإِنَّ اللّٰهَ غَفُورٌ رَّحِيمٌ ۝

116. And say not concerning that which your tongues put forth falsely: "This is lawful and this is forbidden," so as to invent lies against Allâh. Verily, those who invent lies against Allâh will never prosper.

وَلَا تَقُولُوا لِمَا تَصِفُ أَلْسِنَتُكُمُ الْكَذِبَ هَٰذَا حَلَالٌ وَهَٰذَا حَرَامٌ لِّتَفْتَرُوا عَلَى اللّٰهِ الْكَذِبَ ۚ إِنَّ الَّذِينَ يَفْتَرُونَ عَلَى اللّٰهِ الْكَذِبَ لَا يُفْلِحُونَ ۝

117. A passing brief enjoyment (will be theirs), but they will have a painful torment.

مَتَاعٌ قَلِيلٌ وَلَهُمْ عَذَابٌ أَلِيمٌ ۝

118. And unto those who are Jews, We have forbidden such things as We have mentioned to you (O Muhammad صلى الله عليه وسلم) before (see Verse 6:146). And We wronged them not, but they used to wrong themselves.

وَعَلَى الَّذِينَ هَادُوا حَرَّمْنَا مَا قَصَصْنَا عَلَيْكَ مِن قَبْلُ ۖ وَمَا ظَلَمْنَاهُمْ وَلَٰكِن كَانُوا أَنفُسَهُمْ يَظْلِمُونَ ۝

---

[1] (V.16:114) The meat of cattle beast which Allâh has made lawful to you (Muslims) and are slaughtered according to Islâmic way.

119. Then, verily, your Lord — for those who do evil (commit sins and are disobedient to Allâh) in ignorance and afterward repent and do righteous deeds, verily, your Lord thereafter, (to such) is Oft-Forgiving, Most Merciful.

ثُمَّ إِنَّ رَبَّكَ لِلَّذِينَ عَمِلُواْ السُّوٓءَ بِجَهَٰلَةٖ ثُمَّ تَابُواْ مِنۢ بَعۡدِ ذَٰلِكَ وَأَصۡلَحُوٓاْ إِنَّ رَبَّكَ مِنۢ بَعۡدِهَا لَغَفُورٞ رَّحِيمٌ ۝

120. Verily, Ibrâhîm (Abraham) was an *Ummah* (a leader having all the good righteous qualities), or a nation, obedient to Allâh, *Hanîfa* (i.e. to worship none but Allâh), and he was not one of those who were *Al-Mushrikûn* (polytheists, idolaters, disbelievers in the Oneness of Allâh, and those who joined partners with Allâh).

إِنَّ إِبۡرَٰهِيمَ كَانَ أُمَّةٗ قَانِتٗا لِّلَّهِ حَنِيفٗا وَلَمۡ يَكُ مِنَ ٱلۡمُشۡرِكِينَ ۝

121. (He was) thankful for His (Allâh's) favours. He (Allâh) chose him (as an intimate friend) and guided him to a Straight Path (Islâmic Monotheism — neither Judaism nor Christianity)[1].

شَاكِرٗا لِّأَنۡعُمِهِۚ ٱجۡتَبَىٰهُ وَهَدَىٰهُ إِلَىٰ صِرَٰطٖ مُّسۡتَقِيمٖ ۝

---

[1] (V.16:121) (A) Ibrâhîm (Abraham) was neither a Jew nor a Christian, but he was a true Muslim *Hanîfa* (Islâmic Monotheism — to worship none but Allâh Alone) and he joined none in worship with Allâh. [The Qur'ân, Verse 3: 67]

(B) See the footnote (B) of (V.16:71).

(C) Narrated Abu Hurairah رضي الله عنه Ibrâhîm (Abraham) عليه السلام did not tell a lie except on three occasions. Twice for the sake of Allâh عزّ وجلّ when he said, "I am sick," and he said, "(I have not done this but) the big idol has done it."* The (third was) that while Ibrâhîm (Abraham) and Sârah (his wife) were going (on a journey) they passed by (the territory of) a tyrant from among the tyrants. Someone said to the tyrant, "This man (i.e. Ibrâhîm (Abraham) عليه السلام) is accompanied by a very charming lady." So, he sent for Ibrâhîm (Abraham) and asked him about Sârah saying, "Who is this lady?" Ibrâhîm (Abraham) said, "She is my sister." Ibrâhîm

122. And We gave him good in this world, and in the Hereafter he shall be of the righteous.

وَءَاتَيْنَـٰهُ فِى ٱلدُّنْيَا حَسَنَةًۭ ۖ وَإِنَّهُۥ فِى ٱلْءَاخِرَةِ لَمِنَ ٱلصَّـٰلِحِينَ

123. Then, We have sent the revelation to you (O Muhammad صلى الله عليه وسلم saying): "Follow the religion of Ibrâhîm (Abraham) *Hanîfa* (Islâmic Monotheism)[1] — to worship none but

ثُمَّ أَوْحَيْنَآ إِلَيْكَ أَنِ ٱتَّبِعْ مِلَّةَ إِبْرَٰهِيمَ حَنِيفًۭا ۖ وَمَا كَانَ مِنَ ٱلْمُشْرِكِينَ

(Abraham) went to Sârah and said, "O Sârah! There are no believers on the surface of the earth except you and I. This man asked me about you and I have told him that you are my sister, so don't contradict my statement." The tyrant then called Sârah and when she went to him, he tried to take hold of her with his hand, but (his hand got stiff and) he was confounded. He asked Sârah, "Pray to Allâh for me, and I shall not harm you." So Sârah asked Allâh to cure him and he got cured. He tried to take hold of her for the second time, but his hand got as stiff as or stiffer than before) and was more confounded. He again requested Sârah, "Pray to Allâh for me, and I will not harm you," Sârah asked Allâh again and he became all right. He then called one of his guards (who had brought her) and said, "You have not brought me a human being but have brought me a devil." The tyrant then gave Hâjar as a girl-servant to Sârah. Sârah came back [to Ibrâhîm (Abraham)] while he was praying. Ibrâhîm (Abraham), gesturing with his hand, asked, "What has happened?" She replied, "Allâh has spoiled the evil plot of the infidel (or immoral person) and gave me Hâjar for service". (Abu Hurairah then addressed his listeners saying: "That (Hâjar) was your mother, O Banî Mâ'-is-Samâ' (i.e. the Arabs)." (Sahih Al-Bukhari, Vol. 4, *Hadith* No. 578)

* The idolaters invited Ibrâhîm (Abraham) to join them in their celebrations outside the city, but he refused, claiming that he was sick. When he was left alone, he came to their idols and broke them into pieces. When the idolaters questioned him, he claimed that he had not destroyed their idols but the chief idol had, which Ibrâhîm (Abraham) left undisturbed and on whose shoulder he had put an axe to lay the accusation on it.

[1] (V.16:123) See the footnote of (V.2:135).

Allâh) and he was not of the *Mushrikûn* (polytheists, idolaters, disbelievers).

124. The Sabbath was only prescribed for those who differed concerning it, and verily, your Lord will judge between them on the Day of Resurrection about that wherein they used to differ.

إِنَّمَا جُعِلَ السَّبْتُ عَلَى الَّذِينَ اخْتَلَفُوا فِيهِ وَإِنَّ رَبَّكَ لَيَحْكُمُ بَيْنَهُمْ يَوْمَ الْقِيَمَةِ فِيمَا كَانُوا فِيهِ يَخْتَلِفُونَ ٢٤

125. Invite (mankind, O Muhammad صلى الله عليه وسلم) to the Way of your Lord (i.e. Islâm) with wisdom (i.e. with the Divine Revelation and the Qur'ân) and fair preaching, and argue with them in a way that is better. Truly, your Lord knows best who has gone astray from His Path, and He is the Best Aware of those who are guided.

ادْعُ إِلَىٰ سَبِيلِ رَبِّكَ بِالْحِكْمَةِ وَالْمَوْعِظَةِ الْحَسَنَةِ وَجَدِلْهُم بِالَّتِي هِيَ أَحْسَنُ إِنَّ رَبَّكَ هُوَ أَعْلَمُ بِمَن ضَلَّ عَن سَبِيلِهِ وَهُوَ أَعْلَمُ بِالْمُهْتَدِينَ ٢٥

126. And if you punish (your enemy, O' you believers in the Oneness of Allâh), then punish them with the like of that with which you were afflicted. But if you endure patiently, verily, it is better for *As-Sâbirûn* (the patient).[1]

وَإِنْ عَاقَبْتُمْ فَعَاقِبُوا بِمِثْلِ مَا عُوقِبْتُم بِهِ وَلَئِن صَبَرْتُمْ لَهُوَ خَيْرٌ لِّلصَّابِرِينَ ٢٦

---

[1] (V.16:126)

a) The Statement of Allâh: "Only those who are patient shall receive their rewards in full, without reckoning" (V.39:10)

Narrated Abu Mûsâ رضي الله عنه The Prophet صلى الله عليه وسلم said, "None is more patient than Allâh against the harmful saying He hears from the people, they ascribe a son (or offspring) to Him, yet He gives them health and (supplies them with) provision." (*Sahih Al-Bukhari*, Vol. 8, Hadith No. 121)

b) Narrated 'Abdullâh رضي الله عنه The Prophet صلى الله عليه وسلم divided and distributed something as he used to do with some of his distributions. A man from the *Ansâr* said, "By Allâh! in this

127. And endure you patiently (O Muhammad صلى الله عليه وسلم), your patience is not but from Allâh. And grieve not over them (polytheists and pagans), and be not distressed because of what they plot.

وَٱصۡبِرۡ وَمَا صَبۡرُكَ إِلَّا بِٱللَّهِ وَلَا تَحۡزَنۡ عَلَيۡهِمۡ وَلَا تَكُ فِى ضَيۡقٍ مِّمَّا يَمۡكُرُونَ ١٢٧

128. Truly, Allâh is with those who fear Him (keep their duty unto Him),[1] and those who are *Muhsinûn* (good-doers. See the footnote of V.9:120).

إِنَّ ٱللَّهَ مَعَ ٱلَّذِينَ ٱتَّقَوا۟ وَّٱلَّذِينَ هُم مُّحۡسِنُونَ ١٢٨

---

division the pleasure of Allâh has not been intended." I said, "I will definitely tell this to the Prophet صلى الله عليه وسلم." So I went to him while he was sitting with his Companions and told him of it secretly. That was hard upon the Prophet صلى الله عليه وسلم and the colour of his face changed, and he became so angry that I wished I had not told him. The Prophet صلى الله عليه وسلم then said, "Mûsâ (Moses) was harmed with more than this, yet he remained patient." (*Sahih Al-Bukhari*, Vol. 8, *Hadith* No. 122)

[1] (V.16:128) Narrated Abu Hurairah رضي الله عنه Allâh's Messenger صلى الله عليه وسلم said, "The deeds of anyone of you will not save you [from the (Hell) Fire]." They said, "Even you (will not be saved by your deeds), O Allâh's Messenger?" He said, "No, even I (will not be saved) unless and until Allâh bestows His Mercy on me and protects me with His Grace. Therefore, do good deeds properly, sincerely and moderately, and worship Allâh in the forenoon and in the afternoon and during a part of the night, and always adopt a middle, moderate, regular course whereby you will reach your target (Paradise)." (*Sahih Al-Bukhari*, Vol. 8, *Hadith* No. 470)

Sûrat Al-Isrâ'
(The Journey by Night) XVII

بِسمِ اللَّهِ الرَّحْمَٰنِ الرَّحِيمِ

*In the Name of Allâh
the Most Gracious, the Most Merciful*

1. Glorified (and Exalted) is He (Allâh) [above all that (evil) they associate with Him] [*Tafsir Qurtubî*][1]

Who took His slave (Muhammad صلى الله عليه وسلم) for a journey by night from *Al-Masjid Al-Harâm* (at Makkah) to *Al-Masjid Al-Aqsâ* (in Jerusalem), the neighbourhood whereof We have blessed, in order that We might show him (Muhammad صلى الله عليه وسلم) of Our *Ayât* (proofs, evidences, lessons, signs, etc.). Verily, He is the All-Hearer, the All-Seer.[2]

2. And We gave Mûsâ (Moses) the Scripture and made it a guidance for the Children of Israel (saying): "Take none other than Me as (your) *Wakîl* (Protector, Lord, or Disposer of your affairs, etc).

3. "O offspring of those whom We carried (in the ship) with Nûh (Noah)! Verily, he was a grateful slave."

---

[1] (V.17:1) و قد روي طلحة بن عبيدالله أنه قال للنبي صلى الله عليه وسلم ما معنى سبحان الله؟
قال تنزيه الله من كل سوء.

[2] (V.17:1) Narrated Jâbir bin 'Abdullâh رضي الله عنهما that he heard Allâh's Messenger صلى الله عليه وسلم saying, "When the people of Quraish did not believe me [i.e. in the story of my *Isrâ'* — (Night Journey)], I stood up in Al-Hijr and Allâh displayed Jerusalem in front of me, and I began describing it to them while I was looking at it." (*Sahîh Al-Bukhari*, Vol.5, *Hadith* No.226).

4. And We decreed for the Children of Israel in the Scripture: indeed you would do mischief in the land twice and you will become tyrants and extremely arrogant!

وَقَضَيْنَآ إِلَىٰ بَنِىٓ إِسْرَٰٓءِيلَ فِى ٱلْكِتَٰبِ لَتُفْسِدُنَّ فِى ٱلْأَرْضِ مَرَّتَيْنِ وَلَتَعْلُنَّ عُلُوًّا كَبِيرًا ۝

5. So, when the promise came for the first of the two, We sent against you slaves of Ours given to terrible warfare. They entered the very innermost parts of your homes. And it was a promise (completely) fulfilled.

فَإِذَا جَآءَ وَعْدُ أُولَىٰهُمَا بَعَثْنَا عَلَيْكُمْ عِبَادًا لَّنَآ أُولِى بَأْسٍ شَدِيدٍ فَجَاسُوا خِلَٰلَ ٱلدِّيَارِ وَكَانَ وَعْدًا مَّفْعُولًا ۝

6. Then We gave you a return of victory over them. And We helped you with wealth and children and made you more numerous in man-power.

ثُمَّ رَدَدْنَا لَكُمُ ٱلْكَرَّةَ عَلَيْهِمْ وَأَمْدَدْنَٰكُم بِأَمْوَٰلٍ وَبَنِينَ وَجَعَلْنَٰكُمْ أَكْثَرَ نَفِيرًا ۝

7. (And We said: "If you do good, you do good for your ownselves, and if you do evil (you do it) against yourselves." Then, when the second promise came to pass, (We permitted your enemies) to disgrace your faces and to enter the mosque (of Jerusalem) as they had entered it before, and to destroy with utter destruction all that fell in their hands.

إِنْ أَحْسَنتُمْ أَحْسَنتُمْ لِأَنفُسِكُمْ وَإِنْ أَسَأْتُمْ فَلَهَا فَإِذَا جَآءَ وَعْدُ ٱلْءَاخِرَةِ لِيَسُوءُوا وُجُوهَكُمْ وَلِيَدْخُلُوا ٱلْمَسْجِدَ كَمَا دَخَلُوهُ أَوَّلَ مَرَّةٍ وَلِيُتَبِّرُوا مَا عَلَوْا تَتْبِيرًا ۝

8. [And We said in the Taurât (Torah)]: "It may be that your Lord may show mercy unto you, but if you return (to sins), We shall return (to Our punishment). And We have made Hell a prison for the disbelievers.

عَسَىٰ رَبُّكُمْ أَن يَرْحَمَكُمْ وَإِنْ عُدتُّمْ عُدْنَا وَجَعَلْنَا جَهَنَّمَ لِلْكَٰفِرِينَ حَصِيرًا ۝

9. Verily, this Qur'ân guides to that which is most just and right and gives glad tidings to the believers (in the Oneness of Allâh and His Messenger Muhammad صلى الله عليه وسلم), who work

إِنَّ هَٰذَا ٱلْقُرْءَانَ يَهْدِى لِلَّتِى هِىَ أَقْوَمُ وَيُبَشِّرُ ٱلْمُؤْمِنِينَ ٱلَّذِينَ يَعْمَلُونَ ٱلصَّٰلِحَٰتِ أَنَّ

deeds of righteousness, that they shall have a great reward (Paradise).

10. And that those who believe not in the Hereafter, for them We have prepared a painful torment (Hell).

11. And man invokes (Allâh) for evil as he invokes (Allâh) for good and man is ever hasty [i.e., if he is angry with somebody, he invokes (saying): "O Allâh! Curse him," and that one should not do, but one should be patient].

12. And We have appointed the night and the day as two *Ayât* (signs etc.). Then, We have obliterated the sign of the night (with darkness) while We have made the sign of the day illuminating, that you may seek bounty from your Lord, and that you may know the number of the years and the reckoning. And We have explained everything (in detail) with full explanation.

13. And We have fastened every man's deeds[1] to his neck, and on the Day of Resurrection, We shall bring out for him a book which he will find wide open.

---

[1] (V.17:13) Narrated Ibn Mas'ûd رضي الله عنه: A man asked the Prophet صلى الله عليه وسلم: "What deeds are the best?" The Prophet صلى الله عليه وسلم said: "To perform the (daily compulsory) *Salât* (prayers) at their (early) stated fixed times; (2) To be good and dutiful to one's parents (3) and to participate in *Jihâd* in Allâh's Cause." (*Sahih Al-Bukhari*, Vol.9, Hadith No.625).

14. (It will be said to him): "Read your book. You yourself are sufficient as a reckoner against you this Day."

اقْرَأْ كِتَابَكَ كَفَى بِنَفْسِكَ الْيَوْمَ عَلَيْكَ حَسِيبًا ﴿١٤﴾

15. Whoever goes right, then he goes right only for the benefit of his ownself. And whoever goes astray, then he goes astray to his own loss. No one laden with burdens can bear another's burden. And We never punish until We have sent a Messenger (to give warning).

مَّنِ اهْتَدَىٰ فَإِنَّمَا يَهْتَدِي لِنَفْسِهِ وَمَن ضَلَّ فَإِنَّمَا يَضِلُّ عَلَيْهَا وَلَا تَزِرُ وَازِرَةٌ وِزْرَ أُخْرَىٰ وَمَا كُنَّا مُعَذِّبِينَ حَتَّىٰ نَبْعَثَ رَسُولًا ﴿١٥﴾

16. And when We decide to destroy a town (population), We (first) send a definite order (to obey Allâh and be righteous) to those among them [or We (first) increase in number those of its population] who lead a life of luxury. Then, they transgress therein, and thus the word (of torment) is justified against it (them). Then We destroy it with complete destruction.

وَإِذَا أَرَدْنَا أَن نُّهْلِكَ قَرْيَةً أَمَرْنَا مُتْرَفِيهَا فَفَسَقُوا فِيهَا فَحَقَّ عَلَيْهَا الْقَوْلُ فَدَمَّرْنَاهَا تَدْمِيرًا ﴿١٦﴾

17. And how many generations have We destroyed after Nûh (Noah)! And Sufficient is your Lord as an All-Knower and All-Beholder of the sins of His slaves.

وَكَمْ أَهْلَكْنَا مِنَ الْقُرُونِ مِن بَعْدِ نُوحٍ وَكَفَىٰ بِرَبِّكَ بِذُنُوبِ عِبَادِهِ خَبِيرًا بَصِيرًا ﴿١٧﴾

18. Whoever desires the quick-passing (transitory enjoyment of this world), We readily grant him what We will for whom We like. Then, afterwards, We have appointed for him Hell; he will burn therein disgraced and rejected (— far away from Allâh's Mercy).

مَّن كَانَ يُرِيدُ الْعَاجِلَةَ عَجَّلْنَا لَهُ فِيهَا مَا نَشَاءُ لِمَن نُّرِيدُ ثُمَّ جَعَلْنَا لَهُ جَهَنَّمَ يَصْلَاهَا مَذْمُومًا مَّدْحُورًا ﴿١٨﴾ وَمَنْ

19. And whoever desires the Hereafter and strives for it, with the necessary effort due for it (i.e. does righteous deeds of Allâh's obedience)

أَرَادَ الْآخِرَةَ وَسَعَىٰ لَهَا سَعْيَهَا وَهُوَ مُؤْمِنٌ فَأُولَٰئِكَ كَانَ سَعْيُهُم

while he is a believer (in the Oneness of Allâh — Islâmic Monotheism) — then such are the ones whose striving shall be appreciated, [thanked and rewarded (by Allâh)].

20. On each — these as well as those — We bestow from the Bounties of your Lord. And the Bounties of your Lord can never be forbidden.

21. See how We prefer one above another (in this world), and verily, the Hereafter will be greater in degrees and greater in preferment.

22. Set not up with Allâh any other *ilâh* (god), (O man)! (This verse is addressed to Prophet Muhammad صلى الله عليه وسلم, but its implication is general to all mankind), or you will sit down reproved, forsaken (in the Hell-fire).

23. And your Lord has decreed that you worship none but Him. And that you be dutiful to your parents. If one of them or both of them attain old age in your life, say not to them a word of disrespect, nor shout at them but address them in terms of honour.

24. And lower unto them the wing of submission and humility through mercy, and say: "My Lord! Bestow on them Your Mercy as they did bring me up when I was young."

25. Your Lord knows best what is in your inner-selves. If you are righteous, then, verily, He is Ever Most Forgiving to those who turn unto Him again and again in obedience, and in repentance.

26. And give to the kinsman his due and to the *Miskîn*[1] (poor) and to the wayfarer. But spend not wastefully (your wealth) in the manner of a spendthrift.[2] [*Tafsîr At-Tabarî*].

وَءَاتِ ذَا ٱلْقُرْبَىٰ حَقَّهُۥ وَٱلْمِسْكِينَ وَٱبْنَ ٱلسَّبِيلِ وَلَا تُبَذِّرْ تَبْذِيرًا ۝

27. Verily, the spendthrifts are brothers of the *Shayâtîn* (devils), and the *Shaitân* (Devil-Satan) is ever ungrateful to his Lord.

إِنَّ ٱلْمُبَذِّرِينَ كَانُوٓاْ إِخْوَٰنَ ٱلشَّيَٰطِينِ وَكَانَ ٱلشَّيْطَٰنُ لِرَبِّهِۦ كَفُورًا ۝

28. And if you (O Muhammad صلى الله عليه وسلم) turn away from them (kindred, poor, wayfarer, whom We have ordered you to give their rights, but if you have no money at the time they ask you for it) and you are awaiting a mercy from your Lord for which you hope, then, speak unto them a soft, kind word (i.e. Allâh will give me and I shall give you).

وَإِمَّا تُعْرِضَنَّ عَنْهُمُ ٱبْتِغَآءَ رَحْمَةٍ مِّن رَّبِّكَ تَرْجُوهَا فَقُل لَّهُمْ قَوْلًا مَّيْسُورًا ۝

29. And let not your hand be tied (like a miser) to your neck, nor stretch it forth to its utmost reach (like a spendthrift), so that you become blameworthy and in severe poverty.

وَلَا تَجْعَلْ يَدَكَ مَغْلُولَةً إِلَىٰ عُنُقِكَ وَلَا تَبْسُطْهَا كُلَّ ٱلْبَسْطِ فَتَقْعُدَ مَلُومًا مَّحْسُورًا ۝

30. Truly, your Lord enlarges the provision for whom He wills and straitens (for whom He wills). Verily, He is Ever All-Knower, All-Seer of His slaves.

إِنَّ رَبَّكَ يَبْسُطُ ٱلرِّزْقَ لِمَن يَشَآءُ وَيَقْدِرُ إِنَّهُۥ كَانَ بِعِبَادِهِۦ خَبِيرًۢا بَصِيرًا ۝

---

[1] (V.17:26) See the footnote of (V.2:83).

[2] (V.17:26) You have to follow a middle course in your spendings - neither a miser nor a spendthrift, and not to be like those who spend in the disobedience of Allâh and His Messenger صلى الله عليه وسلم.

31. And kill not your children for fear of poverty. We shall provide for them as well as for you. Surely, the killing of them is a great sin.

وَلَا تَقْتُلُوٓا أَوْلَٰدَكُمْ خَشْيَةَ إِمْلَٰقٍ نَّحْنُ نَرْزُقُهُمْ وَإِيَّاكُمْ إِنَّ قَتْلَهُمْ كَانَ خِطْـًٔا كَبِيرًا ﴿٣١﴾

32. And come not near to the unlawful sexual intercourse. Verily, it is a *Fâhishah* (i.e. anything that transgresses its limits), and an evil way (that leads one to Hell unless Allâh forgives him).

وَلَا تَقْرَبُوا الزِّنَىٰٓ إِنَّهُۥ كَانَ فَٰحِشَةً وَسَآءَ سَبِيلًا ﴿٣٢﴾

33. And do not kill anyone whose killing Allâh has forbidden, except for a just cause. And whoever is killed wrongfully (*Mazlûman* intentionally with hostility and oppression and not by mistake), We have given his heir the authority [to demand *Qisâs*, — Law of Equality in punishment — or to forgive, or to take *Diyah* (blood-money)]. But let him not exceed limits in the matter of taking life (i.e. he should not kill except the killer). Verily, he is helped (by the Islâmic law).[1]

وَلَا تَقْتُلُوا النَّفْسَ الَّتِى حَرَّمَ اللَّهُ إِلَّا بِالْحَقِّ وَمَن قُتِلَ مَظْلُومًا فَقَدْ جَعَلْنَا لِوَلِيِّهِۦ سُلْطَٰنًا فَلَا يُسْرِف فِّى الْقَتْلِ إِنَّهُۥ كَانَ مَنصُورًا ﴿٣٣﴾

34. And come not near to the orphan's property except to improve it, until he attains the age of full strength. And fulfil (every) covenant. Verily, the covenant, will be questioned about.

وَلَا تَقْرَبُوا مَالَ الْيَتِيمِ إِلَّا بِالَّتِى هِىَ أَحْسَنُ حَتَّىٰ يَبْلُغَ أَشُدَّهُۥ وَأَوْفُوا بِالْعَهْدِ إِنَّ الْعَهْدَ كَانَ مَسْـُٔولًا ﴿٣٤﴾

35. And give full measure when you measure, and weigh with a balance that is straight. That is good (advantageous) and better in the end.

وَأَوْفُوا الْكَيْلَ إِذَا كِلْتُمْ وَزِنُوا بِالْقِسْطَاسِ الْمُسْتَقِيمِ ذَٰلِكَ خَيْرٌ وَأَحْسَنُ تَأْوِيلًا ﴿٣٥﴾

---

[1] (V.17:33):

a) See the footnote of (V.2:22).

b) See the footnote of (V.5:50).

36. And follow not (O man i.e., say not, or do not or witness not) that of which you have no knowledge.[1] Verily, the hearing, and the sight, and the heart, of each of those ones will be questioned (by Allâh).

وَلَا تَقْفُ مَا لَيْسَ لَكَ بِهِ عِلْمٌ ۚ إِنَّ ٱلسَّمْعَ وَٱلْبَصَرَ وَٱلْفُؤَادَ كُلُّ أُوْلَٰٓئِكَ كَانَ عَنْهُ مَسْـُٔولًا ﴿٣٦﴾

37. And walk not on the earth with conceit and arrogance. Verily, you can neither rend nor penetrate the earth, nor can you attain a stature like the mountains in height.

وَلَا تَمْشِ فِي ٱلْأَرْضِ مَرَحًا ۖ إِنَّكَ لَن تَخْرِقَ ٱلْأَرْضَ وَلَن تَبْلُغَ ٱلْجِبَالَ طُولًا ﴿٣٧﴾

38. All the bad aspects of these (the above mentioned things) are hateful to your Lord.

كُلُّ ذَٰلِكَ كَانَ سَيِّئُهُۥ عِندَ رَبِّكَ مَكْرُوهًا ﴿٣٨﴾

39. This is (part) of Al-Hikmah (wisdom, good manners and high character) which your Lord has revealed to you (O Muhammad صلى الله عليه وسلم). And set not up with Allâh any other ilâh (god) lest you should be thrown into Hell, blameworthy and rejected (from Allâh's Mercy).

ذَٰلِكَ مِمَّآ أَوْحَىٰٓ إِلَيْكَ رَبُّكَ مِنَ ٱلْحِكْمَةِ ۗ وَلَا تَجْعَلْ مَعَ ٱللَّهِ إِلَٰهًا ءَاخَرَ فَتُلْقَىٰ فِي جَهَنَّمَ مَلُومًا مَّدْحُورًا ﴿٣٩﴾

40. Has then your Lord (O pagans of Makkah!) preferred for you sons, and taken for Himself from among the angels daughters? Verily you indeed utter an awful saying.

أَفَأَصْفَىٰكُمْ رَبُّكُم بِٱلْبَنِينَ وَٱتَّخَذَ مِنَ ٱلْمَلَٰٓئِكَةِ إِنَٰثًا ۚ إِنَّكُمْ لَتَقُولُونَ قَوْلًا عَظِيمًا ﴿٤٠﴾

41. And surely, We have explained [Our Promises, Warnings and (set forth many) examples] in this Qur'ân that they (the disbelievers) may take heed, but it increases them in naught save aversion.

وَلَقَدْ صَرَّفْنَا فِي هَٰذَا ٱلْقُرْءَانِ لِيَذَّكَّرُواْ وَمَا يَزِيدُهُمْ إِلَّا نُفُورًا ﴿٤١﴾

---

[1] (V.17:36) You have no knowledge: e.g., one's saying: "I have seen," while in fact he has not seen, or "I have heard," while he has not heard.

42. Say (O Muhammad صلى الله عليه وسلم to these polytheists, pagans): "If there had been other *âlihah* (gods) along with Him as they assert, then they would certainly have sought out a way to the Lord of the Throne (seeking His Pleasures and to be near to Him).

قُل لَّوۡ كَانَ مَعَهُۥٓ ءَالِهَةٌ كَمَا يَقُولُونَ إِذًا لَّٱبۡتَغَوۡاْ إِلَىٰ ذِي ٱلۡعَرۡشِ سَبِيلًا ﴿٤٢﴾

43. Glorified and Exalted is He High above (the great falsehood) that they say! (i.e. forged statements that there are other gods along with Allâh, but He is Allâh, the One, the Self-Sufficient Master, whom all creatures need. He begets not, nor was He begotten, and there is none comparable or coequal unto Him).

سُبۡحَٰنَهُۥ وَتَعَٰلَىٰ عَمَّا يَقُولُونَ عُلُوًّا كَبِيرًا ﴿٤٣﴾

44. The seven heavens and the earth and all that is therein, glorify Him and there is not a thing but glorifies His Praise. But you understand not their glorification. Truly, He is Ever Forbearing, Oft-Forgiving.

تُسَبِّحُ لَهُ ٱلسَّمَٰوَٰتُ ٱلسَّبۡعُ وَٱلۡأَرۡضُ وَمَن فِيهِنَّ ۚ وَإِن مِّن شَيۡءٍ إِلَّا يُسَبِّحُ بِحَمۡدِهِۦ وَلَٰكِن لَّا تَفۡقَهُونَ تَسۡبِيحَهُمۡ ۗ إِنَّهُۥ كَانَ حَلِيمًا غَفُورًا ﴿٤٤﴾

45. And when you (Muhammad صلى الله عليه وسلم) recite the Qur'ân, We put between you and those who believe not in the Hereafter, an invisible veil[1] (or

وَإِذَا قَرَأۡتَ ٱلۡقُرۡءَانَ جَعَلۡنَا بَيۡنَكَ وَبَيۡنَ ٱلَّذِينَ لَا يُؤۡمِنُونَ

---

[1] (V.17:45) It is said in the Book of *Tafsîr* (*Imâm Qurtubî*) as regards this Verse (17:45): Narrated Sa'îd bin Jubair رضي الله عنه: "When the *Sûrah* No.111 (*Tabbat Yadâ*) was revealed, the wife of Abu Lahab came looking for the Prophet صلى الله عليه وسلم while Abu Bakr رضي الله عنه, was sitting beside him. Abu Bakr said to the Prophet صلى الله عليه وسلم: "I wish if you get aside (or go away) as she is coming to us, she may harm you." The Prophet صلى الله عليه وسلم said: "There will be a screen set between me and her." So she did not see him. She said to Abu Bakr: "Your companion is saying poetry against me," Abu Bakr said: "By Allâh, he does not say poetry." She said: "Do you

screen their hearts, so they hear or understand it not).

46. And We have put coverings over their hearts lest they should understand it (the Qur'ân), and in their ears deafness. And when you make mention of your Lord Alone [Lâ ilâha illallâh (none has the right to be worshipped but Allâh) Islâmic Monotheism (توحيد الله)] in the Qur'ân, they turn on their backs, fleeing in extreme dislike.

47. We know best of what they listen to, when they listen to you. And when they take secret counsel, then the Zâlimûn (polytheists and wrongdoers) say: "You follow none but a bewitched man."

48. See what examples they have put forward for you. So they have gone astray, and never can they find a way.

49. And they say: "When we are bones and fragments (destroyed), should we really be resurrected (to be) a new creation?"

50. Say (O Muhammad صلى الله عليه وسلم) "Be you stones or iron,"

---

believe that?" Then she left. Abu Bakr said, "O Allâh's Messenger! She did not see you." The Prophet صلى الله عليه وسلم said: "An angel was screening me from her." [This *Hadith* is quoted in *Musnad Abu Ya'la*.]

It is said that if the above Verse (17:45) is recited by a real believer (of Islâmic Monotheism) he will be screened from a disbeliever. (Allâh knows better). (*Tafsir Al-Qurtubî*).

51. "Or some created thing that is yet greater (or harder) in your breasts (thoughts to be resurrected, even then you shall be resurrected)." Then, they will say: "Who shall bring us back (to life)?" Say: "He Who created you first!" Then, they will shake their heads at you and say: "When will that be?" Say: "Perhaps it is near!"

أَوَخَلْقًا مِّمَّا يَكْبُرُ فِى صُدُورِكُمْ فَسَيَقُولُونَ مَن يُعِيدُنَا قُلِ الَّذِى فَطَرَكُمْ أَوَّلَ مَرَّةٍ فَسَيُنْغِضُونَ إِلَيْكَ رُءُوسَهُمْ وَيَقُولُونَ مَتَىٰ هُوَ قُلْ عَسَىٰ أَن يَكُونَ قَرِيبًا ۝

52. On the Day when He will call you, and you will answer (His Call) with (words of) His praise and obedience, and you will think that you have stayed (in this world) but a little while!

يَوْمَ يَدْعُوكُمْ فَتَسْتَجِيبُونَ بِحَمْدِهِ وَتَظُنُّونَ إِن لَّبِثْتُمْ إِلَّا قَلِيلًا ۝

53. And say to My slaves (i.e. the true believers of Islâmic Monotheism) that they should (only) say those words that are the best. (Because) *Shaitân* (Satan) verily, sows a state of conflict and disagreements among them. Surely, *Shaitân* (Satan) is to man a plain enemy.

وَقُل لِّعِبَادِى يَقُولُوا الَّتِى هِىَ أَحْسَنُ إِنَّ الشَّيْطَانَ يَنزَغُ بَيْنَهُمْ إِنَّ الشَّيْطَانَ كَانَ لِلْإِنسَانِ عَدُوًّا مُّبِينًا ۝

54. Your Lord knows you best; if He wills, He will have mercy on you, or if He wills, He will punish you. And We have not sent you (O Muhammad صلى الله عليه وسلم) as a guardian over them.

رَّبُّكُمْ أَعْلَمُ بِكُمْ إِن يَشَأْ يَرْحَمْكُمْ أَوْ إِن يَشَأْ يُعَذِّبْكُمْ وَمَا أَرْسَلْنَاكَ عَلَيْهِمْ وَكِيلًا ۝

55. And your Lord knows best all who are in the heavens and the earth. And indeed, We have preferred some of the Prophets above others, and to Dawûd (David) We gave the Zabûr (Psalms).

وَرَبُّكَ أَعْلَمُ بِمَن فِى السَّمَاوَاتِ وَالْأَرْضِ وَلَقَدْ فَضَّلْنَا بَعْضَ النَّبِيِّينَ عَلَىٰ بَعْضٍ وَآتَيْنَا دَاوُدَ زَبُورًا ۝

56. Say (O Muhammad صلى الله عليه وسلم): "Call upon those — besides Him — whom you pretend [to be gods like

قُلِ ادْعُوا الَّذِينَ زَعَمْتُم مِّن دُونِهِ

angels, 'Îsâ (Jesus), 'Uzair (Ezra) and others]. They have neither the power to remove the adversity from you nor even to shift it from you to another person."

57. Those whom they call upon [like 'Îsâ (Jesus) - son of Maryam (Mary), 'Uzair (Ezra), angel and others] desire (for themselves) means of access to their Lord (Allâh), as to which of them should be the nearest; and they ['Îsâ (Jesus), 'Uzair (Ezra), angels and others] hope for His Mercy and fear His Torment. Verily, the Torment of your Lord is (something) to be afraid of!

58. And there is not a town (population) but We shall destroy it before the Day of Resurrection, or punish it with a severe torment. That is written in the Book (of our Decrees)[1]

59. And nothing stops Us from sending the Ayât (proofs, evidences, signs) but that the people of old denied them. And We sent the she-camel to Thamûd as a clear sign, but they did her wrong. And We sent not the signs except to warn, and to make them afraid (of destruction).

60. And (remember) when We told you: "Verily, your Lord has encompassed mankind (i.e. they are in His Grip)." And We made not the

---

[1] (V.17:58) It is said by 'Abdullâh bin Mas'ûd رضي الله عنه "If the people of a town indulge in illegal sexual intercourse and practise *Ribâ* (usury of all kinds), Allâh permits its destruction." (*Tafsîr Al-Qurtubî*)

vision which we showed you (O Muhammad as an actual eye-witness and not as a dream on the night of Al-Isrâ'[1]) but a trial for mankind, and (likewise) the accursed tree (Zaqqûm, mentioned) in the Qur'ân. We warn and make them afraid but it only increases them in naught save great disbelief, oppression and disobedience to Allâh.

أَرَيْنَكَ إِلَّا فِتْنَةً لِّلنَّاسِ وَالشَّجَرَةَ الْمَلْعُونَةَ فِي الْقُرْءَانِ وَنُخَوِّفُهُمْ فَمَا يَزِيدُهُمْ إِلَّا طُغْيَنًا كَبِيرًا ٦٠

61. And (remember) when We said to the angels: "Prostrate yourselves unto Adam." They prostrated themselves except Iblîs (Satan). He said: "Shall I prostrate myself to one whom You created from clay?"

وَإِذْ قُلْنَا لِلْمَلَٰٓئِكَةِ ٱسْجُدُوا۟ لِءَادَمَ فَسَجَدُوٓا۟ إِلَّآ إِبْلِيسَ قَالَ ءَأَسْجُدُ لِمَنْ خَلَقْتَ طِينًا ٦١

62. [Iblîs (Satan)] said: "See this one whom You have honoured above me, if You give me respite (keep me alive) to the Day of Resurrection, I will surely, seize and mislead his offspring (by sending them astray) all but a few!"

قَالَ أَرَءَيْتَكَ هَٰذَا ٱلَّذِى كَرَّمْتَ عَلَىَّ لَئِنْ أَخَّرْتَنِ إِلَىٰ يَوْمِ ٱلْقِيَٰمَةِ لَأَحْتَنِكَنَّ ذُرِّيَّتَهُۥٓ إِلَّا قَلِيلًا ٦٢

63. (Allâh) said: "Go, and whosoever of them follows you, surely, Hell will be the recompense of you (all) — an ample recompense.

قَالَ ٱذْهَبْ فَمَن تَبِعَكَ مِنْهُمْ فَإِنَّ جَهَنَّمَ جَزَآؤُكُمْ جَزَآءً مَّوْفُورًا ٦٣

64. "And befool them gradually those whom you can among them with your voice (i.e. songs, music, and any other call for Allâh's disobedience), make assaults on them with your cavalry and your infantry, share with them wealth and children (by tempting them to earn money by illegal ways — usury, or by committing illegal sexual intercourse),

وَٱسْتَفْزِزْ مَنِ ٱسْتَطَعْتَ مِنْهُم بِصَوْتِكَ وَأَجْلِبْ عَلَيْهِم بِخَيْلِكَ وَرَجِلِكَ وَشَارِكْهُمْ فِى ٱلْأَمْوَٰلِ وَٱلْأَوْلَٰدِ وَعِدْهُمْ وَمَا يَعِدُهُمُ ٱلشَّيْطَٰنُ إِلَّا غُرُورًا ٦٤

---

[1] (V.17:60) See footnote of (V.53:12) Al-Mi'râj.

and make promises to them." But Satan promises them nothing but deceit.

65. "Verily, My slaves (i.e. the true believers of Islâmic Monotheism) — you have no authority over them. And All-Sufficient is your Lord as a Guardian."

إِنَّ عِبَادِى لَيْسَ لَكَ عَلَيْهِمْ سُلْطَـٰنٌ وَكَفَىٰ بِرَبِّكَ وَكِيلًا ﴿٦٥﴾

66. Your Lord is He Who drives the ship for you through the sea, in order that you may seek of His Bounty. Truly, He is Ever Most Merciful towards you.

رَّبُّكُمُ ٱلَّذِى يُزْجِى لَكُمُ ٱلْفُلْكَ فِى ٱلْبَحْرِ لِتَبْتَغُوا مِن فَضْلِهِۦٓ إِنَّهُۥ كَانَ بِكُمْ رَحِيمًا ﴿٦٦﴾

67. And when harm touches you upon the sea, those that you call upon vanish from you except Him (Allâh Alone). But when He brings you safe to land, you turn away (from Him). And man is ever ungrateful.[1]

وَإِذَا مَسَّكُمُ ٱلضُّرُّ فِى ٱلْبَحْرِ ضَلَّ مَن تَدْعُونَ إِلَّآ إِيَّاهُ فَلَمَّا نَجَّىٰكُمْ إِلَى ٱلْبَرِّ أَعْرَضْتُمْ وَكَانَ ٱلْإِنسَـٰنُ كَفُورًا ﴿٦٧﴾

---

[1] (V.17:67) Ibn Kathîr in his Book of *Tafsîr* as regards this Verse (17:67) said: 'Ikrimah bin Abî Jahl fled from Allâh's Messenger صلى الله عليه وسلم (at the time) when Makkah was conquered. He rode over the (Red) Sea to cross over to Ethiopia, but (as they proceeded), a heavy stormy wind overtook their boat, and huge waves came to them from all sides, and they thought that they are encircled therein. The people of the boat said to one another: "None can save you except Allâh (the Only True God of the heavens and earth). So invoke (call upon) Him (Allâh) (by making your Faith pure for Him Alone and none else) to deliver you safe (from drowning)." 'Ikrimah said to himself. 'By Allâh if none can benefit in the sea except Allâh (Alone) then no doubt none can benefit over the land except Allâh (Alone). O Allâh! I promise You that if You delivered me safe from this, I will go and put my hands in the hands of (Prophet) Muhammad and surely, I will find him full of pity, kindness and mercy.' So they were delivered safe (by Allâh), and returned to their sea-shore and came out of the sea. 'Ikrimah then proceeded to Allâh's Messenger, Muhammad صلى الله عليه وسلم , (narrated

68. Do you then feel secure that He will not cause a side of the land to swallow you up, or that He will not send against you a violent sand-storm? Then, you shall find no *Wakîl* (guardian — one to guard you from the torment).

أَفَأَمِنتُمْ أَن يَخْسِفَ بِكُمْ جَانِبَ الْبَرِّ أَوْ يُرْسِلَ عَلَيْكُمْ حَاصِبًا ثُمَّ لَا تَجِدُواْ لَكُمْ وَكِيلًا ﴿٦٨﴾

69. Or do you feel secure that He will not send you back a second time to sea and send against you a hurricane of wind and drown you because of your disbelief? Then you will not find any avenger therein against Us.

أَمْ أَمِنتُمْ أَن يُعِيدَكُمْ فِيهِ تَارَةً أُخْرَىٰ فَيُرْسِلَ عَلَيْكُمْ قَاصِفًا مِّنَ الرِّيحِ فَيُغْرِقَكُم بِمَا كَفَرْتُمْ ثُمَّ لَا تَجِدُواْ لَكُمْ عَلَيْنَا بِهِ تَبِيعًا ﴿٦٩﴾

70. And indeed We have honoured the Children of Adam, and We have carried them on land and sea, and have provided them with *At-Tayyibât* (lawful good things), and have preferred them above many of those whom We have created with a marked preferment.

وَلَقَدْ كَرَّمْنَا بَنِي ءَادَمَ وَحَمَلْنَاهُمْ فِي الْبَرِّ وَالْبَحْرِ وَرَزَقْنَاهُم مِّنَ الطَّيِّبَاتِ وَفَضَّلْنَاهُمْ عَلَىٰ كَثِيرٍ مِّمَّنْ خَلَقْنَا تَفْضِيلًا ﴿٧٠﴾

71. (And remember) the Day when We shall call together all human beings with their (respective) *Imâm* [their Prophets, or their records of good and bad deeds, or their Holy Books like the Qur'ân, the Taurât (Torah), the Injeel (Gospel), the leaders whom the people followed in this world]. So whosoever is given his record in his right hand, such will read their records, and they will not be dealt with unjustly in the least.

يَوْمَ نَدْعُواْ كُلَّ أُنَاسٍ بِإِمَامِهِمْ فَمَنْ أُوتِيَ كِتَابَهُ بِيَمِينِهِ فَأُوْلَئِكَ يَقْرَءُونَ كِتَابَهُمْ وَلَا يُظْلَمُونَ فَتِيلًا ﴿٧١﴾

72. And whoever is blind in this world (i.e., does not see Allâh's Signs

وَمَن كَانَ فِي هَٰذِهِ أَعْمَىٰ فَهُوَ

his story), embraced Islâm (just as he promised Allâh), and became a perfect Muslim." (*Tafsir Ibn Kathir*).

and believes not in Him), will be blind in the Hereafter, and more astray from the Path.

73. Verily, they were about to tempt you away from that which We have revealed (the Qur'ân) unto you (O Muhammad صلى الله عليه وسلم), to fabricate something other than it against Us, and then they would certainly have taken you a *Khalîl* (an intimate friend)!

74. And had We not made you stand firm, you would nearly have inclined to them a little.

75. In that case We would have made you taste a double portion (of punishment) in this life and a double portion (of punishment) after death. And then you would have found none to help you against Us.

76. And verily, they were about to frighten you so much as to drive you out from the land. But in that case they would not have stayed (therein) after you, except for a little while.

77. (This was Our) *Sunnah* (rule or way) with the Messengers We sent before you (O Muhammad صلى الله عليه وسلم), and you will not find any alteration in Our *Sunnah* (rule or way).

78. Perform *As-Salât* (*Iqamât-as-Salât*)[1] from mid-day till the darkness of the night (i.e. the *Zuhr*, '*Asr*, *Maghrib*, and '*Ishâ*' prayers), and

وَفِي ٱلْأَخِرَةِ أَعْمَىٰ وَأَضَلُّ سَبِيلًا ﴿٧٢﴾

وَإِن كَادُوا لَيَفْتِنُونَكَ عَنِ ٱلَّذِىٓ أَوْحَيْنَآ إِلَيْكَ لِتَفْتَرِيَ عَلَيْنَا غَيْرَهُۥ وَإِذًا لَّٱتَّخَذُوكَ خَلِيلًا ﴿٧٣﴾

وَلَوْلَآ أَن ثَبَّتْنَٰكَ لَقَدْ كِدتَّ تَرْكَنُ إِلَيْهِمْ شَيْئًا قَلِيلًا ﴿٧٤﴾

إِذًا لَّأَذَقْنَٰكَ ضِعْفَ ٱلْحَيَوٰةِ وَضِعْفَ ٱلْمَمَاتِ ثُمَّ لَا تَجِدُ لَكَ عَلَيْنَا نَصِيرًا ﴿٧٥﴾

وَإِن كَادُوا لَيَسْتَفِزُّونَكَ مِنَ ٱلْأَرْضِ لِيُخْرِجُوكَ مِنْهَا وَإِذًا لَّا يَلْبَثُونَ خِلَٰفَكَ إِلَّا قَلِيلًا ﴿٧٦﴾

سُنَّةَ مَن قَدْ أَرْسَلْنَا قَبْلَكَ مِن رُّسُلِنَا وَلَا تَجِدُ لِسُنَّتِنَا تَحْوِيلًا ﴿٧٧﴾

أَقِمِ ٱلصَّلَوٰةَ لِدُلُوكِ ٱلشَّمْسِ إِلَىٰ غَسَقِ ٱلَّيْلِ وَقُرْءَانَ

---

[1] (V.17:78) See the glossary.

recite the Qur'ân in the early dawn (i.e. the morning prayer). Verily, the recitation of the Qur'ân in the early dawn is ever witnessed (attended by the angels in charge of mankind of the day and the night).[1]

79. And in some parts of the night (also) offer the *Salât* (prayer) with it (i.e. recite the Qur'an in the prayer), as an additional prayer (*Tahajjud* optional prayer — *Nawâfil*) for you (O Muhammad صلى الله عليه وسلم). It may be that your Lord will raise you to *Maqâm Mahmûd* (a station of praise and glory, i.e. the highest degree in Paradise!).[2]

وَمِنَ ٱلَّيْلِ فَتَهَجَّدْ بِهِ نَافِلَةً لَّكَ عَسَى أَن يَبْعَثَكَ رَبُّكَ مَقَامًا مَّحْمُودًا ٧٩

---

[1] (V.17:78):

Narrated Abu Salâmah bin 'Abdur-Rahmân: Abu Hurairah رضي الله عنه said, "I heard Allâh's Messenger صلى الله عليه وسلم saying, 'The reward of a *Salât* (prayer) in congregation is twenty-five times superior in degrees to that of a *Salât* (prayer) offered by a person alone. The angels of the night and the angels of the day gather at the time of *Fajr* prayer.'"

Abu Hurairah then added, "Recite the Holy Book if you wish, for 'Verily, the recitation of the Qur'ân in the early dawn (*Fajr* prayer) is ever witnessed (attended by the angels in charge of mankind of the day and the night)' (V.17:78)". (*Sahih Al-Bukhari*, Vol.1, *Hadith* No. 621).

[2] (V.17:79)

A). Narrated Ibn 'Umar رضي الله عنهما "On the Day of Resurrection the people will fall on their knees and every nation will follow their Prophet and they will say, "O so-and-so! Intercede (for us with Allâh)', till (the right of) intercession will be given to the Prophet (Muhammad صلى الله عليه وسلم) and that will be the day when Allâh will raise him to *Maqâm Mahmûd* (a station of praise and glory)". (*Sahih Al-Bukhari*, Vol. 6, *Hadith* No. 242)

B). Narrated Jâbir bin 'Abdullâh رضي الله عنهما Allâh's Messenger صلى الله عليه وسلم said, "Whoever, after listening to the *Adhân* (call for the prayer)

80. And say (O Muhammad صلى الله عليه وسلم): My Lord! Let my entry (to the city of Al-Madinah) be good, and (likewise) my exit (from the city of Makkah) be good. And grant me from You an authority to help me (or a firm sign or a proof).

وَقُل رَّبِّ أَدْخِلْنِي مُدْخَلَ صِدْقٍ وَأَخْرِجْنِي مُخْرَجَ صِدْقٍ وَاجْعَل لِّي مِن لَّدُنكَ سُلْطَٰنًا نَّصِيرًا ٨٠

81. And say: "Truth (i.e. Islâmic Monotheism or this Qur'ân or Jihâd against polytheists) has come and Bâtil (falsehood, i.e. Satan or polytheism) has vanished. Surely, Bâtil is ever bound to vanish."

وَقُلْ جَآءَ الْحَقُّ وَزَهَقَ الْبَٰطِلُ إِنَّ الْبَٰطِلَ كَانَ زَهُوقًا ٨١

82. And We send down of the Qur'ân that which is a healing and a mercy to those who believe (in Islâmic Monotheism and act on it), and it increases the Zâlimûn (polytheists and wrongdoers) nothing but loss.

وَنُنَزِّلُ مِنَ الْقُرْآنِ مَا هُوَ شِفَآءٌ وَرَحْمَةٌ لِّلْمُؤْمِنِينَ وَلَا يَزِيدُ الظَّٰلِمِينَ إِلَّا خَسَارًا ٨٢

83. And when We bestow Our Grace on man (the disbeliever), he turns away and becomes arrogant (far away from the Right Path). And when evil touches him, he is in great despair.

وَإِذَآ أَنْعَمْنَا عَلَى الْإِنسَٰنِ أَعْرَضَ وَنَأَىٰ بِجَانِبِهِ وَإِذَا مَسَّهُ الشَّرُّ كَانَ يَـُٔوسًا ٨٣

84. Say (O Muhammad صلى الله عليه وسلم to mankind): "Each one does according to Shakilatihi (i.e. his way or his religion or his intentions), and your Lord knows

قُلْ كُلٌّ يَعْمَلُ عَلَىٰ شَاكِلَتِهِ فَرَبُّكُمْ أَعْلَمُ بِمَنْ هُوَ أَهْدَىٰ سَبِيلًا ٨٤

---

says, 'O Allâh, the Lord of this complete call and of this prayer, which is going to be established! Give Muhammad Al-Wasîlah and Al-Fadîlah* and raise him to Maqâm Mahmûd, which You have promised him," and I will be granted my intercession for him on the Day of Resurrection." (Sahih Al-Bukhari, Vol.6, Hadith No. 243).

* Al-Wasîlah is the highest position in Paradise which is granted to the Prophet صلى الله عليه وسلم particularly; Al-Fadîlah* is the extra degree of honour which is bestowed on him above all creation.

best of him whose path (religion) is right."

85. And they ask you (O Muhammad صلى الله عليه وسلم) concerning the *Rûh* (the Spirit); Say: "The *Rûh* (the Spirit) is one of the things, the knowledge of which is only with my Lord. And of knowledge, you (mankind) have been given only a little."

86. And if We willed, We could surely, take away that which We have revealed to you (i.e. this Qur'ân). Then you would find no protector for you against Us in that respect.

87. Except as a Mercy from your Lord. Verily, His Grace unto you (O Muhammad صلى الله عليه وسلم) is ever great.

88. Say: "If the mankind and the jinn were together to produce the like of this Qur'ân, they could not produce the like thereof, even if they helped one another."

89. And indeed We have fully explained to mankind, in this Qur'ân, every kind of similitude, but most of mankind refuse (the truth and accept nothing) but disbelief.

90. And they say: "We shall not believe in you (O Muhammad صلى الله عليه وسلم), until you cause a spring to gush forth from the earth for us;

91. "Or you have a garden of date-palms and grapes, and cause rivers to gush forth in their midst abundantly;

92. "Or you cause the heaven to fall upon us in pieces, as you have pretended, or you bring Allâh and the angels before (us) face to face;

أَوْ تُسْقِطَ السَّمَاءَ كَمَا زَعَمْتَ عَلَيْنَا كِسَفًا أَوْ تَأْتِيَ بِاللَّهِ وَالْمَلَٰٓئِكَةِ قَبِيلًا ۝

93. "Or you have a house of *Zukhruf* (like silver and pure gold), or you ascend up into the sky, and even then we will put no faith in your ascension until you bring down for us a Book that we would read." Say (O Muhammad صلى الله عليه وسلم): "Glorified (and Exalted) is my Lord [(Allâh) above all that evil they (polytheists) associate with Him]! Am I anything but a man, sent as a Messenger?"

أَوْ يَكُونَ لَكَ بَيْتٌ مِّن زُخْرُفٍ أَوْ تَرْقَىٰ فِي السَّمَاءِ وَلَن نُّؤْمِنَ لِرُقِيِّكَ حَتَّىٰ تُنَزِّلَ عَلَيْنَا كِتَٰبًا نَّقْرَؤُهُ قُلْ سُبْحَانَ رَبِّي هَلْ كُنتُ إِلَّا بَشَرًا رَّسُولًا ۝

94. And nothing prevented men from believing when the guidance came to them, except that they said: "Has Allâh sent a man as (His) Messenger?"

وَمَا مَنَعَ النَّاسَ أَن يُؤْمِنُوٓا۟ إِذْ جَآءَهُمُ الْهُدَىٰٓ إِلَّآ أَن قَالُوٓا۟ أَبَعَثَ اللَّهُ بَشَرًا رَّسُولًا ۝

95. Say: "If there were on the earth, angels walking about in peace and security, We should certainly have sent down for them from the heaven an angel as a Messenger."

قُل لَّوْ كَانَ فِي الْأَرْضِ مَلَٰٓئِكَةٌ يَمْشُونَ مُطْمَئِنِّينَ لَنَزَّلْنَا عَلَيْهِم مِّنَ السَّمَاءِ مَلَكًا رَّسُولًا ۝

96. Say: "Sufficient is Allâh for a witness between me and you. Verily, He is Ever the All-Knower, the All-Seer of His slaves."

قُلْ كَفَىٰ بِاللَّهِ شَهِيدًا بَيْنِي وَبَيْنَكُمْ إِنَّهُۥ كَانَ بِعِبَادِهِۦ خَبِيرًۢا بَصِيرًا ۝

97. And he whom Allâh guides, he is led aright; but he whom He sends astray, for such you will find no *Auliyâ'* (helpers and protectors), besides Him, and We shall gather them together on the Day of Resurrection on their faces,[1] blind, dumb and deaf; their

وَمَن يَهْدِ اللَّهُ فَهُوَ الْمُهْتَدِ وَمَن يُضْلِلْ فَلَن تَجِدَ لَهُمْ أَوْلِيَآءَ مِن دُونِهِۦ وَنَحْشُرُهُمْ يَوْمَ الْقِيَٰمَةِ عَلَىٰ وُجُوهِهِمْ عُمْيًا

---

[1] (V.17:97) Narrated Anas bin Mâlik رضي الله عنه: A man said, "O Allâh's Prophet! Will Allâh gather a disbeliever (prone) on his face on the Day of Resurrection?" He صلى الله عليه وسلم said, "Will not the One

abode will be Hell; whenever it abates, We shall increase for them the fierceness of the Fire.

98. That is their recompense, because they denied Our *Ayât* (proofs, evidences, verses, lessons, signs, revelations, etc.) and said: "When we are bones and fragments, shall we really be raised up as a new creation?"

99. See they not that Allâh, Who created the heavens and the earth, is Able to create the like of them. And He has decreed for them an appointed term, whereof there is not doubt. But the *Zâlimûn* (polytheists and wrongdoers) refuse (the truth — the Message of Islâmic Monotheism, and accept nothing) but disbelief.

100. Say (to the disbelievers): "If you possessed the treasure of the Mercy of my Lord (wealth, money, provision), then you would surely, hold back (from spending) for fear of (being exhausted), and man is ever miserly!"

101. And indeed We gave to Mûsâ (Moses) nine clear signs. Ask then the Children of Israel, when he came to

---

Who made him walk on his feet in this world, be able to make him walk on his face on the Day of Resurrection?" (Qatâdah, a subnarrator, said: "Yes, by the Power of Our Lord!") (*Sahih Al-Bukhari*, Vol. 6, Hadith No. 283).

them, then Fir'aun (Pharaoh) said to him: "O Mûsâ (Moses)! I think you are indeed bewitched."

102. [Mûsâ (Moses)] said: "Verily, you know that these signs have been sent down by none but the Lord of the heavens and the earth (as clear evidences i.e. proofs of Allâh's Oneness and His Omnipotence). And I think you are, indeed, O Fir'aun (Pharaoh) doomed to destruction (away from all good)!"

103. So he resolved to turn them out of the land (of Egypt). But We drowned him and all who were with him.

104. And We said to the Children of Israel after him: "Dwell in the land, then, when the final and the last promise comes near [i.e. the Day of Resurrection or the descent of Christ ['Isâ (Jesus), son of Maryam (Mary) عليهما السلام on the earth], We shall bring you altogether as mixed crowd (gathered out of various nations).[*Tafsir Al-Qurtubî*]

105. And with truth We have sent it down (i.e. the Qur'ân), and with truth it has descended. And We have sent you (O Muhammad صلى الله عليه وسلم) as nothing but a bearer of glad tidings (of Paradise, for those who follow your Message of Islâmic Monotheism), and a warner (of Hell-fire for those who refuse to follow your Message of Islâmic Monotheism).[1]

---

[1] (V.17:105)
a) See the footnote of (V.3:85).
b) See the footnote of (V.4:80).

106. And (it is) a Qur'ân which We have divided (into parts), in order that you might recite it to men at intervals. And We have revealed it by stages (in 23 years).

وَقُرْآنًا فَرَقْنَـٰهُ لِتَقْرَأَهُۥ عَلَى ٱلنَّاسِ عَلَىٰ مُكْثٍ وَنَزَّلْنَـٰهُ تَنزِيلًا ﴿١٠٦﴾

107. Say (O Muhammad صلى الله عليه وسلم to them): "Believe in it (the Qur'ân) or do not believe in it). Verily, those who were given knowledge before it (the Jews and the Christians like 'Abdullâh bin Salâm and Salmân Al-Farisî), when it is recited to them, fall down on their faces in humble prostration."

قُلْ ءَامِنُواْ بِهِۦٓ أَوْ لَا تُؤْمِنُوٓاْ إِنَّ ٱلَّذِينَ أُوتُواْ ٱلْعِلْمَ مِن قَبْلِهِۦٓ إِذَا يُتْلَىٰ عَلَيْهِمْ يَخِرُّونَ لِلْأَذْقَانِ سُجَّدًا ﴿١٠٧﴾

108. And they say: "Glory is to our Lord! Truly, the Promise of our Lord must be fulfilled."

وَيَقُولُونَ سُبْحَـٰنَ رَبِّنَآ إِن كَانَ وَعْدُ رَبِّنَا لَمَفْعُولًا ﴿١٠٨﴾

109. And they fall down on their faces weeping and it increases their humility.

وَيَخِرُّونَ لِلْأَذْقَانِ يَبْكُونَ وَيَزِيدُهُمْ خُشُوعًا ۩ ﴿١٠٩﴾

110. Say (O Muhammad صلى الله عليه وسلم): "Invoke Allâh or invoke the Most Gracious (Allâh), by whatever name you invoke Him (it is the same), for to Him belong the Best Names. And offer your Salât (prayer) neither aloud nor in a low voice, but follow a way between."

قُلِ ٱدْعُواْ ٱللَّهَ أَوِ ٱدْعُواْ ٱلرَّحْمَـٰنَ أَيًّا مَّا تَدْعُواْ فَلَهُ ٱلْأَسْمَآءُ ٱلْحُسْنَىٰ وَلَا تَجْهَرْ بِصَلَاتِكَ وَلَا تُخَافِتْ بِهَا وَٱبْتَغِ بَيْنَ ذَٰلِكَ سَبِيلًا ﴿١١٠﴾

111. And say: "All the praises and thanks are to Allâh, Who has not begotten a son (or offspring), and Who has no partner in (His) Dominion, nor He is low to have a Walî (helper, protector or supporter). And magnify Him with all magnificence, [Allâhu-Akbar (Allâh is the Most Great)]."

وَقُلِ ٱلْحَمْدُ لِلَّهِ ٱلَّذِي لَمْ يَتَّخِذْ وَلَدًا وَلَمْ يَكُن لَّهُۥ شَرِيكٌ فِى ٱلْمُلْكِ وَلَمْ يَكُن لَّهُۥ وَلِيٌّ مِّنَ ٱلذُّلِّ وَكَبِّرْهُ تَكْبِيرًۢا ﴿١١١﴾

Sûrat Al-Kahf (The Cave) XVIII

*In the Name of Allâh
the Most Gracious, the Most Merciful*

1. All the praises and thanks are to Allâh, Who has sent down to His slave (Muhammad صلى الله عليه وسلم) the Book (the Qur'ân), and has not placed therein any crookedness.

2. (He has made it) straight to give warning (to the disbelievers) of a severe punishment from Him, and to give glad tidings to the believers (in the Oneness of Allâh — Islâmic Monotheism), who do righteous deeds, that they shall have a fair reward (i.e. Paradise).

3. They shall abide therein for ever.

4. And to warn those (Jews, Christians, and pagans) who say, "Allâh has begotten a son (or offspring or children)."

5. No knowledge have they of such a thing, nor had their fathers. Mighty is the word that comes out of their mouths [i.e. He begot sons and daughters]. They utter nothing but a lie.[1]

6. Perhaps, you, would kill yourself (O Muhammad صلى الله عليه وسلم) in grief, over their footsteps (for their turning away from you), because they believe not in this narration (the Qur'ân).

7. Verily, we have made that which is on earth as an adornment for it, in order that We may test them (mankind) as to which of them are best in deeds. [i.e.

---

[1] (V.18:5) See the footnote of V.2:116.

those who do good deeds in the most perfect manner, that means to do them (deeds) totally for Allâh's sake and in accordance to the legal ways of the Prophet صلى الله عليه وسلم.

8. And verily, We shall make all that is on it (the earth) a bare dry soil (without any vegetation or trees).

9. Do you think that the people of the Cave and the Inscription (the news or the names of the people of the Cave) were a wonder among Our Signs?

10. (Remember) when the young men fled for refuge (from their disbelieving folk) to the Cave. They said: "Our Lord! Bestow on us mercy from Yourself, and facilitate for us our affair in the right way!"

11. Therefore, We covered up their (sense of) hearing (causing them to go in deep sleep) in the Cave for a number of years.

12. Then We raised them up (from their sleep), that We might test which of the two parties was best at calculating the time period that they had tarried.

13. We narrate unto you (O Muhammad صلى الله عليه وسلم) their story with truth: Truly, they were young men who believed in their Lord (Allâh), and We increased them in guidance.

14. And We made their hearts firm and strong (with the light of Faith in Allâh and bestowed upon them patience to bear the separation of their kith and kin and dwellings) when they stood up and said: "Our Lord is the Lord of the heavens and the earth, never shall we call upon any *ilâh* (god) other than Him; if we did, we should indeed have uttered an enormity in disbelief.

15. "These our people have taken for worship *âlihah* (gods) other than Him (Allâh). Why do they not bring for them a clear authority? And who does more wrong than he who invents a lie against Allâh.

16. (The young men said to one another): "And when you withdraw from them, and that which they worship, except Allâh, then seek refuge in the Cave; your Lord will open a way for you from His Mercy and will make easy for you your affair (i.e. will give you what you will need of provision, dwelling)."

17. And you might have seen the sun, when it rose, declining to the right from their Cave, and when it set, turning away from them to the left, while they lay in the midst of the Cave. That is (one) of the *Ayât* (proofs, evidences, signs) of Allâh. He whom Allâh guides, he is the rightly guided; but he whom He sends astray, for him you will find no *Walî* (guiding friend) to lead him (to the Right Path).

18. And you would have thought them awake, whereas they were asleep. And We turned them on their right and on their left sides, and their dog stretching forth his two forelegs at the entrance [of

وَٱلْأَرْضِ لَن نَّدْعُوَا۟ مِن دُونِهِۦٓ
إِلَـٰهًا لَّقَدْ قُلْنَآ إِذًا شَطَطًا ﴿١٤﴾

هَـٰٓؤُلَآءِ قَوْمُنَا ٱتَّخَذُوا۟ مِن
دُونِهِۦٓ ءَالِهَةً لَّوْلَا يَأْتُونَ
عَلَيْهِم بِسُلْطَـٰنٍۭ بَيِّنٍ فَمَنْ
أَظْلَمُ مِمَّنِ ٱفْتَرَىٰ عَلَى ٱللَّهِ
كَذِبًا ﴿١٥﴾

وَإِذِ ٱعْتَزَلْتُمُوهُمْ وَمَا يَعْبُدُونَ
إِلَّا ٱللَّهَ فَأْوُۥٓا۟ إِلَى ٱلْكَهْفِ يَنشُرْ
لَكُمْ رَبُّكُم مِّن رَّحْمَتِهِۦ
وَيُهَيِّئْ لَكُم مِّنْ أَمْرِكُم
مِّرْفَقًا ﴿١٦﴾

۞ وَتَرَى ٱلشَّمْسَ إِذَا طَلَعَت
تَّزَٰوَرُ عَن كَهْفِهِمْ ذَاتَ ٱلْيَمِينِ
وَإِذَا غَرَبَت تَّقْرِضُهُمْ ذَاتَ
ٱلشِّمَالِ وَهُمْ فِى فَجْوَةٍ مِّنْهُ
ذَٰلِكَ مِنْ ءَايَـٰتِ ٱللَّهِ مَن يَهْدِ ٱللَّهُ
فَهُوَ ٱلْمُهْتَدِ وَمَن يُضْلِلْ
فَلَن تَجِدَ لَهُۥ وَلِيًّا مُّرْشِدًا ﴿١٧﴾

وَتَحْسَبُهُمْ أَيْقَاظًا وَهُمْ
رُقُودٌ وَنُقَلِّبُهُمْ ذَاتَ ٱلْيَمِينِ
وَذَاتَ ٱلشِّمَالِ وَكَلْبُهُم
بَـٰسِطٌ ذِرَاعَيْهِ بِٱلْوَصِيدِ

the Cave or in the space near to the entrance of the Cave (as a guard at the gate)]. Had you looked at them, you would certainly have turned back from them in flight, and would certainly have been filled with awe of them.

19. Likewise, We awakened them (from their long deep sleep) that they might question one another. A speaker from among them said: "How long have you stayed (here)?" They said: "We have stayed (perhaps) a day or part of a day." They said: "Your Lord (Alone) knows best how long you have stayed (here). So send one of you with this silver coin of yours to the town, and let him find out which is the good lawful food, and bring some of that to you. And let him be careful and let no man know of you.

20. "For, if they come to know of you, they will stone you (to death or abuse and harm you) or turn you back to their religion; and in that case you will never be successful."

21. And thus We made their case known (to the people), that they might know that the Promise of Allâh is true, and that there can be no doubt about the Hour. (Remember) when they (the people of the city) disputed among themselves about their case, they said: "Construct a building over them; their Lord knows best about them;" (then) those who won their point said (most probably the disbelievers): "We verily, shall build a place of worship over them."

لَوِ اطَّلَعْتَ عَلَيْهِمْ لَوَلَّيْتَ مِنْهُمْ فِرَارًا وَلَمُلِئْتَ مِنْهُمْ رُعْبًا ﴿﴾ وَكَذَٰلِكَ بَعَثْنَاهُمْ لِيَتَسَاءَلُوا بَيْنَهُمْ قَالَ قَائِلٌ مِنْهُمْ كَمْ لَبِثْتُمْ قَالُوا لَبِثْنَا يَوْمًا أَوْ بَعْضَ يَوْمٍ قَالُوا رَبُّكُمْ أَعْلَمُ بِمَا لَبِثْتُمْ فَابْعَثُوا أَحَدَكُمْ بِوَرِقِكُمْ هَٰذِهِ إِلَى الْمَدِينَةِ فَلْيَنْظُرْ أَيُّهَا أَزْكَىٰ طَعَامًا فَلْيَأْتِكُمْ بِرِزْقٍ مِنْهُ وَلْيَتَلَطَّفْ وَلَا يُشْعِرَنَّ بِكُمْ أَحَدًا ﴿١٩﴾ إِنَّهُمْ إِنْ يَظْهَرُوا عَلَيْكُمْ يَرْجُمُوكُمْ أَوْ يُعِيدُوكُمْ فِي مِلَّتِهِمْ وَلَنْ تُفْلِحُوا إِذًا أَبَدًا ﴿٢٠﴾ وَكَذَٰلِكَ أَعْثَرْنَا عَلَيْهِمْ لِيَعْلَمُوا أَنَّ وَعْدَ اللَّهِ حَقٌّ وَأَنَّ السَّاعَةَ لَا رَيْبَ فِيهَا إِذْ يَتَنَازَعُونَ بَيْنَهُمْ أَمْرَهُمْ فَقَالُوا ابْنُوا عَلَيْهِمْ بُنْيَانًا رَبُّهُمْ أَعْلَمُ بِهِمْ قَالَ الَّذِينَ غَلَبُوا عَلَىٰ أَمْرِهِمْ لَنَتَّخِذَنَّ عَلَيْهِمْ مَسْجِدًا ﴿٢١﴾

22. (Some) say they were three, the dog being the fourth among them and (others) say they were five, the dog being the sixth, — guessing at the Unseen; (yet others) say they were seven, and the dog being the eighth. Say (O Muhammad صلى الله عليه وسلم): "My Lord knows best their number; none knows them but a few." So debate not (about their number) except with the clear proof (which We have revealed to you). And consult not any of them (people of the Scripture — Jews and Christians) about (the affair of) the people of the Cave.

سَيَقُولُونَ ثَلَـٰثَةٌ رَّابِعُهُمْ كَلْبُهُمْ وَيَقُولُونَ خَمْسَةٌ سَادِسُهُمْ كَلْبُهُمْ رَجْمًا بِالْغَيْبِ وَيَقُولُونَ سَبْعَةٌ وَثَامِنُهُمْ كَلْبُهُمْ قُل رَّبِّىٓ أَعْلَمُ بِعِدَّتِهِم مَّا يَعْلَمُهُمْ إِلَّا قَلِيلٌ فَلَا تُمَارِ فِيهِمْ إِلَّا مِرَآءً ظَـٰهِرًا وَلَا تَسْتَفْتِ فِيهِم مِّنْهُمْ أَحَدًا ﴿٢٢﴾

23. And never say of anything, "I shall do such and such thing tomorrow."

وَلَا تَقُولَنَّ لِشَا۟ىْءٍ إِنِّى فَاعِلٌ ذَٰلِكَ غَدًا ﴿٢٣﴾

24. Except (with the saying), "If Allâh wills!" And remember your Lord when you forget and say: "It may be that my Lord guides me unto a nearer way of truth than this."

إِلَّآ أَن يَشَآءَ ٱللَّهُ وَٱذْكُر رَّبَّكَ إِذَا نَسِيتَ وَقُلْ عَسَىٰٓ أَن يَهْدِيَنِ رَبِّى لِأَقْرَبَ مِنْ هَـٰذَا رَشَدًا ﴿٢٤﴾

25. And they stayed in their Cave three hundred (solar) years, and adding nine (for lunar years). [*Tafsir Al-Qurtubi*]

وَلَبِثُوا۟ فِى كَهْفِهِمْ ثَلَـٰثَ مِا۟ئَةٍ سِنِينَ وَٱزْدَادُوا۟ تِسْعًا ﴿٢٥﴾

26. Say: "Allâh knows best how long they stayed. With Him is (the knowledge of) the Unseen of the heavens and the earth. How clearly He sees, and hears (everything)! They have no *Walî* (Helper, Disposer of affairs, Protector) other than Him, and He makes none to share in His Decision and His Rule."

قُلِ ٱللَّهُ أَعْلَمُ بِمَا لَبِثُوا۟ لَهُۥ غَيْبُ ٱلسَّمَـٰوَٰتِ وَٱلْأَرْضِ أَبْصِرْ بِهِۦ وَأَسْمِعْ مَا لَهُم مِّن دُونِهِۦ مِن وَلِىٍّ وَلَا يُشْرِكُ فِى حُكْمِهِۦٓ أَحَدًا ﴿٢٦﴾

27. And recite what has been revealed to you (O Muhammad صلى الله عليه وسلم) of the Book (the Qur'ân) of your Lord (i.e. recite it, understand and follow its teachings and act on its orders and preach it to men). None can change His Words, and none will you find as a refuge other than Him.

وَاتْلُ مَا أُوحِيَ إِلَيْكَ مِن كِتَابِ رَبِّكَ لَا مُبَدِّلَ لِكَلِمَٰتِهِ وَلَن تَجِدَ مِن دُونِهِ مُلْتَحَدًا ۝

28. And keep yourself (O Muhammad صلى الله عليه وسلم) patiently with those who call on their Lord (i.e. your companions who remember their Lord with glorification, praising in prayers, and other righteous deeds) morning and afternoon, seeking His Face; and let not your eyes overlook them, desiring the pomp and glitter of the life of the world; and obey not him whose heart We have made heedless of Our Remembrance, and who follows his own lusts, and whose affair (deeds) has been lost.

وَاصْبِرْ نَفْسَكَ مَعَ الَّذِينَ يَدْعُونَ رَبَّهُم بِالْغَدَوٰةِ وَالْعَشِيِّ يُرِيدُونَ وَجْهَهُ وَلَا تَعْدُ عَيْنَاكَ عَنْهُمْ تُرِيدُ زِينَةَ الْحَيَوٰةِ الدُّنْيَا وَلَا تُطِعْ مَنْ أَغْفَلْنَا قَلْبَهُ عَن ذِكْرِنَا وَاتَّبَعَ هَوَىٰهُ وَكَانَ أَمْرُهُ فُرُطًا ۝

29. And say: "The truth is from your Lord." Then whosoever wills, let him believe; and whosoever wills, let him disbelieve. Verily, We have prepared for the Zâlimûn (polytheists and wrongdoers), a Fire whose walls will be surrounding them (disbelievers in the Oneness of Allâh). And if they ask for help (relief, water), they will be granted water like boiling oil, that will scald their faces. Terrible is the drink, and an evil Murtafaq (dwelling, resting place)!

وَقُلِ الْحَقُّ مِن رَّبِّكُمْ فَمَن شَاءَ فَلْيُؤْمِن وَمَن شَاءَ فَلْيَكْفُرْ إِنَّا أَعْتَدْنَا لِلظَّالِمِينَ نَارًا أَحَاطَ بِهِمْ سُرَادِقُهَا وَإِن يَسْتَغِيثُوا يُغَاثُوا بِمَاءٍ كَالْمُهْلِ يَشْوِي الْوُجُوهَ بِئْسَ الشَّرَابُ وَسَاءَتْ مُرْتَفَقًا ۝

30. Verily, as for those who believed and did righteous deeds, certainly We

إِنَّ الَّذِينَ ءَامَنُوا وَعَمِلُوا

shall not make the reward of anyone who does his (righteous) deeds in the most perfect manner to be lost.

31. These! For them will be *'Adn* (Eden) Paradise (everlasting Gardens); wherein rivers flow underneath them; therein they will be adorned with bracelets of gold, and they will wear green garments of fine and thick silk. They will recline therein on raised thrones. How good is the reward, and what an excellent *Murtafaq* (dwelling, resting place)!

32. And put forward to them the example of two men: unto one of them We had given two gardens of grapes, and We had surrounded both with date-palms; and had put between them green crops (cultivated fields).

33. Each of those two gardens brought forth its produce, and failed not in the least therein, and We caused a river to gush forth in the midst of them.

34. And he had property (or fruit) and he said to his companion, in the course of mutual talk: "I am more than you in wealth and stronger in respect of men." [See *Tafsir Qurtubî*].

35. And he went into his garden while in a state (of pride and disbelief), unjust to himself. He said: "I think not that this will ever perish.

36. "And I think not the Hour will ever come, and if indeed I am brought back to my Lord, (on the Day of Resurrection), I surely, shall find better than this when I return to Him."

37. His companion said to him during the talk with him: "Do you disbelieve in Him Who created you out of dust (i.e. your father Adam), then out of *Nutfah* (mixed semen drops of male and female discharge), then fashioned you into a man?

قَالَ لَهُۥ صَاحِبُهُۥ وَهُوَ يُحَاوِرُهُۥٓ أَكَفَرْتَ بِٱلَّذِى خَلَقَكَ مِن تُرَابٍ ثُمَّ مِن نُّطْفَةٍ ثُمَّ سَوَّىٰكَ رَجُلًا ٣٧

38. "But as for my part, (I believe) that He is Allâh, my Lord, and none shall I associate as partner with my Lord.

لَّـٰكِنَّا۠ هُوَ ٱللَّهُ رَبِّى وَلَآ أُشْرِكُ بِرَبِّىٓ أَحَدًا ٣٨

39. "It was better for you to say, when you entered your garden: 'That which Allâh wills (will come to pass)! There is no power but with Allâh!'[1] If you see me less than you in wealth, and children,

وَلَوْلَآ إِذْ دَخَلْتَ جَنَّتَكَ قُلْتَ مَا شَآءَ ٱللَّهُ لَا قُوَّةَ إِلَّا بِٱللَّهِ إِن تَرَنِ أَنَا۠ أَقَلَّ مِنكَ مَالًا وَوَلَدًا ٣٩

40. "It may be that my Lord will give me something better than your garden, and will send on it *Husbân* (torment, bolt) from the sky, then it will be a slippery earth.

فَعَسَىٰ رَبِّىٓ أَن يُؤْتِيَنِ خَيْرًا مِّن جَنَّتِكَ وَيُرْسِلَ عَلَيْهَا حُسْبَانًا مِّنَ ٱلسَّمَآءِ فَتُصْبِحَ صَعِيدًا زَلَقًا ٤٠

---

[1] (V.18:39): What is said regarding the statement: *Lâ haulâ walâ quwwata illa billâh* (i.e. There is neither might nor power except with Allâh).

Narrated Abu Mûsâ Al-Ash'ari: The Prophet صلى الله عليه وسلم started ascending a high place or a hill. A man (amongst his companions) ascended it and shouted in a loud voice. *Lâ ilâha illallahu wallâhu Akbar.** (At that time) Allâh's Messenger صلى الله عليه وسلم was riding his mule. Allâh's Messenger صلى الله عليه وسلم said, "You are not calling upon a deaf or an absent one", and added, "O Abu Mûsâ (or, O 'Abdullâh)! Shall I tell you a sentence from the treasure of Paradise?" I said, "Yes." He said, "*Lâ haulâ walâ quwwata illa billâh.*" (*Sahih Al-Bukhari*, Vol. 8, *Hadith* No. 418).

* None has the right to be worshipped but Allâh, and Allâh is the Most Great.

41. "Or the water thereof (of the gardens) becomes deep-sunken (underground) so that you will never be able to seek it."

أَوْ يُصْبِحَ مَآؤُهَا غَوْرًا فَلَن تَسْتَطِيعَ لَهُ طَلَبًا ﴿٤١﴾

42. So his fruits were encircled (with ruin). And he remained clapping his hands (with sorrow) over what he had spent upon it, while it was all destroyed on its trellises, and he could only say: "Would that I had ascribed no partners to my Lord!" [*Tafsir Ibn Kathîr*]

وَأُحِيطَ بِثَمَرِهِ فَأَصْبَحَ يُقَلِّبُ كَفَّيْهِ عَلَى مَآ أَنفَقَ فِيهَا وَهِيَ خَاوِيَةٌ عَلَى عُرُوشِهَا وَيَقُولُ يَلَيْتَنِى لَمْ أُشْرِكْ بِرَبِّى أَحَدًا ﴿٤٢﴾

43. And he had no group of men to help him against Allâh, nor could he defend (or save) himself.

وَلَمْ تَكُن لَّهُ فِئَةٌ يَنصُرُونَهُ مِن دُونِ اللَّهِ وَمَا كَانَ مُنتَصِرًا ﴿٤٣﴾

44. There (on the Day of Resurrection), *Al-Walâyah* (protection, power, authority and kingdom) will be for Allâh (Alone), the True God. He (Allâh) is the Best for reward and the Best for the final end. (*Lâ ilâha illallâh* — none has the right to be worshipped but Allâh).

هُنَالِكَ الْوَلَايَةُ لِلَّهِ الْحَقِّ هُوَ خَيْرٌ ثَوَابًا وَخَيْرٌ عُقْبًا ﴿٤٤﴾

45. And put forward to them the example of the life of this world: it is like the water (rain) which We send down from the sky, and the vegetation of the earth mingles with it, and becomes fresh and green. But (later) it becomes dry and broken pieces, which the winds scatter. And Allâh is Able to do everything.

وَاضْرِبْ لَهُم مَّثَلَ الْحَيَوةِ الدُّنْيَا كَمَآءٍ أَنزَلْنَاهُ مِنَ السَّمَآءِ فَاخْتَلَطَ بِهِ نَبَاتُ الْأَرْضِ فَأَصْبَحَ هَشِيمًا تَذْرُوهُ الرِّيَاحُ وَكَانَ اللَّهُ عَلَى كُلِّ شَىْءٍ مُّقْتَدِرًا ﴿٤٥﴾

46. Wealth and children are the adornment of the life of this world. But the good righteous deeds[1] that last, are

الْمَالُ وَالْبَنُونَ زِينَةُ الْحَيَوةِ الدُّنْيَا وَالْبَاقِيَاتُ الصَّالِحَاتُ

---

[1] (V.18:46) Good righteous deeds: Five compulsory prayers, deeds of Allâh's obedience, good and nice talk, remembrance of Allâh with glorification, praises and thanks.

better with your Lord for rewards and better in respect of hope.

47. And (remember) the Day We shall cause the mountains to pass away (like clouds of dust), and you will see the earth as a levelled plain, and we shall gather them all together so as to leave not one of them behind.

48. And they will be set before your Lord in (lines as) rows, (and Allâh will say): "Now indeed, you have come to Us as We created you the first time. Nay, but you thought that We had appointed no Meeting for you (with Us)."

49. And the Book (one's Record) will be placed (in the right hand for a believer in the Oneness of Allâh, and in the left hand for a disbeliever in the Oneness of Allâh), and you will see the *Mujrimûn* (criminals, polytheists, sinners), fearful of that which is (recorded) therein. They will say: "Woe to us! What sort of Book is this that leaves neither a small thing nor a big thing, but has recorded it with numbers!" And they will find all that they did, placed before them, and your Lord treats no one with injustice.

50. And (remember) when We said to the angels: "Prostrate yourselves unto Adam." So they prostrated themselves except *Iblîs* (Satan). He was one of the jinn; he disobeyed the Command of his Lord. Will you then take him (*Iblîs*) and his offspring as protectors and helpers rather than Me while they are enemies to you? What an evil is the exchange for the *Zâlimûn* (polytheists, and wrongdoers, etc).

51. I (Allâh) made them (*Iblîs* and his offspring) not to witness (nor took their help in) the creation of the heavens and the earth and not (even) their own creation, nor was I (Allâh) to take the misleaders as helpers.

52. And (remember) the Day He will say:"Call those (so-called) partners of Mine whom you pretended." Then they will cry unto them, but they will not answer them, and We shall put *Maubiq*[1] (a barrier) between them.

53. And the *Mujrimûn* (criminals, polytheists, sinners), shall see the Fire and apprehend that they have to fall therein. And they will find no way of escape from there.

54. And indeed We have put forth every kind of example in this Qur'ân, for mankind. But, man is ever more quarrelsome than anything.

55. And nothing prevents men from believing, (now) when the guidance (the Qur'ân) has come to them, and from asking forgiveness of their Lord, except that the ways of the ancients be repeated with them (i.e. their destruction decreed by Allâh), or the torment be brought to them face to face?

---

[1] (V.18:52) In Arabic, *Maubiq* also means enmity, or destruction, or a valley in Hell.

56. And We send not the Messengers except as givers of glad tidings and warners. But those who disbelieve, dispute with false argument, in order to refute the truth thereby. And they treat My *Ayât* (proofs, evidences, verses, lessons, signs, revelations, etc.), and that with which they are warned, as a jest and mockery!

وَمَا نُرْسِلُ الْمُرْسَلِينَ إِلَّا مُبَشِّرِينَ وَمُنذِرِينَ وَيُجَدِلُ الَّذِينَ كَفَرُوا بِالْبَطِلِ لِيُدْحِضُوا بِهِ الْحَقَّ وَاتَّخَذُوا ءَايَتِى وَمَا أُنذِرُوا هُزُوًا ٥٦

57. And who does more wrong than he who is reminded of the *Ayât* (proofs, evidences, verses, lessons, signs, revelations, etc.) of his Lord, but turns away from them, forgetting what (deeds) his hands have sent forth. Truly, We have set veils over their hearts lest they should understand this (the Qur'ân), and in their ears, deafness. And if you (O Muhammad صلى الله عليه وسلم) call them to guidance, even then they will never be guided.

وَمَنْ أَظْلَمُ مِمَّن ذُكِّرَ بِـَايَتِ رَبِّهِ فَأَعْرَضَ عَنْهَا وَنَسِيَ مَا قَدَّمَتْ يَدَاهُ إِنَّا جَعَلْنَا عَلَى قُلُوبِهِمْ أَكِنَّةً أَن يَفْقَهُوهُ وَفِى ءَاذَانِهِمْ وَقْرًا وَإِن تَدْعُهُمْ إِلَى الْهُدَى فَلَن يَهْتَدُوا إِذًا أَبَدًا ٥٧

58. And your Lord is Most Forgiving, Owner of Mercy. Were He to call them to account for what they have earned, then surely, He would have hastened their punishment. But they have their appointed time, beyond which they will find no escape.

وَرَبُّكَ الْغَفُورُ ذُو الرَّحْمَةِ لَوْ يُؤَاخِذُهُم بِمَا كَسَبُوا لَعَجَّلَ لَهُمُ الْعَذَابَ بَل لَّهُم مَّوْعِدٌ لَّن يَجِدُوا مِن دُونِهِ مَوْئِلًا ٥٨

59. And these towns (population, — 'Âd, Thamûd) We destroyed them when they did wrong. And We appointed a fixed time for their destruction.

وَتِلْكَ الْقُرَى أَهْلَكْنَاهُمْ لَمَّا ظَلَمُوا وَجَعَلْنَا لِمَهْلِكِهِم مَّوْعِدًا ٥٩

60. And (remember) when Mûsâ (Moses) said to his boy-servant: "I will not give up (travelling) until I reach the

وَإِذْ قَالَ مُوسَى لِفَتَاهُ لَا أَبْرَحُ حَتَّى أَبْلُغَ مَجْمَعَ الْبَحْرَيْنِ أَوْ

junction of the two seas or (until) I
spend years and years in travelling."[1]

أَمْضِىَ حُقُبًا ۝

---

[1] (V.18:60) The Story of Mûsâ (Moses) and Khidr عليهما السلام.

Narrated Sa'îd bin Jubair: I said to Ibn 'Abbâs, "Nauf Al-Bikali
claims that Mûsâ (Moses), the companion of Al-Khidr was not the
Mûsâ (Moses) of the Children of Israel." Ibn 'Abbâs said, "The
enemy of Allâh (Nauf) told a lie." Narrated Ubayy bin Ka'b that he
heard Allâh's Messenger صلى الله عليه وسلم saying, "Mûsâ (Moses) got up
to deliver a speech before the Children of Israel and he was asked,
'Who is the most learned person among the people?' Mûsâ (Moses)
replied, 'I (am the most learned).' Allâh admonished him for he did
not ascribe knowledge to Allâh Alone. So Allâh revealed to him:
'At the junction of the two seas there is a slave of Ours who is more
learned than you.' Mûsâ (Moses) asked, 'O my Lord, how can I
meet him?' Allâh said, 'Take a fish and put it in a basket and then
proceed (set out and where you lose the fish, you will find him).' So
Mûsâ (Moses) (took a fish and put it in a basket and) set out, along
with his boy-servant Yûshâ' bin Nûn, till they reached a rock (on
which) they both lay their heads and slept. The fish moved
vigorously in the basket and got out of it and fell into the sea and
there it took its way through the sea (straight) as in a tunnel.
(V.18:61) Allâh stopped the current of water on both sides of the
way created by the fish, and so that way was like a tunnel. When
Mûsâ (Moses) got up, his companion forgot to tell him about the
fish, and so they carried on their journey during the rest of the day
and the whole night. The next morning Mûsâ (Moses) asked his
boy-servant 'Bring us our morning meal; truly, we have suffered
much fatigue in this, our journey.' (V.18:62)

Mûsâ (Moses) did not get tired till he had passed the place which
Allâh had ordered him to seek after. His boy-servant then said to
him, 'Do you remember when we betook ourselves to the rock? I
indeed forgot the fish; none but Satan made me forget to remember
it. It took its course into the sea in a strange way.' (V.18:63)

There was a tunnel for the fish and for Mûsâ (Moses) and his
boy-servant there was astonishment. Mûsâ (Moses) said, 'That is
what we have been seeking'. So they went back retracing their

footsteps. (V.18:64) They both returned, retracing their steps till they reached the rock. Behold! There they found a man covered with a garment. Mûsâ (Moses) greeted him. Al-Khidr said astonishingly. 'Is there such a greeting in your land?' Mûsâ (Moses) said, 'I am Mûsâ (Moses).' He said, 'Are you the Mûsâ (Moses) of the Children of Israel?' Mûsâ (Moses) said, 'Yes'; and added, 'I have come to you so that you may teach me something of that knowledge which you have been taught'.

Al-Khidr said. 'You will not be able to have patience with me.' (V.18:67)

'O Mûsâ (Moses)! I have some of Allâh's Knowledge which He has bestowed upon me but you do not know it; and you too, have some of Allâh's Knowledge which He has bestowed upon you, but I do not know it." Mûsâ (Moses) said, 'If Allâh wills, you will find me patient. and I will not disobey you in aught.' (V.18:69).

Al-Khidr said to him. 'Then, if you follow me, ask me not about anything till I myself mention it to you.' (V.18:70). After that both of them proceeded along the sea coast, till a ship passed by and they requested the crew to let them go on board. The crew recognized Al-Khidr and allowed them to get on board free of charge. When they got on board, suddenly Mûsâ (Moses) saw that Al-Khidr had pulled out one of the planks of the ship with an adze. Mûsâ (Moses) said to him. 'These people gave us a free lift, yet you have scuttled their ship so as to drown its people! Verily, you have committed a thing 'Imr' (a Munkar — evil, bad, dreadful thing).' (V.18:71)

Al-Khidr said. 'Did I not tell you, that you would not be able to have patience with me?' (V.18:72)

Mûsâ (Moses) said, 'Call me not to account for what I forgot and be not hard upon me for my affair (with you).' (V.18:73)."

Allâh's Messenger صلى الله عليه وسلم said, "The first excuse given by Mûsâ (Moses), was that he had forgotten. Then a sparrow came and sat over the edge of the ship and dipped its beak once in the sea. Al-Khidr said to Mûsâ (Moses), 'My knowledge and your knowledge, compared to Allâh's Knowledge is like what this sparrow has taken out of the sea.' Then they both got out of the ship. and while they were walking on the sea shore. Al-Khidr saw a

61. But when they reached the junction of the two seas, they forgot their fish, and it took its way through the sea as in a tunnel.

فَلَمَّا بَلَغَا مَجْمَعَ بَيْنِهِمَا نَسِيَا حُوتَهُمَا فَاتَّخَذَ سَبِيلَهُ فِى الْبَحْرِ سَرَبًا ۞

62. So when they had passed further on (beyond that fixed place), Mûsâ (Moses) said to his boy-servant: "Bring us our morning meal; truly, we have suffered much fatigue in this, our journey."

فَلَمَّا جَاوَزَا قَالَ لِفَتَاهُ ءَاتِنَا غَدَآءَنَا لَقَدْ لَقِينَا مِن سَفَرِنَا هَذَا نَصَبًا ۞

63. He said: "Do you remember when we betook ourselves to the rock? I

قَالَ أَرَءَيْتَ إِذْ أَوَيْنَا إِلَى الصَّخْرَةِ

---

boy playing with other boys. Al-Khidr got hold of the head of that boy and pulled it out with his hands and killed him. Mûsâ (Moses) said, 'Have you killed an innocent person who had killed none! Verily, you have committed a thing 'Nukr' (a great Munkar - prohibited, evil, dreadful thing)!' (V.18:74) He said, 'Did I not tell you that you would not be able to have patience with me?' (V.18:75) (The subnarrator said, 'The second blame was stronger than the first one). Mûsâ (Moses) said, 'If I ask you anything after this, keep me not in your company you have received an excuse from me.' (V.18:76)

Then they both proceeded until they came to the people of a town. They asked them for food but they refused to entertain them. (Then) they found there a wall on the point of falling down. (V.18:77) (Al-Khidr) set it up straight with his own hands. Mûsâ (Moses) said, 'We came to these people, but they neither fed us nor received us as guests. If you had wished, you could surely, have exacted some recompense for it.' (Al-Khidr) said, 'This is the parting between me and you, (please read V.18:79, 80-82) that is the interpretation of those (things) over which you could not hold patience.' (V.18:78-82)."

Allâh's Messenger صلى الله عليه وسلم said, "We wished Mûsâ (Moses) had more patience so that Allâh might have described to us more about their story." (Sahih Al-Bukhari, Vol. 6, Hadith No. 249).

indeed forgot the fish; none but *Shaitân* (Satan) made me forget to remember it. It took its course into the sea in a strange (way)!"

64. [Mûsâ (Moses)] said: "That is what we have been seeking." So they went back retracing their footsteps.

65. Then they found one of Our slaves, on whom We had bestowed mercy from Us, and whom We had taught knowledge from Us.

66. Mûsâ (Moses) said to him (Khidr): "May I follow you so that you teach me something of that knowledge (guidance and true path) which you have been taught (by Allâh)?"

67. He (Khidr) said: "Verily, you will not be able to have patience with me!

68. "And how can you have patience about a thing which you know not?"

69. Mûsâ (Moses) said: "If Allâh wills, you will find me patient, and I will not disobey you in aught."

70. He (Khidr) said: "Then, if you follow me, ask me not about anything till I myself mention of it to you."

71. So they both proceeded, till, when they embarked the ship, he (Khidr) scuttled it. Mûsâ (Moses) said: "Have you scuttled it in order to drown its people? Verily, you have committed a thing *Imr* (a *Munkar* — evil, bad, dreadful thing)."

72. He (Khidr) said: "Did I not tell you, that you would not be able to have patience with me?"

قَالَ أَلَمْ أَقُلْ إِنَّكَ لَن تَسْتَطِيعَ مَعِيَ صَبْرًا ٧٢

73. [Mûsâ (Moses)] said: "Call me not to account for what I forgot,[1] and be not hard upon me for my affair (with you)."

قَالَ لَا تُؤَاخِذْنِي بِمَا نَسِيتُ وَلَا تُرْهِقْنِي مِنْ أَمْرِي عُسْرًا ٧٣

74. Then they both proceeded, till they met a boy, and he (Khidr) killed him. Mûsâ (Moses) said: "Have you killed an innocent person who had killed none? Verily, you have committed a thing *Nukr* (a great *Munkar* — prohibited, evil, dreadful thing)!"

فَانطَلَقَا حَتَّىٰ إِذَا لَقِيَا غُلَامًا فَقَتَلَهُ قَالَ أَقَتَلْتَ نَفْسًا زَكِيَّةً بِغَيْرِ نَفْسٍ لَّقَدْ جِئْتَ شَيْئًا نُّكْرًا ٧٤

---

[1] (V.18:73)

a) If someone does something against his oath due to forgetfulness (should he make expiation?). And the Statement of Allâh:

"And there is no sin on you, if you make a mistake therein." (V.33:5)

And Allâh said:

"[Mûsâ (Moses) said to Khidr]: Call me not to account for what I forgot." (V.18:73)

Narrated Abu Hurairah رضى الله عنه: The Prophet صلى الله عليه وسلم said, "Allâh forgives my followers those (evil deeds) their ownselves may whisper or suggest to them as long as they do not act (on it) or speak." (*Sahih Al-Bukhari*, Vol. 8, *Hadith* No. 657)

b) Narrated Abu Hurairah رضى الله عنه: The Prophet صلى الله عليه وسلم said, "If somebody eats something forgetfully while he is fasting, then he should complete his fast, for Allâh has made him eat and drink." (*Sahih Al-Bukhari*, Vol. 8, *Hadith* No. 662).

75. (Khidr) said: "Did I not tell you that you can have no patience with me?"

قَالَ أَلَمْ أَقُل لَّكَ إِنَّكَ لَن تَسْتَطِيعَ مَعِيَ صَبْرًا ٧٥

76. [Mûsâ (Moses)] said: "If I ask you anything after this, keep me not in your company, you have received an excuse from me."

قَالَ إِن سَأَلْتُكَ عَن شَيْءٍ بَعْدَهَا فَلَا تُصَاحِبْنِي قَدْ بَلَغْتَ مِن لَّدُنِّي عُذْرًا ٧٦

77. Then they both proceeded, till, when they came to the people of a town, they asked them for food, but they refused to entertain them. Then they found therein a wall about to collapse and he (Khidr) set it up straight. [Mûsâ (Moses)] said: "If you had wished, surely, you could have taken wages for it!"

فَانطَلَقَا حَتَّىٰ إِذَا أَتَيَا أَهْلَ قَرْيَةٍ اسْتَطْعَمَا أَهْلَهَا فَأَبَوْا أَن يُضَيِّفُوهُمَا فَوَجَدَا فِيهَا جِدَارًا يُرِيدُ أَن يَنقَضَّ فَأَقَامَهُ قَالَ لَوْ شِئْتَ لَتَّخَذْتَ عَلَيْهِ أَجْرًا ٧٧

78. (Khidr) said: "This is the parting between me and you, I will tell you the interpretation of (those) things over which you were unable to hold patience.

قَالَ هَٰذَا فِرَاقُ بَيْنِي وَبَيْنِكَ سَأُنَبِّئُكَ بِتَأْوِيلِ مَا لَمْ تَسْتَطِع عَّلَيْهِ صَبْرًا ٧٨

79. "As for the ship, it belonged to *Masâkîn* (poor people) working in the sea. So I wished to make a defective damage in it, as there was a king behind them who seized every ship by force.

أَمَّا السَّفِينَةُ فَكَانَتْ لِمَسَاكِينَ يَعْمَلُونَ فِي الْبَحْرِ فَأَرَدتُّ أَنْ أَعِيبَهَا وَكَانَ وَرَاءَهُم مَّلِكٌ يَأْخُذُ كُلَّ سَفِينَةٍ غَصْبًا ٧٩ وَأَمَّا الْغُلَامُ

80. "And as for the boy, his parents were believers, and we feared lest he should oppress them by rebellion and disbelief.

فَكَانَ أَبَوَاهُ مُؤْمِنَيْنِ فَخَشِينَا أَن يُرْهِقَهُمَا طُغْيَانًا وَكُفْرًا ٨٠

81. "So we intended that their Lord should change him for one better in righteousness and nearer to mercy.

فَأَرَدْنَا أَن يُبْدِلَهُمَا رَبُّهُمَا خَيْرًا مِّنْهُ زَكَاةً وَأَقْرَبَ رُحْمًا ٨١

82. "And as for the wall, it belonged to two orphan boys in the town; and there was under it a treasure belonging

وَأَمَّا الْجِدَارُ فَكَانَ لِغُلَامَيْنِ يَتِيمَيْنِ فِي الْمَدِينَةِ وَكَانَ

to them; and their father was a righteous man, and your Lord intended that they should attain their age of full strength and take out their treasure as a mercy from your Lord. And I did them not of my own accord. That is the interpretation of those (things) over which you could not hold patience."

83. And they ask you about Dhul-Qarnain. Say: "I shall recite to you something of his story."

84. Verily, We established him in the earth, and We gave him the means of everything.

85. So he followed a way.

86. Until, when he reached the setting place of the sun, he found it setting in a spring of black muddy (or hot) water. And he found near it a people. We (Allâh) said (by inspiration): "O Dhul-Qarnain! Either you punish them, or treat them with kindness."

87. He said: "As for him (a disbeliever in the Oneness of Allâh) who does wrong, we shall punish him, and then he will be brought back unto his Lord, Who will punish him with a terrible torment (Hell).

88. "But as for him who believes (in Allâh's Oneness) and works righteousness, he shall have the best reward, (Paradise), and we (Dhul-Qarnain) shall speak unto him mild words (as instructions)."

89. Then he followed another way,

تَحْتَهُ كَنْزٌ لَّهُمَا وَكَانَ أَبُوهُمَا صَٰلِحًا فَأَرَادَ رَبُّكَ أَن يَبْلُغَآ أَشُدَّهُمَا وَيَسْتَخْرِجَا كَنزَهُمَا رَحْمَةً مِّن رَّبِّكَ وَمَا فَعَلْتُهُ عَنْ أَمْرِى ذَٰلِكَ تَأْوِيلُ مَا لَمْ تَسْطِع عَّلَيْهِ صَبْرًا ۝

وَيَسْئَلُونَكَ عَن ذِي الْقَرْنَيْنِ قُلْ سَأَتْلُوا۟ عَلَيْكُم مِّنْهُ ذِكْرًا ۝ إِنَّا مَكَّنَّا لَهُ فِي الْأَرْضِ وَءَاتَيْنَٰهُ مِن كُلِّ شَيْءٍ سَبَبًا ۝

فَأَتْبَعَ سَبَبًا ۝

حَتَّىٰٓ إِذَا بَلَغَ مَغْرِبَ الشَّمْسِ وَجَدَهَا تَغْرُبُ فِي عَيْنٍ حَمِئَةٍ وَوَجَدَ عِندَهَا قَوْمًا قُلْنَا يَٰذَا الْقَرْنَيْنِ إِمَّآ أَن تُعَذِّبَ وَإِمَّآ أَن تَتَّخِذَ فِيهِمْ حُسْنًا ۝

قَالَ أَمَّا مَن ظَلَمَ فَسَوْفَ نُعَذِّبُهُۥ ثُمَّ يُرَدُّ إِلَىٰ رَبِّهِۦ فَيُعَذِّبُهُۥ عَذَابًا نُّكْرًا ۝

وَأَمَّا مَنْ ءَامَنَ وَعَمِلَ صَٰلِحًا فَلَهُۥ جَزَآءً الْحُسْنَىٰ وَسَنَقُولُ لَهُۥ مِنْ أَمْرِنَا يُسْرًا ۝

ثُمَّ أَتْبَعَ سَبَبًا ۝

90. Until, when he came to the rising place of the sun, he found it rising on a people for whom We (Allâh) had provided no shelter against the sun.

حَتَّىٰٓ إِذَا بَلَغَ مَطْلِعَ ٱلشَّمْسِ وَجَدَهَا تَطْلُعُ عَلَىٰ قَوْمٍ لَّمْ نَجْعَل لَّهُم مِّن دُونِهَا سِتْرًا ٩٠ كَذَٰلِكَ

91. So (it was)! And We knew all about him (Dhul-Qarnain).

وَقَدْ أَحَطْنَا بِمَا لَدَيْهِ خُبْرًا ٩١

92. Then he followed (another) way,

ثُمَّ أَتْبَعَ سَبَبًا ٩٢

93. Until, when he reached between two mountains, he found, before (near) them (those two mountains), a people who scarcely understood a word.

حَتَّىٰٓ إِذَا بَلَغَ بَيْنَ ٱلسَّدَّيْنِ وَجَدَ مِن دُونِهِمَا قَوْمًا لَّا يَكَادُونَ يَفْقَهُونَ قَوْلًا ٩٣

94. They said: "O Dhul-Qarnain! Verily, Ya'jûj and Ma'jûj (Gog and Magog) [1] are doing great mischief in the land. Shall we then pay you a tribute in order that you might erect a barrier between us and them?"

قَالُوا يَٰذَا ٱلْقَرْنَيْنِ إِنَّ يَأْجُوجَ وَمَأْجُوجَ مُفْسِدُونَ فِي ٱلْأَرْضِ فَهَلْ نَجْعَلُ لَكَ خَرْجًا عَلَىٰٓ أَن تَجْعَلَ بَيْنَنَا وَبَيْنَهُمْ سَدًّا ٩٤

95. He said: "That (wealth, authority and power) in which my Lord had established me is better (than your tribute). So help me with strength (of

قَالَ مَا مَكَّنِّي فِيهِ رَبِّي خَيْرٌ فَأَعِينُونِي بِقُوَّةٍ أَجْعَلْ بَيْنَكُمْ وَبَيْنَهُمْ رَدْمًا ٩٥

---

[1] (V.18:94) Ya'jûj and Ma'jûj [Gog and Magog (people)]: To know about them in detail — please see *Tafsir Al-Qurtubi*.

Narrated Zainab bint Jahsh that one day Allâh's Messenger صلى الله عليه وسلم entered upon her in a state of fear and said, "*Lâ ilâha illallâh* (none has the right to be worshipped but Allâh)! Woe to the Arabs from the great evil that has approached (them). Today a hole has been opened in the dam of Ya'jûj and Ma'jûj (Gog and Magog) like this." The Prophet صلى الله عليه وسلم made a circle with his index finger and thumb. Zainab bint Jahsh added: I said, "O Allâh's Messenger!, Shall we be destroyed though there will be righteous people among us?" The Prophet صلى الله عليه وسلم said: "Yes if *Al-Khabath** (evil persons) increased." (*Sahih Al-Bukhari*, Vol.9, *Hadith* No.249).

* The word *Al-Khabath* is interpreted as illegal sexual intercourse and illegitimate children and every kind of evil deed. (See *Fath Al-Bari*).

men), I will erect between you and them a barrier.

96. "Give me pieces (blocks) of iron;" then, when he had filled up the gap between the two mountain-cliffs, he said: "Blow;" then when he had made them (red as) fire, he said: "Bring me molten copper to pour over them."

ءَاتُونِى زُبَرَ الْحَدِيدِ حَتَّىٰٓ إِذَا سَاوَىٰ بَيْنَ الصَّدَفَيْنِ قَالَ انفُخُوا حَتَّىٰٓ إِذَا جَعَلَهُۥ نَارًا قَالَ ءَاتُونِىٓ أُفْرِغْ عَلَيْهِ قِطْرًا ﴿٩٦﴾

97. So they [Ya'jûj and Ma'jûj (Gog and Magog)] could not scale it or dig through it.

فَمَا اسْطَٰعُوٓا أَن يَظْهَرُوهُ وَمَا اسْتَطَٰعُوا لَهُۥ نَقْبًا ﴿٩٧﴾

98. (Dhul-Qarnain) said: "This is a mercy from my Lord, but when the Promise of my Lord comes, He shall level it down to the ground. And the Promise of my Lord is ever true."

قَالَ هَٰذَا رَحْمَةٌ مِّن رَّبِّى فَإِذَا جَآءَ وَعْدُ رَبِّى جَعَلَهُۥ دَكَّآءَ وَكَانَ وَعْدُ رَبِّى حَقًّا ﴿٩٨﴾

99. And on that Day [i.e. the Day Ya'jûj and Ma'jûj (Gog and Magog) will come out], We shall leave them to surge like waves on one another; and the Trumpet will be blown, and We shall collect them (the creatures) all together.

وَتَرَكْنَا بَعْضَهُمْ يَوْمَئِذٍ يَمُوجُ فِى بَعْضٍ وَنُفِخَ فِى الصُّورِ فَجَمَعْنَٰهُمْ جَمْعًا ﴿٩٩﴾

100. And on that Day We shall present Hell to the disbelievers, plain to view —

وَعَرَضْنَا جَهَنَّمَ يَوْمَئِذٍ لِّلْكَٰفِرِينَ عَرْضًا ﴿١٠٠﴾

101. (To) those whose eyes had been under a covering from My Reminder (this Qur'ân), and who could not bear to hear (it).

الَّذِينَ كَانَتْ أَعْيُنُهُمْ فِى غِطَآءٍ عَن ذِكْرِى وَكَانُوا لَا يَسْتَطِيعُونَ سَمْعًا ﴿١٠١﴾

102. Do then those who disbelieved think that they can take My slaves [i.e., the angels, Allâh's Messengers, 'Îsâ (Jesus), son of Maryam (Mary)] as Auliyâ' (lords, gods, protectors) besides

أَفَحَسِبَ الَّذِينَ كَفَرُوٓا أَن يَتَّخِذُوا عِبَادِى مِن دُونِىٓ أَوْلِيَآءَ إِنَّآ أَعْتَدْنَا جَهَنَّمَ لِلْكَٰفِرِينَ نُزُلًا ﴿١٠٢﴾

Me? Verily, We have prepared Hell as an entertainment for the disbelievers (in the Oneness of Allâh — Islâmic Monotheism).[1]

103. Say (O Muhammad ﷺ): "Shall We tell you the greatest losers in respect of (their) deeds?

104. "Those whose efforts have been wasted in this life while they thought that they were acquiring good by their deeds.[2]

---

[1] (V.18:102) Almighty Allâh says: "They (Jews and Christians) took their rabbis and their monks to be their lords (by obeying them in things that they made lawful or unlawful according to their own desires without being ordered by Allâh) besides Allâh, and (they also took as their Lord) Messiah, son of Maryam (Mary), while they (Jews and Christians) were commanded [in the Taurât (Torah) and the Injeel (Gospel)] to worship none but one Ilâh (God - Allâh), Lâ ilâha illa Huwa (none has the right to be worshipped but He). Praise and glory are to Him, (far above is He) from having the partners they associate (with Him)." [The Qur'ân, Verse 9:31]

Once, while Allâh's Messenger ﷺ was reciting the above Verse, 'Adi bin Hâtim said, "O Allâh's Prophet! They do not worship them (rabbis and monks)." Allâh's Messenger ﷺ said, "They certainly do. They (i.e. rabbis and monks) made legal things illegal, and illegal things legal, and they (i.e. Jews and Christians) followed them, and by doing so they really worshipped them." [Narrated by Ahmad, At-Tirmidhi, and Ibn Jarir. (Tafsîr At-Tabari)]

[2] (V.18:104) For the acceptance of the righteous deeds it is stipulated that the following two basic conditions must be fulfilled:

a) The intentions while doing such deeds must be totally for Allâh's sake only without any show-off or to gain praise or fame.

b) Such a deed must be performed in accordance with the Sunnah of Allâh's Messenger Muhammad bin 'Abdullâh ﷺ, the last of the Prophets and the Messengers.

105. "They are those who deny the *Ayât* (proofs, evidences, verses, lessons, signs, revelations, etc.) of their Lord and the Meeting with Him (in the Hereafter). So their works are in vain, and on the Day of Resurrection, We shall assign no weight for them.

أُوْلَٰٓئِكَ ٱلَّذِينَ كَفَرُواْ بِـَٔايَٰتِ رَبِّهِمْ وَلِقَآئِهِۦ فَحَبِطَتْ أَعْمَٰلُهُمْ فَلَا نُقِيمُ لَهُمْ يَوْمَ ٱلْقِيَٰمَةِ وَزْنًا

106. "That shall be their recompense, Hell; because they disbelieved and took My *Ayât* (proofs, evidences, verses, lessons, signs, revelations, etc.) and My Messengers by way of jest and mockery.

ذَٰلِكَ جَزَآؤُهُمْ جَهَنَّمُ بِمَا كَفَرُواْ وَٱتَّخَذُوٓاْ ءَايَٰتِى وَرُسُلِى هُزُوًا

107. "Verily, those who believe (in the Oneness of Allâh — Islâmic Monotheism) and do righteous deeds, shall have the Gardens of *Al-Firdaus* (Paradise) for their entertainment.

إِنَّ ٱلَّذِينَ ءَامَنُواْ وَعَمِلُواْ ٱلصَّٰلِحَٰتِ كَانَتْ لَهُمْ جَنَّٰتُ ٱلْفِرْدَوْسِ نُزُلًا

108. "Wherein they shall dwell (forever). No desire will they have for removal therefrom."

خَٰلِدِينَ فِيهَا لَا يَبْغُونَ عَنْهَا حِوَلًا

109. Say (O Muhammad صلى الله عليه وسلم to mankind): "If the sea were ink for (writing) the Words of my Lord, surely, the sea would be exhausted before the

قُل لَّوْ كَانَ ٱلْبَحْرُ مِدَادًا لِّكَلِمَٰتِ رَبِّى لَنَفِدَ ٱلْبَحْرُ قَبْلَ أَن تَنفَدَ كَلِمَٰتُ رَبِّى وَلَوْ جِئْنَا

Narrated 'Âishah رضي الله عنها: Allâh's Messenger صلى الله عليه وسلم said, "If somebody innovates something which is not present in our religion (of Islâmic Monotheism), then that thing will be rejected." (*Sahîh Al-Bukhâri*, Vol. 3, *Hadîth* No.861).

In another *Hadîth* narrated 'Âishah رضي الله عنها: The Prophet صلى الله عليه وسلم said: "Whoever performs a (good) deed which we have not ordered (anyone) to do (or is not in accord with our religion of Islâmic Monotheism), then that deed will be rejected and will not be accepted." (*Sahîh Al-Bukhâri*, Vol.9, Chapter No.20 before *Hadîth* No. 449)

بِسْمِ اللَّهِ مَدَدًا

Words of my Lord would be finished, even if We brought (another sea) like it for its aid."

110. Say (O Muhammad صلى الله عليه وسلم): "I am only a man like you. It has been revealed to me that your *Ilâh* (God) is One *Ilâh* (God — i.e. Allâh). So whoever hopes for the Meeting[1] with his Lord, let him work righteousness and associate none as a partner in the worship of his Lord."

قُلْ إِنَّمَا أَنَا بَشَرٌ مِّثْلُكُمْ يُوحَى إِلَيَّ
أَنَّمَا إِلَهُكُمْ إِلَهٌ وَاحِدٌ فَمَن كَانَ
يَرْجُواْ لِقَاءَ رَبِّهِ فَلْيَعْمَلْ عَمَلًا
صَالِحًا وَلَا يُشْرِكْ بِعِبَادَةِ رَبِّهِ
أَحَدَا ۝

Surât Maryam (Mary) XIX

سُورَةُ مَرْيَمَ

In the Name of Allâh
the Most Gracious, the Most Merciful

بِسْمِ اللَّهِ الرَّحْمَٰنِ الرَّحِيمِ

1. *Kâf- Hâ-Yâ-'Aîn-Sâd.*

كهيعص ۝

[These letters are one of the miracles of the Qur'ân, and none but Allâh (Alone) knows their meanings.]

2. (This is) a mention of the mercy of your Lord to His slave Zakariyyâ (Zachariah).

ذِكْرُ رَحْمَتِ رَبِّكَ عَبْدَهُ
زَكَرِيَّا ۝

3. When he called out his Lord (Allâh) a call in secret.

إِذْ نَادَىٰ رَبَّهُ نِدَآءً
خَفِيًّا ۝

4. He said: "My Lord! Indeed my bones have grown feeble, and grey hair has spread on my head, And I have never been unblest in my invocation to You, O my Lord!

قَالَ رَبِّ إِنِّي وَهَنَ الْعَظْمُ مِنِّي
وَاشْتَعَلَ الرَّأْسُ شَيْبًا وَلَمْ
أَكُن بِدُعَآئِكَ رَبِّ شَقِيًّا ۝

5. "And verily, I fear my relatives after me, and my wife is barren. So give me from Yourself an heir.

وَإِنِّي خِفْتُ الْمَوَالِيَ مِن
وَرَآءِي وَكَانَتِ امْرَأَتِي عَاقِرًا
فَهَبْ لِي مِن لَّدُنكَ وَلِيًّا ۝

---

[1] (V.18:110) See the footnote of (V.6:31).

6. "Who shall inherit me, and inherit (also) the posterity of Ya'qûb (Jacob) (inheritance of the religious knowledge and Prophethood, not of wealth). And make him, my Lord, one with whom You are Well-Pleased!"

يَرِثُنِى وَيَرِثُ مِنْ ءَالِ يَعْقُوبَ ۖ وَٱجْعَلْهُ رَبِّ رَضِيًّا ۝

7. (Allâh said) "O Zakariyyâ (Zachariah)! Verily, We give you the glad tidings of a son, whose name will be Yahyâ (John). We have given that name to none before (him)."

يَٰزَكَرِيَّآ إِنَّا نُبَشِّرُكَ بِغُلَٰمٍ ٱسْمُهُۥ يَحْيَىٰ لَمْ نَجْعَل لَّهُۥ مِن قَبْلُ سَمِيًّا ۝

8. He said: "My Lord! How can I have a son, when my wife is barren, and I have reached the extreme old age."

قَالَ رَبِّ أَنَّىٰ يَكُونُ لِى غُلَٰمٌ وَكَانَتِ ٱمْرَأَتِى عَاقِرًا وَقَدْ بَلَغْتُ مِنَ ٱلْكِبَرِ عِتِيًّا ۝

9. He said: "So (it will be). Your Lord says: It is easy for Me. Certainly I have created you before, when you had been nothing!"

قَالَ كَذَٰلِكَ قَالَ رَبُّكَ هُوَ عَلَىَّ هَيِّنٌ وَقَدْ خَلَقْتُكَ مِن قَبْلُ وَلَمْ تَكُ شَيْئًا ۝

10. [Zakariyyâ (Zachariah)] said: "My Lord! Appoint for me a sign." He said: "Your sign is that you shall not speak unto mankind for three nights, though having no bodily defect."

قَالَ رَبِّ ٱجْعَل لِّىٓ ءَايَةً ۖ قَالَ ءَايَتُكَ أَلَّا تُكَلِّمَ ٱلنَّاسَ ثَلَٰثَ لَيَالٍ سَوِيًّا ۝

11. Then he came out to his people from *Al-Mihrâb* (a praying place or a private room) and he told them by signs to glorify Allâh's Praises in the morning and in the afternoon.

فَخَرَجَ عَلَىٰ قَوْمِهِۦ مِنَ ٱلْمِحْرَابِ فَأَوْحَىٰٓ إِلَيْهِمْ أَن سَبِّحُوا بُكْرَةً وَعَشِيًّا ۝

12. (It was said to his son): "O Yahyâ (John)! Hold fast the Scripture [the Taurât (Torah)]." And We gave him wisdom while yet a child.

يَٰيَحْيَىٰ خُذِ ٱلْكِتَٰبَ بِقُوَّةٍ ۖ وَءَاتَيْنَٰهُ ٱلْحُكْمَ صَبِيًّا ۝

13. And (made him) sympathetic to men as a mercy (or a grant) from Us, and pure from sins [i.e. Yahyâ (John)] and he was righteous,

وَحَنَانًا مِّن لَّدُنَّا وَزَكَوٰةً ۖ وَكَانَ تَقِيًّا ۝

14. And dutiful towards his parents, and he was neither arrogant nor disobedient (to Allâh or to his parents).

15. And *Salâmun* (peace) be on him the day he was born, and the day he dies, and the day he will be raised up to life (again)!

16. And mention in the Book (the Qur'ân, O Muhammad صلى الله عليه وسلم, the story of) Maryam (Mary), when she withdrew in seclusion from her family to a place facing east.

17. She placed a screen (to screen herself) from them; then We sent to her Our *Ruh* [angel Jibrael (Gabriel)], and he appeared before her in the form of a man in all respects.

18. She said: "Verily, I seek refuge with the Most Gracious (Allâh) from you, if you do fear Allâh."

19. (The angel) said: "I am only a messenger from your Lord, (to announce) to you the gift of a righteous son."

20. She said: "How can I have a son, when no man has touched me, nor am I unchaste?"

21. He said: "So (it will be), your Lord said: 'That is easy for Me (Allâh): And (We wish) to appoint him as a sign to mankind and a mercy from Us (Allâh), and it is a matter (already) decreed, (by Allâh).'"

22. So she conceived him,[1] and she withdrew with him to a far place (i.e.

---

[1] (V.19:22) "And (remember) she who guarded her chastity [Virgin Maryam (Mary)], We breathed into (the sleeves of) her

Bethlehem valley about 4-6 miles from Jerusalem."

23. And the pains of childbirth drove her to the trunk of a date-palm. She said: "Would that I had died before this, and had been forgotten and out of sight!"

24. Then [the babe 'Îsâ (Jesus) or Jibrael (Gabriel)] cried unto her from below her, saying: "Grieve not: your Lord has provided a water stream under you.

25. "And shake the trunk of date-palm towards you, it will let fall fresh ripe-dates upon you.

26. "So eat and drink and be glad. And if you see any human being, say: 'Verily, I have vowed a fast unto the Most Gracious (Allâh) so I shall not speak to any human being this day.'"

27. Then she brought him (the baby) to her people, carrying him. They said: "O Mary! Indeed you have brought a thing *Fariyy* (a mighty thing). [*Tafsir At-Tabari*]

28. "O sister (i.e. the like) of Hârûn (Aaron)![1] Your father was not a man

---

(shirt or garment) [through Our *Rûh* (Jibrael - Gabriel)]*, and We made her and her son ['Îsâ (Jesus)] a sign for *Al-'Âlamîn* (mankind and jinn)." [The Qur'ân, Verse 21:91]

* It is said that Jibrael (Gabriel) had merely breathed in the sleeve of Maryam's (Mary) shirt, and thus she conceived.

[1] (V.19:28) This Hârûn (Aaron) is not the brother of Mûsâ (Moses), but he was another pious man at the time of Maryam (Mary).

who used to commit adultery, nor your mother was an unchaste woman."

أَمْرَأَ سَوْءٍ وَمَا كَانَتْ أُمُّكِ بَغِيًّا ﴿٢٨﴾

29. Then she pointed to him. They said: "How can we talk to one who is a child in the cradle?[1]"

فَأَشَارَتْ إِلَيْهِ قَالُوا كَيْفَ نُكَلِّمُ مَن كَانَ فِى ٱلْمَهْدِ صَبِيًّا ﴿٢٩﴾

30. He ['Îsâ (Jesus)] said: "Verily, I am a slave of Allâh, He has given me the Scripture and made me a Prophet;[2]"

قَالَ إِنِّى عَبْدُ ٱللَّهِ ءَاتَىٰنِىَ ٱلْكِتَٰبَ وَجَعَلَنِى نَبِيًّا ﴿٣٠﴾

31. "And He has made me blessed wheresoever I be, and has enjoined on me Salât (prayer), and Zakât, as long as I live."

وَجَعَلَنِى مُبَارَكًا أَيْنَ مَا كُنتُ وَأَوْصَٰنِى بِٱلصَّلَوٰةِ وَٱلزَّكَوٰةِ مَا دُمْتُ حَيًّا ﴿٣١﴾

32. "And dutiful to my mother, and made me not arrogant, unblest.

وَبَرًّا بِوَٰلِدَتِى وَلَمْ يَجْعَلْنِى جَبَّارًا شَقِيًّا ﴿٣٢﴾

33. "And Salâm (peace) be upon me the day I was born, and the day I die, and the day I shall be raised alive!"

وَٱلسَّلَٰمُ عَلَىَّ يَوْمَ وُلِدتُّ وَيَوْمَ أَمُوتُ وَيَوْمَ أُبْعَثُ حَيًّا ﴿٣٣﴾

34. Such is 'Îsâ (Jesus), son of Maryam (Mary). (It is) a statement of truth, about which they doubt (or dispute).

ذَٰلِكَ عِيسَى ٱبْنُ مَرْيَمَ قَوْلَ ٱلْحَقِّ ٱلَّذِى فِيهِ يَمْتَرُونَ ﴿٣٤﴾

35. It befits not (the Majesty of) Allâh that He should beget a son [this refers to the slander of Christians against Allâh, by saying that 'Îsâ (Jesus) is the son of Allâh]. Glorified (and Exalted is He above all that they associate with Him). When He decrees a thing, He only says to it: "Be!" — and it is.[3]

مَا كَانَ لِلَّهِ أَن يَتَّخِذَ مِن وَلَدٍ سُبْحَٰنَهُ إِذَا قَضَىٰ أَمْرًا فَإِنَّمَا يَقُولُ لَهُ كُن فَيَكُونُ ﴿٣٥﴾

---

[1] (V.19:29) See the footnote of (V.3:46).

[2] (V.19:30) See the footnote No. 2 of (V.4:171).

[3] (V.19:35) See the footnote of (V.2:116).

36. ['Îsâ (Jesus) said]: "And verily, Allâh is my Lord and your Lord. So worship Him (Alone). That is the Straight Path. (Allâh's religion of Islâmic Monotheism which He did ordain for all of His Prophets." [Tafsir At-Tabarî]

وَإِنَّ ٱللَّهَ رَبِّى وَرَبُّكُمْ فَٱعْبُدُوهُ هَٰذَا صِرَٰطٌ مُّسْتَقِيمٌ ۝

37. Then the sects differed [i.e. the Christians about 'Îsâ (Jesus) عليه السلام], so woe unto the disbelievers [those who gave false witness by saying that 'Îsâ (Jesus) is the son of Allâh] from the Meeting of a great Day (i.e. the Day of Resurrection, when they will be thrown in the blazing Fire).[1]

فَٱخْتَلَفَ ٱلْأَحْزَابُ مِنۢ بَيْنِهِمْ فَوَيْلٌ لِّلَّذِينَ كَفَرُوا۟ مِن مَّشْهَدِ يَوْمٍ عَظِيمٍ ۝

38. How clearly will they (polytheists and disbelievers in the Oneness of Allâh) see and hear, the Day when they will appear before Us! But the Zalimûn (polytheists and wrongdoers) today are in plain error.

أَسْمِعْ بِهِمْ وَأَبْصِرْ يَوْمَ يَأْتُونَنَا لَٰكِنِ ٱلظَّٰلِمُونَ ٱلْيَوْمَ فِى ضَلَٰلٍ مُّبِينٍ ۝

39. And warn them (O Muhammad صلى الله عليه وسلم) of the Day of grief and regrets, when the case has been decided, while (now) they are in a state of carelessness, and they believe not.[2]

وَأَنذِرْهُمْ يَوْمَ ٱلْحَسْرَةِ إِذْ قُضِىَ ٱلْأَمْرُ وَهُمْ فِى غَفْلَةٍ وَهُمْ لَا يُؤْمِنُونَ ۝

---

[1] (V.19:37) See the footnote of (V.3:103).

[2] (V.19:39) Narrated Abu Sa'îd Al-Khudrî رضى الله عنه Allâh's Messenger صلى الله عليه وسلم said, "On the Day of Resurrection, death will be brought forward in the shape of a black and white ram. Then a call-maker will call, 'O people of Paradise!' Thereupon they will stretch their necks and look carefully. The caller will say, 'Do you know this?' They will say: Yes, this is death.' By then all of them would have seen it. Then it will be announced also, 'O people of Hell!' They will stretch their necks and look carefully. The caller

40. Verily, We will inherit the earth and whatsoever is thereon. And to Us they all shall be returned.

إِنَّا نَحْنُ نَرِثُ ٱلْأَرْضَ وَمَنْ عَلَيْهَا وَإِلَيْنَا يُرْجَعُونَ ٤٠

41. And mention in the Book (the Qur'ân) Ibrâhîm (Abraham). Verily, he was a man of truth, a Prophet.

وَٱذْكُرْ فِى ٱلْكِتَٰبِ إِبْرَٰهِيمَ إِنَّهُۥ كَانَ صِدِّيقًا نَّبِيًّا ٤١

42. When he said to his father: "O my father! Why do you worship that which hears not, sees not and cannot avail you in anything?

إِذْ قَالَ لِأَبِيهِ يَٰٓأَبَتِ لِمَ تَعْبُدُ مَا لَا يَسْمَعُ وَلَا يُبْصِرُ وَلَا يُغْنِى عَنكَ شَيْـًٔا ٤٢

43. "O my father! Verily, there has come to me of the knowledge that which came not unto you. So follow me, I will guide you to the Straight Path.

يَٰٓأَبَتِ إِنِّى قَدْ جَآءَنِى مِنَ ٱلْعِلْمِ مَا لَمْ يَأْتِكَ فَٱتَّبِعْنِى أَهْدِكَ صِرَٰطًا سَوِيًّا ٤٣

44. "O my father! Worship not *Shaitân* (Satan). Verily, *Shaitân* (Satan) has been a rebel against the Most Gracious (Allâh).

يَٰٓأَبَتِ لَا تَعْبُدِ ٱلشَّيْطَٰنَ إِنَّ ٱلشَّيْطَٰنَ كَانَ لِلرَّحْمَٰنِ عَصِيًّا ٤٤

45. "O my father! Verily, I fear lest a torment from the Most Gracious (Allâh) should overtake you, so that you become a companion of *Shaitân* (Satan) (in the Hell-fire)." [*Tafsir Al-Qurtubî*]

يَٰٓأَبَتِ إِنِّى أَخَافُ أَن يَمَسَّكَ عَذَابٌ مِّنَ ٱلرَّحْمَٰنِ فَتَكُونَ لِلشَّيْطَٰنِ وَلِيًّا ٤٥

46. He (the father) said: "Do you reject my gods, O Ibrâhîm (Abraham)?

قَالَ أَرَاغِبٌ أَنتَ عَنْ ءَالِهَتِى

---

will say, 'Do you know this?' They will say, 'Yes, this is death.'" And by then all of them would have seen it. Then it (that ram) will be slaughtered and the caller will say. 'O people of Paradise! Eternity for you and no death. O people of Hell! Eternity for you and no death.' Then the Prophet صلى الله عليه وسلم recited: "And warn them (O Muhammad صلى الله عليه وسلم) of the Day of grief and regrets when the case has been decided, while (now) (i.e. the people of the world) are in a state of carelessness and they believe not." (*Sahih Al-Bukhari*, Vol.6, *Hadith* No.254).

If you stop not (this), I will indeed stone you. So get away from me safely (before I punish you)."

47. Ibrâhîm (Abraham) said: "Peace be on you! I will ask forgiveness of my Lord for you. Verily, He is unto me Ever Most Gracious.

48. "And I shall turn away from you and from those whom you invoke besides Allâh. And I shall call upon my Lord and I hope that I shall not be unblest in my invocation to my Lord."

49. So when he had turned away from them and from those whom they worshipped besides Allâh, We gave him Ishâq (Isaac) and Ya'qûb (Jacob), and each one of them We made a Prophet.

50. And We gave them of Our Mercy (a good provision in plenty), and We granted them honour on the tongues (of all the nations, i.e. everybody remembers them with a good praise).[1]

51. And mention in the Book (this Qur'ân) Mûsâ (Moses). Verily, he was chosen and he was a Messenger (and) a Prophet.

52. And We called him from the right side of the Mount, and made him draw near to Us for a talk with him [Mûsâ (Moses)].

---

[1] (V.19:50) See the footnote of (V.2:135) and the footnotes (A, B and C) of (V.16:121)

53. And We granted him his brother Hârûn (Aaron), (also) a Prophet, out of Our Mercy.

54. And mention in the Book (the Qur'ân) Ismâ'îl (Ishmael). Verily, he was true to what he promised, and he was a Messenger, (and) a Prophet.

55. And he used to enjoin on his family and his people As-Salât (the prayers) and the Zakât, and his Lord was pleased with him.

56. And mention in the Book (the Qur'ân) Idrîs (Enoch). Verily, he was a man of truth, (and) a Prophet.

57. And We raised him to a high station.

58. Those were they unto whom Allâh bestowed His Grace from among the Prophets, of the offspring of Adam, and of those whom We carried (in the ship) with Nûh (Noah), and of the offspring of Ibrâhîm (Abraham) and Israel, and from among those whom We guided and chose. When the Verses of the Most Gracious (Allâh) were recited unto them, they fell down prostrate and weeping.[1]

59. Then, there has succeeded them a posterity who have given up As-Salât (the prayers) [i.e. made their Salât (prayers) to be lost, either by not offering them or by not offering them

---

[1] (V.19:58) Prostration: The reciter of the Qur'ân at this place should prostrate himself to Allâh, facing the Ka'bah at Makkah.

perfectly or by not offering them in their proper fixed times) and have followed lusts.[1] So they will be thrown in Hell.

60. Except those who repent and believe (in the Oneness of Allâh and His Messenger Muhammad ﷺ), and work righteousness.[2] Such will enter Paradise and they will not be wronged in aught.

إِلَّا مَن تَابَ وَءَامَنَ وَعَمِلَ صَلِحًا فَأُوْلَئِكَ يَدْخُلُونَ الْجَنَّةَ وَلَا يُظْلَمُونَ شَيْئًا ﴿٦٠﴾

61. (They will enter) 'Adn (Eden) Paradise (everlasting Gardens), which the Most Gracious (Allâh) has promised to His slaves in the Unseen: Verily, His Promise must come to pass.

جَنَّتِ عَدْنٍ الَّتِى وَعَدَ الرَّحْمَنُ عِبَادَهُ بِالْغَيْبِ إِنَّهُ كَانَ وَعْدُهُ مَأْتِيًّا ﴿٦١﴾

62. They shall not hear therein (in Paradise) any Laghw (dirty, false, evil vain talk), but only Salâm (salutations of peace). And they will have therein their sustenance, morning and afternoon. [See (V.40:55)].

لَا يَسْمَعُونَ فِيهَا لَغْوًا إِلَّا سَلَامًا وَلَهُمْ رِزْقُهُمْ فِيهَا بُكْرَةً وَعَشِيًّا ﴿٦٢﴾

63. Such is the Paradise which We shall give as an inheritance to those of Our slaves who have been Al-Muttaqûn (the pious. See V.2:2).

تِلْكَ الْجَنَّةُ الَّتِى نُورِثُ مِنْ عِبَادِنَا مَن كَانَ تَقِيًّا ﴿٦٣﴾

64. And we (angels) descend not except by the Command of your Lord

وَمَا نَتَنَزَّلُ إِلَّا بِأَمْرِ رَبِّكَ

---

[1] (V.19:59) Like drinking alcoholic drinks; giving false witnesses; eating unlawful things - meats of edible animals not slaughtered according to Allâh's Order; taking intoxicants; narcotic drugs like opium, morphine, heroin, cannabis; committing crimes; evil wicked deeds like illegal sexual acts, murdering, taking others' rights unlawfully, robbing, stealing, betraying, backbiting, slandering, telling lies.

[2] (V.19:60) See the footnote of (V.9:121).

(O Muhammad صلى الله عليه وسلم). To Him belongs what is before us and what is behind us, and what is between those two; and your Lord is never forgetful —

لَهُ مَا بَيْنَ أَيْدِينَا وَمَا خَلْفَنَا وَمَا بَيْنَ ذَٰلِكَ وَمَا كَانَ رَبُّكَ نَسِيًّا ٦٤

65. Lord of the heavens and the earth, and all that is between them, so worship Him (Alone) and be constant and patient in His worship. Do you know of any who is similar to Him? (of course none is similar or co-equal or comparable to Him, and He has none as partner with Him). [There is nothing like unto Him and He is the All-Hearer, the All-Seer].[1]

رَبُّ السَّمَاوَاتِ وَالْأَرْضِ وَمَا بَيْنَهُمَا فَاعْبُدْهُ وَاصْطَبِرْ لِعِبَادَتِهِ هَلْ تَعْلَمُ لَهُ سَمِيًّا ٦٥

66. And man (the disbeliever) says: "When I am dead, shall I then be raised up alive?"

وَيَقُولُ الْإِنسَانُ أَءِذَا مَا مِتُّ لَسَوْفَ أُخْرَجُ حَيًّا ٦٦

67. Does not man remember that We created him before, while he was nothing?

أَوَلَا يَذْكُرُ الْإِنسَانُ أَنَّا خَلَقْنَاهُ مِن قَبْلُ وَلَمْ يَكُ شَيْئًا ٦٧

68. So by your Lord, surely, We shall gather them together, and (also) the *Shayâtîn* (devils) with them, then We shall bring them round Hell on their knees.

فَوَرَبِّكَ لَنَحْشُرَنَّهُمْ وَالشَّيَاطِينَ ثُمَّ لَنُحْضِرَنَّهُمْ حَوْلَ جَهَنَّمَ جِثِيًّا ٦٨

69. Then indeed We shall drag out from every sect all those who were worst in obstinate rebellion against the Most Gracious (Allâh).

ثُمَّ لَنَنزِعَنَّ مِن كُلِّ شِيعَةٍ أَيُّهُمْ أَشَدُّ عَلَى الرَّحْمَٰنِ عِتِيًّا ٦٩

70. Then, verily, We know best those who are most worthy of being burnt therein.

ثُمَّ لَنَحْنُ أَعْلَمُ بِالَّذِينَ هُمْ أَوْلَىٰ بِهَا صِلِيًّا ٧٠

---

[1] (V.19:65) See the footnote of (V.3:73).

71. There is not one of you but will pass over it (Hell): this is with your Lord; a Decree which must be accomplished.[1]

وَإِن مِّنكُمْ إِلَّا وَارِدُهَا ۚ كَانَ عَلَىٰ رَبِّكَ حَتْمًا مَّقْضِيًّا ٧١

72. Then We shall save those who use to fear Allâh and were dutiful to Him. And We shall leave the *Zâlimûn* (polytheists and wrongdoers) therein (humbled) to their knees (in Hell).

ثُمَّ نُنَجِّي الَّذِينَ اتَّقَوا وَّنَذَرُ الظَّالِمِينَ فِيهَا جِثِيًّا ٧٢

73. And when Our Clear Verses are recited to them, those who disbelieve (the rich and strong among the pagans of Quraish who live a life of luxury) say to those who believe (the weak, poor companions of Prophet Muhammad صلى الله عليه وسلم who have a hard life): "Which of the two groups (i.e. believers or disbelievers) is best in (point of) position and as regards station (place of council for consultation)."

وَإِذَا تُتْلَىٰ عَلَيْهِمْ ءَايَـٰتُنَا بَيِّنَـٰتٍ قَالَ الَّذِينَ كَفَرُوا لِلَّذِينَ ءَامَنُوا أَيُّ الْفَرِيقَيْنِ خَيْرٌ مَّقَامًا وَأَحْسَنُ نَدِيًّا ٧٣

74. And how many a generation (past nations) have We destroyed before them, who were better in wealth, goods and outward appearance?

وَكَمْ أَهْلَكْنَا قَبْلَهُم مِّن قَرْنٍ هُمْ أَحْسَنُ أَثَـٰثًا وَرِءْيًا ٧٤

75. Say (O Muhammad صلى الله عليه وسلم) whoever is in error, the Most Gracious (Allâh) will extend (the rope) to him, until, when they see that which they were promised, either the torment or the Hour, they will come to know who is worst in position, and who is weaker in forces. [This is the answer to the question in Verse No.19:73]

قُلْ مَن كَانَ فِي الضَّلَـٰلَةِ فَلْيَمْدُدْ لَهُ الرَّحْمَـٰنُ مَدًّا ۚ حَتَّىٰ إِذَا رَأَوْا مَا يُوعَدُونَ إِمَّا الْعَذَابَ وَإِمَّا السَّاعَةَ فَسَيَعْلَمُونَ مَنْ هُوَ شَرٌّ مَّكَانًا وَأَضْعَفُ جُندًا ٧٥

---

[1] (V.19:71) See the footnote (C) of (V.68:42).

76. And Allâh increases in guidance those who walk aright.[1] And the righteous good deeds that last, are better with your Lord, for reward and better for resort.

وَيَزِيدُ اللَّهُ الَّذِينَ اهْتَدَوْا هُدًى وَالْبَاقِيَاتُ الصَّالِحَاتُ خَيْرٌ عِندَ رَبِّكَ ثَوَابًا وَخَيْرٌ مَّرَدًّا ۝

77. Have you seen him who disbelieved in Our *Ayât* (this Qur'ân and Muhammad صلى الله عليه وسلم) and said: "I shall certainly be given wealth and children [if I will be alive (again)]."

أَفَرَأَيْتَ الَّذِى كَفَرَ بِئَايَٰتِنَا وَقَالَ لَأُوتَيَنَّ مَالًا وَوَلَدًا ۝

78. Has he known the Unseen or has he taken a covenant from the Most Gracious (Allâh)?

أَطَّلَعَ الْغَيْبَ أَمِ اتَّخَذَ عِندَ الرَّحْمَٰنِ عَهْدًا ۝

79. Nay, We shall record what he says, and We shall increase his torment (in the Hell);

كَلَّا سَنَكْتُبُ مَا يَقُولُ وَنَمُدُّ لَهُ مِنَ الْعَذَابِ مَدًّا ۝

80. And We shall inherit from him (at his death) all that he talks of (i.e. wealth and children which We have bestowed upon him in this world), and he shall come to Us alone.

وَنَرِثُهُ مَا يَقُولُ وَيَأْتِينَا فَرْدًا ۝

81. And they have taken (for worship) *âlihah* (gods) besides Allâh, that they might give them honour, power and glory (and also protect them from Allâh's punishment).

وَاتَّخَذُوا مِن دُونِ اللَّهِ ءَالِهَةً لِّيَكُونُوا لَهُمْ عِزًّا ۝

82. Nay, but they (the so-called gods) will deny their worship of them, and become opponents to them (on the Day of Resurrection).

كَلَّا سَيَكْفُرُونَ بِعِبَادَتِهِمْ وَيَكُونُونَ عَلَيْهِمْ ضِدًّا ۝

---

[1] (V.19:76) Those who walk aright: True believers in the Oneness of Allâh — who fear Allâh much (abstain from all kinds of sins and evil deeds which He has forbidden), and love Allâh much (perform all kinds of good deeds which He has ordained).

83. See you not that We have sent the *Shayâtîn* (devils) against the disbelievers to push them to do evil.

الَمْ تَرَ أَنَّا أَرْسَلْنَا الشَّيَاطِينَ عَلَى الْكَافِرِينَ تَؤُزُّهُمْ أَزًّا ۝

84. So make no haste against them; We only count out to them (a limited) number (of the days of the life of this world and delay their term so that they may increase in evil and sins).

فَلَا تَعْجَلْ عَلَيْهِمْ إِنَّمَا نَعُدُّ لَهُمْ عَدًّا ۝

85. The Day We shall gather the *Muttaqûn* (the pious. See V.2:2) unto the Most Gracious (Allâh), like a delegation (presented before a king for honour).

يَوْمَ نَحْشُرُ الْمُتَّقِينَ إِلَى الرَّحْمَنِ وَفْدًا ۝

86. And We shall drive the *Mujrimûn* (polytheists, sinners, criminals, disbelievers in the Oneness of Allâh) to Hell, in a thirsty state (like a thirsty herd driven down to water).

وَنَسُوقُ الْمُجْرِمِينَ إِلَى جَهَنَّمَ وِرْدًا ۝

87. None shall have the power of intercession, but such a one as has received permission (or promise) from the Most Gracious (Allâh).

لَا يَمْلِكُونَ الشَّفَاعَةَ إِلَّا مَنِ اتَّخَذَ عِندَ الرَّحْمَنِ عَهْدًا ۝

88. And they say: "The Most Gracious (Allâh) has begotten a son (or offspring or children) [as the Jews say: 'Uzair (Ezra) is the son of Allâh, and the Christians say that He has begotten a son ['Îsâ (Jesus) عليه السلام], and the pagan Arabs say that He has begotten daughters (angels and others)]."

وَقَالُوا اتَّخَذَ الرَّحْمَنُ وَلَدًا ۝

89. Indeed you have brought forth (said) a terrible evil thing.

لَقَدْ جِئْتُمْ شَيْئًا إِدًّا ۝

90. Whereby the heavens are almost torn, and the earth is split asunder, and the mountains fall in ruins,

تَكَادُ السَّمَاوَاتُ يَتَفَطَّرْنَ مِنْهُ وَتَنشَقُّ الْأَرْضُ وَتَخِرُّ الْجِبَالُ هَدًّا ۝

91. That they ascribe a son (or offspring or children) to the Most Gracious (Allâh).

أَن دَعَوْا لِلرَّحْمَنِ وَلَدًا ﴿٩١﴾

92. But it is not suitable for (the Majesty of) the Most Gracious (Allâh) that He should beget a son (or offspring or children).

وَمَا يَنۢبَغِى لِلرَّحْمَنِ أَن يَتَّخِذَ وَلَدًا ﴿٩٢﴾

93. There is none in the heavens and the earth but comes unto the Most Gracious (Allâh) as a slave.

إِن كُلُّ مَن فِى ٱلسَّمَٰوَٰتِ وَٱلْأَرْضِ إِلَّآ ءَاتِى ٱلرَّحْمَٰنِ عَبْدًا ﴿٩٣﴾

94. Verily, He knows each one of them, and has counted them a full counting.

لَّقَدْ أَحْصَىٰهُمْ وَعَدَّهُمْ عَدًّا ﴿٩٤﴾

95. And everyone of them will come to Him alone on the Day of Resurrection (without any helper, or protector or defender).

وَكُلُّهُمْ ءَاتِيهِ يَوْمَ ٱلْقِيَٰمَةِ فَرْدًا ﴿٩٥﴾

96. Verily, those who believe [in the Oneness of Allâh and in His Messenger (Muhammad ﷺ)] and work deeds of righteousness, the Most Gracious (Allâh) will bestow love for them[1] (in the hearts of the believers).

إِنَّ ٱلَّذِينَ ءَامَنُوا۟ وَعَمِلُوا۟ ٱلصَّٰلِحَٰتِ سَيَجْعَلُ لَهُمُ ٱلرَّحْمَٰنُ وُدًّا ﴿٩٦﴾

97. So We have made this (the Qur'ân) easy in your own tongue (O Muhammad ﷺ), only that you

فَإِنَّمَا يَسَّرْنَٰهُ بِلِسَانِكَ لِتُبَشِّرَ بِهِ ٱلْمُتَّقِينَ

---

[1] (V.19:96) Narrated Abu Hurairah رضي الله عنه The Prophet صلى الله عليه وسلم said, "If Allâh loves a person, He calls Jibrael (Gabriel) saying: Allâh loves so-and-so; O Jibrael (Gabriel) love him.' Jibrael (Gabriel) would love him, and then Jibrael (Gabriel) would make an announcement among the residents of the heavens, 'Allâh loves so-and-so, therefore, you should love him also.' So, all the residents of the heavens would love him and then he is granted the pleasure of the people of the earth." (Sahih Al-Bukhari, Vol. 8, Hadith No. 66).

may give glad tidings to the *Muttaqûn* (the pious. See V.2:2), and warn with it the *Ludd*[1] (most quarrelsome) people.

98. And how many a generation before them have We destroyed! Can you (O Muhammad صلى الله عليه وسلم) find a single one of them or hear even a whisper of them?

Sûrat Tâ-Hâ. XX

*In the Name of Allâh
the Most Gracious, the Most Merciful*

1. *Tâ-Hâ.*

[These letters are one of the miracles of the Qur'ân, and none but Allâh (Alone) knows their meanings.]

2. We have not sent down the Qur'ân unto you (O Muhammad صلى الله عليه وسلم) to cause you distress,

3. But only as a Reminder to those who fear (Allâh).

4. A revelation from Him (Allâh) Who has created the earth and high heavens.

5. The Most Gracious (Allâh) rose over (*Istawâ*) the (Mighty) Throne (in a manner that suits His Majesty).

6. To Him belongs all that is in the heavens and all that is on the earth, and

---

[1] (V.19:97) *Ludd*:- The people who don't believe in Allâh's Oneness and His Prophet's message and argue about everything that Allâh has ordained.

all that is between them, and all that is under the soil.

7. And if you (O Muhammad ﷺ) speak (the invocation) aloud, then verily, He knows the secret and that which is yet more hidden.

8. Allâh! Lâ ilâhla illa Huwa (none has the right to be worshipped but He)! To Him belong the Best Names.[1]

9. And has there come to you the story of Mûsâ (Moses)?

10. When he saw a fire, he said to his family: "Wait! Verily, I have seen a fire; perhaps I can bring you some burning brand therefrom, or find some guidance at the fire."

11. And when he came to it (the fire), he was called by name: "O Mûsâ (Moses)!

12. "Verily, I am your Lord! So take off your shoes; you are in the sacred valley, Tuwa.

13. "And I have chosen you. So listen to that which will be revealed (to you).

14. "Verily, I am Allâh! Lâ ilâha illa Ana (none has the right to be worshipped but I), so worship Me, and perform As-Salât (Iqâmat-as-Salât) for My Remembrance.

15. "Verily, the Hour is coming — and I am almost hiding it from Myself — that every person may be rewarded for that which he strives.

---

[1] (V.20:8) See the footnote of (V.7:180).

16. "Therefore, let not the one who believes not therein (i.e. in the Day of Resurrection, Reckoning, Paradise and Hell), but follows his own lusts,[1] divert you therefrom, lest you perish.

17. "And what is that in your right hand, O Mûsâ (Moses)?"

18. He said: "This is my stick, whereon I lean, and wherewith I beat down branches for my sheep, and wherein I find other uses."

19. (Allâh) said: "Cast it down, O Mûsâ (Moses)!"

20. He cast it down, and behold! It was a snake, moving quickly.

21. Allâh said: "Grasp it and fear not; We shall return it to its former state,

22. "And press your (right) hand to your (left) side: it will come forth white (and shining), without any disease as another sign, —

23. "That We may show you (some) of Our Greater Signs.

24. "Go to Fir'aun (Pharaoh)! Verily, he has transgressed (all bounds in disbelief and disobedience, and has behaved as an arrogant and as a tyrant)."

25. [Mûsâ (Moses)] said: "O my Lord! Open for me my chest (grant me self-confidence, contentment, and boldness).

26. "And ease my task for me;

---

[1] (V.20:16) See the footnote of (V.19:59)

27. "And loose the knot (the defect) from my tongue, (i.e. remove the incorrectness from my speech) [That occurred as a result of a brand of fire which Mûsâ (Moses) put in his mouth when he was an infant]. [*Tafsir At-Tabarî*].

28. "That they understand my speech.

29. "And appoint for me a helper from my family,

30. "Hârûn (Aaron), my brother.

31. "Increase my strength with him,

32. "And let him share my task (of conveying Allâh's Message and Prophethood)!

33. "That we may glorify You much,

34. "And remember You much,

35. "Verily, You are Ever a Well-Seer of us."

36. (Allâh) said: "You are granted your request, O Mûsâ (Moses)!

37. "And indeed We conferred a favour on you another time (before).

38. "When We inspired your mother with that which We inspired.

39. "Saying: 'Put him (the child) into the *Tabût* (a box or a case or a chest) and put it into the river (Nile); then the river shall cast it up on the bank, and there, an enemy of Mine and an enemy of his shall take him.' And I endued you with love from Me, in order that you may be brought up under My Eye.

40. "When your sister went and said: 'Shall I show you one who will nurse him?' So We restored you to your mother, that she might cool her eyes and she should not grieve. Then you did kill a man, but We saved you from great distress and tried you with a heavy trial. Then you stayed a number of years with the people of Madyan (Midian). Then you came here according to the fixed term which I ordained (for you), O Mûsâ (Moses)!

أَدُلُّكُمْ عَلَىٰ مَن يَكْفُلُهُۥ
فَرَجَعْنَٰكَ إِلَىٰٓ أُمِّكَ كَىْ تَقَرَّ عَيْنُهَا
وَلَا تَحْزَنَ وَقَتَلْتَ نَفْسًا
فَنَجَّيْنَٰكَ مِنَ ٱلْغَمِّ وَفَتَنَّٰكَ فُتُونًا
فَلَبِثْتَ سِنِينَ فِىٓ أَهْلِ مَدْيَنَ
ثُمَّ جِئْتَ عَلَىٰ قَدَرٍ يَٰمُوسَىٰ ۝

41. "And I have chosen you[1] for Myself.

وَٱصْطَنَعْتُكَ لِنَفْسِى ۝

42. "Go you and your brother with My *Ayât* (proofs, evidences, verses, lessons, signs, revelations, etc.), and do not, you both, slacken and become weak in My Remembrance.

ٱذْهَبْ أَنتَ وَأَخُوكَ بِـَٔايَٰتِى
وَلَا تَنِيَا فِى ذِكْرِى ۝

43. "Go, both of you, to Fir'aun (Pharaoh), verily, he has transgressed (all bounds in disbelief and disobedience and behaved as an arrogant and as a tyrant).

ٱذْهَبَآ إِلَىٰ فِرْعَوْنَ إِنَّهُۥ طَغَىٰ ۝

44. "And speak to him mildly, perhaps he may accept admonition or fear (Allâh)."

فَقُولَا لَهُۥ قَوْلًا لَّيِّنًا لَّعَلَّهُۥ يَتَذَكَّرُ
أَوْ يَخْشَىٰ ۝

45. They said: "Our Lord! Verily, we fear lest he should hasten to punish us or lest he should transgress (all bounds against us)."

قَالَا رَبَّنَآ إِنَّنَا نَخَافُ أَن يَفْرُطَ
عَلَيْنَآ أَوْ أَن يَطْغَىٰ ۝

46. He (Allâh) said: "Fear not, verily, I am with you both, hearing and seeing.

قَالَ لَا تَخَافَآ إِنَّنِى مَعَكُمَآ
أَسْمَعُ وَأَرَىٰ ۝

---

[1] (V.20:41) i.e. chosen you for My Revelation and My Message or created you for Myself or strengthened and taught you as to how to preach My Message to My worshippers. (*Tafsîr Al-Qurtubî*)

47. "So go you both to him, and say: 'Verily, we are Messengers of your Lord, so let the Children of Israel go with us, and torment them not; indeed, we have come with a sign from your Lord! And peace will be upon him who follows the guidance!

48. 'Truly, it has been revealed to us that the torment will be for him who denies [believes not in the Oneness of Allâh, and in His Messengers], and turns away'(from the truth and obedience of Allâh)."

49. Fir'aun (Pharaoh) said: "Who then, O Mûsâ (Moses), is the Lord of you two?"

50. [Mûsâ (Moses)] said: "Our Lord is He Who gave to each thing its form and nature, then guided it aright."

51. [Fir'aun (Pharaoh)] said: "What about the generations of old?"

52. [Mûsâ (Moses)] said: "The knowledge thereof is with my Lord, in a Record. My Lord neither errs nor He forgets."

53. Who has made earth for you like a bed (spread out); and has opened roads (ways and paths) for you therein; and has sent down water (rain) from the sky. And We have brought forth with it various kinds of vegetation.

54. Eat and pasture your cattle (therein); verily, in this are Ayât (proofs and signs) for men of understanding.

55. Thereof (the earth) We created you, and into it We shall return you, and from it We shall bring you out once again.

56. And indeed We showed him [Fir'aun (Pharaoh)] all Our *Ayât* (signs and evidences), but he denied and refused.

57. He [Fir'aun (Pharaoh)] said: "Have you come to drive us out of our land with your magic, O Mûsâ (Moses)?

58. "Then verily, we can produce magic the like thereof; so appoint a meeting between us and you, which neither we nor you shall fail to keep, in an open place where both shall have a just and equal chance (and beholders could witness the competition)."

59. [Mûsâ (Moses)] said: "Your appointed meeting is the day of the festival, and let the people assemble when the sun has risen (forenoon)."

60. So Fir'aun (Pharaoh) withdrew, devised his plot and then came back.

61. Mûsâ (Moses) said to them: "Woe unto you! Invent not a lie against Allâh, lest He should destroy you completely by a torment. And surely, he who invents a lie (against Allâh) will fail miserably."

62. Then they debated one with another what they must do, and they kept their talk secret.

63. They said: "Verily, these are two magicians. Their object is to drive you out from your land with magic, and overcome your chiefs and nobles.

64. "So devise your plot, and then assemble in line. And whoever overcomes this day will be indeed successful."

فَأَجْمِعُوا۟ كَيْدَكُمْ ثُمَّ ٱئْتُوا۟ صَفًّا وَقَدْ أَفْلَحَ ٱلْيَوْمَ مَنِ ٱسْتَعْلَىٰ ٦٤

65. They said:"O Mûsâ (Moses)! Either you throw first or we be the first to throw?"

قَالُوا۟ يَٰمُوسَىٰٓ إِمَّآ أَن تُلْقِىَ وَإِمَّآ أَن نَّكُونَ أَوَّلَ مَنْ أَلْقَىٰ ٦٥

66. [Mûsâ (Moses)] said: "Nay, throw you (first)!" Then behold! their ropes and their sticks, by their magic, appeared to him as though they moved fast.

قَالَ بَلْ أَلْقُوا۟ فَإِذَا حِبَالُهُمْ وَعِصِيُّهُمْ يُخَيَّلُ إِلَيْهِ مِن سِحْرِهِمْ أَنَّهَا تَسْعَىٰ ٦٦

67. So Mûsâ (Moses) conceived fear in himself.

فَأَوْجَسَ فِى نَفْسِهِۦ خِيفَةً مُّوسَىٰ ٦٧

68. We (Allâh) said: "Fear not! Surely, you will have the upper hand.

قُلْنَا لَا تَخَفْ إِنَّكَ أَنتَ ٱلْأَعْلَىٰ ٦٨

69. "And throw that which is in your right hand! It will swallow up that which they have made. That which they have made is only a magician's trick, and the magician will never be successful, to whatever amount (of skill) he may attain.

وَأَلْقِ مَا فِى يَمِينِكَ تَلْقَفْ مَا صَنَعُوٓا۟ إِنَّمَا صَنَعُوا۟ كَيْدُ سَٰحِرٍ وَلَا يُفْلِحُ ٱلسَّاحِرُ حَيْثُ أَتَىٰ ٦٩

70. So the magicians fell down prostrate. They said: "We believe in the Lord of Hârûn (Aaron) and Mûsâ (Moses)."

فَأُلْقِىَ ٱلسَّحَرَةُ سُجَّدًا قَالُوٓا۟ ءَامَنَّا بِرَبِّ هَٰرُونَ وَمُوسَىٰ ٧٠

71. [Fir'aun (Pharaoh)] said: "Believe you in him [Mûsâ (Moses)] before I give you permission? Verily, he is your chief who has taught you magic. So I will surely, cut off your hands and feet on opposite sides, and I will surely, crucify you on the trunks of date-palms, and you shall surely, know

قَالَ ءَامَنتُمْ لَهُۥ قَبْلَ أَنْ ءَاذَنَ لَكُمْ إِنَّهُۥ لَكَبِيرُكُمُ ٱلَّذِى عَلَّمَكُمُ ٱلسِّحْرَ فَلَأُقَطِّعَنَّ أَيْدِيَكُمْ وَأَرْجُلَكُم مِّنْ خِلَٰفٍ وَلَأُصَلِّبَنَّكُمْ فِى جُذُوعِ ٱلنَّخْلِ وَلَتَعْلَمُنَّ أَيُّنَآ

which of us [I (Fir'aun - Pharaoh) or the Lord of Mûsâ (Moses) (Allâh)] can give the severe and more lasting torment."

أَشَدُّ عَذَابًا وَأَبْقَى ۝

72. They said: "We prefer you not over what have come to us of the clear signs and to Him (Allâh) Who created us. So decree whatever you desire to decree, for you can only decree (regarding) this life of the world.

قَالُوا لَن نُّؤْثِرَكَ عَلَى مَا جَاءَنَا مِنَ الْبَيِّنَاتِ وَالَّذِى فَطَرَنَا فَاقْضِ مَا أَنتَ قَاضٍ إِنَّمَا تَقْضِى هَٰذِهِ الْحَيَاةَ الدُّنْيَا ۝

73. "Verily, we have believed in our Lord, that He may forgive us our faults, and the magic to which you did compel us. And Allâh is better as regards reward in comparison to your [Fir'aun's (Pharaoh)] reward, and more lasting (as regards punishment in comparison to your punishment)."

إِنَّا آمَنَّا بِرَبِّنَا لِيَغْفِرَ لَنَا خَطَايَانَا وَمَا أَكْرَهْتَنَا عَلَيْهِ مِنَ السِّحْرِ وَاللَّهُ خَيْرٌ وَأَبْقَى ۝

74. Verily, whoever comes to his Lord as a *Mujrim* (criminal, polytheist, sinner, disbeliever in the Oneness of Allâh and His Messengers), then surely, for him is Hell, wherein he will neither die nor live.

إِنَّهُ مَن يَأْتِ رَبَّهُ مُجْرِمًا فَإِنَّ لَهُ جَهَنَّمَ لَا يَمُوتُ فِيهَا وَلَا يَحْيَىٰ ۝

75. But whoever comes to Him (Allâh) as a believer (in the Oneness of Allâh), and has done righteous good deeds, for such are the high ranks (in the Hereafter), —

وَمَن يَأْتِهِ مُؤْمِنًا قَدْ عَمِلَ الصَّالِحَاتِ فَأُوْلَٰئِكَ لَهُمُ الدَّرَجَاتُ الْعُلَىٰ ۝

76. 'Adn (Eden) Paradise (everlasting Gardens), under which rivers flow, wherein they will abide forever: such is the reward of those who purify themselves (by abstaining from all kinds of sins and evil deeds which Allâh has forbidden and by doing all that Allâh has ordained).

جَنَّاتُ عَدْنٍ تَجْرِى مِن تَحْتِهَا الْأَنْهَارُ خَالِدِينَ فِيهَا وَذَٰلِكَ جَزَاءُ مَن تَزَكَّىٰ ۝

77. And indeed We revealed to Mûsâ (Moses) (saying): "Travel by night with '*Ibâdi* (My slaves) and strike a dry path for them in the sea, fearing neither to be overtaken [by Fir'aun (Pharaoh)] nor being afraid (of drowning in the sea)."

وَلَقَدْ أَوْحَيْنَا إِلَى مُوسَىٰ أَنْ أَسْرِ بِعِبَادِى فَاضْرِبْ لَهُمْ طَرِيقًا فِى الْبَحْرِ يَبَسًا لَّا تَخَافُ دَرَكًا وَلَا تَخْشَىٰ ۞

78. Then Fir'aun (Pharaoh) pursued them with his hosts, but the sea-water completely overwhelmed them and covered them up.

فَأَتْبَعَهُمْ فِرْعَوْنُ بِجُنُودِهِ فَغَشِيَهُم مِّنَ الْيَمِّ مَا غَشِيَهُمْ ۞

79. And Fir'aun (Pharaoh) led his people astray, and he did not guide them.

وَأَضَلَّ فِرْعَوْنُ قَوْمَهُ وَمَا هَدَىٰ ۞

80. O Children of Israel! We delivered you from your enemy, and We made a covenant with you on the right side of the Mount, and We sent down to you *Al-Manna*[1] and quails,

يَبَنِى إِسْرَٰٓءِيلَ قَدْ أَنجَيْنَٰكُم مِّنْ عَدُوِّكُمْ وَوَٰعَدْنَٰكُمْ جَانِبَ الطُّورِ الْأَيْمَنَ وَنَزَّلْنَا عَلَيْكُمُ الْمَنَّ وَالسَّلْوَىٰ ۞

81. (Saying) eat of the *Tayyibât* (good lawful things) wherewith We have provided you, and commit no transgression or oppression therein, lest My Anger should justly descend on you. And he on whom My Anger descends, he is indeed perished. [*Tafsir At-Tabari*]

كُلُوا مِن طَيِّبَٰتِ مَا رَزَقْنَٰكُمْ وَلَا تَطْغَوْا فِيهِ فَيَحِلَّ عَلَيْكُمْ غَضَبِى وَمَن يَحْلِلْ عَلَيْهِ غَضَبِى فَقَدْ هَوَىٰ ۞

82. And verily, I am indeed forgiving to him who repents, believes (in My Oneness, and associates none in worship with Me) and does righteous good deeds, and then remains constant in doing them, (till his death).

وَإِنِّى لَغَفَّارٌ لِّمَن تَابَ وَءَامَنَ وَعَمِلَ صَٰلِحًا ثُمَّ اهْتَدَىٰ ۞

83. "And what made you hasten from your people, O Mûsâ (Moses)?"

وَمَا أَعْجَلَكَ عَن قَوْمِكَ يَٰمُوسَىٰ ۞

---

[1] (V.20:80) See the footnote of (V.2:57).

84. He said: "They are close on my footsteps: and I hastened to You, O my Lord, that You might be pleased."

قَالَ هُمْ أُولَاءِ عَلَىٰ أَثَرِي وَعَجِلْتُ إِلَيْكَ رَبِّ لِتَرْضَىٰ ٨٤

85. (Allâh) said: "Verily, We have tried your people in your absence, and As-Sâmirî has led them astray."

قَالَ فَإِنَّا قَدْ فَتَنَّا قَوْمَكَ مِنۢ بَعْدِكَ وَأَضَلَّهُمُ ٱلسَّامِرِيُّ ٨٥

86. Then Mûsâ (Moses) returned to his people in a state of anger and sorrow. He said: "O my people! Did not your Lord promise you a fair promise? Did then the promise seem to you long in coming? Or did you desire that wrath should descend from your Lord on you, that you broke your promise to me (i.e disbelieving in Allâh and worshipping the calf)?"

فَرَجَعَ مُوسَىٰٓ إِلَىٰ قَوْمِهِۦ غَضْبَٰنَ أَسِفًا قَالَ يَٰقَوْمِ أَلَمْ يَعِدْكُمْ رَبُّكُمْ وَعْدًا حَسَنًا أَفَطَالَ عَلَيْكُمُ ٱلْعَهْدُ أَمْ أَرَدتُّمْ أَن يَحِلَّ عَلَيْكُمْ غَضَبٌ مِّن رَّبِّكُمْ فَأَخْلَفْتُم مَّوْعِدِي ٨٦

87. They said: "We broke not the promise to you, of our own will, but we were made to carry the weight of the ornaments of the [Fir'aun's (Pharaoh)] people, then we cast them (into the fire), and that was what As-Sâmirî suggested."

قَالُوا مَآ أَخْلَفْنَا مَوْعِدَكَ بِمَلْكِنَا وَلَٰكِنَّا حُمِّلْنَآ أَوْزَارًا مِّن زِينَةِ ٱلْقَوْمِ فَقَذَفْنَٰهَا فَكَذَٰلِكَ أَلْقَى ٱلسَّامِرِيُّ ٨٧

88. Then he took out (of the fire) for them (a statue of) a calf which seemed to low. They said: "This is your *ilâh* (god), and the *ilâh* (god) of Mûsâ (Moses), but he [Mûsâ (Moses)] has forgotten (his god).'"

فَأَخْرَجَ لَهُمْ عِجْلًا جَسَدًا لَّهُۥ خُوَارٌ فَقَالُوا هَٰذَآ إِلَٰهُكُمْ وَإِلَٰهُ مُوسَىٰ فَنَسِيَ ٨٨

89. Did they not see that it could not return them a word (for answer), and that it had no power either to harm them or to do them good?

أَفَلَا يَرَوْنَ أَلَّا يَرْجِعُ إِلَيْهِمْ قَوْلًا وَلَا يَمْلِكُ لَهُمْ ضَرًّا وَلَا نَفْعًا ٨٩

90. And Hârûn (Aaron) indeed had said to them beforehand: "O my people! You are being tried in this, and verily, your Lord is (Allâh) the Most Gracious, so follow me and obey my order."

وَلَقَدْ قَالَ لَهُمْ هَٰرُونُ مِن قَبْلُ يَٰقَوْمِ إِنَّمَا فُتِنتُم بِهِۦ وَإِنَّ رَبَّكُمُ ٱلرَّحْمَٰنُ فَٱتَّبِعُونِي وَأَطِيعُوٓا أَمْرِي ٩٠

91. They said: "We will not stop worshipping it (i.e. the calf), until Mûsâ (Moses) returns to us."

قَالُوا۟ لَن نَّبْرَحَ عَلَيْهِ عَٰكِفِينَ حَتَّىٰ يَرْجِعَ إِلَيْنَا مُوسَىٰ ﴿٩١﴾

92. [Mûsâ (Moses) said: "O Hârûn (Aaron)! What prevented you when you saw them going astray;

قَالَ يَٰهَٰرُونُ مَا مَنَعَكَ إِذْ رَأَيْتَهُمْ ضَلُّوٓا۟ ﴿٩٢﴾

93. "That you followed me not (according to my advice to you)? Have you then disobeyed my order?"

أَلَّا تَتَّبِعَنِ أَفَعَصَيْتَ أَمْرِى ﴿٩٣﴾

94. He [Hârûn (Aaron)] said: "O son of my mother! Seize (me) not by my beard, nor by my head! Verily, I feared lest you should say: 'You have caused a division among the Children of Israel, and you have not respected my word!' "

قَالَ يَبْنَؤُمَّ لَا تَأْخُذْ بِلِحْيَتِى وَلَا بِرَأْسِىٓ إِنِّى خَشِيتُ أَن تَقُولَ فَرَّقْتَ بَيْنَ بَنِىٓ إِسْرَٰٓءِيلَ وَلَمْ تَرْقُبْ قَوْلِى ﴿٩٤﴾

95. [Mûsâ (Moses)] said: "And what is the matter with you. O Sâmirî? (i.e. why did you do so?)"

قَالَ فَمَا خَطْبُكَ يَٰسَٰمِرِىُّ ﴿٩٥﴾

96. (Sâmirî) said: "I saw what they saw not, so I took a handful (of dust) from the (hoof) print of the messenger [Jibrael's (Gabriel) horse] and threw it [into the fire in which were put the ornaments of Fir'aun's (Pharaoh) people, or into the calf]. Thus my inner-self suggested to me."

قَالَ بَصُرْتُ بِمَا لَمْ يَبْصُرُوا۟ بِهِ فَقَبَضْتُ قَبْضَةً مِّنْ أَثَرِ الرَّسُولِ فَنَبَذْتُهَا وَكَذَٰلِكَ سَوَّلَتْ لِى نَفْسِى ﴿٩٦﴾

97. Mûsâ (Moses) said: "Then go away! And verily, your (punishment) in this life will be that you will say: "Touch me not (i.e. you will live alone exiled away from mankind); and verily, (for a future torment), you have a promise that will not fail. And look at your *ilâh* (god) to which you have been devoted. We will certainly burn it, and scatter its particles in the sea."

قَالَ فَٱذْهَبْ فَإِنَّ لَكَ فِى ٱلْحَيَوٰةِ أَن تَقُولَ لَا مِسَاسَ وَإِنَّ لَكَ مَوْعِدًا لَّن تُخْلَفَهُۥ وَٱنظُرْ إِلَىٰٓ إِلَٰهِكَ ٱلَّذِى ظَلْتَ عَلَيْهِ عَاكِفًا لَّنُحَرِّقَنَّهُۥ ثُمَّ لَنَنسِفَنَّهُۥ فِى ٱلْيَمِّ نَسْفًا ﴿٩٧﴾

98. Your *Ilâh* (God) is only Allâh, (the One) *Lâ ilâha illa Huwa* (none has the right to be worshipped but He). He has full knowledge of all things.

إِنَّمَا إِلَهُكُمُ ٱللَّهُ ٱلَّذِى لَا إِلَهَ إِلَّا هُوَ وَسِعَ كُلَّ شَىْءٍ عِلْمًا ۝

99. Thus We relate to you (O Muhammad صلى الله عليه وسلم) some information of what happened before. And indeed We have given you from Us a Reminder (this Qur'ân).

كَذَٰلِكَ نَقُصُّ عَلَيْكَ مِنْ أَنۢبَآءِ مَا قَدْ سَبَقَ ۚ وَقَدْ ءَاتَيْنَٰكَ مِن لَّدُنَّا ذِكْرًا ۝

100. Whoever turns away from it (this Qur'ân — i.e. does not believe in it, nor acts on its orders), verily, they will bear a heavy burden (of sins) on the Day of Resurrection,[1]

مَّنْ أَعْرَضَ عَنْهُ فَإِنَّهُۥ يَحْمِلُ يَوْمَ ٱلْقِيَٰمَةِ وِزْرًا ۝

101. They will abide in that (state in the Fire of Hell) — and evil indeed will it be that load for them on the Day of Resurrection;

خَٰلِدِينَ فِيهِ ۖ وَسَآءَ لَهُمْ يَوْمَ ٱلْقِيَٰمَةِ حِمْلًا ۝

102. The Day when the Trumpet will be blown (the second blowing): that Day, We shall gather the *Mujrimûn* (criminals, polytheists, sinners, disbelievers in the Oneness of Allâh) blue or blind-eyed with thirst.[2]

يَوْمَ يُنفَخُ فِى ٱلصُّورِ ۚ وَنَحْشُرُ ٱلْمُجْرِمِينَ يَوْمَئِذٍ زُرْقًا ۝

103. They will speak in a very low voice to each other (saying): "You stayed not longer than ten (days)."

يَتَخَٰفَتُونَ بَيْنَهُمْ إِن لَّبِثْتُمْ إِلَّا عَشْرًا ۝

104. We know very well what they will say, when the best among them in knowledge and wisdom will say: "You stayed no longer than a day!"

نَّحْنُ أَعْلَمُ بِمَا يَقُولُونَ إِذْ يَقُولُ أَمْثَلُهُمْ طَرِيقَةً إِن لَّبِثْتُمْ إِلَّا يَوْمًا ۝

---

[1] (V.20:100) See the footnote of (V.3:85).

[2] (V.20:102) See *Tafsîr Al-Qurtubî.*

105. And they ask you concerning the mountains: say, "My Lord will blast them and scatter them as particles of dust.

وَيَسْـَٔلُونَكَ عَنِ ٱلْجِبَالِ فَقُلْ يَنسِفُهَا رَبِّى نَسْفًا ١٠٥

106. "Then He shall leave it as a level smooth plain.

فَيَذَرُهَا قَاعًا صَفْصَفًا ١٠٦

107. "You will see therein nothing crooked or curved."

لَّا تَرَىٰ فِيهَا عِوَجًا وَلَآ أَمْتًا ١٠٧

108. On that Day mankind will follow strictly (the voice of) Allâh's caller, no crookedness (that is without going to the right or left of that voice) will they show him (Allâh's caller). And all voices shall be humbled for the Most Gracious (Allâh), and nothing shall you hear but the low voice of their footsteps.

يَوْمَئِذٍ يَتَّبِعُونَ ٱلدَّاعِىَ لَا عِوَجَ لَهُۥ وَخَشَعَتِ ٱلْأَصْوَاتُ لِلرَّحْمَٰنِ فَلَا تَسْمَعُ إِلَّا هَمْسًا ١٠٨

109. On that day no intercession shall avail, except the one for whom the Most Gracious (Allâh) has given permission and whose word is acceptable to Him.

يَوْمَئِذٍ لَّا تَنفَعُ ٱلشَّفَٰعَةُ إِلَّا مَنْ أَذِنَ لَهُ ٱلرَّحْمَٰنُ وَرَضِىَ لَهُۥ قَوْلًا ١٠٩

110. He (Allâh) knows what happens to them (His creatures) in this world, and what will happen to them (in the Hereafter) but they will never compass anything of His Knowledge.

يَعْلَمُ مَا بَيْنَ أَيْدِيهِمْ وَمَا خَلْفَهُمْ وَلَا يُحِيطُونَ بِهِۦ عِلْمًا ١١٠

111. And (all) faces shall be humbled before (Allâh), the Ever Living, the One Who sustains and protects all that exists. And he who carried (a burden of) wrongdoing (i.e. he who disbelieved in Allâh, ascribed partners to Him, and did deeds of His disobedience), will be indeed a complete failure (on that Day).

۞ وَعَنَتِ ٱلْوُجُوهُ لِلْحَىِّ ٱلْقَيُّومِ وَقَدْ خَابَ مَنْ حَمَلَ ظُلْمًا ١١١

112. And he who works deeds of righteousness, while he is a believer (in Islâmic Monotheism), then he will have no fear of injustice, nor of any curtailment (of his reward).

ومَن يَعْمَلْ مِنَ الصَّالِحَاتِ وَهُوَ مُؤْمِنٌ فَلَا يَخَافُ ظُلْمًا وَلَا هَضْمًا ۝

113. And thus We have sent it down as a Qur'ân in Arabic, and have explained therein in detail the warnings, in order that they may fear Allâh, or that it may cause them to have a lesson from it (or to have the honour for believing and acting on its teachings).

وَكَذَٰلِكَ أَنزَلْنَاهُ قُرْآنًا عَرَبِيًّا وَصَرَّفْنَا فِيهِ مِنَ الْوَعِيدِ لَعَلَّهُمْ يَتَّقُونَ أَوْ يُحْدِثُ لَهُمْ ذِكْرًا ۝

114. Then High above all be Allâh, the True King. And be not in haste (O Muhammad صلى الله عليه وسلم) with the Qur'ân before its revelation is completed to you, and say: "My Lord! Increase me in knowledge."

فَتَعَالَى اللَّهُ الْمَلِكُ الْحَقُّ وَلَا تَعْجَلْ بِالْقُرْآنِ مِن قَبْلِ أَن يُقْضَىٰ إِلَيْكَ وَحْيُهُ وَقُل رَّبِّ زِدْنِي عِلْمًا ۝

115. And indeed We made a covenant with Adam before, but he forgot, and We found on his part no firm will-power.

وَلَقَدْ عَهِدْنَا إِلَىٰ آدَمَ مِن قَبْلُ فَنَسِيَ وَلَمْ نَجِدْ لَهُ عَزْمًا ۝

116. And (remember) when We said to the angels: "Prostrate yourselves to Adam." They prostrated themselves (all) except Iblîs (Satan); he refused.

وَإِذْ قُلْنَا لِلْمَلَائِكَةِ اسْجُدُوا لِآدَمَ فَسَجَدُوا إِلَّا إِبْلِيسَ أَبَىٰ ۝

117. Then We said: "O Adam! Verily, this is an enemy to you and to your wife. So let him not get you both out of Paradise, so that you will be distressed.

فَقُلْنَا يَا آدَمُ إِنَّ هَٰذَا عَدُوٌّ لَّكَ وَلِزَوْجِكَ فَلَا يُخْرِجَنَّكُمَا مِنَ الْجَنَّةِ فَتَشْقَىٰ ۝

118. Verily, you have (a promise from Us) that you will never be hungry therein nor naked.

إِنَّ لَكَ أَلَّا تَجُوعَ فِيهَا وَلَا تَعْرَىٰ ۝

119. And you (will) suffer not from thirst therein nor from the sun's heat.

وَأَنَّكَ لَا تَظْمَأُ فِيهَا وَلَا تَضْحَىٰ ۝

120. Then *Shaitân* (Satan) whispered to him, saying : "O Adam! Shall I lead you to the Tree of Eternity and to a kingdom that will never waste away?"

فَوَسْوَسَ إِلَيْهِ الشَّيْطَٰنُ قَالَ يَٰٓـَٔادَمُ هَلْ أَدُلُّكَ عَلَىٰ شَجَرَةِ الْخُلْدِ وَمُلْكٍ لَّا يَبْلَىٰ ۝

121. Then they both ate of the tree, and so their private parts became manifest to them, and they began to cover themselves with the leaves of the Paradise for their covering. Thus did Adam disobey his Lord, so he went astray.

فَأَكَلَا مِنْهَا فَبَدَتْ لَهُمَا سَوْءَٰتُهُمَا وَطَفِقَا يَخْصِفَانِ عَلَيْهِمَا مِن وَرَقِ الْجَنَّةِ وَعَصَىٰٓ ءَادَمُ رَبَّهُۥ فَغَوَىٰ ۝

122. Then his Lord chose him, and turned to him with forgiveness, and gave him guidance.

ثُمَّ اجْتَبَٰهُ رَبُّهُۥ فَتَابَ عَلَيْهِ وَهَدَىٰ ۝

123. He (Allâh) said:"Get you down (from the Paradise to the earth), both of you, together, some of you are an enemy to some others. Then if there comes to you guidance from Me, then whoever follows My Guidance he shall neither go astray, nor shall be distressed.

قَالَ اهْبِطَا مِنْهَا جَمِيعًۢا بَعْضُكُمْ لِبَعْضٍ عَدُوٌّ فَإِمَّا يَأْتِيَنَّكُم مِّنِّي هُدًى فَمَنِ اتَّبَعَ هُدَايَ فَلَا يَضِلُّ وَلَا يَشْقَىٰ ۝

124. "But whosoever turns away from My Reminder (i.e. neither believes in this Qur'ân nor acts on its teachings) verily, for him is a life of hardship, and We shall raise him up blind on the Day of Resurrection."

وَمَنْ أَعْرَضَ عَن ذِكْرِي فَإِنَّ لَهُۥ مَعِيشَةً ضَنكًا وَنَحْشُرُهُۥ يَوْمَ الْقِيَٰمَةِ أَعْمَىٰ ۝

125. He will say:"O my Lord! Why have you raised me up blind, while I had sight (before)."

قَالَ رَبِّ لِمَ حَشَرْتَنِيٓ أَعْمَىٰ وَقَدْ كُنتُ بَصِيرًا ۝

126. (Allâh) will say: "Like this: Our *Ayât* (proofs, evidences, verses, lessons, signs, revelations, etc.) came unto you, but you disregarded them (i.e. you left them, did not think deeply in them, and

قَالَ كَذَٰلِكَ أَتَتْكَ ءَايَٰتُنَا فَنَسِيتَهَا وَكَذَٰلِكَ الْيَوْمَ تُنسَىٰ ۝

you turned away from them), and so this Day, you will be neglected (in the Hell-fire, away from Allâh's Mercy)."

127. And thus do We requite him who transgresses beyond bounds [i.e. commits the great sins and disobeys his Lord (Allâh) and believes not in His Messengers, and His revealed Books, like this Qur'ân], and believes not in the *Ayât* (proofs, evidences, verses, lessons, signs, revelations, etc.) of his Lord; and the torment of the Hereafter is far more severe and more lasting.

128. Is it not a guidance for them (to know) how many generations We have destroyed before them, in whose dwellings they walk? Verily, in this are signs indeed for men of understanding.

129. And had it not been for a Word that went forth before from your Lord, and a term determined, (their punishment) must necessarily have come (in this world).

130. So bear patiently (O Muhammad صلى الله عليه وسلم) what they say, and glorify the praises of your Lord before the rising of the sun, and before its setting, and during some hours of the night, and at the ends of the day (an indication for the five compulsory congregational prayers), that you may become pleased with the reward which Allâh shall give you.

131. And strain not your eyes in longing for the things We have given for enjoyment to various groups of them (polytheists and disbelievers in the Oneness of Allâh), the splendour of the life of this world, that We may test them thereby. But the provision (good reward in the Hereafter) of your Lord is better and more lasting.

132. And enjoin *As-Salât* (the prayer) on your family, and be patient in offering them [i.e. the *Salât* (prayers)]. We ask not of you a provision (i.e. to give Us something: money): We provide for you. And the good end (i.e. Paradise) is for the *Muttaqûn* (the pious. See V.2:2).

133. They say: "Why does he not bring us a sign (proof) from his Lord?" Has there not come to them the proof of that which is (written) in the former papers [Scriptures, i.e. the Taurât (Torah), and the Injeel (Gospel), about the coming of the Prophet Muhammad صلى الله عليه وسلم]?

134. And if We had destroyed them with a torment before this (i.e. Messenger Muhammad صلى الله عليه وسلم and the Qur'ân), they would surely, have said: "Our Lord! If only You had sent us a Messenger, we should certainly have followed Your *Ayât* (proofs, evidences, verses, lessons, signs, revelations, etc.), before we were humiliated and disgraced."[1]

---

[1] (V.20:134) Narrated Abu Sa'îd Al-Khudrî رضي الله عنه: 'Alî bin Abî Tâlib sent a piece of gold, not yet taken out of its ore, in a tanned

135. Say (O Muhammad صلى الله عليه وسلم): "Each one (believer and disbeliever) is waiting, so wait you too; and you shall know who are they that are on the Straight and Even Path (i.e. Allâh's religion of Islâmic Monotheism), and who are they that have let themselves be guided (on the Right Path).

قُلْ كُلٌّ مُّتَرَبِّصٌ فَتَرَبَّصُواْ فَسَتَعْلَمُونَ مَنْ أَصْحَٰبُ ٱلصِّرَٰطِ ٱلسَّوِيِّ وَمَنِ ٱهْتَدَىٰ ٱلصِّرَٰطِ

leather container to Allâh's Messenger صلى الله عليه وسلم. Allâh's Messenger صلى الله عليه وسلم distributed that amongst four persons: 'Uyainah bin Badr, Aqra' bin Hâbis, Zaid Al-Khail and the fourth was either 'Alqamah or 'Âmir bin At-Tufail. On that, one of his Companions said, "We are more deserving of this (gold) than these (persons)." When that news reached the Prophet صلى الله عليه وسلم, he said, "Don't you trust me though I am the trustworthy man of the One in the heavens, and I receive the news of heavens (i.e. Divine Revelation) both in the morning and in the evening?" There got up a man with sunken eyes, raised cheek bones, raised forehead, a thick beard, a shaven head and a waist-sheet that was tucked up and he said, "O Allâh's Messenger! Be afraid of Allâh." The Prophet صلى الله عليه وسلم said, "Woe to you! Am I not of all the people of the earth the most entitled to fear Allâh?" Then that man went away. Khâlid bin Al-Walîd said, "O Allâh's Messenger! Shall I chop his neck off?" The Prophet صلى الله عليه وسلم said, "No, may be he offers prayers." Khâlid said, "Numerous are those who offer prayers and say by their tongues (i.e. mouths) what is not in their hearts." Allâh's Messenger صلى الله عليه وسلم said, "I have not been ordered (by Allâh) to search the hearts of the people or cut open their bellies." Then the Prophet صلى الله عليه وسلم looked at him (i.e. that man) while the latter was going away and said, "From the offspring of this (man) there will come out (people) who will recite the Qur'ân continuously and elegantly but it will not exceed their throats. (They will neither understand it nor act upon it). They would go out of the religion (i.e., discard Islâm) as an arrow goes out through a game's body." I think he also said, "If I should be present at their time, I would kill them as the nations of Thamûd were killed." [Sahih Al-Bukhari, Vol. 5, Hadith No. 638].

Sûrat Al-Anbiyâ'
(The Prophets) XXI

سُورَةُ الْأَنْبِيَاءِ

In the Name of Allâh
the Most Gracious, the Most Merciful

بِسْمِ اللهِ الرَّحْمَنِ الرَّحِيمِ

1. Draws near for mankind their reckoning, while they turn away in heedlessness.

اقْتَرَبَ لِلنَّاسِ حِسَابُهُمْ وَهُمْ فِى غَفْلَةٍ مُّعْرِضُونَ ۝

2. Comes not unto them an admonition (a chapter of the Qur'ân) from their Lord as a recent revelation but they listen to it while they play

مَا يَأْتِيهِم مِّن ذِكْرٍ مِّن رَّبِّهِم مُّحْدَثٍ إِلَّا اسْتَمَعُوهُ وَهُمْ يَلْعَبُونَ ۝

3. With their hearts occupied (with evil things). Those who do wrong, conceal their private counsels, (saying): "Is this (Muhammad صلى الله عليه وسلم) more than a human being like you? Will you submit to magic while you see it?"

لَاهِيَةً قُلُوبُهُمْ وَأَسَرُّوا النَّجْوَى الَّذِينَ ظَلَمُوا هَلْ هَذَا إِلَّا بَشَرٌ مِّثْلُكُمْ أَفَتَأْتُونَ السِّحْرَ وَأَنتُمْ تُبْصِرُونَ ۝

4. He (Muhammad صلى الله عليه وسلم) said: "My Lord knows (every) word (spoken) in the heavens and on earth. And He is the All-Hearer, the All-Knower."

قَالَ رَبِّى يَعْلَمُ الْقَوْلَ فِى السَّمَاءِ وَالْأَرْضِ وَهُوَ السَّمِيعُ الْعَلِيمُ ۝

5. Nay, they say:"These (revelations of the Qur'ân which are inspired to Muhammad صلى الله عليه وسلم) are mixed up false dreams! Nay, he has invented it! — Nay, he is a poet! Let him then bring us an *Ayâh* (sign as a proof) like the ones (Prophets) that were sent before (with signs)!"

بَلْ قَالُوا أَضْغَاثُ أَحْلَامٍ بَلِ افْتَرَاهُ بَلْ هُوَ شَاعِرٌ فَلْيَأْتِنَا بِآيَةٍ كَمَا أُرْسِلَ الْأَوَّلُونَ ۝

6. Not one of the towns (populations), of those which We destroyed, believed before them (though We sent them signs): will they then believe?

مَا آمَنَتْ قَبْلَهُم مِّن قَرْيَةٍ أَهْلَكْنَاهَا أَفَهُمْ يُؤْمِنُونَ ۝

7. And We sent not before you (O Muhammad صلى الله عليه وسلم) but men to whom We revealed. So ask the people of the Reminder [Scriptures — the Taurât (Torah), the Injeel (Gospel)] if you do not know.

8. And We did not create them (the Messengers, with) bodies that ate not food, nor were they immortals.

9. Then We fulfilled to them the promise. So We saved them and those whom We willed, but We destroyed Al-Musrifûn (i.e. disbelievers in Allâh, in His Messengers, extravagants, transgressors of Allâh's limits by committing crimes, oppressions, polytheism and sins).

10. Indeed, We have sent down for you (O mankind) a Book (the Qur'ân) in which there is Dhikrukum, (your Reminder or an honour for you i.e. honour for the one who follows the teaching of the Qur'ân and acts on its teachings). Will you not then understand?

11. How many a town (community) given to wrongdoing, have We destroyed, and raised up after them another people!

12. Then, when they perceived (saw) Our Torment (coming), behold, they (tried to) flee from it.

13. Flee not, but return to that wherein you lived a luxurious life, and to your homes, in order that you may be questioned.

14. They cried: "Woe to us! Certainly we have been Zâlimûn (polytheists,

وَمَا أَرْسَلْنَا قَبْلَكَ إِلَّا رِجَالًا نُّوحِىٓ إِلَيْهِمْ فَسْـَٔلُوٓا أَهْلَ الذِّكْرِ إِن كُنتُمْ لَا تَعْلَمُونَ ٧ وَمَا جَعَلْنَٰهُمْ جَسَدًا لَّا يَأْكُلُونَ الطَّعَامَ وَمَا كَانُوا۟ خَٰلِدِينَ ٨ ثُمَّ صَدَقْنَٰهُمُ الْوَعْدَ فَأَنجَيْنَٰهُمْ وَمَن نَّشَآءُ وَأَهْلَكْنَا الْمُسْرِفِينَ ٩ لَقَدْ أَنزَلْنَآ إِلَيْكُمْ كِتَٰبًا فِيهِ ذِكْرُكُمْ أَفَلَا تَعْقِلُونَ ١٠ وَكَمْ قَصَمْنَا مِن قَرْيَةٍ كَانَتْ ظَالِمَةً وَأَنشَأْنَا بَعْدَهَا قَوْمًا ءَاخَرِينَ ١١ فَلَمَّآ أَحَسُّوا۟ بَأْسَنَآ إِذَا هُم مِّنْهَا يَرْكُضُونَ ١٢ لَا تَرْكُضُوا۟ وَارْجِعُوٓا۟ إِلَىٰ مَآ أُتْرِفْتُمْ فِيهِ وَمَسَٰكِنِكُمْ لَعَلَّكُمْ تُسْـَٔلُونَ ١٣ قَالُوا۟ يَٰوَيْلَنَآ إِنَّا كُنَّا ظَٰلِمِينَ ١٤

wrongdoers and disbelievers in the Oneness of Allâh.''

15. And that cry of theirs ceased not, till We made them as a field that is reaped, extinct (dead).

فَمَا زَالَت تِلْكَ دَعْوَىٰهُمْ حَتَّىٰ جَعَلْنَٰهُمْ حَصِيدًا خَٰمِدِينَ ۝

16. We created not the heavens and the earth and all that is between them for a (mere) play.[1]

وَمَا خَلَقْنَا ٱلسَّمَآءَ وَٱلْأَرْضَ وَمَا بَيْنَهُمَا لَٰعِبِينَ ۝

17. Had We intended to take a pastime (i.e. a wife or a son), We could surely, have taken it from Us, if We were going to do (that).

لَوْ أَرَدْنَآ أَن نَّتَّخِذَ لَهْوًا لَّٱتَّخَذْنَٰهُ مِن لَّدُنَّآ إِن كُنَّا فَٰعِلِينَ ۝

18. Nay, We fling (send down) the truth (this Qur'ân) against the falsehood (disbelief), so it destroys it, and behold, it (falsehood) is vanished. And woe to you for that (lie) which you ascribe (to Allâh by uttering that Allâh has a wife and a son).

بَلْ نَقْذِفُ بِٱلْحَقِّ عَلَى ٱلْبَٰطِلِ فَيَدْمَغُهُ فَإِذَا هُوَ زَاهِقٌ وَلَكُمُ ٱلْوَيْلُ مِمَّا تَصِفُونَ ۝

19. To Him belongs whosoever is in the heavens and on earth. And those who are near Him (i.e. the angels) are not too proud to worship Him, nor are they weary (of His worship).

وَلَهُ مَن فِى ٱلسَّمَٰوَٰتِ وَٱلْأَرْضِ وَمَنْ عِندَهُ لَا يَسْتَكْبِرُونَ عَنْ عِبَادَتِهِۦ وَلَا يَسْتَحْسِرُونَ ۝

20. They (i.e. the angels) glorify His Praises night and day, (and) they never slacken (to do so).

يُسَبِّحُونَ ٱلَّيْلَ وَٱلنَّهَارَ لَا يَفْتُرُونَ ۝

21. Or have they taken (for worship) âlihah (gods) from the earth who raise the dead?

أَمِ ٱتَّخَذُوٓا ءَالِهَةً مِّنَ ٱلْأَرْضِ هُمْ يُنشِرُونَ ۝

---

[1] (V.21:16) All the creation of the heavens and the earth is a proof for mankind to learn a lesson and know that the only Creator and the only Organizer of all this universe is One (Allâh), *Lâ ilâha illallâh* (none has the right to be worshipped but Allâh, Who has no partners with Him).

22. Had there been therein (in the heavens and the earth) *âlihah* (gods) besides Allâh, then verily, both would have been ruined. Glorified is Allâh, the Lord of the Throne, (High is He) above all that (evil) they associate with Him!

23. He cannot be questioned as to what He does, while they will be questioned.

24. Or have they taken for worship (other) *âlihah* (gods) besides Him? Say: "Bring your proof." This (the Qur'ân) is the Reminder for those with me and the Reminder for those before me. But most of them know not the Truth, so they are averse.

25. And We did not send any Messenger before you (O Muhammad صلى الله عليه وسلم) but We revealed to him (saying): *Lâ ilâha illa Ana* [none has the right to be worshipped but I (Allâh)], so worship Me (Alone and none else)."

26. And they say: "The Most Gracious (Allâh) has begotten a son (or children)." Glory to Him! They [whom they call children of Allâh i.e. the angels, 'Îsâ (Jesus) — son of Maryam (Mary), 'Uzair (Ezra)], are but honoured slaves.

27. They speak not until He has spoken, and they act on His Command.

28. He knows what is before them, and what is behind them, and they cannot intercede except for him with whom He is pleased. And they stand in awe for fear of Him.

29. And if any of them should say: "Verily, I am an *ilâh* (a god) besides Him (Allâh)," such a one We should recompense with Hell. Thus We recompense the *Zâlimûn* (polytheists and wrongdoers).

۞ وَمَن يَقُلْ مِنْهُمْ إِنِّي إِلَٰهٌ مِّن دُونِهِۦ فَذَٰلِكَ نَجْزِيهِ جَهَنَّمَ كَذَٰلِكَ نَجْزِي ٱلظَّٰلِمِينَ ۝

30. Have not those who disbelieve known that the heavens and the earth were joined together as one united piece, then We parted them? And We have made from water every living thing. Will they not then believe?

أَوَلَمْ يَرَ ٱلَّذِينَ كَفَرُوٓاْ أَنَّ ٱلسَّمَٰوَٰتِ وَٱلْأَرْضَ كَانَتَا رَتْقًا فَفَتَقْنَٰهُمَا وَجَعَلْنَا مِنَ ٱلْمَآءِ كُلَّ شَىْءٍ حَىٍّ أَفَلَا يُؤْمِنُونَ ۝

31. And We have placed on the earth firm mountains, lest it should shake with them, and We placed therein broad highways for them to pass through, that they may be guided.

وَجَعَلْنَا فِى ٱلْأَرْضِ رَوَٰسِىَ أَن تَمِيدَ بِهِمْ وَجَعَلْنَا فِيهَا فِجَاجًا سُبُلًا لَّعَلَّهُمْ يَهْتَدُونَ ۝

32. And We have made the heaven a roof, safe and well guarded. Yet they turn away from its signs (i.e. sun, moon, winds, clouds).

وَجَعَلْنَا ٱلسَّمَآءَ سَقْفًا مَّحْفُوظًا وَهُمْ عَنْ ءَايَٰتِهَا مُعْرِضُونَ ۝

33. And He it is Who has created the night and the day, and the sun and the moon, each in an orbit floating.

وَهُوَ ٱلَّذِى خَلَقَ ٱلَّيْلَ وَٱلنَّهَارَ وَٱلشَّمْسَ وَٱلْقَمَرَ كُلٌّ فِى فَلَكٍ يَسْبَحُونَ ۝

34. And We granted not to any human being immortality before you (O Muhammad صلى الله عليه وسلم): then if you die, would they live forever?

وَمَا جَعَلْنَا لِبَشَرٍ مِّن قَبْلِكَ ٱلْخُلْدَ أَفَإِيْن مِّتَّ فَهُمُ ٱلْخَٰلِدُونَ ۝

35. Everyone is going to taste death, and We shall make a trial of you with evil and with good. And to Us you will be returned.

كُلُّ نَفْسٍ ذَآئِقَةُ ٱلْمَوْتِ وَنَبْلُوكُم بِٱلشَّرِّ وَٱلْخَيْرِ فِتْنَةً وَإِلَيْنَا تُرْجَعُونَ ۝

36. And when those who disbelieved (in the Oneness of Allâh) see you (O Muhammad صلى الله عليه وسلم), they take you

وَإِذَا رَءَاكَ ٱلَّذِينَ كَفَرُوٓاْ إِن يَتَّخِذُونَكَ إِلَّا هُزُوًا

not except for mockery (saying): "Is this the one who talks (badly) about your gods?" While they disbelieve at the mention of the Most Gracious (Allâh). [*Tafsir. Al-Qurtubî*].

37. Man is created of haste. I will show you My *Ayât* (torments, proofs, evidences, verses, lessons, signs, revelations, etc.).So ask Me not to hasten (them).

38. And they say: "When will this promise (come to pass), if you are truthful."

39. If only those who disbelieved knew (the time) when they will not be able to ward off the Fire from their faces, nor from their backs, and they will not be helped.

40. Nay, it (the Fire or the Day of Resurrection) will come upon them all of a sudden and will perplex them, and they will have no power to avert it nor will they get respite.

41. Indeed (many) Messengers were mocked before you (O Muhammad صلى الله عليه وسلم), but the scoffers were surrounded by that, whereat they used to mock.

42. Say: "Who can guard and protect you in the night or in the day from the (punishment of the) Most Gracious (Allâh)?" Nay, but they turn away from the remembrance of their Lord.

43. Or have they *âlihah* (gods) who can guard them from Us? They have no power to help themselves, nor can they be protected from Us (i.e. from Our Torment).

44. Nay, We gave the luxuries of this life to these men and their fathers until the period grew long for them. See they not that We gradually reduce the land (in their control) from its outlying borders? Is it then they who will overcome?[1]

بَلْ مَتَّعْنَا هَٰٓؤُلَآءِ وَءَابَآءَهُمْ حَتَّىٰ طَالَ عَلَيْهِمُ ٱلْعُمُرُۗ أَفَلَا يَرَوْنَ أَنَّا نَأْتِي ٱلْأَرْضَ نَنقُصُهَا مِنْ أَطْرَافِهَآۚ أَفَهُمُ ٱلْغَٰلِبُونَ ﴿٤٤﴾

45. Say (O Muhammad صلى الله عليه وسلم): "I warn you only by the revelation (from Allâh and not by the opinion of the religious scholars and others). But the deaf (who follow the religious scholars and others blindly) will not hear the call, (even) when they are warned [i.e. one should follow only the Qur'ân and the *Sunnah* (legal ways, orders, acts of worship, and the statements of Prophet Muhammad صلى الله عليه وسلم, as the Companions of the Prophet عليه وسلم صلى الله عليه وسلم did)].[2]

قُلْ إِنَّمَآ أُنذِرُكُم بِٱلْوَحْيِۚ وَلَا يَسْمَعُ ٱلصُّمُّ ٱلدُّعَآءَ إِذَا مَا يُنذَرُونَ ﴿٤٥﴾

46. And if a breath (minor calamity) of the Torment of your Lord touches them, they will surely, cry: "Woe unto us! Indeed we have been *Zâlimûn* (polytheists and wrongdoers)."

وَلَئِن مَّسَّتْهُمْ نَفْحَةٌ مِّنْ عَذَابِ رَبِّكَ لَيَقُولُنَّ يَٰوَيْلَنَآ إِنَّا كُنَّا ظَٰلِمِينَ ﴿٤٦﴾

47. And We shall set up balances of justice on the Day of Resurrection, then none will be dealt with unjustly in anything. And if there be the weight of a mustard seed, We will bring it. And Sufficient are We to take account.

وَنَضَعُ ٱلْمَوَٰزِينَ ٱلْقِسْطَ لِيَوْمِ ٱلْقِيَٰمَةِ فَلَا تُظْلَمُ نَفْسٌ شَيْـًٔاۖ وَإِن كَانَ مِثْقَالَ حَبَّةٍ مِّنْ خَرْدَلٍ أَتَيْنَا بِهَاۗ وَكَفَىٰ بِنَا حَٰسِبِينَ ﴿٤٧﴾

---

[1] (V.21:44). "See they not that We gradually reduce the land (of disbelievers, by giving it to the believers, in war victories) from its outlying borders? And Allâh judges, there is none to put back His Judgement and He is Swift at reckoning." [The Qur'ân, Verse 13:41]

[2] (V.21:45) See the footnote of (V.3:103).

48. And indeed We granted to Mûsâ (Moses) and Hârûn (Aaron) the criterion (of right and wrong), and a shining light [i.e. the Taurât (Torah)] and a Reminder for *Al-Muttaqûn* (the pious and righteous persons. See V.2:2).

وَلَقَدْ ءَاتَيْنَا مُوسَىٰ وَهَـٰرُونَ ٱلْفُرْقَانَ وَضِيَآءً وَذِكْرًا لِّلْمُتَّقِينَ ٤٨

49. Those who fear their Lord without seeing Him, and they are afraid of the Hour.

ٱلَّذِينَ يَخْشَوْنَ رَبَّهُم بِٱلْغَيْبِ وَهُم مِّنَ ٱلسَّاعَةِ مُشْفِقُونَ ٤٩

50. And this is a blessed Reminder (the Qur'ân) which We have sent down: will you then (dare to) deny it?[1]

وَهَـٰذَا ذِكْرٌ مُّبَارَكٌ أَنزَلْنَـٰهُ أَفَأَنتُمْ لَهُۥ مُنكِرُونَ ٥٠

51. And indeed We bestowed aforetime on Ibrâhîm (Abraham) his (portion of) guidance, and We were Well-Acquainted with him (as to his Belief in the Oneness of Allâh).

۞ وَلَقَدْ ءَاتَيْنَآ إِبْرَٰهِيمَ رُشْدَهُۥ مِن قَبْلُ وَكُنَّا بِهِۦ عَـٰلِمِينَ ٥١

52. When he said to his father and his people: "What are these images, to which you are devoted?"

إِذْ قَالَ لِأَبِيهِ وَقَوْمِهِۦ مَا هَـٰذِهِ ٱلتَّمَاثِيلُ ٱلَّتِىٓ أَنتُمْ لَهَا عَـٰكِفُونَ ٥٢

53. They said: "We found our fathers worshipping them."

قَالُوا۟ وَجَدْنَآ ءَابَآءَنَا لَهَا عَـٰبِدِينَ ٥٣

54. He said: "Indeed you and your fathers have been in manifest error."

قَالَ لَقَدْ كُنتُمْ أَنتُمْ وَءَابَآؤُكُمْ فِى ضَلَـٰلٍ مُّبِينٍ ٥٤

55. They said: "Have you brought us the truth, or are you one of those who play about?"

قَالُوٓا۟ أَجِئْتَنَا بِٱلْحَقِّ أَمْ أَنتَ مِنَ ٱللَّـٰعِبِينَ ٥٥

56. He said: "Nay, your Lord is the Lord of the heavens and the earth, Who created them and to that I am one of the witnesses.

قَالَ بَل رَّبُّكُمْ رَبُّ ٱلسَّمَـٰوَٰتِ وَٱلْأَرْضِ ٱلَّذِى فَطَرَهُنَّ وَأَنَا۠ عَلَىٰ ذَٰلِكُم مِّنَ ٱلشَّـٰهِدِينَ ٥٦

---

[1] (V.21:50).
a) See the footnote of (V.10:37).
b) See the footnote of (V.3:85).

57. "And by Allâh, I shall plot a plan (to destroy) your idols after you have gone away and turned your backs."

وَتَٱللَّهِ لَأَكِيدَنَّ أَصْنَٰمَكُم بَعْدَ أَن تُوَلُّواْ مُدْبِرِينَ ٥٧

58. So he broke them to pieces, (all) except the biggest of them, that they might turn to it.

فَجَعَلَهُمْ جُذَٰذًا إِلَّا كَبِيرًا لَّهُمْ لَعَلَّهُمْ إِلَيْهِ يَرْجِعُونَ ٥٨

59. They said: "Who has done this to our âlihah (gods)? He must indeed be one of the Zâlimun (wrongdoer)."

قَالُواْ مَن فَعَلَ هَٰذَا بِـَٔالِهَتِنَا إِنَّهُۥ لَمِنَ ٱلظَّٰلِمِينَ ٥٩

60. They said: "We heard a young man talking against them, who is called Ibrâhîm (Abraham)."

قَالُواْ سَمِعْنَا فَتًى يَذْكُرُهُمْ يُقَالُ لَهُۥٓ إِبْرَٰهِيمُ ٦٠

61. They said: "Then bring him before the eyes of the people, that they may testify."

قَالُواْ فَأْتُواْ بِهِۦ عَلَىٰٓ أَعْيُنِ ٱلنَّاسِ لَعَلَّهُمْ يَشْهَدُونَ ٦١

62. They said: "Are you the one who has done this to our gods, O Ibrâhîm (Abraham)?"

قَالُوٓاْ ءَأَنتَ فَعَلْتَ هَٰذَا بِـَٔالِهَتِنَا يَٰٓإِبْرَٰهِيمُ ٦٢

63. [Ibrâhîm (Abraham)] said: "Nay, this one, the biggest of them (idols) did it. Ask them, if they can speak!"[1]

قَالَ بَلْ فَعَلَهُۥ كَبِيرُهُمْ هَٰذَا فَسْـَٔلُوهُمْ إِن كَانُواْ يَنطِقُونَ ٦٣

64. So they turned to themselves and said: "Verily, you are the Zâlimûn (polytheists and wrongdoers)."

فَرَجَعُوٓاْ إِلَىٰٓ أَنفُسِهِمْ فَقَالُوٓاْ إِنَّكُمْ أَنتُمُ ٱلظَّٰلِمُونَ ٦٤

65. Then they turned to themselves (their first thought and said: "Indeed you [Ibrâhîm (Abraham)] know well that these (idols) speak not!"

ثُمَّ نُكِسُواْ عَلَىٰ رُءُوسِهِمْ لَقَدْ عَلِمْتَ مَا هَٰٓؤُلَآءِ يَنطِقُونَ ٦٥

66. [Ibrâhîm (Abraham)] said: "Do you then worship besides Allâh, things that can neither profit you, nor harm you?

قَالَ أَفَتَعْبُدُونَ مِن دُونِ ٱللَّهِ مَا لَا يَنفَعُكُمْ شَيْـًٔا وَلَا يَضُرُّكُمْ ٦٦

---

[1] (V.21:63) See the footnote (C) of (V.16:121).

67. "Fie upon you, and upon that which you worship besides Allâh! Have you then no sense?"

68. They said: "Burn him and help your âlihah (gods), if you will be doing."

69. We (Allâh) said: "O fire! Be you coolness and safety for Ibrâhîm (Abraham)!"

70. And they wanted to harm him, but We made them the worst losers.

71. And We rescued him and Lût (Lot) to the land which We have blessed for the 'Âlamîn (mankind and jinn).

72. And We bestowed upon him Ishâq (Isaac), and (a grandson) Ya'qûb (Jacob). Each one We made righteous.

73. And We made them leaders, guiding (mankind) by Our Command, and We revealed to them the doing of good deeds, performing Salât (Iqâmat-as-Salât), and the giving of Zakât and of Us (Alone) they were the worshippers.

74. And (remember) Lût (Lot), We gave him Hukm (right judgement of the affairs and Prophethood) and (religious) knowledge, and We saved him from the town (folk) who practised Al-Khabâ'ith (evil, wicked and filthy deeds). Verily, they were a people given to evil, and were Fâsiqûn (rebellious, disobedient, to Allâh).

75. And We admitted him to Our Mercy; truly, he was of the righteous.

76. And (remember) Nûh (Noah), when he cried (to Us) aforetime. We answered to his invocation and saved him and his family from the great distress.

77. We helped him against the people who denied Our *Ayât* (proofs, evidences, verses, lessons, signs, revelations, etc.). Verily, they were a people given to evil. So We drowned them all.

78. And (remember) Dâwûd (David) and Sulaimân (Solomon), when they gave judgement in the case of the field in which the sheep of certain people had pastured at night; and We were witness to their judgement.

79. And We made Sulaimân (Solomon) to understand (the case); and to each of them We gave *Hukm* (right judgement of the affairs and Prophethood) and knowledge. And We subjected the mountains and the birds to glorify Our Praises along with Dâwûd (David). And it was We Who were the doer (of all these things).

80. And We taught him the making of metal coats of mail (for battles), to protect you in your fighting. Are you then grateful?

81. And to Sulaimân (Solomon) (We subjected) the wind strongly raging, running by his command towards the land which We had blessed. And of everything We are the All-Knower.

82. And of the *Shayâtîn* (devils from the jinn) were some who dived for him, and did other work besides that; and it was We Who guarded them.

ومِنَ ٱلشَّيَـٰطِينِ مَن يَغُوصُونَ لَهُۥ وَيَعْمَلُونَ عَمَلًا دُونَ ذَٰلِكَ وَكُنَّا لَهُمْ حَٰفِظِينَ ۝

83. And (remember) Ayûb (Job), when he cried to his Lord: "Verily, distress has seized me, and You are the Most Merciful of all those who show mercy."

۞ وَأَيُّوبَ إِذْ نَادَىٰ رَبَّهُۥٓ أَنِّى مَسَّنِىَ ٱلضُّرُّ وَأَنتَ أَرْحَمُ ٱلرَّٰحِمِينَ ۝

84. So We answered to his call, and We removed the distress that was on him, and We restored his family to him (that he had lost) and the like thereof along with them as a mercy from Ourselves and a Reminder for all those who worship Us.

فَٱسْتَجَبْنَا لَهُۥ فَكَشَفْنَا مَا بِهِۦ مِن ضُرٍّ وَءَاتَيْنَٰهُ أَهْلَهُۥ وَمِثْلَهُم مَّعَهُمْ رَحْمَةً مِّنْ عِندِنَا وَذِكْرَىٰ لِلْعَٰبِدِينَ ۝

85. And (remember) Isma'îl (Ishmael), and Idrîs (Enoch) and Dhul-Kifl (Isaiah): all were from among *As-Sâbirûn* (the patient).

وَإِسْمَٰعِيلَ وَإِدْرِيسَ وَذَا ٱلْكِفْلِ كُلٌّ مِّنَ ٱلصَّٰبِرِينَ ۝

86. And We admitted them to Our Mercy. Verily, they were of the righteous.

وَأَدْخَلْنَٰهُمْ فِى رَحْمَتِنَآ إِنَّهُم مِّنَ ٱلصَّٰلِحِينَ ۝

87. And (remember) Dhun-Nûn (Jonah), when he went off in anger, and imagined that We shall not punish him (i.e. the calamities which had befallen him)! But he cried through the darkness (saying): *Lâ ilâha illâ Anta* [none has the right to be worshipped but You (O, Allâh)], Glorified (and Exalted) are You [above all that (evil) they associate with You]! Truly, I have been of the wrongdoers.

وَذَا ٱلنُّونِ إِذ ذَّهَبَ مُغَٰضِبًا فَظَنَّ أَن لَّن نَّقْدِرَ عَلَيْهِ فَنَادَىٰ فِى ٱلظُّلُمَٰتِ أَن لَّآ إِلَٰهَ إِلَّآ أَنتَ سُبْحَٰنَكَ إِنِّى كُنتُ مِنَ ٱلظَّٰلِمِينَ ۝

88. So We answered to his call, and delivered him from the distress. And

فَٱسْتَجَبْنَا لَهُۥ وَنَجَّيْنَٰهُ

thus We do deliver the believers (who believe in the Oneness of Allâh, abstain from evil and work righteousness).

مِنَ ٱلْغَمِّ وَكَذَٰلِكَ نُـجِي ٱلْمُؤْمِنِينَ ۝

89. And (remember) Zakariyyâ (Zachariah), when he cried to his Lord: "O My Lord! Leave me not single (childless), though You are the Best of the inheritors."

وَزَكَرِيَّآ إِذْ نَادَىٰ رَبَّهُۥ رَبِّ لَا تَذَرْنِي فَرْدًا وَأَنتَ خَيْرُ ٱلْوَٰرِثِينَ ۝

90. So We answered his call, and We bestowed upon him Yahyâ (John), and cured his wife (to bear a child) for him. Verily, they used to hasten on to do good deeds, and they used to call on Us with hope and fear, and used to humble themselves before Us.

فَٱسْتَجَبْنَا لَهُۥ وَوَهَبْنَا لَهُۥ يَحْيَىٰ وَأَصْلَحْنَا لَهُۥ زَوْجَهُۥٓ إِنَّهُمْ كَانُوا۟ يُسَٰرِعُونَ فِى ٱلْخَيْرَٰتِ وَيَدْعُونَنَا رَغَبًا وَرَهَبًا ۖ

91. And she who guarded her chastity [Virgin Maryam (Mary)]: We breathed into (the sleeves of) her (shirt or garment) [through Our *Rûh* — Jibraêl (Gabriel)],[1] and We made her and her son ['Îsâ (Jesus)] a sign for *Al-'Âlamîn* (the mankind and jinn).

وَكَانُوا۟ لَنَا خَٰشِعِينَ ۝ وَٱلَّتِىٓ أَحْصَنَتْ فَرْجَهَا فَنَفَخْنَا فِيهَا مِن رُّوحِنَا وَجَعَلْنَٰهَا وَٱبْنَهَآ ءَايَةً لِّلْعَٰلَمِينَ ۝

92. Truly, this, your *Ummah* [*Sharî'ah* or religion (Islâmic Monotheism)] is one religion, and I am your Lord, therefore worship Me (Alone). [*Tafsîr Ibn Kathîr*]

إِنَّ هَٰذِهِۦٓ أُمَّتُكُمْ أُمَّةً وَٰحِدَةً وَأَنَا۠ رَبُّكُمْ فَٱعْبُدُونِ ۝

93. But they have broken up and differed as regards their religion among themselves. (And) they all shall return to Us.

وَتَقَطَّعُوٓا۟ أَمْرَهُم بَيْنَهُمْ ۖ كُلٌّ إِلَيْنَا رَٰجِعُونَ ۝

94. So whoever does righteous good deeds while he is a believer (in the

فَمَن يَعْمَلْ مِنَ ٱلصَّٰلِحَٰتِ وَهُوَ مُؤْمِنٌ فَلَا كُفْرَانَ

---

[1] (V.21:91) It is said that Jibraêl (Gabriel) had merely breathed in the sleeve of Maryam's (Mary) shirt and thus she conceived.

Oneness of Allâh — Islâmic Monotheism), his efforts will not be rejected. Verily, We record it for him (in his Book of deeds).[1]

لِسَعْيِهِ وَإِنَّا لَهُ كَتِبُونَ ﴿٩٤﴾

95. And a ban is laid on every town (population) which We have destroyed that they shall not return (to this world again, nor repent to Us).

وَحَرَمٌ عَلَىٰ قَرْيَةٍ أَهْلَكْنَهَا أَنَّهُمْ لَا يَرْجِعُونَ ﴿٩٥﴾

96. Until, when Ya'jûj and Ma'jûj (Gog and Magog)[2] are let loose (from their barrier), and they swoop down from every mound.

حَتَّىٰٓ إِذَا فُتِحَتْ يَأْجُوجُ وَمَأْجُوجُ وَهُم مِّن كُلِّ حَدَبٍ يَنسِلُونَ ﴿٩٦﴾

97. And the true promise (Day of Resurrection) shall draw near (of fulfilment). Then (when mankind is resurrected from their graves), you shall see the eyes of the disbelievers fixedly staring in horror. (They will say): "Woe to us! We were indeed heedless of this — nay, but we were *Zâlimûn* (polytheists and wrongdoers)."

وَٱقْتَرَبَ ٱلْوَعْدُ ٱلْحَقُّ فَإِذَا هِىَ شَٰخِصَةٌ أَبْصَٰرُ ٱلَّذِينَ كَفَرُوا۟ يَٰوَيْلَنَا قَدْ كُنَّا فِى غَفْلَةٍ مِّنْ هَٰذَا بَلْ كُنَّا ظَٰلِمِينَ ﴿٩٧﴾

98. Certainly you (disbelievers) and that which you are worshipping now besides Allâh, are (but) fuel for Hell! (Surely), you will enter it.[3]

إِنَّكُمْ وَمَا تَعْبُدُونَ مِن دُونِ ٱللَّهِ حَصَبُ جَهَنَّمَ أَنتُمْ لَهَا وَٰرِدُونَ ﴿٩٨﴾

---

[1] (V.21:94) See the footnote of (V.9:121).

[2] (V.21:96) See the footnote of (V.18:94).

[3] (V.21:98) When the following Statement of Allâh عزوجل was revealed: "Certainly you (disbelievers) and that which you are worshipping now besides Allâh are (but) fuel for Hell! (Surely), you will enter it."

The Quraish pagans were delighted and said: "We are pleased to be with our gods in the Hell-fire, as the idols will be with the idolaters (in the Hell-fire), and therefore 'Îsâ (Jesus), the son of Maryam (Mary) will be with his worshippers (i.e. in the Hell-fire) and so on.

99. Had these (idols) been *âlihah* (gods), they would not have entered there (Hell), and all of them will abide therein.

100. Therein they will be breathing out with deep sighs and roaring and therein they will hear not.[1]

101. Verily, those for whom the good has preceded from Us, they will be removed far therefrom (Hell) [e.g. 'Îsâ (Jesus), son of Maryam (Mary); 'Uzair (Ezra)].

102. They shall not hear the slightest sound of it (Hell), while they abide in that which their ownselves desire.

103. The greatest terror (on the Day of Resurrection) will not grieve them, and the angels will meet them, (with the greeting): "This is your Day which you were promised."

104. And (remember) the Day when We shall roll up the heaven like a scroll rolled up for books. As We began the first creation, We shall repeat it. (It is) a

So (to clear the misunderstanding) Allâh عزوجل revealed the following Verse (to deny and reject their claim): "Verily, those for whom the good has preceded from Us, they will be removed far therefrom (Hell). [e.g. 'Îsâ (Jesus), the son of Maryam (Mary); 'Uzair (Ezra)]." [The Qur'ân, Verse 21:101]

[1] (V.21:100) Ibn Mas'ûd رضي الله عنه recited this Verse and then said: "When those (who are destined to remain in the Hell-fire forever) will be thrown in the Hell-fire, each of them will be put in a separate *Tabût* (box) of Fire, so that he will not see anyone punished in the Hell fire except himself." Then Ibn Mas'ûd recited this Verse (21:100). [*Tafsîr Ibn Kathîr, Tabarî* and *Qurtubî*].

promise binding upon Us. Truly, We shall do it.

105. And indeed We have written in *Az-Zabûr* [i.e. all the revealed Holy Books — the Taurât (Torah), the Injeel (Gospel), the Psalms, the Qur'ân] after (We have already written in) *Al-Lauh Al-Mahfûz* (the Book that is in the heaven with Allâh), that My righteous slaves shall inherit the land (i.e. the land of Paradise).

106. Verily, in this (the Qur'ân) there is a plain Message for people who worship Allâh (i.e. the true, real believers of Islâmic Monotheism who act practically on the Qur'ân and the *Sunnah* — legal ways of the Prophet صلى الله عليه وسلم).

107. And We have sent you (O Muhammad صلى الله عليه وسلم) not but as a mercy for the *'Âlamîn* (mankind, jinn and all that exists).

108. Say (O Muhammad صلى الله عليه وسلم): "It is revealed to me that your *Ilâh* (God) is only one *Ilâh* (God - Allâh). Will you then submit to His Will (become Muslims and stop worshipping others besides Allâh)?"

109. But if they (disbelievers, idolaters, Jews, Christians, polytheists) turn away (from Islâmic Monotheism) say (to them O Muhammad صلى الله عليه وسلم): "I give you a notice (of war as) to be known to us all alike. And I know not whether that which you are promised (i.e. the torment or the Day of Resurrection) is near or far.[1]"

110. (Say O Muhammad صلى الله عليه وسلم) Verily, He (Allâh) knows that which is spoken aloud (openly) and that which you conceal.

111. And I know not, perhaps it may be a trial for you, and an enjoyment for a while.

112. He (Muhammad صلى الله عليه وسلم said:"My Lord! Judge You in truth! Our Lord is the Most Gracious, Whose Help is to be sought against that which you attribute (unto Allâh that He has offspring, and unto Muhammad صلى الله عليه وسلم that he is a sorcerer, and unto the Qur'ân that it is poetry)!"

Sûrat Al-Hajj
(The Pilgrimage) XXII

In the Name of Allâh
the Most Gracious, the Most Merciful

1. O mankind! Fear your Lord and be dutiful to Him! Verily, the earthquake of the Hour (of Judgement) is a terrible thing.

2. The Day you shall see it, every nursing mother will forget her nursling, and every pregnant one will drop her load, and you shall see mankind as in a drunken state, yet they will not be drunken, but severe will be the Torment of Allâh.

---

[1] (V.21:109) See the footnote of (V.2:193).

3. And among mankind is he who disputes concerning Allâh, without knowledge, and follows every rebellious (disobedient to Allâh) *Shaitân* (devil) (devoid of every kind of good).

وَمِنَ النَّاسِ مَن يُجَٰدِلُ فِى اللَّهِ بِغَيْرِ عِلْمٍ وَيَتَّبِعُ كُلَّ شَيْطَٰنٍ مَّرِيدٍ ﴿٣﴾

4. For him (the devil) it is decreed that whosoever follows him, he will mislead him, and will drive him to the torment of the Fire. [*Tafsir At-Tabarî*]

كُتِبَ عَلَيْهِ أَنَّهُ مَن تَوَلَّاهُ فَأَنَّهُ يُضِلُّهُ وَيَهْدِيهِ إِلَىٰ عَذَابِ السَّعِيرِ ﴿٤﴾

5. O mankind! If you are in doubt about the Resurrection, then verily, We have created you (i.e. Adam) from dust, then from a *Nutfah* (mixed drops of male and female sexual discharge i.e. the offspring of Adam), then from a clot (a piece of thick coagulated blood) then from a little lump of flesh — some formed and some unformed (as in the case of miscarriage) — that We may make (it) clear to you (i.e. to show you Our Power and Ability to do what We will). And We cause whom We will to remain in the wombs for an appointed term, then We bring you out as infants,[1] then (give you growth) that

يَٰٓأَيُّهَا النَّاسُ إِن كُنتُمْ فِى رَيْبٍ مِّنَ الْبَعْثِ فَإِنَّا خَلَقْنَٰكُم مِّن تُرَابٍ ثُمَّ مِن نُّطْفَةٍ ثُمَّ مِنْ عَلَقَةٍ ثُمَّ مِن مُّضْغَةٍ مُّخَلَّقَةٍ وَغَيْرِ مُخَلَّقَةٍ لِّنُبَيِّنَ لَكُمْ وَنُقِرُّ فِى الْأَرْحَامِ مَا نَشَآءُ إِلَىٰٓ أَجَلٍ مُّسَمًّى ثُمَّ نُخْرِجُكُمْ طِفْلًا ثُمَّ لِتَبْلُغُوٓا أَشُدَّكُمْ وَمِنكُم مَّن يُتَوَفَّىٰ وَمِنكُم مَّن يُرَدُّ إِلَىٰٓ أَرْذَلِ

---

[1] (V.22:5) Narrated 'Abdullâh رضى الله عنه: Allâh's Messenger صلى الله عليه وسلم, the true and truly inspired, said: "(As regards your creation) every one of you is collected in the womb of his mother for the first forty days, and then he becomes a clot for another forty days, and then a piece of flesh for another forty days. Then Allâh sends an angel to write four words: He writes his deeds, time of his death, means of his livelihood, and whether he will be wretched or blessed (in the Hereafter). Then the soul is breathed into his body. So a man may do deeds characteristic of the people of the (Hell) Fire, so much so that there is only the distance of a cubit between him and it, and then what has been written (by the angel) surpasses; and so he starts doing deeds characteristic of the people of Paradise and

you may reach your age of full strength. And among you there is he who dies (young), and among you there is he who is brought back to the miserable old age, so that he knows nothing after having known. And you see the earth barren, but when We send down water (rain) on it, it is stirred (to life), and it swells and puts forth every lovely kind (of growth).

6. That is because Allâh: He is the Truth, and it is He Who gives life to the dead, and it is He Who is Able to do all things.

7. And surely, the Hour is coming, there is no doubt about it; and certainly, Allâh will resurrect those who are in the graves.

8. And among men is he who disputes about Allâh, without knowledge or guidance, or a Book giving light (from Allâh),

9. Bending his neck in pride[1] (far astray from the Path of Allâh), and

---

enters Paradise. Similarly, a person may do deeds characteristic of the people of Paradise, so much so that there is only the distance of a cubit between him and it, and then what has been written (by the angel) surpasses, and he starts doing deeds of the people of the (Hell) Fire and enters the (Hell) Fire." (*Sahih Al-Bukhari*, Vol.4, *Hadith* No.549).

[1] (V.22:9) Narrated Abdullah bin Mas'ûd رضي الله عنه : Allâh's Messenger صلى الله عليه وسلم said, "Whosoever has pride in his heart equal to the weight of an atom (or a small ant) shall not enter Paradise." A person (amongst the audience) said, "Verily, a person loves that his dress should be beautiful, and his shoes should be beautiful." The Prophet صلى الله عليه وسلم remarked, "Verily, Allâh is the Most Beautiful and He loves beauty. (الكبر: بطر الحق وغمط الناس) Pride is to completely

leading (others) too (far) astray from the Path of Allâh. For him there is disgrace in this worldly life, and on the Day of Resurrection We shall make him taste the torment of burning (Fire).

10. That is because of what your hands have sent forth, and verily, Allâh is not unjust to (His) slaves.

11. And among mankind is he who worships Allâh as it were upon the edge (i.e. in doubt): if good befalls him, he is content therewith; but if a trial befalls him he turns back on his face (i.e. reverts to disbelief after embracing Islâm. He loses both this world and the Hereafter. That is the evident loss.

12. He calls besides Allâh unto that which hurts him not, nor profits him. That is a straying far away.

13. He calls unto him whose harm is nearer than his profit: certainly, an evil *Maulâ* (patron) and certainly an evil friend!

14. Truly, Allâh will admit those who believe (in Islâmic Monotheism) and do righteous good deeds (according to the Qur'ân and the *Sunnah*) to Gardens underneath which rivers flow (in Paradise). Verily, Allâh does what He wills.

15. Whoever thinks that Allâh will not help him (Muhammad صلى الله عليه وسلم) in this world and in the Hereafter, let

disregard the truth, and to scorn (to look down upon) the people."
(*Sahih Muslim*, Book of Faith, Vol.1, *Hadîth* No. 164).

him stretch out a rope to the ceiling and let him strangle himself. Then let him see whether his plan will remove that whereat he rages!

16. Thus have We sent it (this Qur'ân) down (to Muhammad صلى الله عليه وسلم) as clear signs, evidences and proofs, and surely, Allâh guides whom He wills.

17. Verily, those who believe (in Allâh and in His Messenger Muhammad صلى الله عليه وسلم), and those who are Jews, and the Sabians, and the Christians, and the Majûs, and those who worship others besides Allâh, truly, Allâh will judge between them on the Day of Resurrection. Verily, Allâh is over all things a Witness.[1]

18. See you not that whoever is in the heavens and whoever is on the earth, and the sun, and the moon, and the stars, and the mountains, and the trees, and *Ad-Dawâbb* [moving (living) creatures, beasts], and many of mankind prostrate themselves to Allâh. But there are many (men) on whom the punishment is justified. And whomsoever Allâh disgraces, none can honour him. Verily, Allâh does what He wills.

19. These two opponents (believers and disbelievers) dispute with each other about their Lord: then as for those who disbelieved, garments of fire will be cut out for them, boiling water will be poured down over their heads.

---

[1] (V.22:17) See (V.2:62) and its footnotes for the explanation of this Verse.

20. With it will melt (or vanish away) what is within their bellies, as well as (their) skins.

يُصْهَرُ بِهِ مَا فِى بُطُونِهِمْ وَالْجُلُودُ

21. And for them are hooked rods of iron (to punish them).

وَلَهُم مَّقَٰمِعُ مِنْ حَدِيدٍ

22. Every time they seek to get away therefrom, from anguish, they will be driven back therein, and (it will be) said to them: "Taste the torment of burning!"

كُلَّمَا أَرَادُوٓا أَن يَخْرُجُوا مِنْهَا مِنْ غَمٍّ أُعِيدُوا فِيهَا وَذُوقُوا عَذَابَ الْحَرِيقِ

23. Truly, Allâh will admit those who believe (in the Oneness of Allâh — Islâmic Monotheism) and do righteous good deeds, to Gardens underneath which rivers flow (in Paradise), wherein they will be adorned with bracelets of gold and pearls and their garments therein will be of silk.

إِنَّ اللَّهَ يُدْخِلُ الَّذِينَ ءَامَنُوا وَعَمِلُوا الصَّٰلِحَٰتِ جَنَّٰتٍ تَجْرِى مِن تَحْتِهَا الْأَنْهَٰرُ يُحَلَّوْنَ فِيهَا مِنْ أَسَاوِرَ مِن ذَهَبٍ وَلُؤْلُؤًا وَلِبَاسُهُمْ فِيهَا حَرِيرٌ

24. And they are guided (in this world) unto goodly speech (i.e. *Lâ ilâha illallâh, Alhamdu lillâh,* recitation of the Qur'ân) and they are guided to the Path of Him (i.e. Allâh's religion of Islâmic Monotheism), Who is Worthy of all praises.

وَهُدُوٓا إِلَى الطَّيِّبِ مِنَ الْقَوْلِ وَهُدُوٓا إِلَىٰ صِرَٰطِ الْحَمِيدِ

25. Verily, those who disbelieved and hinder (men) from the Path of Allâh, and from *Al-Masjid Al-Harâm* (at Makkah) which We have made (open) to (all) men, the dweller in it and the visitor from the country are equal there [as regards its sanctity and pilgrimage (*Hajj* and *'Umrah*)] — and whoever inclines to evil actions therein or to do wrong (i.e. practise polytheism and leave Islâmic Monotheism), him We shall cause to taste from a painful torment.

إِنَّ الَّذِينَ كَفَرُوا وَيَصُدُّونَ عَن سَبِيلِ اللَّهِ وَالْمَسْجِدِ الْحَرَامِ الَّذِى جَعَلْنَٰهُ لِلنَّاسِ سَوَآءً الْعَٰكِفُ فِيهِ وَالْبَادِ وَمَن يُرِدْ فِيهِ بِإِلْحَادٍ بِظُلْمٍ نُذِقْهُ مِنْ عَذَابٍ أَلِيمٍ

26. And (remember) when We showed Ibrâhîm (Abraham) the site of the (Sacred) House (the *Ka'bah* at Makkah) (saying): "Associate not anything (in worship) with Me, [*Lâ ilâha illallâh* (none has the right to be worshipped but Allâh) — Islâmic Monotheism], and sanctify My House for those who circumambulate it, and those who stand up (for prayer), and those who bow (submit themselves with humility and obedience to Allâh), and make prostration (in prayer);"

27. And proclaim to mankind the *Hajj* (pilgrimage). They will come to you on foot and on every lean camel, they will come from every deep and distant (wide) mountain highway (to perform *Hajj*).[1]

28. That they may witness things that are of benefit to them (i.e. reward of *Hajj* in the Hereafter, and also some worldly gain from trade), and mention the Name of Allâh on appointed days (i.e. 10th, 11th, 12th, and 13th day of Dhul-Hijjah), over the beast of cattle that He has provided for them [at the time of their

---

[1] (V.22:27).

a) Narrated Abu Hurairah رضي الله عنه Allâh's Messenger صلى الله عليه وسلم said, "Whoever performs *Hajj* to this House (*Ka'bah*) and does not approach his wife for sexual relations nor commits sins (while performing *Hajj*), he will come out as sinless as a newly-born child (just delivered by his mother)." (*Sahih Al-Bukhari*, Vol.3, Hadith No. 45).

b) See the footnote of (V.2:196).

slaughtering by saying: (Bismillâh, Wallâhu-Akbar, Allâhumma Minka wa Ilaik)]. Then eat thereof and feed therewith the poor who have a very hard time.

29. Then let them complete their prescribed duties (Manâsik of Hajj) and perform their vows, and circumambulate the Ancient House (the Ka'bah at Makkah).[1]

30. That (Manâsik — prescribed duties of Hajj) is the obligation that mankind owes to Allâh) and whoever honours the sacred things of Allâh, then that is better for him with his Lord. The cattle are lawful to you, except those (that will be) mentioned to you (as exceptions). So shun the abomination (worshipping) of idol, and shun lying speech (false statements)[2]

31. Hunafâ' Lillâh (i.e. worshiping none but Allâh), not associating partners (in worship) unto Him; and whoever assigns partners to Allâh, it is as if he had fallen from the sky, and the birds had snatched him, or the wind had thrown him to a far off place.

32. Thus it is [what has been mentioned in the above said Verses (27, 28, 29, 30, 31) is an obligation that mankind owes to Allâh] and whosoever honours the Symbols of Allâh, then it is truly, from the piety of the hearts.

ثُمَّ لِيَقْضُوا تَفَتَهُمْ وَلْيُوفُوا نُذُورَهُمْ وَلْيَطَّوَّفُوا بِالْبَيْتِ الْعَتِيقِ ۝

ذَٰلِكَ وَمَن يُعَظِّمْ حُرُمَٰتِ اللَّهِ فَهُوَ خَيْرٌ لَّهُ عِندَ رَبِّهِ وَأُحِلَّتْ لَكُمُ الْأَنْعَٰمُ إِلَّا مَا يُتْلَىٰ عَلَيْكُمْ فَاجْتَنِبُوا الرِّجْسَ مِنَ الْأَوْثَٰنِ وَاجْتَنِبُوا قَوْلَ الزُّورِ ۝

حُنَفَآءَ لِلَّهِ غَيْرَ مُشْرِكِينَ بِهِۦ وَمَن يُشْرِكْ بِاللَّهِ فَكَأَنَّمَا خَرَّ مِنَ السَّمَآءِ فَتَخْطَفُهُ الطَّيْرُ أَوْ تَهْوِي بِهِ الرِّيحُ فِي مَكَانٍ سَحِيقٍ ۝

ذَٰلِكَ وَمَن يُعَظِّمْ شَعَٰٓئِرَ اللَّهِ فَإِنَّهَا مِن تَقْوَى الْقُلُوبِ ۝

---

[1] (V.22:29) See the footnote of (V.2:128).

[2] (V.22:30) See the footnote of (V.5:32).

33. In them (cattle offered for sacrifice) are benefits for you for an appointed term, and afterwards they are brought for sacrifice unto the ancient House (the *Haram* — sacred territory of Makkah).

لَكُمْ فِيهَا مَنَٰفِعُ إِلَىٰٓ أَجَلٍ مُّسَمًّى ثُمَّ مَحِلُّهَآ إِلَى ٱلْبَيْتِ ٱلْعَتِيقِ ۝

34. And for every nation We have appointed religious ceremonies, that they may mention the Name of Allâh over the beast of cattle that He has given them for food. And your *Ilâh* (God) is One *Ilâh* (God — Allâh), so you must submit to Him Alone (in Islâm). And (O Muhammad صلى الله عليه وسلم) give glad tidings to the *Mukhbitûn* [those who obey Allâh with humility and are humble from among the true believers of Islâmic Monotheism],

وَلِكُلِّ أُمَّةٍ جَعَلْنَا مَنسَكًا لِّيَذْكُرُوا۟ ٱسْمَ ٱللَّهِ عَلَىٰ مَا رَزَقَهُم مِّنۢ بَهِيمَةِ ٱلْأَنْعَٰمِ فَإِلَٰهُكُمْ إِلَٰهٌ وَٰحِدٌ فَلَهُۥٓ أَسْلِمُوا۟ وَبَشِّرِ ٱلْمُخْبِتِينَ ۝

35. Whose hearts are filled with fear when Allâh is mentioned and *As-Sâbirûn* [who patiently bear whatever may befall them (of calamities)]; and who perform *As-Salât* (Iqâmat-as-Salât), and who spend (in Allâh's Cause) out of what We have provided them,

ٱلَّذِينَ إِذَا ذُكِرَ ٱللَّهُ وَجِلَتْ قُلُوبُهُمْ وَٱلصَّٰبِرِينَ عَلَىٰ مَآ أَصَابَهُمْ وَٱلْمُقِيمِى ٱلصَّلَوٰةِ وَمِمَّا رَزَقْنَٰهُمْ يُنفِقُونَ ۝

36. And the *Budn* (cows, oxen, or camels driven to be offered as sacrifices by the pilgrims at the sanctuary of Makkah) We have made them for you as among the Symbols of Allâh, wherein you have much good. So mention the Name of Allâh over them when they are drawn up in lines (for sacrifice). Then, when they are down on their sides (after slaughter), eat thereof, and feed the poor who does not ask (men), and the beggar who asks (men).

وَٱلْبُدْنَ جَعَلْنَٰهَا لَكُم مِّن شَعَٰٓئِرِ ٱللَّهِ لَكُمْ فِيهَا خَيْرٌ فَٱذْكُرُوا۟ ٱسْمَ ٱللَّهِ عَلَيْهَا صَوَآفَّ فَإِذَا وَجَبَتْ جُنُوبُهَا فَكُلُوا۟ مِنْهَا وَأَطْعِمُوا۟ ٱلْقَانِعَ وَٱلْمُعْتَرَّ كَذَٰلِكَ سَخَّرْنَٰهَا لَكُمْ لَعَلَّكُمْ تَشْكُرُونَ ۝

Thus have We made them subject to you that you may be grateful.

37. It is neither their meat nor their blood that reaches Allâh, but it is piety from you that reaches Him. Thus have We made them subject to you that you may magnify Allâh for His Guidance to you. And give glad tidings (O Muhammad صلى الله عليه وسلم) to the *Muhsinûn*[1] (doers of good).

38. Truly, Allâh defends those who believe. Verily, Allâh likes not any treacherous ingrate to Allâh [those who disobey Allâh but obey *Shaitân* (Satan)].

39. Permission to fight (against disbelievers) is given to those (believers) who are fought against, because they have been wronged; and surely, Allâh is Able to give them (believers) victory —

40. Those who have been expelled from their homes unjustly only because they said: "Our Lord is Allâh." For had it not been that Allâh checks one set of people by means of another, monasteries, churches, synagogues, and mosques, wherein the Name of Allâh is mentioned much would surely, have been pulled down. Verily, Allâh will help those who help His (Cause). Truly, Allâh is All-Strong, All-Mighty.

لَن يَنَالَ ٱللَّهَ لُحُومُهَا وَلَا دِمَآؤُهَا وَلَٰكِن يَنَالُهُ ٱلتَّقْوَىٰ مِنكُمْۚ كَذَٰلِكَ سَخَّرَهَا لَكُمْ لِتُكَبِّرُواْ ٱللَّهَ عَلَىٰ مَا هَدَىٰكُمْۗ وَبَشِّرِ ٱلْمُحْسِنِينَ ۝

إِنَّ ٱللَّهَ يُدَٰفِعُ عَنِ ٱلَّذِينَ ءَامَنُوٓاْۗ إِنَّ ٱللَّهَ لَا يُحِبُّ كُلَّ خَوَّانٍ كَفُورٍ ۝

أُذِنَ لِلَّذِينَ يُقَٰتَلُونَ بِأَنَّهُمْ ظُلِمُواْۚ وَإِنَّ ٱللَّهَ عَلَىٰ نَصْرِهِمْ لَقَدِيرٌ ۝

ٱلَّذِينَ أُخْرِجُواْ مِن دِيَٰرِهِم بِغَيْرِ حَقٍّ إِلَّآ أَن يَقُولُواْ رَبُّنَا ٱللَّهُۗ وَلَوْلَا دَفْعُ ٱللَّهِ ٱلنَّاسَ بَعْضَهُم بِبَعْضٍ لَّهُدِّمَتْ صَوَٰمِعُ وَبِيَعٌ وَصَلَوَٰتٌ وَمَسَٰجِدُ يُذْكَرُ فِيهَا ٱسْمُ ٱللَّهِ كَثِيرًاۗ وَلَيَنصُرَنَّ ٱللَّهُ مَن يَنصُرُهُۥٓۗ إِنَّ ٱللَّهَ لَقَوِيٌّ عَزِيزٌ ۝

---

[1] (V.22:37) *Al-Muhsinûn*: The good-doers who perform good deeds totally for Allâh's sake only without any show-off or to gain praise or fame and do them in accordance with the *Sunnah* (legal ways) of Allâh's Messenger Muhammad صلى الله عليه وسلم.

41. Those (Muslim rulers) who, if We give them power in the land, (they) enjoin *Iqamat-as-Salât*[1] [i.e. to perform the five compulsory congregational *Salât* (prayers) (the males in mosques)], to pay the *Zakât* and they enjoin *Al-Ma'rûf* (i.e. Islâmic Monotheism and all that Islâm orders one to do), and forbid *Al-Munkar* (i.e.

الَّذِينَ إِن مَّكَّنَّهُمْ فِي الْأَرْضِ أَقَامُوا الصَّلَوٰةَ وَءَاتَوُا الزَّكَوٰةَ وَأَمَرُوا بِالْمَعْرُوفِ وَنَهَوْا عَنِ الْمُنكَرِ وَلِلَّهِ عَٰقِبَةُ الْأُمُورِ ﴿٤١﴾

---

[1] (V.22:41):

A) *Iqâmat-as-Salât:* Performing of *Salât* (prayers). It means that:

a) Every Muslim, male or female, is obliged to offer his *Salât* (prayers) regularly five times a day at the specified times; the male in the mosque in congregation and the female at home. As the Prophet صلى الله عليه وسلم has said: Order your children to perform *Salât* (prayer) at the age of seven and beat them (about it) at the age of ten. The chief (of a family, town, tribe) and the Muslim rulers of a country are held responsible before Allâh in case of non-fulfilment of this obligation by the Muslims under their authority.

b) One must offer the *Salât* (prayers) as the Prophet صلى الله عليه وسلم used to offer them with all their rules and regulations. i.e., standing, bowing, prostrating and sitting. As he صلى الله عليه وسلم has said: "Offer your *Salât* (prayers) the way you see me offering them (*Hadîth* No. 352, Vol. 9, *Sahîh Al-Bukhârî*)." [For the characteristics of the *Salât* (prayer) of the Prophet صلى الله عليه وسلم see *Sahîh Al-Bukhârî*, Vol.1, *Hadîth* Nos. 702, 703, 704, 723, 786 and 787].

B) Narrated Abu Hurairah رضي الله عنه: The Prophet صلى الله عليه وسلم said, "No *Salât* (prayer) is heavier (harder) for the hypocrites than the *Fajr* and the 'Ishâ prayers, but if they knew the reward for these *Salât* (prayers) at their respective times, they would certainly present themselves (in the mosques) even if they had to crawl." The Prophet صلى الله عليه وسلم added, "Certainly, I intended (or was about) to order the *Mu'adhdhin* (call-maker) to pronounce *Iqâmah* and order a man to lead the *Salât* (prayer) and then take a fire flame to burn all those (men along with their houses) who had not yet left their houses for the *Salât* (prayer) (in the mosques)." (*Sahih Al-Bukhari*, Vol. 1, *Hadith* No. 626)

disbelief, polytheism and all that Islâm has forbidden) [i.e. they make the Qur'ân as the law of their country in all the spheres of life]. And with Allâh rests the end of (all) matters (of creatures).

42. And if they belie you (O Muhammad صلى الله عليه وسلم), so did belie before them, the people of Nûh (Noah), 'Âd and Thamûd (their Prophets).

43. And the people of Ibrâhîm (Abraham) and the people of Lût (Lot),

44. And the dwellers of Madyan (Midian), and belied was Mûsâ (Moses). But I granted respite to the disbelievers for a while, then I seized them, and how (terrible) was My punishment (against their wrong-doing)!

45. And many a township We destroyed while they were given to wrong-doing, so that they lie in ruins (up to this day), and (many) a deserted well and lofty castle!

46. Have they not travelled through the land, and have they hearts wherewith to understand and ears wherewith to hear? Verily, it is not the eyes that grow blind, but it is the hearts which are in the breasts that grow blind.

47. And they ask you to hasten on the torment! And Allâh fails not His Promise. And verily, a day with your Lord is as a thousand years of what you reckon.

وَإِن يُكَذِّبُوكَ فَقَدْ كَذَّبَتْ قَبْلَهُمْ قَوْمُ نُوحٍ وَعَادٌ وَثَمُودُ ﴿٤٢﴾

وَقَوْمُ إِبْرَٰهِيمَ وَقَوْمُ لُوطٍ ﴿٤٣﴾

وَأَصْحَٰبُ مَدْيَنَ وَكُذِّبَ مُوسَىٰ فَأَمْلَيْتُ لِلْكَٰفِرِينَ ثُمَّ أَخَذْتُهُمْ فَكَيْفَ كَانَ نَكِيرِ ﴿٤٤﴾

فَكَأَيِّن مِّن قَرْيَةٍ أَهْلَكْنَٰهَا وَهِيَ ظَالِمَةٌ فَهِيَ خَاوِيَةٌ عَلَىٰ عُرُوشِهَا وَبِئْرٍ مُّعَطَّلَةٍ وَقَصْرٍ مَّشِيدٍ ﴿٤٥﴾ أَفَلَمْ يَسِيرُوا۟ فِى ٱلْأَرْضِ فَتَكُونَ لَهُمْ قُلُوبٌ يَعْقِلُونَ بِهَا أَوْ ءَاذَانٌ يَسْمَعُونَ بِهَا فَإِنَّهَا لَا تَعْمَى ٱلْأَبْصَٰرُ وَلَٰكِن تَعْمَى ٱلْقُلُوبُ ٱلَّتِى فِى ٱلصُّدُورِ ﴿٤٦﴾

وَيَسْتَعْجِلُونَكَ بِٱلْعَذَابِ وَلَن يُخْلِفَ ٱللَّهُ وَعْدَهُ وَإِنَّ يَوْمًا عِندَ رَبِّكَ كَأَلْفِ سَنَةٍ مِّمَّا تَعُدُّونَ ﴿٤٧﴾

48. And many a township did I give respite while it was given to wrong-doing. Then (in the end) I seized it (with punishment). And to Me is the (final) return (of all).

49. Say (O Muhammad صلى الله عليه وسلم): "O mankind! I am (sent) to you only as a plain warner.

50. So those who believe (in the Oneness of Allâh — Islâmic Monotheism) and do righteous good deeds, for them is forgiveness and *Rizqun Karîm* (generous provision, i.e. Paradise).

51. But those who strive against Our *Ayât* (proofs, evidences, verses, lessons, signs, revelations, etc.), to frustrate them, they will be dwellers of the Hell-fire.

52. Never did We send a Messenger or a Prophet before you but when he did recite the revelation or narrated or spoke, *Shaitân* (Satan) threw (some falsehood) in it. But Allâh abolishes that which *Shaitân* (Satan) throws in. Then Allâh establishes His Revelations. And Allâh is All-Knower, All-Wise:

53. That He (Allâh) may make what is thrown in by *Shaitân* (Satan) a trial for those in whose hearts is a disease (of hypocrisy and disbelief) and whose hearts are hardened. And certainly, the *Zalimûn* (polytheists and wrongdoers) are in an opposition far-off (from the truth against Allâh's Messenger and the believers).

54. And that those who have been given knowledge may know that it (this Qur'ân) is the truth from your Lord, so that they may believe therein, and their hearts may submit to it with humility. And verily, Allâh is the Guide of those who believe, to the Straight Path.

55. And those who disbelieved will not cease to be in doubt about it (this Qur'ân) until the Hour comes suddenly upon them, or there comes to them the torment of the Day after which there will be no night (i.e. the Day of Resurrection).

56. The sovereignty on that Day will be that of Allâh (the One Who has no partners). He will judge between them. So those who believed (in the Oneness of Allâh — Islâmic Monotheism) and did righteous good deeds will be in Gardens of delight (Paradise).

57. And those who disbelieved and belied Our Verses (of this Qur'ân), for them will be a humiliating torment (in Hell).

58. Those who emigrated in the Cause of Allâh and after that were killed or died, surely, Allâh will provide a good provision for them. And verily, it is Allâh Who indeed is the Best of those who make provision.

59. Truly, He will make them enter an entrance with which they shall be well-pleased, and verily, Allâh indeed is All-Knowing, Most Forbearing.

60. That is so. And whoever has retaliated with the like of that which he was made to suffer, and then has again been wronged, Allâh will surely help him. Verily, Allâh indeed is Oft-Pardoning, Oft-Forgiving.

61. That is because Allâh merges the night into the day, and He merges the day into the night. And verily, Allâh is All-Hearer, All-Seer.

62. That is because Allâh — He is the Truth (the only True God of all that exists, Who has no partners or rivals with Him), and what they (the polytheists) invoke besides Him, it is Bâtil (falsehood). And verily, Allâh — He is the Most High, the Most Great.

63. See you not that Allâh sends down water (rain) from the sky, and then the earth becomes green? Verily, Allâh is the Most Kind and Courteous, Well-Acquainted with all things.

64. To Him belongs all that is in the heavens and all that is on the earth. And verily, Allâh — He is Rich (Free of all needs), Worthy of all praise.

65. See you not that Allâh has subjected to you (mankind) all that is on the earth, and the ships that sail through the sea by His Command? He withholds the heaven from falling on the earth except by His Leave. Verily, Allâh is, for mankind, full of kindness, Most Merciful.

66. It is He, Who gave you life, and then will cause you to die, and will again give you life (on the Day of Resurrection). Verily, man is indeed an ingrate.

67. For every nation We have ordained religious ceremonies [e.g. slaughtering of the cattle during the three days of stay at Mîna (Makkah) during the *Hajj* (pilgrimage)] which they must follow; so let them (the pagans) not dispute with you on the matter (i.e. to eat of the cattle which you slaughter, and not to eat of the cattle which Allâh kills by its natural death), but invite them to your Lord. Verily, you (O Muhammad صلى الله عليه وسلم) indeed are on the (true) straight guidance (i.e. the true religion of Islâmic Monotheism).

68. And if they argue with you (as regards the slaughtering of the sacrifices), say "Allâh knows best of what you do.

69. "Allâh will judge between you on the Day of Resurrection about that wherein you used to differ."

70. Know you not that Allâh knows all that is in the heaven and on the earth? Verily, it is (all) in the Book (Al-Lauh Al-Mahfûz). Verily, that is easy for Allâh.

71. And they worship besides Allâh others for which He has sent down no authority, and of which they have no knowledge; and for the *Zâlimûn* (wrongdoers, polytheists and disbelievers in the Oneness of Allâh) there is no helper.

72. And when Our Clear Verses are recited to them, you will notice a denial on the faces of the disbelievers! They are nearly ready to attack with violence those who recite Our Verses to them. Say: "Shall I tell you of something worse than that? The Fire (of Hell) which Allâh has promised to those who disbelieved, and worst indeed is that destination!"

73. O mankind! A similitude has been coined, so listen to it (carefully): Verily, those on whom you call besides Allâh, cannot create (even) a fly, even though they combine together for the purpose. And if the fly snatches away a thing from them, they will have no power to release it from the fly. So weak are (both) the seeker and the sought.

74. They have not estimated Allâh His Rightful Estimate. Verily, Allâh is All-Strong, All-Mighty.

75. Allâh chooses Messengers from angels and from men. Verily, Allâh is All-Hearer, All-Seer.

76. He knows what is before them, and what is behind them. And to Allâh return all matters (for decision).

77. O you who have believed! Bow down, and prostrate yourselves, and worship your Lord and do good that you may be successful.

78. And strive hard in Allâh's Cause as you ought to strive (with sincerity and with all your efforts that His Name should be superior). He has chosen you (to convey His Message of Islâmic Monotheism to mankind by inviting them to His religion of Islâm), and has not laid upon you in religion any hardship:[1] it is the religion of your father Ibrâhîm (Abraham) (Islâmic Monotheism). It is He (Allâh) Who has named you Muslims both before and in this (the Qur'ân), that the Messenger (Muhammad صلى الله عليه وسلم) may be a witness over you and you be witnesses over mankind![2] So perform As-Salât (Iqamat-as-Salât), give Zakât and hold fast to Allâh [i.e. have confidence in Allâh, and depend upon Him in all your affairs]. He is your Maulâ (Patron, Lord), what an Excellent Maulâ (Patron, Lord) and what an Excellent Helper!

---

[1] (V.22:78) Religion is very easy. And the statement of the Prophet صلى الله عليه وسلم "The most beloved religion to Allâh عز وجل is the tolerant Hanîfiyyah [i.e., Islâmic Monotheism, i.e., to worship Him (Allâh) Alone and not to worship anything else along with Him.]"

Narrated Abu Hurairah رضى الله عنه: The Prophet صلى الله عليه وسلم said, "Religion is very easy and whoever overburdens himself in his religion will not be able to continue in that way. So you should not be extremists, but try to be near to perfection and receive the good tidings that you will be rewarded; and gain strength by offering the Salât (prayers) in the mornings, afternoons and during the last hours of the nights." (See Fath Al-Bari) (Sahih Al-Bukhari, Vol. 1, Hadith No. 38)

[2] (V.22:78) See the footnote of (V.2:143).

Surat Al-Mu'minûn
(The Believers) XXIII

سُورَةُ الْمُؤْمِنُونَ

*In the Name of Allâh
the Most Gracious, the Most Merciful*

بِسْمِ اللّهِ الرَّحْمَنِ الرَّحِيمِ

1. Successful indeed are the believers.

قَدْ أَفْلَحَ الْمُؤْمِنُونَ ۝

2. Those who offer their *Salât* (prayers) with all solemnity and full submissiveness.

الَّذِينَ هُمْ فِى صَلَاتِهِمْ خَاشِعُونَ ۝

3. And those who turn away from *Al-Laghw* (dirty, false, evil vain talk, falsehood, and all that Allâh has forbidden).

وَالَّذِينَ هُمْ عَنِ اللَّغْوِ مُعْرِضُونَ ۝

4. And those who pay the *Zakât* .

وَالَّذِينَ هُمْ لِلزَّكَوةِ فَاعِلُونَ ۝

5. And those who guard their chastity (i.e. private parts, from illegal sexual acts)

وَالَّذِينَ هُمْ لِفُرُوجِهِمْ حَافِظُونَ ۝

6. Except from their wives or (slaves) that their right hands possess, — for then, they are free from blame;

إِلَّا عَلَى أَزْوَاجِهِمْ أَوْ مَا مَلَكَتْ أَيْمَانُهُمْ فَإِنَّهُمْ غَيْرُ مَلُومِينَ ۝

7. But whoever seeks beyond that, then those are the transgressors;

فَمَنِ ابْتَغَى وَرَاءَ ذَلِكَ فَأُوْلَئِكَ هُمُ الْعَادُونَ ۝

8. Those who are faithfully true to their *Amanât* (all the duties which Allâh has ordained, honesty, moral responsibility and trusts) and to their covenants;

وَالَّذِينَ هُمْ لِأَمَانَاتِهِمْ وَعَهْدِهِمْ رَاعُونَ ۝

9. And those who strictly guard their (five compulsory congregational) *Salawât* (prayers) (at their fixed stated hours).

وَالَّذِينَ هُمْ عَلَى صَلَوَاتِهِمْ يُحَافِظُونَ ۝

10. These are indeed the inheritors

أُوْلَئِكَ هُمُ الْوَارِثُونَ ۝

11. Who shall inherit the *Firdaus* (Paradise). They shall dwell therein forever.

الَّذِينَ يَرِثُونَ الْفِرْدَوْسَ هُمْ فِيهَا خَالِدُونَ ۝

12. And indeed We created man (Adam) out of an extract of clay (water and earth).

13. Thereafter We made him (the offspring of Adam) as a *Nutfah* (mixed drops of the male and female sexual discharge and lodged it) in a safe lodging (womb of the woman).

14. Then We made the *Nutfah* into a clot (a piece of thick coagulated blood), then We made the clot into a little lump of flesh, then We made out of that little lump of flesh bones, then We clothed the bones with flesh, and then We brought it forth as another creation. So Blessed be Allâh, the Best of creators.[1]

15. After that, surely, you will die.

16. Then (again), surely, you will be resurrected on the Day of Resurrection.

17. And indeed We have created above you seven heavens (one over the other), and We are never unaware of the creation.

18. And We sent down from the sky water (rain) in (due) measure, and We gave it lodging in the earth, and verily, We are Able to take it away.

19. Then We brought forth for you therewith gardens of date-palms and grapes, wherein is much fruit for you, and whereof you eat.

20. And a tree (olive) that springs forth from Mount Sinai, that grows (produces) oil, and (it is a) relish for the eaters.

---

[1] (V.23:14) See the footnote of (V.22:5).

21. And verily, in the cattle there is indeed a lesson for you. We give you to drink (milk) of that which is in their bellies. And there are, in them, numerous (other) benefits for you, and of them you eat.

وَإِنَّ لَكُمْ فِي الْأَنْعَامِ لَعِبْرَةً نُّسْقِيكُمْ مِّمَّا فِي بُطُونِهَا وَلَكُمْ فِيهَا مَنَافِعُ كَثِيرَةٌ وَمِنْهَا تَأْكُلُونَ ۝

22. And on them, and on ships you are carried.

وَعَلَيْهَا وَعَلَى الْفُلْكِ تُحْمَلُونَ ۝

23. And indeed We sent Nûh (Noah) to his people, and he said: "O my people! Worship Allâh! You have no other *Ilâh* (God) but Him (Islâmic Monotheism). Will you not then be afraid (of Him i.e. of His punishment because of worshipping others besides Him)?"

وَلَقَدْ أَرْسَلْنَا نُوحًا إِلَى قَوْمِهِ فَقَالَ يَا قَوْمِ اعْبُدُوا اللَّهَ مَا لَكُمْ مِّنْ إِلَهٍ غَيْرُهُ أَفَلَا تَتَّقُونَ ۝

24. But the chiefs of his people who disbelieved said: "He is no more than a human being like you, he seeks to make himself superior to you. Had Allâh willed, He surely, could have sent down angels. Never did we hear such a thing among our fathers of old.

فَقَالَ الْمَلَأُ الَّذِينَ كَفَرُوا مِنْ قَوْمِهِ مَا هَذَا إِلَّا بَشَرٌ مِّثْلُكُمْ يُرِيدُ أَنْ يَتَفَضَّلَ عَلَيْكُمْ وَلَوْ شَاءَ اللَّهُ لَأَنْزَلَ مَلَائِكَةً مَّا سَمِعْنَا بِهَذَا فِي آبَائِنَا الْأَوَّلِينَ ۝

25. "He is only a man in whom is madness, so wait for him for a while."

إِنْ هُوَ إِلَّا رَجُلٌ بِهِ جِنَّةٌ فَتَرَبَّصُوا بِهِ حَتَّى حِينٍ ۝

26. [Nûh (Noah)] said: "O my Lord! Help me because they deny me."

قَالَ رَبِّ انْصُرْنِي بِمَا كَذَّبُونِ ۝

27. So We revealed to him (saying): "Construct the ship under Our Eyes and under Our Revelation (guidance). Then, when Our Command comes, and water gushes forth from the oven, take on board of each kind two (male and female), and your family, except those thereof against whom the Word has already gone forth. And address Me not

فَأَوْحَيْنَا إِلَيْهِ أَنِ اصْنَعِ الْفُلْكَ بِأَعْيُنِنَا وَوَحْيِنَا فَإِذَا جَاءَ أَمْرُنَا وَفَارَ التَّنُّورُ فَاسْلُكْ فِيهَا مِنْ كُلٍّ زَوْجَيْنِ اثْنَيْنِ وَأَهْلَكَ إِلَّا مَنْ سَبَقَ عَلَيْهِ الْقَوْلُ مِنْهُمْ وَلَا

in favour of those who have done wrong. Verily, they are to be drowned.

28. And when you have embarked on the ship, you and whoever is with you, then say: "All the praises and thanks are to Allâh, Who has saved us from the people who are *Zâlimûn* (i.e. oppressors, wrongdoers, polytheists, those who join others in worship with Allâh).

29. And say: "My Lord! Cause me to land at a blessed landing-place, for You are the Best of those who bring to land."

30. Verily, in this [what We did as regards drowning of the people of Nûh (Noah)], there are indeed *Ayât* (proofs, evidences, lessons, signs, etc. for men to understand), for sure We are ever putting (men) to the test.

31. Then, after them, We created another generation.

32. And We sent to them a Messenger from among themselves (saying): "Worship Allâh! You have no other *Ilâh* (God) but Him. Will you not then be afraid (of Him i.e. of His punishment because of worshipping others besides Him)?"

33. And the chiefs of his people who disbelieved and denied the Meeting in the Hereafter, and whom We had given the luxuries and comforts of this life, said: "He is no more than a human being like you, he eats of that which you eat, and drinks of what you drink.

34. "If you were to obey a human being like yourselves, then verily, you indeed would be losers.

35. "Does he promise you that when you have died and have become dust and bones, you shall come out alive (resurrected)?

36. "Far, very far is that which you are promised!

37. "There is nothing but our life of this world! We die and we live! And we are not going to be resurrected!

38. "He is only a man who has invented a lie against Allâh, and we are not going to believe in him."

39. He said: "O my Lord! Help me because they deny me."

40. (Allâh) said: "In a little while, they are sure to be regretful."

41. So As-Saihah (torment — awful cry) overtook them in truth (with justice), and We made them as rubbish of dead plants. So away with the people who are Zâlimûn (polytheists, wrongdoers, disbelievers in the Oneness of Allâh, disobedient to His Messengers).

42. Then, after them, We created other generations.

43. No nation can advance their term, nor can they delay it.

44. Then We sent Our Messengers in succession. Every time there came to a nation their Messenger, they denied him; so We made them follow one another (to destruction), and We made them as *Ahadîth* (the true stories for mankind to learn a lesson from them). So away with a people who believe not!

45. Then We sent Mûsâ (Moses) and his brother Hârûn (Aaron), with Our *Ayât* (proofs, evidences, verses, lessons, signs, revelations, etc.) and manifest authority,

46. To Fir'aun (Pharaoh) and his chiefs, but they behaved insolently and they were people self-exalting (by disobeying their Lord, and exalting themselves over and above the Messenger of Allâh).

47. They said: "Shall we believe in two men like ourselves, and their people are obedient to us with humility (and we use them to serve us as we like)."

48. So they denied them both [Mûsâ (Moses) and Hârûn (Aaron)] and became of those who were destroyed.

49. And indeed We gave Mûsâ (Moses) the Scripture, that they may be guided.

50. And We made the son of Maryam (Mary) and his mother as a sign, and We gave them refuge on high ground, a place of rest, security and flowing streams.

51. O (you) Messengers! Eat of the *Tayyibât* [all kinds of *Halâl* (lawful) foods (meat of slaughtered eatable animals, milk products, fats, vegetables, fruits] and do righteous deeds. Verily, I am Well-Acquainted with what you do.

52. And verily, this your religion (of Islâmic Monotheism) is one religion, and I am your Lord, so keep your duty to Me.

وَإِنَّ هَذِهِۦٓ أُمَّتُكُمۡ أُمَّةً وَٰحِدَةً وَأَنَا۠ رَبُّكُمۡ فَٱتَّقُونِ ٥٢

53. But they (men) have broken their religion among them into sects,[1] each group rejoicing in what is with it (as its beliefs).

فَتَقَطَّعُوٓاْ أَمۡرَهُم بَيۡنَهُمۡ زُبُرًاۖ كُلُّ حِزۡبٍۭ بِمَا لَدَيۡهِمۡ فَرِحُونَ ٥٣

54. So leave them in their error for a time.

فَذَرۡهُمۡ فِي غَمۡرَتِهِمۡ حَتَّىٰ حِينٍ ٥٤

55. Do they think that in wealth and children with which We enlarge them

أَيَحۡسَبُونَ أَنَّمَا نُمِدُّهُم بِهِۦ مِن مَّالٍ وَبَنِينَ ٥٥

56. We hasten unto them with good things. Nay, [it is a *Fitnah* (trial) in this worldly life so that they will have no share of good things in the Hereafter] but they perceive not. [*Tafsir Al-Qurtubi*].

نُسَارِعُ لَهُمۡ فِي ٱلۡخَيۡرَٰتِۚ بَل لَّا يَشۡعُرُونَ ٥٦

57. Verily, those who live in awe for fear of their Lord;

إِنَّ ٱلَّذِينَ هُم مِّنۡ خَشۡيَةِ رَبِّهِم مُّشۡفِقُونَ ٥٧

58. And those who believe in the *Ayât* (proofs, evidences, verses, lessons, signs, revelations, etc.) of their Lord;

وَٱلَّذِينَ هُم بِـَٔايَٰتِ رَبِّهِمۡ يُؤۡمِنُونَ ٥٨

59. And those who join not anyone (in worship) as partners with their Lord;

وَٱلَّذِينَ هُم بِرَبِّهِمۡ لَا يُشۡرِكُونَ ٥٩

60. And those who give that (their charity) which they give (and also do other good deeds) with their hearts full of fear (whether their alms and charities have been accepted or not),[2] because they are sure to return to their Lord (for reckoning).

وَٱلَّذِينَ يُؤۡتُونَ مَآ ءَاتَواْ وَّقُلُوبُهُمۡ وَجِلَةٌ أَنَّهُمۡ إِلَىٰ رَبِّهِمۡ رَٰجِعُونَ ٦٠

---

[1] (V.23:53) See the footnote of (V.3:103).

[2] (V.23:60) Narrated 'Âishah صلى الله عليه وسلم (the wife of the Prophet رضي الله عنها), I asked Allâh's Messenger صلى الله عليه وسلم about this (following

61. It is these who hasten in the good deeds, and they are foremost in them [e.g. offering the compulsory *Salât* (prayers) in their (early) stated, fixed times and so on].

أُوْلَٰئِكَ يُسَٰرِعُونَ فِى ٱلْخَيْرَٰتِ وَهُمْ لَهَا سَٰبِقُونَ ٦١

62. And We task not any person except according to his capacity, and with Us is a Record which speaks the truth, and they will not be wronged.

وَلَا نُكَلِّفُ نَفْسًا إِلَّا وُسْعَهَا وَلَدَيْنَا كِتَٰبٌ يَنطِقُ بِٱلْحَقِّ وَهُمْ لَا يُظْلَمُونَ ٦٢

63. Nay, but their hearts are covered from (understanding) this (the Qur'ân), and they have other (evil) deeds, besides, which they are doing.

بَلْ قُلُوبُهُمْ فِى غَمْرَةٍ مِّنْ هَٰذَا وَلَهُمْ أَعْمَٰلٌ مِّن دُونِ ذَٰلِكَ هُمْ لَهَا عَٰمِلُونَ ٦٣

64. Until when We seize those of them who lead a luxurious life with punishment: behold they make humble invocation with a loud voice.

حَتَّىٰٓ إِذَآ أَخَذْنَا مُتْرَفِيهِم بِٱلْعَذَابِ إِذَا هُمْ يَجْـَٔرُونَ ٦٤

65. Invoke not loudly this day! Certainly you shall not be helped by Us.

لَا تَجْـَٔرُوا ٱلْيَوْمَ إِنَّكُم مِّنَّا لَا تُنصَرُونَ ٦٥

66. Indeed My Verses used to be recited to you, but you used to turn back on your heels (denying them, and refusing with hatred to listen to them).

قَدْ كَانَتْ ءَايَٰتِى تُتْلَىٰ عَلَيْكُمْ فَكُنتُمْ عَلَىٰٓ أَعْقَٰبِكُمْ تَنكِصُونَ ٦٦

67. In pride (they — Quraish pagans and polytheists of Makkah used to feel proud that they are the dwellers of Makkah sanctuary — *Haram*), talking evil about it (the Qur'ân) by night.

مُسْتَكْبِرِينَ بِهِۦ سَٰمِرًا تَهْجُرُونَ ٦٧

Verse): "And those who give that (their charity) which they give (and also do other good deeds) with their hearts full of fear..." (V.23:60).

She added: "Are these who drink alcoholic drinks and steal?" Allâh's Messenger صلى الله عليه وسلم replied: "No! O the daughter of As-Siddîq, but they are those who fast, pray, and practise charity, and they are afraid that (their good) deeds may not be accepted (by Allâh) from them. 'It is these who hasten in good deeds.'" (*Sunan At-Tirmidhi*, Hadith No. 3225), (*Tafsîr Al-Qurtubî*).

68. Have they not pondered over the Word of Allâh (that is sent down to the Prophet صلى الله عليه وسلم), or has there come to them what had not come to their fathers of old?

أَفَلَمْ يَدَّبَّرُوا الْقَوْلَ أَمْ جَآءَهُم مَّا لَمْ يَأْتِ ءَابَآءَهُمُ الْأَوَّلِينَ ﴿٦٨﴾

69. Or is it that they did not recognize their Messenger (Muhammad صلى الله عليه وسلم) so they deny him?

أَمْ لَمْ يَعْرِفُوا رَسُولَهُمْ فَهُمْ لَهُۥ مُنكِرُونَ ﴿٦٩﴾

70. Or say they: There is madness in him? Nay, but he brought them the truth [i.e. *Tauhîd*: Worshipping Allâh Alone in all aspects, the Qur'ân and the religion of Islâm], but most of them (the disbelievers) are averse to the truth.

أَمْ يَقُولُونَ بِهِۦ جِنَّةٌۢ بَلْ جَآءَهُم بِالْحَقِّ وَأَكْثَرُهُمْ لِلْحَقِّ كَٰرِهُونَ ﴿٧٠﴾

71. And if the truth had been in accordance with their desires, verily, the heavens and the earth, and whosoever is therein would have been corrupted! Nay, We have brought them their reminder, but they turn away from their reminder.

وَلَوِ اتَّبَعَ الْحَقُّ أَهْوَآءَهُمْ لَفَسَدَتِ السَّمَٰوَٰتُ وَالْأَرْضُ وَمَن فِيهِنَّ بَلْ أَتَيْنَٰهُم بِذِكْرِهِمْ فَهُمْ عَن ذِكْرِهِم مُّعْرِضُونَ ﴿٧١﴾

72. Or is it that you (O Muhammad صلى الله عليه وسلم) ask them for some wages? But the recompense of your Lord is better, and He is the Best of those who give sustenance.

أَمْ تَسْـَٔلُهُمْ خَرْجًا فَخَرَاجُ رَبِّكَ خَيْرٌ وَهُوَ خَيْرُ الرَّٰزِقِينَ ﴿٧٢﴾

73. And certainly, you (O Muhammad صلى الله عليه وسلم) call them to the Straight Path (true religion — Islâmic Monotheism).

وَإِنَّكَ لَتَدْعُوهُمْ إِلَىٰ صِرَٰطٍ مُّسْتَقِيمٍ ﴿٧٣﴾

74. And verily, those who believe not in the Hereafter are indeed deviating far astray from the Path (true religion — Islâmic Monotheism).

وَإِنَّ الَّذِينَ لَا يُؤْمِنُونَ بِالْءَاخِرَةِ عَنِ الصِّرَٰطِ لَنَٰكِبُونَ ﴿٧٤﴾

75. And though We had mercy on them and removed the distress which is

۞ وَلَوْ رَحِمْنَٰهُمْ وَكَشَفْنَا

on them, still they would obstinately persist in their transgression, wandering blindly.

76. And indeed We seized them with punishment, but they humbled not themselves to their Lord, nor did they invoke (Allâh) with submission to Him.

77. Until, when We open for them the gate of severe punishment, then lo! they will be plunged into destruction with deep regrets, sorrows and in despair.

78. It is He Who has created for you (the sense of) hearing (ears), eyes (sight), and hearts (understanding). Little thanks you give.

79. And it is He Who has created you on the earth, and to Him you shall be gathered back.

80. And it is He Who gives life and causes death, and His is the alternation of night and day. Will you not then understand?

81. Nay, but they say the like of what the men of old said.

82. They said: "When we are dead and have become dust and bones, shall we be resurrected indeed?

83. "Verily, this we have been promised — we and our fathers before (us)! This is only the tales of the ancients!"

84. Say: "Whose is the earth and whosoever is therein? If you know!"

85. They will say: "It is Allâh's!" Say: "Will you not then remember?"

86. Say: "Who is (the) Lord of the seven heavens, and (the) Lord of the Great Throne?"

87. They will say: "Allâh." Say: "Will you not then fear Allâh (believe in His Oneness, obey Him, believe in the Resurrection and Recompense for every good or bad deed)?"

88. Say: "In Whose Hand is the sovereignty of everything (i.e. treasures of everything)? And He protects (all), while against Whom there is no protector, (i.e. if Allâh saves anyone none can punish or harm him, and if Allâh punishes or harms anyone none can save him), if you know?" [Tafsîr Al-Qurtubî]

89. They will say: "(All that belongs to) Allâh." Say: "How then are you deceived and turn away from the truth?"

90. Nay, but We have brought them the truth (Islâmic Monotheism), and verily, they (disbelievers) are liars.

91. No son (or offspring) did Allâh beget, nor is there any ilâh (god) along with Him. (If there had been many gods), then each god would have taken away what he had created, and some would have tried to overcome others! Glorified is Allâh above all that they attribute to Him!

92. All-Knower of the unseen and the seen! Exalted is He over all that they associate as partners to Him!

93. Say (O Muhammad صلى الله عليه وسلم): "My Lord! If You would show me that with which they are threatened (torment),

قُل رَّبِّ إِمَّا تُرِيَنِّي مَا يُوعَدُونَ ۝

94. "My Lord! Then (save me from Your punishment), put me not amongst the people who are the *Zâlimûn* (polytheists and wrongdoers)."

رَبِّ فَلَا تَجْعَلْنِي فِي الْقَوْمِ الظَّالِمِينَ ۝

95. And indeed We are Able to show you (O Muhammad صلى الله عليه وسلم) that with which We have threatened them.

وَإِنَّا عَلَىٰ أَن نُّرِيَكَ مَا نَعِدُهُمْ لَقَادِرُونَ ۝

96. Repel evil with that which is better. We are Best-Acquainted with the things they utter.

ادْفَعْ بِالَّتِي هِيَ أَحْسَنُ السَّيِّئَةَ نَحْنُ أَعْلَمُ بِمَا يَصِفُونَ ۝

97. And say: "My Lord! I seek refuge with You from the whisperings (suggestions) of the *Shayâtîn* (devils).

وَقُل رَّبِّ أَعُوذُ بِكَ مِنْ هَمَزَاتِ الشَّيَاطِينِ ۝

98. "And I seek refuge with You, My Lord! lest they should come near me."

وَأَعُوذُ بِكَ رَبِّ أَن يَحْضُرُونِ ۝

99. Until, when death comes to one of them (those who join partners with Allâh), he says: "My Lord! Send me back,

حَتَّىٰ إِذَا جَاءَ أَحَدَهُمُ الْمَوْتُ قَالَ رَبِّ ارْجِعُونِ ۝

100. "So that I may do good in that which I have left behind!" No! It is but a word that he speaks; and behind them is *Barzakh* (a barrier) until the Day when they will be resurrected.

لَعَلِّي أَعْمَلُ صَالِحًا فِيمَا تَرَكْتُ كَلَّا إِنَّهَا كَلِمَةٌ هُوَ قَائِلُهَا وَمِن وَرَائِهِم بَرْزَخٌ إِلَىٰ يَوْمِ يُبْعَثُونَ ۝

101. Then, when the Trumpet is blown, there will be no kinship among them that Day, nor will they ask of one another.

فَإِذَا نُفِخَ فِي الصُّورِ فَلَا أَنسَابَ بَيْنَهُمْ يَوْمَئِذٍ وَلَا يَتَسَاءَلُونَ ۝

102. Then, those whose scales (of good deeds) are heavy, they are the successful.

فَمَن ثَقُلَتْ مَوَازِينُهُ فَأُولَٰئِكَ هُمُ الْمُفْلِحُونَ ۝

103. And those whose scales (of good deeds) are light, they are those who lose their ownselves, in Hell will they abide.

104. The Fire will burn their faces, and therein they will grin, with displaced lips (disfigured).

105. "Were not My Verses (this Qur'ân) recited to you, and then you used to deny them?"

106. They will say: "Our Lord! Our wretchedness overcame us, and we were (an) erring people.

107. "Our Lord! Bring us out of this. If ever we return (to evil), then indeed we shall be Zâlimûn: (polytheists, oppressors, unjust, and wrongdoers)."

108. He (Allâh) will say: "Remain you in it with ignominy! And speak you not to Me!"

109. Verily, there was a party of My slaves, who used to say: "Our Lord! We believe, so forgive us, and have mercy on us, for You are the Best of all who show mercy!"

110. But you took them for a laughing stock, so much so that they made you forget My Remembrance while you used to laugh at them!

111. Verily, I have rewarded them this Day for their patience: they are indeed the ones that are successful.

112. He (Allâh) will say: "What number of years did you stay on earth?"

113. They will say: "We stayed a day or part of a day. Ask of those who keep account."

قَالُوا لَبِثْنَا يَوْمًا أَوْ بَعْضَ يَوْمٍ فَسْئَلِ الْعَآدِّينَ ﴿١١٣﴾

114. He (Allâh) will say: "You stayed not but a little, if you had only known!

قَالَ إِن لَّبِثْتُمْ إِلَّا قَلِيلًا لَّوْ أَنَّكُمْ كُنتُمْ تَعْلَمُونَ ﴿١١٤﴾

115. "Did you think that We had created you in play (without any purpose), and that you would not be brought back to Us?"

أَفَحَسِبْتُمْ أَنَّمَا خَلَقْنَاكُمْ عَبَثًا وَأَنَّكُمْ إِلَيْنَا لَا تُرْجَعُونَ ﴿١١٥﴾

116. So Exalted is Allâh, the True King: *Lâ ilâha illâ Huwa* (none has the right to be worshipped but He), the Lord of the Supreme Throne!

فَتَعَالَى اللَّهُ الْمَلِكُ الْحَقُّ لَا إِلَٰهَ إِلَّا هُوَ رَبُّ الْعَرْشِ الْكَرِيمِ ﴿١١٦﴾

117. And whoever invokes (or worships), besides Allâh, any other *ilâh* (god), of whom he has no proof; then his reckoning is only with his Lord. Surely, *Al-Kâfirûn* (the disbelievers in Allâh and in the Oneness of Allâh, polytheists, pagans, idolaters) will not be successful.

وَمَن يَدْعُ مَعَ اللَّهِ إِلَٰهًا ءَاخَرَ لَا بُرْهَانَ لَهُۥ بِهِۦ فَإِنَّمَا حِسَابُهُۥ عِندَ رَبِّهِۦٓ إِنَّهُۥ لَا يُفْلِحُ الْكَافِرُونَ ﴿١١٧﴾

118. And say (O Muhammad صلى الله عليه وسلم): "My Lord! Forgive and have mercy, for You are the Best of those who show mercy!"

وَقُل رَّبِّ اغْفِرْ وَارْحَمْ وَأَنتَ خَيْرُ الرَّاحِمِينَ ﴿١١٨﴾

Sûrat An-Nûr (The Light) XXIV

*In the Name of Allâh
the Most Gracious, the Most Merciful*

شُورَةُ النُّورِ

بِسْمِ اللَّهِ الرَّحْمَٰنِ الرَّحِيمِ

1. (This is) a *Sûrah* (chapter of the Qur'ân) which We have sent down and which We have enjoined, (ordained its laws); and in it We have revealed manifest *Ayât* (proofs, evidences,

سُورَةٌ أَنزَلْنَاهَا وَفَرَضْنَاهَا وَأَنزَلْنَا فِيهَآ ءَايَاتٍ بَيِّنَاتٍ لَّعَلَّكُمْ تَذَكَّرُونَ ﴿١﴾

verses, lessons, signs, revelations — lawful and unlawful things, and set boundaries of Islâmic Religion), that you may remember.

2. The woman and the man guilty of illegal sexual intercourse, flog each of them with a hundred stripes. Let not pity withhold you in their case, in a punishment prescribed by Allâh, if you believe in Allâh and the Last Day. And let a party of the believers witness their punishment. (This punishment is for unmarried persons guilty of the above crime, but if married persons commit it, the punishment is to stone them to death, according to Allâh's Law).[1]

اَلزَّانِيَةُ وَالزَّانِي فَاجْلِدُوا كُلَّ وَٰحِدٍ مِّنْهُمَا مِاْئَةَ جَلْدَةٍ وَلَا تَأْخُذْكُم بِهِمَا رَأْفَةٌ فِي دِينِ اللَّهِ إِن كُنتُمْ تُؤْمِنُونَ بِاللَّهِ وَالْيَوْمِ الْآخِرِ وَلْيَشْهَدْ عَذَابَهُمَا طَآئِفَةٌ مِّنَ الْمُؤْمِنِينَ ٢

3. The adulterer marries not but an adulteress or a *Mushrikah* and the adulteress none marries her except an adulterer or a *Muskrik* [and that means that the man who agrees to marry (have a sexual relation with) a *Mushrikah* (female polytheist, pagan or idolatress)

اَلزَّانِي لَا يَنكِحُ إِلَّا زَانِيَةً أَوْ مُشْرِكَةً وَالزَّانِيَةُ لَا يَنكِحُهَا إِلَّا زَانٍ أَوْ مُشْرِكٌ وَحُرِّمَ ذَٰلِكَ عَلَى الْمُؤْمِنِينَ ٣

---

[1] (V.24:2)

a) Narrated Abu Hurairah رضي الله عنه: Allâh's Messenger صلى الله عليه وسلم judged that the unmarried person who was guilty of illegal sexual intercourse be exiled for one year and receive the legal punishment (i.e., be flogged with one hundred stripes). (*Sahih Al-Bukhari*, Vol. 8, *Hadith* No. 819)

b) Narrated Jâbir bin 'Abdullâh Al-Ansâri رضي الله عنها: A man from the tribe of Bani Aslam came to Allâh's Messenger صلى الله عليه وسلم and informed him that he had committed illegal sexual intercourse and he bore witness four times against himself. Allâh's Messenger صلى الله عليه وسلم ordered him to be stoned to death as he was a married person. (*Sahih Al-Bukhari*, Vol. 8, *Hadith* No. 805)

c) See (V.4:25).

or a prostitute, then surely, he is either an adulterer, or a *Mushrik* (polytheist, pagan or idolater). And the woman who agrees to marry (have a sexual relation with) a *Mushrik* (polytheist, pagan or idolater) or an adulterer, then she is either a prostitute or a *Mushrikah* (female polytheist, pagan, or idolatress)]. Such a thing is forbidden to the believers (of Islâmic Monotheism).

4. And those who accuse chaste women, and produce not four witnesses, flog them with eighty stripes, and reject their testimony forever. They indeed are the *Fâsiqûn* (liars, rebellious, disobedient to Allâh).

5. Except those who repent thereafter and do righteous deeds; (for such) verily, Allâh is Oft-Forgiving, Most Merciful.

6. And for those who accuse their wives, but have no witnesses except themselves, let the testimony of one of them be four testimonies (i.e. testifies four times) by Allâh that he is one of those who speak the truth.

7. And the fifth (testimony should be) the invoking of the Curse of Allâh on him if he be of those who tell a lie (against her).

8. But it shall avert the punishment (of stoning to death) from her, if she bears witness four times by Allâh, that he (her husband) is telling a lie.

9. And the fifth (testimony) should be that the Wrath of Allâh be upon her if he (her husband) speaks the truth.

10. And had it not been for the Grace of Allâh and His Mercy on you (He would have hastened the punishment upon you)! And that Allâh is the One Who forgives and accepts repentance, the All-Wise.

وَلَوْلَا فَضْلُ اللَّهِ عَلَيْكُمْ وَرَحْمَتُهُ وَأَنَّ اللَّهَ تَوَّابٌ حَكِيمٌ ۩

11. Verily, those who brought forth the slander (against 'Âishah رضي الله عنها, the wife of the Prophet صلى الله عليه وسلم) are a group among you. Consider it not a bad thing for you. Nay, it is good for you. Unto every man among them will be paid that which he had earned of the sin, and as for him among them who had the greater share therein, his will be a great torment.

إِنَّ الَّذِينَ جَاءُوا بِالْإِفْكِ عُصْبَةٌ مِّنكُمْ لَا تَحْسَبُوهُ شَرًّا لَّكُم بَلْ هُوَ خَيْرٌ لَّكُمْ لِكُلِّ امْرِئٍ مِّنْهُم مَّا اكْتَسَبَ مِنَ الْإِثْمِ وَالَّذِي تَوَلَّىٰ كِبْرَهُ مِنْهُمْ لَهُ عَذَابٌ عَظِيمٌ ۩

12. Why then, did not the believers, men and women, when you heard it (the slander), think good of their own people and say: "This (charge) is an obvious lie?" [1]"

لَّوْلَا إِذْ سَمِعْتُمُوهُ ظَنَّ الْمُؤْمِنُونَ وَالْمُؤْمِنَاتُ بِأَنفُسِهِمْ خَيْرًا وَقَالُوا هَٰذَا إِفْكٌ مُّبِينٌ ۩

13. Why did they not produce four witnesses? Since they (the slanderers) have not produced witnesses! Then with Allâh they are the liars.

لَّوْلَا جَاءُوا عَلَيْهِ بِأَرْبَعَةِ شُهَدَاءَ فَإِذْ لَمْ يَأْتُوا بِالشُّهَدَاءِ فَأُولَٰئِكَ عِندَ اللَّهِ هُمُ الْكَاذِبُونَ ۩

14. Had it not been for the Grace of Allâh and His Mercy unto you in this world and in the Hereafter, a great torment would have touched you for that whereof you had spoken.

وَلَوْلَا فَضْلُ اللَّهِ عَلَيْكُمْ وَرَحْمَتُهُ فِي الدُّنْيَا وَالْآخِرَةِ لَمَسَّكُمْ فِي مَا أَفَضْتُمْ فِيهِ عَذَابٌ عَظِيمٌ ۩

15. When you were propagating it with your tongues, and uttering with

إِذْ تَلَقَّوْنَهُ بِأَلْسِنَتِكُمْ وَتَقُولُونَ بِأَفْوَاهِكُم مَّا لَيْسَ لَكُم بِهِ عِلْمٌ

---

[1] (V.24:12) See *Sahih Al-Bukhari*, Vol.6, *Hadith* No.274 (The story of the slander against 'Âishah رضي الله عنها, the wife of Prophet صلى الله عليه وسلم).

your mouths that whereof you had no knowledge, you counted it a little thing, while with Allâh it was very great.

16. And why did you not, when you heard it, say: "It is not right for us to speak of this. Glory is to You (O Allâh)! This is a great lie."

17. Allâh forbids you from it and warns you not to repeat the like of it forever, if you are believers.

18. And Allâh makes the *Ayât* (proofs, evidences, verses, lessons, signs, revelations, etc.) plain to you, and Allâh is All-Knowing, All-Wise.

19. Verily, those who like that (the crime of) illegal sexual intercourse should be propagated among those who believe, they will have a painful torment in this world and in the Hereafter. And Allâh knows and you know not.

20. And had it not been for the Grace of Allâh and His Mercy on you, (Allâh would have hastened the punishment upon you). And that Allâh is full of kindness, Most Merciful.

21. O you who believe! Follow not the footsteps of *Shaitân* (Satan). And whosoever follows the footsteps of *Shaitân* (Satan), then, verily, he commands *Al-Fahshâ'* [i.e. to commit indecency (illegal sexual intercourse)], and *Al-Munkar* [disbelief and polytheism (i.e. to do evil and wicked deeds; and to speak or to do what is forbidden in Islâm)]. And had it not been for the Grace of Allâh and His Mercy on you, not one of you would ever have been pure from sins. But Allâh purifies (guides to Islâm) whom He wills, and Allâh is All-Hearer, All-Knower.

22. And let not those among you who are blessed with graces and wealth swear not to give (any sort of help) to their kinsmen, *Al-Masâkîn* (the poor), and those who left their homes for Allâh's Cause. Let them pardon and forgive. Do you not love that Allâh should forgive you? And Allâh is Oft-Forgiving, Most Merciful.

23. Verily, those who accuse chaste women, who never even think of anything touching their chastity and are good believers — are cursed in this life and in the Hereafter, and for them will be a great torment —

24. On the Day when their tongues, their hands, and their legs (or feet) will bear witness against them as to what they used to do.

25. On that Day Allâh will pay them the recompense of their deeds in full, and they will know that Allâh, He is the Manifest Truth.

26. Bad statements are for bad people (or bad women for bad men) and bad people for bad statements (or bad men for bad women). Good statements are for good people (or good women for good men) and good people for good statements (or good men for good

women): such (good people) are
innocent of (every) bad statement
which they say; for them is forgiveness,
and *Rizqun Karîm* (generous provision
i.e. Paradise).

27. O you who believe! Enter not
houses other than your own, until you
have asked permission and greeted
those in them; that is better for you, in
order that you may remember.

28. And if you find no one therein,
still, enter not until permission has been
given. And if you are asked to go back,
go back, for it is purer for you. And
Allâh is All-Knower of what you do.

29. There is no sin on you that you
enter (without taking permission)
houses uninhabited (i.e. not possessed
by anybody), (when) you have any
interest in them. And Allâh has
knowledge of what you reveal and what
you conceal.

30. Tell the believing men to lower
their gaze (from looking at forbidden
things), and protect their private parts
(from illegal sexual acts). That is purer
for them. Verily, Allâh is All-Aware of
what they do.

31. And tell the believing women to
lower their gaze (from looking at
forbidden things), and protect their
private parts (from illegal sexual acts)
and not to show off their adornment
except only that which is apparent (like
both eyes for necessity to see the way,
or outer palms of hands or one eye or

dress like veil, gloves, head-cover, apron), and to draw their veils all over Juyûbihinna (i.e. their bodies, faces, necks and bosoms) and not to reveal their adornment except to their husbands, or their fathers, or their husband's fathers, or their sons, or their husband's sons, or their brothers or their brother's sons, or their sister's sons, or their (Muslim) women (i.e. their sisters in Islâm), or the (female) slaves whom their right hands possess, or old male servants who lack vigour, or small children who have no sense of feminine sex. And let them not stamp their feet so as to reveal what they hide of their adornment. And all of you beg Allâh to forgive you all, O believers, that you may be successful.[1]

32. And marry those among you who are single (i.e. a man who has no wife and the woman who has no husband) and (also marry) the *Sâlihûn* (pious, fit and capable ones) of your (male) slaves

---

[1] (V.24:31) "And to draw their veils all over *Juyûbihinna* (i.e. their bodies, faces, necks and bosoms) and not to reveal their adornment..."

Narrated `Âishah رضي الله عنها: 'May Allâh bestow His Mercy on the early emigrant women. When Allâh revealed:

"And to draw their veils all over *Juyûbihinna* (i.e. their bodies, faces, necks, and bosoms)" — they tore their *Murûts* (a woollen dress, or a waist-binding cloth or an apron) and covered their heads and faces with those torn *Murûts*.'

Narrated Safiyah bint Shaibah: `Âishah used to say: 'When the Verse:

"And to draw their veils all over *Juyûbihinna* (i.e. their bodies, faces, necks, and bosoms)" (V.24:31) was revealed, (the ladies) cut their waist sheets at the edges and covered their heads and faces with those cut pieces of cloth.' (*Sahih Al-Bukhari*, Vol.6, Hadith No.282).

and maid-servants (female slaves). If they be poor, Allâh will enrich them out of His Bounty. And Allâh is All-Suffcient for His creatures' needs, All-Knowing (about the state of the people).

33. And let those who find not the financial means for marriage keep themselves chaste, until Allâh enriches them of His Bounty. And such of your slaves as seek a writing (of emancipation), give them such writing, if you find that there is good and honesty in them. And give them something (yourselves) out of the wealth of Allâh which He has bestowed upon you. And force not your maids to prostitution, if they desire chastity, in order that you may make a gain in the (perishable) goods of this worldly life. But if anyone compels them (to prostitution), then after such compulsion, Allâh is Oft-Forgiving, Most Merciful (to those women, i.e. He will forgive them because they have been forced to do this evil act unwillingly).

34. And indeed We have sent down for you Ayât (proofs, evidences, verses, lessons, signs, revelations, etc.) that make things plain, and the example of those who passed away before you, and an admonition for those who are Al-Muttaqûn (the pious and righteous persons. See V.2:2).

35. Allâh is the Light of the heavens and the earth. The parable of His Light is as (if there were) a niche and within

it a lamp: the lamp is in a glass, the glass as it were a brilliant star, lit from a blessed tree, an olive, neither of the east (i.e. neither it gets sun-rays only in the morning) nor of the west (i.e. nor it gets sun-rays only in the afternoon, but it is exposed to the sun all day long), whose oil would almost glow forth (of itself), though no fire touched it. Light upon Light! Allâh guides to His Light whom He wills. And Allâh sets forth parables for mankind, and Allâh is All-Knower of everything.

36. In houses (mosques) which Allâh has ordered to be raised (to be cleaned, and to be honoured], in them His Name is remembered [i.e. Adhân, Iqamah, Salât (prayers), invocations, recitation of the Qur'ân]. Therein glorify Him (Allâh) in the mornings and in the afternoons or the evenings, [1]

---

[1] (V.24:36).

a) Narrated Abu Qatâdah رضي الله عنه Allâh's Messenger صلى الله عليه وسلم said: "If anyone of you enters a mosque, he should pray two Rak'at (Tahiyyat-al-Masjid) before sitting." (Sahih Al-Bukhari, Vol.1, Hadith No.435).

b) Narrated Abu Hurairah رضي الله عنه Allâh's Messenger صلى الله عليه وسلم said: "The reward of the Salât (prayer) offered by a person in congregation is multiplied twenty-five times as much than that of the Salât (prayer) offered in one's house or in the market (alone). And this is because if he performs ablution and does it perfectly and then proceeds to the mosque, with the sole intention of praying; then for every step he takes towards the mosque, he is upgraded one degree in reward and one of his sins is taken off (crossed out) from his accounts (of deeds). When he offers his Salât (prayer), the angels keep on asking Allâh's Blessings and Allâh's Forgiveness for him as long as he is (staying) at his Musallâ (place of prayer). They say: 'O Allâh! Bestow Your Blessings upon him, be

37. Men whom neither trade nor sale (business) diverts from the Remembrance of Allâh (with heart and tongue), nor from performing As-Salât (Iqâmat-as-Salât), nor from giving the Zakât. They fear a Day when hearts and eyes will be overturned (out of the horror of the torment of the Day of Resurrection).

رِجَالٌ لَّا تُلْهِيهِمْ تِجَـٰرَةٌ وَلَا بَيْعٌ عَن ذِكْرِ ٱللَّهِ وَإِقَامِ ٱلصَّلَوٰةِ وَإِيتَآءِ ٱلزَّكَوٰةِ يَخَافُونَ يَوْمًا تَتَقَلَّبُ فِيهِ ٱلْقُلُوبُ وَٱلْأَبْصَـٰرُ ٣٧

38. That Allâh may reward them according to the best of their deeds, and add even more for them out of His Grace. And Allâh provides without measure to whom He wills.[1]

لِيَجْزِيَهُمُ ٱللَّهُ أَحْسَنَ مَا عَمِلُوا۟ وَيَزِيدَهُم مِّن فَضْلِهِۦ وَٱللَّهُ يَرْزُقُ مَن يَشَآءُ بِغَيْرِ حِسَابٍ ٣٨

39. As for those who disbelieved, their deeds are like a mirage in a desert. The thirsty one thinks it to be water, until he comes up to it, he finds it to be nothing; but he finds Allâh with him, Who will pay him his due (Hell). And Allâh is Swift in taking account.[2]

وَٱلَّذِينَ كَفَرُوٓا۟ أَعْمَـٰلُهُمْ كَسَرَابٍ بِقِيعَةٍ يَحْسَبُهُ ٱلظَّمْـَٔانُ مَآءً حَتَّىٰٓ إِذَا جَآءَهُۥ لَمْ يَجِدْهُ شَيْـًٔا وَوَجَدَ ٱللَّهَ عِندَهُۥ فَوَفَّىٰهُ حِسَابَهُۥ وَٱللَّهُ سَرِيعُ ٱلْحِسَابِ ٣٩

40. Or [the state of a disbeliever] is like the darkness in a vast deep sea, overwhelmed with waves topped by waves, topped by dark clouds, (layers of) darkness upon darkness: if a man stretches out his hand, he can hardly see it! And he for whom Allâh has not appointed light, for him there is no light.

أَوْ كَظُلُمَـٰتٍ فِى بَحْرٍ لُّجِّىٍّ يَغْشَىٰهُ مَوْجٌ مِّن فَوْقِهِۦ مَوْجٌ مِّن فَوْقِهِۦ سَحَابٌ ظُلُمَـٰتٌ بَعْضُهَا فَوْقَ بَعْضٍ إِذَآ أَخْرَجَ يَدَهُۥ لَمْ يَكَدْ يَرَىٰهَا وَمَن لَّمْ يَجْعَلِ ٱللَّهُ لَهُۥ نُورًا فَمَا لَهُۥ مِن نُّورٍ ٤٠

---

merciful and kind to him.' And one is regarded in Salât (prayer) as long as one is waiting for the Salât (prayer)." (Sahih Al-Bukhari, Vol.1, Hadith No.620).

[1] (V.24:38) See the footnote of (V.9:121).

[2] (V.24:39) The deeds of a disbeliever are like a mirage for a thirsty person: when he will meet Allâh, he will think that he has a good reward with Allâh of his good deeds, but he will find nothing, like a mirage, and will be thrown in the Fire of Hell.

41. See you not (O Muhammad ﷺ) that Allâh, He it is Whom glorify whosoever is in the heavens and the earth, and the birds with wings outspread (in their flight)? Of each one He (Allâh) knows indeed his *Salât* (prayer) and his glorification, [or everyone knows his *Salât* (prayer) and his glorification]; and Allâh is All-Aware of what they do.

42. And to Allâh belongs the sovereignty of the heavens and the earth, and to Allâh is the return (of all).

43. See you not that Allâh drives the clouds gently, then joins them together, then makes them into a heap of layers, and you see the rain comes forth from between them; and He sends down from the sky hail (like) mountains, (or there are in the heaven mountains of hail from where He sends down hail), and strikes therewith whom He wills, and averts it from whom He wills. The vivid flash of its (clouds) lightning nearly blinds the sight. [*Tafsir At-Tabarî*].

44. Allâh causes the night and the day to succeed each other (i.e. if the day is gone, the night comes, and if the night is gone, the day comes, and so on). Truly, in this is indeed a lesson for those who have insight.

45. Allâh has created every moving (living) creature from water. Of them there are some that creep on their bellies, and some that walk on two legs, and some that walk on four. Allâh creates what He wills. Verily, Allâh is Able to do all things.

إِنَّ ٱللَّهَ عَلَىٰ كُلِّ شَىۡءٍ قَدِيرٌ ۞

46. We have indeed sent down (in this Qur'ân) manifest *Ayât* (proofs, evidences, verses, lessons, signs, revelations, lawful and unlawful things, and the set boundaries of Islâmic religion), that make things clear showing the Right Path of Allâh). And Allâh guides whom He wills to the Straight Path (i.e. to Allâh's religion of Islâmic Monotheism).

لَّقَدۡ أَنزَلۡنَآ ءَايَٰتٍ مُّبَيِّنَٰتٍ وَٱللَّهُ يَهۡدِى مَن يَشَآءُ إِلَىٰ صِرَٰطٍ مُّسۡتَقِيمٍ ۞

47. They (hypocrites) say: "We have believed in Allâh and in the Messenger (Muhammad صلى الله عليه وسلم), and we obey," then a party of them turn away thereafter, such are not believers.

وَيَقُولُونَ ءَامَنَّا بِٱللَّهِ وَبِٱلرَّسُولِ وَأَطَعۡنَا ثُمَّ يَتَوَلَّىٰ فَرِيقٌ مِّنۡهُم مِّنۢ بَعۡدِ ذَٰلِكَ وَمَآ أُوْلَٰٓئِكَ بِٱلۡمُؤۡمِنِينَ ۞

48. And when they are called to Allâh (i.e. His Words, the Qur'ân) and His Messenger (صلى الله عليه وسلم), to judge between them, lo! a party of them refuses (to come) and turns away.

وَإِذَا دُعُوٓاْ إِلَى ٱللَّهِ وَرَسُولِهِۦ لِيَحۡكُمَ بَيۡنَهُمۡ إِذَا فَرِيقٌ مِّنۡهُم مُّعۡرِضُونَ ۞

49. But if the truth is on their side, they come to him willingly with submission.

وَإِن يَكُن لَّهُمُ ٱلۡحَقُّ يَأۡتُوٓاْ إِلَيۡهِ مُذۡعِنِينَ ۞

50. Is there a disease in their hearts? Or do they doubt or fear lest Allâh and His Messenger (صلى الله عليه وسلم) should wrong them in judgement. Nay, it is they themselves who are the *Zâlimûn* (polytheists, hypocrites and wrongdoers).

أَفِى قُلُوبِهِم مَّرَضٌ أَمِ ٱرۡتَابُوٓاْ أَمۡ يَخَافُونَ أَن يَحِيفَ ٱللَّهُ عَلَيۡهِمۡ وَرَسُولُهُۥ بَلۡ أُوْلَٰٓئِكَ هُمُ ٱلظَّٰلِمُونَ ۞

51. The only saying of the faithful believers, when they are called to Allâh (His Words, the Qur'ân) and His Messenger (صلى الله عليه وسلم), to judge between

إِنَّمَا كَانَ قَوۡلَ ٱلۡمُؤۡمِنِينَ إِذَا دُعُوٓاْ إِلَى ٱللَّهِ وَرَسُولِهِۦ لِيَحۡكُمَ بَيۡنَهُمۡ أَن يَقُولُواْ سَمِعۡنَا وَأَطَعۡنَا

them, is that they say: "We hear and we obey." And such are the successful (who will live forever in Paradise).

52. And whosoever obeys Allâh and His Messenger (صلى الله عليه وسلم), fears Allâh, and keeps his duty (to Him), such are the successful.

53. They swear by Allâh their strongest oaths, that if only you would order them, they would leave (their homes for fighting in Allâh's Cause). Say: "Swear not; (this) obedience (of yours) is known (to be false). Verily, Allâh knows well what you do."

54. Say: "Obey Allâh and obey the Messenger, but if you turn away, he (Messenger Muhammad صلى الله عليه وسلم) is only responsible for the duty placed on him (i.e. to convey Allâh's Message) and you for that placed on you. If you obey him, you shall be on the right guidance. The Messenger's duty is only to convey (the message) in a clear way (i.e. to preach in a plain way)."

55. Allâh has promised those among you who believe and do righteous good deeds, that He will certainly grant them succession to (the present rulers) in the land, as He granted it to those before them, and that He will grant them the authority to practise their religion which He has chosen for them (i.e. Islâm). And He will surely, give them in exchange a safe security after their fear (provided) they (believers) worship Me and do not associate anything (in worship) with Me.

But whoever disbelieved after this, they are the *Fâsiqûn* (rebellious, disobedient to Allâh).

56. And perform *As-Salât* (Iqamat-as-Salât), and give *Zakât* and obey the Messenger (Muhammad ﷺ عليه وسلم) that you may receive mercy (from Allâh).

57. Consider not that the disbelievers can escape in the land. Their abode shall be the Fire — and worst indeed is that destination.

58. O you who believe! Let your slaves and slave-girls, and those among you who have not come to the age of puberty ask your permission (before they come to your presence) on three occasions: before *Fajr* (morning) *Salât* (prayer), and while you put off your clothes for the noonday (rest), and after the *'Ishâ'* (late-night) *Salât* (prayer). (These) three times are of privacy for you; other than these times there is no sin on you or on them to move about, attending to each other. Thus Allâh makes clear the *Ayât* (the Verses of this Qur'ân, showing proofs for the legal aspects of permission for visits) to you. And Allâh is All-Knowing, All-Wise.

59. And when the children among you come to puberty, then let them (also) ask for permission, as those senior to them (in age). Thus Allâh makes clear His *Ayât* (Commandments and legal obligations) for you. And Allâh is All-Knowing, All-Wise.

60. And as for women past child-bearing who do not expect wed-lock, it is no sin on them if they discard their (outer) clothing in such a way as not to show their adornment. But to refrain (i.e. not to discard their outer clothing) is better for them. And Allâh is All-Hearer, All-Knower.

61. There is no restriction on the blind, nor any restriction on the lame, nor any restriction on the sick, nor on yourselves, if you eat from your houses, or the houses of your fathers, or the houses of your mothers, or the houses of your brothers, or the houses of your sisters, or the houses of your father's brothers, or the houses of your father's sisters, or the houses of your mother's brothers, or the houses of your mother's sisters, or (from that) whereof you hold keys, or (from the house) of a friend. No sin on you whether you eat together or apart. But when you enter the houses, greet one another with a greeting from Allâh (i.e. say: السلام عليكم *As-Salâmu 'Alaikum* — peace be on you), blessed and good. Thus Allâh makes clear the *Ayât* (these Verses or your religious symbols and signs, etc.) to you that you may understand.

62. The true believers are only those who believe in (the Oneness of) Allâh and His Messenger (Muhammad صلى الله عليه وسلم): and when they are with him on some common matter, they go not away until they have asked his permission. Verily, those who ask your permission, those are they who (really) believe in Allâh and His Messenger. So if they ask your permission for some affairs of theirs, give permission to whom you will of them, and ask Allâh for their forgiveness. Truly, Allâh is Oft-Forgiving, Most Merciful.

63. Make not the calling of the Messenger (Muhammad صلى الله عليه وسلم) among you as your calling one of another. Allâh knows those of you who slip away under shelter (of some excuse without taking the permission to leave, from the Messenger (صلى الله عليه وسلم). And let those who oppose the Messenger's (Muhammad صلى الله عليه وسلم) commandment (i.e. his *Sunnah* — legal ways, orders, acts of worship, statements) (among the sects) beware, lest some *Fitnah* (disbelief, trials, afflictions, earthquakes, killing, overpowered by a tyrant) should befall them or a painful torment be inflicted on them.

64. Certainly, to Allâh belongs all that is in the heavens and the earth. Surely, He knows your condition and (He knows) the Day when they will be brought back to Him, then He will inform them of what they did. And Allâh is All-Knower of everything.

Sûrat Al-Furqân
(The Criterion) XXV

*In the Name of Allâh
the Most Gracious, the Most Merciful.*

1. Blessed is He Who sent down the criterion (of right and wrong, i.e. this Qur'ân) to His slave (Muhammad صلى الله عليه وسلم) that he may be a warner to the *'Âlamîn* (mankind and jinn).

2. He to Whom belongs the dominion of the heavens and the earth, and Who has begotten no son (children or offspring) and for Whom there is no partner in the dominion. He has created everything, and has measured it exactly according to its due measurements.

3. Yet they have taken besides Him other *alîhah* (gods) who created nothing but are themselves created, and possess neither hurt nor benefit for themselves, and possess no power (of causing) death, nor (of giving) life, nor of raising the dead.

4. Those who disbelieve say: "This (the Qur'ân) is nothing but a lie that he (Muhammad صلى الله عليه وسلم) has invented, and others have helped him at it. In fact they have produced an unjust wrong (thing) and a lie."

5. And they say: "Tales of the ancients, which he has written down: and they are dictated to him morning and afternoon."

6. Say: "It (this Qur'ân) has been sent down by Him (Allâh) (the Real Lord of the heavens and earth) Who knows the secret of the heavens and the earth. Truly. He is Oft-Forgiving, Most Merciful."

7. And they say: "Why does this Messenger (Muhammad صلى الله عليه وسلم) eat food, and walk about in the markets (as we). Why is not an angel sent down to him to be a warner with him?

8. "Or (why) has not a treasure been granted to him, or why has he not a garden whereof he may eat?" And the *Zâlimûn* (polytheists and wrongdoers) say: "You follow none but a man bewitched."

9. See how they coin similitudes for you, so they have gone astray, and they cannot find a (Right) Path.

10. Blessed is He Who, if He Wills will assign you better than (all) that — Gardens under which rivers flow (Paradise) and will assign you palaces (i.e. in Paradise).

11. Nay, they deny the Hour (the Day of Resurrection), and for those who deny the Hour, We have prepared a flaming Fire (i.e. Hell).

12. When it (Hell) sees them from a far place, they will hear its raging and its roaring.

13. And when they shall be thrown into a narrow place thereof, chained together, they will exclaim therein for destruction.

14. Exclaim not today for one destruction, but exclaim for many destructions.

15. Say: (O Muhammad صلى الله عليه وسلم) "Is that (torment) better or the Paradise of Eternity which is promised to the *Muttaqûn* (the pious and righteous persons. See V.2:2)?" It will be theirs as a reward and as a final destination.

16. For them there will be therein all that they desire, and they will abide (there forever). It is a promise binding upon your Lord that must be fulfilled.

17. And on the Day when He will gather them together and that which

وَقَالَ ٱلظَّٰلِمُونَ إِن تَتَّبِعُونَ إِلَّا رَجُلًا مَّسۡحُورًا ٨ ٱنظُرۡ كَيۡفَ ضَرَبُواْ لَكَ ٱلۡأَمۡثَٰلَ فَضَلُّواْ فَلَا يَسۡتَطِيعُونَ سَبِيلًا ٩ تَبَارَكَ ٱلَّذِيٓ إِن شَآءَ جَعَلَ لَكَ خَيۡرًا مِّن ذَٰلِكَ جَنَّٰتٍ تَجۡرِي مِن تَحۡتِهَا ٱلۡأَنۡهَٰرُ وَيَجۡعَل لَّكَ قُصُورًا ١٠ بَلۡ كَذَّبُواْ بِٱلسَّاعَةِ وَأَعۡتَدۡنَا لِمَن كَذَّبَ بِٱلسَّاعَةِ سَعِيرًا ١١ إِذَا رَأَتۡهُم مِّن مَّكَانٍ بَعِيدٍ سَمِعُواْ لَهَا تَغَيُّظًا وَزَفِيرًا ١٢ وَإِذَآ أُلۡقُواْ مِنۡهَا مَكَانًا ضَيِّقًا مُّقَرَّنِينَ دَعَوۡاْ هُنَالِكَ ثُبُورًا ١٣ لَّا تَدۡعُواْ ٱلۡيَوۡمَ ثُبُورًا وَٰحِدًا وَٱدۡعُواْ ثُبُورًا كَثِيرًا ١٤ قُلۡ أَذَٰلِكَ خَيۡرٌ أَمۡ جَنَّةُ ٱلۡخُلۡدِ ٱلَّتِي وُعِدَ ٱلۡمُتَّقُونَ كَانَتۡ لَهُمۡ جَزَآءً وَمَصِيرًا ١٥ لَّهُمۡ فِيهَا مَا يَشَآءُونَ خَٰلِدِينَ كَانَ عَلَىٰ رَبِّكَ وَعۡدًا مَّسۡـُٔولًا ١٦ وَيَوۡمَ يَحۡشُرُهُمۡ وَمَا

they worship besides Allâh [idols, angels, pious men, saints, 'Îsâ (Jesus) - son of Maryam (Mary),[1]]. He will say: "Was it you who misled these My slaves or did they (themselves) stray from the (Right) Path?"

18. They will say: "Glorified are You! It was not for us to take any *Auliyâ'* (Protectors, Helpers) besides You, but You gave them and their fathers comfort till they forgot the warning, and became a lost people (doomed to total loss).

19. Thus they (false gods — all deities other than Allâh) will belie you (polytheists) regarding what you say that (that they are gods besides Allâh): then you can neither avert (the punishment), nor get help. And whoever among you does wrong (i.e. sets up rivals to Allâh), We shall make him taste a great torment.

20. And We never sent before you (O Muhammad صلى الله عليه وسلم) any of the Messengers but verily, they ate food and walked in the markets. And We have made some of you as a trial for others: will you have patience? And your Lord is Ever All-Seer (of everything).

---

[1] (V.25:17) Narrated Mu'âdh bin Jabal رضي الله عنه The Prophet صلى الله said, "O Mu'âdh! Do you know what Allâh's Right upon His عليه وسلم slaves is?" I said, "Allâh and His Messenger know better." The Prophet صلى الله عليه وسلم said, "To worship Him (Allâh) Alone and to join none in worship with Him (Allâh). Do you know what their right upon Him is?" I replied, "Allâh and His Messenger know better." The Prophet صلى الله عليه وسلم said, "Not to punish them (if they did so)." (*Sahih Al-Bukhari*, Vol. 9, Hadith No. 470).

21. And those who expect not a Meeting with Us (i.e. those who deny the Day of Resurrection and the life of the Hereafter) said: "Why are not the angels sent down to us, or why do we not see our Lord?" Indeed they think too highly of themselves, and are scornful with great pride.[1]

وَقَالَ ٱلَّذِينَ لَا يَرْجُونَ لِقَآءَنَا لَوْلَآ أُنزِلَ عَلَيْنَا ٱلْمَلَٰٓئِكَةُ أَوْ نَرَىٰ رَبَّنَا لَقَدِ ٱسْتَكْبَرُوا۟ فِىٓ أَنفُسِهِمْ وَعَتَوْ عُتُوًّا كَبِيرًا ﴿٢١﴾

22. On the Day they will see the angels — no glad tidings will there be for the *Mujrimûn* (criminals, disbelievers, polytheists, sinners) that day. And they (angels) will say: "All kinds of glad tidings are forbidden to you," [none will be allowed to enter Paradise except the one who said: *Lâ ilâha illallâh,* "(none has the right to be worshipped but Allâh) and acted practically on its legal orders and obligations — see the footnote of V.2:193].

يَوْمَ يَرَوْنَ ٱلْمَلَٰٓئِكَةَ لَا بُشْرَىٰ يَوْمَئِذٍ لِّلْمُجْرِمِينَ وَيَقُولُونَ حِجْرًا مَّحْجُورًا ﴿٢٢﴾

23. And We shall turn to whatever deeds they (disbelievers, polytheists, sinners) did, and We shall make such deeds as scattered floating particles of dust.

وَقَدِمْنَآ إِلَىٰ مَا عَمِلُوا۟ مِنْ عَمَلٍ فَجَعَلْنَٰهُ هَبَآءً مَّنثُورًا ﴿٢٣﴾

24. The dwellers of Paradise (i.e. those who deserved it through their Islamic Monotheistic Faith and their deeds of righteousness) will, on that Day, have the best abode, and have the fairest of places for repose.

أَصْحَٰبُ ٱلْجَنَّةِ يَوْمَئِذٍ خَيْرٌ مُّسْتَقَرًّا وَأَحْسَنُ مَقِيلًا ﴿٢٤﴾

25. And (remember) the Day when the heaven shall be rent asunder with clouds, and the angels shall be sent down, with a grand descending.

وَيَوْمَ تَشَقَّقُ ٱلسَّمَآءُ بِٱلْغَمَٰمِ وَنُزِّلَ ٱلْمَلَٰٓئِكَةُ تَنزِيلًا ﴿٢٥﴾

---

[1] (V.25:21) See the footnote of (V.22:9).

26. The sovereignty on that Day will be the true (sovereignty), belonging to the Most Gracious (Allâh), and it will be a hard Day for the disbelievers (those who disbelieve in the Oneness of Allâh — Islâmic Monotheism).

ٱلْمُلْكُ يَوْمَئِذٍ ٱلْحَقُّ لِلرَّحْمَنِ وَكَانَ يَوْمًا عَلَى ٱلْكَفِرِينَ عَسِيرًا ۝

27. And (remember) the Day when the Zâlim (wrongdoer, oppressor, polytheist) will bite at his hands, he will say: "Oh! Would that I had taken a path with the Messenger (Muhammad صلى الله عليه وسلم)."[1]

وَيَوْمَ يَعَضُّ ٱلظَّالِمُ عَلَىٰ يَدَيْهِ يَقُولُ يَلَيْتَنِى ٱتَّخَذْتُ مَعَ ٱلرَّسُولِ سَبِيلًا ۝

28. "Ah! Woe to me! Would that I had never taken so-and-so as a Khalîl (an intimate friend)!

يَوَيْلَتَى لَيْتَنِى لَمْ أَتَّخِذْ فُلَانًا خَلِيلًا ۝

29. "He indeed led me astray from the Reminder (this Qur'ân) after it had come to me. And Shaitân (Satan) is to man ever a deserter in the hour of need." [Tafsir Al-Qurtubi]

لَّقَدْ أَضَلَّنِى عَنِ ٱلذِّكْرِ بَعْدَ إِذْ جَآءَنِى وَكَانَ ٱلشَّيْطَنُ لِلْإِنسَنِ خَذُولًا ۝

30. And the Messenger (Muhammad صلى الله عليه وسلم) will say: "O my Lord! Verily, my people deserted this Qur'ân (neither listened to it, nor acted on its laws and teachings).

وَقَالَ ٱلرَّسُولُ يَرَبِّ إِنَّ قَوْمِى ٱتَّخَذُوا۟ هَذَا ٱلْقُرْءَانَ مَهْجُورًا ۝

31. Thus have We made for every Prophet an enemy among the Mujrimûn (disbelievers, polytheists, criminals). But Sufficient is your Lord as a Guide and Helper.

وَكَذَلِكَ جَعَلْنَا لِكُلِّ نَبِىٍّ عَدُوًّا مِّنَ ٱلْمُجْرِمِينَ وَكَفَىٰ بِرَبِّكَ هَادِيًا وَنَصِيرًا ۝

32. And those who disbelieve say: "Why is not the Qur'ân revealed to him all at once?" Thus (it is sent down in parts), that We may strengthen your heart thereby. And We have revealed it to you

وَقَالَ ٱلَّذِينَ كَفَرُوا۟ لَوْلَا نُزِّلَ عَلَيْهِ ٱلْقُرْءَانُ جُمْلَةً وَحِدَةً كَذَلِكَ لِنُثَبِّتَ بِهِ فُؤَادَكَ وَرَتَّلْنَهُ

---

[1] (V.25:27) See the footnote of (V.3:85).

gradually, in stages. (It was revealed to the Prophet صلى الله عليه وسلم in 23 years).

33. And no example or similitude do they bring (to oppose or to find fault in you or in this Qur'ân), but We reveal to you the truth (against that similitude or example), and the better explanation thereof.

34. Those who will be gathered to Hell (prone) on their faces, such will be in an evil state, and most astray from the (Straight) Path.[1]

35. And indeed We gave Mûsâ (Moses) the Scripture [the Taurât (Torah)], and placed his brother Hârûn (Aaron) with him as a helper;

36. And We said: "Go you both to the people who have denied Our Ayât (proofs, evidences, verses, lessons, signs, revelations, etc.)." Then We destroyed them with utter destruction.

37. And Nûh's (Noah) people, when they denied the Messengers, We drowned them, and We made them as a sign for mankind. And We have prepared a painful torment for the Zâlimûn (polytheists and wrongdoers).

38. And (also) 'Âd and Thamûd, and the Dwellers of Ar-Rass, and many generations in between.

39. And for each (of them) We put forward examples (as proofs and lessons), and each (of them) We brought to utter ruin (because of their disbelief and evil deeds).

---

[1] (V.25:34) See the footnote of (V.17:97).

40. And indeed they have passed by the town [of Prophet Lût (Lot)] on which was rained the evil rain. Did they (disbelievers) not then see it (with their own eyes)? Nay ! But they used not to expect any resurrection.

وَلَقَدْ أَتَوْا عَلَى ٱلْقَرْيَةِ ٱلَّتِي أُمْطِرَتْ مَطَرَ ٱلسَّوْءِ أَفَلَمْ يَكُونُوا يَرَوْنَهَا بَلْ كَانُوا لَا يَرْجُونَ نُشُورًا ﴿٤٠﴾

41. And when they see you (O Muhammad صلى الله عليه وسلم), they treat you only in mockery (saying):"Is this the one whom Allâh has sent as a Messenger?

وَإِذَا رَأَوْكَ إِن يَتَّخِذُونَكَ إِلَّا هُزُوًا أَهَٰذَا ٱلَّذِي بَعَثَ ٱللَّهُ رَسُولًا ﴿٤١﴾

42. "He would have nearly misled us from our *âlihah* (gods), had it not been that we were patient and constant in their worship!" And they will know, when they see the torment, who it is that is most astray from the (Right) Path!

إِن كَادَ لَيُضِلُّنَا عَنْ ءَالِهَتِنَا لَوْلَا أَن صَبَرْنَا عَلَيْهَا وَسَوْفَ يَعْلَمُونَ حِينَ يَرَوْنَ ٱلْعَذَابَ مَنْ أَضَلُّ سَبِيلًا ﴿٤٢﴾

43. Have you (O Muhammad صلى الله عليه وسلم) seen him who has taken as his *ilâh* (god) his own vain desire? Would you then be a *Wakîl* (a disposer of his affairs or a watcher) over him?

أَرَءَيْتَ مَنِ ٱتَّخَذَ إِلَٰهَهُ هَوَىٰهُ أَفَأَنتَ تَكُونُ عَلَيْهِ وَكِيلًا ﴿٤٣﴾

44. Or do you think that most of them hear or understand? They are only like cattle — nay, they are even farther astray from the Path (i.e. even worse than cattle).

أَمْ تَحْسَبُ أَنَّ أَكْثَرَهُمْ يَسْمَعُونَ أَوْ يَعْقِلُونَ إِنْ هُمْ إِلَّا كَٱلْأَنْعَٰمِ بَلْ هُمْ أَضَلُّ سَبِيلًا ﴿٤٤﴾

45. Have you not seen how your Lord spread the shadow. If He willed, He could have made it still — But We have made the sun its guide (i.e. after the sunrise, the shadow shrinks and vanishes at midnoon and then again appears in the afternoon with the decline of the sun, and had there been no sunlight, there would have been no shadow.

أَلَمْ تَرَ إِلَىٰ رَبِّكَ كَيْفَ مَدَّ ٱلظِّلَّ وَلَوْ شَاءَ لَجَعَلَهُ سَاكِنًا ثُمَّ جَعَلْنَا ٱلشَّمْسَ عَلَيْهِ دَلِيلًا ﴿٤٥﴾

46. Then We withdraw it to Us — a gradual concealed withdrawal.

ثُمَّ قَبَضْنَاهُ إِلَيْنَا قَبْضًا يَسِيرًا ٤٦

47. And it is He Who makes the night a covering for you, and the sleep (as) a repose, and makes the day *Nushûr* (i.e. getting up and going about here and there for daily work, after one's sleep at night or like resurrection after one's death).

وَهُوَ الَّذِى جَعَلَ لَكُمُ الَّيْلَ لِبَاسًا وَالنَّوْمَ سُبَاتًا وَجَعَلَ النَّهَارَ نُشُورًا ٤٧

48. And it is He Who sends the winds as heralds of glad tidings, going before His Mercy (rain); and We send down pure water from the sky,

وَهُوَ الَّذِى أَرْسَلَ الرِّيَاحَ بُشْرًا بَيْنَ يَدَىْ رَحْمَتِهِ وَأَنْزَلْنَا مِنَ السَّمَاءِ مَاءً طَهُورًا ٤٨

49. That We may give life thereby to a dead land, and We give to drink thereof many of the cattle and men that We had created.

لِنُحْيِىَ بِهِ بَلْدَةً مَّيْتًا وَنُسْقِيَهُ مِمَّا خَلَقْنَا أَنْعَامًا وَأَنَاسِىَّ كَثِيرًا ٤٩

50. And indeed We have distributed it (rain or water) amongst them in order that they may remember the Grace of Allâh, but most men (refuse to accept the Truth or Faith) and accept nothing but disbelief or ingratitude.

وَلَقَدْ صَرَّفْنَاهُ بَيْنَهُمْ لِيَذَّكَّرُوا فَأَبَى أَكْثَرُ النَّاسِ إِلَّا كُفُورًا ٥٠

51. And had We willed, We would have raised a warner in every town.

وَلَوْ شِئْنَا لَبَعَثْنَا فِى كُلِّ قَرْيَةٍ نَّذِيرًا ٥١

52. So obey not the disbelievers, but strive against them (by preaching) with the utmost endeavour with it (the Qur'ân).

فَلَا تُطِعِ الْكَافِرِينَ وَجَاهِدْهُم بِهِ جِهَادًا كَبِيرًا ٥٢

53. And it is He Who has let free the two seas (kinds of water): one palatable and sweet, and the other salt and bitter; and He has set a barrier and a complete partition between them.

وَهُوَ الَّذِى مَرَجَ الْبَحْرَيْنِ هَذَا عَذْبٌ فُرَاتٌ وَهَذَا مِلْحٌ أُجَاجٌ وَجَعَلَ بَيْنَهُمَا بَرْزَخًا وَحِجْرًا مَّحْجُورًا ٥٣

54. And it is He Who has created man from water, and has appointed for

وَهُوَ الَّذِى خَلَقَ مِنَ الْمَاءِ بَشَرًا

him kindred by blood, and kindred by marriage. And your Lord is Ever All-Powerful to do what He wills.

55. And they (disbelievers, polytheists) worship besides Allâh, that which can neither profit them nor harm them; and the disbeliever is ever a helper (of the Satan) against his Lord.

56. And We have sent you (O Muhammad صلى الله عليه وسلم) only as a bearer of glad tidings and a warner.

57. Say: "No reward do I ask of you for this (that which I have brought from my Lord and its preaching), save that whosoever wills, may take a Path to his Lord.

58. And put your trust (O Muhammad صلى الله عليه وسلم) in the Ever Living One Who dies not, and glorify His Praises, and Sufficient is He as the All-Knower of the sins of His slaves,

59. Who created the heavens and the earth and all that is between them in six Days. Then He rose over (*Istawâ*) the Throne (in a manner that suits His Majesty). The Most Gracious (Allâh)! Ask Him (O Prophet Muhammad صلى الله عليه وسلم, concerning His Qualities: His rising over His Throne, His creations), as He is *Al-Khabîr* (The All-Knower of everything i.e. Allâh).

60. And when it is said to them: "Prostrate yourselves to the Most Gracious (Allâh)!" They say: "And what is the Most Gracious? Shall we fall down in prostration to that which you (O Muhammad صلى الله عليه وسلم) command us?" And it increases in them only aversion.

61. Blessed is He Who has placed in the heaven big stars, and has placed therein a great lamp (sun), and a moon giving light.

62. And He it is Who has put the night and the day in succession, for such who desires to remember or desires to show his gratitude.

63. And the (faithful) slaves of the Most Gracious (Allâh) are those who walk on the earth in humility and sedateness, and when the foolish address them (with bad words) they reply back with mild words of gentleness.

64. And those who spend the night in worship of their Lord, prostrate and standing.[1]

65. And those who say: "Our Lord! Avert from us the torment of Hell. Verily, its torment is ever an inseparable, permanent punishment."

66. Evil indeed it (Hell) is as an abode and as a place to rest in.

67. And those who, when they spend, are neither extravagant nor niggardly, but hold a medium (way) between those (extremes).

---

[1] (V.25:64) Ibn 'Abbâs رضي الله عنهما said: "Whosoever prayed two *Rak'at* or more after the *'Isha* (night) prayer, will be considered like those mentioned in this Verse." And Al-Kalabi said: "Whosoever prayed two *Rak'at* after the *Maghrib* (evening) prayer, and four *Rak'at* after the *'Ishâ* (night) prayer will be considered like those mentioned in this Verse." (*Tafsîr Al-Qurtubî*).

68. And those who invoke not any other *ilâh* (god) along with Allâh, nor kill such person as Allâh has forbidden, except for just cause, nor commit illegal sexual intercourse — and whoever does this shall receive the punishment.[1]

69. The torment will be doubled to him on the Day of Resurrection, and he will abide therein in disgrace;

70. Except those who repent and believe (in Islâmic Monotheism), and do righteous deeds; for those, Allâh will change their sins into good deeds, and Allâh is Oft-Forgiving, Most Merciful.[2]

71. And whosoever repents and does righteous good deeds; then verily, he repents towards Allâh with true repentance.

وَٱلَّذِينَ لَا يَدْعُونَ مَعَ ٱللَّهِ إِلَٰهًا ءَاخَرَ وَلَا يَقْتُلُونَ ٱلنَّفْسَ ٱلَّتِي حَرَّمَ ٱللَّهُ إِلَّا بِٱلْحَقِّ وَلَا يَزْنُونَ وَمَن يَفْعَلْ ذَٰلِكَ يَلْقَ أَثَامًا ٦٨

يُضَٰعَفْ لَهُ ٱلْعَذَابُ يَوْمَ ٱلْقِيَٰمَةِ وَيَخْلُدْ فِيهِۦ مُهَانًا ٦٩

إِلَّا مَن تَابَ وَءَامَنَ وَعَمِلَ عَمَلًا صَٰلِحًا فَأُو۟لَٰٓئِكَ يُبَدِّلُ ٱللَّهُ سَيِّـَٔاتِهِمْ حَسَنَٰتٍ وَكَانَ ٱللَّهُ غَفُورًا رَّحِيمًا ٧٠

وَمَن تَابَ وَعَمِلَ صَٰلِحًا فَإِنَّهُۥ يَتُوبُ إِلَى ٱللَّهِ مَتَابًا ٧١

---

[1] (V.25:68)

A) See the footnote of (V.2:22).

B) See the footnote of (V.4:135).

[2] (V.25:70) Islam demolishes all the previous evil deeds and so do migration (for Allâh's sake) and *Hajj* (pilgrimage to Makkah). [*Al-Lu'lu' wal-Marjân*, Vol. 1, Chapter 52, Page 205]

Narrated Ibn 'Abbâs رضى الله عنهما: Some pagans who committed murders in great number and committed illegal sexual intercourse excessively, came to Muhammad صلى الله عليه وسلم and said: "O Muhammad! Whatever you say, and invite people to, is good, but we wish if you could inform us whether we can make an expiation for our (past evil) deeds." So the Divine Verses came: "Those who invoke not with Allâh any other god, nor kill such person as Allâh has forbidden except for just cause, nor commit illegal sexual intercourse." (V.25:68) "... Except those who repent..." (V.25:70).

And there was also revealed: "Say: O My slaves who have transgressed against their onselves! (by committing sins), despair not of the Mercy of Allâh." (V.39:53). (*Sahih Al-Bukhari*, Vol.6, *Hadith* No.334).

72. And those who do not bear witness to falsehood, and if they pass by some evil play or evil talk, they pass by it with dignity.

وَالَّذِينَ لَا يَشْهَدُونَ الزُّورَ وَإِذَا مَرُّوا بِاللَّغْوِ مَرُّوا كِرَامًا ﴿٧٢﴾

73. And those who, when they are reminded of the *Ayât* (proofs, evidences, verses, lessons, signs, revelations, etc.) of their Lord, fall not deaf and blind threat.

وَالَّذِينَ إِذَا ذُكِّرُوا بِآيَاتِ رَبِّهِمْ لَمْ يَخِرُّوا عَلَيْهَا صُمًّا وَعُمْيَانًا ﴿٧٣﴾

74. And those who say: "Our Lord! Bestow on us from our wives and our offspring the comfort of our eyes, and make us leaders of the *Muttaqûn* (the pious. See V.2:2)."

وَالَّذِينَ يَقُولُونَ رَبَّنَا هَبْ لَنَا مِنْ أَزْوَاجِنَا وَذُرِّيَّاتِنَا قُرَّةَ أَعْيُنٍ وَاجْعَلْنَا لِلْمُتَّقِينَ إِمَامًا ﴿٧٤﴾

75. Those will be rewarded with the highest place (in Paradise) because of their patience. Therein they shall be met with greetings and the word of peace and respect.

أُوْلَئِكَ يُجْزَوْنَ الْغُرْفَةَ بِمَا صَبَرُوا وَيُلَقَّوْنَ فِيهَا تَحِيَّةً وَسَلَامًا ﴿٧٥﴾

76. Abiding therein — excellent it is as an abode, and as a place to rest in.

خَالِدِينَ فِيهَا حَسُنَتْ مُسْتَقَرًّا وَمُقَامًا ﴿٧٦﴾

77. Say (O Muhammad صلى الله عليه وسلم to the disbelievers): "My Lord pays attention to you only because of your invocation to Him. But now you have indeed denied (Him). So the torment will be yours for ever (inseparable, permanent punishment)."

قُلْ مَا يَعْبَأُ بِكُمْ رَبِّي لَوْلَا دُعَاؤُكُمْ فَقَدْ كَذَّبْتُمْ فَسَوْفَ يَكُونُ لِزَامًا ﴿٧٧﴾

Sûrat Ash-Shu'arâ'
(The Poets) XXVI

سُورَةُ الشُّعَرَاء

In the Name of Allâh
the Most Gracious, the Most Merciful

بِسْمِ اللَّهِ الرَّحْمَنِ الرَّحِيمِ

1. Tâ-Sîn-Mîm.

طسم ﴿١﴾

[These letters are one of the miracles of the Qur'ân, and none but Allâh (Alone) knows their meanings.]

2. These are the Verses of the manifest Book [(this Qur'ân), which was promised by Allâh in the Taurât (Torah) and the Injeel (Gospel), makes things clear].

تِلْكَ ءَايَـٰتُ ٱلْكِتَـٰبِ ٱلْمُبِينِ ﴿١﴾

3. It may be that you (O Muhammad صلى الله عليه وسلم) are going to kill yourself with grief, that they do not become believers [in your *Risâlah* (Messengership) i.e., in your Message of Islâmic Monotheism].[1]

لَعَلَّكَ بَـٰخِعٌ نَّفْسَكَ أَلَّا يَكُونُوا۟ مُؤْمِنِينَ ﴿٢﴾

4. If We will, We could send down to them from the heaven a sign, to which they would bend their necks in humility.

إِن نَّشَأْ نُنَزِّلْ عَلَيْهِم مِّنَ ٱلسَّمَآءِ ءَايَةً فَظَلَّتْ أَعْنَـٰقُهُمْ لَهَا خَـٰضِعِينَ ﴿٣﴾

5. And never comes there unto them a Reminder as a recent revelation from the Most Gracious (Allâh), but they turn away therefrom.

وَمَا يَأْتِيهِم مِّن ذِكْرٍ مِّنَ ٱلرَّحْمَـٰنِ مُحْدَثٍ إِلَّا كَانُوا۟ عَنْهُ مُعْرِضِينَ ﴿٤﴾

6. So they have indeed denied (the truth — this Qur'ân), then the news of what they mocked at will come to them.

فَقَدْ كَذَّبُوا۟ فَسَيَأْتِيهِمْ أَنۢبَـٰٓؤُا۟ مَا كَانُوا۟ بِهِۦ يَسْتَهْزِءُونَ ﴿٥﴾

7. Do they not observe the earth — how much of every good kind We cause to grow therein?

أَوَلَمْ يَرَوْا۟ إِلَى ٱلْأَرْضِ كَمْ أَنۢبَتْنَا فِيهَا مِن كُلِّ زَوْجٍ كَرِيمٍ ﴿٦﴾

8. Verily, in this is an *Ayâh* (proof or sign), yet most of them (polytheists, pagans, who do not believe in Resurrection) are not believers.

إِنَّ فِى ذَٰلِكَ لَـَٔايَةً وَمَا كَانَ أَكْثَرُهُم مُّؤْمِنِينَ ﴿٧﴾

9. And verily, your Lord, He is truly, the All-Mighty, the Most Merciful.

وَإِنَّ رَبَّكَ لَهُوَ ٱلْعَزِيزُ ٱلرَّحِيمُ ﴿٨﴾

10. And (remember) when your Lord called Mûsâ (Moses) (saying): "Go to

وَإِذْ نَادَىٰ رَبُّكَ مُوسَىٰٓ أَنِ ٱئْتِ ٱلْقَوْمَ

---

[1] (V.26:3) See the footnote of (V.3:85).

the people who are Zâlimûn (polytheists and wrongdoers) — الظَّالِمِينَ

11. "The people of Fir'aun (Pharaoh): Will they not fear Allâh and become righteous?" قَوْمَ فِرْعَوْنَ أَلَا يَتَّقُونَ ١١

12. He said: "My Lord! Verily, I fear that they will belie me, قَالَ رَبِّ إِنِّي أَخَافُ أَن يُكَذِّبُونِ ١٢

13. "And my breast straitens, and my tongue expresses not well. So send for Hârûn (Aaron) (to come along with me). وَيَضِيقُ صَدْرِي وَلَا يَنطَلِقُ لِسَانِي فَأَرْسِلْ إِلَىٰ هَٰرُونَ ١٣

14. "And they have a charge of crime against me, and I fear they will kill me." وَلَهُمْ عَلَىَّ ذَنبٌ فَأَخَافُ أَن يَقْتُلُونِ ١٤

15. (Allâh) said: "Nay! Go you both with Our Signs. Verily, We shall be with you, listening. قَالَ كَلَّا فَاذْهَبَا بِـَٔايَٰتِنَا إِنَّا مَعَكُم مُّسْتَمِعُونَ ١٥

16. "And go both of you to Fir'aun (Pharaoh), and say: 'We are the Messengers of the Lord of the 'Âlamîn (mankind, jinn and all that exists), فَأْتِيَا فِرْعَوْنَ فَقُولَا إِنَّا رَسُولُ رَبِّ الْعَٰلَمِينَ ١٦

17. "So allow the Children of Israel to go with us.'" أَنْ أَرْسِلْ مَعَنَا بَنِي إِسْرَٰٓءِيلَ ١٧

18. [Fir'aun (Pharaoh)] said [to Mûsâ (Moses)]: "Did we not bring you up among us as a child? And you did dwell many years of your life with us. قَالَ أَلَمْ نُرَبِّكَ فِينَا وَلِيدًا وَلَبِثْتَ فِينَا مِنْ عُمُرِكَ سِنِينَ ١٨

19. "And you did your deed, which you did (i.e. the crime of killing a man). While you were one of the ingrates." وَفَعَلْتَ فَعْلَتَكَ الَّتِي فَعَلْتَ وَأَنتَ مِنَ الْكَٰفِرِينَ ١٩

20. Mûsâ (Moses) said: "I did it then, when I was ignorant (as regards my Lord and His Message). قَالَ فَعَلْتُهَا إِذًا وَأَنَا مِنَ الضَّالِّينَ ٢٠

21. "So I fled from you when I feared you. But my Lord has granted me Hukm (i.e. religious knowledge, right judgement فَفَرَرْتُ مِنكُمْ لَمَّا خِفْتُكُمْ فَوَهَبَ

of the affairs and Prophethood), and made me one of the Messengers.

لِى فِي حُكْمًا وَجَعَلَنِى مِنَ الْمُرْسَلِينَ ﴿٢١﴾

22. "And this is the past favour with which you reproach me: that you have enslaved the Children of Israel."

وَتِلْكَ نِعْمَةٌ تَمُنُّهَا عَلَىَّ أَنْ عَبَّدتَّ بَنِى إِسْرَٰٓءِيلَ ﴿٢٢﴾

23. Fir'aun (Pharaoh) said: "And what is the Lord of the 'Âlamîn (mankind, jinn and all that exists)?"

قَالَ فِرْعَوْنُ وَمَا رَبُّ الْعَلَمِينَ ﴿٢٣﴾

24. Mûsâ (Moses) said: "The Lord of the heavens and the earth, and all that is between them, if you seek to be convinced with certainty."

قَالَ رَبُّ السَّمَوَٰتِ وَالْأَرْضِ وَمَا بَيْنَهُمَآ إِن كُنتُم مُّوقِنِينَ ﴿٢٤﴾

25. Fir'aun (Pharaoh) said to those around: "Do you not hear (what he says)?"

قَالَ لِمَنْ حَوْلَهُ أَلَا تَسْتَمِعُونَ ﴿٢٥﴾

26. Mûsâ (Moses) said: "Your Lord and the Lord of your ancient fathers!"

قَالَ رَبُّكُمْ وَرَبُّ ءَابَآئِكُمُ الْأَوَّلِينَ ﴿٢٦﴾

27. [Fir'aun (Pharaoh)] said: "Verily, your Messenger who has been sent to you is a madman!"

قَالَ إِنَّ رَسُولَكُمُ الَّذِىٓ أُرْسِلَ إِلَيْكُمْ لَمَجْنُونٌ ﴿٢٧﴾

28. [Mûsâ (Moses)] said: "Lord of the east and the west, and all that is between them, if you did but understand!"

قَالَ رَبُّ الْمَشْرِقِ وَالْمَغْرِبِ وَمَا بَيْنَهُمَآ إِن كُنتُمْ تَعْقِلُونَ ﴿٢٨﴾

29. [Fir'aun (Pharaoh)] said: "If you choose an *ilâh* (god) other than me, I will certainly put you among the prisoners."

قَالَ لَئِنِ اتَّخَذْتَ إِلَٰهًا غَيْرِى لَأَجْعَلَنَّكَ مِنَ الْمَسْجُونِينَ ﴿٢٩﴾

30. [Mûsâ (Moses)] said: "Even if I bring you something manifest (and convincing)?"

قَالَ أَوَلَوْ جِئْتُكَ بِشَىْءٍ مُّبِينٍ ﴿٣٠﴾

31. [Fir'aun (Pharaoh)] said: "Bring it forth then, if you are of the truthful!"

قَالَ فَأْتِ بِهِ إِن كُنتَ مِنَ الصَّٰدِقِينَ ﴿٣١﴾

32. So [Mûsâ (Moses)] threw his stick, and behold, it was a serpent, manifest.

فَأَلْقَىٰ عَصَاهُ فَإِذَا هِيَ ثُعْبَانٌ مُّبِينٌ ۝

33. And he drew out his hand, and behold, it was white to all beholders!

وَنَزَعَ يَدَهُ فَإِذَا هِيَ بَيْضَآءُ لِلنَّاظِرِينَ ۝

34. [Fir'aun (Pharaoh)] said to the chiefs around him: "Verily, this is indeed a well-versed sorcerer.

قَالَ لِلْمَلَإِ حَوْلَهُ إِنَّ هَٰذَا لَسَٰحِرٌ عَلِيمٌ ۝

35. "He wants to drive you out of your land by his sorcery: what is it then that you command?"

يُرِيدُ أَن يُخْرِجَكُم مِّنْ أَرْضِكُم بِسِحْرِهِ فَمَاذَا تَأْمُرُونَ ۝

36. They said: "Put him off and his brother (for a while), and send callers to the cities;

قَالُوٓا أَرْجِهْ وَأَخَاهُ وَابْعَثْ فِي الْمَدَآئِنِ حَٰشِرِينَ ۝

37. "To bring up to you every well-versed sorcerer."

يَأْتُوكَ بِكُلِّ سَحَّارٍ عَلِيمٍ ۝

38. So the sorcerers were assembled at a fixed time on a day appointed.

فَجُمِعَ السَّحَرَةُ لِمِيقَٰتِ يَوْمٍ مَّعْلُومٍ ۝

39. And it was said to the people: "Are you (too) going to assemble?

وَقِيلَ لِلنَّاسِ هَلْ أَنتُم مُّجْتَمِعُونَ ۝

40. "That we may follow the sorcerers [who were on Fir'aun's (Pharaoh) religion of disbelief] if they are the winners."

لَعَلَّنَا نَتَّبِعُ السَّحَرَةَ إِن كَانُوا هُمُ الْغَٰلِبِينَ ۝

41. So when the sorcerers arrived, they said to Fir'aun (Pharaoh): "Will there surely, be a reward for us if we are the winners?"

فَلَمَّا جَآءَ السَّحَرَةُ قَالُوا لِفِرْعَوْنَ أَئِنَّ لَنَا لَأَجْرًا إِن كُنَّا نَحْنُ الْغَٰلِبِينَ ۝

42. He said: "Yes, and you shall then verily, be of those brought near (to myself)."

قَالَ نَعَمْ وَإِنَّكُمْ إِذًا لَّمِنَ الْمُقَرَّبِينَ ۝

43. Mûsâ (Moses) said to them: "Throw what you are going to throw!"

قَالَ لَهُم مُّوسَىٰٓ أَلْقُوا مَآ أَنتُم مُّلْقُونَ ۝

44. So they threw their ropes and their sticks, and said: "By the might of Fir'aun (Pharaoh), it is we who will certainly win"

فَأَلْقَوْا حِبَالَهُمْ وَعِصِيَّهُمْ وَقَالُوا بِعِزَّةِ فِرْعَوْنَ إِنَّا لَنَحْنُ الْغَالِبُونَ ﴿٤٤﴾

45. Then Mûsâ (Moses) threw his stick, and behold, it swallowed up all that they falsely showed!

فَأَلْقَىٰ مُوسَىٰ عَصَاهُ فَإِذَا هِىَ تَلْقَفُ مَا يَأْفِكُونَ ﴿٤٥﴾

46. And the sorcerers fell down prostrate.

فَأُلْقِىَ السَّحَرَةُ سَاجِدِينَ ﴿٤٦﴾

47. Saying: "We believe in the Lord of the 'Âlamîn (mankind, jinn and all that exists).

قَالُوا ءَامَنَّا بِرَبِّ الْعَالَمِينَ ﴿٤٧﴾

48. "The Lord of Mûsâ (Moses) and Hârûn (Aaron)."

رَبِّ مُوسَىٰ وَهَارُونَ ﴿٤٨﴾

49. [Fir'aun (Pharaoh)] said: "You have believed in him before I give you leave. Surely, he indeed is your chief, who has taught you magic! So verily, you shall come to know. Verily, I will cut off your hands and your feet on opposite sides, and I will crucify you all."

قَالَ ءَامَنتُمْ لَهُ قَبْلَ أَنْ ءَاذَنَ لَكُمْ إِنَّهُ لَكَبِيرُكُمُ الَّذِى عَلَّمَكُمُ السِّحْرَ فَلَسَوْفَ تَعْلَمُونَ لَأُقَطِّعَنَّ أَيْدِيَكُمْ وَأَرْجُلَكُم مِّنْ خِلَافٍ وَلَأُصَلِّبَنَّكُمْ أَجْمَعِينَ ﴿٤٩﴾

50. They said: "No harm! Surely, to our Lord (Allâh) we are to return.

قَالُوا لَا ضَيْرَ إِنَّا إِلَىٰ رَبِّنَا مُنقَلِبُونَ ﴿٥٠﴾

51. "Verily, we really hope that our Lord will forgive us our sins, as we are the first of the believers [in Mûsâ (Moses) and in the Monotheism which he has brought from Allâh]."

إِنَّا نَطْمَعُ أَن يَغْفِرَ لَنَا رَبُّنَا خَطَايَانَا أَن كُنَّا أَوَّلَ الْمُؤْمِنِينَ ﴿٥١﴾

52. And We revealed to Mûsâ (Moses), saying: "Depart by night with My slaves, verily, you will be pursued."

وَأَوْحَيْنَا إِلَىٰ مُوسَىٰ أَنْ أَسْرِ بِعِبَادِي إِنَّكُم مُّتَّبَعُونَ ﴿٥٢﴾

53. Then Fir'aun (Pharaoh) sent callers to (all) the cities.

فَأَرْسَلَ فِرْعَوْنُ فِي الْمَدَائِنِ حَاشِرِينَ ﴿٥٣﴾

54. (Saying): "Verily, these indeed are but a small band.

إِنَّ هَؤُلَاءِ لَشِرْذِمَةٌ قَلِيلُونَ ۝

55. "And verily, they have done what has enraged us.

وَإِنَّهُمْ لَنَا لَغَائِظُونَ ۝

56. "But we are a host all assembled, amply fore-warned."

وَإِنَّا لَجَمِيعٌ حَاذِرُونَ ۝

57. So, We expelled them from gardens and springs,

فَأَخْرَجْنَاهُم مِّن جَنَّاتٍ وَعُيُونٍ ۝

58. Treasures, and every kind of honourable place.

وَكُنُوزٍ وَمَقَامٍ كَرِيمٍ ۝

59. Thus [We turned them (Pharaoh's people) out] and We caused the Children of Israel to inherit them.

كَذَلِكَ وَأَوْرَثْنَاهَا بَنِي إِسْرَائِيلَ ۝

60. So they pursued them at sunrise.

فَأَتْبَعُوهُم مُّشْرِقِينَ ۝

61. And when the two hosts saw each other, the companions of Mûsâ (Moses) said: "We are sure to be overtaken."

فَلَمَّا تَرَاءَى الْجَمْعَانِ قَالَ أَصْحَابُ مُوسَى إِنَّا لَمُدْرَكُونَ ۝

62. [Mûsâ (Moses)] said: "Nay, verily, with me is my Lord. He will guide me."

قَالَ كَلَّا إِنَّ مَعِيَ رَبِّي سَيَهْدِينِ ۝

63. Then We revealed to Mûsâ (Moses) (saying): "Strike the sea with your stick." And it parted, and each separate part (of that sea water) became like huge mountain.

فَأَوْحَيْنَا إِلَى مُوسَى أَنِ اضْرِب بِّعَصَاكَ الْبَحْرَ فَانفَلَقَ فَكَانَ كُلُّ فِرْقٍ كَالطَّوْدِ الْعَظِيمِ ۝

64. Then We brought near the others [Fir'aun's (Pharaoh) party] to that place.

وَأَزْلَفْنَا ثَمَّ الْآخَرِينَ ۝

65. And We saved Mûsâ (Moses) and all those with him.

وَأَنجَيْنَا مُوسَى وَمَن مَّعَهُ أَجْمَعِينَ ۝

66. Then We drowned the others.

ثُمَّ أَغْرَقْنَا الْآخَرِينَ ۝

67. Verily, in this is indeed a sign (or a proof), yet most of them are not believers.

إِنَّ فِي ذَلِكَ لَآيَةً وَمَا كَانَ أَكْثَرُهُم مُّؤْمِنِينَ ۝

68. And verily, your Lord, He is truly, the All-Mighty, the Most Merciful.

وَإِنَّ رَبَّكَ لَهُوَ الْعَزِيزُ الرَّحِيمُ ﴿٦٨﴾

69. And recite to them the story of Ibrâhîm (Abraham).

وَاتْلُ عَلَيْهِمْ نَبَأَ إِبْرَاهِيمَ ﴿٦٩﴾

70. When he said to his father and his people: "What do you worship?"

إِذْ قَالَ لِأَبِيهِ وَقَوْمِهِ مَا تَعْبُدُونَ ﴿٧٠﴾

71. They said: "We worship idols, and to them we are ever devoted."

قَالُوا نَعْبُدُ أَصْنَامًا فَنَظَلُّ لَهَا عَاكِفِينَ ﴿٧١﴾

72. He said: "Do they hear you, when you call on (them)?"

قَالَ هَلْ يَسْمَعُونَكُمْ إِذْ تَدْعُونَ ﴿٧٢﴾

73. "Or do they benefit you or do they harm (you)?"

أَوْ يَنفَعُونَكُمْ أَوْ يَضُرُّونَ ﴿٧٣﴾

74. They said: "(Nay) but we found our fathers doing so."

قَالُوا بَلْ وَجَدْنَا آبَاءَنَا كَذَلِكَ يَفْعَلُونَ ﴿٧٤﴾

75. He said: "Do you observe that which you have been worshipping —

قَالَ أَفَرَأَيْتُم مَّا كُنتُمْ تَعْبُدُونَ ﴿٧٥﴾

76. "You and your ancient fathers?

أَنتُمْ وَآبَاؤُكُمُ الْأَقْدَمُونَ ﴿٧٦﴾

77. "Verily, they are enemies to me, save the Lord of the 'Âlamîn (mankind, jinn and all that exists),

فَإِنَّهُمْ عَدُوٌّ لِّي إِلَّا رَبَّ الْعَالَمِينَ ﴿٧٧﴾

78. "Who has created me, and it is He Who guides me.

الَّذِي خَلَقَنِي فَهُوَ يَهْدِينِ ﴿٧٨﴾

79. "And it is He Who feeds me and gives me to drink.

وَالَّذِي هُوَ يُطْعِمُنِي وَيَسْقِينِ ﴿٧٩﴾

80. "And when I am ill, it is He Who cures me.

وَإِذَا مَرِضْتُ فَهُوَ يَشْفِينِ ﴿٨٠﴾

81. "And Who will cause me to die, and then will bring me to life (again).

وَالَّذِي يُمِيتُنِي ثُمَّ يُحْيِينِ ﴿٨١﴾

82. "And Who, I hope, will forgive me my faults on the Day of Recompense, (the Day of Resurrection)."

وَالَّذِي أَطْمَعُ أَن يَغْفِرَ لِي خَطِيئَتِي يَوْمَ الدِّينِ ﴿٨٢﴾

83. My Lord! Bestow *Hukm* (religious knowledge, right judgement

رَبِّ هَبْ لِي حُكْمًا وَأَلْحِقْنِي

of the affairs and Prophethood) on me, and join me with the righteous.

بِالصَّلِحِينَ ﴿٨٣﴾

84. And grant me an honourable mention in later generations.

وَٱجۡعَل لِّى لِسَانَ صِدۡقٍ فِى ٱلۡأَخِرِينَ ﴿٨٤﴾

85. And make me one of the inheritors of the Paradise of Delight.

وَٱجۡعَلۡنِى مِن وَرَثَةِ جَنَّةِ ٱلنَّعِيمِ ﴿٨٥﴾

86. And forgive my father, verily, he is of the erring.

وَٱغۡفِرۡ لِأَبِىٓ إِنَّهُۥ كَانَ مِنَ ٱلضَّآلِّينَ ﴿٨٦﴾

87. And disgrace me not on the Day when (all the creatures) will be resurrected.

وَلَا تُخۡزِنِى يَوۡمَ يُبۡعَثُونَ ﴿٨٧﴾

88. The Day whereon neither wealth nor sons will avail,

يَوۡمَ لَا يَنفَعُ مَالٌ وَلَا بَنُونَ ﴿٨٨﴾

89. Except him who brings to Allâh a clean heart [clean from *Shirk* (polytheism) and *Nifâq* (hypocrisy)].

إِلَّا مَنۡ أَتَى ٱللَّهَ بِقَلۡبٍ سَلِيمٍ ﴿٨٩﴾

90. And Paradise will be brought near to the *Muttaqûn* (the pious and righteous persons. See V.2:2).

وَأُزۡلِفَتِ ٱلۡجَنَّةُ لِلۡمُتَّقِينَ ﴿٩٠﴾

91. And the (Hell) Fire will be placed in full view of the erring.

وَبُرِّزَتِ ٱلۡجَحِيمُ لِلۡغَاوِينَ ﴿٩١﴾

92. And it will be said to them: "Where are those (the false gods whom you used to set up as rivals with Allâh) that you used to worship.

وَقِيلَ لَهُمۡ أَيۡنَ مَا كُنتُمۡ تَعۡبُدُونَ ﴿٩٢﴾

93. "Instead of Allâh? Can they help you or (even) help themselves?"

مِن دُونِ ٱللَّهِ هَلۡ يَنصُرُونَكُمۡ أَوۡ يَنتَصِرُونَ ﴿٩٣﴾

94. Then they will be thrown on their faces into the (Fire), they and the *Ghâwûn* (devils, and those who were in error).

فَكُبۡكِبُواْ فِيهَا هُمۡ وَٱلۡغَاوُۥنَ ﴿٩٤﴾

95. And the whole hosts of *Iblîs* (Satan) together.

وَجُنُودُ إِبۡلِيسَ أَجۡمَعُونَ ﴿٩٥﴾

96. They say while contending therein,

قَالُواْ وَهُمۡ فِيهَا يَخۡتَصِمُونَ ﴿٩٦﴾

97. By Allâh, we were truly, in a manifest error,

تَاللَّهِ إِن كُنَّا لَفِى ضَلَالٍ مُّبِينٍ ٩٧

98. When We held you (false gods) as equals (in worship) with the Lord of the 'Âlamîn (mankind, jinn and all that exists);

إِذْ نُسَوِّيكُم بِرَبِّ ٱلْعَـٰلَمِينَ ٩٨

99. And none has brought us into error except the Mujrimûn [Iblîs (Satan) and those of human beings who commit crimes, murderers, polytheists, oppressors].

وَمَا أَضَلَّنَا إِلَّا ٱلْمُجْرِمُونَ ٩٩

100. Now we have no intercessors,

فَمَا لَنَا مِن شَـٰفِعِينَ ١٠٠

101. Nor a close friend (to help us).

وَلَا صَدِيقٍ حَمِيمٍ ١٠١

102. (Alas!) If we only had a chance to return (to the world), we shall truly, be among the believers!

فَلَوْ أَنَّ لَنَا كَرَّةً فَنَكُونَ مِنَ ٱلْمُؤْمِنِينَ ١٠٢

103. Verily, in this is indeed a sign, yet most of them are not believers.

إِنَّ فِى ذَٰلِكَ لَـَايَةً وَمَا كَانَ أَكْثَرُهُم مُّؤْمِنِينَ ١٠٣

104. And verily, your Lord, He is truly, the All-Mighty, the Most Merciful.

وَإِنَّ رَبَّكَ لَهُوَ ٱلْعَزِيزُ ٱلرَّحِيمُ ١٠٤

105. The people of Nûh (Noah) belied the Messengers.

كَذَّبَتْ قَوْمُ نُوحٍ ٱلْمُرْسَلِينَ ١٠٥

106. When their brother Nûh (Noah) said to them: "Will you not fear Allâh and obey Him?

إِذْ قَالَ لَهُمْ أَخُوهُمْ نُوحٌ أَلَا تَتَّقُونَ ١٠٦

107. "I am a trustworthy Messenger to you.

إِنِّى لَكُمْ رَسُولٌ أَمِينٌ ١٠٧

108. "So fear Allâh, keep your duty to Him, and obey me.

فَٱتَّقُوا ٱللَّهَ وَأَطِيعُونِ ١٠٨

109. "No reward do I ask of you for it (my Message of Islâmic Monotheism); my reward is only from

وَمَا أَسْـَٔلُكُمْ عَلَيْهِ مِنْ أَجْرٍ إِنْ أَجْرِىَ ١٠٩

the Lord of the 'Âlamîn (mankind, jinn and all that exists).

إِلَّا عَلَىٰ رَبِّ ٱلۡعَٰلَمِينَ ١٥٩

110. "So keep your duty to Allâh, fear Him and obey me."

فَٱتَّقُوا۟ ٱللَّهَ وَأَطِيعُونِ ١١٠

111. They said: "Shall we believe in you, when the meanest (of the people) follow you?"

۞ قَالُوٓا۟ أَنُؤۡمِنُ لَكَ وَٱتَّبَعَكَ ٱلۡأَرۡذَلُونَ ١١١

112. He said: "And what knowledge have I of what they used to do?

قَالَ وَمَا عِلۡمِى بِمَا كَانُوا۟ يَعۡمَلُونَ ١١٢

113. "Their account is only with my Lord, if you could (but) know.

إِنۡ حِسَابُهُمۡ إِلَّا عَلَىٰ رَبِّى لَوۡ تَشۡعُرُونَ ١١٣

114. "And I am not going to drive away the believers.

وَمَآ أَنَا۠ بِطَارِدِ ٱلۡمُؤۡمِنِينَ ١١٤

115. I am only a plain warner."

إِنۡ أَنَا۠ إِلَّا نَذِيرٌ مُّبِينٌ ١١٥

116. They said: "If you cease not, O Nûh (Noah) you will surely, be among those stoned (to death)."

قَالُوا۟ لَئِن لَّمۡ تَنتَهِ يَٰنُوحُ لَتَكُونَنَّ مِنَ ٱلۡمَرۡجُومِينَ ١١٦

117. He said: "My Lord! Verily, my people have belied me.

قَالَ رَبِّ إِنَّ قَوۡمِى كَذَّبُونِ ١١٧

118. Therefore judge You between me and them, and save me and those of the believers who are with me."

فَٱفۡتَحۡ بَيۡنِى وَبَيۡنَهُمۡ فَتۡحًا وَنَجِّنِى وَمَن مَّعِىَ مِنَ ٱلۡمُؤۡمِنِينَ ١١٨

119. And We saved him and those with him in the laden ship.

فَأَنجَيۡنَٰهُ وَمَن مَّعَهُۥ فِى ٱلۡفُلۡكِ ٱلۡمَشۡحُونِ ١١٩

120. Then We drowned the rest (disbelievers) thereafter.

ثُمَّ أَغۡرَقۡنَا بَعۡدُ ٱلۡبَاقِينَ ١٢٠

121. Verily, in this is indeed a sign, yet most of them are not believers.

إِنَّ فِى ذَٰلِكَ لَءَايَةً وَمَا كَانَ أَكۡثَرُهُم مُّؤۡمِنِينَ ١٢١

122. And verily, your Lord, He is indeed the All-Mighty, the Most Merciful.

وَإِنَّ رَبَّكَ لَهُوَ ٱلۡعَزِيزُ ٱلرَّحِيمُ ١٢٢

123. 'Âd (people) belied the Messengers.

كَذَّبَتۡ عَادٌ ٱلۡمُرۡسَلِينَ ١٢٣

124. When their brother Hûd said to them: "Will you not fear Allâh and obey Him?

إِذْ قَالَ لَهُمْ أَخُوهُمْ هُودٌ أَلَا تَتَّقُونَ ۝

125. "Verily, I am a trustworthy Messenger to you.

إِنِّي لَكُمْ رَسُولٌ أَمِينٌ ۝

126. "So fear Allâh, keep your duty to Him, and obey me.

فَاتَّقُوا اللَّهَ وَأَطِيعُونِ ۝

127. "No reward do I ask of you for it (my Message of Islâmic Monotheism); my reward is only from the Lord of the 'Âlamîn (mankind, jinn, and all that exists).

وَمَا أَسْأَلُكُمْ عَلَيْهِ مِنْ أَجْرٍ إِنْ أَجْرِيَ إِلَّا عَلَىٰ رَبِّ الْعَالَمِينَ ۝

128. "Do you build high palaces on every high place, while you do not live in them?

أَتَبْنُونَ بِكُلِّ رِيعٍ آيَةً تَعْبَثُونَ ۝

129. "And do you get for yourselves palaces (fine buildings) as if you will live therein for ever.[1]

وَتَتَّخِذُونَ مَصَانِعَ لَعَلَّكُمْ تَخْلُدُونَ ۝

130. "And when you seize (somebody), seize you (him) as tyrants?

وَإِذَا بَطَشْتُمْ بَطَشْتُمْ جَبَّارِينَ ۝

131. "So fear Allâh, keep your duty to Him, and obey me.

فَاتَّقُوا اللَّهَ وَأَطِيعُونِ ۝

132. "And keep your duty to Him, fear Him Who has aided you with all (good things) that you know.

وَاتَّقُوا الَّذِي أَمَدَّكُم بِمَا تَعْلَمُونَ ۝

133. "He has aided you with cattle and children.

أَمَدَّكُم بِأَنْعَامٍ وَبَنِينَ ۝

134. "And gardens and springs.

وَجَنَّاتٍ وَعُيُونٍ ۝

135. "Verily, I fear for you the torment of a Great Day."

إِنِّي أَخَافُ عَلَيْكُمْ عَذَابَ يَوْمٍ عَظِيمٍ ۝

136. They said: "It is the same to us whether you preach or be not of those who preach.

قَالُوا سَوَاءٌ عَلَيْنَا أَوَعَظْتَ أَمْ لَمْ تَكُن مِّنَ الْوَاعِظِينَ ۝

---

[1] (V.26:129) See the footnote (C) of (V.9:111).

137. "This is no other than the false tales and religion of the ancients, [*Tafsir At-Tabarî*]

إِنْ هَٰذَآ إِلَّا خُلُقُ ٱلْأَوَّلِينَ ﴿١٣٧﴾

138. "And we are not going to be punished."

وَمَا نَحْنُ بِمُعَذَّبِينَ ﴿١٣٨﴾

139. So they belied him, and We destroyed them. Verily, in this is indeed a sign, yet most of them are not believers.

فَكَذَّبُوهُ فَأَهْلَكْنَٰهُمْ إِنَّ فِى ذَٰلِكَ لَءَايَةً وَمَا كَانَ أَكْثَرُهُم مُّؤْمِنِينَ ﴿١٣٩﴾

140. And verily, your Lord, He is indeed the All-Mighty, the Most Merciful.

وَإِنَّ رَبَّكَ لَهُوَ ٱلْعَزِيزُ ٱلرَّحِيمُ ﴿١٤٠﴾

141. Thamûd (people) belied the Messenger.

كَذَّبَتْ ثَمُودُ ٱلْمُرْسَلِينَ ﴿١٤١﴾

142. When their brother Sâlih said to them: "Will you not fear Allâh and obey Him?

إِذْ قَالَ لَهُمْ أَخُوهُمْ صَٰلِحٌ أَلَا تَتَّقُونَ ﴿١٤٢﴾

143. "I am a trustworthy Messenger to you.

إِنِّى لَكُمْ رَسُولٌ أَمِينٌ ﴿١٤٣﴾

144. "So fear Allâh, keep your duty to Him, and obey me.

فَٱتَّقُوا۟ ٱللَّهَ وَأَطِيعُونِ ﴿١٤٤﴾

145. "No reward do I ask of you for it (my Message of Islâmic Monotheism); my reward is only from the Lord of the 'Âlamîn (mankind, jinn and all that exists).

وَمَآ أَسْـَٔلُكُمْ عَلَيْهِ مِنْ أَجْرٍ إِنْ أَجْرِىَ إِلَّا عَلَىٰ رَبِّ ٱلْعَٰلَمِينَ ﴿١٤٥﴾

146. "Will you be left secure in that which you have here?

أَتُتْرَكُونَ فِى مَا هَٰهُنَآ ءَامِنِينَ ﴿١٤٦﴾

147. "In gardens and springs.

فِى جَنَّٰتٍ وَعُيُونٍ ﴿١٤٧﴾

148. And green crops (field) and date-palms with soft spadix.

وَزُرُوعٍ وَنَخْلٍ طَلْعُهَا هَضِيمٌ ﴿١٤٨﴾

149. "And you hew out in the mountains, houses with great skill.

وَتَنْحِتُونَ مِنَ ٱلْجِبَالِ بُيُوتًا فَٰرِهِينَ ﴿١٤٩﴾

150. "So fear Allâh, keep your duty to Him, and obey me.

فَٱتَّقُوا۟ ٱللَّهَ وَأَطِيعُونِ ﴿١٥٠﴾

151. "And follow not the command of *Al-Musrifûn* [i.e. their chiefs: leaders who were polytheists, criminals and sinners],

وَلَا تُطِيعُوٓاْ أَمْرَ ٱلْمُسْرِفِينَ ١٥١

152. "Who make mischief in the land, and reform not."

ٱلَّذِينَ يُفْسِدُونَ فِي ٱلْأَرْضِ وَلَا يُصْلِحُونَ ١٥٢

153. They said: "You are only of those bewitched!

قَالُوٓاْ إِنَّمَآ أَنتَ مِنَ ٱلْمُسَحَّرِينَ ١٥٣

154. "You are but a human being like us. Then bring us a sign if you are of the truthful."

مَآ أَنتَ إِلَّا بَشَرٌ مِّثْلُنَا فَأْتِ بِـَٔايَةٍ إِن كُنتَ مِنَ ٱلصَّٰدِقِينَ ١٥٤

155. He said: "Here is a she-camel: it has a right to drink (water), and you have a right to drink (water) (each) on a day, known.

قَالَ هَٰذِهِۦ نَاقَةٌ لَّهَا شِرْبٌ وَلَكُمْ شِرْبُ يَوْمٍ مَّعْلُومٍ ١٥٥

156. "And touch her not with harm, lest the torment of a Great Day should seize you."

وَلَا تَمَسُّوهَا بِسُوٓءٍ فَيَأْخُذَكُمْ عَذَابُ يَوْمٍ عَظِيمٍ ١٥٦

157. But they killed her, and then they became regretful.

فَعَقَرُوهَا فَأَصْبَحُواْ نَٰدِمِينَ ١٥٧

158. So the torment overtook them. Verily, in this is indeed a sign, yet most of them are not believers.

فَأَخَذَهُمُ ٱلْعَذَابُ إِنَّ فِي ذَٰلِكَ لَءَايَةً وَمَا كَانَ أَكْثَرُهُم مُّؤْمِنِينَ ١٥٨

159. And verily, your Lord, He is indeed the All-Mighty, the Most Merciful.

وَإِنَّ رَبَّكَ لَهُوَ ٱلْعَزِيزُ ٱلرَّحِيمُ ١٥٩

160. The people of Lût (Lot) (— who dwelt in the towns of Sodom in Palestine) belied the Messengers.

كَذَّبَتْ قَوْمُ لُوطٍ ٱلْمُرْسَلِينَ ١٦٠

161. When their brother Lût (Lot) said to them: "Will you not fear Allâh and obey Him?

إِذْ قَالَ لَهُمْ أَخُوهُمْ لُوطٌ أَلَا تَتَّقُونَ ١٦١

162. "Verily, I am a trustworthy Messenger to you.

إِنِّي لَكُمْ رَسُولٌ أَمِينٌ ١٦٢

163. "So fear Allâh, keep your duty to Him, and obey me.

فَٱتَّقُوا۟ ٱللَّهَ وَأَطِيعُونِ ﴿١٦٣﴾

164. "No reward do I ask of you for it (my Message of Islâmic Monotheism); my reward is only from the Lord of the 'Âlamîn (mankind, jinn and all that exists).

وَمَآ أَسْـَٔلُكُمْ عَلَيْهِ مِنْ أَجْرٍ إِنْ أَجْرِيَ إِلَّا عَلَىٰ رَبِّ ٱلْعَٰلَمِينَ ﴿١٦٤﴾

165. "Go you in unto the males of the 'Âlamîn (mankind).

أَتَأْتُونَ ٱلذُّكْرَانَ مِنَ ٱلْعَٰلَمِينَ ﴿١٦٥﴾

166. "And leave those whom Allâh has created for you to be your wives? Nay, you are a trespassing people!"

وَتَذَرُونَ مَا خَلَقَ لَكُمْ رَبُّكُم مِّنْ أَزْوَٰجِكُم ۚ بَلْ أَنتُمْ قَوْمٌ عَادُونَ ﴿١٦٦﴾

167. They said: "If you cease not. O Lût (Lot)! Verily, you will be one of those who are driven out!"

قَالُوا۟ لَئِن لَّمْ تَنتَهِ يَٰلُوطُ لَتَكُونَنَّ مِنَ ٱلْمُخْرَجِينَ ﴿١٦٧﴾

168. He said: "I am, indeed, of those who disapprove with severe anger and fury your (this evil) action (of sodomy).

قَالَ إِنِّي لِعَمَلِكُم مِّنَ ٱلْقَالِينَ ﴿١٦٨﴾

169. "My Lord! Save me and my family from what they do."

رَبِّ نَجِّنِي وَأَهْلِي مِمَّا يَعْمَلُونَ ﴿١٦٩﴾

170. So We saved him and his family, all,

فَنَجَّيْنَٰهُ وَأَهْلَهُۥٓ أَجْمَعِينَ ﴿١٧٠﴾

171. Except an old woman (his wife) among those who remained behind.

إِلَّا عَجُوزًا فِى ٱلْغَٰبِرِينَ ﴿١٧١﴾

172. Then afterward We destroyed the others.

ثُمَّ دَمَّرْنَا ٱلْـَٔاخَرِينَ ﴿١٧٢﴾

173. And We rained on them a rain (of torment). And how evil was the rain of those who had been warned!

وَأَمْطَرْنَا عَلَيْهِم مَّطَرًا ۖ فَسَآءَ مَطَرُ ٱلْمُنذَرِينَ ﴿١٧٣﴾

174. Verily, in this is indeed a sign, yet most of them are not believers.

إِنَّ فِى ذَٰلِكَ لَـَٔايَةً ۖ وَمَا كَانَ أَكْثَرُهُم مُّؤْمِنِينَ ﴿١٧٤﴾

175. And verily, your Lord, He is indeed the All-Mighty, the Most Merciful.

وَإِنَّ رَبَّكَ لَهُوَ ٱلْعَزِيزُ ٱلرَّحِيمُ ﴿١٧٥﴾

176. The dwellers of Al-Aikah [near Madyan (Midian)] belied the Messengers.

كَذَّبَ أَصۡحَٰبُ لۡئَيۡكَةِ لۡمُرۡسَلِينَ ﴿١٧٦﴾

177. When Shu'aib said to them: "Will you not fear Allâh (and obey Him)?

إِذۡ قَالَ لَهُمۡ شُعَيۡبٌ أَلَا تَتَّقُونَ ﴿١٧٧﴾

178. "I am a trustworthy Messenger to you.

إِنِّى لَكُمۡ رَسُولٌ أَمِينٌ ﴿١٧٨﴾

179. "So fear Allâh, keep your duty to Him, and obey me.

فَٱتَّقُوا۟ ٱللَّهَ وَأَطِيعُونِ ﴿١٧٩﴾

180. "No reward do I ask of you for it (my Message of Islâmic Monotheism); my reward is only from the Lord of the 'Âlamîn (mankind, jinn and all that exists).

وَمَآ أَسۡـَٔلُكُمۡ عَلَيۡهِ مِنۡ أَجۡرٍ إِنۡ أَجۡرِىَ إِلَّا عَلَىٰ رَبِّ ٱلۡعَٰلَمِينَ ﴿١٨٠﴾

181. "Give full measure, and cause no loss (to others).

۞ أَوۡفُوا۟ ٱلۡكَيۡلَ وَلَا تَكُونُوا۟ مِنَ ٱلۡمُخۡسِرِينَ ﴿١٨١﴾

182. "And weigh with the true and straight balance.

وَزِنُوا۟ بِٱلۡقِسۡطَاسِ ٱلۡمُسۡتَقِيمِ ﴿١٨٢﴾

183. "And defraud not people by reducing their things, nor do evil, making corruption and mischief in the land.

وَلَا تَبۡخَسُوا۟ ٱلنَّاسَ أَشۡيَآءَهُمۡ وَلَا تَعۡثَوۡا۟ فِى ٱلۡأَرۡضِ مُفۡسِدِينَ ﴿١٨٣﴾

184. "And fear Him Who created you and the generations of the men of old."

وَٱتَّقُوا۟ ٱلَّذِى خَلَقَكُمۡ وَٱلۡجِبِلَّةَ ٱلۡأَوَّلِينَ ﴿١٨٤﴾

185. They said: "You are only one of those bewitched!

قَالُوٓا۟ إِنَّمَآ أَنتَ مِنَ ٱلۡمُسَحَّرِينَ ﴿١٨٥﴾

186. "You are but a human being like us and verily, we think that you are one of the liars!

وَمَآ أَنتَ إِلَّا بَشَرٌ مِّثۡلُنَا وَإِن نَّظُنُّكَ لَمِنَ ٱلۡكَٰذِبِينَ ﴿١٨٦﴾

187. "So cause a piece of the heaven to fall on us, if you are of the truthful!"

فَأَسۡقِطۡ عَلَيۡنَا كِسَفًا مِّنَ ٱلسَّمَآءِ إِن كُنتَ مِنَ ٱلصَّٰدِقِينَ ﴿١٨٧﴾

188. He said: "My Lord is the Best Knower of what you do."

قَالَ رَبِّىٓ أَعۡلَمُ بِمَا تَعۡمَلُونَ ﴿١٨٨﴾

189. But they belied him, so the torment of the day of shadow (a gloomy cloud) seized them. Indeed that was the torment of a Great Day.

فَكَذَّبُوهُ فَأَخَذَهُمْ عَذَابُ يَوْمِ الظُّلَّةِ إِنَّهُ كَانَ عَذَابَ يَوْمٍ عَظِيمٍ ﴿١٨٩﴾

190. Verily, in this is indeed a sign, yet most of them are not believers.

إِنَّ فِى ذَٰلِكَ لَآيَةً وَمَا كَانَ أَكْثَرُهُم مُّؤْمِنِينَ ﴿١٩٠﴾

191. And verily, your Lord, He is indeed the All-Mighty, the Most Merciful.

وَإِنَّ رَبَّكَ لَهُوَ الْعَزِيزُ الرَّحِيمُ ﴿١٩١﴾

192. And truly, this (the Qur'ân) is a revelation from the Lord of the 'Âlamîn (mankind, jinn and all that exists),

وَإِنَّهُ لَتَنزِيلُ رَبِّ الْعَالَمِينَ ﴿١٩٢﴾

193. Which the trustworthy Rûḥ [Jibrael (Gabriel)] has brought down

نَزَلَ بِهِ الرُّوحُ الْأَمِينُ ﴿١٩٣﴾

194. Upon your heart (O Muhammad صلى الله عليه وسلم) that you may be (one) of the warners,

عَلَىٰ قَلْبِكَ لِتَكُونَ مِنَ الْمُنذِرِينَ ﴿١٩٤﴾

195. In the plain Arabic language.

بِلِسَانٍ عَرَبِيٍّ مُّبِينٍ ﴿١٩٥﴾

196. And verily, it (the Qur'ân, and its revelation to Prophet Muhammad صلى الله عليه وسلم) is (announced) in the Scriptures [i.e. the Taurât (Torah) and the Injeel (Gospel)] of former people.

وَإِنَّهُ لَفِى زُبُرِ الْأَوَّلِينَ ﴿١٩٦﴾

197. Is it not a sign to them that the learned scholars (like 'Abdullâh bin Salâm رضي الله عنه who embraced Islâm)[1] of the Children of Israel knew it (as true)?

أَوَلَمْ يَكُن لَّهُمْ آيَةً أَن يَعْلَمَهُ عُلَمَاءُ بَنِى إِسْرَائِيلَ ﴿١٩٧﴾

198. And if We had revealed it (this Qur'ân) unto any of the non-Arabs,

وَلَوْ نَزَّلْنَاهُ عَلَىٰ بَعْضِ الْأَعْجَمِينَ ﴿١٩٨﴾

---

[1] (V.26:197) See the footnote of (V.5:66) [The story about 'Abdullâh bin Salâm رضي الله عنه].

199. And he had recited it unto them, they would not have believed in it.

فَقَرَأَهُۥ عَلَيْهِم مَّا كَانُوا مُؤْمِنِينَ ۝

200. Thus have We caused it (the denial of the Qur'ân) to enter the hearts of the *Mujrimûn* (criminals, polytheists, sinners).

كَذَٰلِكَ سَلَكْنَٰهُ فِى قُلُوبِ ٱلْمُجْرِمِينَ ۝

201. They will not believe in it until they see the painful torment.

لَا يُؤْمِنُونَ بِهِۦ حَتَّىٰ يَرَوُا ٱلْعَذَابَ ٱلْأَلِيمَ ۝

202. It shall come to them of a sudden, while they perceive it not.

فَيَأْتِيَهُم بَغْتَةً وَهُمْ لَا يَشْعُرُونَ ۝

203. Then they will say: "Can we be respited?"

فَيَقُولُوا هَلْ نَحْنُ مُنظَرُونَ ۝

204. Would they then wish for Our Torment to be hastened on?

أَفَبِعَذَابِنَا يَسْتَعْجِلُونَ ۝

205. Tell Me, (even) if We do let them enjoy for years,

أَفَرَءَيْتَ إِن مَّتَّعْنَٰهُمْ سِنِينَ ۝

206. And afterwards comes to them that (punishment) which they had been promised,

ثُمَّ جَآءَهُم مَّا كَانُوا يُوعَدُونَ ۝

207. All that with which they used to enjoy shall not avail them.

مَآ أَغْنَىٰ عَنْهُم مَّا كَانُوا يُمَتَّعُونَ ۝

208. And never did We destroy a township but it had its warners

وَمَآ أَهْلَكْنَا مِن قَرْيَةٍ إِلَّا لَهَا مُنذِرُونَ ۝

209. By way of reminder, and We have never been unjust.

ذِكْرَىٰ وَمَا كُنَّا ظَٰلِمِينَ ۝

210. And it is not the *Shayâtîn* (devils) who have brought it (this Qur'ân) down.

وَمَا تَنَزَّلَتْ بِهِ ٱلشَّيَٰطِينُ ۝

211. Neither would it suit them, nor they can (produce it).

وَمَا يَنۢبَغِى لَهُمْ وَمَا يَسْتَطِيعُونَ ۝

212. Verily, they have been removed far from hearing it.

إِنَّهُمْ عَنِ ٱلسَّمْعِ لَمَعْزُولُونَ ۝

213. So invoke not with Allâh another *ilâh* (god) lest you should be among those who receive punishment. فَلَا تَدْعُ مَعَ اللَّهِ إِلَٰهًا ءَاخَرَ فَتَكُونَ مِنَ الْمُعَذَّبِينَ ۝

214. And warn your tribe (O Muhammad صلى الله عليه وسلم) of near kindred.[1] وَأَنذِرْ عَشِيرَتَكَ الْأَقْرَبِينَ ۝

215. And be kind and humble to the believers who follow you. وَاخْفِضْ جَنَاحَكَ لِمَنِ اتَّبَعَكَ مِنَ الْمُؤْمِنِينَ ۝

216. Then if they disobey you, say: "I am innocent of what you do." فَإِنْ عَصَوْكَ فَقُلْ إِنِّي بَرِيٓءٌ مِّمَّا تَعْمَلُونَ ۝

217. And put your trust in the All-Mighty, the Most Merciful, وَتَوَكَّلْ عَلَى الْعَزِيزِ الرَّحِيمِ ۝

218. Who sees you (O Muhammad صلى الله عليه وسلم) when you stand up (alone at night for *Tahajjud* prayers). الَّذِي يَرَاكَ حِينَ تَقُومُ ۝

219. And your movements among those who fall prostrate (to Allâh in the five compulsory congregational prayers). وَتَقَلُّبَكَ فِي السَّاجِدِينَ ۝

220. Verily, He, only He, is the All-Hearer, the All-Knower. إِنَّهُ هُوَ السَّمِيعُ الْعَلِيمُ ۝

---

[1] (V.26:214) Narrated Ibn 'Abbâs رضي الله عنهما: When the Verse: "And warn your tribe (O Muhammad صلى الله عليه وسلم) of near kindred." (V.26:214) was revealed, Allâh's Messenger صلى الله عليه وسلم went out, and when he had ascended As-Safa mountain, he shouted, "*Ya Sabâhâh!*"* The people said, "Who is that?" Then they gathered around him, whereupon he said, "Do you see? If I inform you that cavalrymen are proceeding up the side of this mountain, will you believe me?" They said, "We have never heard you telling a lie." Then he said, "I am a plain warner to you of a coming severe punishment." Abû Lahab said: "May you perish! You gathered us only for this reason?" Then Abû Lahab went away. So *Sûrat Al-Lahab* "Perish the hands of Abu Lahab!" (V.111:1) was revealed. (*Sahih Al-Bukhari*, Vol.6, *Hadîth* No.495).

* "*Ya Sabâhâh!*" is an Arabic expression used when one appeals for help or draws the attention of others to some danger.

221. Shall I inform you (O people!) upon whom the *Shayâtîn* (devils) descend?

222. They descend on every lying, sinful person.

223. Who gives ear (to the devils and they pour what they may have heard of the Unseen from the angels), and most of them are liars.

224. As for the poets, the erring ones follow them,

225. See you not that they speak about every subject (praising people — right or wrong) in their poetry?

226. And that they say what they do not do.

227. Except those who believe (in the Oneness of Allâh — Islâmic Monotheism) and do righteous deeds, and remember Allâh much and vindicate themselves after they have been wronged (by replying back in poetry) to the unjust poetry (which the pagan poets utter against the Muslims). And those who do wrong will come to know by what overturning they will be overturned.

Sûrat An-Naml
(The Ants) XXVII

In the Name of Allâh
the Most Gracious, the Most Merciful

1. *Tâ-Sîn.*

[These letters are one of the miracles of the Qur'ân, and none but Allâh (Alone) knows their meanings]. These are the Verses of the Qur'ân, and (it is) a Book (that makes things) clear:

2. A guide (to the Right Path) and glad tidings for the believers [who believe in the Oneness of Allâh (i.e. Islâmic Monotheism)].

3. Those who perform As-Salât (Iqâmat-as-Salât) and give Zakât and they believe with certainty in the Hereafter (resurrection, recompense of their good and bad deeds, Paradise and Hell).

4. Verily, those who believe not in the Hereafter, We have made their deeds fair-seeming to them, so that they wander about blindly.

5. They are those for whom there will be an evil torment (in this world). And in the Hereafter they will be the greatest losers.

6. And verily, you (O Muhammad صلى الله عليه وسلم) are being taught the Qur'ân from One, All-Wise, All-Knowing.

7. (Remember) when Mûsâ (Moses) said to his household: "Verily, I have seen a fire; I will bring you from there some information, or I will bring you a burning brand, that you may warm yourselves."

8. But when he came to it, he was called: "Blessed is Whosoever is in the fire, and whosoever is round about it! And glorified is Allâh, the Lord of the 'Âlamîn (mankind, jinn and all that exists).

9. "O Mûsâ (Moses)! Verily, it is I, Allâh, the All-Mighty, the All-Wise.

10. "And throw down your stick!" But when he saw it moving as if it were a snake, he turned in flight, and did not look back. (It was said:) "O Mûsâ (Moses)! Fear not: verily, the Messengers fear not in front of Me.

وَأَلْقِ عَصَاكَ فَلَمَّا رَءَاهَا تَهْتَزُّ كَأَنَّهَا جَآنٌّ وَلَّىٰ مُدْبِرًا وَلَمْ يُعَقِّبْ يَٰمُوسَىٰ لَا تَخَفْ إِنِّي لَا يَخَافُ لَدَيَّ ٱلْمُرْسَلُونَ

11. "Except him who has done wrong and afterwards has changed evil for good; then surely, I am Oft-Forgiving, Most Merciful.

إِلَّا مَن ظَلَمَ ثُمَّ بَدَّلَ حُسْنًا بَعْدَ سُوٓءٍ فَإِنِّي غَفُورٌ رَّحِيمٌ ١١

12. "And put your hand into your bosom, it will come forth white without hurt. (These are) among the nine signs (you will take) to Fir'aun (Pharaoh) and his people. Verily, they are a people who are *Fâsiqûn* (rebellious, disobedient to Allâh).

وَأَدْخِلْ يَدَكَ فِي جَيْبِكَ تَخْرُجْ بَيْضَآءَ مِنْ غَيْرِ سُوٓءٍ فِي تِسْعِ ءَايَٰتٍ إِلَىٰ فِرْعَوْنَ وَقَوْمِهِ إِنَّهُمْ كَانُوا قَوْمًا فَٰسِقِينَ ١٢

13. But when Our *Ayât* (proofs, evidences, verses, lessons, signs, revelations, etc.) came to them, clear to see, they said: "This is a manifest magic."

فَلَمَّا جَآءَتْهُمْ ءَايَٰتُنَا مُبْصِرَةً قَالُوا هَٰذَا سِحْرٌ مُّبِينٌ ١٣

14. And they belied them (those *Ayât*) wrongfully and arrogantly, though their ownselves were convinced thereof [i.e. those (*Ayât*) are from Allâh, and Mûsâ (Moses) is the Messenger of Allâh in truth, but they disliked to obey Mûsâ (Moses), and hated to believe in his Message of Monotheism]. So see what was the end of the *Mufsidûn* (disbelievers, disobedient to Allâh, evil-doers and liars).

وَجَحَدُوا بِهَا وَٱسْتَيْقَنَتْهَآ أَنفُسُهُمْ ظُلْمًا وَعُلُوًّا فَٱنظُرْ كَيْفَ كَانَ عَٰقِبَةُ ٱلْمُفْسِدِينَ ١٤

15. And indeed We gave knowledge to Dâwûd (David) and Sulaimân (Solomon), and they both said: "All the praises and thanks are to Allâh, Who

وَلَقَدْ ءَاتَيْنَا دَاوُۥدَ وَسُلَيْمَٰنَ عِلْمًا وَقَالَا ٱلْحَمْدُ لِلَّهِ ٱلَّذِي فَضَّلَنَا

has preferred us above many of His believing slaves!"

16. And Sulaimân (Solomon) inherited (the knowledge of) Dâwûd (David). He said: "O mankind! We have been taught the language of birds, and on us have been bestowed all things. This, verily, is an evident grace (from Allâh)."

17. And there were gathered before Sulaimân (Solomon) his hosts of jinn and men, and birds, and they all were set in battle order (marching forward).

18. Till, when they came to the valley of the ants, one of the ants said: "O ants! Enter your dwellings, lest Sulaimân (Solomon) and his hosts should crush you, while they perceive not."

19. So he [Sulaimân (Solomon)] smiled, amused at her speech[1] and said: "My Lord! Inspire me and bestow upon me the power and ability that I may be grateful for Your Favours which You have bestowed on me and on my parents, and that I may do righteous good deeds that will please You, and admit me by Your Mercy among Your righteous slaves."

20. He inspected the birds, and said: "What is the matter that I see not the hoopoe? Or is he among the absentees?

21. "I will surely, punish him with a severe torment, or slaughter him, unless he brings me a clear reason."

---

[1] (V.27:19) See the footnote of (V.6:143).

22. But the hoopoe stayed not long: he (came up and) said: "I have grasped (the knowledge of a thing) which you have not grasped and I have come to you from Saba' (Sheba) with true news.

فَمَكَثَ غَيْرَ بَعِيدٍ فَقَالَ أَحَطتُ بِمَا لَمْ تُحِطْ بِهِ وَجِئْتُكَ مِن سَبَإٍ بِنَبَإٍ يَقِينٍ ﴿٢٢﴾

23. "I found a woman ruling over them: she has been given all things that could be possessed by any ruler of the earth, and she has a great throne.

إِنِّي وَجَدتُّ امْرَأَةً تَمْلِكُهُمْ وَأُوتِيَتْ مِن كُلِّ شَيْءٍ وَلَهَا عَرْشٌ عَظِيمٌ ﴿٢٣﴾

24. "I found her and her people worshipping the sun instead of Allâh, and *Shaitân* (Satan) has made their deeds fair-seeming to them, and has barred them from (Allâh's) Way: so they have no guidance."

وَجَدتُّهَا وَقَوْمَهَا يَسْجُدُونَ لِلشَّمْسِ مِن دُونِ اللَّهِ وَزَيَّنَ لَهُمُ الشَّيْطَانُ أَعْمَالَهُمْ فَصَدَّهُمْ عَنِ السَّبِيلِ فَهُمْ لَا يَهْتَدُونَ ﴿٢٤﴾

25. [As *Shaitân* (Satan) has barred them from Allâh's Way] so they do not worship (prostrate themselves before) Allâh, Who brings to light what is hidden in the heavens and the earth, and knows what you conceal and what you reveal. [*Tafsir At-Tabarî*]

أَلَّا يَسْجُدُوا لِلَّهِ الَّذِي يُخْرِجُ الْخَبْءَ فِي السَّمَاوَاتِ وَالْأَرْضِ وَيَعْلَمُ مَا تُخْفُونَ وَمَا تُعْلِنُونَ ﴿٢٥﴾

26. Allâh, *Lâ ilâha illa Huwa* (none has the right to be worshipped but He), the Lord of the Supreme Throne!

اللَّهُ لَا إِلَٰهَ إِلَّا هُوَ رَبُّ الْعَرْشِ الْعَظِيمِ ﴿٢٦﴾

27. [Sulaimân (Solomon)] said: "We shall see whether you speak the truth or you are (one) of the liars.

قَالَ سَنَنظُرُ أَصَدَقْتَ أَمْ كُنتَ مِنَ الْكَاذِبِينَ ﴿٢٧﴾

28. "Go you with this letter of mine, and deliver it to them, then draw back from them, and see what (answer) they return."

اذْهَب بِّكِتَابِي هَٰذَا فَأَلْقِهْ إِلَيْهِمْ ثُمَّ تَوَلَّ عَنْهُمْ فَانظُرْ مَاذَا يَرْجِعُونَ ﴿٢٨﴾

29. She said: "O chiefs! Verily, here is delivered to me a noble letter,

قَالَتْ يَا أَيُّهَا الْمَلَأُ إِنِّي أُلْقِيَ إِلَيَّ كِتَابٌ كَرِيمٌ ﴿٢٩﴾

30. "Verily, it is from Sulaimân (Solomon), and verily, it (reads): In the Name of Allâh, the Most Gracious, the Most Merciful:

إِنَّهُ مِن سُلَيْمَنَ وَإِنَّهُ بِسْمِ اللَّهِ الرَّحْمَنِ الرَّحِيمِ

31. "Be you not exalted against me, but come to me as Muslims (true believers who submit to Allâh with full submission)."

أَلَّا تَعْلُوا عَلَيَّ وَأْتُونِي مُسْلِمِينَ

32. She said: "O chiefs! Advise me in (this) case of mine. I decide no case till you are present with me (and give me your opinions)."

قَالَتْ يَأَيُّهَا الْمَلَؤُا أَفْتُونِي فِي أَمْرِي مَا كُنتُ قَاطِعَةً أَمْرًا حَتَّى تَشْهَدُونِ

33. They said: "We have great strength, and great ability for war, but it is for you to command: so think over what you will command."

قَالُوا نَحْنُ أُوْلُوا قُوَّةٍ وَأُوْلُوا بَأْسٍ شَدِيدٍ وَالْأَمْرُ إِلَيْكِ فَانظُرِي مَاذَا تَأْمُرِينَ

34. She said: "Verily, kings, when they enter a town (country), they despoil it and make the most honourable amongst its people the lowest. And thus they do.

قَالَتْ إِنَّ الْمُلُوكَ إِذَا دَخَلُوا قَرْيَةً أَفْسَدُوهَا وَجَعَلُوا أَعِزَّةَ أَهْلِهَا أَذِلَّةً وَكَذَلِكَ يَفْعَلُونَ

35. "But verily, I am going to send him a present, and see with what (answer) the messengers return."

وَإِنِّي مُرْسِلَةٌ إِلَيْهِم بِهَدِيَّةٍ فَنَاظِرَةٌ بِمَ يَرْجِعُ الْمُرْسَلُونَ

36. So when (the messengers with the present) came to Sulaimân (Solomon), he said: "Will you help me in wealth? What Allâh has given me is better than that which He has given you! Nay, you rejoice in your gift!"

فَلَمَّا جَاءَ سُلَيْمَنَ قَالَ أَتُمِدُّونَنِ بِمَالٍ فَمَا ءَاتَنِيَ اللَّهُ خَيْرٌ مِّمَّا ءَاتَاكُم بَلْ أَنتُم بِهَدِيَّتِكُمْ تَفْرَحُونَ

37. [Then Sulaimân (Solomon) said to the chief of her messengers who brought the present]: "Go back to them. We verily, shall come to them with hosts that they cannot resist, and we

ٱرْجِعْ إِلَيْهِمْ فَلَنَأْتِيَنَّهُم بِجُنُودٍ لَّا قِبَلَ لَهُم بِهَا وَلَنُخْرِجَنَّهُم

shall drive them out from there in disgrace, and they will be abased."

منها أذلة وهم صغرون ۝

38. He said: "O chiefs! Which of you can bring me her throne before they come to me surrendering themselves in obedience?"

قال يأيها الملؤا أيكم يأتينى بعرشها قبل أن يأتونى مسلمين ۝

39. A 'Ifrît (strong one) from the jinn said: "I will bring it to you before you rise from your place (council). And verily, I am indeed strong, and trustworthy for such work."

قال عفريت من الجن أنا ءاتيك به قبل أن تقوم من مقامك وإنى عليه لقوى أمين ۝

40. One with whom was knowledge of the Scripture said: "I will bring it to you within the twinkling of an eye!" Then when he [Sulaimân (Solomon)] saw it placed before him, he said: "This is by the Grace of my Lord — to test me whether I am grateful or ungrateful! And whoever is grateful, truly, his gratitude is for (the good of) his ownself; and whoever is ungrateful, (he is ungrateful only for the loss of his ownself). Certainly my Lord is Rich (Free of all needs), Bountiful."

قال الذى عنده علم من الكتب أنا ءاتيك به قبل أن يرتد إليك طرفك فلما رءاه مستقرا عنده قال هذا من فضل ربى ليبلونى ءأشكر أم أكفر ومن شكر فإنما يشكر لنفسه ومن كفر فإن ربى غنى كريم ۝

41. He said: "Disguise her throne for her that we may see whether she will be guided (to recognise her throne), or she will be one of those not guided."

قال نكروا لها عرشها ننظر أتهتدى أم تكون من الذين لا يهتدون ۝

42. So when she came, it was said (to her): "Is your throne like this?" She said: "(It is) as though it were the very same." And [Sulaimân (Solomon)] said: "Knowledge was bestowed on us before her, and we were submitted to Allâh (in Islâm as Muslims before her)."

فلما جاءت قيل أهكذا عرشك قالت كأنه هو وأوتينا العلم من قبلها وكنا مسلمين ۝

43. And that which she used to worship besides Allâh has prevented her (from Islâm), for she was of a disbelieving people.

وَصَدَّهَا مَا كَانَت تَّعبُدُ مِن دُونِ اللَّهِ إِنَّهَا كَانَت مِن قَومٍ كَفِرِينَ ﴿٤٣﴾

44. It was said to her: "Enter *As-Sarh*" (a glass surface with water underneath it or a palace): but when she saw it, she thought it was a pool, and she (tucked up her clothes) uncovering her legs. Sulaimân (Solomon) said: "Verily, it is a *Sarh* (a glass surface with water underneath it or a palace)." She said: "My Lord! Verily, I have wronged myself, and I submit [in Islâm, together with Sulaimân (Solomon)] to Allâh, the Lord of the *'Âlamîn* (mankind, jinn and all that exists)."

قِيلَ لَهَا ادخُلِى الصَّرحَ فَلَمَّا رَأَتهُ حَسِبَتهُ لُجَّةً وَكَشَفَت عَن سَاقَيهَا قَالَ إِنَّهُ صَرحٌ مُّمَرَّدٌ مِّن قَوَارِيرَ قَالَت رَبِّ إِنِّى ظَلَمتُ نَفسِى وَأَسلَمتُ مَعَ سُلَيمَنَ لِلَّهِ رَبِّ العَلَمِينَ ﴿٤٤﴾

45. And indeed We sent to Thamûd their brother Sâlih, saying: "Worship Allâh (Alone and none else)." Then look! They became two parties (believers and disbelievers) quarreling with each other."

وَلَقَد أَرسَلنَا إِلَى ثَمُودَ أَخَاهُم صَلِحًا أَنِ اعبُدُوا اللَّهَ فَإِذَا هُم فَرِيقَانِ يَختَصِمُونَ ﴿٤٥﴾

46. He said: "O my people! Why do you seek to hasten the evil (torment) before the good (Allâh's Mercy)? Why seek you not the Forgiveness of Allâh, that you may receive mercy?"

قَالَ يَقَومِ لِمَ تَستَعجِلُونَ بِالسَّيِّئَةِ قَبلَ الحَسَنَةِ لَولَا تَستَغفِرُونَ اللَّهَ لَعَلَّكُم تُرحَمُونَ ﴿٤٦﴾

47. They said: "We augur ill omen from you and those with you." He said: "Your ill omen is with Allâh; nay, but you are a people that are being tested."

قَالُوا اطَّيَّرنَا بِكَ وَبِمَن مَّعَكَ قَالَ طَئِرُكُم عِندَ اللَّهِ بَل أَنتُم قَومٌ تُفتَنُونَ ﴿٤٧﴾

48. And there were in the city nine men (from the sons of their chiefs), who

وَكَانَ فِى المَدِينَةِ تِسعَةُ رَهطٍ يُفسِدُونَ فِى الأَرضِ وَلَا

made mischief in the land, and would
not reform.

49. They said: "Swear one to another
by Allâh that we shall make a secret
night attack on him and his household,
and thereafter we will surely, say to his
near relatives: 'We witnessed not the
destruction of his household, and
verily, we are telling the truth.'"

50. So they plotted a plot, and We
planned a plan, while they perceived
not.

51. Then see how was the end of
their plot! Verily, We destroyed them
and their nation, all together.

52. These are their houses in utter
ruin, for they did wrong. Verily, in this
is indeed an *Ayâh* (a lesson or a sign)
for people who know.

53. And We saved those who
believed, and used to fear Allâh, and
keep their duty to Him.

54. And (remember) Lût (Lot)! When
he said to his people.[1] Do you commit
Al-Fâhishah (evil, great sin, every kind
of unlawful sexual intercourse,
sodomy) while you see (one another
doing evil without any screen)?"

55. "Do you practise your lusts on
men instead of women? Nay, but you
are a people who behave senselessly."

---

[1] (V.27:54) i.e. the town of Sodom in Palestine - the place where
the Dead Sea is now. (See the book of history by Ibn Kathir 'The
stories of the Prophets'). (كتاب التاريخ لابن كثير)

56. There was no other answer given by his people except that they said: "Drive out the family of Lût (Lot) from your city. Verily, these are men who want to be clean and pure!"

57. So We saved him and his family, except his wife. We destined her to be of those who remained behind.

58. And We rained down on them a rain (of stones). So evil was the rain of those who were warned.

59. Say (O Muhammad صلى الله عليه وسلم) "Praise and thanks are to Allâh, and peace be on His slaves whom He has chosen (for His Message)! Is Allâh better, or (all) that you ascribe as partners (to Him)?" (Of course, Allâh is Better).[1]

---

[1] (V.27:59)

A) Narrated Anas رضي الله عنه: The Prophet صلى الله عليه وسلم said, "Whoever possesses the following three (qualities) will have the sweetness (delight) of Faith:

1) The one to whom Allâh عز وجل and His Messenger (Muhammad صلى الله عليه وسلم) become dearer than anything else.

2) Who loves a person and he loves him only for Allâh's sake.

3) Who hates to revert to *Kufr* (disbelief) as he hates to be thrown into the fire."

(*Sahih Al-Bukhari*, Vol. 1, *Hadith* No. 15)

B) Narrated Abû Hurairah رضي الله عنه: Allâh's Messenger صلى الله عليه وسلم was asked, "What is the best deed?" He replied, "To believe in Allâh عز وجل and His Messenger Muhammad." The questioner then asked, "What is the next (in goodness)?" He replied, "To participate in *Jihâd* (holy fighting) in Allâh's Cause." The questioner again asked, "What is the next (in goodness)?" He replied, "To perform *Hajj* (pilgrimage to Makkah) *Mabrûr* (which is accepted by Allâh and is performed with the intention of seeking Allâh's Pleasures only and not to show-off and without committing any sin, and in accordance with the legal ways of the Prophet صلى الله عليه وسلم)." (*Sahih Al-Bukhari*, Vol. 1, *Hadith* No. 25)

60. Is not He (better than your gods) Who created the heavens and the earth, and sends down for you water (rain) from the sky, whereby We cause to grow wonderful gardens full of beauty and delight? It is not in your ability to cause the growth of their trees. Is there any *ilâh* (god) with Allâh? Nay, but they are a people who ascribe equals (to Him)!

أَمَّنْ خَلَقَ ٱلسَّمَٰوَٰتِ وَٱلْأَرْضَ وَأَنزَلَ لَكُم مِّنَ ٱلسَّمَآءِ مَآءً فَأَنۢبَتْنَا بِهِۦ حَدَآئِقَ ذَاتَ بَهْجَةٍ مَّا كَانَ لَكُمْ أَن تُنۢبِتُوا۟ شَجَرَهَآ أَءِلَٰهٌ مَّعَ ٱللَّهِ بَلْ هُمْ قَوْمٌ يَعْدِلُونَ ٦٠

61. Is not He (better than your gods) Who has made the earth as a fixed abode, and has placed rivers in its midst, and has placed firm mountains therein, and has set a barrier between the two seas (of salt and sweet water)? Is there any *ilâh* (god) with Allâh? Nay, but most of them know not!

أَمَّن جَعَلَ ٱلْأَرْضَ قَرَارًا وَجَعَلَ خِلَٰلَهَآ أَنْهَٰرًا وَجَعَلَ لَهَا رَوَٰسِىَ وَجَعَلَ بَيْنَ ٱلْبَحْرَيْنِ حَاجِزًا أَءِلَٰهٌ مَّعَ ٱللَّهِ بَلْ أَكْثَرُهُمْ لَا يَعْلَمُونَ ٦١

62. Is not He (better than your gods) Who responds to the distressed one, when he calls on Him, and Who removes the evil, and makes you inheritors of the earth, generations after generations? Is there any *ilâh* (god) with Allâh? Little is that you remember!

أَمَّن يُجِيبُ ٱلْمُضْطَرَّ إِذَا دَعَاهُ وَيَكْشِفُ ٱلسُّوٓءَ وَيَجْعَلُكُمْ خُلَفَآءَ ٱلْأَرْضِ أَءِلَٰهٌ مَّعَ ٱللَّهِ قَلِيلًا مَّا تَذَكَّرُونَ ٦٢

63. Is not He (better than your gods) Who guides you in the darkness of the land and the sea, and Who sends the

أَمَّن يَهْدِيكُمْ فِى ظُلُمَٰتِ ٱلْبَرِّ وَٱلْبَحْرِ وَمَن يُرْسِلُ

C) Narrated 'Abdullâh رضى الله عنه: When the following Verse was revealed: "It is those who believe (in the Oneness of Allâh and worship none but Him Alone) and confuse not their belief with *Zulm* (wrong i.e., by worshipping others besides Allâh.)..." (V.6:82), the Companions of Allâh's Messenger صلى الله عليه وسلم said, "Who is amongst us who had not done *Zulm* (wrong)?" Then Allâh تعالى revealed: "Verily, joining others in worship with Allâh is a great *Zulm* (wrong) indeed." (V.31:13) (*Sahih Al-Bukhari*, Vol. 1, *Hadith* No. 31)

winds as heralds of glad tidings, going before His Mercy (rain)? Is there any *ilâh* (god) with Allâh? High Exalted is Allâh above all that they associate as partners (to Him)!

64. Is not He (better than your so-called gods) Who originates creation, and shall thereafter repeat it, and Who provides for you from heaven and earth? Is there any *ilâh* (god) with Allâh? Say: "Bring forth your proofs, if you are truthful."

65. Say: "None in the heavens and the earth knows the *Ghaib* (Unseen) except Allâh, nor can they perceive when they shall be resurrected."

66. Nay, they have no knowledge of the Hereafter. Nay, they are in doubt about it. Nay, they are in complete blindness about it.

67. And those who disbelieve say: "When we have become dust — we and our fathers — shall we really be brought forth (again)?

68. "Indeed we were promised this — we and our forefathers before (us), verily, these are nothing but tales of ancients."

69. Say to them (O Muhammad صلى الله عليه وسلم) "Travel in the land and see how has been the end of the *Mujrimûn* (criminals, those who denied Allâh's Messengers and disobeyed Allâh)."

70. And grieve you not over them, nor be straitened (in distress) because of what they plot.

71. And they (the disbelievers in the Oneness of Allâh) say: "When (will) this promise (be fulfilled), if you are truthful?"

72. Say: "Perhaps that which you wish to hasten on, may be close behind you.

73. "Verily, your Lord is full of Grace for mankind, yet most of them do not give thanks."

74. And verily, your Lord knows what their breasts conceal and what they reveal.

75. And there is nothing hidden in the heaven and the earth but it is in a Clear Book (i.e. Al-Lauh Al-Mahfûz).

76. Verily, this Qur'ân narrates to the Children of Israel most of that in which they differ.

77. And truly, it (this Qur'ân) is a guide and a mercy for the believers.

78. Verily, your Lord will decide between them (various sects) by His Judgement. And He is the All-Mighty, the All-Knowing.

79. So put your trust in Allâh; surely, you (O Muhammad صلى الله عليه وسلم) are on manifest truth.

80. Verily, you cannot make the dead to hear nor can you make the deaf to hear the call (i.e. benefit them and similarly the disbelievers), when they flee, turning their backs.

81. Nor can you lead the blind out of their error. You can only make to hear those who believe in Our *Ayât* (proofs, evidences, verses, lessons, signs, revelations, etc.), and who have submitted (themselves to Allâh in Islâm as Muslims).

82. And when the Word (of torment) is fulfilled against them, We shall bring out from the earth a beast[1] for them, to speak to them because mankind believed not with certainty in Our *Ayât* (Verses of the Qur'ân and Prophet Muhammad صلى الله عليه وسلم).

83. And (remember) the Day when We shall gather out of every nation a troop of those who denied Our *Ayât* (proofs, evidences, verses, lessons, signs, revelations, etc.), and (then) they (all) shall be set in array (gathered and driven to the place of reckoning).

84. Till, when they come (before their Lord at the place of reckoning), He will say: "Did you deny My *Ayât* (proofs, evidences, verses, lessons, signs, revelations, etc.) whereas you comprehended them not by knowledge (of their truth or falsehood), or what (else) was it that you used to do?"

85. And the Word (of torment) will be fulfilled against them, because they have done wrong, and they will be unable to speak (in order to defend themselves).

86. See they not that We have made the night for them to rest therein, and the day sight-giving? Verily, in this are *Ayât* (proofs, evidences, verses, lessons, signs, revelations, etc.) for the people who believe.

---

[1] (V.27:82) See the footnote of (V.6:158).

87. And (remember) the Day on which the Trumpet will be blown — and all who are in the heavens and all who are on the earth, will be terrified except him whom Allâh will (exempt). And all shall come to Him, humbled.

88. And you will see the mountains and think them solid, but they shall pass away as the passing away of the clouds. The Work of Allâh, Who perfected all things, verily, He is Well-Acquainted with what you do.

89. Whoever brings a good deed (i.e. belief in the Oneness of Allâh along with every deed of righteousness), will have better than its worth; and they will be safe from the terror on that Day.

90. And whoever brings an evil deed (i.e. *Shirk* — polytheism, disbelief in the Oneness of Allâh and every evil sinful deed), they will be cast down (prone) on their faces in the Fire. (And it will be said to them) "Are you being recompensed anything except what you used to do?"

91. I (Muhammad صلى الله عليه وسلم) have been commanded only to worship the Lord of this city (Makkah), Who has sanctified it and to Whom belongs everything. And I am commanded to be from among the Muslims (those who submit to Allâh in Islâm).[1]

---

[1] (V.27:91)

a) Narrated Ibn 'Abbâs رضى الله عنهما: On the day of the conquest of Makkah, Allâh's Messenger صلى الله عليه وسلم said: "Allâh has made this town a sanctuary. Its thorny bushes should not be cut, its game

92. And that I should recite the Qur'ân, then whosoever receives guidance, receives it for the good of his ownself; and whosoever goes astray, say (to him): "I am only one of the warners."

وَأَنْ أَتْلُوَا الْقُرْءَانَ فَمَنِ اهْتَدَىٰ فَإِنَّمَا يَهْتَدِى لِنَفْسِهِ وَمَن ضَلَّ فَقُلْ إِنَّمَآ أَنَا۠ مِنَ الْمُنذِرِينَ ۝

93. And say [(O Muhammad صلى الله عليه وسلم) to these polytheists and pagans]: "All the praises and thanks are to Allâh. He will show you His *Ayât* (signs, in yourselves, and in the universe or punishments), and you shall recognise them. And your Lord is not unaware of what you do."

وَقُلِ الْحَمْدُ لِلَّهِ سَيُرِيكُمْ ءَايَـٰتِهِ فَتَعْرِفُونَهَا وَمَا رَبُّكَ بِغَـٰفِلٍ عَمَّا تَعْمَلُونَ ۝

Sûrat Al-Qasas
(The Narration) XXVIII

سُورَةُ الْقَصَصِ

*In the Name of Allâh
the Most Gracious, the Most Merciful*

بِسْمِ اللَّهِ الرَّحْمَـٰنِ الرَّحِيمِ

1. *Tâ-Sîn-Mîm.*

طسٓمٓ ۝

[These letters are one of the miracles of the Qur'ân, and none but Allâh (Alone) knows their meanings]

2. These are the Verses of the manifest Book (that makes clear truth from falsehood, good from evil).

تِلْكَ ءَايَـٰتُ الْكِتَـٰبِ الْمُبِينِ ۝

3. We recite to you some of the news of Mûsâ (Moses) and Fir'aun (Pharaoh) in truth, for a people who believe (in this Qur'ân, and in the Oneness of Allâh).

نَتْلُوا۟ عَلَيْكَ مِن نَّبَإِ مُوسَىٰ وَفِرْعَوْنَ بِالْحَقِّ لِقَوْمٍ يُؤْمِنُونَ ۝

4. Verily, Fir'aun (Pharaoh) exalted himself in the land and made its people

إِنَّ فِرْعَوْنَ عَلَا فِى الْأَرْضِ

---

should not be chased, and its fallen things should not be picked up except by one who would announce it publicly." (*Sahih Al-Bukhari*, Vol.2, *Hadîth* No.657).

b) See the footnote of (V.2:191).

sects, weakening (oppressing) a group (i.e. Children of Israel) among them: killing their sons, and letting their females live. Verily, he was of the *Mufsidûn* (i.e. those who commit great sins and crimes, oppressors, tyrants).

5. And We wished to do a favour to those who were weak (and oppressed) in the land, and to make them rulers and to make them the inheritors,

6. And to establish them in the land, and We let Fir'aun (Pharaoh) and Hâmân and their hosts receive from them that which they feared.

7. And We inspired the mother of Mûsâ (Moses): (telling): "Suckle him [Mûsâ (Moses)], but when you fear for him, then cast him into the river and fear not, nor grieve. Verily, We shall bring him back to you, and shall make him one of (Our) Messengers." [*Tafsir Al-Qurtubi*]

8. Then the household of Fir'aun (Pharaoh) picked him up, that he might become for them an enemy and a (cause of) grief. Verily, Fir'aun (Pharaoh), Hâmân and their hosts were sinners.

9. And the wife of Fir'aun (Pharaoh) said: "A comfort of the eye for me and for you. Kill him not, perhaps he may be of benefit to us, or we may adopt him as a son." And they perceived not (the result of that).

10. And the heart of the mother of Mûsâ (Moses) became empty [from every thought, except the thought of

Mûsâ (Moses)]. She was very near to disclose his (case, i.e. the child is her son), had We not strengthened her heart (with Faith), so that she might remain as one of the believers.

أَن رَّبَطْنَا عَلَىٰ قَلْبِهَا لِتَكُونَ مِنَ ٱلْمُؤْمِنِينَ ﴿

11. And she said to his [Mûsâ's (Moses)] sister: "Follow him." So she (his sister) watched him from a far place secretly, while they perceived not.

وَقَالَتْ لِأُخْتِهِ قُصِّيهِ فَبَصُرَتْ بِهِ عَن جُنُبٍ وَهُمْ لَا يَشْعُرُونَ ﴿١١﴾

12. And We had already forbidden (other) foster suckling mothers for him, until she (his sister came up and) said: "Shall I direct you to a household who will rear him for you, and look after him in a good manner?"

۞ وَحَرَّمْنَا عَلَيْهِ ٱلْمَرَاضِعَ مِن قَبْلُ فَقَالَتْ هَلْ أَدُلُّكُمْ عَلَىٰٓ أَهْلِ بَيْتٍ يَكْفُلُونَهُۥ لَكُمْ وَهُمْ لَهُۥ نَـٰصِحُونَ ﴿١٢﴾

13. So did We restore him to his mother, that her eye might be comforted, and that she might not grieve, and that she might know that the Promise of Allâh is true. But most of them know not.

فَرَدَدْنَـٰهُ إِلَىٰٓ أُمِّهِۦ كَيْ تَقَرَّ عَيْنُهَا وَلَا تَحْزَنَ وَلِتَعْلَمَ أَنَّ وَعْدَ ٱللَّهِ حَقٌّ وَلَـٰكِنَّ أَكْثَرَهُمْ لَا يَعْلَمُونَ ﴿١٣﴾

14. And when he attained his full strength, and was perfect (in manhood), We bestowed on him *Hukman* (Prophethood, and right judgement of the affairs) and religious knowledge [of the religion of his forefathers i.e. Islâmic Monotheism]. And thus do We reward the *Muhsinûn* (i.e. good doers — See the footnote of V.9:120).

وَلَمَّا بَلَغَ أَشُدَّهُۥ وَٱسْتَوَىٰٓ ءَاتَيْنَـٰهُ حُكْمًا وَعِلْمًا وَكَذَٰلِكَ نَجْزِى ٱلْمُحْسِنِينَ ﴿١٤﴾

15. And he entered the city at a time of unawareness of its people: and he found there two men fighting — one of his party (his religion — from the Children of Israel), and the other of his foes. The man of his (own) party asked him for help against his foe, so Mûsâ

وَدَخَلَ ٱلْمَدِينَةَ عَلَىٰ حِينِ غَفْلَةٍ مِّنْ أَهْلِهَا فَوَجَدَ فِيهَا رَجُلَيْنِ يَقْتَتِلَانِ هَـٰذَا مِن شِيعَتِهِۦ وَهَـٰذَا مِنْ عَدُوِّهِۦ فَٱسْتَغَـٰثَهُ ٱلَّذِى مِن شِيعَتِهِۦ عَلَى ٱلَّذِى مِنْ عَدُوِّهِۦ

(Moses) struck him with his fist and killed him. He said: "This is of *Shaitân's* (Satan) doing: verily, he is a plain misleading enemy."

فَوَكَزَهُۥ مُوسَىٰ فَقَضَىٰ عَلَيۡهِ قَالَ هَٰذَا مِنۡ عَمَلِ ٱلشَّيۡطَٰنِ إِنَّهُۥ عَدُوٌّ مُّضِلٌّ مُّبِينٌ ١٥

16. He said: "My Lord! Verily, I have wronged myself, so forgive me." Then He forgave him. Verily, He is the Oft-Forgiving, the Most Merciful.

قَالَ رَبِّ إِنِّي ظَلَمۡتُ نَفۡسِي فَٱغۡفِرۡ لِي فَغَفَرَ لَهُۥٓ إِنَّهُۥ هُوَ ٱلۡغَفُورُ ٱلرَّحِيمُ ١٦

17. He said: "My Lord! For that with which You have favoured me, I will never more be a helper of the *Mujrimûn* (criminals, disbelievers, polytheists, sinners)!"

قَالَ رَبِّ بِمَآ أَنۡعَمۡتَ عَلَيَّ فَلَنۡ أَكُونَ ظَهِيرًا لِّلۡمُجۡرِمِينَ ١٧

18. So he became afraid, looking about in the city (waiting as to what will be the result of his crime of killing), when behold, the man who had sought his help the day before, called for his help (again). Mûsâ (Moses) said to him: "Verily, you are a plain misleader!"

فَأَصۡبَحَ فِي ٱلۡمَدِينَةِ خَآئِفًا يَتَرَقَّبُ فَإِذَا ٱلَّذِي ٱسۡتَنصَرَهُۥ بِٱلۡأَمۡسِ يَسۡتَصۡرِخُهُۥ قَالَ لَهُۥ مُوسَىٰٓ إِنَّكَ لَغَوِيٌّ مُّبِينٌ ١٨

19. Then when he decided to seize the man who was an enemy to both of them, the man said: "O Mûsâ (Moses)! Is it your intention to kill me as you killed a man yesterday? Your aim is nothing but to become a tyrant in the land, and not to be one of those who do right."

فَلَمَّآ أَنۡ أَرَادَ أَن يَبۡطِشَ بِٱلَّذِي هُوَ عَدُوٌّ لَّهُمَا قَالَ يَٰمُوسَىٰٓ أَتُرِيدُ أَن تَقۡتُلَنِي كَمَا قَتَلۡتَ نَفۡسًۢا بِٱلۡأَمۡسِ إِن تُرِيدُ إِلَّآ أَن تَكُونَ جَبَّارًا فِي ٱلۡأَرۡضِ وَمَا تُرِيدُ أَن تَكُونَ مِنَ ٱلۡمُصۡلِحِينَ ١٩

20. And there came a man running, from the farthest end of the city. He said: "O Mûsâ (Moses)! Verily, the chiefs are taking counsel together about you, to kill you, so escape. Truly, I am one of the good advisers to you."

وَجَآءَ رَجُلٌ مِّنۡ أَقۡصَا ٱلۡمَدِينَةِ يَسۡعَىٰ قَالَ يَٰمُوسَىٰٓ إِنَّ ٱلۡمَلَأَ يَأۡتَمِرُونَ بِكَ لِيَقۡتُلُوكَ فَٱخۡرُجۡ إِنِّي لَكَ مِنَ ٱلنَّٰصِحِينَ ٢٠

21. So he escaped from there, looking about in a state of fear. He said: "My

فَخَرَجَ مِنۡهَا خَآئِفًا يَتَرَقَّبُ قَالَ رَبِّ

Lord! Save me from the people who are *Zâlimûn* (polytheists and wrongdoers)!"

22. And when he went towards (the land of) Madyan (Midian), he said: "It may be that my Lord guides me to the Right Way."

23. And when he arrived at the water (a well) of Madyan (Midian) he found there a group of men watering (their flocks), and besides them he found two women who were keeping back (their flocks). He said: "What is the matter with you?" They said: "We cannot water (our flocks) until the shepherds take (their flocks). And our father is a very old man."

24. So he watered (their flocks) for them, then he turned back to shade, and said: "My Lord! Truly, I am in need of whatever good that You bestow on me!"

25. Then there came to him one of the two women, walking shyly. She said: "Verily, my father calls you that he may reward you for having watered (our flocks) for us." So when he came to him and narrated the story, he said: "Fear not. You have escaped from the people who are *Zâlimûn* (polytheists, disbelievers, and wrongdoers)."

26. And said one of them (the two women): "O my father! Hire him! Verily, the best of men for you to hire is the strong, the trustworthy."

27. He said: "I intend to wed one of these two daughters of mine to you, on condition that you serve me for eight years; but if you complete ten years, it will be (a favour) from you. But I intend not to place you under a difficulty. If Allâh wills, you will find me one of the righteous."

28. He [Mûsâ (Moses)] said: "That (is settled) between me and you: whichever of the two terms I fulfil, there will be no injustice to me, and Allâh is Surety over what we say."

29. Then, when Mûsâ (Moses) had fulfilled the term, and was travelling with his family, he saw a fire in the direction of Tûr (Mount). He said to his family: "Wait, I have seen a fire; perhaps I may bring to you from there some information, or a burning fire-brand that you may warm yourselves."

30. So when he reached it (the fire), he was called from the right side of the valley, in the blessed place, from the tree: "O Mûsâ (Moses)! Verily, I am Allâh, the Lord of the *'Âlamîn* (mankind, jinn and all that exists)!

31. "And throw your stick!" But when he saw it moving as if it were a snake, he turned in flight, and looked not back. (It was said): "O Mûsâ (Moses)! Draw near, and fear not. Verily, you are of those who are secure.

32. "Put your hand in your bosom, it will come forth white without a disease; and draw your hand close to your side to be free from the fear (which you suffered from the snake, and also your hand will return to its original state).

These are two Burhân (signs, miracles, evidences, proofs) from your Lord to Fir'aun (Pharaoh) and his chiefs. Verily, they are the people who are Fâsiqûn (rebellious, disobedient to Allâh).

33. He said: "My Lord! I have killed a man among them, and I fear that they will kill me.

34. "And my brother Hârûn (Aaron) — he is more eloquent in speech than me: so send him with me as a helper to confirm that they may belie me."

35. Allâh said: "We will strengthen your arm through your brother, and give you both power, so they shall not be able to harm you: with Our Ayât (proofs, evidences, verses, lessons, signs, revelations, etc.), you two as well as those who follow you will be the victors."

36. Then when Mûsâ (Moses) came to them with Our Clear Ayât (proofs, evidences, verses, lessons, signs, revelations, etc.), they said: "This is nothing but invented magic. Never did we hear of this among our fathers of old."

37. Mûsâ (Moses) said: "My Lord knows best him who came with guidance from Him, and whose will be the happy end in the Hereafter. Verily, the Zâlimûn (wrongdoers, polytheists and disbelievers in the Oneness of Allâh) will not be successful."

38. Fir'aun (Pharaoh) said: "O chiefs! I know not that you have an ilâh (a god) other than me. So kindle for me (a fire), O Hâmân, to bake (bricks out of) clay, and set up for me a *Sarhan* (a lofty tower, or palace) in order that I may look at (or look for) the *Ilâh* (God) of Mûsâ (Moses): and verily, I think that he [Mûsâ (Moses)] is one of the liars.

39. And he and his hosts were arrogant in the land, without right, and they thought that they would never return to Us.

40. So We seized him and his hosts, and We threw them all into the sea (and drowned them). So behold (O Muhammad صلى الله عليه وسلم) what was the end of the *Zâlimûn* [wrongdoers, polytheists and those who disbelieved in the Oneness of their Lord (Allâh), or rejected the advice of His Messenger Mûsâ (Moses) عليه السلام].

41. And We made them leaders inviting to the Fire: and on the Day of Resurrection, they will not be helped.

42. And We made a curse to follow them in this world, and on the Day of Resurrection, they will be among *Al-Maqbuhûn* (those who are prevented from receiving Allâh's Mercy or any good; despised or destroyed).

43. And indeed We gave Mûsâ (Moses) — after We had destroyed the generations of old — the Scripture [the Taurât (Torah)] as an enlightenment for mankind, and a guidance and a mercy, that they might remember (or receive admonition).

44. And you (O Muhammad صلى الله عليه وسلم) were not on the western side (of the Mount), when We made clear to Mûsâ (Moses) the commandment, and you were not among the witnesses.

45. But We created generations [after generations i.e. after Mûsâ (Moses) عليه السلام], and long were the ages that passed over them. And you (O Muhammad صلى الله عليه وسلم) were not a dweller among the people of Madyan (Midian), reciting Our Verses to them. But it is We Who kept sending (Messengers).

46. And you (O Muhammad صلى الله عليه وسلم) were not at the side of the Tûr (Mount) when We did call: [it is said that Allâh called the followers of Muhammad صلى الله عليه وسلم, and they answered His Call, or that Allâh called Mûsâ (Moses)]. But (you are sent) as a mercy from your Lord, to give warning to a people to whom no warner had come before you: in order that they may remember or receive admonition. [Tafsir At-Tabarî].

47. And if (We had) not (sent you to the people of Makkah) — in case a calamity should seize them for (the deeds) that their hands have sent forth, they would have said: "Our Lord! Why did You not send us a Messenger? We would then have followed Your Ayât (Verses of the Qur'ân) and would have been among the believers."

48. But when the truth (i.e. Muhammad صلى الله عليه وسلم with his

Message) has come to them from Us, they say: "Why is he not given the like of what was given to Mûsâ (Moses)? Did they not disbelieve in that which was given to Mûsâ (Moses) of old? They say: "Two kinds of magic [the Taurât (Torah) and the Qur'ân], each helping the other!" And they say: "Verily, in both we are disbelievers."

49. Say (to them, O Muhammad ﷺ): "Then bring a Book from Allâh, which is a better guide than these two [the Taurât (Torah) and the Qur'ân], that I may follow it, if you are truthful."

50. But if they answer you not (i.e. do not bring the Book nor believe in your doctrine of Islâmic Monotheism), then know that they only follow their own lusts. And who is more astray than one who follows his own lusts, without guidance from Allâh? Verily, Allâh guides not the people who are Zâlimûn (wrongdoers, disobedient to Allâh, and polytheists).

51. And indeed now We have conveyed the Word (this Qur'ân in which is the news of everything) to them, in order that they may remember (or receive admonition).

52. Those to whom We gave the Scripture [i.e. the Taurât (Torah) and the Injeel (Gospel)] before it, they believe in it (the Qur'ân).

53. And when it is recited to them, they say: "We believe in it. Verily, it is the truth from our Lord. Indeed even before it we have been from those who submit themselves to Allâh in Islâm as Muslims (like 'Abdullâh bin Salâm and Salmân Al-Fârisî).[1]

54. These will be given their reward twice over,[2] because they are patient, and repel evil with good, and spend (in charity) out of what We have provided them.

55. And when they hear Al-Laghw (dirty, false, evil vain talk), they withdraw from it and say: "To us our deeds, and to you your deeds. Peace be to you. We seek not (the way of) the ignorant."

56. Verily, you (O Muhammad صلى الله عليه وسلم) guide not whom you like, but Allâh guides whom He wills. And He knows best those who are the guided.[3]

---

[1] (V.28:53): See the footnote of (V.5:66).

[2] (V.28:54)

a) Narrated Abû Burdah's father: Allâh's Messenger صلى الله عليه وسلم said, "Any man who has a slave-girl whom he educates properly, teaches good manners, manumits and marries her, will get a double reward. And if any man of the people of the Scriptures (Jews and Christians) believes in his own Prophet and then believes in me (Muhammad صلى الله عليه وسلم) too, he will (also) get a double reward. And any slave who fulfils his duty to his master and to his Lord (Allâh), will (also) get a double reward." (Sahih Al-Bukhari, Vol.7, Hadîth No.20).

b) See the footnote of (V.3:85).

[3] (V.28:56) Narrated Al-Musaiyyâb: When Abû Tâlib was on his deathbed, the Prophet صلى الله عليه وسلم went to him while Abû Jahl was sitting beside him. The Prophet صلى الله عليه وسلم said: "O my uncle! Say: Lâ ilâha illallâh (none has the right to be worshipped but Allâh), an expression with which I will defend your case, before Allâh." Abû

57. And they say: "If we follow the guidance with you, we would be snatched away from our land." Have We not established for them a secure sanctuary (Makkah), to which are brought fruits of all kinds, a provision from Ourselves, but most of them know not.[1]

58. And how many a town (population) have We destroyed, which was thankless for its means of livelihood (disobeyed Allâh, and His Messengers, by doing evil deeds and crimes) ! And those are their dwellings, which have not been inhabited after

وَقَالُوٓاْ إِن نَّتَّبِعِ ٱلۡهُدَىٰ مَعَكَ نُتَخَطَّفۡ مِنۡ أَرۡضِنَآ أَوَلَمۡ نُمَكِّن لَّهُمۡ حَرَمًا ءَامِنًا يُجۡبَىٰٓ إِلَيۡهِ ثَمَرَٰتُ كُلِّ شَيۡءٖ رِّزۡقٗا مِّن لَّدُنَّا وَلَٰكِنَّ أَكۡثَرَهُمۡ لَا يَعۡلَمُونَ ٥٧

وَكَمۡ أَهۡلَكۡنَا مِن قَرۡيَةِۭ بَطِرَتۡ مَعِيشَتَهَاۖ فَتِلۡكَ مَسَٰكِنُهُمۡ لَمۡ تُسۡكَن مِّنۢ بَعۡدِهِمۡ إِلَّا قَلِيلٗاۖ وَكُنَّا نَحۡنُ ٱلۡوَٰرِثِينَ ٥٨

Jahl and 'Abdullâh bin Umaiyah said: "O Abû Tâlib! Will you leave the religion of 'Abdul Muttalib?" So they kept on saying this to him so that the last statement he said to them (before he died) was: "I am on the religion of 'Abdul Muttalib." Then the Prophet صلى الله عليه وسلم said: "I will keep on asking for Allâh's Forgiveness for you unless I am forbidden to do so." Then the following Verse was revealed: "It is not proper for the Prophet and those who believe to ask Allâh's Forgiveness for the *Mushrikûn* (See V.2:105) even though they be of kin, after it has become clear to them that they are the dwellers of the (Hell) Fire (because they died in a state of disbelief)." (V.9:113).

The other Verse was also revealed: "Verily, you (O Muhammad صلى الله عليه وسلم) guide not whom you like, but Allâh guides whom He wills." (V.28:56). (*Sahih Al-Bukhari*, Vol.5, *Hadîth* No.223).
[1] (V.28:57)

a) Narrated Ibn 'Abbâs رضي الله عنهما: On the day of the conquest of Makkah, Allâh's Messenger صلى الله عليه وسلم said: "Allâh has made this town a sanctuary. Its thorny bushes should not be cut, its game should not be chased, and its fallen things should not be picked up except by one who would announce it publicly." (*Sahih Al-Bukhari*, Vol.2, *Hadîth* No.657).

b) See the footnote of (V.2:191).

them except a little. And verily, We have been the inheritors.

59. And never will your Lord destroy the towns (populations) until He sends to their mother town a Messenger reciting to them Our Verses. And never would We destroy the towns unless the people thereof are *Zâlimûn* (polytheists, wrongdoers, disbelievers in the Oneness of Allâh, oppressors and tyrants).

وَمَا كَانَ رَبُّكَ مُهْلِكَ ٱلْقُرَىٰ حَتَّىٰ يَبْعَثَ فِىٓ أُمِّهَا رَسُولًا يَتْلُوا۟ عَلَيْهِمْ ءَايَٰتِنَا ۚ وَمَا كُنَّا مُهْلِكِى ٱلْقُرَىٰٓ إِلَّا وَأَهْلُهَا ظَٰلِمُونَ ٥٩

60. And whatever you have been given is an enjoyment of the life of (this) world and its adornment, and that (Hereafter) which is with Allâh is better and will remain forever. Have you then no sense?

وَمَآ أُوتِيتُم مِّن شَىْءٍ فَمَتَٰعُ ٱلْحَيَوٰةِ ٱلدُّنْيَا وَزِينَتُهَا ۚ وَمَا عِندَ ٱللَّهِ خَيْرٌ وَأَبْقَىٰٓ ۚ أَفَلَا تَعْقِلُونَ ٦٠

61. Is he whom We have promised an excellent promise (Paradise) — which he will find true — like him whom We have made to enjoy the luxuries of the life of (this) world, then on the Day of Resurrection, he will be among those brought up (to be punished in the Hell-fire)?

أَفَمَن وَعَدْنَٰهُ وَعْدًا حَسَنًا فَهُوَ لَٰقِيهِ كَمَن مَّتَّعْنَٰهُ مَتَٰعَ ٱلْحَيَوٰةِ ٱلدُّنْيَا ثُمَّ هُوَ يَوْمَ ٱلْقِيَٰمَةِ مِنَ ٱلْمُحْضَرِينَ ٦١

62. And (remember) the Day when He will call to them and say: "Where are My (so-called) partners whom you used to assert?"

وَيَوْمَ يُنَادِيهِمْ فَيَقُولُ أَيْنَ شُرَكَآءِىَ ٱلَّذِينَ كُنتُمْ تَزْعُمُونَ ٦٢

63. Those about whom the Word will have come true (to be punished) will say: "Our Lord! These are they whom we led astray. We led them astray, as we were astray ourselves. We declare our innocence (from them) before You. It was not us they worshipped."

قَالَ ٱلَّذِينَ حَقَّ عَلَيْهِمُ ٱلْقَوْلُ رَبَّنَا هَٰٓؤُلَآءِ ٱلَّذِينَ أَغْوَيْنَآ أَغْوَيْنَٰهُمْ كَمَا غَوَيْنَا ۖ تَبَرَّأْنَآ إِلَيْكَ ۖ مَا كَانُوٓا۟ إِيَّانَا يَعْبُدُونَ ٦٣

64. And it will be said (to them): "Call upon your (so-called) partners (of Allâh)", and they will call upon them, but they will give no answer to them, and they will see the torment. (They will then wish) if only they had been guided!

65. And (remember) the Day (Allâh) will call to them, and say: "What answer gave you to the Messengers?"

66. Then the news of a good answer will be obscured to them on that day, and they will not be able to ask one another.

67. But as for him who repented (from polytheism and sins), believed (in the Oneness of Allâh, and in His Messenger Muhammad (صلى الله عليه وسلم), and did righteous deeds (in the life of this world), then he will be among those who are successful.

68. And your Lord creates whatsoever He wills and chooses: no choice have they (in any matter). Glorified is Allâh, and exalted above all that they associate (as partners with Him).

69. And your Lord knows what their breasts conceal, and what they reveal.

70. And He is Allâh: Lâ ilâha illa Huwa (none has the right to be worshipped but He), all praises and thanks be to Him (both) in the first (i.e. in this world) and in the last (i.e.in the Hereafter). And for Him is the Decision, and to Him shall you (all) be returned.

71. Say (O Muhammad صلى الله عليه وسلم): "Tell me! If Allâh made the night continuous for you till the Day of Resurrection, which *ilâh* (a god) besides Allâh could bring you light? Will you not then hear?"

قُلْ أَرَءَيْتُمْ إِن جَعَلَ اللَّهُ عَلَيْكُمُ الَّيْلَ سَرْمَدًا إِلَىٰ يَوْمِ الْقِيَـٰمَةِ مَنْ إِلَـٰهٌ غَيْرُ اللَّهِ يَأْتِيكُم بِضِيَآءٍ أَفَلَا تَسْمَعُونَ ﴿٧١﴾

72. Say (O Muhammad صلى الله عليه وسلم): "Tell me! If Allâh made the day continuous for you till the Day of Resurrection, which *ilâh* (a god) besides Allâh could bring you night wherein you rest? Will you not then see?"

قُلْ أَرَءَيْتُمْ إِن جَعَلَ اللَّهُ عَلَيْكُمُ النَّهَارَ سَرْمَدًا إِلَىٰ يَوْمِ الْقِيَـٰمَةِ مَنْ إِلَـٰهٌ غَيْرُ اللَّهِ يَأْتِيكُم بِلَيْلٍ تَسْكُنُونَ فِيهِ أَفَلَا تُبْصِرُونَ ﴿٧٢﴾

73. It is out of His Mercy that He has made for you the night and the day that you may rest therein (i.e. during the night) and that you may seek of His Bounty (i.e. during the day) — and in order that you may be grateful.

وَمِن رَّحْمَتِهِ جَعَلَ لَكُمُ الَّيْلَ وَالنَّهَارَ لِتَسْكُنُوا فِيهِ وَلِتَبْتَغُوا مِن فَضْلِهِ وَلَعَلَّكُمْ تَشْكُرُونَ ﴿٧٣﴾

74. And (remember) the Day when He (your Lord — Allâh) will call to them (those who worshipped others along with Allâh), and will say: "Where are My (so-called) partners, whom you used to assert?"

وَيَوْمَ يُنَادِيهِمْ فَيَقُولُ أَيْنَ شُرَكَآءِىَ الَّذِينَ كُنتُمْ تَزْعُمُونَ ﴿٧٤﴾

75. And We shall take out from every nation a witness, and We shall say: "Bring your proof." Then they shall know that the truth is with Allâh (Alone), and the lies (false gods) which they invented will disappear from them.

وَنَزَعْنَا مِن كُلِّ أُمَّةٍ شَهِيدًا فَقُلْنَا هَاتُوا بُرْهَـٰنَكُمْ فَعَلِمُوا أَنَّ الْحَقَّ لِلَّهِ وَضَلَّ عَنْهُم مَّا كَانُوا يَفْتَرُونَ ﴿٧٥﴾

76. Verily, Qârûn (Korah) was of Mûsâ's (Moses) people, but he behaved arrogantly towards them. And We gave him of the treasures, that of which the keys would have been a burden to a

۞ إِنَّ قَـٰرُونَ كَانَ مِن قَوْمِ مُوسَىٰ فَبَغَىٰ عَلَيْهِمْ وَءَاتَيْنَـٰهُ مِنَ الْكُنُوزِ مَا إِنَّ مَفَاتِحَهُ لَتَنُوٓأُ

body of strong men. **Remember** when his people said to him: "Do not exult (with riches, being ungrateful to Allâh). Verily, Allâh likes not those who exult (with riches, being ungrateful to Allâh).

بِٱلْعُصْبَةِ أُوْلِى ٱلْقُوَّةِ إِذْ قَالَ لَهُۥ قَوْمُهُۥ لَا تَفْرَحْ إِنَّ ٱللَّهَ لَا يُحِبُّ ٱلْفَرِحِينَ ٧٦

77. "But seek, with that (wealth) which Allâh has bestowed on you, the home of the Hereafter, and forget not your portion of lawful enjoyment in this world; and do good as Allâh has been good to you, and seek not mischief in the land. Verily, Allâh likes not the *Mufsidûn* (those who commit great crimes and sins, oppressors, tyrants, mischief-makers, corrupters)."

وَٱبْتَغِ فِيمَآ ءَاتَىٰكَ ٱللَّهُ ٱلدَّارَ ٱلْأَخِرَةَ وَلَا تَنسَ نَصِيبَكَ مِنَ ٱلدُّنْيَا وَأَحْسِن كَمَآ أَحْسَنَ ٱللَّهُ إِلَيْكَ وَلَا تَبْغِ ٱلْفَسَادَ فِى ٱلْأَرْضِ إِنَّ ٱللَّهَ لَا يُحِبُّ ٱلْمُفْسِدِينَ ٧٧

78. He said: "This has been given to me only because of the knowledge I possess." Did he not know that Allâh had destroyed before him generations, men who were stronger than him in might and greater in the amount (of riches) they had collected? But the *Mujrimûn* (criminals, disbelievers, polytheists, sinners) will not be questioned of their sins (because Allâh knows them well, so they will be punished without being called to account).

قَالَ إِنَّمَآ أُوتِيتُهُۥ عَلَىٰ عِلْمٍ عِندِى أَوَلَمْ يَعْلَمْ أَنَّ ٱللَّهَ قَدْ أَهْلَكَ مِن قَبْلِهِۦ مِنَ ٱلْقُرُونِ مَنْ هُوَ أَشَدُّ مِنْهُ قُوَّةً وَأَكْثَرُ جَمْعًا وَلَا يُسْـَٔلُ عَن ذُنُوبِهِمُ ٱلْمُجْرِمُونَ ٧٨

79. So he went forth before his people in his pomp. Those who were desirous of the life of the world said: "Ah, would that we had the like of what Qârûn (Korah) has been given! Verily, he is the owner of a great fortune.

فَخَرَجَ عَلَىٰ قَوْمِهِۦ فِى زِينَتِهِۦ قَالَ ٱلَّذِينَ يُرِيدُونَ ٱلْحَيَوٰةَ ٱلدُّنْيَا يَٰلَيْتَ لَنَا مِثْلَ مَآ أُوتِىَ قَٰرُونُ إِنَّهُۥ لَذُو حَظٍّ عَظِيمٍ ٧٩

80. But those who had been given (religious) knowledge said: "Woe to

وَقَالَ ٱلَّذِينَ أُوتُوا۟ ٱلْعِلْمَ

you! The Reward of Allâh (in the Hereafter) is better for those who believe and do righteous good deeds, and this none shall attain except those who are As-Sâbirûn (the patient in following the truth)."

وَيۡلَكُمۡ ثَوَابُ ٱللَّهِ خَيۡرٌ لِّمَنۡ ءَامَنَ وَعَمِلَ صَٰلِحًا وَلَا يُلَقَّىٰهَآ إِلَّا ٱلصَّٰبِرُونَ

81. So We caused the earth to swallow him[1] and his dwelling place. Then he had no group or party to help him against Allâh, nor was he one of those who could save themselves.

فَخَسَفۡنَا بِهِۦ وَبِدَارِهِ ٱلۡأَرۡضَ فَمَا كَانَ لَهُۥ مِن فِئَةٍ يَنصُرُونَهُۥ مِن دُونِ ٱللَّهِ وَمَا كَانَ مِنَ ٱلۡمُنتَصِرِينَ ٨١

82. And those who had desired (for a position like) his position the day before, began to say: "Know you not that it is Allâh Who enlarges the provision or restricts it to whomsoever He pleases of His slaves. Had it not been that Allâh was Gracious to us, He could have caused the earth to swallow

وَأَصۡبَحَ ٱلَّذِينَ تَمَنَّوۡاْ مَكَانَهُۥ بِٱلۡأَمۡسِ يَقُولُونَ وَيۡكَأَنَّ ٱللَّهَ يَبۡسُطُ ٱلرِّزۡقَ لِمَن يَشَآءُ مِنۡ عِبَادِهِۦ وَيَقۡدِرُ لَوۡلَآ أَن مَّنَّ ٱللَّهُ عَلَيۡنَا لَخَسَفَ بِنَا وَيۡكَأَنَّهُۥ

---

[1] (V.28:81) Chapter 5. Whoever drags his garment out of pride and arrogance (conceit).

a) Narrated Abû Hurairah رضي الله عنه Allâh's Messenger صلى الله عليه وسلم said, "Allâh will not look, on the Day of Resurrection, at a person who drags his *Izâr** (behind him) out of pride and arrogance." [See the footnote of (V.22:9)]

b) Narrated Abu Hurairah رضي الله عنه The Prophet صلى الله عليه وسلم (or Abul-Qâsim صلى الله عليه وسلم) said, "While a man was walking, clad in a two-piece garment and proud of himself with his hair well-combed, suddenly Allâh made him sink into the earth and he will go on sinking into it till the Day of Resurrection."

c) Narrated 'Abdullâh (bin 'Umar رضي الله عنهما): Allâh's Messenger صلى الله عليه وسلم said, "While a man was dragging his *Izâr** on the ground (behind him), suddenly Allâh made him sink into the earth and he will go on sinking into it till the Day of Resurrection." (*Sahih Al-Bukhari*, Vol. 7, Hadith No. 679, 680, 681).

* *Izâr*: Lower-half bodycover.

us up (also)! Know you not that the disbelievers will never be successful.

يُفْلِحُ الْكَفِرُونَ ٨٢

83. That home of the Hereafter (i.e. Paradise), We shall assign to those who rebel not against the truth with pride [1] and oppression in the land nor do mischief by committing crimes. And the good end is for the *Muttaqûn* (the pious and righteous persons. See V.2:2).

تِلْكَ الدَّارُ الْأَخِرَةُ نَجْعَلُهَا لِلَّذِينَ لَا يُرِيدُونَ عُلُوًّا فِى الْأَرْضِ وَلَا فَسَادًا وَالْعَٰقِبَةُ لِلْمُتَّقِينَ ٨٣

84. Whosoever brings good (Islâmic Monotheism along with righteous deeds), he shall have the better thereof; and whosoever brings evil (polytheism along with evil deeds), then those who do evil deeds will only be requited for what they used to do.

مَن جَآءَ بِالْحَسَنَةِ فَلَهُ خَيْرٌ مِّنْهَا وَمَن جَآءَ بِالسَّيِّئَةِ فَلَا يُجْزَى الَّذِينَ عَمِلُوا السَّيِّئَاتِ إِلَّا مَا كَانُوا يَعْمَلُونَ ٨٤

85. Verily, He Who has given you (O Muhammad صلى الله عليه وسلم) the Qur'ân (i.e. ordered you to act on its laws and to preach it to others) will surely, bring you back to *Ma'âd* (place of return, either to Makkah or to Paradise after your death). Say (O Muhammad صلى الله عليه وسلم): "My Lord is Aware of him who brings guidance, and of him who is in manifest error."

إِنَّ الَّذِى فَرَضَ عَلَيْكَ الْقُرْءَانَ لَرَآدُّكَ إِلَىٰ مَعَادٍ قُل رَّبِّى أَعْلَمُ مَن جَآءَ بِالْهُدَىٰ وَمَنْ هُوَ فِى ضَلَٰلٍ مُّبِينٍ ٨٥

86. And you were not expecting that the Book (this Qur'ân) would be sent down to you, but it is a mercy from your Lord. So never be a supporter of the disbelievers.

وَمَا كُنتَ تَرْجُوا أَن يُلْقَىٰ إِلَيْكَ الْكِتَٰبُ إِلَّا رَحْمَةً مِّن رَّبِّكَ فَلَا تَكُونَنَّ ظَهِيرًا لِّلْكَٰفِرِينَ ٨٦

87. And let them not turn you (O Muhammad صلى الله عليه وسلم) away from (preaching) the *Ayât* (revelations and

وَلَا يَصُدُّنَّكَ عَنْ ءَايَٰتِ اللَّهِ

---

[1] (V.28:83) See the footnote of (V.22:9)

verses) of Allâh after they have been sent down to you: and invite (men) to (believe in) your Lord[1] and be not of *Al-Mushrikûn* (those who associate partners with Allâh, e.g. polytheists, pagans, idolaters, and those who disbelieve in the Oneness of Allâh and deny the Prophethood of Messenger Muhammad صلى الله عليه وسلم).

88. And invoke not any other *ilâh* (god) along with Allâh: *Lâ ilâha illa Huwa* (none has the right to be worshipped but He). Everything will perish save His Face. His is the Decision, and to Him you (all) shall be returned.

Sûrat Al-'Ankabût (The Spider) XXIX

In the Name of Allâh the Most Gracious, the Most Merciful

1. *Alif-Lâm-Mîm.*

[These letters are one of the miracles of the Qur'ân, and none but Allâh (Alone) knows their meanings.]

2. Do people think that they will be left alone because they say: "We believe," and will not be tested.

3. And We indeed tested those who were before them. And Allâh will certainly make (it) known (the truth of) those who are true, and will certainly

---

[1] (V.28:87) i.e: in the Oneness (*Tauhîd*) of Allâh — (1) Oneness of the Lordship of Allâh; (2) Oneness of the worship of Allâh; (3) Oneness of the Names and Qualities of Allâh.

make (it) known (the falsehood) those who are liars, (although Allâh knows all that before putting them to test).

4. Or think those who do evil deeds that they can outstrip Us (i.e. escape Our punishment)? Evil is that which they judge!

5. Whoever hopes for the Meeting[1] with Allâh, then Allâh's Term is surely coming, and He is the All-Hearer, the All-Knower.

6. And whosoever strives, he strives only for himself. Verily, Allâh stands not in need of any of the 'Âlamîn (mankind, jinn, and all that exists).

7. Those who believe [in the Oneness of Allâh (Monotheism) and in Messenger Muhammad صلى الله عليه وسلم , and do not give up their Faith because of the harm they receive from the polytheists], and do righteous good deeds, surely, We shall expiate from them their evil deeds and shall reward them according to the best of that which they used to do.[2]

8. And We have enjoined on man to be good and dutiful to his parents; but if they strive to make you join with Me (in worship) anything (as a partner) of which you have no knowledge, then obey them not. Unto Me is your return and I shall tell you what you used to do.

---

[1] (V.29:5) See (V.6:31) and its footnote.

[2] (V.29:7) See the footnote of (V.9:121).

9. And for those who believe (in the Oneness of Allâh and the other articles of Faith)[11] and do righteous good deeds, surely, We shall make them enter with (in the entrance of) the righteous (in Paradise).

وَالَّذِينَ ءَامَنُوا وَعَمِلُوا الصَّلِحَتِ لَنُدْخِلَنَّهُمْ فِى الصَّلِحِينَ ۞

10. Of mankind are some who say: "We believe in Allâh." But if they are made to suffer for the sake of Allâh, they consider the trial of mankind as Allâh's punishment; and if victory comes from your Lord, (the hypocrites) will say: "Verily, we were with you (helping you)." Is not Allâh Best Aware of what is in the breasts of the 'Âlamîn (mankind and jinn).

وَمِنَ النَّاسِ مَن يَقُولُ ءَامَنَّا بِاللَّهِ فَإِذَآ أُوذِىَ فِى اللَّهِ جَعَلَ فِتْنَةَ النَّاسِ كَعَذَابِ اللَّهِ وَلَئِن جَآءَ نَصْرٌ مِّن رَّبِّكَ لَيَقُولُنَّ إِنَّا كُنَّا مَعَكُمْ أَوَلَيْسَ اللَّهُ بِأَعْلَمَ بِمَا فِى صُدُورِ الْعَٰلَمِينَ ۞

11. Verily, Allâh knows those who believe, and verily, He knows the hypocrites [i.e. Allâh will test the people with good and hard days to discriminate the good from the wicked, although Allâh knows all that before putting them to test].

وَلَيَعْلَمَنَّ اللَّهُ الَّذِينَ ءَامَنُوا وَلَيَعْلَمَنَّ الْمُنَٰفِقِينَ ۞

12. And those who disbelieve say to those who believe: "Follow our way and we will verily, bear your sins." Never will they bear anything of their sins. Surely, they are liars.

وَقَالَ الَّذِينَ كَفَرُوا لِلَّذِينَ ءَامَنُوا اتَّبِعُوا سَبِيلَنَا وَلْنَحْمِلْ خَطَٰيَٰكُمْ وَمَا هُم بِحَٰمِلِينَ مِنْ خَطَٰيَٰهُم مِّن شَىْءٍ إِنَّهُمْ لَكَٰذِبُونَ ۞

13. And verily, they shall bear their own loads, and other loads besides their own; and verily, they shall be questioned on the Day of Resurrection about that which they used to fabricate.

وَلَيَحْمِلُنَّ أَثْقَالَهُمْ وَأَثْقَالًا مَّعَ أَثْقَالِهِمْ وَلَيُسْـَٔلُنَّ يَوْمَ الْقِيَٰمَةِ عَمَّا كَانُوا يَفْتَرُونَ ۞

---

[11] (V.29:9) See the footnote (b) of (V.3:85)

14. And indeed We sent Nûh (Noah) to his people, and he stayed among them a thousand years less fifty years [inviting them to believe in the Oneness of Allâh (Monotheism), and discard the false gods and other deities]; and the Deluge overtook them while they were Zâlimûn (wrongdoers, polytheists, disbelievers).

وَلَقَدْ أَرْسَلْنَا نُوحًا إِلَىٰ قَوْمِهِ فَلَبِثَ فِيهِمْ أَلْفَ سَنَةٍ إِلَّا خَمْسِينَ عَامًا فَأَخَذَهُمُ الطُّوفَانُ وَهُمْ ظَالِمُونَ ﴿١٤﴾

15. Then We saved him and those with him in the ship, and made it (the ship) an Ayâh (a lesson, a warning) for the 'Âlamîn (mankind, jinn and all that exists).

فَأَنجَيْنَاهُ وَأَصْحَابَ السَّفِينَةِ وَجَعَلْنَاهَا آيَةً لِّلْعَالَمِينَ ﴿١٥﴾

16. And (remember) Ibrâhîm (Abraham) when he said to his people: "Worship Allâh (Alone), and fear Him: that is better for you if you did but know.

وَإِبْرَاهِيمَ إِذْ قَالَ لِقَوْمِهِ اعْبُدُوا اللَّهَ وَاتَّقُوهُ ذَٰلِكُمْ خَيْرٌ لَّكُمْ إِن كُنتُمْ تَعْلَمُونَ ﴿١٦﴾

17. "You worship besides Allâh only idols, and you only invent falsehood. Verily, those whom you worship besides Allâh have no power to give you provision: so seek your provision from Allâh (Alone), and worship Him (Alone), and be grateful to Him. To Him (Alone) you will be brought back.

إِنَّمَا تَعْبُدُونَ مِن دُونِ اللَّهِ أَوْثَانًا وَتَخْلُقُونَ إِفْكًا إِنَّ الَّذِينَ تَعْبُدُونَ مِن دُونِ اللَّهِ لَا يَمْلِكُونَ لَكُمْ رِزْقًا فَابْتَغُوا عِندَ اللَّهِ الرِّزْقَ وَاعْبُدُوهُ وَاشْكُرُوا لَهُ إِلَيْهِ تُرْجَعُونَ ﴿١٧﴾

18. "And if you deny, then nations before you have denied (their Messengers). And the duty of the Messenger is only to convey (the Message) plainly."

وَإِن تُكَذِّبُوا فَقَدْ كَذَّبَ أُمَمٌ مِّن قَبْلِكُمْ وَمَا عَلَى الرَّسُولِ إِلَّا الْبَلَاغُ الْمُبِينُ ﴿١٨﴾

19. See they not how Allâh originates the creation, then repeats it. Verily, that is easy for Allâh.

أَوَلَمْ يَرَوْا كَيْفَ يُبْدِئُ اللَّهُ الْخَلْقَ ثُمَّ يُعِيدُهُ إِنَّ ذَٰلِكَ عَلَى اللَّهِ يَسِيرٌ ﴿١٩﴾

20. Say: "Travel in the land and see how (Allâh) originated the creation, and then Allâh will bring forth the creation of the Hereafter (i.e. resurrection after death). Verily, Allâh is Able to do all things."

قُلْ سِيرُوا فِي ٱلْأَرْضِ فَٱنظُرُواْ كَيْفَ بَدَأَ ٱلْخَلْقَ ثُمَّ ٱللَّهُ يُنشِئُ ٱلنَّشْأَةَ ٱلْأَخِرَةَ إِنَّ ٱللَّهَ عَلَىٰ كُلِّ شَىْءٍ قَدِيرٌ ۝

21. He punishes whom He wills, and shows mercy to whom He wills; and to Him you will be returned.

يُعَذِّبُ مَن يَشَآءُ وَيَرْحَمُ مَن يَشَآءُ وَإِلَيْهِ تُقْلَبُونَ ۝

22. And you cannot escape in the earth or in the heaven (from Allâh). And besides Allâh you have neither any *Walî* (Protector or Guardian) nor any Helper.

وَمَآ أَنتُم بِمُعْجِزِينَ فِي ٱلْأَرْضِ وَلَا فِي ٱلسَّمَآءِ وَمَا لَكُم مِّن دُونِ ٱللَّهِ مِن وَلِيٍّ وَلَا نَصِيرٍ ۝

23. And those who disbelieve in the *Ayât* (proofs, evidences, verses, lessons, signs, revelations, etc.) of Allâh and the Meeting with Him, it is they who have no hope of My Mercy: and it is they who will have a painful torment.

وَٱلَّذِينَ كَفَرُوا بِـَٔايَٰتِ ٱللَّهِ وَلِقَآئِهِۦٓ أُوْلَٰٓئِكَ يَئِسُوا مِن رَّحْمَتِى وَأُوْلَٰٓئِكَ لَهُمْ عَذَابٌ أَلِيمٌ ۝

24. So nothing was the answer of [Ibrâhîm's (Abraham)] people except that they said: "Kill him or burn him." Then Allâh saved him from the fire. Verily, in this are indeed signs for a people who believe.[1]

فَمَا كَانَ جَوَابَ قَوْمِهِۦٓ إِلَّآ أَن قَالُوا ٱقْتُلُوهُ أَوْ حَرِّقُوهُ فَأَنجَىٰهُ ٱللَّهُ مِنَ ٱلنَّارِ إِنَّ فِي ذَٰلِكَ لَأَيَٰتٍ لِّقَوْمٍ يُؤْمِنُونَ ۝

25. And [Ibrâhîm (Abraham)] said: "You have taken (for worship) idols instead of Allâh. The love between you is only in the life of this world, but on the Day of Resurrection, you shall disown each other, and curse each other, and your abode will be the Fire, and you shall have no helper."

وَقَالَ إِنَّمَا ٱتَّخَذْتُم مِّن دُونِ ٱللَّهِ أَوْثَٰنًا مَّوَدَّةَ بَيْنِكُمْ فِي ٱلْحَيَوٰةِ ٱلدُّنْيَا ثُمَّ يَوْمَ ٱلْقِيَٰمَةِ يَكْفُرُ بَعْضُكُم بِبَعْضٍ وَيَلْعَنُ بَعْضُكُم بَعْضًا وَمَأْوَىٰكُمُ ٱلنَّارُ وَمَا لَكُم مِّن نَّٰصِرِينَ ۝

---

[1] (V.29:24) See the footnote of (V.3:173).

26. So Lût (Lot) believed in him [Ibrâhîm's (Abraham) Message of Islâmic Monotheism]. He [Ibrâhîm (Abraham)] said: "I will emigrate for the sake of my Lord. Verily, He is the All-Mighty, the All-Wise.[1]"

﴾ فَـَٔامَنَ لَهُۥ لُوطٌ وَقَالَ إِنِّى مُهَاجِرٌ إِلَىٰ رَبِّىٓ إِنَّهُۥ هُوَ ٱلْعَزِيزُ ٱلْحَكِيمُ ﴿

27. And We bestowed on him [Ibrâhîm (Abraham)], Ishâq (Isaac) and Ya'qûb (Jacob), and We ordained among his offspring Prophethood and the Book [i.e. the Taurât (Torah) (to Mûsâ — Moses), the Injeel (Gospel) (to 'Îsâ - Jesus), and the Qur'ân (to Muhammad صلى الله عليه وسلم), all from the offspring of Ibrâhîm (Abraham)], and We granted him his reward in this world; and verily, in the Hereafter he is indeed among the righteous.

﴾ وَوَهَبْنَا لَهُۥٓ إِسْحَـٰقَ وَيَعْقُوبَ وَجَعَلْنَا فِى ذُرِّيَّتِهِ ٱلنُّبُوَّةَ وَٱلْكِتَـٰبَ وَءَاتَيْنَـٰهُ أَجْرَهُۥ فِى ٱلدُّنْيَا وَإِنَّهُۥ فِى ٱلْـَٔاخِرَةِ لَمِنَ ٱلصَّـٰلِحِينَ ﴿

28. And (remember) Lût (Lot), when he said to his people: "You commit Al-Fâhishah (sodomy — the worst sin) which none has preceded you in (committing) it in the 'Âlamîn (mankind and jinn)."

﴾ وَلُوطًا إِذْ قَالَ لِقَوْمِهِۦٓ إِنَّكُمْ لَتَأْتُونَ ٱلْفَـٰحِشَةَ مَا سَبَقَكُم بِهَا مِنْ أَحَدٍ مِّنَ ٱلْعَـٰلَمِينَ ﴿

29. "Verily, you practise sodomy with men, and rob the wayfarer (travellers)! And practise Al-Munkar (disbelief and polytheism and every kind of evil wicked deed) in your meetings." But his people gave no answer except that they said: "Bring Allâh's Torment upon us if you are one of the truthful."

﴾ أَئِنَّكُمْ لَتَأْتُونَ ٱلرِّجَالَ وَتَقْطَعُونَ ٱلسَّبِيلَ وَتَأْتُونَ فِى نَادِيكُمُ ٱلْمُنكَرَ فَمَا كَانَ جَوَابَ قَوْمِهِۦٓ إِلَّآ أَن قَالُوا ٱئْتِنَا بِعَذَابِ ٱللَّهِ إِن كُنتَ مِنَ ٱلصَّـٰدِقِينَ ﴿

---

[1] (V.29:26) See the footnote of (V.9:121).

30. He said: "My Lord! Give me victory over the people who are *Mufsidûn* (those who commit great crimes and sins, oppressors, tyrants, mischief-makers, corrupters).

قَالَ رَبِّ ٱنصُرْنِي عَلَى ٱلْقَوْمِ ٱلْمُفْسِدِينَ ۝

31. And when Our messengers came to Ibrâhîm (Abraham) with the glad tidings they said: "Verily, we are going to destroy the people of this [Lût (Lot's)] town (i.e. the town of Sodom in Palestine); truly, its people have been *Zâlimûn* [wrongdoers, polytheists disobedient to Allâh, and belied their Messenger Lût (Lot)]."

وَلَمَّا جَآءَتْ رُسُلُنَآ إِبْرَٰهِيمَ بِٱلْبُشْرَىٰ قَالُوٓاْ إِنَّا مُهْلِكُوٓاْ أَهْلِ هَٰذِهِ ٱلْقَرْيَةِ إِنَّ أَهْلَهَا كَانُواْ ظَٰلِمِينَ ۝

32. Ibrâhîm (Abraham) said: "But there is Lût (Lot) in it." They said: "We know better who is there. We will verily, save him [Lût (Lot)] and his family except his wife: she will be of those who remain behind (i.e. she will be destroyed along with those who will be destroyed from her folk)."

قَالَ إِنَّ فِيهَا لُوطًا قَالُواْ نَحْنُ أَعْلَمُ بِمَن فِيهَا لَنُنَجِّيَنَّهُۥ وَأَهْلَهُۥٓ إِلَّا ٱمْرَأَتَهُۥ كَانَتْ مِنَ ٱلْغَٰبِرِينَ ۝

33. And when Our messengers came to Lût (Lot), he was grieved because of them, and felt straitened on their account. They said: "Have no fear, and do not grieve! Truly, we shall save you and your family except your wife: she will be of those who remain behind (i.e. she will be destroyed along with those who will be destroyed from her folk).

وَلَمَّآ أَن جَآءَتْ رُسُلُنَا لُوطًا سِيٓءَ بِهِمْ وَضَاقَ بِهِمْ ذَرْعًا وَقَالُواْ لَا تَخَفْ وَلَا تَحْزَنْ إِنَّا مُنَجُّوكَ وَأَهْلَكَ إِلَّا ٱمْرَأَتَكَ كَانَتْ مِنَ ٱلْغَٰبِرِينَ ۝

34. "Verily, we are about to bring down on the people of this town a great torment from the sky, because they have been rebellious (against Allâh's Command)."

إِنَّا مُنزِلُونَ عَلَىٰٓ أَهْلِ هَٰذِهِ ٱلْقَرْيَةِ رِجْزًا مِّنَ ٱلسَّمَآءِ بِمَا كَانُواْ يَفْسُقُونَ ۝

35. And indeed We have left thereof an evident *Ayâh* (a lesson and a warning and a sign — the place where the Dead Sea is now in Palestine)[1] for a folk who understand.

وَلَقَد تَّرَكْنَا مِنْهَآ ءَايَةً بَيِّنَةً لِّقَوْمٍ يَعْقِلُونَ ۝

36. And to (the people of) Madyan (Midian), We sent their brother Shu'aib. He said: "O my people! Worship Allâh (Alone) and hope for (the reward of good deeds by worshipping Allâh Alone, on) the last Day (i.e. the Day of Resurrection), and commit no mischief on the earth as *Mufsidûn* (those who commit great crimes, oppressors, tyrants, mischief-makers, corrupters). [*Tafsir At-Tabari*]

وَإِلَىٰ مَدْيَنَ أَخَاهُمْ شُعَيْبًا فَقَالَ يَـٰقَوْمِ اعْبُدُوا اللَّهَ وَارْجُوا الْيَوْمَ الْآخِرَ وَلَا تَعْثَوْا فِى الْأَرْضِ مُفْسِدِينَ ۝

37. And they belied him (Shu'aib); so the earthquake seized them, and they lay (dead), prostrate in their dwellings.

فَكَذَّبُوهُ فَأَخَذَتْهُمُ الرَّجْفَةُ فَأَصْبَحُوا فِى دَارِهِمْ جَـٰثِمِينَ ۝

38. And 'Ad and Thamûd (people)! And indeed (their destruction) is clearly apparent to you from their (ruined) dwellings. *Shaitân* (Satan) made their deeds fair-seeming to them, and turned them away from the (Right) Path, though they were intelligent.

وَعَادًا وَثَمُودَا۟ وَقَد تَّبَيَّنَ لَكُم مِّن مَّسَـٰكِنِهِمْ وَزَيَّنَ لَهُمُ الشَّيْطَـٰنُ أَعْمَـٰلَهُمْ فَصَدَّهُمْ عَنِ السَّبِيلِ وَكَانُوا مُسْتَبْصِرِينَ ۝

39. And (We destroyed also) Qârûn (Korah), Fir'aun (Pharaoh), and Hâmân. And indeed Mûsâ (Moses) came to them with clear *Ayât* (proofs, evidences, verses, lessons, signs, revelations, etc.), but they were

وَقَـٰرُونَ وَفِرْعَوْنَ وَهَـٰمَـٰنَ وَلَقَدْ جَآءَهُم مُّوسَىٰ بِالْبَيِّنَـٰتِ فَاسْتَكْبَرُوا فِى الْأَرْضِ وَمَا كَانُوا سَـٰبِقِينَ ۝

---

[1] (V.29:35) See the book of history كتاب التاريخ لابن كثير "Stories of the Prophets" by Ibn Kathir (رحمه الله).

arrogant in the land, yet they could not outstrip Us (escape Our punishment).

40. So We punished each (of them) for his sins, of them were some on whom We sent *Hâsib* (a violent wind with shower of stones) [as on the people of Lût (Lot)], and of them were some who were overtaken by *As-Saihah* [torment — awful cry, (as Thamûd or Shu'aib's people)], and of them were some whom We caused the earth to swallow [as Qârûn (Korah)], and of them were some whom We drowned [as the people of Nûh (Noah), or Fir'aun (Pharaoh) and his people]. It was not Allâh Who wronged them, but they wronged themselves.

فَكُلًّا أَخَذْنَا بِذَنْبِهِۦ فَمِنْهُم مَّنْ أَرْسَلْنَا عَلَيْهِ حَاصِبًا وَمِنْهُم مَّنْ أَخَذَتْهُ ٱلصَّيْحَةُ وَمِنْهُم مَّنْ خَسَفْنَا بِهِ ٱلْأَرْضَ وَمِنْهُم مَّنْ أَغْرَقْنَا وَمَا كَانَ ٱللَّهُ لِيَظْلِمَهُمْ وَلَـٰكِن كَانُوٓا أَنفُسَهُمْ يَظْلِمُونَ ۝

41. The likeness of those who take (false deities as) *Auliyâ'* (protectors, helpers) other than Allâh is the likeness of a spider who builds (for itself) a house; but verily, the frailest (weakest) of houses is the spider's house — if they but knew.

مَثَلُ ٱلَّذِينَ ٱتَّخَذُوٓا مِن دُونِ ٱللَّهِ أَوْلِيَآءَ كَمَثَلِ ٱلْعَنكَبُوتِ ٱتَّخَذَتْ بَيْتًا وَإِنَّ أَوْهَنَ ٱلْبُيُوتِ لَبَيْتُ ٱلْعَنكَبُوتِ لَوْ كَانُوا يَعْلَمُونَ ۝

42. Verily, Allâh knows what things they invoke instead of Him. He is the All-Mighty, the All-Wise.[1]

إِنَّ ٱللَّهَ يَعْلَمُ مَا يَدْعُونَ مِن دُونِهِۦ مِن شَىْءٍ وَهُوَ ٱلْعَزِيزُ ٱلْحَكِيمُ ۝

43. And these similitudes We put forward for mankind; but none will understand them except those who have knowledge (of Allâh and His Signs).

وَتِلْكَ ٱلْأَمْثَـٰلُ نَضْرِبُهَا لِلنَّاسِ وَمَا يَعْقِلُهَآ إِلَّا ٱلْعَـٰلِمُونَ ۝

---

[1] (V.29:42) See the footnote of (V.2:165).

44. (Allâh says to His Prophet Muhammad (صلى الله عليه وسلم): "Allâh (Alone) created the heavens and the earth with truth (and none shared Him in their creation)." Verily, therein is surely, a sign for those who believe.

45. Recite (O Muhammad صلى الله عليه وسلم) what has been revealed to you of the Book (the Qur'ân), and perform As-Salât (Iqâmât-as-Salât). Verily, As-Salât (the prayer) prevents from Al-Fahshâ' (i.e. great sins of every kind, unlawful sexual intercourse) and Al-Munkar (i.e. disbelief, polytheism, and every kind of evil wicked deed)[1] and the remembering[2] (praising) of (you by) Allâh (in front of the angels) is greater indeed [than your remembering (praising) of Allâh in prayers]. And Allâh knows what you do.

---

[1] (V.29:45) It is said by Ibn 'Abbâs and 'Abdullâh bin Mas'ûd رضي الله عنهم: If the Salât (prayer) of anyone does not prevent him from Al-Fâhshâ' and Al-Munkar (all kinds of evil, illegal and sinful deeds), then his Salât (prayer) increases him in nothing but loss, and to be far away from his Lord (Allâh) [Tafsir Al-Qurtubî].

[2] (V.29:45) See the footnotes of (V.13:28) and also (B) of (V.2:152).

46. And argue not with the people of the Scripture (Jews and Christians), unless it be in (a way) that is better (with good words and in good manner, inviting them to Islâmic Monotheism with His Verses), except with such of them as do wrong; and say (to them): "We believe in that which has been revealed to us and revealed to you; our *Ilâh* (God) and your *Ilâh* (God) is One (i.e. Allâh), and to Him we have submitted (as Muslims)."

وَلَا تُجَـٰدِلُوٓا۟ أَهۡلَ الۡكِتَـٰبِ إِلَّا بِالَّتِى هِىَ أَحۡسَنُ إِلَّا الَّذِينَ ظَلَمُوا۟ مِنۡهُمۡ وَقُولُوٓا۟ ءَامَنَّا بِالَّذِىٓ أُنزِلَ إِلَيۡنَا وَأُنزِلَ إِلَيۡكُمۡ وَإِلَـٰهُنَا وَإِلَـٰهُكُمۡ وَٰحِدٌ وَنَحۡنُ لَهُۥ مُسۡلِمُونَ ۝

47. And thus We have sent down the Book (i.e. this Qur'an) to you (O Muhammad صلى الله عليه وسلم), and those whom We gave the Scripture [the Taurât (Torah) and the Injeel (Gospel) aforetime] believe therein as also do some of these (who are present with you now like 'Abdullâh bin Salâm)[1] and none but the disbelievers reject Our *Ayât* [(proofs, signs, verses, lessons, etc.,) and deny Our Oneness of Lordship and Our Oneness of worship and Our Oneness of Our Names and Qualities: i.e. Islâmic Monotheism].

وَكَذَٰلِكَ أَنزَلۡنَآ إِلَيۡكَ الۡكِتَـٰبَ فَالَّذِينَ ءَاتَيۡنَـٰهُمُ الۡكِتَـٰبَ يُؤۡمِنُونَ بِهِۦ وَمِنۡ هَـٰٓؤُلَآءِ مَن يُؤۡمِنُ بِهِۦ وَمَا يَجۡحَدُ بِـَٔايَـٰتِنَآ إِلَّا الۡكَـٰفِرُونَ ۝

48. Neither did you (O Muhammad صلى الله عليه وسلم) read any book before it (this Qur'an), nor did you write any book (whatsoever) with your right hand. In that case, indeed, the followers of falsehood might have doubted.

وَمَا كُنتَ تَتۡلُوا۟ مِن قَبۡلِهِۦ مِن كِتَـٰبٍ وَلَا تَخُطُّهُۥ بِيَمِينِكَ إِذًا لَّٱرۡتَابَ الۡمُبۡطِلُونَ ۝

49. Nay, but they, the clear *Ayât* [i.e. the description and the qualities of Prophet Muhammad صلى الله عليه وسلم written in the Taurât (Torah) and the Injeel

بَلۡ هُوَ ءَايَـٰتٌ بَيِّنَـٰتٌ فِى صُدُورِ الَّذِينَ أُوتُوا۟ الۡعِلۡمَ وَمَا يَجۡحَدُ بِـَٔايَـٰتِنَآ إِلَّا

---

[1] (V.29:47) See the footnote of (V.5:66).

الظَّـٰلِمُونَ ۞

(Gospel)] are preserved in the breasts of those who have been given knowledge (among the people of the Scriptures). And none but the *Zâlimûn* (polytheists and wrongdoers) deny Our *Ayât* (proofs, evidences, verses, lessons, signs, revelations, etc.).[1]

وَقَالُوا لَوْلَا أُنزِلَ عَلَيْهِ ءَايَتٌ مِّن رَّبِّهِۦ قُلْ إِنَّمَا الْآيَتُ عِندَ اللَّهِ وَإِنَّمَا أَنَا۠ نَذِيرٌ مُّبِينٌ ۞

50. And they say: "Why are not signs sent down to him from his Lord? Say: "The signs are only with Allâh, and I am only a plain warner."

أَوَلَمْ يَكْفِهِمْ أَنَّا أَنزَلْنَا عَلَيْكَ الْكِتَبَ يُتْلَىٰ عَلَيْهِمْ إِنَّ فِي ذَٰلِكَ لَرَحْمَةً وَذِكْرَىٰ لِقَوْمٍ يُؤْمِنُونَ ۞

51. Is it not sufficient for them that We have sent down to you the Book (the Qur'ân) which is recited to them? Verily, herein is mercy and a reminder (or an admonition) for a people who believe.[2]

قُلْ كَفَىٰ بِاللَّهِ بَيْنِي وَبَيْنَكُمْ

52. Say (to them O Muhammad صلى الله عليه وسلم): "Sufficient is Allâh for a

---

[1] (V.29:49) See the footnote of (V.2:76)

[2] (V.29:51)

a) Narrated Abû Hurairah رضي الله عنه: The Prophet صلى الله عليه وسلم said, "Allâh does not allow for anything as He allows to the Prophet to recite the Qur'ân in a nice, loud and pleasant tone." Sufyân said, "This saying means: The Prophet regards the Qur'ân as something that makes him dispense with many worldly pleasures." (*Sahih Al-Bukhari*, Vol.6, *Hadith* No.542.).

b) Narrated Abû Hurairah رضي الله عنه: Allâh's Messenger صلى الله عليه وسلم said, "Not to wish to be the like of except two men: A man whom Allâh has taught the Qur'ân and he recites it during some hours of the night and during some hours of the day, and his neighbour listens to him and says, 'I wish I had been given what has been given to so-and-so, so that I might do what he does'; and a man whom Allâh has given wealth and he spends it (according to what Allâh has ordained) in a just and right manner, whereupon another man may say, 'I wish I had been given what so-and-so has been given, for then I would do what he does.'" (*Sahih Al-Bukhari*, Vol.6, *Hadith* No.544.)

witness between me and you. He knows what is in the heavens and on earth." And those who believe in *Bâtil* (all false deities other than Allâh), and disbelieve in Allâh and (in His Oneness), it is they who are the losers.

53. And they ask you to hasten on the torment (for them): and had it not been for a term appointed, the torment would certainly have come to them. And surely, it will come upon them suddenly while they perceive not!

54. They ask you to hasten on the torment. And verily, Hell, of a surety, will encompass the disbelievers.

55. On the Day when the torment (Hell-fire) shall cover them from above them and from underneath their feet, and it will be said: "Taste what you used to do."

56. O My slaves who believe! Certainly, spacious is My earth. Therefore worship Me." (Alone).[1]

---

[1] (V.29:56) Narrated Mu'âdh رضي الله عنه While I was riding behind the Prophet صلى الله عليه وسلم as a companion rider, he said, "O Mu'âdh!" I replied, "*Labbaik wa Sa'daik* (I respond to your call and I am obedient to your orders)." He repeated this call three times and then said, "Do you know what Allâh's Right on His slaves is?" I replied "No." He said, "Allâh's Right on His slaves is that they should worship Him (Alone) and should not join partners in worship with Him." He proceeded for a while and then said, "O Mu'âdh!" I replied, "*Labbaik wa Sa'daik* (I respond to your call and I am obedient to your orders)." He said, "Do you know what the right of (Allâh's) slaves on Allâh is, if they do that (worship Him Alone and join none in His worship)? It is that He will not punish them." (*Sahih Al-Bukhari*, Vol. 8, *Hadîth* No.283).

57. Everyone shall taste death. Then unto Us you shall be returned.

كُلُّ نَفْسٍ ذَآئِقَةُ ٱلْمَوْتِ ثُمَّ إِلَيْنَا تُرْجَعُونَ ٥

58. And those who believe (in the Oneness of Allâh — Islâmic Monotheism) and do righteous good deeds, to them We shall surely, give lofty dwellings in Paradise, underneath which rivers flow, to live therein forever. Excellent is the reward for the workers.

وَٱلَّذِينَ ءَامَنُوا وَعَمِلُوا ٱلصَّٰلِحَٰتِ لَنُبَوِّئَنَّهُم مِّنَ ٱلْجَنَّةِ غُرَفًا تَجْرِي مِن تَحْتِهَا ٱلْأَنْهَٰرُ خَٰلِدِينَ فِيهَا نِعْمَ أَجْرُ ٱلْعَٰمِلِينَ ٥

59. Those who are patient, and put their trust (only) in their Lord (Allâh).[1]

ٱلَّذِينَ صَبَرُوا وَعَلَىٰ رَبِّهِمْ يَتَوَكَّلُونَ ٥

60. And so many a moving (living) creature carries not its own provision! Allâh provides for it and for you. And He is the All-Hearer, the All-Knower.

وَكَأَيِّن مِّن دَآبَّةٍ لَّا تَحْمِلُ رِزْقَهَا ٱللَّهُ يَرْزُقُهَا وَإِيَّاكُمْ وَهُوَ ٱلسَّمِيعُ ٱلْعَلِيمُ ٥

61. And if you were to ask them: "Who has created the heavens and the earth and subjected the sun and the moon?" they will surely reply: "Allâh." How then are they deviating (as polytheists and disbelievers)?

وَلَئِن سَأَلْتَهُم مَّنْ خَلَقَ ٱلسَّمَٰوَٰتِ وَٱلْأَرْضَ وَسَخَّرَ ٱلشَّمْسَ وَٱلْقَمَرَ لَيَقُولُنَّ ٱللَّهُ فَأَنَّىٰ يُؤْفَكُونَ ٥

62. Allâh enlarges the provision for whom He wills of His slaves, and straitens it for whom (He wills). Verily, Allâh is the All-Knower of everything.

ٱللَّهُ يَبْسُطُ ٱلرِّزْقَ لِمَن يَشَآءُ مِنْ عِبَادِهِۦ وَيَقْدِرُ لَهُۥٓ إِنَّ ٱللَّهَ بِكُلِّ شَيْءٍ عَلِيمٌ ٥

63. And if you were to ask them: "Who sends down water (rain) from the sky, and gives life therewith to the earth after its death?" they will surely reply: "Allâh." Say: "All the praises and thanks are to Allâh!" Nay, most of them have no sense.

وَلَئِن سَأَلْتَهُم مَّن نَّزَّلَ مِنَ ٱلسَّمَآءِ مَآءً فَأَحْيَا بِهِ ٱلْأَرْضَ مِنۢ بَعْدِ مَوْتِهَا لَيَقُولُنَّ ٱللَّهُ قُلِ ٱلْحَمْدُ لِلَّهِ بَلْ أَكْثَرُهُمْ لَا يَعْقِلُونَ ٥

---

[1] (V.29:59) See the footnote (A) of (V.12:67).

64. And this life of the world is only an amusement and a play! Verily, the home of the Hereafter — that is the life indeed (i.e. the eternal life that will never end), if they but knew.[1]

وَمَا هَذِهِ الْحَيَوٰةُ الدُّنْيَا إِلَّا لَهْوٌ وَلَعِبٌ وَإِنَّ الدَّارَ الْآخِرَةَ لَهِيَ الْحَيَوَانُ لَوْ كَانُوا يَعْلَمُونَ ٦٤

65. And when they embark on a ship, they invoke Allâh, making their Faith pure for Him only: but when He brings them safely to land, behold, they give a share of their worship to others.[2]

فَإِذَا رَكِبُوا فِي الْفُلْكِ دَعَوُا اللَّهَ مُخْلِصِينَ لَهُ الدِّينَ فَلَمَّا نَجَّاهُمْ إِلَى الْبَرِّ إِذَا هُمْ يُشْرِكُونَ ٦٥

66. So that they become ingrate for that which We have given them, and that they take their enjoyment (as a warning and a threat), but they will come to know.

لِيَكْفُرُوا بِمَا آتَيْنَاهُمْ وَلِيَتَمَتَّعُوا فَسَوْفَ يَعْلَمُونَ ٦٦

67. Have they not seen that We have made (Makkah) a secure sanctuary, while men are being snatched away from all around them? Then do they believe in *Bâtil* (falsehood — polytheism, idols and all deities other than Allâh), and deny (become ingrate for) the Graces of Allâh?

أَوَلَمْ يَرَوْا أَنَّا جَعَلْنَا حَرَمًا آمِنًا وَيُتَخَطَّفُ النَّاسُ مِنْ حَوْلِهِمْ أَفَبِالْبَاطِلِ يُؤْمِنُونَ وَبِنِعْمَةِ اللَّهِ يَكْفُرُونَ ٦٧

---

[1] (V.29:64) Narrated Abû Hurairah رضي الله عنه : Allâh's Messenger صلى الله عليه وسلم said,"The first group (of people) who will enter Paradise will be (glittering) like the moon on a full-moon night. They will neither spit therein, nor blow their noses therein nor relieve nature. Their utensils therein will be of gold and their combs of gold and silver; in their censers the aloeswood will be used, and their sweat will smell like musk. Everyone of them will have two wives; the marrow of the bones of the wives' legs will be seen through the flesh out of excessive beauty. They (the people of Paradise) will neither have difference, nor enmity (hatred) amongst themselves; their hearts will be as if one heart, and they will be glorifying Allâh in the morning and in the afternoon." (*Sahih Al-Bukhari*, Vol. 4, *Hadîth* No.468).

[2] (V.29:65) See (V.17:67) and its footnote.

68. And who does more wrong than he who invents a lie against Allâh or denies the truth (Muhammad صلى الله عليه وسلم and his doctrine of Islâmic Monotheism and this Qur'ân), when it comes to him? Is there not a dwelling in Hell for disbelievers (in the Oneness of Allâh and in His Messenger Muhammad صلى الله عليه وسلم)?[1]

69. As for those who strive hard in Us (Our Cause), We will surely, guide them to Our Paths (i.e. Allâh's religion — Islâmic Monotheism). And verily, Allâh is with the *Muhsinûn* (good doers)."[2]

Sûrat Ar-Rûm
(The Romans) XXX

In the Name of Allâh the Most Gracious, the Most Merciful

1. *Alif-Lâm-Mîm.*

[These letters are one of the miracles of the Qur'ân, and none but Allâh (Alone) knows their meanings].

2. The Romans have been defeated.

3. In the nearest land (Syria, Iraq, Jordan, and Palestine), and they, after their defeat, will be victorious.

4. Within three to nine years. The decision of the matter, before and after (these events) is only with Allâh, (before the defeat of the Romans by the Persians, and after the defeat of the

---

[1] (V.29:68) See the footnote of (V.3:85).

[2] (V.29:69) See the footnote of (V.9:120).

Persians by the Romans). And on that Day, the believers (i.e. Muslims) will rejoice (at the victory given by Allâh to the Romans against the Persians) —

5. With the help of Allâh. He helps whom He wills, and He is the All-Mighty, the Most Merciful.

6. (It is) a Promise of Allâh (i.e. Allâh will give victory to the Romans against the Persians), and Allâh fails not in His Promise, but most of men know not.

7. They know only the outside appearance of the life of the world (i.e. the matters of their livelihood, like irrigating or sowing or reaping), and they are heedless of the Hereafter.

8. Do they not think deeply (in their ownselves) about themselves (how Allâh created them from nothing, and similarly He will resurrect them)? Allâh has created not the heavens and the earth, and all that is between them, except with truth and for an appointed term. And indeed many of mankind deny the Meeting with their Lord. [See *Tafsir At-Tabarî*, Part 21, Page 24].

9. Do they not travel in the land, and see what was the end of those before them? They were superior to them in strength, and they tilled the earth and populated it in greater numbers than these (pagans) have done: and there came to them their Messengers with clear proofs. Surely, Allâh wronged them not, but they used to wrong themselves.

10. Then evil was the end of those who did evil, because they belied the *Ayât* (proofs, evidences, verses, lessons, signs, revelations, Messengers, etc.) of Allâh and made a mockery of them.

ثُمَّ كَانَ عَـٰقِبَةَ الَّذِينَ أَسَـٰٓـُٔوا السُّوٓأَىٰٓ أَن كَذَّبُوا بِـَٔايَـٰتِ اللَّهِ وَكَانُوا بِهَا يَسْتَهْزِءُونَ ۝

11. Allâh (Alone) originates the creation, then He will repeat it, then to Him you will be returned.

اللَّهُ يَبْدَؤُا الْخَلْقَ ثُمَّ يُعِيدُهُ ثُمَّ إِلَيْهِ تُرْجَعُونَ ۝

12. And on the Day when the Hour will be established, the *Mujrimûn* (disbelievers, sinners, criminals, polytheists) will be plunged into destruction with (deep regrets, sorrows, and) despair.

وَيَوْمَ تَقُومُ السَّاعَةُ يُبْلِسُ الْمُجْرِمُونَ ۝

13. No intercessors will they have from those whom they made equal with Allâh (partners i.e. their so-called associate gods), and they will (themselves) reject and deny their partners.

وَلَمْ يَكُن لَّهُم مِّن شُرَكَائِهِمْ شُفَعَـٰٓؤُا۟ وَكَانُوا بِشُرَكَائِهِمْ كَـٰفِرِينَ ۝

14. And on the Day when the Hour will be established — that Day shall (all men) be separated (i.e. the believers will be separated from the disbelievers).

وَيَوْمَ تَقُومُ السَّاعَةُ يَوْمَئِذٍ يَتَفَرَّقُونَ ۝

15. Then as for those who believed (in the Oneness of Allâh — Islâmic Monotheism) and did righteous good deeds, such shall be honoured and made to enjoy luxurious life (forever) in a Garden of Delight (Paradise).

فَأَمَّا الَّذِينَ ءَامَنُوا وَعَمِلُوا الصَّـٰلِحَـٰتِ فَهُمْ فِى رَوْضَةٍ يُحْبَرُونَ ۝

16. And as for those who disbelieved and belied Our *Ayât* (proofs, evidences, verses, lessons, signs, revelations, Allâh's Messengers, Resurrection, etc.), and the Meeting of the Hereafter, such

وَأَمَّا الَّذِينَ كَفَرُوا وَكَذَّبُوا بِـَٔايَـٰتِنَا وَلِقَآئِ الْـَٔاخِرَةِ فَأُو۟لَـٰٓئِكَ فِى

shall be brought forth to the torment (in the Hell-fire).

17. So glorify Allâh [above all that (evil) they associate with Him (O believers)], when you come up to the evening [i.e. offer the (*Maghrib*) sunset and ('*Ishâ*') night prayers], and when you enter the morning [i.e. offer the (*Fajr*) morning prayer].

18. And His are all the praises and thanks in the heavens and the earth; and (glorify Him) in the afternoon (i.e. offer '*Asr* prayer) and when you come up to the time, when the day begins to decline (i.e offer *Zuhr* prayer). (Ibn 'Abbâs said: "These are the five compulsory congregational prayers mentioned in the Qur'ân.") [*Tafsir At-Tabari*]

19. He brings out the living from the dead, and brings out the dead from the living. And He revives the earth after its death. And thus shall you be brought out (resurrected).

20. And among His Signs is this, that He created you (Adam) from dust, and then [Hawwâ' (Eve) from Adam's rib, and then] his offspring from the semen, and] — behold you are human beings scattered!

21. And among His Signs is this, that He created for you wives from among yourselves, that you may find repose in them, and He has put between you affection and mercy. Verily, in that are indeed signs for a people who reflect.

22. And among His Signs is the creation of the heavens and the earth, and the difference of your languages and colours. Verily, in that are indeed signs for men of sound knowledge.

وَمِنْ ءَايَـٰتِهِۦ خَلْقُ ٱلسَّمَـٰوَٰتِ وَٱلْأَرْضِ وَٱخْتِلَـٰفُ أَلْسِنَتِكُمْ وَأَلْوَٰنِكُمْ إِنَّ فِى ذَٰلِكَ لَـَٔايَـٰتٍ لِّلْعَـٰلِمِينَ ﴿٢٢﴾

23. And among His Signs is your sleep[1] by night and by day, and your seeking of His Bounty. Verily, in that are indeed signs for a people who listen.

وَمِنْ ءَايَـٰتِهِۦ مَنَامُكُم بِٱلَّيْلِ وَٱلنَّهَارِ وَٱبْتِغَآؤُكُم مِّن فَضْلِهِۦٓ إِنَّ فِى ذَٰلِكَ لَـَٔايَـٰتٍ لِّقَوْمٍ يَسْمَعُونَ ﴿٢٣﴾

24. And among His Signs is that He shows you the lightning, for fear and for hope, and He sends down water (rain) from the sky, and therewith revives the earth after its death. Verily, in that are indeed signs for a people who understand.

وَمِنْ ءَايَـٰتِهِۦ يُرِيكُمُ ٱلْبَرْقَ خَوْفًا وَطَمَعًا وَيُنَزِّلُ مِنَ ٱلسَّمَآءِ مَآءً فَيُحْىِۦ بِهِ ٱلْأَرْضَ بَعْدَ مَوْتِهَآ إِنَّ فِى ذَٰلِكَ لَـَٔايَـٰتٍ لِّقَوْمٍ يَعْقِلُونَ ﴿٢٤﴾

25. And among His Signs is that the heaven and the earth stand by His Command. Then afterwards when He will call you by a single call, behold, you will come out from the earth (i.e. from your graves for reckoning and recompense).

وَمِنْ ءَايَـٰتِهِۦٓ أَن تَقُومَ ٱلسَّمَآءُ وَٱلْأَرْضُ بِأَمْرِهِۦ ثُمَّ إِذَا دَعَاكُمْ دَعْوَةً مِّنَ ٱلْأَرْضِ إِذَآ أَنتُمْ تَخْرُجُونَ ﴿٢٥﴾

26. To Him belongs whatever is in the heavens and the earth. All are obedient to Him.

وَلَهُۥ مَن فِى ٱلسَّمَـٰوَٰتِ وَٱلْأَرْضِ كُلٌّ لَّهُۥ قَـٰنِتُونَ ﴿٢٦﴾

27. And He it is Who originates the creation, then He will repeat it (after it has been perished); and this is easier for

وَهُوَ ٱلَّذِى يَبْدَؤُا۟ ٱلْخَلْقَ ثُمَّ

---

[1] (V.30:23) It is a sign from among the Signs of Allâh that a person goes to sleep; the medical world up to now does not know exactly why a person goes to sleep. There are only theories. So this Qur'ân is a miracle from Allâh, and not an invented tale as the disbelievers (in the Oneness of Allâh) argue.

Him. His is the highest description (i.e. none has the right to be worshipped but He, and there is nothing comparable unto Him) in the heavens and in the earth. And He is the All-Mighty, the All-Wise.

28. He sets forth for you a parable from your ownselves: Do you have partners among those whom your right hands possess (i.e. your slaves) to share as equals in the wealth We have bestowed on you whom you fear as you fear each other? Thus do We explain the signs in detail to a people who have sense.[1]

29. Nay, but those who do wrong follow their own lusts without knowledge. Then who will guide him whom Allâh has sent astray? And for such there will be no helpers.

30. So set you (O Muhammad صلى الله عليه وسلم) your face towards the religion (of pure Islâmic Monotheism) *Hanîf* (worship none but Allâh Alone). Allâh's *Fitrah* (i.e. Allâh's Islâmic Monotheism) with which He has created mankind. No change let there be in *Khalq-illâh* (i.e. the religion of Allâh — Islâmic Monotheism): that is the straight religion, but most of men know not.[2] [Tafsîr At-Tabarî]

---

[1] (V.30:28) That is: How do you join to Us partners of that which We created, while you for yourselves will not accept partners from your slaves?.

[2] (V.30:30) See the footnote of (V.10:19).

31. (And remain always) turning in repentance to Him (only), and be afraid and dutiful to Him; and perform *As-Salât (Iqâmat-as-Salât)* and be not of *Al-Mushrikûn* (the polytheists, idolaters, disbelievers in the Oneness of Allâh).

مُنِيبِينَ إِلَيْهِ وَٱتَّقُوهُ وَأَقِيمُوا۟ ٱلصَّلَوٰةَ وَلَا تَكُونُوا۟ مِنَ ٱلْمُشْرِكِينَ ٣١

32. Of those who split up their religion (i.e. who left the true Islâmic Monotheism), and became sects, [i.e. they invented new things in the religion (*Bid'ah*), and followed their vain desires], each sect rejoicing in that which is with it.[1]

مِنَ ٱلَّذِينَ فَرَّقُوا۟ دِينَهُمْ وَكَانُوا۟ شِيَعًا ۖ كُلُّ حِزْبٍۭ بِمَا لَدَيْهِمْ فَرِحُونَ ٣٢

33. And when harm touches men, they cry sincerely only to their Lord (Allâh), turning to Him in repentance; but when He gives them a taste of His Mercy, behold, a party of them associates partners in worship with their Lord.

وَإِذَا مَسَّ ٱلنَّاسَ ضُرٌّ دَعَوْا۟ رَبَّهُم مُّنِيبِينَ إِلَيْهِ ثُمَّ إِذَآ أَذَاقَهُم مِّنْهُ رَحْمَةً إِذَا فَرِيقٌ مِّنْهُم بِرَبِّهِمْ يُشْرِكُونَ ٣٣

34. So as to be ungrateful for the graces which We have bestowed on them. Then enjoy (your short life); but you will come to know.

لِيَكْفُرُوا۟ بِمَآ ءَاتَيْنَٰهُمْ ۚ فَتَمَتَّعُوا۟ فَسَوْفَ تَعْلَمُونَ ٣٤

35. Or have We revealed to them an authority (a Scripture), which speaks of that which they have been associating with Him?

أَمْ أَنزَلْنَا عَلَيْهِمْ سُلْطَٰنًا فَهُوَ يَتَكَلَّمُ بِمَا كَانُوا۟ بِهِۦ يُشْرِكُونَ ٣٥

36. And when We cause mankind to taste of mercy, they rejoice therein; but when some evil afflicts them because of (evil deeds and sins) that their (own)

وَإِذَآ أَذَقْنَا ٱلنَّاسَ رَحْمَةً فَرِحُوا۟ بِهَا ۖ وَإِن تُصِبْهُمْ سَيِّئَةٌۢ بِمَا

---

[1] (V.30:32) See the footnote of (V.3:103).

hands have sent forth, behold, they are in despair!

37. Do they not see that Allâh enlarges the provision for whom He wills and straitens (it for whom He wills). Verily, in that are indeed signs for a people who believe.

38. So give to the kindred his due, and to Al-Miskîn (the poor) and to the wayfarer. That is best for those who seek Allâh's Countenance; and it is they who will be successful.

39. And that which you give in gift[1] (to others), in order that it may increase (your wealth by expecting to get a better one in return) from other people's property, has no increase with Allâh; but that which you give in Zakât seeking Allâh's Countenance, then those they shall have manifold increase.

40. Allâh is He Who created you, then provided food for you, then will cause you to die, then (again) He will give you life (on the Day of Resurrection). Is there any of your (so-called) partners (of Allâh) that do anything of that? Glory is to Him! And Exalted is He above all that (evil) they associate (with Him).

41. Evil (sins and disobedience to Allâh) has appeared on land and sea because of what the hands of men have earned (by oppression and evil deeds),

---

[1] (V.30:39) See *Tafsîr Ibn Kathîr*.

that He (Allâh) may make them taste a part of that which they have done, in order that they may return (by repenting to Allâh, and begging His Pardon).

42. Say (O Muhammad صلى الله عليه وسلم): "Travel in the land and see what was the end of those before (you)! Most of them were *Mushrikûn* (polytheists, idolaters, disbelievers in the Oneness of Allâh)."

43. So set you (O Muhammad صلى الله عليه وسلم) your face (in obedience to Allâh, your Lord) to the straight and right religion (Islâmic Monotheism), before there comes from Allâh a Day which none can avert. On that Day men shall be divided [(in two groups), a group in Paradise and a group in Hell].

44. Whosoever disbelieves will suffer from his disbelief, and whosoever does righteous good deeds (by practising Islâmic Monotheism), then such will prepare a good place (in Paradise) for themselves (and will be saved by Allâh from His Torment).

45. That He may reward those who believe (in the Oneness of Allâh — Islâmic Monotheism), and do righteous good deeds, out of His Bounty. Verily, He likes not the disbelievers.

46. And among His Signs is this, that He sends the winds as glad tidings, giving you a taste of His Mercy (i.e. rain), and that the ships may sail at His Command, and that you may seek of His Bounty, in order that you may be thankful.

47. And indeed We did send Messengers before you (O Muhammad صلى الله عليه وسلم) to their own peoples. They came to them with clear proofs, then, We took vengeance on those who committed crimes (disbelief, setting partners in worship with Allâh, sins); and (as for) the believers, it was incumbent upon Us to help (them).

وَلَقَدْ أَرْسَلْنَا مِن قَبْلِكَ رُسُلًا إِلَىٰ قَوْمِهِمْ فَجَآءُوهُم بِالْبَيِّنَـٰتِ فَانتَقَمْنَا مِنَ الَّذِينَ أَجْرَمُوا ۖ وَكَانَ حَقًّا عَلَيْنَا نَصْرُ الْمُؤْمِنِينَ ٤٧

48. Allâh is He Who sends the winds, so that they raise clouds, and spread them along the sky as He wills, and then break them into fragments, until you see rain drops come forth from their midst! Then when He has made them fall on whom of His slaves as He wills, lo, they rejoice!

اللَّهُ الَّذِي يُرْسِلُ الرِّيَاحَ فَتُثِيرُ سَحَابًا فَيَبْسُطُهُ فِى السَّمَاءِ كَيْفَ يَشَاءُ وَيَجْعَلُهُ كِسَفًا فَتَرَى الْوَدْقَ يَخْرُجُ مِنْ خِلَالِهِ ۖ فَإِذَا أَصَابَ بِهِ مَن يَشَاءُ مِنْ عِبَادِهِ إِذَا هُمْ يَسْتَبْشِرُونَ ٤٨

49. And verily, before that (rain) — just before it was sent down upon them — they were in despair!

وَإِن كَانُوا مِن قَبْلِ أَن يُنَزَّلَ عَلَيْهِم مِّن قَبْلِهِ لَمُبْلِسِينَ ٤٩

50. Look then at the effects (results) of Allâh's Mercy: how He revives the earth after its death. Verily, that (Allâh) (Who revived the earth after its death) shall indeed raise the dead (on the Day of Resurrection), and He is Able to do all things.

فَانظُرْ إِلَىٰ آثَارِ رَحْمَتِ اللَّهِ كَيْفَ يُحْيِ الْأَرْضَ بَعْدَ مَوْتِهَا ۚ إِنَّ ذَٰلِكَ لَمُحْيِ الْمَوْتَىٰ ۖ وَهُوَ عَلَىٰ كُلِّ شَيْءٍ قَدِيرٌ ٥٠

51. And if We send a wind [which would spoil the green growth (tilth) brought up by the previous rain], and they see (their tilth) turn yellow — behold, they then (after their being glad), would become unthankful (to their Lord Allâh as) disbelievers.
[Tafsir At-Tabari]

وَلَئِنْ أَرْسَلْنَا رِيحًا فَرَأَوْهُ مُصْفَرًّا لَّظَلُّوا مِنۢ بَعْدِهِ يَكْفُرُونَ ٥١

52. So verily, you (O Muhammad صلى الله عليه وسلم) cannot make the dead to hear (i.e. the disbelievers), nor can you make the deaf to hear the call, when they show their backs and turn away.

فَإِنَّكَ لَا تُسْمِعُ الْمَوْتَىٰ وَلَا تُسْمِعُ الصُّمَّ الدُّعَآءَ إِذَا وَلَّوْا مُدْبِرِينَ ﴿٥٢﴾

53. And you (O Muhammad صلى الله عليه وسلم) cannot guide the blind from their straying; you can make to hear only those who believe in Our *Ayât* (proofs, evidences, verses, lessons, signs, revelations, etc.), and have submitted to Allâh in Islâm (as Muslims).

وَمَآ أَنتَ بِهَٰدِ الْعُمْىِ عَن ضَلَٰلَتِهِمْ إِن تُسْمِعُ إِلَّا مَن يُؤْمِنُ بِآيَٰتِنَا فَهُم مُّسْلِمُونَ ﴿٥٣﴾

54. Allâh is He Who created you in (a state of) weakness, then gave you strength after weakness, then after strength gave (you) weakness and grey hair. He creates what He wills. And it is He Who is the All-Knowing, the All-Powerful (i.e. Able to do all things).

۞ اللَّهُ الَّذِى خَلَقَكُم مِّن ضَعْفٍ ثُمَّ جَعَلَ مِنۢ بَعْدِ ضَعْفٍ قُوَّةً ثُمَّ جَعَلَ مِنۢ بَعْدِ قُوَّةٍ ضَعْفًا وَشَيْبَةً يَخْلُقُ مَا يَشَآءُ وَهُوَ الْعَلِيمُ الْقَدِيرُ ﴿٥٤﴾

55. And on the Day that the Hour will be established, the *Mujrimûn* (criminals, disbelievers, polytheists, sinners) will swear that they stayed not but an hour — thus were they ever deluded [away from the truth (i.e. they used to tell lies and take false oaths, and turn away from the truth) in this life of the world)].

وَيَوْمَ تَقُومُ السَّاعَةُ يُقْسِمُ الْمُجْرِمُونَ مَا لَبِثُوا غَيْرَ سَاعَةٍ كَذَٰلِكَ كَانُوا يُؤْفَكُونَ ﴿٥٥﴾

56. And those who have been bestowed with knowledge and Faith will say: "Indeed you have stayed according to the Decree of Allâh, until the Day of Resurrection: so this is the Day of Resurrection, but you knew not."

وَقَالَ الَّذِينَ أُوتُوا الْعِلْمَ وَالْإِيمَٰنَ لَقَدْ لَبِثْتُمْ فِى كِتَٰبِ اللَّهِ إِلَىٰ يَوْمِ الْبَعْثِ فَهَٰذَا يَوْمُ الْبَعْثِ وَلَٰكِنَّكُمْ كُنتُمْ لَا تَعْلَمُونَ ﴿٥٦﴾

57. So on that Day no excuse of theirs will avail those who did wrong (by associating partners in worship with

فَيَوْمَئِذٍ لَّا يَنفَعُ الَّذِينَ ظَلَمُوا

Allâh, and by denying the Day of Resurrection), nor will they be allowed (then) to return to seek Allâh's Pleasure (by having Islâmic Faith with righteous deeds and by giving up polytheism, sins and crimes with repentance).

58. And indeed We have set forth for mankind, in this Qur'ân every kind of parable. But if you (O Muhammad الله صلى عليه وسلم) bring to them any sign or proof (as an evidence for the truth of your Prophethood), the disbelievers are sure to say (to the believers): "You follow nothing but falsehood, and magic."

59. Thus does Allâh seal up the hearts of those who know not [the proofs and evidence of the Oneness of Allâh i.e. those who try to understand true facts that which you (Muhammad صلى الله عليه وسلم) have brought to them].

60. So be patient (O Muhammad صلى الله عليه وسلم). Verily, the Promise of Allâh is true; and let not those who have no certainty of faith discourage you from conveying Allâh's Message (which you are obliged to convey).

Sûrat Luqmân
(Luqmân) XXXI

*In the Name of Allâh
the Most Gracious, the Most Merciful*

1. *Alif-Lâm-Mîm.*

[These letters are one of the miracles of the Qur'ân, and none but Allâh (Alone) knows their meanings].

2. These are Verses of the Wise Book (the Qur'ân).

تِلْكَ ءَايَـٰتُ ٱلْكِتَـٰبِ ٱلْحَكِيمِ ۝

3. A guide and a mercy for the *Muhsinûn* (good-doers).[1]

هُدًى وَرَحْمَةً لِّلْمُحْسِنِينَ ۝

4. Those who perform *As-Salât* (Iqamat-as-Salât) and give *Zakât* and they have faith in the Hereafter with certainty.

ٱلَّذِينَ يُقِيمُونَ ٱلصَّلَوٰةَ وَيُؤْتُونَ ٱلزَّكَوٰةَ وَهُم بِٱلْأَخِرَةِ هُمْ يُوقِنُونَ ۝

5. Such are on guidance from their Lord, and such are the successful.

أُوْلَـٰئِكَ عَلَىٰ هُدًى مِّن رَّبِّهِمْ وَأُوْلَـٰئِكَ هُمُ ٱلْمُفْلِحُونَ ۝

6. And of mankind is he who purchases idle talks (i.e. music, singing) to mislead (men) from the Path of Allâh without knowledge, and takes it (the Path of Allâh, or the Verses of the Qur'ân) by way of mockery. For such there will be a humiliating torment (in the Hell-fire).[2]

وَمِنَ ٱلنَّاسِ مَن يَشْتَرِى لَهْوَ ٱلْحَدِيثِ لِيُضِلَّ عَن سَبِيلِ ٱللَّهِ بِغَيْرِ عِلْمٍ وَيَتَّخِذَهَا هُزُوًا أُوْلَـٰئِكَ لَهُمْ عَذَابٌ مُّهِينٌ ۝

7. And when Our Verses (of the Qur'ân) are recited to such a one, he

وَإِذَا تُتْلَىٰ عَلَيْهِ ءَايَـٰتُنَا وَلَّىٰ مُسْتَكْبِرًا كَأَن لَّمْ يَسْمَعْهَا

---

[1] (V.31:3) See the footnote of (V.9:120).

[2] (V.31:6) What is said regarding the one who regards an alcoholic drink lawful to drink, and calls it by another name.

Narrated Abu 'Âmir or Abu Malik Al-Ash'ari that he heard the Prophet صلى الله عليه وسلم saying: "From among my followers there will be some people who will consider illegal sexual intercourse, the wearing of silk, the drinking of alcoholic drinks, and the use of musical instruments as lawful. And (from them), there will be some who will stay near the side of a mountain, and in the evening their shepherd will come to them with their sheep and ask them for something, but they will say to him: 'Return to us tomorrow.' Allâh will destroy them during the night and will let the mountain fall on them, and He will transform the rest of them into monkeys and pigs; and they will remain so till the Day of Resurrection." (*Sahih Al-Bukhari*, Vol. 7, *Hadith* No. 494B)

turns away in pride,[1] as if he heard them not — as if there were deafness in his ear. So announce to him a painful torment.

8. Verily, those who believe (in Islâmic Monotheism) and do righteous good deeds, for them are Gardens of Delight (Paradise).

9. To abide therein. It is a Promise of Allâh in truth. And He is the All-Mighty, the All-Wise.

10. He has created the heavens without any pillars that you see, and has set on the earth firm mountains lest it should shake with you. And He has scattered therein moving (living) creatures of all kinds. And We send down water (rain) from the sky, and We cause (plants) of every goodly kind to grow therein.

11. This is the creation of Allâh. So show Me that which those (whom you worship) besides Him have created. Nay, the Zâlimûn (polytheists, wrongdoers and those who do not believe in the Oneness of Allâh) are in plain error.

12. And indeed We bestowed upon Luqmân Al-Hikmah (wisdom and religious understanding) saying: "Give thanks to Allâh." And whoever gives thanks, he gives thanks for (the good of) his ownself. And whoever is unthankful, then verily, Allâh is All-Rich (Free of all needs), Worthy of all praise.

---

[1] (V.31:7): See the footnote of (V.22:9).

13. And (remember) when Luqmân said to his son when he was advising him: "O my son! Join not in worship others with Allâh. Verily, joining others in worship with Allâh is a great *Zûlm* (wrong) indeed.[1]

وَإِذْ قَالَ لُقْمَنُ لِأَبْنِهِۦ وَهُوَ يَعِظُهُۥ يَبُنَىَّ لَا تُشْرِكْ بِٱللَّهِ إِنَّ ٱلشِّرْكَ لَظُلْمٌ عَظِيمٌ ۝

14. And We have enjoined on man (to be dutiful and good) to his parents. His mother bore him in weakness and hardship upon weakness and hardship, and his weaning is in two years — give thanks to Me and to your parents. Unto Me is the final destination.[2]

وَوَصَّيْنَا ٱلْإِنسَنَ بِوَٰلِدَيْهِ حَمَلَتْهُ أُمُّهُۥ وَهْنًا عَلَىٰ وَهْنٍ وَفِصَلُهُۥ فِى عَامَيْنِ أَنِ ٱشْكُرْ لِى وَلِوَٰلِدَيْكَ إِلَىَّ ٱلْمَصِيرُ ۝

15. But if they (both) strive with you to make you join in worship with Me others that of which you have no knowledge, then obey them not; but behave with them in the world kindly, and follow the path of him who turns to Me in repentance and in obedience. Then to Me will be your return, and I shall tell you what you used to do.

وَإِن جَهَدَاكَ عَلَىٰٓ أَن تُشْرِكَ بِى مَا لَيْسَ لَكَ بِهِۦ عِلْمٌ فَلَا تُطِعْهُمَا وَصَاحِبْهُمَا فِى ٱلدُّنْيَا مَعْرُوفًا وَٱتَّبِعْ سَبِيلَ مَنْ أَنَابَ إِلَىَّ ثُمَّ إِلَىَّ مَرْجِعُكُمْ فَأُنَبِّئُكُم بِمَا كُنتُمْ تَعْمَلُونَ ۝

---

[1] (V.31:13)

a) See the footnote (C) of (V.27:59).

b) See the footnote of (V.2:22).

[2] (V.31:14).

a) See the footnote of (V.17:13).

b) Narrated 'Âishah رضى الله عنها : (that she said), "O Allâh's Messenger! We consider *Jihâd* as the best deed. Should we not fight in Allâh's Cause?" He said, "The best *Jihâd* (for women) is *Hajj-Mabrur* [i.e. *Hajj* (pilgrimage to Makkah) which is performed according to the Prophet's *Sunnah* (legal ways), and is accepted by Allâh]." (See *Sahih Al-Bukhari*, Vol.3, *Hadîth* No.84." and *Sahih Al-Bukhari*, Vol.4, *Hadîth* No.43).

16. "O my son! If it be (anything) equal to the weight of a grain of mustard seed, and though it be in a rock, or in the heavens or in the earth, Allâh will bring it forth. Verily, Allâh is Subtle (in bringing out that grain), Well-Aware (of its place).

بُنَيَّ إِنَّهَآ إِن تَكُ مِثْقَالَ حَبَّةٍ مِّنْ خَرْدَلٍ فَتَكُن فِى صَخْرَةٍ أَوْ فِى ٱلسَّمَٰوَٰتِ أَوْ فِى ٱلْأَرْضِ يَأْتِ بِهَا ٱللَّهُ إِنَّ ٱللَّهَ لَطِيفٌ خَبِيرٌ ۝

17. "O my son! *Aqim-is-Salât* (perform *As-Salât*), enjoin (on people) *Al-Ma'rûf* — (Islâmic Monotheism and all that is good), and forbid (people) from *Al-Munkar* (i.e. disbelief in the Oneness of Allâh, polytheism of all kinds and all that is evil and bad), and bear with patience whatever befalls you. Verily, these are some of the important commandments (ordered by Allâh with no exemption).

بُنَيَّ أَقِمِ ٱلصَّلَوٰةَ وَأْمُرْ بِٱلْمَعْرُوفِ وَٱنْهَ عَنِ ٱلْمُنكَرِ وَٱصْبِرْ عَلَىٰ مَآ أَصَابَكَ إِنَّ ذَٰلِكَ مِنْ عَزْمِ ٱلْأُمُورِ ۝

18. "And turn not your face away from men with pride, nor walk in insolence through the earth. Verily, Allâh likes not any arrogant boaster.[1]

وَلَا تُصَعِّرْ خَدَّكَ لِلنَّاسِ وَلَا تَمْشِ فِى ٱلْأَرْضِ مَرَحًا إِنَّ ٱللَّهَ لَا يُحِبُّ كُلَّ مُخْتَالٍ فَخُورٍ ۝

19. "And be moderate (or show no insolence) in your walking, and lower your voice. Verily, the harshest of all voices is the braying of the ass."

وَٱقْصِدْ فِى مَشْيِكَ وَٱغْضُضْ مِن صَوْتِكَ إِنَّ أَنكَرَ ٱلْأَصْوَٰتِ لَصَوْتُ ٱلْحَمِيرِ ۝

20. See you not (O men) that Allâh has subjected for you whatsoever is in the heavens and whatsoever is in the earth, and has completed and perfected His Graces upon you, (both) apparent (i.e. Islâmic Monotheism, and the lawful pleasures of this world, including health, good looks) and hidden [i.e. one's Faith in Allâh (of

أَلَمْ تَرَوْا أَنَّ ٱللَّهَ سَخَّرَ لَكُم مَّا فِى ٱلسَّمَٰوَٰتِ وَمَا فِى ٱلْأَرْضِ وَأَسْبَغَ عَلَيْكُمْ نِعَمَهُۥ ظَٰهِرَةً وَبَاطِنَةً

---

[1] (V.31:18): See the footnote of (V.22:9).

Islâmic Monotheisrı), knowledge, wisdom, guidance for doing righteous deeds, and also the pleasures and delights of the Hereafter in Paradise]? Yet of mankind is he who disputes about Allâh without knowledge or guidance or a Book giving light!

21. And when it is said to them: "Follow that which Allâh has sent down", they say: "Nay, we shall follow that which we found our fathers (following)." (Would they do so) even if *Shaitân* (Satan) invites them to the torment of the Fire?

22. And whosoever submits his face (himself) to Allâh,[1] while he is a *Muhsin* (good-doer i.e. performs good deeds totally for Allâh's sake without any show off or to gain praise or fame and does them in accordance with the *Sunnah* of Allâh's Messenger Muhammad (صلى الله عليه وسلم), then he has grasped the most trustworthy handhold [*Lâ ilâha illallâh* (none has the right to be worshipped but Allâh)]. And to Allâh return all matters for decision.

23. And whoever disbelieves, let not his disbelief grieve you (O Muhammad صلى الله عليه وسلم). To Us is their return, and We shall inform them what they have done. Verily, Allâh is the All-Knower of what is in the breasts (of men).

---

[1] (V.31:22) His face to Allâh: i.e. follows Allâh's religion of Islâmic Monotheism, worships Allâh (Alone) with sincere Faith in the (1) Oneness of His Lordship, (2) Oneness of His worship, and (3) Oneness of His Names and Qualities.

24. We let them enjoy for a little while, but in the end We shall oblige them to (enter) a great torment.

نُمَتِّعُهُمْ قَلِيلًا ثُمَّ نَضْطَرُّهُمْ إِلَىٰ عَذَابٍ غَلِيظٍ ﴿٢٤﴾

25. And if you (O Muhammad صلى الله عليه وسلم) ask them: "Who has created the heavens and the earth," they will certainly say: "Allâh." Say: "All the praises and thanks be to Allâh!" But most of them know not.

وَلَئِن سَأَلْتَهُم مَّنْ خَلَقَ ٱلسَّمَـٰوَٰتِ وَٱلْأَرْضَ لَيَقُولُنَّ ٱللَّهُ قُلِ ٱلْحَمْدُ لِلَّهِ بَلْ أَكْثَرُهُمْ لَا يَعْلَمُونَ ﴿٢٥﴾

26. To Allâh belongs whatsoever is in the heavens and the earth. Verily, Allâh, He is Al-Ghanî (Rich, Free of all needs), Worthy of all praise.

لِلَّهِ مَا فِى ٱلسَّمَـٰوَٰتِ وَٱلْأَرْضِ إِنَّ ٱللَّهَ هُوَ ٱلْغَنِىُّ ٱلْحَمِيدُ ﴿٢٦﴾

27. And if all the trees on the earth were pens and the sea (were ink wherewith to write), with seven seas behind it to add to its (supply), yet the Words of Allâh would not be exhausted. Verily, Allâh is All-Mighty, All-Wise.

وَلَوْ أَنَّمَا فِى ٱلْأَرْضِ مِن شَجَرَةٍ أَقْلَـٰمٌ وَٱلْبَحْرُ يَمُدُّهُ مِنۢ بَعْدِهِ سَبْعَةُ أَبْحُرٍ مَّا نَفِدَتْ كَلِمَـٰتُ ٱللَّهِ إِنَّ ٱللَّهَ عَزِيزٌ حَكِيمٌ ﴿٢٧﴾

28. The creation of you all and the resurrection of you all are only as (the creation and resurrection of) a single person. Verily, Allâh is All-Hearer, All-Seer.

مَّا خَلْقُكُمْ وَلَا بَعْثُكُمْ إِلَّا كَنَفْسٍ وَٰحِدَةٍ إِنَّ ٱللَّهَ سَمِيعٌ بَصِيرٌ ﴿٢٨﴾

29. See you not (O Muhammad صلى الله عليه وسلم) that Allâh merges the night into the day (i.e. the decrease in the hours of the night are added to the hours of the day), and merges the day into the night (i.e. the decrease in the hours of day are added to the hours of night), and has subjected the sun and the moon, each running its course for a term appointed; and that Allâh is All-Aware of what you do.

أَلَمْ تَرَ أَنَّ ٱللَّهَ يُولِجُ ٱلَّيْلَ فِى ٱلنَّهَارِ وَيُولِجُ ٱلنَّهَارَ فِى ٱلَّيْلِ وَسَخَّرَ ٱلشَّمْسَ وَٱلْقَمَرَ كُلٌّ يَجْرِى إِلَىٰٓ أَجَلٍ مُّسَمًّى وَأَنَّ ٱللَّهَ بِمَا تَعْمَلُونَ خَبِيرٌ ﴿٢٩﴾

30. That is because Allâh, He is the Truth, and that which they invoke besides Him[1] is Al-Bâtil (falsehood, Satan and all other false deities); and that Allâh, He is the Most High, the Most Great.

31. See you not that the ships sail through the sea by Allâh's Grace that He may show you of His Signs? Verily, in this are signs for every patient, grateful (person).

32. And when a wave covers them like shades (i.e. like clouds or the mountains of sea-water), they invoke Allâh, making their invocations for Him only. But when He brings them safe to land, there are among them those that stop in between (Belief and disbelief). But none denies Our Signs except every perfidious ingrate.[2]

33. O mankind! Be afraid of your Lord (by keeping your duty to Him and avoiding all evil), and fear a Day when no father can avail aught for his son, nor a son avail aught for his father. Verily, the Promise of Allâh is true: let not then this (worldly) present life deceive you, nor let the chief deceiver (Satan) deceive you about Allâh.

34. Verily, Allâh, with Him (Alone) is the knowledge of the Hour, He sends down the rain, and knows that which is in the wombs. No person knows what he will

---

[1] (V.31:30) See the footnote of (V.2:165).

[2] (V.31:32) See the footnote of (V.17:67).

earn tomorrow, and no person knows in what land he will die. Verily, Allâh is All-Knower, All-Aware (of things).[1]

Sûrat As-Sajdah
(The Prostration) XXXII

In the Name of Allâh
the Most Gracious, the Most Merciful

1. *Alif-Lâm-Mîm.*

[These letters are one of the miracles of the Qur'ân, and none but Allâh (Alone) knows their meanings].

2. The revelation of the Book (this Qur'ân) in which there is no doubt, is from the Lord of the *'Âlamîn* (mankind, jinn and all that exists)?

3. Or say they: "He (Muhammad صلى الله عليه وسلم) has fabricated it?" Nay, it is the truth from your Lord, so that you may warn a people to whom no warner has come before you (O Muhammad صلى الله عليه وسلم): in order that they may be guided.

4. Allâh it is He Who has created the heavens and the earth, and all that is between them in six Days. Then He rose over (*Istawâ*) the Throne (in a manner that suits His Majesty). You (mankind) have none, besides Him, as a *Walî* (protector or helper) or an intercessor. Will you not then remember (or receive admonition)?

5. He manages and regulates (every) affair from the heavens to the earth;

---

[1] (V.31:34) See the footnote of (V.7:187).

then it (affair) will go up to Him, in one Day, the space whereof is a thousand years of your reckoning (i.e. reckoning of our present world's time).

6. That is He: the All-Knower of the unseen and the seen, the All-Mighty, the Most Merciful.

7. Who made everything He has created good and He began the creation of man from clay.

8. Then He made his offspring from semen of despised water (male and female sexual discharge).

9. Then He fashioned him in due proportion, and breathed into him the soul (created by Allâh for that person); and He gave you hearing (ears), sight (eyes) and hearts. Little is the thanks you give!

10. And they say: "When we are (dead and become) lost in the earth, shall we indeed be created anew?" Nay, but they deny the Meeting with their Lord!

11. Say: "The angel of death, who is set over you, will take your souls. Then you shall be brought to your Lord."

12. And if you only could see when the *Mujrimûn* (criminals, disbelievers, polytheists, sinners) shall hang their heads before their Lord (saying): "Our Lord! We have now seen and heard, so send us back (to the world), that we will do righteous good deeds. Verily, we now believe with certainty."

الأَرْضِ ثُمَّ يَعْرُجُ إِلَيْهِ فِى يَوْمٍ كَانَ مِقْدَارُهُۥ أَلْفَ سَنَةٍ مِّمَّا تَعُدُّونَ ٥

ذَٰلِكَ عَٰلِمُ ٱلْغَيْبِ وَٱلشَّهَٰدَةِ ٱلْعَزِيزُ ٱلرَّحِيمُ ٦

ٱلَّذِىٓ أَحْسَنَ كُلَّ شَىْءٍ خَلَقَهُۥ وَبَدَأَ خَلْقَ ٱلْإِنسَٰنِ مِن طِينٍ ٧

ثُمَّ جَعَلَ نَسْلَهُۥ مِن سُلَٰلَةٍ مِّن مَّآءٍ مَّهِينٍ ٨

ثُمَّ سَوَّىٰهُ وَنَفَخَ فِيهِ مِن رُّوحِهِۦ وَجَعَلَ لَكُمُ ٱلسَّمْعَ وَٱلْأَبْصَٰرَ وَٱلْأَفْـِٔدَةَ قَلِيلًا مَّا تَشْكُرُونَ ٩

وَقَالُوٓا۟ أَءِذَا ضَلَلْنَا فِى ٱلْأَرْضِ أَءِنَّا لَفِى خَلْقٍ جَدِيدٍ بَلْ هُم بِلِقَآءِ رَبِّهِمْ كَٰفِرُونَ ١٠

۞ قُلْ يَتَوَفَّىٰكُم مَّلَكُ ٱلْمَوْتِ ٱلَّذِى وُكِّلَ بِكُمْ ثُمَّ إِلَىٰ رَبِّكُمْ تُرْجَعُونَ ١١

وَلَوْ تَرَىٰٓ إِذِ ٱلْمُجْرِمُونَ نَاكِسُوا۟ رُءُوسِهِمْ عِندَ رَبِّهِمْ رَبَّنَآ أَبْصَرْنَا وَسَمِعْنَا فَٱرْجِعْنَا نَعْمَلْ صَٰلِحًا إِنَّا مُوقِنُونَ ١٢

13. And if We had willed, surely, We would have given every person his guidance, but the Word from Me took effect (about evil-doers), that I will fill Hell with jinn and mankind together.

14. Then taste you (the torment of the Fire) because of your forgetting the Meeting of this Day of yours. Surely, We too will forget you: so taste you the abiding torment for what you used to do.

15. Only those believe in Our *Ayât* (proofs, evidences, verses, lessons, signs, revelations, etc.), who, when they are reminded of them, fall down prostrate, and glorify the Praises of their Lord, and they are not proud.[1]

16. Their sides forsake their beds, to invoke their Lord in fear and hope, and they spend (in charity in Allâh's Cause) out of what We have bestowed on them.[2]

17. No person knows what is kept hidden for them of joy as a reward for what they used to do.

---

[1] (V.32:15): See the footnote of (V.22:9).

[2] (V.32:16) Narrated Mu'âdh bin Jabal ‏رضي الله عنه‏ The Prophet (Allâh's Messenger ‏صلى الله عليه وسلم‏) said to him: "May I show you the gates of goodness? (They are): (1) Fasting is a screen from Hell. (2) *As-Sadaqâh* (deeds of charity in Allâh's Cause) extinguishes (removes) the sins, as the water extinguishes the fire. (3) Standing in *Salât* (performing of prayers) by a person during the middle (or the last third) part of a night." Then Prophet ‏صلى الله عليه وسلم‏ recited: "Their sides forsake their beds." (V.32:16) (*Abû Dâwûd* and *Tirmidhi*) (*Tafsîr Al-Qurtubî*).

18. Is then he who is a believer like him who is a *Fâsiq* (disbeliever and disobedient to Allâh)? Not equal are they.

أَفَمَن كَانَ مُؤْمِنًا كَمَن كَانَ فَاسِقًا لَّا يَسْتَوُونَ ۝

19. As for those who believe (in the Oneness of Allâh — Islâmic Monotheism) and do righteous good deeds, for them are Gardens (Paradise) as an entertainment for what they used to do.

أَمَّا الَّذِينَ ءَامَنُوا وَعَمِلُوا الصَّـٰلِحَـٰتِ فَلَهُمْ جَنَّـٰتُ الْمَأْوَىٰ نُزُلًا بِمَا كَانُوا يَعْمَلُونَ ۝

20. And as for those who are *Fâsiqûn* (disbelievers and disobedient to Allâh), their abode will be the Fire, everytime they wish to get away therefrom, they will be put back thereto, and it will be said to them: "Taste you the torment of the Fire which you used to deny."

وَأَمَّا الَّذِينَ فَسَقُوا فَمَأْوَىٰهُمُ النَّارُ كُلَّمَآ أَرَادُوا أَن يَخْرُجُوا مِنْهَآ أُعِيدُوا فِيهَا وَقِيلَ لَهُمْ ذُوقُوا عَذَابَ النَّارِ الَّذِي كُنتُم بِهِۦ تُكَذِّبُونَ ۝

21. And verily, We will make them taste of the near torment (i.e. the torment in the life of this world, i.e. disasters, calamities) prior to the supreme torment (in the Hereafter), in order that they may (repent and) return (i.e. accept Islâm).

وَلَنُذِيقَنَّهُم مِّنَ الْعَذَابِ الْأَدْنَىٰ دُونَ الْعَذَابِ الْأَكْبَرِ لَعَلَّهُمْ يَرْجِعُونَ ۝

22. And who does more wrong than he who is reminded of the *Ayât* (proofs, evidences, verses, lessons, signs, revelations, etc.) of his Lord, then turns aside therefrom? Verily, We shall exact retribution from the *Mujrimûn* (criminals, disbelievers, polytheists, sinners).

وَمَنْ أَظْلَمُ مِمَّن ذُكِّرَ بِـَٔايَـٰتِ رَبِّهِۦ ثُمَّ أَعْرَضَ عَنْهَآ إِنَّا مِنَ الْمُجْرِمِينَ مُنتَقِمُونَ ۝

23. And indeed We gave Mûsâ (Moses) the Scripture [the Taurât (Torah)]. So be not you in doubt of

وَلَقَدْ ءَاتَيْنَا مُوسَى الْكِتَـٰبَ

meeting him [i.e. when you met Mûsâ (Moses) during the night of *Al-Isrâ'* and *Al-Mi'râj*[1] over the heavens]. And We made it [the Taurât (Torah)] a guide to the Children of Israel.

24. And We made from among them (Children of Israel), leaders, giving guidance under Our Command, when they were patient and used to believe with certainty in Our *Ayât* (proofs, evidences, verses, lessons, signs, revelations, etc.).

25. Verily, your Lord will judge between them, on the Day of Resurrection, concerning that wherein they used to differ.

26. Is it not a guidance for them: how many generations We have destroyed before them in whose dwellings they do walk about? Verily, therein indeed are signs. Would they not then listen?

27. Have they not seen how We drive water to the dry land that has no vegetation, and therewith bring forth crops providing food for their cattle and themselves? Will they not then see?

28. They say: "When will this *Fath* (Decision) be (between us and you, i.e. the Day of Resurrection), if you are telling the truth?

29. Say: "On the Day of *Al-Fath* (Decision), no profit will it be to those who disbelieve

فَلَا تَكُن فِي مِرْيَةٍ مِّن لِّقَآئِهِۦ وَجَعَلْنَٰهُ هُدًى لِّبَنِىٓ إِسْرَٰٓءِيلَ ٢٣

وَجَعَلْنَا مِنْهُمْ أَئِمَّةً يَهْدُونَ بِأَمْرِنَا لَمَّا صَبَرُواْ وَكَانُواْ بِـَٔايَٰتِنَا يُوقِنُونَ ٢٤

إِنَّ رَبَّكَ هُوَ يَفْصِلُ بَيْنَهُمْ يَوْمَ ٱلْقِيَٰمَةِ فِيمَا كَانُواْ فِيهِ يَخْتَلِفُونَ ٢٥

أَوَلَمْ يَهْدِ لَهُمْ كَمْ أَهْلَكْنَا مِن قَبْلِهِم مِّنَ ٱلْقُرُونِ يَمْشُونَ فِى مَسَٰكِنِهِمْ إِنَّ فِى ذَٰلِكَ لَـَٔايَٰتٍ أَفَلَا يَسْمَعُونَ ٢٦

أَوَلَمْ يَرَوْاْ أَنَّا نَسُوقُ ٱلْمَآءَ إِلَى ٱلْأَرْضِ ٱلْجُرُزِ فَنُخْرِجُ بِهِۦ زَرْعًا تَأْكُلُ مِنْهُ أَنْعَٰمُهُمْ وَأَنفُسُهُمْ أَفَلَا يُبْصِرُونَ ٢٧

وَيَقُولُونَ مَتَىٰ هَٰذَا ٱلْفَتْحُ إِن كُنتُمْ صَٰدِقِينَ ٢٨

قُلْ يَوْمَ ٱلْفَتْحِ لَا يَنفَعُ ٱلَّذِينَ كَفَرُواْ إِيمَٰنُهُمْ

---

[1] (V.32:23): [*Al-Mi'râj* المعراج — See the footnote of (V.53:12), *Hadîth* No. 429].

who disbelieve if they (then) believe! Nor will they be granted a respite."

30. So turn aside from them (O Muhammad صلى الله عليه وسلم) and await: verily, they (too) are awaiting.

Sûrat Al-Ahzâb
(The Confederates) XXXIII

*In the Name of Allâh
the Most Gracious, the Most Merciful*

1. O Prophet (Muhammad صلى الله عليه وسلم)! Keep your duty to Allâh, and obey not the disbelievers and the hypocrites (i.e., do not follow their advice). Verily, Allâh is Ever All-Knower, All-Wise.

2. And follow that which is revealed to you from your Lord. Verily, Allâh is Well-Acquainted with what you do.

3. And put your trust in Allâh, and Sufficient is Allâh as a *Wakîl* (Trustee or Disposer of affairs).

4. Allâh has not made for any man two hearts inside his body. Neither has He made your wives whom you declare to be like your mothers' backs, your real mothers [*Az-Zihâr* is the saying of a husband to his wife, "You are to me like the back of my mother" i.e. You are unlawful for me],[1] nor has He made your adopted sons your real sons. That is but your saying with your mouths.

---

[1] (V.33:4):See the Qur'ân (V.58:3 & 4).

But Allâh says the truth, and He guides to the (Right) Way.

5. Call them (adopted sons) by (the names of) their fathers: that is more just with Allâh. But if you know not their father's (names, call them) your brothers in Faith and *Mawâlîkum* (your freed slaves). And there is no sin on you concerning that in which you made a mistake, except in regard to what your hearts deliberately intend. And Allâh is Ever Oft-Forgiving, Most Merciful.

6. The Prophet is closer to the believers than their ownselves,[1] and his wives are their (believers') mothers (as regards respect and marriage). And blood relations among each other have closer personal ties in the Decree of Allâh (regarding inheritance) than (the brotherhood of) the believers and the *Muhâjirûn* (emigrants from Makkah), except that you do kindness to those brothers (when the Prophet صلى الله عليه وسلم joined them in brotherhood ties). This has been written in the (Allâh's Book of Divine) Decrees — (*Al-Lauh Al-Mahfûz*)."

---

[1] (V.33:6) Narrated 'Abdullâh bin Hishâm رضي الله عنه: We were with the Prophet صلى الله عليه وسلم and he was holding the hand of 'Umar bin Al-Khattâb. 'Umar said to Him, "O Allâh's Messenger! You are dearer to me than everything except my ownself." The Prophet صلى الله عليه وسلم said, "No, by Him in Whose Hand my soul is, (you will not have complete Faith) till I am dearer to you than your ownself." Then 'Umar said to him, "Now, by Allâh, you are dearer to me than my ownself." The Prophet صلى الله عليه وسلم said, "Now, O 'Umar, (now you are a believer)." (*Sahih Al-Bukhari*, Vol.8, *Hadîth* No.628).

7. And (remember) when We took from the Prophets their covenant, and from you (O Muhammad صلى الله عليه وسلم), and from Nûh (Noah), Ibrâhîm (Abraham), Mûsâ (Moses), and 'Îsâ (Jesus) son of Maryam (Mary). We took from them a strong covenant.[1]

وَإِذۡ أَخَذۡنَا مِنَ ٱلنَّبِيِّـۧنَ مِيثَٰقَهُمۡ وَمِنكَ وَمِن نُّوحٖ وَإِبۡرَٰهِيمَ وَمُوسَىٰ وَعِيسَى ٱبۡنِ مَرۡيَمَۖ وَأَخَذۡنَا مِنۡهُم مِّيثَٰقًا غَلِيظٗا ٧

8. That He may ask the truthful (Allâh's Messengers and His Prophets) about their truth (i.e. the conveyance of Allâh's Message that which they were charged with). And He has prepared for the disbelievers a painful torment (Hell-fire).

لِّيَسۡـَٔلَ ٱلصَّٰدِقِينَ عَن صِدۡقِهِمۡۚ وَأَعَدَّ لِلۡكَٰفِرِينَ عَذَابًا أَلِيمٗا ٨

9. O you who believe! Remember Allâh's Favour to you, when there came against you hosts, and We sent against them a wind and forces that you saw not [i.e. troops of angels during the battle of *Al-Ahzâb* (the Confederates)]. And Allâh is Ever All-Seer of what you do.

يَٰٓأَيُّهَا ٱلَّذِينَ ءَامَنُواْ ٱذۡكُرُواْ نِعۡمَةَ ٱللَّهِ عَلَيۡكُمۡ إِذۡ جَآءَتۡكُمۡ جُنُودٞ فَأَرۡسَلۡنَا عَلَيۡهِمۡ رِيحٗا وَجُنُودٗا لَّمۡ تَرَوۡهَاۚ وَكَانَ ٱللَّهُ بِمَا تَعۡمَلُونَ بَصِيرًا ٩

10. When they came upon you from above you and from below you, and when the eyes grew wild and the hearts reached to the throats, and you were harbouring doubts about Allâh.

إِذۡ جَآءُوكُم مِّن فَوۡقِكُمۡ وَمِنۡ أَسۡفَلَ مِنكُمۡ وَإِذۡ زَاغَتِ ٱلۡأَبۡصَٰرُ وَبَلَغَتِ ٱلۡقُلُوبُ ٱلۡحَنَاجِرَ وَتَظُنُّونَ بِٱللَّهِ ٱلظُّنُونَا۠ ١٠

11. There, the believers were tried and shaken with a mighty shaking.

هُنَالِكَ ٱبۡتُلِيَ ٱلۡمُؤۡمِنُونَ وَزُلۡزِلُواْ زِلۡزَالٗا شَدِيدٗا ١١

12. And when the hypocrites and those in whose hearts is a disease (of

وَإِذۡ يَقُولُ ٱلۡمُنَٰفِقُونَ وَٱلَّذِينَ فِي

---

[1] (V.33:7) There are many Prophets and Messengers of Allâh. About twenty-five of them are mentioned in the Qur'ân; out of these twenty-five, only five are of strong will: namely Muhammad صلى الله عليه وسلم , Nûh (Noah), Ibrâhîm (Abraham), Mûsâ (Moses) and 'Îsâ (Jesus), son of Maryam (Mary). عليهم السلام.

doubts) said: "Allâh and His Messenger (صلى الله عليه وسلم) promised us nothing but delusion!"

13. And when a party of them said: "O people of Yathrib (Al-Madinah)! There is no stand (possible) for you (against the enemy attack!) Therefore go back!" And a band of them ask for permission of the Prophet (صلى الله عليه وسلم) saying: "Truly, our homes lie open (to the enemy)." And they lay not open. They but wished to flee.

14. And if the enemy had entered from all sides (of the city), and they had been exhorted to *Al-Fitnah* (i.e. to renegade from Islâm to polytheism), they would surely, have committed it and would have hesitated thereupon but little.

15. And indeed they had already made a covenant with Allâh not to turn their backs, and a covenant with Allâh must be answered for.

16. Say (O Muhammad صلى الله عليه وسلم to these hypocrites who ask your permission to run away from you): "Flight will not avail you if you flee from death or killing and then you will enjoy no more than a little while!"

17. Say: "Who is he who can protect you from Allâh if He intends to harm you, or intends mercy on you?" And they will not find, besides Allâh, for themselves any *Walî* (protector, supporter) or any helper.

18. Allâh already knows those among you who keep back (men) from fighting in Allâh's Cause, and those who say to their brethren "Come here towards us," while they (themselves) come not to the battle except a little,

قَدْ يَعْلَمُ اللَّهُ الْمُعَوِّقِينَ مِنكُمْ
وَالْقَائِلِينَ لِإِخْوَانِهِمْ هَلُمَّ إِلَيْنَا
وَلَا يَأْتُونَ الْبَأْسَ إِلَّا قَلِيلاً ۝

19. Being miserly towards you (as regards help and aid in Allâh's Cause). Then when fear comes, you will see them looking to you, their eyes revolving like (those of) one over whom hovers death; but when the fear departs, they will smite you with sharp tongues, miserly towards (spending anything in any) good (and only covetous of booty and wealth). Such have not believed. Therefore Allâh makes their deeds fruitless and that is ever easy for Allâh.

أَشِحَّةً عَلَيْكُمْ فَإِذَا جَاءَ الْخَوْفُ
رَأَيْتَهُمْ يَنظُرُونَ إِلَيْكَ تَدُورُ
أَعْيُنُهُمْ كَالَّذِي يُغْشَى عَلَيْهِ مِنَ
الْمَوْتِ فَإِذَا ذَهَبَ الْخَوْفُ
سَلَقُوكُم بِأَلْسِنَةٍ حِدَادٍ
أَشِحَّةً عَلَى الْخَيْرِ أُوْلَئِكَ لَمْ
يُؤْمِنُوا فَأَحْبَطَ اللَّهُ أَعْمَالَهُمْ
وَكَانَ ذَلِكَ عَلَى اللَّهِ يَسِيراً ۝

20. They think that Al-Ahzâb (the Confederates) have not yet withdrawn; and if Al-Ahzâb (the Confederates) should come (again), they would wish they were in the deserts (wandering) among the bedouins, seeking news about you (from a far place); and if they (happen) to be among you, they would not fight but little.

يَحْسَبُونَ الْأَحْزَابَ لَمْ يَذْهَبُوا
وَإِن يَأْتِ الْأَحْزَابُ يَوَدُّوا لَوْ
أَنَّهُم بَادُونَ فِي الْأَعْرَابِ
يَسْأَلُونَ عَنْ أَنبَائِكُمْ وَلَوْ
كَانُوا فِيكُم مَّا قَاتَلُوا إِلَّا
قَلِيلاً ۝

21. Indeed in the Messenger of Allâh (Muhammad صلى الله عليه وسلم) you have a good example to follow for him who hopes for (the Meeting with) Allâh and the Last Day, and remembers Allâh much.

لَّقَدْ كَانَ لَكُمْ فِي رَسُولِ اللَّهِ
أُسْوَةٌ حَسَنَةٌ لِّمَن كَانَ يَرْجُو
اللَّهَ وَالْيَوْمَ الْآخِرَ وَذَكَرَ اللَّهَ
كَثِيراً ۝

22. And when the believers saw Al-Ahzâb (the Confederates), they said: "This is what Allâh and His Messenger

وَلَمَّا رَأَى الْمُؤْمِنُونَ الْأَحْزَابَ

(Muhammad صلى الله عليه وسلم) had promised us; and Allâh and His Messenger (Muhammad صلى الله عليه وسلم) had spoken the truth. And it only added to their Faith and to their submissiveness (to Allâh).

قَالُوا هَذَا مَا وَعَدَنَا اللَّهُ وَرَسُولُهُ وَصَدَقَ اللَّهُ وَرَسُولُهُ وَمَا زَادَهُمْ إِلَّا إِيمَانًا وَتَسْلِيمًا ٢٢

23. Among the believers are men who have been true to their covenant with Allâh [i.e. they have gone out for *Jihâd* (holy fighting), and showed not their backs to the disbelievers]; of them some have fulfilled their obligations (i.e. have been martyred); and some of them are still waiting, but they have never changed [i.e. they never proved treacherous to their covenant which they concluded with Allâh] in the least.[1]

مِنَ الْمُؤْمِنِينَ رِجَالٌ صَدَقُوا مَا عَاهَدُوا اللَّهَ عَلَيْهِ فَمِنْهُم مَّن قَضَى نَحْبَهُ وَمِنْهُم مَّن يَنتَظِرُ وَمَا بَدَّلُوا تَبْدِيلًا ٢٣

---

[1] (V.33:23) Narrated Anas رضى الله عنه: My uncle Anas bin An-Nadr was absent from the battle of Badr. He said, "O Allâh's Messenger (صلى الله عليه وسلم)! I was absent from the first battle you fought against the pagans. (By Allâh) if Allâh gives me a chance to fight the pagans, no doubt, Allâh will see how (bravely) I will fight." On the day of Uhud when the Muslims turned their backs and fled, he said, "O Allâh! I apologise to You for what these (i.e. his companions) have done, and I denounce what these (i.e. the pagans) have done." Then he advanced and Sa'd bin Mu'âdh met him. He said "O Sa'd bin Mu'âdh! By the Lord of An-Nadr, Paradise! I am smelling its aroma coming from before (the mountain of) Uhud," Later on, Sa'd said, "O Allâh's Messenger! I cannot achieve or do what he (i.e. Anas bin An-Nadr) did. We found more than eighty wounds by swords and arrows on his body. We found him dead and his body was mutilated so badly that none except his sister could recognise him by his fingers." We used to think that the following Verse was revealed concerning him and other men of his sort: "Among the believers are men who have been true to their covenant with Allâh." (V.33:23).

24. That Allâh may reward the men of truth for their truth (i.e. for their patience at the accomplishment of that which they covenanted with Allâh), and punish the hypocrites, if He wills, or accept their repentance by turning to them (in Mercy). Verily, Allâh is Oft-Forgiving, Most Merciful.

لِيَجْزِيَ اللّٰهُ الصّٰدِقِينَ بِصِدْقِهِمْ وَيُعَذِّبَ الْمُنَٰفِقِينَ إِن شَآءَ أَوْ يَتُوبَ عَلَيْهِمْ إِنَّ اللّٰهَ كَانَ غَفُورًا رَّحِيمًا ۝

25. And Allâh drove back those who disbelieved in their rage: they gained no advantage (booty). Allâh sufficed for the believers in the fighting (by sending against the disbelievers a severe wind and troops of angels). And Allâh is Ever All-Strong, All-Mighty.

وَرَدَّ اللّٰهُ الَّذِينَ كَفَرُوا بِغَيْظِهِمْ لَمْ يَنَالُوا خَيْرًا وَكَفَى اللّٰهُ الْمُؤْمِنِينَ الْقِتَالَ وَكَانَ اللّٰهُ قَوِيًّا عَزِيزًا ۝

26. And those of the people of the Scripture who backed them (the disbelievers), Allâh brought them down from their forts and cast terror into their hearts, (so that) a group (of them) you killed, and a group (of them) you made captives.

وَأَنزَلَ الَّذِينَ ظَٰهَرُوهُم مِّنْ أَهْلِ الْكِتَٰبِ مِن صَيَاصِيهِمْ وَقَذَفَ فِي قُلُوبِهِمُ الرُّعْبَ فَرِيقًا تَقْتُلُونَ وَتَأْسِرُونَ فَرِيقًا ۝

27. And He caused you to inherit their lands, and their houses, and their riches, and a land which you had not trodden (before). And Allâh is Able to do all things.

وَأَوْرَثَكُمْ أَرْضَهُمْ وَدِيَٰرَهُمْ وَأَمْوَٰلَهُمْ وَأَرْضًا لَّمْ تَطَئُوهَا وَكَانَ اللّٰهُ عَلَىٰ كُلِّ شَيْءٍ قَدِيرًا ۝

His sister Ar-Rubaiyi' broke a front tooth of a woman and Allâh's Messenger صلى الله عليه وسلم ordered for retaliation. On that Anas (bin An-Nadr) said, "O Allâh's Messenger! By Him Who has sent you with the truth, my sister's tooth shall not be broken, then the opponents of Anas's sister accepted the compensation and gave up the claim of retaliation. So Allâh's Messenger صلى الله عليه وسلم said, "There are some people amongst Allâh's slaves whose oaths are fulfilled by Allâh when they take them." (Sahih Al-Bukhari, Vol.4, Hadith No.61).

28. O Prophet (Muhammad صلى الله عليه وسلم)! Say to your wives: "If you desire the life of this world, and its glitter, then come! I will make a provision for you and set you free in a handsome manner (divorce).[1]

29. "But if you desire Allâh and His Messenger, and the home of the Hereafter, then verily, Allâh has prepared for *Al-Muhsinât* (good-doers) amongst you an enormous reward."

30. O wives of the Prophet! Whoever of you commits an open illegal sexual intercourse, the torment for her will be doubled, and that is ever easy for Allâh.

يَتَأَيُّهَا ٱلنَّبِيُّ قُل لِّأَزْوَٰجِكَ إِن كُنتُنَّ تُرِدْنَ ٱلْحَيَوٰةَ ٱلدُّنْيَا وَزِينَتَهَا فَتَعَالَيْنَ أُمَتِّعْكُنَّ وَأُسَرِّحْكُنَّ سَرَاحًا جَمِيلًا ۝ وَإِن كُنتُنَّ تُرِدْنَ ٱللَّهَ وَرَسُولَهُ وَٱلدَّارَ ٱلْآخِرَةَ فَإِنَّ ٱللَّهَ أَعَدَّ لِلْمُحْسِنَٰتِ مِنكُنَّ أَجْرًا عَظِيمًا ۝ يَٰنِسَآءَ ٱلنَّبِيِّ مَن يَأْتِ مِنكُنَّ بِفَٰحِشَةٍ مُّبَيِّنَةٍ يُضَٰعَفْ لَهَا ٱلْعَذَابُ ضِعْفَيْنِ وَكَانَ ذَٰلِكَ عَلَى ٱللَّهِ يَسِيرًا ۝

---

[1] (V.33:28)

a) Narrated `Âishah رضي الله عنها the wife of the Prophet صلى الله عليه وسلم: When Allâh's Messenger صلى الله عليه وسلم was ordered to give option to his wives, he started with me, saying, "I am going to mention to you something, but you shall not hasten (to give your reply) unless you consult your parents." The Prophet صلى الله عليه وسلم knew that my parents would not order me to leave him. Then he said, "Allâh says:

"O Prophet (Muhammad صلى الله عليه وسلم)! Say to your wives: 'If you desire the life of this world and its glitter … an enormous reward.' " (V.33:28,29)

I said, "Then why consult I my parents? Verily, I desire Allâh, His Messenger and the Home of the Hereafter." Then all the other wives of the Prophet did the same as I did. (Sahih Al-Bukhari, Vol. 6, Hadith No. 309)

b) Narrated `Âishah رضي الله عنها: Allâh's Messenger صلى الله عليه وسلم gave us the option (to remain with him or to be divorced) and we chose Allâh and His Messenger. So, giving us that option was not regarded as divorce. (Sahih Al-Bukhari, Vol. 7, Hadith No. 188)

31. And whosoever of you is obedient to Allâh and His Messenger (صلى الله عليه وسلم), and does righteous good deeds, We shall give her, her reward twice over, and We have prepared for her *Rizqan Karîm* (a noble provision — Paradise).

﴾ وَمَن يَقْنُتْ مِنكُنَّ لِلَّهِ وَرَسُولِهِۦ وَتَعْمَلْ صَـٰلِحًا نُّؤْتِهَآ أَجْرَهَا مَرَّتَيْنِ وَأَعْتَدْنَا لَهَا رِزْقًا كَرِيمًا ﴿٣١﴾

32. O wives of the Prophet! You are not like any other women. If you keep your duty (to Allâh), then be not soft in speech, lest he in whose heart is a disease (of hypocrisy, or evil desire for adultery) should be moved with desire, but speak in an honourable manner.

يَـٰنِسَآءَ ٱلنَّبِىِّ لَسْتُنَّ كَأَحَدٍ مِّنَ ٱلنِّسَآءِ إِنِ ٱتَّقَيْتُنَّ فَلَا تَخْضَعْنَ بِٱلْقَوْلِ فَيَطْمَعَ ٱلَّذِى فِى قَلْبِهِۦ مَرَضٌ وَقُلْنَ قَوْلًا مَّعْرُوفًا ﴿٣٢﴾

33. And stay in your houses, and do not display yourselves like that of the times of ignorance, and perform *As-Salât (Iqâmat-as-Salât)*, and give *Zakât* and obey Allâh and His Messenger. Allâh wishes only to remove *Ar-Rijs* (evil deeds and sins) from you, O members of the family (of the Prophet صلى الله عليه وسلم), and to purify you with a thorough purification.

وَقَرْنَ فِى بُيُوتِكُنَّ وَلَا تَبَرَّجْنَ تَبَرُّجَ ٱلْجَـٰهِلِيَّةِ ٱلْأُولَىٰ وَأَقِمْنَ ٱلصَّلَوٰةَ وَءَاتِينَ ٱلزَّكَوٰةَ وَأَطِعْنَ ٱللَّهَ وَرَسُولَهُۥٓ إِنَّمَا يُرِيدُ ٱللَّهُ لِيُذْهِبَ عَنكُمُ ٱلرِّجْسَ أَهْلَ ٱلْبَيْتِ وَيُطَهِّرَكُمْ تَطْهِيرًا ﴿٣٣﴾

34. And remember (O you the members of the Prophet's family, the Graces of your Lord), that which is recited in your houses of the Verses of Allâh and *Al-Hikmah* (i.e. Prophet's *Sunnah* — legal ways, so give your thanks to Allâh and glorify His Praises for this Qur'an and the *Sunnah*). Verily, Allâh is Ever Most Courteous, Well-Acquainted with all things.

وَٱذْكُرْنَ مَا يُتْلَىٰ فِى بُيُوتِكُنَّ مِنْ ءَايَـٰتِ ٱللَّهِ وَٱلْحِكْمَةِ إِنَّ ٱللَّهَ كَانَ لَطِيفًا خَبِيرًا ﴿٣٤﴾

35. Verily, the Muslims (those who submit to Allâh in Islâm) men and

إِنَّ ٱلْمُسْلِمِينَ وَٱلْمُسْلِمَـٰتِ

women, the believers men and women (who believe in Islâmic Monotheism), the men and the women who are obedient (to Allâh), the men and women who are truthful (in their speech and deeds), the men and the women who are patient (in performing all the duties which Allâh has ordered and in abstaining from all that Allâh has forbidden), the men and the women who are humble (before their Lord — Allâh), the men and the women who give *Sadaqât* (i.e. *Zakât* and alms), the men and the women who observe *Saum* (fast) (the obligatory fasting during the month of Ramadân, and the optional *Nawâfil* fasting), the men and the women who guard their chastity (from illegal sexual acts) and the men and the women who remember Allâh much with their hearts and tongues.[1] Allâh has prepared for them forgiveness and a great reward (i.e. Paradise).

36. It is not for a believer, man or woman, when Allâh and His Messenger have decreed a matter that they should have any option in their decision. And whoever disobeys Allâh and His Messenger, he has indeed strayed into a plain error.

37. And (remember) when you said to him (Zaid bin Hârithah رضي الله عنه

---

[1] (V.33:35) Remember Allâh while sitting, standing, for more than 300 times extra over the remembrance of Allâh during the five compulsory congregational prayers or praying extra additional *Nawâfil* prayers of night in the last part of night.

the freed-slave of the Prophet صلى الله عليه وسلم on whom Allâh has bestowed Grace (by guiding him to Islâm) and you (O Muhammad صلى الله عليه وسلم too) have done favour (by manumitting him): "Keep your wife to yourself, and fear Allâh." But you did hide in yourself (i.e. what Allâh has already made known to you that He will give her to you in marriage) that which Allâh will make manifest, you did fear the people (i.e., their saying that Muhammad صلى الله عليه وسلم married the divorced wife of his manumitted slave) whereas Allâh had a better right that you should fear Him. So when Zaid had accomplished his desire from her (i.e. divorced her), We gave her to you in marriage, so that (in future) there may be no difficulty to the believers in respect of (the marriage of) the wives of their adopted sons when the latter have no desire to keep them (i.e. they have divorced them). And Allâh's Command must be fulfilled.

38. There is no blame on the Prophet (صلى الله عليه وسلم) in that which Allâh has made legal for him. That has been Allâh's Way with those who have passed away of (the Prophets of) old. And the Command of Allâh is a decree determined.

39. Those who convey the Message of Allâh and fear Him, and fear none save Allâh. And Sufficient is Allâh as a Reckoner.

40. Muhammad (صلى الله عليه وسلم) is not the father of any of your men, but he is

وَخَاتَمَ النَّبِيِّنَ ۗ وَكَانَ اللَّهُ بِكُلِّ

the Messenger of Allâh and the last (end) of the Prophets.[1] And Allâh is Ever All-Aware of everything.

شَىْءٍ عَلِيمًا ٤٠

يَتأَيُّهَا الَّذِينَ ءَامَنُوا اذْكُرُوا اللَّهَ

41. O you who believe! Remember Allâh with much remembrance.[2]

ذِكْرًا كَثِيرًا ٤١

42. And glorify His Praises morning and afternoon [the early morning (Fajr) and 'Asr prayers].

وَسَبِّحُوهُ بُكْرَةً وَأَصِيلًا ٤٢

43. He it is Who sends Salât (His blessings) on you, and His angels too (ask Allâh to bless and forgive you), that He may bring you out from darkness (of disbelief and polytheism) into light (of Belief and Islâmic Monotheism). And He is Ever Most Merciful to the believers.

هُوَ الَّذِى يُصَلِّى عَلَيْكُمْ
وَمَلَٰٓئِكَتُهُۥ لِيُخْرِجَكُم مِّنَ
الظُّلُمَٰتِ إِلَى النُّورِ ۚ وَكَانَ
بِالْمُؤْمِنِينَ رَحِيمًا ٤٣

44. Their greeting on the Day they shall meet Him will be "Salâm: Peace (i.e. the angels will say to them: Salâmun 'Alaikum)!" And He has prepared for them a generous reward (i.e. Paradise).

تَحِيَّتُهُمْ يَوْمَ يَلْقَوْنَهُۥ سَلَٰمٌ ۚ وَأَعَدَّ
لَهُمْ أَجْرًا كَرِيمًا ٤٤

45. O Prophet (Muhammad صلى الله عليه وسلم)! Verily, We have sent you as witness, and a bearer of glad tidings, and a warner,

يَٰٓأَيُّهَا النَّبِىُّ إِنَّآ أَرْسَلْنَٰكَ
شَٰهِدًا وَمُبَشِّرًا وَنَذِيرًا ٤٥

46. And as one who invites to Allâh [Islâmic Monotheism, i.e. to worship none but Allâh (Alone)] by His Leave, and as a lamp spreading light (through your instructions from the Qur'ân and the Sunnah — the legal ways of the Prophet صلى الله عليه وسلم).[3]

وَدَاعِيًا إِلَى اللَّهِ بِإِذْنِهِۦ وَسِرَاجًا
مُّنِيرًا ٤٦

---

[1] (V.33:40) See the footnote (B) of (V.2:252).

[2] (V.33:41) See the footnote of (V.13:28).

[3] (V.33:46) See the footnote of [(V.3:164), *Hadîth* No.385 and 387]

47. And announce to the believers (in the Oneness of Allâh and in His Messenger Muhammad صلى الله عليه وسلم) the glad tidings, that they will have from Allâh a Great Bounty.

وَبَشِّرِ ٱلْمُؤْمِنِينَ بِأَنَّ لَهُم مِّنَ ٱللَّهِ فَضْلًا كَبِيرًا ﴿٤٧﴾

48. And obey not the disbelievers and the hypocrites, and harm them not (in revenge for their harming you till you are ordered). And put your trust in Allâh, and Sufficient is Allâh as a *Wakîl* (Trustee, or Disposer of affairs). [*Tafsir Al-Qurtubi*]

وَلَا تُطِعِ ٱلْكَٰفِرِينَ وَٱلْمُنَٰفِقِينَ وَدَعْ أَذَىٰهُمْ وَتَوَكَّلْ عَلَى ٱللَّهِ وَكَفَىٰ بِٱللَّهِ وَكِيلًا ﴿٤٨﴾

49. O you who believe! When you marry believing women, and then divorce them before you have sexual intercourse with them, no *'Iddah* [divorce prescribed period, see (V.65:4)] have you to count in respect of them. So give them a present, and set them free (i.e. divorce), in a handsome manner.

يَٰٓأَيُّهَا ٱلَّذِينَ ءَامَنُوٓا إِذَا نَكَحْتُمُ ٱلْمُؤْمِنَٰتِ ثُمَّ طَلَّقْتُمُوهُنَّ مِن قَبْلِ أَن تَمَسُّوهُنَّ فَمَا لَكُمْ عَلَيْهِنَّ مِنْ عِدَّةٍ تَعْتَدُّونَهَا فَمَتِّعُوهُنَّ وَسَرِّحُوهُنَّ سَرَاحًا جَمِيلًا ﴿٤٩﴾

50. O Prophet (Muhammad صلى الله عليه وسلم)! Verily, We have made lawful to you your wives, to whom you have paid their *Mahr* (bridal-money given by the husband to his wife at the time of marriage), and those (slaves) whom your right hand possesses — whom Allâh has given to you, and the daughters of your *'Amm* (paternal uncles) and the daughters of your *'Ammât* (paternal aunts) and the daughters of your *Khâl* (maternal uncles) and the daughters of your *Khâlât* (maternal aunts) who migrated (from Makkah) with you, and a believing woman if she offers herself to the Prophet, and the Prophet wishes to

يَٰٓأَيُّهَا ٱلنَّبِيُّ إِنَّآ أَحْلَلْنَا لَكَ أَزْوَٰجَكَ ٱلَّٰتِىٓ ءَاتَيْتَ أُجُورَهُنَّ وَمَا مَلَكَتْ يَمِينُكَ مِمَّآ أَفَآءَ ٱللَّهُ عَلَيْكَ وَبَنَاتِ عَمِّكَ وَبَنَاتِ عَمَّٰتِكَ وَبَنَاتِ خَالِكَ وَبَنَاتِ خَٰلَٰتِكَ ٱلَّٰتِى هَاجَرْنَ مَعَكَ وَٱمْرَأَةً مُّؤْمِنَةً إِن وَهَبَتْ نَفْسَهَا لِلنَّبِىِّ إِنْ أَرَادَ ٱلنَّبِىُّ أَن يَسْتَنكِحَهَا خَالِصَةً لَّكَ مِن دُونِ ٱلْمُؤْمِنِينَ قَدْ عَلِمْنَا مَا فَرَضْنَا عَلَيْهِمْ فِىٓ أَزْوَٰجِهِمْ

marry her — a privilege for you only, not for the (rest of) the believers. Indeed We know what We have enjoined upon them about their wives and those (slaves) whom their right hands possess, in order that there should be no difficulty on you. And Allâh is Ever Oft-Forgiving, Most Merciful.

51. You (O Muhammad صلى الله عليه وسلم) can postpone (the turn of) whom you will of them (your wives), and you may receive whom you will. And whomsoever you desire of those whom you have set aside (her turn temporarily), it is no sin on you (to receive her again): that is better that they may be comforted and not grieved, and may all be pleased with what you give them. Allâh knows what is in your hearts. And Allâh is Ever All-Knowing, Most Forbearing.

52. It is not lawful for you (to marry other) women after this, nor to change them for other wives even though their beauty attracts you, except those (slaves) whom your right hand possesses. And Allâh is Ever a Watcher over all things.

53. O you who believe! Enter not the Prophet's houses, unless permission is given to you for a meal, (and then) not (so early as) to wait for its preparation. But when you are invited, enter, and when you have taken your meal, disperse without sitting for a talk. Verily, such (behaviour) annoys the

Prophet, and he is shy of (asking) you
(to go); but Allâh is not shy of (telling
you) the truth. And when you ask (his
wives) for anything you want, ask them
from behind a screen: that is purer for
your hearts and for their hearts. And it
is not (right) for you that you should
annoy Allâh's Messenger, nor that you
should ever marry his wives after him
(his death). Verily, with Allâh that shall
be an enormity.

54. Whether you reveal anything or
conceal it, verily, Allâh is Ever
All-Knower of everything.

55. It is no sin on them (the Prophet's
wives, if they appear unveiled) before
their fathers, or their sons, or their
brothers, or their brother's sons, or the
sons of their sisters, or their own
(believing) women, or their (female)
slaves. And (O ladies), keep your duty
to Allâh. Verily, Allâh is Ever
All-Witness over everything.

56. Allâh sends His *Salât* (Graces,
Honours, Blessings, Mercy) on the
Prophet (Muhammad صلى الله عليه وسلم), and
also His angels (ask Allâh to bless and
forgive him). O you who believe! Send
your *Salât*[1] on (ask Allâh to bless) him
(Muhammad صلى الله عليه وسلم), and (you
should) greet (salute) him with the
Islâmic way of greeting (salutation i.e.
As-Salâmu 'Alaikum).

---

[1] (V.33:56). Narrated 'Abdur-Rahmân bin Abî Laila: Ka'b bin 'Ujrah
met me and said, "Shall I not give you a present I got from the Prophet
صلى الله عليه وسلم ?" 'Abdur-Rahmân said, "Yes, give it to me." He said, "We

57. Verily, those who annoy Allâh and His Messenger [1] Allâh has cursed them in this world, and in the Hereafter, and has prepared for them a humiliating torment.

58. And those who annoy believing men and women undeservedly, they bear (on themselves) the crime of slander and plain sin.

59. O Prophet! Tell your wives and your daughters and the women of the believers to draw their cloaks (veils) all over their bodies (i.e. screen themselves completely except the eyes or one eye to see the way). That will be better, that they should be known (as free

إِنَّ ٱلَّذِينَ يُؤْذُونَ ٱللَّهَ وَرَسُولَهُۥ لَعَنَهُمُ ٱللَّهُ فِى ٱلدُّنْيَا وَٱلْأَخِرَةِ وَأَعَدَّ لَهُمْ عَذَابًا مُّهِينًا ۝ وَٱلَّذِينَ يُؤْذُونَ ٱلْمُؤْمِنِينَ وَٱلْمُؤْمِنَتِ بِغَيْرِ مَا ٱكْتَسَبُوا۟ فَقَدِ ٱحْتَمَلُوا۟ بُهْتَنًا وَإِثْمًا مُّبِينًا ۝ يَـٰٓأَيُّهَا ٱلنَّبِىُّ قُل لِّأَزْوَجِكَ وَبَنَاتِكَ وَنِسَآءِ ٱلْمُؤْمِنِينَ يُدْنِينَ عَلَيْهِنَّ مِن جَلَبِيبِهِنَّ ذَٰلِكَ أَدْنَىٰٓ أَن يُعْرَفْنَ فَلَا يُؤْذَيْنَ

asked Allâh's Messenger صلى الله عليه وسلم saying, 'O Allâh's Messenger! How should one (ask Allâh to) send As-Salât upon you and Ahl-al-Bait أهل البيت (the members of the family of the Prophet صلى الله عليه وسلم), for Allâh has taught us how to greet you?' He said, 'Say *Allâhumma salli 'alâ Muhammadin wa'alâ ali Muhammadin, kama sal-laita 'alâ Ibrâhîma wa 'alâ âli Ibrâhîm, Innaka Hamîdun Majîd. Allâhumma bârik 'alâ Muhammadin wa 'alâ âli Muhâmmadîn kama bârakta 'alâ Ibrâhîma wa 'alâ âli Ibrâhîm, Innaka Hamîdun Majîd.'* [O Allâh! Send Your Salât (Graces, Honours and Mercy) on Muhammad and on the family or the followers of Muhammad, as You sent Your Salât (Graces, Honours and Mercy) on Abraham and on the family or the followers of Abraham, for You are the Most Praiseworthy, the Most Gracious. O Allâh! Send Your Blessings on Muhammad, and on the family or the followers of Muhammad as You sent your Blessings on Abraham and on the family or the followers of Abraham, for You are the Most Praiseworthy, the Most Gracious.' " (*Sahih Al-Bukhari*, Vol. 4, *Hadîth* No.589).

[1] (V.33:57)

(A) By abusing or telling lies against Allâh and His Messenger صلى الله عليه وسلم , by making pictures — imitating Allâh's creations, and by disobeying Allâh and His Messenger صلى الله عليه وسلم .

(B) See the footnote of (V.2:278).

respectable women) so as not to be annoyed. And Allâh is Ever Oft-Forgiving, Most Merciful.[1]

60. If the hypocrites, and those in whose hearts is a disease (evil desire for adultery), and those who spread false news among the people in Al-Madinah stop not, We shall certainly let you overpower them: then they will not be able to stay in it as your neighbours but a little while.

61. Accursed, they shall be seized wherever found, and killed with a (terrible) slaughter.

62. That was the Way of Allâh in the case of those who passed away of old: and you will not find any change in the Way of Allâh.

63. People ask you concerning the Hour, say: "The knowledge of it is with Allâh only. What do you know? It may be that the Hour is near!"

64. Verily, Allâh has cursed the disbelievers, and has prepared for them a flaming Fire (Hell).

65. Wherein they will abide for ever, and they will find neither a Walî (a protector) nor a helper.

66. On the Day when their faces will be turned over in the Fire, they will say: "Oh, would that we had obeyed Allâh and obeyed the Messenger (Muhammad صلى الله عليه وسلم)."

---

[1] (V.33:59) See the footnote of (V.24:31).

67. And they will say: "Our Lord! Verily, we obeyed our chiefs and our great ones, and they misled us from the (Right) Way."

وَقَالُوا رَبَّنَآ إِنَّآ أَطَعْنَا سَادَتَنَا وَكُبَرَآءَنَا فَأَضَلُّونَا السَّبِيلَا ۝

68. "Our Lord! Give them double torment and curse them with a mighty curse!"

رَبَّنَآ ءَاتِهِمْ ضِعْفَيْنِ مِنَ الْعَذَابِ وَالْعَنْهُمْ لَعْنًا كَبِيرًا ۝

69. O you who believe! Be not like those who annoyed Mûsâ (Moses), but Allâh cleared him of that which they alleged, and he was honourable before Allâh.[1]

يَٰٓأَيُّهَا الَّذِينَ ءَامَنُوا لَا تَكُونُوا كَالَّذِينَ ءَاذَوْا مُوسَىٰ فَبَرَّأَهُ اللَّهُ مِمَّا قَالُوا وَكَانَ عِندَ اللَّهِ وَجِيهًا ۝

70. O you who believe! Keep your duty to Allâh and fear Him, and speak (always) the truth.

يَٰٓأَيُّهَا الَّذِينَ ءَامَنُوا اتَّقُوا اللَّهَ وَقُولُوا قَوْلًا سَدِيدًا ۝

---

[1] (V.33:69) Narrated Abû Hurairah رضي الله عنه: Allâh's Messenger صلى الله عليه وسلم said, "(Prophet) Mûsâ (Moses) was a shy person and used to cover his body completely because of his extensive shyness. One of the Children of Israel hurt him by saying, 'He covers his body in this way only because of some defect in his skin, either leprosy or scrotal hernia, or he had some other defect.' Allâh wished to clear Mûsâ (Moses) of what they said about him: so one day while Mûsâ (Moses) was in seclusion, he took off his clothes and put them on a stone and started taking a bath. When he had finished the bath, he moved towards his clothes so as to take them, but the stone took his clothes and fled. Mûsâ (Moses) picked up his stick and ran after the stone saying, 'O stone! give me my clothes!' till he reached a group of Banî Israel who saw him naked then, and found him the best of what Allâh had created; and Allâh cleared him of what they had accused him of. The stone stopped there and Mûsâ (Moses) took and put his garment on and started hitting the stone with his stick. By Allâh, the stone still has some traces of the hitting: three, four or five marks. This was what Allâh عز وجل refers to in His Saying: 'O you who believe! Be not like those, who annoyed Mûsâ (Moses), but Allâh cleared him of that which they alleged and he was honourable before Allâh...' (V.33:69) (Sahih Al-Bukhari, Vol.4, Hadîth No.616).

71. He will direct you to do righteous good deeds and will forgive you your sins. And whosoever obeys Allâh and His Messenger (صلى الله عليه وسلم), he has indeed achieved a great achievement (i.e. he will be saved from the Hell-fire and will be admitted to Paradise).

72. Truly, We did offer Al-Amânah (the trust or moral responsibility or honesty and all the duties which Allâh has ordained) to the heavens and the earth, and the mountains, but they declined to bear it and were afraid of it (i.e. afraid of Allâh's Torment). But man bore it. Verily, he was unjust (to himself) and ignorant (of its results).[1]

73. So that Allâh will punish the hypocrites, men and women, and the men and women who are Al-Mushrikûn (polytheists, idolaters, pagans, disbelievers, in the Oneness of Allâh, and His Messenger Muhammad صلى الله عليه وسلم). And Allâh will pardon (accept the repentance of) the true believers of the Islâmic Monotheism, men and women. And Allâh is Ever Oft-Forgiving, Most Merciful.

Sûrat Saba'
(Sheba) XXXIV

In the Name of Allâh
the Most Gracious, the Most Merciful

1. All the praises and thanks are to Allâh, to Whom belongs all that is in

---

[1] (V.33:72): See the footnote of the (V.3:164).

the heavens and all that is in the earth.
His is all the praises and thanks in the
Hereafter, and He is the All-Wise, the
All-Aware.

2. He knows that which goes into the
earth and that which comes forth from
it, and that which descends from the
heaven and that which ascends to it.
And He is the Most Merciful, the
Oft-Forgiving.

3. Those who disbelieve say: "The
Hour will not come to us." Say: "Yes,
by my Lord, the All-Knower of the
Unseen, it will come to you; not even
the weight of an atom (or a small ant) or
less than that or greater escapes His
Knowledge in the heavens or in the
earth but it is in a Clear Book (Al-Lauh
Al-Mahfûz)."

4. That He may recompense those
who believe (in the Oneness of Allâh
—Islâmic Monotheism) and do
righteous good deeds. Those, theirs is
forgiveness and *Rizq Karîm* (generous
provision, i.e. Paradise).

5. But those who strive against Our
Ayât (proofs, evidences, verses, lessons,
signs, revelations, etc.) to frustrate them
— those, for them will be a severe
painful torment.[1]

6. And those who have been given
knowledge see that what is revealed to
you (O Muhammad ﷺ) from
your Lord is the truth, and that it guides

---

[1] (V.34:5) See the footnote of (V.3:91).

to the Path of the Exalted in might, Owner of all praise.

7. Those who disbelieve say: "Shall we direct you to a man (Muhammad صلى الله عليه وسلم who will tell you (that) when you have become fully disintegrated into dust with full dispersion, then you will be created (again) anew?"

8. Has he (Muhammad صلى الله عليه وسلم invented a lie against Allâh, or is there a madness in him? Nay, but those who disbelieve in the Hereafter are (themselves) in a torment, and in far error.

9. See they not what is before them and what is behind them, of the heaven and the earth? If We will, We shall sink the earth with them, or cause a piece of the heaven to fall upon them. Verily, in this is a sign for every slave who turns to Allâh in repentance (i.e. the one who believes in the Oneness of Allâh and performs deeds of His obedience and always begs His Pardon).

10. And indeed We bestowed grace on Dâwûd (David) from Us (saying): "O you mountains. Glorify (Allâh) with him! And you birds (also)! And We made the iron soft for him."

11. Saying: "Make you perfect coats of mail, and balance well the rings of chain armour, and work you (men) righteousness. Truly, I am All-Seer of what you do."

12. And to Solomon (We subjected) the wind, its morning (stride from sunrise till midnoon) was a month's (journey), and its afternoon (stride from the midday decline of the sun to sunset) was a month's (journey i.e. in one day he could travel two months' journey). And We caused a fount of (molten) brass to flow for him, and there were jinn that worked in front of him, by the Leave of his Lord. And whosoever of them turned aside from Our Command, We shall cause him to taste of the torment of the blazing Fire.

ورداجها شهرا وأسلنا له عين القطر ومن الجن من يعمل بين يديه بإذن ربه ومن يزغ منهم عن أمرنا نذقه من عذاب السعير ﴿١٢﴾

13. They worked for him as he desired, (making) high rooms, images, basins as large as reservoirs, and (cooking) cauldrons fixed (in their places). "Work you, O family of Dâwûd (David), with thanks!" But few of My slaves are grateful.

يعملون له ما يشاء من محريب وتماثيل وجفان كالجواب وقدور راسيت اعملوا ءال داود شكرا وقليل من عبادي الشكور ﴿١٣﴾

14. Then when We decreed death for him [Sulaimân (Solomon)], nothing informed them (jinn) of his death except a little worm of the earth which kept (slowly) gnawing away at his stick. So when he fell down, the jinn saw clearly that if they had known the Unseen, they would not have stayed in the humiliating torment.

فلما قضينا عليه الموت ما دلهم على موته إلا دآبة الأرض تأكل منسأته فلما خر تبينت الجن أن لو كانوا يعلمون الغيب ما لبثوا في العذاب المهين ﴿١٤﴾

15. Indeed there was for Saba' (Sheba) a sign in their dwelling-place — two gardens on the right hand and on the left; (and it was said to them:) "Eat of the provision of your Lord, and be grateful to Him." A fair land and an Oft-Forgiving Lord!

لقد كان لسبإ في مسكنهم ءاية جنتان عن يمين وشمال كلوا من رزق ربكم واشكروا له بلدة طيبة ورب غفور ﴿١٥﴾

16. But they turned away (from the obedience of Allâh), so We sent against them *Sail Al-'Arim* (flood released from the dam), and We converted their two gardens into gardens producing bitter bad fruit, and tamarisks, and some few lote-trees.

17. Like this We requited them because they were ungrateful disbelievers. And never do We requit in such a way except those who are ungrateful (disbelievers).

18. And We placed, between them and the towns which We had blessed, towns easy to be seen, and We made the stages (of journey) between them easy (saying): "Travel in them safely both by night and day."

19. But they said: "Our Lord! Make the stages between our journey longer," and they wronged themselves; so We made them as tales (in the land), and We dispersed them all totally. Verily, in this are indeed signs for every steadfast, grateful (person).

20. And indeed *Iblîs* (Satan) did prove true his thought about them: so they followed him, all except a group of true believers (in the Oneness of Allâh).

21. And he (*Iblîs* - Satan) had no authority over them, — except that We might test him who believes in the Hereafter from him who is in doubt about it. And your Lord is a *Hafîz* (Watchful) over everything. (All-Knower of everything i.e. He

حَفِيظٌ ۝

keeps record of every person as regards deeds, and then He will reward them accordingly)

22. Say: (O Muhammad صلى الله عليه وسلم to polytheists, pagans) "Call upon those whom you assert (to be associate gods) besides Allâh, they possess not even an atom's (or a small ant's) weight either in the heavens or on the earth, nor have they any share in either, nor there is for Him any supporter from among them.

قُلِ ادْعُوا الَّذِينَ زَعَمْتُم مِّن دُونِ اللَّهِ لَا يَمْلِكُونَ مِثْقَالَ ذَرَّةٍ فِي السَّمَوَاتِ وَلَا فِي الْأَرْضِ وَمَا لَهُمْ فِيهِمَا مِن شِرْكٍ وَمَا لَهُ مِنْهُم مِّن ظَهِيرٍ ۝

23. Intercession with Him profits not except for him whom He permits. So much so that when fear is banished from their (angels') hearts, they (angels) say: "What is it that your Lord has said?" They say: "The truth. And He is the Most High, the Most Great."

وَلَا تَنفَعُ الشَّفَاعَةُ عِندَهُ إِلَّا لِمَنْ أَذِنَ لَهُ حَتَّى إِذَا فُزِّعَ عَن قُلُوبِهِمْ قَالُوا مَاذَا قَالَ رَبُّكُمْ قَالُوا الْحَقَّ وَهُوَ الْعَلِيُّ الْكَبِيرُ ۝

24. Say (O Muhammad صلى الله عليه وسلم to polytheists, pagans) "Who gives you provision from the heavens and the earth?" Say: "Allâh. And verily, (either) we or you are rightly guided or in plain error."

۞ قُلْ مَن يَرْزُقُكُم مِّنَ السَّمَوَاتِ وَالْأَرْضِ قُلِ اللَّهُ وَإِنَّا أَوْ إِيَّاكُمْ لَعَلَى هُدًى أَوْ فِي ضَلَالٍ مُّبِينٍ ۝

25. Say (O Muhammad صلى الله عليه وسلم to polytheists, pagans) "You will not be asked about our sins, nor shall we be asked of what you do."

قُل لَّا تُسْأَلُونَ عَمَّا أَجْرَمْنَا وَلَا نُسْأَلُ عَمَّا تَعْمَلُونَ ۝

26. Say: "Our Lord will assemble us all together (on the Day of Resurrection), then He will judge between us with truth. And He is the Just Judge, the All-Knower of the true state of affairs." [Tafsir Ibn Kathir]

قُلْ يَجْمَعُ بَيْنَنَا رَبُّنَا ثُمَّ يَفْتَحُ بَيْنَنَا بِالْحَقِّ وَهُوَ الْفَتَّاحُ الْعَلِيمُ ۝

27. Say (O Muhammad صلى الله عليه وسلم to polytheists and pagans): "Show me

قُلْ أَرُونِيَ الَّذِينَ أَلْحَقْتُم بِهِ

those whom you have joined with Him as partners. Nay (there are not at all any partners with Him)! But He is Allâh (Alone), the All-Mighty, the All-Wise.

28. And We have not sent you (O Muhammad صلى الله عليه وسلم) except as a giver of glad tidings and a warner to all mankind, but most of men know not.[1]

29. And they say: "When is this promise (i.e. the Day of Resurrection) if you are truthful?"

30. Say (O Muhammad صلى الله عليه وسلم): "The appointment to you is for a Day, which you cannot put back for an hour (or a moment) nor put forward."

31. And those who disbelieve say: "We believe not in this Qur'ân nor in that which was before it." But if you could see when the *Zâlimûn* (polytheists and wrongdoers) will be made to stand before their Lord, how they will cast the (blaming) word one to another! Those who were deemed weak will say to those who were arrogant: "Had it not been for you, we should certainly have been believers!"

32. And those who were arrogant will say to those who were deemed weak: "Did we keep you back from guidance after it had come to you? Nay, but you were *Mujrimûn* (polytheists, sinners, disbelievers, criminals)."

33. Those who were deemed weak will say to those who were arrogant:

---

[1] (V.34:28) See the footnote of (V.2:252).

"Nay, but it was your plotting by night and day: when you ordered us to disbelieve in Allâh and set up rivals to Him!" And each of them (parties) will conceal their own regrets (for disobeying Allâh during this worldly life), when they behold the torment. And We shall put iron collars round the necks of those who disbelieved. Are they requited aught except what they used to do?

34. And We did not send a warner to a township but those who were given the worldly wealth and luxuries among them said: "We believe not in the (Message) with which you have been sent."

35. And they say: "We are more in wealth and in children, and we are not going to be punished."

36. Say (O Muhammad صلى الله عليه وسلم): "Verily, my Lord enlarges the provision to whom He wills and restricts, but most men know not."

37. And it is not your wealth, nor your children that bring you nearer to Us (i.e. please Allâh), but only he who believes (in the Islâmic Monotheism), and does righteous deeds (will please Us); as for such, there will be twofold reward for what they did, and they will reside in the high dwellings (Paradise) in peace and security.

38. And those who strive against Our *Ayât* (proofs, evidences, verses, lessons, signs, revelations, etc.), to frustrate them, they will be brought to the torment.

39. Say: "Truly, my Lord enlarges the provision for whom He wills of His slaves, and (also) restricts (it) for him, and whatsoever you spend of anything (in Allâh's Cause), He will replace it. And He is the Best of providers."

40. And (remember) the Day when He will gather them all together, then He will say to the angels: "Was it you that these people used to worship?"

41. They (the angels) will say: "Glorified are You! You are our *Walî* (Lord) instead of them. Nay, but they used to worship the jinn; most of them were believers in them."

42. So Today (i.e. the Day of Resurrection), none of you can profit or harm one another. And We shall say to those who did wrong [i.e. worshipped others (like the angels, jinn, prophets, saints, righteous persons) along with Allâh]: "Taste the torment of the Fire which you used to belie."[1]

---

[1] (V.34:42) Almighty Allâh says: "They (Jews and Christians) took their rabbis and their monks to be their lords (by obeying them in things that they made lawful or unlawful according to their own desires without being ordered by Allâh) besides Allâh, and (they also took as their Lord) Messiah, son of Maryam (Mary), while they (Jews and Christians) were commanded [in the Taurât (Torah) and the Injeel (Gospel)] to worship none but one *Ilâh* (God - Allâh), *Lâ ilâha illâ Huwa* (none has the right to be worshipped but He). Praise and Glory is to Him, (far above is He) from having the partners they associate (with Him)." [The Qur'ân, Verse 9:31]

Once, while Allâh's Messenger صلى الله عليه وسلم was reciting the above Verse, 'Adi bin Hâtim said, "O Allâh's Prophet! They do not worship them (rabbis and monks)." Allâh's Messenger صلى الله عليه وسلم said, "They certainly

43. And when Our Clear Verses are recited to them, they say: "This (Muhammad صلى الله عليه وسلم) is naught but a man who wishes to hinder you from that which your fathers used to worship." And they say: "This (the Qur'ân) is nothing but an invented lie." And those who disbelieve say of the truth when it has come to them (i.e. Prophet Muhammad صلى الله عليه وسلم when Allâh sent him as a Messenger with proofs, evidences, verses of this Qur'ân, lessons, signs, etc.): "This is nothing but evident magic!"

وَإِذَا تُتۡلَىٰ عَلَيۡهِمۡ ءَايَٰتُنَا بَيِّنَٰتٍ قَالُواْ مَا هَٰذَآ إِلَّا رَجُلٞ يُرِيدُ أَن يَصُدَّكُمۡ عَمَّا كَانَ يَعۡبُدُ ءَابَآؤُكُمۡ وَقَالُواْ مَا هَٰذَآ إِلَّآ إِفۡكٞ مُّفۡتَرٗى وَقَالَ ٱلَّذِينَ كَفَرُواْ لِلۡحَقِّ لَمَّا جَآءَهُمۡ إِنۡ هَٰذَآ إِلَّا سِحۡرٞ مُّبِينٞ ٤٣

44. And We had not given them Scriptures which they could study, nor sent to them before you (O Muhammad صلى الله عليه وسلم) any warner (Messenger).

وَمَآ ءَاتَيۡنَٰهُم مِّن كُتُبٖ يَدۡرُسُونَهَاۖ وَمَآ أَرۡسَلۡنَآ إِلَيۡهِمۡ قَبۡلَكَ مِن نَّذِيرٖ ٤٤

45. And those before them belied; these have not received even a tenth of what We had granted to those (of old); yet they belied My Messengers. Then how (terrible) was My denial (punishment)!

وَكَذَّبَ ٱلَّذِينَ مِن قَبۡلِهِمۡ وَمَا بَلَغُواْ مِعۡشَارَ مَآ ءَاتَيۡنَٰهُمۡ فَكَذَّبُواْ رُسُلِيۖ فَكَيۡفَ كَانَ نَكِيرِ ٤٥

46. Say (to them O Muhammad صلى الله عليه وسلم): "I exhort you to one (thing) only: that you stand up for Allâh's sake in pairs and singly, and reflect (within yourselves) the life history of the Prophet صلى الله عليه وسلم: there is no madness in your companion

۞ قُلۡ إِنَّمَآ أَعِظُكُم بِوَٰحِدَةٍۖ أَن تَقُومُواْ لِلَّهِ مَثۡنَىٰ وَفُرَٰدَىٰ ثُمَّ تَتَفَكَّرُواْۚ مَا بِصَاحِبِكُم مِّن جِنَّةٍۚ إِنۡ هُوَ إِلَّا نَذِيرٞ لَّكُم بَيۡنَ يَدَيۡ عَذَابٖ شَدِيدٖ ٤٦

---

do. They (i.e. rabbis and monks) made legal things illegal, and illegal things legal, and they (i.e. Jews and Christians) followed them, and by doing so they really worshipped them." [Narrated by Ahmad, At-Tirmidhi, and Ibn Jarîr. (*Tafsîr At-Tabari*)]

(Muhammad صلى الله عليه وسلم). He is only a warner to you in face of a severe torment."

47. Say (O Muhammad صلى الله عليه وسلم) "Whatever wage I might have asked of you is yours. My wage is from Allâh only, and He is a Witness over all things."

قُلْ مَا سَأَلْتُكُم مِّنْ أَجْرٍ فَهُوَ لَكُمْ إِنْ أَجْرِيَ إِلَّا عَلَى اللَّهِ وَهُوَ عَلَى كُلِّ شَىْءٍ شَهِيدٌ ٤٧

48. Say (O Muhammad صلى الله عليه وسلم) "Verily, my Lord sends down (Revelation and makes apparent) the truth (i.e. this Revelation that had come to me), the All-Knower of the *Ghaib* (Unseen).

قُلْ إِنَّ رَبِّى يَقْذِفُ بِالْحَقِّ عَلَّامُ الْغُيُوبِ ٤٨

49. Say (O Muhammad صلى الله عليه وسلم) "*Al-Haqq* (the truth i.e. the Qur'ân and Allâh's Revelation) has come, and *Al-Bâtil* [falsehood — *Iblîs* (Satan)] can neither create anything nor resurrect (anything)."

قُلْ جَاءَ الْحَقُّ وَمَا يُبْدِئُ الْبَاطِلُ وَمَا يُعِيدُ ٤٩

50. Say: "If (even) I go astray, I shall stray only to my own loss. But if I remain guided, it is because of the Revelation of my Lord to me. Truly, He is All-Hearer, Ever Near (to all things)."

قُلْ إِن ضَلَلْتُ فَإِنَّمَا أَضِلُّ عَلَى نَفْسِى وَإِنِ اهْتَدَيْتُ فَبِمَا يُوحِى إِلَىَّ رَبِّى إِنَّهُ سَمِيعٌ قَرِيبٌ ٥٠

51. And if you could but see, when they will be terrified with no escape (for them), and they will be seized from a near place.

وَلَوْ تَرَى إِذْ فَزِعُوا فَلَا فَوْتَ وَأُخِذُوا مِن مَّكَانٍ قَرِيبٍ ٥١

52. And they will say (in the Hereafter): "We do believe (now);" but how could they receive (Faith and the acceptance of their repentance by Allâh) from a place so far off (i.e. to return to the worldly life again).

وَقَالُوا ءَامَنَّا بِهِ وَأَنَّى لَهُمُ التَّنَاوُشُ مِن مَّكَانٍ بَعِيدٍ ٥٢

53. Indeed they did disbelieve (in the Oneness of Allâh, Islâm, the Qur'ân and Muhammad (صلى الله عليه وسلم) before (in this world), and they (used to) conjecture about the Unseen [i.e. the Hereafter, Hell, Paradise, Resurrection and the Promise of Allâh, (by saying) all that is untrue], from a far place.

54. And a barrier will be set between them and that which they desire [i.e. At-Taubah (turning to Allâh in repentance) and the accepting of Faith], as was done in the past with the people of their kind. Verily, they have been in grave doubt.

Sûrat Fâtir or Al-Malâ'ikah (The Originator of Creation, or The Angels) XXXV

In the Name of Allâh the Most Gracious, the Most Merciful

1. All the praises and thanks are to Allâh, the (only) Originator [or the (Only) Creator] of the heavens and the earth, Who made the angels messengers with wings, two or three or four. He increases in creation what He wills. Verily, Allâh is Able to do all things.

2. Whatever of mercy (i.e. of good), Allâh may grant to mankind, none can withhold it; and whatever He may withhold, none can grant it thereafter. And He is the All-Mighty, the All-Wise.

3. O mankind! Remember the Grace of Allâh upon you! Is there any creator other than Allâh who provides for you from the sky (rain) and the earth? *Lâ ilâha illâ Huwa* (none has the right to be worshipped but He). How then are you turning away (from Him)?

4. And if they belie you (O Muhammad صلى الله عليه وسلم), so were Messengers belied before you. And to Allâh return all matters (for decision).

5. O mankind! Verily, the Promise of Allâh is true. So let not this present life deceive you, and let not the chief deceiver (Satan) deceive you about Allâh.

6. Surely, *Shaitân* (Satan) is an enemy to you, so take (treat) him as an enemy. He only invites his *Hizb* (followers) that they may become the dwellers of the blazing Fire.

7. Those who disbelieve, theirs will be a severe torment; and those who believe (in the Oneness of Allâh — Islâmic Monotheism) and do righteous good deeds, theirs will be forgiveness and a great reward (i.e. Paradise).

8. Is he, then, to whom the evil of his deeds is made fair-seeming, so that he considers it as good (equal to one who is rightly guided)? Verily, Allâh sends astray whom He wills, and guides whom He wills. So destroy not yourself (O Muhammad صلى الله عليه وسلم) in sorrow for them. Truly, Allâh is the All-Knower of what they do!

9. And it is Allâh Who sends the winds, so that they raise up the clouds, and We drive them to a dead land, and revive therewith to the earth after its death. As such (will be) the Resurrection!

10. Whosoever desires honour, (power and glory), then to Allâh belong all honour, power and glory [and one can get honour, power and glory only by obeying and worshipping Allâh (Alone)]. To Him ascend (all) the goodly words, and the righteous deeds exalt it (i.e. the goodly words are not accepted by Allâh unless and until they are followed by good deeds), but those who plot evils, theirs will be severe torment. And the plotting of such will perish.

11. And Allâh did create you (Adam) from dust, then from *Nutfah* (male and female discharge semen drops i.e. Adam's offspring), then He made you pairs (male and female). And no female conceives or gives birth but with His Knowledge. And no aged man is granted a length of life nor is a part cut off from his life (or another man's life), but is in a Book (*Al-Lauh Al-Mahfûz*) Surely, that is easy for Allâh.

12. And the two seas (kinds of water) are not alike: this is fresh sweet and pleasant to drink, and that is salt and bitter. And from them both you eat fresh tender meat (fish), and derive the ornaments that you wear. And you see the ships cleaving (the sea-water as they sail through it), that you may seek of His Bounty, and that you may give thanks.

13. He merges the night into the day (i.e. the decrease in the hours of the night is added to the hours of the day), and He merges the day into the night (i.e. the decrease in the hours of the day is added to the hours of the night). And He has subjected the sun and the moon: each runs its course for a term appointed. Such is Allâh, your Lord; His is the kingdom. And those, whom you invoke or call upon instead of Him, own not even a *Qitmîr* (the thin membrane over the date-stone).

14. If you invoke (or call upon) them, they hear not your call; and if (in case) they were to hear, they could not grant it (your request) to you. And on the Day of Resurrection, they will disown your worshipping them. And none can inform you (O Muhammad صلى الله عليه وسلم) like Him Who is the All-Knower (of everything).[1]

15. O mankind! it is you who stand in need of Allâh. But Allâh is Rich (Free of all needs), Worthy of all praise.

16. If He willed, He could destroy you and bring about a new creation.

17 And that is not hard for Allâh.

18. And no bearer of burdens shall bear another's burden; and if one heavily laden calls another to (bear) his load, nothing of it will be lifted even

مَوَاخِرَ لِتَبْتَغُوا مِن فَضْلِهِۦ وَلَعَلَّكُمْ تَشْكُرُونَ ۝

يُولِجُ ٱلَّيْلَ فِى ٱلنَّهَارِ وَيُولِجُ ٱلنَّهَارَ فِى ٱلَّيْلِ وَسَخَّرَ ٱلشَّمْسَ وَٱلْقَمَرَ كُلٌّ يَجْرِى لِأَجَلٍ مُّسَمًّى ذَٰلِكُمُ ٱللَّهُ رَبُّكُمْ لَهُ ٱلْمُلْكُ وَٱلَّذِينَ تَدْعُونَ مِن دُونِهِۦ مَا يَمْلِكُونَ مِن قِطْمِيرٍ ۝

إِن تَدْعُوهُمْ لَا يَسْمَعُوا دُعَآءَكُمْ وَلَوْ سَمِعُوا مَا ٱسْتَجَابُوا لَكُمْ وَيَوْمَ ٱلْقِيَٰمَةِ يَكْفُرُونَ بِشِرْكِكُمْ وَلَا يُنَبِّئُكَ مِثْلُ خَبِيرٍ ۝

۞ يَٰٓأَيُّهَا ٱلنَّاسُ أَنتُمُ ٱلْفُقَرَآءُ إِلَى ٱللَّهِ وَٱللَّهُ هُوَ ٱلْغَنِىُّ ٱلْحَمِيدُ ۝

إِن يَشَأْ يُذْهِبْكُمْ وَيَأْتِ بِخَلْقٍ جَدِيدٍ ۝

وَمَا ذَٰلِكَ عَلَى ٱللَّهِ بِعَزِيزٍ ۝

وَلَا تَزِرُ وَازِرَةٌ وِزْرَ أُخْرَىٰ وَإِن

---

[1] (V.35:14) See the footnote of (V.2:165).

though he be near of kin. You (O Muhammad صلى الله عليه وسلم) can warn only those who fear their Lord unseen and perform As-Salât (Iqâmat-as-Salât). And he who purifies himself (from all kinds of sins), then he purifies only for the benefit of his ownself. And to Allâh is the (final) Return (of all).

19. Not alike are the blind (disbelievers in Islâmic Monotheism) and the seeing (believers in Islâmic Monotheism).

20. Nor are (alike) darkness (disbelief) and light (belief in Islâmic Monotheism).

21. Nor are (alike) the shade and the sun's heat.

22. Nor are (alike) the living (i.e., the believers) and the dead (i.e., the disbelievers). Verily, Allâh makes whom He wills to hear, but you cannot make hear those who are in graves.

23. You (O Muhammad صلى الله عليه وسلم) are only a warner (i.e. your duty is to convey Allâh's Message to mankind but the guidance is Allâh's).

24. Verily, We have sent you with the truth, a bearer of glad tidings and a warner. And there never was a nation but a warner had passed among them.

25. And if they belie you, those before them also belied. Their Messengers came to them with clear signs, and with the Scriptures, and the book giving light.

26. Then I took hold of those who disbelieved: and how terrible was My denial (punishment)!

ثُمَّ أَخَذْتُ الَّذِينَ كَفَرُوا فَكَيْفَ كَانَ نَكِيرِ ۝

27. See you not that Allâh sends down water (rain) from the sky, and We produce therewith fruits of various colours, and among the mountains are streaks white and red, of varying colours and (others) very black.

أَلَمْ تَرَ أَنَّ اللَّهَ أَنزَلَ مِنَ السَّمَاءِ مَاءً فَأَخْرَجْنَا بِهِ ثَمَرَاتٍ مُّخْتَلِفًا أَلْوَانُهَا وَمِنَ الْجِبَالِ جُدَدٌ بِيضٌ وَحُمْرٌ مُّخْتَلِفٌ أَلْوَانُهَا وَغَرَابِيبُ سُودٌ ۝

28. And likewise of men and Ad-Dawâbb [moving (living) creatures, beasts], and cattle, are of various colours. It is only those who have knowledge among His slaves that fear Allâh. Verily, Allâh is All-Mighty, Oft-Forgiving.

وَمِنَ النَّاسِ وَالدَّوَابِّ وَالْأَنْعَامِ مُخْتَلِفٌ أَلْوَانُهُ كَذَلِكَ إِنَّمَا يَخْشَى اللَّهَ مِنْ عِبَادِهِ الْعُلَمَاءُ إِنَّ اللَّهَ عَزِيزٌ غَفُورٌ ۝

29. Verily, those who recite the Book of Allâh (this Qur'ân), and perform As-Salât (Iqâmat-as-Salât), and spend (in charity) out of what We have provided for them, secretly and openly, they hope for a (sure) trade-gain that will never perish.

إِنَّ الَّذِينَ يَتْلُونَ كِتَابَ اللَّهِ وَأَقَامُوا الصَّلَاةَ وَأَنفَقُوا مِمَّا رَزَقْنَاهُمْ سِرًّا وَعَلَانِيَةً يَرْجُونَ تِجَارَةً لَّن تَبُورَ ۝

30. That He may pay them their wages in full, and give them (even) more, out of His Grace. Verily, He is Oft-Forgiving, Most Ready to appreciate (good deeds and to recompense).

لِيُوَفِّيَهُمْ أُجُورَهُمْ وَيَزِيدَهُم مِّن فَضْلِهِ إِنَّهُ غَفُورٌ شَكُورٌ ۝

31. And what We have revealed to you (O Muhammad صلى الله عليه وسلم), of the Book (the Qur'ân), it is the (very) truth [that you Muhammad صلى الله عليه وسلم and your followers must act on its instructions], confirming that which was (revealed) before it. Verily, Allâh

وَالَّذِي أَوْحَيْنَا إِلَيْكَ مِنَ الْكِتَابِ هُوَ الْحَقُّ مُصَدِّقًا لِّمَا بَيْنَ يَدَيْهِ إِنَّ اللَّهَ بِعِبَادِهِ لَخَبِيرٌ بَصِيرٌ ۝

is indeed All-Aware, and All-Seer of His slaves.

32. Then We gave the Book (the Qur'ân) as inheritance to such of Our slaves whom We chose (the followers of Muhammad (صلى الله عليه وسلم). Then of them are some who wrong their ownselves, and of them are some who follow a middle course, and of them are some who are, by Allâh's Leave, foremost in good deeds. That (inheritance of the Qur'ân) — that is indeed a great grace.

ثُمَّ أَوْرَثْنَا الْكِتَابَ الَّذِينَ اصْطَفَيْنَا مِنْ عِبَادِنَا فَمِنْهُمْ ظَالِمٌ لِّنَفْسِهِۦ وَمِنْهُم مُّقْتَصِدٌ وَمِنْهُمْ سَابِقٌ بِالْخَيْرَاتِ بِإِذْنِ اللَّهِ ذَٰلِكَ هُوَ الْفَضْلُ الْكَبِيرُ ٣٢

33. 'Adn (Eden) Paradise (everlasting Gardens) will they enter, therein will they be adorned with bracelets of gold and pearls, and their garments therein will be of silk.

جَنَّاتُ عَدْنٍ يَدْخُلُونَهَا يُحَلَّوْنَ فِيهَا مِنْ أَسَاوِرَ مِن ذَهَبٍ وَلُؤْلُؤًا وَلِبَاسُهُمْ فِيهَا حَرِيرٌ ٣٣

34. And they will say: "All the praises and thanks are to Allâh Who has removed from us (all) grief. Verily, our Lord is indeed Oft-Forgiving, Most Ready to appreciate (good deeds and to recompense).

وَقَالُوا الْحَمْدُ لِلَّهِ الَّذِي أَذْهَبَ عَنَّا الْحَزَنَ إِنَّ رَبَّنَا لَغَفُورٌ شَكُورٌ ٣٤

35. Who, out of His Grace, has lodged us in a home that will last forever, where toil will touch us not nor weariness will touch us."

الَّذِي أَحَلَّنَا دَارَ الْمُقَامَةِ مِن فَضْلِهِۦ لَا يَمَسُّنَا فِيهَا نَصَبٌ وَلَا يَمَسُّنَا فِيهَا لُغُوبٌ ٣٥

36. But those who disbelieve (in the Oneness of Allâh — Islâmic Monotheism), for them will be the Fire of Hell. Neither will it have a complete killing effect on them so that they die, nor shall its torment be lightened for them. Thus do We requite every disbeliever!

وَالَّذِينَ كَفَرُوا لَهُمْ نَارُ جَهَنَّمَ لَا يُقْضَىٰ عَلَيْهِمْ فَيَمُوتُوا وَلَا يُخَفَّفُ عَنْهُم مِّنْ عَذَابِهَا كَذَٰلِكَ نَجْزِي كُلَّ كَفُورٍ ٣٦

37. Therein they will cry: "Our Lord! Bring us out, we shall do righteous good deeds, not (the evil deeds) that we used to do." (Allâh will reply): "Did We not give you lives long enough, so that whosoever would receive admonition could receive it? And the warner came to you. So taste you (the evil of your deeds). For the *Zâlimûn* (polytheists and wrongdoers) there is no helper."

38. Verily, Allâh is the All-Knower of the Unseen of the heavens and the earth. Verily, He is the All-Knower of that is in the breasts.

39. He it is Who has made you successors generations after generations in the earth, so whosoever disbelieves (in Islâmic Monotheism) on him will be his disbelief. And the disbelief of the disbelievers adds nothing but hatred of their Lord. And the disbelief of the disbelievers adds nothing but loss.[1]

40. Say (O Muhammad صلى الله عليه وسلم): "Tell me or inform me (what) do you think about your (so-called) partner-gods to whom you call upon besides Allâh? Show me, what they have created of the earth? Or have they any share in the heavens? Or have We given them a Book, so that they act on clear proof therefrom? Nay, the *Zâlimûn* (polytheists and wrongdoers) promise one another nothing but delusions."

---

[1] (V.35:39) See the footnote of (V.3:85).

41. Verily, Allâh grasps the heavens and the earth lest they should move away from their places, and if they were to move away from their places, there is not one that could grasp them after Him. Truly, He is Ever Most Forgearing, Oft-Forgiving.[1]

42. And they swore by Allâh their most binding oath that if a warner came to them, they would be more guided than any of the nations (before them); yet when a warner (Muhammad صلى الله عليه وسلم) came to them, it increased in them nothing but flight (from the truth).

43. (They took to flight because of their) arrogance in the land and their plotting of evil. But the evil plot encompasses only him who makes it. Then, can they expect anything (else) but the *Sunnah* (way of dealing) of the peoples of old? So no change will you find in Allâh's *Sunnah* (way of dealing), and no turning off will you find in Allâh's *Sunnah* (way of dealing).

44. Have they not travelled in the land, and seen what was the end of those before them — though they were superior to them in power? Allâh is not such that anything in the heavens or in

بِسۡمِ ٱللَّهِ يُمۡسِكُ ٱلسَّمَٰوَٰتِ وَٱلۡأَرۡضَ أَن تَزُولَاۚ وَلَئِن زَالَتَآ إِنۡ أَمۡسَكَهُمَا مِنۡ أَحَدٍ مِّنۢ بَعۡدِهِۦٓ إِنَّهُۥ كَانَ حَلِيمًا غَفُورًا ﴿٤١﴾

وَأَقۡسَمُواْ بِٱللَّهِ جَهۡدَ أَيۡمَٰنِهِمۡ لَئِن جَآءَهُمۡ نَذِيرٌ لَّيَكُونُنَّ أَهۡدَىٰ مِنۡ إِحۡدَى ٱلۡأُمَمِۖ فَلَمَّا جَآءَهُمۡ نَذِيرٌ مَّا زَادَهُمۡ إِلَّا نُفُورًا ﴿٤٢﴾

ٱسۡتِكۡبَارًا فِى ٱلۡأَرۡضِ وَمَكۡرَ ٱلسَّيِّئِ وَلَا يَحِيقُ ٱلۡمَكۡرُ ٱلسَّيِّئُ إِلَّا بِأَهۡلِهِۦۚ فَهَلۡ يَنظُرُونَ إِلَّا سُنَّتَ ٱلۡأَوَّلِينَۚ فَلَن تَجِدَ لِسُنَّتِ ٱللَّهِ تَبۡدِيلًاۖ وَلَن تَجِدَ لِسُنَّتِ ٱللَّهِ تَحۡوِيلًا ﴿٤٣﴾

أَوَلَمۡ يَسِيرُواْ فِى ٱلۡأَرۡضِ فَيَنظُرُواْ كَيۡفَ كَانَ عَٰقِبَةُ ٱلَّذِينَ مِن قَبۡلِهِمۡ وَكَانُوٓاْ أَشَدَّ مِنۡهُمۡ قُوَّةًۚ وَمَا كَانَ ٱللَّهُ لِيُعۡجِزَهُۥ مِن شَىۡءٍ فِى

---

[1] (V.35:41) Narrated Abû Hurairah رضي الله عنه I heard Allâh's Messenger صلى الله عليه وسلم saying, "(On the Day of Resurrection) Allâh will grasp the whole planet of earth (by His Hand), and roll all the heavens up with His Right Hand, and then He will say, 'I am the King; where are the kings of the earth?' " (*Sahih Al-Bukhari*, Vol.6, *Hadith* No.336).

the earth escapes Him. Verily, He is All-Knowing, All-Omnipotent.

45. And if Allâh were to punish men for that which they earned, He would not leave a moving (living) creature on the surface of the earth; but He gives them respite to an appointed term: and when their term comes, then verily, Allâh is Ever All-Seer of His slaves.

Sûrat Yâ-Sîn XXXVI

*In the Name of Allâh
the Most Gracious, the Most Merciful*

1. Yâ-Sîn.

[These letters are one of the miracles of the Qur'ân, and none but Allâh (Alone) knows their meanings].

2. By the Qur'ân, full of wisdom (i.e. full of laws, evidences, and proofs),

3. Truly, you (O Muhammad صلى الله عليه وسلم) are one of the Messengers,

4. On the Straight Path (i.e. on Allâh's religion of Islâmic Monotheism).

5. (This is a Revelation) sent down by the All-Mighty, the Most Merciful,

6. In order that you may warn a people whose forefathers were not warned, so they are heedless.

7. Indeed the Word (of punishment) has proved true against most of them, so they will not believe.

8. Verily, We have put on their necks iron collars reaching to the chins, so that their heads are raised up.

9. And We have put a barrier before them, and a barrier behind them, and We have covered them up, so that they cannot see.

وَجَعَلۡنَا مِنۢ بَيۡنِ أَيۡدِيهِمۡ سَدًّا وَمِنۡ خَلۡفِهِمۡ سَدًّا فَأَغۡشَيۡنَٰهُمۡ فَهُمۡ لَا يُبۡصِرُونَ ٩

10. It is the same to them whether you warn them or you warn them not, they will not believe.

وَسَوَآءٌ عَلَيۡهِمۡ ءَأَنذَرۡتَهُمۡ أَمۡ لَمۡ تُنذِرۡهُمۡ لَا يُؤۡمِنُونَ

11. You can only warn him who follows the Reminder (the Qur'ân), and fears the Most Gracious (Allâh) unseen. Bear you to such one the glad tidings of forgiveness, and a generous reward (i.e. Paradise).

إِنَّمَا تُنذِرُ مَنِ ٱتَّبَعَ ٱلذِّكۡرَ وَخَشِيَ ٱلرَّحۡمَٰنَ بِٱلۡغَيۡبِ فَبَشِّرۡهُ بِمَغۡفِرَةٍ وَأَجۡرٍ كَرِيمٍ ١١

12. Verily, We give life to the dead, and We record that which they send before (them), and their traces[1] and all things We have recorded with numbers (as a record) in a Clear Book.

إِنَّا نَحۡنُ نُحۡيِ ٱلۡمَوۡتَىٰ وَنَكۡتُبُ مَا قَدَّمُوا۟ وَءَاثَٰرَهُمۡ وَكُلَّ شَيۡءٍ أَحۡصَيۡنَٰهُ فِىٓ إِمَامٍ مُّبِينٍ ١٢

13. And put forward to them a similitude: the (story of the) Dwellers of the Town, [it is said that the town was Antioch (Antâkiya)], when there came Messengers to them.

وَٱضۡرِبۡ لَهُم مَّثَلًا أَصۡحَٰبَ ٱلۡقَرۡيَةِ إِذۡ جَآءَهَا ٱلۡمُرۡسَلُونَ ١٣

14. When We sent to them two Messengers, they belied them both; so We reinforced them with a third, and they said: "Verily, we have been sent to you as Messengers."

إِذۡ أَرۡسَلۡنَآ إِلَيۡهِمُ ٱثۡنَيۡنِ فَكَذَّبُوهُمَا فَعَزَّزۡنَا بِثَالِثٍ فَقَالُوٓا۟ إِنَّآ إِلَيۡكُم مُّرۡسَلُونَ ١٤

15. They (people of the town) said: "You are only human beings like ourselves, and the Most Gracious

قَالُوا۟ مَآ أَنتُمۡ إِلَّا بَشَرٌ مِّثۡلُنَا وَمَآ أَنزَلَ ٱلرَّحۡمَٰنُ مِن شَىۡءٍ إِنۡ

---

[1] (V.36:12) Traces: Their footsteps and walking on the earth with their legs to the mosques for the five compulsory congregational prayers, *Jihâd* (holy fighting in Allâh's Cause) and all other good and evil they did, and that which they leave behind.

(Allâh) has revealed nothing. You are only telling lies."

16. The Messengers said: "Our Lord knows that we have been sent as Messengers to you,

17. "And our duty is only to convey plainly (the Message)."

18. They (people) said: "For us, we see an evil omen from you: if you cease not, we will surely, stone you, and a painful torment will touch you from us."

19. They (Messengers) said: "Your evil omens be with you! (Do you call it "evil omen") because you are admonished? Nay, but you are a people *Musrifûn* (transgressing all bounds by committing all kinds of great sins, and by disobeying Allâh)."

20. And there came a man running from the farthest part of the town. He said: "O my people! Obey the Messengers.

21. "Obey those who ask no wages of you (for themselves), and who are rightly guided.

22. "And why should I not worship Him (Allâh Alone) Who has created me and to Whom you shall be returned.

23. "Shall I take besides Him *âlihah* (gods)? If the Most Gracious (Allâh) intends me any harm, their intercession will be of no use for me whatsoever, nor can they save me?

24. "Then verily, I should be in plain error.

25. "Verily, I have believed in your Lord, so listen to me!"

إِنِّى ءَامَنتُ بِرَبِّكُمْ فَاسْمَعُونِ ۝

26. It was said (to him when the disbelievers killed him): "Enter Paradise." He said: "Would that my people knew[1]

قِيلَ ادْخُلِ الْجَنَّةَ قَالَ يَالَيْتَ قَوْمِى يَعْلَمُونَ ۝

27. "That my Lord (Allâh) has forgiven me, and made me of the honoured ones!"

بِمَا غَفَرَ لِى رَبِّى وَجَعَلَنِى مِنَ الْمُكْرَمِينَ ۝

---

[1] (V.36:26)

a) Narrated Abu Mûsâ رضي الله عنه : Allâh's Messenger صلى الله عليه وسلم said, "My example and the example of the Message with which Allâh has sent me is like that of a man who came to some people and said, 'I have seen with my own eyes the enemy forces, and I am a naked warner (to you) so save yourself, save yourself!' A group of them obeyed him and went out at night, slowly and stealthily and were safe, while another group did not believe him and thus the army took them in the morning and destroyed them." (Sahih Al-Bukhari, Vol. 8, Hadith No. 489).

b) Narrated Anas bin Mâlik رضي الله عنه : The Prophet صلى الله عليه وسلم said, "Nobody who enters Paradise likes to go back to the world even if he got everything on the earth, except a martyr who wishes to return to the world so that he may be martyred ten times because of the honour and dignity he received (from Allâh)." (Sahih Al-Bukhari, Vol. 4, Hadith No.72)

c) Narrated 'Abdullah bin Abî Aufâ رضي الله عنهما : Allâh's Messenger صلى الله عليه وسلم said, "Know that Paradise is under the shades of swords (Jihâd in Allâh's Cause)." (Sahih Al-Bukhari, Vol. 4, Hadith No. 73)

d) Narrated Anas bin Mâlik رضي الله عنه : The Prophet صلى الله عليه وسلم used to say, "O Allâh! I seek refuge with You from helplessness, laziness, cowardice and senile old age; I seek refuge with You from Fitan (trials and afflictions) of life and death and seek refuge with You from the punishment in the grave." (Sahih Al-Bukhari, Vol. 4, Hadith No. 77)

e) Narrated Abdullah bin Umar رضي الله عنهما : I heard Allâh's Messenger صلى الله عليه وسلم saying, "People are just like camels: out of one hundred, one can hardly find a single camel suitable to ride." (Sahih Al-Bukhari, Vol. 8, Hadith No. 505).

28. And We sent not against his people after him a host from the heaven, nor was it needful for Us to send (such a thing).

وَمَآ أَنزَلْنَا عَلَىٰ قَوْمِهِ مِنۢ بَعْدِهِۦ مِن جُندٍ مِّنَ ٱلسَّمَآءِ وَمَا كُنَّا مُنزِلِينَ ٢٨

29. It was but one *Saihah* (shout) and lo! they (all) were still (silent, dead, destroyed).

إِن كَانَتْ إِلَّا صَيْحَةً وَٰحِدَةً فَإِذَا هُمْ خَٰمِدُونَ ٢٩

30. Alas for mankind! There never came a Messenger to them but they used to mock at him.

يَٰحَسْرَةً عَلَى ٱلْعِبَادِ مَا يَأْتِيهِم مِّن رَّسُولٍ إِلَّا كَانُوا۟ بِهِۦ يَسْتَهْزِءُونَ ٣٠

31. Do they not see how many of the generations We have destroyed before them? Verily, they will not return to them.

أَلَمْ يَرَوْا۟ كَمْ أَهْلَكْنَا قَبْلَهُم مِّنَ ٱلْقُرُونِ أَنَّهُمْ إِلَيْهِمْ لَا يَرْجِعُونَ ٣١

32. And surely, all — everyone of them will be brought before Us.

وَإِن كُلٌّ لَّمَّا جَمِيعٌ لَّدَيْنَا مُحْضَرُونَ ٣٢

33. And a sign for them is the dead land. We give it life, and We bring forth from it grains, so that they eat thereof.

وَءَايَةٌ لَّهُمُ ٱلْأَرْضُ ٱلْمَيْتَةُ أَحْيَيْنَٰهَا وَأَخْرَجْنَا مِنْهَا حَبًّا فَمِنْهُ يَأْكُلُونَ ٣٣

34. And We have made therein gardens of date-palms and grapes, and We have caused springs of water to gush forth therein.

وَجَعَلْنَا فِيهَا جَنَّٰتٍ مِّن نَّخِيلٍ وَأَعْنَٰبٍ وَفَجَّرْنَا فِيهَا مِنَ ٱلْعُيُونِ ٣٤

35. So that they may eat of the fruit thereof — and their hands made it not. Will they not, then, give thanks?

لِيَأْكُلُوا۟ مِن ثَمَرِهِۦ وَمَا عَمِلَتْهُ أَيْدِيهِمْ أَفَلَا يَشْكُرُونَ ٣٥

36. Glory is to Him Who has created all the pairs of that which the earth produces, as well as of their own (human) kind (male and female), and of that which they know not.

سُبْحَٰنَ ٱلَّذِى خَلَقَ ٱلْأَزْوَٰجَ كُلَّهَا مِمَّا تُنۢبِتُ ٱلْأَرْضُ وَمِنْ أَنفُسِهِمْ وَمِمَّا لَا يَعْلَمُونَ ٣٦

37. And a sign for them is the night. We withdraw therefrom the day, and behold, they are in darkness.

وَءَايَةٌ لَّهُمُ ٱلَّيْلُ نَسْلَخُ مِنْهُ ٱلنَّهَارَ فَإِذَا هُم مُّظْلِمُونَ ٣٧

38. And the sun runs on its fixed course for a term (appointed). That is

وَٱلشَّمْسُ تَجْرِى لِمُسْتَقَرٍّ لَّهَا

the Decree of the All-Mighty, the All-Knowing.

39. And the moon, We have measured for it mansions (to traverse) till it returns like the old dried curved date stalk.

40. It is not for the sun to overtake the moon, nor does the night outstrip the day. They all float, each in an orbit.

41. And an *Ayâh* (sign) for them is that We bore their offspring in the laden ship [of Nûh (Noah)].

42. And We have created for them of the like thereunto, on which they ride.

43. And if We will, We shall drown them, and there will be no shout (or helper) for them (to hear their cry for help), nor will they be saved.

44. Unless it be a mercy from Us, and as an enjoyment for a while.

45. And when it is said to them: "Beware of that which is before you (worldly torments), and that which is behind you (torments in the Hereafter), in order that you may receive Mercy (i.e. if you believe in Allâh's religion — Islâmic Monotheism, and avoid polytheism, and obey Allâh with righteous deeds).

46. And never came an *Ayâh* from among the *Ayât* (proofs, evidences, verses, lessons, signs, revelations, etc.) of their Lord to them, but they did turn away from it.

47. And when it is said to them: "Spend of that with which Allâh has provided you," those who disbelieve say to those who believe: "Shall we feed those whom, if Allâh willed, He (Himself) would have fed? You are only in a plain error."

وَإِذَا قِيلَ لَهُمْ أَنفِقُوا مِمَّا رَزَقَكُمُ اللَّهُ قَالَ الَّذِينَ كَفَرُوا لِلَّذِينَ ءَامَنُوٓا أَنُطْعِمُ مَن لَّوْ يَشَآءُ اللَّهُ أَطْعَمَهُۥٓ إِنْ أَنتُمْ إِلَّا فِى ضَلَٰلٍ مُّبِينٍ

48. And they say: "When will this promise (i.e. Resurrection) be fulfilled, if you are truthful?"

وَيَقُولُونَ مَتَىٰ هَٰذَا الْوَعْدُ إِن كُنتُمْ صَٰدِقِينَ

49. They await only but a single *Saihah* (shout) which will seize them while they are disputing!

مَا يَنظُرُونَ إِلَّا صَيْحَةً وَٰحِدَةً تَأْخُذُهُمْ وَهُمْ يَخِصِّمُونَ

50. Then they will not be able to make bequest, nor they will return to their family.

فَلَا يَسْتَطِيعُونَ تَوْصِيَةً وَلَآ إِلَىٰٓ أَهْلِهِمْ يَرْجِعُونَ

51. And the Trumpet will be blown (i.e. the second blowing) and behold from the graves they will come out quickly to their Lord.

وَنُفِخَ فِى الصُّورِ فَإِذَا هُم مِّنَ الْأَجْدَاثِ إِلَىٰ رَبِّهِمْ يَنسِلُونَ

52. They will say: "Woe to us! Who has raised us up from our place of sleep." (It will be said to them): "This is what the Most Gracious (Allâh) had promised, and the Messengers spoke truth!"

قَالُوا يَٰوَيْلَنَا مَن بَعَثَنَا مِن مَّرْقَدِنَا هَٰذَا مَا وَعَدَ الرَّحْمَٰنُ وَصَدَقَ الْمُرْسَلُونَ

53. It will be but a single *Saihah* (shout), so behold they will all be brought up before Us!

إِن كَانَتْ إِلَّا صَيْحَةً وَٰحِدَةً فَإِذَا هُمْ جَمِيعٌ لَّدَيْنَا مُحْضَرُونَ

54. This Day (Day of Resurrection), none will be wronged in anything, nor will you be requited anything except that which you used to do.

فَالْيَوْمَ لَا تُظْلَمُ نَفْسٌ شَيْـًٔا وَلَا تُجْزَوْنَ إِلَّا مَا كُنتُمْ تَعْمَلُونَ

55. Verily, the dwellers of the Paradise, that Day, will be busy with joyful things.

إِنَّ أَصْحَٰبَ الْجَنَّةِ الْيَوْمَ فِى شُغُلٍ فَٰكِهُونَ

56. They and their wives will be in pleasant shade, reclining on thrones.

57. They will have therein fruits (of all kinds) and all that they ask for.

58. (It will be said to them): *Salâm* (peace be on you) — a Word from the Lord (Allâh), Most Merciful.

59. (It will be said): "And O you *Mujrimûn* (criminals, polytheists, sinners, disbelievers in the Islâmic Monotheism, wicked evil ones)! Get you apart this Day (from the believers).

60. Did I not command you, O Children of Adam, that you should not worship *Shaitân* (Satan). Verily, he is a plain enemy to you.

61. And that you should worship Me [Alone — Islâmic Monotheism, and set up not rivals, associate-gods with Me]. That is the Straight Path.[1]

62. And indeed he (Satan) did lead astray a great multitude of you. Did you not, then, understand?

63. This is Hell which you were promised!

64. Burn therein this Day, for that you used to disbelieve.[2]

65. This Day, We shall seal up their mouths, and their hands will speak to Us, and their legs will bear witness to what they used to earn. (It is said that

---

[1] (V.36:61) See the footnote of (V.2:22).

[2] (V.36:64) See the footnote of (V.3:91).

one's left thigh will be the first to bear the witness). [Tafsir At-Tabarî]

66. And if it had been Our Will, We would surely, have wiped out (blinded) their eyes, so that they would struggle for the Path, how then would they see?

67. And if it had been Our Will, We could have transformed them (into animals or lifeless objects) in their places. Then they would have been unable to go forward (move about) nor they could have turned back.[1]

68. And he whom We grant long life — We reverse him in creation (weakness after strength). Will they not then understand?

69. And We have not taught him (Muhammad صلى الله عليه وسلم) poetry, nor is it suitable for him. This is only a Reminder and a plain Qur'ân.

70. That he or it (Muhammad صلى الله عليه وسلم or the Qur'ân) may give warning to him who is living (a healthy minded — the believer), and that Word (charge) may be justified against the disbelievers (dead, as they reject the warnings).

71. Do they not see that We have created for them of what Our Hands have created, the cattle, so that they are their owners.

72. And We have subdued them unto them so that some of them they have for riding and some they eat.

---

[1] (V.36:67) See (V.7:166) and the footnote of (V.5:90).

73. And they have (other) benefits from them, and they get (milk) to drink. Will they not then be grateful?

وَلَهُمْ فِيهَا مَنَـٰفِعُ وَمَشَارِبُ أَفَلَا يَشْكُرُونَ ۝

74. And they have taken besides Allâh *âlihah* (gods), hoping that they might be helped (by those so-called gods).

وَٱتَّخَذُوا۟ مِن دُونِ ٱللَّهِ ءَالِهَةً لَّعَلَّهُمْ يُنصَرُونَ ۝

75. They cannot help them, but they will be brought forward as a troop against those who worshipped them (at the time of Reckoning).

لَا يَسْتَطِيعُونَ نَصْرَهُمْ وَهُمْ لَهُمْ جُندٌ مُّحْضَرُونَ ۝

76. So let not their speech, then, grieve you (O Muhammad صلى الله عليه وسلم). Verily, We know what they conceal and what they reveal.

فَلَا يَحْزُنكَ قَوْلُهُمْ إِنَّا نَعْلَمُ مَا يُسِرُّونَ وَمَا يُعْلِنُونَ ۝

77. Does not man see that We have created him from *Nutfah* (mixed male and female sexual discharge — semen drops). Yet behold he (stands forth) as an open opponent.

أَوَلَمْ يَرَ ٱلْإِنسَـٰنُ أَنَّا خَلَقْنَـٰهُ مِن نُّطْفَةٍ فَإِذَا هُوَ خَصِيمٌ مُّبِينٌ ۝

78. And he puts forth for Us a parable, and forgets his own creation. He says: "Who will give life to these bones after they are rotten and have become dust?"

وَضَرَبَ لَنَا مَثَلًا وَنَسِىَ خَلْقَهُۥ قَالَ مَن يُحْىِ ٱلْعِظَـٰمَ وَهِىَ رَمِيمٌ ۝

79. Say: (O Muhammad صلى الله عليه وسلم) "He will give life to them Who created them for the first time! And He is the All-Knower of every creation!"

قُلْ يُحْيِيهَا ٱلَّذِىٓ أَنشَأَهَآ أَوَّلَ مَرَّةٍ وَهُوَ بِكُلِّ خَلْقٍ عَلِيمٌ ۝

80. He Who produces for you fire out of the green tree, when behold you kindle therewith.

ٱلَّذِى جَعَلَ لَكُم مِّنَ ٱلشَّجَرِ ٱلْأَخْضَرِ نَارًا فَإِذَآ أَنتُم مِّنْهُ تُوقِدُونَ ۝

81. Is not He Who created the heavens and the earth, Able to create

أَوَلَيْسَ ٱلَّذِى خَلَقَ ٱلسَّمَـٰوَٰتِ وَٱلْأَرْضَ بِقَـٰدِرٍ عَلَىٰٓ أَن يَخْلُقَ مِثْلَهُم بَلَىٰ وَهُوَ ٱلْخَلَّـٰقُ ٱلْعَلِيمُ ۝

the like of them? Yes, indeed! He is the All-Knowing Supreme Creator.

82. Verily, His Command, when He intends a thing, is only that He says to it, "Be!" — and it is!

إِنَّمَا أَمْرُهُۥ إِذَآ أَرَادَ شَيْئًا أَن يَقُولَ لَهُۥ كُن فَيَكُونُ ۝

83. So glorified is He and exalted above all that they associate with Him, and in Whose Hands is the dominion of all things: and to Him you shall be returned.

فَسُبْحَٰنَ ٱلَّذِى بِيَدِهِۦ مَلَكُوتُ كُلِّ شَىْءٍ وَإِلَيْهِ تُرْجَعُونَ ۝

Sûrat As-Sâffât
(Those Ranged in Ranks) XXXVII

سُورَةُ الصَّافَّات

In the Name of Allâh
. the Most Gracious, the Most Merciful

بِسْمِ ٱللَّهِ ٱلرَّحْمَٰنِ ٱلرَّحِيمِ

1. By those (angels) ranged in ranks (or rows).

وَٱلصَّٰٓفَّٰتِ صَفًّا ۝

2. By those (angels) who drive the clouds in a good way.

فَٱلزَّٰجِرَٰتِ زَجْرًا ۝

3. By those (angels) who bring the Book and the Qur'ân from Allâh to mankind [Tafsir Ibn Kathîr].

فَٱلتَّٰلِيَٰتِ ذِكْرًا ۝

4. Verily, your Ilâh (God) is indeed One (i.e. Allâh):

إِنَّ إِلَٰهَكُمْ لَوَٰحِدٌ ۝

5. Lord of the heavens and of the earth, and all that is between them, and Lord of every point of the sun's risings.[1]

رَبُّ ٱلسَّمَٰوَٰتِ وَٱلْأَرْضِ وَمَا بَيْنَهُمَا وَرَبُّ ٱلْمَشَٰرِقِ ۝

6. Verily, We have adorned the near heaven with the stars (for beauty).[2]

إِنَّا زَيَّنَّا ٱلسَّمَآءَ ٱلدُّنْيَا بِزِينَةٍ ٱلْكَوَاكِبِ ۝

---

[1] (V.37:5) The sun has approx. 365 points for its rising and 365 points for its setting (i.e. the number of days of a solar year). Every day it rises and sets in a new point, till the end of the year, then it comes back to the same point after a year. [See Tafsir Al-Qurtubi].

[2] (V.37:6) See the footnote of (V.6:97).

7. And to guard against every rebellious devil.

وَحِفْظًا مِّن كُلِّ شَيْطَٰنٍ مَّارِدٍ ۝

8. They cannot listen to the higher group (angels) for they are pelted from every side.

لَّا يَسَّمَّعُونَ إِلَى ٱلْمَلَإِ ٱلْأَعْلَىٰ وَيُقْذَفُونَ مِن كُلِّ جَانِبٍ ۝

9. Outcast, and theirs is a constant (or painful) torment.

دُحُورًا وَلَهُمْ عَذَابٌ وَاصِبٌ ۝

10. Except such as snatch away something by stealing, and they are pursued by a flaming fire of piercing brightness.

إِلَّا مَنْ خَطِفَ ٱلْخَطْفَةَ فَأَتْبَعَهُ شِهَابٌ ثَاقِبٌ ۝

11. Then ask them (i.e. these polytheists, O Muhammad صلى الله عليه وسلم): "Are they stronger as creation, or those (others like the heavens and the earth and the mountains) whom We have created?" Verily, We created them of a sticky clay.

فَٱسْتَفْتِهِمْ أَهُمْ أَشَدُّ خَلْقًا أَم مَّنْ خَلَقْنَآ إِنَّا خَلَقْنَٰهُم مِّن طِينٍ لَّازِبٍ ۝

12. Nay, you (O Muhammad صلى الله عليه وسلم) wondered (at their insolence) while they mock (at you and at the Qur'ân).

بَلْ عَجِبْتَ وَيَسْخَرُونَ ۝

13. And when they are reminded, they pay no attention.

وَإِذَا ذُكِّرُوا لَا يَذْكُرُونَ ۝

14. And when they see an Ayâh (a sign, or an evidence) from Allâh, they mock at it.

وَإِذَا رَأَوْا ءَايَةً يَسْتَسْخِرُونَ ۝

15. And they say: "This is nothing but evident magic!

وَقَالُوٓا إِنْ هَٰذَآ إِلَّا سِحْرٌ مُّبِينٌ ۝

16. "When we are dead and have become dust and bones, shall we (then) verily, be resurrected?

أَءِذَا مِتْنَا وَكُنَّا تُرَابًا وَعِظَٰمًا أَءِنَّا لَمَبْعُوثُونَ ۝

17. "And also our fathers of old?"

أَوَءَابَآؤُنَا ٱلْأَوَّلُونَ ۝

18. Say (O Muhammad صلى الله عليه وسلم) "Yes, and you shall then be humiliated."

قُلْ نَعَمْ وَأَنتُمْ دَٰخِرُونَ ۝

19. It will be a single *Zajrah* [shout (i.e. the second blowing of the Trumpet)], and behold, they will be staring!

فَإِنَّمَا هِيَ زَجْرَةٌ وَاحِدَةٌ فَإِذَا هُمْ يَنظُرُونَ ۝

20. They will say: "Woe to us! This is the Day of Recompense!"

وَقَالُوا يَٰوَيْلَنَا هَٰذَا يَوْمُ الدِّينِ ۝

21. (It will be said): "This is the Day of Judgement which you used to deny."

هَٰذَا يَوْمُ الْفَصْلِ الَّذِي كُنتُم بِهِۦ تُكَذِّبُونَ ۝

22. (It will be said to the angels): "Assemble those who did wrong, together with their companions (from the devils) and what they used to worship,

۞ احْشُرُوا الَّذِينَ ظَلَمُوا وَأَزْوَٰجَهُمْ وَمَا كَانُوا يَعْبُدُونَ ۝

23. "Instead of Allâh, and lead them on to the way of flaming Fire (Hell);

مِن دُونِ اللَّهِ فَاهْدُوهُمْ إِلَىٰ صِرَٰطِ الْجَحِيمِ ۝

24. "But stop them, verily, they are to be questioned.

وَقِفُوهُمْ إِنَّهُم مَّسْئُولُونَ ۝

25. "What is the matter with you? Why do you not help one another (as you used to do in the world)?"

مَا لَكُمْ لَا تَنَاصَرُونَ ۝

26. Nay, but that Day they shall surrender.

بَلْ هُمُ الْيَوْمَ مُسْتَسْلِمُونَ ۝

27. And they will turn to one another and question one another.

وَأَقْبَلَ بَعْضُهُمْ عَلَىٰ بَعْضٍ يَتَسَاءَلُونَ ۝

28. They will say: "It was you who used to come to us from the right side (i.e., from the right side of one of us and beautify for us every evil, join on us polytheism, and stop us from the truth i.e. Islâmic Monotheism and from every good deed)."

قَالُوا إِنَّكُمْ كُنتُمْ تَأْتُونَنَا عَنِ الْيَمِينِ ۝

29. They will reply: "Nay, you yourselves were not believers.

قَالُوا بَل لَّمْ تَكُونُوا مُؤْمِنِينَ ۝

30. "And we had no authority over you. Nay! But you were *Tâghûn*

وَمَا كَانَ لَنَا عَلَيْكُم مِّن سُلْطَٰنٍ

(transgressing) people (polytheists, and disbelievers).

بَلْ كُنتُمْ قَوْمًا طَٰغِينَ ﴿٣٠﴾

31. "So now the Word of our Lord has been justified against us, that we shall certainly (have to) taste (the torment).

فَحَقَّ عَلَيْنَا قَوْلُ رَبِّنَآ إِنَّا لَذَآئِقُونَ ﴿٣١﴾

32. "So we led you astray because we were ourselves astray."

فَأَغْوَيْنَٰكُمْ إِنَّا كُنَّا غَٰوِينَ ﴿٣٢﴾

33. Then verily, that Day, they will (all) share in the torment.

فَإِنَّهُمْ يَوْمَئِذٍ فِي ٱلْعَذَابِ مُشْتَرِكُونَ ﴿٣٣﴾

34. Certainly, that is how We deal with *Al-Mujrimûn* (polytheists, sinners, disbelievers, criminals, the disobedient to Allâh).

إِنَّا كَذَٰلِكَ نَفْعَلُ بِٱلْمُجْرِمِينَ ﴿٣٤﴾

35. Truly, when it was said to them: *Lâ ilâha illallâh* (none has the right to be worshipped but Allâh)," they puffed themselves up with pride[1] (i.e. denied it).

إِنَّهُمْ كَانُوٓا۟ إِذَا قِيلَ لَهُمْ لَآ إِلَٰهَ إِلَّا ٱللَّهُ يَسْتَكْبِرُونَ ﴿٣٥﴾

36. And (they) said: "Are we going to abandon our *âlihah* (gods) for the sake of a mad poet?

وَيَقُولُونَ أَئِنَّا لَتَارِكُوٓا۟ ءَالِهَتِنَا لِشَاعِرٍ مَّجْنُونٍ ﴿٣٦﴾

37. Nay! he (Muhammad صلى الله عليه وسلم) has come with the truth (i.e. Allâh's religion — Islâmic Monotheism and this Qur'ân) and he confirms the Messengers (before him who brought Allâh's religion — Islâmic Monotheism).

بَلْ جَآءَ بِٱلْحَقِّ وَصَدَّقَ ٱلْمُرْسَلِينَ ﴿٣٧﴾

38. Verily, you (pagans of Makkah) are going to taste the painful torment;

إِنَّكُمْ لَذَآئِقُوا۟ ٱلْعَذَابِ ٱلْأَلِيمِ ﴿٣٨﴾

39. And you will be requited nothing except for what you used to do (evil

وَمَا تُجْزَوْنَ إِلَّا مَا كُنتُمْ تَعْمَلُونَ ﴿٣٩﴾

---

[1] (V.37:35): See the footnote of (V.22:9).

deeds, sins, and Allâh's disobedience which you used to do in this world)

40. Save the chosen slaves of Allâh (i.e. the true believers of Islâmic Monotheism).

إِلَّا عِبَادَ اللَّهِ ٱلۡمُخۡلَصِينَ ﴿٤٠﴾

41. For them there will be a known provision (in Paradise),

أُوْلَٰٓئِكَ لَهُمۡ رِزۡقٌ مَّعۡلُومٌ ﴿٤١﴾

42. Fruits; and they shall be honoured,

فَوَٰكِهُ وَهُم مُّكۡرَمُونَ ﴿٤٢﴾

43. In the Gardens of delight (Paradise),

فِى جَنَّٰتِ ٱلنَّعِيمِ ﴿٤٣﴾

44. Facing one another on thrones.

عَلَىٰ سُرُرٍ مُّتَقَٰبِلِينَ ﴿٤٤﴾

45. Round them will be passed a cup of pure wine —

يُطَافُ عَلَيۡهِم بِكَأۡسٍ مِّن مَّعِينِۭ ﴿٤٥﴾

46. White, delicious to the drinkers.

بَيۡضَآءَ لَذَّةٍ لِّلشَّٰرِبِينَ ﴿٤٦﴾

47. Neither will they have *Ghoul* (any kind of hurt, abdominal pain, headache, a sin) from that, nor will they suffer intoxication therefrom.

لَا فِيهَا غَوۡلٌ وَلَا هُمۡ عَنۡهَا يُنزَفُونَ ﴿٤٧﴾

48. And beside them will be *Qâsirât-at-Tarf* [chaste females (wives), restraining their glances (desiring none except their husbands)], with wide and beautiful eyes.[1]

وَعِندَهُمۡ قَٰصِرَٰتُ ٱلطَّرۡفِ عِينٌ ﴿٤٨﴾

49. (Delicate and pure) as if they were (hidden) eggs (well) preserved.

كَأَنَّهُنَّ بَيۡضٌ مَّكۡنُونٌ ﴿٤٩﴾

50. Then they will turn to one another, mutually questioning.

فَأَقۡبَلَ بَعۡضُهُمۡ عَلَىٰ بَعۡضٍ يَتَسَآءَلُونَ ﴿٥٠﴾

51. A speaker of them will say: "Verily, I had a companion (in the world),

قَالَ قَآئِلٌ مِّنۡهُمۡ إِنِّى كَانَ لِى قَرِينٌ ﴿٥١﴾

52. Who used to say: "Are you among those who believe (in resurrection after death).

يَقُولُ أَءِنَّكَ لَمِنَ ٱلۡمُصَدِّقِينَ ﴿٥٢﴾

---

[1] (V.37:48) See the footnote of (V.29:64).

53. "(That) when we die and become dust and bones, shall we indeed (be raised up) to receive reward or punishment (according to our deeds)?"

أَءِذَا مِتْنَا وَكُنَّا تُرَابًا وَعِظَمًا أَءِنَّا لَمَدِينُونَ ۝

54. (The speaker) said: "Will you look down?"

قَالَ هَلْ أَنتُم مُّطَّلِعُونَ ۝

55. So he looked down and saw him in the midst of the Fire.

فَاطَّلَعَ فَرَءَاهُ فِى سَوَآءِ الْجَحِيمِ ۝

56. He said: "By Allâh! You have nearly ruined me.

قَالَ تَاللَّهِ إِن كِدتَّ لَتُرْدِينِ ۝

57. "Had it not been for the Grace of my Lord, I would certainly have been among those brought forth (to Hell)."

وَلَوْلَا نِعْمَةُ رَبِّى لَكُنتُ مِنَ الْمُحْضَرِينَ ۝

58. "(The dwellers of Paradise will say) Are we then not to die (any more)?

أَفَمَا نَحْنُ بِمَيِّتِينَ ۝

59. "Except our first death, and we shall not be punished? (after we have entered Paradise)."

إِلَّا مَوْتَتَنَا الْأُولَىٰ وَمَا نَحْنُ بِمُعَذَّبِينَ ۝

60. Truly, this is the supreme success!

إِنَّ هَٰذَا لَهُوَ الْفَوْزُ الْعَظِيمُ ۝

61. For the like of this let the workers work.

لِمِثْلِ هَٰذَا فَلْيَعْمَلِ الْعَامِلُونَ ۝

62. Is that (Paradise) better entertainment or the tree of *Zaqqûm* (a horrible tree in Hell)?

أَذَٰلِكَ خَيْرٌ نُّزُلًا أَمْ شَجَرَةُ الزَّقُّومِ ۝

63. Truly, We have made it (as) a trail for the *Zâlimûn* (polytheists, disbelievers, wrongdoers).

إِنَّا جَعَلْنَاهَا فِتْنَةً لِّلظَّالِمِينَ ۝

64. Verily, it is a tree that springs out of the bottom of Hell-fire,

إِنَّهَا شَجَرَةٌ تَخْرُجُ فِى أَصْلِ الْجَحِيمِ ۝

65. The shoots of its fruit-stalks are like the heads of *Shayâtîn* (devils);

طَلْعُهَا كَأَنَّهُ رُءُوسُ الشَّيَاطِينِ ۝

66. Truly, they will eat thereof and fill their bellies therewith.

فَإِنَّهُمْ لَآكِلُونَ مِنْهَا فَمَالِئُونَ مِنْهَا الْبُطُونَ ۝

67. Then on the top of that they will be given boiling water to drink so that it becomes a mixture (of boiling water and *Zaqqûm* in their bellies).

ثُمَّ إِنَّ لَهُمْ عَلَيْهَا لَشَوْبًا مِّنْ حَمِيمٍ ۝

68. Then thereafter, verily, their return is to the flaming fire of Hell.

ثُمَّ إِنَّ مَرْجِعَهُمْ لَإِلَى ٱلْجَحِيمِ ۝

69. Verily, they found their fathers on the wrong path;

إِنَّهُمْ أَلْفَوْا ءَابَآءَهُمْ ضَآلِّينَ ۝

70. So they (too) hastened in their footsteps!

فَهُمْ عَلَىٰٓ ءَاثَٰرِهِمْ يُهْرَعُونَ ۝

71. And indeed most of the men of old went astray before them;

وَلَقَدْ ضَلَّ قَبْلَهُمْ أَكْثَرُ ٱلْأَوَّلِينَ ۝

72. And indeed We sent among them warners (Messengers);

وَلَقَدْ أَرْسَلْنَا فِيهِم مُّنذِرِينَ ۝

73. Then see what was the end of those who were warned (but heeded not).

فَٱنظُرْ كَيْفَ كَانَ عَٰقِبَةُ ٱلْمُنذَرِينَ ۝

74. Except the chosen slaves of Allâh (faithful, obedient, and true believers of Islâmic Monotheism).

إِلَّا عِبَادَ ٱللَّهِ ٱلْمُخْلَصِينَ ۝

75. And indeed Nûh (Noah) invoked Us, and We are the Best of those who answer (the request).

وَلَقَدْ نَادَىٰنَا نُوحٌ فَلَنِعْمَ ٱلْمُجِيبُونَ ۝

76. And We rescued him and his family from the great distress (i.e. drowning),

وَنَجَّيْنَٰهُ وَأَهْلَهُ مِنَ ٱلْكَرْبِ ٱلْعَظِيمِ ۝

77. And, his progeny, them We made the survivors (i.e. Shem, Ham and Japheth).

وَجَعَلْنَا ذُرِّيَّتَهُۥ هُمُ ٱلْبَاقِينَ ۝

78. And left for him (a goodly remembrance) among the later generations:

وَتَرَكْنَا عَلَيْهِ فِى ٱلْءَاخِرِينَ ۝

79. "Salâm (peace) be upon Nûh (Noah) (from Us) among the *'Âlamîn* (mankind, jinn and all that exists)!"

سَلَٰمٌ عَلَىٰ نُوحٍ فِى ٱلْعَٰلَمِينَ ۝

80. Verily, thus We reward the *Muhsinûn* (good-doers — See V.2:112).

إِنَّا كَذَٰلِكَ نَجْزِي ٱلْمُحْسِنِينَ ﴿٨٠﴾

81. Verily, he [Nûh (Noah)] was one of Our believing slaves.

إِنَّهُۥ مِنْ عِبَادِنَا ٱلْمُؤْمِنِينَ ﴿٨١﴾

82. Then We drowned the others (disbelievers and polytheists).

ثُمَّ أَغْرَقْنَا ٱلْآخَرِينَ ﴿٨٢﴾

83. And, verily, among those who followed his [Nûh's (Noah)] way (Islâmic Monotheism) was Ibrâhîm (Abraham).

۞ وَإِنَّ مِن شِيعَتِهِۦ لَإِبْرَٰهِيمَ ﴿٨٣﴾

84. When he came to his Lord with a pure heart [attached to Allâh Alone and none else, worshipping none but Allâh Alone — true Islâmic Monotheism, pure from the filth of polytheism].

إِذْ جَآءَ رَبَّهُۥ بِقَلْبٍ سَلِيمٍ ﴿٨٤﴾

85. When he said to his father and to his people: "What is it that which you worship?

إِذْ قَالَ لِأَبِيهِ وَقَوْمِهِۦ مَاذَا تَعْبُدُونَ ﴿٨٥﴾

86. "Is it a falsehood — *âlihah* (gods) other than Allâh — that you desire?

أَئِفْكًا ءَالِهَةً دُونَ ٱللَّهِ تُرِيدُونَ ﴿٨٦﴾

87. "Then what think you about the Lord of the *'Âlamîn* (mankind, jinn, and all that exists)?"

فَمَا ظَنُّكُم بِرَبِّ ٱلْعَٰلَمِينَ ﴿٨٧﴾

88. Then he cast a glance at the stars,

فَنَظَرَ نَظْرَةً فِى ٱلنُّجُومِ ﴿٨٨﴾

89. And he said: "Verily, I am sick[1] (with plague). [He did this trick to remain in their temple of idols to destroy them and not to accompany them to the pagan feast)].

فَقَالَ إِنِّى سَقِيمٌ ﴿٨٩﴾

90. So they turned away from him, and departed (for fear of the disease).

فَتَوَلَّوْا عَنْهُ مُدْبِرِينَ ﴿٩٠﴾

---

[1] (V.37:89) See the footnote (C) of (V.16:121).

91. Then he turned to their *âlihah* (gods) and said: "Will you not eat (of the offering before you)?

فَرَاغَ إِلَىٰ ءَالِهَتِهِمْ فَقَالَ أَلَا تَأْكُلُونَ ٩١

92. "What is the matter with you that you speak not?"

مَا لَكُمْ لَا تَنطِقُونَ ٩٢

93. Then he turned upon them, striking (them) with (his) right hand.

فَرَاغَ عَلَيْهِمْ ضَرْبًۢا بِٱلْيَمِينِ ٩٣

94. Then they (the worshippers of idols) came, towards him, hastening.

فَأَقْبَلُوٓا۟ إِلَيْهِ يَزِفُّونَ ٩٤

95. He said: "Worship you that which you (yourselves) carve?

قَالَ أَتَعْبُدُونَ مَا تَنْحِتُونَ ٩٥

96. "While Allâh has created you and what you make!"

وَٱللَّهُ خَلَقَكُمْ وَمَا تَعْمَلُونَ ٩٦

97. They said: "Build for him a building (it is said that the building was like a furnace) and throw him into the blazing fire!"

قَالُوا۟ ٱبْنُوا۟ لَهُۥ بُنْيَٰنًا فَأَلْقُوهُ فِى ٱلْجَحِيمِ ٩٧

98. So they plotted a plot against him, but We made them the lowest.

فَأَرَادُوا۟ بِهِۦ كَيْدًا فَجَعَلْنَٰهُمُ ٱلْأَسْفَلِينَ ٩٨

99. And he said (after his rescue from the fire): "Verily, I am going to my Lord. He will guide me!"

وَقَالَ إِنِّى ذَاهِبٌ إِلَىٰ رَبِّى سَيَهْدِينِ ٩٩

100. "My Lord! Grant me (offspring) from the righteous."

رَبِّ هَبْ لِى مِنَ ٱلصَّٰلِحِينَ ١٠٠

101. So We gave him the glad tidings of a forbearing boy.

فَبَشَّرْنَٰهُ بِغُلَٰمٍ حَلِيمٍ ١٠١

102. And, when he (his son) was old enough to walk with him, he said: "O my son! I have seen in a dream that I am slaughtering you (offering you in sacrifice to Allâh). So look what you think!" He said: "O my father! Do that which you are commanded, *Inshâ' Allâh* (if Allâh wills), you shall find me of *As-Sâbirûn* (the patient)."

فَلَمَّا بَلَغَ مَعَهُ ٱلسَّعْىَ قَالَ يَٰبُنَىَّ إِنِّىٓ أَرَىٰ فِى ٱلْمَنَامِ أَنِّىٓ أَذْبَحُكَ فَٱنظُرْ مَاذَا تَرَىٰ قَالَ يَٰٓأَبَتِ ٱفْعَلْ مَا تُؤْمَرُ سَتَجِدُنِىٓ إِن شَآءَ ٱللَّهُ مِنَ ٱلصَّٰبِرِينَ ١٠٢

103. Then, when they had both submitted themselves (to the Will of Allâh), and he had laid him prostrate on his forehead (or on the side of his forehead for slaughtering);

فَلَمَّا أَسْلَمَا وَتَلَّهُ لِلْجَبِينِ ﴿١٠٣﴾

104. We called out to him: "O Abraham!

وَنَادَيْنَهُ أَن يَٰإِبْرَٰهِيمُ ﴿١٠٤﴾

105. You have fulfilled the dream!" Verily, thus do We reward the *Muhsinûn* (good-doers — See 2:112).

قَدْ صَدَّقْتَ ٱلرُّءْيَآ إِنَّا كَذَٰلِكَ نَجْزِي ٱلْمُحْسِنِينَ ﴿١٠٥﴾

106. Verily, that indeed was a manifest trial.

إِنَّ هَٰذَا لَهُوَ ٱلْبَلَٰٓؤُاْ ٱلْمُبِينُ ﴿١٠٦﴾

107. And We ransomed him with a great sacrifice (i.e. كبش — a ram);

وَفَدَيْنَٰهُ بِذِبْحٍ عَظِيمٍ ﴿١٠٧﴾

108. And We left for him (a goodly remembrance) among the later generations.

وَتَرَكْنَا عَلَيْهِ فِي ٱلْءَاخِرِينَ ﴿١٠٨﴾

109. "Salâm (peace) be upon Ibrâhîm (Abraham)!"

سَلَٰمٌ عَلَىٰٓ إِبْرَٰهِيمَ ﴿١٠٩﴾

110. Thus indeed do We reward the *Muhsinûn* (good-doers — See V.2:112).

كَذَٰلِكَ نَجْزِي ٱلْمُحْسِنِينَ ﴿١١٠﴾

111. Verily, he was one of Our believing slaves.

إِنَّهُۥ مِنْ عِبَادِنَا ٱلْمُؤْمِنِينَ ﴿١١١﴾

112. And We gave him the glad tidings of Ishâq (Isaac) — a Prophet from the righteous.

وَبَشَّرْنَٰهُ بِإِسْحَٰقَ نَبِيًّا مِّنَ ٱلصَّٰلِحِينَ ﴿١١٢﴾

113. We blessed him and Ishâq (Isaac). And of their progeny are (some) that do right, and some that plainly wrong themselves.

وَبَٰرَكْنَا عَلَيْهِ وَعَلَىٰٓ إِسْحَٰقَ وَمِن ذُرِّيَّتِهِمَا مُحْسِنٌ وَظَالِمٌ لِّنَفْسِهِۦ مُبِينٌ ﴿١١٣﴾

114. And, indeed We gave Our Grace to Mûsâ (Moses) and Hârûn (Aaron).

وَلَقَدْ مَنَنَّا عَلَىٰ مُوسَىٰ وَهَٰرُونَ ﴿١١٤﴾

115. And We saved them and their people from the great distress,

وَنَجَّيْنَٰهُمَا وَقَوْمَهُمَا مِنَ ٱلْكَرْبِ ٱلْعَظِيمِ ﴿١١٥﴾

116. And helped them, so that they became the victors;

وَنَصَرْنَهُمْ ﴿١١٦﴾

فَكَانُوا هُمُ ٱلْغَلِبِينَ ﴿١١٧﴾

117. And We gave them the clear Scripture;

وَءَاتَيْنَهُمَا ٱلْكِتَبَ ٱلْمُسْتَبِينَ ﴿١١٧﴾

118. And guided them to the Right Path.

وَهَدَيْنَهُمَا ٱلصِّرَطَ ٱلْمُسْتَقِيمَ ﴿١١٨﴾

119. And We left for them (a goodly remembrance) among the later generations.

وَتَرَكْنَا عَلَيْهِمَا فِى ٱلْءَاخِرِينَ ﴿١١٩﴾

120. "Salâm (peace) be upon Mûsâ (Moses) and Hârûn (Aaron)!"

سَلَمٌ عَلَىٰ مُوسَىٰ وَهَرُونَ ﴿١٢٠﴾

121. Verily, thus do We reward the Muhsinûn (good-doers — See V.2:112).

إِنَّا كَذَلِكَ نَجْزِى ٱلْمُحْسِنِينَ ﴿١٢١﴾

122. Verily, they were two of Our believing slaves.

إِنَّهُمَا مِنْ عِبَادِنَا ٱلْمُؤْمِنِينَ ﴿١٢٢﴾

123. And verily, Iliyâs (Elias) was one of the Messengers.

وَإِنَّ إِلْيَاسَ لَمِنَ ٱلْمُرْسَلِينَ ﴿١٢٣﴾

124. When he said to his people: "Will you not fear Allâh?

إِذْ قَالَ لِقَوْمِهِ أَلَا تَتَّقُونَ ﴿١٢٤﴾

125. "Will you call upon Ba'l (a well-known idol of his nation whom they used to worship) and forsake the Best of creators,

أَتَدْعُونَ بَعْلًا وَتَذَرُونَ أَحْسَنَ ٱلْخَلِقِينَ ﴿١٢٥﴾

126. "Allâh, your Lord and the Lord of your forefathers?"

ٱللَّهَ رَبَّكُمْ وَرَبَّ ءَابَائِكُمُ ٱلْأَوَّلِينَ ﴿١٢٦﴾

127. But they denied him [Iliyâs (Elias)], so they will certainly be brought forth (to the punishment),

فَكَذَّبُوهُ فَإِنَّهُمْ لَمُحْضَرُونَ ﴿١٢٧﴾

128. Except the chosen slaves of Allâh.

إِلَّا عِبَادَ ٱللَّهِ ٱلْمُخْلَصِينَ ﴿١٢٨﴾

129. And We left for him (a goodly remembrance) among the later generations.

وَتَرَكْنَا عَلَيْهِ فِى ٱلْءَاخِرِينَ ﴿١٢٩﴾

130. "Salâm (peace) be upon Ilyâsîn (Elias)!"

سَلَامٌ عَلَىٰٓ إِلْ يَاسِينَ ﴿١٣٠﴾

131. Verily, thus do We reward the Muhsinûn (good-doers, who perform good deeds totally for Allâh's sake only — See V.2:112).

إِنَّا كَذَٰلِكَ نَجْزِى ٱلْمُحْسِنِينَ ﴿١٣١﴾

132. Verily, he was one of Our believing slaves.

إِنَّهُۥ مِنْ عِبَادِنَا ٱلْمُؤْمِنِينَ ﴿١٣٢﴾

133. And verily, Lût (Lot) was one of the Messengers.

وَإِنَّ لُوطًا لَّمِنَ ٱلْمُرْسَلِينَ ﴿١٣٣﴾

134. When We saved him and his family, all,

إِذْ نَجَّيْنَٰهُ وَأَهْلَهُۥٓ أَجْمَعِينَ ﴿١٣٤﴾

135. Except an old woman (his wife) who was among those who remained behind.

إِلَّا عَجُوزًا فِى ٱلْغَٰبِرِينَ ﴿١٣٥﴾

136. Then We destroyed the rest (the town of Sodom at the place of the Dead Sea now in Palestine).

ثُمَّ دَمَّرْنَا ٱلْءَاخَرِينَ ﴿١٣٦﴾

137. Verily, you pass by them in the morning

وَإِنَّكُمْ لَتَمُرُّونَ عَلَيْهِم مُّصْبِحِينَ ﴿١٣٧﴾

138. And at night; will you not then reflect?

وَبِٱلَّيْلِ أَفَلَا تَعْقِلُونَ ﴿١٣٨﴾

139. And, verily, Yûnus (Jonah) was one of the Messengers.

وَإِنَّ يُونُسَ لَمِنَ ٱلْمُرْسَلِينَ ﴿١٣٩﴾

140. When he ran to the laden ship:

إِذْ أَبَقَ إِلَى ٱلْفُلْكِ ٱلْمَشْحُونِ ﴿١٤٠﴾

141. Then he (agreed to) cast lots, and he was among the losers.

فَسَاهَمَ فَكَانَ مِنَ ٱلْمُدْحَضِينَ ﴿١٤١﴾

142. Then a (big) fish swallowed him as he had done an act worthy of blame.

فَٱلْتَقَمَهُ ٱلْحُوتُ وَهُوَ مُلِيمٌ ﴿١٤٢﴾

143. Had he not been of them who glorify Allâh,

فَلَوْلَآ أَنَّهُۥ كَانَ مِنَ ٱلْمُسَبِّحِينَ ﴿١٤٣﴾

144. He would have indeed remained inside its belly (the fish) till the Day of Resurrection.

لَلَبِثَ فِى بَطْنِهِۦٓ إِلَىٰ يَوْمِ يُبْعَثُونَ ﴿١٤٤﴾

145. But We cast him forth on the naked shore while he was sick,

فَنَبَذْنَهُ بِٱلْعَرَاءِ وَهُوَ سَقِيمٌ ﴿١٤٥﴾

146. And We caused a plant of gourd to grow over him.

وَأَنۢبَتْنَا عَلَيْهِ شَجَرَةً مِّن يَقْطِينٍ ﴿١٤٦﴾

147. And We sent him to a hundred thousand (people) or even more.

وَأَرْسَلْنَٰهُ إِلَىٰ مِائَةِ أَلْفٍ أَوْ يَزِيدُونَ ﴿١٤٧﴾

148. And they believed; so We gave them enjoyment for a while.

فَـَٔامَنُوا فَمَتَّعْنَٰهُمْ إِلَىٰ حِينٍ ﴿١٤٨﴾

149. Now ask them (O Muhammad صلى الله عليه وسلم): "Are there (only) daughters for your Lord and sons for them?"

فَٱسْتَفْتِهِمْ أَلِرَبِّكَ ٱلْبَنَاتُ وَلَهُمُ ٱلْبَنُونَ ﴿١٤٩﴾

150. Or did We create the angels female while they were witnesses?

أَمْ خَلَقْنَا ٱلْمَلَٰئِكَةَ إِنَٰثًا وَهُمْ شَٰهِدُونَ ﴿١٥٠﴾

151. Verily, it is of their falsehood that they (Quraish pagans) say:

أَلَا إِنَّهُم مِّنْ إِفْكِهِمْ لَيَقُولُونَ ﴿١٥١﴾

152. "Allâh has begotten (offspring — the angels being the daughters of Allâh)?" And, verily, they are liars!

وَلَدَ ٱللَّهُ وَإِنَّهُمْ لَكَٰذِبُونَ ﴿١٥٢﴾

153. Has He (then) chosen daughters rather than sons?

أَصْطَفَى ٱلْبَنَاتِ عَلَى ٱلْبَنِينَ ﴿١٥٣﴾

154. What is the matter with you? How do you decide?

مَا لَكُمْ كَيْفَ تَحْكُمُونَ ﴿١٥٤﴾

155. Will you not then remember?

أَفَلَا تَذَكَّرُونَ ﴿١٥٥﴾

156. Or is there for you a plain authority?

أَمْ لَكُمْ سُلْطَٰنٌ مُّبِينٌ ﴿١٥٦﴾

157. Then bring your Book if you are truthful!

فَأْتُوا بِكِتَٰبِكُمْ إِن كُنتُمْ صَٰدِقِينَ ﴿١٥٧﴾

158. And they have invented a kinship between Him and the jinn, but the jinn know well that they have indeed to appear (before Him) (i.e. they will be called to account.

وَجَعَلُوا بَيْنَهُ وَبَيْنَ ٱلْجِنَّةِ نَسَبًا وَلَقَدْ عَلِمَتِ ٱلْجِنَّةُ إِنَّهُمْ لَمُحْضَرُونَ ﴿١٥٨﴾

159. Glorified is Allâh! (He is free) from what they attribute unto Him!

سُبْحَٰنَ ٱللَّهِ عَمَّا يَصِفُونَ ﴿١٥٩﴾

160. Except the slaves of Allâh, whom He chooses (for His Mercy i.e. true believers of Islâmic Monotheism who do not attribute false things unto Allâh).

إِلَّا عِبَادَ ٱللَّهِ ٱلۡمُخۡلَصِينَ ١٦٠

161. So, verily, you (pagans) and those whom you worship (idols)

فَإِنَّكُمۡ وَمَا تَعۡبُدُونَ ١٦١

162. Cannot lead astray [turn away from Him (Allâh) anyone of the believers],

مَآ أَنتُمۡ عَلَيۡهِ بِفَٰتِنِينَ ١٦٢

163. Except those who are predestined to burn in Hell!

إِلَّا مَنۡ هُوَ صَالِ ٱلۡجَحِيمِ ١٦٣

164. And there is not one of us (angels) but has his known place (or position);

وَمَا مِنَّآ إِلَّا لَهُۥ مَقَامٌ مَّعۡلُومٌ ١٦٤

165. And verily, we (angels), we stand in rows (for the prayers as you Muslims stand in rows for your prayers);

وَإِنَّا لَنَحۡنُ ٱلصَّآفُّونَ ١٦٥

166. And verily, we (angels), indeed are those who glorify (Allâh's Praises i.e. perform prayers).

وَإِنَّا لَنَحۡنُ ٱلۡمُسَبِّحُونَ ١٦٦

167. And indeed they (Arab pagans) used to say:

وَإِن كَانُواْ لَيَقُولُونَ ١٦٧

168. "If we had a reminder as had the men of old (before the coming of Prophet Muhammad صلى الله عليه وسلم as a Messenger of Allâh),

لَوۡ أَنَّ عِندَنَا ذِكۡرًا مِّنَ ٱلۡأَوَّلِينَ ١٦٨

169. "We would have indeed been the chosen slaves of Allâh (true believers of Islâmic Monotheism)!"

لَكُنَّا عِبَادَ ٱللَّهِ ٱلۡمُخۡلَصِينَ ١٦٩

170. But (now that the Qur'ân has come) they disbelieve therein (i.e. in the Qur'ân and in Prophet Muhammad صلى الله عليه وسلم, and all that he brought, — the Divine Revelation), so they will come to know! [1]

فَكَفَرُواْ بِهِۦ فَسَوۡفَ يَعۡلَمُونَ ١٧٠

---

[1] (V.37:170) See the footnote (A) of (V.3:85).

171. And, verily, Our Word has gone forth of old for Our slaves, the Messengers,

وَلَقَدْ سَبَقَتْ كَلِمَتُنَا لِعِبَادِنَا الْمُرْسَلِينَ ﴿١٧١﴾

172. That they verily, would be made triumphant,

إِنَّهُمْ لَهُمُ الْمَنصُورُونَ ﴿١٧٢﴾

173. And that Our hosts! they verily, would be the victors.

وَإِنَّ جُندَنَا لَهُمُ الْغَالِبُونَ ﴿١٧٣﴾

174. So turn away (O Muhammad صلى الله عليه وسلم) from them for a while,

فَتَوَلَّ عَنْهُمْ حَتَّى حِينٍ ﴿١٧٤﴾

175. And watch them and they shall see (the punishment)!

وَأَبْصِرْهُمْ فَسَوْفَ يُبْصِرُونَ ﴿١٧٥﴾

176. Do they seek to hasten on Our Torment?

أَفَبِعَذَابِنَا يَسْتَعْجِلُونَ ﴿١٧٦﴾

177. Then, when it descends in their courtyard (i.e. near to them), evil will be the morning for those who had been warned!

فَإِذَا نَزَلَ بِسَاحَتِهِمْ فَسَاءَ صَبَاحُ الْمُنذَرِينَ ﴿١٧٧﴾

178. So turn (O Muhammad صلى الله عليه وسلم) away from them for a while,

وَتَوَلَّ عَنْهُمْ حَتَّى حِينٍ ﴿١٧٨﴾

179. And watch and they shall see (the torment)!

وَأَبْصِرْ فَسَوْفَ يُبْصِرُونَ ﴿١٧٩﴾

180. Glorified is your Lord, the Lord of Honour and Power! (He is free) from what they attribute unto Him!

سُبْحَانَ رَبِّكَ رَبِّ الْعِزَّةِ عَمَّا يَصِفُونَ ﴿١٨٠﴾

181. And peace be on the Messengers!

وَسَلَامٌ عَلَى الْمُرْسَلِينَ ﴿١٨١﴾

182. And all the praises and thanks are to Allâh, Lord of the 'Âlamîn (mankind, jinn and all that exists).

وَالْحَمْدُ لِلَّهِ رَبِّ الْعَالَمِينَ ﴿١٨٢﴾

Sûrat Sâd XXXVIII   سورة ص

*In the Name of Allâh
the Most Gracious, the Most Merciful*   بسم الله الرحمن الرحيم

1. Sâd

[These letters (*Sâd*, etc.) are one of the miracles of the Qur'ân, and none but Allâh (Alone) knows their meanings].

By the Qur'ân full of reminding (explanations and honour for the one who believes in it).

2. Nay, those who disbelieve are in false pride and opposition.

3. How many a generation have We destroyed before them! And they cried out when there was no longer time for escape.

4. And they (Arab pagans) wonder that a warner (Prophet Muhammad صلى الله عليه وسلم) has come to them from among themselves. And the disbelievers say: "This (Prophet Muhammad صلى الله عليه وسلم) is a sorcerer, a liar.

5. "Has he made the *âlihah* (gods) (all) into One *Ilâh* (God — Allâh). Verily, this is a curious thing!"

6. And the leaders among them went about (saying): "Go on, and remain constant to your *âlihah* (gods)! Verily, this is a thing designed (against you)!

7. "We have not heard (the like) of this in the religion of these later days (i.e. Christianity). This is nothing but an invention! [*Tafsir Al-Qurtubî*]

8. "Has the Reminder been sent down to him (alone) from among us?" Nay, but they are in doubt about My Reminder (this Qur'ân)! Nay, but they have not tasted (My) Torment!

9. Or have they the treasures of the Mercy of your Lord, the All-Mighty, the Real Bestower?

10. Or is it that the dominion of the heavens and the earth and all that is between them is theirs? If so, let them ascend up with means (to the heavens)!

11. (As they denied Allâh's Message) they will be a defeated host like the Confederates of the old times (who were defeated).

12. Before them (were many who) belied (Messengers) — the people of Nûh (Noah); and 'Âd; and Fir'aun (Pharaoh) the man of stakes (with which he used to punish the people),

13. And Thamûd, and the people of Lût (Lot), and the Dwellers of the Wood: such were the Confederates.

14. Not one of them but belied the Messengers; therefore My Torment was justified.

15. And these only wait for a single *Saihah* [shout (i.e. the blowing of the Trumpet by the angel *Isrâfîl*)] there will be no pause or ending thereto [till everything will perish except Allâh (the only God full of majesty, bounty and honour)].

16. They say: "Our Lord! Hasten to us *Qittanâ* (i.e. our Record of good and bad deeds so that we may see it) before the Day of Reckoning!"

17. Be patient (O Muhammad صلى الله عليه وسلم) of what they say, and remember Our slave Dâwûd (David), endued with power. Verily, he was ever oft-returning in all matters and in repentance (toward Allâh).

الْحِسَابِ ٦

أَصْبِرْ عَلَىٰ مَا يَقُولُونَ وَاذْكُرْ عَبْدَنَا دَاوُۥدَ ذَا الْأَيْدِ إِنَّهُۥ أَوَّابٌ ١٧

18. Verily, We made the mountains to glorify Our Praises with him [Dâwûd (David)] in the 'Ashî (i.e. after the mid-day till sunset) and Ishrâq (i.e. after the sunrise till mid-day).

إِنَّا سَخَّرْنَا الْجِبَالَ مَعَهُۥ يُسَبِّحْنَ بِالْعَشِيِّ وَالْإِشْرَاقِ ١٨

19. And (so did) the birds assembled: all obedient to him [Dâwûd (David)] [i.e. they came and glorified Allâh's Praises along with him]. (Tafsîr Al-Qurtubî).

وَالطَّيْرَ مَحْشُورَةً كُلٌّ لَّهُۥ أَوَّابٌ ١٩

20. We made his kingdom strong and gave him Al-Hikmah (Prophethood) and sound judgement in speech and decision.

وَشَدَدْنَا مُلْكَهُۥ وَآتَيْنَاهُ الْحِكْمَةَ وَفَصْلَ الْخِطَابِ ٢٠

21. And has the news of the litigants reached you? When they climbed over the wall into (his) Mihrâb (a praying place or a private room);

وَهَلْ أَتَاكَ نَبَؤُا الْخَصْمِ إِذْ تَسَوَّرُوا الْمِحْرَابَ ٢١

22. When they entered in upon Dâwûd (David), he was terrified of them. They said: "Fear not! (We are) two litigants, one of whom has wronged the other, therefore judge between us with truth, and treat us not with injustice, and guide us to the Right Way.

إِذْ دَخَلُوا عَلَىٰ دَاوُۥدَ فَفَزِعَ مِنْهُمْ قَالُوا لَا تَخَفْ خَصْمَانِ بَغَىٰ بَعْضُنَا عَلَىٰ بَعْضٍ فَاحْكُم بَيْنَنَا بِالْحَقِّ وَلَا تُشْطِطْ وَاهْدِنَا إِلَىٰ سَوَاءِ الصِّرَاطِ ٢٢

23. Verily, this my brother (in religion) has ninety-nine ewes, while I

إِنَّ هَٰذَا أَخِي لَهُۥ تِسْعٌ وَتِسْعُونَ نَعْجَةً

have (only) one ewe, and he says: "Hand it over to me, and he overpowered me in speech."

24. [Dâwûd (David)] said (immediately without listening to the opponent): "He has wronged you in demanding your ewe in addition to his ewes. And, verily, many partners oppress one another, except those who believe and do righteous good deeds, and they are few." And Dâwûd (David) guessed that We have tried him and he sought forgiveness of his Lord, and he fell down prostrate and turned (to Allâh) in repentance.

25. So We forgave him that, and verily, for him is a near access to Us, and a good place of (final) return (Paradise).

26. O Dâwûd (David)! Verily, We have placed you as a successor on the earth; so judge you between men in truth (and justice) and follow not your desire — for it will mislead you from the Path of Allâh. Verily, those who wander astray from the Path of Allâh (shall) have a severe torment, because they forgot the Day of Reckoning.

27. And We created not the heaven and the earth and all that is between them without purpose! That is the consideration of those who disbelieve! Then woe to those who disbelieve (in Islâmic Monotheism) from the Fire!

28. Shall We treat those who believe (in the Oneness of Allâh — Islâmic **Monotheism**) and do righteous

وَلِيَ نَعْجَةٌ وَٰحِدَةٌ فَقَالَ أَكْفِلْنِيهَا وَعَزَّنِي فِي ٱلْخِطَابِ ٢٣

قَالَ لَقَدْ ظَلَمَكَ بِسُؤَالِ نَعْجَتِكَ إِلَىٰ نِعَاجِهِۦ وَإِنَّ كَثِيرًا مِّنَ ٱلْخُلَطَآءِ لَيَبْغِى بَعْضُهُمْ عَلَىٰ بَعْضٍ إِلَّا ٱلَّذِينَ ءَامَنُوا۟ وَعَمِلُوا۟ ٱلصَّٰلِحَٰتِ وَقَلِيلٌ مَّا هُمْ وَظَنَّ دَاوُۥدُ أَنَّمَا فَتَنَّٰهُ فَٱسْتَغْفَرَ رَبَّهُۥ وَخَرَّ رَاكِعًا وَأَنَابَ ۩ ٢٤

فَغَفَرْنَا لَهُۥ ذَٰلِكَ وَإِنَّ لَهُۥ عِندَنَا لَزُلْفَىٰ وَحُسْنَ مَـَٔابٍ ٢٥

يَٰدَاوُۥدُ إِنَّا جَعَلْنَٰكَ خَلِيفَةً فِى ٱلْأَرْضِ فَٱحْكُم بَيْنَ ٱلنَّاسِ بِٱلْحَقِّ وَلَا تَتَّبِعِ ٱلْهَوَىٰ فَيُضِلَّكَ عَن سَبِيلِ ٱللَّهِ إِنَّ ٱلَّذِينَ يَضِلُّونَ عَن سَبِيلِ ٱللَّهِ لَهُمْ عَذَابٌ شَدِيدٌۢ بِمَا نَسُوا۟ يَوْمَ ٱلْحِسَابِ ٢٦

وَمَا خَلَقْنَا ٱلسَّمَآءَ وَٱلْأَرْضَ وَمَا بَيْنَهُمَا بَٰطِلًا ذَٰلِكَ ظَنُّ ٱلَّذِينَ كَفَرُوا۟ فَوَيْلٌ لِّلَّذِينَ كَفَرُوا۟ مِنَ ٱلنَّارِ ٢٧

أَمْ نَجْعَلُ ٱلَّذِينَ ءَامَنُوا۟ وَعَمِلُوا۟ ٱلصَّٰلِحَٰتِ كَٱلْمُفْسِدِينَ فِى

good deeds as *Mufsidûn* (those who associate partners in worship with Allâh and commit crimes) on earth? Or shall We treat the *Muttaqûn* (the pious. See V.2:2) as the *Fujjâr* (criminals, disbelievers, the wicked)?

29. (This is) a Book (the Qur'ân) which We have sent down to you, full of blessings, that they may ponder over its Verses, and that men of understanding may remember.

30. And to Dâwûd (David) We gave Sulaimân (Solomon). How excellent a slave! Verily, he was ever oft-returning in repentance (to Us)!

31. When there were displayed before him, in the afternoon, well trained horses of the highest breed [for *Jihâd* (holy fighting in Allâh's Cause)].

32. He said: "I did love the good (these horses) instead of remembering my Lord (in my 'Asr prayer)" till the time was over, and (the sun) had hidden in the veil (of night).

33. Then he said "Bring them (horses) back to me." Then he began to pass his hand over their legs and their necks (till the end of the display).

34. And indeed, We did try Sulaimân (Solomon) and We placed on his throne *Jasad* (a devil, so he lost his kingdom for a while) and he did return (to Allâh with obedience and in repentance, and to his throne and kingdom by the Grace of Allâh).

35. He said: "My Lord! Forgive me, and bestow upon me a kingdom such as shall not belong to any other after me: Verily, You are the Bestower."

قَالَ رَبِّ اغْفِرْ لِى وَهَبْ لِى مُلْكًا لَّا يَنۢبَغِى لِأَحَدٍ مِّنۢ بَعْدِىٓ إِنَّكَ أَنتَ الْوَهَّابُ ﴿٣٥﴾

36. So, We subjected to him the wind; it blew gently by his order whithersoever he willed,

فَسَخَّرْنَا لَهُ الرِّيحَ تَجْرِى بِأَمْرِهِ رُخَآءً حَيْثُ أَصَابَ ﴿٣٦﴾

37. And also the *Shayâtîn* (devils) from the jinn (including) every kind of builder and diver,

وَالشَّيَـٰطِينَ كُلَّ بَنَّآءٍ وَغَوَّاصٍ ﴿٣٧﴾

38. And also others bound in fetters.

وَءَاخَرِينَ مُقَرَّنِينَ فِى الْأَصْفَادِ ﴿٣٨﴾

39. [Allâh said to Sulaimân (Solomon)]: "This is Our gift: so spend you or withhold, no account will be asked of you."

هَـٰذَا عَطَآؤُنَا فَامْنُنْ أَوْ أَمْسِكْ بِغَيْرِ حِسَابٍ ﴿٣٩﴾

40. And verily, for him is a near access to Us, and a good (final) return (Paradise).

وَإِنَّ لَهُۥ عِندَنَا لَزُلْفَىٰ وَحُسْنَ مَـَٔابٍ ﴿٤٠﴾

41. And remember Our slave Ayûb (Job), when he invoked his Lord (saying): "Verily, *Shaitân* (Satan) has touched me with distress (by ruining my health) and torment (by ruining my wealth)!

وَاذْكُرْ عَبْدَنَآ أَيُّوبَ إِذْ نَادَىٰ رَبَّهُۥٓ أَنِّى مَسَّنِىَ الشَّيْطَـٰنُ بِنُصْبٍ وَعَذَابٍ ﴿٤١﴾

42. (Allâh said to him): "Strike the ground with your foot: This is (a spring of) water to wash in, cool and a (refreshing) drink."

ارْكُضْ بِرِجْلِكَ هَـٰذَا مُغْتَسَلٌۢ بَارِدٌ وَشَرَابٌ ﴿٤٢﴾

43. And We gave him (back) his family, and along with them the like thereof, as a Mercy from Us, and a Reminder for those who understand.

وَوَهَبْنَا لَهُۥٓ أَهْلَهُۥ وَمِثْلَهُم مَّعَهُمْ رَحْمَةً مِّنَّا وَذِكْرَىٰ لِأُولِى الْأَلْبَـٰبِ ﴿٤٣﴾

44. "And take in your hand a bundle of thin grass and strike therewith (your wife), and break not

وَخُذْ بِيَدِكَ ضِغْثًا فَاضْرِب بِّهِۦ وَلَا

your oath.[1] Truly, We found him patient. How excellent a slave! Verily, he was ever oft-returning in repentance (to Us)!

45. And remember Our slaves, Ibrâhîm (Abraham), Ishâq (Isaac), and Ya'qûb (Jacob), (all) owners of strength (in worshipping Us) and (also) of religious understanding.

46. Verily, We did choose them by granting them (a good thing, — i.e.) the remembrance of the home [in the Hereafter and they used to make the people remember it, and also they used to invite the people to obey Allâh and to do good deeds for the Hereafter].

47. And they are with Us, verily, of the chosen and the best!

48. And remember Ismâ'îl (Ishmael), Alyasaa' (Elisha), and Dhul-Kifl (Isaiah), all are among the best.

49. This is a Reminder. And verily, for the *Muttaqûn* (the pious and righteous persons. See V.2:2) is a good final return (Paradise), —

50. 'Adn (Eden) Paradise (everlasting Gardens), whose doors will be opened for them.

51. Therein they will recline; therein they will call for fruits in abundance and drinks;

---

[1] (V.38:44) During the ailment of Ayûb (Job), his wife used to beg for him, and Satan told her a word of disbelief to say and she told her husband [Ayûb (Job)]; so he became angry with her and took an oath to strike her one hundred lashes. So Allâh ordered Ayûb (Job) to fulfil his oath by striking her with the bundle of thin grass. [*Tafsîr Al-Qurtubî*]

52. And beside them will be *Qâsirât-at-Tarf* [chaste females (wives) restraining their glances (desiring none except their husbands)], (and) of equal ages.

۞ وَعِندَهُمۡ قَـٰصِرَٰتُ ٱلطَّرۡفِ أَتۡرَابٌ ۝

53. This is what you (*Al-Muttaqûn* — the pious. See V.2:2) are promised for the Day of Reckoning!

هَـٰذَا مَا تُوعَدُونَ لِيَوۡمِ ٱلۡحِسَابِ ۝

54. (It will be said to them)! Verily, this is Our provision which will never finish.

إِنَّ هَـٰذَا لَرِزۡقُنَا مَا لَهُۥ مِن نَّفَادٍ ۝

55. This is so! And for the *Tâghûn* (transgressors, the disobedient to Allâh and His Messenger — disbelievers in the Oneness of Allâh, criminals) will be an evil final return (Fire).

هَـٰذَا وَإِنَّ لِلطَّـٰغِينَ لَشَرَّ مَـَٔابٍ ۝

56. Hell! Where they will burn, and worst (indeed) is that place to rest!

جَهَنَّمَ يَصۡلَوۡنَهَا فَبِئۡسَ ٱلۡمِهَادُ ۝

57. This is so! Then let them taste it — a boiling fluid and dirty wound discharges.

هَـٰذَا فَلۡيَذُوقُوهُ حَمِيمٌ وَغَسَّاقٌ ۝

58. And other (torments) of similar kind — all together!

وَءَاخَرُ مِن شَكۡلِهِۦٓ أَزۡوَٰجٌ ۝

59. This is a troop entering with you (in Hell), no welcome for them! Verily, they shall burn in the Fire!

هَـٰذَا فَوۡجٌ مُّقۡتَحِمٌ مَّعَكُمۡ لَا مَرۡحَبَۢا بِهِمۡ إِنَّهُمۡ صَالُوا ٱلنَّارِ ۝

60. (The followers of the misleaders will say): "Nay, you (too)! No welcome for you! It is you (misleaders) who brought this upon us (because you misled us in the world), so evil is this place to stay in!"

قَالُوا بَلۡ أَنتُمۡ لَا مَرۡحَبَۢا بِكُمۡ أَنتُمۡ قَدَّمۡتُمُوهُ لَنَا فَبِئۡسَ ٱلۡقَرَارُ ۝

61. They will say: "Our Lord! Whoever brought this upon us, add to him a double torment in the Fire!"

قَالُوا رَبَّنَا مَن قَدَّمَ لَنَا هَـٰذَا فَزِدۡهُ عَذَابًا ضِعۡفًا فِى ٱلنَّارِ ۝

62. And they will say: "What is the matter with us that we see not men whom we used to count among the bad ones?"

وَقَالُوا۟ مَا لَنَا لَا نَرَىٰ رِجَالًا كُنَّا نَعُدُّهُم مِّنَ ٱلْأَشْرَارِ ٦٢

63. Did we take them as an object of mockery, or have (our) eyes failed to perceive them?"

أَتَّخَذْنَـٰهُمْ سِخْرِيًّا أَمْ زَاغَتْ عَنْهُمُ ٱلْأَبْصَـٰرُ ٦٣

64. Verily, that is the very truth — the mutual dispute of the people of the Fire!

إِنَّ ذَٰلِكَ لَحَقٌّ تَخَاصُمُ أَهْلِ ٱلنَّارِ ٦٤

65. Say (O Muhammad صلى الله عليه وسلم): "I am only a warner and there is no *Ilâh* (God) except Allâh (none has the right to be worshipped but Allâh) the One, the Irresistible,

قُلْ إِنَّمَا أَنَا۠ مُنذِرٌ وَمَا مِنْ إِلَـٰهٍ إِلَّا ٱللَّهُ ٱلْوَٰحِدُ ٱلْقَهَّارُ ٦٥

66. "The Lord of the heavens and the earth and all that is between them, the All-Mighty, the Oft-Forgiving."

رَبُّ ٱلسَّمَـٰوَٰتِ وَٱلْأَرْضِ وَمَا بَيْنَهُمَا ٱلْعَزِيزُ ٱلْغَفَّـٰرُ ٦٦

67. Say: "That (this Qur'ân) is a great news,

قُلْ هُوَ نَبَؤٌا۟ عَظِيمٌ ٦٧

68. "From which you turn away!

أَنتُمْ عَنْهُ مُعْرِضُونَ ٦٨

69. "I had no knowledge of the chiefs (angels) on high when they were disputing and discussing (about the creation of Adam).

مَا كَانَ لِيَ مِنْ عِلْمٍ بِٱلْمَلَإِ ٱلْأَعْلَىٰٓ إِذْ يَخْتَصِمُونَ ٦٩

70. "Only this has been revealed to me, that I am a plain warner."

إِن يُوحَىٰٓ إِلَيَّ إِلَّآ أَنَّمَآ أَنَا۠ نَذِيرٌ مُّبِينٌ ٧٠

71. (Remember) when your Lord said to the angels: "Truly, I am going to create man from clay".

إِذْ قَالَ رَبُّكَ لِلْمَلَـٰٓئِكَةِ إِنِّى خَـٰلِقٌۢ بَشَرًا مِّن طِينٍ ٧١

72. So when I have fashioned him and breathed into him (his) soul created by Me, then you fall down prostrate to him."

فَإِذَا سَوَّيْتُهُۥ وَنَفَخْتُ فِيهِ مِن رُّوحِى فَقَعُوا۟ لَهُۥ سَـٰجِدِينَ ٧٢

73. So the angels prostrated themselves, all of them:

فَسَجَدَ ٱلْمَلَٰٓئِكَةُ كُلُّهُمْ أَجْمَعُونَ ۝

74. Except *Iblîs* (Satan): he was proud[1] and was one of the disbelievers.

إِلَّآ إِبْلِيسَ ٱسْتَكْبَرَ وَكَانَ مِنَ ٱلْكَٰفِرِينَ ۝

75. (Allâh) said: "O *Iblîs* (Satan)! What prevents you from prostrating yourself to one whom I have created with Both My Hands.[2] Are you too proud (to fall prostrate to Adam) or are you one of the high exalted?"

قَالَ يَٰٓإِبْلِيسُ مَا مَنَعَكَ أَن تَسْجُدَ لِمَا خَلَقْتُ بِيَدَيَّ أَسْتَكْبَرْتَ أَمْ كُنتَ مِنَ ٱلْعَالِينَ ۝

76. [*Iblîs* (Satan)] said: "I am better than he. You created me from fire, and You created him from clay."

قَالَ أَنَا۠ خَيْرٌ مِّنْهُ خَلَقْتَنِي مِن نَّارٍ وَخَلَقْتَهُۥ مِن طِينٍ ۝

77. (Allâh) said: "Then get out from here; for verily, you are outcast.

قَالَ فَٱخْرُجْ مِنْهَا فَإِنَّكَ رَجِيمٌ ۝

78. "And verily, My Curse is on you till the Day of Recompense."

وَإِنَّ عَلَيْكَ لَعْنَتِيٓ إِلَىٰ يَوْمِ ٱلدِّينِ ۝

79. [*Iblîs* (Satan)] said: "My Lord! Give me then respite till the Day the (dead) are resurrected."

قَالَ رَبِّ فَأَنظِرْنِيٓ إِلَىٰ يَوْمِ يُبْعَثُونَ ۝

80. (Allâh) said: "Verily, you are of those allowed respite,

قَالَ فَإِنَّكَ مِنَ ٱلْمُنظَرِينَ ۝

81. "Till the Day of the time appointed."

إِلَىٰ يَوْمِ ٱلْوَقْتِ ٱلْمَعْلُومِ ۝

82. [*Iblîs* (Satan)] said: "By Your Might, then I will surely, mislead them all,

قَالَ فَبِعِزَّتِكَ لَأُغْوِيَنَّهُمْ أَجْمَعِينَ ۝

83. "Except Your chosen slaves amongst them (i.e. faithful, obedient, true believers of Islâmic Monotheism)."

إِلَّا عِبَادَكَ مِنْهُمُ ٱلْمُخْلَصِينَ ۝

84. (Allâh) said: "The truth is — and the truth I say —

قَالَ فَٱلْحَقُّ وَٱلْحَقَّ أَقُولُ ۝

---

[1] (V.38:74): See the footnote of (V.22:9).

[2] (V.38:75) See the footnote of (V.3:73).

85. That I will fill Hell with you [*Iblîs* (Satan)] and those of them (mankind) that follow you, together."

لَأَمْلَأَنَّ جَهَنَّمَ مِنكَ وَمِمَّن تَبِعَكَ مِنْهُمْ أَجْمَعِينَ ﴿٨٥﴾

86. Say (O Muhammad صلى الله عليه وسلم): "No wage do I ask of you for this (the Qur'ân), nor am I one of the *Mutakallifûn* (those who pretend and fabricate things which do not exist).

قُلْ مَآ أَسْأَلُكُمْ عَلَيْهِ مِنْ أَجْرٍ وَمَآ أَنَا۠ مِنَ ٱلْمُتَكَلِّفِينَ ﴿٨٦﴾

87. "It (this Qur'ân) is only a Reminder for all the *'Âlamîn* (mankind and jinn).

إِنْ هُوَ إِلَّا ذِكْرٌ لِّلْعَـٰلَمِينَ ﴿٨٧﴾

88. "And you shall certainly know the truth of it after a while".

وَلَتَعْلَمُنَّ نَبَأَهُۥ بَعْدَ حِينٍۭ ﴿٨٨﴾

Sûrat Az-Zumar
(The Groups) XXXIX

سُورَةُ ٱلزُّمَرِ

In the Name of Allâh
the Most Gracious, the Most Merciful

بِسْمِ ٱللَّهِ ٱلرَّحْمَٰنِ ٱلرَّحِيمِ

1. The revelation of this Book (the Qur'ân) is from Allâh, the All-Mighty, the All-Wise.

تَنزِيلُ ٱلْكِتَٰبِ مِنَ ٱللَّهِ ٱلْعَزِيزِ ٱلْحَكِيمِ ﴿١﴾

2. Verily, We have sent down the Book to you (O Muhammad صلى الله عليه وسلم) in truth: So worship Allâh (Alone) by doing religious deeds sincerely for Allâh's sake only.

إِنَّآ أَنزَلْنَآ إِلَيْكَ ٱلْكِتَٰبَ بِٱلْحَقِّ فَٱعْبُدِ ٱللَّهَ مُخْلِصًا لَّهُ ٱلدِّينَ ﴿٢﴾

3. Surely, the religion (i.e. the worship and the obedience) is for Allâh only. And those who take *Auliyâ'* (protectors, helpers, lords, gods) besides Him (say): "We worship them only that they may bring us near to Allâh." Verily, Allâh will judge between them concerning that wherein they differ. Truly, Allâh guides not him who is a liar, and a disbeliever.

أَلَا لِلَّهِ ٱلدِّينُ ٱلْخَالِصُ وَٱلَّذِينَ ٱتَّخَذُوا۟ مِن دُونِهِۦٓ أَوْلِيَآءَ مَا نَعْبُدُهُمْ إِلَّا لِيُقَرِّبُونَآ إِلَى ٱللَّهِ زُلْفَىٰٓ إِنَّ ٱللَّهَ يَحْكُمُ بَيْنَهُمْ فِي مَا هُمْ فِيهِ يَخْتَلِفُونَ إِنَّ ٱللَّهَ لَا يَهْدِي مَنْ هُوَ كَٰذِبٌ كَفَّارٌ ﴿٣﴾

4. Had Allâh willed to take a son (or offspring), He could have chosen whom He willed out of those whom He created. But glory is to Him! (He is above such things). He is Allâh, the One, the Irresistible.[1]

5. He has created the heavens and the earth with truth. He makes the night to go in the day and makes the day to go in the night. And He has subjected the sun and the moon. Each running (on a fixed course) for an appointed term. Verily, He is the All-Mighty, the Oft-Forgiving.

6. He created you (all) from a single person (Adam); then made from him his wife [Hawwâ' (Eve)]. And He has sent down for you of cattle eight pairs (of the sheep, two, male and female; of the goats, two, male and female; of the oxen, two, male and female; and of the camels, two, male and female). He creates you in the wombs of your mothers: creation after creation in three veils of darkness. Such is Allâh your Lord. His is the kingdom. *Lâ ilâha illâ Huwa* (none has the right to be worshipped but He). How then are you turned away?

7. If you disbelieve, then verily, Allâh is not in need of you; He likes not disbelief for His slaves. And if you are grateful (by being believers), He is pleased therewith for you. No

---

[1] (V.39:4) See the footnote of (V.2:116).

bearer of burdens shall bear the burden of another. Then to your Lord is your return, and He will inform you what you used to do. Verily, He is the All-Knower of that which is in (men's) breasts.

8. And when some hurt touches man, he cries to his Lord (Allâh Alone), turning to Him in repentance. But when He bestows a favour upon him from Himself, he forgets that for which he cried for before, and he sets up rivals to Allâh, in order to mislead others from His Path. Say: "Take pleasure in your disbelief for a while: surely, you are (one) of the dwellers of the Fire!"

9. Is one who is obedient to Allâh, prostrating himself or standing (in prayer) during the hours of the night, fearing the Hereafter and hoping for the Mercy of his Lord (like one who disbelieves)? Say: "Are those who know equal to those who know not?" It is only men of understanding who will remember (i.e. get a lesson from Allâh's Signs and Verses).

10. Say (O Muhammad صلى الله عليه وسلم): "O My slaves who believe (in the Oneness of Allâh — Islâmic Monotheism), be afraid of your Lord (Allâh) and keep your duty to Him. Good is (the reward) for those who do good in this world, and Allâh's earth is spacious (so if you cannot worship Allâh at a place, then go to another)! Only those who are patient shall receive their reward in full, without reckoning.[1]"

11. Say (O Muhammad صلى الله عليه وسلم): "Verily, I am commanded to worship Allâh (Alone) by obeying Him and doing religious deeds sincerely for His sake only.

قُلۡ إِنِّيٓ أُمِرۡتُ أَنۡ أَعۡبُدَ ٱللَّهَ مُخۡلِصًا لَّهُ ٱلدِّينَ ۝

12. "And I am commanded (this) in order that I may be the first of those who submit themselves to Allâh (in Islâm) as Muslims."

وَأُمِرۡتُ لِأَنۡ أَكُونَ أَوَّلَ ٱلۡمُسۡلِمِينَ ۝

13. Say (O Muhammad صلى الله عليه وسلم): "Verily, if I disobey my Lord, I am afraid of the torment of a great Day."

قُلۡ إِنِّيٓ أَخَافُ إِنۡ عَصَيۡتُ رَبِّي عَذَابَ يَوۡمٍ عَظِيمٍ ۝

14. Say (O Muhammad صلى الله عليه وسلم): "Allâh Alone I worship by doing religious deeds sincerely for His sake only (and not to show off, and not to set up rivals with Him in worship)."

قُلِ ٱللَّهَ أَعۡبُدُ مُخۡلِصًا لَّهُ دِينِي ۝

15. So worship what you like besides Him. Say (O Muhammad صلى الله عليه وسلم): "The losers are those who will lose themselves and their families on the Day of Resurrection. Verily, that will be a manifest loss!"

فَٱعۡبُدُوا۟ مَا شِئۡتُم مِّن دُونِهِۦ قُلۡ إِنَّ ٱلۡخَٰسِرِينَ ٱلَّذِينَ خَسِرُوٓا۟ أَنفُسَهُمۡ وَأَهۡلِيهِمۡ يَوۡمَ ٱلۡقِيَٰمَةِ أَلَا ذَٰلِكَ هُوَ ٱلۡخُسۡرَانُ ٱلۡمُبِينُ ۝

16. They shall have coverings of Fire, above them and covering (of Fire) beneath them. With this Allâh does frighten His slaves: "O My slaves, therefore fear Me!"

لَهُم مِّن فَوۡقِهِمۡ ظُلَلٌ مِّنَ ٱلنَّارِ وَمِن تَحۡتِهِمۡ ظُلَلٌ ذَٰلِكَ يُخَوِّفُ ٱللَّهُ بِهِۦ عِبَادَهُۥ يَٰعِبَادِ فَٱتَّقُونِ ۝

17. Those who avoid At-Tâghût[2] (false deities) by not worshipping

وَٱلَّذِينَ ٱجۡتَنَبُوا۟ ٱلطَّٰغُوتَ أَن

---

[1] (V.39:10) See the footnote of (V.16:126).

[2] (V.39:17) See the footnote of (V.2:256).

them and turn to Allâh (in repentance), for them are glad tidings; so announce the good news to My slaves —

بَعِدُوهَا وَأَنَابُوٓاْ إِلَى ٱللَّهِ لَهُمُ ٱلْبُشْرَىٰ فَبَشِّرْ عِبَادِ ٧

18. Those who listen to the Word [good advice Lâ ilâha illallâh — (none has the right to be worshipped but Allâh) and Islâmic Monotheism] and follow the best thereof (i.e. worship Allâh Alone, repent to Him and avoid Tâghût) those are (the ones) whom Allâh has guided and those are men of understanding.[1]

ٱلَّذِينَ يَسْتَمِعُونَ ٱلْقَوْلَ فَيَتَّبِعُونَ أَحْسَنَهُۥٓ أُوْلَٰٓئِكَ ٱلَّذِينَ هَدَىٰهُمُ ٱللَّهُ وَأُوْلَٰٓئِكَ هُمْ أُوْلُواْ ٱلْأَلْبَٰبِ ١٨

19. Is, then one against whom the Word of punishment is justified (equal to the one who avoids evil)? Will you (O Muhammad صلى الله عليه وسلم) rescue him who is in the Fire?

أَفَمَنْ حَقَّ عَلَيْهِ كَلِمَةُ ٱلْعَذَابِ أَفَأَنتَ تُنقِذُ مَن فِى ٱلنَّارِ ١٩

20. But those who fear their Lord (Allâh) and keep their duty to Him, for them are built lofty rooms, one above another under which rivers flow (i.e. Paradise). (This is) the Promise of Allâh: and Allâh does not fail in (His) Promise.

لَٰكِنِ ٱلَّذِينَ ٱتَّقَوْاْ رَبَّهُمْ لَهُمْ غُرَفٌ مِّن فَوْقِهَا غُرَفٌ مَّبْنِيَّةٌ تَجْرِى مِن تَحْتِهَا ٱلْأَنْهَٰرُ وَعْدَ ٱللَّهِ لَا يُخْلِفُ ٱللَّهُ ٱلْمِيعَادَ ٢٠

21. See you not that Allâh sends down water (rain) from the sky, and causes it to penetrate the earth, (and then makes it to spring up) as water-springs, and afterward thereby

أَلَمْ تَرَ أَنَّ ٱللَّهَ أَنزَلَ مِنَ ٱلسَّمَآءِ مَآءً فَسَلَكَهُۥ يَنَٰبِيعَ فِى ٱلْأَرْضِ ثُمَّ يُخْرِجُ بِهِۦ زَرْعًا مُّخْتَلِفًا أَلْوَٰنُهُۥ ثُمَّ

---

[1] (V.39:18) Like Zaid bin ʿAmr bin Nufail, Salmân Al-Fârisi and Abû Dharr Al-Ghifârî. [*Tafsir Al-Qurtubi*, also see the footnote of (V.2:135)]

produces crops of different colours, and afterward they wither and you see them turn yellow; then He makes them dry and broken pieces. Verily, in this is a Reminder for men of understanding.

22. Is he whose breast Allâh has opened to Islâm, so that he is in light from His Lord (as he who is a non-Muslim)? So woe to those whose hearts are hardened against remembrance of Allâh! They are in plain error!

23. Allâh has sent down the Best Statement, a Book (this Qur'ân), its parts resembling each other (in goodness and truth) (and) oft-repeated. The skins of those who fear their Lord shiver from it (when they recite it or hear it). Then their skin and their heart soften to the remembrance of Allâh. That is the guidance of Allâh. He guides therewith whom He wills; and whomever Allâh sends astray, for him there is no guide.

24. Is he then, who will confront with his face the awful torment on the Day of Resurrection (as he who enters peacefully in Paradise)? And it will be said to the Zâlimûn (polytheists and wrongdoers): "Taste what you used to earn!"

25. Those before them belied, and so the torment came on them from directions they perceived not.

كَذَّبَ الَّذِينَ مِن قَبْلِهِمْ فَأَتَنهُمُ الْعَذَابُ مِنْ حَيْثُ لَا يَشْعُرُونَ ۝

26. So Allâh made them to taste the disgrace in the present life, but greater is the torment of the Hereafter if they only knew!

فَأَذَاقَهُمُ اللَّهُ الْخِزْيَ فِي الْحَيَوٰةِ الدُّنْيَا وَلَعَذَابُ الْآخِرَةِ أَكْبَرُ لَوْ كَانُوا يَعْلَمُونَ ۝

27. And indeed We have put forth for men, in this Qur'ân every kind of similitude in order that they may remember.

وَلَقَدْ ضَرَبْنَا لِلنَّاسِ فِي هَٰذَا الْقُرْآنِ مِن كُلِّ مَثَلٍ لَّعَلَّهُمْ يَتَذَكَّرُونَ ۝

28. An Arabic Qur'ân, without any crookedness (therein) in order that they may avoid all evil which Allâh has ordered them to avoid, fear Him and keep their duty to Him.

قُرْآنًا عَرَبِيًّا غَيْرَ ذِي عِوَجٍ لَّعَلَّهُمْ يَتَّقُونَ ۝

29. Allâh puts forth a similitude: a (slave) man belonging to many partners (like those who worship others along with Allâh) disputing with one another, and a (slave) man belonging entirely to one master (like those who worship Allâh Alone). Are those two equal in comparison? All the praises and thanks are to Allâh! But most of them know not.

ضَرَبَ اللَّهُ مَثَلًا رَّجُلًا فِيهِ شُرَكَاءُ مُتَشَاكِسُونَ وَرَجُلًا سَلَمًا لِّرَجُلٍ هَلْ يَسْتَوِيَانِ مَثَلًا الْحَمْدُ لِلَّهِ بَلْ أَكْثَرُهُمْ لَا يَعْلَمُونَ ۝

30. Verily, you (O Muhammad صلى الله عليه وسلم) will die, and verily, they (too) will die.

إِنَّكَ مَيِّتٌ وَإِنَّهُم مَّيِّتُونَ ۝

31. Then, on the Day of Resurrection, you will be disputing before your Lord.

ثُمَّ إِنَّكُمْ يَوْمَ الْقِيَامَةِ عِندَ رَبِّكُمْ تَخْتَصِمُونَ ۝

32. Then, who does more wrong than one who utters a lie against Allâh,[1] and denies the truth [this Qur'ân, the Prophet (Muhammad صلى الله عليه وسلم) and the Islâmic Monotheism] when it comes to him! Is there not in Hell an abode for the disbelievers?

33. And he (Muhammad صلى الله عليه وسلم) who has brought the truth (this Qur'ân and Islâmic Monotheism) and (those who) believed therein (i.e. the true believers of Islâmic Monotheism), those are Al-Muttaqûn (the pious and righteous persons. See V.2:2).

34. They shall have all that they will desire with their Lord. That is the reward of Muhsinûn (good-doers — see the footnote of V.9:120).

35. So that Allâh may expiate from them the evil of what they did and give them the reward, according to the best of what they used to do.[2]

36. Is not Allâh Sufficient for His slave? Yet they try to frighten you with those (whom they worship) besides Him! And whom Allâh sends astray, for him there will be no guide.

37. And whomsoever Allâh guides, for him there will be no misleader. Is not Allâh All-Mighty, Possessor of Retribution?

38. And verily, if you ask them: "Who created the heavens and the

---

[1] (V.39:32) See the footnote of (V.6:101).

[2] (V.39:35) See the footnote of (V.9:121).

earth?" Surely, they will say: "Allâh (has created them)." Say: "Tell me then, the things that you invoke besides Allâh — if Allâh intended some harm for me, could they remove His harm? Or if He (Allâh) intended some mercy for me, could they withhold His Mercy?" Say : "Sufficient for me is Allâh; in Him those who trust (i.e. believers) must put their trust.[1]"

39. Say: (O Muhammad صلى الله عليه وسلم) "O My people! Work according to your way, I am working (according to my way). Then you will come to know

40. "To whom comes a disgracing torment, and on whom descends an everlasting torment."

41. Verily, We have sent down to you (O Muhammad صلى الله عليه وسلم) the Book (this Qur'ân) for mankind in truth. So whosoever accepts the guidance, it is only for his ownself, and whosoever goes astray, he goes astray only for his (own) loss. And you (O Muhammad صلى الله عليه وسلم) are not a *Wakîl* (trustee or disposer of affairs, or guardian) over them.[2]

42. It is Allâh Who takes away the souls at the time of their death, and those that die not during their sleep. He keeps those (souls) for which He has ordained death and sends the rest for a term appointed. Verily, in this are signs for a people who think deeply.

---

[1] (V.39:38) See the footnote of (V.12:67).
[2] (V.39:41) See the footnote of (V.3:85).

43. Have they taken (others) as intercessors besides Allâh? Say: "Even if they have power over nothing whatever and have no intelligence?"

أَمِ ٱتَّخَذُوا مِن دُونِ ٱللَّهِ شُفَعَآءَ قُلْ أَوَلَوْ كَانُوا لَا يَمْلِكُونَ شَيْئًا وَلَا يَعْقِلُونَ ٤٣

44. Say: "To Allâh belongs all intercession. His is the Sovereignty of the heavens and the earth. Then to Him you shall be brought back."

قُل لِّلَّهِ ٱلشَّفَعَةُ جَمِيعًا لَّهُۥ مُلْكُ ٱلسَّمَوَتِ وَٱلْأَرْضِ ثُمَّ إِلَيْهِ تُرْجَعُونَ ٤٤

45. And when Allâh Alone is mentioned, the hearts of those who believe not in the Hereafter are filled with disgust (from the Oneness of Allâh توحيد الله) and when those (whom they obey or worship) besides Him [like all false deities other than Allâh, — it may be a Messenger, an angel, a pious man, a jinni, or any other creature even idols, graves of religious people, saints, priests, monks and others] are mentioned, behold, they rejoice![1]

وَإِذَا ذُكِرَ ٱللَّهُ وَحْدَهُ ٱشْمَأَزَّتْ قُلُوبُ ٱلَّذِينَ لَا يُؤْمِنُونَ بِٱلْآخِرَةِ وَإِذَا ذُكِرَ ٱلَّذِينَ مِن دُونِهِۦٓ إِذَا هُمْ يَسْتَبْشِرُونَ ٤٥

46. Say (O Muhammad صلى الله عليه وسلم): "O Allâh! Creator of the heavens and the earth! All-Knower of the *Ghaib* (Unseen) and the seen! You will judge between your slaves about that wherein they used to differ."

قُلِ ٱللَّهُمَّ فَاطِرَ ٱلسَّمَوَتِ وَٱلْأَرْضِ عَلِمَ ٱلْغَيْبِ وَٱلشَّهَدَةِ أَنتَ تَحْكُمُ بَيْنَ عِبَادِكَ فِي مَا كَانُوا فِيهِ يَخْتَلِفُونَ ٤٦

47. And those who did wrong (the polytheists and disbelievers in the Oneness of Allâh), if they had all that is in earth and therewith as much again, they verily, would offer it to ransom themselves therewith on the Day of Resurrection from the evil torment; and there will become apparent to them

وَلَوْ أَنَّ لِلَّذِينَ ظَلَمُوا مَا فِي ٱلْأَرْضِ جَمِيعًا وَمِثْلَهُۥ مَعَهُۥ لَٱفْتَدَوْا بِهِۦ مِن سُوٓءِ ٱلْعَذَابِ يَوْمَ ٱلْقِيَمَةِ وَبَدَا لَهُم مِّنَ ٱللَّهِ مَا لَمْ يَكُونُوا يَحْتَسِبُونَ ٤٧

---

[1] (V.39:45) See the footnote of (V.2:165).

from Allâh what they had not been reckoning.[1]

48. And the evils of that which they earned will become apparent to them, and that which they used to mock at will encircle them.

49. When harm touches man, he calls to Us (for help); then when We have (rescued him from that harm and) changed it into a favour from Us, he says: "Only because of knowledge (that I possess) I obtained it." Nay, it is only a trial, but most of them know not!

50. Verily, those before them said it, yet (all) that they had earned availed them not.

51. So, the evil results of that which they earned overtook them. And those who did wrong of these [people to whom (Muhammad صلى الله عليه وسلم) have been sent] will also be overtaken by the evil results (torment) for that which they earned; and they will never be able to escape.[2]

52. Do they not know that Allâh enlarges the provision for whom He wills, and straitens it (for whom He wills). Verily, in this are signs for the folk who believe!

53. Say: "O *'Ibâdî* (My slaves) who have transgressed against themselves (by committing evil deeds and sins)!

وَبَدَا لَهُم سَيِّئَاتُ مَا كَسَبُواْ وَحَاقَ بِهِم مَّا كَانُواْ بِهِۦ يَسْتَهْزِءُونَ ﴿٤٨﴾

فَإِذَا مَسَّ ٱلْإِنسَٰنَ ضُرٌّ دَعَانَا ثُمَّ إِذَا خَوَّلْنَٰهُ نِعْمَةً مِّنَّا قَالَ إِنَّمَآ أُوتِيتُهُۥ عَلَىٰ عِلْمٍ بَلْ هِيَ فِتْنَةٌ وَلَٰكِنَّ أَكْثَرَهُمْ لَا يَعْلَمُونَ ﴿٤٩﴾

قَدْ قَالَهَا ٱلَّذِينَ مِن قَبْلِهِمْ فَمَآ أَغْنَىٰ عَنْهُم مَّا كَانُواْ يَكْسِبُونَ ﴿٥٠﴾

فَأَصَابَهُمْ سَيِّئَاتُ مَا كَسَبُواْ وَٱلَّذِينَ ظَلَمُواْ مِنْ هَٰٓؤُلَآءِ سَيُصِيبُهُمْ سَيِّئَاتُ مَا كَسَبُواْ وَمَا هُم بِمُعْجِزِينَ ﴿٥١﴾

أَوَلَمْ يَعْلَمُوٓاْ أَنَّ ٱللَّهَ يَبْسُطُ ٱلرِّزْقَ لِمَن يَشَآءُ وَيَقْدِرُ إِنَّ فِي ذَٰلِكَ لَءَايَٰتٍ لِّقَوْمٍ يُؤْمِنُونَ ﴿٥٢﴾

۞ قُلْ يَٰعِبَادِيَ ٱلَّذِينَ أَسْرَفُواْ عَلَىٰٓ أَنفُسِهِمْ لَا تَقْنَطُواْ مِن

---

[1] (V.39:47) See the footnote of (V.3:91).

[2] (V.39:51) See the footnote of (V.5:90).

Despair not of the Mercy of Allâh:
verily, Allâh forgives all sins. Truly, He
is Oft-Forgiving, Most Merciful.[1]

54. "And turn in repentance and in
obedience with true Faith (Islâmic
Monotheism) to your Lord and submit
to Him (in Islâm) before the torment
comes upon you, (and) then you will
not be helped.

55. "And follow the best of that
which is sent down to you from your
Lord (i.e. this Qur'ân, do what it orders
you to do and keep away from what it
forbids), before the torment comes on
you suddenly while you perceive not!"

56. Lest a person should say: "Alas,
my grief that I was undutiful to Allâh
(i.e. I have not done what Allâh has
ordered me to do), and I was indeed
among those who mocked [at the truth!
i.e. Lâ ilâha illallâh (none has the right
to be worshipped but Allâh), the
Qur'ân, and Muhammad صلى الله عليه وسلم and
at the faithful believers]

57. Or (lest) he should say: "If only
Allâh had guided me, I should indeed
have been among the Muttaqûn (the pious
and righteous persons. See V.2:2)."

58. Or (lest) he should say when he
sees the torment: "If only I had another

---

[1] (V.39:53)

A) See the footnote of (V.9:121).

B) See the footnote of (V.22:27).

C) See the footnote of (V.25:70).

chance (to return to the world), then I should indeed be among the *Muhsinûn* (good-doers — See V.2:112)."

أَن لِى كَرَّةً فَأَكُونَ مِنَ ٱلْمُحْسِنِينَ ٥٨

59. Yes! Verily, there came to you My *Ayât* (proofs, evidences, verses, lessons, signs, revelations, etc.) and you denied them, and were proud[1] and were among the disbelievers.

بَلَىٰ قَدْ جَآءَتْكَ ءَايَنِي فَكَذَّبْتَ بِهَا وَٱسْتَكْبَرْتَ وَكُنتَ مِنَ ٱلْكَٰفِرِينَ ٥٩

60. And on the Day of Resurrection you will see those who lied against Allâh (i.e. attributed to Him sons, partners) — their faces will be black. Is there not in Hell an abode for the arrogant?

وَيَوْمَ ٱلْقِيَٰمَةِ تَرَى ٱلَّذِينَ كَذَبُوا۟ عَلَى ٱللَّهِ وُجُوهُهُم مُّسْوَدَّةٌ أَلَيْسَ فِى جَهَنَّمَ مَثْوًى لِّلْمُتَكَبِّرِينَ ٦٠

61. And Allâh will deliver those who are the *Muttaqûn* (the pious. See V.2:2) to their places of success (Paradise). Evil shall touch them not, nor shall they grieve.

وَيُنَجِّى ٱللَّهُ ٱلَّذِينَ ٱتَّقَوْا۟ بِمَفَازَتِهِمْ لَا يَمَسُّهُمُ ٱلسُّوٓءُ وَلَا هُمْ يَحْزَنُونَ ٦١

62. Allâh is the Creator of all things, and He is the *Wakîl* (Trustee, Disposer of affairs, Guardian) over all things.

ٱللَّهُ خَٰلِقُ كُلِّ شَىْءٍ وَهُوَ عَلَىٰ كُلِّ شَىْءٍ وَكِيلٌ ٦٢

63. To Him belong the keys of the heavens and the earth. And those who disbelieve in the *Ayât* (proofs, evidences, verses, signs, revelations, etc.) of Allâh, such are they who will be the losers.

لَّهُۥ مَقَالِيدُ ٱلسَّمَٰوَٰتِ وَٱلْأَرْضِ وَٱلَّذِينَ كَفَرُوا۟ بِـَٔايَٰتِ ٱللَّهِ أُو۟لَٰٓئِكَ هُمُ ٱلْخَٰسِرُونَ ٦٣

64. Say (O Muhammad ﷺ to the polytheists): "Do you order me to worship other than Allâh? O you fools!"

قُلْ أَفَغَيْرَ ٱللَّهِ تَأْمُرُوٓنِّىٓ أَعْبُدُ أَيُّهَا ٱلْجَٰهِلُونَ ٦٤

65. And indeed it has been revealed to you (O Muhammad ﷺ), as it was to those (Allâh's Messengers)

وَلَقَدْ أُوحِىَ إِلَيْكَ وَإِلَى ٱلَّذِينَ مِن قَبْلِكَ لَئِنْ أَشْرَكْتَ لَيَحْبَطَنَّ

---

[1] (V.39:59) See the footnote of (V.22:9)

before you: "If you join others in worship with Allâh, (then) surely, (all) your deeds will be in vain, and you will certainly be among the losers.[1]"

66. Nay! But worship Allâh (Alone and none else), and be among the grateful.

67. They made not a just estimate of Allâh such as is due to Him. And on the Day of Resurrection the whole of the earth will be grasped by His Hand[2] and the heavens will be rolled up in His Right Hand. Glorified is He, and High is He above all that they associate as partners with Him!

68. And the Trumpet will be blown, and all who are in the heavens and all who are on the earth will swoon away, except him whom Allâh wills. Then it will be blown a second time, and behold they will be standing, looking on (waiting).[3]

---

[1] (V.39:65)

A) See the footnote of (V.2:165).

B) See the footnote of (V.4:135).

[2] (V.39:67) See the footnote of (V.35:41).

[3] (V.39:68).

a) Narrated Abû Hurairah رضي الله عنه The Prophet صلى الله عليه وسلم said, "I will be the first to raise my head after the second blowing of the Trumpet and will see Mûsâ (Moses) holding or clinging to the Throne; and I will not know whether he had been in that state all the time or after the blowing of the Trumpet." (Sahih Al-Bukhari, Vol.6, Hadîth No.337).

b) Narrated Abû Hurairah رضي الله عنه The Prophet صلى الله عليه وسلم said, "Between the two blowings of the Trumpet there will be forty." The people said, "O Abû Hurairah! Forty days?" I refused to reply. They said, "Forty years?" I refused to reply. They said, "Forty Months?" I

69. And the earth will shine with the light of its Lord (Allâh, when He will come to judge among men): and the Book will be placed (open); and the Prophets and the witnesses will be brought forward; and .it will be judged between them with truth, and they will not be wronged.

وَأَشْرَقَتِ ٱلْأَرْضُ بِنُورِ رَبِّهَا وَوُضِعَ ٱلْكِتَٰبُ وَجِايٓءَ بِٱلنَّبِيِّـۧنَ وَٱلشُّهَدَآءِ وَقُضِيَ بَيْنَهُم بِٱلْحَقِّ وَهُمْ لَا يُظْلَمُونَ ٦٩

70. And each person will be paid in full of what he did; and He is Best Aware of what they do.

وَوُفِّيَتْ كُلُّ نَفْسٍ مَّا عَمِلَتْ وَهُوَ أَعْلَمُ بِمَا يَفْعَلُونَ ٧٠

71. And those who disbelieved will be driven to Hell in groups till, when they reach it, the gates thereof will be opened (suddenly like a prison at the arrival of the prisoners). And its keepers will say, "Did not the Messengers come to you from yourselves, reciting to you the Verses of your Lord, and warning you of the Meeting of this Day of yours?" They will say: "Yes," but the Word of torment has been justified against the disbelievers![1]

وَسِيقَ ٱلَّذِينَ كَفَرُوٓاْ إِلَىٰ جَهَنَّمَ زُمَرًا حَتَّىٰٓ إِذَا جَآءُوهَا فُتِحَتْ أَبْوَٰبُهَا وَقَالَ لَهُمْ خَزَنَتُهَآ أَلَمْ يَأْتِكُمْ رُسُلٌ مِّنكُمْ يَتْلُونَ عَلَيْكُمْ ءَايَٰتِ رَبِّكُمْ وَيُنذِرُونَكُمْ لِقَآءَ يَوْمِكُمْ هَٰذَا قَالُواْ بَلَىٰ وَلَٰكِنْ حَقَّتْ كَلِمَةُ ٱلْعَذَابِ عَلَى ٱلْكَٰفِرِينَ ٧١

72. It will be said (to them): "Enter you the gates of Hell, to abide therein. And (indeed) what an evil abode of the arrogant!"

قِيلَ ٱدْخُلُوٓاْ أَبْوَٰبَ جَهَنَّمَ خَٰلِدِينَ فِيهَا فَبِئْسَ مَثْوَى ٱلْمُتَكَبِّرِينَ ٧٢

73. And those who kept their duty to their Lord will be led to Paradise in

وَسِيقَ ٱلَّذِينَ ٱتَّقَوْاْ رَبَّهُمْ إِلَى

---

refused to reply and added: Everything of a human body will waste away, perish or decay except the last coccyx bone (of the tail) and from that bone Allâh will reconstruct the whole body. (*Sahih Al-Bukhari*, Vol.6, *Hadith* No.338).

[1] (V.39:71) See the footnote of (V.3:85).

groups, till, when they reach it, and its gates will be opened (before their arrival for their reception) and its keepers will say: *Salâmun 'Alaikum* (peace be upon you)! You have done well, so enter here to dwell therein."

74. And they will say: "All the praises and thanks are to Allâh Who has fulfilled His Promise to us and has made us inherit (this) land. We can dwell in Paradise where we will; how excellent a reward for the (pious, good) workers!"

75. And you will see the angels surrounding the Throne (of Allâh) from all round, glorifying the praises of their Lord (Allâh). And they (all the creatures) will be judged with truth. And it will be said, "All the praises and thanks are to Allâh, the Lord of the *'Âlamîn* (mankind, jinn and all that exists)."

Surat Ghâfir or Al-Mû'min (The Forgiver or The Believer) XL

In the Name of Allâh the Most Gracious, the Most Merciful

1. *Hâ. Mîm.*

[These letters are one of the miracles of the Qur'ân, and none but Allâh (Alone) knows their meanings].

2. The revelation of the Book (this Qur'ân) is from Allâh, the All-Mighty, the All-Knower.

3. The Forgiver of sin, the Acceptor of repentance, the Severe in punishment, the Bestower (of favours). *Lâ ilâha illâ Huwa* (none has the right to be worshipped but He), to Him is the final return.

4. None disputes in the *Ayât* (proofs, evidences, verses, lessons, signs, revelations, etc.) of Allâh but those who disbelieve. So let not their ability of going about here and there through the land (for their purposes) deceive you [O Muhammad صلى الله عليه وسلم, for their ultimate end will be the Fire of Hell!]

5. The people of Nûh (Noah) and the Confederates after them denied (their Messengers) before these; and every (disbelieving) nation plotted against their Messenger to seize him, and disputed by means of falsehood to refute therewith the truth. So I seized them (with punishment), and how (terrible) was My punishment!

6. Thus has the Word of your Lord been justified against those who disbelieved, that they will be the dwellers of the Fire.[1]

7. Those (angels) who bear the Throne (of Allâh) and those around it glorify the praises of their Lord, and believe in Him, and ask forgiveness for those who believe in the Oneness of Allâh (saying): "Our Lord! You comprehend all things in mercy and knowledge, so forgive those who repent

---

[1] (V.40:6) See the footnote of (V.3:85).

and follow Your Way, and save them from the torment of the blazing Fire!

8. "Our Lord! And make them enter the 'Adn (Eden) Paradise (everlasting Gardens) which you have promised them — and to the righteous among their fathers, their wives, and their offspring! Verily, You are the All-Mighty, the All-Wise.

9. "And save them from (the punishment for what they did of) the sins, and whomsoever You save from (the punishment for what he did of) the sins (i.e. pardon him) that Day, him verily, You have taken into mercy." And that is the supreme success.

10. Those who disbelieve will be addressed (at the time of entering the Fire): "Allâh's aversion was greater towards you (in the worldly life when you used to reject the Faith) than your aversion towards one another (now in the Fire of Hell, as you are now enemies to one another), when you were called to the Faith but you used to refuse."

11. They will say: "Our Lord! You have made us to die twice (i.e. we were dead in the loins of our fathers and dead after our life in this world), and You have given us life twice (i.e. life when we were born and life when we are Resurrected)! Now we confess our sins, then is there any way to get out (of the Fire)?" [See *Tafsir Al-Qurtubi*].

12. (It will be said:) "This is because, when Allâh Alone was invoked (in worship) you disbelieved (denied), but when partners were joined to Him, you believed! So the judgement is only with Allâh, the Most High, the Most Great![1]"

ذَٰلِكُم بِأَنَّهُۥٓ إِذَا دُعِىَ ٱللَّهُ وَحْدَهُۥ كَفَرْتُمْ وَإِن يُشْرَكْ بِهِۦ تُؤْمِنُواْ فَٱلْحُكْمُ لِلَّهِ ٱلْعَلِىِّ ٱلْكَبِيرِ ۝

13. It is He Who shows you His *Ayât* (proofs, evidences, lessons, signs, revelations, etc.) and sends down (rain with which grows) provision for you from the sky. And none remembers but those who turn (to Allâh in obedience and) in repentance (by begging His Pardon and by worshipping and obeying Him Alone and none else).

هُوَ ٱلَّذِى يُرِيكُمْ ءَايَٰتِهِۦ وَيُنَزِّلُ لَكُم مِّنَ ٱلسَّمَآءِ رِزْقًا وَمَا يَتَذَكَّرُ إِلَّا مَن يُنِيبُ ۝

14. So, call you (O Muhammad صلى الله عليه وسلم and the believers) upon (or invoke) Allâh making (your) worship pure for Him (Alone) (by worshipping none but Him and by doing religious deeds sincerely for Allâh's sake only and not to show off and not to set up rivals with Him in worship), however much the disbelievers (in the Oneness of Allâh) may hate (it).

فَٱدْعُواْ ٱللَّهَ مُخْلِصِينَ لَهُ ٱلدِّينَ وَلَوْ كَرِهَ ٱلْكَٰفِرُونَ ۝

15. (He is Allâh) Owner of High Ranks and Degrees, the Owner of the Throne. He sends the revelation by His Command to

رَفِيعُ ٱلدَّرَجَٰتِ ذُو ٱلْعَرْشِ

---

[1] (V.40:12) Narrated 'Abdullâh رضى الله عنه "The Prophet صلى الله عليه وسلم said one statement and I said another. The Prophet صلى الله عليه وسلم said: 'Whoever dies while still invoking anything other than Allâh as a rival to Allâh, will enter Hell (Fire).' And I said, 'Whoever dies without invoking anything as a rival to Allâh, will enter Paradise.'" (Sahih Al-Bukhari, Vol. 6, Hadith No. 24).

any of His slaves He wills, that he (the person who receives revelation) may warn (men) of the Day of Mutual Meeting (i.e. the Day of Resurrection).

16. The Day when they will (all) come out, nothing of them will be hidden from Allâh. Whose is the kingdom this Day? (Allâh Himself will reply to His Question): It is Allâh's the One, the Irresistible!

17. This Day shall every person be recompensed for what he earned. This Day no injustice (shall be done to anybody). Truly, Allâh is Swift in reckoning.

18. And warn them (O Muhammad ﷺ (صلى الله عليه وسلم) of the Day that is drawing near (i.e. the Day of Resurrection), when the hearts will be choking the throats, and they can neither return them (hearts) to their chests nor can they throw them out. There will be no friend, nor an intercessor for the *Zâlimûn* (polytheists and wrongdoers), who could be given heed to.

19. Allâh knows the fraud of the eyes, and all that the breasts conceal.

20. And Allâh judges with truth, while those to whom they invoke besides Him, cannot judge anything. Certainly, Allâh! He is the All-Hearer, the All-Seer.

21. Have they not travelled in the land and seen what was the end of those who were before them? They were superior to them in strength, and in the traces (which they left) in the land. But Allâh seized them with punishment for their sins. And none had they to protect them from Allâh.

22. That was because there came to them their Messengers with clear evidences (proofs and signs) but they disbelieved (in them). So Allâh seized them (with punishment). Verily, He is All-Strong, Severe in punishment.

23. And indeed We sent Mûsâ (Moses) with Our *Ayât* (proofs, evidences, verses, lessons, signs, revelations, etc.), and a manifest authority,

24. To Fir'aun (Pharaoh), Hâmân and Qârûn (Korah), but they called (him): "A sorcerer, a liar!"

25. Then, when he brought them the Truth from Us, they said: "Kill the sons of those who believe with him and let their women live"; but the plots of disbelievers are nothing but in vain!

26. Fir'aun (Pharaoh) said: "Leave me to kill Mûsâ (Moses), and let him call his Lord (to stop me from killing him)! I fear that he may change your religion, or that he may cause mischief to appear in the land!"

27. Mûsâ (Moses) said: "Verily, I seek refuge in my Lord and your Lord from every arrogant who believes not in the Day of Reckoning!"

28. And a believing man of Fir'aun's (Pharaoh) family, who hid his faith said: "Would you kill a man because he says: My Lord is Allâh, and he has come to you with clear signs (proofs) from your Lord? And if he is (the sin of) his lie; but if he is telling the truth, then some of that (calamity) wherewith he threatens you will befall on you." Verily, Allâh guides not one who is a *Musrif* (a polytheist, or a murderer who shed blood without a right, or those who commit great sins, oppressor, transgressor), a liar!

29. "O my people! Yours is the kingdom today, you being dominant in the land. But who will save us from the Torment of Allâh, should it befall us?" Fir'aun (Pharaoh) said: "I show you only that which I see (correct), and I guide you only to the path of right policy!"

30. And he who believed said: "O my people! Verily, I fear for you a fate like that day (of disaster) of the Confederates (of old)!

31. "Like the fate of the people of Nûh (Noah), and 'Âd, and Thamûd and those who came after them. And Allâh wills no injustice for (His) slaves.

32. "And, O my people! Verily, I fear for you the Day when there will be mutual calling (between the people of Hell and of Paradise)."

33. A Day when you will turn your backs and flee having no protector from Allâh. And whomsoever Allâh sends astray, for him there is no guide.

34. And indeed Yûsuf (Joseph) did come to you, in times gone by, with clear signs, but you ceased not to doubt

in that which he did bring to you: till
when he died you said: "No Messenger
will Allâh send after him." Thus Allâh
leaves astray him who is a *Musrif* (a
polytheist, an oppressor, a criminal, a
sinner who commits great sins) and a
Murtâb (one who doubts Allâh's
Warning and His Oneness).

35. Those who dispute about the *Ayât*
(proofs, evidences, verses, lessons,
signs, revelations, etc.) of Allâh,
without any authority that has come to
them, it is greatly hateful and disgusting
to Allâh and to those who believe. Thus
does Allâh seal up the heart of every
arrogant, tyrant. (So they cannot guide
themselves to the Right Path).

36. And Fir'aun (Pharaoh) said: "O
Hâmân! Build me a tower that I may
arrive at the ways —

37. "The ways of the heavens, and I
may look upon the *Ilâh* (God) of Mûsâ
(Moses): But verily, I think him to be a
liar." Thus it was made fair-seeming, in
Fir'aun's (Pharaoh) eyes, the evil of his
deeds, and he was hindered from the
(Right) Path; and the plot of Fir'aun
(Pharaoh) led to nothing but loss and
destruction (for him).

38. And the man who believed said:
"O my people! Follow me, I will guide
you to the way of right conduct [i.e.
guide you to Allâh's religion of Islâmic
Monotheism with which Mûsâ (Moses)
has been sent].

39. "O my people! Truly, this life of the world is nothing but a (quick passing) enjoyment, and verily, the Hereafter that is the home that will remain forever."

يَقَوْمِ إِنَّمَا هَذِهِ ٱلْحَيَوٰةُ ٱلدُّنْيَا مَتَٰعٌ وَإِنَّ ٱلْءَاخِرَةَ هِيَ دَارُ ٱلْقَرَارِ

40. "Whosoever does an evil deed, will not be requited except the like thereof; and whosoever does a righteous deed, whether male or female and is a true believer (in the Oneness of Allâh), such will enter Paradise, where they will be provided therein (with all things in abundance) without limit.

مَنْ عَمِلَ سَيِّئَةً فَلَا يُجْزَىٰٓ إِلَّا مِثْلَهَا وَمَنْ عَمِلَ صَٰلِحًا مِّن ذَكَرٍ أَوْ أُنثَىٰ وَهُوَ مُؤْمِنٌ فَأُوْلَٰٓئِكَ يَدْخُلُونَ ٱلْجَنَّةَ يُرْزَقُونَ فِيهَا بِغَيْرِ حِسَابٍ

41. "And O my people! How is it that I call you to salvation while you call me to the Fire!

وَيَٰقَوْمِ مَا لِىٓ أَدْعُوكُمْ إِلَى ٱلنَّجَوٰةِ وَتَدْعُونَنِىٓ إِلَى ٱلنَّارِ

42. "You invite me to disbelieve in Allâh (and in His Oneness), and to join partners in worship with Him of which I have no knowledge; and I invite you to the All-Mighty, the Oft-Forgiving!

تَدْعُونَنِى لِأَكْفُرَ بِٱللَّهِ وَأُشْرِكَ بِهِۦ مَا لَيْسَ لِى بِهِۦ عِلْمٌ وَأَنَا۠ أَدْعُوكُمْ إِلَى ٱلْعَزِيزِ ٱلْغَفَّٰرِ

43. "No doubt you call me to (worship) one who cannot grant (me) my request or respond to my invocation) in this world or in the Hereafter. And our return will be to Allâh, and *Al-Musrifûn* (i.e. polytheists and arrogants, those who commit great sins, the transgressors of Allâh's set limits): they shall be the dwellers of the Fire!

لَا جَرَمَ أَنَّمَا تَدْعُونَنِىٓ إِلَيْهِ لَيْسَ لَهُۥ دَعْوَةٌ فِى ٱلدُّنْيَا وَلَا فِى ٱلْءَاخِرَةِ وَأَنَّ مَرَدَّنَآ إِلَى ٱللَّهِ وَأَنَّ ٱلْمُسْرِفِينَ هُمْ أَصْحَٰبُ ٱلنَّارِ

44. "And you will remember what I am telling you, and my affair I leave it to Allâh. Verily, Allâh is the All-Seer of (His) slaves."

فَسَتَذْكُرُونَ مَآ أَقُولُ لَكُمْ وَأُفَوِّضُ أَمْرِىٓ إِلَى ٱللَّهِ إِنَّ ٱللَّهَ بَصِيرٌۢ بِٱلْعِبَادِ

45. So Allâh saved him from the evils that they plotted (against him),

فَوَقَىٰهُ ٱللَّهُ سَيِّئَاتِ مَا مَكَرُواْ

while an evil torment encompassed Fir'aun's (Pharaoh) people.

46. The Fire, they are exposed to it, morning and afternoon. And on the Day when the Hour will be established (it will be said to the angels): "Cause Fir'aun's (Pharaoh) people to enter the severest torment!"

47. And, when they will dispute in the Fire, the weak will say to those who were arrogant: "Verily, we followed you: can you then take from us some portion of the Fire?"

48. Those who were arrogant will say: "We are all (together) in this (Fire)! Verily, Allâh has judged between (His) slaves!"

49. And those in the Fire will say to the keepers (angels) of Hell: "Call upon your Lord to lighten for us the torment for a day!"

50. They will say: "Did there not come to you, your Messengers with (clear) evidences (and signs)?" They will say: "Yes." They will reply: "Then call (as you like)! And the invocation of the disbelievers is nothing but in vain (as it will not be answered by Allâh)!"

51. Verily, We will indeed make victorious Our Messengers and those who believe (in the Oneness of Allâh — Islâmic Monotheism) in this world's life and on the Day when the witnesses will stand forth, (i.e. Day of Resurrection)—

52. The Day when their excuses will be of no profit to Zâlimûn (polytheists, wrongdoers and disbelievers in the Oneness of Allâh). Theirs will be the curse, and theirs will be the evil abode (i.e. painful torment in Hell-fire).

53. And, indeed We gave Mûsâ (Moses) the guidance, and We caused the Children of Israel to inherit the Scripture [i.e. the Taurât (Torah)] —

54. A guide and a reminder for men of understanding.

55. So be patient (O Muhammad صلى الله عليه وسلم). Verily, the Promise of Allâh is true, and ask forgiveness for your fault,[1] and glorify the praises of your Lord in the *'Ashî* (i.e. the time period after the midnoon till sunset) and in the *Ibkâr* (i.e. the time period from early morning or sunrise till before midnoon) [it is said that, that means the five compulsory congregational *Salât* (prayers) or the *'Asr* and *Fajr* prayers].

56. Verily, those who dispute about the *Ayât* (proofs, evidences, verses, lessons, signs, revelations, etc.) of Allâh, without any authority having come to them, there is nothing else in their breasts except pride [to accept you (Muhammad صلى الله عليه وسلم as a Messenger of Allâh and to obey you).][2] They will never have it (i.e. Prophethood which Allâh has bestowed upon you). So seek refuge in Allâh (O Muhammad صلى الله عليه وسلم from the arrogants). Verily, it is He Who is the All-Hearer, the All-Seer.

---

[1] (V.40:55) See the footnote of (V.4:106).

[2] (V.40:56) See the footnote of (V.3:85).

57. The creation of the heavens and the earth is indeed greater than the creation of mankind; yet, most of mankind know not.

58. And not equal are the blind and those who see; nor are (equal) those who believe (in the Oneness of Allâh — Islâmic Monotheism), and do righteous good deeds, and those who do evil. Little do you remember!

59. Verily, the Hour (Day of Judgement) is surely coming, there is no doubt about it, yet most men believe not.

60. And your Lord said: "Invoke Me, [i.e. believe in My Oneness (Islâmic Monotheism) and ask Me for anything] I will respond to your (invocation). Verily, those who scorn My worship [i.e. do not invoke Me, and do not believe in My Oneness, (Islâmic Monotheism)] they will surely, enter Hell in humiliation!"

61. Allâh, it is He Who has made the night for you that you may rest therein and the day for you to see. Truly, Allâh is full of bounty to mankind; yet, most of mankind give no thanks.

62. That is Allâh, your Lord, the Creator of all things: *Lâ ilâha illâ Huwa* (none has the right to be worshipped but He). How then are you turning away (from Allâh, by worshipping others instead of Him)?

63. Thus were turned away those who used to deny the Ayât (proofs, evidences, verses, lessons, signs, revelations, etc.) of Allâh.

بِئَايَٰتِ ٱللَّهِ يَجۡحَدُونَ ٦٣

64. Allâh, it is He Who has made for you the earth as a dwelling place and the sky as a canopy, and has given you shape and made your shapes good (looking) and has provided you with good things. That is Allâh, your Lord: so Blessed is Allâh, the Lord of the *'Âlamîn* (mankind, jinn and all that exists).

ٱللَّهُ ٱلَّذِي جَعَلَ لَكُمُ ٱلۡأَرۡضَ قَرَارًا وَٱلسَّمَآءَ بِنَآءً وَصَوَّرَكُمۡ فَأَحۡسَنَ صُوَرَكُمۡ وَرَزَقَكُم مِّنَ ٱلطَّيِّبَٰتِ ذَٰلِكُمُ ٱللَّهُ رَبُّكُمۡ فَتَبَارَكَ ٱللَّهُ رَبُّ ٱلۡعَٰلَمِينَ ٦٤

65. He is the Ever Living, *Lâ ilâha illâ Huwa* (none has the right to be worshipped but He); so invoke Him making your worship pure for Him Alone (by worshipping Him Alone, and none else, and by doing righteous deeds sincerely for Allâh's sake only, and not to show off, and not setting up rivals with Him in worship). All the praises and thanks are to Allâh, the Lord of the *'Âlamîn* (mankind, jinn and all that exists).

هُوَ ٱلۡحَيُّ لَآ إِلَٰهَ إِلَّا هُوَ فَٱدۡعُوهُ مُخۡلِصِينَ لَهُ ٱلدِّينَ ٱلۡحَمۡدُ لِلَّهِ رَبِّ ٱلۡعَٰلَمِينَ ٦٥

66. Say (O Muhammad صلى الله عليه وسلم): "I have been forbidden to worship those whom you worship besides Allâh, since there have come to me evidences from my Lord; and I am commanded to submit (in Islâm) to the Lord of the *'Âlamîn* (mankind, jinn and all that exists).

۞ قُلۡ إِنِّي نُهِيتُ أَنۡ أَعۡبُدَ ٱلَّذِينَ تَدۡعُونَ مِن دُونِ ٱللَّهِ لَمَّا جَآءَنِيَ ٱلۡبَيِّنَٰتُ مِن رَّبِّي وَأُمِرۡتُ أَنۡ أُسۡلِمَ لِرَبِّ ٱلۡعَٰلَمِينَ ٦٦

67. It is He, Who has created you (Adam) from dust, then from a *Nutfah* [mixed semen drops of male and female sexual discharge (i.e. Adam's offspring)] then from a clot (a piece of coagulated blood), then brings you forth as an infant, then (makes you

هُوَ ٱلَّذِي خَلَقَكُم مِّن تُرَابٍ ثُمَّ مِن نُّطۡفَةٍ ثُمَّ مِنۡ عَلَقَةٍ ثُمَّ يُخۡرِجُكُمۡ طِفۡلًا ثُمَّ لِتَبۡلُغُوٓاْ أَشُدَّكُمۡ ثُمَّ لِتَكُونُواْ

grow) to reach the age of full strength, and afterwards to be old (men and women) — though some among you die before — and that you reach an appointed term in order that you may understand.[1]

68. It is He Who gives life and causes death. And when He decides upon a thing He says to it only: "Be!" — and it is.

69. See you not those who dispute about the *Ayât* (proofs, evidences, verses, lessons, signs, revelations, etc.) of Allâh? How are they turning away [from the truth, (i.e. Islâmic Monotheism to the falsehood (i.e. polytheism)]?

70. Those who deny the Book (this Qur'ân), and that with which We sent Our Messengers (i.e. to worship none but Allâh Alone sincerely, and to reject all false deities and to confess resurrection after the death for recompense) they will come to know (when they will be cast into the Fire of Hell).

71. When iron collars will be rounded over their necks, and the chains, they shall be dragged along,[2]

72. In the boiling water, then they will be burned in the Fire.[3]

73. Then it will be said to them: "Where are (all) those whom you used to join in worship as partners[4]

---

[1] (V.40:67) See the footnote of (V.22:5).

[2] (V.40:71) See the footnote of (V.17:97).

[3] (V.40:72) See the footnote of (V.3:85).

[4] (V.40:73) See the footnote of (V.4:135).

74. "Besides Allâh"? They will say: "They have vanished from us: Nay, we did not invoke (worship) anything before." Thus Allâh leads astray the disbelievers.[1]

75. That was because you had been exulting in the earth without any right (by worshipping others instead of Allâh and by committing crimes), and that you used to rejoice extremely (in your error).

76. Enter the gates of Hell to abide therein: and (indeed) what an evil abode of the arrogant!

77. So be patient (O Muhammad صلى الله عليه وسلم); verily, the Promise of Allâh is true and whether We show you (O Muhammad صلى الله عليه وسلم in this world) some part of what We have promised them, or We cause you to die then still it is to Us they all shall be returned.

78. And, indeed We have sent Messengers before you (O Muhammad صلى الله عليه وسلم): of some of them We have related to you their story.[2] And of some We have not related to you their story, and it was not given to any Messenger that he should bring a sign except by the Leave of Allâh. But, when comes the Commandment of Allâh, the matter will be decided with

---

[1] (V.40:74) See the footnote of (V.2:165).

[2] (V.40:78) There are many Prophets and Messengers of Allâh. About twenty-five of them are mentioned in the Qur'ân; out of these twenty-five, only five are of strong will, namely: Muhammad صلى الله عليه وسلم, Nûh (Noah), Ibrâhîm (Abraham), Mûsâ (Moses), and 'Îsâ (Jesus) — son of Maryam (Mary) عليهم السلام

truth, and the followers of falsehood
will then be lost.

79. Allâh, it is He Who has made
cattle for you, that you may ride on
some of them, and of some you eat.

اللَّهُ الَّذِى جَعَلَ لَكُمُ الْأَنْعَـٰمَ
لِتَرْكَبُوا مِنْهَا وَمِنْهَا
تَأْكُلُونَ ٧٩

80. And you have (many other)
benefits from them, and that you may
reach by their means a desire that is in
your breasts (i.e. carry your goods,
loads), and on them and on ships you
are carried.

وَلَكُمْ فِيهَا مَنَـٰفِعُ وَلِتَبْلُغُوا
عَلَيْهَا حَاجَةً فِى صُدُورِكُمْ
وَعَلَيْهَا وَعَلَى الْفُلْكِ
تُحْمَلُونَ ٨٠

81. And He shows you His Ayât
(signs and proofs) (of His Oneness in
all the above-mentioned things).
Which, then of the Ayât (signs and
proofs) of Allâh do you deny?

وَيُرِيكُمْ ءَايَـٰتِهِ فَأَىَّ ءَايَـٰتِ
اللَّهِ تُنكِرُونَ ٨١

82. Have they not travelled through
the earth and seen what was the end of
those before them? They were more in
number than them and mightier in
strength, and in the traces (they have
left behind them) in the land; yet all
that they used to earn availed them not.

أَفَلَمْ يَسِيرُوا فِى الْأَرْضِ فَيَنظُرُوا
كَيْفَ كَانَ عَـٰقِبَةُ الَّذِينَ مِن
قَبْلِهِمْ كَانُوا أَكْثَرَ مِنْهُمْ وَأَشَدَّ
قُوَّةً وَءَاثَارًا فِى الْأَرْضِ فَمَا
أَغْنَىٰ عَنْهُم مَّا كَانُوا يَكْسِبُونَ ٨٢

83. Then when their Messengers
came to them with clear proofs, they
were glad (and proud) with that which
they had of the knowledge (of worldly
things). And that at which they used to
mock, surrounded them (i.e. the
punishment).

فَلَمَّا جَاءَتْهُمْ رُسُلُهُم بِالْبَيِّنَـٰتِ
فَرِحُوا بِمَا عِندَهُم مِّنَ الْعِلْمِ
وَحَاقَ بِهِم مَّا كَانُوا بِهِ
يَسْتَهْزِءُونَ ٨٣

84. So when they saw Our
punishment, they said: "We believe in
Allâh Alone and reject (all) that we
used to associate with Him as (His)
partners.

فَلَمَّا رَأَوْا بَأْسَنَا قَالُوا ءَامَنَّا
بِاللَّهِ وَحْدَهُ وَكَفَرْنَا بِمَا
كُنَّا بِهِ مُشْرِكِينَ ٨٤

85. Then their Faith (in Islâmic Monotheism) could not avail them when they saw Our punishment. (Like) this has been the way of Allâh in dealing with His slaves. And there the disbelievers lost utterly (when Our Torment covered them).

فَلَمْ يَكُ يَنفَعُهُمْ إِيمَـٰنُهُمْ لَمَّا رَأَوْا بَأْسَنَا سُنَّتَ ٱللَّهِ ٱلَّتِى قَدْ خَلَتْ فِى عِبَادِهِۦ وَخَسِرَ هُنَالِكَ ٱلْكَـٰفِرُونَ ۝

Sûrat Fussilat
(They are explained in detail) XLI

سُورَةُ فُصِّلَتْ

In the Name of Allâh
the Most Gracious, the Most Merciful

بِسْمِ ٱللَّهِ ٱلرَّحْمَـٰنِ ٱلرَّحِيمِ

1. *Hâ-Mîm.*

[These letters are one of the miracles of the Qur'ân, and none but Allâh (Alone) knows their meanings.]

حمٓ ۝

2. A revelation from (Allâh) the Most Gracious, the Most Merciful.

تَنزِيلٌ مِّنَ ٱلرَّحْمَـٰنِ ٱلرَّحِيمِ

3. A Book whereof the Verses are explained in detail — a Qur'ân in Arabic for people who know.

كِتَـٰبٌ فُصِّلَتْ ءَايَـٰتُهُۥ قُرْءَانًا عَرَبِيًّا لِّقَوْمٍ يَعْلَمُونَ

4. Giving glad tidings [of Paradise to the one who believes in the Oneness of Allâh (i.e. Islâmic Monotheism) and fears Allâh much (abstains from all kinds of sins and evil deeds) and loves Allâh much (performing all kinds of good deeds which He has ordained)], and warning (of punishment in the Hell-fire to the one who disbelieves in the Oneness of Allâh), but most of them turn away, so they hear not.

بَشِيرًا وَنَذِيرًا فَأَعْرَضَ أَكْثَرُهُمْ فَهُمْ لَا يَسْمَعُونَ ۝

5. And they say: "Our hearts are under coverings (screened) from that to which you invite us; and in our ears is

وَقَالُوا قُلُوبُنَا فِىٓ أَكِنَّةٍ مِّمَّا تَدْعُونَآ إِلَيْهِ وَفِىٓ ءَاذَانِنَا وَقْرٌ

deafness, and between us and you is a screen: so work you (on your way); verily, we are working (on our way)."

6. Say (O Muhammad صلى الله عليه وسلم): "I am only a human being like you. It is revealed to me that your *Ilâh* (God) is One *Ilâh* (God — Allâh), therefore take Straight Path to Him (with true Faith — Islâmic Monotheism) and obedience to Him, and seek forgiveness of Him. And woe to *Al-Mushrikûn* (the polytheists, idolaters, disbelievers in the Oneness of Allâh).

7. Those who give not the *Zakât* and they are disbelievers in the Hereafter.

8. Truly, those who believe (in the Oneness of Allâh, and in His Messenger Muhammad — صلى الله عليه وسلم — Islâmic Monotheism) and do righteous good deeds, for them will be an endless reward that will never stop (i.e. Paradise).

9. Say (O Muhammad صلى الله عليه وسلم): "Do you verily, disbelieve in Him Who created the earth in two Days? And you set up rivals (in worship) with Him? That is the Lord of the *'Âlamîn* (mankind, jinn and all that exists).

10. He placed therein (i.e. the earth) firm mountains from above it, and He blessed it, and measured therein its sustenance (for its dwellers) in four Days equal (i.e. all these four 'days' were equal in the length of time) for all those who ask (about its creation).

11. Then He rose over (*Istawâ*) towards the heaven when it was smoke, and said to it and to the earth: "Come both of you willingly or unwillingly." They both said: "We come willingly."

12. Then He completed and finished from their creation (as) seven heavens in two Days and He made in each heaven its affair. And We adorned the nearest (lowest) heaven with lamps (stars)[1] to be an adornment as well as to guard (from the devils by using them as missiles against the devils). Such is the Decree of Him the All-Mighty, the All-Knower.

13. But if they turn away, then say (O Muhammad صلى الله عليه وسلم): "I have warned you of a *Sâ'iqah* (a destructive awful cry, torment, hit, a thunderbolt) like the *Sâ'iqah* which overtook 'Âd and Thamûd (people)."

14. When the Messengers came to them, from before them and behind them (saying): "Worship none but Allâh", they said: "If our Lord had so willed, He would surely, have sent down the angels. So indeed we disbelieve in that with which you have been sent."

15. As for 'Âd, they were arrogant in the land without right, and they said: "Who is mightier than us in strength?" See they not that Allâh Who created them was mightier in strength than them. And they used to deny Our *Ayât* (proofs, evidences, verses, lessons, revelations, etc.)!

---

[1] (V.41:12) See the footnote of (V.6:97).

16. So We sent upon them a furious wind in days of evil omen (for them) that We might give them a taste of disgracing torment ⌊in this present worldly life. But surely, the torment of the Hereafter will be more disgracing, and they will never be helped.

فَأَرْسَلْنَا عَلَيْهِمْ رِيحًا صَرْصَرًا فِى أَيَّامٍ نَّحِسَاتٍ لِّنُذِيقَهُمْ عَذَابَ الْخِزْىِ فِى الْحَيَوٰةِ الدُّنْيَا وَلَعَذَابُ الْءَاخِرَةِ أَخْزَىٰ وَهُمْ لَا يُنصَرُونَ ١٦

17. And as for Thamûd, We showed and made clear to them the Path of Truth (Islâmic Monotheism) through Our Messenger, (i.e. showed them the way of success), but they preferred blindness to guidance; so the *Sâ'iqah* (a destructive awful cry, torment, hit, a thunderbolt) of disgracing torment seized them because of what they used to earn.

وَأَمَّا ثَمُودُ فَهَدَيْنَٰهُمْ فَاسْتَحَبُّوا الْعَمَىٰ عَلَى الْهُدَىٰ فَأَخَذَتْهُمْ صَٰعِقَةُ الْعَذَابِ الْهُونِ بِمَا كَانُوا يَكْسِبُونَ ١٧

18. And We saved those who believed and used to fear Allâh, keep their duty to Him and avoid evil.

وَنَجَّيْنَا الَّذِينَ ءَامَنُوا وَكَانُوا يَتَّقُونَ ١٨

19. And (remember) the Day that the enemies of Allâh will be gathered to the Fire, then they will be driven [(to the Fire), former ones being withheld till their later ones will join them].

وَيَوْمَ يُحْشَرُ أَعْدَآءُ اللَّهِ إِلَى النَّارِ فَهُمْ يُوزَعُونَ ١٩

20. Till, when they reach it (Hell-fire), their hearing (ears) and their eyes, and their skins will testify against them as to what they used to do.

حَتَّىٰ إِذَا مَا جَآءُوهَا شَهِدَ عَلَيْهِمْ سَمْعُهُمْ وَأَبْصَٰرُهُمْ وَجُلُودُهُم بِمَا كَانُوا يَعْمَلُونَ ٢٠

21. And they will say to their skins, "Why do you testify against us?" They will say: "Allâh has caused us to speak — He causes all things to speak: and He created you the first time, and to Him you are made to return."

وَقَالُوا لِجُلُودِهِمْ لِمَ شَهِدتُّمْ عَلَيْنَا قَالُوا أَنطَقَنَا اللَّهُ الَّذِى أَنطَقَ كُلَّ شَىْءٍ وَهُوَ خَلَقَكُمْ أَوَّلَ مَرَّةٍ وَإِلَيْهِ تُرْجَعُونَ ٢١

22. And you have not been hiding yourselves (in the world), lest your ears,

وَمَا كُنتُمْ تَسْتَتِرُونَ أَن يَشْهَدَ عَلَيْكُمْ سَمْعُكُمْ وَلَا أَبْصَٰرُكُمْ

and your eyes, and your skins should testify against you; but you thought that Allâh knew not much of what you were doing.

23. And that thought of yours which you thought about your Lord, has brought you to destruction; and you have become (this Day) of those utterly lost!

24. Then, if they bear the torment patiently, then the Fire is the home for them, and if they seek to please Allâh, yet they are not of those who will ever be allowed to please Allâh.

25. And We have assigned for them (devils) intimate companions (in this world), who have made fair-seeming to them, what was before them (evil deeds which they were doing in the present worldly life and disbelief in the Reckoning and the Resurrection) and what was behind them (denial of the matters in the coming life of the Hereafter as regards punishment or reward). And the Word (i.e. the torment) is justified against them as it was justified against those who were among the previous generations of jinn and men that had passed away before them. Indeed they (all) were the losers.

26. And those who disbelieve say: "Listen not to this Qur'ân, and make noise in the midst of its (recitation) that you may overcome."

27. But surely, We shall cause those who disbelieve to taste a severe torment, and certainly, We shall requite them the worst of what they used to do.

ولا جُلُودُكُمْ وَلَٰكِن ظَنَنتُمْ أَنَّ اللَّهَ لا يَعْلَمُ كَثِيرًا مِّمَّا تَعْمَلُونَ ۝

وَذَٰلِكُمْ ظَنُّكُمُ الَّذِي ظَنَنتُم بِرَبِّكُمْ أَرْدَىٰكُمْ فَأَصْبَحْتُم مِّنَ الْخَاسِرِينَ ۝

فَإِن يَصْبِرُوا فَالنَّارُ مَثْوًى لَّهُمْ وَإِن يَسْتَعْتِبُوا فَمَا هُم مِّنَ الْمُعْتَبِينَ ۝

۞ وَقَيَّضْنَا لَهُمْ قُرَنَآءَ فَزَيَّنُوا لَهُم مَّا بَيْنَ أَيْدِيهِمْ وَمَا خَلْفَهُمْ وَحَقَّ عَلَيْهِمُ الْقَوْلُ فِي أُمَمٍ قَدْ خَلَتْ مِن قَبْلِهِم مِّنَ الْجِنِّ وَالْإِنسِ إِنَّهُمْ كَانُوا خَاسِرِينَ ۝

وَقَالَ الَّذِينَ كَفَرُوا لَا تَسْمَعُوا لِهَٰذَا الْقُرْآنِ وَالْغَوْا فِيهِ لَعَلَّكُمْ تَغْلِبُونَ ۝

فَلَنُذِيقَنَّ الَّذِينَ كَفَرُوا عَذَابًا شَدِيدًا وَلَنَجْزِيَنَّهُمْ أَسْوَأَ الَّذِي كَانُوا يَعْمَلُونَ ۝

28. That is the recompense of the enemies of Allâh: the Fire. Therein will be for them the eternal home, a (deserving) recompense for that they used to deny Our *Ayât* (proofs, evidences, verses, lessons, signs, revelations, etc.).

29. And those who disbelieve will say: "Our Lord! Show us those among jinn and men who led us astray: that we may crush them under our feet so that they become the lowest."

30. Verily, those who say: "Our Lord is Allâh (Alone)," and then they stand firm,[1] on them the angels will descend (at the time of their death) (saying): "Fear not, nor grieve! But receive the glad tidings of Paradise which you have been promised!

31. "We have been your friends in the life of this world and are (so) in the Hereafter. Therein you shall have (all) that your inner-selves desire, and therein you shall have (all) for which you ask.

32. "An entertainment from (Allâh), the Oft-Forgiving, Most Merciful."

33. And who is better in speech than he who [says: "My Lord is Allâh (believes in His Oneness)," and then stands firm (acts upon His Order), and]

---

[1] (V.41:30) In Arabic *Istaqâmû*: stand firm, i.e. they followed (really) the religion of Islâmic Monotheism, believed in the Oneness of Allâh, and worshipped none but Him (Alone), and performed all that was ordained by Allâh (good deeds) and abstained from all that was forbidden by Allâh (sins and evil deeds).

invites (men) to Allâh's (Islâmic Monotheism), and does righteous deeds, and says: "I am one of the Muslims."

34. The good deed and the evil deed cannot be equal. Repel (the evil) with one which is better (i.e. Allâh orders the faithful believers to be patient at the time of anger,[1] and to excuse those who treat them badly) then verily he, between whom and you there was enmity, (will become) as though he was a close friend.

35. But none is granted it (the above quality) except those who are patient — and none is granted it except the owner of the great portion (of happiness in the Hereafter i.e. Paradise and of a high moral character) in this world.

36. And if an evil whisper from *Shaitân* (Satan) tries to turn you away (O Muhammad (صلى الله عليه وسلم)) (from doing good), then seek refuge in Allâh. Verily, He is the All-Hearer, the All-Knower.

37. And from among His Signs are the night and the day, and the sun and the moon. Prostrate yourselves not to the sun nor to the moon, but prostrate yourselves to Allâh Who created them, if you (really) worship Him.

38. But if they are too proud[2] (to do so), then there are those who are with

---

[1] (V.41:34) See the footnote of (V.3:134).

[2] (V.41:38): See the footnote of (V.22:9).

your Lord (angels) glorify Him night and day, and never are they tired.

وَهُمْ لَا يَسْأَمُونَ ۩

39. And among His Signs (in this), that you see the earth barren; but when We send down water (rain) to it, it is stirred to life and growth (of vegetations). Verily, He Who gives it life, surely, He is Able to give life to the dead (on the Day of Resurrection). Indeed He is Able to do all things.

وَمِنْ ءَايَٰتِهِۦٓ أَنَّكَ تَرَى ٱلْأَرْضَ خَٰشِعَةً فَإِذَآ أَنزَلْنَا عَلَيْهَا ٱلْمَآءَ ٱهْتَزَّتْ وَرَبَتْ إِنَّ ٱلَّذِىٓ أَحْيَاهَا لَمُحْىِ ٱلْمَوْتَىٰٓ إِنَّهُۥ عَلَىٰ كُلِّ شَىْءٍ قَدِيرٌ ۝

40. Verily, those who turn away from Our *Ayât* (proofs, evidences, verses, lessons, signs, revelations, etc. by attacking, distorting and denying them) are not hidden from Us. Is he who is cast into the Fire better or he who comes secure on the Day of Resurrection? Do what you will. Verily, He is All-Seer of what you do (this is a severe threat to the disbelievers[1]).

إِنَّ ٱلَّذِينَ يُلْحِدُونَ فِىٓ ءَايَٰتِنَا لَا يَخْفَوْنَ عَلَيْنَآ أَفَمَن يُلْقَىٰ فِى ٱلنَّارِ خَيْرٌ أَم مَّن يَأْتِىٓ ءَامِنًا يَوْمَ ٱلْقِيَٰمَةِ ٱعْمَلُوا۟ مَا شِئْتُمْ إِنَّهُۥ بِمَا تَعْمَلُونَ بَصِيرٌ ۝

41. Verily, those who disbelieved in the Reminder (i.e. the Qur'ân) when it came to them (shall receive the punishment). And verily, it is an honourable well-fortified respected Book (because it is Allâh's Speech, and He has protected it from corruption, (See V.15:9)

إِنَّ ٱلَّذِينَ كَفَرُوا۟ بِٱلذِّكْرِ لَمَّا جَآءَهُمْ وَإِنَّهُۥ لَكِتَٰبٌ عَزِيزٌ ۝

42. Falsehood cannot come to it from before it or behind it: (it is) sent down by the All-Wise, Worthy of all praise (Allâh) (عَزَّ وَجَلَّ).

لَّا يَأْتِيهِ ٱلْبَٰطِلُ مِنۢ بَيْنِ يَدَيْهِ وَلَا مِنْ خَلْفِهِۦ تَنزِيلٌ مِّنْ حَكِيمٍ حَمِيدٍ ۝

---

[1] (V.41:40) See the footnote of (V.17:97).

43. Nothing is said to you (O Muhammad صلى الله عليه وسلم) except what was said to the Messengers before you. Verily, your Lord is the Possessor of forgiveness, and (also) the Possessor of painful punishment.[1]

مَا يُقَالُ لَكَ إِلَّا مَا قَدْ قِيلَ لِلرُّسُلِ مِن قَبْلِكَ إِنَّ رَبَّكَ لَذُو مَغْفِرَةٍ وَذُو عِقَابٍ أَلِيمٍ ۝

44. And if We had sent this as a Qur'ân in a foreign language (other than Arabic), they would have said: "Why are not its verses explained in detail (in our language)? What! (A Book) not in Arabic and the Messenger an Arab?" Say: "It is for those who believe, a guide and a healing. And as for those who disbelieve, there is heaviness (deafness) in their ears, and it (the Qur'ân) is blindness for them. They are those who are called from a place far away (so they neither listen nor understand)."

وَلَوْ جَعَلْنَاهُ قُرْآنًا أَعْجَمِيًّا لَّقَالُوا لَوْلَا فُصِّلَتْ ءَايَٰتُهُۥٓ ءَاعْجَمِيٌّ وَعَرَبِيٌّ قُلْ هُوَ لِلَّذِينَ ءَامَنُوا هُدًى وَشِفَآءٌ وَالَّذِينَ لَا يُؤْمِنُونَ فِىٓ ءَاذَانِهِمْ وَقْرٌ وَهُوَ عَلَيْهِمْ عَمًى أُوْلَٰٓئِكَ يُنَادَوْنَ مِن مَّكَانٍۭ بَعِيدٍ ۝

45. And indeed We gave Mûsâ (Moses) the Scripture, but dispute arose therein. And had it not been for a Word that went forth before from your Lord, (the torment would have overtaken them) and the matter would have been settled between them. But truly, they are in grave doubt thereto (i.e. about the Qur'ân). [Tafsir Al-Qurtubi].

وَلَقَدْ ءَاتَيْنَا مُوسَى الْكِتَٰبَ فَاخْتُلِفَ فِيهِ وَلَوْلَا كَلِمَةٌ سَبَقَتْ مِن رَّبِّكَ لَقُضِىَ بَيْنَهُمْ وَإِنَّهُمْ لَفِى شَكٍّ مِّنْهُ مُرِيبٍ ۝

46. Whosoever does righteous good deed, it is for (the benefit of) his ownself; and whosoever does evil, it is

مَنْ عَمِلَ صَٰلِحًا فَلِنَفْسِهِۦ وَمَنْ أَسَآءَ فَعَلَيْهَا وَمَا رَبُّكَ بِظَلَّٰمٍ

---

[1] (V.41:43) See the footnote of (V.3:85).

against his ownself. And your Lord is
not at all unjust to (His) slaves.[1]

لِّلْعَبِيدِ

---

[1] (V.41:46)

a) See the footnote of (V.6:160).

b) See the footnote of (V.3:85).

c) Narrated Abu Mûsâ رضى الله عنه The Prophet صلى الله عليه وسلم said, "The
example of Muslims, Jews and Christians is like the example of a
man who employed labourers to work for him from morning till
night for specific wages. They worked till mid-day and then said,
'We do not need your money which you have fixed for us and let
whatever we have done be annulled.' The man said to them, 'Don't
quit the work, but complete the rest of it and take your full wages.'
But they refused and went away (like the Jews who refused to
believe in the Message of Jesus عليه السلام). The man employed another
batch after them and said to them, 'Complete the rest of the day and
yours will be the wages I had fixed for the first batch.' So, they
worked till the time of 'Asr prayer. They said, 'Let what we have
done be annulled and keep the wages you have promised us for
yourself!' The man said to them, 'Complete the rest of the work, as
only a little of the day remains': but they refused (like the Christians
who refused to believe in the Message of Muhammad صلى الله عليه وسلم).
Thereafter, he employed another batch to work for the rest of the
day and they worked for the rest of the day till the sunset, and they
received the wages of the two former batches. So that was the
example of these people (Muslims) and the example of this light
[Islamic Monotheism, the Qur'ân, the Sunnah (legal ways of the
Prophet Muhammad صلى الله عليه وسلم) and the guidance which Prophet Muhammad
الله عليه وسلم brought] which they have accepted willingly."* (Sahih
Al-Bukhari, Vol. 3, Hadith No. 471)

* The Jews refused to believe in the Message of 'Îsâ (Jesus), so all
their work was annulled; similarly, the Christians refused to accept
the Message of Muhammad صلى الله عليه وسلم and thus their work was
annulled too. Such people were not rewarded, because they refused
to have true Faith for the rest of their lives and died as disbelievers.
They should have believed in the latest Message; for their insistence
on keeping their old religion deprived them of the reward which
they would have got for their previous good deeds achieved before
the advent of the new religion. On the other hand, Muslims
accepted and believed in all the three Messages and deserved a full
reward for their complete surrender to Allâh (Al-Qastalâni).

47. To Him (Alone) is referred the knowledge of the Hour.[1] No fruit comes out of its sheath, nor does a female conceive nor brings forth (young), except by His Knowledge. And on the Day when He will call unto them (polytheists) (saying): "Where are My (so-called) partners (whom you did invent)?" They will say: "We inform You that none of us bears witness to it (that they are Your partners)!"

48. And those whom they used to invoke before (in this world) shall disappear from them, and they will perceive that they have no place of refuge (from Allâh's punishment).[2]

49. Man (the disbeliever) does not get tired of asking good (things from Allâh); but if an evil touches him, then he gives up all hope and is lost in despair.

50. And truly, if We give him a taste of mercy from Us, after some adversity (severe poverty or disease) has touched him, he is sure to say: "This is due to my (merit); I think not that the Hour will be established. But if I am brought back to my Lord, surely, there will be for me the best (wealth) with Him. Then, We verily, will show to the disbelievers what they have done, and We shall make them taste a severe torment.

51. And when We show favour to man, he withdraws and turns away; but

---

[1] (V.41:47) See the footnote of (V.7:187).

[2] (V.41:48) See the footnote of (V.2:165).

when evil touches him, then he has recourse to long supplications.

52. Say: "Tell me, if it (the Qur'ân) is from Allâh, and you disbelieve in it? Who is more astray than one who is in opposition far away (from Allâh's Right Path and His obedience).

53. We will show them Our Signs in the universe, and in their own selves, until it becomes manifest to them that this (the Qur'ân) is the truth. Is it not sufficient in regard to your Lord that He is a Witness over all things?

54. Verily, they are in doubt concerning the Meeting with their Lord? (i.e. Resurrection after their death, and their return to their Lord). Verily, He it is Who is surrounding all things!

Sûrat Ash-Shûra
(The Consultation) XLII

*In the Name of Allâh
the Most Gracious, the Most Merciful*

1. *Hâ-Mîm.*

2. *'Aîn-Sîn-Qâf.*

[These letters are one of the miracles of the Qur'ân, and none but Allâh (Alone) knows their meanings].

3. Likewise Allâh, the All-Mighty, the All-Wise sends Revelation to you (O Muhammad صلى الله عليه وسلم) as (He sent Revelation to) those before you.[1]

---

[1] (V.42:3) See the footnote of (V.4:163).

4. To Him belongs all that is in the heavens and all that is in the earth, and He is the Most High, the Most Great.

لَهُۥ مَا فِى ٱلسَّمَٰوَٰتِ وَمَا فِى ٱلْأَرْضِ ۖ وَهُوَ ٱلْعَلِىُّ ٱلْعَظِيمُ ﴿٤﴾

5. Nearly the heavens might be rent asunder from above them (by His Majesty): and the angels glorify the praises of their Lord, and ask for forgiveness for those on the earth. Verily, Allâh is the Oft-Forgiving, the Most Merciful.

تَكَادُ ٱلسَّمَٰوَٰتُ يَتَفَطَّرْنَ مِن فَوْقِهِنَّ ۚ وَٱلْمَلَٰٓئِكَةُ يُسَبِّحُونَ بِحَمْدِ رَبِّهِمْ وَيَسْتَغْفِرُونَ لِمَن فِى ٱلْأَرْضِ ۗ أَلَآ إِنَّ ٱللَّهَ هُوَ ٱلْغَفُورُ ٱلرَّحِيمُ ﴿٥﴾

6. And as for those who take as *Auliyâ'* (guardians, supporters, helpers, lords, gods, protectors) others besides Him [i.e. they take false deities other than Allâh as protectors, and they worship them] — Allâh is *Hafiz* (Protector, Watcher) over them (i.e. takes care of their deeds and will recompense them), and you (O Muhammad صلى الله عليه وسلم) are not a *Wakîl* (guardian or a disposer of their affairs) over them (to protect their deeds).

وَٱلَّذِينَ ٱتَّخَذُوا۟ مِن دُونِهِۦٓ أَوْلِيَآءَ ٱللَّهُ حَفِيظٌ عَلَيْهِمْ وَمَآ أَنتَ عَلَيْهِم بِوَكِيلٍ ﴿٦﴾

7. And thus We have revealed to you (O Muhammad صلى الله عليه وسلم) a Qur'ân in Arabic that you may warn the Mother of the Towns (Makkah) and all around it, and warn (them) of the Day of Assembling of which there is no doubt: when a party will be in Paradise (those who believed in Allâh and followed what Allâh's Messenger صلى الله عليه وسلم brought them) and a party in the blazing Fire (Hell) (those who disbelieved in Allâh and followed not what Allâh's Messenger صلى الله عليه وسلم brought them).[1]

وَكَذَٰلِكَ أَوْحَيْنَآ إِلَيْكَ قُرْءَانًا عَرَبِيًّا لِّتُنذِرَ أُمَّ ٱلْقُرَىٰ وَمَنْ حَوْلَهَا وَتُنذِرَ يَوْمَ ٱلْجَمْعِ لَا رَيْبَ فِيهِ ۚ فَرِيقٌ فِى ٱلْجَنَّةِ وَفَرِيقٌ فِى ٱلسَّعِيرِ ﴿٧﴾

---

[1] (V.42:7) See the footnote of (V.3:85).

8. And if Allâh had willed, He could have made them one nation, but He admits whom He wills to His Mercy. And the *Zâlimûn* (polytheists and wrongdoers) will have neither a *Walî* (protector or guardian) nor a helper.

وَلَوْ شَاءَ ٱللَّهُ لَجَعَلَهُمْ أُمَّةً وَٰحِدَةً وَلَٰكِن يُدْخِلُ مَن يَشَاءُ فِى رَحْمَتِهِۦ ۚ وَٱلظَّٰلِمُونَ مَا لَهُم مِّن وَلِيٍّ وَلَا نَصِيرٍ ٨

9. Or have they taken (for worship) *Auliyâ'* (guardians, supporters, helpers, protectors, lords, gods) besides Him? But Allâh — He Alone is the *Walî* (Lord, God, Protector). And it is He Who gives life to the dead, and He is Able to do all things.

أَمِ ٱتَّخَذُوا۟ مِن دُونِهِۦٓ أَوْلِيَآءَ ۖ فَٱللَّهُ هُوَ ٱلْوَلِىُّ وَهُوَ يُحْىِ ٱلْمَوْتَىٰ وَهُوَ عَلَىٰ كُلِّ شَىْءٍ قَدِيرٌ ٩

10. And in whatsoever you differ, the decision thereof is with Allâh (He is the ruling Judge). (And say O Muhammad صلى الله عليه وسلم to these polytheists:) Such is Allâh, my Lord in Whom I put my trust, and to Him I turn (in all of my affairs and) in repentance.

وَمَا ٱخْتَلَفْتُمْ فِيهِ مِن شَىْءٍ فَحُكْمُهُۥٓ إِلَى ٱللَّهِ ۚ ذَٰلِكُمُ ٱللَّهُ رَبِّى عَلَيْهِ تَوَكَّلْتُ وَإِلَيْهِ أُنِيبُ ١٠

11. The Creator of the heavens and the earth. He has made for you mates from yourselves, and for the cattle (also) mates. By this means He creates you (in the wombs). There is nothing like Him; and He is the All-Hearer, the All-Seer.

فَاطِرُ ٱلسَّمَٰوَٰتِ وَٱلْأَرْضِ ۚ جَعَلَ لَكُم مِّنْ أَنفُسِكُمْ أَزْوَٰجًا وَمِنَ ٱلْأَنْعَٰمِ أَزْوَٰجًا يَذْرَؤُكُمْ فِيهِ ۚ لَيْسَ كَمِثْلِهِۦ شَىْءٌ ۖ وَهُوَ ٱلسَّمِيعُ ٱلْبَصِيرُ ١١

12. To Him belong the keys of the heavens and the earth. He enlarges provision for whom He wills, and straitens (it for whom He wills). Verily, He is the All-Knower of everything.

لَهُۥ مَقَالِيدُ ٱلسَّمَٰوَٰتِ وَٱلْأَرْضِ ۖ يَبْسُطُ ٱلرِّزْقَ لِمَن يَشَاءُ وَيَقْدِرُ ۚ إِنَّهُۥ بِكُلِّ شَىْءٍ عَلِيمٌ ١٢

13. He (Allâh) has ordained for you the same religion (Islâmic Monotheism) which He ordained for Nûh (Noah), and that which We have revealed to you (O

شَرَعَ لَكُم مِّنَ ٱلدِّينِ مَا وَصَّىٰ بِهِۦ نُوحًا وَٱلَّذِىٓ أَوْحَيْنَا

Muhammad (صلى الله عليه وسلم), and that which We ordained for Ibrâhîm (Abraham), Mûsâ (Moses) and 'Îsâ (Jesus) saying you should establish religion (i.e. to do what it orders you to do practically), and make no divisions[1] in it (religion) (i.e. various sects in religion). Intolerable for the *Mushrikûn*[2] is that (Islamic Monotheism) to which you (O Muhammad صلى الله عليه وسلم) call them. Allâh chooses for Himself whom He wills, and guides unto Himself who turns to Him in repentance and in obedience.

إِلَيْكَ وَمَا وَصَّيْنَا بِهِۦٓ إِبْرَٰهِيمَ وَمُوسَىٰ وَعِيسَىٰٓ أَنْ أَقِيمُوا۟ ٱلدِّينَ وَلَا تَتَفَرَّقُوا۟ فِيهِ ۚ كَبُرَ عَلَى ٱلْمُشْرِكِينَ مَا تَدْعُوهُمْ إِلَيْهِ ۚ ٱللَّهُ يَجْتَبِىٓ إِلَيْهِ مَن يَشَآءُ وَيَهْدِىٓ إِلَيْهِ مَن يُنِيبُ ١٣

14. And they divided not till after knowledge had come to them, through (selfish) transgression between themselves. And had it not been for a Word that went forth before from your Lord for an appointed term, the matter would have been settled between them. And verily, those who were made to inherit the Scripture [i.e. the Taurâh (Torah) and the Injeel (Gospel)] after them (i.e. Jews and Christians) are in grave doubt concerning it (i.e. Allâh's true religion — Islâm or the Qur'ân).

وَمَا تَفَرَّقُوٓا۟ إِلَّا مِنۢ بَعْدِ مَا جَآءَهُمُ ٱلْعِلْمُ بَغْيًۢا بَيْنَهُمْ ۚ وَلَوْلَا كَلِمَةٌ سَبَقَتْ مِن رَّبِّكَ إِلَىٰٓ أَجَلٍ مُّسَمًّى لَّقُضِىَ بَيْنَهُمْ ۚ وَإِنَّ ٱلَّذِينَ أُورِثُوا۟ ٱلْكِتَٰبَ مِنۢ بَعْدِهِمْ لَفِى شَكٍّ مِّنْهُ مُرِيبٍ ١٤

15. So unto this (religion of Islâm alone and this Qur'ân) then invite (people) (O Muhammad صلى الله عليه وسلم), and stand firm on Islâmic Monotheism [by performing all that is ordained by Allâh (good deeds)], and by abstaining

فَلِذَٰلِكَ فَٱدْعُ ۖ وَٱسْتَقِمْ كَمَآ أُمِرْتَ ۖ وَلَا تَتَّبِعْ أَهْوَآءَهُمْ ۖ وَقُلْ ءَامَنتُ بِمَآ أَنزَلَ ٱللَّهُ مِن كِتَٰبٍ ۖ وَأُمِرْتُ لِأَعْدِلَ

---

[1] (V.42:13) See the footnote of (V.3:103).

[2] (V.42:13) *Mushrikun*: Polytheists, pagans, idolaters, and disbelievers in the Oneness of Allâh, those who worship others along with Allâh or set up rivals or partners to Allâh.

from all that is forbidden by Allâh (sins and evil deeds)], as you are commanded, and follow not their desires but say: "I believe in whatsoever Allâh has sent down of the Book [all the holy Books, — this Qur'ân and the Books of the old from the Taurât (Torah), or the Injeel (Gospel) or the Pages of Ibrâhîm (Abraham)] and I am commanded to do justice among you. Allâh is our Lord and your Lord. For us our deeds and for you your deeds. There is no dispute between us and you. Allâh will assemble us (all), and to Him is the final return."

16. And those who dispute concerning Allâh (His religion of Islâmic Monotheism with which Muhammad صلى الله عليه وسلم has been sent), after it has been accepted (by the people), of no use is their dispute before their Lord and on them is wrath, and for them will be a severe torment.[1]

17. It is Allâh Who has sent down the Book (the Qur'ân) in truth, and the Balance (i.e. to act justly). And what can make you know that perhaps the Hour is close at hand?

18. Those who believe not therein seek to hasten it, while those who believe are fearful of it, and know that it is the very truth. Verily, those who dispute concerning the Hour are certainly in error far away.

---

[1] (V.42:16) See the footnote of (V.3:85).

19. Allâh is very Gracious and Kind to His slaves. He gives provisions to whom He wills. And He is the All-Strong, the All-Mighty.

اللَّهُ لَطِيفٌ بِعِبَادِهِ يَرْزُقُ مَن يَشَآءُ وَهُوَ الْقَوِيُّ الْعَزِيزُ ١٩

20. Whosoever desires (by his deeds) the reward of the Hereafter, We give him increase in his reward, and whosoever desires the reward of this world (by his deeds), We give him thereof (what is decreed for him), and he has no portion in the Hereafter.

مَن كَانَ يُرِيدُ حَرْثَ الْأَخِرَةِ نَزِدْ لَهُ فِي حَرْثِهِ وَمَن كَانَ يُرِيدُ حَرْثَ الدُّنْيَا نُؤْتِهِ مِنْهَا وَمَا لَهُ فِي الْأَخِرَةِ مِن نَّصِيبٍ ٢٠

21. Or have they partners with Allâh (false gods) who have instituted for them a religion which Allâh has not ordained? And had it not been for a decisive Word (gone forth already), the matter would have been judged between them. And verily, for the *Zâlimûn* (polytheists and wrongdoers) there is a painful torment.

أَمْ لَهُمْ شُرَكَٰٓؤُا۟ شَرَعُوا۟ لَهُم مِّنَ الدِّينِ مَا لَمْ يَأْذَن بِهِ اللَّهُ وَلَوْلَا كَلِمَةُ الْفَصْلِ لَقُضِيَ بَيْنَهُمْ وَإِنَّ الظَّٰلِمِينَ لَهُمْ عَذَابٌ أَلِيمٌ ٢١

22. You will see (on the Day of Resurrection), the *Zâlimûn* (polytheists and wrongdoers) fearful of that which they have earned, and it (Allâh's Torment) will surely, befall them. But those who believe (in the Oneness of Allâh — Islâmic Monotheism) and do righteous deeds (will be) in the flowering meadows of the Gardens (Paradise). They shall have whatsoever they desire with their Lord. That is the supreme Grace, (Paradise).

تَرَى الظَّٰلِمِينَ مُشْفِقِينَ مِمَّا كَسَبُوا۟ وَهُوَ وَاقِعٌ بِهِمْ وَالَّذِينَ ءَامَنُوا۟ وَعَمِلُوا۟ الصَّٰلِحَٰتِ فِي رَوْضَاتِ الْجَنَّاتِ لَهُم مَّا يَشَآءُونَ عِندَ رَبِّهِمْ ذَٰلِكَ هُوَ الْفَضْلُ الْكَبِيرُ ٢٢

23. That is (the Paradise) whereof Allâh gives glad tidings to His slaves who believe (in the Oneness of Allâh — Islâmic Monotheism) and do righteous good deeds. Say (O Muhammad صلى الله عليه وسلم): "No reward do I ask of you for this except to be kind to me for my kinship with you."[1] And whoever earns a good righteous deed, We shall give him an increase of good in respect thereof. Verily, Allâh is Oft-Forgiving, Most Ready to appreciate (the deeds of those who are obedient to Him).

24. Or say they: "He has invented a lie against Allâh?" If Allâh willed, He could have sealed up your heart (so that you forget all that you know of the Qur'ân). And Allâh wipes out falsehood, and establishes the truth (Islâm) by His Word (this Qur'ân). Verily, He knows well what (secrets) are in the breasts (of mankind).

25. And He it is Who accepts repentance from His slaves, and forgives sins, and He knows what you do.[2]

---

[1] (V.42:23) i.e. I do not ask for any reward from you (in the form of wealth and money) for my preaching of Islamic Monotheism, but I only request you not to harm me for the kinship between you and me, as you are my tribesmen, and you have more right to obey me and follow me in my doctrine of Islamic Monotheism.

[2] (V.42:25)
Narrated Shaddâd bin Aus رضي الله عنه: The Prophet صلى الله عليه وسلم said, "The most superior way of asking for forgiveness from Allâh is: *Allâhumma Anta Rabbi, lâ ilâha illa Anta. Anta khalaqtani wa ana 'abduka, wa ana alâ 'ahdika wa wa'dika mastata' tu. A'udhu bika min sharri ma sanatu, abu'u laka bini'matika 'alaiya, wa abu'u laka bidhanbi faghfirli fa innahu la yaghfiru adhdhunûba illa Anta.*" The Prophet صلى الله عليه وسلم added: "If somebody recites them during the day with firm faith in it, and dies on the same day before

26. And He answers (the invocation of) those who believe (in the Oneness of Allâh — Islâmic Monotheism) and do righteous good deeds, and gives them increase of His Bounty. And as for the disbelievers, theirs will be a severe torment.

وَيَسۡتَجِيبُ ٱلَّذِينَ ءَامَنُوا۟ وَعَمِلُوا۟ ٱلصَّٰلِحَٰتِ وَيَزِيدُهُم مِّن فَضۡلِهِۦ وَٱلۡكَٰفِرُونَ لَهُمۡ عَذَابٌ شَدِيدٌ ۝

27. And if Allâh were to enlarge the provision for His slaves, they would surely, rebel in the earth, but He sends down by measure as He wills. Verily, He is, in respect of His slaves, the Well-Aware, the All-Seer (of things that benefit them).

۞ وَلَوۡ بَسَطَ ٱللَّهُ ٱلرِّزۡقَ لِعِبَادِهِۦ لَبَغَوۡا۟ فِى ٱلۡأَرۡضِ وَلَٰكِن يُنَزِّلُ بِقَدَرٍ مَّا يَشَآءُ إِنَّهُۥ بِعِبَادِهِۦ خَبِيرٌۢ بَصِيرٌ ۝

28. And He it is Who sends down the rain after they have despaired, and spreads His Mercy. And He is the Walî (Helper, Supporter, Protector, Lord), Worthy of all Praise.

وَهُوَ ٱلَّذِى يُنَزِّلُ ٱلۡغَيۡثَ مِنۢ بَعۡدِ مَا قَنَطُوا۟ وَيَنشُرُ رَحۡمَتَهُۥ وَهُوَ ٱلۡوَلِىُّ ٱلۡحَمِيدُ ۝

29. And among His Ayât (proofs, evidences, lessons, signs, etc.) is the creation of the heavens and the earth, and whatever moving (living) creatures He has dispersed in them both. And He is All-Potent over their assembling (i.e.

وَمِنۡ ءَايَٰتِهِۦ خَلۡقُ ٱلسَّمَٰوَٰتِ وَٱلۡأَرۡضِ وَمَا بَثَّ فِيهِمَا مِن دَآبَّةٍ وَهُوَ عَلَىٰ جَمۡعِهِمۡ إِذَا يَشَآءُ قَدِيرٌ ۝

---

the evening, he will be from the people of Paradise; and if somebody recites it at night with firm faith in it, and dies before the morning, he will be from the people of Paradise." (*Sahih Al-Bukhari*, Vol.8, *Hadîth* No.318).

* O Allâh, You are my Lord! None has the right to be worshipped but You. You created me and I am Your slave, and I am faithful to my covenant and my promise (to You) as much as I can. I seek refuge with You from all the evil I have done. I acknowledge before You all the blessings You have bestowed upon me, and I confess to You all my sins. So I entreat You to forgive my sins, for nobody can forgive sins except You.

resurrecting them on the Day of Resurrection after their death, and dispersion of their bodies) whenever He wills.

30. And whatever of misfortune befalls you, it is because of what your hands have earned. And He pardons much. (See the Qur'ân Verse 35:45).

وَمَآ أَصَـٰبَكُم مِّن مُّصِيبَةٍ فَبِمَا كَسَبَتْ أَيْدِيكُمْ وَيَعْفُواْ عَن كَثِيرٍ ۞

31. And you cannot escape from Allâh (i.e. His punishment) in the earth, and besides Allâh you have neither any *Walî* (guardian or a protector, helper) nor any helper.

وَمَآ أَنتُم بِمُعْجِزِينَ فِى ٱلْأَرْضِ وَمَا لَكُم مِّن دُونِ ٱللَّهِ مِن وَلِيٍّ وَلَا نَصِيرٍ ۞

32. And among His Signs are the ships in the sea like mountains.

وَمِنْ ءَايَـٰتِهِ ٱلْجَوَارِ فِى ٱلْبَحْرِ كَٱلْأَعْلَـٰمِ ۞

33. If He wills, He causes the wind to cease, then they would become motionless on the back (of the sea). Verily, in this are signs for everyone patient and grateful.

إِن يَشَأْ يُسْكِنِ ٱلرِّيحَ فَيَظْلَلْنَ رَوَاكِدَ عَلَىٰ ظَهْرِهِۦٓ إِنَّ فِى ذَٰلِكَ لَأَيَـٰتٍ لِّكُلِّ صَبَّارٍ شَكُورٍ ۞

34. Or He may destroy them (by shipwreck) because of that which their (people) have earned. And He pardons much.

أَوْ يُوبِقْهُنَّ بِمَا كَسَبُواْ وَيَعْفُ عَن كَثِيرٍ ۞

35. And those who dispute (polytheists, with Our Messenger Muhammad صلى الله عليه وسلم) as regards Our *Ayât* (proofs, signs, verses of Islâmic Monotheism) may know that there is no place of refuge for them (from Allâh's punishment)[1] [*Tafsir At-Tabari*].

وَيَعْلَمَ ٱلَّذِينَ يُجَـٰدِلُونَ فِىٓ ءَايَـٰتِنَا مَا لَهُم مِّن مَّحِيصٍ ۞

36. So whatever you have been given is but (a passing) enjoyment for this

فَمَآ أُوتِيتُم مِّن شَىْءٍ فَمَتَـٰعُ ٱلْحَيَوٰةِ

---

[1] (V.42:35) See the footnote of (V.3:85).

worldly life, but that which is with Allâh (Paradise) is better and more lasting for those who believe (in the Oneness of Allâh — Islâmic Monotheism) and put their trust in their Lord (concerning all of their affairs).

37. And those who avoid the greater sins,[1] and Al-Fawâhish (illegal sexual intercourse), and when they are angry, forgive.[2]

38. And those who answer the Call of their Lord [i.e. to believe that He is the only One Lord (Allâh), and to worship none but Him Alone], and perform As-Salât (Iqâmat-as-Salât), and who (conduct) their affairs by mutual consultation, and who spend of what We have bestowed on them.

39. And those who, when an oppressive wrong is done to them, take revenge.

40. The recompense for an evil is an evil like thereof; but whoever forgives and makes reconciliation, his reward is with Allâh. Verily, He likes not the Zâlimûn (oppressors, polytheists, and wrongdoers).

---

[1] (V.42:37) e.g. to join partners in worship with Allâh, to be undutiful to one's parents, to commit murder, to give false statements and witnesses, to steal, (See Verses 6:151 and 6:152).

[2] (V.42:37)

a) See the footnote (B) of (V.3:130) and (V.3:134).

b) See the footnote of (V.2:22).

c) See the footnote of (V.4:135).

d) See the footnote of (V.2:278).

41. And indeed whosoever takes revenge after he has suffered wrong, for such there is no way (of blame) against them.

ولَمَنِ ٱنتَصَرَ بَعۡدَ ظُلۡمِهِۦ فَأُوْلَٰٓئِكَ مَا عَلَيۡهِم مِّن سَبِيلٍ ٤١

42. The way (of blame) is only against those who oppress men and rebel in the earth without justification; for such there will be a painful torment.

إِنَّمَا ٱلسَّبِيلُ عَلَى ٱلَّذِينَ يَظۡلِمُونَ ٱلنَّاسَ وَيَبۡغُونَ فِى ٱلۡأَرۡضِ بِغَيۡرِ ٱلۡحَقِّ أُوْلَٰٓئِكَ لَهُمۡ عَذَابٌ أَلِيمٌ ٤٢

43. And verily, whosoever shows patience and forgives, that would truly, be from the things recommended by Allâh.

ولَمَن صَبَرَ وَغَفَرَ إِنَّ ذَٰلِكَ لَمِنۡ عَزۡمِ ٱلۡأُمُورِ ٤٣

44. And whomsoever Allâh sends astray, for him there is no *Walî* (protector, helper, guardian) after Him. And you will see the *Zâlimûn* (polytheists, wrongdoers, oppressors): when they behold the torment, they will say: "Is there any way of return (to the world)?"

ومَن يُضۡلِلِ ٱللَّهُ فَمَا لَهُۥ مِن وَلِيٍّ مِّنۢ بَعۡدِهِۦ وَتَرَى ٱلظَّٰلِمِينَ لَمَّا رَأَوُاْ ٱلۡعَذَابَ يَقُولُونَ هَلۡ إِلَىٰ مَرَدٍّ مِّن سَبِيلٍ ٤٤

45. And you will see them brought forward to it (Hell) made humble by disgrace,[1] (and) looking with stealthy glance. And those who believe will say: "Verily, the losers are they who lose themselves and their families on the Day of Resurrection. Verily, the *Zâlimûn* [i.e. *Al-Kâfirûn* (disbelievers in Allâh, in His Oneness and in His Messenger صلى الله عليه وسلم, polytheists,

وتَرَىٰهُمۡ يُعۡرَضُونَ عَلَيۡهَا خَٰشِعِينَ مِنَ ٱلذُّلِّ يَنظُرُونَ مِن طَرۡفٍ خَفِيٍّ وَقَالَ ٱلَّذِينَ ءَامَنُوٓاْ إِنَّ ٱلۡخَٰسِرِينَ ٱلَّذِينَ خَسِرُوٓاْ أَنفُسَهُمۡ وَأَهۡلِيهِمۡ يَوۡمَ ٱلۡقِيَٰمَةِ أَلَآ إِنَّ ٱلظَّٰلِمِينَ فِى عَذَابٍ مُّقِيمٍ ٤٥

---

[1] (V.42:45) Narrated Anas bin Mâlik رضى الله عنه: A man said, "O Allâh's Prophet (صلى الله عليه وسلم)! Will Allâh gather a disbeliever prone on his face on the Day of Resurrection?" He صلى الله عليه وسلم said, "Will not the One Who made him walk on his feet in this world, be able to make him walk on his face on the Day of Resurrection?" (Qatâdah, a subnarrator, said: "Yes, by the Power of Our Lord!") (*Sahih Al-Bukhari*, Vol.6, *Hadîth* No.283).

wrongdoers)] will be in a lasting torment. (*Tafsir At-Tabari*)

46. And they will have no *Auliyâ'* (protectors, helpers, guardians, lords) to help them other than Allâh. And he whom Allâh sends astray, for him there is no way.

وَمَاكَانَ لَهُم مِّنْ أَوْلِيَاءَ يَنصُرُونَهُم مِّن دُونِ ٱللَّهِ وَمَن يُضْلِلِ ٱللَّهُ فَمَا لَهُۥ مِن سَبِيلٍ ٤٦

47. Answer the Call of your Lord (i.e. accept the Islâmic Monotheism, O mankind and jinn) before there comes from Allâh a Day which cannot be averted (i.e. the Day of Resurrection). You will have no refuge on that Day nor there will be for you any denying (of your crimes as they are all recorded in the Book of your deeds).

ٱسْتَجِيبُواْ لِرَبِّكُم مِّن قَبْلِ أَن يَأْتِيَ يَوْمٌ لَّا مَرَدَّ لَهُۥ مِنَ ٱللَّهِ مَا لَكُم مِّن مَّلْجَإٍ يَوْمَئِذٍ وَمَا لَكُم مِّن نَّكِيرٍ ٤٧

48. But if they turn away (O Muhammad ﷺ from the Islâmic Monotheism, which you have brought to them). We have not sent you (O Muhammad ﷺ) as a *Hafiz* (watcher, protector) over them (i.e. to take care of their deeds and to recompense them). Your duty is to convey (the Message). And verily, when We cause man to taste of Mercy from Us, he rejoices thereat; but when some ill befalls them because of the deeds which their hands have sent forth, then verily, man (becomes) ingrate!

فَإِنْ أَعْرَضُواْ فَمَا أَرْسَلْنَاكَ عَلَيْهِمْ حَفِيظًا إِنْ عَلَيْكَ إِلَّا ٱلْبَلَاغُ وَإِنَّا إِذَا أَذَقْنَا ٱلْإِنسَانَ مِنَّا رَحْمَةً فَرِحَ بِهَا وَإِن تُصِبْهُمْ سَيِّئَةٌ بِمَا قَدَّمَتْ أَيْدِيهِمْ فَإِنَّ ٱلْإِنسَانَ كَفُورٌ ٤٨

49. To Allâh belongs the kingdom of the heavens and the earth. He creates what He wills. He bestows female (offspring) upon whom He wills, and bestows male (offspring) upon whom He wills.

لِّلَّهِ مُلْكُ ٱلسَّمَاوَاتِ وَٱلْأَرْضِ يَخْلُقُ مَا يَشَاءُ يَهَبُ لِمَن يَشَاءُ إِنَاثًا وَيَهَبُ لِمَن يَشَاءُ ٱلذُّكُورَ

50. Or He bestows both males and females, and He renders barren whom He wills. Verily, He is the All-Knower and is Able to do all things.

51. It is not given to any human being that Allâh should speak to him unless (it be) by Revelation, or from behind a veil, or (that) He sends a Messenger to reveal what He wills by His Leave. Verily, He is Most High, Most Wise.[1]

52. And thus We have sent to you (O Muhammad صلى الله عليه وسلم) Rûh (a Revelation, and a Mercy) of Our Command. You knew not what is the Book, nor what is Faith? But We have made it (this Qur'ân) a light wherewith We guide whosoever of Our slaves We will. And verily, you (O Muhammad صلى الله عليه وسلم) are indeed guiding (mankind) to the Straight Path (i.e. Allâh's religion of Islâmic Monotheism).

53. The Path of Allâh to Whom belongs all that is in the heavens and all that is in the earth. Verily, all matters at the end go to Allâh (for decision).

Sûrat Az-Zukhruf
(The Gold Adornments) XLIII

In the Name of Allâh
the Most Gracious, the Most Merciful

1. Hâ-Mîm.

[These letters are one of the miracles of the Qur'ân, and none but Allâh (Alone) knows their meanings].

---

[1] (V.42:51) See the footnote of (V.4:163).

2. By the manifest Book (i.e. this Qur'ân that makes things clear).

3. Verily, We have made it a Qur'ân in Arabic that you may be able to understand (its meanings and its admonitions).

4. And verily, it (this Qur'ân) is in the Mother of the Book (i.e. *Al-Lauh Al-Mahfûz*) with Us, indeed exalted, full of wisdom.

5. Shall We then (warn you not and) take away the Reminder (this Qur'ân) from you, because you are a people *Musrifûn*.[1]

6. And how many a Prophet have We sent amongst the men of old.

7. And never came there a Prophet to them but they used to mock at him.

8. Then We destroyed men stronger (in power) than these — and the example of the ancients has passed away (before them).

9. And indeed if you ask them, "Who has created the heavens and the earth?" They will surely say: "The All-Mighty, the All-Knower created them."

10. Who has made for you the earth like a bed, and has made for you roads therein, in order that you may find your way.

11. And Who sends down water (rain) from the sky in due measure, then

---

[1] (V.43:5) *Musrifun:* Those who transgress the limits, as sinners, polytheists, pagans, idolaters and disbelievers in the Oneness of Allâh and in His Messenger Muhammad صلى الله عليه وسلم.

We revive a dead land therewith, and even so you will be brought forth (from the graves).

12. And Who has created all the pairs and has appointed for you ships and cattle on which you ride:

13. In order that you may mount on their backs, and then may remember the Favour of your Lord when you mount thereon, and say: "Glory to Him Who has subjected this to us, and we could never have it (by our efforts).

14. And verily, to Our Lord we indeed are to return!"

15. Yet, they assign to some of His slaves a share with Him (by pretending that He has children, and considering them as equals or co-partners in worship with Him). Verily, man is indeed a manifest ingrate!

16. Or has He taken daughters out of what He has created, and He has selected for you sons?

17. And if one of them is informed of the news of (the birth of a girl) that which he sets forth as a parable to the Most Gracious (Allâh), his face becomes dark, and he is filled with grief!

18. (Like they then for Allâh) a creature who is brought up in adornments (wearing silk and gold ornaments, i.e. women), and who in dispute cannot make herself clear?

19. And they make the angels who themselves are slaves of the Most

بِقَدَرٍ فَأَنشَرْنَا بِهِ بَلْدَةً مَّيْتًا كَذَٰلِكَ تُخْرَجُونَ ١١

وَالَّذِى خَلَقَ الْأَزْوَاجَ كُلَّهَا وَجَعَلَ لَكُم مِّنَ الْفُلْكِ وَالْأَنْعَامِ مَا تَرْكَبُونَ ١٢

لِتَسْتَوُا عَلَىٰ ظُهُورِهِ ثُمَّ تَذْكُرُوا نِعْمَةَ رَبِّكُمْ إِذَا اسْتَوَيْتُمْ عَلَيْهِ وَتَقُولُوا سُبْحَانَ الَّذِى سَخَّرَ لَنَا هَٰذَا وَمَا كُنَّا لَهُ مُقْرِنِينَ ١٣

وَإِنَّا إِلَىٰ رَبِّنَا لَمُنقَلِبُونَ ١٤

وَجَعَلُوا لَهُ مِنْ عِبَادِهِ جُزْءًا إِنَّ الْإِنسَانَ لَكَفُورٌ مُّبِينٌ ١٥

أَمِ اتَّخَذَ مِمَّا يَخْلُقُ بَنَاتٍ وَأَصْفَاكُم بِالْبَنِينَ ١٦

وَإِذَا بُشِّرَ أَحَدُهُم بِمَا ضَرَبَ لِلرَّحْمَٰنِ مَثَلًا ظَلَّ وَجْهُهُ مُسْوَدًّا وَهُوَ كَظِيمٌ ١٧

أَوَمَن يُنَشَّأُ فِى الْحِلْيَةِ وَهُوَ فِى الْخِصَامِ غَيْرُ مُبِينٍ ١٨

وَجَعَلُوا الْمَلَائِكَةَ الَّذِينَ هُمْ

Gracious (Allâh) females. Did they witness their creation? Their testimony will be recorded, and they will be questioned!

20. And they said: "If it had been the Will of the Most Gracious (Allâh), we should not have worshipped them (false deities)." They have no knowledge whatsoever of that. They do nothing but lie!

21. Or have We given them any Book before this (the Qur'ân) to which they are holding fast?

22. Nay! They say: "We found our fathers following a certain way and religion, and we guide ourselves by their footsteps."

23. And similarly, We sent not a warner before you (O Muhammad صلى الله عليه وسلم) to any town (people) but the luxurious ones among them said: "We found our fathers following a certain way and religion, and we will indeed follow their footsteps."

24. (The warner) said: "Even if I bring you better guidance than that which you found your fathers following?" They said: "Verily, we disbelieve in that with which you have been sent."

25. So We took revenge on them, then see what was the end of those who denied (Islâmic Monotheism).

26. And (remember) when Ibrâhîm (Abraham) said to his father and his people: "Verily, I am innocent of what you worship,

إِنَّنِي بَرَآءٌ مِّمَّا تَعْبُدُونَ ۝

27. "Except Him (i.e. Allâh Alone I worship none) Who did create me; and verily, He will guide me."

إِلَّا الَّذِي فَطَرَنِي فَإِنَّهُ سَيَهْدِينِ ۝

28. And he made it [i.e. Lâ ilâha illallâh (none has the right to be worshipped but Allâh Alone)] a Word lasting among his offspring, that they may turn back (i.e. to repent to Allâh or receive admonition).

وَجَعَلَهَا كَلِمَةً بَاقِيَةً فِي عَقِبِهِ لَعَلَّهُمْ يَرْجِعُونَ ۝

29. Nay, but I gave (the good things of this life) to these (polytheists) and their fathers to enjoy, till there came to them the truth (the Qur'ân), and a Messenger (Muhammad صلى الله عليه وسلم) making things clear.

بَلْ مَتَّعْتُ هَٰٓؤُلَآءِ وَءَابَآءَهُمْ حَتَّىٰ جَآءَهُمُ الْحَقُّ وَرَسُولٌ مُّبِينٌ ۝

30. And when the truth (this Qur'ân) came to them, they (the disbelievers in this Qur'ân) said: "This is magic, and we disbelieve therein."

وَلَمَّا جَآءَهُمُ الْحَقُّ قَالُوا هَٰذَا سِحْرٌ وَإِنَّا بِهِۦ كَٰفِرُونَ ۝

31. And they say: "Why is not this Qur'ân sent down to some great man of the two towns (Makkah and Tâ'if)?"

وَقَالُوا لَوْلَا نُزِّلَ هَٰذَا الْقُرْءَانُ عَلَىٰ رَجُلٍ مِّنَ الْقَرْيَتَيْنِ عَظِيمٍ ۝

32. Is it they who would portion out the Mercy of your Lord? It is We Who portion out between them their livelihood in this world, and We raised some of them above others in ranks, so that some may employ others in their work. But the Mercy (Paradise) of your Lord (O Muhammad صلى الله عليه وسلم) is better than the (wealth of this world) which they amass.

أَهُمْ يَقْسِمُونَ رَحْمَتَ رَبِّكَ نَحْنُ قَسَمْنَا بَيْنَهُم مَّعِيشَتَهُمْ فِي الْحَيَوٰةِ الدُّنْيَا وَرَفَعْنَا بَعْضَهُمْ فَوْقَ بَعْضٍ دَرَجَٰتٍ لِّيَتَّخِذَ بَعْضُهُم بَعْضًا سُخْرِيًّا وَرَحْمَتُ رَبِّكَ خَيْرٌ مِّمَّا يَجْمَعُونَ ۝

33. And were it not that mankind would have become of one community (all disbelievers desiring worldly life only), We would have provided for those who disbelieve in the Most Gracious (Allâh), silver roofs for their houses, and elevators whereby they ascend,

34. And for their houses, doors (of silver), and thrones (of silver) on which they could recline,

35. And adornments of gold. Yet all this (i.e. the roofs, doors, stairs, elevators, thrones of their houses) would have been nothing but an enjoyment of this world. And the Hereafter with your Lord is (only) for the *Muttaqûn*.[1]

36. And whosoever turns away blindly from the remembrance of the Most Gracious (Allâh) (i.e. this Qur'ân and worship of Allâh), We appoint for him *Shaitân* (Satan - devil) to be a *Qarîn* (companion) to him.

37. And verily, they (Satans / devils) hinder them from the Path (of Allâh), but they think that they are guided aright!

38. Till, when (such a one) comes to Us, he says [to his *Qarîn* (Satan / devil companion)] "Would that between me and you were the distance of the two

---

[1] (V.43:35) *Al-Muttaqûn*: means the pious and righteous persons who fear Allâh much (abstain from all kinds of sins and evil deeds which He has forbidden) and love Allâh much (perform all kinds of good deeds which He has ordained).

easts (or the east and west)" — a worst (type of) companion (indeed)!

39. It will profit you not this Day (O you who turn away from Allâh's remembrance and His worship) as you did wrong, (and) that you will be sharers (you and your *Qarîn*) in the punishment.

40. Can you (O Muhammad صلى الله عليه وسلم) make the deaf to hear, or can you guide the blind or him who is in manifest error?

41. And even if We take you (O Muhammad صلى الله عليه وسلم) away, We shall indeed take vengeance on them.

42. Or (if) We show you that wherewith We threaten them: then verily, We have perfect command over them.

43. So hold you (O Muhammad صلى الله عليه وسلم) fast to that which is revealed to you. Verily, you are on the Straight Path.

44. And verily, this (the Qur'ân) is indeed a Reminder for you (O Muhammad صلى الله عليه وسلم) and your people (Quraish people, or your followers), and you will be questioned (about it).

45. And ask (O Muhammad صلى الله عليه وسلم) those of Our Messengers whom We sent before you: "Did We ever appoint *âlihah* (gods) to be worshipped besides the Most Gracious (Allâh)?"

وَلَن يَنفَعَكُمُ ٱلْيَوْمَ إِذ ظَّلَمْتُمْ أَنَّكُمْ فِي ٱلْعَذَابِ مُشْتَرِكُونَ ۝

أَفَأَنتَ تُسْمِعُ ٱلصُّمَّ أَوْ تَهْدِي ٱلْعُمْىَ وَمَن كَانَ فِي ضَلَٰلٍ مُّبِينٍ ۝

فَإِمَّا نَذْهَبَنَّ بِكَ فَإِنَّا مِنْهُم مُّنتَقِمُونَ ۝

أَوْ نُرِيَنَّكَ ٱلَّذِي وَعَدْنَٰهُمْ فَإِنَّا عَلَيْهِم مُّقْتَدِرُونَ ۝

فَٱسْتَمْسِكْ بِٱلَّذِي أُوحِيَ إِلَيْكَ إِنَّكَ عَلَىٰ صِرَٰطٍ مُّسْتَقِيمٍ ۝

وَإِنَّهُۥ لَذِكْرٌ لَّكَ وَلِقَوْمِكَ وَسَوْفَ تُسْـَٔلُونَ ۝

وَسْـَٔلْ مَنْ أَرْسَلْنَا مِن قَبْلِكَ مِن رُّسُلِنَآ أَجَعَلْنَا مِن دُونِ ٱلرَّحْمَٰنِ ءَالِهَةً يُعْبَدُونَ ۝

46. And indeed We did send Mûsâ (Moses) with Our *Ayât* (proofs, evidences, verses, lessons, signs, revelations, etc.) to Fir'aun (Pharaoh) and his chiefs (inviting them to Allâh's religion of Islâm) He said: "Verily, I am a Messenger of the Lord of the *'Âlamîn* (mankind, jinn and all that exists)."

وَلَقَدْ أَرْسَلْنَا مُوسَىٰ بِـَٔايَٰتِنَآ إِلَىٰ فِرْعَوْنَ وَمَلَإِيْهِۦ فَقَالَ إِنِّى رَسُولُ رَبِّ ٱلْعَٰلَمِينَ ٤٦

47. But when he came to them with Our *Ayât* (proofs, evidences, verses, lessons, signs, revelations, etc.) behold, they laughed at them.

فَلَمَّا جَآءَهُم بِـَٔايَٰتِنَآ إِذَا هُم مِّنْهَا يَضْحَكُونَ ٤٧

48. And not an *Ayâh* (sign, etc.) We showed them but it was greater than its fellow preceding it, and We seized them with torment, in order that they might turn [from their polytheism to Allâh's religion (Islâmic Monotheism)].

وَمَا نُرِيهِم مِّنْ ءَايَةٍ إِلَّا هِىَ أَكْبَرُ مِنْ أُخْتِهَا وَأَخَذْنَٰهُم بِٱلْعَذَابِ لَعَلَّهُمْ يَرْجِعُونَ ٤٨

49. And they said [to Mûsâ (Moses)]: "O you sorcerer! Invoke your Lord for us according to what He has covenanted with you. Verily, We shall guide ourselves (aright)."

وَقَالُوا يَٰٓأَيُّهَ ٱلسَّاحِرُ ٱدْعُ لَنَا رَبَّكَ بِمَا عَهِدَ عِندَكَ إِنَّنَا لَمُهْتَدُونَ ٤٩

50. But when We removed the torment from them, behold, they broke their covenant (that they will believe if We remove the torment from them).

فَلَمَّا كَشَفْنَا عَنْهُمُ ٱلْعَذَابَ إِذَا هُمْ يَنكُثُونَ ٥٠

51. And Fir'aun (Pharaoh) proclaimed among his people (saying): "O my people! Is not mine the dominion of Egypt, and these rivers flowing underneath me. See you not then?

وَنَادَىٰ فِرْعَوْنُ فِى قَوْمِهِۦ قَالَ يَٰقَوْمِ أَلَيْسَ لِى مُلْكُ مِصْرَ وَهَٰذِهِ ٱلْأَنْهَٰرُ تَجْرِى مِن تَحْتِىٓ أَفَلَا تُبْصِرُونَ ٥١

52. "Am I not better than this one [Mûsâ (Moses)] who is despicable and can scarcely express himself clearly?

أَمْ أَنَا خَيْرٌ مِّنْ هَٰذَا ٱلَّذِى هُوَ مَهِينٌ وَلَا يَكَادُ يُبِينُ ٥٢

53. "Why then are not golden bracelets bestowed on him, or angels sent along with him?"

فَلَوْلَا أُلْقِيَ عَلَيْهِ أَسْوِرَةٌ مِّن ذَهَبٍ أَوْ جَآءَ مَعَهُ الْمَلَٰٓئِكَةُ مُقْتَرِنِينَ ٥٣

54. Thus he [Fir'aun (Pharaoh)] befooled (and misled) his people, and they obeyed him. Verily, they were ever a people who were Fâsiqûn (rebellious, disobedient to Allâh).

فَاسْتَخَفَّ قَوْمَهُ فَأَطَاعُوهُ إِنَّهُمْ كَانُوا قَوْمًا فَٰسِقِينَ ٥٤

55. So when they angered Us, We punished them, and drowned them all.

فَلَمَّآ ءَاسَفُونَا انتَقَمْنَا مِنْهُمْ فَأَغْرَقْنَٰهُمْ أَجْمَعِينَ ٥٥

56. And We made them a precedent (as a lesson for those coming after them), and an example to later generations.

فَجَعَلْنَٰهُمْ سَلَفًا وَمَثَلًا لِّلْءَاخِرِينَ ٥٦

57. And when the son of Maryam (Mary) is quoted as an example [i.e. 'Îsâ (Jesus) is worshipped like their idols], behold, your people cry aloud (laugh out at the example).

۞ وَلَمَّا ضُرِبَ ابْنُ مَرْيَمَ مَثَلًا إِذَا قَوْمُكَ مِنْهُ يَصِدُّونَ ٥٧

58. And say: "Are our âlihah (gods) better or is he ['Îsâ (Jesus)]?" They quoted not the above example except for argument. Nay! But they are a quarrelsome people. (See V.21:98-101)

وَقَالُوٓا ءَأَٰلِهَتُنَا خَيْرٌ أَمْ هُوَ مَا ضَرَبُوهُ لَكَ إِلَّا جَدَلًا بَلْ هُمْ قَوْمٌ خَصِمُونَ ٥٨

59. He ['Îsâ (Jesus)] was not more than a slave. We granted Our Favour to him, and We made him an example for the Children of Israel (i.e. his creation without a father).

إِنْ هُوَ إِلَّا عَبْدٌ أَنْعَمْنَا عَلَيْهِ وَجَعَلْنَٰهُ مَثَلًا لِّبَنِيٓ إِسْرَٰٓءِيلَ ٥٩

60. And if it were Our Will, We would have [destroyed you (mankind) all, and] made angels to replace you on the earth. [Tafsir At-Tabarî, Vol:25, Page 89].

وَلَوْ نَشَآءُ لَجَعَلْنَا مِنكُم مَّلَٰٓئِكَةً فِى الْأَرْضِ يَخْلُفُونَ ٦٠

61. And he ['Îsâ (Jesus), son of Maryam (Mary)] shall be a known sign for (the coming of) the Hour (Day of Resurrection) [i.e. 'Îsâ's (Jesus) descent on the earth].[1] Therefore have no doubt concerning it (i.e. the Day of Resurrection). And follow Me (Allâh) (i.e. be obedient to Allâh and do what He orders you to do, O mankind)! This is the Straight Path (of Islâmic Monotheism, leading to Allâh and to His Paradise).

62. And let not *Shaitân* (Satan) hinder you (from the right religion, i.e. Islâmic Monotheism). Verily, he (Satan) to you is a plain enemy.

63. And when 'Îsâ (Jesus) came with (Our) clear Proofs, he said: "I have come to you with *Al-Hikmah* (Prophethood), and in order to make clear to you some of the (points) in which you differ. Therefore fear Allâh and obey me.

64. "Verily, Allâh! He is my Lord (God) and your Lord (God). So worship Him (Alone). This is the (only) Straight Path (i.e. Allâh's religion of true Islâmic Monotheism)."

65. But the sects from among themselves differed. So woe to those who do wrong [by ascribing things to 'Îsâ (Jesus) that are not true] from the torment of a painful Day (i.e. the Day of Resurrection)!

---

[1] (V.43:61) See the footnote of (V.3:55).

66. Do they only wait for the Hour that it shall come upon them suddenly while they perceive not?

هَلۡ يَنظُرُونَ إِلَّا ٱلسَّاعَةَ أَن تَأۡتِيَهُم بَغۡتَةً وَهُمۡ لَا يَشۡعُرُونَ ٦٦

67. Friends on that Day will be foes one to another except Al-Muttaqûn (the pious. See V.2:2).

ٱلۡأَخِلَّآءُ يَوۡمَئِذِۭ بَعۡضُهُمۡ لِبَعۡضٍ عَدُوٌّ إِلَّا ٱلۡمُتَّقِينَ ٦٧

68. (It will be said to the true believers of Islâmic Monotheism): My worshippers! No fear shall be on you this Day, nor shall you grieve,

يَٰعِبَادِ لَا خَوۡفٌ عَلَيۡكُمُ ٱلۡيَوۡمَ وَلَآ أَنتُمۡ تَحۡزَنُونَ ٦٨

69. (You) who believed in Our Ayât (proofs, verses, lessons, signs, revelations, etc.) and were Muslims (i.e. who submit totally to Allâh's Will, and believe in the Oneness of Allâh — Islâmic Monotheism).

ٱلَّذِينَ ءَامَنُوا بِـَٔايَٰتِنَا وَكَانُوا مُسۡلِمِينَ ٦٩

70. Enter Paradise, you and your wives, in happiness.

ٱدۡخُلُوا ٱلۡجَنَّةَ أَنتُمۡ وَأَزۡوَٰجُكُمۡ تُحۡبَرُونَ ٧٠

71. Trays of gold and cups will be passed round them; (there will be) therein all that inner-selves could desire, and all that eyes could delight in and you will abide therein forever.

يُطَافُ عَلَيۡهِم بِصِحَافٍ مِّن ذَهَبٍ وَأَكۡوَابٍ وَفِيهَا مَا تَشۡتَهِيهِ ٱلۡأَنفُسُ وَتَلَذُّ ٱلۡأَعۡيُنُ وَأَنتُمۡ فِيهَا خَٰلِدُونَ ٧١

72. This is the Paradise which you have been made to inherit because of your deeds which you used to do (in the life of the world).

وَتِلۡكَ ٱلۡجَنَّةُ ٱلَّتِيٓ أُورِثۡتُمُوهَا بِمَا كُنتُمۡ تَعۡمَلُونَ ٧٢

73. Therein for you will be fruits in plenty, of which you will eat (as you desire).

لَكُمۡ فِيهَا فَٰكِهَةٌ كَثِيرَةٌ مِّنۡهَا تَأۡكُلُونَ ٧٣

74. Verily, the Mujrimûn (criminals, sinners, disbelievers) will be in the torment of Hell to abide therein forever.

إِنَّ ٱلۡمُجۡرِمِينَ فِي عَذَابِ جَهَنَّمَ خَٰلِدُونَ ٧٤

75. (The torment) will not be lightened for them, and they will be plunged into destruction with deep regrets, sorrows and in despair therein.

لَا يُفَتَّرُ عَنْهُمْ وَهُمْ فِيهِ مُبْلِسُونَ ٧٥

76. We wronged them not, but they were the *Zâlimûn* (polytheists, wrongdoers).

وَمَا ظَلَمْنَـٰهُمْ وَلَـٰكِن كَانُوا۟ هُمُ ٱلظَّـٰلِمِينَ ٧٦

77. And they will cry: "O Malik (Keeper of Hell)! Let your Lord make an end of us." He will say: "Verily, you shall abide forever."

وَنَادَوْا۟ يَـٰمَـٰلِكُ لِيَقْضِ عَلَيْنَا رَبُّكَ قَالَ إِنَّكُم مَّـٰكِثُونَ ٧٧

78. Indeed We have brought the truth (Muhammad ﷺ with the Qur'ân) to you, but most of you have a hatred for the truth.[1]

لَقَدْ جِئْنَـٰكُم بِٱلْحَقِّ وَلَـٰكِنَّ أَكْثَرَكُمْ لِلْحَقِّ كَـٰرِهُونَ ٧٨

79. Or have they plotted some plan? Then We too are planning.

أَمْ أَبْرَمُوٓا۟ أَمْرًا فَإِنَّا مُبْرِمُونَ ٧٩

80. Or do they think that We hear not their secrets and their private counsel? (Yes We do) and Our messengers (appointed angels in charge of mankind) are by them, to record.

أَمْ يَحْسَبُونَ أَنَّا لَا نَسْمَعُ سِرَّهُمْ وَنَجْوَىٰهُم بَلَىٰ وَرُسُلُنَا لَدَيْهِمْ يَكْتُبُونَ ٨٠

81. Say (O Muhammad ﷺ): "If the Most Gracious (Allâh) had a son (or children as you pretend), then I am the first of (Allâh's) worshippers [who deny and refute this claim of yours (and the first to believe in Allâh Alone and testify that He has no children)]." [*Tafsir At-Tabari*].

قُلْ إِن كَانَ لِلرَّحْمَـٰنِ وَلَدٌ فَأَنَا۠ أَوَّلُ ٱلْعَـٰبِدِينَ ٨١

82. Glorified is the Lord of the heavens and the earth, the Lord of the

سُبْحَـٰنَ رَبِّ ٱلسَّمَـٰوَٰتِ وَٱلْأَرْضِ رَبِّ ٱلْعَرْشِ عَمَّا يَصِفُونَ ٨٢

---

[1] (V.43:78) See the footnote of (V.3:85).

Throne! Exalted is He from all that they ascribe (to Him).

83. So leave them (alone) to speak nonsense and play until they meet the Day of theirs which they have been promised.

فَذَرْهُمْ يَخُوضُوا وَيَلْعَبُوا حَتَّىٰ يُلَٰقُوا يَوْمَهُمُ ٱلَّذِى يُوعَدُونَ ۝

84. It is He (Allâh) Who is the only *Ilâh* (God to be worshipped) in the heaven and the only *Ilâh* (God to be worshipped) on the earth. And He is the All-Wise, the All-Knower.

وَهُوَ ٱلَّذِى فِى ٱلسَّمَآءِ إِلَٰهٌ وَفِى ٱلْأَرْضِ إِلَٰهٌ وَهُوَ ٱلْحَكِيمُ ٱلْعَلِيمُ ۝

85. And Blessed is He to Whom belongs the kingdom of the heavens and the earth, and all that is between them, and with Whom is the knowledge of the Hour, and to Whom you (all) will be returned.

وَتَبَارَكَ ٱلَّذِى لَهُۥ مُلْكُ ٱلسَّمَٰوَٰتِ وَٱلْأَرْضِ وَمَا بَيْنَهُمَا وَعِندَهُۥ عِلْمُ ٱلسَّاعَةِ وَإِلَيْهِ تُرْجَعُونَ ۝

86. And those whom they invoke instead of Him have no power of intercession — except for those who bear witness to the truth knowingly (i.e. believed in the Oneness of Allâh, and obeyed His Orders), and they know (the facts about the Oneness of Allâh).[1]

وَلَا يَمْلِكُ ٱلَّذِينَ يَدْعُونَ مِن دُونِهِ ٱلشَّفَٰعَةَ إِلَّا مَن شَهِدَ بِٱلْحَقِّ وَهُمْ يَعْلَمُونَ ۝

87. And if you ask them who created them, they will surely, say: "Allâh." How then are they turned away (from the worship of Allâh Who created them)?

وَلَئِن سَأَلْتَهُم مَّنْ خَلَقَهُمْ لَيَقُولُنَّ ٱللَّهُ فَأَنَّىٰ يُؤْفَكُونَ ۝

88. (And Allâh has the knowledge) of (Prophet Muhammad's) saying: "O my Lord! Verily, these are a people who believe not!"

وَقِيلِهِ يَٰرَبِّ إِنَّ هَٰٓؤُلَآءِ قَوْمٌ لَّا يُؤْمِنُونَ ۝

---

[1] (V.43:86) See the footnote of (V.2:165).

89. So turn away from them (O Muhammad (صلى الله عليه وسلم)), and say: *Salâm* (peace)! But they will come to know.[1]

فَٱصْفَحْ عَنْهُمْ وَقُلْ سَلَـٰمٌ فَسَوْفَ يَعْلَمُونَ ﴿٨٩﴾

Sûrat Ad-Dukhân (The Smoke) XLIV

سُورَةُ الدُّخَانِ

In the Name of Allâh the Most Gracious, the Most Merciful

بِسْمِ اللَّهِ الرَّحْمَٰنِ الرَّحِيمِ

1. *Hâ-Mîm.*

[These letters are one of the miracles of the Qur'ân and none but Allâh (Alone) knows their meanings].

حمٓ ﴿١﴾

2. By the manifest Book (this Qur'ân) that makes things clear.

وَٱلْكِتَٰبِ ٱلْمُبِينِ ﴿٢﴾

3. We sent it (this Qur'ân) down on a blessed night [(i.e. the night of *Al-Qadr*, *Sûrah* No. 97) in the month of Ramadân — the 9th month of the Islâmic calendar]. Verily, We are ever warning [mankind that Our Torment will reach those who disbelieve in Our Oneness of Lordship and in Our Oneness of worship].

إِنَّآ أَنزَلْنَٰهُ فِى لَيْلَةٍ مُّبَٰرَكَةٍ إِنَّا كُنَّا مُنذِرِينَ ﴿٣﴾

4. Therein (that night) is decreed every matter of ordainments.[2]

فِيهَا يُفْرَقُ كُلُّ أَمْرٍ حَكِيمٍ ﴿٤﴾

5. As a Command (or this Qur'ân or the Decree of every matter) from Us. Verily, We are ever sending (the Messengers),

أَمْرًا مِّنْ عِندِنَآ إِنَّا كُنَّا مُرْسِلِينَ ﴿٥﴾

---

[1] (V.43:89) The provision of this Verse was abrogated by the revelation of the Verse of fighting against them (V.9:5).

[2] (V.44:4) i.e. the matters of deaths, births, provisions, calamities, for the whole (coming) year as decreed by Allâh.

6. (As) a Mercy from your Lord. Verily, He is the All-Hearer, the All-Knower.

7. The Lord of the heavens and the earth and all that is between them, if you (but) have a faith with certainty.

8. *Lâ ilaha illâ Huwa* (none has the right to be worshipped but He). It is He Who gives life and causes death — your Lord and the Lord of your forefathers.

9. Nay! They play about in doubt.

10. Then wait you for the Day when the sky will bring forth a visible smoke,

11. Covering the people: this is a painful torment.

12. (They will say): "Our Lord! Remove the torment from us, really we shall become believers!"

13. How can there be for them an admonition (at the time when the torment has reached them), when a Messenger explaining things clearly has already come to them.

14. Then they had turned away from him (Messenger Muhammad صلى الله عليه وسلم) and said: (He is one Muhammad) taught (by a human being), a madman!"

15. Verily, We shall remove the torment for a while. Verily, We will revert (to disbelief).

16. On the Day when We shall seize you with the greatest seizure (punishment). Verily, We will exact retribution.

17. And indeed We tried before them Fir'aun's (Pharaoh) people, when there came to them a noble Messenger [i.e. Mûsâ (Moses) , [عليه السلام]],

18. Saying: "Deliver to me the slaves of Allâh (i.e. the Children of Israel). Verily, I am to you a Messenger worthy of all trust.

19. "And exalt not yourselves against Allâh. Truly, I have come to you with a manifest authority.

20. "And truly, I seek refuge with my Lord and your Lord, lest you should stone me (or call me a sorcerer or kill me).

21. "But if you believe me not, then keep away from me and leave me alone."

22. (But they were aggressive), so he [Mûsâ (Moses)] called upon his Lord (saying): "These are indeed the people who are *Mujrimûn* (disbelievers, polytheists, sinners, criminals)."

23. (Allâh said): "Depart you with My slaves by night. Surely, you will be pursued.

24. "And leave the sea as it is (quiet and divided). Verily, they are a host to be drowned."

25. How many of gardens and springs that they [Fir'aun's (Pharaoh) people] left behind,

26. And green crops (fields) and goodly places,

﴿ وَلَقَدْ فَتَنَّا قَبْلَهُمْ قَوْمَ فِرْعَوْنَ وَجَآءَهُمْ رَسُولٌ كَرِيمٌ ﴿١٧﴾

أَنْ أَدُّوٓا۟ إِلَىَّ عِبَادَ ٱللَّهِ إِنِّى لَكُمْ رَسُولٌ أَمِينٌ ﴿١٨﴾

وَأَن لَّا تَعْلُوا۟ عَلَى ٱللَّهِ إِنِّىٓ ءَاتِيكُم بِسُلْطَٰنٍ مُّبِينٍ ﴿١٩﴾

وَإِنِّى عُذْتُ بِرَبِّى وَرَبِّكُمْ أَن تَرْجُمُونِ ﴿٢٠﴾

وَإِن لَّمْ تُؤْمِنُوا۟ لِى فَٱعْتَزِلُونِ ﴿٢١﴾

فَدَعَا رَبَّهُۥٓ أَنَّ هَٰٓؤُلَآءِ قَوْمٌ مُّجْرِمُونَ ﴿٢٢﴾

فَأَسْرِ بِعِبَادِى لَيْلًا إِنَّكُم مُّتَّبَعُونَ ﴿٢٣﴾

وَٱتْرُكِ ٱلْبَحْرَ رَهْوًا إِنَّهُمْ جُندٌ مُّغْرَقُونَ ﴿٢٤﴾

كَمْ تَرَكُوا۟ مِن جَنَّٰتٍ وَعُيُونٍ ﴿٢٥﴾

وَزُرُوعٍ وَمَقَامٍ كَرِيمٍ ﴿٢٦﴾

27. And comforts of life wherein they used to take delight!

وَنَعْمَةٍ كَانُوا فِيهَا فَٰكِهِينَ ٢٧

28. Thus (it was)! And We made other people inherit them (i.e. We made the Children of Israel to inherit the kingdom of Egypt).

كَذَٰلِكَ وَأَوْرَثْنَٰهَا قَوْمًا ءَاخَرِينَ ٢٨

29. And the heavens and the earth wept not for them,[1] nor were they given a respite.

فَمَا بَكَتْ عَلَيْهِمُ السَّمَآءُ وَالْأَرْضُ وَمَا كَانُوا مُنظَرِينَ ٢٩

30. And indeed We saved the Children of Israel from the humiliating torment:

وَلَقَدْ نَجَّيْنَا بَنِىٓ إِسْرَٰٓءِيلَ مِنَ الْعَذَابِ الْمُهِينِ ٣٠

31. From Fir'aun (Pharaoh); verily, he was arrogant and was of the *Musrifûn* (those who transgress beyond bound in spending and other things and commit great sins).

مِن فِرْعَوْنَ إِنَّهُۥ كَانَ عَالِيًا مِّنَ الْمُسْرِفِينَ ٣١

32. And We chose them (the Children of Israel) above the *'Âlamîn* (mankind and jinn) [during the time of Mûsâ (Moses)] with knowledge,

وَلَقَدِ اخْتَرْنَٰهُمْ عَلَىٰ عِلْمٍ عَلَى الْعَٰلَمِينَ ٣٢

33. And granted them signs in which there was a plain trial.

وَءَاتَيْنَٰهُم مِّنَ الْءَايَٰتِ مَا فِيهِ بَلَٰٓؤٌا۟ مُّبِينٌ ٣٣

34. Verily, these (Quraish) people are saying:

إِنَّ هَٰٓؤُلَآءِ لَيَقُولُونَ ٣٤

35. "There is nothing but our first death, and we shall not be resurrected.

إِنْ هِىَ إِلَّا مَوْتَتُنَا الْأُولَىٰ وَمَا نَحْنُ بِمُنشَرِينَ ٣٥

---

[1] (V.44:29) Narrated Ibn Jarîr At-Tabari: Ibn 'Abbâs رضي الله عنهما said, "When a believer dies, the place of earth on which he used to prostrate himself in his *Salât* (prayer), and the gate in the heaven through which his good deeds used to ascend, weep for him, while they do not weep for the disbeliever." [*Tafsir At-Tabari*, V.25, P.125].

36. "Then bring back our forefathers, if you speak the truth!"

37. Are they better or the people of Tubba' and those before them? We destroyed them because they were indeed *Mujrimûn* (disbelievers, polytheists, sinners, criminals).

38. And We created not the heavens and the earth, and all that is between them, for mere play.

39. We created them not except with truth (i.e. to examine and test those who are obedient and those who are disobedient and then reward the obedient ones and punish the disobedient ones), but most of them know not.

40. Verily, the Day of Judgement (when Allâh will judge between the creatures) is the time appointed for all of them —

41. The Day when a *Maulâ* (a near relative) cannot avail a *Maulâ* (a near relative) in aught, and no help can they receive,

42. Except him on whom Allâh has Mercy. Verily, He is the All-Mighty, the Most Merciful.

43. Verily, the tree of *Zaqqûm*

44. Will be the food of the sinners.

45. Like boiling oil, it will boil in the bellies,

46. Like the boiling of scalding water.

47. (It will be said) "Seize him and drag him into the midst of blazing Fire,

خُذُوهُ فَاعْتِلُوهُ إِلَىٰ سَوَآءِ الْجَحِيمِ ۝

48. "Then pour over his head the torment of boiling water.

ثُمَّ صُبُّوا فَوْقَ رَأْسِهِۦ مِنْ عَذَابِ الْحَمِيمِ ۝

49. "Taste you (this)! Verily, you were (pretending to be) the mighty, the generous!

ذُقْ إِنَّكَ أَنتَ الْعَزِيزُ الْكَرِيمُ ۝

50. "Verily, this is that whereof you used to doubt!"

إِنَّ هَٰذَا مَا كُنتُم بِهِۦ تَمْتَرُونَ ۝

51. Verily, the *Muttaqûn* (the pious. See V.2:2), will be in place of Security (Paradise).

إِنَّ الْمُتَّقِينَ فِى مَقَامٍ أَمِينٍ ۝

52. Among Gardens and Springs,

فِى جَنَّٰتٍ وَعُيُونٍ ۝

53. Dressed in fine silk and (also) in thick silk, facing each other,

يَلْبَسُونَ مِن سُندُسٍ وَإِسْتَبْرَقٍ مُّتَقَٰبِلِينَ ۝

54. So (it will be). And We shall marry them to *Hûr*[1] (fair females) with wide, lovely eyes.

كَذَٰلِكَ وَزَوَّجْنَٰهُم بِحُورٍ عِينٍ ۝

55. They will call therein for every kind of fruit in peace and security;

يَدْعُونَ فِيهَا بِكُلِّ فَٰكِهَةٍ ءَامِنِينَ ۝

56. They will never taste death therein except the first death (of this world), and He will save them from the torment of the blazing Fire,

لَا يَذُوقُونَ فِيهَا الْمَوْتَ إِلَّا الْمَوْتَةَ الْأُولَىٰ وَوَقَىٰهُمْ عَذَابَ الْجَحِيمِ ۝

57. As a Bounty from your Lord! That will be the supreme success!

فَضْلًا مِّن رَّبِّكَ ذَٰلِكَ هُوَ الْفَوْزُ الْعَظِيمُ ۝

58. Certainly, We have made this (Qur'ân) easy in your tongue, in order that they may remember.

فَإِنَّمَا يَسَّرْنَٰهُ بِلِسَانِكَ لَعَلَّهُمْ يَتَذَكَّرُونَ ۝

---

[1] (V.44:54) *Hûr* (houris): Very fair females created by Allâh as such not from the offspring of Adam عليه السلام , with intense black irises of their eyes and intense white scleras. [For details see the book *Hadi Al-Arwâh* by Ibn Al-Qaiyim, Chapter 54, Page 147].

59. Wait then (O Muhammad صلى الله عليه وسلم); verily, they (too) are waiting.

فَٱرْتَقِبْ إِنَّهُم مُّرْتَقِبُونَ ۝

Sûrat Al-Jâthiyah
(The Kneeling) (XLV)

In the Name of Allâh
the Most Gracious, the Most Merciful

بِسْمِ ٱللَّهِ ٱلرَّحْمَٰنِ ٱلرَّحِيمِ

1. *Hâ-Mîm.*

حم ۝

[These letters are one of the miracles of the Qur'ân and none but Allâh (Alone) knows their meanings].

2. The revelation of the Book (this Qur'ân) is from Allâh, the All-Mighty, the All-Wise.

تَنزِيلُ ٱلْكِتَٰبِ مِنَ ٱللَّهِ ٱلْعَزِيزِ ٱلْحَكِيمِ ۝

3. Verily, in the heavens and the earth are signs for the believers.

إِنَّ فِى ٱلسَّمَٰوَٰتِ وَٱلْأَرْضِ لَءَايَٰتٍ لِّلْمُؤْمِنِينَ ۝

4. And in your creation, and what He scattered (through the earth) of moving (living) creatures are signs for people who have Faith with certainty.

وَفِى خَلْقِكُمْ وَمَا يَبُثُّ مِن دَآبَّةٍ ءَايَٰتٌ لِّقَوْمٍ يُوقِنُونَ ۝

5. And in the alternation of night and day, and the provision (rain) that Allâh sends down from the sky, and revives therewith the earth after its death, and in the turning about of the winds (i.e. sometimes towards the east or north, and sometimes towards the south or west sometimes bringing glad tidings of rain and sometimes bringing the torment), are signs for a people who understand.

وَٱخْتِلَٰفِ ٱلَّيْلِ وَٱلنَّهَارِ وَمَا أَنزَلَ ٱللَّهُ مِنَ ٱلسَّمَآءِ مِن رِّزْقٍ فَأَحْيَا بِهِ ٱلْأَرْضَ بَعْدَ مَوْتِهَا وَتَصْرِيفِ ٱلرِّيَٰحِ ءَايَٰتٌ لِّقَوْمٍ يَعْقِلُونَ ۝

6. These are the *Ayât* (proofs, evidences, verses, lessons, revelations, etc.) of Allâh, which We recite to you (O Muhammad وسلم الله عليه صلى) with truth.

تِلْكَ ءَايَٰتُ ٱللَّهِ نَتْلُوهَا عَلَيْكَ بِٱلْحَقِّ فَبِأَىِّ حَدِيثٍ بَعْدَ ٱللَّهِ وَءَايَٰتِهِۦ

Then in which speech after Allâh and His *Ayât* will they believe?

7. Woe to every sinful liar

8. Who hears the Verses of Allâh (being) recited to him, yet persists with pride as if he heard them not. So announce to him a painful torment!

9. And when he learns something of Our Verses (this Qur'ân), he makes them a jest. For such there will be a humiliating torment.

10. In front of them there is Hell. And that which they have earned will be of no profit to them, nor (will be of any profit to them) those whom they have taken as *Auliyâ'* (protectors, helpers) besides Allâh. And theirs will be a great torment.

11. This (Qur'ân) is a guidance. And those who disbelieve in the *Ayât* (proofs, evidences, verses, lessons, signs, revelations, etc.) of their Lord, for them there is a painful torment of *Rijz* (a severe kind of punishment).

12. Allâh, it is He Who has subjected to you the sea, that ships may sail through it by His Command, and that you may seek of His Bounty, and that you may be thankful.

13. And has subjected to you all that is in the heavens and all that is in the earth; it is all as a favour and kindness from Him. Verily, in it are signs for a people who think deeply.

قُل لِّلَّذِينَ ءَامَنُوا يَغْفِرُوا لِلَّذِينَ لَا يَرْجُونَ أَيَّامَ ٱللَّهِ لِيَجْزِيَ قَوْمًا بِمَا كَانُوا يَكْسِبُونَ ١٤

14. Say (O Muhammad صلى الله عليه وسلم to the believers to forgive those who (harm them and) hope not for the Days of Allâh (i.e. His Recompense), that He may recompense people, according to what they have earned (i.e. to punish these disbelievers who harm the believers).[1]

مَنْ عَمِلَ صَـٰلِحًا فَلِنَفْسِهِۦ وَمَنْ أَسَآءَ فَعَلَيْهَا ثُمَّ إِلَىٰ رَبِّكُمْ تُرْجَعُونَ ١٥

15. Whosoever does a good deed, it is for his ownself, and whosoever does evil, it is against (his ownself). Then to your Lord you will be made to return.

وَلَقَدْ ءَاتَيْنَا بَنِىٓ إِسْرَٰٓءِيلَ ٱلْكِتَـٰبَ وَٱلْحُكْمَ وَٱلنُّبُوَّةَ وَرَزَقْنَـٰهُم مِّنَ ٱلطَّيِّبَـٰتِ وَفَضَّلْنَـٰهُمْ عَلَى ٱلْعَـٰلَمِينَ ١٦

16. And indeed We gave the Children of Israel the Scripture, and the understanding of the Scripture and its laws, and the Prophethood; and provided them with good things, and preferred them above the *'Âlamîn* (mankind and jinn of their time, during that period).

وَءَاتَيْنَـٰهُم بَيِّنَـٰتٍ مِّنَ ٱلْأَمْرِ فَمَا ٱخْتَلَفُوٓا إِلَّا مِنۢ بَعْدِ مَا جَآءَهُمُ ٱلْعِلْمُ بَغْيًۢا بَيْنَهُمْ إِنَّ رَبَّكَ يَقْضِى بَيْنَهُمْ يَوْمَ ٱلْقِيَـٰمَةِ فِيمَا كَانُوا فِيهِ يَخْتَلِفُونَ ١٧

17. And gave them clear proofs in matters [by revealing to them the Taurât (Torah)]. And they differed not until after the knowledge came to them, through envy among themselves. Verily, Your Lord will judge between them on the Day of Resurrection about that wherein they used to differ.

ثُمَّ جَعَلْنَـٰكَ عَلَىٰ شَرِيعَةٍ مِّنَ ٱلْأَمْرِ فَٱتَّبِعْهَا وَلَا تَتَّبِعْ أَهْوَآءَ ٱلَّذِينَ لَا يَعْلَمُونَ ١٨

18. Then We have put you (O Muhammad صلى الله عليه وسلم on a (plain) way of (Our) commandment [like the one which We commanded Our Messengers before you (i.e. legal ways

[1] (V.45:14) The provision of this Verse was abrogated by the Verse of *Jihâd* (holy fighting) (V.9:36) against the polytheists.

and laws of the Islâmic Monotheism)].
So follow you that (Islâmic
Monotheism and its laws), and follow
not the desires of those who know not.
[Tafsir At-Tabarî].

19. Verily, they can avail you
nothing against Allâh (if He wants to
punish you). Verily, the Zâlimûn
(polytheists, wrongdoers) are Auliyâ'
(protectors, helpers) of one another, but
Allâh is the Walî (Helper, Protector) of
the Muttaqûn (the pious. See V.2:2).

إِنَّهُمْ لَن يُغْنُواْ عَنكَ مِنَ اللَّهِ
شَيْئًا وَإِنَّ الظَّٰلِمِينَ بَعْضُهُمْ
أَوْلِيَآءُ بَعْضٍ وَاللَّهُ وَلِيُّ
الْمُتَّقِينَ ﴿١٩﴾

20. This (Qur'ân) is a clear insight
and evidence for mankind, and a
guidance and a mercy for people who
have Faith with certainty.[1]

هَٰذَا بَصَٰٓئِرُ لِلنَّاسِ وَهُدًى
وَرَحْمَةٌ لِّقَوْمٍ يُوقِنُونَ ﴿٢٠﴾

21. Or do those who earn evil deeds
think that We shall hold them equal
with those who believe (in the Oneness
of Allâh — Islâmic Monotheism) and
do righteous good deeds, in their
present life and after their death? Worst
is the judgement that they make.

أَمْ حَسِبَ الَّذِينَ اجْتَرَحُوا
السَّيِّئَاتِ أَن نَّجْعَلَهُمْ كَالَّذِينَ
ءَامَنُوا وَعَمِلُوا الصَّٰلِحَٰتِ
سَوَآءً مَّحْيَاهُمْ وَمَمَاتُهُمْ سَآءَ
مَا يَحْكُمُونَ ﴿٢١﴾

22. And Allâh has created the
heavens and the earth with truth, in
order that each person may be
recompensed what he has earned, and
they will not be wronged.[2]

وَخَلَقَ اللَّهُ السَّمَٰوَٰتِ وَالْأَرْضَ
بِالْحَقِّ وَلِتُجْزَىٰ كُلُّ نَفْسٍ بِمَا
كَسَبَتْ وَهُمْ لَا يُظْلَمُونَ ﴿٢٢﴾

23. Have you seen him who takes his
own lust (vain desires) as his ilâh

أَفَرَءَيْتَ مَنِ اتَّخَذَ إِلَٰهَهُ هَوَىٰهُ
وَأَضَلَّهُ اللَّهُ عَلَىٰ عِلْمٍ وَخَتَمَ عَلَىٰ سَمْعِهِ

---

[1] (V.45:20)
a) See the footnote of (V.10:37).
b) See the footnote of (V.3:85).
[2] (V.45:22) See the footnote of (V.15:23).

(god)? And Allâh knowing (him as such), left him astray, and sealed his hearing and his heart, and put a cover on his sight. Who then will guide him after Allâh? Will you not then remember?

وَقَلْبِهِ وَجَعَلَ عَلَىٰ بَصَرِهِ غِشَوَةٌ فَمَن يَهْدِيهِ مِنۢ بَعْدِ ٱللَّهِ أَفَلَا تَذَكَّرُونَ ۝

24. And they say: "There is nothing but our life of this world, we die and we live and nothing destroys us except Ad-Dahr (time). [1] And they have no knowledge of it: they only conjecture.

وَقَالُوا مَا هِيَ إِلَّا حَيَاتُنَا ٱلدُّنْيَا نَمُوتُ وَنَحْيَا وَمَا يُهْلِكُنَا إِلَّا ٱلدَّهْرُ وَمَا لَهُم بِذَٰلِكَ مِنْ عِلْمٍ إِنْ هُمْ إِلَّا يَظُنُّونَ ۝

25. And when Our Clear Verses are recited to them, their argument is no other than that they say: "Bring back our (dead) fathers, if you are truthful!"

وَإِذَا تُتْلَىٰ عَلَيْهِمْ ءَايَٰتُنَا بَيِّنَٰتٍ مَّا كَانَ حُجَّتَهُمْ إِلَّا أَن قَالُوا ٱئْتُوا بِـَٔابَآئِنَآ إِن كُنتُمْ صَٰدِقِينَ ۝

26. Say (to them): "Allâh gives you life, then causes you to die, then He will assemble you on the Day of Resurrection about which there is no doubt. But most of mankind know not."

قُلِ ٱللَّهُ يُحْيِيكُمْ ثُمَّ يُمِيتُكُمْ ثُمَّ يَجْمَعُكُمْ إِلَىٰ يَوْمِ ٱلْقِيَٰمَةِ لَا رَيْبَ فِيهِ وَلَٰكِنَّ أَكْثَرَ ٱلنَّاسِ لَا يَعْلَمُونَ ۝

27. And to Allâh belongs the kingdom of the heavens and the earth. And on the Day that the Hour will be established — on that Day the followers of falsehood (polytheists, disbelievers, worshippers of false deities) shall lose (everything).

وَلِلَّهِ مُلْكُ ٱلسَّمَٰوَٰتِ وَٱلْأَرْضِ وَيَوْمَ تَقُومُ ٱلسَّاعَةُ يَوْمَئِذٍ يَخْسَرُ ٱلْمُبْطِلُونَ ۝

---

[1] (V.45:24) Narrated Abu Hurairah رضى الله عنه: Allâh's Messenger صلى الله عليه وسلم said: "Allâh said, 'The son of Adam annoys Me for he abuses Ad-Dahr* (Time) though I am Ad-Dahr (Time); in My Hands are all things, and I cause the revolution of day and night.' " (Sahih Al-Bukhari, Vol.6, Hadîth No.351).

* 'I am Ad-Dahr' means 'I am the Creator of Time, and I manage the affairs of all creation including Time.' One should not **attribute** anything whether cheerful or disastrous to Time, for everything is in the Hands of Allâh and only He is the Disposer of everything.

28. And you will see each nation humbled to their knees (kneeling): each nation will be called to its Record (of deeds). This Day you shall be recompensed for what you used to do.

وَتَرَىٰ كُلَّ أُمَّةٍ جَاثِيَةً كُلُّ أُمَّةٍ تُدْعَىٰ إِلَىٰ كِتَـٰبِهَا ٱلْيَوْمَ تُجْزَوْنَ مَا كُنتُمْ تَعْمَلُونَ ﴿٢٨﴾

29. This Our Record speaks about you with truth. Verily, We were recording what you used to do (i.e. Our angels used to record your deeds).

هَـٰذَا كِتَـٰبُنَا يَنطِقُ عَلَيْكُم بِٱلْحَقِّ إِنَّا كُنَّا نَسْتَنسِخُ مَا كُنتُمْ تَعْمَلُونَ ﴿٢٩﴾

30. Then, as for those who believed (in the Oneness of Allâh — Islâmic Monotheism) and did righteous good deeds, their Lord will admit them to His Mercy. That will be the evident success.

فَأَمَّا ٱلَّذِينَ ءَامَنُوا وَعَمِلُوا ٱلصَّـٰلِحَـٰتِ فَيُدْخِلُهُمْ رَبُّهُمْ فِى رَحْمَتِهِ ذَٰلِكَ هُوَ ٱلْفَوْزُ ٱلْمُبِينُ ﴿٣٠﴾

31. But as for those who disbelieved (it will be said to them): "Were not Our Verses recited to you? But you were proud, and you were a people who were Mujrimûn (polytheists, disbelievers, sinners, criminals)."

وَأَمَّا ٱلَّذِينَ كَفَرُوا أَفَلَمْ تَكُنْ ءَايَـٰتِى تُتْلَىٰ عَلَيْكُمْ فَٱسْتَكْبَرْتُمْ وَكُنتُمْ قَوْمًا مُّجْرِمِينَ ﴿٣١﴾

32. And when it was said: "Verily, Allâh's Promise is the truth, and there is no doubt about the coming of the Hour," you said: "We know not what is the Hour: we do not think it but as a conjecture, and we have no firm convincing belief (therein)."

وَإِذَا قِيلَ إِنَّ وَعْدَ ٱللَّهِ حَقٌّ وَٱلسَّاعَةُ لَا رَيْبَ فِيهَا قُلْتُم مَّا نَدْرِى مَا ٱلسَّاعَةُ إِن نَّظُنُّ إِلَّا ظَنًّا وَمَا نَحْنُ بِمُسْتَيْقِنِينَ ﴿٣٢﴾

33. And the evil of what they did will appear to them, and that which they used to mock at will completely encircle them.

وَبَدَا لَهُمْ سَيِّئَاتُ مَا عَمِلُوا وَحَاقَ بِهِم مَّا كَانُوا بِهِۦ يَسْتَهْزِءُونَ ﴿٣٣﴾

34. And it will be said: "This Day We will forget you as you forgot the Meeting of this Day of yours. And your abode is the Fire, and there is none to help you."

وَقِيلَ ٱلْيَوْمَ نَنسَىٰكُمْ كَمَا نَسِيتُمْ لِقَآءَ يَوْمِكُمْ هَـٰذَا وَمَأْوَىٰكُمُ ٱلنَّارُ وَمَا لَكُم مِّن نَّـٰصِرِينَ ﴿٣٤﴾

35. This, because you took the revelations of Allâh (this Qur'ân) in mockery, and the life of the world deceived you. So this Day, they shall not be taken out from there (Hell),[1] nor shall they be returned to the worldly life (so that they repent to Allâh, and beg His Pardon for their sins).

ذَٰلِكُم بِأَنَّكُمُ ٱتَّخَذۡتُمۡ ءَايَٰتِ ٱللَّهِ هُزُوٗا وَغَرَّتۡكُمُ ٱلۡحَيَوٰةُ ٱلدُّنۡيَاۚ فَٱلۡيَوۡمَ لَا يُخۡرَجُونَ مِنۡهَا وَلَا هُمۡ يُسۡتَعۡتَبُونَ ۝

36. So all the praises and thanks be to Allâh, the Lord of the heavens and the Lord of the earth, and the Lord of the 'Âlamîn (mankind, jinn and all that exists).

فَلِلَّهِ ٱلۡحَمۡدُ رَبِّ ٱلسَّمَٰوَٰتِ وَرَبِّ ٱلۡأَرۡضِ رَبِّ ٱلۡعَٰلَمِينَ ۝

37. And His (Alone) is the Majesty in the heavens and the earth, and He is the All-Mighty, the All-Wise.

وَلَهُ ٱلۡكِبۡرِيَآءُ فِي ٱلسَّمَٰوَٰتِ وَٱلۡأَرۡضِۖ وَهُوَ ٱلۡعَزِيزُ ٱلۡحَكِيمُ ۝

---

[1] (V.45:35)

a) Narrated Anas bin Mâlik رضى الله عنه: Allâh's Messenger صلى الله عليه وسلم said, "When carried to his grave, a dead person is followed by three, two of which return (after his burial) and one remains with him: his relatives, his property and his deeds follow him; relatives and his property return back while his deeds remain with him." (*Sahih Al-Bukhari*, Vol. 8, Hadith No. 521)

b) Narrated Anas رضى الله عنه: The Prophet صلى الله عليه وسلم said. "The people will be thrown into Hell (Fire) and it will keep on saying, 'Is there any more?' till the Lord of the 'Âlamîn (mankind, jinn and all that exists) puts His Foot over it, whereupon its different sides will come close to each other, and it will say, 'Qat! Qat! (enough! enough!) By Your 'Izzat (Honour and Power) and Your *Karam* (Generosity)!' Paradise will remain spacious enough to accommodate more people until Allâh will create some more people and let them dwell in the superfluous (empty) space of Paradise." (*Sahih Al-Bukhari*, Vol. 9, *Hadith* No. 481).

c) Narrated Ibn 'Abbâs رضى الله عنهما: The Prophet صلى الله عليه وسلم used to say, "I seek refuge (with You) by Your 'Izzat (Honour and Power). *Lâ ilâha illâ Anta* (none has the right to be worshipped but You), Who does not die, while the jinn and the human beings die." (*Sahih Al-Bukhari*, Vol. 9, *Hadith* No. 480).

Sûrat Al-Ahqâf
(The Curved Sand-hills) (XLVI)

سُورَةُ الأَحْقَافِ

*In the Name of Allâh
the Most Gracious, the Most Merciful*

بِسۡمِ ٱللَّهِ ٱلرَّحۡمَٰنِ ٱلرَّحِيمِ

1. Hâ-Mîm.

حمٓ ١

[These letters are one of the miracles of the Qur'ân, and none but Allâh (Alone) knows their meanings].

2. The revelation of the Book (this Qur'ân) is from Allâh, the All-Mighty, the All-Wise.

تَنزِيلُ ٱلۡكِتَٰبِ مِنَ ٱللَّهِ ٱلۡعَزِيزِ ٱلۡحَكِيمِ ٢

3. We created not the heavens and the earth and all that is between them except with truth, and for an appointed term. But those who disbelieve turn away from that whereof they are warned.

مَا خَلَقۡنَا ٱلسَّمَٰوَٰتِ وَٱلۡأَرۡضَ وَمَا بَيۡنَهُمَآ إِلَّا بِٱلۡحَقِّ وَأَجَلٍ مُّسَمًّى وَٱلَّذِينَ كَفَرُواْ عَمَّآ أُنذِرُواْ مُعۡرِضُونَ ٣

4. Say (O Muhammad صلى الله عليه وسلم to these pagans): "Think you about all that you invoke besides Allâh? Show me. What have they created of the earth? Or have they a share in (the creation of) the heavens? Bring me a Book (revealed before this), or some trace of knowledge (in support of your claims), if you are truthful!"

قُلۡ أَرَءَيۡتُم مَّا تَدۡعُونَ مِن دُونِ ٱللَّهِ أَرُونِي مَاذَا خَلَقُواْ مِنَ ٱلۡأَرۡضِ أَمۡ لَهُمۡ شِرۡكٌ فِي ٱلسَّمَٰوَٰتِ ٱئۡتُونِي بِكِتَٰبٍ مِّن قَبۡلِ هَٰذَآ أَوۡ أَثَٰرَةٍ مِّنۡ عِلۡمٍ إِن كُنتُمۡ صَٰدِقِينَ ٤

5. And who is more astray than one who calls on (invokes) besides Allâh, such as will not answer him till the Day of Resurrection, and who are (even) unaware of their calls (invocations) to them?[1]

وَمَنۡ أَضَلُّ مِمَّن يَدۡعُواْ مِن دُونِ ٱللَّهِ مَن لَّا يَسۡتَجِيبُ لَهُۥٓ إِلَىٰ يَوۡمِ ٱلۡقِيَٰمَةِ وَهُمۡ عَن دُعَآئِهِمۡ غَٰفِلُونَ ٥

---

[1] (V.46:5) See the footnote of (V.2:165).

6. And when mankind are gathered (on the Day of Resurrection), they (false deities) will become their enemies and will deny their worshipping.

وَإِذَا حُشِرَ ٱلنَّاسُ كَانُوٓا لَهُمْ أَعْدَآءً وَكَانُوا بِعِبَادَتِهِمْ كَٰفِرِينَ ٦

7. And when Our Clear Verses are recited to them, the disbelievers say of the truth (this Qur'ân) when it reaches them: "This is plain magic!"

وَإِذَا تُتْلَىٰ عَلَيْهِمْ ءَايَٰتُنَا بَيِّنَٰتٍ قَالَ ٱلَّذِينَ كَفَرُوا لِلْحَقِّ لَمَّا جَآءَهُمْ هَٰذَا سِحْرٌ مُّبِينٌ ٧

8. Or say they: "He (Muhammad صلى الله عليه وسلم) has fabricated it." Say: "If I have fabricated it, still you have no power to support me against Allâh. He knows best of what you say among yourselves concerning it (i.e. this Qur'ân)! Sufficient is He as a witness between me and you! And He is the Oft-Forgiving, the Most Merciful."

أَمْ يَقُولُونَ ٱفْتَرَىٰهُ قُلْ إِنِ ٱفْتَرَيْتُهُ فَلَا تَمْلِكُونَ لِي مِنَ ٱللَّهِ شَيْئًا هُوَ أَعْلَمُ بِمَا تُفِيضُونَ فِيهِ كَفَىٰ بِهِۦ شَهِيدًۢا بَيْنِي وَبَيْنَكُمْ وَهُوَ ٱلْغَفُورُ ٱلرَّحِيمُ ٨

9. Say (O Muhammad صلى الله عليه وسلم): "I am not a new thing among the Messengers (of Allâh i.e. I am not the first Messenger) nor do I know what will be done with me or with you. I only follow that which is revealed to me, and I am but a plain warner."

قُلْ مَا كُنتُ بِدْعًا مِّنَ ٱلرُّسُلِ وَمَآ أَدْرِي مَا يُفْعَلُ بِي وَلَا بِكُمْ إِنْ أَتَّبِعُ إِلَّا مَا يُوحَىٰ إِلَيَّ وَمَآ أَنَا۠ إِلَّا نَذِيرٌ مُّبِينٌ ٩

10. Say: "Tell me! If this (Qur'ân) is from Allâh and you deny it, and a witness from among the Children of Israel ('Abdullâh bin Salâm رضى الله عنه) testifies that this Qur'ân is from Allâh [like the Taurât (Torah)], and he believed (embraced Islâm)[1] while you are too proud (to believe)." Verily, Allâh guides not the people who are Zâlimûn (polytheists, disbelievers and wrong-doing).

قُلْ أَرَءَيْتُمْ إِن كَانَ مِنْ عِندِ ٱللَّهِ وَكَفَرْتُم بِهِۦ وَشَهِدَ شَاهِدٌ مِّنۢ بَنِىٓ إِسْرَٰٓءِيلَ عَلَىٰ مِثْلِهِۦ فَـَٔامَنَ وَٱسْتَكْبَرْتُمْ إِنَّ ٱللَّهَ لَا يَهْدِي ٱلْقَوْمَ ٱلظَّٰلِمِينَ ١٠

---

[1] (V.46:10) See the footnote of (V.5:66).

11. And those who disbelieve (the strong and wealthy) say of those who believe (the weak and poor): "Had it (Islâmic Monotheism to which Muhammad صلى الله عليه وسلم is inviting mankind) been a good thing, they (the weak and poor) would not have preceded us thereto!" And when they have not let themselves be guided by it (this Qur'ân), they say: "This is an ancient lie!"

وَقَالَ ٱلَّذِينَ كَفَرُوا لِلَّذِينَ ءَامَنُوا لَوْ كَانَ خَيْرًا مَّا سَبَقُونَا إِلَيْهِ وَإِذْ لَمْ يَهْتَدُوا بِهِۦ فَسَيَقُولُونَ هَذَآ إِفْكٌ قَدِيمٌ ﴿١١﴾

12. And before this was the Scripture of Mûsâ (Moses) as a guide and a mercy. And this is a confirming Book (the Qur'ân) in the Arabic language, to warn those who do wrong, and as glad tidings to the *Muhsinûn* (good-doers). See the footnote of V.9:120).

وَمِن قَبْلِهِۦ كِتَابُ مُوسَىٰٓ إِمَامًا وَرَحْمَةً وَهَذَا كِتَابٌ مُّصَدِّقٌ لِّسَانًا عَرَبِيًّا لِّيُنذِرَ ٱلَّذِينَ ظَلَمُوا وَبُشْرَىٰ لِلْمُحْسِنِينَ ﴿١٢﴾

13. Verily, those who say: "Our Lord is (only) Allâh," and thereafter stand firm and straight on the Islâmic Faith of Monotheism[1] on them shall be no fear, nor shall they grieve.

إِنَّ ٱلَّذِينَ قَالُوا رَبُّنَا ٱللَّهُ ثُمَّ ٱسْتَقَامُوا فَلَا خَوْفٌ عَلَيْهِمْ وَلَا هُمْ يَحْزَنُونَ ﴿١٣﴾

14. Such shall be the dwellers of Paradise, abiding therein (forever) — a reward for what they used to do.

أُوْلَٰٓئِكَ أَصْحَابُ ٱلْجَنَّةِ خَالِدِينَ فِيهَا جَزَآءًۢ بِمَا كَانُوا يَعْمَلُونَ ﴿١٤﴾

15. And We have enjoined on man to be dutiful and kind to his parents. His mother bears him with hardship. And she brings him forth with hardship, and the bearing of him, and the weaning of him is thirty months, till when he attains full strength and reaches forty

وَوَصَّيْنَا ٱلْإِنسَانَ بِوَالِدَيْهِ إِحْسَانًا حَمَلَتْهُ أُمُّهُۥ كُرْهًا وَوَضَعَتْهُ كُرْهًا وَحَمْلُهُۥ وَفِصَالُهُۥ ثَلَاثُونَ شَهْرًا حَتَّىٰٓ إِذَا بَلَغَ أَشُدَّهُۥ وَبَلَغَ

---

[1] (V.46:13) Stand firm on the Islamic Monotheism: i.e. by abstaining from all kinds of sins and evil deeds which Allâh has forbidden and by performing all kinds of good deeds which He has ordained.

years, he says: "My Lord! Grant me the power and ability that I may be grateful for Your Favour which You have bestowed upon me and upon my parents, and that I may do righteous good deeds, such as please You, and make my offspring good. Truly, I have turned to You in repentance, and truly, I am one of the Muslims (submitting to Your Will)."

أَرْبَعِينَ سَنَةً قَالَ رَبِّ أَوْزِعْنِىٓ أَنْ أَشْكُرَ نِعْمَتَكَ ٱلَّتِىٓ أَنْعَمْتَ عَلَىَّ وَعَلَىٰ وَٰلِدَىَّ وَأَنْ أَعْمَلَ صَٰلِحًا تَرْضَىٰهُ وَأَصْلِحْ لِى فِى ذُرِّيَّتِىٓ إِنِّى تُبْتُ إِلَيْكَ وَإِنِّى مِنَ ٱلْمُسْلِمِينَ ﴿١٥﴾

16. They are those from whom We shall accept the best of their deeds and overlook their evil deeds. (They shall be) among the dwellers of Paradise — a promise of truth, which they have been promised.

أُوْلَٰٓئِكَ ٱلَّذِينَ نَتَقَبَّلُ عَنْهُمْ أَحْسَنَ مَا عَمِلُوا۟ وَنَتَجَاوَزُ عَن سَيِّـَٔاتِهِمْ فِىٓ أَصْحَٰبِ ٱلْجَنَّةِ وَعْدَ ٱلصِّدْقِ ٱلَّذِى كَانُوا۟ يُوعَدُونَ ﴿١٦﴾

17. But he who says to his parents: "Fie upon you both! Do you hold out the promise to me that I shall be raised up (again) when generations before me have passed away (without rising)?" While they (father and mother) invoke Allâh for help (and rebuke their son): "Woe to you! Believe! Verily, the Promise of Allâh is true." But he says: "This is nothing but the tales of the ancient."

وَٱلَّذِى قَالَ لِوَٰلِدَيْهِ أُفٍّ لَّكُمَآ أَتَعِدَانِنِىٓ أَنْ أُخْرَجَ وَقَدْ خَلَتِ ٱلْقُرُونُ مِن قَبْلِى وَهُمَا يَسْتَغِيثَانِ ٱللَّهَ وَيْلَكَ ءَامِنْ إِنَّ وَعْدَ ٱللَّهِ حَقٌّ فَيَقُولُ مَا هَٰذَآ إِلَّآ أَسَٰطِيرُ ٱلْأَوَّلِينَ ﴿١٧﴾

18. They are those against whom the Word (of torment) is justified among the previous generations of jinn and mankind that have passed away. Verily, they are ever the losers.

أُوْلَٰٓئِكَ ٱلَّذِينَ حَقَّ عَلَيْهِمُ ٱلْقَوْلُ فِىٓ أُمَمٍ قَدْ خَلَتْ مِن قَبْلِهِم مِّنَ ٱلْجِنِّ وَٱلْإِنسِ إِنَّهُمْ كَانُوا۟ خَٰسِرِينَ ﴿١٨﴾

19. And for all, there will be degrees according to that which they did, that He (Allâh) may recompense them in full for their deeds. And they will not be wronged.

وَلِكُلٍّ دَرَجَٰتٌ مِّمَّا عَمِلُوا۟ وَلِيُوَفِّيَهُمْ أَعْمَٰلَهُمْ وَهُمْ لَا يُظْلَمُونَ ﴿١٩﴾

20. On the Day when those who disbelieve (in the Oneness of Allâh — Islâmic Monotheism) will be exposed to the Fire (it will be said): "You received your good things in the life of the world, and you took your pleasure therein. Now this Day you shall be recompensed with a torment of humiliation, because you were arrogant in the land without a right, and because you used to rebel against Allâh's Command (disobey Allâh).

21. And remember (Hûd) the brother of 'Âd, when he warned his people in Al-Ahqâf (the curved sand-hills in the southern part of Arabian Peninsula). And surely, there have passed away warners before him and after him (saying): "Worship none but Allâh; truly, I fear for you the torment of a mighty Day (i.e. the Day of Resurrection)."

22. They said: "Have you come to turn us away from our âlihah (gods)? Then bring us that with which you threaten us, if you are one of the truthful!"

23. He said: "The knowledge (of the time of its coming) is with Allâh only. And I convey to you that wherewith I have been sent, but I see that you are a people given to ignorance!"

24. Then, when they saw it as a dense cloud coming towards their valleys, they said: "This is a cloud bringing us rain!" Nay, but it is that (torment) which you were asking to be hastened — a wind wherein is a painful torment!

25. Destroying everything by the Command of its Lord! So they became such that nothing could be seen except their dwellings! Thus do We recompense the people who are *Mujrimûn* (polytheists, disbelievers, sinners)!

قُدَمِّرُ كُلَّ شَيْءٍ بِأَمْرِ رَبِّهَا فَأَصْبَحُوا لَا يُرَىٰٓ إِلَّا مَسَٰكِنُهُمْ كَذَٰلِكَ نَجْزِى ٱلْقَوْمَ ٱلْمُجْرِمِينَ ۝

26. And indeed We had firmly established them with that wherewith We have not established you (O Quraish)! And We had assigned them the (faculties of) hearing (ears), seeing (eyes), and hearts; but their hearing (ears), seeing (eyes), and their hearts availed them nothing since they used to deny the *Ayât* (Allâh's Prophets and their Prophethood, proofs, evidences, verses, signs, revelations, etc.) of Allâh, and they were completely encircled by that which they used to mock at!

وَلَقَدْ مَكَّنَّٰهُمْ فِيمَآ إِن مَّكَّنَّٰكُمْ فِيهِ وَجَعَلْنَا لَهُمْ سَمْعًا وَأَبْصَٰرًا وَأَفْـِٔدَةً فَمَآ أَغْنَىٰ عَنْهُمْ سَمْعُهُمْ وَلَآ أَبْصَٰرُهُمْ وَلَآ أَفْـِٔدَتُهُم مِّن شَيْءٍ إِذْ كَانُوا۟ يَجْحَدُونَ بِـَٔايَٰتِ ٱللَّهِ وَحَاقَ بِهِم مَّا كَانُوا۟ بِهِۦ يَسْتَهْزِءُونَ ۝

27. And indeed We have destroyed towns (populations) round about you, and We have (repeatedly) shown (them) the *Ayât* (proofs, evidences, verses, lessons, signs, revelations, etc.) in various ways that they might return (to the truth and believe in the Oneness of Allâh — Islâmic Monotheism).

وَلَقَدْ أَهْلَكْنَا مَا حَوْلَكُم مِّنَ ٱلْقُرَىٰ وَصَرَّفْنَا ٱلْـَٔايَٰتِ لَعَلَّهُمْ يَرْجِعُونَ ۝

28. Then why did those whom they had taken for *âlihah* (gods) besides Allâh, as a way of approach (to Allâh) not help them? Nay, but they vanished completely from them (when there came the torment). And that was their lie, and their inventions which they had been inventing (before their destruction).

فَلَوْلَا نَصَرَهُمُ ٱلَّذِينَ ٱتَّخَذُوا۟ مِن دُونِ ٱللَّهِ قُرْبَانًا ءَالِهَةً ۖ بَلْ ضَلُّوا۟ عَنْهُمْ ۚ وَذَٰلِكَ إِفْكُهُمْ وَمَا كَانُوا۟ يَفْتَرُونَ ۝

29. And (remember) when We sent towards you (Muhammad صلى الله عليه وسلم) a

وَإِذْ صَرَفْنَآ إِلَيْكَ نَفَرًا مِّنَ ٱلْجِنِّ

group (three to ten persons) of the jinn, (quietly) listening to the Qur'ân. When they stood in the presence thereof, they said: "Listen in silence!" And when it was finished, they returned to their people, as warners.

30. They said: "O our people! Verily, we have heard a Book (this Qur'ân) sent down after Mûsâ (Moses), confirming what came before it: it guides to the truth and to the Straight Path (i.e. Islâm).

31. O our people! Respond (with obedience) to Allâh's Caller (i.e. Allâh's Messenger Muhammad صلى الله عليه وسلم), and believe in him (i.e. believe in that which Muhammad صلى الله عليه وسلم has brought from Allâh and follow him). He (Allâh) will forgive you of your sins, and will save you from a painful torment (i.e. Hell-fire).[1]

32. And whosoever does not respond to Allâh's Caller, he cannot escape on earth, and there will be no *Auliyâ'* (lords, helpers, supporters, protectors) for him besides Allâh (from Allâh's punishment). Those are in manifest error.

33. Do they not see that Allâh, Who created the heavens and the earth, and was not wearied by their creation, is Able to give life to the dead? Yes, He surely, is Able to do all things.

34. And on the Day when those who disbelieve will be exposed to the Fire (it

---

[1] (V.46:31) See the footnote of (V.3:85).

النَّارِ أَلَيْسَ هَٰذَا بِٱلْحَقِّ قَالُواْ بَلَىٰ
وَرَبِّنَا قَالَ فَذُوقُواْ ٱلْعَذَابَ
بِمَا كُنتُمْ تَكْفُرُونَ ٣٤

will be said to them): "Is this not the truth?" They will say: "Yes, By our Lord!" He will say: "Then taste the torment, because you used to disbelieve!"

35. Therefore be patient (O Muhammad (صلى الله عليه وسلم) as did the Messengers of strong will[1] and be in no haste about them (disbelievers). On the Day when they will see that (torment) with which they are promised (i.e. threatened, it will be) as if they had not stayed more than an hour in a single day. (O mankind! this Qur'ân is sufficient (as) a clear Message (or proclamation) to save yourself from destruction). But shall any be destroyed except the people who are Al-Fâsiqûn (the rebellious against Allâh's Command, the disobedient to Allâh).

فَٱصْبِرْ كَمَا صَبَرَ أُوْلُواْ ٱلْعَزْمِ مِنَ
ٱلرُّسُلِ وَلَا تَسْتَعْجِل لَّهُمْ كَأَنَّهُمْ
يَوْمَ يَرَوْنَ مَا يُوعَدُونَ لَمْ يَلْبَثُواْ
إِلَّا سَاعَةً مِّن نَّهَارٍ بَلَٰغٌ فَهَلْ
يُهْلَكُ إِلَّا ٱلْقَوْمُ ٱلْفَٰسِقُونَ ٣٥

Sûrat Muhammad or Sûrat Al-Qitâl (Muhammad (صلى الله عليه وسلم) or (The Fighting) (XLVII)

سُورَةُ مُحَمَّدٍ

In the Name of Allâh the Most Gracious, the Most Merciful

بِسْمِ ٱللَّهِ ٱلرَّحْمَٰنِ ٱلرَّحِيمِ

1. Those who disbelieve [in the Oneness of Allâh, and in the Message of Prophet Muhammad صلى الله عليه وسلم], and hinder (men) from the Path of Allâh (Islâmic Monotheism), He will render their deeds vain.[2]

ٱلَّذِينَ كَفَرُواْ وَصَدُّواْ عَن سَبِيلِ ٱللَّهِ
أَضَلَّ أَعْمَٰلَهُمْ ١

---

[1] (V.46:35) There are many Prophets and Messengers of Allâh, about twenty-five of them are mentioned in the Qur'ân; out of these twenty-five, only five are of strong will: namely, Muhammad صلى الله عليه وسلم, Nûh (Noah), Ibrâhîm (Abraham), Mûsâ (Moses) and 'Îsâ (Jesus), son of Maryam (Mary) عليهم السلام.

[2] (V.47:1) It is obligatory to have Belief in the Messengership of the Prophet (Muhammad صلى الله عليه وسلم).

2. But those who believe and do righteous good deeds, and believe in that which is sent down to Muhammad (صلى الله عليه وسلم) — for it is the truth from their Lord — He will expiate from them their sins, and will make good their state.

وَٱلَّذِينَ ءَامَنُوا۟ وَعَمِلُوا۟ ٱلصَّـٰلِحَـٰتِ وَءَامَنُوا۟ بِمَا نُزِّلَ عَلَىٰ مُحَمَّدٍ وَهُوَ ٱلْحَقُّ مِن رَّبِّهِمْ كَفَّرَ عَنْهُمْ سَيِّـَٔاتِهِمْ وَأَصْلَحَ بَالَهُمْ ۝

3. That is because those who disbelieve follow falsehood, while those who believe follow the truth from their Lord. Thus does Allâh set forth for mankind their parables.

ذَٰلِكَ بِأَنَّ ٱلَّذِينَ كَفَرُوا۟ ٱتَّبَعُوا۟ ٱلْبَـٰطِلَ وَأَنَّ ٱلَّذِينَ ءَامَنُوا۟ ٱتَّبَعُوا۟ ٱلْحَقَّ مِن رَّبِّهِمْ كَذَٰلِكَ يَضْرِبُ ٱللَّهُ لِلنَّاسِ أَمْثَـٰلَهُمْ ۝

4. So, when you meet (in fight — *Jihâd* in Allâh's Cause) those who disbelieve, smite (their) necks till when you have killed and wounded many of them, then bind a bond firmly (on them, i.e. take them as captives). Thereafter (is the time) either for generosity (i.e. free them without ransom), or ransom (according to what benefits Islâm), until the war lays down its burden. Thus [you are ordered by Allâh to continue in carrying out *Jihâd* against the disbelievers till they embrace Islâm and are saved from the punishment in the Hell-fire or at least come under your protection], but if it had been Allâh's Will, He Himself could certainly have punished them (without you). But (He

فَإِذَا لَقِيتُمُ ٱلَّذِينَ كَفَرُوا۟ فَضَرْبَ ٱلرِّقَابِ حَتَّىٰٓ إِذَآ أَثْخَنتُمُوهُمْ فَشُدُّوا۟ ٱلْوَثَاقَ فَإِمَّا مَنًّۢا بَعْدُ وَإِمَّا فِدَآءً حَتَّىٰ تَضَعَ ٱلْحَرْبُ أَوْزَارَهَا ذَٰلِكَ وَلَوْ يَشَآءُ ٱللَّهُ لَٱنتَصَرَ مِنْهُمْ وَلَـٰكِن لِّيَبْلُوَا۟ بَعْضَكُم بِبَعْضٍ وَٱلَّذِينَ قُتِلُوا۟ فِى سَبِيلِ ٱللَّهِ فَلَن يُضِلَّ أَعْمَـٰلَهُمْ ۝

Narrated Abu Hurairah (رضي الله عنه): Allâh's Messenger (صلى الله عليه وسلم) said, "By Him (Allâh) in Whose Hand Muhammad's soul is, there is none from amongst the Jews and the Christians (of these present nations) who hears about me and then dies without believing in the Message with which I have been sent (i.e. Islâmic Monotheism), but he will be from the dwellers of the (Hell) Fire." (*Sahih Muslim*, the Book of Faith, Vol. 1, Chapter No. 240). See also (V.3:85) and (V.3:116).

lets you fight) in order to test some of you with others. But those who are killed in the Way of Allâh, He will never let their deeds be lost.[1]

5. He will guide them and set right their state.

سَيَهْدِيهِمْ وَيُصْلِحُ بَالَهُمْ ۝

6. And admit them to Paradise which He has made known to them (i.e. they will know their places in Paradise better than they used to know their homes in the world).[2] [Tafsir Ibn Kathir]

وَيُدْخِلُهُمُ ٱلْجَنَّةَ عَرَّفَهَا لَهُمْ ۝

7. O you who believe! If you help (in the cause of) Allâh, He will help you, and make your foothold firm.

يَأَيُّهَا ٱلَّذِينَ ءَامَنُوٓاْ إِن تَنصُرُواْ ٱللَّهَ يَنصُرْكُمْ وَيُثَبِّتْ أَقْدَامَكُمْ ۝

8. But those who disbelieve (in the Oneness of Allâh — Islâmic Monotheism), for them is destruction, and (Allâh) will make their deeds vain.

وَٱلَّذِينَ كَفَرُواْ فَتَعْسًا لَّهُمْ وَأَضَلَّ أَعْمَالَهُمْ ۝

9. That is because they hate that which Allâh has sent down (this Qur'ân and Islâmic laws); so He has made their deeds fruitless.

ذَٰلِكَ بِأَنَّهُمْ كَرِهُواْ مَآ أَنزَلَ ٱللَّهُ فَأَحْبَطَ أَعْمَالَهُمْ ۝

10. Have they not travelled through the earth and seen what was the end of

أَفَلَمْ يَسِيرُواْ فِى ٱلْأَرْضِ فَيَنظُرُواْ كَيْفَ كَانَ عَٰقِبَةُ ٱلَّذِينَ مِن قَبْلِهِمْ

---

[1] (V.47:4) See the footnote of (V.2:190) and (V.9:20).

[2] (V.47:6) Narrated Abû Sa'îd Al-Khudrî رضى الله عنه : Allâh's Messenger صلى الله عليه وسلم said, "The believers, after being saved from the (Hell) Fire, will be stopped at a bridge between Paradise and Hell and mutual retaliation will take place among them regarding the wrongs they have committed in the world against one another. After they are cleansed and purified (through the retaliation), they will be admitted into Paradise; and by Him in Whose Hand Muhammad's soul is, everyone of them will know his dwelling in Paradise better than he knew his dwelling in this world." (Sahih Al-Bukhari, Vol. 8, Hadith No. 542)

those before them? Allâh destroyed them completely, and a similar (fate awaits) the disbelievers.

11. That is because Allâh is the *Maulâ* (Lord, Master, Helper, Protector) of those who believe, and the disbelievers have no *Maulâ* (lord, master, helper, protector).

12. Certainly Allâh will admit those who believe (in the Oneness of Allâh — Islâmic Monotheism) and do righteous good deeds, to Gardens under which rivers flow (Paradise); while those who disbelieve enjoy themselves and eat as cattle eat; and the Fire will be their abode.

13. And many a town, stronger than your town (Makkah) (O Muhammad صلى الله عليه وسلم) which has driven you out We have destroyed. And there was none to help them.

14. Is he who is on a clear proof from his Lord, like those for whom their evil deeds that they do are beautified for them, while they follow their own lusts (evil desires)?

15. The description of Paradise which the *Muttaqûn* (the pious. See V.2:2) have been promised (is that) in it are rivers of water the taste and smell of which are not changed, rivers of milk of which the taste never changes, rivers of wine delicious to those who drink, and rivers of clarified honey (clear and pure) therein for them is every kind of fruit, and forgiveness from their Lord. (Are these) like those who shall dwell for ever in the Fire and be given to drink boiling water so that it cuts up their bowels?

16. And among them are some who listen to you (O Muhammad صلى الله عليه وسلم) till when they go out from you, they say to those who have received knowledge: "What has he said just now? Such are men whose hearts Allâh has sealed, and they follow their lusts (evil desires).

17. While as for those who accept guidance, He increases their guidance and bestows on them their piety.

18. Do they then await (anything) other than the Hour that it should come upon them suddenly? But some of its portents (indications and signs) have already come; and when it (actually) is on them, how can they benefit then by their reminder?[1]

19. So know (O Muhammad صلى الله عليه وسلم) that Lâ ilâha illallâh (none has the right to be worshipped but Allâh),[2] and ask forgiveness for your sin, and also for (the sin of) believing men and believing women. And Allâh knows well your moving about, and your place of rest (in your homes).

20. Those who believe say: "Why is not a Sûrah (chapter of the Qur'ân) sent down (for us)? But when a decisive

---

[1] (V.47:18) See the footnote of (V.6:158).

[2] (V.47:19) It is essential to know a thing first before saying or acting upon it as Allâh's Statement: "So know..." (V.47:19). Please see also the footnote of (V.6:125).

Sûrah (explaining and ordering things) is sent down, and fighting (*Jihâd* — holy fighting in Allâh's cause) is mentioned (i.e. ordained) therein, you will see those in whose hearts is a disease (of hypocrisy) looking at you with a look of one fainting to death. But it was better for them (hypocrites, to listen to Allâh and to obey Him).

21. Obedience (to Allâh) and good words (were better for them). And when the matter (preparation for *Jihâd*) is resolved on, then if they had been true to Allâh, it would have been better for them.

22. Would you then, if you were given the authority, do mischief in the land, and sever your ties of kinship?[1]

23. Such are they whom Allâh has cursed, so that He has made them deaf and blinded their sight.

24. Do they not then think deeply in the Qur'ân, or are their hearts locked up (from understanding it)?

---

[1] (V.47:22).

a) Narrated Abû Hurairah رضى الله عنه : The Prophet صلى الله عليه وسلم said, "Allâh created His creation, and when He finished it, the womb got up and caught hold of Allâh whereupon Allâh said, 'What is the matter?' On that, it said, 'I seek refuge with you from *Al-Qatîah* (those who sever the ties of kith and kin).' On that Allâh said, 'Will you accept (be satisfied) if I bestow My Favours on him who keeps your ties, and withhold My Favours from him who severs your ties?' On that it said, 'Yes, O my Lord!' Then Allâh said, 'That is for you.' " Abu Hurairah added: If you wish, you can recite: "Would you then, if you were given the authority, do mischief in the land and sever your ties of kinship?" (V.47:22). (*Sahih Al-Bukhari*, Vol.6, *Hadith* No.354).

b) See the footnote of (V.2:27).

25. Verily, those who have turned back (have apostatised) as disbelievers after the guidance has been manifested to them — *Shaitân* (Satan) has beautified for them (their false hopes), and (Allâh) prolonged their term (age).

26. This is because they said to those who hate what Allâh has sent down: "We will obey you in part of the matter." But Allâh knows their secrets.

27. Then how (will it be) when the angels will take their souls at death, smiting their faces and their backs?

28. That is because they followed that which angered Allâh and hated that which pleased Him. So He made their deeds fruitless.

29. Or do those in whose hearts is a disease (of hypocrisy), think that Allâh will not bring to light all their hidden ill-wills?

30. Had We willed, We could have shown them to you, and you should have known them by their marks; but surely, you will know them by the tone of their speech! And Allâh knows (all) your deeds.

31. And surely, We shall try you till We test those who strive hard (for the Cause of Allâh) and *As-Sâbirûn* (the patient), and We shall test your facts (i.e. the one who is a liar, and the one who is truthful).

32. Verily, those who disbelieve, and hinder (men) from the Path of Allâh (i.e. Islâm), and oppose the Messenger (صلى الله عليه وسلم) (by standing against him and hurting him), after the guidance[1] has been clearly shown to them, they will not hurt Allâh in the least, but He will make their deeds fruitless,

33. O you who believe! Obey Allâh, and obey the Messenger (Muhammad صلى الله عليه وسلم) and render not vain your deeds.

34. Verily, those who disbelieve, and hinder (men) from the Path of Allâh (i.e. Islâm); then die while they are disbelievers — Allâh will not forgive them.[2]

35. So be not weak and ask not for peace (from the enemies of Islâm) while

---

[1] (V.47:32) A. Narrated Abû Mûsâ رضي الله عنه: The Prophet صلى الله عليه وسلم said, "The example of guidance and knowledge (the Qur'ân and the Sunnah) with which Allâh has sent me, is like abundant rain falling on the earth, some of which was fertile soil that absorbed rain water and brought forth vegetation and grass in abundance. (And) another portion of it was hard and held the rain water and Allâh benefited the people with it and they utilized it for drinking, making their animals drink from it and irrigating the land for cultivation. (And) a portion of it was barren which could neither hold the water nor bring forth vegetation (then that land gave no benefits). The first is the example of the person who comprehends Allâh's religion (Islam) and gets benefit (from the knowledge) which Allâh عز و جل has revealed through me (the Prophet صلى الله عليه وسلم) and learns and then teaches it to others. The last example is that of a person who does not care for it and does not take Allâh's Guidance revealed through me: (He is like that barren land)." (Sahih Al-Bukhari, Vol.1, Hadîth No.79).

B: Guidance is of two kinds:

a) Guidance of Taufîq and it is totally from Allâh, i.e. Allâh opens one's heart to receive the truth (from disbelief to Belief in Islamic Monotheism).

b) Guidance of Irshâd i.e. through preaching by Allâh's Messengers and pious preachers who preach the truth i.e. Islamic Monotheism.

[2] (V.47:34) See the footnote of (V.3:85).

you are having the upper hand. Allâh is with you, and He will never decrease the reward of your good deeds.

36. The life of this world is but play and pastime; but if you believe (in the Oneness of Allâh — Islâmic Monotheism), and fear Allâh, and avoid evil, He will grant you your wages, and will not ask you your wealth.

37. If He were to ask you of it, and press you, you would covetously withhold, and He will bring out all your (secret) ill-wills.

38. Behold! You are those who are called to spend in the Cause of Allâh, yet among you are some who are niggardly. And whoever is niggardly, it is only at the expense of his ownself. But Allâh is Rich (Free of all needs), and you (mankind) are poor. And if you turn away (from Islâm and the obedience to Allâh), He will exchange you for some other people and they will not be your likes.

Sûrat Al-Fath
(The Victory) (XLVIII)

*In the Name of Allâh
the Most Gracious, the Most Merciful*

1. Verily, We have given you (O Muhammad صلى الله عليه وسلم) a manifest victory.

2. That Allâh may forgive you your sins of the past and the future,[1] and

---

[1] (V.48:2) Narrated Al-Mughîrah: The Prophet صلى الله عليه وسلم used to offer night prayers till his feet became swollen. Somebody said to

complete His Favour on you, and guide you on the Straight Path.

3. And that Allâh may help you with strong help.

4. He it is Who sent down *As-Sakînah* (calmness and tranquillity) into the hearts of the believers, that they may grow more in Faith along with their (present) Faith. And to Allâh belong the hosts of the heavens and the earth, and Allâh is Ever All-Knower, All-Wise.

5. That He may admit the believing men and the believing women to Gardens under which rivers flow (i.e. Paradise) to abide therein forever, and He may expiate from them their sins; and that is with Allâh a supreme success,

6. And that He may punish the *Munâfiqûn* (hypocrites), men and women, and also the *Mushrikûn*[1] men and women, who think evil thoughts about Allâh: for them is a disgraceful torment. And the Anger of Allâh is upon them, and He has cursed them and prepared Hell for them — and worst indeed is that destination.

7. And to Allâh belong the hosts of the heavens and the earth. And Allâh is Ever All-Knower, All-Wise.

---

him, "Allâh has forgiven you your sins of the past and the future." On that, He said, "Shouldn't I be a thankful slave of Allâh?" (*Sahih Al-Bukhari*, Vol.6, *Hadîth* No.360).

[1] (V.48:6) *Al-Mushrikûn*: Polytheists, pagans, idolaters, and disbelievers in the Oneness of Allâh and in His Messenger Muhammad صلى الله عليه وسلم.

8. Verily, We have sent you (O Muhammad ﷺ) as a witness, as a bearer of glad tidings, and as a warner.[1]

9. In order that you (O mankind) may believe in Allâh and His Messenger (الله ﷺ), and that you assist and honour him (عليه وسلم), and (that you) glorify (Allâh's) praises morning and afternoon.

10. Verily, those who give *Bai'ah* (pledge) to you (O Muhammad صلى الله عليه وسلم) they are giving *Bai'ah* (pledge) to Allâh. The Hand of Allâh is over their hands. Then whosoever breaks his pledge, breaks it only to his own harm; and whosoever fulfils what he has covenanted with Allâh, He will bestow on him a great reward.

11. Those of the bedouins who lagged behind will say to you: "Our possessions and our families occupied us, so ask forgiveness for us." They say with their tongues what is not in their hearts. Say: "Who then has any power at all (to intervene) on your behalf with Allâh, if He intends you hurt or intends you benefit? Nay, but Allâh is Ever All-Aware of what you do.

12. "Nay, but you thought that the Messenger (صلى الله عليه وسلم) and the believers would never return to their families, and that was made fair-seeming in your hearts, and you did think an evil thought and you became a useless people going for destruction."

---

[1] (V.48:8) See the footnote of (V.2:42).

13. And whosoever does not believe in Allâh and His Messenger (Muhammad صلى الله عليه وسلم), then verily, We have prepared for the disbelievers a blazing Fire.[1]

وَمَن لَّمْ يُؤْمِنۢ بِٱللَّهِ وَرَسُولِهِۦ فَإِنَّآ أَعْتَدْنَا لِلْكَٰفِرِينَ سَعِيرًا ١٣

14. And to Allâh belongs the sovereignty of the heavens and the earth. He forgives whom He wills, and punishes whom He wills. And Allâh is Ever Oft-Forgiving, Most Merciful.

وَلِلَّهِ مُلْكُ ٱلسَّمَٰوَٰتِ وَٱلْأَرْضِ يَغْفِرُ لِمَن يَشَآءُ وَيُعَذِّبُ مَن يَشَآءُ وَكَانَ ٱللَّهُ غَفُورًا رَّحِيمًا ١٤

15. Those who lagged behind will say, when you set forth to take the spoils, "Allow us to follow you." They want to change Allâh's Words. Say: "You shall not follow us; thus Allâh has said beforehand." Then they will say: "Nay, you envy us." Nay, but they understand not except a little.

سَيَقُولُ ٱلْمُخَلَّفُونَ إِذَا ٱنطَلَقْتُمْ إِلَىٰ مَغَانِمَ لِتَأْخُذُوهَا ذَرُونَا نَتَّبِعْكُمْ يُرِيدُونَ أَن يُبَدِّلُوا۟ كَلَٰمَ ٱللَّهِ قُل لَّن تَتَّبِعُونَا كَذَٰلِكُمْ قَالَ ٱللَّهُ مِن قَبْلُ فَسَيَقُولُونَ بَلْ تَحْسُدُونَنَا بَلْ كَانُوا۟ لَا يَفْقَهُونَ إِلَّا قَلِيلًا ١٥

16. Say (صلى الله عليه وسلم O Muhammad) to the bedouins who lagged behind: "You shall be called to fight against a people given to great warfare, then you shall fight them, or they shall surrender. Then if you obey, Allâh will give you a fair reward; but if you turn away as you did turn away before, He will punish you with a painful torment."

قُل لِّلْمُخَلَّفِينَ مِنَ ٱلْأَعْرَابِ سَتُدْعَوْنَ إِلَىٰ قَوْمٍ أُو۟لِى بَأْسٍ شَدِيدٍ تُقَٰتِلُونَهُمْ أَوْ يُسْلِمُونَ فَإِن تُطِيعُوا۟ يُؤْتِكُمُ ٱللَّهُ أَجْرًا حَسَنًا وَإِن تَتَوَلَّوْا۟ كَمَا تَوَلَّيْتُم مِّن قَبْلُ يُعَذِّبْكُمْ عَذَابًا أَلِيمًا ١٦

17. No blame or sin is there upon the blind, nor is there blame or sin upon the lame, nor is there blame or sin upon the sick (that they go not for fighting). And whosoever obeys Allâh and His Messenger (صلى الله عليه وسلم Muhammad), He will admit him to Gardens beneath which rivers flow (Paradise); and

لَّيْسَ عَلَى ٱلْأَعْمَىٰ حَرَجٌ وَلَا عَلَى ٱلْأَعْرَجِ حَرَجٌ وَلَا عَلَى ٱلْمَرِيضِ حَرَجٌ وَمَن يُطِعِ ٱللَّهَ وَرَسُولَهُۥ يُدْخِلْهُ جَنَّٰتٍ تَجْرِى مِن تَحْتِهَا ٱلْأَنْهَٰرُ وَمَن يَتَوَلَّ يُعَذِّبْهُ عَذَابًا أَلِيمًا ١٧

---

[1] (V.48:13) See the footnote of (V.3:85).

whosoever turns back. He will punish him with a painful torment.

18. Indeed. Allâh was pleased with the believers when they gave the *Bai'ah* (pledge) to you (O Muhammad صلى الله عليه وسلم) under the tree: He knew what was in their hearts. and He sent down *As-Sakînah* (calmness and tranquillity) upon them, and He rewarded them with a near victory.

۞ لَّقَدْ رَضِىَ ٱللَّهُ عَنِ ٱلْمُؤْمِنِينَ إِذْ يُبَايِعُونَكَ تَحْتَ ٱلشَّجَرَةِ فَعَلِمَ مَا فِى قُلُوبِهِمْ فَأَنزَلَ ٱلسَّكِينَةَ عَلَيْهِمْ وَأَثَٰبَهُمْ فَتْحًا قَرِيبًا ١٨

19. And abundant spoils that they will capture. And Allâh is Ever All-Mighty, All-Wise.

وَمَغَانِمَ كَثِيرَةً يَأْخُذُونَهَا وَكَانَ ٱللَّهُ عَزِيزًا حَكِيمًا ١٩

20. Allâh has promised you abundant spoils that you will capture, and He has hastened for you this, and He has restrained the hands of men from you: that it may be a sign for the believers, and that He may guide you to the Straight Path.

وَعَدَكُمُ ٱللَّهُ مَغَانِمَ كَثِيرَةً تَأْخُذُونَهَا فَعَجَّلَ لَكُمْ هَٰذِهِۦ وَكَفَّ أَيْدِىَ ٱلنَّاسِ عَنكُمْ وَلِتَكُونَ ءَايَةً لِّلْمُؤْمِنِينَ وَيَهْدِيَكُمْ صِرَٰطًا مُّسْتَقِيمًا ٢٠

21. And other (victories and much booty He promises you) which are not yet within your power; indeed Allâh compasses them. And Allâh is Ever Able to do all things.

وَأُخْرَىٰ لَمْ تَقْدِرُوا عَلَيْهَا قَدْ أَحَاطَ ٱللَّهُ بِهَا وَكَانَ ٱللَّهُ عَلَىٰ كُلِّ شَىْءٍ قَدِيرًا ٢١

22. And if those who disbelieve fight against you, they certainly would have turned their backs; then they would have found neither a *Walî* (protector, guardian) nor a helper.

وَلَوْ قَٰتَلَكُمُ ٱلَّذِينَ كَفَرُوا لَوَلَّوُا ٱلْأَدْبَٰرَ ثُمَّ لَا يَجِدُونَ وَلِيًّا وَلَا نَصِيرًا ٢٢

23. That has been the Way of Allâh already with those who passed away before. And you will not find any change in the Way of Allâh.

سُنَّةَ ٱللَّهِ ٱلَّتِى قَدْ خَلَتْ مِن قَبْلُ وَلَن تَجِدَ لِسُنَّةِ ٱللَّهِ تَبْدِيلًا ٢٣

24. And He it is Who has withheld their hands from you and your hands

وَهُوَ ٱلَّذِى كَفَّ أَيْدِيَهُمْ عَنكُمْ وَأَيْدِيَكُمْ عَنْهُم بِبَطْنِ مَكَّةَ مِنۢ

from them in the midst of Makkah, after He had made you victors over them. And Allâh is Ever the All-Seer of what you do.

بَعْدِ أَنْ أَظْفَرَكُمْ عَلَيْهِمْ وَكَانَ اللَّهُ بِمَا تَعْمَلُونَ بَصِيرًا ﴿٢٤﴾

25. They are the ones who disbelieved (in the Oneness of Allâh — Islâmic Monotheism) and hindered you from *Al-Masjid Al-Harâm* (at Makkah) and detained the sacrificial animals, from reaching their place of sacrifice. Had there not been believing men and believing women whom you did not know, that you may kill them and on whose account a sin would have been committed by you without (your) knowledge, that Allâh might bring into His Mercy whom He wills — if they (the believers and the disbelievers) had been apart, We verily, would have punished those of them who disbelieved with painful torment.

هُمُ الَّذِينَ كَفَرُوا وَصَدُّوكُمْ عَنِ الْمَسْجِدِ الْحَرَامِ وَالْهَدْىَ مَعْكُوفًا أَن يَبْلُغَ مَحِلَّهُ وَلَوْلَا رِجَالٌ مُّؤْمِنُونَ وَنِسَاءٌ مُّؤْمِنَاتٌ لَّمْ تَعْلَمُوهُمْ أَن تَطَئُوهُمْ فَتُصِيبَكُم مِّنْهُم مَّعَرَّةٌ بِغَيْرِ عِلْمٍ لِّيُدْخِلَ اللَّهُ فِى رَحْمَتِهِ مَن يَشَاءُ لَوْ تَزَيَّلُوا لَعَذَّبْنَا الَّذِينَ كَفَرُوا مِنْهُمْ عَذَابًا أَلِيمًا ﴿٢٥﴾

26. When those who disbelieve had put in their hearts pride and haughtiness — the pride and haughtiness of the time of ignorance, — then Allâh sent down His *Sakînah* (calmness and tranquillity) upon His Messenger (ﷺ) and upon the believers, and made them stick to the word of piety (i.e. none has the right to be worshipped but Allâh); and they were well entitled to it and worthy of it. And Allâh is the All-Knower of everything.

إِذْ جَعَلَ الَّذِينَ كَفَرُوا فِى قُلُوبِهِمُ الْحَمِيَّةَ حَمِيَّةَ الْجَاهِلِيَّةِ فَأَنزَلَ اللَّهُ سَكِينَتَهُ عَلَىٰ رَسُولِهِ وَعَلَى الْمُؤْمِنِينَ وَأَلْزَمَهُمْ كَلِمَةَ التَّقْوَىٰ وَكَانُوا أَحَقَّ بِهَا وَأَهْلَهَا وَكَانَ اللَّهُ بِكُلِّ شَىْءٍ عَلِيمًا ﴿٢٦﴾

27. Indeed Allâh shall fulfil the true vision which He showed to His Messenger (ﷺ) [i.e. the Prophet ﷺ saw a dream that he has entered Makkah along with his Companions, having their (head) hair

لَّقَدْ صَدَقَ اللَّهُ رَسُولَهُ الرُّؤْيَا بِالْحَقِّ لَتَدْخُلُنَّ الْمَسْجِدَ الْحَرَامَ إِن شَاءَ اللَّهُ ءَامِنِينَ مُحَلِّقِينَ رُءُوسَكُمْ وَمُقَصِّرِينَ

shaved and cut short] in very truth. Certainly, you shall enter *Al-Masjid Al-Harâm*, if Allâh wills, secure, (some) having your heads shaved, and (some) having your head hair cut short, having no fear. He knew what you knew not, and He granted besides that a near victory.

لَا تَخَافُونَ فَعَلِمَ مَا لَمْ تَعْلَمُوا فَجَعَلَ مِن دُونِ ذَٰلِكَ فَتْحًا قَرِيبًا ٢٧

28. He it is Who has sent His Messenger (Muhammad ﷺ) with guidance and the religion of truth (Islâm), that He may make it (Islâm) superior to all religions. And All-Sufficient is Allâh as a Witness.

هُوَ ٱلَّذِىٓ أَرْسَلَ رَسُولَهُۥ بِٱلْهُدَىٰ وَدِينِ ٱلْحَقِّ لِيُظْهِرَهُۥ عَلَى ٱلدِّينِ كُلِّهِۦ وَكَفَىٰ بِٱللَّهِ شَهِيدًا ٢٨

29. Muhammad (ﷺ) is the Messenger of Allâh. And those who are with him are severe against disbelievers, and merciful among themselves. You see them bowing and falling down prostrate (in prayer), seeking Bounty from Allâh and (His) Good Pleasure. The mark of them (i.e. of their Faith) is on their faces (foreheads) from the traces of prostration (during prayers). This is their description in the Taurât (Torah). But their description in the Injeel (Gospel) is like a (sown) seed which sends forth its shoot, then makes it strong, and becomes thick and it stands straight on its stem, delighting the sowers, that He may enrage the disbelievers with them. Allâh has promised those among them who believe (i.e. all those who follow Islâmic Monotheism, the religion of Prophet Muhammad ﷺ till the Day of Resurrection) and do righteous good deeds, forgiveness and a mighty reward (i.e. Paradise).

مُّحَمَّدٌ رَّسُولُ ٱللَّهِ وَٱلَّذِينَ مَعَهُۥٓ أَشِدَّآءُ عَلَى ٱلْكُفَّارِ رُحَمَآءُ بَيْنَهُمْ تَرَىٰهُمْ رُكَّعًا سُجَّدًا يَبْتَغُونَ فَضْلًا مِّنَ ٱللَّهِ وَرِضْوَٰنًا سِيمَاهُمْ فِى وُجُوهِهِم مِّنْ أَثَرِ ٱلسُّجُودِ ذَٰلِكَ مَثَلُهُمْ فِى ٱلتَّوْرَىٰةِ وَمَثَلُهُمْ فِى ٱلْإِنجِيلِ كَزَرْعٍ أَخْرَجَ شَطْـَٔهُۥ فَـَٔازَرَهُۥ فَٱسْتَغْلَظَ فَٱسْتَوَىٰ عَلَىٰ سُوقِهِۦ يُعْجِبُ ٱلزُّرَّاعَ لِيَغِيظَ بِهِمُ ٱلْكُفَّارَ وَعَدَ ٱللَّهُ ٱلَّذِينَ ءَامَنُوا وَعَمِلُوا ٱلصَّٰلِحَٰتِ مِنْهُم مَّغْفِرَةً وَأَجْرًا عَظِيمًا ٢٩

Sûrat Al-Hujurât
(The Dwellings) XLIX

سُورَةُ الْحُجُرَاتِ

*In the Name of Allâh
the Most Gracious, the Most Merciful*

بِسْمِ اللَّهِ الرَّحْمَنِ الرَّحِيمِ

1. O you who believe! Make not (a decision) in advance[1] before Allâh and His Messenger (صلى الله عليه وسلم), and fear Allâh. Verily, Allâh is All-Hearing, All-Knowing.

يَتَأَيُّهَا الَّذِينَ ءَامَنُوا لَا تُقَدِّمُوا بَيْنَ يَدَيِ اللَّهِ وَرَسُولِهِ وَاتَّقُوا اللَّهَ إِنَّ اللَّهَ سَمِيعٌ عَلِيمٌ

2. O you who believe! Raise not your voices above the voice of the Prophet (صلى الله عليه وسلم), nor speak aloud to him in talk as you speak aloud to one another, lest your deeds should be rendered fruitless while you perceive not.

يَتَأَيُّهَا الَّذِينَ ءَامَنُوا لَا تَرْفَعُوا أَصْوَاتَكُمْ فَوْقَ صَوْتِ النَّبِيِّ وَلَا تَجْهَرُوا لَهُ بِالْقَوْلِ كَجَهْرِ بَعْضِكُمْ لِبَعْضٍ أَن تَحْبَطَ أَعْمَالُكُمْ وَأَنتُمْ لَا تَشْعُرُونَ

3. Verily, those who lower their voices in the presence of Allâh's Messenger (صلى الله عليه وسلم), they are the ones whose hearts Allâh has tested for piety. For them is forgiveness and a great reward.

إِنَّ الَّذِينَ يَغُضُّونَ أَصْوَاتَهُمْ عِندَ رَسُولِ اللَّهِ أُوْلَئِكَ الَّذِينَ امْتَحَنَ اللَّهُ قُلُوبَهُمْ لِلتَّقْوَى لَهُم مَّغْفِرَةٌ وَأَجْرٌ عَظِيمٌ

4. Verily, those who call you from behind the dwellings, most of them have no sense.

إِنَّ الَّذِينَ يُنَادُونَكَ مِن وَرَاءِ الْحُجُرَاتِ أَكْثَرُهُمْ لَا يَعْقِلُونَ

5. And if they had patience till you could come out to them, it would have been better for them. And Allâh is Oft-Forgiving, Most Merciful.

وَلَوْ أَنَّهُمْ صَبَرُوا حَتَّى تَخْرُجَ إِلَيْهِمْ لَكَانَ خَيْرًا لَّهُمْ وَاللَّهُ غَفُورٌ رَّحِيمٌ

6. O you who believe! If a *Fâsiq* (liar — evil person) comes to you with a

يَتَأَيُّهَا الَّذِينَ ءَامَنُوا إِن جَاءَكُمْ

---

[1] (V.49:1) [i.e. hasten not to decide] in matters of war or religion before Allâh and His Messenger صلى الله عليه وسلم, that you may decide the contrary to what Allâh and His Messenger صلى الله عليه وسلم may decide.

news, verify it, lest you should harm people in ignorance, and afterwards you become regretful for what you have done.

7. And know that among you there is the Messenger of Allâh (صلى الله عليه وسلم). If he were to obey you (i.e. follow your opinions and desires) in much of the matter, you would surely, be in trouble. But Allâh has endeared the Faith to you and has beautified it in your hearts, and has made disbelief, wickedness and disobedience (to Allâh and His Messenger صلى الله عليه وسلم) hateful to you. Such are they who are the rightly guided.

8. (This is) a Grace from Allâh and His Favour. And Allâh is All-Knowing, All-Wise.

9. And if two parties or groups among the believers fall to fighting, then make peace between them both. But if one of them outrages against the other, then fight you (all) against the one that which outrages till it complies with the Command of Allâh. Then if it complies, then make reconciliation between them justly, and be equitable. Verily, Allâh loves those who are the equitable.

10. The believers are nothing else than brothers (in Islâmic religion). So make reconciliation between your brothers, and fear Allâh, that you may receive mercy.

11. O you who believe! Let not a group scoff at another group, it may be that the latter are better than the former. Nor let (some) women scoff at other women, it may be that the latter are better than the former. Nor defame one another, nor insult one another by nicknames. How bad is it to insult one's brother after having Faith [i.e. to call your Muslim brother (a faithful believer) as: "O sinner", or "O wicked"]. And whosoever does not repent, then such are indeed *Zâlimûn* (wrongdoers).

12. O you who believe! Avoid much suspicion; indeed some suspicions are sins. And spy not, neither backbite one another. Would one of you like to eat the flesh of his dead brother? You would hate it (so hate backbiting).[1]

---

[1] (V.49:12).

a) Narrated Abû Hurairah رضي الله عنه Allâh's Messenger صلى الله عليه وسلم said, "Beware of suspicion, for suspicion is the worst of false tales; and do not look for other's faults, and do not do spying on one another, and do not practise *Najsh** and do not be jealous of one another and do not hate one another, and do not desert (stop talking to) one another. And O Allâh's worshippers! Be brothers!" (*Sahih Al-Bukhari*, Vol. 8, *Hadith* No.92).

b) Narrated Hudhaifah رضي الله عنه I heard the Prophet صلى الله عليه وسلم saying, "A *Qattât*** will not enter Paradise." (*Sahih Al-Bukhari*, Vol.8, *Hadith* No.82).

c) Backbiting and the Statement of Allâh: عز وجل "And spy not, neither backbite one another."

Narrated Ibn 'Abbâs رضي الله عنهما Allâh's Messenger صلى الله عليه وسلم passed by two graves and said, "Both of them (persons in the grave) are being tortured, and they are not being tortured for a major sin. This one used not to save himself from being soiled with his urine, and the other used to go about with calumnies (among the people to rouse hostilities, e.g., one goes to a person and tells him that

And fear Allâh. Verily, Allâh is the One Who forgives and accepts repentance, Most Merciful.

13. O mankind! We have created you from a male and a female, and made you into nations and tribes, that you may know one another. Verily, the most honourable of you with Allâh is that (believer) who has *At-Taqwâ* [he is one of the *Muttaqûn* (the pious. See V.2:2). Verily, Allâh is All-Knowing, All-Aware.

14. The bedouins say: "We believe." Say: "You believe not but you only say, 'We have surrendered (in Islâm),' for Faith has not yet entered your hearts. But if you obey Allâh and His Messenger (صلى الله عليه وسلم), He will not decrease anything in reward for your deeds. Verily, Allâh is Oft-Forgiving, Most Merciful."

15. Only those are the believers who have believed in Allâh and His Messenger, and afterward doubt not but strive with their wealth and their lives

---

so-and-so says about him such and such evil things)." The Prophet صلى الله عليه وسلم then asked for a green branch of a date-palm tree, split it into two pieces and planted one on each grave and said, "It is hoped that their punishment may be abated till those two pieces of the branch get dried."*** (*Sahih Al-Bukhari*, Vol.8, *Hadîth* No.78).

* *Najsh* means to offer a high price for something in order to allure another customer who is interested in the thing.

**A *Qattât* is a person who conveys disagreeable, false information from one person to another with the intention of causing harm and enmity between them.

***This action was a kind of invocation on the part of the Prophet صلى الله عليه وسلم for the deceased persons. [*Fath Al-Bari*, Vol. I, Page 332].

for the Cause of Allâh. Those! They are the truthful.

16. Say: "Will you inform Allâh of your religion while Allâh knows all that is in the heavens and all that is in the earth, and Allâh is All-Aware of everything.

17. They regard as favour to you (O Muhammad صلى الله عليه وسلم) that they have embraced Islâm. Say: "Count not your Islâm as a favour to me. Nay, but Allâh has conferred a favour upon you that He has guided you to the Faith if you indeed are true.

18. Verily, Allâh knows the Unseen of the heavens and the earth. And Allâh is the All-Seer of what you do.

Sûrat Qâf .L

In the Name of Allâh the Most Gracious, the Most Merciful

1. Qâf.

[These letters (*Qâf*, etc.) are one of the miracles of the Qur'ân, and none but Allâh (Alone) knows their meanings].

By the Glorious Qur'ân.

2. Nay, they wonder that there has come to them a warner (Muhammad صلى الله عليه وسلم) from among themselves. So the disbelievers say: "This is a strange thing!

3. "When we are dead and have become dust (shall we be resurrected?) That is a far return."

4. We know that which the earth takes of them (their dead bodies), and with Us is a Book preserved (i.e. the Book of Decrees).

5. Nay, but they have denied the truth (this Qur'ân) when it has come to them, so they are in a confused state (cannot differentiate between right and wrong).

6. Have they not looked at the heaven above them, how We have made it and adorned it, and there are no rifts in it?

7. And the earth! We have spread it out, and set thereon mountains standing firm, and have produced therein every kind of lovely growth (plants).

8. An insight and a Reminder for every slave who turns to Allâh in repentance (i.e. the one who believes in the Oneness of Allâh and performs deeds of His obedience, and always begs His pardon).

9. And We send down blessed water (rain) from the sky, then We produce therewith gardens and grain (every kind of harvests) that are reaped.

10. And tall date-palms, with ranged clusters.

11. A provision for (Allâh's) slaves. And We give life therewith to a dead land. Thus will be the resurrection (of the dead).

12. Denied before them (i.e. these pagans of Makkah) the people of Nûh (Noah), and the Dwellers of Rass, and Thamûd;

13. And 'Âd, and Fir'aun (Pharaoh), and the brethren of Lût (Lot);

وَعَادٌ وَفِرْعَوْنُ وَإِخْوَٰنُ لُوطٍ ۝

14. And the Dwellers of the Wood, and the people of Tubba'. Everyone of them denied (their) Messengers, so My Threat took effect.

وَأَصْحَٰبُ ٱلْأَيْكَةِ وَقَوْمُ تُبَّعٍ ۚ كُلٌّ كَذَّبَ ٱلرُّسُلَ فَحَقَّ وَعِيدِ ۝

15. Were We then tired with the first creation? Nay, they are in confused doubt about a new creation (i.e. Resurrection).

أَفَعَيِينَا بِٱلْخَلْقِ ٱلْأَوَّلِ ۚ بَلْ هُمْ فِى لَبْسٍ مِّنْ خَلْقٍ جَدِيدٍ ۝

16. And indeed We have created man, and We know what his ownself whispers to him. And We are nearer to him than his jugular vein (by Our Knowledge).

وَلَقَدْ خَلَقْنَا ٱلْإِنسَٰنَ وَنَعْلَمُ مَا تُوَسْوِسُ بِهِۦ نَفْسُهُۥ ۖ وَنَحْنُ أَقْرَبُ إِلَيْهِ مِنْ حَبْلِ ٱلْوَرِيدِ ۝

17. (Remember) that the two receivers (recording angels) receive (each human being), one sitting on the right and one on the left (to note his or her actions).[1]

إِذْ يَتَلَقَّى ٱلْمُتَلَقِّيَانِ عَنِ ٱلْيَمِينِ وَعَنِ ٱلشِّمَالِ قَعِيدٌ ۝

18. Not a word does he (or she) utter but there is a watcher by him ready (to record it).[2]

مَّا يَلْفِظُ مِن قَوْلٍ إِلَّا لَدَيْهِ رَقِيبٌ عَتِيدٌ ۝

19. And the stupor of death will come in truth: "This is what you have been avoiding!"

وَجَآءَتْ سَكْرَةُ ٱلْمَوْتِ بِٱلْحَقِّ ۖ ذَٰلِكَ مَا كُنتَ مِنْهُ تَحِيدُ ۝

---

[1] (V.50:17)

a) Narrated Âishah رضى الله عنها the Prophet صلى الله عليه وسلم said: "The deeds of the following three persons are not recorded by the pen: (1) a sleeping person till he wakes up (2) a child till he reaches the age of puberty (3) an insane person till he becomes sane." This *Hadîth* is quoted by Nasâ'i, the Book of Divorce, chapter 21.

b) See the footnote (B) of (V.6:61).

[2] (V.50:18) See the footnote (A) of (V.6:61).

20. And the Trumpet will be blown — that will be the Day whereof warning (had been given) (i.e. the Day of Resurrection).

وَنُفِخَ فِي ٱلصُّورِ ذَلِكَ يَوْمُ ٱلْوَعِيدِ ﴿٢٠﴾

21. And every person will come forth along with an (angel) to drive (him) and an (angel) to bear witness.

وَجَآءَتْ كُلُّ نَفْسٍ مَّعَهَا سَآئِقٌ وَشَهِيدٌ ﴿٢١﴾

22. (It will be said to the sinners): "Indeed you were heedless of this. Now We have removed from you, your covering, and sharp is your sight this Day!"

لَّقَدْ كُنتَ فِي غَفْلَةٍ مِّنْ هَذَا فَكَشَفْنَا عَنكَ غِطَآءَكَ فَبَصَرُكَ ٱلْيَوْمَ حَدِيدٌ ﴿٢٢﴾

23. And his companion (angel) will say: "Here is (this Record) ready with me!"

وَقَالَ قَرِينُهُ هَذَا مَا لَدَيَّ عَتِيدٌ ﴿٢٣﴾

24. Allâh will say to the angels: "Both of you throw into Hell every stubborn disbeliever (in the Oneness of Allâh, in His Messengers) —

أَلْقِيَا فِي جَهَنَّمَ كُلَّ كَفَّارٍ عَنِيدٍ ﴿٢٤﴾

25. "Hinderer of good, transgressor, doubter,

مَّنَّاعٍ لِّلْخَيْرِ مُعْتَدٍ مُّرِيبٍ ﴿٢٥﴾

26. "Who set up another · *ilâh* (god) with Allâh. Then both of you cast him in the severe torment."

ٱلَّذِي جَعَلَ مَعَ ٱللَّهِ إِلَهًا ءَاخَرَ فَأَلْقِيَاهُ فِي ٱلْعَذَابِ ٱلشَّدِيدِ ﴿٢٦﴾

27. His companion (Satan — devil) will say: "Our Lord! I did not push him to transgression, (in disbelief, oppression, and evil deeds), but he was himself in error far astray."

۞ قَالَ قَرِينُهُ رَبَّنَا مَآ أَطْغَيْتُهُ وَلَكِن كَانَ فِي ضَلَالٍ بَعِيدٍ ﴿٢٧﴾

28. Allâh will say: "Dispute not in front of Me, I had already in advance sent you the threat.

قَالَ لَا تَخْتَصِمُوا لَدَيَّ وَقَدْ قَدَّمْتُ إِلَيْكُم بِٱلْوَعِيدِ ﴿٢٨﴾

29. The Sentence that comes from Me cannot be changed, and I am not unjust to the slaves."

مَا يُبَدَّلُ ٱلْقَوْلُ لَدَيَّ وَمَآ أَنَا۠ بِظَلَّامٍ لِّلْعَبِيدِ ﴿٢٩﴾

30. On the Day when We will say to Hell: "Are you filled?" It will say: "Are there any more (to come)?"[1]

31. And Paradise will be brought near to the *Muttaqûn* (the pious. See V.2:2), not far off.

32. (It will be said): "This is what you were promised — (it is) for those oft-returning (to Allâh) in sincere repentance, and those who preserve their covenant with Allâh (by obeying Him in all what He has ordered, and worshipping none but Allâh Alone, i.e. follow Allâh's religion — Islâmic Monotheism).

33. "Who feared the Most Gracious (Allâh) in the *Ghaib* (Unseen) and brought a heart turned in repentance (to Him and absolutely free from every kind of polytheism).

34. "Enter you therein in peace and security — this is a Day of eternal life!"

35. There they will have all that they desire — and We have more (for them, i.e. a glance at the All-Mighty, All-Majestic جل جلاله).

36. And how many a generation We have destroyed before them who were

---

[1] (V.50:30) Allâh's Statement: "It (Hell) will say: 'Are there any more (to come)?'"

Narrated Anas رضي الله عنه: The Prophet صلى الله عليه وسلم said, "The people will be thrown into the (Hell) Fire and it will say: 'Are there any more (to come)?' till Allâh will put His Foot over it and it will say: 'Qat! Qat! (Enough! Enough!)'" (*Sahih Al-Bukhari*, Vol.6, *Hadith* No.371).

stronger in power than they. And (when Our Torment came), they ran for a refuge in the land! Could they find any place of refuge (for them to save themselves from destruction)?

الْبِلَادِ هَلْ مِن مَّحِيصٍ ۝

37. Verily, therein is indeed a reminder for him who has a heart or gives ear while he is heedful.

إِنَّ فِى ذَٰلِكَ لَذِكْرَىٰ لِمَن كَانَ لَهُ قَلْبٌ أَوْ أَلْقَى السَّمْعَ وَهُوَ شَهِيدٌ ۝

38. And indeed We created the heavens and the earth and all between them in six Days and nothing of fatigue touched Us.

وَلَقَدْ خَلَقْنَا السَّمَٰوَٰتِ وَالْأَرْضَ وَمَا بَيْنَهُمَا فِى سِتَّةِ أَيَّامٍ وَمَا مَسَّنَا مِن لُّغُوبٍ ۝

39. So bear with patience (O Muhammad ﷺ) all that they say, and glorify the Praises of your Lord, before the rising of the sun and before (its) setting (i.e. the *Fajr*, *Zuhr*, and '*Asr* prayers).[1]

فَاصْبِرْ عَلَىٰ مَا يَقُولُونَ وَسَبِّحْ بِحَمْدِ رَبِّكَ قَبْلَ طُلُوعِ الشَّمْسِ وَقَبْلَ الْغُرُوبِ ۝

40. And during a part of the night (also) glorify His praises (i.e. *Maghrib* and '*Isha* prayers) and (so likewise) after the prayers [*As-Sunnah*, *Nawâfil* — optional and additional prayers. And

وَمِنَ الَّيْلِ فَسَبِّحْهُ وَأَدْبَارَ السُّجُودِ ۝

---

[1] (V.50:39).

a) Narrated Qais: Jarîr said, "We were with the Prophet ﷺ and he looked at the moon on a full-moon night and said: "Certainly you will see your Lord as you see this moon and you will have no trouble in seeing Him. So if you can avoid missing (through sleep or business) a prayer before the sunrise (*Fajr*) and a prayer before sunset ('*Asr*), you must do so". 'He then recited Allâh's Statement: "And glorify the praises of your Lord before the rising of the sun and before (its) setting." (V.50:39).

Ismâ'îl said: "Offer those prayers and do not miss them." (*Sahih Al-Bukhari*, Vol.1, *Hadîth* No.529)

b) See the footnote of (V.32:16).

also glorify, praise and magnify Allâh — *Subhân Allâh, Alhamdu lillâh, Allâhu Akbar*].

41. And listen on the Day when the caller will call from a near place.

وَٱسۡتَمِعۡ يَوۡمَ يُنَادِ ٱلۡمُنَادِ مِن مَّكَانٖ قَرِيبٖ ﴿٤١﴾

42. The Day when they will hear *As-Saihah* (shout) in truth: that will be the Day of coming out (from the graves, i.e. the Day of Resurrection).

يَوۡمَ يَسۡمَعُونَ ٱلصَّيۡحَةَ بِٱلۡحَقِّ ذَٰلِكَ يَوۡمُ ٱلۡخُرُوجِ ﴿٤٢﴾

43. Verily, We it is Who give life and cause death; and to Us is the final return.

إِنَّا نَحۡنُ نُحۡيِۦ وَنُمِيتُ وَإِلَيۡنَا ٱلۡمَصِيرُ ﴿٤٣﴾

44. On the Day when the earth shall be cleft, from off them, (they will come out) hastening forth. That will be a gathering, quite easy for Us.

يَوۡمَ تَشَقَّقُ ٱلۡأَرۡضُ عَنۡهُمۡ سِرَاعٗاۚ ذَٰلِكَ حَشۡرٌ عَلَيۡنَا يَسِيرٞ ﴿٤٤﴾

45. We know best what they say. And you (O Muhammad صلى الله عليه وسلم) are not the one to force them (to Belief). But warn by the Qur'ân; him who fears My Threat.

نَّحۡنُ أَعۡلَمُ بِمَا يَقُولُونَۖ وَمَآ أَنتَ عَلَيۡهِم بِجَبَّارٖۖ فَذَكِّرۡ بِٱلۡقُرۡءَانِ مَن يَخَافُ وَعِيدِ ﴿٤٥﴾

Sûrat Adh-Dhâriyât (The Winds that Scatter) LI

سُورَةُ الذَّارِيَات

In the Name of Allâh the Most Gracious, the Most Merciful

بِسۡمِ ٱللَّهِ ٱلرَّحۡمَٰنِ ٱلرَّحِيمِ

1. By (the winds) that scatter dust.

وَٱلذَّٰرِيَٰتِ ذَرۡوٗا ﴿١﴾

2. And (the clouds) that bear heavy weight of water.

فَٱلۡحَٰمِلَٰتِ وِقۡرٗا ﴿٢﴾

3. And (the ships) that float with ease and gentleness.

فَٱلۡجَٰرِيَٰتِ يُسۡرٗا ﴿٣﴾

4. And those (angels) who distribute (provisions, rain, and other blessings) by (Allâh's) Command.

فَٱلۡمُقَسِّمَٰتِ أَمۡرٗا ﴿٤﴾

5. Verily, that which you are promised (i.e. Resurrection in the Hereafter and receiving the reward or punishment of good or bad deeds) is surely true.

إِنَّمَا تُوعَدُونَ لَصَادِقٌ ﴿٥﴾

6. And verily, the Recompense is sure to happen.

وَإِنَّ ٱلدِّينَ لَوَقِعٌ ﴿٦﴾

7. By the heaven full of paths,

وَٱلسَّمَآءِ ذَاتِ ٱلۡحُبُكِ ﴿٧﴾

8. Certainly, you have different ideas (about Muhammad صلى الله عليه وسلم and the Qur'ân).

إِنَّكُمۡ لَفِى قَوۡلٍ مُّخۡتَلِفٍ ﴿٨﴾

9. Turned aside therefrom (i.e. from Muhammad صلى الله عليه وسلم and the Qur'ân) is he who is turned aside (by the Decree and Preordainment القضاء والقدر of Allâh).

يُؤۡفَكُ عَنۡهُ مَنۡ أُفِكَ ﴿٩﴾

10. Cursed be the liars

قُتِلَ ٱلۡخَرَّٰصُونَ ﴿١٠﴾

11. Who are under a cover of heedlessness (think not about the gravity of the Hereafter),

ٱلَّذِينَ هُمۡ فِى غَمۡرَةٍ سَاهُونَ ﴿١١﴾

12. They ask: "When will be the Day of Recompense?"

يَسۡـَٔلُونَ أَيَّانَ يَوۡمُ ٱلدِّينِ ﴿١٢﴾

13. (It will be) a Day when they will be tried (punished i.e. burnt) over the Fire!

يَوۡمَ هُمۡ عَلَى ٱلنَّارِ يُفۡتَنُونَ ﴿١٣﴾

14. "Taste you your trial (punishment i.e. burning)! This is what you used to ask to be hastened!"

ذُوقُواْ فِتۡنَتَكُمۡ هَٰذَا ٱلَّذِى كُنتُم بِهِۦ تَسۡتَعۡجِلُونَ ﴿١٤﴾

15. Verily, the Muttaqûn (the pious. See V.2:2) will be in the midst of Gardens and Springs (in the Paradise).

إِنَّ ٱلۡمُتَّقِينَ فِى جَنَّٰتٍ وَعُيُونٍ ﴿١٥﴾

16. Taking joy in the things which their Lord has given them. Verily, they were before this Muhsinûn (good-doers — See V.2:112).

ءَاخِذِينَ مَآ ءَاتَىٰهُمۡ رَبُّهُمۡ إِنَّهُمۡ كَانُواْ قَبۡلَ ذَٰلِكَ مُحۡسِنِينَ ﴿١٦﴾

17. They used to sleep but little by night [invoking their Lord (Allâh) and praying, with fear and hope].

كَانُوا قَلِيلًا مِّنَ ٱلَّيۡلِ مَا يَهۡجَعُونَ ۝

18. And in the hours before. dawn, they were (found) asking (Allâh) for forgiveness.

وَبِٱلۡأَسۡحَارِ هُمۡ يَسۡتَغۡفِرُونَ ۝

19. And in their properties there was the right of the *Sâ'il* (the beggar who asked) and the *Mahrûm* (the poor who does not ask others).[1]

وَفِىٓ أَمۡوَٰلِهِمۡ حَقٌّ لِّلسَّآئِلِ وَٱلۡمَحۡرُومِ ۝

20. And on the earth are signs for those who have Faith with certainty.

وَفِى ٱلۡأَرۡضِ ءَايَٰتٌ لِّلۡمُوقِنِينَ ۝

21. And also in your ownselves. Will you not then see?

وَفِىٓ أَنفُسِكُمۡ أَفَلَا تُبۡصِرُونَ ۝

22. And in the heaven is your provision, and that which you are promised.

وَفِى ٱلسَّمَآءِ رِزۡقُكُمۡ وَمَا تُوعَدُونَ ۝

23. Then by the Lord of the heaven and the earth, it is the truth (i.e. what has been promised to you), just as it is the truth that you can speak.

فَوَرَبِّ ٱلسَّمَآءِ وَٱلۡأَرۡضِ إِنَّهُۥ لَحَقٌّ مِّثۡلَ مَآ أَنَّكُمۡ تَنطِقُونَ ۝

24. Has the story reached you, of the honoured guests [three angels; Jibrael (Gabriel) along with another two] of Ibrâhîm (Abraham)?

هَلۡ أَتَىٰكَ حَدِيثُ ضَيۡفِ إِبۡرَٰهِيمَ ٱلۡمُكۡرَمِينَ ۝

25. When they came in to him and said: "*Salâm*, (peace be upon you)!" He answered: "*Salâm*, (peace be upon you)," and said: "You are a people unknown to me."

إِذۡ دَخَلُوا عَلَيۡهِ فَقَالُوا سَلَٰمًا قَالَ سَلَٰمٌ قَوۡمٌ مُّنكَرُونَ ۝

---

[1] (V.51:19) See the footnote of (V.4:37).

26. Then he turned to his household, and brought out a roasted calf [as the property of Ibrâhîm (Abraham) was mainly cows].

فَرَاغَ إِلَىٰٓ أَهْلِهِۦ فَجَآءَ بِعِجْلٍ سَمِينٍ ۝

27. And placed it before them, (saying): "Will you not eat?"

فَقَرَّبَهُۥٓ إِلَيْهِمْ قَالَ أَلَا تَأْكُلُونَ ۝

28. Then he conceived fear of them (when they ate not). They said: "Fear not."[1] And they gave him glad tidings of a son having knowledge (about Allâh and His religion of True Monotheism).

فَأَوْجَسَ مِنْهُمْ خِيفَةً قَالُوا لَا تَخَفْ وَبَشَّرُوهُ بِغُلَٰمٍ عَلِيمٍ ۝

29. Then his wife came forward with a loud voice: she smote her face, and said: "A barren old woman!"[2]

فَأَقْبَلَتِ ٱمْرَأَتُهُۥ فِى صَرَّةٍ فَصَكَّتْ وَجْهَهَا وَقَالَتْ عَجُوزٌ عَقِيمٌ ۝

30. They said: "Even so says your Lord.[3] Verily, He is the All-Wise, the All-Knower."

قَالُوا كَذَٰلِكِ قَالَ رَبُّكِ إِنَّهُۥ هُوَ ٱلْحَكِيمُ ٱلْعَلِيمُ ۝

---

[1] (V.51:28) i.e. when the angels noticed some fear over the face of Abraham, they told him that they are Allâh's messengers. And they also gave the glad news to his wife Sarah that she will give birth to a son (Isaac).

[2] (V.51:29) "How can I bear a child." At that time she (Sarah) was approximately 99 years old. (*Tafsîr Al-Qurtubi*, Vol. 17, Page 47).

[3] (V.51:30)

a) The Statement of Allâh عز وجل:

'Verily, Our Word (Command) unto a thing, when We intend it, is only that We say unto it: "Be!" — and it is.' (V.16:40)

Narrated Mu'âwiyyah رضي الله عنه : I heard the Prophet صلى الله عليه وسلم saying, "A group of my followers will keep on following Allâh's Orders [i.e., following strictly Allâh's Book (the Qur'ân) and the Prophet's *Sunnah* (legal ways)] strictly and they will not be harmed by those who will belie (disbelieve) them or desert (stand against) them till Allâh's Order (the Hour) will come while they will be in that state." (*Sahih Al-Bukhari*, Vol. 9, *Hadith* No. 552).

b) Narrated Abu Hurairah رضى الله عنه: Allâh's Messenger صلى الله عليه وسلم said, "Allâh said, 'I have prepared for My pious slaves things which have never been seen by an eye, nor heard by an ear, or (even) imagined by a human being.' " (*Sahih Al-Bukhari*, Vol. 4, *Hadith* No. 467)

c) Narrated Abû Sa'îd Al-Khudrî رضى الله عنه: The Prophet صلى الله عليه وسلم said, "The people of Paradise will look at the dwellers of *Al-Ghuraf* (the lofty mansions i.e. a superior place in Paradise) in the same way as one looks at a brilliant star far away in the east or in the west on the horizon; all that is because of their superiority over one another (in rewards)." On that the people said, "O Allâh's Messenger! Are these residences (lofty mansions) for the Prophets which nobody else can reach?" The Prophet صلى الله عليه وسلم replied, "No! By Him (Allâh) in Whose Hand my soul is, these are for the men who believed in Allâh and also believed in the Messengers." (*Sahih Al-Bukhari*, Vol. 4, *Hadith* No. 478)

d) Narrated Abu Hurairah رضى الله عنه: Allâh's Messenger صلى الله عليه وسلم said, "The first batch (of people) who will enter Paradise will be (glittering) like the moon on a full-moon night and those who will enter next will be glittering like the brightest star. Their hearts will be as if the heart of a single man for they will have neither difference nor any enmity amongst themselves, and everyone of them shall have two wives, each of whom will be so beautiful, pure and transparent that the marrow of the bones of their legs will be seen through the flesh. They will be glorifying Allâh in the morning and afternoon, and will never fall ill, and they will neither blow their noses nor spit. Their utensils will be of gold and silver, and their combs will be of gold and the fuel used in their censers will be of aloes-wood and their sweat will smell like musk." ... (*Sahih Al-Bukhari*, Vol. 4, *Hadith* No. 469)

31. [Ibrâhîm (Abraham)] said: "Then for what purpose you have come, O messengers?"

قَالَ فَمَا خَطْبُكُمْ أَيُّهَا الْمُرْسَلُونَ ۝

32. They said: "We have been sent to a people who are *Mujrimûn* (polytheists, sinners, criminals, disbelievers in Allâh)

قَالُوٓا إِنَّآ أُرْسِلْنَآ إِلَىٰ قَوْمٍ مُّجْرِمِينَ ۝

33. To send down upon them stones of baked clay.

لِنُرْسِلَ عَلَيْهِمْ حِجَارَةً مِّن طِينٍ ۝

34. Marked by your Lord for the *Musrifûn* (polytheists, criminals, sinners — those who trespass Allâh's set limits in evil-doings by committing great sins).

مُّسَوَّمَةً عِندَ رَبِّكَ لِلْمُسْرِفِينَ ۝

35. So We brought out from therein the believers.

فَأَخْرَجْنَا مَن كَانَ فِيهَا مِنَ الْمُؤْمِنِينَ ۝

36. But We found not there any household of the Muslims except one [of Lût (Lot) and his two daughters].

فَمَا وَجَدْنَا فِيهَا غَيْرَ بَيْتٍ مِّنَ الْمُسْلِمِينَ ۝

37. And We have left there a sign (i.e. the place of the Dead Sea[1] in Palestine) for those who fear the painful torment.

وَتَرَكْنَا فِيهَآ ءَايَةً لِّلَّذِينَ يَخَافُونَ الْعَذَابَ الْأَلِيمَ ۝

38. And in Mûsâ (Moses) (too, there is a sign), when We sent him to Fir'aun (Pharaoh) with a manifest authority.

وَفِي مُوسَىٰٓ إِذْ أَرْسَلْنَاهُ إِلَىٰ فِرْعَوْنَ بِسُلْطَانٍ مُّبِينٍ ۝

39. But [Fir'aun (Pharaoh)] turned away (from Belief in might) along with his hosts, and said: "A sorcerer, or a madman."

فَتَوَلَّىٰ بِرُكْنِهِۦ وَقَالَ سَاحِرٌ أَوْ مَجْنُونٌ ۝

40. So We took him and his hosts, and dumped them into the sea, for he was blameworthy.

فَأَخَذْنَاهُ وَجُنُودَهُۥ فَنَبَذْنَاهُمْ فِي الْيَمِّ وَهُوَ مُلِيمٌ ۝

---

[1] (V.51:37) See the book of history "The Stories of the Prophets" by Ibn Kathir الله رحمة.

41. And in 'Âd (there is also a sign) when We sent against them the barren wind;

وَفِى عَادٍ إِذْ أَرْسَلْنَا عَلَيْهِمُ الرِّيحَ الْعَقِيمَ ۝

42. It spared nothing that it reached, but blew it into broken spreads of rotten ruins.

مَا تَذَرُ مِن شَىْءٍ أَتَتْ عَلَيْهِ إِلَّا جَعَلَتْهُ كَالرَّمِيمِ ۝

43. And in Thamûd (there is also a sign), when they were told: "Enjoy yourselves for a while!"

وَفِى ثَمُودَ إِذْ قِيلَ لَهُمْ تَمَتَّعُوا حَتَّىٰ حِينٍ ۝

44. But they insolently defied the Command of their Lord, so the Sâ'iqah[1] overtook them while they were looking.

فَعَتَوْا عَنْ أَمْرِ رَبِّهِمْ فَأَخَذَتْهُمُ الصَّاعِقَةُ وَهُمْ يَنظُرُونَ ۝

45. Then they were unable to rise up, nor could they help themselves.

فَمَا اسْتَطَاعُوا مِن قِيَامٍ وَمَا كَانُوا مُنتَصِرِينَ ۝

46. (So were) the people of Nûh (Noah) before them. Verily, they were a people who were Fâsiqûn (rebellious, disobedient to Allâh).

وَقَوْمَ نُوحٍ مِّن قَبْلُ إِنَّهُمْ كَانُوا قَوْمًا فَاسِقِينَ ۝

47. With power did We construct the heaven. Verily, We are Able to extend the vastness of space thereof.

وَالسَّمَاءَ بَنَيْنَاهَا بِأَيْدٍ وَإِنَّا لَمُوسِعُونَ ۝

48. And We have spread out the earth: how Excellent Spreader (thereof) are We!

وَالْأَرْضَ فَرَشْنَاهَا فَنِعْمَ الْمَاهِدُونَ ۝

49. And of everything We have created pairs, that you may remember (the Grace of Allâh).

وَمِن كُلِّ شَىْءٍ خَلَقْنَا زَوْجَيْنِ لَعَلَّكُمْ تَذَكَّرُونَ ۝

50. So flee to Allâh (from His Torment to His Mercy — Islâmic Monotheism). Verily, I (Muhammad صلى الله عليه وسلم) am a plain warner to you from Him.[2]

فَفِرُّوا إِلَى اللَّهِ إِنِّي لَكُم مِّنْهُ نَذِيرٌ مُّبِينٌ ۝

---

[1] (V.51:44) *Sâ'iqah*: A destructive awful cry, torment, hit, a thunderbolt. See (V.41:13).

[2] (V.51:50) See the footnote of (V.3:85).

51. And set not up (or worship not) any other *ilâh* (god) along with Allâh [Glorified is He He (Alone), Exalted above all that they associate as partners with Him]. Verily, I (Muhammad صلى الله عليه وسلم) am a plain warner to you from Him.

ولَا تَجْعَلُوا مَعَ ٱللَّهِ إِلَـٰهًا ءَاخَرَ إِنِّي لَكُم مِّنْهُ نَذِيرٌ مُّبِينٌ ۞

52. Likewise, no Messenger came to those before them but they said: "A sorcerer or a madman!"

كَذَٰلِكَ مَآ أَتَى ٱلَّذِينَ مِن قَبْلِهِم مِّن رَّسُولٍ إِلَّا قَالُوا سَاحِرٌ أَوْ مَجْنُونٌ ۞

53. Have they (the people of the past) transmitted this saying to these (Quraish pagans)? Nay, they are themselves a people transgressing beyond bounds (in disbelief)!

أَتَوَاصَوْا بِهِۦ بَلْ هُمْ قَوْمٌ طَاغُونَ ۞

54. So turn away (O Muhammad صلى الله عليه وسلم) from them (Quraish pagans), you are not blameworthy (as you have conveyed Allâh's Message).

فَتَوَلَّ عَنْهُمْ فَمَآ أَنتَ بِمَلُومٍ ۞

55. And remind (by preaching the Qur'ân, O Muhammad صلى الله عليه وسلم), for verily, the reminding profits the believers.

وَذَكِّرْ فَإِنَّ ٱلذِّكْرَىٰ تَنفَعُ ٱلْمُؤْمِنِينَ ۞

56. And I (Allâh) created not the jinn and mankind except that they should worship Me (Alone).

وَمَا خَلَقْتُ ٱلْجِنَّ وَٱلْإِنسَ إِلَّا لِيَعْبُدُونِ ۞

57. I seek not any provision from them (i.e. provision for themselves or for My creatures) nor do I ask that they should feed Me (i.e. feed themselves or My creatures).

مَآ أُرِيدُ مِنْهُم مِّن رِّزْقٍ وَمَآ أُرِيدُ أَن يُطْعِمُونِ ۞

58. Verily, Allâh is the All-Provider, Owner of Power, the Most Strong.

إِنَّ ٱللَّهَ هُوَ ٱلرَّزَّاقُ ذُو ٱلْقُوَّةِ ٱلْمَتِينُ ۞

59. And verily, for those who do wrong, there is a portion of torment like to the evil portion of torment (which

فَإِنَّ لِلَّذِينَ ظَلَمُوا ذَنُوبًا مِّثْلَ

came for) their likes (of old); so let them not ask Me to hasten on!

60. Then woe to those who disbelieve (in Allâh and His Oneness — Islâmic Monotheism) from their Day which they have been promised (for their punishment).[1]

ذَنُوبًا أَصْحَـٰبِهِمْ فَلَا يَسْتَعْجِلُونِ ۝

فَوَيْلٌ لِّلَّذِينَ كَفَرُوا مِنْ يَوْمِهِمُ ٱلَّذِي يُوعَدُونَ ۝

Sûrat At-Tûr
(The Mount) LII

سُورَةُ الطُّورِ

*In the Name of Allâh
the Most Gracious, the Most Merciful*

بِسْمِ اللَّهِ الرَّحْمَنِ الرَّحِيمِ

1. By the Tûr (Mount)

وَٱلطُّورِ ۝

2. And by the Book Inscribed

وَكِتَابٍ مَّسْطُورٍ ۝

3. In parchment unrolled.

فِى رَقٍّ مَّنْشُورٍ ۝

4. And by Al-Bait-ul-Ma'mûr[2] (the house over the heavens parallel to the Ka'bah at Makkah, continuously visited by the angels).

وَٱلْبَيْتِ ٱلْمَعْمُورِ ۝

5. And by the roof raised high (i.e. the heaven).

وَٱلسَّقْفِ ٱلْمَرْفُوعِ ۝

6. And by the sea kept filled (or it will be fire kindled on the Day of Resurrection).

وَٱلْبَحْرِ ٱلْمَسْجُورِ ۝

---

[1] (V.51:60)

A) See the footnote of (V.3:85).

B) Narrated Anas رضي الله عنه : The Prophet صلى الله عليه وسلم said, "Allâh will say to that person of the (Hell) Fire who will receive the least punishment, 'If you had everything on the earth, would you give it as a ransom to free yourself (i.e., save yourself from this Fire)?' He will say, 'Yes.' Then Allâh will say, 'While you were in the backbone of Adam, I asked you much less than this, (i.e., not to worship others besides Me), but you insisted on worshipping others besides me.'" (Sahih Al-Bukhari, Vol. 4, Hadith No. 551)

[2] (V.52:4) See the footnote of (V.53:12).

7. Verily, the Torment of your Lord will surely, come to pass.

إِنَّ عَذَابَ رَبِّكَ لَوَاقِعٌ ۝

8. There is none that can avert it.

مَّا لَهُ مِن دَافِعٍ ۝

9. On the Day when the heaven will shake with a dreadful shaking,

يَوْمَ تَمُورُ السَّمَآءُ مَوْرًا ۝

10. And the mountains will move away with a (horrible) movement.

وَتَسِيرُ الْجِبَالُ سَيْرًا ۝

11. Then woe that Day to the beliers.[1]

فَوَيْلٌ يَوْمَئِذٍ لِّلْمُكَذِّبِينَ ۝

12. Who are playing in falsehood.[2]

الَّذِينَ هُمْ فِي خَوْضٍ يَلْعَبُونَ ۝

13. The Day when they will be pushed down by force to the Fire of Hell, with a horrible, forceful pushing.

يَوْمَ يُدَعُّونَ إِلَىٰ نَارِ جَهَنَّمَ دَعًّا ۝

14. This is the Fire which you used to belie.

هَٰذِهِ النَّارُ الَّتِي كُنتُم بِهَا تُكَذِّبُونَ ۝

15. Is this magic or do you not see?

أَفَسِحْرٌ هَٰذَآ أَمْ أَنتُمْ لَا تُبْصِرُونَ ۝

16. Taste you therein its heat and whether you are patient of it or impatient of it, it is all the same. You are only being requited for what you used to do.

اصْلَوْهَا فَاصْبِرُوٓا أَوْ لَا تَصْبِرُوا سَوَآءٌ عَلَيْكُمْ إِنَّمَا تُجْزَوْنَ مَا كُنتُمْ تَعْمَلُونَ ۝

17. Verily, the *Muttaqûn* (the pious. See V.2:2) will be in Gardens (Paradise) and Delight.

إِنَّ الْمُتَّقِينَ فِي جَنَّاتٍ وَنَعِيمٍ ۝

18. Enjoying in that which their Lord has bestowed on them, and (the fact that) their Lord saved them from the torment of the blazing Fire.

فَكِهِينَ بِمَآ ءَاتَاهُمْ رَبُّهُمْ وَوَقَاهُمْ رَبُّهُمْ عَذَابَ الْجَحِيمِ ۝

19. "Eat and drink with happiness because of what you used to do."

كُلُوا وَاشْرَبُوا هَنِيٓئًا بِمَا كُنتُمْ تَعْمَلُونَ ۝

---

[1] (V.52:11) See the footnote of (V.17:97).

[2] (V.52:12) Busy in disbelief and evil deeds in this world, that are trials (for mankind), and they are ignoring their eternal end (i.e. punishment in the Fire of Hell, forever)

20. They will recline (with ease) on thrones arranged in ranks. And We shall marry them to *Hûr* (fair female) with wide lovely eyes.[1]

مُتَّكِئِينَ عَلَىٰ سُرُرٍ مَّصْفُوفَةٍ وَزَوَّجْنَـٰهُم بِحُورٍ عِينٍ ٢٠

21. And those who believe and whose offspring follow them in Faith: to them shall We join their offspring, and We shall not decrease the reward of their deeds in anything. Every person is a pledge for that which he has earned.

وَالَّذِينَ ءَامَنُوا وَاتَّبَعَتْهُمْ ذُرِّيَّتُهُم بِإِيمَـٰنٍ أَلْحَقْنَا بِهِمْ ذُرِّيَّتَهُمْ وَمَآ أَلَتْنَـٰهُم مِّنْ عَمَلِهِم مِّن شَيْءٍ كُلُّ امْرِئٍ بِمَا كَسَبَ رَهِينٌ ٢١

22. And We shall provide them with fruit and meat such as they desire.

وَأَمْدَدْنَـٰهُم بِفَـٰكِهَةٍ وَلَحْمٍ مِّمَّا يَشْتَهُونَ ٢٢

23. There they shall pass from hand to hand a (wine) cup, free from any *Laghw* (dirty, false, evil vain talk between them), and free from sin[2] (because it will be lawful for them to drink).

يَتَنَـٰزَعُونَ فِيهَا كَأْسًا لَّا لَغْوٌ فِيهَا وَلَا تَأْثِيمٌ ٢٣

24. And there will go round boy-servants of theirs, to serve them as if they were preserved pearls.

۞ وَيَطُوفُ عَلَيْهِمْ غِلْمَانٌ لَّهُمْ كَأَنَّهُمْ لُؤْلُؤٌ مَّكْنُونٌ ٢٤

25. And some of them draw near to others, questioning.

وَأَقْبَلَ بَعْضُهُمْ عَلَىٰ بَعْضٍ يَتَسَآءَلُونَ ٢٥

26. Saying: "Aforetime, we were afraid (of the punishment of Allâh) in the midst of our families.

قَالُوٓا إِنَّا كُنَّا قَبْلُ فِىٓ أَهْلِنَا مُشْفِقِينَ ٢٦

27. "So Allâh has been gracious to us, and has saved us from the torment of the Fire.

فَمَنَّ اللَّهُ عَلَيْنَا وَوَقَىٰنَا عَذَابَ السَّمُومِ ٢٧

---

[1] (V.52:20) *Hûr* (houris): Very fair females created by Allâh as such, not from the offspring of Adam عليه السلام with intense black irises of their eyes and intense white scleras. [See the footnote of (V.44:54)]

[2] (V.52:23) See Footnote b, c and d of (V.2:219).

28. "Verily, We used to invoke Him (Alone and none else) before. Verily, He is *Al-Barr* (the Most Subtle, Kind, Courteous, and Generous), the Most Merciful."[1]

إِنَّا كُنَّا مِن قَبْلُ نَدْعُوهُ إِنَّهُ هُوَ ٱلْبَرُّ ٱلرَّحِيمُ ﴿٢٨﴾

29. Therefore, remind (mankind of Islâmic Monotheism, O Muhammad صلى الله عليه وسلم). By the Grace of Allâh, you are neither a soothsayer, nor a madman.

فَذَكِّرْ فَمَآ أَنتَ بِنِعْمَتِ رَبِّكَ بِكَاهِنٍ وَلَا مَجْنُونٍ ﴿٢٩﴾

30. Or do they say: "(Muhammad صلى الله عليه وسلم is) a poet! We await for him some calamity by time!"

أَمْ يَقُولُونَ شَاعِرٌ نَّتَرَبَّصُ بِهِ رَيْبَ ٱلْمَنُونِ ﴿٣٠﴾

31. Say (O Muhammad صلى الله عليه وسلم to them): "Wait! I am with you among the waiters!"

قُلْ تَرَبَّصُوا فَإِنِّي مَعَكُم مِّنَ ٱلْمُتَرَبِّصِينَ ﴿٣١﴾

32. Do their minds command them this [i.e. to tell a lie against you (Muhammad صلى الله عليه وسلم)] or are they people transgressing all bounds?

أَمْ تَأْمُرُهُمْ أَحْلَامُهُم بِهَذَآ أَمْ هُمْ قَوْمٌ طَاغُونَ ﴿٣٢﴾

33. Or do they say: "He (Muhammad صلى الله عليه وسلم) has forged it (this Qur'ân)?" Nay! They believe not!

أَمْ يَقُولُونَ تَقَوَّلَهُ بَل لَّا يُؤْمِنُونَ ﴿٣٣﴾

34. Let them then produce a recital like unto it (the Qur'ân) if they are truthful.

فَلْيَأْتُوا بِحَدِيثٍ مِّثْلِهِ إِن كَانُوا صَادِقِينَ ﴿٣٤﴾

35. Were they created by nothing? Or were they themselves the creators?

أَمْ خُلِقُوا مِنْ غَيْرِ شَىْءٍ أَمْ هُمُ ٱلْخَالِقُونَ ﴿٣٥﴾

36. Or did they create the heavens and the earth? Nay, but they have no firm Belief.

أَمْ خَلَقُوا ٱلسَّمَاوَاتِ وَٱلْأَرْضَ بَل لَّا يُوقِنُونَ ﴿٣٦﴾

---

[1] (V.52:28) See the footnote of (V.2:165).

37. Or are with them the treasures of your Lord? Or are they the tyrants with the authority to do as they like?

أَمْ عِندَهُمْ خَزَآئِنُ رَبِّكَ أَمْ هُمُ ٱلْمُصَيْطِرُونَ ۝

38. Or have they a stairway (to heaven), by means of which they listen (to the talks of the angels)? Then let their listener produce some manifest proof.

أَمْ لَهُمْ سُلَّمٌ يَسْتَمِعُونَ فِيهِ فَلْيَأْتِ مُسْتَمِعُهُم بِسُلْطَنٍ مُّبِينٍ ۝

39. Or has He (Allâh) only daughters and you have sons?

أَمْ لَهُ ٱلْبَنَـٰتُ وَلَكُمُ ٱلْبَنُونَ ۝

40. Or is it that you (O Muhammad صلى الله عليه وسلم) ask a wage from them (for your preaching of Islâmic Monotheism) so that they are burdened with a load of debt?

أَمْ تَسْـَٔلُهُمْ أَجْرًا فَهُم مِّن مَّغْرَمٍ مُّثْقَلُونَ ۝

41. Or that the *Ghaib* (Unseen) is with them, and they write it down?

أَمْ عِندَهُمُ ٱلْغَيْبُ فَهُمْ يَكْتُبُونَ ۝

42. Or do they intend a plot (against you O Muhammad صلى الله عليه وسلم)? But those who disbelieve (in the Oneness of Allâh — Islâmic Monotheism) are themselves plotted against!

أَمْ يُرِيدُونَ كَيْدًا فَٱلَّذِينَ كَفَرُوا هُمُ ٱلْمَكِيدُونَ ۝

43. Or have they an *ilâh* (a god) other than Allâh? Glorified is Allâh from all that they ascribe as partners (to Him)[1]

أَمْ لَهُمْ إِلَـٰهٌ غَيْرُ ٱللَّهِ سُبْحَـٰنَ ٱللَّهِ عَمَّا يُشْرِكُونَ ۝

44. And if they were to see a piece of the heaven falling down, they would say: "Clouds gathered in heaps!"

وَإِن يَرَوْا كِسْفًا مِّنَ ٱلسَّمَآءِ سَاقِطًا يَقُولُوا سَحَابٌ مَّرْكُومٌ ۝

45. So leave them alone till they meet their Day, in which they will sink into a fainting (with horror).

فَذَرْهُمْ حَتَّىٰ يُلَـٰقُوا يَوْمَهُمُ ٱلَّذِي فِيهِ يُصْعَقُونَ ۝

---

[1] (V.52:43)
a) See the footnote (B) of (V.3:130).
b) See the footnote of (V.2:278)

46. The Day when their plotting shall not avail them at all nor will they be helped (i.e. they will receive their torment in Hell).

يَوْمَ لَا يُغْنِى عَنْهُمْ كَيْدُهُمْ شَيْئًا وَلَا هُمْ يُنصَرُونَ ۝

47. And verily, for those who do wrong, there is another punishment (i.e. the torment in this world and in their graves)[1] before this; but most of them know not. [Tafsîr At-Tabarî].

وَإِنَّ لِلَّذِينَ ظَلَمُوا عَذَابًا دُونَ ذَٰلِكَ وَلَٰكِنَّ أَكْثَرَهُمْ لَا يَعْلَمُونَ ۝

48. So wait patiently (O Muhammad صلى الله عليه وسلم) for the Decision of your Lord, for verily, you are under Our Eyes[2]; and glorify the Praises of your Lord when you get up from sleep.

وَاصْبِرْ لِحُكْمِ رَبِّكَ فَإِنَّكَ بِأَعْيُنِنَا وَسَبِّحْ بِحَمْدِ رَبِّكَ حِينَ تَقُومُ ۝

49. And in the nighttime also glorify His Praises — and at the setting of the stars. [3]

وَمِنَ الَّيْلِ فَسَبِّحْهُ وَإِدْبَٰرَ النُّجُومِ ۝

Sûrat An-Najm
(The Star) LIII

سُوْرَةُ النَّجْمِ

*In the Name of Allâh
the Most Gracious, the Most Merciful*

بِسْمِ اللَّهِ الرَّحْمَٰنِ الرَّحِيمِ

1. By the star when it goes down (or vanishes).

وَالنَّجْمِ إِذَا هَوَىٰ ۝

2. Your companion (Muhammad صلى الله عليه وسلم) has neither gone astray nor has erred.

مَا ضَلَّ صَاحِبُكُمْ وَمَا غَوَىٰ ۝

3. Nor does he speak of (his own) desire.

وَمَا يَنطِقُ عَنِ الْهَوَىٰ ۝

---

[1] (V.52:47) See the footnote of (B) of (V.6:93).

[2] (V.52:48) See the footnote of (V.3:73).

[3] (V.52:49) It is said that glorifying Allâh's Praises here means: all the five compulsory and additional *Nawâfil* prayers.

4. It is only a Revelation revealed.

إِنْ هُوَ إِلَّا وَحْىٌ يُوحَىٰ ٤

5. He has been taught (this Qur'ân) by one mighty in power [Jibrael (Gabriel)].

عَلَّمَهُۥ شَدِيدُ ٱلْقُوَىٰ ٥

6. One free from any defect in body and mind then he (Jibrael — Gabriel in his real shape as created by Allâh) rose and became stable.

ذُو مِرَّةٍ فَٱسْتَوَىٰ ٦

7. While he [Jibrael (Gabriel)] was in the highest part of the horizon, [*Tafsir Ibn Kathir*]

وَهُوَ بِٱلْأُفُقِ ٱلْأَعْلَىٰ ٧

8. Then he [Jibrael (Gabriel)] approached and came closer,

ثُمَّ دَنَا فَتَدَلَّىٰ ٨

9. And was at a distance of two bows' length or (even) nearer.

فَكَانَ قَابَ قَوْسَيْنِ أَوْ أَدْنَىٰ ٩

10. So (Allâh) revealed to His slave [Muhammad صلى الله عليه وسلم] through Jibrael (Gabriel) عليه السلام whatever He revealed.

فَأَوْحَىٰ إِلَىٰ عَبْدِهِۦ مَا أَوْحَىٰ ١٠

11. The (Prophet's) heart lied not in what he (Muhammad صلى الله عليه وسلم) saw.

مَا كَذَبَ ٱلْفُؤَادُ مَا رَأَىٰ ١١

12. Will you then dispute with him (Muhammad صلى الله عليه وسلم) about what he saw [during the *Mi'râj*: Ascent of the Prophet صلى الله عليه وسلم to the seven heavens].[1]

أَفَتُمَـٰرُونَهُۥ عَلَىٰ مَا يَرَىٰ ١٢

---

[1] (V.53:12) Al-Mi'râj [i.e. Ascent of Prophet Muhammad صلى الله عليه وسلم to the heavens with his body and soul (بالروح والجسم)].

Narrated Mâlik bin Sa'sa'ah رضي الله عنه: The Prophet صلى الله عليه وسلم said, "While I was at the house in a state midway between sleep and wakefulness, (an angel recognized me) as the man lying between two men. A golden tray full of wisdom and belief was brought to me and my body was cut open from the throat to the lower part of the abdomen and then my abdomen was washed with *Zamzam* water and (my heart was) filled with wisdom and belief. Al-Burâq, a white animal smaller than a mule and bigger than a donkey was brought to me and I set out with Jibrael (Gabriel). When I reached the nearest heaven, Jibrael said to the gate-keeper of the heaven, 'Open the gate.' The gate-keeper asked, 'Who is it?' He said, 'Jibrael.' The gate-keeper, said 'Who is accompanying you?' Jibrael said, 'Muhammad صلى الله عليه وسلم: The gate-keeper said, 'Has he been called?' Jibrael said, 'Yes'. Then it was said, 'He is welcome. What a wonderful visit his is!' Then I met Adam and greeted him and he said, 'You are welcome O son and a Prophet.' Then we ascended to the second heaven. It was asked, 'Who is it?' Jibrael said, 'Jibrael.' It was said, 'Who is with you? He said, 'Muhammad صلى الله عليه وسلم'. It was asked, 'Has he been sent for?' He said, 'Yes.'It was said, 'He is welcome. What a wonderful visit his is.' Then I met 'Îsâ (Jesus) and Yahyâ (John) who said, 'You are welcome, O brother and a Prophet.' Then we ascended to the third heaven. It was asked, 'Who is it?' Jibrael said, 'Jibrael.' It was asked, 'Who is with you?' Jibrael said, 'Muhammad صلى الله عليه وسلم' It was asked, 'Has he been sent for?' Jibrael said, 'Yes.' It was said 'He is welcome. What a wonderful visit his is!' (The Prophet صلى الله عليه وسلم added:). There I met Yûsuf (Joseph) and greeted him, and he replied, 'You are welcome, O brother and a Prophet!' Then we ascended to the fourth heaven and again the same questions and answers were exchanged as in the previous heavens. There I met Idrîs (Enoch) and greeted him. He said, 'You are welcome, O brother and Prophet.' Then we ascended to the fifth heaven and again the same questions and answers were exchanged as in the previous heavens. There I met and greeted Hârûn (Aaron) who said, 'You are welcome, O brother and a Prophet.' Then we ascended to the sixth heaven and again the same questions and answers were exchanged as in the previous heavens. There I met and greeted Mûsâ (Moses) who said, 'You are welcome, O brother and a Prophet.' When I proceeded on, he started weeping and on being asked why he was weeping, he said, 'O Lord! followers of this youth who was sent after me will enter Paradise in greater number than my followers.' Then we ascended to the seventh heaven and again the same questions and answers were exchanged as in the previous heavens. There I met and greeted Ibrâhîm (Abraham) who said, 'You are welcome, O son and a Prophet.' Then I was shown Al-Bait Al-Ma'mûr (i.e. Allâh's House). I asked Jibrael about it and he said, 'This is Al-Bait

13. And indeed he (Muhammad الله صلى (وسلم عليه saw him [Jibrael (Gabriel)] at a second descent (i.e. another time). وَلَقَدْ رَءَاهُ نَزْلَةً أُخْرَى ١٣

14. Near *Sidrat-ul-Muntahâ* (a lote-tree of the utmost boundary over the seventh heaven beyond which none can pass). عِندَ سِدْرَةِ ٱلْمُنتَهَى ١٤

15. Near it is the Paradise of Abode. عِندَهَا جَنَّةُ ٱلْمَأْوَى ١٥

Al-Ma'mûr where 70,000 angels perform prayers daily; and when they leave they never return to it (but always a fresh batch comes into it daily).' Then I was shown *Sidrat-ul Muntaha* (i.e. the lote-tree of the utmost boundary over the seventh heaven) and I saw its *Nabiq* fruits which resembled the clay jugs of Hijar (a town in Arabia), and its leaves were like the ears of elephants, and four rivers originated at its root: two of them were apparent and two were hidden. I asked Jibrael about those rivers and he said, 'The two hidden rivers are in Paradise and the apparent ones are the Nile and the Euphrates.' Then fifty prayers were enjoined on me. I descended till I met Mûsâ who asked me, 'What have you done?' I said, 'Fifty prayers have been enjoined on me.' He said, 'I know the people better than you, because I had the hardest experience to bring Banî Israel to obedience. Your followers cannot put up with such obligation. So, return to your Lord and request Him (to reduce the number of prayers).' I returned and requested Allâh (for reduction) and He made it forty. I returned and [met Mûsâ] and had a similar discussion, and then returned again to Allâh for reduction and He made it thirty, then twenty, then ten; and then I came to Mûsâ who repeated the same advice. Ultimately Allâh reduced it to five. When I came to Mûsâ again, he said, 'What have you done?' I said, 'Allâh has made it five only.' He repeated the same advice but I said that I surrendered (to Allâh's Final Order)" Allâh's Messenger وسلم عليه الله صلى was addressed by Allâh, "I have decreed My Obligation and have reduced the burden on My slaves, and I shall reward a single good deed as if it were ten good deeds." (*Sahih Al-Bukhari*, Vol.4, *Hadîth* No.429).

16. When that covered the lote-tree which did cover it![1]

إِذْ يَغْشَى السِّدْرَةَ مَا يَغْشَى ۞

17. The sight (of Prophet Muhammad صلى الله عليه وسلم) turned not aside (right or left), nor it transgressed beyond the limit (ordained for it).

مَا زَاغَ الْبَصَرُ وَمَا طَغَىٰ ۞

18. Indeed he (Muhammad صلى الله عليه وسلم) did see of the Greatest Signs, of his Lord (Allâh).

لَقَدْ رَأَى مِنْ ءَايَٰتِ رَبِّهِ الْكُبْرَىٰٓ ۞

19. Have you then considered Al-Lât, and Al-'Uzzâ (two idols of the pagan Arabs)[2]

أَفَرَءَيْتُمُ اللَّٰتَ وَالْعُزَّىٰ ۞

20. And Manât (another idol of the pagan Arabs), the other third?

وَمَنَاةَ الثَّالِثَةَ الْأُخْرَىٰٓ ۞

21. Is it for you the males and for Him the females?

أَلَكُمُ الذَّكَرُ وَلَهُ الْأُنثَىٰ ۞

22. That indeed is a division most unfair!

تِلْكَ إِذًا قِسْمَةٌ ضِيزَىٰٓ ۞

23. They are but names which you have named — you and your fathers — for which Allâh has sent down no authority. They follow but a guess and that which they themselves desire, whereas there has surely, come to them the Guidance from their Lord!

إِنْ هِيَ إِلَّآ أَسْمَآءٌ سَمَّيْتُمُوهَآ أَنتُمْ وَءَابَآؤُكُم مَّآ أَنزَلَ اللَّهُ بِهَا مِن سُلْطَٰنٍ إِن يَتَّبِعُونَ إِلَّا الظَّنَّ وَمَا تَهْوَى الْأَنفُسُ وَلَقَدْ جَآءَهُم مِّن رَّبِّهِمُ الْهُدَىٰٓ ۞

24. Or shall man have what he wishes?

أَمْ لِلْإِنسَٰنِ مَا تَمَنَّىٰ ۞

25. But to Allâh belongs the last (Hereafter) and the first (the world).

فَلِلَّهِ الْآخِرَةُ وَالْأُولَىٰ ۞

---

[1] (53:16) It is said that the lote-tree was covered with the light of Allâh along with the angels and also with different kinds of colours. [Please see *Tafsir Ibn Kathir*]

[2] (V.53:19) See the footnote of (A) of (V.2:219).

26. And there are many angels in the heavens, whose intercession will avail nothing except after Allâh has given leave for whom He wills and is pleased with.

27. Verily, those who believe not in the Hereafter, name the angels with female names.

28. But they have no knowledge thereof. They follow but a guess, and verily, guess is no substitute for the truth.

29. Therefore withdraw (O Muhammad صلى الله عليه وسلم) from him who turns away from Our Reminder (this Qur'ân) and desires nothing but the life of this world.

30. That is what they could reach of knowledge. Verily, your Lord it is He Who knows best him who goes astray from His Path, and He knows best him who receives guidance.

31. And to Allâh belongs all that is in the heavens and all that is in the earth, that He may requite those who do evil with that which they have done (i.e. punish them in Hell), and reward those who do good, with what is best (i.e. Paradise).

32. Those who avoid great sins (See the Qur'ân, Verses: 6:152,153) and Al-Fawâhish (illegal sexual intercourse) except the small faults, — verily, your Lord is of Vast Forgiveness. He knows you well when He created you from the earth (Adam), and when you were fetuses in your mothers' wombs. So ascribe not purity to yourselves. He knows best him who fears Allâh and keep his duty to Him [i.e. those who are *Al-Muttaqûn* (the pious. See V.2:2)].

33. Did you (O Muhammad صلى الله عليه وسلم) observe him who turned away (from Islâm)?

34. And gave a little, then stopped (giving)?

35. Is with him the knowledge of the Unseen so that he sees?

36. Or is he not informed with what is in the Pages (Scripture) of Mûsâ (Moses),

37. And of Ibrâhîm (Abraham) who fulfilled (or conveyed) all that (Allâh ordered him to do or convey):

38. That no burdened person (with sins) shall bear the burden (sins) of another.

39. And that man can have nothing but what he does (good or bad).[1]

40. And that his deeds will be seen.

41. Then he will be recompensed with a full and the best recompense.[2]

42. And that to your Lord (Allâh) is the End (Return of everything).

---

[1] (V.53:39) Narrated Abû Hurairah رضي الله عنه Allâh's Messenger صلى الله عليه وسلم said: "When a person is dead, his deeds cease (are stopped) except from three:

a) Deeds of continuous *Sadaqah* (act of charity): e.g. an orphan home (orphanage) or a well for giving water to drink.

b) (Written) knowledge with which mankind gets benefit.

c) A righteous, pious son (or daughter) who begs Allâh to forgive his (or her) parents."

(Sahih Muslim. The Book of *Wasâyâ* (Wills and Testaments).

[2] (V.53:41) See the footnote (A) of (V.6:61).

43. And that it is He (Allâh) Who makes (whom He wills) laugh, and makes (whom He wills) weep.

وَأَنَّهُۥ هُوَ أَضْحَكَ وَأَبْكَىٰ ٤٣

44. And that it is He (Allâh) Who causes death and gives life.

وَأَنَّهُۥ هُوَ أَمَاتَ وَأَحْيَا ٤٤

45. And that it is He (Allâh) creates the pairs, male and female,

وَأَنَّهُۥ خَلَقَ ٱلزَّوْجَيْنِ ٱلذَّكَرَ وَٱلْأُنثَىٰ ٤٥

46. From *Nutfah* (drops of semen — male and female discharges) when it is emitted.

مِن نُّطْفَةٍ إِذَا تُمْنَىٰ ٤٦

47. And that upon Him (Allâh) is another bringing forth (Resurrection).

وَأَنَّ عَلَيْهِ ٱلنَّشْأَةَ ٱلْأُخْرَىٰ ٤٧

48. And that it is He (Allâh) Who gives much or a little (of wealth and contentment)

وَأَنَّهُۥ هُوَ أَغْنَىٰ وَأَقْنَىٰ ٤٨

49. And that He (Allâh) is the Lord of Sirius (the star which the pagan Arabs used to worship).

وَأَنَّهُۥ هُوَ رَبُّ ٱلشِّعْرَىٰ ٤٩

50. And that it is He (Allâh) Who destroyed the former 'Âd (people),

وَأَنَّهُۥ أَهْلَكَ عَادًا ٱلْأُولَىٰ ٥٠

51. And Thamûd (people): He spared none of them.

وَثَمُودَ فَمَا أَبْقَىٰ ٥١

52. And the people of Nûh (Noah) aforetime. Verily, they were more unjust and more rebellious and transgressing [in disobeying Allâh and His Messenger Nûh (Noah) عليه السلام].

وَقَوْمَ نُوحٍ مِّن قَبْلُ إِنَّهُمْ كَانُوا هُمْ أَظْلَمَ وَأَطْغَىٰ ٥٢

53. And He destroyed the overthrown cities [of Sodom to which Prophet Lût (Lot) was sent].

وَٱلْمُؤْتَفِكَةَ أَهْوَىٰ ٥٣

54. So there covered them that which did cover (i.e. torment with stones).

فَغَشَّىٰهَا مَا غَشَّىٰ ٥٤

55. Then which of the Graces of your Lord (O man!) will you doubt?

فَبِأَيِّ ءَالَآءِ رَبِّكَ تَتَمَارَىٰ ٥٥

56. This (Muhammad صلى الله عليه وسلم) is a warner (Messenger) of the (series of) warners (Messengers) of old.[1]

57. The Day of Resurrection draws near.

58. None besides Allâh can avert it (or advance it or delay it).

59. Do you then wonder at this recitation (the Qur'ân)?

60. And you laugh at it and weep not,

61. Wasting your (precious) lifetime in pastime and amusements (singing).

62. So fall you down in prostration to Allâh and worship Him (Alone).

Sûrat Al-Qamar
(The Moon) LIV

*In the Name of Allâh
the Most Gracious, the Most Merciful*

1. The Hour has drawn near, and the moon has been cleft asunder (the people of Makkah requested Prophet Muhammad صلى الله عليه وسلم to show them a miracle, so he showed them the splitting of the moon).[2]

2. And if they see a sign, they turn away, and say: "This is continuous magic."

---

[1] (V.53:56) See the footnote of (V.2:252).

[2] (V.54:1) Narrated Anas رضي الله عنه: The people of Makkah asked the Prophet صلى الله عليه وسلم to show them a sign (miracle). So he showed them (the miracle) of the cleaving of the moon. (*Sahih Al-Bukhari*, Vol.6, *Hadîth* No.390).

3. They belied (the Verses of Allâh — this Qur'ân), and followed their own lusts. And every matter will be settled (according to the kind of deeds: good deeds will take their doers to Paradise, and similarly evil deeds will take their doers to Hell).

وَكَذَّبُواْ وَٱتَّبَعُوٓاْ أَهْوَآءَهُمْ وَكُلُّ أَمْرٍ مُّسْتَقِرٌّ ٣

4. And indeed there has come to them news (in this Qur'ân) wherein there is (enough warning) to check (them from evil),

وَلَقَدْ جَآءَهُم مِّنَ ٱلْأَنۢبَآءِ مَا فِيهِ مُزْدَجَرٌ ٤

5. Perfect wisdom (this Qur'ân), but (the preaching of) warners benefit them not.

حِكْمَةٌۢ بَٰلِغَةٌ فَمَا تُغْنِ ٱلنُّذُرُ ٥

6. So (O Muhammad صلى الله عليه وسلم) withdraw from them. The Day that the caller will call (them) to a terrible thing.

فَتَوَلَّ عَنْهُمْ يَوْمَ يَدْعُ ٱلدَّاعِ إِلَىٰ شَىْءٍ نُّكُرٍ ٦

7. They will come forth, with humbled eyes from (their) graves as if they were locusts spread abroad,

خُشَّعًا أَبْصَٰرُهُمْ يَخْرُجُونَ مِنَ ٱلْأَجْدَاثِ كَأَنَّهُمْ جَرَادٌ مُّنتَشِرٌ ٧

8. Hastening towards the caller. The disbelievers will say: "This is a hard Day."

مُّهْطِعِينَ إِلَى ٱلدَّاعِ يَقُولُ ٱلْكَٰفِرُونَ هَٰذَا يَوْمٌ عَسِرٌ ٨

9. The people of Nûh (Noah) denied (their Messenger) before them. They rejected Our slave, and said: "A madman!" and he was insolently rebuked and threatened.

كَذَّبَتْ قَبْلَهُمْ قَوْمُ نُوحٍ فَكَذَّبُواْ عَبْدَنَا وَقَالُواْ مَجْنُونٌ وَٱزْدُجِرَ ٩

10. Then he invoked his Lord (saying): "I have been overcome, so help (me)!"

فَدَعَا رَبَّهُۥٓ أَنِّي مَغْلُوبٌ فَٱنتَصِرْ ١٠

11. So We opened the gates of the heaven with water pouring forth.

فَفَتَحْنَآ أَبْوَٰبَ ٱلسَّمَآءِ بِمَآءٍ مُّنْهَمِرٍ ١١

12. And We caused springs to gush forth from the earth. So the waters of

وَفَجَّرْنَا ٱلْأَرْضَ عُيُونًا فَٱلْتَقَى

the heaven and the earth) met for a matter predestined.

ٱلسَّمَآءَ عَلَىٰ أَمْرٍ قَدْ قُدِرَ ١٢

13. And We carried him on a (ship) made of planks and nails,

وَحَمَلْنَٰهُ عَلَىٰ ذَاتِ أَلْوَٰحٍ وَدُسُرٍ ١٣

14. Floating under Our Eyes: a reward for him who had been rejected!

تَجْرِى بِأَعْيُنِنَا جَزَآءً لِّمَن كَانَ كُفِرَ ١٤

15. And indeed, We have left this as a sign. Then is there any that will remember (or receive admonition)?

وَلَقَد تَّرَكْنَٰهَآ ءَايَةً فَهَلْ مِن مُّدَّكِرٍ ١٥

16. Then how (terrible) was My Torment and My Warnings?

فَكَيْفَ كَانَ عَذَابِى وَنُذُرِ ١٦

17. And We have indeed made the Qur'ân easy to understand and remember; then is there any one who will remember (or receive admonition)?

وَلَقَدْ يَسَّرْنَا ٱلْقُرْءَانَ لِلذِّكْرِ فَهَلْ مِن مُّدَّكِرٍ ١٧

18. 'Âd (people) belied (their Prophet, Hûd); then how (terrible) was My Torment and My Warnings?

كَذَّبَتْ عَادٌ فَكَيْفَ كَانَ عَذَابِى وَنُذُرِ ١٨

19. Verily, We sent against them a furious wind of harsh voice on a day of evil omen and continuous calamity.

إِنَّآ أَرْسَلْنَا عَلَيْهِمْ رِيحًا صَرْصَرًا فِى يَوْمِ نَحْسٍ مُّسْتَمِرٍّ ١٩

20. Plucking out men as if they were uprooted stems of date-palms.

تَنزِعُ ٱلنَّاسَ كَأَنَّهُمْ أَعْجَازُ نَخْلٍ مُّنقَعِرٍ ٢٠

21. Then, how (terrible) was My Torment and My Warnings?

فَكَيْفَ كَانَ عَذَابِى وَنُذُرِ ٢١

22. And We have indeed made the Qur'ân easy to understand and remember; then is there any that will remember (or receive admonition)?

وَلَقَدْ يَسَّرْنَا ٱلْقُرْءَانَ لِلذِّكْرِ فَهَلْ مِن مُّدَّكِرٍ ٢٢

23. Thamûd (people also) belied the warnings.

كَذَّبَتْ ثَمُودُ بِٱلنُّذُرِ ٢٣

24. And they said: "A man, alone among us — shall we follow him?

فَقَالُوٓا أَبَشَرًا مِّنَّا وَٰحِدًا نَّتَّبِعُهُ

Truly, then we should be in error and distress (or madness)!"

إِنَّا إِذًا لَّفِى ضَلَالٍ وَسُعُرٍ ۝

25. "Is it that the Reminder is sent to him (Prophet Sâlih عليه السلام) alone from among us? Nay, he is an insolent liar!"

أَءُلْقِىَ ٱلذِّكْرُ عَلَيْهِ مِنۢ بَيْنِنَا بَلْ هُوَ كَذَّابٌ أَشِرٌ ۝

26. Tomorrow they will come to know who is the liar, the insolent one!

سَيَعْلَمُونَ غَدًا مَّنِ ٱلْكَذَّابُ ٱلْأَشِرُ ۝

27. Verily, We are sending the she-camel as a test for them. So watch them (O Sâlih عليه السلام), and be patient!

إِنَّا مُرْسِلُوا ٱلنَّاقَةِ فِتْنَةً لَّهُمْ فَٱرْتَقِبْهُمْ وَٱصْطَبِرْ ۝

28. And inform them that the water is to be shared between (her and) them, each one's right to drink being established (by turns).

وَنَبِّئْهُمْ أَنَّ ٱلْمَآءَ قِسْمَةٌۢ بَيْنَهُمْ كُلُّ شِرْبٍ مُّحْتَضَرٌ ۝

29. But they called their comrade and he took (a sword) and killed (her).

فَنَادَوْا صَاحِبَهُمْ فَتَعَاطَىٰ فَعَقَرَ ۝

30. Then, how (terrible) was My Torment and My Warnings?

فَكَيْفَ كَانَ عَذَابِى وَنُذُرِ ۝

31. Verily, We sent against them a single *Saihah* (torment — awful cry), and they became like the stubble of a fold-builder.

إِنَّا أَرْسَلْنَا عَلَيْهِمْ صَيْحَةً وَٰحِدَةً فَكَانُوا كَهَشِيمِ ٱلْمُحْتَظِرِ ۝

32. And indeed, We have made the Qur'ân easy to understand and remember; then is there any that will remember (or receive admonition)?

وَلَقَدْ يَسَّرْنَا ٱلْقُرْءَانَ لِلذِّكْرِ فَهَلْ مِن مُّدَّكِرٍ ۝

33. The people of Lût (Lot) belied the warnings.

كَذَّبَتْ قَوْمُ لُوطٍۭ بِٱلنُّذُرِ ۝

34. Verily, We sent against them a violent storm of stones (which destroyed them all), except the family of Lût (Lot), them We saved in the last hour of the night,

إِنَّا أَرْسَلْنَا عَلَيْهِمْ حَاصِبًا إِلَّا ءَالَ لُوطٍ نَّجَّيْنَٰهُم بِسَحَرٍ ۝

35. As a Favour from Us. Thus do We reward him who gives thanks (by obeying Us).

نِعْمَةً مِّنْ عِندِنَا كَذَٰلِكَ نَجْزِى مَن شَكَرَ ۝

36. And he [Lût (Lot)] indeed had warned them of Our Seizure (punishment), but they did doubt the warnings!

وَلَقَدْ أَنذَرَهُم بَطْشَتَنَا فَتَمَارَوْا بِٱلنُّذُرِ ۝

37. And they indeed sought to shame his guest (by asking to commit sodomy with them). So We blinded their eyes (saying), "Then taste you My Torment and My Warnings."

وَلَقَدْ رَٰوَدُوهُ عَن ضَيْفِهِۦ فَطَمَسْنَآ أَعْيُنَهُمْ فَذُوقُوا عَذَابِى وَنُذُرِ ۝

38. And verily, an abiding torment seized them early in the morning.

وَلَقَدْ صَبَّحَهُم بُكْرَةً عَذَابٌ مُّسْتَقِرٌّ ۝

39. "Then taste you My Torment and My Warnings."

فَذُوقُوا عَذَابِى وَنُذُرِ ۝

40. And indeed, We have made the Qur'ân easy to understand and remember; then is there any that will remember (or receive admonition)?

وَلَقَدْ يَسَّرْنَا ٱلْقُرْءَانَ لِلذِّكْرِ فَهَلْ مِن مُّدَّكِرٍ ۝

41. And indeed, warnings came to the people of Fir'aun (Pharaoh) [through Mûsâ (Moses) and Hârûn (Aaron)].

وَلَقَدْ جَآءَ ءَالَ فِرْعَوْنَ ٱلنُّذُرُ ۝

42. (They) belied all Our Signs, so We seized them with a Seizure of the All-Mighty, All-Capable (Omnipotent).

كَذَّبُوا بِـَٔايَٰتِنَا كُلِّهَا فَأَخَذْنَٰهُمْ أَخْذَ عَزِيزٍ مُّقْتَدِرٍ ۝

43. Are your disbelievers (O Quraish!) better than these [nations of Nûh (Noah), Lût (Lot), Sâlih, and the people of Fir'aun (Pharaoh), who were destroyed)? Or have you an immunity (against Our Torment) in the Divine Scriptures?

أَكُفَّارُكُمْ خَيْرٌ مِّنْ أُوْلَٰٓئِكُمْ أَمْ لَكُم بَرَآءَةٌ فِى ٱلزُّبُرِ ۝

44. Or say they: "We are a great multitude, victorious?"

أَمْ يَقُولُونَ نَحْنُ جَمِيعٌ مُّنتَصِرٌ ۝

45. Their multitude will be put to flight, and they will show their backs.

سَيُهْزَمُ الْجَمْعُ وَيُوَلُّونَ الدُّبُرَ ٤٥

46. Nay, but the Hour is their appointed time (for their full recompense), and the Hour will be more grievous and more bitter.

بَلِ السَّاعَةُ مَوْعِدُهُمْ وَالسَّاعَةُ أَدْهَىٰ وَأَمَرُّ ٤٦

47. Verily, the *Mujrimûn* (polytheists, disbelievers, sinners, criminals) are in error (in this world) and will burn (in the Hell-fire in the Hereafter).

إِنَّ الْمُجْرِمِينَ فِي ضَلَالٍ وَسُعُرٍ ٤٧

48. The Day they will be dragged on their faces into the Fire (it will be said to them): "Taste you the touch of Hell!"[1]

يَوْمَ يُسْحَبُونَ فِي النَّارِ عَلَىٰ وُجُوهِهِمْ ذُوقُوا مَسَّ سَقَرَ ٤٨

49. Verily, We have created all things with *Qadar* (Divine Preordainments of all things before their creation as written in the Book of Decrees — *Al-Lauh Al-Mahfûz*).

إِنَّا كُلَّ شَيْءٍ خَلَقْنَاهُ بِقَدَرٍ ٤٩

50. And Our Commandment is but one as the twinkling of an eye.

وَمَا أَمْرُنَا إِلَّا وَاحِدَةٌ كَلَمْحٍ بِالْبَصَرِ ٥٠

51. And indeed, We have destroyed your likes; then is there any that will remember (or receive admonition)?

وَلَقَدْ أَهْلَكْنَا أَشْيَاعَكُمْ فَهَلْ مِنْ مُدَّكِرٍ ٥١

52. And everything they have done is noted in (their) Records (of deeds).

وَكُلُّ شَيْءٍ فَعَلُوهُ فِي الزُّبُرِ ٥٢

53. And everything, small and big, is written down (in *Al-Lauh Al-Mahfûz* already beforehand i.e. before it befalls, or is done by its doer: الإيمان بالقدر) (See the Qur'ân V.57:22 and its footnote).

وَكُلُّ صَغِيرٍ وَكَبِيرٍ مُسْتَطَرٌ ٥٣

---

[1] (V.54:48) See (V.25:34) and the footnote of (V.17:97).

54. Verily, the *Muttaqûn* (the pious. See V.2:2), will be in the midst of Gardens and Rivers (Paradise).

إِنَّ ٱلْمُتَّقِينَ فِي جَنَّتٍ وَنَهَرٍ ۝

55. In a seat of truth (i.e. Paradise), near the Omnipotent King (Allâh, the One, the All-Blessed, the Most High, the Owner of Majesty and Honour).

فِى مَقْعَدِ صِدْقٍ عِندَ ۝

مَلِيكٍ مُّقْتَدِرٍ ۝

Sûrat Ar-Rahmân
(The Most Gracious) LV

سورة الرحمن

*In the Name of Allâh
the Most Gracious, the Most Merciful*

بِسْمِ ٱللَّهِ ٱلرَّحْمَنِ ٱلرَّحِيمِ

1. The Most Gracious (Allâh)!

ٱلرَّحْمَنُ ۝

2. He has taught (you mankind) the Qur'ân (by His Mercy).

عَلَّمَ ٱلْقُرْءَانَ ۝

3. He created man.

خَلَقَ ٱلْإِنسَنَ ۝

4. He taught him eloquent speech.

عَلَّمَهُ ٱلْبَيَانَ ۝

5. The sun and the moon run on their fixed courses (exactly) calculated with measured out stages for each (for reckoning).

ٱلشَّمْسُ وَٱلْقَمَرُ بِحُسْبَانٍ ۝

6. And the herbs (or stars) and the trees both prostrate themselves (to Allâh — See V.22:18). [Tafsîr Ibn Kathîr]

وَٱلنَّجْمُ وَٱلشَّجَرُ يَسْجُدَانِ ۝

7. And the heaven: He has raised it high, and He has set up the Balance.

وَٱلسَّمَآءَ رَفَعَهَا وَوَضَعَ ٱلْمِيزَانَ ۝

8. In order that you may not transgress (due) balance.

أَلَّا تَطْغَوْا فِى ٱلْمِيزَانِ ۝

9. And observe the weight with equity and do not make the balance deficient.

وَأَقِيمُوا ٱلْوَزْنَ بِٱلْقِسْطِ وَلَا تُخْسِرُوا ٱلْمِيزَانَ ۝

10. And the earth: He has put down (laid) for the creatures.

وَٱلْأَرْضَ وَضَعَهَا لِلْأَنَامِ ۝

11. Therein are fruits, date-palms producing sheathed fruit-stalks (enclosing dates).

فِيهَا فَكِهَةٌ وَالنَّخْلُ ذَاتُ الْأَكْمَامِ ۝

12. And also corn, with (its) leaves and stalk for fodder, and sweet-scented plants.

وَالْحَبُّ ذُو الْعَصْفِ وَالرَّيْحَانُ ۝

13. Then which of the Blessings of your Lord will you both (jinn and men) deny?

فَبِأَيِّ آلَاءِ رَبِّكُمَا تُكَذِّبَانِ ۝

14. He created man (Adam) from sounding clay like the clay of pottery.

خَلَقَ الْإِنْسَانَ مِن صَلْصَالٍ كَالْفَخَّارِ ۝

15. And the jinn: He created from a smokeless flame of fire.

وَخَلَقَ الْجَانَّ مِن مَّارِجٍ مِّن نَّارٍ ۝

16. Then which of the Blessings of your Lord will you both (jinn and men) deny?

فَبِأَيِّ آلَاءِ رَبِّكُمَا تُكَذِّبَانِ ۝

17. (He is) the Lord of the two easts (places of sunrise during early summer and early winter) and the Lord of the two wests (places of sunset during early summer and early winter).

رَبُّ الْمَشْرِقَيْنِ وَرَبُّ الْمَغْرِبَيْنِ ۝

18. Then which of the Blessings of your Lord will you both (jinn and men) deny?

فَبِأَيِّ آلَاءِ رَبِّكُمَا تُكَذِّبَانِ ۝

19. He has let loose the two seas (the salt and fresh water) meeting together.

مَرَجَ الْبَحْرَيْنِ يَلْتَقِيَانِ ۝

20. Between them is a barrier which none of them can transgress.

بَيْنَهُمَا بَرْزَخٌ لَّا يَبْغِيَانِ ۝

21. Then which of the Blessings of your Lord will you both (jinn and men) deny?

فَبِأَيِّ آلَاءِ رَبِّكُمَا تُكَذِّبَانِ ۝

22. Out of them both come out pearl and coral.

يَخْرُجُ مِنْهُمَا اللُّؤْلُؤُ وَالْمَرْجَانُ ۝

23. Then which of the Blessings of your Lord will you both (jinn and men) deny?

فَبِأَيِّ ءَالَآءِ رَبِّكُمَا تُكَذِّبَانِ ۝

24. And His are the ships going and coming in the seas, like mountains.

وَلَهُ الْجَوَارِ الْمُنشَئَاتُ فِي الْبَحْرِ كَالْأَعْلَامِ ۝

25. Then which of the Blessings of your Lord will you both (jinn and men) deny?

فَبِأَيِّ ءَالَآءِ رَبِّكُمَا تُكَذِّبَانِ ۝

26. Whatsoever is on it (the earth) will perish.

كُلُّ مَنْ عَلَيْهَا فَانٍ ۝

27. And the Face of your Lord full of Majesty and Honour will remain forever.

وَيَبْقَى وَجْهُ رَبِّكَ ذُو الْجَلَالِ وَالْإِكْرَامِ ۝

28. Then which of the Blessings of your Lord will you both (jinn and men) deny?

فَبِأَيِّ ءَالَآءِ رَبِّكُمَا تُكَذِّبَانِ ۝

29. Whosoever is in the heavens and on earth begs of Him (its needs from Him). Every day He is (engaged) in some affair (such as giving honour or disgrace to some, life or death to some)!

يَسْأَلُهُ مَن فِي السَّمَوَاتِ وَالْأَرْضِ كُلَّ يَوْمٍ هُوَ فِي شَأْنٍ ۝

30. Then which of the Blessings of your Lord will you both (jinn and men) deny?

فَبِأَيِّ ءَالَآءِ رَبِّكُمَا تُكَذِّبَانِ ۝

31. We shall attend to you, O you two classes (jinn and men)!

سَنَفْرُغُ لَكُمْ أَيُّهَ الثَّقَلَانِ ۝

32. Then which of the Blessings of your Lord will you both (jinn and men) deny?

فَبِأَيِّ ءَالَآءِ رَبِّكُمَا تُكَذِّبَانِ ۝

33. O assembly of jinn and men! If you have power to pass beyond the zones of the heavens and the earth, then pass beyond (them)! But you will never be able to pass them, except with authority (from Allâh)!

يَا مَعْشَرَ الْجِنِّ وَالْإِنسِ إِنِ اسْتَطَعْتُمْ أَن تَنفُذُوا مِنْ أَقْطَارِ السَّمَوَاتِ وَالْأَرْضِ فَانفُذُوا لَا تَنفُذُونَ إِلَّا بِسُلْطَانٍ ۝

34. Then which of the Blessings of your Lord will you both (jinn and men) deny?

فَبِأَيِّ ءَالَآءِ رَبِّكُمَا تُكَذِّبَانِ ۝

35. There will be sent against you both, smokeless flames of fire and (molten) brass, and you will not be able to defend yourselves.

يُرْسَلُ عَلَيْكُمَا شُوَاظٌ مِّن نَّارٍ وَنُحَاسٌ فَلَا تَنتَصِرَانِ ۝

36. Then which of the Blessings of your Lord will you both (jinn and men) deny?

فَبِأَيِّ ءَالَآءِ رَبِّكُمَا تُكَذِّبَانِ ۝

37. Then when the heaven is rent asunder, and it becomes rosy or red like red-oil, or red hide — [See V.70:8]

فَإِذَا انشَقَّتِ السَّمَاءُ فَكَانَتْ وَرْدَةً كَالدِّهَانِ ۝

38. Then which of the Blessings of your Lord will you both (jinn and men) deny?

فَبِأَيِّ ءَالَآءِ رَبِّكُمَا تُكَذِّبَانِ ۝

39. So on that Day no question will be asked of man or jinn as to his sin, (because they have already been known from their faces either white (dwellers of Paradise — true believers of Islamic Monotheism) or black (dwellers of Hell — polytheists; disbelievers, criminals).

فَيَوْمَئِذٍ لَّا يُسْـَٔلُ عَن ذَنبِهِۦٓ إِنسٌ وَلَا جَانٌّ ۝

40. Then which of the Blessings of your Lord will you both (jinn and men) deny?

فَبِأَيِّ ءَالَآءِ رَبِّكُمَا تُكَذِّبَانِ ۝

41. The *Mujrimûn* (polytheists, criminals, sinners) will be known by their marks (black faces), and they will be seized by their forelocks and their feet.

يُعْرَفُ الْمُجْرِمُونَ بِسِيمَٰهُمْ فَيُؤْخَذُ بِالنَّوَاصِي وَالْأَقْدَامِ ۝

42. Then which of the Blessings of your Lord will you both (jinn and men) deny?

فَبِأَيِّ ءَالَآءِ رَبِّكُمَا تُكَذِّبَانِ ۝

43. This is the Hell which the *Mujrimûn* (polytheists, criminals, sinners) denied.

هَٰذِهِۦ جَهَنَّمُ الَّتِى يُكَذِّبُ بِهَا الْمُجْرِمُونَ ۝

44. They will go between it (Hell) and the fierce boiling water!

يَطُوفُونَ بَيْنَهَا وَبَيْنَ حَمِيمٍ ءَانٍ ۞

45. Then which of the Blessings of your Lord will you both (jinn and men) deny?

فَبِأَىِّ ءَالَاءِ رَبِّكُمَا تُكَذِّبَانِ ۞

46. But for him who[1] fears the standing before his Lord, there will be two Gardens (i.e. in Paradise).

وَلِمَنْ خَافَ مَقَامَ رَبِّهِۦ جَنَّتَانِ ۞

47. Then which of the Blessings of your Lord will you both (jinn and men) deny?

فَبِأَىِّ ءَالَاءِ رَبِّكُمَا تُكَذِّبَانِ ۞

48. With spreading branches.

ذَوَاتَا أَفْنَانٍ ۞

49. Then which of the Blessings of your Lord will you both (jinn and men) deny?

فَبِأَىِّ ءَالَاءِ رَبِّكُمَا تُكَذِّبَانِ ۞

50. In them (both) will be two springs flowing (free).

فِيهِمَا عَيْنَانِ تَجْرِيَانِ ۞

51. Then which of the Blessings of your Lord will you both (jinn and men) deny?

فَبِأَىِّ ءَالَاءِ رَبِّكُمَا تُكَذِّبَانِ ۞

52. In them (both) will be every kind of fruit in pairs.

فِيهِمَا مِن كُلِّ فَٰكِهَةٍ زَوْجَانِ ۞

53. Then which of the Blessings of your Lord will you both (jinn and men) deny?

فَبِأَىِّ ءَالَاءِ رَبِّكُمَا تُكَذِّبَانِ ۞

54. Reclining upon the couches lined with silk brocade, and the fruits of the two Gardens will be near at hand.

مُتَّكِئِينَ عَلَىٰ فُرُشٍ بَطَائِنُهَا مِنْ إِسْتَبْرَقٍ وَجَنَى ٱلْجَنَّتَيْنِ دَانٍ ۞

---

[1] (V.55:46)

a) For him who: the true believer of Islâmic Monotheism who performs all the duties ordained by Allâh and His Messenger Muhammad صلى الله عليه وسلم, and abstain from all kinds of sin and evil deeds prohibited in Islâm.

b) See the footnote of (V.23:60)

55. Then which of the Blessings of your Lord will you both (jinn and men) deny?

فَبِأَىِّ ءَالَآءِ رَبِّكُمَا تُكَذِّبَانِ ۝

.56. Wherein both will be *Qâsirât-ut-Tarf* [chaste females (wives) restraining their glances, desiring none except their husbands], with whom no man or jinni has had *Tamth*[11] before them.

فِيهِنَّ قَصِرَتُ ٱلطَّرْفِ لَمْ يَطْمِثْهُنَّ إِنسٌ قَبْلَهُمْ وَلَا جَآنٌّ ۝

57. Then which of the Blessings of your Lord will you both (jinn and men) deny?

فَبِأَىِّ ءَالَآءِ رَبِّكُمَا تُكَذِّبَانِ ۝

58. (In beauty) they are like rubies and coral.

كَأَنَّهُنَّ ٱلْيَاقُوتُ وَٱلْمَرْجَانُ ۝

59. Then which of the Blessings of your Lord will you both (jinn and men) deny?

فَبِأَىِّ ءَالَآءِ رَبِّكُمَا تُكَذِّبَانِ ۝

60. Is there any reward for good other than good?

هَلْ جَزَآءُ ٱلْإِحْسَـٰنِ ۝

61. Then which of the Blessings of your Lord will you both (jinn and men) deny?

إِلَّا ٱلْإِحْسَـٰنُ ۝ فَبِأَىِّ ءَالَآءِ رَبِّكُمَا تُكَذِّبَانِ ۝

62. And besides these two, there are two other Gardens (i.e. in Paradise).

وَمِن دُونِهِمَا جَنَّتَانِ ۝

63. Then which of the Blessings of your Lord will you both (jinn and men) deny?

فَبِأَىِّ ءَالَآءِ رَبِّكُمَا تُكَذِّبَانِ ۝

64. Dark green (in colour).

مُدْهَآمَّتَانِ ۝

65. Then which of the Blessings of your Lord will you both (jinn and men) deny?

فَبِأَىِّ ءَالَآءِ رَبِّكُمَا تُكَذِّبَانِ ۝

---

[11] (V.55:56) *Tamth* means: Opening their hymens with sexual intercourse.

66. In them (both) will be two springs gushing forth. فِيهِمَا عَيۡنَانِ نَضَّاخَتَانِ ۝

67. Then which of the Blessings of your Lord will you both (jinn and men) deny? فَبِأَىِّ ءَالَآءِ رَبِّكُمَا تُكَذِّبَانِ ۝

68. In them (both) will be fruits, and date-palms and pomegranates. فِيهِمَا فَٰكِهَةٌ وَنَخۡلٌ وَرُمَّانٌ ۝

69. Then which of the Blessings of your Lord will you both (jinn and men) deny? فَبِأَىِّ ءَالَآءِ رَبِّكُمَا تُكَذِّبَانِ ۝

70. Therein (Gardens) will be *Khairâtun-Hisân* [fair (wives) good and beautiful]; فِيهِنَّ خَيۡرَٰتٌ حِسَانٌ ۝

71. Then which of the Blessings of your Lord will you both (jinn and men) deny? فَبِأَىِّ ءَالَآءِ رَبِّكُمَا تُكَذِّبَانِ ۝

72. *Hûr*[1] (beautiful, fair females) guarded in pavilions; حُورٌ مَّقۡصُورَٰتٌ فِى الۡخِيَامِ ۝

73. Then which of the Blessings of your Lord will you both (jinn and men) deny? فَبِأَىِّ ءَالَآءِ رَبِّكُمَا تُكَذِّبَانِ ۝

74. With whom no man or jinni has had *Tamth*[2] before them. لَمۡ يَطۡمِثۡهُنَّ إِنسٌ قَبۡلَهُمۡ وَلَا جَانٌّ ۝

75. Then which of the Blessings of your Lord will you both (jinn and men) deny? فَبِأَىِّ ءَالَآءِ رَبِّكُمَا تُكَذِّبَانِ ۝

76. Reclining on green cushions and rich beautiful mattresses. مُتَّكِئِينَ عَلَىٰ رَفۡرَفٍ خُضۡرٍ وَعَبۡقَرِىٍّ حِسَانٍ ۝

---

[1] (V.55:72) See footnote of (V.52:20).

[2] (V.55:74) *Tamth* means: Opening their hymens with sexual intercourse.

77. Then which of the Blessings of your Lord will you both (jinn and men) deny?

فَبِأَيِّ ءَالَآءِ رَبِّكُمَا تُكَذِّبَانِ ۝

78. Blessed is the Name of your Lord (Allâh), the Owner of Majesty and Honour.

تَبَـٰرَكَ ٱسۡمُ رَبِّكَ ذِي ٱلۡجَلَـٰلِ وَٱلۡإِكۡرَامِ ۝

Sûrat Al-Wâqi'ah
(The Event) LVI

سُورَةُ الْوَاقِعَةِ

*In the Name of Allâh
the Most Gracious, the Most Merciful*

بِسۡمِ ٱللَّهِ ٱلرَّحۡمَـٰنِ ٱلرَّحِيمِ

1. When the Event (i.e. the Day of Resurrection) befalls —

إِذَا وَقَعَتِ ٱلۡوَاقِعَةُ ۝

2. And there can be no denial of its befalling —

لَيۡسَ لِوَقۡعَتِهَا كَاذِبَةٌ ۝

3. Bringing low (some — those who will enter Hell) exalting (others — those who will enter Paradise). [*Tafsir Ibn Kathir*]

خَافِضَةٌ رَّافِعَةٌ ۝

4. When the earth will be shaken with a terrible shake.

إِذَا رُجَّتِ ٱلۡأَرۡضُ رَجًّا ۝

5. And the mountains will be powdered to dust,

وَبُسَّتِ ٱلۡجِبَالُ بَسًّا ۝

6. So that they will become floating dust particles.

فَكَانَتۡ هَبَآءً مُّنۢبَثًّا ۝

7. And you (all) will be in three groups.

وَكُنتُمۡ أَزۡوَٰجًا ثَلَـٰثَةً ۝

8. So those on the Right Hand (i.e. those who will be given their Records in their right hands) — how (fortunate) will be those on the Right Hand! (As a respect for them, because they will enter Paradise).

فَأَصۡحَـٰبُ ٱلۡمَيۡمَنَةِ مَآ أَصۡحَـٰبُ ٱلۡمَيۡمَنَةِ ۝

9. And those on the Left Hand (i.e. those who will be given their Record in

وَأَصۡحَـٰبُ ٱلۡمَشۡـَٔمَةِ مَآ أَصۡحَـٰبُ

their left hands) — how (unfortunate) will be those on the Left Hand! (As a disgrace for them, because they will enter Hell).

ٱلْمَشْئَمَةِ ۝

10. And those foremost [(in Islâmic Faith of Monotheism and in performing righteous deeds) in the life of this world on the very first call for to embrace Islâm] will be foremost (in Paradise).

وَٱلسَّٰبِقُونَ ٱلسَّٰبِقُونَ ۝

11. These will be the nearest (to Allâh).

أُوْلَٰٓئِكَ ٱلْمُقَرَّبُونَ ۝

12. In the Gardens of Delight (Paradise).

فِى جَنَّٰتِ ٱلنَّعِيمِ ۝

13. A multitude of those (foremost) will be from the first generations (who embraced Islâm).

ثُلَّةٌ مِّنَ ٱلْأَوَّلِينَ ۝

14. And a few of those (foremost) will be from the later generations.

وَقَلِيلٌ مِّنَ ٱلْءَاخِرِينَ ۝

15. (They will be) on thrones woven with gold and precious stones.

عَلَىٰ سُرُرٍ مَّوْضُونَةٍ ۝

16. Reclining thereon, face to face.

مُّتَّكِئِينَ عَلَيْهَا مُتَقَٰبِلِينَ ۝

17. Immortal boys will go around them (serving),

يَطُوفُ عَلَيْهِمْ وِلْدَٰنٌ مُّخَلَّدُونَ ۝

18. With cups, and jugs, and a glass of flowing wine,

بِأَكْوَابٍ وَأَبَارِيقَ وَكَأْسٍ مِّن مَّعِينٍ ۝

19. Wherefrom they will get neither any aching of the head, nor any intoxication.

لَّا يُصَدَّعُونَ عَنْهَا وَلَا يُنزِفُونَ ۝

20. And with fruit that they may choose.

وَفَٰكِهَةٍ مِّمَّا يَتَخَيَّرُونَ ۝

21. And with the flesh of fowls that they desire.

وَلَحْمِ طَيْرٍ مِّمَّا يَشْتَهُونَ ۝

22. And (there will be) *Hûr* (fair females) with wide, lovely eyes (as wives for the pious),

وَحُورٌ عِينٌ ۝

23. Like unto preserved pearls.

كَأَمْثَلِ ٱللُّؤْلُؤِ ٱلْمَكْنُونِ ۝

24. A reward for what they used to do.

جَزَآءً بِمَا كَانُوا۟ يَعْمَلُونَ ۝

25. No *Laghw* (dirty, false, evil vain talk) will they hear therein, nor any sinful speech (like backbiting).

لَا يَسْمَعُونَ فِيهَا لَغْوًا وَلَا تَأْثِيمًا ۝

26. But only the saying of: *Salâm! Salâm!* (greetings with peace)[1]

إِلَّا قِيلًا سَلَـٰمًا سَلَـٰمًا ۝

27. And those on the Right Hand — how (fortunate) will be those on the Right Hand?

وَأَصْحَـٰبُ ٱلْيَمِينِ مَآ أَصْحَـٰبُ ٱلْيَمِينِ ۝

28. (They will be) among thornless lote-trees,

فِى سِدْرٍ مَّخْضُودٍ ۝

29. And among *Talh* (banana-trees) with fruits piled one above another,

وَطَلْحٍ مَّنضُودٍ ۝

30. And in shade long-extended,

وَظِلٍّ مَّمْدُودٍ ۝

31. And by water flowing constantly,

وَمَآءٍ مَّسْكُوبٍ ۝

32. And fruit in plenty,

وَفَـٰكِهَةٍ كَثِيرَةٍ ۝

33. Whose supply is not cut off (by change of season) nor are they out of reach.

لَّا مَقْطُوعَةٍ وَلَا مَمْنُوعَةٍ ۝

34. And on couches or thrones, raised high.

وَفُرُشٍ مَّرْفُوعَةٍ ۝

35. Verily, We have created them (maidens) of special creation.

إِنَّآ أَنشَأْنَـٰهُنَّ إِنشَآءً ۝

36. And made them virgins.

فَجَعَلْنَـٰهُنَّ أَبْكَارًا ۝

37. Loving (their husbands only), (and) of equal age.

عُرُبًا أَتْرَابًا ۝

38. For those on the Right Hand.

لِّأَصْحَـٰبِ ٱلْيَمِينِ ۝

39. A multitude of those (on the Right Hand) will be from the first generation (who embraced Islâm).

ثُلَّةٌ مِّنَ ٱلْأَوَّلِينَ ۝

---

[1] (V.56:26) See the footnote (A) of (V.29:64).

40. And a multitude of those (on the Right Hand) will be from the later generations.

وَثُلَّةٌ مِّنَ الْآخِرِينَ ۝

41. And those on the Left Hand — how (unfortunate) will be those on the Left Hand?

وَأَصْحَابُ الشِّمَالِ مَا أَصْحَابُ الشِّمَالِ ۝

42. In fierce hot wind and boiling water,

فِي سَمُومٍ وَحَمِيمٍ ۝

43. And shadow of black smoke,

وَظِلٍّ مِّن يَحْمُومٍ ۝

44. (That shadow) neither cool, nor (even) pleasant.

لَّا بَارِدٍ وَلَا كَرِيمٍ ۝

45. Verily, before that, they indulged in luxury,

إِنَّهُمْ كَانُوا قَبْلَ ذَٰلِكَ مُتْرَفِينَ ۝

46. And were persisting in great sin (joining partners in worship along with Allâh, committing murder and other crimes)[1]

وَكَانُوا يُصِرُّونَ عَلَى الْحِنثِ الْعَظِيمِ ۝

47. And they used to say: "When we die and become dust and bones, shall we then indeed be resurrected?

وَكَانُوا يَقُولُونَ أَئِذَا مِتْنَا وَكُنَّا تُرَابًا وَعِظَامًا أَءِنَّا لَمَبْعُوثُونَ ۝

48. "And also our forefathers?"

أَوَآبَاؤُنَا الْأَوَّلُونَ ۝

49. Say (O Muhammad صلى الله عليه وسلم): "(Yes) verily, those of old, and those of later times.

قُلْ إِنَّ الْأَوَّلِينَ وَالْآخِرِينَ ۝

50. "All will surely, be gathered together for appointed Meeting of a known Day.

لَمَجْمُوعُونَ إِلَىٰ مِيقَاتِ يَوْمٍ مَّعْلُومٍ ۝

51. "Then moreover, verily, you the erring-ones, the deniers (of Resurrection)!

ثُمَّ إِنَّكُمْ أَيُّهَا الضَّالُّونَ الْمُكَذِّبُونَ ۝

52. "You verily, will eat of the trees of Zaqqûm.

لَآكِلُونَ مِن شَجَرٍ مِّن زَقُّومٍ ۝

---

[1] (V.56:46) See the footnote (B) of (V.3:130).

53. "Then you will fill your bellies therewith,

قَالِرُونَ مِنْهَا ٱلْبُطُونَ ﴿٥٣﴾

54. "And drink boiling water on top of it.

فَشَٰرِبُونَ عَلَيْهِ مِنَ ٱلْحَمِيمِ ﴿٥٤﴾

55. "And you will drink (that) like thirsty camels!"

فَشَٰرِبُونَ شُرْبَ ٱلْهِيمِ ﴿٥٥﴾

56. That will be their entertainment on the Day of Recompense!

هَٰذَا نُزُلُهُمْ يَوْمَ ٱلدِّينِ ﴿٥٦﴾

57. We created you: then why do you believe not?

نَحْنُ خَلَقْنَٰكُمْ فَلَوْلَا تُصَدِّقُونَ ﴿٥٧﴾

58. Then tell Me (about) the (human) semen that you emit.

أَفَرَءَيْتُم مَّا تُمْنُونَ ﴿٥٨﴾

59. Is it you who create it (i.e. make this semen into a perfect human being), or are We the Creator?

ءَأَنتُمْ تَخْلُقُونَهُۥٓ أَمْ نَحْنُ ٱلْخَٰلِقُونَ ﴿٥٩﴾

60. We have decreed death to you all, and We are not outstripped,

نَحْنُ قَدَّرْنَا بَيْنَكُمُ ٱلْمَوْتَ وَمَا نَحْنُ بِمَسْبُوقِينَ ﴿٦٠﴾

61. To transfigure you and create you in (forms) that you know not.

عَلَىٰٓ أَن نُّبَدِّلَ أَمْثَٰلَكُمْ وَنُنشِئَكُمْ فِى مَا لَا تَعْلَمُونَ ﴿٦١﴾

62. And indeed, you have already known the first form of creation (i.e. the creation of Adam): why then do you not remember (or take heed)?

وَلَقَدْ عَلِمْتُمُ ٱلنَّشْأَةَ ٱلْأُولَىٰ فَلَوْلَا تَذَكَّرُونَ ﴿٦٢﴾

63. Then tell Me about the seed that you sow in the ground.

أَفَرَءَيْتُم مَّا تَحْرُثُونَ ﴿٦٣﴾

64. Is it you that make it grow, or are We the Grower?

ءَأَنتُمْ تَزْرَعُونَهُۥٓ أَمْ نَحْنُ ٱلزَّٰرِعُونَ ﴿٦٤﴾

65. Were it Our Will, We could crumble it to dry pieces, and you would be regretful (or left in wonderment). [*Tafsir Ibn Kathîr*]

لَوْ نَشَآءُ لَجَعَلْنَٰهُ حُطَٰمًا فَظَلْتُمْ تَفَكَّهُونَ ﴿٦٥﴾

66. (Saying): "We are indeed *Mughramûn* (i.e. ruined or have lost the money without any profit, or punished

إِنَّا لَمُغْرَمُونَ ﴿٦٦﴾

by the loss of all that we spend for cultivation)! [See *Tafsir Al-Qurtubî*]

67. "Nay, but we are deprived!"

بَلْ نَحْنُ مَحْرُومُونَ ۝

68. Then tell Me about the water that you drink.

أَفَرَءَيْتُمُ الْمَآءَ الَّذِى تَشْرَبُونَ ۝

69. Is it you who cause it from the rain-clouds to come down, or are We the Causer of it to come down?

ءَأَنتُمْ أَنزَلْتُمُوهُ مِنَ الْمُزْنِ أَمْ نَحْنُ الْمُنزِلُونَ ۝

70. If We willed, We verily, could make it salt (and undrinkable): why then do you not give thanks (to Allâh)?

لَوْ نَشَآءُ جَعَلْنَـٰهُ أُجَاجًا فَلَوْلَا تَشْكُرُونَ ۝

71. Then tell Me about the fire which you kindle.

أَفَرَءَيْتُمُ النَّارَ الَّتِى تُورُونَ ۝

72. Is it you who made the tree thereof to grow, or are We the Grower?

ءَأَنتُمْ أَنشَأْتُمْ شَجَرَتَهَآ أَمْ نَحْنُ الْمُنشِئُونَ ۝

73. We have made it a Reminder (of the Hell-fire in the Hereafter), and an article of use for the travellers (and all the others, in this world).

نَحْنُ جَعَلْنَـٰهَا تَذْكِرَةً وَمَتَـٰعًا لِّلْمُقْوِينَ ۝

74. Then glorify with praises the Name of your Lord, the Most Great.

فَسَبِّحْ بِاسْمِ رَبِّكَ الْعَظِيمِ ۝

75. So I swear by the setting of the stars.[1]

فَلَآ أُقْسِمُ ۝

76. And verily, that is indeed a great oath, if you but know.

بِمَوَٰقِعِ النُّجُومِ ۝
وَإِنَّهُ لَقَسَمٌ لَّوْ تَعْلَمُونَ ۝

77. That (this) is indeed an honourable recitation (the Noble Qur'ân).

عَظِيمٌ ۝
إِنَّهُ لَقُرْءَانٌ كَرِيمٌ ۝

78. In a Book well-guarded (with Allâh in the heaven i.e. *Al-Lauh Al-Mahfûz*).

فِى كِتَـٰبٍ مَّكْنُونٍ ۝

---

[1] (V.56:75) In Arabic *Mawâqi'i An-Nujûm*: This word has many interpretations, it may mean the setting or the rising (or the mansions) of the stars, or the Qur'ân and its gradual revelation in stages. Please see *Tafsir At-Tabari* for detail.

79. Which (that Book with Allâh) none can touch but the purified (i.e. the angels).

لَا يَمَسُّهُ إِلَّا ٱلْمُطَهَّرُونَ ٧٩

80. A Revelation (this Qur'ân) from the Lord of the 'Âlamîn (mankind, jinn and all that exists).

تَنزِيلٌ مِّن رَّبِّ ٱلْعَٰلَمِينَ ٨٠

81. Is it such a talk (this Qur'ân) that you (disbelievers) deny?

أَفَبِهَٰذَا ٱلْحَدِيثِ أَنتُم مُّدْهِنُونَ ٨١

82. And instead (of thanking Allâh) for the provision He gives you, you deny (Him by disbelief)!

وَتَجْعَلُونَ رِزْقَكُمْ أَنَّكُمْ تُكَذِّبُونَ ٨٢

83. Then why do you not (intervene) when (the soul of a dying person) reaches the throat?

فَلَوْلَا إِذَا بَلَغَتِ ٱلْحُلْقُومَ ٨٣

84. And you at the moment are looking on,

وَأَنتُمْ حِينَئِذٍ تَنظُرُونَ ٨٤

85. But We (i.e. Our angels who take the soul) are nearer to him than you, but you see not, [Tafsir At-Tabarî]

وَنَحْنُ أَقْرَبُ إِلَيْهِ مِنكُمْ وَلَٰكِن لَّا تُبْصِرُونَ ٨٥

86. Then why do you not — if you are exempt from the reckoning and recompense (punishment) —

فَلَوْلَا إِن كُنتُمْ غَيْرَ مَدِينِينَ ٨٦

87. Bring back the soul (to its body), if you are truthful?

تَرْجِعُونَهَا إِن كُنتُمْ صَٰدِقِينَ ٨٧

88. Then, if he (the dying person) be of the Muqarrabûn (those brought near to Allâh),

فَأَمَّا إِن كَانَ مِنَ ٱلْمُقَرَّبِينَ ٨٨

89. (There is for him) rest and provision, and a Garden of Delights (Paradise).

فَرَوْحٌ وَرَيْحَانٌ وَجَنَّتُ نَعِيمٍ ٨٩

90. And if he (the dying person) be of those on the Right Hand,

وَأَمَّا إِن كَانَ مِنْ أَصْحَٰبِ ٱلْيَمِينِ ٩٠

91. Then there is safety and peace (from the punishment of Allâh) for those on the Right Hand.

فَسَلَٰمٌ لَّكَ مِنْ أَصْحَٰبِ ٱلْيَمِينِ ٩١

92. But if he (the dying person) be of the denying (of the Resurrection), the

وَأَمَّا إِن كَانَ مِنَ ٱلْمُكَذِّبِينَ

erring (away from the Right Path of Islâmic Monotheism),

93. Then for him is an entertainment with boiling water.

94. And burning in Hell-fire.

95. Verily, this! This is an absolute Truth with certainty.

96. So glorify with praises the Name of your Lord, the Most Great.

Sûrat Al-Hadîd
(Iron) LVII

*In the Name of Allâh
the Most Gracious, the Most Merciful*

1. Whatsoever is in the heavens and the earth glorifies Allâh — and He is the All-Mighty, All-Wise.

2. His is the kingdom of the heavens and the earth. It is He Who gives life and causes death: and He is Able to do all things.

3. He is the First (nothing is before Him) and the Last (nothing is after Him), the Most High (nothing is above Him) and the Most Near (nothing is nearer than Him). And He is the All-Knower of every thing.

4. He it is Who created the heavens and the earth in six Days and then rose over (*Istawâ*) the Throne (in a manner that suits His Majesty). He knows what goes into the earth and what comes forth from it, and what descends from the heaven and what ascends thereto. And He is with you (by His Knowledge) wheresoever you may be. And Allâh is the All-Seer of what you do.

5. His is the kingdom of the heavens and the earth. And to Allâh return all the matters (for decision).

أَلَهُ مُلْكُ ٱلسَّمَٰوَٰتِ وَٱلْأَرْضِ وَإِلَى ٱللَّهِ تُرْجَعُ ٱلْأُمُورُ ٥

6. He merges night into day (i.e. the decrease in the hours of the night is added into the hours of the day), and merges day into night (i.e. the decrease in the hours of the day is added into the hours of the night), and He has full knowledge of whatsoever is in the breasts.

يُولِجُ ٱلَّيْلَ فِى ٱلنَّهَارِ وَيُولِجُ ٱلنَّهَارَ فِى ٱلَّيْلِ وَهُوَ عَلِيمٌ بِذَاتِ ٱلصُّدُورِ ٦

7. Believe in Allâh and His Messenger (Muhammad صلى الله عليه وسلم), and spend of that whereof He has made you trustees.[1] And such of you as believe and spend (in Allâh's Way), theirs will be a great reward.

ءَامِنُوا۟ بِٱللَّهِ وَرَسُولِهِۦ وَأَنفِقُوا۟ مِمَّا جَعَلَكُم مُّسْتَخْلَفِينَ فِيهِ فَٱلَّذِينَ ءَامَنُوا۟ مِنكُمْ وَأَنفَقُوا۟ لَهُمْ أَجْرٌ كَبِيرٌ ٧

8. And what is the matter with you that you believe not in Allâh! While the Messenger (Muhammad صلى الله عليه وسلم) invites you to believe in your Lord (Allâh); and He (Allâh) has indeed taken your covenant, if you are real believers.

وَمَا لَكُمْ لَا تُؤْمِنُونَ بِٱللَّهِ وَٱلرَّسُولُ يَدْعُوكُمْ لِتُؤْمِنُوا۟ بِرَبِّكُمْ وَقَدْ أَخَذَ مِيثَٰقَكُمْ إِن كُنتُم مُّؤْمِنِينَ ٨

9. It is He Who sends down manifest *Ayât* (proofs, evidences, verses, lessons, signs, revelations, etc.) to His slave (Muhammad صلى الله عليه وسلم) that He may bring you out from darkness into light. And verily, Allâh is to you full of kindness, Most Merciful.

هُوَ ٱلَّذِى يُنَزِّلُ عَلَىٰ عَبْدِهِۦ ءَايَٰتٍۭ بَيِّنَٰتٍ لِّيُخْرِجَكُم مِّنَ ٱلظُّلُمَٰتِ إِلَى ٱلنُّورِ وَإِنَّ ٱللَّهَ بِكُمْ لَرَءُوفٌ رَّحِيمٌ ٩

10. And what is the matter with you that you spend not in the Cause of Allâh? And to Allâh belongs the heritage of the heavens and the earth. Not equal among you are those who

وَمَا لَكُمْ أَلَّا تُنفِقُوا۟ فِى سَبِيلِ ٱللَّهِ وَلِلَّهِ مِيرَٰثُ ٱلسَّمَٰوَٰتِ وَٱلْأَرْضِ لَا يَسْتَوِى مِنكُم مَّنْ أَنفَقَ مِن قَبْلِ ٱلْفَتْحِ وَقَٰتَلَ أُو۟لَٰٓئِكَ أَعْظَمُ

---

[1] (V.57:7) See the footnote of (V.4:37).

spent and fought before the conquering (of Makkah, with those among you who did so later). Such are higher in degree than those who spent and fought afterwards. But to all Allâh has promised the best (reward). And Allâh is All-Aware of what you do.

درَجَةً مِّنَ ٱلَّذِينَ أَنفَقُواْ مِنۢ بَعْدُ وَقَٰتَلُواْ وَكُلًّا وَعَدَ ٱللَّهُ ٱلْحُسْنَىٰ وَٱللَّهُ بِمَا تَعْمَلُونَ خَبِيرٌ ١٠

11. Who is he that will lend to Allâh a goodly loan: then (Allâh) will increase it manifold to his credit (in repaying), and he will have (besides) a good reward (i.e. Paradise).

مَّن ذَا ٱلَّذِى يُقْرِضُ ٱللَّهَ قَرْضًا حَسَنًا فَيُضَٰعِفَهُۥ لَهُۥ وَلَهُۥٓ أَجْرٌ كَرِيمٌ ١١

12. On the Day you shall see the believing men and the believing women: their light running forward before them and by their right hands. Glad tidings for you this Day! Gardens under which rivers flow (Paradise), to dwell therein forever! Truly, this is the great success!

يَوْمَ تَرَى ٱلْمُؤْمِنِينَ وَٱلْمُؤْمِنَٰتِ يَسْعَىٰ نُورُهُم بَيْنَ أَيْدِيهِمْ وَبِأَيْمَٰنِهِم بُشْرَىٰكُمُ ٱلْيَوْمَ جَنَّٰتٌ تَجْرِى مِن تَحْتِهَا ٱلْأَنْهَٰرُ خَٰلِدِينَ فِيهَا ذَٰلِكَ هُوَ ٱلْفَوْزُ ٱلْعَظِيمُ ١٢

13. On the Day when the hypocrites — men and women — will say to the believers: "Wait for us! Let us get something from your light!" It will be said: "Go back to your rear! Then seek a light!" So a wall will be put up between them, with a gate therein. Inside it will be mercy, and outside it will be torment."

يَوْمَ يَقُولُ ٱلْمُنَٰفِقُونَ وَٱلْمُنَٰفِقَٰتُ لِلَّذِينَ ءَامَنُوا ٱنظُرُونَا نَقْتَبِسْ مِن نُّورِكُمْ قِيلَ ٱرْجِعُواْ وَرَآءَكُمْ فَٱلْتَمِسُواْ نُورًا فَضُرِبَ بَيْنَهُم بِسُورٍ لَّهُۥ بَابٌ بَاطِنُهُۥ فِيهِ ٱلرَّحْمَةُ وَظَٰهِرُهُۥ مِن قِبَلِهِ ٱلْعَذَابُ ١٣

14. (The hypocrites) will call the believers: "Were we not with you?" The believers will reply: "Yes! But you led yourselves into temptations, you looked forward for our destruction; you doubted (in Faith) and you were deceived by false desires, till the Command of Allâh came to pass. And

يُنَادُونَهُمْ أَلَمْ نَكُن مَّعَكُمْ قَالُواْ بَلَىٰ وَلَٰكِنَّكُمْ فَتَنتُمْ أَنفُسَكُمْ وَتَرَبَّصْتُمْ وَٱرْتَبْتُمْ وَغَرَّتْكُمُ ٱلْأَمَانِىُّ حَتَّىٰ جَآءَ أَمْرُ ٱللَّهِ وَغَرَّكُم بِٱللَّهِ ٱلْغَرُورُ ١٤

the chief deceiver (Satan) deceived you in respect of Allâh."

15. So this Day no ransom shall be taken from you (hypocrites), nor of those who disbelieved (in the Oneness of Allâh — Islâmic Monotheism). Your abode is the Fire. That is your *maulâ* (friend — proper place), and worst indeed is that destination.

فَالْيَوْمَ لَا يُؤْخَذُ مِنكُمْ فِدْيَةٌ وَلَا مِنَ الَّذِينَ كَفَرُوا مَأْوَىٰكُمُ النَّارُ هِيَ مَوْلَىٰكُمْ وَبِئْسَ الْمَصِيرُ ﴿١٥﴾

16. Has not the time come for the hearts of those who believe (in the Oneness of Allâh — Islâmic Monotheism) to be affected by Allâh's Reminder (this Qur'ân), and that which has been revealed of the truth, lest they become as those who received the Scripture [the Taurât (Torah) and the Injeel (Gospel)] before (i.e. Jews and Christians), and the term was prolonged for them and so their hearts were hardened? And many of them were *Fâsiqûn* (the rebellious, the disobedient to Allâh).

۞ أَلَمْ يَأْنِ لِلَّذِينَ ءَامَنُوا أَن تَخْشَعَ قُلُوبُهُمْ لِذِكْرِ اللَّهِ وَمَا نَزَلَ مِنَ الْحَقِّ وَلَا يَكُونُوا كَالَّذِينَ أُوتُوا الْكِتَـٰبَ مِن قَبْلُ فَطَالَ عَلَيْهِمُ الْأَمَدُ فَقَسَتْ قُلُوبُهُمْ وَكَثِيرٌ مِّنْهُمْ فَـٰسِقُونَ ﴿١٦﴾

17. Know that Allâh gives life to the earth after its death! Indeed We have made clear the *Ayât* (proofs, evidences, verses, lessons, signs, revelations, etc.) to you, if you but understand.

اعْلَمُوا أَنَّ اللَّهَ يُحْيِ الْأَرْضَ بَعْدَ مَوْتِهَا قَدْ بَيَّنَّا لَكُمُ الْآيَـٰتِ لَعَلَّكُمْ تَعْقِلُونَ ﴿١٧﴾

18. Verily, those who give *Sadaqât* (i.e. *Zakât* and alms), men and women, and lend to Allâh a goodly loan, it shall be increased manifold (to their credit), and theirs shall be an honourable good reward (i.e. Paradise).

إِنَّ الْمُصَّدِّقِينَ وَالْمُصَّدِّقَاتِ وَأَقْرَضُوا اللَّهَ قَرْضًا حَسَنًا يُضَاعَفُ لَهُمْ وَلَهُمْ أَجْرٌ كَرِيمٌ ﴿١٨﴾

19. And those who believe in (the Oneness of) Allâh and His Messengers — they are the *Siddîqûn* (i.e. those

وَالَّذِينَ ءَامَنُوا بِاللَّهِ وَرُسُلِهِ أُوْلَـٰئِكَ هُمُ الصِّدِّيقُونَ وَالشُّهَدَاءُ

followers of the Prophets who were
first and foremost to believe in them),
and the martyrs with their Lord. They
shall have their reward and their light.
But those who disbelieve (in the
Oneness of Allâh — Islâmic
Monotheism) and deny Our *Ayât*
(proofs, evidences, verses, lessons,
signs, revelations, etc.) — they shall be
the dwellers of the blazing Fire.

عِندَ رَبِّهِمْ لَهُمْ أَجْرُهُمْ وَنُورُهُمْ
وَالَّذِينَ كَفَرُوا وَكَذَّبُوا
بِـَٔايَٰتِنَآ أُوْلَٰٓئِكَ أَصْحَٰبُ
الْجَحِيمِ ﴿١٩﴾

20. Know that the life of this world is
only play and amusement, pomp and
mutual boasting among you, and rivalry
in respect of wealth and children. (It is)
as the likeness of vegetation after rain,
thereof the growth is pleasing to the
tiller; afterwards it dries up and you see
it turning yellow; then it becomes
straw. But in the Hereafter (there is) a
severe torment (for the disbelievers —
evil-doers), and (there is) Forgiveness
from Allâh and (His) Good Pleasure
(for the believers — good-doers). And
the life of this world is only a deceiving
enjoyment.

اعْلَمُوٓا أَنَّمَا الْحَيَوٰةُ الدُّنْيَا لَعِبٌ
وَلَهْوٌ وَزِينَةٌ وَتَفَاخُرٌۢ بَيْنَكُمْ
وَتَكَاثُرٌ فِى الْأَمْوَٰلِ وَالْأَوْلَٰدِ
كَمَثَلِ غَيْثٍ أَعْجَبَ الْكُفَّارَ
نَبَاتُهُۥ ثُمَّ يَهِيجُ فَتَرَىٰهُ مُصْفَرًّا
ثُمَّ يَكُونُ حُطَٰمًا وَفِى الْأَخِرَةِ
عَذَابٌ شَدِيدٌ وَمَغْفِرَةٌ مِّنَ اللَّهِ
وَرِضْوَٰنٌ وَمَا الْحَيَوٰةُ الدُّنْيَآ إِلَّا
مَتَٰعُ الْغُرُورِ ﴿٢٠﴾

21. Race with one another in hastening
towards forgiveness from your Lord
(Allâh), and Paradise the width whereof
is as the width of the heaven and the
earth, prepared for those who believe in
Allâh and His Messengers. That is the
Grace of Allâh which He bestows on
whom He is pleased with. And Allâh is
the Owner of Great Bounty.

سَابِقُوٓا إِلَىٰ مَغْفِرَةٍ مِّن رَّبِّكُمْ
وَجَنَّةٍ عَرْضُهَا كَعَرْضِ السَّمَآءِ
وَالْأَرْضِ أُعِدَّتْ لِلَّذِينَ ءَامَنُوا
بِاللَّهِ وَرُسُلِهِۦ ذَٰلِكَ فَضْلُ اللَّهِ
يُؤْتِيهِ مَن يَشَآءُ وَاللَّهُ ذُو الْفَضْلِ
الْعَظِيمِ ﴿٢١﴾

22. No calamity befalls on the earth
or in yourselves but it is inscribed in the
Book of Decrees (*Al-Lauh Al-Mahfûz*)

مَآ أَصَابَ مِن مُّصِيبَةٍ فِى الْأَرْضِ
وَلَا فِىٓ أَنفُسِكُمْ إِلَّا فِى

before We bring it into existence. Verily, that is easy for Allâh.[1]

23. In order that you may not grieve at the things over that you fail to get, nor rejoice that which has been given to you. And Allâh likes not prideful boasters.

24. Those who are misers and enjoin upon people miserliness — (Allâh is not in need of their charity). And whosoever turns away (from Faith — Allâh's Monotheism), then Allâh is Rich (Free of all needs), Worthy of all praise.

25. Indeed We have sent Our Messengers with clear proofs, and revealed with them the Scripture and the Balance (justice) that mankind may keep up justice. And We brought forth iron wherein is mighty power (in

---

[1] (V.57:22) Narrated Ibn 'Abbas رضي الله عنهما : Once I was behind the Prophet صلى الله عليه وسلم and he said: "O boy, I will teach you a few words:

(a) Be loyal and obedient to Allâh [worship Him (Alone)], remember Him always, obey His Orders. He will save you from every evil and will take care of you in all the spheres of life.

(b) Be loyal and obedient to Allâh, you will find Him near (infront of you) i.e. He will respond to your requests.

(c) If you ask, ask Allâh.

(d) If you seek help, seek help from Allâh.

(e) Know that if all the people get together in order to benefit you with something, they will not be able to benefit you in anything except what Allâh has decreed for you. And if they all get together in order to harm you with something, they will not be able to harm you in anything except what Allâh has decreed for you.

The pens have stopped writings [Divine (Allâh's) Preordainments]. And (the ink over) the papers (Book of Decrees) have dried." [This *Hadith* is quoted in *Sahih At-Tirmidhi*]

matters of war[1]), as well as many benefits for mankind, that Allâh may test who it is that will help Him (His religion) and His Messengers in the unseen. Verily, Allâh is All-Strong, All-Mighty.

26. And indeed, We sent Nûh (Noah) and Ibrâhîm (Abraham), and placed in their offspring Prophethood and Scripture. And among them there are some who are guided; but many of them are *Fâsiqûn* (rebellious, disobedient to Allâh).

27. Then, We sent after them Our Messengers, and We sent 'Îsâ (Jesus) - son of Maryam (Mary), and gave him the Injeel (Gospel). And We ordained in the hearts of those who followed him, compassion and mercy. But the monasticism which they invented for themselves, We did not prescribe for them, but (they sought it) only to please Allâh therewith, but that they did not observe it with the right observance. So

بَأْسٌ شَدِيدٌ وَمَنَـٰفِعُ لِلنَّاسِ وَلِيَعْلَمَ ٱللَّهُ مَن يَنصُرُهُۥ وَرُسُلَهُۥ بِٱلْغَيْبِ إِنَّ ٱللَّهَ قَوِيٌّ عَزِيزٌ ۝

وَلَقَدْ أَرْسَلْنَا نُوحًا وَإِبْرَٰهِيمَ وَجَعَلْنَا فِى ذُرِّيَّتِهِمَا ٱلنُّبُوَّةَ وَٱلْكِتَـٰبَ فَمِنْهُم مُّهْتَدٍ وَكَثِيرٌ مِّنْهُمْ فَـٰسِقُونَ ۝

ثُمَّ قَفَّيْنَا عَلَىٰٓ ءَاثَـٰرِهِم بِرُسُلِنَا وَقَفَّيْنَا بِعِيسَى ٱبْنِ مَرْيَمَ وَءَاتَيْنَـٰهُ ٱلْإِنجِيلَ وَجَعَلْنَا فِى قُلُوبِ ٱلَّذِينَ ٱتَّبَعُوهُ رَأْفَةً وَرَحْمَةً وَرَهْبَانِيَّةً ٱبْتَدَعُوهَا مَا كَتَبْنَـٰهَا عَلَيْهِمْ إِلَّا ٱبْتِغَآءَ رِضْوَٰنِ ٱللَّهِ فَمَا رَعَوْهَا حَقَّ رِعَايَتِهَا فَـَٔاتَيْنَا ٱلَّذِينَ ءَامَنُوا

---

[1] (V.57:25) Paradise is under the blades of swords (*Jihâd* in Allâh's cause).

a) Narrated Al-Mughîrah bin Shu'bah رضي الله عنه: Our Prophet صلى الله عليه وسلم, told us about the Message of our Lord that ..."whoever amongst us is killed (in *Jihâd* in Allâh's cause) will go to Paradise". 'Umar asked the Prophet صلى الله عليه وسلم, "Is it not true that our men who are killed (in *Jihâd* in Allâh's cause) will go to Paradise and their's (i.e. those of the pagan's) will go to the (Hell) Fire?" The Prophet الله said, "Yes".

b) Narrated 'Abdullâh bin Abî Aufâ رضي الله عنهما! Allâh's Messenger صلى الله عليه وسلم said, "Know that Paradise is under the shades of sword (*Jihâd* in Allâh's cause)." (*Sahih Al-Bukhari*, Vol.4, *Hadîth* **No.73** and its chapter No.22).

We gave those among them who believed, their (due) reward; but many of them are Fâsiqûn (rebellious, disobedient to Allâh).

28. O you who believe [in Mûsâ (Moses) (i.e. Jews) and 'Îsâ (Jesus) (i.e. Christians)]! Fear Allâh, and believe in His Messenger (Muhammad صلى الله عليه وسلم), He will give you a double portion of His Mercy, and He will give you a light by which you shall walk (straight). And He will forgive you. And Allâh is Oft-Forgiving, Most Merciful.[1]

29. So that the people of the Scripture (Jews and Christians) may know that they have no power whatsoever over the Grace of Allâh, and that (His) Grace is (entirely) in His Hand to bestow it on whomsoever He wills. And Allâh is the Owner of Great Bounty.

---

[1] (V.57:28) (a) Narrated Abû Buradah's father: Allâh's Messenger صلى الله عليه وسلم said, "Any man who has a slave-girl whom he educates properly, teaches good manners, manumits and marries her will get a double reward. And if any man of the people of the Scriptures (Jews and Christians) believes in his own Prophet and then believes in me (Muhammad صلى الله عليه وسلم) too, he will (also) get a double reward. And any slave who fulfils his duty to his master and to his Lord (Allâh) will (also) get a double reward." (Sahih Al-Bukhari, Vol.7, Hadîth No.20).

(b) It is obligatory to have Belief in the Messengership of the Prophet (Muhammad صلى الله عليه وسلم).

Narrated Abu Hurairah رضي الله عنه Allâh's Messenger صلى الله عليه وسلم said, "By Him (Allâh) in Whose Hand Muhammad's soul is, there is none from amongst the Jews and the Christians (of these present nations) who hears about me and then dies without believing in the Message with which I have been sent (i.e. Islâmic Monotheism), but he will be from the dwellers of the (Hell) Fire." (Sahih Muslim, the Book of Faith, Vol. 1, Chapter No. 240) See also (V.3:85) and (V.3:116).

Sûrat Al-Mujâdilah
(The Disputation) LVIII

*In the Name of Allâh
the Most Gracious, the Most Merciful*

1. Indeed Allâh has heard the statement of her (Khaulah bint Tha'labah) that disputes with you (O Muhammad ﷺ) concerning her husband (Aus bin As-Sâmit), and complains to Allâh. And Allâh hears the argument between you both. Verily, Allâh is All-Hearer, All-Seer.

2. Those among you who make their wives unlawful to them by *Zihâr*[1] (i.e., by saying to them "You are like my mother's back,") they cannot be their mothers. None can be their mothers except those who gave them birth. And verily, they utter an ill word and a lie. And verily, Allâh is Oft-Pardoning, Oft-Forgiving.

3. And those who make unlawful to them (their wives) by *Zihâr* الظهار and wish to free themselves from what they uttered, (the penalty) in that case is the freeing of a slave before they touch each other. That is an admonition to you (so that you may not repeat such an ill thing). And Allâh is All-Aware of what you do.

---

[1] (V.58:2) *Zihâr* الظهار is the saying of a husband to his wife: You are to me like the back of my mother (i.e. unlawful for me to approach).

4. And he who finds not (the money for freeing a slave) must fast two successive months before they both touch each other. And he who is unable to do so, should feed sixty *Masâkins* (poor). That is in order that you may have perfect Faith in Allâh and His Messenger. These are the limits set by Allâh. And for disbelievers, there is a painful torment.

فَمَن لَّمْ يَجِدْ فَصِيَامُ شَهْرَيْنِ مُتَتَابِعَيْنِ مِن قَبْلِ أَن يَتَمَآسَّا فَمَن لَّمْ يَسْتَطِعْ فَإِطْعَامُ سِتِّينَ مِسْكِينًا ذَٰلِكَ لِتُؤْمِنُوا بِاللَّهِ وَرَسُولِهِۦ وَتِلْكَ حُدُودُ اللَّهِ وَلِلْكَٰفِرِينَ عَذَابٌ أَلِيمٌ ﴿٤﴾

5. Verily, those who oppose Allâh and His Messenger (Muhammad صلى الله عليه وسلم)[1] will be disgraced, as those before them (among the past nation), were disgraced. And We have sent down clear *Ayât* (proofs, evidences, verses, lessons, signs, revelations, etc.). And for the disbelievers is a disgracing torment

إِنَّ الَّذِينَ يُحَآدُّونَ اللَّهَ وَرَسُولَهُۥ كُبِتُوا كَمَا كُبِتَ الَّذِينَ مِن قَبْلِهِمْ وَقَدْ أَنزَلْنَآ ءَايَٰتٍ بَيِّنَٰتٍ وَلِلْكَٰفِرِينَ عَذَابٌ مُّهِينٌ ﴿٥﴾

6. On the Day when Allâh will resurrect them all together (i.e. on the Day of Resurrection) and inform them of what they did. Allâh has kept account of it, while they have forgotten it. And Allâh is Witness over all things.

يَوْمَ يَبْعَثُهُمُ اللَّهُ جَمِيعًا فَيُنَبِّئُهُم بِمَا عَمِلُوٓا أَحْصَىٰهُ اللَّهُ وَنَسُوهُ وَاللَّهُ عَلَىٰ كُلِّ شَىْءٍ شَهِيدٌ ﴿٦﴾

7. Have you not seen that Allâh knows whatsoever is in the heavens and whatsoever is on the earth? There is no *Najwâ*[2] (secret counsel) of three but He is their fourth (with His Knowledge, while He Himself is over the Throne, over the seventh heaven), nor of five but He is their sixth (with His

أَلَمْ تَرَ أَنَّ اللَّهَ يَعْلَمُ مَا فِي السَّمَٰوَٰتِ وَمَا فِي الْأَرْضِ مَا يَكُونُ مِن نَّجْوَىٰ ثَلَٰثَةٍ إِلَّا هُوَ رَابِعُهُمْ وَلَا خَمْسَةٍ إِلَّا هُوَ سَادِسُهُمْ وَلَآ أَدْنَىٰ مِن ذَٰلِكَ وَلَآ أَكْثَرَ إِلَّا هُوَ مَعَهُمْ أَيْنَ مَا كَانُوٓا ثُمَّ يُنَبِّئُهُم

---

[1] (V.58:5) See the footnote of (V.3:85).

[2] (V.58:7) See the footnote of (V.11:18)

Knowledge), nor of less than that or more than that or He is with them (with His Knowledge) wheresoever they may be. And afterwards on the Day of Resurrection He will inform them of what they did. Verily, Allâh is the All-Knower of everything.

8. Have you not seen those who were forbidden to hold secret counsels, and afterwards returned to that which they had been forbidden, and conspired together for sin and wrong doing and disobedience to the Messenger (Muhammad صلى الله عليه وسلم). And when they come to you, they greet you with a greeting wherewith Allâh greets you not, and say within themselves: "Why should Allâh punish us not for what we say?" Hell will be sufficient for them; they will burn therein. And worst indeed is that destination!

9. O you who believe! When you hold secret counsel, do it not for sin and wrong-doing, and disobedience towards the Messenger (Muhammad صلى الله عليه وسلم), but do it for *Al-Birr* (righteousness) and *Taqwâ* (virtues and piety); and fear Allâh unto Whom you shall be gathered.

10. Secret counsels (conspiracies) are only from *Shaitân* (Satan), in order that he may cause grief to the believers. But he cannot harm them in the least, except as Allâh permits. And in Allâh let the believers put their trust.[1]

---

[1] (V.58:10) See the footnote (A) of (V.12:67).

11. O you who believe! When you are told to make room in the assemblies, (spread out and) make room. Allâh will give you (ample) room (from His Mercy). And when you are told to rise up [for prayers, or *Jihâd* (holy fighting in Allâh's cause), or for any other good deed], rise up. Allâh will exalt in degree those of you who believe, and those who have been granted knowledge. And Allâh is Well-Acquainted with what you do.

12. O you who believe! When you (want to) consult the Messenger (Muhammad صلى الله عليه وسلم) in private, spend something in charity before your private consultation. That will be better and purer for you. But if you find not (the means for it), then verily, Allâh is Oft-Forgiving, Most Merciful.

13. Are you afraid of spending in charity before your private consultation (with him)? If then you do it not, and Allâh has forgiven you, then (at least) perform *Salât* (*Iqâmat-as-Salât*) and give *Zakât* and obey Allâh (i.e. do all that Allâh and His Messenger صلى الله عليه وسلم order you to do). And Allâh is All-Aware of what you do.

14. Have you (O Muhammad صلى الله عليه وسلم) not seen those (hypocrites) who take as friends a people upon whom is the Wrath of Allâh (i.e. Jews)? They are neither of you (Muslims) nor of them (Jews), and they swear to a lie while they know.

15. Allâh has prepared for them a severe torment. Evil indeed is that which they used to do.

أَعَدَّ ٱللَّهُ لَهُمْ عَذَابًا شَدِيدًا إِنَّهُمْ سَآءَ مَا كَانُوا۟ يَعْمَلُونَ ١٥

16. They have made their oaths a screen (for their evil actions). Thus they hinder (men) from the Path of Allâh: so they shall have a humiliating torment.

ٱتَّخَذُوٓا۟ أَيْمَـٰنَهُمْ جُنَّةً فَصَدُّوا۟ عَن سَبِيلِ ٱللَّهِ فَلَهُمْ عَذَابٌ مُّهِينٌ ١٦

17. Their children and their wealth will avail them nothing against Allâh. They will be the dwellers of the Fire to dwell therein forever.

لَّن تُغْنِىَ عَنْهُمْ أَمْوَٰلُهُمْ وَلَآ أَوْلَـٰدُهُم مِّنَ ٱللَّهِ شَيْـًٔا أُو۟لَـٰٓئِكَ أَصْحَـٰبُ ٱلنَّارِ هُمْ فِيهَا خَـٰلِدُونَ ١٧

18. On the Day when Allâh will resurrect them all together (for their account); then they will swear to Him as they swear to you (O Muslims). And they think that they have something (to stand upon). Verily, they are liars!

يَوْمَ يَبْعَثُهُمُ ٱللَّهُ جَمِيعًا فَيَحْلِفُونَ لَهُۥ كَمَا يَحْلِفُونَ لَكُمْ وَيَحْسَبُونَ أَنَّهُمْ عَلَىٰ شَىْءٍ أَلَآ إِنَّهُمْ هُمُ ٱلْكَـٰذِبُونَ ١٨

19. *Shaitân* (Satan) has overpowered them. So he has made them forget the remembrance of Allâh. They are the party of *Shaitân* (Satan). Verily, it is the party of *Shaitân* (Satan) that will be the losers!

ٱسْتَحْوَذَ عَلَيْهِمُ ٱلشَّيْطَـٰنُ فَأَنسَىٰهُمْ ذِكْرَ ٱللَّهِ أُو۟لَـٰٓئِكَ حِزْبُ ٱلشَّيْطَـٰنِ أَلَآ إِنَّ حِزْبَ ٱلشَّيْطَـٰنِ هُمُ ٱلْخَـٰسِرُونَ ١٩

20. Those who oppose Allâh and His Messenger (Muhammad ﷺ), they will be among the lowest (most humiliated).

إِنَّ ٱلَّذِينَ يُحَآدُّونَ ٱللَّهَ وَرَسُولَهُۥٓ أُو۟لَـٰٓئِكَ فِى ٱلْأَذَلِّينَ ٢٠

21. Allâh has decreed: "Verily, it is I and My Messengers who shall be the victorious." Verily, Allâh is All-Powerful, All-Mighty.

كَتَبَ ٱللَّهُ لَأَغْلِبَنَّ أَنَا۠ وَرُسُلِىٓ إِنَّ ٱللَّهَ قَوِىٌّ عَزِيزٌ ٢١

22. You (O Muhammad ﷺ) will not find any people who believe in Allâh and the Last Day, making friendship with those who oppose Allâh

لَّا تَجِدُ قَوْمًا يُؤْمِنُونَ بِٱللَّهِ وَٱلْيَوْمِ ٱلْءَاخِرِ يُوَآدُّونَ مَنْ حَآدَّ ٱللَّهَ وَرَسُولَهُۥ وَلَوْ كَانُوٓا۟

and His Messenger (Muhammad صلى الله عليه وسلم), even though they were their fathers or their sons or their brothers or their kindred (people). For such He has written Faith in their hearts, and strengthened them with *Rûh* (proofs, light and true guidance) from Himself. And We will admit them to Gardens (Paradise) under which rivers flow to dwell therein (forever). Allâh is pleased with them, and they with Him. They are the Party of Allâh. Verily, it is the Party of Allâh that will be the successful.

دَابَآءَهُمْ أَوْ أَبْنَآءَهُمْ أَوْ إِخْوَٰنَهُمْ أَوْ عَشِيرَتَهُمْ أُوْلَٰٓئِكَ كَتَبَ فِى قُلُوبِهِمُ ٱلْإِيمَٰنَ وَأَيَّدَهُم بِرُوحٍ مِّنْهُ وَيُدْخِلُهُمْ جَنَّٰتٍ تَجْرِى مِن تَحْتِهَا ٱلْأَنْهَٰرُ خَٰلِدِينَ فِيهَا رَضِىَ ٱللَّهُ عَنْهُمْ وَرَضُوا۟ عَنْهُ أُوْلَٰٓئِكَ حِزْبُ ٱللَّهِ أَلَآ إِنَّ حِزْبَ ٱللَّهِ هُمُ ٱلْمُفْلِحُونَ ٢٢

Sûrat Al-Hashr
(The Gathering) LIX

سُورَةُ الْحَشْرِ

In the Name of Allâh the Most Gracious, the Most Merciful

بِسْمِ ٱللَّهِ ٱلرَّحْمَٰنِ ٱلرَّحِيمِ

1. Whatsoever is in the heavens and whatsoever is on the earth glorifies Allâh. And He is the All-Mighty, the All-Wise.

سَبَّحَ لِلَّهِ مَا فِى ٱلسَّمَٰوَٰتِ وَمَا فِى ٱلْأَرْضِ وَهُوَ ٱلْعَزِيزُ ٱلْحَكِيمُ ١

2. He it is Who drove out the disbelievers among the people of the Scripture (i.e. the Jews of the tribe of Banû An-Nadîr) from their homes at the first gathering. You did not think that they would get out. And they thought that their fortresses would defend them from Allâh! But Allâh's (Torment) reached them from a place whereof they expected it not, and He cast terror into their hearts so that they destroyed their own dwellings with their own hands and the hands of the believers. Then take admonition, O you with eyes (to see).

هُوَ ٱلَّذِىٓ أَخْرَجَ ٱلَّذِينَ كَفَرُوا۟ مِنْ أَهْلِ ٱلْكِتَٰبِ مِن دِيَٰرِهِمْ لِأَوَّلِ ٱلْحَشْرِ مَا ظَنَنتُمْ أَن يَخْرُجُوا۟ وَظَنُّوٓا۟ أَنَّهُم مَّانِعَتُهُمْ حُصُونُهُم مِّنَ ٱللَّهِ فَأَتَىٰهُمُ ٱللَّهُ مِنْ حَيْثُ لَمْ يَحْتَسِبُوا۟ وَقَذَفَ فِى قُلُوبِهِمُ ٱلرُّعْبَ يُخْرِبُونَ بُيُوتَهُم بِأَيْدِيهِمْ وَأَيْدِى ٱلْمُؤْمِنِينَ فَٱعْتَبِرُوا۟ يَٰٓأُو۟لِى ٱلْأَبْصَٰرِ ٢

3. And had it not been that Allâh had decreed exile for them, He would certainly have punished them in this world; and in the Hereafter theirs shall be the torment of the Fire.

وَلَوۡلَآ أَن كَتَبَ ٱللَّهُ عَلَيۡهِمُ ٱلۡجَلَآءَ لَعَذَّبَهُمۡ فِى ٱلدُّنۡيَا وَلَهُمۡ فِى ٱلۡأٓخِرَةِ عَذَابُ ٱلنَّارِ ۞

4. That is because they opposed Allâh and His Messenger (Muhammad صلى الله عليه وسلم). And whosoever opposes Allâh, then verily, Allâh is Severe in punishment.

ذَٰلِكَ بِأَنَّهُمۡ شَآقُّوا۟ ٱللَّهَ وَرَسُولَهُۥ وَمَن يُشَآقِّ ٱللَّهَ فَإِنَّ ٱللَّهَ شَدِيدُ ٱلۡعِقَابِ ۞

5. What you (O Muslims) cut down of the palm-trees (of the enemy), or you left them standing on their stems, it was by Leave of Allâh, and in order that He might disgrace the Fâsiqûn (the rebellious, the disobedient to Allâh).

مَا قَطَعۡتُم مِّن لِّينَةٍ أَوۡ تَرَكۡتُمُوهَا قَآئِمَةً عَلَىٰٓ أُصُولِهَا فَبِإِذۡنِ ٱللَّهِ وَلِيُخۡزِىَ ٱلۡفَٰسِقِينَ ۞

6. And what Allâh gave as booty (Fai') to His Messenger (Muhammad صلى الله عليه وسلم) from them — for this you made no expedition with either cavalry or camelry. But Allâh gives power to His Messengers over whomsoever He wills. And Allâh is Able to do all things.

وَمَآ أَفَآءَ ٱللَّهُ عَلَىٰ رَسُولِهِۦ مِنۡهُمۡ فَمَآ أَوۡجَفۡتُمۡ عَلَيۡهِ مِنۡ خَيۡلٍ وَلَا رِكَابٍ وَلَٰكِنَّ ٱللَّهَ يُسَلِّطُ رُسُلَهُۥ عَلَىٰ مَن يَشَآءُ وَٱللَّهُ عَلَىٰ كُلِّ شَىۡءٍ قَدِيرٌ ۞

7. What Allâh gave as booty (Fai') to His Messenger (Muhammad صلى الله عليه وسلم) from the people of the townships — it is for Allâh, His Messenger (Muhammad صلى الله عليه وسلم), the kindred (of Messenger Muhammad صلى الله عليه وسلم), the orphans, Al-Masâkin (the poor), and the wayfarer, in order that it may not become a fortune used by the rich among you. And whatsoever the Messenger (Muhammad صلى الله عليه وسلم) gives you, take it; and whatsoever he

مَّآ أَفَآءَ ٱللَّهُ عَلَىٰ رَسُولِهِۦ مِنۡ أَهۡلِ ٱلۡقُرَىٰ فَلِلَّهِ وَلِلرَّسُولِ وَلِذِى ٱلۡقُرۡبَىٰ وَٱلۡيَتَٰمَىٰ وَٱلۡمَسَٰكِينِ وَٱبۡنِ ٱلسَّبِيلِ كَىۡ لَا يَكُونَ دُولَةَۢ بَيۡنَ ٱلۡأَغۡنِيَآءِ مِنكُمۡ وَمَآ ءَاتَىٰكُمُ ٱلرَّسُولُ فَخُذُوهُ وَمَا نَهَىٰكُمۡ عَنۡهُ فَٱنتَهُوا۟ وَٱتَّقُوا۟ ٱللَّهَ إِنَّ ٱللَّهَ شَدِيدُ ٱلۡعِقَابِ

forbids you, abstain (from it).[1] And fear Allâh; verily, Allâh is Severe in punishment.

8. (And there is also a share in this booty) for the poor emigrants, who were expelled from their homes and their property, seeking Bounties from Allâh and to please Him, and helping Allâh (i.e. helping His religion) and His Messenger (Muhammad صلى الله عليه وسلم).

لِلْفُقَرَآءِ ٱلْمُهَٰجِرِينَ ٱلَّذِينَ أُخْرِجُوا۟ مِن دِيَٰرِهِمْ وَأَمْوَٰلِهِمْ يَبْتَغُونَ فَضْلًا مِّنَ ٱللَّهِ وَرِضْوَٰنًا وَيَنصُرُونَ ٱللَّهَ وَرَسُولَهُۥٓ أُو۟لَٰٓئِكَ هُمُ ٱلصَّٰدِقُونَ ٨

---

[1] (V.59:7) Narrated 'Alqamah: 'Abdullâh (bin Mas'ûd) said."Allâh curses those ladies who practise tatooing and those who get themselves tatooed, and those ladies who get their hair removed from their eyebrows and faces except the beard and moustache, and those who make artificial spaces between their teeth in order to look more beautiful whereby they change Allâh's creation." His saying reached a lady from Banû Asad, called Umm Ya'qûb, who came (to 'Abdullâh) and said, "I have come to know that you have cursed such and such (ladies)?" He replied, "Why should I not curse these whom Allâh's Messenger صلى الله عليه وسلم has cursed and who are (cursed) in Allâh's Book!" Umm Ya'qûb said, "I have read the whole Qur'ân, but I did not find in it what you say." He said, "Verily, if you have read it (i.e. the Qur'ân), you have found it. Didn't you read:

"And whatsoever the Messenger (Muhammad صلى الله عليه وسلم) gives you, take it, and whatsoever he forbids you, abstain (from it)." (V.59:7).

She replied, "Yes, I did". He said, "Verily, Allâh's Messenger صلى الله عليه وسلم forbade such things." She said, "But I see your wife doing these things?" He said, "Go and watch her". She went and watched her but could not see anything in support of her statement. On that he said, "If my wife was as you thought, I would not keep her in my company (i.e., I would divorce her)." (Sahih Al-Bukhari, Vol.6, Hadîth No.408).

Narrated 'Abdullâh (bin Mas'ûd) رضي الله عنه: Allâh's Messenger صلى الله عليه وسلم has cursed the lady who uses false hair. (See Sahih Al-Bukhari, Vol.6, Hadîth No.409).

Such are indeed the truthful (to what they say).

9. And (it is also for) those who, before them, had homes (in Al-Madinah) and had adopted the Faith, love those who emigrate to them, and have no jealousy in their breasts for that which they have been given (from the booty of Banû An-Nadîr), and give them (emigrants) preference over themselves even though they were in need of that. And whosoever is saved from his own covetousness, such are they who will be the successful.

10. And those who came after them say: "Our Lord! Forgive us and our brethren who have preceded us in Faith, and put not in our hearts any hatred against those who have believed. Our Lord! You are indeed full of kindness, Most Merciful.

11. Have you (O Muhammad صلى الله عليه وسلم) not observed the hypocrites who say to their friends among the people of the Scripture who disbelieve: "(By Allâh) If you are expelled, we (too) indeed will go out with you, and we shall never obey any one against you; and if you are attacked (in fight), we shall indeed help you." But Allâh is Witness that they verily, are liars.

12. Surely, if they (the Jews) are expelled, never will they (hypocrites) go out with them; and if they are attacked, they will never help them. And (even) if they do help them, they

وَالَّذِيْنَ تَبَوَّؤُا الدَّارَ وَالْإِيْمَانَ
مِنْ قَبْلِهِمْ يُحِبُّوْنَ مَنْ هَاجَرَ إِلَيْهِمْ
وَلَا يَجِدُوْنَ فِيْ صُدُوْرِهِمْ
حَاجَةً مِّمَّا أُوْتُوْا وَيُؤْثِرُوْنَ
عَلَى أَنْفُسِهِمْ وَلَوْ كَانَ بِهِمْ
خَصَاصَةٌ ۚ وَمَنْ يُّوْقَ شُحَّ نَفْسِهِ
فَأُولٰٓئِكَ هُمُ
الْمُفْلِحُوْنَ ۝

وَالَّذِيْنَ جَآءُوْ مِنْ بَعْدِهِمْ
يَقُوْلُوْنَ رَبَّنَا اغْفِرْ لَنَا
وَلِإِخْوَانِنَا الَّذِيْنَ سَبَقُوْنَا
بِالْإِيْمَانِ وَلَا تَجْعَلْ فِيْ قُلُوْبِنَا
غِلًّا لِّلَّذِيْنَ آمَنُوْا رَبَّنَا إِنَّكَ
رَءُوْفٌ رَّحِيْمٌ ۝

۞ أَلَمْ تَرَ إِلَى
الَّذِيْنَ نَافَقُوْا يَقُوْلُوْنَ
لِإِخْوَانِهِمُ الَّذِيْنَ كَفَرُوْا مِنْ
أَهْلِ الْكِتَابِ لَئِنْ أُخْرِجْتُمْ
لَنَخْرُجَنَّ مَعَكُمْ وَلَا نُطِيْعُ
فِيْكُمْ أَحَدًا أَبَدًا وَّإِنْ قُوْتِلْتُمْ
لَنَنْصُرَنَّكُمْ ۖ وَاللّٰهُ يَشْهَدُ إِنَّهُمْ
لَكَاذِبُوْنَ ۝

لَئِنْ أُخْرِجُوْا لَا يَخْرُجُوْنَ مَعَهُمْ
وَلَئِنْ قُوْتِلُوْا لَا يَنْصُرُوْنَهُمْ وَلَئِنْ

(hypocrites) will turn their backs, and they will not be victorious.

13. Verily, you (believers in the Oneness of Allâh — Islâmic Monotheism) are more fearful in their (Jews of Banû An-Nadîr) breasts than Allâh. That is because they are a people who comprehend not (the Majesty and Power of Allâh).

14. They fight not against you even together, except in fortified townships, or from behind walls. Their enmity among themselves is very great. You would think they were united, but their hearts are divided. That is because they are a people who understand not.

15. They are like their immediate predecessors (the Jews of Banû Qainûqâ', who suffered); they tasted the evil result of their conduct, and (in the Hereafter, there is) for them a painful torment.

16. (Their allies deceived them) like Shaitân (Satan), when he says to man: "Disbelieve in Allâh." But when (man) disbelieves in Allâh, Shaitân (Satan) says: "I am free of you, I fear Allâh, the Lord of the 'Âlamîn (mankind, jinn and all that exists)!"

17. So the end of both will be that they will be in the Fire, abiding therein. Such is the recompense of the Zâlimûn (i.e. polytheists, wrongdoers, disbelievers in Allâh and His Oneness).

18. O you who believe! Fear Allâh and keep your duty to Him. And let every person look to what he has sent forth for the morrow, and fear Allâh. Verily, Allâh is All-Aware of what you do.[1]

يَـٰٓأَيُّهَا ٱلَّذِينَ ءَامَنُوا۟ ٱتَّقُوا۟ ٱللَّهَ وَلْتَنظُرْ نَفْسٌ مَّا قَدَّمَتْ لِغَدٍۢ وَٱتَّقُوا۟ ٱللَّهَ إِنَّ ٱللَّهَ خَبِيرٌۢ بِمَا تَعْمَلُونَ ۝

19. And be not like those who forgot Allâh (i.e. became disobedient to Allâh), and He caused them to forget their ownselves, (let them to forget to do righteous deeds). Those are the *Fâsiqûn* (rebellious, disobedient to Allâh).

وَلَا تَكُونُوا۟ كَٱلَّذِينَ نَسُوا۟ ٱللَّهَ فَأَنسَىٰهُمْ أَنفُسَهُمْ أُو۟لَـٰٓئِكَ هُمُ ٱلْفَـٰسِقُونَ ۝

20. Not equal are the dwellers of the Fire and the dwellers of the Paradise. It is the dwellers of Paradise that will be successful.

لَا يَسْتَوِىٓ أَصْحَـٰبُ ٱلنَّارِ وَأَصْحَـٰبُ ٱلْجَنَّةِ أَصْحَـٰبُ ٱلْجَنَّةِ هُمُ ٱلْفَآئِزُونَ ۝

21. Had We sent down this Qur'ân on a mountain, you would surely, have seen it humbling itself and rent asunder by the fear of Allâh. Such are the parables which We put forward to mankind that they may reflect.[2]

لَوْ أَنزَلْنَا هَـٰذَا ٱلْقُرْءَانَ عَلَىٰ جَبَلٍۢ لَّرَأَيْتَهُۥ خَـٰشِعًۭا مُّتَصَدِّعًۭا مِّنْ خَشْيَةِ ٱللَّهِ وَتِلْكَ ٱلْأَمْثَـٰلُ نَضْرِبُهَا لِلنَّاسِ لَعَلَّهُمْ يَتَفَكَّرُونَ ۝

---

[1] (V.59:18).
a) See the footnote of (V.32:16).
b) See the footnote of (V.15:23).
c) See the footnote (C) of (V.9:111).

[2] (V.59:21) Narrated Jâbir bin 'Abdullâh رضي الله عنهما: The Prophet صلى الله عليه وسلم used to stand by a tree or a date-palm on Friday. Then an *Ansâri* woman or man said, "O Allâh's Messenger! Shall we make a pulpit for you?" He replied, "If you wish." So they made a pulpit for him and when it was Friday, he proceeded towards the pulpit [for delivering the *Khutbah* (religious talk)]. The date-palm cried like a child! The Prophet صلى الله عليه وسلم descended (from the pulpit) and embraced it while it continued moaning like a child being

22. He is Allâh, beside Whom *Lâ ilâha illa Huwa* (none has the right to be worshipped but He) the All-Knower of the unseen and the seen. He is the Most Gracious, the Most Merciful.

23. He is Allâh beside Whom *Lâ ilâha illa Huwa* (none has the right to be worshipped but He), the King, the Holy, the One Free from all defects, the Giver of security, the Watcher over His creatures, the All-Mighty, the Compeller, the Supreme. Glory is to Allâh! (High is He) above all that they associate as partners with Him.

24. He is Allâh, the Creator, the Inventor of all things, the Bestower of forms. To Him belong the Best Names.[1] All that is in the heavens and the earth glorify Him. And He is the All-Mighty, the All-Wise.

Sûrat Al-Mumtahinah
(The Woman to be examined) LX

*In the Name of Allâh
the Most Gracious, the Most Merciful*

1. O you who believe! Take not My enemies and your enemies (i.e. disbelievers and polytheists) as friends, showing affection towards them, while they have disbelieved in what has come to you of the truth (i.e. Islâmic

---

quietened. The Prophet صلى الله عليه وسلم said, "It was crying for (missing) what it used to hear of religious knowledge given near it." (*Sahih Al-Bukhari*, Vol.4, *Hadîth* No.784).

[1] (V.59:24) See the footnote of (V.7:180).

Monotheism, this Qur'ân, and Muhammad (ﷺ), and have driven out the Messenger (Muhammad ﷺ) and yourselves (from your homeland) because you believe in Allâh your Lord! If you have come forth to strive in My Cause and to seek My Good Pleasure, (then take not these disbelievers and polytheists, as your friends). You show friendship to them in secret, while I am All-Aware of what you conceal and what you reveal. And whosoever of you (Muslims) does that, then indeed he has gone (far) astray from the Straight Path.[1]

أَن تُؤْمِنُواْ بِٱللَّهِ رَبِّكُمْ إِن كُنتُمْ خَرَجْتُمْ جِهَٰدًا فِى سَبِيلِى وَٱبْتِغَآءَ مَرْضَاتِى تُسِرُّونَ إِلَيْهِم بِٱلْمَوَدَّةِ وَأَنَا۠ أَعْلَمُ بِمَآ أَخْفَيْتُمْ وَمَآ أَعْلَنتُمْ وَمَن يَفْعَلْهُ مِنكُمْ فَقَدْ ضَلَّ سَوَآءَ ٱلسَّبِيلِ ﴿١﴾

2. Should they gain the upper hand over you, they would behave to you as enemies, and stretch forth their hands and their tongues against you with evil, and they desire that you should disbelieve.

إِن يَثْقَفُوكُمْ يَكُونُواْ لَكُمْ أَعْدَآءً وَيَبْسُطُوٓاْ إِلَيْكُمْ أَيْدِيَهُمْ وَأَلْسِنَتَهُم بِٱلسُّوٓءِ وَوَدُّواْ لَوْ تَكْفُرُونَ ﴿٢﴾

3. Neither your relatives nor your children will benefit you on the Day of Resurrection (against Allâh). He will judge between you. And Allâh is the All-Seer of what you do.

لَن تَنفَعَكُمْ أَرْحَامُكُمْ وَلَآ أَوْلَٰدُكُمْ يَوْمَ ٱلْقِيَٰمَةِ يَفْصِلُ بَيْنَكُمْ وَٱللَّهُ بِمَا تَعْمَلُونَ بَصِيرٌ ﴿٣﴾

4. Indeed there has been an excellent example for you in Ibrâhîm (Abraham) and those with him, when they said to their people: "Verily, we are free from you and whatever you worship besides Allâh: we have rejected you, and there has started between us and you, hostility and hatred for ever until you

قَدْ كَانَتْ لَكُمْ أُسْوَةٌ حَسَنَةٌ فِىٓ إِبْرَٰهِيمَ وَٱلَّذِينَ مَعَهُۥٓ إِذْ قَالُواْ لِقَوْمِهِمْ إِنَّا بُرَءَٰٓؤُاْ مِنكُمْ وَمِمَّا تَعْبُدُونَ مِن دُونِ ٱللَّهِ كَفَرْنَا بِكُمْ وَبَدَا بَيْنَنَا وَبَيْنَكُمُ ٱلْعَدَٰوَةُ

---

[1] (V.60:1) See V.3:149 and its footnote.

believe in Allâh Alone" — except the saying of Ibrâhîm (Abraham) to his father: "Verily, I will ask forgiveness (from Allâh) for you, but I have no power to do anything for you before Allâh.[1]" "Our Lord! In You (Alone) we put our trust, and to You (Alone) we turn in repentance, and to You (Alone) is (our) final Return.

5. "Our Lord! Make us not a trial for the disbelievers, and forgive us, Our Lord! Verily, You, only You, are the All-Mighty, the All-Wise."

6. Certainly, there has been in them an excellent example for you to follow — for those who look forward to (the Meeting with) Allâh and the Last Day. And whosoever turns away, then verily, Allâh is Rich (Free of all needs), Worthy of all praise.

7. Perhaps Allâh will make friendship between you and those whom you hold as enemies. And Allâh has power (over all things), and Allâh is Oft-Forgiving, Most Merciful.

8. Allâh does not forbid you to deal justly and kindly with those who fought not against you on account of religion nor drove you out of your homes. Verily, Allâh loves those who deal with equity.

9. It is only as regards those who fought against you on account of

---

[1] (V.60:4) See the Qur'ân Verses (V.9:114), (V.19:41-49) and (V.26:70-86)

religion, and have driven you out of your homes, and helped to drive you out, that Allâh forbids you to befriend them. And whosoever will befriend them, then such are the *Zâlimûn* (wrongdoers — those who disobey Allâh).

10. O you who believe! When believing women come to you as emigrants, examine them; Allâh knows best as to their Faith; then if you ascertain that they are true believers send them not back to the disbelievers. They are not lawful (wives) for the disbelievers nor are the disbelievers lawful (husbands) for them. But give them (disbelievers) that (amount of money) which they have spent [as their *Mahr*[1]] to them. And there will be no sin on you to marry them if you have paid their *Mahr* to them. Likewise hold not the disbelieving women as wives, and ask for (the return of) that which you have spent (as *Mahr*) and let them (the disbelievers) ask back for that which they have spent. That is the Judgement of Allâh, He judges between you. And Allâh is All-Knowing, All-Wise.

11. And if any of your wives have gone from you to the disbelievers, (as apostates and you asked them to return

---

[1] (V.60:10) *Mahr*: Bridal-money given by the husband to his wife at the time of wedding.

back your *Mahr* but they refused) —
then you went out for a *Ghazwah*
(military expedition) (against them) and
gained booty; then pay from that booty
to those whose wives have gone, the
equivalent of what they had spent (on
their *Mahr*). And fear Allâh in Whom
you believe.

ذَهَبَتْ أَزْوَٰجُهُمْ مِّثْلَ مَآ أَنفَقُوا ۚ
وَٱتَّقُوا ٱللَّهَ ٱلَّذِىٓ أَنتُم بِهِۦ
مُؤْمِنُونَ ﴿١١﴾

12. O Prophet! When believing
women come to you to give you the
Bai'ah (pledge), that they will not
associate anything in worship with
Allâh, that they will not steal, that they
will not commit illegal sexual
intercourse; that they will not kill their
children, that they will not utter slander,
intentionally forging falsehood (i.e. by
making illegal children belonging to
their husbands), and that they will not
disobey you in *Ma'rûf* (Islâmic
Monotheism and all that which Islâm
ordains), then accept their *Bai'ah*
(pledge), and ask Allâh to forgive them.
Verily, Allâh is Oft-Forgiving, Most
Merciful.

يَٰٓأَيُّهَا ٱلنَّبِىُّ إِذَا جَآءَكَ ٱلْمُؤْمِنَٰتُ
يُبَايِعْنَكَ عَلَىٰٓ أَن لَّا يُشْرِكْنَ
بِٱللَّهِ شَيْئًا وَلَا يَسْرِقْنَ وَلَا يَزْنِينَ
وَلَا يَقْتُلْنَ أَوْلَٰدَهُنَّ وَلَا يَأْتِينَ
بِبُهْتَٰنٍ يَفْتَرِينَهُۥ بَيْنَ أَيْدِيهِنَّ
وَأَرْجُلِهِنَّ وَلَا يَعْصِينَكَ
فِى مَعْرُوفٍ فَبَايِعْهُنَّ وَٱسْتَغْفِرْ
لَهُنَّ ٱللَّهَ ۖ إِنَّ ٱللَّهَ غَفُورٌ رَّحِيمٌ ﴿١٢﴾

13. O you who believe! Take not as
friends the people who incurred the
Wrath of Allâh (i.e. the Jews). Surely,
they have despaired of (receiving any
good in) the Hereafter, just as the
disbelievers have despaired of those
(buried) in graves (that they will not be
resurrected on the Day of Resurrection).

يَٰٓأَيُّهَا ٱلَّذِينَ ءَامَنُوا لَا تَتَوَلَّوْا
قَوْمًا غَضِبَ ٱللَّهُ عَلَيْهِمْ
قَدْ يَئِسُوا مِنَ ٱلْءَاخِرَةِ كَمَا يَئِسَ
ٱلْكُفَّارُ مِنْ أَصْحَٰبِ ٱلْقُبُورِ ﴿١٣﴾

Sûrat As-Saff
(The Row or the Rank) LXI

سُورَةُ الصَّفِّ

*In the Name of Allâh
the Most Gracious, the Most Merciful*

بِسْمِ اللَّهِ الرَّحْمَٰنِ الرَّحِيمِ

1. Whatsoever is in the heavens and whatsoever is on the earth glorifies Allâh. And He is the All-Mighty, the All-Wise.

سَبَّحَ لِلَّهِ مَا فِى السَّمَوَٰتِ وَمَا فِى الْأَرْضِ وَهُوَ الْعَزِيزُ الْحَكِيمُ ۞

2. O you who believe! Why do you say that which you do not do?

يَٰٓأَيُّهَا الَّذِينَ ءَامَنُوا لِمَ تَقُولُونَ مَا لَا تَفْعَلُونَ ۞

3. Most hateful it is with Allâh that you say that which you do not do.

كَبُرَ مَقْتًا عِندَ اللَّهِ أَن تَقُولُوا مَا لَا تَفْعَلُونَ ۞

4. Verily, Allâh loves those who fight in His Cause in rows (ranks) as if they were a solid structure.[1]

إِنَّ اللَّهَ يُحِبُّ الَّذِينَ يُقَٰتِلُونَ فِى سَبِيلِهِ صَفًّا كَأَنَّهُم بُنْيَٰنٌ مَّرْصُوصٌ ۞

5. And (remember) when Mûsâ (Moses) said to his people: "O my people! Why do you annoy me while you know certainly that I am the Messenger of Allâh to you? So when they turned away (from the Path of Allâh), Allâh turned their hearts away (from the Right Path). And Allâh guides not the people who are *Fâsiqûn* (the rebellious, the disobedient to Allâh).

وَإِذْ قَالَ مُوسَىٰ لِقَوْمِهِ يَٰقَوْمِ لِمَ تُؤْذُونَنِى وَقَد تَّعْلَمُونَ أَنِّى رَسُولُ اللَّهِ إِلَيْكُمْ فَلَمَّا زَاغُوٓا أَزَاغَ اللَّهُ قُلُوبَهُمْ وَاللَّهُ لَا يَهْدِى الْقَوْمَ الْفَٰسِقِينَ ۞

---

[1] (V.61:4)

a) Narrated Abû Sa'îd Al-Khudrî رضى الله عنه: Somebody asked, "O Allâh's Messenger! Who is the best among the people?" Allâh's Messenger صلى الله عليه وسلم replied, "A believer who strives his utmost in Allâh's Cause with his life and property." They asked, "Who is next?" He replied, "A believer who stays in one of the mountain paths worshipping Allâh and leaving the people secure from his mischief." (*Sahih Al-Bukhari*, Vol.4, *Hadîth* No.45).

b) See the footnote (A) of (V.9:111).

6. And (remember) when 'Îsâ (Jesus), son of Maryam (Mary), said: "O Children of Israel! I am the Messenger of Allâh unto you, confirming the Taurât [(Torah) which came] before me, and giving glad tidings of a Messenger to come after me, whose name shall be Ahmad.[1] But when he (Ahmad i.e. Muhammad صلى الله عليه وسلم) came to them with clear proofs, they said: "This is plain magic.[2]"

وَإِذْ قَالَ عِيسَى ٱبْنُ مَرْيَمَ يَٰبَنِىٓ إِسْرَٰٓءِيلَ إِنِّى رَسُولُ ٱللَّهِ إِلَيْكُم مُّصَدِّقًا لِّمَا بَيْنَ يَدَىَّ مِنَ ٱلتَّوْرَىٰةِ وَمُبَشِّرًۢا بِرَسُولٍ يَأْتِى مِنۢ بَعْدِى ٱسْمُهُۥٓ أَحْمَدُ فَلَمَّا جَآءَهُم بِٱلْبَيِّنَٰتِ قَالُوا۟ هَٰذَا سِحْرٌ مُّبِينٌ ٦

---

[1] (V.61:6) i.e. the second name of Prophet Muhammad صلى الله عليه وسلم and it (Ahmad) literally means: "One who praises Allâh more than others".

[2] (V.61:6)

A) Narrated Jubair bin Mut'im رضى الله عنه: Allâh's Messenger صلى الله عليه وسلم said, "I have five names: I am Muhammad and Ahmad; I am Al-Mahî through whom Allâh will eliminate Al-Kufr (infidelity); I am Al-Hâshir who will be the first to be resurrected, the people being resurrected thereafter; and I am also Al-'Âqib (i.e. there will be no Prophet after me)." (Sahih Al-Bukhari, Vol. 4, Hadîth No. 732).

B) Narrated Abû Hurairah رضى الله عنه: Allâh's Messenger صلى الله عليه وسلم said, "By Him (Allâh) in Whose Hand my soul is, surely, the son of Mary ['Îsâ (Jesus)] عليه السلام* will shortly descend amongst you people (Muslims), and will judge mankind justly by the Law of the Qur'ân (as a just ruler), and will break the Cross and kill the pigs and abolish the Jizyah [a tax taken from the people of the Scriptures (Jews and Christians), who are under the protection of a Muslim government. This Jizyah tax will not be accepted by 'Îsâ (Jesus) عليه السلام and all mankind will be required to embrace Islam with no other alternative]. Then there will be abundance of money and nobody will accept charitable gifts." (See Fath Al-Bari, Page No.304 and 305, Vol.7), (Sahih Al-Bukhari, Vol.3, Hadîth No.425).

* 'Îsâ (Jesus), the son of Maryam (Mary) عليهما السلام will descend as a leader of the Muslims and it is a severe warning to the Christians who claim to be the followers of 'Îsâ (Jesus) and he will break the Cross and kill the pigs, and he will abolish the Jizyah (tax); and all

7. And who does more wrong than the one who invents a lie against Allâh, while he is being invited to Islâm? And Allâh guides not the people who are *Zâlimûn* (polytheists, wrongdoers and disbelievers) folk.

وَمَنْ أَظْلَمُ مِمَّنِ ٱفْتَرَىٰ عَلَى ٱللَّهِ ٱلْكَذِبَ وَهُوَ يُدْعَىٰٓ إِلَى ٱلْإِسْلَٰمِ وَٱللَّهُ لَا يَهْدِى ٱلْقَوْمَ ٱلظَّٰلِمِينَ ٧

8. They intend to put out the Light of Allâh (i.e. the Religion of Islâm, this Qur'ân, and the Prophet Muhammad صلى الله عليه وسلم) with their mouths. But Allâh will bring His Light to perfection even though the disbelievers hate (it).

يُرِيدُونَ لِيُطْفِـُٔوا۟ نُورَ ٱللَّهِ بِأَفْوَٰهِهِمْ وَٱللَّهُ مُتِمُّ نُورِهِۦ وَلَوْ كَرِهَ ٱلْكَٰفِرُونَ ٨

9. He it is Who has sent His Messenger (Muhammad صلى الله عليه وسلم) with guidance and the religion of truth (Islâmic Monotheism) to make it victorious over all (other) religions even though the *Mushrikûn* (polytheists, pagans, idolaters, and disbelievers in the Oneness of Allâh and in His Messenger Muhammad صلى الله عليه وسلم) hate (it).

هُوَ ٱلَّذِىٓ أَرْسَلَ رَسُولَهُۥ بِٱلْهُدَىٰ وَدِينِ ٱلْحَقِّ لِيُظْهِرَهُۥ عَلَى ٱلدِّينِ كُلِّهِۦ وَلَوْ كَرِهَ ٱلْمُشْرِكُونَ ٩

10. O you who believe! Shall I guide you to a trade that will save you from a painful torment?

يَٰٓأَيُّهَا ٱلَّذِينَ ءَامَنُوا۟ هَلْ أَدُلُّكُمْ عَلَىٰ تِجَٰرَةٍ تُنجِيكُم مِّنْ عَذَابٍ أَلِيمٍ ١٠

11. That you believe in Allâh and His Messenger (Muhammad صلى الله عليه وسلم), and that you strive hard and fight in the Cause of Allâh with your wealth and your lives: that will be better for you, if you but know!

تُؤْمِنُونَ بِٱللَّهِ وَرَسُولِهِۦ وَتُجَٰهِدُونَ فِى سَبِيلِ ٱللَّهِ بِأَمْوَٰلِكُمْ وَأَنفُسِكُمْ ذَٰلِكُمْ خَيْرٌ لَّكُمْ إِن كُنتُمْ تَعْلَمُونَ ١١

---

mankind will be required to embrace Islam with no other alternative.

12. (If you do so) He will forgive you your sins, and admit you into Gardens under which rivers flow, and pleasant dwellings in *'Adn* (Eden) Paradise; that is indeed the great success.

13. And also (He will give you) another (blessing) which you love, — help from Allâh (against your enemies) and a near victory. And give glad tidings (O Muhammad صلى الله عليه وسلم) to the believers.

14. O you who believe! Be you helpers (in the Cause) of Allâh as said 'Îsâ (Jesus), son of Maryam (Mary), to the *Hawâriyyûn* (the disciples): "Who are my helpers (in the Cause) of Allâh?" The *Hawâriyyûn* (the disciples) said: "We are Allâh's helpers" (i.e. we will strive in His Cause!). Then a group of the Children of Israel believed and a group disbelieved. So We gave power to those who believed against their enemies, and they became the victorious (uppermost).

Sûrat Al-Jumu'ah
(Friday) LXII

In the Name of Allâh
the Most Gracious, the Most Merciful

1. Whatsoever is in the heavens and whatsoever is on the earth glorifies Allâh, the King (of everything), the Holy, the All-Mighty, the All-Wise.

2. He it is Who sent among the unlettered ones a Messenger (Muhammad صلى الله عليه وسلم) from among themselves, reciting to them His Verses, purifying them (from the filth of disbelief and polytheism), and teaching them the Book (this Qur'ân, Islâmic laws and Islâmic jurisprudence) and *Al-Hikmah* (*As-Sunnah*: legal ways, orders, acts of worship of Prophet Muhammad صلى الله عليه وسلم). And verily, they had been before in manifest error;

3. And [He has sent him (Prophet Muhammad صلى الله عليه وسلم) also to] others among them (Muslims) who have not yet joined them (but they will come). And He (Allâh) is the All-Mighty, the All-Wise.

4. That is the Grace of Allâh, which He bestows on whom He wills. And Allâh is the Owner of Mighty Grace.

5. The likeness of those who were entrusted with the (obligation of the) Taurât (Torah) (i.e. to obey its commandments and to practise its laws), but who subsequently failed in those (obligations), is as the likeness of a donkey which carries huge burdens of books (but understands nothing from them). How bad is the example of people who deny the *Ayât* (proofs, evidences, verses, signs, revelations, etc.) of Allâh. And Allâh guides not the people who are *Zâlimûn* (polytheists, wrongdoers, disbelievers).

6. Say (O Muhammad صلى الله عليه وسلم): "O you Jews! If you pretend that you are friends of Allâh, to the exclusion of (all) other mankind, then long for death if you are truthful."

7. But they will never long for it (death), because of what (deeds) their hands have sent before them! And Allâh knows well the *Zâlimûn* (polytheists, wrongdoers, disbelievers).

ولَن يَتَمَنَّوْهُ أَبَدًۢا بِمَا قَدَّمَتْ أَيْدِيهِمْ وَٱللَّهُ عَلِيمٌۢ بِٱلظَّـٰلِمِينَ ٧

8. Say (to them): "Verily, the death from which you flee will surely, meet you, then you will be sent back to (Allâh), the All-Knower of the unseen and the seen, and He will tell you what you used to do."

قُلْ إِنَّ ٱلْمَوْتَ ٱلَّذِى تَفِرُّونَ مِنْهُ فَإِنَّهُۥ مُلَـٰقِيكُمْ ثُمَّ تُرَدُّونَ إِلَىٰ عَـٰلِمِ ٱلْغَيْبِ وَٱلشَّهَـٰدَةِ فَيُنَبِّئُكُم بِمَا كُنتُمْ تَعْمَلُونَ ٨

9. O you who believe (Muslims)! When the call is proclaimed for the *Salât* (prayer) on Friday (*Jumu'ah* prayer), come to the remembrance of Allâh [*Jumu'ah* religious talk (*Khutbah*) and *Salât* (prayer)] and leave off business (and every other thing). That is better for you if you did but know!

يَـٰٓأَيُّهَا ٱلَّذِينَ ءَامَنُوٓا۟ إِذَا نُودِىَ لِلصَّلَوٰةِ مِن يَوْمِ ٱلْجُمُعَةِ فَٱسْعَوْا۟ إِلَىٰ ذِكْرِ ٱللَّهِ وَذَرُوا۟ ٱلْبَيْعَ ذَٰلِكُمْ خَيْرٌ لَّكُمْ إِن كُنتُمْ تَعْلَمُونَ ٩

10. Then when the (*Jumu'ah*) *Salât* (prayer) is ended, you may disperse through the land, and seek the Bounty of Allâh (by working), and remember Allâh much: that you may be successful.

فَإِذَا قُضِيَتِ ٱلصَّلَوٰةُ فَٱنتَشِرُوا۟ فِى ٱلْأَرْضِ وَٱبْتَغُوا۟ مِن فَضْلِ ٱللَّهِ وَٱذْكُرُوا۟ ٱللَّهَ كَثِيرًا لَّعَلَّكُمْ تُفْلِحُونَ ١٠

11. And when they see some merchandise or some amusement [beating of *Tambur* (drum)] they disperse headlong to it, and leave you (Muhammad صلى الله عليه وسلم) standing [while delivering *Jumu'ah* religious talk (*Khutbah*)]. Say: "That which Allâh has is better than any amusement or merchandise! And Allâh is the Best of providers."

وَإِذَا رَأَوْا۟ تِجَـٰرَةً أَوْ لَهْوًا ٱنفَضُّوٓا۟ إِلَيْهَا وَتَرَكُوكَ قَآئِمًا قُلْ مَا عِندَ ٱللَّهِ خَيْرٌ مِّنَ ٱللَّهْوِ وَمِنَ ٱلتِّجَـٰرَةِ وَٱللَّهُ خَيْرُ ٱلرَّٰزِقِينَ ١١

Sûrat Al-Munâfiqûn
(The Hypocrites) LXIII

*In the Name of Allâh
the Most Gracious, the Most Merciful*

1. When the hypocrites come to you (O Muhammad صلى الله عليه وسلم), they say: "We bear witness that you are indeed the Messenger of Allâh." Allâh knows that you are indeed His Messenger, and Allâh bears witness that the hypocrites are liars indeed.

2. They have made their oaths a screen (for their hypocrisy). Thus they hinder (men) from the Path of Allâh. Verily, evil is what they used to do.

3. That is because they believed, and then disbelieved; therefore their hearts are sealed, so they understand not.

4. And when you look at them, their bodies please you; and when they speak, you listen to their words. They are as blocks of wood propped up. They think that every cry is against them. They are the enemies, so beware of them. May Allâh curse them! How are they denying (or deviating from) the Right Path?

5. And when it is said to them: "Come, so that the Messenger of Allâh may ask forgiveness from Allâh for you," they twist their heads, and you would see them turning away their faces in pride.[1]

---

[1] (V.63:5) See the footnote of (V.22:9).

6. It is equal to them whether you (Muhammad صلى الله عليه وسلم) ask forgiveness or ask not forgiveness for them. Verily, Allâh guides not the people who are the *Fâsiqûn* (the rebellious, the disobedient to Allâh).[1]

سَوَآءٌ عَلَيْهِمْ أَسْتَغْفَرْتَ لَهُمْ أَمْ لَمْ تَسْتَغْفِرْ لَهُمْ لَن يَغْفِرَ اللَّهُ لَهُمْ إِنَّ اللَّهَ لَا يَهْدِى الْقَوْمَ الْفَٰسِقِينَ ٦

7. They are the ones who say: "Spend not on those who are with Allâh's Messenger, until they desert him." And to Allâh belong the treasures of the heavens and the earth, but the hypocrites comprehend not.

هُمُ الَّذِينَ يَقُولُونَ لَا تُنفِقُوا عَلَىٰ مَنْ عِندَ رَسُولِ اللَّهِ حَتَّىٰ يَنفَضُّوا وَلِلَّهِ خَزَآئِنُ السَّمَٰوَٰتِ وَالْأَرْضِ وَلَٰكِنَّ الْمُنَٰفِقِينَ لَا يَفْقَهُونَ ٧

8. They (hypocrites) say: "If we return to Al-Madinah, indeed the more honourable ('Abdûllah bin Ubai bin Salûl, the chief of hypocrites at Al-Madinah) will expel therefrom the meaner (i.e. Allâh's Messenger صلى الله عليه وسلم)." But honour, power and glory belong to Allâh, and to His Messenger (Muhammad صلى الله عليه وسلم), and to the believers, but the hypocrites know not.

يَقُولُونَ لَئِن رَّجَعْنَآ إِلَى الْمَدِينَةِ لَيُخْرِجَنَّ الْأَعَزُّ مِنْهَا الْأَذَلَّ وَلِلَّهِ الْعِزَّةُ وَلِرَسُولِهِ وَلِلْمُؤْمِنِينَ وَلَٰكِنَّ الْمُنَٰفِقِينَ لَا يَعْلَمُونَ ٨

9. O you who believe! Let not your properties or your children divert you from the remembrance of Allâh. And whosoever does that, then they are the losers.

يَٰٓأَيُّهَا الَّذِينَ ءَامَنُوا لَا تُلْهِكُمْ أَمْوَٰلُكُمْ وَلَآ أَوْلَٰدُكُمْ عَن ذِكْرِ اللَّهِ وَمَن يَفْعَلْ ذَٰلِكَ فَأُوْلَٰٓئِكَ هُمُ الْخَٰسِرُونَ ٩

10. And spend (in charity) of that with which We have provided you before death comes to one of you, and he says: "My Lord! If only You would give me respite for a little while (i.e. return to the worldly life), then I would give *Sadaqah* (i.e. *Zakât*) of my

وَأَنفِقُوا مِن مَّا رَزَقْنَٰكُم مِّن قَبْلِ أَن يَأْتِيَ أَحَدَكُمُ الْمَوْتُ فَيَقُولَ رَبِّ لَوْلَآ أَخَّرْتَنِيٓ إِلَىٰٓ أَجَلٍ قَرِيبٍ

---

[1] (V.63:6) See the Qur'ân (V.4:138-145).

wealth,[1] and be among the righteous [i.e. perform *Hajj* (pilgrimage to Makkah) and other good deeds].

11. And Allâh grants respite to none when his appointed time (death) comes. And Allâh is All-Aware of what you do.

Sûrat At-Taghâbun (Mutual Loss and Gain) LXIV

In the Name of Allâh the Most Gracious, the Most Merciful

1. Whatsoever is in the heavens and whatsoever is on the earth glorifies Allâh. His is the dominion, and to Him belong all the praises and thanks, and He is Able to do all things.

---

[1] (V.63:10).

A) Narrated Abu Hurairah رضي الله عنه: The Prophet صلى الله عليه وسلم said, "Everyday two angels come down from heaven and one of them says, 'O Allâh! Compensate every person who spends in Your Cause,' and the other (angel) says, 'O Allâh! Destroy every miser.'" (*Sahih Al-Bukhari*, Vol. 2, Hadith No. 522).

B) The performance of *Hajj* is an enjoined duty and its superiority, and the Statement of Allâh عز وجل: "*Hajj* (pilgrimage) to the House (*Ka'bah*), is a duty that mankind owes to Allâh, those who can afford the expenses (for one's conveyance, provision and residence) and whoever disbelieves [i.e. denies *Hajj* (pilgrimage to Makkah), then he is a disbeliever of Allâh], then Allâh stands not in need of any of the *'Âlamîn* (mankind and jinn)." (V.3:97).

C) Islam demolishes all the previous evil deeds and so do migration (for Allâh's sake) and *Hajj* (pilgrimage to Makkah) [*Al-Lû'lû' wal-Marjân*, Vol. 1, Chapter 52, Page 205] (*Sahih Muslim*, Vol. 1, Chapter 52, Page 78)

D) See the footnote of (V.3:180).

2. He it is Who created you, then some of you are disbelievers and some of you are believers. And Allâh is All-Seer of what you do.

هُوَ ٱلَّذِى خَلَقَكُمْ فَمِنكُمْ كَافِرٌ وَمِنكُم مُّؤْمِنٌ وَٱللَّهُ بِمَا تَعْمَلُونَ بَصِيرٌ ۝

3. He has created the heavens and the earth with truth, and He shaped you and made good your shapes. And to Him is the final Return.

خَلَقَ ٱلسَّمَٰوَٰتِ وَٱلْأَرْضَ بِٱلْحَقِّ وَصَوَّرَكُمْ فَأَحْسَنَ صُوَرَكُمْ وَإِلَيْهِ ٱلْمَصِيرُ ۝

4. He knows what is in the heavens and on earth, and He knows what you conceal and what you reveal. And Allâh is the All-Knower of what is in the breasts (of men).

يَعْلَمُ مَا فِى ٱلسَّمَٰوَٰتِ وَٱلْأَرْضِ وَيَعْلَمُ مَا تُسِرُّونَ وَمَا تُعْلِنُونَ وَٱللَّهُ عَلِيمٌۢ بِذَاتِ ٱلصُّدُورِ ۝

5. Has not the news reached you of those who disbelieved aforetime? And so they tasted the evil result of their disbelief, and theirs will be a painful torment.

أَلَمْ يَأْتِكُمْ نَبَؤُاْ ٱلَّذِينَ كَفَرُواْ مِن قَبْلُ فَذَاقُواْ وَبَالَ أَمْرِهِمْ وَلَهُمْ عَذَابٌ أَلِيمٌ ۝

6. That was because there came to them their Messengers with clear proofs (signs), but they said: "Shall mere men guide us?" So they disbelieved and turned away (from the truth). But Allâh was not in need (of them). And Allâh is Rich (Free of all needs), Worthy of all praise.

ذَٰلِكَ بِأَنَّهُۥ كَانَت تَّأْتِيهِمْ رُسُلُهُم بِٱلْبَيِّنَٰتِ فَقَالُوٓاْ أَبَشَرٌ يَهْدُونَنَا فَكَفَرُواْ وَتَوَلَّواْ وَٱسْتَغْنَى ٱللَّهُ وَٱللَّهُ غَنِيٌّ حَمِيدٌ ۝

7. The disbelievers pretend that they will never be resurrected (for the Account). Say (O Muhammad صلى الله عليه وسلم): Yes! By my Lord, you will certainly be resurrected, then you will be informed of (and recompensed for) what you did; and that is easy for Allâh.

زَعَمَ ٱلَّذِينَ كَفَرُوٓاْ أَن لَّن يُبْعَثُواْ قُلْ بَلَىٰ وَرَبِّى لَتُبْعَثُنَّ ثُمَّ لَتُنَبَّؤُنَّ بِمَا عَمِلْتُمْ وَذَٰلِكَ عَلَى ٱللَّهِ يَسِيرٌ ۝

8. Therefore, believe in Allâh and His Messenger (Muhammad صلى الله عليه وسلم) and

فَـَٔامِنُواْ بِٱللَّهِ وَرَسُولِهِۦ وَٱلنُّورِ

in the Light (this Qur'ân) which We have sent down. And Allâh is All-Aware of what you do.

9. (And remember) the Day when He will gather you (all) on the Day of Gathering, — that will be the Day of mutual loss and gain (i.e. loss for the disbelievers as they will enter the Hell-fire and gain for the believers as they will enter Paradise). And whosoever believes in Allâh and performs righteous good deeds, He will expiate from him his sins, and will admit him to Gardens under which rivers flow (Paradise) to dwell therein forever; that will be the great success.

10. But those who disbelieved (in the Oneness of Allâh – Islâmic Monotheism) and denied Our Ayât (proofs, evidences, verses, lessons, signs, revelations, etc.), they will be the dwellers of the Fire, to dwell therein forever. And worst indeed is that destination.[1]

11. No calamity befalls, but by the Leave [i.e. Decision and Qadar (Divine Preordainments)] of Allâh, and whosoever believes in Allâh, He guides his heart [to the true Faith with certainty, i.e. what has befallen him was already written for him by Allâh from the Qadar (Divine Preordainments)]. And Allâh is the All-Knower of everything.[2]

---

[1] (V.64:10) See the footnote of (V.3:85):

[2] (V.64:11) See the footnote of (V.57:22).

12. Obey Allâh, and obey the Messenger (Muhammad ﷺ); but if you turn away, then the duty of Our Messenger is only to convey (the Message) clearly.

وَأَطِيعُوا۟ ٱللَّهَ وَأَطِيعُوا۟ ٱلرَّسُولَ فَإِن تَوَلَّيْتُمْ فَإِنَّمَا عَلَىٰ رَسُولِنَا ٱلْبَلَٰغُ ٱلْمُبِينُ ﴿١٢﴾

13. Allâh! *Lâ ilâha illâ Huwa* (none has the right to be worshipped but He). And in Allâh (Alone) therefore let the believers put their trust.

ٱللَّهُ لَآ إِلَٰهَ إِلَّا هُوَ وَعَلَى ٱللَّهِ فَلْيَتَوَكَّلِ ٱلْمُؤْمِنُونَ ﴿١٣﴾

14. O you who believe! Verily, among your wives and your children are your enemies (who may stop you from the obedience of Allâh); therefore beware of them! But if you pardon (them) and overlook, and forgive (their faults), then verily, Allâh is Oft-Forgiving, Most Merciful.

يَٰٓأَيُّهَا ٱلَّذِينَ ءَامَنُوٓا۟ إِنَّ مِنْ أَزْوَٰجِكُمْ وَأَوْلَٰدِكُمْ عَدُوًّا لَّكُمْ فَٱحْذَرُوهُمْ وَإِن تَعْفُوا۟ وَتَصْفَحُوا۟ وَتَغْفِرُوا۟ فَإِنَّ ٱللَّهَ غَفُورٌ رَّحِيمٌ ﴿١٤﴾

15. Your wealth and your children are only a trial, whereas Allâh! With Him is a great reward (Paradise).

إِنَّمَآ أَمْوَٰلُكُمْ وَأَوْلَٰدُكُمْ فِتْنَةٌ وَٱللَّهُ عِندَهُۥٓ أَجْرٌ عَظِيمٌ ﴿١٥﴾

16. So keep your duty to Allâh and fear Him as much as you can; listen and obey, and spend in charity; that is better for yourselves. And whosoever is saved from his own covetousness, then they are the successful ones.

فَٱتَّقُوا۟ ٱللَّهَ مَا ٱسْتَطَعْتُمْ وَٱسْمَعُوا۟ وَأَطِيعُوا۟ وَأَنفِقُوا۟ خَيْرًا لِّأَنفُسِكُمْ وَمَن يُوقَ شُحَّ نَفْسِهِۦ فَأُو۟لَٰٓئِكَ هُمُ ٱلْمُفْلِحُونَ ﴿١٦﴾

17. If you lend to Allâh a goodly loan (i.e. spend in Allâh's Cause), He will double it for you, and will forgive you. And Allâh is Most Ready to appreciate and to reward, Most Forbearing,

إِن تُقْرِضُوا۟ ٱللَّهَ قَرْضًا حَسَنًا يُضَٰعِفْهُ لَكُمْ وَيَغْفِرْ لَكُمْ وَٱللَّهُ شَكُورٌ حَلِيمٌ ﴿١٧﴾

18. All-Knower of the unseen and seen, the All-Mighty, the All-Wise.

عَٰلِمُ ٱلْغَيْبِ وَٱلشَّهَٰدَةِ ٱلْعَزِيزُ ٱلْحَكِيمُ ﴿١٨﴾

Sûrat At-Talâq
(The Divorce) LXV

سُورَةُ الطَّلاقِ

*In the Name of Allâh
the Most Gracious, the Most Merciful*

بِسْمِ اللهِ الرَّحْمَنِ الرَّحِيمِ

1. O Prophet (صلى الله عليه وسلم)! When you divorce women, divorce them at their 'Iddah (prescribed periods) and count (accurately) their 'Iddah (periods)[1]. And fear Allâh your Lord (O Muslims). And turn them not out of their (husband's) homes nor shall they (themselves) leave, except in case they are guilty of some open illegal sexual intercourse. And those are the set limits of Allâh. And whosoever transgresses the set limits of Allâh, then indeed he has wronged himself. You (the one who divorces his wife) know not it may be that Allâh will afterward bring some new thing to pass (i.e. to return her back to you if that was the first or second divorce).

يَٰٓأَيُّهَا ٱلنَّبِىُّ إِذَا طَلَّقْتُمُ ٱلنِّسَآءَ فَطَلِّقُوهُنَّ لِعِدَّتِهِنَّ وَأَحْصُوا۟ ٱلْعِدَّةَ وَٱتَّقُوا۟ ٱللَّهَ رَبَّكُمْ لَا تُخْرِجُوهُنَّ مِنۢ بُيُوتِهِنَّ وَلَا يَخْرُجْنَ إِلَّآ أَن يَأْتِينَ بِفَٰحِشَةٍ مُّبَيِّنَةٍ وَتِلْكَ حُدُودُ ٱللَّهِ وَمَن يَتَعَدَّ حُدُودَ ٱللَّهِ فَقَدْ ظَلَمَ نَفْسَهُ لَا تَدْرِى لَعَلَّ ٱللَّهَ يُحْدِثُ بَعْدَ ذَٰلِكَ أَمْرًا ﴿١﴾

2. Then when they are about to attain their term appointed, either take them

فَإِذَا بَلَغْنَ أَجَلَهُنَّ فَأَمْسِكُوهُنَّ

---

[1] (V.65:1) Narrated 'Abdullâh bin 'Umar رضى الله عنهما that he had divorced his wife while she was menstruating during the lifetime of Allâh's Messenger صلى الله عليه وسلم. 'Umar bin Al-Khattâb رضى الله عنه asked Allâh's Messenger صلى الله عليه وسلم about that. Allâh's Messenger صلى الله عليه وسلم said, "Order him (your son) to take her back and keep her till she is clean from her menses and then to wait till she gets her next period and becomes clean again, whereupon, if he wishes to keep her, he can do so, and if he wishes to divorce her he can divorce her before having sexual intercourse with her; and that is the 'Iddah (prescribed period) which Allâh has fixed for the women meant to be divorced." (Sahih Al-Bukhari, Vol.7, Hadîth No.178).

back in a good manner or part with them in a good manner. And take as witness two just persons from among you (Muslims). And establish the testimony for Allâh. That will be an admonition given to him who believes in Allâh and the Last Day. And whosoever fears Allâh and keeps his duty to Him, He will make a way for him to get out (from every difficulty).

3. And He will provide him from (sources) he never could imagine. And whosoever puts his trust in Allâh, then He will suffice him. Verily, Allâh will accomplish his purpose. Indeed Allâh has set a measure for all things.

4. And those of your women as have passed the age of monthly courses, for them the 'Iddah (prescribed period), if you have doubt (about their periods), is three months; and for those who have no courses [(i.e. they are still immature) their 'Iddah (prescribed period) is three months likewise, except in case of death].[1] And for those who are pregnant (whether they are divorced or their husbands are dead), their 'Iddah (prescribed period) is until they lay down their burden; and whosoever fears Allâh and keeps his duty to Him, He will make his matter easy for him.

5. That is the Command of Allâh, which He has sent down to you; and whosoever fears Allâh and keeps his

---

[1] (V.65:4) See the Qur'an, Verse 2:234.

duty to Him, He will expiate from him his sins, and will enlarge his reward.

6. Lodge them (the divorced women) where you dwell, according to your means, and do not harm them so as to straiten them (that they be obliged to leave your house). And if they are pregnant, then spend on them till they lay down their burden. Then if they give suck to the children for you, give them their due payment, and let each of you accept the advice of the other in a just way. But if you make difficulties for one another, then some other woman may give suck for him (the father of the child).

7. Let the rich man spend according to his means; and the man whose resources are restricted, let him spend according to what Allâh has given him. Allâh puts no burden on any person beyond what He has given him. Allâh will grant after hardship, ease.

8. And many a town (population) revolted against the Command of its Lord and His Messengers; and We called it to a severe account (i.e. torment in this worldly life), and We shall punish it with a horrible torment (in Hell in the Hereafter).

9. So it tasted the evil result of its affair (disbelief), and the consequence of its affair (disbelief) was loss (destruction in this life and an eternal punishment in the Hereafter).

10. Allâh has prepared for them a severe torment. So fear Allâh and keep your duty to Him, O men of understanding who have believed! Allâh has indeed sent down to you a Reminder (this Qur'ân).

11. (And has also sent to you) a Messenger (Muhammad صلى الله عليه وسلم), who recites to you the Verses of Allâh (the Qur'ân) containing clear explanations, that He may take out those who believe and do righteous good deeds, from the darkness (of polytheism and disbelief) to the light (of Islamic Monotheism). And whosoever believes in Allâh and performs righteous good deeds, He will admit him into Gardens under which rivers flow (Paradise) to dwell therein forever. Allâh has indeed granted for him an excellent provision.

12. It is Allâh Who has created seven heavens and of the earth the like thereof (i.e. seven). His Command descends between them (heavens and earth), that you may know that Allâh has power over all things, and that Allâh surrounds all things in (His) Knowledge.

Sûrat At-Tahrîm
(The Prohibition) LXVI

*In the Name of Allâh
the Most Gracious, the Most Merciful*

1. O Prophet! Why do you forbid (for yourself) that which Allâh has allowed to you, seeking to please your wives? And Allâh is Oft-Forgiving, Most Merciful.

2. Allâh has already ordained for you (O men) the absolution from your oaths. And Allâh is your *Maulâ* (Lord, or Master, or Protector) and He is the All-Knower, the All-Wise.

قَدْ فَرَضَ ٱللَّهُ لَكُمْ تَحِلَّةَ أَيْمَـٰنِكُمْ وَٱللَّهُ مَوْلَىٰكُمْ وَهُوَ ٱلْعَلِيمُ ٱلْحَكِيمُ ﴿٢﴾

3. And (remember) when the Prophet (صلى الله عليه وسلم) disclosed a matter in confidence to one of his wives (Hafsah), then she told it (to another i.e. 'Âishah). And Allâh made it known to him; he informed part thereof and left a part. Then when he told her (Hafsah) thereof, she said: "Who told you this?" He said: "The All-Knower, the All-Aware (Allâh) has told me."

وَإِذْ أَسَرَّ ٱلنَّبِيُّ إِلَىٰ بَعْضِ أَزْوَٰجِهِۦ حَدِيثًا فَلَمَّا نَبَّأَتْ بِهِۦ وَأَظْهَرَهُ ٱللَّهُ عَلَيْهِ عَرَّفَ بَعْضَهُۥ وَأَعْرَضَ عَنۢ بَعْضٍ فَلَمَّا نَبَّأَهَا بِهِۦ قَالَتْ مَنْ أَنۢبَأَكَ هَـٰذَا قَالَ نَبَّأَنِيَ ٱلْعَلِيمُ ٱلْخَبِيرُ ﴿٣﴾

4. If you two (wives of the Prophet صلى الله عليه وسلم : 'Âishah and Hafsah رضي الله عنهما) turn in repentance to Allâh, (it will be better for you), your hearts are indeed so inclined (to oppose what the Prophet صلى الله عليه وسلم likes); but if you help one another against him (Muhammad صلى الله عليه وسلم), then verily, Allâh is his *Maulâ* (Lord, or Master, or Protector), and Jibrael (Gabriel), and the righteous among the believers; and furthermore, the angels are his helpers.

إِن تَتُوبَآ إِلَى ٱللَّهِ فَقَدْ صَغَتْ قُلُوبُكُمَا وَإِن تَظَـٰهَرَا عَلَيْهِ فَإِنَّ ٱللَّهَ هُوَ مَوْلَىٰهُ وَجِبْرِيلُ وَصَـٰلِحُ ٱلْمُؤْمِنِينَ وَٱلْمَلَـٰٓئِكَةُ بَعْدَ ذَٰلِكَ ظَهِيرٌ ﴿٤﴾

5. It may be if he divorced you (all) that his Lord will give him instead of you, wives better than you — Muslims (who submit to Allâh), believers, obedient (to Allâh), turning to Allâh in repentance, worshipping Allâh sincerely, given to fasting or emigrants

عَسَىٰ رَبُّهُۥٓ إِن طَلَّقَكُنَّ أَن يُبْدِلَهُۥٓ أَزْوَٰجًا خَيْرًا مِّنكُنَّ مُسْلِمَـٰتٍ مُّؤْمِنَـٰتٍ قَـٰنِتَـٰتٍ تَـٰٓئِبَـٰتٍ عَـٰبِدَٰتٍ سَـٰٓئِحَـٰتٍ ثَيِّبَـٰتٍ وَأَبْكَارًا ﴿٥﴾

(for Allâh's sake), previously married and virgins.

6. O you who believe! Ward off yourselves and your families against a Fire (Hell) whose fuel is men and stones, over which are (appointed) angels stern (and) severe, who disobey not, (from executing) the Commands they receive from Allâh, but do that which they are commanded.

يَـٰٓأَيُّهَا ٱلَّذِينَ ءَامَنُوا۟ قُوٓا۟ أَنفُسَكُمْ وَأَهْلِيكُمْ نَارًا وَقُودُهَا ٱلنَّاسُ وَٱلْحِجَارَةُ عَلَيْهَا مَلَـٰٓئِكَةٌ غِلَاظٌ شِدَادٌ لَّا يَعْصُونَ ٱللَّهَ مَآ أَمَرَهُمْ وَيَفْعَلُونَ مَا يُؤْمَرُونَ ٦

7. (It will be said in the Hereafter) O you who disbelieve (in the Oneness of Allâh — Islâmic Monotheism)! Make no excuses this Day! You are being requited only for what you used to do.[1]

يَـٰٓأَيُّهَا ٱلَّذِينَ كَفَرُوا۟ لَا تَعْتَذِرُوا۟ ٱلْيَوْمَ إِنَّمَا تُجْزَوْنَ مَا كُنتُمْ تَعْمَلُونَ ٧

8. O you who believe! Turn to Allâh with sincere repentance! It may be that your Lord will expiate from you your sins, and admit you into Gardens under which rivers flow (Paradise) — the Day that Allâh will not disgrace the Prophet (Muhammad صلى الله عليه وسلم) and those who believe with him. Their Light will run forward before them and (with their Records — Books of deeds) in their right hands. They will say: "Our Lord! Keep perfect our Light for us [and do not put it off till we cross over the *Sirât* (a slippery bridge over the Hell) safely]

يَـٰٓأَيُّهَا ٱلَّذِينَ ءَامَنُوا۟ تُوبُوٓا۟ إِلَى ٱللَّهِ تَوْبَةً نَّصُوحًا عَسَىٰ رَبُّكُمْ أَن يُكَفِّرَ عَنكُمْ سَيِّـَٔاتِكُمْ وَيُدْخِلَكُمْ جَنَّـٰتٍ تَجْرِى مِن تَحْتِهَا ٱلْأَنْهَـٰرُ يَوْمَ لَا يُخْزِى ٱللَّهُ ٱلنَّبِىَّ وَٱلَّذِينَ ءَامَنُوا۟ مَعَهُۥ نُورُهُمْ يَسْعَىٰ بَيْنَ أَيْدِيهِمْ وَبِأَيْمَـٰنِهِم يَقُولُونَ رَبَّنَآ أَتْمِمْ لَنَا نُورَنَا وَٱغْفِرْ لَنَآ إِنَّكَ عَلَىٰ كُلِّ شَىْءٍ قَدِيرٌ ٨

---

[1] (V.66:7) See the footnote of (V.3:85).

and grant us forgiveness. Verily, You are Able to do all things."[1]

9. O Prophet (Muhammad صلى الله عليه وسلم)! Strive hard against the disbelievers and the hypocrites, and be severe against them; their abode will be Hell, and worst indeed is that destination.[2]

10. Allâh sets forth an example for those who disbelieve: the wife of Nûh (Noah) and the wife of Lût (Lot). They were under two of our righteous slaves, but they both betrayed them (their husbands by rejecting their doctrine). So they [Nûh (Noah) and Lût (Lot) عليهما السلام] availed them (their respective wives) not against Allâh and it was said: "Enter the Fire along with those who enter!"

11. And Allâh has set forth an example for those who believe: the wife of Fir'aun (Pharaoh), when she said: "My Lord! Build for me a home with You in Paradise, and save me from Fir'aun (Pharaoh) and his work, and save me from the people who are Zâlimûn (polytheists, wrongdoers and disbelievers in Allâh).

12. And Maryam (Mary), the daughter of 'Imrân who guarded her

بَأَيُّهَا ٱلنَّبِىُّ جَهِدِ ٱلْكُفَّارَ وَٱلْمُنَفِقِينَ وَٱغْلُظْ عَلَيْهِمْ وَمَأْوَىٰهُمْ جَهَنَّمُ وَبِئْسَ ٱلْمَصِيرُ ۝

ضَرَبَ ٱللَّهُ مَثَلًا لِّلَّذِينَ كَفَرُواْ ٱمْرَأَتَ نُوحٍ وَٱمْرَأَتَ لُوطٍ كَانَتَا تَحْتَ عَبْدَيْنِ مِنْ عِبَادِنَا صَالِحَيْنِ فَخَانَتَاهُمَا فَلَمْ يُغْنِيَا عَنْهُمَا مِنَ ٱللَّهِ شَيْئًا وَقِيلَ ٱدْخُلَا ٱلنَّارَ مَعَ ٱلدَّاخِلِينَ ۝

وَضَرَبَ ٱللَّهُ مَثَلًا لِّلَّذِينَ ءَامَنُواْ ٱمْرَأَتَ فِرْعَوْنَ إِذْ قَالَتْ رَبِّ ٱبْنِ لِي عِندَكَ بَيْتًا فِي ٱلْجَنَّةِ وَنَجِّنِي مِن فِرْعَوْنَ وَعَمَلِهِ وَنَجِّنِي مِنَ ٱلْقَوْمِ ٱلظَّالِمِينَ ۝

وَمَرْيَمَ ٱبْنَتَ عِمْرَانَ ٱلَّتِي أَحْصَنَتْ

---

[1] (V.66:8).

a) See the footnote of (V.4:106).

b) See the footnote of (V.5:74).

c) See the footnote of (V.68:42).

[2] (V.66:9) See the footnote of (V.8:39).

chastity. And We breathed into (the sleeve of her shirt or her garment) through Our *Rûh* [i.e. Jibrael (Gabriel)][1], and she testified to the truth of the Words of her Lord [i.e. believed in the Words of Allâh: "Be!" — and he was; that is 'Îsâ (Jesus), son of Maryam (Mary) as a Messenger of Allâh], and (also believed in) His Scriptures, and she was of the *Qanitûn* (i.e. obedient to Allâh).[2]

فَرَجَهَا فَنَفَخْنَا فِيهِ مِن رُّوحِنَا وَصَدَّقَتْ بِكَلِمَٰتِ رَبِّهَا وَكُتُبِهِ وَكَانَتْ مِنَ ٱلْقَٰنِتِينَ ۝

---

[1] (V.66:12) "And (remember) she who guarded her chastity [Virgin Maryam (Mary)], We breathed into (the sleeves of) her (shirt or garment) [through Our *Rûh* (Jibrael - Gabriel)]*, and We made her and her son (Jesus) a sign for *Al-'Âlamîn* (mankind and jinn)." [The Qur'ân, (V.21:91)]

* It is said that Jibrael (Gabriel) had merely breathed in the sleeve of Maryam's (Mary) shirt, and thus she conceived.

[2] (V.66:12) The Statement of Allâh عَزَّ وَجَلَّ:

'And Allâh has set forth an example for those who believe: the wife of Pharaoh … (up to) … and she was of the obedient to Allâh.' (V.66:11 and 12).

Narrated Abu Mûsâ رَضِيَ اللهُ عَنْهُ: Allâh's Messenger صَلَّى اللهُ عَلَيْهِ وَسَلَّمَ said, "Many amongst men reached (the level of) perfection but none amongst the women reached this level except Asiyah, Pharaoh's wife, and Maryam (Mary), the daughter of 'Imrân. And no doubt, the superiority of 'Âishah to other women is like the superiority of *Tharid* (i.e. a meat and bread dish) to other meals." (*Sahih Al-Bukhari*, 4, *Hadith* No. 623).

Sûrat Al-Mulk
(Dominion) LXVII

سُورَةُ الملكِ

In the Name of Allâh
the Most Gracious, the Most Merciful

بِسۡمِ اللهِ الرَّحۡمٰنِ الرَّحِيمِ

1. Blessed is He in Whose Hand is the dominion; and He is Able to do all things.

تَبَـٰرَكَ الَّذِى بِيَدِهِ الۡمُلۡكُ وَهُوَ عَلَىٰ كُلِّ شَىۡءٍ قَدِيرٌ ۝

2. Who has created death and life that He may test you which of you is best in deed.[1] And He is the All-Mighty, the Oft-Forgiving;

الَّذِى خَلَقَ الۡمَوۡتَ وَالۡحَيَوٰةَ لِيَبۡلُوَكُمۡ أَيُّكُمۡ أَحۡسَنُ عَمَلًا وَهُوَ الۡعَزِيزُ الۡغَفُورُ ۝

3. Who has created the seven heavens one above another; you can see no fault in the creation of the Most Gracious. Then look again: "Can you see any rifts?"

الَّذِى خَلَقَ سَبۡعَ سَمَٰوَٰتٍ طِبَاقًا مَّا تَرَىٰ فِى خَلۡقِ الرَّحۡمَٰنِ مِن تَفَٰوُتٍ فَارۡجِعِ الۡبَصَرَ هَلۡ تَرَىٰ مِن فُطُورٍ ۝

4. Then look again and yet again: your sight will return to you in a state of humiliation and worn out.

ثُمَّ ارۡجِعِ الۡبَصَرَ كَرَّتَيۡنِ يَنقَلِبۡ إِلَيۡكَ الۡبَصَرُ خَاسِئًا وَهُوَ حَسِيرٌ ۝

5. And indeed We have adorned the nearest heaven with lamps, and We have made such lamps (as) missiles to drive away the *Shayâtîn* (devils), and have prepared for them the torment of the blazing Fire.

وَلَقَدۡ زَيَّنَّا السَّمَاءَ الدُّنۡيَا بِمَصَٰبِيحَ وَجَعَلۡنَٰهَا رُجُومًا لِّلشَّيَٰطِينِ وَأَعۡتَدۡنَا لَهُمۡ عَذَابَ السَّعِيرِ ۝

6. And for those who disbelieve in their Lord (Allâh) is the torment of Hell, and worst indeed is that destination.

وَلِلَّذِينَ كَفَرُوا بِرَبِّهِمۡ عَذَابُ جَهَنَّمَ وَبِئۡسَ الۡمَصِيرُ ۝

7. When they are cast therein, they will hear the (terrible) drawing in of its breath as it blazes forth.

إِذَا أُلۡقُوا فِيهَا سَمِعُوا لَهَا شَهِيقًا وَهِىَ تَفُورُ ۝

---

[1] (V.67:2) i.e. who amongst you do the good deeds in the most perfect manner, that means to do them (deeds) totally for Allâh's sake and in accordance with the legal ways of Prophet Muhammad صلى الله عليه وسلم .

8. It almost bursts up with fury. Every time a group is cast therein, its keeper will ask: "Did no warner come to you?"

تَكَادُ تَمَيَّزُ مِنَ ٱلْغَيْظِ كُلَّمَا أُلْقِىَ فِيهَا فَوْجٌ سَأَلَهُمْ خَزَنَتُهَا أَلَمْ يَأْتِكُمْ نَذِيرٌ ﴿٨﴾

9. They will say: "Yes, indeed a warner did come to us, but we belied him and said: 'Allâh never sent down anything (of revelation); you are only in great error.'"

قَالُوا بَلَىٰ قَدْ جَاءَنَا نَذِيرٌ فَكَذَّبْنَا وَقُلْنَا مَا نَزَّلَ ٱللَّهُ مِن شَىْءٍ إِنْ أَنتُمْ إِلَّا فِى ضَلَٰلٍ كَبِيرٍ ﴿٩﴾

10. And they will say: "Had we but listened or used our intelligence, we would not have been among the dwellers of the blazing Fire!"

وَقَالُوا لَوْ كُنَّا نَسْمَعُ أَوْ نَعْقِلُ مَا كُنَّا فِىٓ أَصْحَٰبِ ٱلسَّعِيرِ ﴿١٠﴾

11. Then they will confess their sin. So, away with the dwellers of the blazing Fire!

فَٱعْتَرَفُوا بِذَنۢبِهِمْ فَسُحْقًا لِّأَصْحَٰبِ ٱلسَّعِيرِ ﴿١١﴾

12. Verily, those who fear their Lord unseen (i.e. they do not see Him, nor His punishment in the Hereafter), theirs will be forgiveness and a great reward (i.e. Paradise).

إِنَّ ٱلَّذِينَ يَخْشَوْنَ رَبَّهُم بِٱلْغَيْبِ لَهُم مَّغْفِرَةٌ وَأَجْرٌ كَبِيرٌ ﴿١٢﴾

13. And whether you keep your talk secret or disclose it, verily, He is the All-Knower of what is in the breasts (of men).

وَأَسِرُّوا قَوْلَكُمْ أَوِ ٱجْهَرُوا بِهِۦٓ إِنَّهُۥ عَلِيمٌۢ بِذَاتِ ٱلصُّدُورِ ﴿١٣﴾

14. Should not He Who has created know? And He is the Most Kind and Courteous (to His slaves), All-Aware (of everything).

أَلَا يَعْلَمُ مَنْ خَلَقَ وَهُوَ ٱللَّطِيفُ ٱلْخَبِيرُ ﴿١٤﴾

15. He it is Who has made the earth subservient to you (i.e. easy for you to walk, to live and to do agriculture on it); so walk in the path thereof and eat of His provision. And to Him will be the Resurrection.

هُوَ ٱلَّذِى جَعَلَ لَكُمُ ٱلْأَرْضَ ذَلُولًا فَٱمْشُوا فِى مَنَاكِبِهَا وَكُلُوا مِن رِّزْقِهِۦ وَإِلَيْهِ ٱلنُّشُورُ ﴿١٥﴾

16. Do you feel secure that He, Who is over the heaven (Allâh), will not cause the earth to sink with you, and then it should quake?

17. Or do you feel secure that He, Who is over the heaven (Allâh), will not send against you a violent whirlwind? Then you shall know how (terrible) has been My Warning.

18. And indeed those before them belied (the Messengers of Allâh), then how terrible was My denial (punishment)?

19. Do they not see the birds above them, spreading out their wings and folding them in? None upholds them except the Most Gracious (Allâh). Verily, He is the All-Seer of everything.

20. Who is he besides the Most Gracious that can be an army to you to help you? The disbelievers are in nothing but delusion.

21. Who is he that can provide for you if He should withhold His provision? Nay, but they continue to be in pride, and (they) flee (from the truth).

22. Is he who walks prone (without seeing) on his face, more rightly guided, or he who (sees and) walks upright on the Straight Way (i.e. Islâmic Monotheism)?

23. Say it is He Who has created you, and endowed you with hearing (ears) and seeing (eyes), and hearts. Little thanks you give.

24. Say: "It is He Who has created you from the earth, and to Him shall you be gathered (in the Hereafter)."

25. They say: "When will this promise (i.e. the Day of Resurrection) come to pass if you are telling the truth?"

26. Say (O Muhammad صلى الله عليه وسلم): "The knowledge (of its exact time) is with Allâh only, and I am only a plain warner."

27. But when they will see it (the torment on the Day of Resurrection) approaching, the faces of those who disbelieve will change and turn black with sadness and in grief and it will be said (to them): "This is (the promise) which you were calling for!"

28. Say (O Muhammad صلى الله عليه وسلم): "Tell me! If Allâh destroys me, and those with me, or He bestows His Mercy on us — who can save the disbelievers from a painful torment?"

29. Say: "He is the Most Gracious (Allâh), in Him we believe, and in Him we put our trust. So you will come to know who is it that is in manifest error."

30. Say (O Muhammad صلى الله عليه وسلم): "Tell me! If (all) your water were to sink away, who then can supply you with flowing (spring) water?"

Sûrat Al-Qalam or Nûn (The Pen) LXVIII

سورة القلم

In the Name of Allâh the Most Gracious, the Most Merciful

بسم الله الرحمن الرحيم

1. *Nûn.*

[These letters (*Nûn*, etc.) are one of the miracles of the Qur'ân, and none but Allâh (Alone) knows their meanings].

By the pen and by what they (the angels) write (in the Records of men).

2. You (O Muhammad صلى الله عليه وسلم), by the Grace of your Lord, are not mad.

مَآ أَنتَ بِنِعْمَةِ رَبِّكَ بِمَجْنُونٍ ﴿٢﴾

3. And verily, for you (O Muhammad صلى الله عليه وسلم) will be an endless reward.

وَإِنَّ لَكَ لَأَجْرًا غَيْرَ مَمْنُونٍ ﴿٣﴾

4. And verily, you (O Muhammad صلى الله عليه وسلم) are on an exalted (standard of) character.

وَإِنَّكَ لَعَلَىٰ خُلُقٍ عَظِيمٍ ﴿٤﴾

5. You will see, and they will see,

فَسَتُبْصِرُ وَيُبْصِرُونَ ﴿٥﴾

6. Which of you is afflicted with madness.

بِأَيِّكُمُ ٱلْمَفْتُونُ ﴿٦﴾

7. Verily, your Lord is the Best Knower of him who has gone astray from His Path, and He is the Best Knower of those who are guided.

إِنَّ رَبَّكَ هُوَ أَعْلَمُ بِمَن ضَلَّ عَن سَبِيلِهِ وَهُوَ أَعْلَمُ بِٱلْمُهْتَدِينَ ﴿٧﴾

8. So (O Muhammad صلى الله عليه وسلم) obey you not the deniers [(of Islâmic Monotheism — those who belie the Verses of Allâh), the Oneness of Allâh, and the Messengership of Muhammad صلى الله عليه وسلم]^[1]

فَلَا تُطِعِ ٱلْمُكَذِّبِينَ ﴿٨﴾

9. They wish that you should compromise (in religion out of courtesy) with them: so they (too) would compromise with you.

وَدُّوا لَوْ تُدْهِنُ فَيُدْهِنُونَ ﴿٩﴾

10. And (O Muhammad صلى الله عليه وسلم) obey you not everyone *Hallâf Mahîn* (the one who swears much and is a liar or is worthless). [*Tafsir At-Tabari*]

وَلَا تُطِعْ كُلَّ حَلَّافٍ مَّهِينٍ ﴿١٠﴾

11. A slanderer, going about with calumnies,

هَمَّازٍ مَّشَّاءٍ بِنَمِيمٍ ﴿١١﴾

---

[1] (V.68:8) See the footnote of (V.3:85).

12. Hinderer of the good, transgressor, sinful,

مَنَّاعٍ لِلْخَيْرِ مُعْتَدٍ أَثِيمٍ ﴿١٢﴾

13. Cruel, and moreover base-born (of illegitimate birth).

عُتُلٍّ بَعْدَ ذَٰلِكَ زَنِيمٍ ﴿١٣﴾

14. (He was so) because he had wealth and children.

أَن كَانَ ذَا مَالٍ وَبَنِينَ ﴿١٤﴾

15. When Our Verses (of the Qur'ân) are recited to him, he says: "Tales of the men of old!"

إِذَا تُتْلَىٰ عَلَيْهِ آيَاتُنَا قَالَ أَسَاطِيرُ الْأَوَّلِينَ ﴿١٥﴾

16. We shall brand him on the snout (nose)!

سَنَسِمُهُ عَلَى الْخُرْطُومِ ﴿١٦﴾

17. Verily, We have tried them as We tried the People of the Garden, when they swore to pluck the fruits of the (garden) in the morning,

إِنَّا بَلَوْنَاهُمْ كَمَا بَلَوْنَا أَصْحَابَ الْجَنَّةِ إِذْ أَقْسَمُوا لَيَصْرِمُنَّهَا مُصْبِحِينَ ﴿١٧﴾

18. Without saying: *Inshâ' Allâh* (If Allâh wills).

وَلَا يَسْتَثْنُونَ ﴿١٨﴾

19. Then there passed by on the (garden) a visitation (fire) from your Lord at night and burnt it while they were asleep.

فَطَافَ عَلَيْهَا طَائِفٌ مِّن رَّبِّكَ وَهُمْ نَائِمُونَ ﴿١٩﴾

20. So the (garden) became black by the morning, like a pitch dark night (in complete ruins).

فَأَصْبَحَتْ كَالصَّرِيمِ ﴿٢٠﴾

21. Then they called out one to another as soon as the morning broke.

فَتَنَادَوْا مُصْبِحِينَ ﴿٢١﴾

22. Saying: "Go to your tilth in the morning, if you would pluck the fruits."

أَنِ اغْدُوا عَلَىٰ حَرْثِكُمْ إِن كُنتُمْ صَارِمِينَ ﴿٢٢﴾

23. So they departed, conversing in secret low tones (saying):

فَانطَلَقُوا وَهُمْ يَتَخَافَتُونَ ﴿٢٣﴾

24. No *Miskin* (poor man) shall enter upon you into it today.

أَن لَّا يَدْخُلَنَّهَا الْيَوْمَ عَلَيْكُم مِّسْكِينٌ ﴿٢٤﴾

25. And they went in the morning with strong intention, thinking that they

وَغَدَوْا عَلَىٰ حَرْدٍ قَادِرِينَ ﴿٢٥﴾

have power (to prevent the poor taking anything of the fruits therefrom).

26. But when they saw the (garden), they said: "Verily, we have gone astray."

فَلَمَّا رَأَوْهَا قَالُوٓاْ إِنَّا لَضَآلُّونَ ۝

27. (Then they said): "Nay! Indeed we are deprived of (the fruits)!"

بَلْ نَحْنُ مَحْرُومُونَ ۝

28. The best among them said: "Did I not tell you: why say you not: Inshâ' Allâh (If Allâh wills)."

قَالَ أَوْسَطُهُمْ أَلَمْ أَقُل لَّكُمْ لَوْلَا تُسَبِّحُونَ ۝

29. They said: "Glory to Our Lord! Verily, we have been Zâlimûn (wrongdoers)."

قَالُواْ سُبْحَٰنَ رَبِّنَآ إِنَّا كُنَّا ظَٰلِمِينَ ۝

30. Then they turned one against another, blaming.

فَأَقْبَلَ بَعْضُهُمْ عَلَىٰ بَعْضٍ يَتَلَٰوَمُونَ ۝

31. They said: "Woe to us! Verily, we were Tâghûn (transgressors and disobedient).

قَالُواْ يَٰوَيْلَنَآ إِنَّا كُنَّا طَٰغِينَ ۝

32. We hope that our Lord will give us in exchange a better (garden) than this. Truly, we turn to our Lord (wishing for good that He may forgive our sins and reward us in the Hereafter).

عَسَىٰ رَبُّنَآ أَن يُبْدِلَنَا خَيْرًا مِّنْهَآ إِنَّآ إِلَىٰ رَبِّنَا رَٰغِبُونَ ۝

33. Such is the punishment (in this life), but truly, the punishment of the Hereafter is greater if they but knew.

كَذَٰلِكَ ٱلْعَذَابُ وَلَعَذَابُ ٱلْءَاخِرَةِ أَكْبَرُ لَوْ كَانُواْ يَعْلَمُونَ ۝

34. Verily, for the Muttaqûn (the pious. See V.2:2) are Gardens of delight (Paradise) with their Lord.

إِنَّ لِلْمُتَّقِينَ عِندَ رَبِّهِمْ جَنَّٰتِ ٱلنَّعِيمِ ۝

35. Shall We then treat the Muslims (believers of Islamic Monotheism, doers of righteous deeds) like the Mujrimûn (criminals, polytheists and disbelievers)?

أَفَنَجْعَلُ ٱلْمُسْلِمِينَ كَٱلْمُجْرِمِينَ ۝

36. What is the matter with you? How judge you?

مَا لَكُمْ كَيْفَ تَحْكُمُونَ ۝

37. Or have you a Book wherein you learn, أَمْ لَكُمْ كِتَبٌ فِيهِ تَدْرُسُونَ ﴿٣٧﴾

38. That you shall therein have all that you choose? إِنَّ لَكُمْ فِيهِ لَمَا تَخَيَّرُونَ ﴿٣٨﴾

39. Or you have oaths from Us, reaching to the Day of Resurrection, that yours will be what you judge? أَمْ لَكُمْ أَيْمَـٰنٌ عَلَيْنَا بَـٰلِغَةٌ إِلَىٰ يَوْمِ الْقِيَـٰمَةِ إِنَّ لَكُمْ لَمَا تَحْكُمُونَ ﴿٣٩﴾

40. Ask them, which of them will stand surety for that! سَلْهُمْ أَيُّهُم بِذَٰلِكَ زَعِيمٌ ﴿٤٠﴾

41. Or have they "partners"? Then let them bring their "partners" if they are truthful! أَمْ لَهُمْ شُرَكَاءُ فَلْيَأْتُوا بِشُرَكَائِهِمْ إِن كَانُوا صَـٰدِقِينَ ﴿٤١﴾

42. (Remember) the Day when the Shin[1] shall be laid bare (i.e. the Day of يَوْمَ يُكْشَفُ عَن سَاقٍ وَيُدْعَوْنَ إِلَى

---

[1] (V.68:42).

a) Narrated Abû-Sa'îd رضي الله عنه I heard the Prophet صلى الله عليه وسلم saying, "Allâh will lay bare His Shin and then all the believers, men and women, will prostrate themselves before Him; but there will remain those who used to prostrate themselves in the world for showing off and for gaining good reputation. Such a one will try to prostrate himself (on the Day of Judgement) but his back (bones) will become a single (vertebra) bone (so he will not be able to prostrate). (Sahih Al-Bukhari, Vol.6, Hadîth No.441).

b) See the footnote of (V.3:73). صفات الله عنه.

c) Narrated Abû Sa'îd Al-Khudrî رضي الله عنه We said, "O Allâh's Messenger! Shall we see our Lord on the Day of Resurrection?" He said, "Do you have any difficulty in seeing the sun and the moon when the sky is clear?" We said, "No." He said, "So you will have no difficulty in seeing your Lord on that Day as you have no difficulty in seeing the sun and the moon (in a clear sky)." The Prophet صلى الله عليه وسلم then said, "Somebody will then announce, 'Let every nation follow what they used to worship.' So the people of the Cross will go with their Cross, and the idolaters (will go) with their idols, and the worshippers of every god (false deities) (will go) with their god: till there remain those who used to worship Allâh, from the righteous pious ones and the mischievous ones, and some of the people of the Scripture (Jews and Christians). Then Hell will be presented to them as if it were a mirage. Then it will be said to the Jews, 'What did you use to worship?' They will reply, 'We used to worship 'Uzair (Ezra), the son of Allâh.' It will be said to them, 'You are liars, for Allâh has neither a wife nor a son. What do you want (now)?' They will reply, 'We want You to provide us with water.' Then it will be said to them 'Drink', and they will fall down in Hell (instead). Then it will be said to the Christians, 'What did you use to worship?' They will reply, 'We used to worship Messiah, the son of Allâh.' It will be said, 'You are liars, for Allâh has neither a wife nor a son. What do you want (now)?' They will say, 'We want You to provide us with water.' It will be said to them, 'Drink,' and they will fall down in Hell (instead): till there remain only those who used to worship Allâh (Alone), from the righteous pious ones and the mischievous evil ones, it will be said to them, 'What keeps you here when all the people have gone?' They will say, 'We left them (in the world) when we were in greater need of them than we are today; we heard the call of one proclaiming — Let every nation follow what they used to worship, - and now we are waiting for our Lord.' Then the Almighty will come to them in a shape other than the one which they saw the first time, and He will say, 'I am your Lord,' and they will say, 'You are our Lord.' And none will speak to Him then but the Prophets. And then it will be said to them, 'Do you know any sign by which you can recognise Him?' They will say, 'The Shin', and so Allâh will then uncover His Shin whereupon every believer will prostrate himself before Him and there will remain those who used to prostrate themselves before Him just for showing off and for gaining good reputation. Such a one will try to prostrate himself but his back (bones) will become a single (vertebra) bone [like one piece of wood and he will not be able to prostrate]. Then the bridge will be brought and laid across Hell." We (the Companions of the Prophet ﷺ) said, "O Allâh's Messenger! What is the bridge?" He said, "It is a slippery (bridge) on which there are clamps and (hooks like) a thorny seed that is wide at one side and narrow at the other and has thorns with bent ends. Such a thorny seed is found in Najd and is called As-Sa'dân. Some of the believers will cross the bridge as quickly as the wink of an eye, some others as quick as lightning, or a strong wind, or fast horses or she-camels. So some will be safe without any harm; some will be safe after receiving some scratches and some will fall down into Hell (Fire). The last person will cross as if being dragged (over the bridge)." The Prophet صلى الله عليه وسلم said, "You (Muslims) cannot be more pressing in claiming from me a right that has been clearly proved to be yours than the believers in interceding with Almighty for their (Muslim) brothers on that Day, when they see themselves safe. They will say, 'O Allâh! (Save) our brothers (for they) used to pray with us, fast with us and also do good deeds with us.' Allâh will say, 'Go and take out (of Hell) anyone in whose heart you find Faith equal to the weight of one (gold) Dinar.' Allâh will forbid the Fire to burn the faces of those sinners. They will go to them and find some of them in Hell (Fire) up to their feet, and some up to the middle of their legs. So, they will take out those whom they will recognise and then they will return. And Allâh will say (to them), 'Go and take out (of Hell) anyone in whose heart you find Faith equal to the weight of one-half Dinar.' They will take out whomever they will recognise and return. And then Allâh will say, 'Go and take out (of Hell) anyone in whose heart you find Faith equal to the weight of an atom (or a small ant), and so they will take out all those whom they will recognise." Abû Sa'îd said: "If you do not believe me then read the Holy Verse: 'Surely, Allâh wrongs not even of the weight of an atom (or a small ant) but if there is any good (done), He doubles it.' (V.4:40)."

The Prophet صلى الله عليه وسلم added: "Then the Prophets and angels and the believers will intercede, and (last of all) the Almighty (Allâh) will say, 'Now remains My Intercession. He will then hold a handful of the Fire from which He will take out some people whose bodies have been burnt, and they will be thrown into a river at the entrance of Paradise, called the Water of Life. They will grow on its banks, as a seed carried by the torrent grows. You have noticed how it grows beside a rock or beside a tree, and how the side facing the sun is usually green while the side facing the shade is white. Those people will come out (of the River of Life) like pearls, and they will have (golden) necklaces, and then they will enter Paradise whereupon the people of Paradise will say, 'These are the people emancipated by the Gracious. He has admitted them into Paradise without (them) having done any good deed and without sending forth any good (for themselves).' Then it will be said to them, 'For

Resurrection) and they shall be called to prostrate themselves (to Allâh), but they (hypocrites) shall not be able to do so.

43. Their eyes will be cast down and ignominy will cover them; they used to be called to prostrate themselves (offer prayers), while they were healthy and good (in the life of the world, but they did not).

44. Then leave Me Alone with such as belie this Qur'ân. We shall punish them gradually from directions they perceive not.

45. And I will grant them a respite. Verily, My Plan is strong.

46. Or is it that you (O Muhammad صلى الله عليه وسلم) ask them a wage, so that they are heavily burdened with debt?

47. Or that the *Ghaib* (the Unseen — here in this Verse it means *Al-Lauh Al-Mahfûz*) is in their hands, so that they can write it down?

48. So wait with patience for the Decision of your Lord, and be not like the Companion of the Fish — when he cried out (to Us) while he was in deep sorrow. (See the Qur'ân, Verse 21:87).

49. Had not a Grace from his Lord reached him, he would indeed have been (left in the stomach of the fish, but We forgave him): so he was cast off on the naked shore, while he was to be blamed.

---

you is what you have seen and its equivalent as well.' " (***Sahih Al-Bukhari***, Vol. 9, *Hadîth* No. 532B).

50. Then his Lord chose him and made him of the righteous.

51. And verily, those who disbelieve would almost make you slip with their eyes (through hatred) when they hear the Reminder (the Qur'ân), and they say: "Verily, he (Muhammad صلى الله عليه وسلم) is a madman!"

52. But it is nothing else than a Reminder to all the 'Âlamîn (mankind, jinn and all that exists).

Sûrat Al-Hâqqah
(The Inevitable) LXIX

*In the Name of Allâh
the Most Gracious, the Most Merciful*

1. The Inevitable (i.e. the Day of Resurrection)!

2. What is the Inevitable?

3. And what will make you know what the Inevitable is?

4. Thamûd and 'Âd people denied the *Qâri'ah* (the striking Hour of Judgement)!

5. As for Thamûd, they were destroyed by the awful cry!

6. And as for 'Âd, they were destroyed by a furious violent wind!

7. Which Allâh imposed on them for seven nights and eight days in succession, so that you could see men lying overthrown (destroyed), as if they were hollow trunks of date-palms!

8. Do you see any remnants of them?

9. And Fir'aun (Pharaoh), and those before him, and the cities overthrown [the towns of the people of [Lût (Lot)] committed sin.

‏وَجَآءَ فِرْعَوْنُ وَمَن قَبْلَهُۥ وَالْمُؤْتَفِكَتُ بِالْخَاطِئَةِ ۝‏

10. And they disobeyed their Lord's Messenger, so He seized them with a strong punishment.

‏فَعَصَوْا۟ رَسُولَ رَبِّهِمْ فَأَخَذَهُمْ أَخْذَةً رَّابِيَةً ۝‏

11. Verily, when the water rose beyond its limits [Nûh's (Noah) Flood], We carried you (mankind) in the floating [ship that was constructed by Nûh (Noah)].

‏إِنَّا لَمَّا طَغَا الْمَآءُ حَمَلْنَكُمْ فِى الْجَارِيَةِ ۝‏

12. That We might make it (Noah's ship) an admonition for you and that it might be retained by the retaining ears.

‏لِنَجْعَلَهَا لَكُمْ تَذْكِرَةً وَتَعِيَهَآ أُذُنٌ وَعِيَةٌ ۝‏

13. Then when the Trumpet will be blown with one blowing (the first one).

‏فَإِذَا نُفِخَ فِى الصُّورِ نَفْخَةٌ وَحِدَةٌ ۝‏

14. And the earth and the mountains shall be removed from their places, and crushed with a single crushing.

‏وَحُمِلَتِ الْأَرْضُ وَالْجِبَالُ فَدُكَّتَا دَكَّةً وَحِدَةً ۝‏

15. Then on that Day shall the (Great) Event befall.

‏فَيَوْمَئِذٍ وَقَعَتِ الْوَاقِعَةُ ۝‏

16. And the heaven will be rent asunder, for that Day it (the heaven) will be frail and torn up.

‏وَانشَقَّتِ السَّمَآءُ فَهِىَ يَوْمَئِذٍ وَاهِيَةٌ ۝‏

17. And the angels will be on its sides, and eight angels will, that Day, bear the Throne of your Lord above them.

‏وَالْمَلَكُ عَلَىٰٓ أَرْجَآئِهَا وَيَحْمِلُ عَرْشَ رَبِّكَ فَوْقَهُمْ يَوْمَئِذٍ ثَمَنِيَةٌ ۝‏

18. That Day shall you be brought to Judgement, not a secret of you will be hidden.

‏يَوْمَئِذٍ تُعْرَضُونَ لَا تَخْفَىٰ مِنكُمْ خَافِيَةٌ ۝‏

19. Then as for him who will be given his Record in his right hand will say: "Here! read my Record!

‏فَأَمَّا مَنْ أُوتِىَ كِتَبَهُۥ بِيَمِينِهِۦ فَيَقُولُ هَآؤُمُ اقْرَءُوا۟ كِتَبِيَهْ ۝‏

20. "Surely, I did believe that I shall meet my Account!"

إِنِّى ظَنَنتُ أَنِّى مُلَـٰقٍ حِسَابِيَهْ ٢٠

21. So he shall be in a life, well-pleasing,

فَهُوَ فِى عِيشَةٍ رَّاضِيَةٍ ٢١

22. In a lofty Paradise,

فِى جَنَّةٍ عَالِيَةٍ ٢٢

23. The fruits in bunches whereof will be low and near at hand.

قُطُوفُهَا دَانِيَةٌ ٢٣

24. Eat and drink at ease for that which you have sent on before you in days past!

كُلُوا وَٱشْرَبُوا هَنِيٓـًٔا بِمَآ أَسْلَفْتُمْ فِى ٱلْأَيَّامِ ٱلْخَالِيَةِ ٢٤

25. But as for him who will be given his Record in his left hand, will say: "I wish that I had not been given my Record!

وَأَمَّا مَنْ أُوتِىَ كِتَـٰبَهُۥ بِشِمَالِهِۦ فَيَقُولُ يَـٰلَيْتَنِى لَمْ أُوتَ كِتَـٰبِيَهْ ٢٥

26. "And that I had never known how my Account is?

وَلَمْ أَدْرِ مَا حِسَابِيَهْ ٢٦

27. "Would that it had been my end (death)!

يَـٰلَيْتَهَا كَانَتِ ٱلْقَاضِيَةَ ٢٧

28. "My wealth has not availed me;

مَآ أَغْنَىٰ عَنِّى مَالِيَهْ ٢٨

29. "My power (and arguments to defend myself) have gone from me!"

هَلَكَ عَنِّى سُلْطَـٰنِيَهْ ٢٩

30. (It will be said): "Seize him and fetter him;

خُذُوهُ فَغُلُّوهُ ٣٠

31. Then throw him in the blazing Fire.

ثُمَّ ٱلْجَحِيمَ صَلُّوهُ ٣١

32. "Then fasten him with a chain whereof the length is seventy cubits!"

ثُمَّ فِى سِلْسِلَةٍ ذَرْعُهَا سَبْعُونَ ذِرَاعًا فَٱسْلُكُوهُ ٣٢

33. Verily, he used not to believe in Allâh, the Most Great,

إِنَّهُۥ كَانَ لَا يُؤْمِنُ بِٱللَّهِ ٱلْعَظِيمِ ٣٣

34. And urged not on the feeding of *Al-Miskîn* (the poor).[1]

وَلَا يَحُضُّ عَلَىٰ طَعَامِ ٱلْمِسْكِينِ ٣٤

---

[1] (V.69:34)

a) See the footnote of (V.2:83).

b) Narrated 'Abdullâh bin 'Amr رضي الله عنه A man asked the Prophet صلى الله عليه وسلم "What sort of deeds (or what qualities) of Islâm are

35. So no friend has he here this Day,

36. Nor any food except filth from the washing of wounds.

37. None will eat it except the *Khâti'ûn* (sinners, disbelievers, polytheists).

38. So I swear by whatsoever you see,

39. And by whatsoever you see not,

40. That this is verily, the word of an honoured Messenger [i.e. Jibrael (Gabriel) or Muhammad صلى الله عليه وسلم which he has brought from Allâh].

41. It is not the word of a poet: little is that you believe!

42. Nor is it the word of a soothsayer (or a foreteller): little is that you remember!

43. This is the Revelation sent down from the Lord of the *'Âlamîn* (mankind, jinn and all that exists).

44. And if he (Muhammad صلى الله عليه وسلم) had forged a false saying concerning Us (Allâh جل جلاله),

45. We surely, would have seized him by his right hand (or with power and might),

46. And then We certainly would have cut off his life artery (aorta),

47. And none of you could have withheld Us from (punishing) him.

---

good?" The Prophet صلى الله عليه وسلم replied, "To feed (the poor) and greet those whom you know and those whom you do not know" (*Sahih Al-Bukhari*, Vol.1, *Hadith* No. 11).

48. And verily, this (Qur'ân) is a Reminder for the *Muttaqûn* (the pious. See V.2:2).

49. And verily, We know that there are some among you that belie (this Qur'ân). [*Tafsir At-Tabarî*, V.29, Page 68]

50. And indeed it (this Qur'ân) will be an anguish for the disbelievers (on the Day of Resurrection).[1]

51. And verily, it (this Qur'ân) is an absolute truth with certainty.[2]

52. So glorify the Name of your Lord, the Most Great.[3]

Sûrat Al-Ma'ârij
(The Ways of Ascent) LXX

*In the Name of Allâh
the Most Gracious, the Most Merciful*

1. A questioner asked concerning a torment about to befall

2. Upon the disbelievers, which none can avert,

3. From Allâh, the Lord of the ways of ascent.

4. The angels and the *Rûh* [Jibrael (Gabriel)] ascend to Him in a Day the measure whereof is fifty thousand years.

---

[1] (V.69:50) See the footnote of (V.3:85).

[2] (V.69:51) See the footnote of (V.10:37).

[3] (V.69:52) See footnotes of (V.13:28).

5. So be patient (O Muhammad صلى الله عليه وسلم), with a good patience.

فَاصْبِرْ صَبْرًا جَمِيلًا ﴿٥﴾

6. Verily, they see it (the torment) afar off.

إِنَّهُمْ يَرَوْنَهُ بَعِيدًا ﴿٦﴾

7. But We see it (quite) near.

وَنَرَاهُ قَرِيبًا ﴿٧﴾

8. The Day that the sky will be like the boiling filth of oil, (or molten copper or silver or lead).

يَوْمَ تَكُونُ السَّمَاءُ كَالْمُهْلِ ﴿٨﴾

9. And the mountains will be like flakes of wool.

وَتَكُونُ الْجِبَالُ كَالْعِهْنِ ﴿٩﴾

10. And no friend will ask a friend (about his condition),

وَلَا يَسْأَلُ حَمِيمٌ حَمِيمًا ﴿١٠﴾

11. Though they shall be made to see one another [(i.e. on the Day of Resurrection), there will be none but see his father, children and relatives, but he will neither speak to them nor will ask them for any help]. The *Mujrim*, (criminal, sinner, disbeliever) would desire to ransom himself from the punishment of that Day by his children.

يُبَصَّرُونَهُمْ يَوَدُّ الْمُجْرِمُ لَوْ يَفْتَدِي مِنْ عَذَابِ يَوْمِئِذٍ بِبَنِيهِ ﴿١١﴾

12. And his wife and his brother,

وَصَاحِبَتِهِ وَأَخِيهِ ﴿١٢﴾

13. And his kindred who sheltered him,

وَفَصِيلَتِهِ الَّتِي تُؤْوِيهِ ﴿١٣﴾

14. And all that are in the earth, so that it might save him.[1]

وَمَنْ فِي الْأَرْضِ جَمِيعًا ثُمَّ يُنْجِيهِ ﴿١٤﴾

15. By no means! Verily, it will be the Fire of Hell,

كَلَّا إِنَّهَا لَظَى ﴿١٥﴾

16. Taking away (burning completely) the head skin!

نَزَّاعَةً لِلشَّوَى ﴿١٦﴾

17. Calling[2] (all) such as turn their backs and turn away their faces (from

تَدْعُو مَنْ أَدْبَرَ وَتَوَلَّى ﴿١٧﴾

---

[1] (V.70:14) See the footnote (B) of (V.51:60).

[2] (V.70:17) Calling: i.e. the Hell will call out): "[O *Kafir* (O

Faith) [picking and swallowing them up from that great gathering of mankind on the Day of Resurrection just as a bird picks up a food-grain from the earth with its beak and swallows it up] [Tafsir Al-Qurtubî]

18. And collect (wealth) and hide it (from spending it in the Cause of Allâh).

19. Verily, man (disbeliever) was created very impatient;

20. Irritable (discontented) when evil touches him;

21. And niggardly when good touches him.

22. Except those who are devoted to Salât (prayers).[1]

23. Those who remain constant in their Salât (prayers);

24. And those in whose wealth there is a recognised right

25. For the beggar who asks, and for the unlucky who has lost his property and wealth, (and his means of living has been straitened).

26. And those who believe in the Day of Recompense.

27. And those who fear the torment of their Lord.

---

disbeliever in Allâh, His angels, His Book, His Messengers, Day of Resurrection and in Al-Qadar (Divine Preordainments), O Mushrik (O polytheist, disbeliever in the Oneness of Allâh)].

[1] (V.70:22) See the footnote of (V.9:91).

28. Verily, the torment of their Lord is that before which none can feel secure.

إِنَّ عَذَابَ رَبِّهِمْ غَيْرُ مَأْمُونٍ ﴿٢٨﴾

29. And those who guard their chastity (i.e. private parts from illegal sexual acts).[1]

وَٱلَّذِينَ هُمْ لِفُرُوجِهِمْ حَٰفِظُونَ ﴿٢٩﴾

30. Except with their wives and the (women slaves) whom their right hands possess — for (then) they are not blameworthy.

إِلَّا عَلَىٰٓ أَزْوَٰجِهِمْ أَوْ مَا مَلَكَتْ أَيْمَٰنُهُمْ فَإِنَّهُمْ غَيْرُ مَلُومِينَ ﴿٣٠﴾

31. But whosoever seeks beyond that, then it is those who are trespassers.[2]

فَمَنِ ٱبْتَغَىٰ وَرَآءَ ذَٰلِكَ فَأُوْلَٰٓئِكَ هُمُ ٱلْعَادُونَ ﴿٣١﴾

32. And those who keep their trusts and covenants.

وَٱلَّذِينَ هُمْ لِأَمَٰنَٰتِهِمْ وَعَهْدِهِمْ رَٰعُونَ ﴿٣٢﴾

33. And those who stand firm in their testimonies.

وَٱلَّذِينَ هُم بِشَهَٰدَٰتِهِمْ قَآئِمُونَ ﴿٣٣﴾

---

[1] (V.70:29) Narrated Sahl bin Sa'd رضي الله عنه Allâh's Messenger صلى said, "Whoever can guarantee (the chastity of) what is الله عليه وسلم between his two jaw-bones and what is between his two legs (i.e. his mouth, tongue and his private parts),* I guarantee Paradise for him." (Sahih Al-Bukhari, Vol. 8, Hadith No. 481).

* i.e., whoever protects his tongue from illegal talk like telling lies, or backbiting, etc., and his mouth from eating and drinking of forbidden illegal things, etc., and his private parts from illegal sexual acts.

[2] (V.70:31) Narrated Anas رضي الله عنه I will narrate to you a Hadith I heard from Allâh's Messenger صلى الله عليه وسلم and none other than I will tell of it. I heard Allâh's Messenger صلى الله عليه وسلم saying, "From among the portents of the Hour are the following: Religious knowledge will be taken away; General ignorance (in religious matters) will increase; Illegal sexual intercourse will prevail; Drinking of alcoholic drinks will be very common; Men will decrease in number, and women will increase in number, so much so that fifty women will be looked after by one man." (Sahih Al-Bukhari, Vol.7, Hadith No.158).

34. And those who guard their *Salât* (prayers) well.[1]

وَٱلَّذِينَ هُمْ عَلَىٰ صَلَاتِهِمْ يُحَافِظُونَ ٣٤

35. Such shall dwell in the Gardens (i.e. Paradise), honoured.

أُوْلَٰٓئِكَ فِى جَنَّٰتٍ مُّكْرَمُونَ ٣٥

36. So what is the matter with those who disbelieve that they hasten to listen from you [O Muhammad وسلم عليه الله صلى), in order to belie you and to mock at you, and at Allâh's Book (this Qur'ân)].

فَمَالِ ٱلَّذِينَ كَفَرُواْ قِبَلَكَ مُهْطِعِينَ ٣٦

37. (Sitting) in groups on the right and on the left (of you, O Muhammad وسلم عليه الله صلى)?

عَنِ ٱلْيَمِينِ وَعَنِ ٱلشِّمَالِ عِزِينَ ٣٧

38. Does every man of them hope to enter the Paradise of Delight?

أَيَطْمَعُ كُلُّ ٱمْرِئٍ مِّنْهُمْ أَن يُدْخَلَ جَنَّةَ نَعِيمٍ ٣٨

39. No, that is not like that! Verily, We have created them out of that which they know!

كَلَّآ إِنَّا خَلَقْنَٰهُم مِّمَّا يَعْلَمُونَ ٣٩

40. So I swear by the Lord of all the [three hundred and sixty-five (365)] points of sunrise and sunset in the east and the west that surely, We are Able

فَلَآ أُقْسِمُ بِرَبِّ ٱلْمَشَٰرِقِ وَٱلْمَغَٰرِبِ إِنَّا لَقَٰدِرُونَ ٤٠

41. To replace them by (others) better than them; and We are not to be outrun.

عَلَىٰٓ أَن نُّبَدِّلَ خَيْرًا مِّنْهُمْ وَمَا نَحْنُ بِمَسْبُوقِينَ ٤١

42. So leave them to plunge in vain talk[2] and play about, until they meet their Day which they are promised —

فَذَرْهُمْ يَخُوضُواْ وَيَلْعَبُواْ حَتَّىٰ يُلَٰقُواْ يَوْمَهُمُ ٱلَّذِى يُوعَدُونَ ٤٢

43. The Day when they will come out of the graves quickly as racing to a goal,

يَوْمَ يَخْرُجُونَ مِنَ ٱلْأَجْدَاثِ سِرَاعًا كَأَنَّهُمْ إِلَىٰ نُصُبٍ يُوفِضُونَ ٤٣

44. With their eyes lowered in fear and humility, ignominy covering them

خَٰشِعَةً أَبْصَٰرُهُمْ تَرْهَقُهُمْ ذِلَّةٌ ذَٰلِكَ

---

[1] (V.70:34) See (V.2:238) and its footnote.

[2] (V.70:42) See the footnote of (V.4:5).

(all over)! That is the Day which they were promised!

آلْيَوْمَ الَّذِى كَانُوا يُوعَدُونَ ٤٤

Sûrat Nûh
(Noah) LXXI

سُورَةُ نُوحٍ

In the Name of Allâh
the Most Gracious, the Most Merciful

بِسْمِ اللَّهِ الرَّحْمَنِ الرَّحِيمِ

1. Verily, We sent Nûh (Noah) to his people (saying): "Warn your people before there comes to them a painful torment."

إِنَّا أَرْسَلْنَا نُوحًا إِلَىٰ قَوْمِهِ أَنْ أَنذِرْ قَوْمَكَ مِن قَبْلِ أَن يَأْتِيَهُمْ عَذَابٌ أَلِيمٌ ١

2. He said: "O my people! Verily, I am a plain warner to you,

قَالَ يَٰقَوْمِ إِنِّى لَكُمْ نَذِيرٌ مُّبِينٌ ٢

3. "That you should worship Allâh (Alone), be dutiful to Him, and obey me,

أَنِ اعْبُدُوا اللَّهَ وَاتَّقُوهُ وَأَطِيعُونِ ٣

4. "He (Allâh) will forgive you of your sins and respite you to an appointed term. Verily, the term of Allâh when it comes, cannot be delayed, if you but knew."

يَغْفِرْ لَكُم مِّن ذُنُوبِكُمْ وَيُؤَخِّرْكُمْ إِلَىٰ أَجَلٍ مُّسَمًّى إِنَّ أَجَلَ اللَّهِ إِذَا جَاءَ لَا يُؤَخَّرُ لَوْ كُنتُمْ تَعْلَمُونَ ٤

5. He said: "O my Lord! Verily, I have called to my people night and day (i.e. secretly and openly to accept the doctrine of Islâmic Monotheism),[1]

قَالَ رَبِّ إِنِّى دَعَوْتُ قَوْمِى لَيْلًا وَنَهَارًا ٥

6. "But all my calling added nothing but to (their) flight (from the truth).

فَلَمْ يَزِدْهُمْ دُعَائِى إِلَّا فِرَارًا ٦

7. And verily, every time I called unto them that You might forgive them, they thrust their fingers into their ears, covered themselves up with their garments, and persisted (in their refusal), and magnified themselves in pride.

وَإِنِّى كُلَّمَا دَعَوْتُهُمْ لِتَغْفِرَ لَهُمْ جَعَلُوا أَصَابِعَهُمْ فِى آذَانِهِمْ وَاسْتَغْشَوْا ثِيَابَهُمْ وَأَصَرُّوا وَاسْتَكْبَرُوا اسْتِكْبَارًا ٧

---

[1] (V.71:5) See the footnote of (V.2:143).

8. "Then verily, I called to them openly (aloud).

ثُمَّ إِنِّى دَعَوْتُهُمْ جِهَارًا ﴿٨﴾

9. "Then verily, I proclaimed to them in public, and I have appealed to them in private.

ثُمَّ إِنِّى أَعْلَنتُ لَهُمْ وَأَسْرَرْتُ لَهُمْ إِسْرَارًا ﴿٩﴾

10. "I said (to them): 'Ask forgiveness from your Lord, verily, He is Oft-Forgiving;

فَقُلْتُ اسْتَغْفِرُوا رَبَّكُمْ إِنَّهُ كَانَ غَفَّارًا ﴿١٠﴾

11. 'He will send rain to you in abundance,

يُرْسِلِ السَّمَاءَ عَلَيْكُم مِّدْرَارًا ﴿١١﴾

12. 'And give you increase in wealth and children, and bestow on you gardens and bestow on you rivers.'"

وَيُمْدِدْكُم بِأَمْوَالٍ وَبَنِينَ وَيَجْعَل لَّكُمْ جَنَّاتٍ وَيَجْعَل لَّكُمْ أَنْهَارًا ﴿١٢﴾

13. What is the matter with you, that [you fear not Allâh (His punishment), and] you hope not for reward (from Allâh or you believe not in His Oneness).

مَّا لَكُمْ لَا تَرْجُونَ لِلَّهِ وَقَارًا ﴿١٣﴾

14. While He has created you in (different) stages [i.e. first *Nutfah*, then *'Alaqah* and then *Mudghah*, see (V.23:13,14)].

وَقَدْ خَلَقَكُمْ أَطْوَارًا ﴿١٤﴾

15. See you not how Allâh has created the seven heavens one above another?

أَلَمْ تَرَوْا كَيْفَ خَلَقَ اللَّهُ سَبْعَ سَمَاوَاتٍ طِبَاقًا ﴿١٥﴾

16. And has made the moon a light therein, and made the sun a lamp?

وَجَعَلَ الْقَمَرَ فِيهِنَّ نُورًا وَجَعَلَ الشَّمْسَ سِرَاجًا ﴿١٦﴾

17. And Allâh has brought you forth from the (dust of) earth? [Tafsir At-Tabarî].

وَاللَّهُ أَنبَتَكُم مِّنَ الْأَرْضِ نَبَاتًا ﴿١٧﴾

18. Afterwards He will return you into it (the earth), and bring you forth (again on the Day of Resurrection)?

ثُمَّ يُعِيدُكُمْ فِيهَا وَيُخْرِجُكُمْ إِخْرَاجًا ﴿١٨﴾

19. And Allâh has made for you the earth a wide expanse.

وَاللَّهُ جَعَلَ لَكُمُ الْأَرْضَ بِسَاطًا ﴿١٩﴾

20. That you may go about therein in broad roads.

لِّتَسْلُكُوا مِنْهَا سُبُلًا فِجَاجًا ۝

21. Nûh (Noah) said: "My Lord! They have disobeyed me, and followed one whose wealth and children give him no increase but loss.

قَالَ نُوحٌ رَّبِّ إِنَّهُمْ عَصَوْنِي وَاتَّبَعُوا مَن لَّمْ يَزِدْهُ مَالُهُ وَوَلَدُهُ إِلَّا خَسَارًا ۝

22. "And they have plotted a mighty plot.

وَمَكَرُوا مَكْرًا كُبَّارًا ۝

23. "And they have said: 'You shall not leave your gods: nor shall you leave Wadd, nor Suwâ', nor Yaghûth, nor Ya'ûq nor Nasr' (these are the names of their idols).

وَقَالُوا لَا تَذَرُنَّ آلِهَتَكُمْ وَلَا تَذَرُنَّ وَدًّا وَلَا سُوَاعًا وَلَا يَغُوثَ وَيَعُوقَ وَنَسْرًا ۝

24. "And indeed they have led many astray. And (O Allâh): 'Grant no increase to the Zâlimûn (polytheists, wrongdoers, and disbelievers) save error.' "

وَقَدْ أَضَلُّوا كَثِيرًا وَلَا تَزِدِ الظَّالِمِينَ إِلَّا ضَلَالًا ۝

25. Because of their sins they were drowned, then were made to enter the Fire. And they found none to help them instead of Allâh.

مِمَّا خَطِيئَاتِهِمْ أُغْرِقُوا فَأُدْخِلُوا نَارًا فَلَمْ يَجِدُوا لَهُم مِّن دُونِ اللَّهِ أَنصَارًا ۝

26. And Nûh (Noah) said: "My Lord! Leave not one of the disbelievers on the earth!

وَقَالَ نُوحٌ رَّبِّ لَا تَذَرْ عَلَى الْأَرْضِ مِنَ الْكَافِرِينَ دَيَّارًا ۝

27. "If You leave them, they will mislead Your slaves, and they will beget none but wicked disbelievers.

إِنَّكَ إِن تَذَرْهُمْ يُضِلُّوا عِبَادَكَ وَلَا يَلِدُوا إِلَّا فَاجِرًا كَفَّارًا ۝

28. "My Lord! Forgive me, and my parents, and him who enters my home as a believer, and all the believing men and women. And to the Zâlimûn (polytheists, wrongdoers, and disbelievers) grant You no increase but destruction!"

رَّبِّ اغْفِرْ لِي وَلِوَالِدَيَّ وَلِمَن دَخَلَ بَيْتِيَ مُؤْمِنًا وَلِلْمُؤْمِنِينَ وَالْمُؤْمِنَاتِ وَلَا تَزِدِ الظَّالِمِينَ إِلَّا تَبَارًا ۝

Sûrat Al-Jinn
(The Jinn) LXXII

سُورَةُ الجِنّ

*In the Name of Allâh
the Most Gracious, the Most Merciful*

بِسْمِ اللهِ الرَّحْمَنِ الرَّحِيمِ

1. Say (O Muhammad ﷺ): "It has been revealed to me that a group (from three to ten in number) of jinn[1] listened (to this Qur'ân). They said: 'Verily, we have heard a wonderful Recitation (this Qur'ân)!

قُلْ أُوحِيَ إِلَيَّ أَنَّهُ ٱسْتَمَعَ نَفَرٌ مِّنَ ٱلْجِنِّ فَقَالُوٓاْ إِنَّا سَمِعْنَا قُرْءَانًا عَجَبًا ١

2. 'It guides to the Right Path, and we have believed therein, and we shall never join (in worship) anything with our Lord (Allâh).

يَهْدِىٓ إِلَى ٱلرُّشْدِ فَـَامَنَّا بِهِۦ وَلَن نُّشْرِكَ بِرَبِّنَآ أَحَدًا ٢

3. 'And He, exalted is the Majesty of our Lord, has taken neither a wife nor a son (or offspring or children).[2]

وَأَنَّهُۥ تَعَٰلَىٰ جَدُّ رَبِّنَا مَا ٱتَّخَذَ صَٰحِبَةً وَلَا وَلَدًا ٣

4. 'And that the foolish among us [i.e. *Iblis* (Satan) or the polytheists amongst the jinn] used to utter against Allâh that which was an enormity in falsehood.

وَأَنَّهُۥ كَانَ يَقُولُ سَفِيهُنَا عَلَى ٱللَّهِ شَطَطًا ٤

5. 'And verily, we thought that men and jinn would not utter a lie against Allâh.

وَأَنَّا ظَنَنَّآ أَن لَّن تَقُولَ ٱلْإِنسُ وَٱلْجِنُّ عَلَى ٱللَّهِ كَذِبًا ٥

6. 'And verily, there were men among mankind who took shelter with the males among the jinn, but they (jinn) increased them (mankind) in sin and transgression.

وَأَنَّهُۥ كَانَ رِجَالٌ مِّنَ ٱلْإِنسِ يَعُوذُونَ بِرِجَالٍ مِّنَ ٱلْجِنِّ فَزَادُوهُمْ رَهَقًا ٦

---

[1] (V.72:1) Jinn: A creation, created by Allâh from fire like human beings from dust, and angels from light.

[2] (V.72:3)

A) See the footnote of (V.2:116) and (V.6:101).

B) See the footnote of (C) of (V.68:42).

7. 'And they thought as you thought, that Allâh will not send any Messenger (to mankind or jinn).

وَأَنَّهُمْ ظَنُّوا كَمَا ظَنَنتُمْ أَن لَّن يَبْعَثَ
اللَّهُ أَحَدًا ۝

8. 'And we have sought to reach the heaven; but found it filled with stern guards and flaming fires.

وَأَنَّا لَمَسْنَا السَّمَآءَ فَوَجَدْنَٰهَا
مُلِئَتْ حَرَسًا شَدِيدًا
وَشُهُبًا ۝

9. 'And verily, we used to sit there in stations, to (steal) a hearing, but any who listens now will find a flaming fire watching him in ambush.

وَأَنَّا كُنَّا نَقْعُدُ مِنْهَا
مَقَٰعِدَ لِلسَّمْعِ فَمَن يَسْتَمِعِ
الْآنَ يَجِدْ لَهُۥ شِهَابًا رَّصَدًا ۝

10. 'And we know not whether evil is intended for those on earth, or whether their Lord intends for them a Right Path.

وَأَنَّا لَا نَدْرِى أَشَرٌّ أُرِيدَ بِمَن فِى
الْأَرْضِ أَمْ أَرَادَ بِهِمْ رَبُّهُمْ رَشَدًا ۝

11. 'There are among us some that are righteous, and some the contrary; we are groups having different ways (religious sects).

وَأَنَّا مِنَّا الصَّٰلِحُونَ وَمِنَّا دُونَ
ذَٰلِكَ كُنَّا طَرَآئِقَ قِدَدًا ۝

12. 'And we think that we cannot escape (the punishment of) Allâh in the earth, nor can we escape Him by flight.

وَأَنَّا ظَنَنَّا أَن لَّن نُّعْجِزَ اللَّهَ فِى
الْأَرْضِ وَلَن نُّعْجِزَهُۥ هَرَبًا ۝

13. 'And indeed when we heard the Guidance (this Qur'ân), we believed therein (Islâmic Monotheism), and whosoever believes in his Lord shall have no fear, either of a decrease in the reward of his good deeds or an increase in the punishment for his sins.

وَأَنَّا لَمَّا سَمِعْنَا الْهُدَىٰ ءَامَنَّا
بِهِۦ فَمَن يُؤْمِنۢ بِرَبِّهِۦ فَلَا يَخَافُ
بَخْسًا وَلَا رَهَقًا ۝

14. 'And of us some are Muslims (who have submitted to Allâh, after listening to this Qur'ân), and of us some are Al-Qâsitûn (disbelievers — those who have deviated from the Right Path)'. And whosoever has embraced Islâm (i.e. has become a Muslim by

وَأَنَّا مِنَّا الْمُسْلِمُونَ وَمِنَّا
الْقَٰسِطُونَ فَمَنْ أَسْلَمَ فَأُوْلَٰٓئِكَ
تَحَرَّوْا رَشَدًا ۝

submitting to Allâh), then such have sought the Right Path."

15. And as for the *Qâsitûn* (disbelievers who deviated from the Right Path), they shall be firewood for Hell,

وَأَمَّا ٱلْقَٰسِطُونَ فَكَانُوا لِجَهَنَّمَ حَطَبًا ﴿١٥﴾

16. If they (non-Muslims) had believed in Allâh, and went on the Right Way (i.e. Islâm) We would surely, have bestowed on them water (rain) in abundance.

وَأَلَّوِ ٱسْتَقَٰمُوا عَلَى ٱلطَّرِيقَةِ لَأَسْقَيْنَٰهُم مَّآءً غَدَقًا ﴿١٦﴾

17. That We might try them thereby. And whosoever turns away from the Reminder of his Lord (i.e. this Qur'ân, — and practise not its laws and orders), He will cause him to enter in a severe torment (i.e. Hell).

لِنَفْتِنَهُمْ فِيهِ وَمَن يُعْرِضْ عَن ذِكْرِ رَبِّهِ يَسْلُكْهُ عَذَابًا صَعَدًا ﴿١٧﴾

18. And the mosques are for Allâh (Alone): so invoke not anyone along with Allâh.[1]

وَأَنَّ ٱلْمَسَٰجِدَ لِلَّهِ فَلَا تَدْعُوا مَعَ ٱللَّهِ أَحَدًا ﴿١٨﴾

19. And when the slave of Allâh (Muhammad صلى الله عليه وسلم) stood up invoking Him (his Lord — Allâh) in prayer they (the jinn) just made round him a dense crowd as if sticking one over the other (in order to listen to the Prophet's recitation).

وَأَنَّهُۥ لَمَّا قَامَ عَبْدُ ٱللَّهِ يَدْعُوهُ كَادُوا يَكُونُونَ عَلَيْهِ لِبَدًا ﴿١٩﴾

20. Say (O Muhammad صلى الله عليه وسلم): "I invoke only my Lord (Allâh Alone), and I associate none as partners along with Him."

قُلْ إِنَّمَآ أَدْعُوا رَبِّي وَلَآ أُشْرِكُ بِهِۦٓ أَحَدًا ﴿٢٠﴾

21. Say: "It is not in my power to cause you harm, or to bring you to the Right Path."

قُلْ إِنِّي لَآ أَمْلِكُ لَكُمْ ضَرًّا وَلَا رَشَدًا ﴿٢١﴾

---

[1] (V.72:18) See the footnote of (V.2:165).

22. Say (O Muhammad صلى الله عليه وسلم): "None can protect me from Allâh's punishment (if I were to disobey Him), nor can I find refuge except in Him.

قُلْ إِنِّى لَن يُجِيرَنِى مِنَ اللَّهِ أَحَدٌ وَلَنْ أَجِدَ مِن دُونِهِ مُلْتَحَدًا ۝

23. "(Mine is) but conveyance (of the truth) from Allâh and His Messages (of Islâmic Monotheism), and whosoever disobeys Allâh and His Messenger, then verily, for him is the Fire of Hell, he shall dwell therein forever."[1]

إِلَّا بَلَٰغًا مِّنَ اللَّهِ وَرِسَٰلَٰتِهِۦ وَمَن يَعْصِ اللَّهَ وَرَسُولَهُۥ فَإِنَّ لَهُۥ نَارَ جَهَنَّمَ خَٰلِدِينَ فِيهَآ أَبَدًا ۝

24. Till, when they see that which they are promised, then they will know who it is that is weaker concerning helpers and less important concerning numbers.

حَتَّىٰٓ إِذَا رَأَوْا مَا يُوعَدُونَ فَسَيَعْلَمُونَ مَنْ أَضْعَفُ نَاصِرًا وَأَقَلُّ عَدَدًا ۝

25. Say (O Muhammad صلى الله عليه وسلم): "I know not whether (the punishment) which you are promised is near or whether my Lord will appoint for it a distant term.

قُلْ إِنْ أَدْرِىٓ أَقَرِيبٌ مَّا تُوعَدُونَ أَمْ يَجْعَلُ لَهُۥ رَبِّىٓ أَمَدًا ۝

26. "(He Alone is) the All-Knower of the *Ghaib* (Unseen), and He reveals to none His *Ghaib* (Unseen)."

عَٰلِمُ ٱلْغَيْبِ فَلَا يُظْهِرُ عَلَىٰ غَيْبِهِۦٓ أَحَدًا ۝

27. Except to a Messenger (from mankind) whom He has chosen (He informs him of the Unseen as much as He likes), and then He makes a band of watching guards (angels) to march before him and behind him.

إِلَّا مَنِ ٱرْتَضَىٰ مِن رَّسُولٍ فَإِنَّهُۥ يَسْلُكُ مِنۢ بَيْنِ يَدَيْهِ وَمِنْ خَلْفِهِۦ رَصَدًا ۝

28. [He (Allâh) protects them (the Messengers)], till He sees that they (the Messengers) have conveyed the Messages of their Lord (Allâh). And He

لِّيَعْلَمَ أَن قَدْ أَبْلَغُوا۟ رِسَٰلَٰتِ رَبِّهِمْ وَأَحَاطَ بِمَا لَدَيْهِمْ وَأَحْصَىٰ

---

[1] (V.72:23) See the footnote of (V.3:85).

(Allâh) surrounds all that which is with them, and He (Allâh) keeps count of all things (i.e. He knows the exact number of everything).

كُلَّ شَىۡءٍ عَدَدًۢا ۞

Sûrat Al-Muzzammil (The One wrapped in Garments) LXXIII

سُوۡرَةُ الۡمُزَّمِّلِ

In the Name of Allâh the Most Gracious, the Most Merciful

بِسۡمِ اللهِ الرَّحۡمَٰنِ الرَّحِيمِ

1. O you wrapped in garments (i.e. Prophet Muhammad صلى الله عليه وسلم)!

يَـٰٓأَيُّهَا الۡمُزَّمِّلُ ۞

2. Stand (to pray) all night, except a little —

قُمِ الَّيۡلَ إِلَّا قَلِيلًا ۞

3. Half of it or a little less than that,

نِّصۡفَهُۥٓ أَوِ انقُصۡ مِنۡهُ قَلِيلًا ۞

4. Or a little more. And recite the Qur'ân (aloud) in a slow, (pleasant tone and) style.[1]

أَوۡ زِدۡ عَلَيۡهِ وَرَتِّلِ الۡقُرۡءَانَ تَرۡتِيلًا ۞

5. Verily, We shall send down to you a weighty Word (i.e. obligations, laws).

إِنَّا سَنُلۡقِي عَلَيۡكَ قَوۡلًا ثَقِيلًا ۞

6. Verily, the rising by night (for *Tahajjud* prayer) is very hard and most potent and good for governing oneself, and most suitable for (understanding) the Word (of Allâh).

إِنَّ نَاشِئَةَ الَّيۡلِ هِيَ أَشَدُّ وَطۡـًٔا وَأَقۡوَمُ قِيلًا ۞

7. Verily, there is for you by day prolonged occupation with ordinary duties.

إِنَّ لَكَ فِي النَّهَارِ سَبۡحًا طَوِيلًا ۞

8. And remember the Name of your Lord and devote yourself to Him with a complete devotion.

وَاذۡكُرِ اسۡمَ رَبِّكَ وَتَبَتَّلۡ إِلَيۡهِ تَبۡتِيلًا ۞

9. (He Alone is) the Lord of the east and the west; *Lâ ilâha illâ Huwa* (none

رَّبُّ الۡمَشۡرِقِ وَالۡمَغۡرِبِ لَآ إِلَٰهَ إِلَّا

---

[1] (V.73:4) See the footnote of (V.29:51).

has the right to be worshipped but He). So take Him Alone as *Wakîl* (Disposer of your affairs).[1]

10. And be patient (O Muhammad صلى الله عليه وسلم) with what they say, and keep away from them in a good way.

11. And leave Me Alone to deal with the beliers (those who deny My Verses), those who are in possession of good things of life. And give them respite for a little while.

12. Verily, with Us are fetters (to bind them), and a raging Fire.

13. And a food that chokes, and a painful torment.

14. On the Day when the earth and the mountains will be in violent shake, and the mountains will be a heap of sand poured out.

15. Verily, We have sent to you (O men) a Messenger (Muhammad صلى الله عليه وسلم) to be a witness over you, as We did send a Messenger [Mûsâ (Moses)] to Fir'aun (Pharaoh).[2]

16. But Fir'aun (Pharaoh) disobeyed the Messenger [Mûsâ (Moses)]; so We seized him with a severe punishment.

17. Then how can you avoid the punishment, if you disbelieve, on a Day (i.e. the Day of Resurrection) that will make the children grey-headed?

---

[1] (V.73:9) See the (V.3:173) and its footnotes.

[2] (V.73:15) See the footnotes of (V.2:252).

18. Whereon the heaven will be cleft asunder? His Promise is certainly to be accomplished.

19. Verily, this is an admonition: therefore whosoever will, let him take a Path to His Lord!

20. Verily, your Lord knows that you do stand (to pray at night) a little less than two thirds of the night, or half the night, or a third of the night, and also a party of those with you. And Allâh measures the night and the day. He knows that you are unable to pray the whole night, so He has turned to you (in mercy). So, recite you of the Qur'ân as much as may be easy for you. He knows that there will be some among you sick, others travelling through the land, seeking of Allâh's Bounty, yet others fighting in Allâh's Cause. So recite as much of the Qur'ân as may be easy (for you), and perform As-Salât (Iqâmat-as-Salât) and give Zakât, and lend to Allâh a goodly loan. And whatever good you send before you for yourselves (i.e. Nawâfil — non-obligatory acts of worship: prayers, charity, fasting, Hajj and 'Umrah), you will certainly find it with Allâh, better and greater in reward. And seek Forgiveness of Allâh. Verily, Allâh is Oft-Forgiving, Most-Merciful.[1]

---

[1] (V.73:20) See the footnotes of (V.50:39).

Sûrat Al-Muddaththir
(The One Enveloped) LXXIV

سُوْرَةُ الْمُدَّثِّر

*In the Name of Allâh
the Most Gracious, the Most Merciful*

بِسْمِ اللهِ الرَّحْمَنِ الرَّحِيمِ

1. O you (Muhammad صلى الله عليه وسلم) enveloped in garments!

يَٰٓأَيُّهَا الْمُدَّثِّرُ ۝

2. Arise and warn!

قُمْ فَأَنذِرْ ۝

3. And magnify your Lord (Allâh)!

وَرَبَّكَ فَكَبِّرْ ۝

4. And purify your garments!

وَثِيَابَكَ فَطَهِّرْ ۝

5. And keep away from *Ar-Rujz* (the idols)!

وَالرُّجْزَ فَاهْجُرْ ۝

6. And give not a thing in order to have more (or consider not your deeds of obedience to Allâh as a favour to Him).

وَلَا تَمْنُن تَسْتَكْثِرُ ۝

7. And be patient for the sake of your Lord (i.e. perform your duty to Allâh)!

وَلِرَبِّكَ فَاصْبِرْ ۝

8. Then, when the Trumpet is sounded (i.e. the second blowing of the horn).

فَإِذَا نُقِرَ فِي النَّاقُورِ ۝

9. Truly, that Day will be a Hard Day —

فَذَٰلِكَ يَوْمَئِذٍ يَوْمٌ عَسِيرٌ ۝

10. Far from easy for the disbelievers.

عَلَى الْكَٰفِرِينَ غَيْرُ يَسِيرٍ ۝

11. Leave Me Alone (to deal with) whom I created Alone (without any means, i.e. Al-Walîd bin Al-Mughîrah Al-Makhzûmî).

ذَرْنِي وَمَنْ خَلَقْتُ وَحِيدًا ۝

12. And then granted him resources in abundance.

وَجَعَلْتُ لَهُ مَالًا مَّمْدُودًا ۝

13. And children to be by his side.

وَبَنِينَ شُهُودًا ۝

14. And made life smooth and comfortable for him.

وَمَهَّدتُّ لَهُ تَمْهِيدًا ۝

15. After all that he desires that I should give him;

ثُمَّ يَطْمَعُ أَنْ أَزِيدَ ۝

16. Nay! Verily, he has been opposing Our *Ayât* (proofs, evidences, verses, lessons, signs, revelations, etc.).

كَلَّآ إِنَّهُۥ كَانَ لِأَيَٰتِنَا عَنِيدًا ۝

17. I shall oblige him to (climb a slippery mountain in the Hell-fire called *As-Sa'ûd*, or) face a severe torment!

سَأُرْهِقُهُۥ صَعُودًا ۝

18. Verily, he thought and plotted.

إِنَّهُۥ فَكَّرَ وَقَدَّرَ ۝

19. So let him be cursed: how he plotted!

فَقُتِلَ كَيْفَ قَدَّرَ ۝

20. And once more let him be cursed: how he plotted!

ثُمَّ قُتِلَ كَيْفَ قَدَّرَ ۝

21. Then he thought.

ثُمَّ نَظَرَ ۝

22. Then he frowned and he looked in a bad tempered way;

ثُمَّ عَبَسَ وَبَسَرَ ۝

23. Then he turned back, and was proud.

ثُمَّ أَدْبَرَ وَٱسْتَكْبَرَ ۝

24. Then he said: "This is nothing but magic from that of old,

فَقَالَ إِنْ هَٰذَآ إِلَّا سِحْرٌ يُؤْثَرُ ۝

25. "This is nothing but the word of a human being!"

إِنْ هَٰذَآ إِلَّا قَوْلُ ٱلْبَشَرِ ۝

26. I will cast him into Hell-fire.[1]

سَأُصْلِيهِ سَقَرَ ۝

27. And what will make you know (exactly) what Hell-fire is?

وَمَآ أَدْرَىٰكَ مَا سَقَرُ ۝

28. It spares not (any sinner), nor does it leave (anything unburnt)!

لَا تُبْقِى وَلَا تَذَرُ ۝

29. Burning and blackening the skins!

لَوَّاحَةٌ لِّلْبَشَرِ ۝

30. Over it are nineteen (angels as guardians and keepers of Hell).

عَلَيْهَا تِسْعَةَ عَشَرَ ۝

---

[1] (V.74:26) See the footnote of (V.17:97).

31. And We have set none but angels as guardians of the Fire. And We have fixed their number (19) only as a trial for the disbelievers, in order that the people of the Scripture (Jews and Christians) may arrive at a certainty [that this Qur'ân is the truth as it agrees with their Books regarding the number (19) which is written in the Taurât (Torah) and the Injeel (Gospel)] and that the believers may increase in Faith (as this Qur'ân is the truth), and that no doubt may be left for the people of the Scripture and the believers, and that those in whose hearts is a disease (of hypocrisy) and the disbelievers may say: "What Allâh intends by this (curious) example?" Thus Allâh leads astray whom He wills and guides whom He wills. And none can know the hosts of your Lord but He. And this (Hell) is nothing else than a (warning) reminder to mankind.

وَمَا جَعَلْنَا أَصْحَابَ النَّارِ إِلَّا مَلَائِكَةً وَمَا جَعَلْنَا عِدَّتَهُمْ إِلَّا فِتْنَةً لِّلَّذِينَ كَفَرُوا لِيَسْتَيْقِنَ الَّذِينَ أُوتُوا الْكِتَابَ وَيَزْدَادَ الَّذِينَ آمَنُوا إِيمَانًا وَلَا يَرْتَابَ الَّذِينَ أُوتُوا الْكِتَابَ وَالْمُؤْمِنُونَ وَلِيَقُولَ الَّذِينَ فِي قُلُوبِهِم مَّرَضٌ وَالْكَافِرُونَ مَاذَا أَرَادَ اللَّهُ بِهَٰذَا مَثَلًا كَذَٰلِكَ يُضِلُّ اللَّهُ مَن يَشَاءُ وَيَهْدِي مَن يَشَاءُ وَمَا يَعْلَمُ جُنُودَ رَبِّكَ إِلَّا هُوَ وَمَا هِيَ إِلَّا ذِكْرَىٰ لِلْبَشَرِ ۝

32. Nay! And by the moon

كَلَّا وَالْقَمَرِ ۝

33. And by the night when it withdraws.

وَاللَّيْلِ إِذْ أَدْبَرَ ۝

34. And by the dawn when it brightens.

وَالصُّبْحِ إِذَا أَسْفَرَ ۝

35. Verily, it (Hell, or their denial of Prophet Muhammad صلى الله عليه وسلم, or the Day of Resurrection) is but one of the greatest (signs).

إِنَّهَا لَإِحْدَى الْكُبَرِ ۝

36. A warning to mankind —

نَذِيرًا لِّلْبَشَرِ ۝

37. To any of you that chooses to go forward (by working righteous deeds), or to remain behind (by commiting sins).

لِمَن شَاءَ مِنكُمْ أَن يَتَقَدَّمَ أَوْ يَتَأَخَّرَ ۝

38. Every person is a pledge for what he has earned,

كُلُّ نَفْسٍ بِمَا كَسَبَتْ رَهِينَةٌ ٣٨

39. Except those on the Right, (i.e. the pious true believers of Islâmic Monotheism).

إِلَّا أَصْحَابَ الْيَمِينِ ٣٩

40. In Gardens (Paradise) they will ask one another,

فِى جَنَّاتٍ يَتَسَاءَلُونَ ٤٠

41. About *Al-Mujrimûn* (polytheists, criminals, disbelievers), (And they will say to them):

عَنِ الْمُجْرِمِينَ ٤١

42. "What has caused you to enter Hell?"

مَا سَلَكَكُمْ فِى سَقَرَ ٤٢

43. They will say: "We were not of those who used to offer the *Salât* (prayers),[1]

قَالُوا لَمْ نَكُ مِنَ الْمُصَلِّينَ ٤٣

44. "Nor we used to feed *Al-Miskîn* (the poor);

وَلَمْ نَكُ نُطْعِمُ الْمِسْكِينَ ٤٤

45. "And we used to talk falsehood (all that which Allâh hated) with vain talkers.[2]

وَكُنَّا نَخُوضُ مَعَ الْخَائِضِينَ ٤٥

46. And we used to belie the Day of Recompense,[3]

وَكُنَّا نُكَذِّبُ بِيَوْمِ الدِّينِ ٤٦

47. "Until there came to us (the death) that is certain."

حَتَّى أَتَانَا الْيَقِينُ ٤٧

48. So no intercession of intercessors will be of any use to them.

فَمَا تَنْفَعُهُمْ شَفَاعَةُ الشَّافِعِينَ ٤٨

49. Then what is wrong with them (i.e. the polytheists, the disbelievers) that they turn away from (receiving) admonition?

فَمَا لَهُمْ عَنِ التَّذْكِرَةِ مُعْرِضِينَ ٤٩

---

[1] (V.74:43) See the footnote of (V.8:39).

[2] (V.74:45) See the footnote of (V.4:5).

[3] (V.74:46) See the footnotes of (V.3:85).

50. As if they were (frightened) wild donkeys. كَأَنَّهُمْ حُمُرٌ مُّسْتَنفِرَةٌ ۝

51. Fleeing from a hunter, or a lion, or a beast of prey. فَرَّتْ مِن قَسْوَرَةٍ ۝

52. Nay, everyone of them desires that he should be given pages spread out (coming from Allâh with a writing that Islâm is the right religion, and Muhammad صلى الله عليه وسلم has come with the truth from Allâh, the Lord of the heavens and earth). بَلْ يُرِيدُ كُلُّ امْرِئٍ مِّنْهُمْ أَن يُؤْتَى صُحُفًا مُّنَشَّرَةً ۝

53. Nay! But they fear not the Hereafter (from Allâh's punishment). كَلَّا بَل لَّا يَخَافُونَ الْآخِرَةَ ۝

54. Nay, verily, this (Qur'ân) is an admonition, كَلَّا إِنَّهُ تَذْكِرَةٌ ۝

55. So whosoever will (let him read it), and receive admonition (from it)! فَمَن شَاءَ ذَكَرَهُ ۝

56. And they will not receive admonition unless Allâh wills; He (Allâh) is the One, deserving that mankind should be afraid of, and should be dutiful to Him, and should not take any Ilâh (god) along with Him, and He is the One Who forgives (sins). وَمَا يَذْكُرُونَ إِلَّا أَن يَشَاءَ اللَّهُ هُوَ أَهْلُ التَّقْوَى وَأَهْلُ الْمَغْفِرَةِ ۝

Sûrat Al-Qiyâmah (The Resurrection) LXXV
سورة القيامة

In the Name of Allâh the Most Gracious, the Most Merciful بِسْمِ اللَّهِ الرَّحْمَٰنِ الرَّحِيمِ

1. I swear by the Day of Resurrection. لَا أُقْسِمُ بِيَوْمِ الْقِيَامَةِ ۝

2. And I swear by the self-reproaching person (a believer). وَلَا أُقْسِمُ بِالنَّفْسِ اللَّوَّامَةِ ۝

3. Does man (a disbeliever) think that We shall not assemble his bones? أَيَحْسَبُ الْإِنسَانُ أَلَّن نَّجْمَعَ عِظَامَهُ ۝

4. Yes, We are Able to put together in perfect order the tips of his fingers.[1]

بَلَىٰ قَـٰدِرِينَ عَلَىٰٓ أَن نُّسَوِّيَ بَنَانَهُۥ ٤

5. Nay! Man (denies Resurrection and Reckoning. So he) desires to continue committing sins.

بَلْ يُرِيدُ ٱلْإِنسَـٰنُ لِيَفْجُرَ أَمَامَهُۥ ٥

6. He asks: "When will be this Day of Resurrection?"

يَسْـَٔلُ أَيَّانَ يَوْمُ ٱلْقِيَـٰمَةِ ٦

7. So, when the sight shall be dazed.

فَإِذَا بَرِقَ ٱلْبَصَرُ ٧

8. And the moon will be eclipsed.

وَخَسَفَ ٱلْقَمَرُ ٨

9. And the sun and moon will be joined together (by going one into the other or folded up or deprived of their light).[2]

وَجُمِعَ ٱلشَّمْسُ وَٱلْقَمَرُ ٩

10. On that Day man will say: "Where (is the refuge) to flee?"

يَقُولُ ٱلْإِنسَـٰنُ يَوْمَئِذٍ أَيْنَ ٱلْمَفَرُّ ١٠

11. No! There is no refuge!

كَلَّا لَا وَزَرَ ١١

12. Unto your Lord (Alone) will be the place of rest that Day.

إِلَىٰ رَبِّكَ يَوْمَئِذٍ ٱلْمُسْتَقَرُّ ١٢

13. On that Day man will be informed of what he sent forward (of his evil or good deeds), and what he left behind (of his good or evil traditions).

يُنَبَّؤُا۟ ٱلْإِنسَـٰنُ يَوْمَئِذٍ بِمَا قَدَّمَ وَأَخَّرَ ١٣

14. Nay! Man will be a witness against himself [as his body parts (skin,

بَلِ ٱلْإِنسَـٰنُ عَلَىٰ نَفْسِهِۦ بَصِيرَةٌ ١٤

---

[1] (V.75:4) Each human being has his or her own special finger prints not resembling anyone else, indicating that our Lord (Allâh) is the Most Superior Creator of everything: *Lâ ilâha illa Huwa* (none has the right to be worshipped but He).

[2] (V.75:9) Narrated Abu Hurairah صلى الله عليه وسلم The Prophet رضي الله عنه said, "The sun and the moon will be folded up (or joined together or deprived of their lights) on the Day of Resurrection." (See the Qur'ân 75:9) (*Sahih Al-Bukhari*, Vol. 4, *Hadith* No. 422).

hands, legs) will speak about his deeds],

15. Though he may put forth his excuses (to cover his evil deeds).

وَلَوْ أَلْقَىٰ مَعَاذِيرَهُۥ ﴿١٥﴾

16. Move not your tongue concerning (the Qur`ân, O Muhammad صلى الله عليه وسلم) to make haste therewith.

لَا تُحَرِّكْ بِهِۦ لِسَانَكَ لِتَعْجَلَ بِهِۦٓ ﴿١٦﴾

17. It is for Us to collect it and to give you (O Muhammad صلى الله عليه وسلم) the ability to recite it (the Qur`ân).

إِنَّ عَلَيْنَا جَمْعَهُۥ وَقُرْءَانَهُۥ ﴿١٧﴾

18. And when We have recited it to you [O Muhammad صلى الله عليه وسلم through Jibrael (Gabriel)], then follow its (the Qur`ân's) recital.

فَإِذَا قَرَأْنَٰهُ فَٱتَّبِعْ قُرْءَانَهُۥ ﴿١٨﴾

19. Then it is for Us (Allâh) to make it clear (to you).

ثُمَّ إِنَّ عَلَيْنَا بَيَانَهُۥ ﴿١٩﴾

20. Not [as you think, that you (mankind) will not be resurrected and recompensed for your deeds], but you (men) love the present life of this world,

كَلَّا بَلْ تُحِبُّونَ ٱلْعَاجِلَةَ ﴿٢٠﴾

21. And neglect the Hereafter.

وَتَذَرُونَ ٱلْءَاخِرَةَ ﴿٢١﴾

22 Some faces that Day shall be *Nâdirah* (shining and radiant).

وُجُوهٌ يَوْمَئِذٍ نَّاضِرَةٌ ﴿٢٢﴾

23. Looking at their Lord (Allâh).

إِلَىٰ رَبِّهَا نَاظِرَةٌ ﴿٢٣﴾

24. And some faces, that Day, will be *Bâsirah* (dark, gloomy, frowning, and sad),

وَوُجُوهٌ يَوْمَئِذٍ بَاسِرَةٌ ﴿٢٤﴾

25. Thinking that some calamity is about to fall on them.

تَظُنُّ أَن يُفْعَلَ بِهَا فَاقِرَةٌ ﴿٢٥﴾

26. Nay, when (the soul) reaches to the collar bone (i.e. up to the throat in its exit),

كَلَّا إِذَا بَلَغَتِ ٱلتَّرَاقِيَ ﴿٢٦﴾

27. And it will be said: "Who can cure him (and save him from death)?"

وَقِيلَ مَنْ رَاقٍ ﴿٢٧﴾

28. And he (the dying person) will conclude that it was (the time) of parting (death);

وَظَنَّ أَنَّهُ ٱلْفِرَاقُ ۝

29. And one leg will be joined with another leg (shrouded).[1]

وَٱلْتَفَّتِ ٱلسَّاقُ بِٱلسَّاقِ ۝

30. The drive will be, on that Day, to your Lord (Allâh)!

إِلَىٰ رَبِّكَ يَوْمَئِذٍ ٱلْمَسَاقُ ۝

31. So he (the disbeliever) neither believed (in this Qur'ân and in the Message of Muhammad صلى الله عليه وسلم) nor prayed!

فَلَا صَدَّقَ وَلَا صَلَّىٰ ۝

32. But on the contrary, he belied (this Qur'ân and the Message of Muhammad صلى الله عليه وسلم) and turned away!

وَلَٰكِن كَذَّبَ وَتَوَلَّىٰ ۝

33. Then he walked in conceit (full pride) to his family admiring himself!

ثُمَّ ذَهَبَ إِلَىٰ أَهْلِهِ يَتَمَطَّىٰ ۝

34. Woe to you [O man (disbeliever)]! And then (again) woe to you!

أَوْلَىٰ لَكَ فَأَوْلَىٰ ۝

35. Again, woe to you [O man (disbeliever)]! And then (again) woe to you!

ثُمَّ أَوْلَىٰ لَكَ فَأَوْلَىٰ ۝

36. Does man think that he will be left neglected (without being punished or rewarded for the obligatory duties enjoined by his Lord Allâh on him)?

أَيَحْسَبُ ٱلْإِنسَٰنُ أَن يُتْرَكَ سُدًى ۝

37. Was he not a *Nutfah* (mixed male and female sexual discharge) of semen emitted (poured forth)?

أَلَمْ يَكُ نُطْفَةً مِّن مَّنِيٍّ يُمْنَىٰ ۝

38. Then he became an *'Alaqah* (a clot); then (Allâh) shaped and fashioned (him) in due proportion.[2]

ثُمَّ كَانَ عَلَقَةً فَخَلَقَ فَسَوَّىٰ ۝

---

[1] (V.75:29) Or it may mean: hardship and distress will be joined with another hardship and distress (i.e. distress of death, and of the thought as to what is going to happen to him in the Hereafter). (*Tafsîr At-Tabari*).

[2] (V.75:38) See the footnote of (V.22:5).

39. And made of him two sexes, male and female. ﴿٣٩﴾

40. Is not He (Allâh Who does that) Able to give life to the dead? (Yes! He is Able to do all things).

Sûrat Al-Insân or Ad-Dahr
(Man or Time) LXXVI

سُوۡرَةُ الإِنسَان

*In the Name of Allâh
the Most Gracious, the Most Merciful*

بِسۡمِ اللهِ الرَّحۡمٰنِ الرَّحِيۡمِ

1. Has there not been over man a period of time, when he was not a thing worth mentioning?

2. Verily, We have created man from *Nutfah* (drops of mixed semen (sexual discharge of man and woman), in order to try him: so We made him hearer and seer.

3. Verily, We showed him the way, whether he be grateful or ungrateful.

4. Verily, We have prepared for the disbelievers iron chains, iron collars, and a blazing Fire.

5. Verily, the *Abrâr* (the pious and righteous), shall drink of a cup (of wine) mixed with (water from a spring in Paradise called) *Kâfûr*.

6. A spring wherefrom the slaves of Allâh will drink, causing it to gush forth abundantly.

7. They (are those who) fulfil (their) vows, and they fear a Day whose evil will be wide-spreading.

8. And they give food, inspite of their love for it (or for the love of Him), to the *Miskîn*[1] (the poor), the orphan, and the captive

9. (Saying): "We feed you seeking Allâh's Countenance only. We wish for no reward, nor thanks from you.

10. "Verily, We fear from our Lord a Day, hard and distressful, that will make the faces look horrible (from extreme dislike to it)."

11. So Allâh saved them from the evil of that Day, and gave them *Nadrah* (a light of beauty) and joy.

12. And their recompense shall be Paradise, and silken garments, because they were patient.

13. Reclining therein on raised thrones, they will see there neither the excessive heat of the sun, nor the excessive bitter cold, (as in Paradise there is no sun and no moon).

14. And the shade thereof is close upon them, and the bunches of fruit thereof will hang low within their reach.

15. And amongst them will be passed round vessels of silver and cups of crystal —

16. Crystal-clear, made of silver. They will determine the measure thereof (according to their wishes).

17. And they will be given to drink there of a cup (of wine) mixed with *Zanjabîl* (ginger),

---

[1] (V.76:8) See the footnote of (V.2:83).

18. A spring there, called *Salsabîl.*

عَيْنًا فِيهَا تُسَمَّىٰ سَلْسَبِيلًا ۝

19. And round about them will (serve) boys of everlasting youth. If you see them, you would think them scattered pearls.

وَيَطُوفُ عَلَيْهِمْ وِلْدَٰنٌ مُّخَلَّدُونَ ۝ إِذَا رَأَيْتَهُمْ حَسِبْتَهُمْ لُؤْلُؤًا مَّنثُورًا ۝

20. And when you look there (in Paradise), you will see a delight (that cannot be imagined), and a great dominion.

وَإِذَا رَأَيْتَ ثَمَّ رَأَيْتَ نَعِيمًا وَمُلْكًا كَبِيرًا ۝

21. Their garments will be of fine green silk, and gold embroidery. They will be adorned with bracelets of silver, and their Lord will give them a pure drink.

عَٰلِيَهُمْ ثِيَابُ سُندُسٍ خُضْرٌ وَإِسْتَبْرَقٌ وَحُلُّوٓا أَسَاوِرَ مِن فِضَّةٍ وَسَقَاهُمْ رَبُّهُمْ شَرَابًا طَهُورًا ۝

22. (And it will be said to them): "Verily, this is a reward for you, and your endeavour has been accepted."

إِنَّ هَٰذَا كَانَ لَكُمْ جَزَآءً وَكَانَ سَعْيُكُم مَّشْكُورًا ۝

23. Verily, it is We Who have sent down the Qur'ân to you (O Muhammad صلى الله عليه وسلم) by stages.

إِنَّا نَحْنُ نَزَّلْنَا عَلَيْكَ ٱلْقُرْءَانَ تَنزِيلًا ۝

24. Therefore be patient (O Muhammad صلى الله عليه وسلم) with constancy to the Command of your Lord (Allâh, by doing your duty to Him and by conveying His Message to mankind), and obey neither a sinner nor a disbeliever among them.

فَٱصْبِرْ لِحُكْمِ رَبِّكَ وَلَا تُطِعْ مِنْهُمْ ءَاثِمًا أَوْ كَفُورًا ۝

25. And remember the Name of your Lord every morning and afternoon [i.e. offering of the Morning (*Fajr*), *Zuhr*, and *'Asr* prayers].

وَٱذْكُرِ ٱسْمَ رَبِّكَ بُكْرَةً وَأَصِيلًا ۝

26. And during night, prostrate yourself to Him (i.e. the offering of *Maghrib* and *'Ishâ* prayers), and

وَمِنَ ٱلَّيْلِ فَٱسْجُدْ لَهُۥ وَسَبِّحْهُ لَيْلًا طَوِيلًا ۝

glorify Him a long night through (i.e. *Tahajjud* prayer).

27. Verily, these (disbelievers) love the present life of this world, and put behind them a heavy Day (that will be hard).

إِنَّ هَٰٓؤُلَآءِ يُحِبُّونَ ٱلْعَاجِلَةَ وَيَذَرُونَ وَرَآءَهُمْ يَوْمًا ثَقِيلًا ۝

28. It is We Who created them, and We have made them of strong built. And when We will, We can replace them with others like them with a complete replacement.

نَّحْنُ خَلَقْنَٰهُمْ وَشَدَدْنَآ أَسْرَهُمْ وَإِذَا شِئْنَا بَدَّلْنَآ أَمْثَٰلَهُمْ تَبْدِيلًا ۝

29. Verily, this (Verses of the Qur'ân) is an admonition, so whosoever wills, let him take a Path to his Lord (Allâh).

إِنَّ هَٰذِهِۦ تَذْكِرَةٌ فَمَن شَآءَ ٱتَّخَذَ إِلَىٰ رَبِّهِۦ سَبِيلًا ۝

30. But you cannot will, unless Allâh wills. Verily, Allâh is Ever All-Knowing, All-Wise.

وَمَا تَشَآءُونَ إِلَّآ أَن يَشَآءَ ٱللَّهُ إِنَّ ٱللَّهَ كَانَ عَلِيمًا حَكِيمًا ۝

31. He will admit to His Mercy whom He wills and as for the *Zâlimûn* — (polytheists, wrongdoers) He has prepared a painful torment.

يُدْخِلُ مَن يَشَآءُ فِي رَحْمَتِهِۦ وَٱلظَّٰلِمِينَ أَعَدَّ لَهُمْ عَذَابًا أَلِيمًا ۝

Sûrat Al-Mursalât
(Those sent forth) LXXVII

سُورَةُ الْمُرْسَلَاتِ

*In the Name of Allâh
the Most Gracious, the Most Merciful*

بِسْمِ ٱللَّهِ ٱلرَّحْمَٰنِ ٱلرَّحِيمِ

1. By the winds (or angels or the Messengers of Allâh) sent forth one after another.

وَٱلْمُرْسَلَٰتِ عُرْفًا ۝

2. And by the winds that blow violently.

فَٱلْعَٰصِفَٰتِ عَصْفًا ۝

3. And by the winds that scatter clouds and rain.

وَٱلنَّٰشِرَٰتِ نَشْرًا ۝

4. And by the Verses (of the Qur`ân) that separate the right from the wrong.

فَالْفَارِقَاتِ فَرْقًا ٤

5. And by the angels that bring the revelations to the Messengers,

فَالْمُلْقِيَاتِ ذِكْرًا ٥

6. To cut off all excuses or to warn.

عُذْرًا أَوْ نُذْرًا ٦

7. Surely, what you are promised must come to pass.

إِنَّمَا تُوعَدُونَ لَوَاقِعٌ ٧

8. Then when the stars lose their lights.

فَإِذَا النُّجُومُ طُمِسَتْ ٨

9. And when the heaven is cleft asunder.

وَإِذَا السَّمَاءُ فُرِجَتْ ٩

10. And when the mountains are blown away.

وَإِذَا الْجِبَالُ نُسِفَتْ ١٠

11. And when the Messengers are gathered to their time appointed.

وَإِذَا الرُّسُلُ أُقِّتَتْ ١١

12. For what Day are these signs postponed?

لِأَيِّ يَوْمٍ أُجِّلَتْ ١٢

13. For the Day of Sorting Out (the men of Paradise from the men destined for Hell).

لِيَوْمِ الْفَصْلِ ١٣

14. And what will explain to you what is the Day of Sorting Out?

وَمَا أَدْرَاكَ مَا يَوْمُ الْفَصْلِ ١٤

15. Woe that Day to the deniers (of the Day of Resurrection)!

وَيْلٌ يَوْمَئِذٍ لِّلْمُكَذِّبِينَ ١٥

16. Did We not destroy the ancients?

أَلَمْ نُهْلِكِ الْأَوَّلِينَ ١٦

17. So shall We make later generations to follow them.

ثُمَّ نُتْبِعُهُمُ الْآخِرِينَ ١٧

18. Thus do We deal with the *Mujrimûn* (polytheists, disbelievers, sinners, criminals).

كَذَلِكَ نَفْعَلُ بِالْمُجْرِمِينَ ١٨

19. Woe that Day to the deniers (of the Day of Resurrection)!

وَيْلٌ يَوْمَئِذٍ لِّلْمُكَذِّبِينَ ١٩

20. Did We not create you from a despised water (semen)?

أَلَمْ نَخْلُقكُّم مِّن مَّآءٍ مَّهِينٍ ﴿٢٠﴾

21. Then We placed it in a place of safety (womb),

فَجَعَلْنَهُ فِى قَرَارٍ مَّكِينٍ ﴿٢١﴾

22. For a known period (determined by gestation)?

إِلَىٰ قَدَرٍ مَّعْلُومٍ ﴿٢٢﴾

23. So We did measure; and We are the Best to measure (the things).

فَقَدَرْنَا فَنِعْمَ الْقَٰدِرُونَ ﴿٢٣﴾

24. Woe that Day to the deniers (of the Day of Resurrection)!

وَيْلٌ يَوْمَئِذٍ لِّلْمُكَذِّبِينَ ﴿٢٤﴾

25. Have We not made the earth a receptacle

أَلَمْ نَجْعَلِ الْأَرْضَ كِفَاتًا ﴿٢٥﴾

26. For the living and the dead?

أَحْيَآءً وَأَمْوَٰتًا ﴿٢٦﴾

27. And have placed therein firm, and tall mountains, and have given you to drink sweet water?

وَجَعَلْنَا فِيهَا رَوَٰسِىَ شَٰمِخَٰتٍ وَأَسْقَيْنَٰكُم مَّآءً فُرَاتًا ﴿٢٧﴾

28. Woe that Day to the deniers (of the Day of Resurrection)!

وَيْلٌ يَوْمَئِذٍ لِّلْمُكَذِّبِينَ ﴿٢٨﴾

29. (It will be said to the disbelievers): "Depart you to that which you used to deny!

انطَلِقُوا إِلَىٰ مَا كُنتُم بِهِۦ تُكَذِّبُونَ ﴿٢٩﴾

30. "Depart you to a shadow (of Hell-Fire smoke ascending) in three columns,

انطَلِقُوا إِلَىٰ ظِلٍّ ذِى ثَلَٰثِ شُعَبٍ ﴿٣٠﴾

31. Neither shady, nor of any use against the fierce flame of the Fire."

لَّا ظَلِيلٍ وَلَا يُغْنِى مِنَ اللَّهَبِ ﴿٣١﴾

32. Verily, it (Hell) throws sparks (huge) as Al-Qasr (a fort or a huge log of wood),

إِنَّهَا تَرْمِى بِشَرَرٍ كَالْقَصْرِ ﴿٣٢﴾

33. As if they were yellow camels or bundles of ropes.

كَأَنَّهُۥ جِمَٰلَتٌ صُفْرٌ ﴿٣٣﴾

34. Woe that Day to the deniers (of the Day of Resurrection)!

وَيْلٌ يَوْمَئِذٍ لِّلْمُكَذِّبِينَ ﴿٣٤﴾

35. That will be a Day when they shall not speak (during some part of it),

هَٰذَا يَوْمُ لَا يَنطِقُونَ ٣٥

36. And they will not be permitted to put forth any excuse.

وَلَا يُؤْذَنُ لَهُمْ فَيَعْتَذِرُونَ ٣٦

37. Woe that Day to the deniers (of the Day of Resurrection)!

وَيْلٌ يَوْمَئِذٍ لِّلْمُكَذِّبِينَ ٣٧

38. That will be a Day of Decision! We have brought you and the men of old together!

هَٰذَا يَوْمُ الْفَصْلِ جَمَعْنَٰكُمْ وَالْأَوَّلِينَ ٣٨

39. So if you have a plot, use it against Me (Allâh جل جلاله)!

فَإِن كَانَ لَكُمْ كَيْدٌ فَكِيدُونِ ٣٩

40. Woe that Day to the deniers (of the Day of Resurrection)!

وَيْلٌ يَوْمَئِذٍ لِّلْمُكَذِّبِينَ ٤٠

41. Verily, the *Muttaqûn* (the pious. See V.2:2) shall be amidst shades and springs.

إِنَّ الْمُتَّقِينَ فِي ظِلَٰلٍ وَعُيُونٍ ٤١

42. And fruits, such as they desire.

وَفَوَٰكِهَ مِمَّا يَشْتَهُونَ ٤٢

43. "Eat and drink comfortably for that which you used to do."

كُلُوا وَاشْرَبُوا هَنِيٓـًٔا بِمَا كُنتُمْ تَعْمَلُونَ ٤٣

44. Verily, thus We reward the *Muhsinûn* (good-doers. See V.2:112).

إِنَّا كَذَٰلِكَ نَجْزِي الْمُحْسِنِينَ ٤٤

45. Woe that Day to the deniers (of the Day of Resurrection)!

وَيْلٌ يَوْمَئِذٍ لِّلْمُكَذِّبِينَ ٤٥

46. (O you disbelievers)! Eat and enjoy yourselves (in this worldly life) for a little while. Verily, you are the *Mujrimûn* (polytheists, disbelievers, sinners, criminals).

كُلُوا وَتَمَتَّعُوا قَلِيلًا إِنَّكُم مُّجْرِمُونَ ٤٦

47. Woe that Day to the deniers (of the Day of Resurrection)!

وَيْلٌ يَوْمَئِذٍ لِّلْمُكَذِّبِينَ ٤٧

48. And when it is said to them: "Bow down yourself (in prayer)!" They bow not down (offer not their prayers).[1]

وَإِذَا قِيلَ لَهُمُ ٱرْكَعُواْ لَا يَرْكَعُونَ ٤٨

49. Woe that Day to the deniers (of the Day of Resurrection)!

وَيْلٌ يَوْمَئِذٍ لِّلْمُكَذِّبِينَ ٤٩

50. Then in what statement after this (the Qur'ân) will they believe?

فَبِأَيِّ حَدِيثٍ بَعْدَهُ يُؤْمِنُونَ ٥٠

---

[1] (V.77:48)

A) Narrated Anas bin Mâlik رضي الله عنه: Allâh's Messenger صلى الله عليه وسلم said, "I have been ordered to fight the people till they say: *Lâ ilâha illallâh* (none has the right to be worshipped but Allâh). And if they say so, perform *As-Salât* (the prayer) like our *Salât* (prayers), face our *Qiblah* and slaughter as we slaughter, then their blood and property will be sacred to us and we will not interfere with them except legally and their reckoning will be with Allâh." Narrated Maimûn bin Siyâh that he asked Anas bin Mâlik, "O Abu Hamzah! What makes the life and property of a person sacred?" He replied, "Whoever says, *Lâ ilâha illallâh* (none has the right to be worshipped but Allâh), faces our *Qiblah* during the *Salât* (prayers), perform *As-Salât* (the prayer) like us, and eat our slaughtered animals then he is a Muslim and has got the same rights and obligations as other Muslims have." (*Sahih Al-Bukhari*, Vol. 1, *Hadith* No. 387).

B) Narrated Abu Hurairah رضي الله عنه: Allâh's Messenger صلى الله عليه وسلم said, "If the people knew (the reward for) pronouncing the *Adhân* and for standing in the first row (in congregational prayers) and found no other way to get that except by drawing lots, they would draw lots, and if they knew (the reward of) the *Zuhr* prayer (in the early moments of its stated time) they would race for it (go early) and if they knew (the reward of) *'Ishâ* (night and morning) prayers in congregation, they would come to offer them even if they had to crawl." (*Sahih Al-Bukhârî*, Vol. 1, *Hadith* No. 589).

Sûrat An-Naba'
(The Great News) LXXVIII

سُوْرَةُ النَّبَا

بِسْمِ اللهِ الرَّحْمٰنِ الرَّحِيمِ

In the Name of Allâh
the Most Gracious, the Most Merciful

1. What are they asking (one another) about?

عَمَّ يَتَسَآءَلُوْنَ ۞

2. About the great news, (i.e. Islâmic Monotheism, the Qur'ân, which Prophet Muhammad صلى الله عليه وسلم brought and the Day of Resurrection)

عَنِ النَّبَإِ الْعَظِيْمِ ۞

3. About which they are in disagreement.

الَّذِي هُمْ فِيْهِ مُخْتَلِفُوْنَ ۞

4. Nay, they will come to know!

كَلَّا سَيَعْلَمُوْنَ ۞

5. Nay, again, they will come to know!

ثُمَّ كَلَّا سَيَعْلَمُوْنَ ۞

6. Have We not made the earth as a bed,

أَلَمْ نَجْعَلِ الْأَرْضَ مِهَادًا ۞

7. And the mountains as pegs?

وَالْجِبَالَ أَوْتَادًا ۞

8. And We have created you in pairs (male and female, tall and short, good and bad).

وَخَلَقْنَاكُمْ أَزْوَاجًا ۞

9. And We have made your sleep as a thing for rest.

وَجَعَلْنَا نَوْمَكُمْ سُبَاتًا ۞

10. And We have made the night as a covering (through its darkness),

وَجَعَلْنَا اللَّيْلَ لِبَاسًا ۞

11. And We have made the day for livelihood,

وَجَعَلْنَا النَّهَارَ مَعَاشًا ۞

12. And We have built above you seven strong (heavens),

وَبَنَيْنَا فَوْقَكُمْ سَبْعًا شِدَادًا ۞

13. And We have made (therein) a shining lamp (sun).

وَجَعَلْنَا سِرَاجًا وَهَّاجًا ۞

14. And We have sent down from the rainy clouds abundant water.

وَأَنْزَلْنَا مِنَ الْمُعْصِرَاتِ مَآءً ثَجَّاجًا ۞

15. That We may produce therewith corn and vegetations,

لِّنُخْرِجَ بِهِ حَبًّا وَنَبَاتًا ۝

16. And gardens of thick growth.

وَجَنَّاتٍ أَلْفَافًا ۝

17. Verily, the Day of Decision is a fixed time.

إِنَّ يَوْمَ الْفَصْلِ كَانَ مِيقَاتًا ۝

18. The Day when the Trumpet will be blown, and you shall come forth in crowds (groups after groups). [Tafsir At-Tabari]

يَوْمَ يُنفَخُ فِي الصُّورِ فَتَأْتُونَ أَفْوَاجًا ۝

19. And the heaven shall be opened, and it will become as gates,

وَفُتِحَتِ السَّمَاءُ فَكَانَتْ أَبْوَابًا ۝

20. And the mountains shall be moved away from their places and they will be as if they were a mirage.

وَسُيِّرَتِ الْجِبَالُ فَكَانَتْ سَرَابًا ۝

21. Truly, Hell is a place of ambush

إِنَّ جَهَنَّمَ كَانَتْ مِرْصَادًا ۝

22. A dwelling place for the *Tâghûn* (those who transgress the boundary limits set by Allâh like polytheists, disbelievers in the Oneness of Allâh, hypocrites, sinners, criminals),

لِّلطَّاغِينَ مَآبًا ۝

23. They will abide therein for ages.

لَّابِثِينَ فِيهَا أَحْقَابًا ۝

24. Nothing cool shall they taste therein, nor any drink.

لَّا يَذُوقُونَ فِيهَا بَرْدًا وَلَا شَرَابًا ۝

25. Except boiling water, and dirty wound discharges —

إِلَّا حَمِيمًا وَغَسَّاقًا ۝

26. An exact recompense (according to their evil crimes).

جَزَاءً وِفَاقًا ۝

27. For verily, they used not to look for a reckoning.

إِنَّهُمْ كَانُوا لَا يَرْجُونَ حِسَابًا ۝

28. But they belied Our *Ayât* (proofs, evidences, verses, lessons, signs, revelations, and that which Our Prophet صلى الله عليه وسلم brought) completely.

وَكَذَّبُوا بِآيَاتِنَا كِذَّابًا ۝

29. And all things We have recorded in a Book.

وَكُلَّ شَىْءٍ أَحْصَيْنَٰهُ كِتَٰبًا ۝

30. So taste you (the results of your evil actions). No increase shall We give you, except in torment.

فَذُوقُوا فَلَن نَّزِيدَكُمْ إِلَّا عَذَابًا ۝

31. Verily, for the *Muttaqûn*,[1] there will be a success (Paradise);

إِنَّ لِلْمُتَّقِينَ مَفَازًا ۝

32. Gardens and vineyards,

حَدَآئِقَ وَأَعْنَٰبًا ۝

33. And young full-breasted (mature) maidens of equal age,

وَكَوَاعِبَ أَتْرَابًا ۝

34. And a full cup (of wine).

وَكَأْسًا دِهَاقًا ۝

35. No *Laghw* (dirty, false, evil talk) shall they hear therein, nor lying;

لَّا يَسْمَعُونَ فِيهَا لَغْوًا وَلَا كِذَّٰبًا ۝

36. A reward from your Lord, an ample calculated gift (according to the best of their good deeds),[2]

جَزَآءً مِّن رَّبِّكَ عَطَآءً حِسَابًا ۝

---

[1] (V.78:31) *Muttaqûn*: means pious and righteous persons who fear Allâh much (abstain from all kinds of sins and evil deeds which He has forbidden) and love Allâh much (perform all kinds of good deeds which He has ordained).

[2] (V.78:36)

a) Islâm demolishes all the previous evil deeds and so do migration (for Allâh's sake) and *Hajj* (pilgrimage to Makkah). (*Sahih Muslim*, Vol. 1, Chapter 52, Page 18).

b) What is said regarding the superiority of a person who embraces Islâm sincerely:

Narrated Abu Sa'îd Al-Khudri رضى الله عنه: Allâh's Messenger صلى الله عليه وسلم said, "If a person embraces Islâm sincerely, then Allâh shall forgive all his past sins, and after that starts the settlement of accounts: the reward of his good deeds will be ten times to seven hundred times for each good deed, and an evil deed will be recorded as it is unless Allâh forgives it." (*Sahih Al-Bukhari*, Vol. 1, *Hadith* No. 40A).

Narrated Abu Hurairah رضى الله عنه: Allâh's Messenger صلى الله عليه وسلم said: "If anyone of you improves (follows strictly) his Islâmic religion,

رَبِّ ٱلسَّمَٰوَٰتِ وَٱلْأَرْضِ وَمَا بَيْنَهُمَا ٱلرَّحْمَٰنِ لَا يَمْلِكُونَ مِنْهُ خِطَابًا ۝

37. (From) the Lord of the heavens and the earth, and whatsoever is in between them, the Most Gracious, with Whom they cannot dare to speak (on the Day of Resurrection except by His Leave).

يَوْمَ يَقُومُ ٱلرُّوحُ وَٱلْمَلَٰئِكَةُ صَفًّا لَّا يَتَكَلَّمُونَ إِلَّا مَنْ أَذِنَ لَهُ ٱلرَّحْمَٰنُ وَقَالَ صَوَابًا ۝

38. The Day that Ar-Rûh [Jibrael (Gabriel) or another angel] and the angels will stand forth in rows, they will not speak except him whom the Most Gracious (Allâh) allows, and he will speak what is right.

ذَٰلِكَ ٱلْيَوْمُ ٱلْحَقُّ فَمَن شَآءَ ٱتَّخَذَ إِلَىٰ رَبِّهِ مَـَٔابًا ۝

39. That is (without doubt) the True Day. So, whosoever wills, let him seek a place with (or a way to) His Lord (by obeying Him in this worldly life)!

إِنَّآ أَنذَرْنَٰكُمْ عَذَابًا قَرِيبًا يَوْمَ يَنظُرُ ٱلْمَرْءُ مَا قَدَّمَتْ يَدَاهُ وَيَقُولُ ٱلْكَافِرُ يَٰلَيْتَنِى كُنتُ تُرَٰبًۢا ۝

40. Verily, We have warned you of a near torment — the Day when man will see that (the deeds) which his hands have sent forth, and the disbeliever will say: "Woe to me! Would that I were dust!"

Sûrat An-Nâzi'ât
(Those Who Pull Out) LXXIX

سُورَةُ ٱلنَّازِعَاتِ

*In the Name of Allâh
the Most Gracious, the Most Merciful*

بِسْمِ ٱللَّهِ ٱلرَّحْمَٰنِ ٱلرَّحِيمِ

وَٱلنَّٰزِعَٰتِ غَرْقًا ۝

1. By those (angels) who pull out (the souls of the disbelievers and the wicked) with great violence.

وَٱلنَّٰشِطَٰتِ نَشْطًا ۝

2. By those (angels) who gently take out (the souls of the believers).

---

then his good deeds will be rewarded ten times to seven hundred times for each good deed and a bad deed will be recorded as it is." (Sahih Al-Bukhari, Vol. 1, Hadith No. 40B).

3. And by those that swim along (i.e. angels or planets in their orbits).

وَالسَّٰبِحَٰتِ سَبْحًا ﴿٣﴾

4. And by those that press forward as in a race (i.e. the angels or stars or the horses).

فَالسَّٰبِقَٰتِ سَبْقًا ﴿٤﴾

5. And by those angels who arrange to do the Commands of their Lord, (so verily, you disbelievers will be called to account).

فَالْمُدَبِّرَٰتِ أَمْرًا ﴿٥﴾

6. On the Day (when the first blowing of the Trumpet is blown), the earth and the mountains will shake violently (and everybody will die).

يَوْمَ تَرْجُفُ الرَّاجِفَةُ ﴿٦﴾

7. The second blowing of the Trumpet follows it (and everybody will be resurrected).

تَتْبَعُهَا الرَّادِفَةُ ﴿٧﴾

8. (Some) hearts that Day will shake with fear and anxiety.

قُلُوبٌ يَوْمَئِذٍ وَاجِفَةٌ ﴿٨﴾

9. Their eyes will be downcast.

أَبْصَٰرُهَا خَٰشِعَةٌ ﴿٩﴾

10. They say: "Shall we indeed be returned to (our) former state of life?

يَقُولُونَ أَءِنَّا لَمَرْدُودُونَ فِي الْحَافِرَةِ ﴿١٠﴾

11. "Even after we are crumbled bones?"

أَءِذَا كُنَّا عِظَٰمًا نَّخِرَةً ﴿١١﴾

12. They say: "It would in that case, be a return with loss!"

قَالُوا تِلْكَ إِذًا كَرَّةٌ خَاسِرَةٌ ﴿١٢﴾

13. But it will be only a single *Zajrah* [shout (i.e. the second blowing of the Trumpet)], (See Verse 37:19).

فَإِنَّمَا هِيَ زَجْرَةٌ وَٰحِدَةٌ ﴿١٣﴾

14. When behold, they find themselves on the surface of the earth alive after their death,

فَإِذَا هُم بِالسَّاهِرَةِ ﴿١٤﴾

15. Has there come to you the story of Mûsâ (Moses)?

هَلْ أَتَاكَ حَدِيثُ مُوسَىٰ ﴿١٥﴾

16. When his Lord called him in the sacred valley of Tuwâ,

إِذْ نَادَاهُ رَبُّهُ بِالْوَادِ الْمُقَدَّسِ طُوًى ۝

17. Go to Fir'aun (Pharaoh); verily, he has transgressed all bounds (in crimes, sins, polytheism, disbelief).

اذْهَبْ إِلَىٰ فِرْعَوْنَ إِنَّهُ طَغَىٰ ۝

18. And say to him: "Would you purify yourself (from the sin of disbelief by becoming a believer)?"

فَقُلْ هَل لَّكَ إِلَىٰ أَن تَزَكَّىٰ ۝

19. "And that I guide you to your Lord, so you should fear Him?"

وَأَهْدِيَكَ إِلَىٰ رَبِّكَ فَتَخْشَىٰ ۝

20. Then [Mûsâ (Moses)] showed him the great sign (miracles).

فَأَرَاهُ الْآيَةَ الْكُبْرَىٰ ۝

21. But [Fir'aun (Pharaoh)] belied and disobeyed.

فَكَذَّبَ وَعَصَىٰ ۝

22. Then he turned his back, striving (against Allâh).

ثُمَّ أَدْبَرَ يَسْعَىٰ ۝

23. Then he gathered (his people) and cried aloud,

فَحَشَرَ فَنَادَىٰ ۝

24. Saying: "I am your lord, most high."

فَقَالَ أَنَا رَبُّكُمُ الْأَعْلَىٰ ۝

25. So Allâh, seized him with punishment for his last [1] and first [2] transgression. [Tafsir At-Tabari]

فَأَخَذَهُ اللَّهُ نَكَالَ الْآخِرَةِ وَالْأُولَىٰ ۝

26. Verily, in this is an instructive admonition for whosoever fears Allâh.

إِنَّ فِي ذَٰلِكَ لَعِبْرَةً لِّمَن يَخْشَىٰ ۝

27. Are you more difficult to create or is the heaven that He constructed?

أَأَنتُمْ أَشَدُّ خَلْقًا أَمِ السَّمَاءُ بَنَاهَا ۝

28. He raised its height, and has perfected it.

رَفَعَ سَمْكَهَا فَسَوَّاهَا ۝

---

[1] (V.79:25) Last: i.e. his saying: "I am your lord, most high" (See Verse 79:24).

[2] (V.79:25) First: i.e. his saying, "O chiefs! I know not that you have a god other than I" (See Verse 28:38)

29. Its night He covers with darkness and its forenoon He brings out (with light).

وَأَغْطَشَ لَيْلَهَا وَأَخْرَجَ ضُحَىٰهَا ۝

30. And after that He spread the earth,

وَالْأَرْضَ بَعْدَ ذَٰلِكَ دَحَىٰهَا ۝

31. And brought forth therefrom its water and its pasture.

أَخْرَجَ مِنْهَا مَاءَهَا وَمَرْعَىٰهَا ۝

32. And the mountains He has fixed firmly,

وَالْجِبَالَ أَرْسَىٰهَا ۝

33. (To be) a provision and benefit for you and your cattle.

مَتَٰعًا لَّكُمْ وَلِأَنْعَٰمِكُمْ ۝

34. But when there comes the greatest catastrophe (i.e. the Day of Recompense)

فَإِذَا جَاءَتِ الطَّامَّةُ الْكُبْرَىٰ ۝

35. The Day when man shall remember what he strove for.

يَوْمَ يَتَذَكَّرُ الْإِنسَٰنُ مَا سَعَىٰ ۝

36. And Hell-fire shall be made apparent in full view for (every) one who sees.

وَبُرِّزَتِ الْجَحِيمُ لِمَن يَرَىٰ ۝

37. Then for him who transgressed all bounds, (in disbelief, oppression and evil deeds of disobedience to Allâh).

فَأَمَّا مَن طَغَىٰ ۝

38. And preferred the life of this world (by following his evil desires and lusts),

وَءَاثَرَ الْحَيَوٰةَ الدُّنْيَا ۝

39. Verily, his abode will be Hell-fire;

فَإِنَّ الْجَحِيمَ هِيَ الْمَأْوَىٰ ۝

40. But as for him who feared standing before his Lord, and restrained himself from impure evil desires and lusts.

وَأَمَّا مَنْ خَافَ مَقَامَ رَبِّهِ وَنَهَى النَّفْسَ عَنِ الْهَوَىٰ ۝

41. Verily, Paradise will be his abode.

فَإِنَّ الْجَنَّةَ هِيَ الْمَأْوَىٰ ۝

42. They ask you (O Muhammad صلى الله عليه وسلم) about the Hour — when will be its appointed time?

يَسْتَلُونَكَ عَنِ السَّاعَةِ أَيَّانَ مُرْسَىٰهَا ۝

43. You have no knowledge to say anything about it.

فِيمَ أَنتَ مِن ذِكْرَىٰهَا ۝

44. To your Lord belongs (the knowledge of) the term thereof?

إِلَىٰ رَبِّكَ مُنتَهَىٰهَا ۝

45. You (O Muhammad صلى الله عليه وسلم) are only a warner for those who fear it,

إِنَّمَآ أَنتَ مُنذِرُ مَن يَخْشَىٰهَا ۝

46. The Day they see it, (it will be) as if they had not tarried (in this world) except an afternoon or a morning.

كَأَنَّهُمْ يَوْمَ يَرَوْنَهَا لَمْ يَلْبَثُوٓا إِلَّا عَشِيَّةً أَوْ ضُحَىٰهَا ۝

**Sûrat 'Abasa
(He Frowned) LXXX**

سورة عبس

*In the Name of Allâh
the Most Gracious, the Most Merciful*

بِسْمِ اللهِ الرَّحْمَٰنِ الرَّحِيمِ

1. (The Prophet صلى الله عليه وسلم) frowned and turned away.

عَبَسَ وَتَوَلَّىٰٓ ۝

2. Because there came to him the blind man (i.e. 'Abdullâh bin Umm-Maktûm, who came to the Prophet صلى الله عليه وسلم while he was preaching to one or some of the Quraish chiefs).

أَن جَآءَهُ الْأَعْمَىٰ ۝

3. And how can you know that he might become pure (from sins)?

وَمَا يُدْرِيكَ لَعَلَّهُۥ يَزَّكَّىٰٓ ۝

4. Or he might receive admonition, and the admonition might profit him?

أَوْ يَذَّكَّرُ فَتَنفَعَهُ الذِّكْرَىٰٓ ۝

5. As for him who thinks himself self-sufficient, .

أَمَّا مَنِ اسْتَغْنَىٰ ۝

6. To him you attend;

فَأَنتَ لَهُۥ تَصَدَّىٰ ۝

7. What does it matter to you if he will not become pure (from disbelief: you are only a Messenger, your duty is to convey the Message of Allâh).

وَمَا عَلَيْكَ أَلَّا يَزَّكَّىٰ ۝

8. But as to him who came to you running,

وَأَمَّا مَن جَآءَكَ يَسْعَىٰ ۝

9. And is afraid (of Allâh and His punishment).

وَهُوَ يَخْشَىٰ ۝

10. Of him you are neglectful and divert your attention to another,

فَأَنتَ عَنْهُ تَلَهَّىٰ ۝

11. Nay, (do not do like this); indeed it (this Qur'ân) is an admonition.

كَلَّآ إِنَّهَا تَذْكِرَةٌ ۝

12. So whoever wills, let him pay attention to it.

فَمَن شَآءَ ذَكَرَهُ ۝

13. (It is) in Records held (greatly) in honour (Al-Lauh Al-Mahfûz),

فِى صُحُفٍ مُّكَرَّمَةٍ ۝

14. Exalted (in dignity), purified,

مَّرْفُوعَةٍ مُّطَهَّرَةٍ ۝

15. In the hands of scribes (angels).

بِأَيْدِى سَفَرَةٍ ۝

16. Honourable and obedient.

كِرَامٍ بَرَرَةٍ ۝

17. Be cursed (the disbelieving) man! How ungrateful he is!

قُتِلَ ٱلْإِنسَـٰنُ مَآ أَكْفَرَهُ ۝

18. From what thing did He create him?

مِنْ أَىِّ شَىْءٍ خَلَقَهُ ۝

19. From *Nutfah* (male and female semen drops) He created him and then set him in due proportion.

مِن نُّطْفَةٍ خَلَقَهُ فَقَدَّرَهُ ۝

20. Then He makes the Path easy for him.

ثُمَّ ٱلسَّبِيلَ يَسَّرَهُ ۝

21. Then He causes him to die and puts him in his grave.

ثُمَّ أَمَاتَهُ فَأَقْبَرَهُ ۝

22. Then when it is His Will, He will resurrect him (again).

ثُمَّ إِذَا شَآءَ أَنشَرَهُ ۝

23. Nay, but (man) has not done what He commanded him.   كَلَّا لَمَّا يَقْضِ مَا أَمَرَهُ ۝

24. Then let man look at his food·   فَلْيَنظُرِ الْإِنسَانُ إِلَىٰ طَعَامِهِ ۝

25. We pour forth water in abundance.   أَنَّا صَبَبْنَا الْمَاءَ صَبًّا ۝

26. And We split the earth in clefts.   ثُمَّ شَقَقْنَا الْأَرْضَ شَقًّا ۝

27. And We cause therein the grain to grow,   فَأَنبَتْنَا فِيهَا حَبًّا ۝

28. And grapes and clover plants (i.e. green fodder for the cattle),   وَعِنَبًا وَقَضْبًا ۝

29. And olives and date-palms,   وَزَيْتُونًا وَنَخْلًا ۝

30. And gardens dense with many trees,   وَحَدَائِقَ غُلْبًا ۝

31. And fruits and herbage.   وَفَاكِهَةً وَأَبًّا ۝

32. (To be) a provision and benefit for you and your cattle.   مَّتَاعًا لَّكُمْ وَلِأَنْعَامِكُمْ ۝

33. Then when there comes As-Sâkhkhah (on the Day of Resurrection second blowing of the Trumpet) —   فَإِذَا جَاءَتِ الصَّاخَّةُ ۝

34. That Day shall a man flee from his brother,   يَوْمَ يَفِرُّ الْمَرْءُ مِنْ أَخِيهِ ۝

35. And from his mother and his father,   وَأُمِّهِ وَأَبِيهِ ۝

36. And from his wife and his children.   وَصَاحِبَتِهِ وَبَنِيهِ ۝

37. Every man that Day will have enough to make him careless of others.   لِكُلِّ امْرِئٍ مِّنْهُمْ يَوْمَئِذٍ شَأْنٌ يُغْنِيهِ ۝

38. Some faces that Day will be bright (true believers of Islâmic Monotheism),   وُجُوهٌ يَوْمَئِذٍ مُّسْفِرَةٌ ۝

39. Laughing, rejoicing at good news (of Paradise).   ضَاحِكَةٌ مُّسْتَبْشِرَةٌ ۝

40. And other faces, that Day, will be dust-stained.

وَوُجُوهٌ يَوْمَئِذٍ عَلَيْهَا غَبَرَةٌ ﴿٤٠﴾

41. Darkness will cover them.

تَرْهَقُهَا قَتَرَةٌ ﴿٤١﴾

42. Such will be the *Kafarah* (disbelievers in Allâh, in His Oneness, and in His Messenger Muhammad صلى الله عليه وسلم), the *Fajarah* (wicked evil doers).

أُولَٰئِكَ هُمُ الْكَفَرَةُ الْفَجَرَةُ ﴿٤٢﴾

Sûrat At-Takwîr (Wound Round and Lost its Light) LXXXI

سُورَةُ التَّكْوِيرِ

In the Name of Allâh the Most Gracious, the Most Merciful

بِسْمِ اللَّهِ الرَّحْمَٰنِ الرَّحِيمِ

1. When the sun shall be wound round and its light is lost and is overthrown[1].

إِذَا الشَّمْسُ كُوِّرَتْ ﴿١﴾

2. And when the stars shall fall.

وَإِذَا النُّجُومُ انكَدَرَتْ ﴿٢﴾

3. And when the mountains shall be made to pass away;

وَإِذَا الْجِبَالُ سُيِّرَتْ ﴿٣﴾

4. And when the pregnant she-camels shall be neglected;

وَإِذَا الْعِشَارُ عُطِّلَتْ ﴿٤﴾

5. And when the wild beasts shall be gathered together.

وَإِذَا الْوُحُوشُ حُشِرَتْ ﴿٥﴾

6. And when the seas shall become as blazing Fire or shall overflow.

وَإِذَا الْبِحَارُ سُجِّرَتْ ﴿٦﴾

7. And when the souls shall be joined with their bodies (the good with the good and the bad with the bad).

وَإِذَا النُّفُوسُ زُوِّجَتْ ﴿٧﴾

---

[1] (V.81:1) Narrated Abu Hurairah رضي الله عنه: The Prophet صلى الله عليه وسلم said, "The sun and the moon will be folded up (or joined together or deprived of their lights) on the Day of Resurrection." [See the Qur'ân (V.75:9)] (*Sahih Al-Bukhari*, Vol. 4, *Hadith* No. 422).

8. And when the female (infant) buried alive (as the pagan Arabs used to do) shall be questioned:[1]

وَإِذَا الْمَوْءُۥدَةُ سُئِلَتْ ۝

9. For what sin was she killed?

بِأَىِّ ذَنبٍ قُتِلَتْ ۝

10. And when the (written) pages [of deeds (good and bad) of every person] shall be laid open.

وَإِذَا الصُّحُفُ نُشِرَتْ ۝

11. And when the heaven shall be stripped off and taken away from its place;

وَإِذَا السَّمَآءُ كُشِطَتْ ۝

12. And when Hell-fire shall be set ablaze.

وَإِذَا الْجَحِيمُ سُعِّرَتْ ۝

13. And when Paradise shall be brought near.

وَإِذَا الْجَنَّةُ أُزْلِفَتْ ۝

14. (Then) every person will know what he has brought (of good and evil).

عَلِمَتْ نَفْسٌ مَّآ أَحْضَرَتْ ۝

15. So verily, I swear by the planets that recede (i.e. disappear during the day and appear during the night).

فَلَآ أُقْسِمُ بِالْخُنَّسِ ۝

16. And by the planets that move swiftly and hide themselves.

الْجَوَارِ الْكُنَّسِ ۝

17. And by the night as it departs.

وَالَّيْلِ إِذَا عَسْعَسَ ۝

18. And by the dawn as it brightens.

وَالصُّبْحِ إِذَا تَنَفَّسَ ۝

19. Verily, this is the Word (this Qur'ân brought by) a most honourable

إِنَّهُ لَقَوْلُ رَسُولٍ كَرِيمٍ ۝

---

[1] (V.81:8) Narrated Al-Mughîrah bin Shu'bah رضى الله عنه The Prophet صلى الله عليه وسلم said, "Allâh has forbidden for you: (1) to be undutiful to your mothers, (2) to bury your daughters alive, (3) not to pay the rights of the others (e.g., charity), and (4) to beg of men (i.e., begging). And Allâh hates for you: (1) sinful and useless talk like backbiting, or that you talk too much about others, (2) to ask too many questions (in disputed religious matters), and (3) to waste the wealth (by extravagance with lack of wisdom and thinking)." (Sahih Al-Bukhari, Vol. 3, Hadith No. 591).

messenger [Jibrael (Gabriel), from Allâh to Prophet Muhammad صلى الله عليه وسلم].

20. Owner of power, (and high rank) with (Allâh), the Lord of the Throne,

ذِى قُوَّةٍ عِندَ ذِى ٱلْعَرْشِ مَكِينٍ ٢٠

21. Obeyed (by the angels in the heavens) and trustworthy.

مُّطَاعٍ ثَمَّ أَمِينٍ ٢١

22. And (O people) your companion (Muhammad صلى الله عليه وسلم) is not a madman.

وَمَا صَاحِبُكُم بِمَجْنُونٍ ٢٢

23. And indeed he (Muhammad صلى الله عليه وسلم) saw him [Jibrael (Gabriel)] in the clear horizon (towards the east).

وَلَقَدْ رَءَاهُ بِٱلْأُفُقِ ٱلْمُبِينِ ٢٣

24. And he (Muhammad صلى الله عليه وسلم) withholds not a knowledge of the Unseen.

وَمَا هُوَ عَلَى ٱلْغَيْبِ بِضَنِينٍ ٢٤

25. And it (the Qur'ân) is not the word of the outcast Shaitân (Satan).

وَمَا هُوَ بِقَوْلِ شَيْطَانٍ رَّجِيمٍ ٢٥

26. Then where are you going?

فَأَيْنَ تَذْهَبُونَ ٢٦

27. Verily, this (the Qur'ân) is no less than a Reminder to (all) the 'Âlamîn (mankind and jinn)[1]

إِنْ هُوَ إِلَّا ذِكْرٌ لِّلْعَالَمِينَ ٢٧

---

[1] (V.81:27)

a) Narrated Abu Hurairah رضي الله عنه: The Prophet صلى الله عليه وسلم said, "There was no Prophet among the Prophets but was given miracles because of which people had security or had belief, but what I have been given is the Divine Revelation which Allâh has revealed to me. So I hope that my followers will be more than those of any other Prophet on the Day of Resurrection." (Sahih Al-Bukhari, Vol. 9, Hadith No. 379)

b) It is obligatory to have Belief in the Messengership of the Prophet (Muhammad صلى الله عليه وسلم). Narrated Abu Hurairah رضي الله عنه: Allâh's Messenger صلى الله عليه وسلم said: "By Him (Allâh) in Whose Hand Muhammad's soul is, there is none from amongst the Jews and Christians (of these present nations) who hears about me and

28. To whomsoever among you who wills to walk straight.

لِمَن شَآءَ مِنكُمْ أَن يَسْتَقِيمَ ۝

29. And you cannot will unless (it be) that Allâh wills — the Lord of the 'Âlamîn (mankind, jinn and all that exists).

وَمَا تَشَآءُونَ إِلَّآ أَن يَشَآءَ ٱللَّهُ رَبُّ ٱلْعَٰلَمِينَ ۝

Sûrat Al-Infitâr
(The Cleaving) LXXXII

سُورَةُ الانفِطَار

*In the Name of Allâh
the Most Gracious, the Most Merciful*

بِسْمِ ٱللَّهِ ٱلرَّحْمَٰنِ ٱلرَّحِيمِ

1. When the heaven is cleft asunder.

إِذَا ٱلسَّمَآءُ ٱنفَطَرَتْ ۝

2. And when the stars have fallen and scattered.

وَإِذَا ٱلْكَوَاكِبُ ٱنتَثَرَتْ ۝

3. And when the seas are burst forth.

وَإِذَا ٱلْبِحَارُ فُجِّرَتْ ۝

4. And when the graves are turned upside down (and bring out their contents).

وَإِذَا ٱلْقُبُورُ بُعْثِرَتْ ۝

5. (Then) a person will know what he has sent forward and (what he has) left behind (of good or bad deeds).

عَلِمَتْ نَفْسٌ مَّا قَدَّمَتْ وَأَخَّرَتْ ۝

6. O man! What has made you careless about your Lord, the Most Generous?

يَٰٓأَيُّهَا ٱلْإِنسَٰنُ مَا غَرَّكَ بِرَبِّكَ ٱلْكَرِيمِ ۝

7. Who created you, fashioned you perfectly, and gave you due proportion.

ٱلَّذِي خَلَقَكَ فَسَوَّىٰكَ فَعَدَلَكَ ۝

8. In whatever form He willed, He put you together.

فِىٓ أَىِّ صُورَةٍ مَّا شَآءَ رَكَّبَكَ ۝

9. Nay! But you deny Ad-Dîn (i.e. the Day of Recompense).

كَلَّا بَلْ تُكَذِّبُونَ بِٱلدِّينِ ۝

---

then dies without believing in the Message with which I have been sent (i.e. Islâmic Monotheism), but he will be from the dwellers of the (Hell) Fire." (*Sahih Muslim*, the Book of Faith, Vol. 1, Chapter No.240). See also (V.3:85) and (V.3:116).

10. But verily, over you (are appointed angels in charge of mankind) to watch you,[1]

وَإِنَّ عَلَيْكُمْ لَحَٰفِظِينَ ١٠

11. Kirâman (Honourable) Kâtibîn writing down (your deeds),[2]

كِرَامًا كَٰتِبِينَ ١١

12. They know all that you do.

يَعْلَمُونَ مَا تَفْعَلُونَ ١٢

13. Verily, the Abrâr (the pious and righteous) will be in Delight (Paradise);

إِنَّ ٱلْأَبْرَارَ لَفِى نَعِيمٍ ١٣

14. And verily, the Fujjâr (the wicked, disbelievers, polytheists, sinners and evil-doers) will be in the blazing Fire (Hell),

وَإِنَّ ٱلْفُجَّارَ لَفِى جَحِيمٍ ١٤

---

[1] (V.82:10) Narrated Abu Hurairah رضي الله عنه: The Prophet صلى الله عليه وسلم said: "Angels come (to you) in succession by night and day, and all of them get together at the time of the *Fajr* and *'Asr* prayers. Then those who have stayed with you overnight, ascend unto Allâh, Who asks them (and He knows the answer better than they): "How have you left My slaves?" They reply, "We left them while they were praying and we came to them while they were praying." The Prophet صلى الله عليه وسلم added: "If anyone of you says *Amîn* (during the prayer at the end of the recitation of *Sûrat Al-Fâtihah*), and the angels in heaven say the same, and the two saying coincide, all his past sins will be forgiven." (*Sahih Al-Bukhari*, Vol. 4, Hadith No. 446).

[2] (V.82:11) Whoever intended to do a good deed or a bad deed.

Narrated Ibn 'Abbâs رضي الله عنهما: The Prophet صلى الله عليه وسلم narrating about his Lord عز وجل said, "Allâh ordered (the angels appointed over you) that the good and the bad deeds be written, and He then showed (the way) how (to write). If somebody intends to do a good deed and he does not do it, then Allâh will write for him a full good deed (in his account with Him); and if he intends to do a good deed and actually does it, then Allâh will write for him (in his account) with Him (its reward equal) from ten to seven hundred times, to many more times; and if somebody intended to do a bad deed and he does not do it, then Allâh will write a full good deed (in his account) with Him, and if he intended to do it (a bad deed) and actually does it, then Allâh will write one bad deed (in his account)." (*Sahih Al-Bukhari*, Vol. 8, Hadith No. 498)

15. Therein they will enter, and taste its burning flame on the Day of Recompense,

صَلَوْا بِهَا يَوْمَ الدِّينِ ﴿١٥﴾

16. And they (Al-Fujjâr) will not be absent therefrom.

وَمَا هُمْ عَنْهَا بِغَآئِبِينَ ﴿١٦﴾

17. And what will make you know what the Day of Recompense is?

وَمَآ أَدْرَىٰكَ مَا يَوْمُ الدِّينِ ﴿١٧﴾

18. Again, what will make you know what the Day of Recompense is?

ثُمَّ مَآ أَدْرَىٰكَ مَا يَوْمُ الدِّينِ ﴿١٨﴾

19. (It will be) the Day when no person shall have power (to do) anything for another, and the Decision, that Day, will be (wholly) with Allâh.

يَوْمَ لَا تَمْلِكُ نَفْسٌ لِّنَفْسٍ شَيْئًا وَالْأَمْرُ يَوْمَئِذٍ لِّلَّهِ ﴿١٩﴾

Sûrat Al-Mutaffifin
(Those Who Deal in Fraud)
LXXXIII

سُورَةُ الْمُطَفِّفِينَ

In the Name of Allâh
the Most Gracious, the Most Merciful

بِسْمِ اللَّهِ الرَّحْمَٰنِ الرَّحِيمِ

1. Woe to Al-Mutaffifûn (those who give less in measure and weight).

وَيْلٌ لِّلْمُطَفِّفِينَ ﴿١﴾

2. Those who, when they have to receive by measure from men, demand full measure,

الَّذِينَ إِذَا اكْتَالُوا عَلَى النَّاسِ يَسْتَوْفُونَ ﴿٢﴾

3. And when they have to give by measure or weight to (other) men, give less than due.

وَإِذَا كَالُوهُمْ أَو وَّزَنُوهُمْ يُخْسِرُونَ ﴿٣﴾

4. Do they not think that they will be resurrected (for reckoning),

أَلَا يَظُنُّ أُولَٰئِكَ أَنَّهُم مَّبْعُوثُونَ ﴿٤﴾

5. On a Great Day?

لِيَوْمٍ عَظِيمٍ ﴿٥﴾

6. The Day when (all) mankind will stand before the Lord of the ʿÂlamîn (mankind, jinn and all that exists)?

يَوْمَ يَقُومُ النَّاسُ لِرَبِّ الْعَالَمِينَ ﴿٦﴾

7. Nay! Truly, the Record (writing of the deeds) of the *Fujjâr* (disbelievers, polytheists, sinners, evil-doers and the wicked) is (preserved) in *Sijjîn*.

كَلَّا إِنَّ كِتَـٰبَ ٱلۡفُجَّارِ لَفِى سِجِّينٍ ۝

8. And what will make you know what *Sijjîn* is?

وَمَآ أَدۡرَىٰكَ مَا سِجِّينٌ ۝

9. A Register inscribed.

كِتَـٰبٌ مَّرۡقُومٌ ۝

10. Woe, that Day, to those who deny.

وَيۡلٌ يَوۡمَئِذٍ لِّلۡمُكَذِّبِينَ ۝

11. Those who deny the Day of Recompense.

ٱلَّذِينَ يُكَذِّبُونَ بِيَوۡمِ ٱلدِّينِ ۝

12. And none can deny it except every transgressor beyond limits, (in disbelief, oppression and disobedience to Allâh) the sinner!

وَمَا يُكَذِّبُ بِهِۦٓ إِلَّا كُلُّ مُعۡتَدٍ أَثِيمٍ ۝

13. When Our Verses (of the Qur'ân) are recited to him he says: "Tales of the ancients!"

إِذَا تُتۡلَىٰ عَلَيۡهِ ءَايَـٰتُنَا قَالَ أَسَـٰطِيرُ ٱلۡأَوَّلِينَ ۝

14. Nay! But on their hearts is the *Rân* (covering of sins and evil deeds) which they used to earn.[1]

كَلَّا بَلۡ رَانَ عَلَىٰ قُلُوبِهِم مَّا كَانُواْ يَكۡسِبُونَ ۝

15. Nay! Surely, they (evil-doers) will be veiled from seeing their Lord that Day.

كَلَّا إِنَّهُمۡ عَن رَّبِّهِمۡ يَوۡمَئِذٍ لَّمَحۡجُوبُونَ ۝

---

[1] (V.83:14) Narrated Abu Hurairah رضي الله عنه Allâh's Messenger صلى said, "When a slave (a person) commits a sin (an evil deed) الله عليه وسلم a black dot is dotted on his heart. Then if that person gives up that evil deed (sin), begs Allâh to forgive him, and repents, then his heart is cleared (from that heart covering dot); but if he repeats the evil deed (sin), then that covering is increased till his heart is completely covered with it. And that is *Ar-Rân* which Allâh mentioned in the Qur'ân), "Nay! but on their hearts is the *Rân* (covering of sins and evil deeds) which they used to earn." (At-Tirmidhi).

16. Then verily, they will indeed enter (and taste) the burning flame of Hell.

ثُمَّ إِنَّهُمْ لَصَالُواْ الْجَحِيمِ ۝

17. Then, it will be said to them: "This is what you used to deny!"

ثُمَّ يُقَالُ هَٰذَا الَّذِى كُنتُم بِهِۦ تُكَذِّبُونَ ۝

18. Nay! Verily, the Record (writing of the deeds) of Al-Abrâr (the pious and righteous) is (preserved) in 'Illiyyûn

كَلَّآ إِنَّ كِتَٰبَ الْأَبْرَارِ لَفِى عِلِّيِّينَ ۝

19. And what will make you know what 'Illiyyûn is?

وَمَآ أَدْرَىٰكَ مَا عِلِّيُّونَ ۝

20. A Register inscribed,

كِتَٰبٌ مَّرْقُومٌ ۝

21. To which bear witness those nearest (to Allâh, i.e. the angels).

يَشْهَدُهُ الْمُقَرَّبُونَ ۝

22. Verily, Al-Abrâr (the pious and righteous) will be in Delight (Paradise).

إِنَّ الْأَبْرَارَ لَفِى نَعِيمٍ ۝

23. On thrones, looking (at all things).

عَلَى الْأَرَآئِكِ يَنظُرُونَ ۝

24. You will recognise in their faces the brightness of delight.

تَعْرِفُ فِى وُجُوهِهِمْ نَضْرَةَ النَّعِيمِ ۝

25. They will be given to drink of pure sealed wine.

يُسْقَوْنَ مِن رَّحِيقٍ مَّخْتُومٍ ۝

26. The last thereof (that wine) will be the smell of Musk, and for this let (all) those strive who want to strive (i.e. hasten earnestly to the obedience of Allâh).

خِتَٰمُهُۥ مِسْكٌ وَفِى ذَٰلِكَ فَلْيَتَنَافَسِ الْمُتَنَافِسُونَ ۝

27. It (that wine) will be mixed with Tasnîm:

وَمِزَاجُهُۥ مِن تَسْنِيمٍ ۝

28. A spring whereof drink those nearest to Allâh.

عَيْنًا يَشْرَبُ بِهَا الْمُقَرَّبُونَ ۝

29. Verily, (during the worldly life) those who committed crimes used to laugh at those who believed.

إِنَّ الَّذِينَ أَجْرَمُواْ كَانُواْ مِنَ الَّذِينَ ءَامَنُواْ يَضْحَكُونَ ۝

30. And, whenever they passed by them, used to wink one to another (in mockery).

وَإِذَا مَرُّواْ بِهِمْ يَتَغَامَزُونَ ۝

31. And when they returned to their own people, they would return jesting;

وَإِذَا ٱنقَلَبُوٓاْ إِلَىٰٓ أَهْلِهِمُ ٱنقَلَبُواْ فَكِهِينَ ۝

32. And when they saw them, they said: "Verily, these have indeed gone astray!"

وَإِذَا رَأَوْهُمْ قَالُوٓاْ إِنَّ هَـٰٓؤُلَآءِ لَضَآلُّونَ ۝

33. But they (disbelievers, sinners) had not been sent as watchers over them (the believers).

وَمَآ أُرْسِلُواْ عَلَيْهِمْ حَٰفِظِينَ ۝

34. But this Day (the Day of Resurrection) those who believe will laugh at the disbelievers[1]

فَٱلْيَوْمَ ٱلَّذِينَ ءَامَنُواْ مِنَ ٱلْكُفَّارِ يَضْحَكُونَ ۝

35. On (high) thrones, looking (at all things).

عَلَى ٱلْأَرَآئِكِ يَنظُرُونَ ۝

36. Are not the disbelievers paid (fully) for what they used to do?

هَلْ ثُوِّبَ ٱلْكُفَّارُ مَا كَانُواْ يَفْعَلُونَ ۝

Sûrat Al-Inshiqâq
(The Splitting Asunder) LXXXIV

سُورَةُ الإنْشِقَاق

In the Name of Allâh
the Most Gracious, the Most Merciful

بِسْمِ ٱللَّهِ ٱلرَّحْمَٰنِ ٱلرَّحِيمِ

1. When the heaven is split asunder,

إِذَا ٱلسَّمَآءُ ٱنشَقَّتْ ۝

2. And listens to and obeys its Lord — and it must do so.

وَأَذِنَتْ لِرَبِّهَا وَحُقَّتْ ۝

---

[1] (V.83:34) Narrated Anas bin Mâlik رضى الله عنه A man said, "O Allâh's Prophet! Will Allâh gather a disbeliever (prone) on his face on the Day of Resurrection?" He صلى الله عليه وسلم said, "Will not the One Who made him walk on his feet in this world, be able to make him walk on his face on the Day of Resurrection?" (Qatâdah, a subnarrator, said: "Yes, By the Power of Our Lord!") (*Sahih Al-Bukhari*, Vol. 6, *Hadith* No.283).

3. And when the earth is stretched forth,

وَإِذَا الْأَرْضُ مُدَّتْ ﴿٣﴾

4. And has cast out all that was in it and became empty.

وَأَلْقَتْ مَا فِيهَا وَتَخَلَّتْ ﴿٤﴾

5. And listens to and obeys its Lord — and it must do so.

وَأَذِنَتْ لِرَبِّهَا وَحُقَّتْ ﴿٥﴾

6. O man! Verily, you are returning towards your Lord with your deeds and actions (good or bad), a sure returning, and you will meet (the results of your deeds which you did).

يَأَيُّهَا الْإِنسَانُ إِنَّكَ كَادِحٌ إِلَى رَبِّكَ كَدْحًا فَمُلَقِيهِ ﴿٦﴾

7. Then as for him who will be given his Record in his right hand,

فَأَمَّا مَنْ أُوتِيَ كِتَابَهُ بِيَمِينِهِ ﴿٧﴾

8. He surely, will receive an easy reckoning,

فَسَوْفَ يُحَاسَبُ حِسَابًا يَسِيرًا ﴿٨﴾

9. And will return to his family in joy!

وَيَنقَلِبُ إِلَى أَهْلِهِ مَسْرُورًا ﴿٩﴾

10. But whosoever is given his Record behind his back,

وَأَمَّا مَنْ أُوتِيَ كِتَابَهُ وَرَاءَ ظَهْرِهِ ﴿١٠﴾

11. He will invoke (for his) destruction,

فَسَوْفَ يَدْعُو ثُبُورًا ﴿١١﴾

12. And he shall enter a blazing Fire, and made to taste its burning.

وَيَصْلَى سَعِيرًا ﴿١٢﴾

13. Verily, he was among his people in joy!

إِنَّهُ كَانَ فِي أَهْلِهِ مَسْرُورًا ﴿١٣﴾

14. Verily, he thought that he would never come back (to Us)!

إِنَّهُ ظَنَّ أَن لَّن يَحُورَ ﴿١٤﴾

15. Yes! Verily, his Lord has been ever beholding him!

بَلَى إِنَّ رَبَّهُ كَانَ بِهِ بَصِيرًا ﴿١٥﴾

16. So I swear by the afterglow of sunset;

فَلَا أُقْسِمُ بِالشَّفَقِ ﴿١٦﴾

17. And by the night and whatever it gathers in its darkness,

وَالَّيْلِ وَمَا وَسَقَ ﴿١٧﴾

18. And by the moon when it is at the full.

وَالْقَمَرِ إِذَا اتَّسَقَ ﴿١٨﴾

19. You shall certainly travel from stage to stage (in this life and in the Hereafter).

20. What is the matter with them, that they believe not?

21. And when the Qur'ân is recited to them, they fall not prostrate.

22. Nay, those who disbelieve belie (Prophet Muhammad صلى الله عليه وسلم and whatever he brought, i.e. this Qur'ân and Islâmic Monotheism).[1]

23. And Allâh knows best what they gather (of good and bad deeds),

24. So announce to them a painful torment,

25. Save those who believe and do righteous good deeds, for them is a reward that will never come to an end (i.e. Paradise).

Sûrat Al-Burûj
(The Big Stars "Burûj") LXXXV

*In the Name of Allâh
the Most Gracious, the Most Merciful*

1. By the heaven holding the big stars.[2]

---

[1] (V.84:22) It is obligatory to have belief in the Messengership of the Prophet (Muhammad صلى الله عليه وسلم). Narrated Abu Hurairah رضى الله عنه: Allâh's Messenger صلى الله عليه وسلم said: "By Him (Allâh) in Whose Hand Muhammad's soul is, there is none from amongst the Jews and Christians (of these present nations) who hears about me and then dies without believing in the Message with which I have been sent (i.e. Islâmic Monotheism), but he will be from the dwellers of the (Hell) Fire." (*Sahih Muslim*, the Book of Faith, Vol. 1, Chapter No.240). See also (V.3:85) and (V.3:116).

[2] (V.85:1) (About the) Stars, Abu Qatâdah mentioning Allâh's Statement:

2. And by the Promised Day (i.e. the Day of Resurrection). وَالْيَوْمِ الْمَوْعُودِ

3. And by the Witnessing day (i.e. Friday), and by the Witnessed day [i.e. the day of 'Arafah (Hajj) the ninth of Dhul-Hijjah]; وَشَاهِدٍ وَمَشْهُودٍ

4. Cursed were the People of the Ditch (in the story of the Boy and the King).[1] قُتِلَ أَصْحَابُ الْأُخْدُودِ

"And We have adorned the nearest heaven with lamps," and said, "The creation of these stars is for three purposes, i.e., as decoration of the heaven, as missiles to hit the devils, and as signs to guide travellers. So, if anybody tries to find a different interpretation, he is mistaken and just wastes his efforts, and troubles himself with what is beyond his limited knowledge." (Sahih Al-Bukhari, Vol. 4, Chapter 3).

[1] (V.85:4) The Story of the Boy and the King

Narrated Shu'aib رضي الله عنه Allâh's Messenger صلى الله عليه وسلم said: "Among the people before you, there was a king and he had a sorcerer. When the sorcerer became old, he said to the king: 'I have now become an old man, get me a boy so that I may teach him sorcery.' So the king sent him a boy to teach him sorcery. Whenever the boy proceeded to the sorcerer, he sat with a monk who was on the way and listened to his talks and used to admire them (those talks). So when he went to the sorcerer, he passed by the monk and sat there with him. And on visiting the sorcerer, the latter thrashed him. So the boy complained about that to the monk. The monk said to him: Whenever you are afraid of the sorcerer, say to him: 'My people kept me busy'; and whenever you are afraid of your people, say to them: 'The sorcerer kept me busy.' So the boy carried on like that (for a period).

"There came (on the main road) a huge creature (animal), and the people were unable to pass by. The boy said: 'Today I will know whether the sorcerer is better or the monk'. So he took a stone and said: 'O Allâh! If the deeds and actions of the sorcerer are liked by You better than those of the sorcerer, then kill this creature so that the people can cross (the road).' Then he hit (it) with the stone, and

it was killed and the people passed (the road). The boy came to the
monk and informed him about it. The monk said to him: 'O my son!
Today you are better than I; you have achieved what I see! And you
will be put to trial. And in case you are put to trial, do not inform
(them) about me.' The boy used to treat the people suffering from
born-blindness, leprosy, leucoderma, and other diseases. A blind
courtier of the king heard about the boy. He came and brought a
number of gifts for the boy and said: 'All these gifts are for you on
condition that you cure me'.The boy said: 'I do not cure anybody; it
is only Allâh (Alone) Who cures (people). So if you believe in
Allâh, and invoke Allâh, He will cure you'. He then believed in
Allâh, and Allâh cured him. Later the courtier came to the king, and
sat at the place where he used to sit before. The king asked him:
'Who has given you your sight back?' The courtier replied:'My
Lord (Allâh)!' The king said: 'Have you got another lord than I?'
The courtier said: 'My Lord and your Lord is Allâh!' The king got
hold of him and kept on tormenting him till he informed him about
the boy. So the boy was brought. The king said to the boy: 'O boy!
Has your (knowledge of) sorcery reached to the extent that you cure
born-blinds, lepers, leucodermic patients and do such and such?'
The boy replied: 'I do not cure anybody; it is only Allâh (Alone)
Who does cure'. Then the king got hold of him, and kept on
tormenting him till he informed him about the monk. And the monk
was brought, and it was said to him: 'Give up your religion (turn
apostate)!' The monk refused to turn apostate. Then the king
ordered a saw (to be brought), and it was put in the middle of his
scalp and was sawn, till he fell, cut in two pieces. Then that courtier
was brought, and it was said to him: 'Give up your religion (turn
apostate)!' The courtier refused to turn apostate. So the saw was put
in the middle of his scalp, and was sawn till he fell, cut in two
pieces. Then the boy was brought, and it was said to him: 'Give up
your religion (turn apostate)!' The boy refused to turn apostate. So
the king ordered some of his courtiers to take the boy to such and
such a mountain saying, 'Then ascend up the mountain with him till
you reach its top, and see if he turns apostate (from his religion);
well and good); otherwise throw him down from its top.' They took
him, ascended up the mountain, and the boy said: 'O Allâh! Save
me from them by anything You wish!' So the mountain shook and
all of them fell down, and the boy came walking to the king. The

5. Of fire fed with fuel,

6. When they sat by it (fire),

النَّارِ ذَاتِ الْوَقُودِ ﴿٥﴾
إِذْ هُمْ عَلَيْهَا قُعُودٌ ﴿٦﴾

---

king asked him: 'What did your companions do?' The boy said:
'Allâh has saved me from them.' The king then ordered some of his
courtiers to take the boy on board a boat into the middle of the sea,
saying, 'Then if he turns apostate (from his religion, well and
good), otherwise cast him into the sea.' So they took him, and he
said: 'O Allâh! Save me from them by anything You wish.' So the
boat capsized, and (all the accompanying courtiers) were drowned.
The boy then came walking to the king. The king said: 'What did
your companions do?' The boy replied: 'Allâh saved me from
them', and he further said to the king: 'You cannot kill me till you
do what I command!' The king said: 'What is that (command of
yours)?' The boy said: 'Gather all the people in an upland place,
and fasten me to the stem (of a tree); then take an arrow from my
quiver and fix it in the bow, and say: — In the Name of Allâh, the
Lord of the boy, — and shoot (me). If you do that, you will kill me.'
So the king gathered the people in an upland place, and fastened the
boy to the stem, took an arrow from his quiver, fixed it in the bow,
and said: 'In the Name of Allâh, the Lord of the boy', and shot the
arrow. The arrow hit the temporal region of the skull of the boy, and
the boy put his hand over the temporal region of his skull at the
point where the arrow hit, and then died. The people proclaimed:
'We have believed in the Lord of the boy! We have believed in the
Lord of the boy! We have believed in the Lord of the boy!' The
king came, and it was said to him: 'That is the thing which you
were afraid of. By Allâh! The thing which you were afraid of, has
fallen upon you, the people have believed (in Allâh).' So he ordered
(deep) ditches to be dug at the entrances of the roads, and it was
done, then fire was kindled in those ditches, and the king ordered
that whoever did not turn apostate (from his religion) be cast into
the ditches, and it was done. Then there came a woman with her
babe. She nearly retreated back from the ditch but the babe said
(spoke): 'O mother! Be patient, you are on the Truth,' (So she threw
herself in the ditch of the fire alongwith her child to be with the
martyrs in the Paradise)." (*Sahih Muslim*, Vol. 4, *Hadith* No. 7148).

7. And they witnessed what they were doing against the believers (i.e. burning them).

وَهُمْ عَلَىٰ مَا يَفْعَلُونَ بِالْمُؤْمِنِينَ شُهُودٌ ﴿٧﴾

8. And they had no fault except that they believed in Allâh, the All-Mighty, Worthy of all praise!

وَمَا نَقَمُوا مِنْهُمْ إِلَّا أَن يُؤْمِنُوا بِاللَّهِ الْعَزِيزِ الْحَمِيدِ ﴿٨﴾

9. To Whom belongs the dominion of the heavens and the earth! And Allâh is Witness over everything.

الَّذِي لَهُ مُلْكُ السَّمَاوَاتِ وَالْأَرْضِ وَاللَّهُ عَلَىٰ كُلِّ شَيْءٍ شَهِيدٌ ﴿٩﴾

10. Verily, those who put into trial the believing men and believing women (by torturing them and burning them), and then do not turn in repentance (to Allâh), then they will have the torment of Hell, and they will have the punishment of the burning Fire.

إِنَّ الَّذِينَ فَتَنُوا الْمُؤْمِنِينَ وَالْمُؤْمِنَاتِ ثُمَّ لَمْ يَتُوبُوا فَلَهُمْ عَذَابُ جَهَنَّمَ وَلَهُمْ عَذَابُ الْحَرِيقِ ﴿١٠﴾

11. Verily, those who believe and do righteous good deeds, for them will be Gardens under which rivers flow (Paradise). That is the great success.

إِنَّ الَّذِينَ آمَنُوا وَعَمِلُوا الصَّالِحَاتِ لَهُمْ جَنَّاتٌ تَجْرِي مِن تَحْتِهَا الْأَنْهَارُ ذَٰلِكَ الْفَوْزُ الْكَبِيرُ ﴿١١﴾

12. Verily, (O Muhammad صلى الله عليه وسلم) the Seizure (punishment) of your Lord is severe and painful. [See V.11:102].

إِنَّ بَطْشَ رَبِّكَ لَشَدِيدٌ ﴿١٢﴾

13. Verily, He it is Who begins (punishment) and repeats (punishment in the Hereafter) (or originates the creation of everything, and then repeats it on the Day of Resurrection).

إِنَّهُ هُوَ يُبْدِئُ وَيُعِيدُ ﴿١٣﴾

14. And He is Oft-Forgiving, full of love (towards the pious who are real true believers of Islâmic Monotheism),

وَهُوَ الْغَفُورُ الْوَدُودُ ﴿١٤﴾

15. Owner of the throne, the Glorious,

ذُو الْعَرْشِ الْمَجِيدُ ﴿١٥﴾

16. (He is the) Doer of whatsoever He intends (or wills).

فَعَّالٌ لِّمَا يُرِيدُ ١٦

17. Has the story reached you of the hosts,

هَلۡ أَتَىٰكَ حَدِيثُ ٱلۡجُنُودِ ١٧

18. Of Fir'aun (Pharaoh) and Thamûd?

فِرۡعَوۡنَ وَثَمُودَ ١٨

19. Nay! The disbelievers (persisted) in denying (Prophet Muhammad صلى الله عليه وسلم and his Message of Islâmic Monotheism).

بَلِ ٱلَّذِينَ كَفَرُواْ فِى تَكۡذِيبٍ ١٩

20. And Allâh encompasses them from behind! (i.e. all their deeds are within His Knowledge, and He will requite them for their deeds).

وَٱللَّهُ مِن وَرَآئِهِم مُّحِيطُۢ ٢٠

21. Nay! This is a Glorious Qur'ân,

بَلۡ هُوَ قُرۡءَانٌ مَّجِيدٌ ٢١

22. (Inscribed) in Al-Lauh Al-Mahfûz (The Preserved Tablet)!

فِى لَوۡحٍ مَّحۡفُوظِۭ ٢٢

Sûrat At-Târiq
(The Night-Comer) LXXXVI

سُورَةُ الطَّارِقِ

In the Name of Allâh the Most Gracious, the Most Merciful

بِسۡمِ ٱللَّهِ ٱلرَّحۡمَٰنِ ٱلرَّحِيمِ

1. By the heaven, and *At-Târiq* (the night-comer, i.e. the bright star);

وَٱلسَّمَآءِ وَٱلطَّارِقِ ١

2. And what will make you to know what *At-Târiq* (night-comer) is?

وَمَآ أَدۡرَىٰكَ مَا ٱلطَّارِقُ ٢

3. (It is) the star of piercing brightness;

ٱلنَّجۡمُ ٱلثَّاقِبُ ٣

4. There is no human being but has a protector over him (or her) (i.e. angels in charge of each human being guarding him, writing his good and bad deeds).[1]

إِن كُلُّ نَفۡسٍ لَّمَّا عَلَيۡهَا حَافِظٌ ٤

---

[1] (V.86:4)

a) Whoever intended to do a good deed or a bad deed:.

5. So let man see from what he is created! فَلْيَنظُرِ ٱلإِنسَـٰنُ مِمَّ خُلِقَ ۞

6. He is created from a water gushing forth, خُلِقَ مِن مَّآءٍ دَافِقٍ ۞

7. Proceeding from between the backbone and the ribs. يَخْرُجُ مِنۢ بَيْنِ ٱلصُّلْبِ وَٱلتَّرَآئِبِ ۞

8. Verily, (Allâh) is Able to bring him back (to life)! إِنَّهُۥ عَلَىٰ رَجْعِهِۦ لَقَادِرٌ ۞

9. The Day when all the secrets (deeds, prayers, fasting) will be examined (as to their truth). يَوْمَ تُبْلَى ٱلسَّرَآئِرُ ۞

Narrated Ibn 'Abbâs رضي الله عنهما: The Prophet صلى الله عليه وسلم narrating about his Lord عزّ وجلّ said, "Allâh ordered (the appointed angels over you) that the good and the bad deeds be written, and He then showed (the way) how (to write). If somebody intends to do a good deed and he does not do it, then Allâh will write for him a full good deed (in his account with Him); and if he intends to do a good deed and actually does it, then Allâh will write for him (in his account) with Him (its reward equal) from ten to seven hundred times, to many more times; and if somebody intended to do a bad deed and he does not do it, then Allâh will write a full good deed (in his account) with Him, and if he intended to do it (a bad deed) and actually does it, then Allâh will write one bad deed (in his account)." (Sahih Al-Bukhari, Vol. 8, Hadith No. 498)

b) Narrated Abu Hurairah رضي الله عنه: The Prophet صلى الله عليه وسلم said: "Angels come (to you) in succession by night and day, and all of them get together (to you) at the time of, the Fajr and 'Asr prayers. Then those who have stayed with you overnight, ascend unto Allâh, Who asks them (and He knows the answer better than they): "How have you left My slaves?" They reply, "We left them while they were praying and we came to them while they were praying." The Prophet صلى الله عليه وسلم added: "If anyone of you says Amîn (during the prayer at the end of the recitation of Sûrat Al-Fâtihah), and the angels in heaven say the same, and the two sayings coincide, all his past sins will be forgiven." (Sahih Al-Bukhari, Vol. 4, Hadith No. 446).

10. Then he will have no power, nor any helper.

قَالَهُمِنْ قُوَّةٍ وَلَانَاصِرٍ ۝

11. By the sky (having rain clouds) which gives rain, again and again.

وَالسَّمَآءِ ذَاتِ الرَّجْعِ ۝

12. And the earth which splits (with the growth of trees and plants).

وَالْأَرْضِ ذَاتِ الصَّدْعِ ۝

13. Verily, this (the Qur'ân) is the Word that separates (the truth from falsehood, and commands strict laws for mankind to cut the roots of evil).

إِنَّهُۥ لَقَوْلٌ فَصْلٌ ۝

14. And it is not a thing for amusement.

وَمَاهُوَ بِالْهَزْلِ ۝

15. Verily, they are but plotting a plot (against you O Muhammad ﷺ).

إِنَّهُمْ يَكِيدُونَ كَيْدًا ۝

16. And I (too) am planning a plan.

وَأَكِيدُ كَيْدًا ۝

17. So give a respite to the disbelievers; deal gently with them for a while.

فَمَهِّلِ الْكَٰفِرِينَ أَمْهِلْهُمْ رُوَيْدًا ۝

Sûrat Al-A'lâ
(The Most High) LXXXVII

سُورَةُ الْأَعْلَىٰ

In the Name of Allâh
the Most Gracious, the Most Merciful

بِسْمِ اللَّهِ الرَّحْمَٰنِ الرَّحِيمِ

1. Glorify the Name of your Lord, the Most High,

سَبِّحِ اسْمَ رَبِّكَ الْأَعْلَى ۝

2. Who has created (everything), and then proportioned it.

الَّذِى خَلَقَ فَسَوَّىٰ ۝

3. And Who has measured (preordainments for everything even to be blessed or wretched); and then guided (i.e. showed mankind the right as well as the wrong paths, and guided the animals to pasture).

وَالَّذِى قَدَّرَ فَهَدَىٰ ۝

4. And Who brings out the pasturage,

وَٱلَّذِىٓ أَخْرَجَ ٱلْمَرْعَىٰ ﴿٤﴾

5. And then makes it dark stubble.

فَجَعَلَهُۥ غُثَآءً أَحْوَىٰ ﴿٥﴾

6. We shall make you to recite (the Qur'ân), so you (O Muhammad صلى الله عليه وسلم) shall not forget (it),

سَنُقْرِئُكَ فَلَا تَنسَىٰٓ ﴿٦﴾

7. Except what Allâh may will. He knows what is apparent and what is hidden.

إِلَّا مَا شَآءَ ٱللَّهُ إِنَّهُۥ يَعْلَمُ ٱلْجَهْرَ وَمَا يَخْفَىٰ ﴿٧﴾

8. And We shall make easy for you (O Muhammad صلى الله عليه وسلم) the easy way (i.e. the doing of righteous deeds).

وَنُيَسِّرُكَ لِلْيُسْرَىٰ ﴿٨﴾

9. Therefore remind (men) in case the reminder profits (them).

فَذَكِّرْ إِن نَّفَعَتِ ٱلذِّكْرَىٰ ﴿٩﴾

10. The reminder will be received by him who fears (Allâh),

سَيَذَّكَّرُ مَن يَخْشَىٰ ﴿١٠﴾

11. But it will be avoided by the wretched,

وَيَتَجَنَّبُهَا ٱلْأَشْقَى ﴿١١﴾

12. Who will enter the great Fire (and will be made to taste its burning).

ٱلَّذِى يَصْلَى ٱلنَّارَ ٱلْكُبْرَىٰ ﴿١٢﴾

13. There he will neither die (to be in rest) nor live (a good living).

ثُمَّ لَا يَمُوتُ فِيهَا وَلَا يَحْيَىٰ ﴿١٣﴾

14. Indeed whosoever purifies himself (by avoiding polytheism and accepting Islâmic Monotheism) shall achieve success,

قَدْ أَفْلَحَ مَن تَزَكَّىٰ ﴿١٤﴾

15. And remembers (glorifies) the Name of his Lord (worships none but Allâh), and prays (five compulsory prayers and *Nawâfil* — additional prayers).

وَذَكَرَ ٱسْمَ رَبِّهِۦ فَصَلَّىٰ ﴿١٥﴾

16. Nay, you prefer the life of this world,

بَلْ تُؤْثِرُونَ ٱلْحَيَوٰةَ ٱلدُّنْيَا ﴿١٦﴾

17. Although the Hereafter is better and more lasting.

وَٱلْءَاخِرَةُ خَيْرٌ وَأَبْقَىٰٓ ﴿١٧﴾

18. Verily, this is in the former Scriptures —

إِنَّ هَٰذَا لَفِى ٱلصُّحُفِ ٱلْأُولَىٰ ﴿١٨﴾

19. The Scriptures of Ibrâhîm (Abraham) and Mûsâ (Moses) (عليهما السلام).

صُحُفِ إِبْرَٰهِيمَ وَمُوسَىٰ ﴿١٩﴾

Sûrat Al-Ghâshiyah
(The Overwhelming) LXXXVIII

شورة الغاشية

In the Name of Allâh
the Most Gracious, the Most Merciful

بِسْمِ ٱللَّهِ ٱلرَّحْمَٰنِ ٱلرَّحِيمِ

1. Has there come to you the narration of the overwhelming (i.e. the Day of Resurrection)?

هَلْ أَتَىٰكَ حَدِيثُ ٱلْغَٰشِيَةِ ﴿١﴾

2. Some faces, that Day will be humiliated (in the Hell-fire, i.e. the faces of all disbelievers, Jews and Christians).[1]

وُجُوهٌ يَوْمَئِذٍ خَٰشِعَةٌ ﴿٢﴾

3. Labouring (hard in the worldly life by worshipping others besides Allâh), weary (in the Hereafter with humility and disgrace).[2]

عَامِلَةٌ نَّاصِبَةٌ ﴿٣﴾

---

[1] (V.88:2) It is obligatory to have belief in the Messengership of the Prophet (Muhammad صلى الله عليه وسلم). Narrated Abu Hurairah رضى الله عنه: Allâh's Messenger صلى الله عليه وسلم said: "By Him (Allâh) in Whose Hand Muhammad's soul is, there is none from amongst the Jews and Christians (of these present nations) who hears about me and then dies without believing in the Message with which I have been sent (i.e. Islâmic Monotheism), but he will be from the dwellers of the (Hell) Fire." (*Sahih Muslim*, the Book of Faith, Vol. 1, Chapter No. 240). See also the footnotes of (V.3:85) and (V.41:46).

[2] (V.88:3) Narrated 'Abdullâh رضى الله عنه: "The Prophet صلى الله عليه وسلم said one statement and I said another. The Prophet صلى الله عليه وسلم said: 'Whoever dies while still invoking anything other than Allâh as a rival to Allâh, will enter Hell (Fire).' And I said, 'Whoever dies without invoking anything as a rival to Allâh, will enter Paradise.'" (*Sahih Al-Bukhari*, Vol. 6, Hadith No. 24).

4. They will enter in the hot blazing Fire. تَصۡلَىٰ نَارًا حَامِيَةً ٤

5. They will be given to drink from a boiling spring. تُسۡقَىٰ مِنۡ عَيۡنٍ ءَانِيَةٍ ٥

6. No food there will be for them but a poisonous thorny plant, لَّيۡسَ لَهُمۡ طَعَامٌ إِلَّا مِن ضَرِيعٍ ٦

7. Which will neither nourish nor avail against hunger. لَّا يُسۡمِنُ وَلَا يُغۡنِى مِن جُوعٍ ٧

8. (Other) faces that Day will be joyful. وُجُوهٌ يَوۡمَئِذٍ نَّاعِمَةٌ ٨

9. Glad with their endeavour (for their good deeds which they did in this world, along with the true Faith of Islâmic Monotheism).[1] لِّسَعۡيِهَا رَاضِيَةٌ ٩

10. In a lofty Paradise. فِى جَنَّةٍ عَالِيَةٍ ١٠

11. Where they shall neither hear harmful speech nor falsehood. لَّا تَسۡمَعُ فِيهَا لَٰغِيَةً ١١

12. Therein will be a running spring. فِيهَا عَيۡنٌ جَارِيَةٌ ١٢

13. Therein will be thrones raised high. فِيهَا سُرُرٌ مَّرۡفُوعَةٌ ١٣

14. And cups set at hand. وَأَكۡوَابٌ مَّوۡضُوعَةٌ ١٤

15. And cushions set in rows. وَنَمَارِقُ مَصۡفُوفَةٌ ١٥

16. And rich carpets (all) spread out. وَزَرَابِىُّ مَبۡثُوثَةٌ ١٦

17. Do they not look at the camels, how they are created? أَفَلَا يَنظُرُونَ إِلَى ٱلۡإِبِلِ كَيۡفَ خُلِقَتۡ ١٧

18. And at the heaven, how it is raised? وَإِلَى ٱلسَّمَاءِ كَيۡفَ رُفِعَتۡ ١٨

19. And at the mountains, how they are rooted (and fixed firm)? وَإِلَى ٱلۡجِبَالِ كَيۡفَ نُصِبَتۡ ١٩

20. And at the earth, how it is outspread? وَإِلَى ٱلۡأَرۡضِ كَيۡفَ سُطِحَتۡ ٢٠

[1] (V.88:9) See footnote of (V.18:104).

21. So remind them (O Muhammad صلى الله عليه وسلم — you are only one who reminds.

فَذَكِّرْ إِنَّمَآ أَنتَ مُذَكِّرٌ ﴿٢١﴾

22. You are not a dictator over them —

لَّسْتَ عَلَيْهِم بِمُصَيْطِرٍ ﴿٢٢﴾

23. Save the one who turns away and disbelieves.[1]

إِلَّا مَن تَوَلَّىٰ وَكَفَرَ ﴿٢٣﴾

24. Then Allâh will punish him with the greatest punishment.

فَيُعَذِّبُهُ ٱللَّهُ ٱلْعَذَابَ ٱلْأَكْبَرَ ﴿٢٤﴾

25. Verily, to Us will be their return;

إِنَّ إِلَيْنَآ إِيَابَهُمْ ﴿٢٥﴾

26. Then verily, for Us will be their reckoning.

ثُمَّ إِنَّ عَلَيْنَا حِسَابَهُم ﴿٢٦﴾

Sûrat Al-Fajr (The Break of Day or the Dawn) LXXXIX

سُورَةُ الْفَجْرِ

In the Name of Allâh
the Most Gracious, the Most Merciful

بِسْمِ ٱللَّهِ ٱلرَّحْمَٰنِ ٱلرَّحِيمِ

1. By the dawn;

وَٱلْفَجْرِ ﴿١﴾

2. By the ten nights (i.e. the first ten days of the month of Dhul-Hijjah),[2]

وَلَيَالٍ عَشْرٍ ﴿٢﴾

3. And by the even and the odd (of all the creations of Allâh).[3]

وَٱلشَّفْعِ وَٱلْوَتْرِ ﴿٣﴾

---

[1] (V.88:23) See footnote of (V.8:39).

[2] (V.89:2) Narrated Ibn 'Abbâs رضي الله عنهما : The Prophet صلى الله عليه وسلم said, "No good deeds done on other days are superior to those done on these (first ten days of Dhul-Hijjah)." Then some Companions of the Prophet صلى الله عليه وسلم said, "Not even *Jihâd*?" He replied, "Not even *Jihâd*, except that of a man who does it by putting himself and his property in danger (for Allâh's sake) and does not return with any of those things." (*Sahih Al-Bukhari*, Vol. 2, Hadith No.86).

[3] (V.89:3) "Even" and "Odd" is interpreted differently by different religious scholars. Some say: Even is the Day of Slaughtering of the Sacrifices, i.e. 10th of Dhul-Hijjah, and Odd is the Day of 'Arafah (*Hajj*), i.e. 9th of Dhul-Hijjah. Others say: Even is all the creatures

4. And by the night when it departs.

وَالَّيْلِ إِذَا يَسْرِ ﴿٤﴾

5. There is indeed in them (the above oaths) sufficient proofs for men of understanding (and that, they should avoid all kinds of sins and disbeliefs)!

هَلْ فِى ذَلِكَ قَسَمٌ لِّذِى حِجْرٍ ﴿٥﴾

6. Saw you (O Muhammad صلى الله عليه وسلم) not how your Lord dealt with 'Ad (people)

أَلَمْ تَرَ كَيْفَ فَعَلَ رَبُّكَ بِعَادٍ ﴿٦﴾

7. Of Iram (who were very tall) like (lofty) pillars,

إِرَمَ ذَاتِ الْعِمَادِ ﴿٧﴾

8. The like of which were not created in the land?

الَّتِى لَمْ يُخْلَقْ مِثْلُهَا فِى الْبِلَدِ ﴿٨﴾

9. And (with) Thamûd (people), who hewed out rocks in the valley (to make dwellings)?[1]

وَثَمُودَ الَّذِينَ جَابُوا الصَّخْرَ بِالْوَادِ ﴿٩﴾

10. And (with) Fir'aun (Pharaoh) who had the stakes (to torture men by binding them to the stakes)?

وَفِرْعَوْنَ ذِى الْأَوْتَادِ ﴿١٠﴾

11. Who did transgress beyond bounds in the lands (in the disobedience of Allâh),

الَّذِينَ طَغَوْا فِى الْبِلَدِ ﴿١١﴾

12. And made therein much mischief.

فَأَكْثَرُوا فِيهَا الْفَسَادَ ﴿١٢﴾

13. So your Lord poured on them different kinds of severe torment.

فَصَبَّ عَلَيْهِمْ رَبُّكَ سَوْطَ عَذَابٍ ﴿١٣﴾

14. Verily, your Lord is Ever Watchful (over them).

إِنَّ رَبَّكَ لَبِالْمِرْصَادِ ﴿١٤﴾

15. As for man, when his Lord tries him by giving him honour and bounties,

فَأَمَّا الْإِنْسَنُ إِذَا مَا ابْتَلَيهُ رَبُّهُ فَأَكْرَمَهُ وَنَعَّمَهُ فَيَقُولُ رَبِّ ﴿١٥﴾

---

and Odd is Allâh. Some say it is the compulsory congregational prayer, i.e. *Maghrib* is *Witr*, and the other four prayers are *Shaf'*.

[1] (V.89:9) "And you hew out in the mountains, houses with great skill." [The Qur'ân, Verse 26:149]

then he says (in exultation): "My Lord has honoured me."   أَكْرَمَنِ ۝

16. But when He tries him by straitening his means of life, he says: "My Lord has humiliated me!"   وَأَمَّا إِذَا مَا ابْتَلَاهُ فَقَدَرَ عَلَيْهِ رِزْقَهُ فَيَقُولُ رَبِّي أَهَانَنِ ۝

17. Nay! But you treat not the orphans with kindness and generosity (i.e. you neither treat them well, nor give them their exact right of inheritance)!   كَلَّا بَل لَّا تُكْرِمُونَ الْيَتِيمَ ۝

18. And urge not one another on the feeding of *Al-Miskîn* (the poor)!   وَلَا تَحَاضُّونَ عَلَىٰ طَعَامِ الْمِسْكِينِ ۝

19. And you devour the inheritance all with greed.   وَتَأْكُلُونَ التُّرَاثَ ۝

20. And you love wealth with much love.   وَتُحِبُّونَ الْمَالَ حُبًّا جَمًّا ۝

21. Nay! When the earth is ground to powder.   كَلَّا إِذَا دُكَّتِ الْأَرْضُ ۝

22. And your Lord comes with the angels in rows.   وَجَاءَ رَبُّكَ وَالْمَلَكُ صَفًّا صَفًّا ۝

23. And Hell will be brought near that Day. On that Day will man remember, but how will that remembrance (then) avail him?   وَجِيءَ يَوْمَئِذٍ بِجَهَنَّمَ يَوْمَئِذٍ يَتَذَكَّرُ الْإِنسَانُ ۝

24. He will say: "Alas! Would that I had sent forth (good deeds) for (this) my life!"   يَقُولُ يَا لَيْتَنِي قَدَّمْتُ لِحَيَاتِي ۝

25. So, on that Day none will punish as He will punish.   فَيَوْمَئِذٍ لَّا يُعَذِّبُ عَذَابَهُ أَحَدٌ ۝

26. And none will bind (the wicked, disbelievers and polytheists) as He will bind.   وَلَا يُوثِقُ وَثَاقَهُ أَحَدٌ ۝

27. (It will be said to the pious believers of Islamic Monotheism): "O (you) the one in (complete) rest and satisfaction! يَٰٓأَيَّتُهَا ٱلنَّفْسُ ٱلْمُطْمَئِنَّةُ ٢٧

28. "Come back to your Lord — well-pleased (yourself) and well-pleasing (unto Him)! ٱرْجِعِىٓ إِلَىٰ رَبِّكِ رَاضِيَةً مَّرْضِيَّةً ٢٨

29. "Enter you then among My (honoured) slaves, فَٱدْخُلِى فِى عِبَٰدِى ٢٩

30. "And enter you My Paradise!" وَٱدْخُلِى جَنَّتِى ٣٠

Sûrat Al-Balad
(The City) XC

سُورَةُ البَلَد

*In the Name of Allâh
the Most Gracious, the Most Merciful*

بِسْمِ ٱللَّهِ ٱلرَّحْمَٰنِ ٱلرَّحِيمِ

1. I swear by this city (Makkah); لَآ أُقْسِمُ بِهَٰذَا ٱلْبَلَدِ ١

2. And you are free (from sin, and to punish the enemies of Islâm on the Day of the conquest) in this city (Makkah).[1] وَأَنتَ حِلٌّ بِهَٰذَا ٱلْبَلَدِ ٢

3. And by the begetter (i.e. Adam عليه السلام) and that which he begot (i.e. his progeny), وَوَالِدٍ وَمَا وَلَدَ ٣

4. Verily, We have created man in toil. لَقَدْ خَلَقْنَا ٱلْإِنسَٰنَ فِى كَبَدٍ ٤

5. Does he think that none can overcome him? أَيَحْسَبُ أَن لَّن يَقْدِرَ عَلَيْهِ أَحَدٌ ٥

---

[1] (V.90:2)

a) Narrated Ibn 'Abbâs رضي الله عنهما : On the day of the conquest of Makkah, Allâh's Messenger صلى الله عليه وسلم said, "Allâh has made this town a sanctuary. Its thorny bushes should not be cut, its game should not be chased, and its fallen things should not be picked up except by one who would announce it publicly." (Sahih Al-Bukhari, Vol. 2, Hadith No. 657)

b) See the footnote of (V.2:191)

6. He says (boastfully): "I have wasted wealth in abundance!"

يَقُولُ أَهْلَكْتُ مَالًا لُّبَدًا ۝

7. Does he think that none sees him?

أَيَحْسَبُ أَن لَّمْ يَرَهُۥٓ أَحَدٌ ۝

8. Have We not made for him a pair of eyes,

أَلَمْ نَجْعَل لَّهُۥ عَيْنَيْنِ ۝

9. And a tongue and a pair of lips?

وَلِسَانًا وَشَفَتَيْنِ ۝

10. And shown him the two ways (good and evil)?

وَهَدَيْنَـٰهُ النَّجْدَيْنِ ۝

11. But he has not attempted to pass on the path that is steep (i.e. the path which will lead to goodness and success).

فَلَا ٱقْتَحَمَ ٱلْعَقَبَةَ ۝

12. And what will make you know the path that is steep?

وَمَآ أَدْرَىٰكَ مَا ٱلْعَقَبَةُ ۝

13. (It is) freeing a neck (slave)[1]

فَكُّ رَقَبَةٍ ۝

14. Or giving food in a day of hunger (famine),

أَوْ إِطْعَٰمٌ فِى يَوْمٍ ذِى مَسْغَبَةٍ ۝

15. To an orphan near of kin.

يَتِيمًا ذَا مَقْرَبَةٍ ۝

16. Or to a *Miskîn* (poor) cleaving to dust (out of misery).

أَوْ مِسْكِينًا ذَا مَتْرَبَةٍ ۝

17. Then he became one of those who believed (in the Islamic Monotheism) and recommended one another to perseverance and patience, and (also) recommended one another to pity and compassion.

ثُمَّ كَانَ مِنَ ٱلَّذِينَ ءَامَنُوا۟ وَتَوَاصَوْا۟ بِٱلصَّبْرِ وَتَوَاصَوْا۟ بِٱلْمَرْحَمَةِ ۝

18. They are those on the Right Hand (i.e. the dwellers of Paradise),

أُو۟لَـٰٓئِكَ أَصْحَـٰبُ ٱلْمَيْمَنَةِ ۝

19. But those who disbelieved in Our *Ayât* (proofs, evidences, verses, lessons,

وَٱلَّذِينَ كَفَرُوا۟ بِـَٔايَـٰتِنَا هُمْ أَصْحَـٰبُ ٱلْمَشْـَٔمَةِ ۝

---

[1] (V.90:13) Narrated Abu Hurairah رضى الله عنه: The Prophet صلى الله عليه وسلم said: "Whoever frees a Muslim slave, Allâh will save all the parts of his body from the (Hell) Fire, as he has freed the body-parts of the slave." (*Sahih Al-Bukhari*, Vol.3, *Hadith* No.693)

signs, revelations, etc.), they are those on the Left Hand (the dwellers of Hell).

20. The Fire will be shut over them (i.e. they will be enveloped by the Fire without any opening or window or outlet.[1]

عَلَيْهِم نَارٌ مُّؤْصَدَةٌ ۝

Sûrat Ash-Shams
(The Sun) XCI

سُورَةُ الشَّمْسِ

*In the Name of Allâh
the Most Gracious, the Most Merciful*

بِسْمِ اللَّهِ الرَّحْمَنِ الرَّحِيمِ

1. By the sun and its brightness.

وَالشَّمْسِ وَضُحَىٰهَا ۝

2. By the moon as it follows it (the sun).

وَالْقَمَرِ إِذَا تَلَىٰهَا ۝

3. By the day as it shows up (the sun's) brightness.

وَالنَّهَارِ إِذَا جَلَّىٰهَا ۝

4. By the night as it conceals it (the sun).

وَاللَّيْلِ إِذَا يَغْشَىٰهَا ۝

5. By the heaven and Him Who built it.

وَالسَّمَاءِ وَمَا بَنَىٰهَا ۝

6. By the earth and Him Who spread it.

وَالْأَرْضِ وَمَا طَحَىٰهَا ۝

7. By *Nafs* (Adam or a person or a soul), and Him Who perfected him in proportion;

وَنَفْسٍ وَمَا سَوَّىٰهَا ۝

---

[1] (V.90:20) "Therein breathing out with deep sighs and roaring will be their portion, and therein they will hear not.**" [The Qur'ân, Verse 21:100]

**Ibn Mas'ûd رضي الله عنه recited this Verse and then said: "When those (who are destined to remain in the Hell-fire forever) will be thrown in the Hell-fire, each of them will be put in a separate *Tabût* (Box) of Fire, so that he will not see anyone punished in the Hell-fire except he himself." Then Ibn Mas'ûd recited this Verse (V.21:100). [*Tafsîr Ibn Kathir*, *Tabarî* and *Qurtubî*].

8. Then He showed him what is wrong for him and what is right for him.

فَأَلْهَمَهَا فُجُورَهَا وَتَقْوَاهَا ۝

9. Indeed he succeeds who purifies his ownself (i.e. obeys and performs all that Allâh ordered, by following the true Faith of Islâmic Monotheism and by doing righteous good deeds).

قَدْ أَفْلَحَ مَن زَكَّاهَا ۝

10. And indeed he fails who corrupts his ownself (i.e. disobeys what Allah has ordered by rejecting the true Faith of Islâmic Monotheism or by following polytheism, or by doing every kind of evil wicked deeds).

وَقَدْ خَابَ مَن دَسَّاهَا ۝

11. Thamûd (people) denied (their Prophet) through their transgression (by rejecting the true Faith of Islâmic Monotheism, and by following polytheism, and by committing every kind of sin).

كَذَّبَتْ ثَمُودُ بِطَغْوَاهَا ۝

12. When the most wicked man among them went forth (to kill the she-camel).

إِذِ انبَعَثَ أَشْقَاهَا ۝

13. But the Messenger of Allâh [Sâlih (عليه السلام)] said to them: "Be cautious! (Fear the evil end). That is the she-camel of Allâh! (Do not harm it) and bar it not from having its drink!"

فَقَالَ لَهُمْ رَسُولُ اللَّهِ نَاقَةَ اللَّهِ وَسُقْيَاهَا ۝

14. Then they denied him and they killed it. So their Lord destroyed them because of their sin, and made them equal in destruction (i.e. all grades of people, rich and poor, strong and weak)!

فَكَذَّبُوهُ فَعَقَرُوهَا فَدَمْدَمَ عَلَيْهِمْ رَبُّهُم بِذَنبِهِمْ فَسَوَّاهَا ۝

15. And He (Allâh) feared not the consequences thereof.

وَلَا يَخَافُ عُقْبَاهَا ۝

Sûrat Al-Lail
(The Night) XCII

سُورَةُ الَّيْلِ

In the Name of Allâh
the Most Gracious, the Most Merciful

بِسْمِ اللّٰهِ الرَّحْمٰنِ الرَّحِيْمِ

1. By the night as it envelops.

وَالَّيْلِ إِذَا يَغْشَىٰ ١

2. By the day as it appears in brightness.

وَالنَّهَارِ إِذَا تَجَلَّىٰ ٢

3. By Him Who created male and female.

وَمَا خَلَقَ الذَّكَرَ وَالْأُنْثَىٰ ٣

4. Certainly, your efforts and deeds are diverse (different in aims and purposes);

إِنَّ سَعْيَكُمْ لَشَتَّىٰ ٤

5. As for him who gives (in charity) and keeps his duty to Allâh and fears Him,

فَأَمَّا مَنْ أَعْطَىٰ وَاتَّقَىٰ ٥

6. And believes Al-Husnâ.[1]

وَصَدَّقَ بِالْحُسْنَىٰ ٦

7. We will make smooth for him the path of ease (goodness).

فَسَنُيَسِّرُهُ لِلْيُسْرَىٰ ٧

8. But he who is greedy miser and thinks himself self-sufficient.[2]

وَأَمَّا مَنْ بَخِلَ وَاسْتَغْنَىٰ ٨

---

[1] (V.92:6)

(A) *Al-Husnâ*: The Best (i.e. either *Lâ ilâha illallâh*: none has the right to be worshipped but Allâh) or a reward from Allâh (i.e. Allâh will compensate him for what he will spend in Allâh's Way or bless him with Paradise).

(B) See the footnote of (V.4:37).

[2] (V.92:8) Narrated 'Alî رضي الله عنه: We were in the company of the Prophet صلى الله عليه وسلم and he said, "There is none among you but has his place written for him, either in Paradise or in the Hell-fire." We said, "O Allâh's Messenger! Shall we depend (on this fact and give up work)?" He replied, "No! Carry on doing good deeds, for everybody will find easy (to do) such deeds as will lead him to his destined place." Then the Prophet صلى الله عليه وسلم recited: "As for him who gives (in charity) and keeps his duty to Allâh and fears Him, and believes in *Al-Husnâ*. We will make smooth for him the path of ease ..." (V.92: 5-10) (*Sahih Al-Bukhari*, Vol.6, *Hadith* No.472).

9. And belies *Al-Husnâ* (See the footnote of the Verse No: 6).

وَكَذَّبَ بِٱلْحُسْنَىٰ ٩

10. We will make smooth for him the path for evil.

فَسَنُيَسِّرُهُۥ لِلْعُسْرَىٰ ١٠

11. And what will his wealth avail him when he goes down (in destruction)?

وَمَا يُغْنِى عَنْهُ مَالُهُۥٓ إِذَا تَرَدَّىٰٓ ١١

12. Truly, on Us is (to give) guidance.

إِنَّ عَلَيْنَا لَلْهُدَىٰ ١٢

13. And truly, unto Us (belong) the last (Hereafter) and the first (this world).

وَإِنَّ لَنَا لَلْأٓخِرَةَ وَٱلْأُولَىٰ ١٣

14. Therefore I have warned you of a blazing Fire (Hell).

فَأَنذَرْتُكُمْ نَارًا تَلَظَّىٰ ١٤

15. None shall enter it save the most wretched.

لَا يَصْلَىٰهَآ إِلَّا ٱلْأَشْقَى ١٥

16. Who denies and turns away.

ٱلَّذِى كَذَّبَ وَتَوَلَّىٰ ١٦

17. And *Al-Muttaqûn* (the pious. See V.2:2) will be far removed from it (Hell).

وَسَيُجَنَّبُهَا ٱلْأَتْقَى ١٧

18. He who spends his wealth for increase in self-purification,

ٱلَّذِى يُؤْتِى مَالَهُۥ يَتَزَكَّىٰ ١٨

19. And who has (in mind) no favour from anyone to be paid back,

وَمَا لِأَحَدٍ عِندَهُۥ مِن نِّعْمَةٍ تُجْزَىٰٓ ١٩

20. Except to seek the Countenance of his Lord, the Most High.

إِلَّا ٱبْتِغَآءَ وَجْهِ رَبِّهِ ٱلْأَعْلَىٰ ٢٠

21. He surely, will be pleased (when he will enter Paradise).

وَلَسَوْفَ يَرْضَىٰ ٢١

Sûrat Ad-Duha (The Forenoon —
After Sunrise) XCIII

سُورَةُ الضُّحَىٰ

In the Name of Allâh
the Most Gracious, the Most Merciful

بِسْمِ اللَّهِ الرَّحْمَٰنِ الرَّحِيمِ

1. By the forenoon (after sunrise).[1]

وَالضُّحَىٰ ١

2. By the night when it darkens (and stand still).

وَالَّيْلِ إِذَا سَجَىٰ ٢

3. Your Lord (O Muhammad صلى الله عليه وسلم) has neither forsaken you nor hates you.

مَا وَدَّعَكَ رَبُّكَ وَمَا قَلَىٰ ٣

4. And indeed the Hereafter is better for you than the present (life of this world).

وَلَلْآخِرَةُ خَيْرٌ لَّكَ مِنَ الْأُولَىٰ ٤

5. And verily, your Lord will give you (all good) so that you shall be well-pleased.

وَلَسَوْفَ يُعْطِيكَ رَبُّكَ فَتَرْضَىٰ ٥

6. Did He not find you (O Muhammad صلى الله عليه وسلم) an orphan and gave you a refuge?

أَلَمْ يَجِدْكَ يَتِيمًا فَآوَىٰ ٦

---

[1] (V.93:1)

a) Narrated Ibn Abî Lailâ: Only Umm Hanî told us that she had seen the Prophet صلى الله عليه وسلم offering the *Duha* (Forenoon prayer). She said. "On the day of the conquest of Makkah, the Prophet صلى الله عليه وسلم took a bath in my house and offered eight *Raka'at*. I never saw him praying such a light prayer but he performed perfect prostrations and bowings". (*Sahih Al-Bukhari*, Vol.2, *Hadith* No.207A).

b) Narrated Abu Hurairah رضي الله عنه: My friend (the Prophet) advised me to observe three things:

(1) to fast three days a month;

(2) to pray two *Raka'at* of *Duha* prayer (Forenoon prayer); and

(3) to pray *Witr* before sleeping.

(*Sahih Al-Bukhari*, Vol.3, *Hadith* No.202).

7. And He found you unaware (of the Qur'ân, its legal laws and Prophethood) and guided you?

وَوَجَدَكَ ضَالًّا فَهَدَىٰ ۞

8. And He found you poor and made you rich (self-sufficient with self-contentment)?

وَوَجَدَكَ عَآئِلًا فَأَغْنَىٰ ۞

9. Therefore, treat not the orphan with oppression.

فَأَمَّا ٱلْيَتِيمَ فَلَا تَقْهَرْ ۞

10. And repulse not the beggar.

وَأَمَّا ٱلسَّآئِلَ فَلَا تَنْهَرْ ۞

11. And proclaim the Grace of your Lord (i.e. the Prophethood and all other Graces).

وَأَمَّا بِنِعْمَةِ رَبِّكَ فَحَدِّثْ ۞

Sûrat Ash-Sharh
(The Opening Forth) XCIV

سورة الشرح

In the Name of Allâh
the Most Gracious, the Most Merciful

بِسْمِ ٱللَّهِ ٱلرَّحْمَٰنِ ٱلرَّحِيمِ

1. Have We not opened your breast for you (O Muhammad صلى الله عليه وسلم)?

أَلَمْ نَشْرَحْ لَكَ صَدْرَكَ ۞

2. And removed from you your burden.

وَوَضَعْنَا عَنكَ وِزْرَكَ ۞

3. Which weighed down your back?

ٱلَّذِىٓ أَنقَضَ ظَهْرَكَ ۞

4. And have We not raised high your fame?

وَرَفَعْنَا لَكَ ذِكْرَكَ ۞

5. Verily, along with every hardship is relief,

فَإِنَّ مَعَ ٱلْعُسْرِ يُسْرًا ۞

6. Verily, along with every hardship is relief (i.e. there is one hardship with two reliefs, so one hardship cannot overcome two reliefs).

إِنَّ مَعَ ٱلْعُسْرِ يُسْرًا ۞

7. So when you have finished (your occupation), devote yourself for Allâh's worship.

فَإِذَا فَرَغْتَ فَٱنصَبْ ۞

8. And to your Lord (Alone) turn (all your) intentions and hopes.

وَإِلَىٰ رَبِّكَ فَٱرْغَب ۝

Sûrat At-Tin
(The Fig) XCV

سُورَةُ التِّينِ

In the Name of Allâh
the Most Gracious, the Most Merciful

بِسْمِ ٱللَّهِ ٱلرَّحْمَٰنِ ٱلرَّحِيمِ

1. By the fig, and the olive.

وَٱلتِّينِ وَٱلزَّيْتُونِ ۝

2. By Mount Sinai.

وَطُورِ سِينِينَ ۝

3. By this city of security (Makkah).[1]

وَهَٰذَا ٱلْبَلَدِ ٱلْأَمِينِ ۝

4. Verily, We created man in the best stature (mould).

لَقَدْ خَلَقْنَا ٱلْإِنسَٰنَ فِىٓ أَحْسَنِ تَقْوِيمٍ ۝

5. Then We reduced him to the lowest of the low.

ثُمَّ رَدَدْنَٰهُ أَسْفَلَ سَٰفِلِينَ ۝

6. Save those who believe (in Islâmic Monotheism) and do righteous deeds. Then they shall have a reward without end (Paradise).

إِلَّا ٱلَّذِينَ ءَامَنُوا۟ وَعَمِلُوا۟ ٱلصَّٰلِحَٰتِ فَلَهُمْ أَجْرٌ غَيْرُ مَمْنُونٍ ۝

7. Then what (or who) causes you (O disbelievers) to deny the Recompense (i.e. the Day of Resurrection)?

فَمَا يُكَذِّبُكَ بَعْدُ بِٱلدِّينِ ۝

8. Is not Allâh the Best of judges?

أَلَيْسَ ٱللَّهُ بِأَحْكَمِ ٱلْحَٰكِمِينَ ۝

Sûrat Al-'Alaq
(The Clot) XCVI

سُورَةُ الْعَلَقِ

In the Name of Allâh
the Most Gracious, the Most Merciful

بِسْمِ ٱللَّهِ ٱلرَّحْمَٰنِ ٱلرَّحِيمِ

1. Read! In the Name of your Lord Who has created (all that exists).

ٱقْرَأْ بِٱسْمِ رَبِّكَ ٱلَّذِى خَلَقَ ۝

2. He has created man from a clot (a piece of thick coagulated blood).

خَلَقَ ٱلْإِنسَٰنَ مِنْ عَلَقٍ ۝

---

[1] (V.95:3) See footnote of (V.2:191).

3. Read! And your Lord is the Most Generous.

اقْرَأْ وَرَبُّكَ الْأَكْرَمُ ۞

4. Who has taught (the writing) by the pen.

الَّذِي عَلَّمَ بِالْقَلَمِ ۞

5. He has taught man that which he knew not.

عَلَّمَ الْإِنسَانَ مَا لَمْ يَعْلَمْ ۞

6. Nay! Verily, man does transgress (in disbelief and evil deed).

كَلَّا إِنَّ الْإِنسَانَ لَيَطْغَىٰ ۞

7. Because he considers himself self-sufficient.

أَن رَّءَاهُ اسْتَغْنَىٰ ۞

8. Surely, unto your Lord is the return.

إِنَّ إِلَىٰ رَبِّكَ الرُّجْعَىٰ ۞

9. Have you (O Muhammad صلى الله عليه وسلم) seen him (i.e. Abû Jahl) who prevents

أَرَءَيْتَ الَّذِي يَنْهَىٰ ۞

10. A slave (Muhammad صلى الله عليه وسلم) when he prays?

عَبْدًا إِذَا صَلَّىٰ ۞

11. Tell me if he (Muhammad صلى الله عليه وسلم) is on the guidance (of Allâh)

أَرَءَيْتَ إِن كَانَ عَلَى الْهُدَىٰ ۞

12. Or enjoins piety?

أَوْ أَمَرَ بِالتَّقْوَىٰ ۞

13. Tell me if he (Abû Jahl) denies (the truth, i.e. this Qur'ân) and turns away?

أَرَءَيْتَ إِن كَذَّبَ وَتَوَلَّىٰ ۞

14. Knows he not that Allâh does see (what he does)?

أَلَمْ يَعْلَم بِأَنَّ اللَّهَ يَرَىٰ ۞

15. Nay! If he (Abû Jahl) ceases not, We will catch him by the forelock —

كَلَّا لَئِن لَّمْ يَنتَهِ لَنَسْفَعًا بِالنَّاصِيَةِ ۞

16. A lying, sinful forelock!

نَاصِيَةٍ كَاذِبَةٍ خَاطِئَةٍ ۞

17. Then let him call upon his council (of helpers).

فَلْيَدْعُ نَادِيَهُ ۞

18. We will call out the guards of Hell (to deal with him)!

سَنَدْعُ الزَّبَانِيَةَ ۞

19. Nay! (O Muhammad صلى الله عليه وسلم! Do not obey him (Abû Jahl). Fall prostrate and draw near to Allâh!

Sûrat Al-Qadr
(The Night of Decree) XCVII

In the Name of Allâh
the Most Gracious, the Most Merciful

1. Verily, We have sent it (this Qur'ân) down in the night of *Al-Qadr* (Decree).[1]

2. And what will make you know what the night of *Al-Qadr* (Decree) is?

3. The night of *Al-Qadr* (Decree) is better than a thousand months (i.e. worshipping Allâh in that night is better than worshipping Him a thousand months, i.e. 83 years and 4 months).

4. Therein descend the angels and the *Rûh* [Jibrael (Gabriel)] by Allâh's Permission with all Decrees,

5. (All that night), there is Peace (and Goodness from Allâh to His believing slaves) until the appearance of dawn.[2]

---

[1] (V.97:1)"Therein (that night) is decreed every matter of ordainments." [The Qur'ân, Verse 44:4)]**

** i.e., the matters of deaths, births, provisions, calamities, etc. for the whole (coming) year as decreed by Allâh.

[2] (V.97:5) Narrated 'Âishah رضي الله عنها Allâh's Messenger صلى الله عليه وسلم said, "Search for the Night of *Qadr* in the odd nights of the last ten nights of Ramadân." (*Sahih Al-Bukhari*, Vol 3, Hadith No.234).

Sûrat Al-Bayyinah
(The Clear Evidence) XCVIII

سُورَةُ الْبَيِّنَة

*In the Name of Allâh
the Most Gracious, the Most Merciful*

بِسْمِ اللَّهِ الرَّحْمَنِ الرَّحِيمِ

1. Those who disbelieve from among the people of the Scripture (Jews and Christians) and *Al-Mushrikûn*,[1] were not going to leave (their disbelief) until there came to them clear evidence.

لَمْ يَكُنِ الَّذِينَ كَفَرُوا مِنْ أَهْلِ الْكِتَبِ وَالْمُشْرِكِينَ مُنفَكِّينَ حَتَّى تَأْتِيَهُمُ الْبَيِّنَةُ ﴿١﴾

2. A Messenger (Muhammad صلى الله عليه وسلم) from Allâh, reciting (the Qur'ân) purified pages [purified from *Al-Bâtil* (falsehood)].

رَسُولٌ مِّنَ اللَّهِ يَتْلُوا صُحُفًا مُّطَهَّرَةً ﴿٢﴾

3. Wherein are correct and straight laws from Allâh.

فِيهَا كُتُبٌ قَيِّمَةٌ ﴿٣﴾

4. And the people of the Scripture (Jews and Christians) differed not until after there came to them clear evidence. (i.e. Prophet Muhammad صلى الله عليه وسلم and whatever was revealed to him).

وَمَا تَفَرَّقَ الَّذِينَ أُوتُوا الْكِتَبَ إِلَّا مِنْ بَعْدِ مَا جَاءَتْهُمُ الْبَيِّنَةُ ﴿٤﴾

5. And they were commanded not, but that they should worship Allâh, and worship none but Him Alone (abstaining from ascribing partners to Him), and perform *As-Salât (Iqâmat-as-Salât)* and give *Zakât*, and that is the right religion.

وَمَا أُمِرُوا إِلَّا لِيَعْبُدُوا اللَّهَ مُخْلِصِينَ لَهُ الدِّينَ حُنَفَاءَ وَيُقِيمُوا الصَّلَوٰةَ وَيُؤْتُوا الزَّكَوٰةَ وَذَلِكَ دِينُ الْقَيِّمَةِ ﴿٥﴾

6. Verily, those who disbelieve (in the religion of Islâm, the Qur'ân and Prophet Muhammad صلى الله عليه وسلم) from

إِنَّ الَّذِينَ كَفَرُوا مِنْ أَهْلِ الْكِتَبِ وَالْمُشْرِكِينَ فِي نَارِ جَهَنَّمَ خَالِدِينَ

---

[1] (V.98:1,6) *Al-Mushrikûn:* polytheists, pagans, idolaters and disbelievers in the Oneness of Allâh and His Messenger Muhammad صلى الله عليه وسلم.

among the people of the Scripture (Jews and Christians) and *Al-Mushrikûn* will abide in the Fire of Hell. They are the worst of creatures.[1]

فِيهَا أُوْلَٰٓئِكَ هُمْ شَرُّ ٱلْبَرِيَّةِ

7. Verily, those who believe [in the Oneness of Allâh, and in His Messenger (Muhammad صلى الله عليه وسلم) including all obligations ordered by Islâm] and do righteous good deeds, they are the best of creatures.

إِنَّ ٱلَّذِينَ ءَامَنُواْ وَعَمِلُواْ ٱلصَّٰلِحَٰتِ أُوْلَٰٓئِكَ هُمْ خَيْرُ ٱلْبَرِيَّةِ

8. Their reward with their Lord is *'Adn* (Eden) Paradise (Gardens of Eternity), underneath which rivers flow. They will abide therein forever, Allâh will be pleased with them, and they with Him. That is for him who fears his Lord.

جَزَآؤُهُمْ عِندَ رَبِّهِمْ جَنَّٰتُ عَدْنٍ تَجْرِى مِن تَحْتِهَا ٱلْأَنْهَٰرُ خَٰلِدِينَ فِيهَآ أَبَدًا رَّضِىَ ٱللَّهُ عَنْهُمْ وَرَضُواْ عَنْهُ ذَٰلِكَ لِمَنْ خَشِىَ رَبَّهُۥ

Sûrat Az-Zalzalah
(The Earthquake) XCIX

سورة الزلزلة

*In the Name of Allâh
the Most Gracious, the Most Merciful*

بِسْمِ ٱللَّهِ ٱلرَّحْمَٰنِ ٱلرَّحِيمِ

1. When the earth is shaken with its (final) earthquake.

إِذَا زُلْزِلَتِ ٱلْأَرْضُ زِلْزَالَهَا

2. And when the earth throws out its burdens.

وَأَخْرَجَتِ ٱلْأَرْضُ أَثْقَالَهَا

---

[1] (V.98:6) It is obligatory to have belief in the Messengership of the Prophet (Muhammad صلى الله عليه وسلم). Narrated Abu Hurairah رضي الله عنه: Allâh's Messenger صلى الله عليه وسلم said: "By Him (Allâh) in Whose Hand Muhammad's soul is, there is none from amongst the Jews and Christians (of these present nations) who hears about me and then dies without believing in the Message with which I have been sent (i.e. Islâmic Monotheism) but he will be from the dwellers of the (Hell) Fire." (*Sahih Muslim*, the Book of Faith, Vol. 1, Chapter No.240). See also (V.3:85) and (V.3:116).

3. And man will say: "What is the matter with it?"

وَقَالَ ٱلْإِنسَـٰنُ مَا لَهَا ۝

4. That Day it will declare its information (about all that happened over it of good or evil).

يَوْمَئِذٍ تُحَدِّثُ أَخْبَارَهَا ۝

5. Because your Lord will inspire it.

بِأَنَّ رَبَّكَ أَوْحَىٰ لَهَا ۝

6. That Day mankind will proceed in scattered groups that they may be shown their deeds.[1]

يَوْمَئِذٍ يَصْدُرُ ٱلنَّاسُ أَشْتَاتًا لِّيُرَوْا أَعْمَـٰلَهُمْ ۝

7. So whosoever does good equal to the weight of an atom (or a small ant) shall see it.

فَمَن يَعْمَلْ مِثْقَالَ ذَرَّةٍ خَيْرًا يَرَهُۥ ۝

8. And whosoever does evil equal to the weight of an atom (or a small ant) shall see it.

وَمَن يَعْمَلْ مِثْقَالَ ذَرَّةٍ شَرًّا يَرَهُۥ ۝

Sûrat Al-'Âdiyât
(Those That Run) C

سُورَةُ العَادِيَاتِ

In the Name of Allâh the Most Gracious, the Most Merciful.

بِسْمِ ٱللَّهِ ٱلرَّحْمَـٰنِ ٱلرَّحِيمِ

1. By the (steeds) that run, with panting.

وَٱلْعَـٰدِيَـٰتِ ضَبْحًا ۝

2. Striking sparks of fire (by their hooves).

فَٱلْمُورِيَـٰتِ قَدْحًا ۝

3. And scouring to the raid at dawn.

فَٱلْمُغِيرَٰتِ صُبْحًا ۝

4. And raise the dust in clouds the while.

فَأَثَرْنَ بِهِۦ نَقْعًا ۝

5. And penetrating forthwith as one into the midst (of the foe).

فَوَسَطْنَ بِهِۦ جَمْعًا ۝

6. Verily,. man (disbeliever) is ungrateful to his Lord.

إِنَّ ٱلْإِنسَـٰنَ لِرَبِّهِۦ لَكَنُودٌ ۝

---

[1] (V.99:6) See footnote of (V.11:18).

7. And to that he bears witness (by his deeds).

وَإِنَّهُۥ عَلَىٰ ذَٰلِكَ لَشَهِيدٌ ۞

8. And verily, he is violent in the love of wealth.

وَإِنَّهُۥ لِحُبِّ ٱلْخَيْرِ لَشَدِيدٌ ۞

9. Knows he not that when the contents of the graves are poured forth (all mankind is resurrected)?

۞ أَفَلَا يَعْلَمُ إِذَا بُعْثِرَ مَا فِى ٱلْقُبُورِ ۞

10. And that which is in the breasts (of men) shall be made known?

وَحُصِّلَ مَا فِى ٱلصُّدُورِ ۞

11. Verily, that Day (i.e. the Day of Resurrection) their Lord will be Well-Acquainted with them (as to their deeds and will reward them for their deeds).

إِنَّ رَبَّهُم بِهِمْ يَوْمَئِذٍ لَّخَبِيرٌ ۞

Sûrat Al-Qâri'ah
(The Striking Hour) CI

سُورَةُ ٱلْقَارِعَةِ

*In the Name of Allâh
the Most Gracious, the Most Merciful*

بِسْمِ ٱللَّهِ ٱلرَّحْمَٰنِ ٱلرَّحِيمِ

1. Al-Qâri'ah (the striking Hour i.e. the Day of Resurrection).

ٱلْقَارِعَةُ ۞

2. What is the striking (Hour)?

مَا ٱلْقَارِعَةُ ۞

3. And what will make you know what the striking (Hour) is?

وَمَآ أَدْرَىٰكَ مَا ٱلْقَارِعَةُ ۞

4. It is a Day whereon mankind will be like moths scattered about.

يَوْمَ يَكُونُ ٱلنَّاسُ كَٱلْفَرَاشِ ٱلْمَبْثُوثِ ۞

5. And the mountains will be like carded wool.

وَتَكُونُ ٱلْجِبَالُ كَٱلْعِهْنِ ٱلْمَنفُوشِ ۞

6. Then as for him whose balance (of good deeds) will be heavy,[1]

فَأَمَّا مَن ثَقُلَتْ مَوَٰزِينُهُۥ ۞

---

[1] (V.101:6) See footnote of (V.7:8).

7. He will live a pleasant life (in Paradise).

8. But as for him whose balance (of good deeds) will be light,

9. He will have his home in *Hâwiyah* (pit, i.e. Hell).

10. And what will make you know what it is?

11. (It is) a fiercely blazing Fire!

Sûrat At-Takâthur (The piling Up — The Emulous Desire) CII

*In the Name of Allâh
the Most Gracious, the Most Merciful*

1. The mutual rivalry (for piling up of worldly things) diverts you,

2. Until you visit the graves (i.e. till you die).

3. Nay! You shall come to know!

4. Again nay! You shall come to know!

5. Nay! If you knew with a sure knowledge (the end result of piling up, you would not have been occupied yourselves in worldly things).

6. Verily, you shall see the blazing Fire (Hell)!

7. And again, you shall see it with certainty of sight!

8. Then on that Day you shall be asked about the delights[1] (you indulged in, in this world)!

---

[1] (V.102:8) Narrated Abu Hurairah رضي الله عنه: Once during a day or a night Allâh's Messenger صلى الله عليه وسلم came out and found Abu

Sûrat Al-'Asr
(The Time) CIII

سُوْرَةُ الْعَصْرِ

*In the Name of Allâh
the Most Gracious, the Most Merciful*

بِسْمِ اللهِ الرَّحْمَنِ الرَّحِيمِ

1. By *Al-'Asr* (the time).

وَالْعَصْرِ ۞

2. Verily, man is in loss,

إِنَّ الْإِنسَانَ لَفِى خُسْرٍ ۞

3. Except those who believe (in Islâmic Monotheism) and do righteous good deeds, and recommend one another to the truth [i.e. order one

إِلَّا الَّذِينَ ءَامَنُوا وَعَمِلُوا الصَّالِحَاتِ

Bakr and 'Umar رضى الله عنهما, he said: "What has brought you out of your homes at this hour?" They replied: "Hunger, O Allâh's Messenger." He said: "By Him (Allâh) in Whose Hand my soul is, I too have come out for the same reason for which you have come out." Then he صلى الله عليه وسلم said to them (both): "Come along!" And he went along with them to a man from the *Ansâr* but they did not find him in his house. The wife of that man saw the Prophet صلى الله عليه وسلم and said: "You are welcome." Allâh's Messenger صلى الله عليه وسلم asked her (saying): "Where is so-and-so?" She replied: "He has gone to fetch some water for us." In the mean time the *Ansârî* man came, saw Allâh's Messenger صلى الله عليه وسلم with his two Companions and said: "All the praise and thanks be to Allâh: today there is none superior to me as regards guests." Then he went and brought a part of a bunch of date-fruit, having dates, some still green, some ripe and some fully ripe and requested them to eat from it. He then took his knife (to slaughter a sheep for them). Allâh's Messenger صلى الله عليه وسلم said to him: "Beware! Do not slaughter a milch sheep". So he slaughtered a sheep (prepared the meals from its meat). They ate from that sheep and that bunch of dates and drank water. After they had finished eating and drinking to their fill, Allâh's Messenger صلى الله عليه وسلم said to Abu Bakr and 'Umar رضى الله عنهما: "By Him in Whose Hand my soul is, you will be asked about this treat on the Day of Resurrection. He (Allâh) brought you out of your homes with hunger and you are not returning to your homes till you have been blessed with this treat." (*Sahih Muslim*, Vol.6, The Book of Drinks, Chapter 20, Pages 116,117).

another to perform all kinds of good deeds (Al-Ma'rûf) which Allâh has ordained, and abstain from all kinds of sins and evil deeds (Al-Munkar) which Allâh has forbidden], and recommend one another to patience (for the sufferings, harms, and injuries which one may encounter in Allâh's Cause during preaching His religion of Islâmic Monotheism or Jihâd).

وَتَوَاصَوْا بِالْحَقِّ وَتَوَاصَوْا بِالصَّبْرِ ۝

Sûrat Al-Humazah (The Slanderer) CIV

سُورَةُ الْهُمَزَةِ

In the Name of Allâh the Most Gracious, the Most Merciful

بِسْمِ اللَّهِ الرَّحْمَٰنِ الرَّحِيمِ

1. Woe to every slanderer and backbiter.[1]

وَيْلٌ لِّكُلِّ هُمَزَةٍ لُّمَزَةٍ ۝

2. Who has gathered wealth and counted it.

الَّذِي جَمَعَ مَالًا وَعَدَّدَهُ ۝

3. He thinks that his wealth will make him last forever!

يَحْسَبُ أَنَّ مَالَهُ أَخْلَدَهُ ۝

4. Nay! Verily, he will be thrown into the crushing Fire.

كَلَّا لَيُنْبَذَنَّ فِي الْحُطَمَةِ ۝

5. And what will make you know what the crushing Fire is?

وَمَا أَدْرَاكَ مَا الْحُطَمَةُ ۝

6. The fire of Allâh kindled,

نَارُ اللَّهِ الْمُوقَدَةُ ۝

7. Which leaps up over the hearts,

الَّتِي تَطَّلِعُ عَلَى الْأَفْئِدَةِ ۝

8. Verily, it shall be closed upon them,

إِنَّهَا عَلَيْهِمْ مُؤْصَدَةٌ ۝

9. In pillars stretched forth (i.e. they will be punished in the Fire with pillars).

فِي عَمَدٍ مُمَدَّدَةٍ ۝

---

[1] (V.104:1) See the footnotes A, B, C, of (V.49:12).

Sûrat Al-Fîl
(The Elephant) CV

سُوْرَةُ الفِيلِ

In the Name of Allâh
the Most Gracious, the Most Merciful

بِسْمِ اللهِ الرَّحْمٰنِ الرَّحِيمِ

1. Have you (O Muhammad ﷺ) not seen how your Lord dealt with the owners of the Elephant? [The Elephant army which came from Yemen under the command of Abrahah Al-Ashram intending to destroy the *Ka'bah* at Makkah.]

أَلَمْ تَرَ كَيْفَ فَعَلَ رَبُّكَ بِأَصْحَابِ الْفِيلِ ۝

2. Did He not make their plot go astray?

أَلَمْ يَجْعَلْ كَيْدَهُمْ فِي تَضْلِيلٍ ۝

3. And He sent against them birds, in flocks,

وَأَرْسَلَ عَلَيْهِمْ طَيْرًا أَبَابِيلَ ۝

4. Striking them with stones of *Sijjîl* (baked clay).

تَرْمِيهِمْ بِحِجَارَةٍ مِّن سِجِّيلٍ ۝

5. And He made them like an empty field of stalks (of which the corn has been eaten up by cattle).[1]

فَجَعَلَهُمْ كَعَصْفٍ مَّأْكُولٍ ۝

---

[1] (V.105:5) The story of the army of the Elephants (the Qur'ân 105:1-5). This incident happened during the period of the birth-year of Prophet Muhammad ﷺ. Abrahah Al-Ashram was the governor of Yemen on behalf of the king of Ethiopia (as Yemen was a part of the Ethiopian kingdom). He (Abrahah) thought to build a house (like the *Ka'bah* at Makkah) in San'a (the capital of Yemen) and call the Arabs to perform the pilgrimage there in San'a instead of the *Ka'bah* (Al-Bait Al-Harâm) in Makkah, with the intention of diverting the trade and benefits from Makkah to Yemen. He presented his idea to the king of Ethiopia who agreed to his idea. So the house (church) was built and he named it *Al-Qullais*; there was no church of its like at that time. Then a man from the Quraish tribe of Makkah came there and was infuriated by it, so he relieved his nature (stools and urine) in it, soiled its walls

Sûrat Quraish
(Quraish) CVI

سُورَةُ قُرَيْشٍ

In the Name of Allâh
the Most Gracious, the Most Merciful

بِسْمِ اللَّهِ الرَّحْمَٰنِ الرَّحِيمِ

1. (It is a great Grace and Protection from Allâh) for the taming of the Quraish,

لِإِيلَٰفِ قُرَيْشٍ

2. (And with all those Allâh's Grace and Protections for their taming, We

إِلَٰفِهِمْ رِحْلَةَ الشِّتَآءِ

---

and went away. When Abrahah Al-Ashram saw that, he could not control his anger and raised an army to invade Makkah and demolish the *Ka'bah*. He had in that army thirteen elephants and amongst them was an elephant called Mahmûd which was the biggest of them. So that army proceeded and none amongst the Arab tribes that faced them (fought against them) but was killed and defeated, till it approached near Makkah. Then there took place negotiations between Abrahah Al-Ashram and the chief of Makkah (Abdul Muttalib bin Hashim, the grandfather of the Prophet صلى الله عليه وسلم), and it was concluded that Abrahah would restore the camels of Abdul Muttalib which he had taken away, and then he (Abrahah Al-Ashram) would decide himself as regards the *Ka'bah*. Abdul Muttalib ordered the men of Makkah to evacuate the city and go to the top of the mountains along with their wives and children in case some harm should come to them from the invading oppressors. Then that army moved towards Makkah till they reached Muhassir valley. While the army was marching towards Makkah, in the middle of the valley, suddenly it was overtaken by flocks of birds, flocks after flocks, air-raiding that army with small stones slightly bigger than a lentil seed. There never fell a stone on a soldier except it dissolved his flesh and burst it into pieces. So they perished with a total destruction. Abrahah Al-Ashram fled away while his flesh was bursting into pieces till he died on the way (back to Yemen). Such was the victory bestowed by Allâh, (the All-Majestic, All-Powerful) to the people of Makkah and such was the protection provided by Him for His House (*Ka'bah* in Makkah). (See *Tafsîr Ibn Kathîr, Sûrah Al-Fîl*).

cause) the (Quraish) caravans to set forth safe in winter (to the south) and in summer (to the north without any fear),

3. So let them worship (Allâh) the Lord of this House (the *Ka'bah* in Makkah),

4. (He) Who has fed them against hunger, and has made them safe from fear.

Sûrat Al-Mâ'ûn
(The Small Kindnesses) CVII

*In the Name of Allâh
the Most Gracious, the Most Merciful*

1. Have you seen him who denies the Recompense?

2. That is he who repulses the orphan (harshly),[1]

3. And urges not on the feeding of *Al-Miskîn* (the poor),[2]

4. So woe unto those performers of *Salât* (prayers) (hypocrites),

5. Those who delay their *Salât* (prayer from their stated fixed times).

---

[1] (V.107:2) Narrated Sahl bin Sa'd رضي الله عنهما : The Prophet صلى الله عليه وسلم said, "I and the person who looks after an orphan and provides for him, will be in Paradise like this," putting his index and middle fingers together. (*Sahih Al-Bukhari*, Vol.8, Hadith No.34).

[2] (V.107:3) Narrated Abu Hurairah رضي الله عنه : The Prophet صلى الله عليه وسلم said, "The one who looks after a widow or a poor person is like a *Mujâhid* (fighter) who fights for Allâh's Cause, or like him who performs prayers all the night and fasts all the day." (*Sahih Al-Bukhari*, Vol.7, Hadith No.265).

6. Those who do good deeds only to be seen (of men),

ٱلَّذِينَ هُمْ يُرَآءُونَ ٦

7. And withhold Al-Mâ'ûn (small kindnesses like salt, sugar, water).

وَيَمْنَعُونَ ٱلْمَاعُونَ ٧

Sûrat Al-Kauthar
(A River in Paradise) CVIII

سُورَةُ الكَوْثَر

*In the Name of Allâh
the Most Gracious, the Most Merciful*

بِسْمِ ٱللَّهِ ٱلرَّحْمَٰنِ ٱلرَّحِيمِ

1. Verily, We have granted you (O Muhammad صلى الله عليه وسلم) Al-Kauthar (a river in Paradise).[1]

إِنَّآ أَعْطَيْنَٰكَ ٱلْكَوْثَرَ ١

2. Therefore turn in prayer to your Lord and sacrifice (to Him only).

فَصَلِّ لِرَبِّكَ وَٱنْحَرْ ٢

3. For he who hates you (O Muhammad صلى الله عليه وسلم), he will be cut off (from posterity and every good thing in this world and in the Hereafter).[2]

إِنَّ شَانِئَكَ هُوَ ٱلْأَبْتَرُ ٣

Sûrat Al-Kâfirûn
(The Disbelievers) CIX

سُورَةُ الكَافِرُون

*In the Name of Allâh
the Most Gracious, the Most Merciful*

بِسْمِ ٱللَّهِ ٱلرَّحْمَٰنِ ٱلرَّحِيمِ

1. Say: (O Muhammad صلى الله عليه وسلم to these Mushrikûn and Kâfirûn): "O Al-Kâfirûn (disbelievers in Allâh, in

قُلْ يَٰٓأَيُّهَا ٱلْكَٰفِرُونَ ١

---

[1] (V.108:1) Narrated Anas رضى الله عنه: When the Prophet صلى الله عليه وسلم was made to ascend to the heavens. He صلى الله عليه وسلم said (after his return), "I came upon a river (in Paradise) the banks of which were made of tents of hollow pearls. I asked Jibrael (Gabriel), 'What is this (river)?' He replied, 'This is the Kauthar.'" (Sahih Al-Bukhari, Vol.6, Hadith No. 488).

[2] (V.108:3) Narrated Anas رضى الله عنه: The Prophet صلى الله عليه وسلم said, "None of you will have Faith till he loves me more than his father, his children and all mankind." (Sahih Al-Bukhari, Vol.1, Hadith No.14).

His Oneness, in His Angels, in His Books, in His Messengers, in the Day of Resurrection, and in *Al-Qadar*)!

2. "I worship not that which you worship, لَا أَعْبُدُ مَا تَعْبُدُونَ ②

3. "Nor will you worship that which I worship. وَلَا أَنتُمْ عَـٰبِدُونَ مَا أَعْبُدُ ③

4. "And I shall not worship that which you are worshipping. وَلَا أَنَا عَابِدٌ مَّا عَبَدتُّمْ ④

5. "Nor will you worship that which I worship. وَلَا أَنتُمْ عَـٰبِدُونَ مَا أَعْبُدُ ⑤

6. "To you be your religion, and to me my religion (Islâmic Monotheism)." لَكُمْ دِينُكُمْ وَلِىَ دِينِ ⑥

Sûrat An-Nasr (The Help) CX
سُورَةُ النَّصْرِ

*In the Name of Allâh
the Most Gracious, the Most Merciful*
بِسْمِ اللَّهِ الرَّحْمَٰنِ الرَّحِيمِ

1. When there comes the Help of Allâh (to you, O Muhammad صلى الله عليه وسلم against your enemies) and the conquest (of Makkah). إِذَا جَاءَ نَصْرُ اللَّهِ وَالْفَتْحُ ①

2. And you see that the people enter Allâh's religion (Islâm) in crowds. وَرَأَيْتَ النَّاسَ يَدْخُلُونَ فِى دِينِ اللَّهِ أَفْوَاجًا ②

3. So glorify the Praises of your Lord, and ask His Forgiveness. Verily, He is the One Who accepts the repentance and Who forgives. فَسَبِّحْ بِحَمْدِ رَبِّكَ وَاسْتَغْفِرْهُ إِنَّهُ كَانَ تَوَّابًا ③

Sûrat Al-Masad (The Palm Fibre) CXI
سُورَةُ المَسَدِ

*In the Name of Allâh
the Most Gracious, the Most Merciful*
بِسْمِ اللَّهِ الرَّحْمَٰنِ الرَّحِيمِ

1. Perish the two hands of Abû Lahab (an uncle of the Prophet) and perish he![1] تَبَّتْ يَدَا أَبِى لَهَبٍ وَتَبَّ ①

---

[1] (V.111:1) Narrated Ibn 'Abbâs رضي الله عنهما : "When the Verse, 'And warn your tribe (O Muhammad صلى الله عليه وسلم) of near kindred.'

2. His wealth and his children will not benefit him! مَآ أَغْنَىٰ عَنْهُ مَالُهُ وَمَا كَسَبَ

3. He will be burnt in a Fire of blazing flames! سَيَصْلَىٰ نَارًا ذَاتَ لَهَبٍ

4. And his wife, too, who carries wood (thorns of Sa'dân which she used to put on the way of the Prophet صلى الله عليه وسلم, or use to slander him).[1] وَامْرَأَتُهُ حَمَّالَةَ الْحَطَبِ

5. In her neck is a twisted rope of Masad (palm fibre).[2] فِى جِيدِهَا حَبْلٌ مِّن مَّسَدٍ

(V.26:214) was revealed, Allâh's Messenger صلى الله عليه وسلم went out, and when he had ascended As-Safâ mountain, he shouted, 'Ya Sabâhâh!'* The people said, 'What is that?' Then they gathered around him, whereupon he said, 'Do you see? If I inform you that cavalrymen are proceeding up the side of this mountain, will you believe me?' They said, 'We have never heard you telling a lie.' Then he said, 'I am a plain warner to you of a coming severe punishment.' Abu Lahab said, 'May you perish! You gathered us only for this reason?' Then Abu Lahab went away. So *Sûrat Al-Masad* 'Perish the hands of Abu Lahab!' was revealed. (V.111:1). (*Sahih Al-Bukhari*, Vol. 6, *Hadith* No. 495).

* "*Ya Sabâhâh!*" is an Arabic expression used when one appeals for help or draws the attention of others to some danger.

[1] (V.111:4) 'And his wife too, who carries wood.' Mujâhid said, 'Carries the wood' means that she used to slander (the Prophet صلى الله عليه وسلم) and goes about with calumnies.

[2] (V.111:5) "In her neck is a twisted rope of palm fibre, [i.e. the chain which is in the Fire (of Hell)]." (*Sahih Al-Bukhari*, Vol.6, Chapter 356, Page 469).

[Imâm Qurtubî says in the *Tafsîr* of the (V.17:45)]:

Narrated Sa'îd bin Jubâir رضي الله عنه : "When *Sûrah* No.111 (*Sûrat Al-Masad*) was revealed, the wife of Abu Lahab came looking for the Prophet صلى الله عليه وسلم while Abu Bakr رضي الله عنه was sitting him. Abu Bakr said to the Prophet صلى الله عليه وسلم : 'I wish if you get aside (or go away) as she is coming, to us, she may harm you'. The Prophet said: 'There will be a screen set between me and her'. So

Sûrat Al-Ikhlâs or At-Tauhîd **(The Purity) CXII**	سُورَةُ الإِخْلاصِ

In the Name of Allâh
the Most Gracious, the Most Merciful

بِسْمِ اللَّهِ الرَّحْمَنِ الرَّحِيمِ

1. Say (O Muhammad صلى الله عليه وسلم):
"He is Allâh, (the) One.[1]

قُلْ هُوَ اللَّهُ أَحَدٌ ١

2. *"Allâh-us-Samad* السيد الذي يصمد اليه في
الحاجات) [Allâh — the Self-Sufficient
Master, Whom all creatures need, (He
neither eats nor drinks)].

اللَّهُ الصَّمَدُ ٢

3. "He begets not, nor was He
begotten.[2]

لَمْ يَلِدْ وَلَمْ يُولَدْ ٣

---

she did not see him صلى الله عليه وسلم . She said to Abu Bakr: 'Your
companion is saying poetry against me.' Abu Bakr said: 'By Allâh
he does not say poetry.' She said: 'Do you believe that'. Then she
left. Abu Bakr said, 'O Allâh's Messenger! She did not see you'.
The Prophet صلى الله عليه وسلم said: 'An angel was screening me from
her.' " [This *Hadîth* is quoted in *Masnad Abû Ya'la*]

It is said that if the Verse [(17:45) The Qur'ân] is recited by a real
believer (of Islâmic Monotheism) he will be screened from a
disbeliever. (Allâh knows best). (*Tafsîr Al-Qurtubî*, Vol.10, Page 269).

[1] (V.112:1) See *Tauhîd* in the Glossary (Appendix).

[2] (V.112:3)

A) Narrated Mu'âdh bin Jabal رضي الله عنه : The Prophet صلى الله عليه وسلم
said, "O Mu'âdh! Do you know what Allâh's Right upon His slaves
is?" I said, "Allâh and His Messenger know better." The Prophet صلى
الله عليه وسلم said, "To worship Him (Allâh) Alone and to join none in
worship with Him (Allâh). Do you know what their right upon Him
is?" I replied, "Allâh and His Messenger know better." The Prophet
صلى الله عليه وسلم said, "Not to punish them (if they did so)." [*Sahih
Al-Bukhari*, Vol. 9, Hadith No. 470].

B) Narrated Abu Sa'îd Al-Khudrî رضي الله عنه : A man heard another
man reciting: 'Say (O Muhammad): "He is Allâh, (the) One."
(112:1) And he recited it repeatedly. When it was morning, he went
to the Prophet صلى الله عليه وسلم and informed him about that as if he
considered that the recitation of that *Sûrah* by itself was not enough.

4. "And there is none co-equal or comparable unto Him."

Sûrat Al-Falaq
(The Daybreak) CXIII

*In the Name of Allâh
the Most Gracious, the Most Merciful*

1. Say: "I seek refuge with (Allâh), the Lord of the daybreak,

2. "From the evil of what He has created,

3. "And from the evil of the darkening (night) as it comes with its darkness; (or the moon as it sets or goes away),

4. "And from the evil of those who practise witchcrafts when they blow in the knots,

5. "And from the evil of the envier when he envies."

Allâh's Messenger صلى الله عليه وسلم said, "By Him in Whose Hand my soul is, it is equal to one-third of the Qur'ân." [*Sahih Al-Bukhari*, Vol. 9, *Hadith* No. 471].

C) Narrated 'Âishah رضي الله عنها: The Prophet صلى الله عليه وسلم sent (an army unit) under the command of a man who used to lead his companions in the prayers and would finish his recitation with (the *Sûrah* 112): 'Say (O Muhammad): "He is Allâh, (the) One."' (112:1). When they returned (from the battle), they mentioned that to the Prophet صلى الله عليه وسلم. He said (to them), "Ask him why he does so." They asked him and he said, "I do so because it mentions the Qualities of the Most Gracious and I love to recite it (in my prayer)." The Prophet صلى الله عليه وسلم said (to them). "Tell him that Allâh loves him." [*Sahih Al-Bukhari*, Vol. 9, *Hadith* No. 472].

Sûrat An-Nâs
(Mankind) CXIV

سُورَةُ النَّاسِ

*In the Name of Allâh
the Most Gracious, the Most Merciful*

بِسْمِ اللَّهِ الرَّحْمَٰنِ الرَّحِيمِ

1. Say: "I seek refuge with (Allâh) the Lord of mankind,

قُلْ أَعُوذُ بِرَبِّ النَّاسِ ۝

2. "The King of mankind — [1]

مَلِكِ النَّاسِ ۝

3. "The *Ilâh* (God) of mankind,

إِلَٰهِ النَّاسِ ۝

4. "From the evil of the whisperer (devil who whispers evil in the hearts of men) who withdraws (from his whispering in one's heart after one remembers Allâh).[2]

مِن شَرِّ الْوَسْوَاسِ الْخَنَّاسِ ۝

5. "Who whispers in the breasts of mankind.

الَّذِي يُوَسْوِسُ فِي صُدُورِ النَّاسِ ۝

6. "Of jinn and men."

مِنَ الْجِنَّةِ وَالنَّاسِ ۝

---

[1] (V.114:2) The Statement of Allâh عزّ وجلّ : 'The King of mankind.' Narrated Abu Hurairah رضي الله عنه The Prophet صلى الله عليه وسلم said, "On the Day of Resurrection Allâh will grasp the whole (planet of) earth (by His Hand) and shall roll up the heaven with His Right Hand and say, 'I am the King. Where are the kings of the earth?'" (*Sahih Al-Bukhari*, Vol. 9, *Hadith* No. 479).

[2] (V.114:4) Narrated Abu Hurairah رضي الله عنه : Allâh's Messenger صلى الله عليه وسلم said, "The (Hell) Fire is surrounded by all kinds of desires and passions, while Paradise is surrounded by all kinds of disliked undesirable things."* (*Sahih Al-Bukhari*, Vol. 8, *Hadith* No. 494).

* Inordinate desires and animalistic passions lead to the Fire while self-control, perseverance, chastity and all other virtues, the obedience to Allâh and His Messenger صلى الله عليه وسلم lead to Paradise. What leads to Hell is easy to do while what leads to Paradise is difficult to do.

INDEX OF SURAH — CHAPTERS

Sûrah	No.	Page	Makki / Madani	Sûrah	No.	Page	Makki / Madani
Al-Fâtihah	1	9	Makki	Ar-Rûm	30	731	Makki
Al-Baqarah	2	13	Madani	Luqmân	31	742	Makki
Al-'Imran	3	105	Madani	As-Sajdah	32	750	Makki
An-Nisâ'	4	158	Madani	Al-Ahzâb	33	755	Madani
Al-Mâ'idah	5	205	Madani	Saba'	34	773	Makki
Al-An'âm	6	243	Makki	Fâtir	35	784	Makki
Al-A'râf	7	284	Makki	Yâ-Sîn	36	793	Makki
Al-Anfâl	8	327	Madani	As-Sâffât	37	803	Makki
At-Taubah	9	343	Madani	Sâd	38	818	Makki
Yûnus	10	378	Makki	Az-Zumar	39	828	Makki
Hûd	11	401	Makki	Ghâfir	40	843	Makki
Yûsuf	12	424	Makki	Fussilat	41	859	Makki
Ar-Ra'd	13	444	Madani	Ash-Shûra	42	870	Makki
Ibrâhîm	14	455	Makki	Az-Zukhruf	43	882	Makki
Al-Hijr	15	470	Makki	Ad-Dukhân	44	895	Makki
An-Nahl	16	481	Makki	Al-Jâthiyah	45	901	Makki
Al-Isrâ'	17	509	Makki	Al-Ahqâf	46	908	Makki
Al-Kahf	18	532	Makki	Muhammad	47	915	Madani
Maryam	19	555	Makki	Al-Fath	48	923	Madani
Tâ-Hâ	20	570	Makki	Al-Hujurât	49	930	Madani
Al-Anbiyâ'	21	589	Makki	Qâf	50	934	Makki
Al-Hajj	22	605	Madani	Adh-Dhâriyât	51	940	Makki
Al-Mu'minûn	23	623	Makki	At-Tûr	52	948	Makki
An-Nûr	24	636	Madani	An-Najm	53	953	Makki
Al-Furqân	25	652	Makki	Al-Qamar	54	961	Makki
Ash-Shu'arâ	26	664	Makki	Ar-Rahmân	55	967	Madani
An-Naml	27	683	Makki	Al-Wâqi'ah	56	974	Makki
Al-Qasas	28	698	Makki	Al-Hadîd	57	981	Madani
Al-'Ankabûh	29	716	Makki	Al-Mujâdilah	58	989	Madani

INDEX OF SURAH — CHAPTERS

Sûrah	No.	Page	Makki / Madani	Sûrah	No.	Page	Makki / Madani
Al-Hashr	59	994	Madani	Al-A'lâ	87	1098	Makki
Al-Mumtahinah	60	1000	Madani	Al-Ghâshiyah	88	1100	Makki
As-Saff	61	1005	Madani	Al-Fajr	89	1102	Makki
Al-Jumu'ah	62	1008	Madani	Al-Balad	90	1105	Makki
Al-Munâfiqûn	63	1011	Madani	Ash-Shams	91	1107	Makki
At-Taghâbun	64	1013	Madani	Al-Lail	92	1109	Makki
At-Talâq	65	1017	Madani	Ad-Duhâ	93	1111	Makki
At-Tahrîm	66	1020	Madani	Ash-Sharh	94	1112	Makki
Al-Mulk	67	1025	Makki	At-Tîn	95	1113	Makki
Al-Qalam	68	1028	Makki	Al-'Alaq	96	1113	Makki
Al-Hâqqah	69	1036	Makki	Al-Qadr	97	1115	Makki
Al-Ma'ârij	70	1040	Makki	Al-Baiyinah	98	1116	Madani
Nûh	71	1045	Makki	Az-Zalzalah	99	1117	Madani
Al-Jinn	72	1048	Makki	Al-'Adiyât	100	1118	Makki
Al-Muzzammil	73	1052	Makki	Al-Qâri'ah	101	1119	Makki
Al-Muddaththir	74	1055	Makki	At-Takâthur	102	1120	Makki
Al-Qiyâmah	75	1059	Makki	Al-'Asr	103	1121	Makki
Al-Insân	76	1063	Madani	Al-Humazah	104	1122	Makki
Al-Mursalât	77	1066	Makki	Al-Fîl	105	1123	Makki
An-Naba'	78	1071	Makki	Quraish	106	1124	Makki
An-Nâzi'ât	79	1074	Makki	Al-Mâ'ûn	107	1125	Makki
Abasa	80	1078	Makki	Al-Kauthar	108	1126	Makki
At-Takwîr	81	1081	Makki	Al-Kâfirûn	109	1126	Makki
Al-Infitâr	82	1084	Makki	An-Nasr	110	1127	Madani
Al-Mutaffifîn	83	1086	Makki	Al-Masad	111	1127	Makki
Al-Inshiqâq	84	1089	Makki	Al-Ikhlâs	112	1129	Makki
Al-Burûj	85	1091	Makki	Al-Falaq	113	1130	Makki
At-Tarîq	86	1096	Makki	An-Nâs	114	1131	Makki

LIST OF PROSTRATION PLACES IN THE QUR'ÂN

It is a good practice to prostrate at the following places while reciting the Qur'ân.

No.	Part No.	Name of Sûrah	Sûrah No.	Verse No.
1.	9	Al-A'râf	7	206
2.	13	Ar-Ra'd	13	15
3.	14	An-Nahl	16	50
4.	15	Al-Isrâ'	17	100
5.	16	Maryam	19	58
6.	17	Al-Hajj	22	18
7.	17	Al-Hajj	22	77*
8.	19	Al-Furqân	25	60
9.	19	An-Naml	27	26
10.	21	As-Sajdah	32	15
11.	23	Sâd	38	24
12.	24	Fussilat	41	38
13.	27	An-Najm	53	62
14.	30	Al-Inshiqâq	84	21
15.	30	Al-'Alaq	96	19

*In all, fourteen places of prostration are agreed upon by all Muslim religious scholars and *Ulama,* while Imâm Shâf'i suggests prostration at this place also..

The following invocation is usually recited during the prostration:

سَجَدَ وَجْهِيَ لِلَّذِي خَلَقَهُ وَصَوَّرَهُ وَشَقَّ سَمْعَهُ وَبَصَرَهُ تَبَارَكَ اللهُ أَحْسَنُ الْخَالِقِينَ

Sajada wajhiya lilladhi khalaqahu wa sawwarahu, wa shaqqa sam'ahu wa basarahu, tabarak-Allâhu Ahsan-ul-Khaliqueen. [Sahih Muslim, Vol. 4, Hadith No.201].

PROPHETS MENTIONED IN THE QUR'ÂN

Many Prophets came before the last Prophet Muhammad صلى الله عليه وسلم , the names of some are mentioned in the Qur'ân. In this translation the Biblical names of these Prophets are used so as to make their identification easier for the non-Muslim readers. The list of the names is as follows:

S.No.	Qur'ânic Name	Name used in Noble Qur'ân	Arabic
1.	Al-Yas'	Elisha	اليسع عليه السلام
2.	Ayub	Job	ايوب عليه السلام
3.	Dawûd	David	داود عليه السلام
4.	Dhul-Kifl	Dhul-kifl	ذوالكفل عليه السلام
5.	Harûn	Aaron	هارون عليه السلام
6.	Hûd	Hud	هود عليه السلام
7.	Ibrâhîm	Abraham	ابراهيم عليه السلام
8.	Idris	Enoch	ادريس عليه السلام
9.	Iliyâs	Elias	الياس عليه السلام
10.	'Îsâ	Jesus	عيسى عليه السلام
11.	Ishâq	Isaac	اسحق عليه السلام
12.	Ismâ'îl	Ishmael	اسماعيل عليه السلام
13.	Lût	Lot	لوط عليه السلام
14.	Mûsâ	Moses	موسى عليه السلام
15.	Nûh	Noah	نوح عليه السلام
16.	Sâleh	Salih	صالح عليه السلام
17.	Shu'aib	Shuaib	شعيب عليه السلام
18.	Sulaimân	Solomon	سليمان عليه السلام
19.	'Uzair	Ezra	عزير عليه السلام
20.	Ya'qûb	Jacob	يعقوب عليه السلام
21.	Yahyâ	John	يحيى عليه السلام
22.	Yunus	Jonah	يونس عليه السلام
23.	Yusuf	Joseph	يوسف عليه السلام
24.	Zakariyâ	Zachariya	زكريا عليه السلام
25.	Muhammad	Muhammad or Ahmad	محمد او احمد صلى الله عليه وسلم

بِسْمِ اللّٰهِ الرَّحْمٰنِ الرَّحِيْمِ

In the Name of Allâh, the Most Gracious, the Most Merciful

The Noble Qur'ân - A Miracle from Allâh
(to Prophet Muhammad صلى الله عليه وسلم)

وَمَا كَانَ هٰذَا الْقُرْآنُ أَن يُفْتَرَىٰ مِن دُونِ اللّٰهِ وَلٰكِن تَصْدِيقَ الَّذِى بَيْنَ يَدَيْهِ وَتَفْصِيلَ الْكِتَابِ لَا رَيْبَ فِيهِ مِن رَّبِّ الْعَالَمِينَ ۝

"And this Qur'ân is not such as could ever be produced by other than Allâh (Lord of the heavens and the earth), but (on the contrary), it is a confirmation of (revelation) that was before it (i.e. the Torah and the Gospel etc.) and a full explanation of the Book (i.e. laws and orders, etc., decreed for mankind) — wherein there is no doubt — from the Lord of the *Al-'Alamîn* (mankind and jinns and all that exists)." (V.10:37)

وَمَن يَبْتَغِ غَيْرَ الْإِسْلَامِ دِينًا فَلَن يُقْبَلَ مِنْهُ وَهُوَ فِى الْآخِرَةِ مِنَ الْخَاسِرِينَ ۝

"And whoever seeks a religion other than Islam, it will never be accepted of him, and in the Hereafter he will be one of the losers." (V.3:85)

Narrated Abû Hurairah رضى الله عنه: The Prophet صلى الله عليه وسلم said, "There was no Prophet among the Prophets but was given miracles because of which people had security or had belief, but what I have been given is the Divine Inspiration which Allâh has revealed to me. So I hope that my followers will be more than those of any other Prophet on the Day of Resurrection."(*Hadîth* No.379, Vol. No.9, *Sahih Al-Bukhari*)

Narrated Jâbir bin 'Abdullâh رضى الله عنهما: Some angels came to the Prophet (Muhammad صلى الله عليه وسلم) while he was sleeping. Some of them said, "He is sleeping." Others said, "His eyes are sleeping but his heart is awake." Then they said, "There is an example for this companion of yours." One of them said, "Then set forth an example for him." One of them said, "He is sleeping." Another said, "His eyes are sleeping but his heart is awake." Then they said, "His example is that of a man who built a house and then offered therein a banquet and sent an inviter (messenger) to invite the people. So whoever accepted the invitation of the inviter, entered the house and ate of the banquet, and whoever did not accept the invitation of the inviter, did not enter the house, nor did he eat of the banquet." Then the angels said, "Interpret this parable to him so that he may understand it." One of them said, "He is sleeping." The others said, "His eyes are sleeping but his heart is awake." And then they said, "The house stands for Paradise and the callmaker is Muhammad صلى الله عليه وسلم and whoever obeys Muhammad, obeys Allâh; and whoever disobeys Muhammad, disobeys Allâh. Muhammad separated the people (i.e., through his message, the good is distinguished from the bad, and the believers from the disbelievers)." (Hadîth No. 385, Vol. No.9, Sahih Al-Bukhari).

Narrated Abu Hurairah رضي الله عنه: Allâh's Messenger صلى الله عليه وسلم said, "Both in this world and in the Hereafter, I am the nearest of all the people to 'Iesa (Jesus), the son of Maryam (Mary). The Prophets are paternal brothers; their mothers are different, but their religion is one (i.e., Islamic Monotheism)." (Hadîth No. 652, Vol. No.4, Sahih Al-Bukhari).

It is obligatory to have belief in the Messengership of the Prophet (Muhammad صلى الله عليه وسلم). Narrated Abu Hurairah رضي الله عنه: Allâh's Messenger صلى الله عليه وسلم said: "By Him (Allâh) in Whose Hand Muhammad's soul is, there is none from amongst the Jews and the Christians (of these present nations) who hears about me and then dies without believing in the Message with which I have been sent (i.e., Islamic Monotheism), but he will be from the dwellers of the (Hell) Fire." (Sahih Muslim, the Book of Faith, Vol.1, Chapter No. 24). [See also (V.3:116)]

APPENDIX-I
GLOSSARY

'Abd : (العبد) A male slave, a slave of Allâh.

'Âd : (عاد) An ancient tribe that lived after Nûh (Noah). It was prosperous, but disobedient to Allâh, so Allâh destroyed it with a violent destructive westerly wind.

Adhân : (الأذان) The call to Salât (prayer) pronounced loudly to indicate that the time of praying is due. And it is as follows: *Allâhu Akbar, Allâhu-Akbar; Allâhu-Akbar, Allâhu-Akbar; Ash-hadu an lâ ilâha illallâh, Ash-hadu an lâ ilâha illallâh; Ash-hadu anna Muhammadan Rasûl-Ullâh, Ash-hadu anna Muhammadan Rasûl-Ullâh; Haiya 'alas-Salâ(h), Haiya'alas-Salâ(h); Haiya 'alal-Falâh, Haiya 'alal-Falâh; Allâhu-Akbar, Allâhu-Akbar; Lâ ilâha illallâh.* (See *Sahîh Al-Bukhâri*, Vol.1, Page 334).

Ahkâm : (الأحكام) "Legal status". According to Islâmic law, there are five kinds of Ahkâm:
1. Compulsory (Wâjib) (الواجب)
2. Desirable but not compulsory (Mustahab) (المستحب)
3. Forbidden (Muharram) (المحرم)
4. Disliked but not forbidden (Makrûh) (المكروه)
5. Lawful and allowed (Halâl) (الحلال)

Al-Ahzâb : (الأحزاب) The Confederates. The term is used for the disbelievers of Quraish and the Jews residing at Al-Madînah and some other Arab tribes who invaded the Muslims of Al-Madînah but were forced to withdraw.

'Ajwah : (العجوة) A kind of dates.

Âlim : (العالم) A knowledgeable person or a religious scholar in Islâm.

Allâhu-Akbar : (الله أكبر) Allâh is the Most Great.

'Amah : (الأمة) A female slave.

Al-'Amânah : (الأمانة) The trust or the moral responsibility or honesty, and all the duties which Allâh has ordained.

Amîn : (آمين) O Allâh, accept our invocation.

Amma Ba'du : (أما بعد) An expression used for separating an introductory from the main topics in a speech; the introductory being usually concerned with Allâh's Praises and Glorification. Literally it means, "whatever comes after." It is generally translated as "then after" or "to proceed."

Ansâr	:	(الأنصار) صلى الله عليه وسلم The Companions of the Prophet from the inhabitants of Al-Madînah, who embraced Islâm and supported it and who received and entertained the Muslim emigrants from Makkah and other places.
Al-'Aqîq	:	(العقيق) A valley in Al-Madînah about seven kilometers west of Al-Madînah.
'Aqîqah	:	(العقيقة) It is the sacrificing of one or two sheep on the occasion of the birth of a child, as a token of gratitude to Allâh. (See *Sahîh Al-Bukhâri*, The Book of *'Aqîqa*, Vol. 7, Page No. 272).
'Aqrâ Halqâ	:	(عقرى حلقى) It is just an exclamatory expression, the literal meaning of which is not meant always. It expresses disapproval.
'Arafah (day of)	:	(عرفة) The ninth day of the month Dhul-Hijjah, on which the pilgrims stay in Arafât plain till sunset.
'Arafât	:	(عرفات) A famous place of pilgrimage on the southeast of Makkah about twenty-five kilometers from it.
Arâk	:	(الأراك) A tree from which *Siwâk* (سواك) (tooth brush) is made.
Al-Arba'ah	:	(الأربعة) The four compilers of *Ahadith* — Abu Da'ud, Nasâ'i, Tirmidhi, Ibn Mâjah.
'Asabah	:	(العصبة) All male relatives of a deceased person from the father's side.
'Asb	:	(العصب) A kind of Yemeni cloth that is very coarse.
Ashâb As-Suffah	:	(أصحاب الصفة) They were about eighty or more men who used to stay and have religious teachings in the Prophet's mosque in Al-Madînah, and they were very poor people.
Ashâb As-Sunan	:	(أصحاب السنن) The compilers of the prophetic *Ahadith* on Islamic jurisprudence.
'Ashûra	:	(العاشوراء) The 10th of the month of Muharram (the first month in the Islâmic calendar).
'Asr	:	(العصر) Afternoon, *'Asr* prayer time.
'Aurah	:	(العورة) That part of the body which is illegal to expose to others.
Awsuq	:	(أوسق) Plural of *Wasq*, which is a measure equal to 60 *Sâ'* = 135 kgms. (approx). It may be less or more.
Ayât	:	(الآيات) Proofs, evidences, verses, lessons, signs, revelations, etc.
Ayat-ul-Kursi	:	(آية الكرسي) Qur'ânic Verse No. 255 of *Sûrat Al-Baqarah*.
Ayyâm At-Tashriq	:	(أيام التشريق) It is a term used for the eleventh, twelfth and thirteenth of Dhul-Hijjah.

Ayyim	:	(الأيم) A woman who already has had a sexual experience, she may be a widow or a divorced.
'Azl	:	(العزل) Coitus interruptus, i.e., pulling out the penis from vagina at the time of ejaculation of semen for the purpose of birth control.
Azlâm	:	(الأزلام) Literally means "arrows". Here it means arrows used to seek good luck or a decision, practised by the 'Arabs of Pre-Islamic Period of Ignorance.
Badanah	:	(بدنة) (Plural : *Budn*). A camel or a cow or an ox driven to be offered as a sacrifice, by the pilgrims at the sanctuary of Makkah.
Badr	:	(البدر) A place about 150 kilometers to the south of Al-Madînah, where the first great battle in Islâmic history took place between the early Muslims and the infidels of Quraish.
Al-Bahîrah	:	(البحيرة) A milking she-camel, whose milk used to be spared for idols and other false deities.
Bai'ah	:	(البيعة) A pledge given by the citizens etc. to their *Imâm* (Muslim ruler) to be obedient to him according to the Islâmic religion.
Bai' As-Salaf:		(بيع السلف) See *Salaf*.
Bai' As-Salam:		(بيع السلم) See *Salam*.
Al-Bait-ul-Ma'mûr:		(البيت المعمور) Allâh's House over the seventh heaven.
Bait-ul-Maqdis :		(بيت القدس) *Bait* literally means 'House': a mosque is frequently called *Baitullâh* (the House of Allâh). Bait-ul-Maqdis is the famous mosque in Jerusalem which is regarded as the third sacred mosque in Islâm, the first and second being *Al-Masjid-al-Harâm* at Makkah and the mosque of the Prophet صلى الله عليه وسلم at Al-Madînah, respectively.
Bait-ul-Midras :		(بيت المدراس) A place in Al-Madînah (and it was a Jewish centre).
Bai'at-ur-Ridwân :		(بيعة الرضوان) The oath and pledge taken by the *Sahâbah* at Al-Hudaibiyah in the year 6 H to fight Quraish in case they harmed 'Uthmân رضي الله عنه who had gone to negotiate with them and reported to have been taken captive.
Bâlam	:	(بالام) Means an ox.
Banû Al-Asfar :		(بنو الأصفر) The Byzantines.
Baqi'	:	(البقيع) The cemetery of the people of Al-Madînah; many of the Companions of the Prophet صلى الله عليه وسلم are buried in it.

Barr	:	(البَرّ) Pious.
Bid'ah	:	(البِدعة) Any innovated practice in religion.
Bint Labûn	:	(بنت لبون) Two-year-old she-camel.
Bint Makhâd	:	(بنت مخاض) One-year-old she-camel.
Burâq	:	(بُراق) An animal bigger than a donkey and smaller than a horse on which the Prophet صلى الله عليه وسلم went for the *Mi'râj*. (The Ascent of the Prophet صلى الله عليه وسلم to the heavens.)
Burd, Burda	:	(البُرد، البُردة) A black square narrow dress.
Burnus	:	(البُرنس) A hooded cloak.
Burud	:	(البُرُد) Plural of *Barîd*. One *Barid* is equal to 4 *Farsakh* = 12 miles = 19.31 kilometers.
Buthan	:	(بطحان) A valley in Al-Madînah.
Ad-Dabûr	:	(الدبور) Westerly wind.
Daghâbis	:	(الدغابيس) Snake cucumbers.It is a plural of *Daghbûs*.
Dajjâl	:	(الدجّال) Pseudo Messiah (*Al-Masîh-ad-Dajjâl*) or Antichrist. Literally a liar, quack, deceiver. (See the footnote of V.6:158 the Qur'ân and also *Hadîth* No.649 and 650, Vol.4, *Sahih Al-Bukhâri*.)
Dâniq	:	(دانق) A coin equal to one-sixth of a Dirham.
Dâr-al-Qadâ'	:	(دارالقضاء) Justice House (court).
Dayyân	:	(الديّان) Allâh; it literally means the One Who judges people from their deeds after calling them to account.
Dhât-'Irq	:	(ذات عرق) *Miqât* for the pilgrims coming from Iraq.
Dhât-un-Nitâqain	:	(ذات النطاقين) Asmâ', the daughter of Abû Bakr رضي الله عنهما. It literally means a woman with two belts. She was named so by the Prophet صلى الله عليه وسلم.
Dhaw-ul-Arhâm	:	(ذوو الأرحام) Relatives on the maternal side.
Dhimmî	:	(الذمي) A non-Muslim living under the protection of an Islâmic government.
Dhûl-Farâ'id	:	(ذوالفرائض) Those persons whose share of inheritance is described in the Qur'ân are called *Dhûl-Farâid*, and the rest are *Asabah* (العصبة).
Dhûl-Hijjah	:	(ذوالحجة) The twelfth month in the Islâmic calendar.
Dhûl-Hulaifah	:	(ذوالحليفة) The *Miqât* of the people of Al-Madînah now called 'Abyâr 'Alî.
Dhûl-Khalasah	:	(ذو الخلصة) Al-Ka'bah Al-Yamaniyah. (A house in Yemen where idols used to be worshipped. It belonged to the tribe of Khath'am and Bujailah.)

Dhûl-Qa'dah	:	(ذو القعدة) The eleventh month of the Islâmic calendar.
Dhûl-Qarnain	:	(ذو القرنين) A great ruler in the past who ruled all over the world, and was a true believer. His story is mentioned in the Qur'ân. (V.18:83)
Dhû-Mahram	:	(ذو محرم) A man, whom a woman can never marry because of close relationship (e.g. a brother, a father, an uncle); or her own husband.
Dhû-Tuwa	:	(ذي طوى) It is one of the valleys (districts) of Makkah and there is a well-known well in it. In the lifetime of the Prophet ﷺ Makkah was a small city and this well was outside its precincts. Nowadays Makkah is a larger city and the well is within its boundaries.
Dîbâj	:	(الديباج) Pure silk cloth.
Dînâr	:	(الدينار) An ancient gold coin.
Dirham	:	(الدرهم) A silver coin weighing 50 grains of barley with cut ends. It equals to $^1/_{12}$ of one *Uqiyyah* of gold in value.
Diyah	:	(الدية) (Plural: *Dîyât*) Blood money (for wounds, killing etc.), compensation paid by the killer to the relatives of the victim (in unintentional cases).
Duha	:	(الضحى) Forenoon.
Fadak	:	(فدك) A town near Al-Madînah.
Fâhish	:	(الفاحش) One who talks evil.
Fai'	:	(الفيء) War booty gained without fighting.
Fajr	:	(الفجر) Dawn or early morning before sunrise, or morning *Salât* (prayer).
Faqîh	:	(الفقيه) A learned man who can give religious verdicts.
Farâ'id	:	(الفرائض) Share fixed for the relatives of a deceased. Such shares are prescribed in the Qur'ân ($^1/_2$, $^1/_4$, $^1/_3$, $^1/_6$ $^1/_8$, $^2/_3$). [V.4:11, 12, 176]
Fard 'Ain	:	(فرض العين) It is an individual duty — an obligation essentially to be performed by each individual.
Fard Kifâyah	:	(فرض الكفاية) It is a collective duty — an obligation which, if performed by one person, suffices for the rest; as it does not have to be performed essentially by all.
Farîdah	:	(الفريضة) (Plural: *Farâ'id*) An enjoined duty.
Farsakh	:	(الفرسخ) (Parasang — Persian unit of distance) A distance of three miles (approx). 1 mile = 6000 *Dora* = 1760 yards = 1.6 kilometer.
Fatât	:	(الفتاة) A female slave or a young lady.

Al-Fâtihah	:	(الفاتحة) The first *Sûrah* in the Qur'ân.
Fidyah	:	(الفدية) Compensation for a missed or wrongly practised religious obligation (like in *Hajj*), usually in the form of money or foodstuff or offering (animal by slaughtering it).
Fiqh	:	(الفقه) Islamic jurisprudence.
Al-Firdaus	:	(الفردوس) The middle and the highest part of Paradise.
Fitnah	:	(الفتنة) (Plural: *Fitan*) Trials, persecution, confusion in the religion, conflicts and strifes among the Muslims.
Ghairah	:	(الغيرة) This word covers a wide meaning : jealousy as regards women, and also it is a feeling of great fury and anger when one's honour and prestige is injured or challenged.
Ghâzî	:	(الغازي) A Muslim fighter returning after participation in *Jihâd* (Islâmic holy fighting).
Ghazwah	:	(الغزوة) (Plural : *Ghazawât*). A holy battle or fighting in the Cause of Allâh consisting of a large army unit with the Prophet صلى الله عليه وسلم himself leading the army.
Ghazwat-ul-Khandaq	:	(غزوة الخندق) The name of a battle between the early Muslims and the infidels in which the Muslims dug a *Khandaq* (trench) round Al-Madînah to prevent any advance by the enemies.
Ghulûl	:	(الغلول) Stealing from the war booty before its distribution.
Ghuraf	:	(الغرف) Special abodes.
Al-Ghurr-ul-Muhajjalûn	:	(الغر المحجلون) A name that will be given on the Day of Resurrection to the Muslims because the parts of their bodies which they used to wash in ablution will shine then.
Ghusl	:	(الغسل) A ceremonial bath. This is necessary for one who is *Junub*, and also on other occasions. This expression 'taking a bath' is used with the special meaning of *Ghusl* mentioned here.
Habal-ul-Habalah	:	(حبل الحبلة) There were two forms of this trade called *Habal-ul-Habalah*. The example of first form is that to buy an offspring of an animal which itself is yet to be born by making the payment in advance. Second form is to sell an animal on condition to have the offspring of the sold animal. Both forms of this kind of transaction are prohibited.
Al-Hadath Al-Akbar	:	(الحدث الأكبر) State of uncleanliness because of sexual discharge.
Al-Hadath Al-Asghar	:	(الحدث الأصغر) Passing wind or urine or answering the call of nature.

Hadîth : (الحديث) (Plural: *Ahadith* أحاديث) The sayings, deeds and approvals accurately narrated from the Prophet صلى الله عليه وسلم . Following are the few classifications of *Ahadith*:

(الضعيف) *Da'if* (weak) — An inaccurate narration which does not qualify to be either *Sahih* (sound) or *Hasan* (fair), and hence cannot be used as a basis of an Islamic opinion.

(الغريب) *Gharib* (unfamiliar or rare) — A *Hadith* or version reported by one reliable or unreliable narrator which differs in context with another *Hadith* or version reported by a group of reliable narrators. A *Gharib Hadith* can be *Sahih* (sound) or *Da'if* (weak).

(الحسن) *Hasan* (fair) — A *Musnad Hadith* narrated by a reliable chain, but not reaching the grade of *Sahih* (sound) *Hadith*.

(المجهول) *Majhul* (unknown) — If there is an unknown person in the chain of narrators of a *Hadith*.

(المقطوع) *Maqtu'* (disconnected) — (i) A *Hadith* ending at a *Tabi'i* by both action and words. (ii) A *Hadith* with incomplete chain of narrators. (iii) A *Hadith* in which a *Sahâbi* describes about something by saying, 'we used to do ....'.

(المرفوع) *Marfu'* (traceable) — A *Hadith* referred to the Prophet صلى الله عليه وسلم, be it a saying or an action, whether *Muttasil* (connected), *Munqata'* (interrupted) or *Mursal* (disreferred).

(الموقوف) *Mauqûf* (untraceable) — It is a *Hadith* about a *Sahâbi* (Companion of the Prophet صلى الله عليه وسلم). A description, report or an information given by a *Sahâbi*. A *Mauquf* is also called an *Athar*.

(المضطرب) *Mudtarib* (confounding) — A *Hadith* in which the narrators disagree on a particular source or on any other aspect with equally strong grounds with no possibility of preponderating one opinion against the other. This difference could be either on the chain of narrators or in the text.

(المنقطع) *Munqati'* (disconnected) — A *Hadith* with incomplete chain of narrators or containing in its chain an unknown reporter.

(المرسل) *Mursal* (disreferred) — A *Hadith* with the chain of narrators ending at a *Tabi'i*, without the reference of the Companion, quoting from the Prophet صلى الله عليه وسلم .

(المسند) *Musnad* (subjective) — (i) A *Hadith* with a

complete **chain** of narrators reaching the Prophet صلى الله عليه وسلم (ii) A *Hadîth* collection in which all the narrations of a reporter are gathered together.

(المتصل) *Muttasil* (connected) or *Mausul* (الموصول) — A *Hadîth* with a complete chain of narrators until it reaches its source. It can either be a *Marfu'* (traceable) referring to the Prophet صلى الله عليه وسلم, or a *Mauquf* (untraceable) ending at a *Sahâbi*.

(الصحيح) *Sahih* (sound) — A *Musnad Hadîth* with an unbroken chain of narrators, one narrated from are and all reliable reporters with good memory up to the source without being a *Shâdh* (شاذ -odd) or a *Mu'allal* (المعلل -faulty).

Hady	:	(الهدى) An animal (a camel, a cow, a sheep or a goat) offered as a sacrifice by the pilgrims.
Hais	:	(الحيس) A dish made of cooking-butter, dates and cheese.
Hajj	:	(الحج) Pilgrimage to Makkah.
Hajj-al-Akbar	:	(الحج الأكبر) The day of *Nahr* (i.e the 10th of Dhul-Hijjah).
Hajj-al-Asghar	:	(الحج الأصغر) *Umrah*.
Hajj-al-Ifrâd	:	(حج الإفراد) In it, a pilgrim enters in the state of *Ihrâm* with the intention of performing *Hajj* only.
Hajj-al-Qirân	:	(حج القران) In it, a pilgrim enters in the state of *Ihrâm* with the intention of performing *Umrah* and *Hajj* together.
Hajj-at-Tamattu'	:	(حج التمتع) In it a pilgrim enters in the state of *Ihrâm* with the intention of performing *Umrah*, and then after performing *Tawâf* and *Sa'y*, he comes out of his *Ihrâm*. With the commencement of *Hajj* days, he enters in the state of *Ihrâm* again and performs *Hajj*.
Hajjat-ul-Wadâ'	:	(حجة الوداع) The last *Hajj* of the Prophet صلى الله عليه وسلم the year before he died.
Hajj Mabrûr	:	(الحج المبرور) *Hajj* accepted by Allâh for being perfectly performed according to the Prophet's *Sunnah* and with legally earned money.
Halâl	:	(الحلال) Lawful.
Hanîf	:	(الحنيف) Pure Islâmic Monotheism (worshipping Allâh Alone and nothing else).
Hantâh	:	(هنتاه) An expression used when you don't want to call somebody by her name. (It is used for calling a female).
Hanût	:	(الحنوط) A kind of scent used for embalming the dead.
Harâm	:	(الحرام) Unlawful, forbidden and punishable from the viewpoint of religion.

Haram	:	(الحرم) Sanctuaries of Makkah and Al-Madînah.
Harbah	:	(الحربة) A short spear.
Harj	:	(الهرج) Killing.
Harrah	:	(الحرة) A well-known rocky place in Al-Madînah covered with black stones.
Al-Harûriyyah:		(الحرورية) A special unorthodox religious sect.
Al-Hasbâ'	:	(الحصباء) A place outside Makkah where pilgrims go after finishing all the ceremonies of *Hajj*.
Hawâlah	:	(الحوالة) The transference of a debt from one person to another. It is an agreement whereby a debtor is released from a debt by another becoming responsible for it.
Hawâzin	:	(الهوازن) A tribe of Quraish.
Hayâ'	:	(الحياء) This term covers a large number of concepts. It may mean 'modesty', 'self-respect', 'bashfulness', 'honour', etc. *Hayâ'* is of two kinds: good and bad; the good *Hayâ'* is to be ashamed to commit a crime or a thing which Allâh صلى الله عليه وسلم and His Messenger عز وجل has forbidden, and bad *Hayâ'* is to be ashamed to do a thing, which Allâh and His Messenger صلى الله عليه وسلم ordered to do. (See *Sahîh Al-Bukhâri*, Vol. 1, *Hadith* No.8).
Hibah	:	(الهبة) It means to present something to someone as a gift for Allâh's sake.
Al-Hidanah	:	(الحضانة) The nursing and caretaking of children.
Hijâb	:	(الحجاب) A long dress prescribed for Muslim women to cover their whole body from head to feet.
Al-Hijr	:	(الحجر) The unroofed portion of the Ka'bah which at present is in the form of a compound towards the north of the Ka'bah.
Hijrah	:	(الهجرة) Literally it means 'migration'. This term is used for: (i) the migration of Muslims from an enemy land to a secure place for religious causes, (ii) the first Muslims migration from Makkah to Abyssinia (Ethiopia) and later to Al-Madînah, (iii) the Prophet's migration journey from Makkah to Al-Madînah, and (iv) the Islamic calendar year which started from the Prophet's migration journey from Makkah to Al-Madînah.
Hilâb	:	(حلاب) A kind of scent.
Hima	:	(الحمى) A private pasture.
Himyân	:	(حميان) A kind of belt, part of which serves as a purse to keep money in it.

Hinna	:	(الحناء) (Henna) A kind of plant used for dyeing hair etc.
Hiqqah	:	(الحقة) A three-year-old she-camel.
Hirâ'	:	(الحراء) A well-known cave in a mountain near Makkah.
Hubal	:	(هبل) The name of an idol in the Ka'bah in the Pre-Islâmic Period of Ignorance.
Hublâ	:	(الحبلى) A kind of desert tree.
Hudâ	:	(الحداء) Chanting of camel-drivers keeping time of camel's walk.
Al-Hudaibiyyah:	(الحديبية) A well-known place about 16 kilometers from Makkah on the way to Jeddah. At this place a treaty was made in 6 H. between the Prophet صلى الله عليه وسلم and the Quraish who stopped him and his Companions from performing *'Umrah*.
Hudûd	:	(الحدود) (Plural of *Hadd*) Allâh's boundary limits for *Halâl* (lawful) and *Harâm* (unlawful).
Hujrah	:	(الحجرة) Courtyard or a room.
Hukm	:	(الحكم) A judgement of legal decision (especially of Allâh)
Hums	:	(حمس) The tribe of Quraish, their offspring and their allies were called *Hums*. This word implies enthusiasm and strictness. The *Hums* used to say, "We are the people of Allâh and we shall not go out of the sanctuary of Makkah." They thought themselves superior to the other people.
Hunain	:	(الحنين) A valley between Makkah and Tâ'if where the battle took place between the Prophet صلى الله عليه وسلم and Quraish pagans.
Hûr	:	(الحور) Very fair females created by Allâh as such not from the offspring of Adam, with intense black irises of their eyes and intense white scleras. [For details see the book *Hâdi Al-Arwâh* by Ibn Al-Qaiyim, Chapter 54, Page 147].
'Îd-al-Adha	(	(عيد الأضحى) The four days' festival of Muslims starting on the tenth day of Dhul-Hijjah (month).
'Îd-al-Fitr	:	(عيد الفطر) The three days' festival of Muslims starting from the first day of Shawwâl, the month that follows Ramadân. *Fitr* literally means 'breaking the *Saum* (fast).' Muslims observe *Saum* (fast) the whole of Ramadân, the ninth month of the Islâmic calendar and when Shawwâl comes, they break their *Saum* (fast) .
'Iddah	:	(العدة) Allâh's prescribed waiting period for a woman after divorce or death of her husband, after the expiry of

which she can remarry another person. (See the Qur'ân, *Sûrat* 65).

Idkhkhir : (الإذخر) It is a kind of grass which is used in the process of melting of the metals. The same is laid down on the roofs and floors of houses, and is also used in spreading in the graves.

Iftâr : (الإفطار) The opposite of *Saum* (fasting), (breaking the fast).

Al-Ihdâd : (الإحداد) Mourning for a deceased husband.

Ihrâm : (الإحرام) A state in which one is prohibited to practise certain deeds that are lawful at other times. The duties of *'Umrah* and *Hajj* are performed during such state. When one assumes this state, the first thing one should do is to express mentally and orally one's intention to assume this state for the purpose of performing *Hajj* or *'Umrah*. Then *Talbîyah* is recited, two sheets of unstitched clothes are the only clothes one wears, (1) *Izâr*: worn below one's waist; and the other (2) *Ridâ'* : worn round the upper part of the body.

Ihsân : (الإحسان) The highest level of deeds and worship, (perfection i.e. when you worship Allâh or do deeds, consider yourself as if you see Him and if you cannot achieve this feeling or attitude, then you must bear in mind that He sees you).

Al-Ihtibâ' : (الاحتباء) A sitting posture, putting one's arms around one's legs while sitting on the hips.

'Ilâ' : (الإيلاء) The oath taken by a husband that he would not approach his wife for a certain period.

Iliyâ' : (إيليا) Jerusalem.

Imâm : (الإمام) The person who leads others in the *Salât* (prayer) or the Muslim caliph (or ruler).

Imlâs : (الإملاص) An abortion caused by being beaten over one's (a pregnant wife's) abdomen.

'Inah : (العينة) A kind of transaction One form of it is that if a person asks someone to lend him a certain amount of money, he refuses the money in cash, but instead offers him an article at a higher price than his demand of the required money, and later on buys the same article from him at a less price i.e., equal to the money he wants. In this way he makes him indebted for the difference. It shows that two things are the causes of Muslim disgrace — one is giving up of *Jihâd* and the second is fraud and swindling.

Iqâmah	:	(الإقامة) The wording of *Adhân* is reduced so that the wording that is repeated twice in the *Adhân* is said once in *Iqâmah*, except the last phrase of *Allâhu Akbar*, and the prayer is offered immediately after the *Iqâmah*.
Iqamat-as-Salât	:	(إقامة الصلاة) The performing of *As-Salât* (the prayers). This is not understood by many Muslims. It means:

(A) Each and every Muslim, male or female, is obliged to offer his *Salât* (prayers) regularly five times a day at the specified times; the male in the mosque in congregation and the female at home. As the Prophet صلى الله عليه وسلم has said: "Order your children to offer *Salât* (prayers) at the age of seven and beat them (about it) at the age of ten". The chief (of a family, town, tribe, etc.) and the Muslim ruler of a country are held responsible before Allâh in case of non-fulfillment of this obligation by the Muslims under his authority.

(B) To perform the *Salât* (prayers) in a way just as Prophet Muhammad صلى الله عليه وسلم used to perform it with all its rules and regulations, i.e. standing, bowing, prostrating, sitting etc: as he صلى الله عليه وسلم has said: "Perform your *Salât* (prayer) the way you see me performing it." *[9:352 — O.B.]* Please see Ahâdîth Nos. 702, 703, 704, 723, 786, 787 Vol. 1, *Sahîh Al-Bukhâri* for the Prophet's way of offering *Salât* (prayer), in the Book of Characteristics of the *Salât* (prayer) and that the *Salât* (prayer) begins with *Takbîr* (*Allâhu-Akbar*) with the recitation of *Sûrat Al-Fâtihah* etc. along with its various postures, standing, bowing, prostrations, sitting etc. and it ends with *Taslîm*.

'Ishâ'	:	(العشاء) Late evening *Salât* (prayer). Its time starts about one and a half hour after sunset, till the middle of the night.
Istabraq	:	(استبرق) Thick *Dîbâj* (pure silk cloth).
Istihâdah	:	(الاستحاضة) Any bleeding from the womb of a woman in between her normal periods. (See *Sahîh Al-Bukhâri*, Vol. 1, *Hadîth* No. 303 and Chapter No. 10, Page No. 183).
Istihsân	:	(الاستحسان) To give a verdict with a proof from one's heart (only) with satisfaction, and one cannot express it [only Abû Hanîfah and his pupils say so but the rest of the Muslim religious scholars of *Sunnah* (and they are the majority) do not agree to it].

Istikhârah	:	(الاستخارة) A *Salât* (prayer) consisting of two *Rak'ah* in which the praying person appeals to Allâh to guide him on the right way, regarding a certain matter he wants to undertake. (See *Hadîth* No. 263, Vol. 2, *Hadîth* No.391, Vol. 8, *Hadîth* No. 487, Vol 9, *Sahîh Al-Bukhâri*).
Istisqâ'	:	(الاستسقاء) A *Salât* (prayer) consisting of two *Rak'ah*, invoking Allâh for rain in seasons of drought.
I'tikâf	:	(الاعتكاف) Seclusion in a mosque for the purpose of worshipping Allâh only. The one in such a state should not have sexual relations with his wife, and one is not allowed to leave the mosque except for a very short period, and that is only for very urgent necessity e.g. answering the call of nature or joining a funeral procession etc.
Izâr	:	(الإزار) A sheet worn below the waist to cover the lower-half of the body.
Jadha'ah	:	(الجذعة) A four-year-old she-camel.
Jahannam	:	(جهنم) Hell-fire.
Jahiliya	:	(الجاهلية) (i) Ignorance belonging to the period before the advent of the Prophet صلى الله عليه وسلم . (ii) Un-Islamic practices which either existed or were inherited from the era before the advent of the Prophet صلى الله عليه وسلم .
Jalsat-ul-Istirâhah	:	(جلسة الاستراحة) The brief sitting between rising up from a prostration position to the standing position in a prayer.
Jam'	:	(الجمع) Al-Muzdalifah, a well-known place near Makkah.
Jamrah	:	(الجمرة) A small stone-built pillar in a walled place. There are three *Jamrah* situated at Mina. One of the ceremonies of *Hajj* is to throw pebbles at these *Jamrah* on the four days of *'Îd-al-Adha* at Mina.
Jamrat-al-'Aqabah	:	(جمرة العقبة) One of the three stone-built pillars situated at Mina. It is situated at the entrance of Mina from the direction of Makkah.
Janâbah	:	(الجنابة) The state of a person after having sexual intercourse with his wife or after having a sexual discharge in a wet dream. A person in such a state should perform *Ghusl* (i.e. have a bath) or do *Tayammum*, if a bath is not possible.
Janâzah	:	(الجنازة) [Plural: *Janâ'iz* الجنائز) Funeral.
Jannah	:	(الجنة) Paradise.
Jihâd	:	(الجهاد) Holy fighting in the Cause of Allâh or any other kind of effort to make Allâh's Word (i.e. Islâm) superior. *Jihâd* is regarded as one of the fundamentals of Islâm. [See the footnote of (V.2:190) The Noble Qur'ân].

Jimâr	:	(الجمار) Plural of *Jamrah*.
Jinn	:	(الجن) A creation, created by Allâh from fire, like human beings from dust, and angels from light.
Al-Ji'rânah	:	(الجعرانة) A place, few kilometers from Makkah. The Prophet صلى الله عليه وسلم distributed the war booty of the battle of Hunain there, and from there he assumed the state of *Ihrâm* to perform *'Umrah*.
Jizyah	:	(الجزية) Head tax imposed by Islâm on all non-Muslims living under the protection of an Islâmic government. [See *Sahih Al-Bukhâri*, Vol. 4, Page No. 251, Chapter 21, and *Ahâdith* No. 384, 385 and 386.]
Al-Juhfah	:	(الجحفة) The *Miqât* of the people of Shâm.
Jumu'ah	:	(الجمعة) Friday.
Junub	:	(الجنب) A person who is in a state of *Janâba*.
Jurhum	:	(جرهم) Name of an Arab tribe.
Ka'bah	:	(الكعبة) A square stone building in *Al-Masjid-al-Harâm* (the great mosque at Makkah) towards which all Muslims face in *Salât* (prayer).
Kafâlah	:	(الكفالة) The pledge given by somebody to a creditor to guarantee that the debtor will be present at a certain specific place to pay his debt or fine, or to undergo a punishment etc.
Kaffârah	:	(الكفارة) Making atonement for uttering or committing an unlawful thing in Islam.
Kâfir	:	(الكافر) (Plural: *Kuffâr* الكفار). The one who disbelieves in Allâh, His Messengers, all the angels, all the holy Books, Day of Resurrection and in the *Al-Qadar* (Divine Preordainments).
Kanz	:	(الكنز) Hoarded up gold, silver and money, the *Zakât* of which has not been paid. (See the Qur'ân V. 9:34).
Katm	:	(الكتم) A plant used for dyeing hair.
Al-Kauthar	:	(الكوثر) A river in Paradise (see the Qur'ân, *Sûrah* No.108).
Al-Khamsah	:	(الخمسة) The five compilers of *Ahadith* — Abu Dâwûd, Nasâ'i, Tirmidhi, Ibn Mâjah and Ahmad.
Khaibar	:	(خيبر) An oasis and date-growing village, about 100 kilometers from Al-Madînah. During the Prophet's time, it was inhabited by a Jewish tribe called Banû Nadîr. It was conquered by the Muslims in 5 H.
Khalifah	:	(الخليفة) (Plural: *Khulafâ'* الخلفاء) Caliph. a successor, an Islamic term used for the first four rulers after the death of the Prophet صلى الله عليه وسلم.

Khalîl	:	(الخليل) The one whose love is mixed with one's heart and it is superior to a friend or beloved. The Prophet صلى الله عليه وسلم had only one *Khalîl*, i.e. Allâh, but he had many friends.
Khamr	:	(الخمر) Wine, Alcohol, intoxicant etc.
Khamîsah	:	(الخميصة) A black woollen square blanket with marks on it.
Khandaq	:	(الخندق) See *Ghazwat-ul-Khandaq.*
Kharâj	:	(الخراج) *Zakât* imposed on the yield of the land ($^1/_{10}$th or $^1/_{20}$th).
Khasuf	:	(الخسوف) Lunar eclipse.
Khawârij	:	(الخوارج) The people who dissented from the religion and disagreed with the rest of the Muslims.
Khazîr or *Khazîrah*	:	(الخزير، الخزيرة) A special type of dish prepared from barley-flour, meat-soup, fat etc.
Khilafah	:	(الخلافة) (i) Succession. (ii) Islamic leadership.
Khimâr	:	(الخمار) A piece of cloth with which a woman covers her head and neck area.
Khuff	:	(الخف) Leather socks.
Khul'	:	(الخلع) A kind of divorce in which a wife seeks divorce from her husband by giving him a certain compensation, or returning back the *Mahr* which he gave her.
Khumrah	:	(خمرة) A small mat just sufficient for the face and the hands [on prostrating during *Salât* (prayers)].
Khumus	:	(الخمس) One-fifth of war booty given in Allâh's Cause etc. (The Qur'ân, V.8:41).
Khushû'	:	(الخشوع) Humility before Allâh.
Khutbah	:	(الخطبة) Religious talk (sermon).
Khutbat-un-Nikâh	:	(خطبة النكاح) A speech delivered at the time of concluding the marriage contract.
Khuzâ'ah	:	(الخزاعة) Banu Khuzâ'ah, an Arabian tribe.
Kohl	:	(الكحل) Antimony eye powder.
Kûfah	:	(الكوفة) A town in 'Irâq.
Kufr	:	(الكفر) It is basically disbelief in any of the articles of Islâmic Faith and they are: to believe in Allâh (God), His angels, His Messengers, His revealed Books, the Day of Resurrection, and *Al-Qadar* (i.e. Divine Preordainments whatever Allâh has ordained must come to pass).
Kunyah	:	(الكنية) Calling a man, 'O father of so-and-so!' or calling a woman, 'O mother of so-and-so!' This is a custom of the Arabs.

Kusûf	:	(الكسوف) Solar eclipse.
Labbaika wa sa'daika	:	(لبيك وسعديك) I respond to your call and I am obedient to your orders.
Lâ ilâha illallâh	:	(لا إله إلا الله) None has the right to be worshipped but Allâh.
Lailat-ul-Qadr	:	(ليلة القدر) One of the odd last ten nights of the month of Saum (fasting) (i.e. Ramadân), Allâh تعالى describes it as better than one thousand months, and the one who worships Allâh during it by performing optional prayers and reciting the Noble Qur'ân, etc. will get a reward better than that of worshipping Him for one thousand months (i.e. 83 years and four months).[See the Qur'ân Sûrat 97 (VV.97: 1-5)]. (See Sahih Al-Bukhâri, Vol. 3, Hadîth No. 231 and Chapter No.2).
Lât & Uzza	:	(اللات والعزى) Well-known idols in Hijâz which used to be worshipped during the Pre-Islâmic Period of Ignorance.
Li'ân	:	(اللعان) An oath which is taken by both the wife and the husband when the husband accuses his wife of committing illegal sexual intercourse. (The Qur'ân, Sûrat Nûr,24 :6,7,8,9,).
Luqatah	:	(اللقطة) Article or a thing (a pouch or a purse tied with a string) found by somebody other than the owner who has lost it.
Ma'âfiri	:	(معافري) A type of garment of Yemen origin.
Al-Madînah	:	(المدينة) Well-known city in Saudi Arabia, where the Prophet's mosque is situated. It was formerly called Yathrib.
Maghâfir	:	(المغافير) A bad smelling gum.
Al-Maghâzi	:	(المغازي) Plural of Maghza, i.e. holy battle; or the place where the battle took place; or the deeds and virtues of Ghâzi (fighters in Allâh's Cause)
Maghrib	:	(المغرب) Sunset, evening Salât (prayer).
Mahr	:	(المهر) Bridal money given by the husband to the wife at the time of marriage.
Mahram	:	(المحرم) See Dhu-Mahram.
Makrûh	:	(المكروه) Not approved of, undesirable from the point of view of religion, although not punishable.
Mamlûk	:	(المملوك) A male slave.
Al-Manâsî'	:	(المناصع) A vast plateau on the outskirts of Al-Madînah.
Manâsik Al-Hajj	:	(مناسك الحج والعمرة) Acts connected with Hajj like Ihrâm; Tawâf of the Ka'bah and Sa'y of As-Safa and

wal-'Umrah		Al-Marwah; stay at 'Arafat, Muzdalifah and Mina; *Ramy* (throwing pebbles) of *Jamarât*; slaughtering of *Hady* (animal) etc. For details, see The Book of *Hajj* and *'Umrah, Sahih Al-Bukhâri*, Vol.2-3.
Manîhah	:	(المنيحة Plural:*Manâ'ih* المنائح) A sort of gift in the form of a she-camel or a sheep which is given to somebody temporarily so that its milk may be used and then the animal is returned to its owner.
Maqâm Ibrâhîm	:	(مقام إبراهيم) The stone on which Ibrâhîm (Abraham) عليه السلام stood while he and Ismâ'îl (Ishmael) عليه السلام were building the Ka'bah.
Maqâm Mahmûd	:	(المقام المحمود) The highest place in Paradise, which will be granted to Prophet Muhammad صلى الله عليه وسلم and none else. (See *Hadîth* No. 242, Vol.6, *Sahih Al-Bukhâri*).
Al-Marwah	:	(المروة) A mountain in Makkah, neighbouring the sacred mosque (i.e. *Al-Masjid-al-Harâm*).
Mâ shâ' Allâh	:	(ما شاء الله) An Arabic expression meaning literally, "What Allâh wills," and it indicates a good omen.
Al-Mash'ar-al-Harâm	:	(المشعر الحرام) A sacred place at *Muzdalifah*.
Al-Masîh-ad-Dajjâl	:	(المسيح الدجال) Pseudo Messiah or Antichrist (see the footnote of V.6:158 the *Qur'ân* and also *Hadîth* No.649 and 650, Vol.4, *Sahih Al-Bukhâri*).
Al-Masjid-al-Aqsa	:	(المسجد الأقصى) The most sacred mosque in Jerusalem.
Al-Masjid-al-Harâm	:	(المسجد الحرام) The most sacred mosque in Makkah. The Ka'bah is situated in it.
Mathânî	:	(المثاني) Oft repeated Verses of the *Qur'ân*, and that is *Sûrat Al-Fâtihah*, recited repeatedly in the *Salât* (prayer).
Maulâ	:	(المولى) It has many meanings. Some are: a manumitted slave, or a patron, protector, supporter, or master of the *Rabb* [Lord (Allâh)].
Maulâya	:	(مولاي) My lord, my master (an expression used when a slave addresses his master) (also used for freed slave).
Mauqûdhah	:	(الموقوذة) An animal beaten to death with a stick, a stone or the like without proper slaughtering.
Mawâlî	:	(الموالي) Non-Arabs and originally former slaves.
Mayâthir	:	(الميائر) Silk cushions.
Mihjan	:	(المحجن) A walking stick with a bent handle.

Mijanna	:	(المجن) A place at Makkah.
Mina	:	(منى) A pilgrimage place outside Makkah on the road to 'Arafât. It is eight kilometers away from Makkah and about sixteen kilometers from 'Arafât.
Mîqât	:	(الميقات) (Plural: *Mawâqît* المواقيت) One of the several places specified by the Prophet صلى الله عليه وسلم for the people to assume *Ihrâm* at, on their way to Makkah, when intending to perform *Hajj* or 'Umrah.
Mi'râj	:	(المعراج) The Ascent of the Prophet صلى الله عليه وسلم to the heavens (by soul and body). (See *Hadîth* No. 345, Vol. 1, *Hadîth* No. 429, Vol.4 and *Hadîth* No.227, Vol 5, *Sahih Al-Bukhâri*). [Also see (V.53:12) the Qur'ân]
Miswâk	:	(السواك) A tooth brush made of *Arâk*-tree roots.
Mithqâl	:	(المثقال) A special kind of weight (equals 4⅓ grams approx., used for weighing gold). It may be less or more. [20 *Mithqâl* = 94 grams approx.]
Mu'adhdhin	:	(المؤذن) A call-maker who pronounces the *Adhân* loudly calling people to come and perform the *Salât* (prayer).
Mu'allafat-ul-Qulûb	:	(مؤلفة القلوب) New Muslims who were given *Sadaqah* by the Prophet صلى الله عليه وسلم to keep them firm in the fold of Islam.
Mu'arras	:	(المعرس) A place nearer to Mina than Ash-Shajarah.
Mu'awwidhât	:	(المعوذات) i.e. *Sûrat Al-Falaq* (113) and *Sûrat An-Nâs* (114). [The Qur'ân].
Mubashshirât	:	(المبشرات) Glad tidings. [See the footnote of (V. 10:64). *Sahih Al-Bukhâri*, Vol. 9, *Hadîth* No. 119].
Mûbiqât	:	(الموبقات) Great destructive sins.
Mudabbar	:	(المدبر) A slave who is promised by his master to be manumitted after the latter's death.
Mudd	:	(المد) A measure of two-thirds of a kilogram (approx.) It may be less or more.
Mufassal or *Mufassalât*	:	(المفصل، المفصلات) The *Sûrah* starting from *Qâf* to the end of the Noble Qur'ân (i.e. from No. 50 to the end of the Qur'ân, No. 114).
Muhâjir	:	(المهاجر) Anyone of the early Muslims who had migrated from any place to Al-Madînah in the lifetime of the Prophet صلى الله عليه وسلم before the conquest of Makkah and also the one who emigrates for the sake of Allâh and Islâm and also the one who quits all those things which Allâh has forbidden.

Muhâqala : (المحاقلة) It is selling un-harvested grain in the field with an already harvested grain like wheat.

Muharram : (المحرم) The first month of the Islâmic calendar.

Al-Muhassab : (المحصب) A valley outside Makkah sometimes called Khaif Banî Kinanah.

Muhkam : (المحكم) Qur'ânic Verses the contents of which are not abrogated.

Muhrim : (المحرم) One who assumes the state of *Ihrâm* for the purpose of performing the *Hajj* or *'Umrah*.

Muhrimah : (المحرمة) A female in the state of *Ihrâm*.

Muhsar : (المحصر) A *Muhrim* who intends to perform the *Hajj* or *'Umrah* but cannot because of some obstacle.

Mujâhid : (المجاهد) (Plural: *Mujâhidûn*) A Muslim fighter in *Jihâd*.

Mujazziz : (المجزز) A *Qâ'if* : a learned man who reads the foot and hand marks.

Mujtahidûn : (المجتهدون) Independent religious scholars who do not follow religious opinions except with proof from the Qur'ân and the Prophet's *Sunnah*.

Mukâtab : (المكاتب) A slave (male or female) who makes an agreement with the master to pay a certain ransom for his (or her) freedom.

Mukhadram : (المخضرم) (Plural: *Mukhadramun*) A person who became a Muslim during the Prophet's lifetime but did not see him.

Mulâ'anah : (الملاعنة) The act of performing *Li'ân*.

Mulhidûn : (الملحدون) Heretics.

Musalla : (المصلى) A praying place.

Mushrikûn : (المشركون) Polytheists, pagans, idolaters and disbelievers in the Oneness of Allâh and His Messenger Muhammad صلى الله عليه وسلم.

Mustahadah : (المستحاضة) A woman who has bleeding from the womb in between her normal periods.

Mutafahhish : (المتفحش) A person who conveys evil talk.

Mut'ah : (المتعة) A temporary marriage which was allowed in the early period of Islâm when one was away from his home, but later on it was cancelled (abrogated).

Mu'takif : (المعتكف) One who is in a state of *I'tikâf*.

Mutashâbihât : (المتشابهات) Qur'ânic Verses which are not clear and are difficult to understand.

Mutras : (مترس) A Persian word meaning "don't be afraid."

| Muttafaq 'Alaih | : | (متفق عليه) Meaning 'Agreed upon'. The term is used for such *Ahadith* which are found in both the collection of *Ahadith*: *Bukhari* and *Muslim*. |

| Muttaqûn | : | (المتقون) Pious and righteous persons who fear Allâh much (abstain from all kinds of sins and evil deeds which He has forbidden) and love Allâh much (perform all kinds of good deeds which He has ordained). |

| Muwatta' | : | (الموطأ) A *Hadîth* book compiled by Imâm Mâlik bin Anas, one of the four *Fiqh Imâm*. |

| Muzaffat | : | (المزفت) A name of a pot in which alcoholic drinks used to be prepared. |

| Muzâra'ah | : | (المزارعة) *Al-Muzâra'ah* means to give the land for cultivation to someone and divide the produce. The Prophet صلى الله عليه وسلم did not stop or prevent from this, however when land was less and *Ansâr* and *Muhâjirîn* were more in number, he ordered as a measure of expediency to cultivate the land as much as one can, and not to give the rest of the land on produce-share basis or *Muzâra'ah*, but to give the land on *Ijârah* or on rent, because *Ijrârah* provided some ease to the tenants. Afterwards when land was enough for all, this restriction was lifted. |

| Muzdalifah | : | (المزدلفة) A place between 'Arafât and Mina where the pilgrims while returning from 'Arafât, have to stop and stay for the whole night or greater part of it (the night), between the ninth and tenth of Dhul-Hijjah and to perform the *Maghrib* and *'Ishâ'* prayers (together) there. |

| Nabîdh | : | (النبيذ) Water in which dates or grapes etc. are soaked and is not yet fermented. |

| An-Najâshi | : | (النجاشي) (Title for the) king of Ethiopia (Abyssinia) — Negus. |

| An-Najsh | : | (النجش) A trick (of offering a very high price) for something without the intention of buying it but just to allure and cheat somebody else who really wants to buy it although it is not worth such a high price. |

| An-Najwa | : | (النجوى) The private talk between Allâh and each of His slaves on the Day of Resurrection. It also means a secret counsel or conference or consultation. [See the Qur'ân (VV.58: 7-13), and also see the footnote of (V.11:18)].(See *Sahîh Al-Bukhâri*, Vol.3, *Hadîth* No. 621). |

| Namîmah | : | (النميمة) (Calumnies) conveyance of disagreeable false |

information from one person to another to create hostility between them.

Naqîb	:	(النقيب) A person heading a group of six persons in an expedition; a tribal chief.
Nash	:	(النش) A measure of weight equal to ½ *Uqiyah* (64 grams approximately).
Nawâfil	:	(النوافل) (Plural of *Nâfila*) Optional practice of worship in contrast to obligatory (*Farîdah*).
Nikâh	:	(النكاح) Marriage (wedlock) according to Islâmic law.
Nisâb	:	(النصاب) Minimum amount of property liable to payment of the *Zakât* e.g. *Nisâb* of gold is twenty (20) *Mithqâl* i.e. approx. 94 grams; *Nisâb* of silver is two hundred (200) dirhams, i.e. approx. 640 grams; *Nisâb* of food-grains and fruit is 5 *Awsuq* i.e. 673.5 kgms. *Nisâb* of camels is 5 camels; *Nisâb* of cows is 5 cows; and *Nisâb* of sheep is 40 sheep, etc.
Nûn	:	(نون) Fish.
Nusub	:	(النصب) (Singular of *Ansâb*) *An-Nusub* were stone alters at fixed places or graves, etc., whereon sacrifices were slaughtered during fixed periods of occasions and seasons in the name of idols, jinns, angels, pious men, saints, etc., in order to honour them, or to expect some benefit from them.
Nusuk	:	(النسك) Religious act of worship.
Qadar	:	(القدر) Divine Preordainment.
Qadi	:	(القاضي) A Muslim judge.
Qalîb	:	(القليب) A well.
Qâri'	:	(القارئ) Early Muslim religious scholars were called *Qurrâ'* (plural of *Qâri'* — this word is also used for a person who knows the Qur'ân by heart). The plural is *Qurrâ'*. The *Qurrâ'* were teachers of the early Muslims.
Qârin	:	(القارن) One who performs *Hajj-al-Qirân*.
Qarn-al-Manâzil	:	(قرن المنازل) The *Mîqât* of the people of Najd. It is situated on the way to Makkah. (Now it is known as As-Sail-al-Kabeer)
Qasab	:	(القصب) Pipes made of gold, pearls and other precious stones.
Qatîfa	:	(القطيفة) Thick soft cloth.
Quttât	:	(القتات) A person who conveys information from someone to another with the intention of causing harm and enmity between them. (*Sahîh Al-Bukhâri*, Vol. 8, *Hadîth* No.82).

Qiblah	:	(القبلة) The direction towards all Muslims face in *Salât* (prayers) and that direction is towards the Ka'bah in Makkah (Saudi Arabia).
Qîl wa Qâl	:	(قيل وقال) Sinful, useless talk (e.g. backbiting, lies, etc.).
Qintâr	:	(القنطار) A weight-measure for food-grains, etc., e.g. wheat, maize, oat, barley.
Qîrât	:	(القيراط) A special weight; sometimes a very great weight like Uhud mountain. 1 *Qîrat* = ½ *Dâniq* & 1 *Dâniq* = ⅙ Dirham.
Al-Qisâs	:	(القصاص) Laws of equality in punishment for wounds etc. in retaliation.
Qissî	:	(القسّي) A kind of cloth containing silk; some say it is called so because it is manufactured in Egypt at a place called *Qiss*.
Qithâm	:	(القثام) A plant disease which causes fruit to fall before ripening.
Qiyâm	:	(القيام) The standing posture in *Salât* (prayer).
Qiyâs	:	(القياس) Verdicts and judgements given by the Islâmic religious scholars. These are given on the following proofs respectively:- (A) From the Qur'ân; (B) From the Prophet's *Sunnah*. (C) From the unanimously accepted verdict of the *Mujtahidûn*; (D) *Qiyâs*: i.e. the verdict given by a *Mujtahid* who considered the case similar in comparison with a case judged by the Prophet صلى الله عليه وسلم. *Qiyâs* is not to be practised except if the judgement of the case is not found in the first three above mentioned proofs, A, B and C.
Qubâ'	:	(القباء) A place on the outskirts of Al-Madînah. The Prophet صلى الله عليه وسلم established a mosque there, which bears the same name. A visit to that mosque on Saturday forenoon and offering a two *Rak'ah Salât* (prayer) is regarded as a performance of *'Umrah* in reward according to the Prophet's saying.
Qumqum	:	(قمقم) A narrow - headed vessel.
Qunût	:	(القنوت) An invocation in the *Salât* (prayer).
Quraish	:	(القريش) One of the greatest tribes in Arabia in the Pre-Islâmic Period of Ignorance. Prophet Muhammad صلى الله عليه وسلم belonged to this tribe, which had great powers spiritually and financially both before and after Islâm came.
Quraishi	:	(القريشي) A person belonging to the Quraish (well-known Arab) tribe.

Rabb	:	(الرب) There is no proper equivalent for *Rabb* in English language. It means the One and the Only Lord for all the universe, its Creator, Owner, Organizer, Provider, Master, Planner, Sustainer, Cherisher, and Giver of security. *Rabb* is also one of the Names of Allâh. We have used the word "Lord" as nearest to *Rabb*. All occurances of "Lord" actually mean *Rabb* and should be understood as such..
Rabbuka	:	(ربك) Your Lord, Your Master.
Rabî'-ul-Awwal	:	(ربيع الأول) Third month of the Islâmic calendar.
Râhilah	:	(الراحلة) A she-camel used for riding. (Literally means: a mount to ride).
Rahn	:	(الرهن) According to *Shari'ah*, *Ar-Rahn* (mortgage) means to give some property or belonging to a creditor as a security for payment of a loan or debt.
Raiyyân	:	(الريان) The name of one of the gates of Paradise through which the people who often observe *Saum* (fasts) will enter.
Rajab	:	(رجب) The seventh month of the Islâmic calendar.
Ar-Raj'ah	:	(الرجعة) The bringing back of a wife by the husband after the first or second divorce.
Rajaz	:	(الرجز) Name of poetic metre.
Ar-Rajm	:	(الرجم) To stone to death those married persons who commit the crime of illegal sexual intercourse.
Rak'ah	:	(الركعة) The *Salât* (prayer) of Muslims consists of *Rak'ât* (singular-*Rak'ah*, which is a unit of prayer and consists of one standing, one bowing and two prostrations.
Ramadân	:	(رمضان) The month of observing *Saum* (fasts). It is the ninth month of the Islamic calendar. In it the Noble Qur'ân started to be revealed to our Prophet صلى الله عليه وسلم and in it occurs the night of *Qadr* and in it also occurred the great decisive battle of Badr.
Ramal	:	(الرمل) Fast walking accompanied by the movements of the arms and legs to show one's physical strength. This is to be observed in the first three rounds of the *Tawâf* around the Ka'bah, and is to be done by the men only and not by the women.
Ramy	:	(الرمي) The throwing of pebbles at the *Jimar* at Mina.
Riba	:	(الربا) Usury, which is of two major kinds: (a) *Riba Nasî'ah*, i.e. interest on, lent money; (b) *Riba Fadl*, i.e.

taking a superior thing of the same kind of goods by giving more of the same kind of goods of inferior quality, e.g., dates of superior quality for dates of inferior quality in greater amount. Islâm strictly forbids all kinds of usury.

Ridâ' : (الرداء) A piece of cloth (sheet etc.) worn around the upper part of the body.

Rikâz : (الركاز) Buried wealth.

Rûh-ullah : (روح الله) According to the early religious scholars from among the Companions of the Prophet صلى الله عليه وسلم and their students and the *Mujtahidûn*, there is a rule to distinguish between the two nouns in the genitive construction:

(A) When one of the two nouns is Allâh, and the other is a person or a thing, e.g., (i) Allâh's House (*Bait-ullah* بيت الله), (ii) Allâh's Messenger; (iii) Allâh's slave ('*Abdullah* عبدالله); (iv) Allâh's spirit (*Rûh-ullah* روح الله) etc.

The rule of the above words is that the second noun, e.g., House, Messenger, slave, spirit, etc. is created by Allâh and is honourable with Him and similarly Allâh's spirit may be understood as the spirit of Allâh, in fact, it is a soul created by Allâh, i.e. 'Îsâ (Jesus), and it was His Word: "Be!" — and he was created (like the creation of Adam).

(B) But when one of the two is Allâh and the second is neither a person nor a thing, then it is not a created thing but is a quality of Allâh, e.g., (i) Allâh's Knowledge ('*Ilmullâh* علم الله); (ii) Allâh's Life (*Hayatullâh* حياة الله); (iii) Allâh's Statement (*Kalâmullâh* كلام الله); (iv) Allâh's Self (*Dhâtullâh* ذات الله)etc.

Ruqba : (رقبى) It is the house which is gifted to someone for lifetime only to live at, and not as a belonging.

Ar-Ruqyah : (الرقية) Divine Speech recited as a means of curing disease. (It is a kind of treatment, i.e. to recite *Sûrat Al-Fâtihah* or any other *Sûrah* of the Qur'ân and then blow one's breath with saliva over a sick person's body-part).

Sâ' : (الصاع) A measure that equals four *Mudd* (3 kg. approx.)

As-Saba : (الصبا) Easterly wind.

Sab'a-al-Mathânî : (سبع المثاني) The seven repeatedly recited Verses i.e. *Sûrat Al-Fâtihah*.[See the Noble Qur'ân (V.15:87)].

As-Sab'ah : (السبعة) The seven compilers of *Ahadith* — Bukhari, Muslim, Abû Dâwûd, Nasâ'i, Tirmidhi, Ibn Mâjah and Ahmad.

Sabâhâh	:	(صباحاه) An exclamation indicating an appeal for help.
Sâbi'ûn	:	(الصابئون) A people who lived in Iraq and used to say *Lâ ilâha illallâh* (none has the right to be worshipped but Allâh) and used to read *Az-Zabûr* (the Psalms of the *Sâbi'ûn*) and they were neither Jews nor Christians.
Sa'dân	:	(السعدان) A thorny plant suitable for grazing animals.
Sadaqah	:	(الصدقة) Anything given in charity.
Safa and Marwah	:	(الصفا والمروة) Two mountains at Makkah neighbouring *Al-Masjid-al-Harâm* (the sacred mosque) to the east. One who performs '*Umrah* and *Hajj* should walk seven times between these two mountains and that is called *Sa'y*.
Sahbâ'	:	(صهباء) A place near Khaibar.
Sahihain	:	(الصحيحين) The two *Hadîth* books of Imam Bukhari and Muslim.
Sahûr	:	(السحور) A meal taken at night before the *Fajr* (morning) prayer by a person observing *Saum* (fast).
Sahw	:	(السهو) Forgetting (here it means forgetting how many *Rak'at* a person has prayed in which case he should perform two prostrations of *Sahw*).
As-Sâ'ibah	:	(السائبة) A she-camel which used to be let loose for free pastures in the name of idols, gods, and false deities. (See the Noble Qur'ân V.5:103).
Sakînah	:	(السكينة) Tranquillity, calmness, peace and reassurance etc.
Salab	:	(السلب) Belongings (arms, horse, etc.) of a deceased warrior killed in a battle.
As-Salât	:	(الصلاة) See *Iqâmat-as-Salât*.
Sami Allâhu liman hamidah	:	(سمع الله لمن حمده) Allâh hears him who praises Him.
Samur	:	(السمر) A kind of tree.
Sarif	:	(سرف) A place about ten kilometers away from Makkah.
Sarîyah	:	(السرية) A small army-unit sent by the Prophet صلى الله عليه وسلم for *Jihâd*, without his participation in it.
As-Saum	:	(الصوم) The fasting i.e., not to eat or drink or have sexual relations etc. from before the *Adhân* of the *Fajr* (early morning) prayer till the sunset.
Sawîq	:	(السويق) A kind of mash made of powdered roasted wheat or barley grain (also with sugar and dates).
Sa'y	:	(السعي) The going for seven times between the mountains of As-Safâ and Al-Marwah in Makkah during the performance of *Hajj* and '*Umrah*.

Sha`bân	:	(شعبان) The eighth month of the Islâmic calendar.
Ash-Shahâdah	:	(الشهادة) (i) Testimony of Faith. (ii) "None has the right to be worshipped but Allâh, and Muhammad صلى الله عليه وسلم is the Messenger of Allâh."
Shâm	:	(الشام) The region comprising Syria, Palestine, Lebanon and Jordan.
Shawwâl	:	(شوال) The tenth month of the Islâmic calendar.
Shighâr	:	(الشغار) A type of marriage in which persons exchange their daughters or sisters in marriage without *Mahr*.
Ash-Shiqâq	:	(الشقاق) Difference between husband and wife or any two persons.
Shirk	:	(الشرك) Polytheism and it is to worship others along with Allâh.
Shuf`ah	:	(الشفعة) Pre-emption.
Siddîq and *Siddîqûn*	:	(الصديق والصديقون) Those followers of the Prophets who were first and foremost to believe in them (See the Qur`ân, V.4:69).
Sidr	:	(السدر) Lote tree (or *Nibk* tree).
Sidrat-ul-Muntaha	:	(سدرة المنتهى) A *Nabk* tree over the seventh heaven near the Paradise (the lote tree of the utmost boundary)
Siffîn (battle of)	:	(صفين) A battle that took place at Siffin between `Alî's followers and Mu`âwiyah's followers after the killing of `Uthmân رضى الله عنه.
As-Sihah *As-Sittah*	:	(الصحاح الستة) The six books of *Ahadith*: Compiled by Bukhari, Muslim, Abû Dâwûd, Nasâ`i, Tirmldhi and Ibn Mâjah.
As-Sirât	:	(الصراط) *Sirât* originally means 'a road'; it also means the bridge that will be laid across Hell-fire for the people to pass over on the Day of Judgement. It is described as sharper than a sword and thinner than a hair. It will have hooks over it to snatch the people.
As-Sittah	:	(الستة) The six compilers of *Ahadith* — Bukhari, Muslim, Abû Dâwûd, Nasâ`i, Tirmidhi, Ibn Mâjah; and their six collections are called *Sihah Sittah*.
Siwâk	:	(السواك) A piece of a root of a tree called *Al-Arâk*, used as a toothbrush.
Subhân Allâh	:	(سبحان الله) Glorified is Allâh.
Sundus	:	(السندس) A kind of silk cloth.
Sunnah	:	(السنة) The legal way or ways, orders, acts of worship and statements of the Prophet صلى الله عليه وسلم, that have become models to be followed by the Muslims.

Sutrah	:	(السترة) An object like a pillar, wall or stick, a spear etc., the height of which should not be less than a foot and it should be in front of a person offering *Salât* (prayer) to act as a symbolical barrier between him and the others.
Tâbah	:	(الطابة) Another name for Al-Madînah Al-Munawwarah.
Tâbi'i	:	One who has met or accompanied any Companion of the Prophet ﷺ.
Tabûk	:	(تبوك) A well-known town about 700 kilometers north of Al-Madînah.
Tâghût	:	(الطاغوت) The word *Tâghût* covers a wide range of meanings: it means anything worshipped other than the Real God (Allâh), i.e. all the false deities. It may be Satan, devils, idols, stones, sun, stars, angels, human beings e.g. Messengers of Allâh, who were falsely worshipped and taken as *Tâghût*. Likewise saints, graves, rulers, leaders, are falsely worshipped, and wrongly followed. [See *Tafsir Ibn Kathir*, Vol. 1, page 512; and (V.2:51)].
Tahajjud	:	(التهجد) Night optional prayer offered at any time after *'Ishâ'* prayer and before the *Fajr* prayer.
Tahnîk	:	(التحنيك) It is the Islâmic customary process of chewing a piece of date etc.and putting a part of its juice in the child's mouth and pronouncing *Adhân* in child's ears, etc. (See *Sahîh Al-Bukhâri*, the Book of *'Aqîqah*, Vol. 7, Page No. 272).
Taiba	:	(الطيبة) One of the names of Al-Madînah city.
Tâ'if	:	(الطائف) A well-known town near Makkah.
Takbîr	:	(التكبير) Saying *Allâhu-Akbar* (Allâh is the Most Great).
Takbîrah	:	(التكبيرة) A single utterance of *Allâhu-Akbar*
Talbînah	:	(التلبينة) A dish prepared from flour and honey.
Talbiyah	:	(التلبية) Saying *Labbaik, Allâhumma Labbaik* (O Allâh! I am obedient to Your Orders, I respond to Your Call).
At-Tan'îm	:	(التنعيم) A place towards the north of Makkah outside the sanctuary from where Makkans may assume the state of *Ihrâm* to perform *'Umrah*.
Taqlîd	:	(التقليد) Putting coloured garlands around the necks of *Budn* (animals for sacrifice).
Tarâwîh	:	(التراويح) Optional *Salât* (prayers) offered after the *'Ishâ'* prayers on the nights of Ramadân. These may be performed individually or in congregation.

Tarji'	:	(الترجيع) Repetition of the words of the *Adhân* twice by the *Mu'adhdhin* (call-maker).
Tashahhud	:	(التشهد) The recitation of the invocation: *At-tahiyâtu lillâhi*... (up to) ... *wa ash-hadu anna Muhammadan Rasûl-ullâh*", while in *Qu'ûd*, i.e. sitting posture in *Salât* (prayer). [See *Sahîh Al-Bukhâri*, Vol. 1, *Hadith* No. 794, and it also means: to testify *Lâ ilâha illallâh Muhammadun Rusûl Allâh* (none has the right to be worshipped but Allâh and Muhammad is the Messenger of Allâh).
Taslîm	:	(التسليم) On finishing the *Salât* (prayer), one turns one's face to the right and then to the left saying, *Assalamu 'Alaikum wa Rahmatullâh* (Peace and Mercy of Allâh be on you), and this action is called *Taslîm*.
Tauhîd (Islâmic Monotheism)	:	(التوحيد) *Tauhid* means declaring Allâh to be the only God. It has three aspects:

(A) Oneness of the Lordship of Allâh; *Tauhîd-ar-Rubûbiyyah*: To believe that there is only one Lord for all the universe and He is its Creator, Organizer, Planner, Sustainer, and the Giver of security, and that is Allâh.

(B) Oneness of the worship of Allâh; *Tauhîd-al-Uluhiyyah*: To believe that none has the right to be worshipped [e.g. praying, invoking, asking for help (from the unseen), swearing, slaughtering sacrifices, giving charity, fasting, pilgrimage, etc.], but Allâh.

(C) Oneness of the Names and the Qualities of Allâh; *Tauhîd-al-Asmâ' was-Sifât*: To believe that : (i) we must not name or qualify Allâh except with what He or His Messenger صلى الله عليه وسلم has named or qualified Him; (ii) none can be named or qualified with the Names or Qualifications of Allâh; e.g. *Al-Karîm*; (iii) we must believe in all the qualities of Allâh which Allâh has stated in His Book (the Qur'ân) or mentioned through His Messenger (Muhammad صلى الله عليه وسلم) without changing their meaning or ignoring them completely or twisting the meanings or giving resemblance to any of the created things; e.g. Allâh is present over His Throne as mentioned in the Qur'ân. (V.20: 5): "The Most Gracious (i.e. Allâh) rose over (*Istawa*) the (Mighty) Throne" over the seventh heaven; and He comes down over the first (nearest) heaven (to us) during the day of 'Arafâh (*Hajj*, i.e. 9th Dhul-Hijjah) and also during the last third part of the night, as mentioned by the Prophet صلى الله عليه وسلم , but He is with us by His Knowledge, not by His Personal Self (*Bi-Dhâtihi*), "There is nothing like unto Him, and He is the All-Hearer, the All-Seer." (The Qur'ân, V. 42:11).

This Noble Verse proves the quality of hearing and the quality of sight for Allâh without likening it (or giving resemblance) to others; and likewise He also says: "To one whom I have created with Both My Hands," (V. 38:75); and He also says: "The Hand of Allâh is over their hands.": (V. 48:10, the Qur'ân). This confirms two Hands for Allâh, but there is no similarity for them.

This is the Faith of all true believers, and was the Faith of all the Prophets of Allâh from Nûh (Noah), Ibrâhîm (Abraham), Mûsa (Moses) and 'Îsâ (Jesus) till the last of the Prophets, Muhammad صلى الله عليه وسلم. It is not like as some people think that Allâh is present everywhere, here, there and even inside the breasts of men.

These three aspects of *Tauhîd* are included in the meanings of *Lâ ilâha ill-Allâh* (none has the right to be worshipped but Allâh).

It is also essential to follow Allâh's Messenger Muhammad صلى الله عليه وسلم: *Wajûb Al-Ittibâ'* and it is a part of *Tauhîd-al-Ulûhiyyah*. This is included in the meaning: "I testify that Muhammad صلى الله عليه وسلم is the Messenger of Allâh" and this means, "None has the right to be followed after Allâh's Book (the Qur'ân), but Allâh's Messenger صلى الله عليه وسلم ". [See the Qur'ân (V.59:7) and (V. 3:31)].

Tawâf	:	(الطواف) The circumambulation of the Ka'bah.
Tawâf-al-Ifâdah	:	(طواف الإفاضة) The circumambulation of the Ka'bah by the pilgrims after they come from Mina on the tenth day of Dhul-Hijjah. This *Tawâf* is one of the essential ceremonies (*Rukn*) of the Hajj.
Tawâf-ul-Wadâ'	:	(طواف الوداع) The *Tawâf* made before leaving Makkah after performing Hajj or '*Umrah*.
Tayammum	:	(التيمم) To put or strike lightly the hands over clean earth and then pass the palm of each on the back of the other, blow off the dust and then pass them on the face. This is performed instead of ablution (*Wudû'*) and *Ghusl* (in case of *Janaba*).
Ath-Thalathah:		(الثلاثة) The three compilers of *Ahadith* — Abû Dâwûd, Nasâ'I and Tirmidhi.

Thaniyat-al-Wadâ	:	(ثنية الوداع) A place near Al-Madînah.
Tharîd	:	(الثريد) A kind of meal, prepared from meat and bread.
Thaur	:	(الثور) A well-known mountain in Al-Madînah.
Tulaqâ'	:	(الطلقاء) Those persons who had embraced Islâm on the day of the conquest of Makkah.
Tûr	:	(الطور) A mountain.
Uhud	:	(أحد) A well-known mountain in Al-Madînah. One of the great battles in the Islâmic history took place at its foot. This battle is called Ghazwah Uhud.
'Umrah	:	(العمرة) A visit to Makkah during which one performs the Tawâf around the Ka'bah and the Sa'y between As-Safâ and Al-Marwah. It is also called 'lesser Hajj'. (See Sahih Al-Bukhâri, Vol. 3, Page 1).
'Urfut	:	(العرفط) The tree which produces Maghâfir.
'Ushr	:	(العشر) One-tenth of the yield of land to be levied for public assistance (Zakât). (See Sahîh Al-Bukhâri, Vol. 2, Hadîth No. 560).
Wahy	:	(الوحي) The Revelation or Inspiration of Allâh to His Prophets.
Waihaka	:	(ويحك) 'May Allâh be Merciful to you.'
Wailaka	:	(ويلك) 'Woe upon you!'
Walâ'	:	(الولاء) Al-Walâ is a right to inherit the property of a freed slave to the person who has freed him. Ahadîth has made it clear that Wâla' is a part like a lineage. It cannot be sold or gifted, so selling it or offering it as a gift is prohibited.
Walî	:	(الولي) (Plural Auliyâ') Protector, guardian, supporter, helper, friend.
Walîmah	:	(الوليمة) The marriage feast.
Waqf	:	(الوقف) Religious endowment.
Wars	:	(الورس) A kind of shrub used for colouring yellow.
Wasâyâ	:	(الوصايا) Wills or testaments. (Singular: Wasiyyah الوصية)
Al-Wâsil	:	(الواصل) One who keeps good relations with his kith and kin.
Wasilah	:	(الوسيلة) The means of approach or achieving closeness to Allâh by getting His favours.
Wasq	:	(الوسق) (Plural: Awsaq or Awsuq) A measure equal to 60 Sa = 135 kg. approx. It may be less or more.
Wisâl	:	(الوصال) Observing Saum (fast) for more than one day continuously.

Witr	:	(الوتر) An odd number of *Rak'at* with which one finishes one's *Salât* (prayers) at night after the night prayer or the *Ishâ* prayer.
Wudû'	:	(الوضوء) Ablution, which is washing the face and the hands up to the elbows, wiping the head and ears with wet fingers, and washing the feet up to ankles for the purpose of offering prayers or doing circumambulation round the Ka'bah.
Yalamlam	:	(يلملم) The *Mîqât* of the people of Yemen.
Yaqîn	:	(اليقين) Perfect absolute Faith.
Yarmûk	:	(اليرموك) A place in Shâm.
Yathrib	:	(يثرب) One of the names of Al-Madînah.
Yaum An-Nafr:		(يوم النفر) The 12th or 13th of Dhul-Hijjah when the pilgrims leave Mina after performing all the ceremonies of *Hajj* at 'Arafât, Al-Muzdalifah and Mina.
Yaum An-Nahr:		(يوم النحر) The day of slaughtering the sacrificial animals, i.e., the 10th of Dhul-Hijjah.
Yaum Ar-Ru'ûs:		(يوم الرؤوس) Meaning 'day of heads'. It is the name of the day following the *'Îd* day (*'Îd-al-Adha*).
Yaum At-Tarwiyah	:	(يوم التروية) The eighth day of the month of Dhul-Hijjah, when the pilgrims leave Makkah for Mina.
Zakât	:	(الزكاة) A certain fixed proportion of the wealth and of every kind of the property liable to *Zakât* of a Muslim to be paid yearly for the benefit of the poor in the Muslim community. The payment of *Zakât* is obligatory as it is one of the five pillars of Islâm. *Zakât* is the major economic means for establishing social justice and leading the Muslim society to prosperity and security..
Zakât-ul-Fitr	:	(زكاة الفطر) An obligatory *Sadaqa* to be given by Muslims before the prayer of *'Îd-ul-Fitr* (See *Sahîh Al-Bukhâri*, Vol. 2, The Book of *Zakât-al-Fitr*, Page No. 339).
Zamzam	:	(زمزم) The sacred well inside the *Haram* (the grand mosque) at Makkah.
Zanâdiqah	:	(الزنادقة) Atheists.
Zarnab	:	(زرنب) A kind of good smelling grass.
Az-Zihâr	:	(الظهار) One's telling to his wife, "You are unlawful to me for cohabitation like my mother."
Zuhr	:	(الظهر) Noon, mid-day *Salât* (prayer) is called *Zuhr* prayer.

APPENDIX II

TAUHID — (ISLAMIC MONOTHEISM)

Tauhîd (Islamic Monotheism) has three aspects:

(A) Oneness of the Lordship of Allâh; *Tauhîd-ar-Rubûbiyyah*: To believe that there is only one Lord for all the universe and He is, its Creator, Organizer, Planner, Sustainer, and the Giver of security, and that is Allâh.

(B) Oneness of the worship of Allâh; *Tauhîd-al-Ulûhiyyah*: To believe that none has the right to be worshipped [e.g. praying, invoking, asking for help (from the unseen), swearing, slaughtering sacrifices, giving charity, fasting, pilgrimage] but Allâh.

(C) Oneness of the Names and the Qualities of Allâh: *Tauhîd-al-Asmâ was-Sifât*: To believe that:

(i) We must not name or qualify Allâh except with what He or His Messenger صلى الله عليه وسلم has named or qualified Him;

(ii) None can be named or qualified with the Names or Qualifications of Allâh; e.g. *Al-Karîm*;

(iii) We must believe in all the Qualities of Allâh which Allâh has stated in His Book (the Qur'ân) or mentioned through His Messenger (Muhammad صلى الله عليه وسلم) without changing their meaning or ignoring them completely or twisting the meanings or giving resemblance to any of the created things [e.g. Allâh is present over His Throne as mentioned in the Qur'ân (V. 20:5):-

"The Most Gracious (Allâh) rose over (*Istawa*) the (Mighty) Throne (in a manner that suits His Majesty)," over the seventh heaven; and He comes down over the first (nearest) heaven to us during the last third part of every night and also on the day of 'Arafât (*Hajj*, i.e. the 9th of Dhul-Hijja), as mentioned by the Prophet صلى الله عليه وسلم , but He is with us by His Knowledge, not by His Personal-Self (*Bi-Dhâtihi*).

Also Allâh says:

"There is nothing like unto Him and He is the All-Hearer, the All-Seer" (V.42:11).

This holy Verse proves the quality of hearing and the quality of sight for Allâh without likening it (or giving resemblance) to any of the created things, and likewise He عز وجل also says:

"To one whom I have created with Both My Hands," (V.38:75);

and He also says:

"The Hand of Allâh is over their hands." (V.48:10).

This confirms two Hands for Allâh, but there is no similarity for them. This is the Faith of all true believers, and was the Faith of all the Prophets of Allâh, from Nûh (Noah), Ibrâhîm (Abraham), Mûsâ (Moses) and 'Isâ (Jesus) till the last of the Prophets, Muhammad صلى الله عليه وسلم. [It is not like as some people think that Allâh is present everywhere — here, there and even inside the breasts of men].

These three aspects of *Tauhîd* are included in the meaning of *Lâ ilâha illallâh* (none has the right to be worshipped but Allâh).

It is also essential to follow Allâh's Messenger, Muhammad صلى الله عليه وسلم : *Wajûb al-Ittibâ'* and it is a part of *Tauhîd-al-Ulûhiyyah.*

This is included in the meaning, "I testify that Muhammad صلى الله عليه وسلم is Allâh's Messenger," and this means, "None has the right to be followed after Allâh's Book (the Qur'ân), but Allâh's Messenger; صلى الله عليه وسلم".

Allâh says:

"And whatsoever the Messenger (Muhammad صلى الله عليه وسلم) gives you, take it, and whatsoever he forbids you, abstain (from it)." (V.59:7)

And also Allâh says:

"Say (O Muhammad صلى الله عليه وسلم to mankind), 'If you (really) love Allâh then follow me [i.e. accept Islâmic Monotheism, follow the Qur'ân and the *Sunnah* (legal ways of the Prophet صلى الله عليه وسلم)], Allâh will love you and forgive you of your sins.' " (V.3:31)

SHAHADAH — CONFESSION OF A MUSLIM

لاإله إلا الله محمد رسول الله

Lâ ilâha illallâh, Muhammad-ur-Rasûl-Allâh

(None has the right to be worshipped but Allâh,
and Muhammad صلى الله عليه وسلم is the Messenger of Allâh).

I have noticed that most of mankind, who embrace Islam, do not understand the reality of the meaning of the first fundamental principle of Islam, i.e. *Lâ ilâha illallâh, Muhammad-ur-Rasûl-Allâh* (none has the right to be worshipped but Allâh, and Muhammad صلى الله عليه وسلم is the Messenger of Allâh). So I consider it essential to explain something of the meanings of this great sentence (principle) in some detail:

لاإله إلا الله محمد رسول الله

Lâ ilâha illallâh, Muhammad-ur- Rasûl-Allâh

"None has the right to be worshipped but Allâh... and Muhammad صلى الله عليه وسلم is the Messenger of Allâh" has three aspects: A,B and C.

A. It is that, you have to pledge a covenant with (Allâh), the Creator of the heavens and earth, the Ruler of all that exists, the Lord of Majesty and Highness, on four points (or conditions):

Point I: A confession with your heart that the Creator (of everything) is Allâh, it is that you have to say: "I testify that the Creator of all the universe including the stars, the sun, the moon, the heavens, the earth with all its known and unknown forms of life, is Allâh. He is the Organizer and Planner of all its affairs. It is He Who gives life and death, and He (i.e. Allâh Alone) is the Sustainer, and the Giver of security." And this is called (your confession for the) "Oneness of the Lordship of Allâh," — *Tauhid-ar-Rubûbiyyah*.

Point II: A confession with your heart that you have to say: "I testify that none has the right to be worshipped but Allâh Alone." The word "Worship" (i.e. *'Ibadah*) carries a great number of meanings in the Arabic language: It conveys that all kinds of worship are meant for Allâh Alone [and none else, whether it be an angel, Messenger, Prophet 'Îsâ (Jesus) – son of Maryam (Mary),

'Uzair (Ezra), Muhammad, saint, idol, the sun, the moon and all other kinds of false deities]. So pray to none but Allâh, invoke none but Allâh, ask for help from none (unseen) but Allâh, swear by none but Allâh, offer an animal as sacrifice to none but Allâh,....etc, and that means, — all that Allâh and His Messenger Muhammad صلى الله عليه وسلم order you to do, (in the Qur'ân and in the *Sunnah* (legal ways of Prophet Muhammad صلى الله عليه وسلم) you must do, and all that Allâh and His Messenger صلى الله عليه وسلم forbid you, you must not do. And this is called (your confession for the) "Oneness of the worship of Allâh," — *Tauhid-al-Ulûhiyyah*. And that you (mankind) worship none but Allâh.

Point III: A confession with your heart that you have to say: "O Allâh! I testify that all the best of names and the most perfect qualities with which You have named or qualified Yourself in Your Book (i.e. the Qur'ân) or as Your Prophet Muhammad صلى الله عليه وسلم has named or qualified You, with his statement, I believe that all those (names and qualities) are for You without changing their meanings or neglecting them completely or likening them (giving resemblance) to others." As Allâh says:

"There is nothing like unto Him and He is the All-Hearer, the All-Seer." (V.42:11).

This holy Verse confirms the quality of hearing and the quality of sight for Allâh without likening them (giving resemblance) to others, and He also says:

"To one whom I have created with Both My Hands," (V.38:75)

and He also said:

"The Hand of Allâh is over their hands." (V.48:10)

This confirms two Hands for Allâh, but there is no similarity for them. Similarly Allâh says:

"The Most Gracious (Allâh) rose over (*Istawa*) the (Mighty) Throne." (V.20:5).

So He rose over the Throne really in a manner that suits His Majesty. And Allâh is over His Throne over the seventh heaven, as the slave-girl pointed towards the heavens, when Allâh's Messenger (Muhammad صلى الله عليه وسلم) asked her as to where Allâh is. He only comes down over the first (nearest) heaven to us during the last third part of every night and also on the day of 'Arafâh (*Hajj*, i.e. the 9th of Dhul-Hijjah), as mentioned by the Prophet صلى الله عليه وسلم, but He is with us by His Knowledge only, not by His Personal-Self (*Bi-Dhâtihi*). It is not like that, as some people say that Allâh is present everywhere — here, there, and even inside the breasts of men. He sees and hears all that we do or utter. And this is called (your confession for the) "Oneness of the Names and Qualities of Allâh" — *Tauhîd-al-Asmâ was-Sifât* and this is the right Faith, the Faith which was followed by the Messengers of Allâh [from Nûh (Noah), Ibrâhîm (Abraham), Mûsa (Moses), Dâwûd (David), Sulaimân (Solomon), 'Isâ (Jesus) to Muhammad عليهم الصلاة والسلام and the Companions of Prophet Muhammad صلى الله عليه وسلم] and the righteous followers of these Messengers عليهم السلام.

Point IV: A confession with your heart that you have to say: "O Allâh! I testify that Muhammad صلى الله عليه وسلم is Your Messenger." That means that none has the right to be followed after Allâh, but the Prophet Muhammad صلى الله عليه وسلم as he is the last of His Messengers. As Allâh says:

"Muhammad (صلى الله عليه وسلم) is not the father of any man among you, but he is the Messenger of Allâh and the last (end) of the Prophets. And Allâh is Ever All-Aware of everything." (V.33:40).

"And whatsoever the Messenger (Muhammad صلى الله عليه وسلم) gives you, take it, and whatsoever he forbids you, abstain from it,"(V.59:7).

And Allâh says:

"Say (O Muhammad صلى الله عليه وسلم to mankind): 'If you (really) love Allâh, then follow me i.e. accept Islamic Monotheism, follow the Qur'ân and the *Sunnah*.' " (V.3:31)

As for others than Muhammad صلى الله عليه وسلم, their statements are to be taken or rejected as to whether these are in accordance with Allâh's Book (i.e. the Qur'ân) or with the *Sunnah* (legal ways, orders, acts of worship, statements, etc.) of the Prophet صلى الله عليه وسلم or not. As the Divine Revelation has stopped after the death of Prophet Muhammad صلى الله عليه وسلم and it will not resume except at the time of the Descent of 'Isâ (Jesus) — son of Maryam (Mary) and he (i.e.

Jesus) will rule with justice according to the Islamic laws, during the last days of the world as it has been mentioned in the authentic *Hadîth* (i.e. narration of Prophet Muhammad صلى الله عليه وسلم). (*Sahih-Al-Bukhari*, Vol. 3, *Hadith* No. 425).

B. It is essential to utter: *Lâ ilâha illallâh, Muhammad-ur-Rasûl Allâh* (none has the right to be worshipped but Allâh, and Muhammad صلى الله عليه وسلم is the Messenger of Allâh.) As it has come in the statement of the Prophet Muhammad صلى الله عليه وسلم to his uncle Abû Tâlib at the time of the latter's death: "O uncle, if you utter it (*Lâ ilâh illallâh, Muhammad-ur-Rasûl Allâh*, none has the right to be worshipped but Allâh, and Muhammad صلى الله عليه وسلم is the Messenger of Allâh), then I shall be able to argue on your behalf before Allâh, on the Day of Resurrection." Similarly, when Abû Dharr Al-Ghifârî embraced Islam, he went to *Al-Masjid-al-Harâm* and he proclaimed it loudly in front of the Quraish infidels until he was beaten severely.

C. It is essential that the limbs and all the other parts and organs of one's body testify to it, and this is very important as regards its meaning (i.e., the meaning of *Lâ ilâha illallâh Muhammad Rasul Allâh* — none has the right to be worshipped but Allâh, and Muhammad صلى الله عليه وسلم is the Messenger of Allâh). So whoever has confessed this (with his Lord), he shall not commit sins like robbing, killing, stealing, illegal sexual intercourse, eating pig meat, drinking alcoholic beverages, taking undue advantage of orphan's property, cheating in trade, bribery and earning money through illegal means, telling lies, backbiting etc., or otherwise the limbs and all the other parts and organs of his body will testify against him that he was a liar in his words which he pledged to Allâh. In case he commits the above sins, he should know that it is a sin that obliges him to repent to Allâh, and ask His Forgiveness, as (his) body parts (i.e. skin, private parts, hands, tongue, ears, etc.)will testify to the above mentioned crimes (i.e. actions) against himself on the Day of Resurrection.

And with the confession of this great sentence (i.e. principle) a person enters in the fold of (i.e. embraces) the Islamic religion accordingly, it is essential for him to believe in all the Messengers of Allâh and not to differentiate between them. As it is mentioned in His Book, Allâh says:

"Do then those who disbelieve think that they can take My slaves [i.e. the angels; Allâh's Messengers; 'Îsâ (Jesus), son of Maryam (Mary), etc.] as *Auliyâ'* (lords, gods, protectors) besides Me? Verily, We have prepared Hell as an entertainment for the disbelievers (in the Oneness of Allâh — Islamic Monotheism).

"Say (O Muhammad صلى الله عليه وسلم): 'Shall We tell you the greatest losers in respect of (their) deeds?'

"Those whose efforts have been wasted in this life, while they thought they were acquiring good by their deeds!

"They are those who deny the *Ayât* (proofs, evidences, verses, lessons, signs, revelations, etc.) of their Lord and the Meeting with Him (in the Hereafter). So their works are in vain, and on the Day of Resurrection, We shall not give them any weight.

"That shall be their recompense, Hell; because they disbelieved and took My *Ayât* (proofs, evidences, verses, lessons, revelations, etc.) and My Messengers by way of jest and mockery.

"Verily! Those who believe (in the Oneness of Allâh — Islamic Monotheism), and do righteous deeds, shall have the Gardens of *Al-Firdaus* (Paradise) for their entertainment.

"Wherein they shall dwell (forever). No desire will they have to be removed therefrom.

"Say (O Muhammad صلى الله عليه وسلم to mankind): If the sea were ink for (writing) the Words of my Lord, surely the sea would be exhausted, before the Words of my Lord would be finished even if we brought (another sea) like it for its aid.

"Say (O Muhammad صلى الله عليه وسلم): I am only a man like you, it has been inspired to me that your *Ilâh* (God) is One *Ilâh* (God, — i.e. Allâh). So whoever hopes for the Meeting with his Lord, let him work righteousness and associate none as a partner in the worship of his Lord." (V. 18:102-110).

This introduction is necessary for anyone who wishes to embrace Islam. After this confession he (or she) should take a bath (i.e. *Ghusl*) and then offer a two *Rak'at* prayer, and act upon the five principles of Islam, as narrated by Ibn 'Umar رضي الله عنه, in the Book, *Sahih Al-Bukhari*, Vol.1 *Hadith* No.7:-

Narrated Ibn 'Umar رضي الله عنه : Allâh's Messenger صلى الله عليه وسلم said: Islam is based on the following five (principles):

1. To testify *Lâ ilâha illallâh wa anna Muhammad-ur-Rasul-Allâh* (none has the right to be worshipped but Allâh and that Muhammad is the Messenger of Allâh).
2. Perform (*Iqâmat*) *As-Salât*[1].
3. To pay *Zakât*[2].
4. To perform *Hajj*. (i.e. pilgrimage to Makkah).
5. To observe *Saum* (fast) during the month of Ramadân.
[and must believe in the six articles of Faith, i.e. to believe in:

(1) Allâh, (2) His angels, (3) His Messengers, (4) His revealed Books, (5) the Day of Resurrection, and (6) *Al-Qadar* (Divine Preordainments i.e. whatever Allâh has ordained must come to pass)]

IMPORTANT NOTE:

The acceptance of the righteous deeds depends on the following two basic conditions which must be fulfilled:

(1) The intentions while doing such deeds must be totally for Allâh's sake only without any show off or gaining praise or fame, etc.

(2) Such a deed must be performed in accordance with the *Sunna* (legal ways, orders, acts of worship, statements, etc.) of Allâh's Messenger Muhammad bin 'Abdullah, the last (end) of all the Prophets and the Messengers عليهم السلام .

---

[1] See the Glossary.

[2] See the Glossary.

Shirk and *Kufr*
POLYTHEISM AND DISBELIEF

Salvation of all mankind from the greatest sin against Allâh

I consider it essential to mention here some details of the greatest sin which will not be forgiven by Allâh. This unpardonable sin is *Shirk*

Shirk implies ascribing partners to Allâh or ascribing divine attributes to others besides Allâh and believing that the source of power, harm and blessings comes from another besides Allâh.

Almighty Allâh says:

"Verily, Allâh forgives not that partners should be set up with Him in worship, but He forgives except that (anything else) to whom He pleases; and whoever sets up partners to Allâh in worship, he has indeed invented a tremendous sin."(V. 4:48).

Almighty Allâh says:

"Then when the Trumpet is blown, there will be no kinship among them that Day, nor will they ask of one another.

"Then those whose scales (of good deeds) are heavy, — these! they are the successful.

"And those whose scales (of good deeds) are light, — they are those who lose their ownselves; in Hell will they abide."

"The Fire will burn their faces, and they will grin with displaced lips (disfigured)."

"(It will be said) 'Were not My Verses (this Qur'ân) recited to you and then you used to deny them?'

"They will say: 'Our Lord! Our wretchedness overcame us and we were (an) erring people.

"Our Lord! Bring us out of this; if ever we return (to evil) then indeed we shall be *Zâlimûn* (polytheists, oppressors, unjust, and wrongdoers etc.).'

"He (Allâh) will say: 'Remain you in it with ignominy! And speak you not to Me!' (V. 23:101-108).

"And whoever invokes (or worships) besides Allâh, any other *ilâh* (god), of whom he has no proof, then his reckoning is only with his Lord. Surely! *Al-Kâfirûn* (disbelievers in Allâh and in the Oneness of Allâh, polytheists, pagans, idolaters) will not be successful." (V. 23:117).

ASH-SHIRK
POLYTHEISM AND ITS VARIOUS MANIFESTATIONS

Definition: *Shirk* basically is polytheism, i.e., the worship of others along with Allâh. It also implies attributing divine attributes to any other besides Allâh. It particularly implies associating partners in worship with Allâh or to believe that the source of power, harm or blessings is from others besides Allâh.

Types: There are three types of *Shirk*, namely:

(1) *Ash-Shirk-al-Akbar*, i.e. major *Shirk*

(2) *Ash-Shirk-al-Asghar*, i.e. minor *Shirk*

(3) *Ash-Shirk-al-Khafi*, i.e. inconspicuous *Shirk*.

Manifestations: (1) *Ash-Shirk-al-Akbar* (The major *Shirk*): The major and serious polytheistic form, it has four aspects:

(a) *Shirk-ad-Du'â*, i.e. invocation. This aspect implies invoking, supplicating or praying to other deities besides Allâh.

Almighty Allâh says:

"And when they embark on a ships they invoke Allâh, making their Faith pure for Him only, but when He brings them safely to land, behold, they give a share of their worship to others," (V.29:65)

(b) *Shirk-al-Niyyah wal-Iradah wal-Qasd*. This aspect implies intentions, purpose and determination in acts of worship or religious deeds not for the sake of Allâh but directed towards other deities.

Almighty Allâh says:

"Whosoever desires the life of the world and its glitter, to them We shall pay in full (the wages of) their deeds therein, and they will have no diminution therein. They are those for whom there is nothing in the Hereafter but Fire; and vain are the deeds they did therein. And of no effect is that which they used to do."(V. 11:15,16)

(c) *Shirk-at-Tâ'ah*. This aspect implies rendering obedience to any authority against the Order of Allâh.

Almighty Allâh says:

> "They (Jews and Christians) took their *Rabbis* and their monks to be their lords besides Allâh (by obeying them in things which they made lawful or unlawful according to their own desires without being ordered by Allâh), and (they also took as their lord) Messiah, son of Maryam (Mary), while they (Jews and Christians) were commanded (in the Torah and the Gospel) to worship none but One *Ilâh* (God i.e., Allâh), *Lâ ilâha illâ Huwa* (none has the right to be worshipped but He). Praise and Glory is to Him (far above is He) from having the partners they associate with Him)." (V.9:31).

Once, while Allâh's Messenger صلى الله عليه وسلم was reciting the above Verse, 'Adi bin Hatim said, "O Allâh's Prophet! They do not worship them (*rabbis* and monks)." Allâh's Messenger said, "They certainly do. They (i.e. *Rabbis* and monks) made legal things illegal, and illegal things legal, and they (i.e. Jews and Christians) followed them; and by doing so they really worshipped them."(Narrated by *Ahmad, At-Tirmidhi,* and *Ibn Jarir*). (*Tafsir At-Tabari*, Vol.10, Page No. 114).

(d) *Shirk-al-Mahabbah*. This implies showing the love which is due to Allâh Alone, to others than Him.

Almighty Allâh says:

> "And of mankind are some who take (for worship) others besides Allâh as rivals (to Allâh). They love them as they love Allâh. But those who believe, love Allâh more (than anything else). If only those who do wrong could see, when they will see the torment, that all power belongs to Allâh and that Allâh is Severe in punishment." (V. 2:165)

(2) *Ash-Shirk-al-Asghar Ar-Riyâ'* (The minor *Shirk*, i.e. acts performed to show off). Any act of worship or any religious deed done in order to gain praise, fame or for worldly purposes, falls under this category.

Almighty Allâh says:

> "Say (O Muhammad صلى الله عليه وسلم) : 'I am only a man like you, it has been inspired to me that your *Ilâh* (God) is One *Ilâh*

(God — i.e Allâh). So whoever hopes for the meeting with his Lord, let him work righteousness and associate none as a partner in the worship of his Lord.' " (V. 18:110)

(3) *Ash-Shirk-al-Khafi* (The inconspicuous *Shirk*). This type implies being inwardly dissatisfied with the inevitable condition that has been ordained for one by Allâh; conscientiously lamenting that had you done or not done such and such or had you approached such and such you would have had a better status, etc.

The Noble Prophet Muhammad صلى الله عليه وسلم said:

"*Ash-Shirk-al-Khafi* in the Muslim nation is more inconspicuous than the creeping of black ant on black rock in the pitch-darkness of the night." And this inconspicuous *Shirk* is expiated by saying thrice the following sentences within a day and a night: "O Allâh! I take Your refuge from that I should ascribe anything as partner in Your worship, being conscious of that, and I beg Your pardon for that sin which I am not aware of."

JESUS AND MUHAMMAD
(peace be upon them)
IN THE BIBLE AND THE QUR'AN

BIBLICAL EVIDENCE OF JESUS BEING A SERVANT OF GOD AND HAVING NO SHARE IN DIVINITY

By Dr. M.T. Al-Hilali, Ph.D.
Professor of Islamic Faith and Teachings, Islamic University, Al-Madinah Al-Munawarrah.
(Rendered into English by Adam M. Makda)

INTRODUCTION

All praise is to the One to Whom all Dignity, Honour and Glory are due; the Unique with perfect attributes, Who begets not, nor is He begotten. He has no equal but He is the Almighty, Omnipotent. He sent His Messengers and Prophets to guide humanity towards monotheism; to worship Him Alone, the only One Worthy of worship, and to warn them of the eternal dire consequences of polytheism; associating partners with One Allâh and the worship of creatures.

Peace and Blessings of Allâh be upon all the Prophets and Messengers, especially on Muhammad, the last of the Prophets, and on all who follow him in righteousness until the Day of Recompense.

CHRISTIANITY: MEN WITHOUT RELIGION
ISLAM: RELIGION WITHOUT MEN

A Muslim never lacks proofs about the purity and truthfulness of his religion, but what he lacks are those truthful brothers who stand for Allâh and His Prophet صلى الله عليه وسلم testifying to the truth. Indeed, in this age, Islam is a religion without men (custodians and propagators) whereas Christianity is men without a religion; yet, by their endeavour, adventurous spirit, patience and monetary contributions they are able to falsify truth and make falsehood appear true. In this materialistic age most of humanity have become slaves to wealth, fashions, and mansions.

There is none worthy of worship but Allâh and in Him (Alone) do I put my trust; and towards Him am I destined.

JESUS AND THE DEVIL IN THE BIBLE

In the New Testament of the Bible, in the fourth chapter of the Gospel according to Matthew, the sixth and seventh verses clearly indicate that Jesus is an obedient mortal and God is the Master and Lord according to his saying in the seventh verse:

"It is written again, Thou shalt not tempt the Lord, thy God."

In this chapter we read that the Devil actually carried the Messiah, and took him from place to place. How can the Devil carry God? Glory be to Allâh; He is above such blasphemy!

Then the Devil orders him to prostrate before him and worship him, even tempting him with worldly possessions. How can the Devil even dare such an audacity with God? When the Devil wanted Jesus to comply with his orders, he (Jesus) replied by saying that it was written (in the previous Books):

"Thou shalt worship the Lord, thy God; And Him only shalt thou serve."

— Matthew 4:10.

CHILDREN OF GOD

Jesus never called himself *Son of God* as far as I know — but he used to call himself the 'Son of Man' (ref. Mark 2:10) although he heard himself being called by that name he did not object — as assumed in the Bible — and did not consider the title exclusively for him.

According to the Biblical term in the Old and New Testaments, every God- fearing righteous person is called 'Son of God'. In Matthew 5:9 we read:

"Blessed are the peace-makers, for they shall be called the children of God."

In Matthew 5:45 —

"That ye may be children of your Father which is in heaven..."

GOD THE FATHER

In Matthew 5:48 —

"Be ye therefore perfect, even as your Father which is in heaven is perfect."

In Matthew 6:1 —

> "... otherwise ye have no reward of your Father which is in heaven."

Matthew 7:21 —

> "Not every one that sayeth unto me (Jesus), Lord, Lord, shall enter into the kingdom of heaven: but he that doeth the will of my Father, which is in heaven."

N.B. The word 'Lord' here was translated as *Rabb* in the Arabic version of the Bible so that people may be convinced that Jesus is God! But if one studies the rest of the verse, one will note that the verse bears testimony to the subservience (to God's Will) of the Messiah (Jesus). Therefore the correct translation should be:

> "Not every one that sayeth to me, O my Master, shall enter into the kingdom of heaven, but he that doeth the will of my Father which is in heaven."

It is obvious from the above readings from the Bible that the term 'Father' is used for God in numerous places in the Bible. It is never used exclusively for Jesus.

Matthew 11:25 —

> "At that time Jesus answered and said, 'I thank Thee, O Father, Lord of heaven and earth, because Thou hast hid these things from the wise and prudent and has revealed them unto babes.'"

JESUS THE WORSHIPPER

Matthew 14:23 —

> "And when he had sent the multitudes away, he went up into a mountain apart to pray....."

I say: If he (Jesus) is God or a part of God then why did he pray? In fact, prayer is always from a submitting, needy and dependent one for the Mercy of Almighty Allâh as mentioned in the Qur'ân:

> "O mankind! it is you who stand in need of Allâh but Allâh is Rich (Free of all wants and needs), Worthy of all praise" (V.35:15).

And in (V.19:93) of Qur'ân:-

"There is none in the heavens and the earth but comes unto the Most Gracious (Allâh) as a slave."

A BIBLICAL STORY

Matthew 15:22-28 —

"And, behold, a woman of Canaan came out of the same coasts and cried unto him, saying, 'Have mercy on me, O Lord, thou son of David: my daughter is grievously vexed with a devil.' But he answered her not a word. And his disciples came and besought him, saying; 'Send her away, for she crieth after us.' But he answered and said, 'I am not sent but unto the lost sheep of the house of Israel.'

Then came she and worshipped him, saying, 'Lord, help me.' But he answered and said, 'It is not meet to take the children's bread and to cast it to dogs.'

And she said, 'Truth, Lord: yet the dogs eat of the crumbs which fall from their masters' table.'

Then Jesus answered and said unto her, 'O woman, great is thy faith: be it unto thee even as thou wilt. And her daughter was made whole from that very hour.' "

In this story about a woman from Canaan there are noteworthy points:

(1) Lack of mercy and love charged against Jesus (if the incident is reported correctly).

(2) Degraded discrimination in regard to the uplifting of his tribe and not for the others.

(3) Tribal pride of descendance and prejudice against others and calling them dogs.

(4) An ignorant polytheist woman debated with him and won him over.

JESUS: A PROPHET OF ALLÂH.

Matthew 19:16-17 —

"And behold, one came and said unto him, 'Good master, what good thing shall I do that I may have eternal life?' And he said unto him, 'Why callest thou me good? (There is) none good but one, (i.e.) God, but if thou wilt enter into life, keep the commandments.' "

In the above verses we note this acknowledgment of his submissiveness (to Allâh's Will).

Matthew 21:45-46 —

"And when the chief priests and pharisees had heard his parable, they perceived that he spoke of them. But when they sought to lay hands on him, they feared the multitude because they took him for a Prophet."

Here it is proved that all those who believed in Jesus during his life-time did not believe in him being God or the Son of God or one in the doctrine of Trinity; but they believed in him as being a Prophet only. This is indeed one of the strongest points of evidence against those who believe in the Divinity of Jesus (Incarnation of God) if only they pondered.

JESUS: A SERVANT OF ALLÂH.

Matthew 23:8 —

'But be not ye called Rabbi: for one is your master, even Jesus, and all ye are brethren.'

Here it is clearly proved that Jesus was servant of Allâh, and that there is only One Master and He is Allâh. In the Arabic version of the Bible this verse has been translated so that Jesus is meant to be the master whereas the English rendering is nearer the original sense.

Matthew 23:9 —

"And call no man your father upon the earth: for one is your Father which is in heaven."

From this you will note that fatherhood and sonship is meant to be the relationship between the Lord and His servants: it is meant in a general sense and not specifically for Jesus.

Matthew 24:36 —

"But of that day and hour knoweth no man, no, not the angels of heaven, but my Father only."

This is a definite proof that the Final Hour is unknown to any but Allâh, thus Jesus' knowledge is imperfect like all other men; Allâh Alone is All-Knowing, Omniscient.

Matthew 26:39 —

> "And he (Jesus) went a little farther, and fell on his face and prayed, saying, 'O my Father, if it be possible, let this cup pass from me: nevertheless not as I will, but as Thou wilt.' "

We note here that the person speaking is unaware of Allâh's Will and realizes the fact that he is a servant of Allâh. He (Allâh) Alone can cause the change.

THE COMPILATION OF THE BIBLE

Matthew 27:7-8 —

> "And they took counsel and bought with them the potter's field to bury strangers in. Wherefore that field was called the Field of Blood, unto this day."

From these verses we understand that the Bible (the New Testament) was not written during Jesus' life-time but long after the occurrence of the events described, having been retained in the memory of the people.

Matthew 27:46 —

> "And about the ninth hour Jesus cried with a loud voice, saying, 'Eli,Eli, lama sabachthani? (My God, My God, why hast thou forsaken me?')"

This is according to their (Christians') assumption that Jesus cried in a loud voice saying the above words while he was being crucified. This is a great insult as such words could only come from unbelievers in Allâh. Further, it is incredible that such words should come out from a Prophet of Allâh because Allâh never breaks His Promise and His Prophets never complained against His Promise.

JESUS: PREACHER OF MONOTHEISM (TAUHID)

In John 17:3 —

> "And this is life eternal, that they might know Thee, the only true God, and Jesus Christ whom thou has sent."

In Mark 12:28-30 —

"And one of the scribes came, and having heard them reasoning together, and perceiving that he had answered them well, asked him, 'Which is the first commandment of all?' And Jesus answered him: 'The first of all the commandments is; hear O Israel, the Lord thy God is One Lord: and thou shalt love the Lord, thy God with all thy heart, and with all thy soul, and with all thy mind, and with all thy strength: this is the first commandment.' "

In Mark 12:32 —

"And the scribe said unto him, 'Well, Master, thou hast said the truth: for there is One God; and there is none other but He.' "

In Mark 12:34 —

"...he (Jesus) said unto him, 'Thou art not far from the kingdom of God...' "

In these verses, Jesus (peace be upon him) himself had testified that Allâh is the One God, there is none other than Him, and that whoever believes in His Oneness, he is near the Kingdom of Allâh. Therefore whoever associates partners with Allâh or believes in the Trinity is far away from the Kingdom of Allâh, and whoever is far away from the Kingdom of Allâh he is the enemy of Allâh.

In Matthew 24:36 —

"But of that day and hour knoweth no man, no, not the angels of the heaven, but my Father only."

I say: A similar text was quoted from S.Matthew which is exactly as proclaimed by the Qur'ân in that none knows when the Hour will come except Allâh. This establishes the fact that Jesus was subservient to Allâh and that he had no share in Divinity; that he was an incarnation of God, was an innovation by the people of Canaan.

In John 20:16 —

"Jesus said unto her, 'Mary'. She turned herself, and sayeth unto him, 'Rabboni', which is to say, Master, Jesus saith unto her, 'Touch me not: For I am not yet ascended to my Father; but go to my brethren, and say unto them, I ascend unto my

Father and your Father; and to my God and your God.' Mary Magdalene came and told the disciples that she has seen the Lord, and that He had spoken these things unto her."

In the above narrative Jesus clearly testified that Allâh is his God and their God, making no difference between him and them in the worship of the One Allâh. Whoever believes that Jesus is God has indeed blasphemed against Allâh and betrayed Jesus and all the Prophets and Messengers of Allâh.

BIBLICAL PROPHECY ON THE ADVENT OF MUHAMMAD (peace be upon him) (صلى الله عليه وسلم)

John 14:15-16 —

"If you love me, keep my commandments. And I will pray the Father and He shall give you another Comforter that he may abide with you forever."

Muslim theologians have said that "another Comforter" is Muhammad, the Messenger of Allâh; and him to "abide forever" means the perpetuity of his laws and way of life (*Shari'ah*) and the Book (Qur'ân) which was revaled to him.

John 15:26-27 —

"But when the Comforter is come, whom I will send unto you from the Father, even the Spirit of truth, which proceedeth from the Father, he shall testify of me: And ye also shall bear witness, because ye have been with me from the beginning."

John 16:5-8 —

"But now I go my way to Him that sent me and none of you asketh me 'Whither goest thou?' But because I have said these things unto you, sorrow hath filled your heart. Nevertheless I tell you the truth; for if I go not away, the Comforter will not come unto you; but if I depart, I will send him unto you. And when he is come, he will reprove the world of sin, and approve righteousness and judgment."

John 16:12-14 —

"I have yet many things to say unto you, but you cannot bear them now. How be it when he, the Spirit of truth, is come, he will guide you into all truth: for he shall not speak of himself; but whatsoever he shall hear, that shall he speak; and he will shew you things to come. He shall glorify me: for he shall receive of mine, and he shall shew it unto you."

John 16:16 —

"A little while and ye shall not see me: and again a little while, ye shall see me, because I go to the Father."

Muslim theologians have stated that the person who is described by Jesus to come after him — in the above verses — does not comply with any other person but Muhammad صلى الله عليه وسلم the Messenger of Allâh. This 'person' whom Jesus prophesied will come after him is called in the Bible 'Parqaleeta' This word was deleted by later interpreters and translators and changed at times to 'Spirit of Truth', and at other times, to 'Comforter' and sometimes to 'Holy Spirit'. The original word is Greek and its meaning is 'one whom people praise exceedingly.' The sense of the word is applicable to the word 'Muhammad' (in Arabic).

FINALITY ON PROOFS ON THE FABRICATION OF THE STORY OF THE CROSS

(1) The Bible testifies to the fact that Jesus was known among the Jews; he used to preach and deliver sermons in the Temple of Solomon in Jerusalem. It was therefore, unnecessary to hire a Jew for thirty pieces of silver to direct them to him as related in Matthew.

(2) It is related that one of the twelve disciples named Judas Iscariot was hired to direct the Jews to Jesus. They then sentenced him after which Judas was greatly ashamed and dissociated himself from their act and then committed suicide. All this took place within twenty four hours. The contradictions are obvious.

(3) The clearest proof which alone is sufficient to discredit this story is when the Jews passed the sentence of death against Jesus and intended to get the approval of the governor, Pontious Pilate.

Matthew 27:11-14 —

'And Jesus stood before the governor: The governor asked him, saying, 'Art thou the king of the Jews!' And Jesus said unto him, 'Thou sayeth (sayest)': And when he was accused of (by) the chief priests and elders. He answered nothing. Then said Pilate unto him, 'Hearest thou not how many things they witness against thee?' And he answered him never (to) a word..."

The Christians will interpret the above verse to mean that Jesus wanted to die on the Cross for the redemption of mankind and for the forgiveness of their sins: if so, then why did he ask to turn away that cup from him (i.e. death)? Why did he cry out while on the Cross (as they assume): "O Lord, why hast thou forsaken me?" How could he have remained silent when the truth was being challenged? He was known for his soul-inspiring sermons challenging the learned Jewish *Rabbis*. No sane person can believe in this. If the story of the Cross is disproved then the very foundation on which Christianity is based, will be demolished.

Muslims believe that Jesus was not crucified by the Jews as revealed in the Holy Qur'ân by Allâh in a crystal clear manner: V. 4:157,158.—

"And because of their saying (in boast): 'We killed Messiah Jesus, son of Mary, the Messenger of Allâh'; — but they killed him not, nor crucified him, but the resemblance of Jesus was put over another man (and they killed that man), and those who differ therein are full of doubts. They have no (certain) knowledge, they follow nothing but conjecture. For surely, they killed him not (i.e., Jesus, son of Mary). But Allâh raised him (Jesus) up (with his body and soul) unto Himself (and he عليه السلام is in the heavens).. And Allâh is Ever All-Powerful, All-Wise."

The Jews themselves, together with the entire Christian world, believe that he was crucified. As proofs against their views and to prove the truth of the Muslim verdict through the Bible, I prepared the following set of questions based on the Book of S. Matthew in the New Testament of Bible. (Chapters 26 and 27):

(1) Did those who captured Jesus (according to their assumption) know him in person? or did they not know him?

Matthew testifies that they did not know him.

(2) Was it during the day or night that he was captured?

Matthew says — it was during the night.

(3) Who was the one that directed them to him?

Matthew says: He was one of his twelve disciples called Judas Iscariot.

(4) Did he direct them free of charge or for a fixed reward which they specified, for him?

Matthew says: He directed them to him for a fixed reward of thirty pieces of silver.

(5) What was the condition of Jesus during that night?

Matthew says: He was fearful and prostrated in prayer saying: "O God, if it is possible for You to let this cup pass from me, then let it pass." It is incredible that such words could come from a believer in God, let alone a Prophet of God, because all believers believe that God has power over all things.

(6) What was the condition of his eleven disciples?

Matthew says: Sleep overcame them that night together with their teacher (according to their assumption) out of fear.

(7) Was Jesus contented with their condition?

Matthew says (verses 40-46): He was not satisfied. He used to come to them to wake them up saying: "Watch and pray, that ye enter not into temptation; the spirit indeed is willing but the flesh is weak." Then he would come again to find them asleep and he would again wake them up and say the same thing. This weakness could not have been spoken of righteous pupils even if they were pupils of an ordinary pious teacher, let alone the disciples of Jesus, son of Mary.

(8) Did they help him when those ruffians captured him?

Matthew says: They forsook him and fled.

(9) Did Jesus have confidence in his disciples that night?

Matthew says: Jesus informed them that they will all forsake him. Then Jesus said unto them: "Verily I say unto thee that this night before the cock crows, thou shalt deny me — thrice." Peter said unto him, "Although I should die with thee, yet will I not deny thee." Likewise also said all the disciples. And so it happened.

(10) How did those ruffians capture him?

Matthew says: They came to him with swords and staves after they were directed to him by a Jew, then they captured him as described in verse 57:

"And they that had laid hold on Jesus, led him away to Caiaphas the high priest, where the elders were assembled."

There they passed the sentence of death on him. The ruffians then took him away, spat on his face and struck him with their hands after which they stripped him of his clothes and clad him in scarlet robes, then placed a crown of thorns on his head and took him about, teasing and mocking him. They said to him: 'You are the king of Israel according to your claim.' They severely degraded him.

(11) Who finally decided to pass the death sentence against him?

Matthew says: He was Pontious Pilate, a Greek Roman, who was at that time the governor of Palestine.

(12) When the ruffians brought that man before the governor and informed him that the priest of the Jews passed the sentence of death by crucifixion according to their law (Torah), did he believe in them without investigation?

Matthew says: He did not believe them but asked that man: "Is it true what they have said?" He remained silent. The question was repeated and he continued to remain silent. He remained silent in view of the truth; it was essential for him even if he was not a Prophet to clarify the truth and deny the false accusation of the Jews. The governor's wife went to the governor and she said to him: "Have thou nothing to do with that just man? for I have suffered many things this day in a dream because of him."

The Bible states that Jesus delivered lengthy speeches to the Jews rebuking and warning them which amounted to defaming them. Then why was he silent that day? The governor's intention for asking him was to stand for the truth.

(13) How was he crucified according to their assumption?

Matthew says: They crucified him between two thieves both of whom abused him by saying to him, "If you are truthful then save yourself."

(14) This was a great calamity. What did he say while on the cross (according to their assumption)?

Matthew says (27:46):

> Jesus cried with a loud voice, saying, "Eli, Eli, lama sabachthani? (that is to say,) my God, my God, why has Thou forsaken me?"

This is a blatant declaration of disbelief according to all theological authorities. Whoever relates it to a Prophet is a disbeliever according to the revealed religions.

Almighty Allâh, in the Qur'ân warns, the Jews and the Christians against their blasphemy; that Jesus is an incarnation of God (Allâh) or the son of God (Allâh) or in rejecting him totally; and that they must believe in him as a Messenger of Allâh only:

> "And there is none of the people of the Scripture (Jews and Christians) but must believe in him (Jesus, son of Mary, as only a Messenger of Allâh and a human being) before his (Jesus عليه السلام or a Jew's or a Christian's) death (at the time of the appearance of the angel of death). And on the Day of Resurrection, he (Jesus) will be a witness against them." (V.4:159).

BRIEF INDEX

(Bold numericals in the reference numbers denote Sûrah No. while other numericals show the Ayât Nos.)

Aaron (Harûn) 2:248; 4:163; 6:84; 7:122,142; 10:75; 19:28,53; 20:30,70, 90,92; 21:48; 23:45; 25:35; 26:13,48; 28:34; 37:114,120.

'Abasa, S.80; 74:22

Ablutions (Wûdû), 4:43; 5:6

Abraham (Ibrâhîm) S.14; 2:124-127, 130, 132, 133, 135, 136, 148, 258, 260; 3:33, 65, 67, 68, 84, 95, 97; 4:54, 125, 163; 6:74, 75, 83, 161; 9:70, 114; 11:69, 74-76; 12:6, 38; 14: 35; 15:51; 16:120,123; 19:41, 46, 58; 21:51,60,62,69; 22:26, 43, 78; 26:69; 29:16, 31; 33:7; 37:83,104,109; 38:45; 42:13; 43:26; 51:24; 53:37; 57:26; 60:4; 87:19

Abrar, 3:193, 198; 76:5; 82:13; 83:18-22

Abû Lahab (Father of Flame), 111:1-5

'Ad people, 7:65-74; 9:70; 11:59; 14:9; 22:42; 25:38; 26:123; 29:38; 38:12; 40:31; 41:13,15; 46:21; 50:13; 51:41; 53:50; 54:18; 69:4-6; 89:6

Âdam, 2:31, 33, 34, 35, 37; 3:33,59; 5:27; 7:11, 19, 26, 27, 31, 35, 172; 17:61, 70; 18:50; 19:58; 20:116, 117,120,121; 36:60

'Âdiyât, S.100

'Adn Paradise, 9:72; 13:23;16:31; 18:31; 19:61; 20:76; 35:33; 38:50; 40:8; 61:12; 98:8

Ahmad, 61:6

Ahqâf, S.46; 46:21

Ahzâb, S. 33; 11:17; 13:36; 19:37; 38:11,13; 40: 5,30; 43:65

Aiykah, dwellers of, 15:78; 26:176; 38:13; 50:14

Â'lâ S. 87, 87:1; 92:20

Alaq, S.96

Âl-'Imrân, S.3

Allâh. The word Allâh has occured in the Qur'ân more than 3000 times.

Amânah, Trust and Allâh prescribed duties etc., 2:283; 4:58; 8:27; see Trust

Angel or Angels. These words occur more than 100 times.

'Ankabût, S.29

Apostates, 47:25

A'râf; S.7; 7:266,48

Arafât, 2:198

Argue, not on behalf of those who deceive themselves, 4:107 you argued for them in this world, but who will on the Day of Resurrection, 4:109

'Asr, S.103

Ayat Al-Kursi, 2:255

Backbiter, 49:12; 104:1

Badr (battle of), 3:13 lessons from, 8:5-19, 42-48

Bait-ul-Ma'mûr, 52:4

Bakkah (Makkah), 3:96

B'al, 37:125

Balad, S. 90

Balance, 7:8,9; 17:35; 21:47; 55:7-9; 57:25; 101:6-9

Banî An-Nadîr, 59:2-6, 13.

Baqarah, S.2

Barâ'a (See Taubah), S.9

Barzakh, (Barrier), **23**:100; **25**:53; **55**:20; also see **18**:94-97; **34**:54; **36**:9 (barrier)

Baiyinah, S.**98**

Beast (of the Last Days), **27**:82

Bedouins, **9**:90,97-99,101,120; **48**:11, 16; **49**:14

Bee, **16**:68,69

Believers. This word occurs more than 200 times in Noble Qur'ân. Mentioning every place will make the Index very big.

Bequest, **2**:180,240; **4**:7,12; **36**:50;

Betray (deceive, fraud), **2**:187; **4**:107; **5**:13; **8**:27,58,71; **12**:52; **22**:38; **66**:10

Birds, **2**:260; **3**:49; **5**:110; **6**:38; **12**:36,41; **16**:79; **21**:79; **22**:31; **24**:41; **27**:16,17,20; **34**:10; **38**:19; **56**:21; **67**:19; **105**:3.

Blood-money (*Diya*), **2**:178,179; **4**:92; **17**:33

Book. This word occurs more than 300 times in Noble Qur'ân. Mentioning every place will make the Index very big.

Booty, war, **4**:94. **8**:41; *Fai*, **59**:6-8; *Ghulul*, **3**:161 (See spoils) taking illegally, **3**:162

Bribery, **2**:188

Budn, **22**:36

Burden
of another, no bearer of burdens shall bear the, **35**:18; **39**:7; **53**:38
disbelievers will bear also the burdens of others, **16**:25; **29**:13
evil indeed are the burdens that they will bear, **6**:31,164
Allâh burdens not a person beyond his scope, **2**:286; **7**:42; **23**:62

Burûj (Big stars). S. **85**; **85**:1;

15:16; **25**:61

Camel, **6**:144; **7**:40; **77**:33; **88**:17

Captives, **4**:25; **8**:67, 70, 71; **9**:60; **33**:26,27;**76**:8 (see also Prisoners of war)

Cattle, **3**:14; **4**:119; **5**:1; **6**:136,138, 139,142; **7**:179; **10**:24; **16**:5-8,10,66,80; **20**:54; **22**:28,30,34; **23**:21; **25**:44,49; **26**:133; **32**:27; **35**:28; **36**:71-73; **39**:6; **40**:79; **42**:11; **43**:12,13; **47**:12; **79**:33; **80**:32.

Cave of Thawr, **9**:40

Cave, people of the **18**:9-22, 25,26

Certainty with truth, **56**:95; **69**:51;

Charity, (*Sadaqah*), **2**:196,263, 264, 270, 271,273; **4**:114; **9**:58,75,76-79,103,104; **57**:18; **58**:12,13
objects of charity and *Zakât*, **2**:273; **9**:60

Children **2**:233; **42**:49,50
lost are they who have killed their, from folly, without knowledge, **6**:140

Christ, (see Jesus)

Christians. This word occurs more than 600 times in Noble Qur'ân. Mentioning every place will make the Index very big.

Cities overthrown, **69**:9

City of security, **95**:3

Confederates, **33**:9, 22 — see *Ahzâb*.

Consultation, mutual, **42**:38

Creation,
begins and repeated, **10**:4; **21**:104; **27**:64; **29**:19,20
a new, **17**:49, 98; **35**:16
with truth, **15**:85; **16**:3; **29**:44; **39**:5; **44**:39; **45**:22; **46**:3
not for play, **21**:16,17; **24**:115

every living thing made from, 21:30; 24:45; 25:54

of man, 4:1; 6:2; 15:26,28,33; 16:4; 21:30; 22:5;23:12-14; 25:54; 32:7-9; 35:11; 36:77,78; 37:11; 39:6; 40:67; 49:13; 55:14; 56:57-59; 75:37-40; 76:1,2; 77:20-23; 80:18,19; 86:5-8; 96:2

the first form of 56:62

in six Days, 7:54; 11:7; 32:4; 50:38; 57:4

in pairs, 13:3; 30:8; 36:36; 42:11; 43:12; 51:9,49; 53:45

variety in, 35:27,28

Allâh commands "Be!" — and it is, 2:117; 16:40; 36:82; 40:68

as the twinkling of an eye, 54:50

night and day, sun and moon, 39:5

of heaven and earth greater than, of mankind, 40:57; 79:27

purpose of, 51:56

Crow, 5:31

Criterion, 2:53,185; 3:4; 8:29,41; 21:48; 25:1

Dahr.(see Insân,) S. 76; 45:24

time, 76:1; 103:1

David (Dâwûd), 4:163; 6:84; 21:78-80; 5:78; 34:10,13; 38:17-30; 17:55

fights Goliath, 2:251

Dawâb or Daba (moving living creature etc.) 2:164; 6:38; 8:22, 55; 11:6, 56; 16:49,61; 22:18; 24:45; 27:82; 29:60; 31:10; 34:14; 35:28,45; 42:29; 45:4

Days. This word occurs more than 500 times in Noble Qur'ân. Mentioning every place will make the Index very big.

Dead will be raised up, 6:36

Death. This word occurs more than 200 times in Noble Qur'ân. Mentioning every place will make the Index very big.

Debts, 2:280, 282; 4:11,12

Decree,

for each and every matter, there is a, 13:38

never did We destroy a township but there was a known, for it, 15:4

of every matter is from Allâh, 44:5

when He decrees a matter, He says only, "Be!" — and it is, 2:117; 36:82; 40:68

Deeds,

evil, beautified for them, 47:14

to us our, to you your deeds, 28:55; 42:15; 45:15

good and bad, are for and against his ownself, 41:46

fastened man's, to his own neck, 17:13

Degrees, according to what they did, 6:132

Desire, those follow their evil, 47:14,16

who has taken as his god his own, 25:43

Despair not of the Mercy of Allâh, 39:53

Dhan-Nûn (Companion of the Fish), 21:87,88; 68:48-50 (see also Jonah)

Dhâriyât, (Zâriyât) S. 51

Dhikr, 8:205; 15:6,9

Dhûl-Kifl, 21:85, 38:48

Dhûl-Qarnain, 18:83-98

Disbelievers. This word occurs more than 200 times in Noble Qur'ân. Mentioning every place will make the Index very big.

Disease in the hearts of hypocrites and disbelievers, 2:10; 5:52; 8:49; 9:125;22:53; 24:50; 33:12, 32, 60; 47:20, 29; 74:31

Distress, after it there is security, 3:154

Distribution of war-booty, 8:41; *Fai* (booty), 59:7-8

Ditch, people of the, 85:4-10

Divorce, 2:228-232, 236,237, 241; 65:1-7; see also 4:35 (see also *Zihâr*).

Donkeys (Ass), 2:259; 16: 8; 31:19; 62:5; 74:50

Drink, alcoholic, 2:219; 5:90 pure, 37:45; 76:21 pure sealed wine, 83:25 white delicious, 37:46

Duhâ, S .93

Dukhân, S. 44

Earth. This word occurs more than 200 times in Noble Qur'ân. Mentioning every place will make the Index very big.

Elephant army, 105:1-5

Elias (Elijah; Ilyâsîn) 6:85; 37:123-132

Elisha, 6:86; 38:48

Enoch, (see Idris)

Event, 56:1; 69:15

Evil, 4:123; 10:27-30; 19:83; 59:15 should not be uttered in public, 4:148 comes from ourselves, but good from Allâh, 4:79; 42:48 pardon an, 4:149 recompensed, 6:160; 42:40 who devise, plots, 16:45-47 was the end, 30:10 has appeared on land and sea, 30:41 repel/defend, with good, 13:22; 23:96; 41:34 changed, for the good, 7:95 those follow their, desires,

47:14,16 deeds beautified for them, 47:14

Excess, forbidden in food, 5:87 in religion, 4:171; 5:77-81

Eyes, ears and skins will bear witness against sinners, 41:20-23

Ezra, 9:30

Face or Countenance of Allâh, 2:115,272; 6:52; 13:22; 18:28; 28:88; 30:38,39; 55:27; 76:9; 92:20

Fair-seeming, Allâh has made, to each people its own doings, 6:108

Faith (Belief), 2:108; 3:167,177,193; 5:5; 9:23; 16:106; 30:56; 40:10; 42:52; 49:7,11,14; 52:21; 58:22; 59:9,10 rejectors of, 3:116 increase in, 3:173 with certainty, 44:7; 45:4,20; 51:20 He has guided you to the, 49:17

Fajr, S.89

Falaq, S. 113

False conversation about Verses of Qur'ân, 6:68

False gods, besides Allâh, idols and so-called partners 7:194-198; 16:20,21, 72,86; 21:22,24; 34:22,27; 41:47,48; 46:5,6; 53:19-24; 71:23,24 insult not those whom they worship besides Allâh, 6:108

Falsehood (*Bâtil*), 2:42; 3:71; 8:8; 9:24; 13:17; 17:81; 21:18; 22:62; 29:52,67; 31:30; 34:49; 40:5; 41:42; 42:24; 47:3

Fastened man's deeds to his own neck, 17:13

Fasting, 2:178,183,184,185, 187, 196; 4:92; 5:89,95; 19:26; 33:35
eat and drink until white thread appears distinct from the black thread, 2:187

Fath, S. 48

Fâtihah, S. 1

Fâtir, S. 35

Fear. This word occurs more than 1000 times in Noble Qur'ân. Mentioning every place will make the Index very big.

Fidyah (ransom),
of fast, 2:196
for freeing the captives, 8:67
ransom offered by disbelievers. 3:91; 5:36,37; 10:54; 13:18

Fig, 95:1

Fighting,
in the way of Allâh, against disbelievers, 2:190-193,244; 4:84,95; 8:72,74,75; 9:12-16,20,24,36,123; 47:4; 61:11
ordained, 2:216
in sacred months, 2:217; 9:5
by Children of Israel, 2:246-251
in the Cause of Allâh, and oppressed men and women, 4:74-76
till no more Fitnah, 8:39
twenty overcoming two hundred, 8:65
against those who believe not in Allâh, 9:29
permission against those who are wronged, 39:39-41
and the hypocrites, 47:20
exemptions from, 48:17

Fîl, S. 105

Firdaus Paradise, 18:160; 23:11

Fire. This word occurs more than 200 times in Noble Qur'ân. Mentioning every place will make the Index very big.

Fly, 22:73

Food,
lawful and unlawful, (Halâl and Harâm), 2:168,172,173; 5:1,3-5,88; 6:118, 119,121, 145,146; 16:114-118; 23:51
no sin for what ate in the past, 5:93
transgress not, 5:87
make not unlawful which Allâh has made lawful, 5:87; 7:32; 16:116

Forbidden conduct, 6:151,152; 7:33

Forgiveness, 2:109; 4:48,110,116; 7:199; 39:53; 42:5,40-43; 45:14; 53:32; 57:21
a duty of Believers, 42:37; 45:14
by Believers, for people of the Scripture, 2:109
Allâh forgives to whom He pleases, 4:48
Allâh forgives not setting up partners in worship with Him, 4:48,116
whoever seeks Allâh's, 4:110
not to ask Allâh's, for the Mushrikûn, 9:113
Allâh forgives all sins, 39:53
angels ask for, for those on the earth, 42:5
forgive, when they are angry, 42:37
forgive and make reconciliation, 42:40
Believers to forgive those who hope not for the Days of Allâh, 45:14
for those who avoid great sins and the Fawâhish, 53:32
race one with another in hastening towards, 57:21

Fraud, 83:1-6 (see Betray)

Free will,

limited by Allâh's Will, 6:107;
  10:99; 74:56; 76:31; 81:28,29
whosoever wills, let him:
  believe and disbelieve, 18:29
  take a path to his Lord, 76:29
  walk straight, 81:28
Friday prayers, 62:9-11
Fruits, 6:41; 16:11
  in Paradise, in plenty, 43:73
  every kind of, 47:15
  as they desire, 77:42
Fujjâr, 82:14-16; 83:7
Furqân, S.25
Fussilat (see Hâ Mîm), S.41

Gabriel, 2:97,98; 26:193; 66:4;
  81:19-21
  Rûh, 26:193; 67:12; 70:4; 78:38;
  97:4
  Rûh-ul-Qudus, 2:87, 253; 5:110;
  16:102
Gambling, 2:219; 5:90
Game, in a state of Ihrâm, 5: 94-96
Ghâfir (see Mu'min), S. 40
Ghâshiyah, S. 88
Ghûsl, 4:43; 5:6
Gifts, 30:39
Goliath, 2: 249-251
Good (Days), 3:140
  you dislike a thing which is, and
    like which is bad, 2:216
  to be rewarded, 4:85; 28:54
  rewarded double, 4:40; 28:54
  rewarded ten times, 6:160
  increased, 42:23
  for those who do, there is good
    and the home of Hereafter, 16:30
  is for those who do good in this
    world, 39:10
  Allâh rewards those who do,
    with what is best, 53:31
  is there any reward for, other
    than good, 55:60
  do, as Allâh has been good to

you, 28:77
Good and Evil,
  good is from Allâh and evil is
    from yourself, 4:79
  if you do good, for your
    ownselves and if you do evil,
    against yourselves, 17:7; 41:46
  repel evil with good, 23:96;
    28:54; 41:34
  good and the evil deed cannot
    be equal, 41:34
  every person will be confronted
    with all the, he has done, 3:30
  (see also Muhsinûn)
Good deed,
  disclose or conceal it, 4:149
  strive as in a race in, 5:48
Gospel, 3:3,48,65;
  5:46,47,66,68,110; 7:157;
  9:111; 48:29; 57:27.
Great News, 78:1-5
Greeting, 4:86; 10:10; 14:23;
  33:44; 25:75; 24:61

Hadîd, S. 57
Hady (animal for sacrifice),
  2:196,200
Hajj (Pilgrimage), 2:158, 196-203;
  3:97; 5:2; 22:30
Hajj, S. 22
Hâmân, 28:6, 38; 29:39;
  40:24,36,37
Hands and legs will bear witness,
  36:65·
Hâqqah, S.69
Hardship, there is relief with
  every, 94:56
Hârût, 2:102
Hashr, S.59
Hearts,
  hardened, 2:74; 22:53; 39:22;
    57:16
  sealed, 7:100,101; 40:35; 47:16;
    63:3

covered, **17**:46; **41**:5
locked up, **47**:24
divided, **59**:14
filled with fear, **22**:35
in whose, there is a disease,
2:10; **5**:52; **8**:49; **9**:125; **22**:53;
24:50; **33**:12,32,60; **47**:20,29;
74:31
Heavens,
to Allâh belong the unseen of
the, **16**:77
created not for a play, **21**:16
and the earth were joined
together, **21**:30
there is nothing hidden in the,
27:75
created without any pillars,
31:10
will be rolled up in His Right
Hand, **39**:67
creation of seven heavens in two
days, **41**:12
adorned nearest heaven with
lamps, **41**:12
to Allâh belong all that is in the,
45:27; **53**:31
seven heavens, one above
another, **67**:3
Hell. This word occurs more than
200 times in Noble Qur'ân.
Mentioning every place will
make the Index very big.
Hereafter,
better is the house in the, **6**:32;
7:169
which will be the end in the,
6:135
Zâlimûn will not be successful
(in), **6**:135
home of the, **12**:109; **16**:30;
28:83; **29**:64
who believe not in the, **17**:10
reward of the, **42**:20
better than silver and gold,

43:33-35
only for the *Muttaqûn*, **43**:35
punishment of, **68**:33
better and more lasting, **87**:17
better than the present, **93**:4
Highways, broad, **21**:31
Hijr (Rocky Tract), **15**:80-85
Hijr, S.**15**
Horses, **16**:8
Hour,
the knowledge of it is with
Allâh only, **7**:187; **33**:63;
41:47; **68**:26
all of a sudden it is on them,
6:31; **7**:187; **12**:107; **43**:66
comes upon you, **6**:40; **12**:107;
20:15; **34**:3
has drawn near, **54**:1-5
as a twinkling of the eye, or
even nearer, **16**: 77
earthquake of the, **22**:1
will be established, on the Day,
30:12,14
surely coming, there is no doubt,
40:59; **45**:32; **51**:5,6
Hûr (females in Paradise), **44**:54;
52:20
Houses, manners about entering,
24:27-29
Hûd, **7**:65-72; **11**:50-60; **26**:123-
140; **46**:21-26
Hûd, S.**11**
Hujurât, S.**49**
Humazah, S.**104**
Hunain (battle), **9**:25
Hypocrites,
say: we believe in Allâh and the
Last Day, but in fact believe
not, **2**:8
deceive themselves, **2**:9
disease in their hearts, **2**:10;
8:49; **22**:53; **33**:12; **47**:29
make mischief, **2**:11,12
fools and mockers, **2**:13-15

purchased error for guidance, 2:16

deaf, dumb and blind, 2:17,18

in fear of death and darkness, 2:19,20

pleasing speech, 2:204-206

refuse to fight, 3:167,168

Allâh knows what is in their hearts, 3:167; 4:63

go for judgement to false judges, turn away from Revelation, come when a catastrophe befalls, 4:60-62

in misfortune and in a great success, 4:72, 73

Allâh has cast them back, 4:88

not to be taken as friends, 4:89; 58:14-19

if they turn back, kill them wherever you find them, 4:89

they wait and watch for your victory or disbelievers success, 4:141

seek to deceive Allâh, 4:142

they pray with laziness and to be seen of men, 4:142

belong neither to these nor to those, 4:143

in lowest depths of Fire; no helper, 4:145

afraid of being found out, 9:64,65

not to pray for, 9:84

men and women are from one another; losers; Curse of Allâh, 9:67-69

in bedouins, 9:101

wherever found, they shall be seized and killed, 33:61

Allâh will punish the, 33:73

liars; turning their backs; there hearts are divided, 59:11-14

liars; made their oaths a screen; their hearts are sealed; beware of them, 63:1-4

comprehend not, know not, 63:7,8

to strive hard against, 66:9

Iblîs (Satan), 2:34; 7:11-18; 15:31-44; 17:61-65; 18:50; 20:116-120; 34:20,21; 38:71-85 (see also Satan)

Ibrâhîm, (see Abraham)

Ibrâhîm, S. 14

'Iddah (divorce prescribed period of women), 2:228, 231, 232, 234, 235; 33:49; 65:1-7

Idrîs (Enoch), 19:56,57; 21:85; 96:4

Ihrâm, 2:197; 5:2,95

Ihsan, 16:90

Ikhlâs, S.112

Ilâh, only One, 2:163; 6:19; 16:22,51; 23:91; 37:4; 38:65

Illegal sexual intercourse; evidence of witnesses, 4:15-18; 24:2,19

'Illiyyûn, 83:18-21

Impure (Najasun) — See 9:28 and its footnote.

'Imrân, wife of, 3:35; daughter of, 66:12

Infitâr, S.82

Inheritance, 2:180,240; 4:7-9,11, 12,19, 33, 176; 5:106-108

Injustice, to whom has been done, 4:30, 148

Insân (see Dahr), S. 76

Inshiqâq, S. 84

Inshirâh (see Sharh), S.94

Inspiration, 6:93; 10:2,109; 12:102; 17:86; 40:15; 42:3,7,51,52; 53:4,10

Intercession/Intercessor, 6:51,70,93,94; 10:3; 19:87; 20:106,109; 30:13; 34:23; 39:44; 40:18; 43:86; 53:26; 74:48

Intoxicants, **5**:90 (see also **2**:219)

Iqamat-as-Salat,
2:3,43,83,110,177, 277; **4**:77,
102,103; **5**:12,55; **6**:72; **7**:170;
8:3; **9**:5,11,18,71; 10:87;
11:114; **13**:22; **14**:31,37;
17:78; **20**:14; **22**:41,78; **24**:56;
27:3; **29**:45; **30**:31; **31**:4,17;
33:33; **35**:18,29; **42**:38; **58**:13;
73:20; **98**:5.

Iqra' (see *'Alaq*), S. **96**

Iram, **89**:7

Isaac, **2**:133; **4**:163; **6**:84; **19**:49;
21:72; **29**:27; **37**:112,113

Ishmael (Isma'il), **2**:125-129, 133;
4:163; **6**:86; **19**:54,55; **21**:85;
38:48

Islâm, **3**:19,85; **5**:3; **6**:125; **39**:22;
61:7
first of those who submit as
Muslims, **6**:14,163; **39**:12
first to embrace, **9**:100
breast opened to, **39**:22
as a favour, **49**:17

Isrâ'. S. **17**

Israel, Children of, **2**:40-86
favour bestowed, **2**:47-53, 60,
122; **45**:16,17
rebelling against Allâh's
obedience, **2**:54-59, 61,63-74;
5:71; **7**:138-141
their relations with Muslims,
2:75-79
their arrogance, **2**:80,88,91
their covenants, **2**:80,83-
86,93,100; **5**:12,13,70
bought the life of this world at
the price of Hereafter, **2**:86
greediest of mankind for life,
2:96
ask for a king, **2**:246-251
exceeded the limits; broken into
various groups; monkeys,
7:161-171

promised twice, **17**:4-8
delivered from enemy, **20**:80-82
given Scripture and leaders,
32:23-25; **40**:53,54
the learned scholars of, knew it
(Qur'ân as true), **26**:197

Istawâ (rose over), **2**:29; **7**:54; **10**:3;
13:2; **20**:5; **32**:4; **41**:11; **57**:4

I'tikâf. **2**:187

Jacob, **2**:132,133; **4**:163; **6**:84;
12:18; **19**:49; **21**:72; **29**:27
Asbât (twelve sons of Jacob),
2:140; **3**:84; **4**:163

Jamarât, **2**:200

Jâthiyyah, S. **45**

Jesus, son of Mary,
glad tidings of birth, **3**:45-47;
19:22,23
Messenger to the Children of
Israel, **3**:49-51
disciples, **3**:52,53; **5**:111-115
disciples as Allâh's helpers,
3:52; **61**:14
raised up, **3**:55-58; **4**:157-159
likeness of Adam, **3**:59
not crucified, **4**:157
inspired, **4**:163
no more than Messenger, **4**:171;
5:75; **43**:63,64
they have disbelieved who say,
5:17,72; **9**:30
Our Messenger (Muhammad
صلى الله عليه وسلم) has come, **5**:19
gave the Gospel, **5**:46
disciples said: we are Muslims,
5:111
Table spread with food, **5**:114
taught no false worship, **5**:116-118
a righteous Prophet, **6**:85
as a Sign, **23**:50; **43**:61
no more than a slave and an
example to the Children of
Israel, **43**:59

glad tidings of a Messenger
whose name shall be Ahmed,
61:6

Jews,
and Christians, **2**:140; **4**:153-
161,171; **5**:18
listen to falsehood, **5**:41,42
accursed for what they uttered,
5:64
enmity to the believers
(Muslims), **5**:82
who embraced Islâm, **26**:197;
28:53; **29**:47

Jihâd, **2**:216; **9**:24; **22**:78; **25**:52
(see also Fighting; Striving)

Jinn, S.**72**

Jinn, **6**:100,112; **15**:27; **34**:41;
38:37; **46**:18,29; **55**:15,33,39;
72:1-15

Job, **4**:163; **6**:84; **21**:83,84; **38**:41-44

John, Yahyâ,
glad tidings of, **3**:39; **21**:90
righteous, **6**:85
wise, sympathetic, dutiful,
19:12-15

Jonah (Jonas or Yûnus), **4**:163; **6**:86;
10:98; **21**:87; **37**:139-148;
(Dhan-Nûn) **21**:87; **68**:48-50

Joseph (Yûsuf), **6**:84; **12**:4-101

Jûdi, Mount, **11**:44

Jumu'ah, S.**62**

Justice (Adl), **2**:282; **4**:58,135;
7:29; **16**:90; **57**:25 (see also
4:65,105)

Ka'bah,
built by Abraham, **2**:125-127
no killing of game, **5**:94-96
asylum of security, **5**:97
going round in naked state, **7**:28
while praying and going round,
2:200; **7**:29,31

Kâfirûn. S. **109**

Kâfûr, cup mixed with, **76**:5

Kahf, S.**18**

Kanz, **9**:34,35.

Kauthar (river in Paradise), **108**:1

Kauthar, S.**108**

Keys,
of the heavens and the earth,
39:63; **42**:12
of the Ghaib, **6**:59

Khaulah bint Tha'labah, **58**:1

Killing,
if anyone killed a person, he
killed all mankind, **5**:32
do not kill anyone, **17**:33

Kind words are better than charity,
2:263

Kindred, rights of, **2**:83, 177, 215;
4:7-9,36; **8**:41; **16**:90; **17**:26;
24:22; **29**:8; **30**:38; **42**:23

Kirâman-Katibîn, **82**:11

Knowledge,
not a leaf falls, but He knows it,
6:59
lost are they who have killed
their children from folly,
without, **6**:140
of five things, with Allâh Alone,
31:34
with certainty, **102**:5-7

Korah (Qârûn), **28**:76-82; **29**:39;
40:24

Kursi, **2**:255

Lahab (See Masad), S.**111**

Lail, S.**92**

Lamp, **25**:61; **67**:5; **71**:16; **78**:13

Languages, difference in, and
colours of men, **30**:22

Lât, **53**:19

Law, prescribed, **5**:48

Laws from Allâh, **2**:219; **98**:3

Liars, **26**:221-223

Life, if anyone saved a, he saved
the life of all mankind, **5**:32

Life of this world,
bought the, at the price of
Hereafter, 2:86
is only the enjoyment of
deception, 3:185
sell the, for the Hereafter, 4:74
is nothing but amusement and
play, 6:32; 29:64; 47:36; 57:20
deceives, 6:130
little is the enjoyment of the,
than the Hereafter, 9:38; 13:26;
28:60
likeness of, is as the rain, 10:24
glad tidings in the, 10:64
whoever desires, gets therein;
but then there will be no
portion in the Hereafter,
11:15,16; 17:18; 42:20
who love the present, and
neglect the Hereafter,
75:20,21; 76:27
you prefer the, 87:16

Light,
manifest, 4:174
and darkness, 6:1
parable of, 24:35
goes before and with the
Believers, 57:12-15; 66:8
given by Allâh, that the
Believers may walk straight,
57:2

Limits set by Allâh,
2:173,187,190,230; 9:112;
58:4; 65:1; 78:22
these are the, 2:187; 229, 230;
4:13; 58:4; 65:1
transgress not the, 2:190,229
whosoever transgresses, 2:229;
4:14; 78:22
but forced by necessity, nor
transgressing the, 2:173; 6:145
do not exceed the, in your
religion, 4:171; 5:77
when they eexceeded the,

(became monkeys), 7:166
who observe the, 9:112

Lion, 74:51

Loan,
lend to Allâh a goodly, 2:245;
73:20
increased manifold, 57:11,18
doubled, 64:17

Loss, manifest, 39:15

Lot, 6:86; 7:80; 11:70,74,77,81,89;
15:59,61; 21:71,74; 22:43;
26:160, 161,167; 27:54-56;
29:26,28,32,33; 37:133; 38:13;
50:13; 54:33,34; 66:10
his disobedient wife, 11:81;
15:60; 66:10

Lote tree, 34:16; 53:14-16; 56:28

Luqmân, 31:12-14
Luqmân, S.31

Ma'ârij, S.70

Madînah (Yathrib), 9:120;
33:13,60; 63:8

Madyan, 7:85-93; 11:84-95;
20:40; 22:44; 28:22,23;
29:36,37 (see also Aiyka;
Wood)

Mahr (bridal-money),
2:229,236,237; 4:4,19-21,24,
25; 5:5; 33:50; 60:10,11

Mâ'idah, S.5

Makkah (Bakkah), 3:96; 90:1,2;
City of Security, 95:3

Man,
generations after generations on
earth, 2:30; 6:165;
made necessor, 35:39
duty, 2:83,84,88,177; 4:1-36;
8:41; 16:90; 17:23-39; 24:22;
29:8,9; 30:38; 33:33; 42:23;
64:14; 70:22-35
tested by Allâh, 2:155; 3:186;
47:31; 57:25
things men covet, 3:14

created from, **4**:1; **6**:2;
15:26,28,33; **16**:4; **21**:30; **22**:5;
23:12-14; **25**:54; **30**:20; **32**:7-9;
35:11; **36**:77,78; **37**:11; **39**:6;
40:67; **49**:13; **55**:14; **56**:57-59;
75:37-40; **76**:1,2; **77**:20-23;
80:18,19; **86**:5-8; **96**:2

created and decreed a stated
term, **6**:2; **15**:26

reconciliation between, and
wife, **4**:35

losers who denied their Meeting
with Allâh, **6**:31

the return, **6**:60,72,164;
10:45,46

plots against ownself, **6**:123

shall not bear the burden of
another, **6**:164

is ungrateful, **7**:10; **11**:9; **30**:34;
32:9; **80**:17; **100**:6

warned against Satan, **7**:27

wife and children, **7**:189,190

when harm or evil touches,
10:12; **11**:9,10; **16**:53-55;
17:67; **29**:10; **30**:33; **31**:32;
39:8,49; **41**:49-51; **42**:48;
70:19-21; **89**:16

returning towards the Lord,
10:23; **84**:6; **96**:8

wrong themselves, **10**:44

is exultant and boastful, **11**:10

invokes for evil, **17**:11

is ever hasty, **17**:11

his deeds fastened to his neck,
17:13

whoever goes astray, to his own
loss and goes right, only for his
ownself, **17**:15

not be dealt unjustly, **17**:71

death and resurrection, **23**:15,16

have broken their religion into
sects, each rejoicing in its
belief, **23**:53

tongues, hands and feet will

bear witness against, **24**:24

witness against himself, **75**:14

who has taken as his god his
own desire, **25**:43

kindred by blood and marriage,
25:54

Allâh has subjected for you
whatsoever is in the heaven
and earth, **31**:20

whosoever submits his face to
Allâh, **31**:22

not two hearts inside his body,
33:4

to worship Allâh, **39**:64-66

misfortunes because of what his
hands have earned, **42**:30,48

angels recording his doings,
50:17,18,23; **85**:11

angels guarding him, **13**:11;
86:4

sorted out into three classes,
56:7-56

those nearest to Allâh, **56**:10,11

companions of Right Hand,
56:27-40

companions of Left Hand,
56:41-56

to be transfigured and created in
forms unknown, **56**:60-62

made shapes good, **64**:3

wealth and children are only a
trial, **64**:15

created and endowed with,
67:23,24; **74**:12-15; **90**:8-10

is impatient, **70**:19-21

devoted to prayers, **70**:22-35

desires more, **74**:15

witness against himself,
75:14,15

his arrogance, **75**:31-40; **90**:5-7

loves the present life of this
world, **76**:27

more difficult to create, or is the
heaven, **79**:28

careless concerning the Lord,
82:6-12

fashioned perfectly and given
due proportion, 82:7

travels from stage to stage,
84:19

love of wealth, 89:20

created in toil, 90:4

efforts and deeds are diverse,
92:4

smooth for him the path of Ease,
and Evil, 92:7,10

created of the best stature
(moulds), 95:4

then reduced to the lowest of the
low, 96:5

transgresses all bounds, 96:6,7

Manâsik (duties) of *Hajj*,
2:128,200; 22:30

Manât, 53:20

Mankind,

witnesses over, 2:143

one community, 2:213; 10:19

created from single pair, 4:1;
39:6; 49:13

rebellion against ownselves,
10:23

heedless though Reckoning is
near, 21:1-3

created on *Fitrah*, 30:30

most honourable of, 49:13

made into nations and tribes,
49:13

Manna and the quails, 2:57

Manners,

about entering houses, 24:27-29

in the home, 24:58-61

in the Prophet's houses, 33:53

to greet and send *Salât* on the
Prophet, 33:56

not to annoy Allâh and His
Messenger or believing men or
women, 33:57,58

verify news before belief, 49:6

not to scoff another, 49:11

in assemblies, 58:11

Marriage, 2:232,234

to disbelievers or slaves, 2:221

to how many, lawful, 4:3

Mahr not to be taken back (in
case of divorce), 4:20,21

forbidden are for, 4:22-24

if no means to wed free
believing women, 4:25

if breach feared, two arbitrators
to be appointed, 4:35

if wife fears cruelty or desertion,
make terms of peace, 4:128

not incline too much to one wife
so as to leave the other
hanging, 4:129

of adulterers, 24:3

to those who are poor, 24:32

those who find not the financial
means for marriage, 24:33

wives made lawful to the
Prophet, 33:50-52

before sexual intercourse, no
'*Iddah* on divorce, 33:49

Martyrs,

not dead, 2:154; 3:169

rejoice in Grace and Bounty
from Allâh, 3:170,171

receive forgiveness and mercy,
3:157,158

will receive good provision,
22:58,59

Mârût, 2:102

Mary (mother of Jesus),

birth, 3:35-7

glad tidings of Jesus, 3:42-51;
19:16-21

in childbirth, 19:23-26

brought the babe to her people,
19:27-33

false charge, 4:156

guarded her chastity, 21:91;
66:12

Maryam, S.**19**
Masad, S.**111**
Masjid-al-Aqsa, **17**:1
Masjid-al-Harâm, ·
    2:144,149,150,191,196,217;
    5:2; **9**:19,28; **17**:1; **48**:25,27
Mash'ar-il-Harâm, **2**:198
Ma'ûn, S.**107**
Mava Paradise, **53**:15
Measure and weight, give full,
    11:85;**17**:35; **83**:3:1-5
Meeting,
    with Allâh, **6**:31
    of Great Day, **19**:37
    of the Hereafter, **30**:16
Messengers, **2**:253; **4**:164,165;
    40:78; **57**:27
    succession of, **2**:87
    series of, **5**:19; **23**:44
    killed, **3**:183
    threatened, **14**:13
    mocked, **6**:10; **13**:32; **15**:11;
    21:41
    denied and rejected, **3**:184;
    6:34; **25**:37; **34**:45; **51**:52
    believing in some and rejecting
    others, **4**:150-152
    gathering of the, **5**:109
    sent as givers of glad tidings and
    warners, **6**:48; **14**:4-8
    as a witness from every nation,
    16:89
    for every nation, there is a,
    10:47; **16**:36
    reciting Allâh's Verses, **7**:35,36
    an angel as a, **17**:95; **25**:7
    no more than human beings,
    14:10-12; **17**:94; **21**:8;
    25:7,8,20
    and their wives and offspring,
    13:38
    (see also Prophets)
M'irâj, **17**:1; **53**:12
Miserliness/Misers, **57**:24

Misfortune, because of your hands,
    42:30
Monasticism, not prescribed,
    57:27
Monkeys, transgressors became as,
    2:65; **5**:60; **7**:166
Months, number of, **9**:36,37
Moon, **7**:54; **10**:5; **16**:12; **22**:18;
    25:61; **36**:39,40; **71**:16; **91**:2
    spliting of: **54**:1
Moses (Mûsâ),
    and his people, **2**:51-61; **5**:20-29;
    7:138-141,159-162; **14**:5-8; **61**:5
    and Pharaoh, **2**:49,50; **7**:103-
    137; **10**:75-92; **11**:96-99;
    17:101-103; **20**:17-53,56-79;
    23:45-49; **25**:35,36; **26**:10-69;
    28:4-21,31-42; **40**:23-46;
    43:46-56; **51**:38-40; **73**:16;
    79:15-26
    guided by Allâh, **6**:84
    mountain and Lord's
    appearance, **7**:142-145
    and calf-worship of his people,
    7:148-156; **20**:86-98
    his Book, differences arose
    therein, **11**:110
    given the Scripture, **17**:2
    nine Clear Signs, **7**:133; **17**:101
    to the junction of the two seas,
    18:60-82
    called and given Messengership,
    19:51-53; **20**:9-56; **28**:29-35
    his childhood, mother and sister,
    20:38-40; **28**:7-13
    magicians converted, **20**:70-73;
    26:46-52
    in Madyan, **20**:40; **28**:22-28
    granted the Criterion, **21**:48
    and the mystic fire, **27**:7-12;
    28:29-35
    his mishap in the city, **28**:15-21
    came with clear *Ayat*, **29**:39
    guided to the Right Path,

37:114-122
Scripture of, **53**:36; **87**:19
Mosque (of Jerusalem), **17**:7
Mosque (of Qubâ), **9**:107,108
Mosques, **2**:187; **9**:17-19
to maintain, of Allâh, **9**:17,18
Mosquito, a parable, **2**:26
Mountains, **15**:19; **16**:15; **20**:105-107; **21**:31; **22**:18; **31**:10; **42**:32,33; **59**:21; **73**:14; **77**:10,27; **81**:3; **101**:5
Muddaththir, S.74
Muhâjir (Emigrants), **4**:100; **9**:100, 107,117; **22**:58,59; **24**:22;**33**:6; **59**:8,9
women, **60**:10-12
Muhammad صلى الله عليه وسلم
mocked, **2**:104; **4**:46; **25**:41,42; **34**:78
respect the Messenger, **2**:104; **4**:46; **49**:1-5
covenant to believe in, **3**:81
a witnesses over believers, **2**:143
no more than a Messenger, **3**:144
dealing gently, **3**:159
his work, **3**:164; **7**:157; **36**:6; **52**:29; **74**:1-7
sent as a great favour to the believers, **3**:164
sent with the truth, **4**:170
not made a watcher, **6**:107
unlettered, **7**:157; **62**:2
sent to the mankind as the Messenger of Allâh, **7**:158; **48**:9,29
a plain warner, **7**:184,188; **11**:2; **15**:89; **53**:56
not a madman, **7**:184; **68**:2; **81**:22
who accuse you, **9**:58
men who hurt the Prophet, **9**:61
a mercy to the Believers, **9**:61
only follow that which is

revealed, **10**:15,16; **11**:12-14; **46**:9
his sayings, **11**:2-4; **12**:108; **34**:46-50
Allâh is Witness over him, **13**:43; **29**:52; **46**:8
sent as a witness, bearer of glad tidings and a warner, **11**:2; **15**:89; **26**:194; **33**:45; **34**:28; **48**:8
not to be distressed, **15**:97; **16**:127; **18**:6
sent to be a witness, **16**:89; **22**:78; **73**:15
to invite with wisdom and fair preaching, and argue in a better way, **16**:125
Maqâman Mahmûdâ, **17**:79
inspired, **18**:110
mercy for the '*Alamin*, **21**:107
asks no reward, **25**:57; **38**:86; **42**:23
has been commanded to, **27**:91-93; **30**:30; **66**:9
as a mercy from Allâh, **28**:46,47
close to the believers, **33**:6
good example to follow, **33**:21
last of the Prophets, **33**:40
send *Salât* on, **33**:56
sent to all mankind, **34**:28
wage is from Allâh only, **34**:47
only a human being, **41**:6
sent as a protector, **42**:48
not a new thing in the Messengers, **46**:9
witness from among the Children of Israel, **46**:10
Bai'âh (pledge) to him is *Bai'âh* (pledge) to Allâh, **48**:10,18
saw Gabriel, **53**:4-18; **81**:22-25
oppose him not, **58**:20-22
foretold by Jesus, **61**:6
to make Religion of Truth victorious overall religions, **61**:9

from the darkness to the light, 65:11

to strive hard against disbelievers and hypocrites, 66:9

exalted standard of character, 68:4

not a poet or soothsayer, 69:41,42

devoted to prayer, 73:1-8,20; 74:3

and the blind man, 80:1-12

to prostrate and draw near to Allâh, 96:19

reciting pure pages, 98:2

Ayât regarding family of, 24:11-17; 33:28-34,50-53,55,59; 66:1,3-6; 108:3

(see also Messengers; Prophets)

Muhammad, S.47

Muhsinûn (Good-doers), 2:117,195; 4:125,128; 10:126; 16:128

Allâh loves the, 3:134,148; 5:93

Allâh loses not the reward of the, 5:85; 9:120; 11:115; 18:30

We reward the, 12:22; 37:80,105,110; 39:34; 77:44

glad tidings to the, 22:37; 46:12

Allâh's Mercy is near to the, 7:56

Allâh is with the, 29:69

dutiful and good to parents, 2:83

patient in performing duties to Allâh, 16:90

(see also Good and Evil)

Mujâdilah, S.58

Mules, 16:8

Mulk, S.67

Mu'min (see Ghâfir), S.40

Mu'minûn, S.23

Mumtahinah, S.60

Munâfiqûn, S.63

Murder, 2:178,179

Mursalât, S.77

Muslims,
first of the, 6:14,163; 9:100; 39:12

Who has named, 22:78

forgiveness and a great reward for them who, 33:35,36

Mutaffifîn, S.83

Muzzammil, S.73

Naba', S.78

Nadîr, Banî-An-,(Jews), 59:2,9,13

Nahl, S.16

Najasun (impure) 9:28 and its footnote.

Najm, S.53

Najwa (See Secret)

Names,
to Him belong the Most Beautiful, 7:180

to Him belong the Best, 17:110; 20:8; 59:24

Naml, S.27

Nas, S.114

Nasr, 71:23

Nasr, S.110

Naziat, S.79

Necessity, if one is forced by, 2:173; 6:145

Neighbour, 4:36

New moons, 2:189

News, to be tested, 4:83

Niggards condemned, 17:29; 47:38; 48:38

Night, (as a symbol), 79:29; 92:1; 93:2;

for rest, 10:67

as a covering, 13:3; 78:10

to be of service, 14:32

Night of Al-Qadr (Decree), 44:3,4; 97:1-5

Nisa', S.4

Noah, 3:33; 4:163; 6:84; 7:59-69; 9:70; 10:71;

11:25,32,36,42,45,46,48,89;
17:3; **21**:76; **23**:23; **25**:37;
26:105; **29**:14; **37**:75; **51**:46;
54:9; **69**:11; **71**:1-28

the Deluge, **29**:14

unrighteous son not saved,
  11:45-47

unrighteous wife, **14**:9; **17**:3,17;
  19:58; **21**:76; **22**:42; **26**:105,
  106,116; **33**:7; **37**:75,79;**38**:12;
  42:13; **40**:5,31; **42**:13; **50**:12;
  53:52; **57**:26; **66**:10;**71**:1,21,26

Nuh, S.**71**

Nur, S.**24**

Oath, **2**:224-227; **3**:77; **5**:89;
  6:109; **16**:38,91,92,94;
  24:22,53; **66**:2; **68**:10,39; **77**:3

Obedience, **3**:132;
  4:59,64,66,80,81; **5**:95; **18**:46;
  24:51,52,54; **47**:33; **64**:12

Obligations to be fulfilled, **5**:1

Offspring, **4**:9; **42**:49,50

He bestows male and female, upon
  whom He wills, **42**:49

Olive, **6**:141; **16**:11; **23**:20; **24**:35;
  95:1

Only One *'Ilah.*, **2**:163; **6**:19;
  16:22,51; **23**:91; **37**: 4; **38**:65

Orphans, **2**:83, 177, 215,220;
  4:2,3,6,8,10,36,127; **6**:152;
  8:41; **17**:34; **18**:82; **59**:7; **76**:8;
  89:17; **90**:15; **93**:6; **107**:2

guardians of, **4**:6

Own doings, made fair-seeming to
  each people, **6**:108

Pairs, in all creatures, **13**:3; **30**:8;
  36:36; **42**:11; **43**:12; **51**:9,49;
  53:45

Palm tree, **13**:4; **19**:25; **20**:71; **59**:5

Parables, (likeness, example,
  similitudes)
  who kindled a fire, **2**:17,18
  rain storm from the sky, **2**:19,20

mosquito, **2**:26

who shout, **2**:171

a town all in utter ruins, **2**:259

grain of corn, **2**:261

smooth rock, **2**:264

garden, **2**:265,266

rope, **3**:103

cold wind, **3**:117

dog who lolls his tongue out,
  7:176

brink of a precipice, **9**:109,110

rain, **10**:24

clean-mown harvest, **10**:24

blind and deaf, **11**:24

ashes on which the wind blows
  furiously, **14**:18

goodly tree, **14**:24,25

evil tree, **14**:26

slave and a man, **16**:75

dumb man who is a burden to
  his master, **16**:76

woman undoing the thread,
  16:92

township, secure and well
  content, **16**:112,113

two men with gardens of grapes,
  18:32-44

life of this world like water from
  the sky, **18**:45

fallen from the sky and snatched
  by birds, **22**:31

a fly, **22**:73

Light is as a niche, **24**:35,36

mirage, **24**:39

darkness in a vast deep sea,
  24:40

spider, **29**:41

partners, **30**:28

dwellers of the town, **36**:13-32

a man belonging to many
  partners, **39**:29

seed growing, **48**:29

vegetation after rain, **57**:20

mountain humbling itself, **59**:21

donkey, **62**:5

water were to be sunk away, **67**:30

people of the garden, **68**:17-33

Paradise,
of Abode, (*Mava* Paradise), **53**:15

Firdaus Paradise, **18**:107; **23**:11

Gardens under which rivers flow, **3**:15,198; **4**:57; **5**:119; **7**:43; **9**:72; **18**:31; **22**:23; **39**:20; **57**:12; **64**:9; **98**:8

Everlasting Gardens ('*Adn* Paradise) **9**:72; **13**:23; **18**:31; **19**:61; **20**:76

Gardens of Eternity ('*Adn* Paradise), **16**:31; **35**:33; **98**:8

Gardens of delight, **37**:43; **56**:12,89

Gardens with everlasting delights, **9**:21

Gardens and grapeyards, **78**:32

fruits of two gardens, **55**:54,62

fruits of all kinds as desired, in plenty, **36**:57; **37**:42; **43**:73; **44**:55; **47**:15; **55**:52,68; **56**:20,29,32; **77**:42

fruits will be near at hand, **55**:54; **69**:23

fruit and meat, **52**:22

flesh of fowls, **56**:21

thornless lote trees and *Talh* (banana trees), **56**:28,29

a running spring, **88**:12

spring called *Salsabîl*, **76**:18

a spring called *Kâfûr*, **76**:5

a spring *Tasnim*, **83**:27,28

a river in Paradise, *Kauthar*, **108**:1

rivers of wine, milk, clarified honey, **47**:15

pure sealed wine, white, delicious, **37**:45,46; **56**:18; **76**:21; **83**:25

cup, mixed with, *Zanjabil*,

76:17; **78**:34; water, **76**:5

trays of gold and cups, **43**:71

vessels of silver and cups of crystal, **76**:15,16

green garments of fine and thick silk, **18**:31; **22**:23; **35**:33; **44**:53; **76**:12,21

adorned with bracelets of gold and pearls, **18**:31; **22**:23; **35**:33; **76**:21

coaches lined with silk brocade, **55**:54

green cushions and rich beautiful mattresses, set in row, **55**:76; **88**:15

thrones woven with gold and precious stones, raised high **56**:15; **88**:13

rich carpets spread out, **88**:16

beautiful mansions, lofty rooms, one above another, **9**:72; **39**:20

abiding therein forever, **3**:198; **4**:57; **5**:119; **9**:22,72; **11**:108; **43**:71; **57**:12; **98**:8

eternal home, **3**:15; **35**:35

facing one another on thrones, **15**:47; **37**:44; **44**:53; **56**:16

never taste death therein, **44**:56

nor they (ever) be asked to leave it, **15**:48

hatred or sense of injury removed from their hearts, **7**:43; **15**:47

all grief removed, **35**:34

no sense of fatigue, toil or weariness, **15**:48; **35**:35

neither will be any hurt, abdominal pain, headache nor intoxication, **37**:47; **56**:19

no vain speaking nor sinful speech, **19**:62; **56**:25

neither harmful speech nor falsehood, **78**:35; **88**:11

free from sin, **37**:47; **52**:23

neither excessive heat nor bitter cold, **76**:13

there will be a known provision, **37**:41; **56**:89

in peace and security, **15**:46; **44**:51,55; **50**:34

home of peace, **6**:127

greetings in, **7**:46; **10**:10; **13**:24; **14**:23; **16**:32; **19**:62; **36**:58; **39**:73; **56**:26

whoever does righteous deeds will enter, **4**:124; **42**:22; **44**:51

who kept their duty to their Lord will be led in groups, **39**:73

been made to inherit because of deeds, **43**:72

Allâh is pleased with them and they with Him, **5**:119

My Paradise, **89**:30

the greatest bliss, **9**:72

the great success, **57**:12; **64**:9

the supreme success, **9**:72; **44**:57

for believers are Gardens as an entertainment, **32**:19

dwellers of Paradise will be busy in joyful things that Day, **36**:35

will be amidst gardens and water springs, **15**:45; **19**:63; **44**:52; **52**:17; **54**:54; **55**:46

see the angels surrounding the Throne, **39**:75

near the Omnipotent King, **54**:55

they will have all that they desire, **50**:35

Hûr, chaste females with wide and beautiful eyes, as if preserved eggs, **37**:48,49; **44**:54; **52**:20; **55**:58,70; **56**:22,23

pure wives, **3**:15

wives in pleasant shade,

reclining on thrones, **36**:55

young full-breasted maidens of equal age, **78**:33

immoral boy-servants to serve them, as scattered pearls, **52**:24; **56**:17; **76**:19

Parents, kindness to, **2**:83,215; **4**:36; **16**:90; **17**:23; **29**:8; **31**:14; **46**:15-17

'Partners' of Allâh, a falsehood, **4**:116; **10**:34,35,66; **16**:86; **28**:62-64, 71-75; **30**:40; **42**:21

Pasturage, **87**:4,5

Path, **5**:77; **16**:94; **42**:52,53; **43**:43; **90**:11,12 (see also Way)

Patience, **3**:186,200; **10**:109; **11**:115; **16**:126,127; **20**:130; **40**:55,77; **42**:43; **46**:35; **70**:5; **73**:10

seek help in, and prayer, **2**:45,153; **20**:132; **50**:39

Patient,

will receive reward in full, **39**:10

Allâh is with those who are, **8**:46

and be, **11**:115

in performing duties to Allâh, **16**:90

to be, at the time of anger, **41**:34

Peace, incline to, **8**:61

Pearl and coral, preserved, **52**:24; **55**:22; **56**:23

Pen, **68**:1; **96**:4

Person,

Allâh burdens not a, beyond his scope, **2**:286; **7**:42

Allâh tax not any, except according to his capacity, **23**:62

no, knows what he will earn tomorrow and in what land he will die, **31**:34

every, will be confronted with all the good and evil he has

done **3**:30

every, will come up pleading for himself, **16**:111

every, is a pledge for what he has earned, **74**:38

Allâh swears by the self-reproaching, **75**:2

Pharaoh, **28**:6; **40**:24

people of, **2**:49; **3**:11, **7**:141; **44**:17-33

drowned, **2**:50

dealings with Moses, **7**:103-137; **10**:75-92 (see also Moses and Pharaoh)

dead body out from sea, **10**:90-92

transgressed beyond bounds; committed sins and disobeyed, **20**:24; **69**:9; **73**:16; **85**:17-20; **89**:10-14

righteous wife, **28**:8,9

claims to be god, **28**:38; **79**:24

destroyed, **29**:39

a believing man from Pharaoh's family, **40**:28-44

building of a tower, **40**:36,37

Piling up of the worldly things, **102**:1-4

Pledge (*Bai'ah*),

for Islam, **16**:91

to the Messenger is *Bai'ah* (pledge) to Allâh, **48**:10

of the Believers, **48**:18; **60**:12

Pledge (Mortgaging),

let there be a, **2**:283

every person is a, for that which he has earned, **52**:21; **74**:38

Poetry, **36**:69

Poets, **26**:224-227; **69**:41

Pomegranates, **6**:141

Poor, **2**:88,177,215,273; **4**:8,36; **8**:41; **9**:60; **17**:26; **24**:22,32; **30**:38; **47**:38; **51**:19; **59**:7,8; **69**:34; **74**:44; **76**:8; **89**:18; **90**:16; **93**:8; **107**:3

Prayer, **1**:1-7; **3**:8,26,27,147,191-194; **4**:103; **17**:80; **23**:118

neither aloud nor in a low voice, **17**:110

invocation for disbelievers, **9**:113,114

invocation of disbelievers, **13**:14

He answers (the invocation of) those, **42**:26

Prayers, five obligatory,

seek help in patience and, **2**:45,153; **20**:132; **50**:39

perform *Iqâmat-as-Salât*, (see *Iqamat-as-Salat*)

facing towards *Qiblah*, **2**:142-145, 149,150

guard strictly the, **2**:238

in travel and attack, **2**:239; **4**:101,102

approach not when in a drunken state, **4**:43

nor in a state of *Janâba*, **4**:43

purifying for, **4**:43; **5**:6

when finished the, **4**:103

times of, **11**:114; **17**:78,79; **20**:130; **30**:17,18; **50**:39,40; **52**:48,49; **73**:1-6,20

prostration for Allâh Alone, **13**:15

Prayers, Friday, **62**:9-11

Precautions in danger, **4**:71

Prisoners of war, **8**:67-71 (see also Captives)

Promise of Truth, **46**:16,17

Property, **2**:188; **3**:186; **4**:5,7,29; **51**:19; **59**:7-9; **70**:25

Prophets, **3**:33, 34,146; **4**:163; **5**:20; **6**:84-90; **23**:23-50; **57**:26

covenants of the, **3**:81; **33**:7-8

illegal for, **3**:161

an enemy for every, **6**:112; **25**:31 (see also Messengers)

Prostration, unto Allâh falls in, whoever in the heavens and the earth and so do their shadows, **13**:15

Provision, **10**:59; **13**:26; **14**:32; **16**:73; **34**:36,39; **42**:12; **51**:57; **67**:21; **79**:33

Psalms, **4**:163

Punishment,
postponing of, **3**:178
cutting of hands or feet, **5**:33
punish them with the like of that with which you were afflicted, **16**:126
of this life and Hereafter, **24**:19; **68**:33

Purifying, bodily, **4**:43; **5**:6; spiritually (from impurities), **87**:14; **91**:9 (please also see the footnote of **9**:28)

Qadr, S.**97**
Qudar, **5**:5; **64**:11
Qaf, S.**50**
Qalam, S. **68**
Qamar, S. **54**
Qari'ah, S. **101**.
Qârûn (Korah) **28**:76-82; **29**:39
Qasas, S.**28**.
Qiblah, **2**:142-145,149
Qisâs (Law of equality in punishment), **2**:178,179,194; **5**:45; **16**:126; **17**:33; **22**:60; **42**:40

Qur'ân,
described, **13**:31,36,37; **14**:1; **56**:77-80
is not such as could ever be produced by other than Allâh, **2**:23; **10**:38; **11**:13; **17**:88
had it been from other than Allâh, therein have been much contradictions, **4**:82
a manifest light, **4**:174; **42**:52
revealed, **6**:19
Allâh is Witness to it, **6**:19

clear proof, **6**:157
false conversation about Verses of, **6**:68
a Reminder, **7**:63; **12**:104; **18**:101; **20**:3,99,124; **25**:29; **36**:11,69; **43**:44; **50**:8; **65**:10; **72**:17
when recited, listen and be silent, **7**:204
Dhikr, **7**:205; **15**:6,9
Book of Wisdom, **10**:1; **31**:2; **36**:2
inspired Message, **10**:2, 109; **42**:52
those reject it, **11**:17
in Arabic, **12**:2; **13**:37; **16**:103; **20**:113;**26**:195; **39**:28;**41**:3,44; **42**:7; **43**:3; **44**:58; **46**:12
made into parts, and revealed in stages, **15**:91; **17**:106; **25**:32; **76**:23
change of a Verse, **16**:10
when you want to recite the, **16**:98
guides, **17**:9
glad tidings and warning, **17**:9,10
and the disbelievers, **17**:45-47
recitation in the early dawn is ever witnessed (by the angels), **17**:78
healing and mercy, **17**:82
fully explained to mankind, every kind of similitude and example, but most refuse, **17**:89; **18**:54; **39**:27
easy, **19**:97; **44**:58; **54**:17,22,32,40
"my people deserted this Qur'ân", **25**:30
confirmed by the Scriptures, **26**:196
narrates to the Children of Israel about which they differ, **27**:76
recite and pray, **29**:45

Truth from Allâh, **32**:3; **35**:31
on a blessed Night, **44**:3
therein is decreed every matter
of ordainments, **44**:4
think deeply in the, **47**:24
warn by the, **50**:45
taught by Allâh, **55**:1
and honourable recital, well-
guarded, **56**:77,78
non can touch but who are pure,
56:79
if sent down on a mountain,
59:21
an anguish for the disbelievers,
69:50
an absolute truth with certainty,
69:51
recite in a slow style, **73**:4
in Records held in honour, kept
pure and holy, **80**:13-16
a Reminder to (all) the '*Âlamîn*,
81:27
disbelievers belie, **84**:22
in Tablet preserved, **85**:22
Word that separates the truth
from falsehood, **86**:13
reciting pure pages, **98**:2
(see also Book; Revelation)
Quraish, S.**106**
Quraish,
disbelievers of, **54**:43-46,51
taming of, **106**:1-4

Rabbis and monks, **9**:31,34
Race, strive as in a, in good deeds,
5:48
Ra'd, S.**13**
Rahmân, S.**55**
Raiment of righteousness is better,
7:26
Rain,
Allâh's Gift, **56**:68-70
of stones, **27**:58
Ramadân, **2**:185

Ramy, **2**:200
Ransom,
no, shall be taken, **57**:15
offered by disbelievers, **3**:91;
10:54; **13**:18
Fidyah, of fast, **2**:196; for
freeing the captives, **8**:67
Rass, dwellers of the, **25**:38; **50**:12
Reality, **69**:1-3
Recompense,
the Day of, **1**:4; **37**:20; **51**:12;
56:56; **82**:17,18; **96**:7
deniers of, **107**:1-7
of an evil is an evil like thereof,
42:40
Reconciliation,
whoever forgives and makes,
42:40
between man and wife, **4**:35
between believers, **49**:9,10

Record,
a Register inscribed, **83**:7-9,18-21
each nation will be called to its,
45:28,29
written pages of deeds of every
person, **81**:10
which speaks the truth, **23**:62
in right hand, **69**:19; **84**:7-9
in left hand, **69**:25
behind the back, **84**:10-15
Recording angels, **50**:17,18,23;
85:11
Relief, with the hardship, **94**:5,6
Religion,
no compulsion in, **2**:256
is Islâm, **3**:19
of Allâh, **3**:83,84
other than Islâm, **3**:85
do not exceed the limits in,
4:171;**5**:77
perfected, **5**:3
who take, as play and
amusement, **6**:70

who divide their, and break up into sects, 6:159; 30:32 (see also 42:13,14; 43:65; 45:17)

men have broken their, into sects, each group rejoicing in its belief, 23:53; 30:32

not laid in, any hardship, 22:78

mankind created on the, 30:30

same, for all Prophets, 42:13-15

ancestral, 43:22-24

Remembrance of Allâh, 63:9

in the, hearts find rest, 13:28

Repentance,

accepted if evil done in ignorance and repent soon afterwards, 4:17; 6:54

and of no effect is the, if evil deeds are continued, 4:18

He accepts, and forgives sins, 4:25

Respite for evil, 3:178; 10:11; 12:110; 14:42,44; 29:53-55; 86:15-17

Resurrection, 7:53; 14:21; 16:38-40; 17:49-52; 19:66-72; 22:5; 23:15,16; 46:33-34; 50:3,20-29,41-44; 75:1-15; 79:10-12; 86:5-8

Resurrection Day, 7:89; 20:100,101,124

the True Day, 78:39

paid your wages in full 3:185

written pages of deeds shall be laid open, 81:11

every person will know what he has brought, 81:14

every person will be confronted with all the good and evil he has done, 3:30

a person will know what he has sent forward and left behind, 82:5

no fear of injustice, 20:112

balances of justice, 21:47

scales of deeds, 23:102,103

whosoever does good or evil equal to the weight of an atom, shall see it, 100:7,8

all the secrets will be examined, 86:9

Record given in right hand, 69:19; 84:7-9

Record given in left hand, 69:25

Record given behind back, 84:10-15

hard day, for the disbelievers, 25:26; 54:8; 74:9

a heavy day, 76:27

bear a heavy burden, 20:100,101

not permitted to put forth any excuse, 77:36

wrong-doer will bite at his hands, 25:27

wrong-doer assembled with their companions and idols, 37:22

destruction with deep regrets, sorrows and despair, 30:12

the female buried alive shall be questioned, 81:8,9

the greatest terror, 21:103

the caller will call, to a terrible thing, 50:41; 54:6-8

a single (shout), 36:29,49,53; 38:15; 50:42

Zajrah (shout), 37:19; 79:13

a near torment, 78:40

the heaven will shake with a dreadful shaking, 52:9; 56:4

heaven is split asunder, 84:1,2

heaven cleft asunder, 77:9; 82:1

heaven shall be rent asunder with clouds, 25:25

heaven will be rolled up, in His Right Hand, 21:104; 39:67

all in heaven and on the earth will swoon away, 39:68

heaven shall be opened, it will

become as gates, **78**:19

sky will be like the boiling filth of oil, **70**:8

stars shall fall, **81**:2; **82**:2

stars will lose their lights, **77**:8

sun will lost its light, **81**:1

seas shall become as blazing Fire, **81**:6

seas are burst forth, **82**:3

earthquake of the Hour, **22**:1; **99**:1

mountains will move away, **18**:47; **27**:88; **52**:10; **77**:9; **78**:20; **81**:3; powdered to dust **20**:105; **56**:5; like flakes of wool, **70**:9; **101**:5

earth and the mountains will be shaken violently, **73**:14; **79**:6

earth is ground to powder, **89**:21

earth will be changed to another earth and so will be the heavens, **14**:48

earth is stretched forth, **84**:3-5

earth as a levelled plain **18**:47; **20**:106

earth throws out its burdens, **84**:4; **99**:2

graves turned upside down, **82**:4

resurrection from the graves, **21**:97; **70**:43

over the earth alive after death, **79**:14

wild beasts shall be gathered together, **81**:5

raised up blind, **20**:124,125

Trumpet will be blown, **6**:73; **18**:99; **20**:102; **23**:101; **27**:87; **36**:51; **39**:68; **50**:20; **69**:13; **74**:8; **78**:18; **79**:7; *Sakhkhah*, **80**:33

the souls shall be joined with their bodies, **81**:7

stay not longer than ten days, **20**:103

stay no longer than a day, **20**:104; or part of a day, **24**:112-114

Day of Gathering, **64**: 9

Day of Judgement, **37**:21

Day of Decision, **77**:38; **78**:17

Day of Sorting out, **77**:13,14

Day of Grief and Regrets, **19**:39

deniers of, **77**:15-50

mankind will be like moths scattered about, **101**:4

mankind will proceed in scattered groups, **100**:6

mankind as in a drunken state, **22**:2

pregnant she-camels shall be neglected, **81**:4

nursing mother will forget her nursling, **22**:2

every pregnant will drop her load, **22**:2

relatives shall be made to see one another, **70**:11

shall a man flee from his relatives, **81**:34-37

no friend will ask of a friend, **70**:10

there will be no friend nor an intercessor, **40**:18

no person shall have power to do anything for another, **82**:19

will have no power, nor any helper, **87**:10

no fear on believers, **43**:68

believers will be amidst shades and springs, and fruits, **77**:41-43

dwellers of the Paradise and their wives, **36**:55-58

angels will be sent down with a grand descending, **25**:25

Shin shall be laid bare, **68**:42,43

Paradise shall be brought near, **81**:13

Hell will be brought near, **89**:23

Hell-Fire shall be stripped off, kindled to fierce ablaze, **81**:11,12

Retaliation by way of charity will be an expiation, **5**:45

Revelation,
  if you are in doubt, **2**:23,24
  abrogated or forgotten Verse, **2**:106
  right guidance, **3**:73
  from the Lord, so be not of those who doubt, **6**:114
  for people who understand, **6**:98
  a Guidance and a Mercy, **7**:203; **16**:64; **31**:3
  through *Rûh-ul-Qudus*, **16**:102; **26**:192,193
  explained in detail, **6**:98; **41**:2-4
  of the Book is from Allâh, **46**:2
  (see also Book and Qur'ân)

Revenge of oppressive wrong, **42**:39-43

Reward,
  according to the best of deeds, and even more, **24**:38; **29**:7; **39**:35
  as a, **25**:15
  Allâh rewards those who do good, with what is best, **53**:31
  for good, no reward other than good, **55**:60

Riba (See usury)

Righteous,
  company of the, **4**:69
  shall inherit the land, **21**:105
  in Paradise, **51**:15-19; **76**:5-12
  (see also Good)

Righteousness,
  2:177,207,208,212;
  3:16,17,92,133-135,191-195;
  4:36,125; **5**:93; **7**:42,43; **16**:97
  steep path of, **90**:11-18

Right guidance is the Guidance of Allâh, **3**:73

Roads, way, **43**:10

Rocky Tract (*Hijr*), dwellers of, **15**:80-85

Romans, **30**:2-5

Roof, the heaven, **21**:32

Rûh (Gabriel), **26**:193; **67**:12; **70**:4; **78**:38; **97**:4
  Rûh-ul-Qudus, **2**:87,253; **5**:110; **16**:102 (see also Gabriel)

Rûh (soul, spirit), **15**:29; **17**:85; **58**:22

Rûm, S.**30**

Saba' (Sheba), **27**:22-44; **34**:15-21

Sabâ', S.**34**

Sabbath,
  transgressors of, **2**:65; **4**:154; **7**:163-166
  prescribed only for, **16**:124

Sabians, **5**:69; **22**:17

Sacrifice, **2**:196,200; **22**:34-37

Sâd, S.**38**

Sadaqah (Charity),
  2:196,263,264,270 271, 273;
  4:114; **9**:60,75,76,79, 103,104;
  57:18; **58**:12,13
  concealing is better than showing, **2**:271

Safa and Marwah, **2**:158

Saff, S.**61**

Sâffât, S.**37**

Sail Al-'Arim (flood released from Ma'arib Dam), **34**:16

Sajdah, S. **32**

Sakînah (calmness and tranquillity), **2**:248; **9**:26,40; **48**:4,18,26

Sâlih, **7**:73-79; **11**:61-68; **26**:141-159; **27**:45-53; **91**:13

Salsabîl (spring in Paradise), **76**:18

Samîrî, **20**:85,95-97

Samuel, **2**:247

Satan, **2**:36,168,208,268,275;

3:36,155, 175;
4:38,60,76,83,119,120; 5:80,
91; 6:43, 68,142;
7:20,22,27,175, 200,201; 8:48;
16:63,98; 20:120; 24:21;
25:29; 27:24; 41:36; 58:10, 19;
82:25

excites enmity and hatred, 5:91
evil whispers from, 7:200,201
deceives, 8:48
betrayed, 14:22
has no power over believers,
16:99,100
throws falsehood, 22:52,53
is an enemy, 12:5; 35:6; 36:60
(see also Iblîs)

Scale, successful, whose will be
heavy, 7:8,9 (See also balance)

Scripture,
people of the, (Jews and
Christians), 2:109;
3:64,65,69,70,71,72,75,98,
99,110,113,199; 4:47,153-161;
5:59,60,68; 98:1
what they were hiding, 5:61-63
among them who are on the
right course, 5:66
they recognise but not believe,
6:20

Seas, 42:32,33; 45:12
the two, 18:60; 25:53; 35:12;
55:19,20
when, are burst forth, 82:3

Secret (Najwa),
talks, 4:114 (See the footnote of
11:18)
counsel of three, 58:7
counsels, 58:8,10
private consultation, 58:12,13

Sects and divisions in religion,
6:15; 23:53; 30:32; 42:13,14;
43:65; 45:17

Security, after the distress, He sent
down, 3:154

Seed, Who makes it grow, 56:63-67
Senses, 23:78
Seven, created,
heavens, 2:29; 23:17; 65:12;
67:3; 71:15
and of the earth like there of,
65:12
Shadow,
unto Allâh falls in prostration,
13:15; 16:48
spread of, 25:45
Shams, S.91
She-camel as a clear sign to
Thamûd people, 7:73; 17:59;
26:155-158
Ship, sailing of, as a Sign; to be of
service; to be grateful; to seek
His Bounty, 2:164; 14:32;
16:14; 17:66; 22:65; 31:31;
35:12; 42:32,33; 43:12; 45:12;
55:24
Shu'aib, 7:85-93; 11:84-95;
29:36,37
Shu'arâ', S.26
Shûrâ, S.42
Sidrat-ul-Muntaha, 53:14
Siege of Al-Madînah, 33:9-27
Signs of Allâh (Ayât). This word
occurs more than 300 times in
Noble Qur'ân. Mentioning
every place will make the
Index very big.
Sijjîn, 88:7-9
Sin, 7:100; 74:43-6
illegal sexual intercourse,
4:15,16; 24:2,19
if greater, are avoided, small
sins are remitted, 4:31
they may hide from men, but
cannot hide from Allâh, 4:108
whoever earns, he earns it only
against himself, 4:111
whoever earns a, and then
throws on to someone

innocent, 4:112

Allâh forgives not setting up partners in worship with Him, but forgives whom He pleases other sins than that, 4:116

those who commit, will get due recompense, 6:120

sinners will never be successful, 10:17

Allâh forgives all, 39:53 greater sins, 42:37

Sinai, Mount, 19:52; 23:20; 95:2

Sinners, their ears, eyes, and skins will testify against them, 41:20-23

Sirât Bridge, 66:8

Slanderer, 68:11,12; 104:1

Slaves, 2:177,178; 4:25,36,92; 5:89; 24:33; 58:3; 90:13 (see also Prisoners of war; Captives)

Sleep, a thing for rest, 78:9

Sodom, 29:31; 37:136

Sodomy, 7:80-82; 11:77-83; 15:61-77; 29:28,29

Solomon, 2:102; 4:163; 6:84; 21:78-82; 27:15-44; 34:12-14; 38:30-40

and the ants, 27:18,19

and the hoopoe, 27:22-26

and the Queen of Sabâ', 27:22-44; 34:15

Son, adopted, 33:4,5

Soul (spirit, Rûh), 15:29; 17:85; 58:22

Spend,

in Allâh's Cause, 2:195,215,254,262,265,267, 274; 3:92,134; 8:3; 9:99; 13:22; 14:31; 22:35; 32:16; 35:29; 36:47; 47:38; 57:7; 63:10; 64:16

which is beyond your needs, 2:219

likeness of those who, their wealth in the Way of Allâh, 2:261

to be seen of men, 2:264; 4:38

whatever you, in Allâh's cause it will be repaid to you, 2:272; 8:60; 34:39

not with extravagance, or wastefully, 6:141; 17:26

neither extravagant nor niggardly, 25:67

who close hands from spending in Allâh's Cause, 9:67

Spirit (soul, Rûh), 15:29

its knowledge is with Allâh, 17:85

Allâh strengthens believers with, 58:22

Spoils of war, 8:41,69; 48:15,19,20; 48:15 (see also Booty)

Spying, 49:12

Star, 53:1,49; 86:1-4

Stars, 7:54; 15:16; 16:12,16; 22:18; 25:61; 37:6-10; 56:75; 77:8; 81:2; 82:2

Straight, Way, 1:6 etc; Path, 6:153 etc.

Striving, 4:95; 8:72,74,75; 9:20,24,81; 22:78; 25:52; 29:69:69; 47:3; 60:1; 61:11

Suckling, the term of, foster mother, 2:233

Suffering, poverty, loss of health and calamities; prosperity and wealth, 7:94-96

Sun, 7:54; 10:5; 14:32; 16:12; 22:18; 25:61; 36:38,40; 71:16; 81:1; 91:1

Supreme canopy, 9:72; 44:57

Sûrah, 10:38; 11:13; 47:20; its revelation increases faith, 9:124-127

Suspicions, 49:12

Sustenance, **19**:62 (see also
    Provision; Providence)
Suwâ', **71**:23

Tabûk, **9**:40-59, 81-99,
    117,118,120-122
Taghâbûn, S.**64**
Taghût, **2**:256,257; **4**:51,60,76;
    5:60; **16**:36; **17**:39.
Tâ-Hâ, S.**20**
Tahrîm, S.**66**
Takâthur, S.**102**
Takwîr, S.**81**
Talâq, S.**65**
Talh (banana tree), **56**:29
Tâlût (Saul), **2**:247-249
Târiq, S.**86**
Tasnîm (spring), **83**:27,28
Taubah, S.**9**
Tawâf (going round the Ka'ba),
    2:200; **7**:29,31
Tayammum, **4**:43; **5**:6
Term, every nation has its
    appointed, no can anticipate
    nor delay it, **7**:34; **10**:49;
    15:4,5; **16**:61; **20**:129
Territory, guard your, by army
    units, **3**:200
Test, by Allâh, **3**:154; **34**:21
Thamûd, **7**:73-79; **11**:61-68;
    17:59; **25**:38; **26**:141-159;
    27:45-53; **29**:38; **41**:17; **51**:43-
    45; **54**:23-31; **69**:4-8; **85**:17-
    20; **89**:9-14; **91**:11-15
Thief, punishment, **5**:38,39
Throne, **7**:54,58; **9**:129; **10**:3;
    13:2; **20**:5; **23**:86,116; **32**:4;
    40:15; **57**:4; **85**:15
    on water, **11**:7
    eight angels bearing the,**39**:75;
    40:7; **69**:17
Time, **45**:24; **76**:1; **103**:1
Tin, S.**95**
Torment, **3**:188; **6**:15,16; **10**:50-

53; **11**:10; **13**:34; **16**:88; **46**:20;
    70:1,2
Township, never did We destroy a,
    but there was a known decree
    for it, **15**:4
Trade and property, **4**:29
Travel, have they not travelled
    through the earth, **6**:11; **10**:22;
    12:109; **22**:46; **27**:69; **29**:20;
    30:9,42; **34**:18; **35**:44;
    40:21,82; **47**:10
Treachery, **8**:58; **22**:38 (See Betray)
Treasure hoarded, **9**:35 and its
    footnote.
Treasures of Allâh, **6**:50
Tree of Eternity, **20**:120
Trees, **22**:18
Trials, **2**:214-218; **64**:15
Trumpet, on the Day of
    Resurrection, **6**:73; **18**:99;
    20:102; **23**:101; **27**:87; **36**:51;
    39:68; **50**:20; **69**:13; **74**:8;
    78:18; **79**:7; *Sakhkhah*, **80**:33
Trust offered to heavens, earth and
    mountains, but undertaken by
    man, **33**:72,73
Trusts (*Amânah*), **2**:283; **4**:58;
    8:27; **23**:8; **33**:72; **70**:32 (see
    Amânah)
Truth, **5**:48; **23**:70,71,90; **25**:33;
    69:51
    mix not with falsehood nor
    conceal, **2**:42
    has come and falsehood has
    vanished, **17**:81
    promise of, **46**:16,17
Tubba', people of, **44**:37;**50**:14
Tûr (Mount), **28**:29,46
Tur, S.**52**
Tûwa, valley of, **20**:12; **79**:16

Uhud, battle of, **3**:121-128, 140-
    180
Ummah (community, nation),

2:143, 144; 10:47,49;
11:118;16:36,120

'Umrah, 2:128,158,196

Usury (Riba), 2:275,276,278-280;
3:130; 4:161, 30:39

'Uzzâ, 53:19

Veil, an invisible, 17:45,46

Veiling, 24:31; 33:59

Verses, Sabâ' Al-Mathâni, 15:87

Victory,
given by Allâh, 48:1
through help from Allâh, 61:13

Virtues, (see Righteousness;
Believers)

Wadd, 71:23

"Wait you, we too are waiting",
7:71; 9:52; 10:102; 11:122;
20:135; 44:59; 52:31

Wâqi'a, S.56

War against Allâh, 5:33,34

Waste not by extravagance, 6:141;
7:31; 17:26

Water, every living thing made
from, 21:30; 24:45; 25:54
two seas, 18:60; 25:53; 35:12;
55:19,20
Allâh's Throne on the, 11:7
rain, 23:18

Way, the, 1:6; 42:52,53; 90:10 etc.
easy, make easy, 87:8
(see also Path)

Wayfarer, 2:177,215; 8:41; 17:26;
29:29; 30: 38; 59:7

Wealth,
who has gathered, 104:2-4
spending in Allâh's Cause (see
Spend)

Wealth and children, adornment of
the life of this world, 18:46

Weight and Measure, give full,
11:85;17:35; 83:1-5

Widows, 2:234,235,240

Will of Allâh, 10:99,100; 30:5;
81:29; 82:8

Will of man, to walk straight,
unless Allâh wills, 28:29

Winds, 77:1-3
as heralds of glad tidings, 7:57;
30:46
raising clouds, causing water,
15:22; 30:48
turning yellow, 30:51

Wine (in Paradise),
pure drinks, 37:45; 76:21
white, delicious, 37:46
rivers of, 47:15
pure sealed, 83:25

Wish not for the things in which
Allâh has made some to excel
others, 4:32

Witnesses,
to covenant of the Prophets, 3:81
over mankind, 2:143; 22:78
for a contract, 2:282
two women against one man,
2:282
to illegal sexual intercourse,
4:16; 24:2
be just, 5:8
hands and legs will bear
witness, 36:65
man against himself, 75:14

Witnessing Day and Witnessed
Day, 85:3

Wives,
are a tilth for you, 2:223
cover for you, 2:187
of your own kind, 16:72

Woman, the disputing, 58:1,2

Women, 2:222,223; 4:15,19-
22,34,127
who accuse chaste, 24:4,5,11-
17,23-26
veiling, 24:31; 33:59
believing, as emigrants, 60:10-12
not making clear herself in

dispute, **43**:17,18

Wood, dwellers of the, **15**:78;
38:13; **50**:14 (see also *Aiykah*;
Madyan) **26**:176-191
World, life of this,
is nothing but play and
amusement, **6**:32; **29**:64;
47:36; **57**:20
deceives men, **6**:130
little is the enjoyment of the,
than the Hereafter, **9**:38; **13**:26;
28:60,61
whoever desires, gets therein,
but then there will be no
portion in the Hereafter,
11:15,16; **17**:18; **42**:20
wealth and children, adornment
of the, **18**:46
who love the present, and leave
the Hereafter, **75**:20,21; **76**:27
Writing, for contracts, **2**:282
Wrongdoers, **11**:18-22,101-
104,116,117; **39**:47 (see also
Disbelievers)
Wûdû' (Ablutions), **4**:43; **5**:6

Yaghûth, **71**:23
Yahyâ (John, the Baptist),
glad tidings of, **3**:39; **21**:90
righteous, **6**:85

wise; sympathetic; dutiful,
19:12-15
Yâ-Sîn, S.**36**
Yathrib (Al-Madinah), people of,
33:13
Ya'ûq, **71**:23
Yûnus, S.**10** (see Jonah)
Yûsuf, S.**12** (see Joseph)

Zabur, **21**:105
Zachariah (Zakariyâ), **3**:37-41;
6:85; **19**:2-11; **21**:89,90
Zaid Ibn Harithah, slave of the
Prophet, **33**:37,38
Zakât, **2**:3,43,83,110,177,277;
3:85; **4**:77,162; **5**:12,55; **6**:141;
7:156; **9**:5, 11,18,71; **19**:31,55;
21:73; **22**:41,78; **23**:4;
24:37,56; **27**:3; **30**:39; **31**:4;
33:33; **41**:7; **58**:13; **73**:20; **98**:5
objects of *Zakât* and charity,
2:273; **9**:60
Zanjabîl, **76**:17
Zalzalah, S.**99**
Zamzam, footnote of **14**:37.
Zaqqûm, **17**:60; **37**:62-66; **44**:43-
46; **56**:52
Zâriyât (Dhâriyât), S. **51**
Zihâr, **33**:4; **58**:2-4
Zukhruf, S.**43**
Zumar, S.**39**

APPENDIX-IV

In the Name of Allâh, the Most Gracious, the Most Merciful

THE CALL TO *JIHÂD*
(HOLY FIGHTING IN ALLÂH'S CAUSE)
IN THE QUR'ÂN

Praise is to Allâh تعالى who has ordained *Al-Jihâd* (the holy fighting in Allâh's Cause):

1. With the heart (intentions or feelings),
2. With the hand (weapons, etc.),
3. With the tongue (speeches, etc., in the Cause of Allâh).

Allâh has rewarded the one who performs it with lofty dwellings in the Gardens (of Paradise).

I testify that there is none who has the right to be worshipped but Allâh تعالى Alone and He has no partners (with Him). I (also) testify that Muhammad صلى الله عليه وسلم is His slave and His Messenger, the one sent by Allâh تعالى as mercy for the *'Alamîn* (mankind and jinn); the one commanded by Allâh تعالى to fight against the *Mushrikûn*[1] (and all those who ascribe partners with Allâh). He fought in Allâh's Cause with all his power and ability — may Allâh's Peace and Blessings be upon him, upon his followers and upon his Companions who believed in him, and honoured him, helped him and followed the light (the Qur'ân) and his *As-Sunnah* (the legal ways, orders, acts of worship, statements) which was revealed to him...those who emigrated and fought in the Cause of Allâh with their wealth and their lives, they were the supreme conquerors and the masters.

It is well-known how the Messenger صلى الله عليه وسلم was fighting against the *Mushrikûn* (and all those who ascribe partners with Allâh تعالى) since Allâh the Most Respectful, the All-Majestic sent him and honoured him with the Messengership till Allâh تعالى caused him to die and selected for him what was with Him (Paradise and all that is good).

The Prophet صلى الله عليه وسلم used to visit the people in their gatherings during the *Hajj* and *Umrah* season and other occasions (too). He used to go to their market places, recite the Qur'ân, invite them to Allâh تعالى, the Most Respectful, the All-Majestic. He used to say, "Who will give me a safe shelter, and who will support me till I convey the Message of my Lord (Allâh) in return for having Paradise?" But he would not find anyone to support him or to give him a safe shelter.

---

[1] *Al-Mushrikûn*: polytheists, pagans, idolaters, and disbelievers in the Oneness of Allâh and in His Messenger Muhammad صلى الله عليه وسلم.

Prophet Muhammad صلى الله عليه وسلم carried on his mission of inviting people to Allâh تعالى (Islâmic Religion) and persevered in his mission of invitation for 13 years in spite of the harm and injuries (which he suffered), and he used to forgive the ignorant... in order that Allâh's Proof be established against the disbelievers and that His Promise (be fulfilled to them which He assured them with His Statement):

"And We never punish until We have sent a Messenger (to give warning)." (V.17:15)

The people continued in their transgression and they did not take guidance from the manifest proof. The people of Quraish oppressed and harmed all those who followed him (Muhammad صلى الله عليه وسلم), put them to trials and afflictions in order to keep them away from their religion (Islâm), even to the extent that they exiled them from their homeland; some of them fled to Ethiopia, some went to Al-Madînah (Al-Munawwarah) and some remained patient (at Makkah) in spite of the harm they suffered; by being imprisoned, made to suffer from hunger and thirst and by being beaten (in a horrible manner)... so much so that some of them were not able to sit straight from the severity (of the injuries) sustained from the beatings.

They used to tie a rope around the neck of Bilâl (may Allâh be pleased with him) and give the end of that rope in the hands of boys to play and drag him through the pathways of Makkah... And what Yâsir's family suffered from the torment was beyond what a normal human being can endure.

The people of Quraish harmed Allâh's Messenger (Muhammad صلى الله عليه وسلم) (too). They besieged him in Ash-Shi'b. Once 'Uqbah bin Abi Mu'ait tried to strangle him and he kept on squeezing the Prophet's clothes round his neck till the eyes of the Prophet صلى الله عليه وسلم bulged out, and Abû Bakr rushed at 'Uqbah and released the Prophet صلى الله عليه وسلم from him and said, "Would you kill a man because he says: My Lord is Allâh تعالى ?"

Abû Jahl also tried to kill the Messenger صلى الله عليه وسلم, while the latter was in prostration praying in the Al-Masjid-al-Harâm, he carried a huge stone to throw it on the Prophet's head. But when he (Abû Jahl) tried to throw it he turned on his heels frightened saying: "I am being prevented from going near to Muhammad (صلى الله عليه وسلم) by a huge stallion camel intending to swallow me."

And when Allâh تعالى wanted to reveal His Religion (Islâm) and to fulfil His Promise and to make His Prophet صلى الله عليه وسلم victorious. So, Allâh تعالى the Most High ordered him to emigrate to Al-Madînah. So he stayed there and Allâh supported him with His Victory and with His slaves, the faithful believers —the Islamic army unit composed of different sorts of people (black, white, and red). They strove hard for him with all their efforts, and preferred his love to the love of (their) fathers, offspring and wives.

Muhammad صلى الله عليه وسلم was dearer to the believers than their ownselves. The (pagan) Arabs and Jews had formed a united front against them (Muhammad صلى الله عليه وسلم and his followers) and had put up all their efforts of enmity, standing and fighting against them... and (in fact) they shouted against them from every corner. Then, at that time Allâh permitted them (Muhammad صلى الله عليه وسلم and his followers) to fight but He did not make it obligatory. He said:

"Permission to fight is given to those (i.e. believers against disbelievers) who are fighting them (and) because they (believers) have been wronged, and surely Allâh is Able to give them (believers) victory." (V.22:39)

"Those who have been expelled from their homes unjustly only because they said: Our Lord is Allâh." (V.22:39,40)

The above Verses clearly state that Allâh عز وجل is Able to give victory to His worshippers (the believers) without fighting, but Allâh wants from His worshippers obedience with all their efforts as it is evident from the following Divine Verse:

"So when you meet (in fight... Jihâd in Allâh's Cause) those who disbelieve smite at their necks till when you have killed and wounded many of them, then bind a bond firmly (on them, i.e. take them as captives). Thereafter (is the time) either for generosity (i.e. free them without ransom) or ransom (according to what benefits Islâm), until war lays down its burden. Thus [you are ordered by Allâh to continue in carrying out Jihâd against the disbelievers till they embrace Islâm (i.e. are saved from the punishment in the Hell-fire) or at least come under your protection] but if it had been Allâh's Will, He Himself could certainly have punished them (without you). But (He lets you fight) in order to test you, some with others. But those who are killed in the Way of Allâh, He will never let their deeds be lost.

"He will guide them and set right their state.

"And admit them to Paradise which He has made known to them (i.e. they will know their places in Paradise better than they used to know their homes in this world)." (V.47:4,5,6)

Then after that He made fighting (Jihâd) obligatory against all those who fight you (Muslims); not against those who didn't fight you. So Allâh ordered:

"And fight in the way of Allâh those who fight you..." (V.2:190)

Then Allâh عز وجل revealed in Sûrat At-Taubah (Bara'ah) (Repentance, IX) the order to discard (all) the obligations (covenants, etc.) and commanded the Muslims to fight against all the Mushrikûn as well as against the people of the Scriptures (Jews and Christians) if they do not embrace Islâm, till they pay the *Jizyah* (a tax levied on the non-Muslims who do not embrace Islâm and are under the protection of an Islâmic government) with willing submission and feel themselves subdued (as it is revealed in the Verse 9:29). So Muslims were not permitted to abandon "the fighting" against them (Pagans, Jews and Christians) and to reconcile with them and to suspend hostilities against them for an unlimited period while they are strong and are able to fight against them (non-Muslims).

As it is now obvious, at first "the fighting" was forbidden, then it was permitted and after that it was made obligatory— (1) against them who start "the fighting" against you (Muslims)... (2) and against all those who worship others along with Allâh... as mentioned in *Sûrat Al-Baqarah* (II), *Al-Imran* (III) and *Taubah* (IX)... and other *Sûrah* (Chapters of the Qur'ân).

Allâh عز وجل made the fighting (*Jihâd*) obligatory for the Muslims and gave importance to the subject-matter of *Jihâd* in all the Surah (Chapters of the Qur'ân) which were revealed (at Al-Madinah) as in Allâh's Statement:

"March forth whether you are light (being healthy, young and wealthy) or heavy (being ill, old and poor), and strive hard with your wealth and your lives in the Cause of Allâh. This is better for you if you but knew." (V.9:41).

And He (Allâh) said:

"*Jihâd* (holy fighting in Allâh's Cause) is ordained for you (Muslims) though you dislike it, and it may be that you dislike a thing which is good for you and that you like a thing which is bad for you. Allâh knows but you do not know." (V.2:216).

Fighting, even though by its nature is disliked by the human soul because of the liability, of being killed, or being taken as a captive, or being injured, with the wasting of the wealth, the damage to the industries, the destruction of the country, the spreading of fear and awe in the souls and the (possibility) of being exiled from one's homeland, Allâh had made ready an immensely good reward that cannot be imagined by a human soul.

'Ikrimah (a religious scholar) said: At first Muslims disliked it (*Jihâd*), but later they loved it and said: "We listen and obey." And that is because the submission to the order to fight means hardship, but if the reward is made known it becomes clear to compare the hardship involved and its reward.

The Verses of the Qur'ân and the *Sunnah* (the Prophet's legal ways, orders) exhort Muslims greatly to take part in *Jihâd* and have made quite clear its rewards, and praised greatly those who perform *Jihâd* (the holy fighting in Allâh's Cause) and explained to them various kinds of honours which they will receive from their Lord (Allâh عز وجل). This is because they — *Mujâhidin* are Allâh's troops. Allâh عز وجل will establish His religion (Islâm), with them (*Mujâhidin*). He will repel the might of His enemies, and with them He will protect Islâm and guard the religion safely.

And it is they, (Mujâhidin) who fight against the enemies of Allâh in order that the worship should be all for Allâh (Alone and not for any other deity) and that the Word of Allâh تعالى (i.e. none has the right to be worshipped but Allâh تعالى and His religion Islâm) should be superior. Allâh has made them (Mujâhidin) partners in reward along with all those who guard Islam with their weapons, along with their good deeds which they performed even if they sleep in their homes.

And the Law-Giver (Allâh) has made one who leads another to do a deed equal to the doer of the deed himself, both in reward (for a good deed) and in punishment (for a crime). So the inviter to a good deed and the inviter to an evil deed both will have a reward (good or bad) equal to the reward of the one who has done that deed.

And sufficient is Allâh's Statement in this matter:

"O you who believe! Shall I guide you to a commerce that will save you from a painful torment?" (V.61:10)

After this Verse was revealed the souls became filled with the yearning for this profitable commerce with Allâh تعالى , the Lord of 'Alamîn (mankind, jinn and all that exists), the All-Knower, the All-Wise Himself directed the people towards it. Allâh تعالى says:

"That you believe in Allâh and His Messenger (Muhammad صلى الله عليه وسلم) and that you strive hard and fight in the Cause of Allâh تعالى with your wealth and your lives... (V.61:11)

Allâh تعالى further says:

"That will be better for you if you but know." (V.61:11)

i.e. Jihâd (holy fighting in Allâh's Cause) is better for you than your staying (back at home). Regarding the reward Allâh says:

"(If you do so) He will forgive you your sins, and admit you into Gardens under which rivers flow and pleasant dwellings in Gardens of Eternity ('Adn Paradise) — that is indeed the great success." (V.61:12)

So it was as if they (the souls) said (as regards the above Verse): This is for us in the Hereafter and there is nothing for us in this world. Then Allâh تعالى said:

"And also (He will give you) another (blessing) which you love, — help from Allâh (against your enemies) and a near victory. And give glad tidings (O Muhammad صلى الله عليه وسلم) to the believers." (V.61:13)

Good-gracious (indeed) how beautiful are these Words (of Allâh) and how they appeal to human hearts. How great is the attraction for them and how they lead one towards one's Lord (Allâh تعالى). How soothing are they for the hearts of every lover of good. How great is the contentment of the heart and a happy life when one understands their meaning. We supplicate Allâh تعالى to bestow upon us His Blessings.

And Allâh تعالى says:

"Do you consider the providing of drinking water to pilgrims and the maintenance of Al-Masjid-al-Harâm (at Makkah) as equal to the worth of those who believe in Allâh and the Last Day, and strive hard and fight in the Cause of Allâh? They are not equal before Allâh! And Allâh guides not those people who are the Zalimûn (polytheists and wrong-doers)." (V.9:19).

"Those who believed (in the Oneness of Allâh — Islâmic Monotheism) and emigrated and strove hard and fought in Allâh's Cause with their wealth and their lives are far higher in degree with Allâh. They are the successful." (V.9:20).

"Their Lord gives them glad tidings of Mercy from Him, and His being pleased (with them) and of Gardens (Paradise) for them wherein are everlasting delights.(V.9:21).

"They will dwell therein for ever. Verily, with Allâh is a great reward." (V.9:22).

In the above Verses Allâh تعالى the Most High, Who is above all that they ascribe to Him, informs that those who maintain Al-Masjid-al-Harâm (at Makkah) [and their maintenance of the mosque means to do I'tikâf in it, the Tawâf (circumambulation) of the Ka'bah, and the offering of Salât (prayers) in it, etc.] mentioned in the above said Verse — and those who provide drinking water to the pilgrims are not equal to those who did Jihâd in Allâh's Cause. Allâh تعالى informed that the believers who fight in Allâh's Cause (Mujâhidîn) are far superior in grades before Him and it is they who will be successful.

And they are the ones who have received the glad tidings of : (1) His Mercy, (2) His being pleased with them, (3) and Gardens (Paradise).

Hence Allâh تعالى denied the equality between the Mujâhidîn (those who fight in Allâh's Cause) and those who maintain the Al-Masjid-al-Harâm (at Makkah) along with the various kinds of worship, in spite of His praising those who maintain the mosques in His Statement:

"The Mosques of Allâh shall be maintained only by those who believe in Allâh تعالى and the Last Day, perform Iqâmat-as-Salât, and give Zakât and fear none but Allâh. It is they who are expected to be on true guidance." (V.9:18).

So it is they (above said people) who are called by Allâh تعالى as "the maintainers of the mosques" — And in spite of all this, still the people who do Jihâd are far superior in grade than them (maintainers of the mosques) before Allâh تعالى.

Allâh تعالى says:

"Not equal are those of the believers who sit (at home) except those who are disabled (by injury, or are blind, or lame, etc.) and those who strive hard and fight in the Cause of Allâh with their wealth and their lives. Allâh has preferred in grades those who strive hard and fight with their wealth and lives above those who sit (at home). Unto each Allâh has promised good (Paradise), but Allâh has preferred those who strive hard and fight, above those who sit (at home) by a huge reward." (V.4:95).

"Degrees of (higher) grades from Him, and Forgiveness and Mercy. And Allâh is Ever Oft-Forgiving, Most Merciful." (V.4:96).

Allâh تعالى (the All-Mighty) denied the equality between the believers who sit (at home) and join not in *Jihâd* — and the *Mujâhidin* (those who fight in Allâh's Cause), — then He mentioned the superiority of the *Mujâhidin* over those (believers) who sit (at home) by a grade and then later on mentioned their (*Mujâhidin's*) superiority over them (believers who sit at home) by degrees of grades.

Ibn Zaid (a religious scholar) said: The degrees of grades with which Allâh تعالى preferred the *Mujâhidin* over those (believers) who sit (at home) are seven and these Allâh تعالى mentioned in His Statement:

"... That is because they suffer neither thirst, nor fatigue, nor hunger in the Cause of Allâh, تعالى, nor they take any step to raise the anger of disbelievers nor inflict any injury upon an enemy, but is written to their credit as a deed of righteousness. Surely Allâh loses not the reward of the *Muhsinûn*." (V.9:120).

These are five — then Allâh says:

"Nor do they spend anything (in Allâh's Cause) — small or great, — nor cross a valley, but is written to their credit..." (V.9:121).

So these are two bringing the total to seven.

Ibn Qayyim after mentioning the statement of Ibn Zaid said: True! Indeed the degrees of grades mentioned are reported in *Sahih Al-Bukhari*:

Narrated Abû Hurairah رضي الله عنه said, : The Prophet صلى الله عليه وسلم said, "Whoever believes in Allâh and His Messenger, performs *Iqâmat-as-Salât* and observes *Saum* (fasts) in the month of Ramadân, then it will be a promise binding upon Allâh to admit him to Paradise no matter whether he fights in Allâh's Cause or remains in the land where he is born." The people said, "O Allâh's Messenger! Shall we inform the people of this good news?" He صلى الله عليه وسلم said, "Paradise has one hundred grades which Allâh has reserved for the *Mujâhidin* who fight in His Cause, and the distance between each of the two grades is like the distance between the heaven and the earth. So, when you ask Allâh (for something), ask for *Al-Firdaus* which is the middle (best) and highest part of Paradise." [The subnarrator added, "I think the Prophet صلى الله عليه وسلم also said: 'Above it (i.e. *Al-Firdaus*) is the Throne of the Gracious (i.e. Allâh), and from it originate the rivers of Paradise.' "] (*Hadîth* No. 48, Vol. 4).

Ibn Qayyim said as regards the Statement of Allâh (تعالى):-

"Verily, Allâh has purchased of the believers their lives and their properties; for (the price) that theirs shall be the Paradise. They fight in Allâh's Cause, so they kill (others) and are killed. It is a promise in truth which is binding on Him in the Torah and the Gospel and the Qur'ân. And who is truer to his covenant than Allâh? Then rejoice in the bargain which you have concluded. That is the supreme success." (V.9:١11).

So Allâh (سبحانه) has put Paradise as the price of the believers and their properties, so if they sacrifice their lives and properties for His Cause, then they deserve the prize (Paradise) and the bargain which they concluded with Him. He reassured them with a number of assurances:

1. Allâh informed the believers with the word of emphasis: "Surely."

2. By using the past tense which denotes that the thing has already happened, and was confirmed and it remained as it was.

3. Moreover, He took upon Himself the responsibility of this convenant as He Himself bought the deal.

4. He informed that He has promised to give this price (Paradise) and shall neither break His Promise, nor shall neglect it.

5. The Arabic word *'alâ* used in this Divine Verse denotes obligation to convey to His worshippers that it is a binding on Him.

6. He confirmed that it is indeed a binding on Him.

7. He has informed that it (this bargain) is written in the Best Books revealed from the heavens (i.e. the Torah, the Gospel, and the Qur'ân).

8. He used the interrogative form to emphasize the fact that there is none Truer to his convenant than Him (Allâh).

9. He the Glorified, the Most High ordered them to receive the glad tidings of this contract (bargain) and give the good news to one another regarding a contract which has been ratified and has come to stay and admits of no choice or abrogation.

10. He informed them of a truly sure news that there is a supreme success in the bargain (contract) which they have concluded. And bargain here means the thing which they shall receive with this price (their lives and properties) is Paradise.

And His (Allâh's) Statement "Bargain which you have concluded" i.e. the price with which you have exchanged the deal, Allâh the Glorified mentioned the kinds of people who have concluded this contract (deal) and not any other (as mentioned in His Statement):

"(The believers whose lives Allâh has purchased are) those who turn to Allâh in repentance (from polytheism and hypocrisy), who worship (Him), who praise (Him), who observe Saum (fast) (or go out in Allâh's Cause), who bow down [in Salât (prayer)], who prostrate themselves [in Salât (prayer)], who enjoin (people) Al-Ma'rûf (i.e. Islâmic Monotheism and all that Islâm has ordained) and forbid (people) from Al-Munkar (i.e. disbelief, polytheism of all kinds and all that Islâm has forbidden), and who observe the limits· set by Allâh (do all that Allâh has ordained and abstain from all kinds of sins and evil deeds which Allâh has forbidden). And give glad tidings to the believers." (V.9:112)

And sufficient is this excellence — (for a Mujâhid which he will receive) honour and high degrees of grade — along with other things which Allâh تعالى has made clear in the Qur'ân: about the description of the reward of Mujâhidin, their magnificent state, moving of feelings and sentiments, the demanding of sacrifice in the cause of inviting others to Islâm, to put strength and courage in the souls and to urge them to go forward, to be stable and firm, and Allâh تعالى will grant them victory and support them with the angels, as it is evident from the Statement of Allâh:

"Remember when you ·(Muhammad صلى الله عليه وسلم) said to the believers: 'Is it not enough for you that your Lord (Allâh) should help you with three thousand angels sent down?' Yes, if you hold on to patience and piety and the enemy comes rushing at you; your Lord will help you with five thousand angels having marks (of distinction). Allâh made it not but as a message of good news for you and as an assurance to your hearts, and there is no victory except from Allâh the All-Mighty, the All-Wise." (V.3:124, 125, 126).

"So do not become weak (against your enemy), nor be sad and you will be superior (in victory) if you are indeed (true) believers. If a wound (and killing) has touched you, be sure a similar wound (and killing) has touched the others. And so are the days (good and not so good) We give to men by turns, that Allâh may test those who believe, and that He may take martyrs from among you. And Allâh likes not the Zalimûn (polytheists and wrongdoers). And that Allâh may test (or purify) the believers (from sins) and destroy the disbelievers. Do you think that you will enter Paradise before Allâh tests those of you who fought (in His Cause) and (also) tests those who are patient?" (V.3:139, 140, 141, 142).

And Allâh informed about those who are martyred in His Way. They are alive and that they are with their Lord Allâh تعالى finding what they wish of provisions and their faces are delighted with glad tidings. As Allâh تعالى says:

"Think not of those who are killed in the Way of Allâh as dead. Nay, they are alive with their Lord and they have provision.

"They rejoice in what Allâh has bestowed upon them of His Bounty, rejoicing for the sake of those who have not yet joined them, but are left behind (not yet martyred) that on them no fear shall come, nor shall they grieve.

"They rejoice in a Grace and a Bounty from Allâh and that Allâh will not waste the reward of the believers.

"Those who answered (the Call of) Allâh and the Messenger (Muhammad صلى الله عليه وسلم) after being wounded; for those of them who did good deeds and feared Allâh, there is a great reward." (V.3:169-172)

And He (Allâh تعالى) says:

"Those who believe, fight in the Cause of Allâh, and those who disbelieve, fight in the cause of Tâghût (Satan etc.). So fight you against the friends of Satan; ever feeble indeed is the plot of Satan." (V.4:76).

"Then fight, (O Muhammad صلى الله عليه وسلم), in the Cause of Allâh, you are not tasked (held responsible) except for yourself, and incite the believers (to fight along with you), it may be that Allâh will restrain the evil might of the disbelievers. And Allâh is Stronger in might and Stronger in punishing." (V.4:84).

And He (Allâh تعالى) says:

"Let those (believers) who sell the life of this world for the Hereafter, fight in the Cause of Allâh; and whoso fights in the Cause of Allâh and is killed or gets victory, We shall bestow on him a great reward." (V.4:74).

And so on — there are other similar Verses (in the Qur'ân) — besides these.

Think deeply, dear brother in Islâm, how Allâh تعالى encourages the spirit to make His Word superior and to protect the weak, and to rescue the oppressed ones.

Also think deeply how Jihâd is connected with Salât (prayers) and Saum (fasting). It is made obvious that Jihâd is similar to both of them, and all the three (Jihâd, Salât and Saum) are ordained (by Allâh) for the believers.

See how Allâh has encouraged the cowardly men to plunge themselves into the battles, to face death with an open heart, and to run madly for it (Jihâd) with great encouragement, showing clearly to them that death will certainly overtake them, and in case they die as Mujâhidin (Martyrs) they will be compensated for their worldly life with a mighty compensation and they will not be dealt with unjustly in the very least.

Jihâd is a great deed indeed and there is no deed whose reward or blessing is as that of it, and for this reason, it is the best thing that one can volunteer for. All the Muslim religious scholars unanimously agree that

Jihâd is superior to *Hajj* and *'Umrah* (pilgrimage) and also superior to non-obligatory *Salât* (prayer) and *Saum* (fasting) as mentioned in the Qur'ân and Prophet's *Sunnah*. It is obvious that the benefits of *Jihâd* for us are extensive and comprehensive; it (*Jihâd*) includes all kinds of worship both hidden and open, it also includes (a great) love for Allâh تعالى and it shows one's sincerity to Him and it also shows one's trust in Him, and it indicates the handing over of one's soul and property to Him — it (*Jihâd*) shows one's patience, one's devotion to Islâm, one's remembrance to Allâh تعالى and there are other kinds of good deeds that are present in *Jihâd* and are not present in any other act of worship.

For these above mentioned degrees of grades of various kinds of worship one should race for *Jihâd*. It is confirmed in the two authentic books (of *Hadîth*). Narrated Abû Hurairah (may Allâh be pleased with him): I heard Allâh's Messenger صلى الله عليه وسلم saying: "By Him in Whose Hand my soul is! Were it not for some men amongst the believers who dislike to be left behind me, and whom I cannot provide with means of conveyance, I would certainly never remain behind any *Sariyyah* (army unit) going out for *Jihâd* in Allâh's Cause. By Him in Whose Hand my life is! I would love to be martyred in Allâh's Cause and then come back to life and then be martyred and then come back to life again and then be martyred and then come back to life again and then be martyred." (*Sahih Al-Bukhari*, Vol 4, *Hadith* No. 54).

So the Prophet صلى الله عليه وسلم, through his ways of life, his firmness, his courage, and his patience has deeply encouraged the *Mujâhidin* for Allâh's Cause.

He صلى الله عليه وسلم informed them the immediate and deferred reward of *Jihâd* for them, and how different kinds of evils Allâh تعالى repels with it; and what a great honour, power, dignity and high grade is obtained through it and he صلى الله عليه وسلم has placed *Jihâd* at the top in Islâm. The Prophet صلى الله عليه وسلم says:

"Paradise has one hundred grades, the distance between each of the two grades is like the distance between the heaven and the earth, and these grades Allâh تعالى has reserved for the *Mujâhidin* who fight in His Cause" [as mentioned in the two authentic books (*Al-Bukhâri* and *Muslim*)]. [See *Sahih Al-Bukhari*, Vol 4, *Hadîth* No. 48].

It is narrated in *Sahih Al-Bukhâri*, Allâh's Messenger صلى الله عليه وسلم said:

"Anyone whose both feet get covered with dust in Allâh's Cause will not be touched by the Hell-fire." (Vol. 4, *Hadîth* No. 66).

It is also narrated in the two books (*Al-Bukhâri* and *Muslim*):

A man said, "O Messenger of Allâh! Inform me of a thing that is equal to *Jihâd* (in Allâh's Cause)!" Allâh's Messenger صلى الله عليه وسلم said, "You cannot (do that)." The man said, "Inform me of that." Allâh's Messenger صلى الله عليه وسلم said, "Can you observe *Saum* (fast) continuously without eating or drinking (at all) and stand continuously in *Salât* (prayer) from the time the *Mujâhidîn* go out for *Jihâd* (till the time they return back home)?" The man replied, "No." Allâh's Messenger صلى الله عليه وسلم said, "That is (the thing) which is equal to *Jihâd*."

Likewise Allâh's Messenger صلى الله عليه وسلم said:

1) The souls of the martyrs are in the green birds dwelling in Paradise wherever they like.

2) That all their sins and faults are forgiven.

3) That each of them can intercede with Allâh تعالى for seventy of his family members.

4) That he will come secure on the Day of Resurrection from the great terror.

5) That he will not feel the agonies and distress of death.

6) That he will not be horrified by the (great) Gathering (on the Day of Resurrection).

7) That he does not feel the pain of "the killing" except like that of a pinch.

And how many agonies and distresses are there for a person who dies on his bed — and a standing (praying) or a sleeping person in *Jihâd* is better than a fasting or standing (praying) person not in *Jihâd* — and whosoever acted as a guard or escort in Allâh's Cause, his eyes will never witness the Fire (Hell) and that a day spent while one is in *Jihâd* for Allâh's Cause is better than the world and whatsoever is in it.

If one has understood (all) that, then Allâh تعالى has reproached those who remained behind from Allâh's Messenger صلى الله عليه وسلم during the battle of Tabuk (i.e. they did not join in it) — they who clung heavily to the luxuries of this world — they who lagged behind from hastening onwards to march forth (for the battle of Tabuk) — Allâh تعالى says:

"O you who believe! What is the matter with you, that when you are asked to march forth in the Cause of Allâh تعالى (i.e. go for *Jihâd*), you cling heavily to the earth? Are you pleased with the life of this world rather than the Hereafter? But little is the enjoyment of the life of this world as compared to the Hereafter." (V.9:38)

Similarly Allâh تعالى disapproved of those who abandoned *Jihâd* (i.e. they did not go for *Jihâd*) and attributed to them hypocrisy and disease in their hearts, and threatened (all) those who remain behind from *Jihâd* and sit (at home) with horrible punishment. He (Allâh تعالى) referred to them with the most ugly descriptions, rebuked them for their cowardice and spoke against them (about their weakness and their remaining behind) as He said:

"If you march not forth, He will punish you with a painful torment and will replace you by another people and you cannot harm Him at all, and Allâh is Able to do all things." (V.9:39)

And there are many Verses of the Qur'ân besides this Verse (that threaten the Muslim nation if they give up *Jihâd*).

And you will not find any organization past or present, religious or non-religious as regards (*Jihâd* and military) (ordering) the whole nation to march forth and mobilize all of them into active military service as a single row for *Jihâd* in Allâh's Cause so as to make superior the Word of Allâh (i.e. none has the right to be worshipped but Allâh, as you will find in the Islâmic Religion and its teachings.

The Qur'ân and *As-Sunnah* (the legal ways of Prophet Muhammad صلى الله عليه وسلم) have clearly given (wonderful explanation for) every act concering *Jihâd*. The Book has distributed its different actions and its great number of responsibilities on its special units a most accurate distribution that excels above all the modern organizations and the military teachings. And in fact these modern organizations and military teachings are only a small portion (drop) of the military laws of the Qur'ân and *As-Sunnah*.

The Verses of Qur'ân and *As-Sunnah* of Allâh's Messenger Muhammad صلى الله عليه وسلم are both flooded with these high meanings, calling with eloquent phrases in a crystal clear way.

The Muslims were ordered to take all precautions against the enemies of Allâh تعالى and to get ready against them with all they can of power — because that is the first step for *Jihâd* (fighting) and the supreme way for the defence. To get ready (for *Jihâd*) includes various kinds of preparations and weapons [tanks, missiles, artillery, aeroplanes (air force), ships (navy), etc., and the training of the soldiers in these weapons] are all included under (the meaning) of the word "force (i.e land-force, navy and air-force)." And to look after (take care of) the permanent forces as well as the stationed forces similar to looking after the mobile forces. And to take care of the army in peace-time as well as during war-time.

The foundation of the military spirit as they say is: obedience and military discipline. Allâh تعالى has mentioned the two elements of this foundation in the Verses of His Book (the Qur'ân).

As to the obdience, Allâh تعالى says:

"Those who believe say: 'Why is not a *Sûrah* (Chapter of the Qur'ân) sent down (for us)?' But when a decisive *Sûrah* (explaining things) is sent down, and fighting (*Jihâd* — holy fighting in Allâh's Cause) is mentioned (i.e. ordained) therein, you will see those in whose hearts there is a disease (of hypocrisy) looking at you with a look of one fainting to death. But it was better for them (hypocrites to listen to Allâh and to obey Him). Obedience (to Allâh) and good words (were better for them)." (V.47:20,21).

And as to the military discipline, Allâh تعالى said in *Sûrah As-Saff* (Rows or Ranks):

"Verily! Allâh loves those who fight in His Cause in rows (ranks) as if they were a solid structure." (V.61:4).

Similarly the Islamic armed forces are exhorted to give their *Bai'ah* (pledge) to listen and obey, both in hard times and in ease, and in what they like and in what they dislike. Allâh تعالى says:

"Verily, those who give the *Bai'ah* (pledge) to you (O Muhammad), they are (in fact) giving the *Bai'ah* (pledge) to Allâh." (V.48:10).

And Allâh تعالى praised those who are true to (their) covenant and who fulfill their covenant by His Statement:

"Among the believers are men who have been true to their covenant with Allâh, [i.e. they have gone out for *Jihâd* (holy fighting), and showed not their backs to the disbelievers], of them some have fulfilled their obligations, (i.e. have been martyred) and some still are waiting, but they have never changed [i.e. they never proved treacherous to their covenant which they concluded with Allâh] in the least." (V.33:23)

And He ordered the believers to take a firm stand against the enemy when you (believers) meet their force, and to remember Allâh تعالى (much) at the time of horror, as He said:

"O you who believe! When you meet (an enemy) force take a firm stand against them and remember the Name of Allâh much (both with tongue and mind), so that you may be successful." (V.8:45).

And He (Allâh تعالى) encouraged the *Mujâhidîn* in His Cause to take a firm stand without any (kind) of fear and to display true bravery (against the enemy) from the start of the battle to the end — as He said:

"So when you meet (in fight — *Jihâd* in Allâh's Cause) those who disbelieve, smite at their necks till you have killed and wounded many of them, then bind a bond firmly (on them i.e. take them as captives). Thereafter (is the time for) either generosity (i.e. free them without ransom) or ransom (according to what benefits Islam), until war lays down its burdens..." (V.47:4)

"And don't be weak in the pursuit of the enemy; if you are suffering (hardships) then surely they (too) are suffering (hardships) as you are suffering, but you have a hope from Allâh (for the Reward i.e. Paradise) that for which they hope not; and Allâh is Ever All-Knowing, All-Wise." (V.4:104)

"And many a Prophet (i.e. many men from amongst the Prophets) fought (in Allâh's Cause) and along with them (fought) large bands of religious learned men. But they never lost heart for that which did befall them in Allâh's Way, nor did they weaken, nor degrade themselves. And Allâh loves the patient ones." (V.3:146)

Similarly, He ordered (the *Mujâhidûn*) to have confidence, to keep their composure and to expel (from their minds) all wrong conceptions, weakness and sadness — as He said:

"So do not become weak (against your enemy), nor be sad, and you will be superior (in victory), if you are indeed (true) believers." (V.3:139)

And Allâh تعالى informed that He has given a guarantee of victory to those who will defend Allâh's religion (true Islâm). And there is no consideration for the number of men or for the equipment with weapons but (the most important thing) is: true faith in Allâh تعالى and that the victory is (always) from Allâh تعالى — as Allâh تعالى said:

"If Allâh helps you, none can overcome you; and if He forsakes you, who is there after Him that can help you? And in Allâh (Alone) let believers put their trust." (V.3:160)

"How often a small group overcame a mighty host by Allâh's leave? And Allâh is with the patient." (V.2:249)

"O you who believe! If you help (in the cause of) Allâh, He will help you and make your foothold firm." (V.47:7)

"And, verily Our Word has gone forth of old for Our slaves, — Messengers, that they verily would be made triumphant. And that Our hosts, they verily would be victors." (V.37:171-173)

"... And (as for) the believers it was incumbent upon Us to help (them)." (V.30:47)

Similarly the Qur'ân points out the well-known fact that the battle is by turns, (one) day (victory) is for you — (the other) day (victory) is for others — as Allâh تعالى said:

"If a wound (and killing) has touched you, be sure a similar wound (and killing) has touched the others. And so are the days (good and not so good) that We give to men by turns..." (V.3:140)

And He made "the mutual consultation" as one of the legal foundations in order to make an exact decision, particularly in important matters like *Jihâd* and dealing with enemies, etc. and He praised His believers — slaves for this quality by His Statement:

"... And who (conduct) their affairs by mutual consultaion." (V.42:38)

And in spite of the perfection of the intelligence of Allâh's Messenger صلى الله عليه وسلم and along with his being helped by Divine Inspiration still Allâh ordered him (saying):

"... And consult them in the affairs..." (V.3:159)

So that his followers may follow his example after him.

Similarly, the Qur'ân warned (the believers) from committing sins (both in open and in secret) small sins or great sins... and He informed them that Allâh's Help does not descend upon the disobedient sinners:

"Those of you who turned back on the day, the two hosts met (i.e. battle of Uhud), it was Satan who caused them to backslide (run away from the battlefield) because of some (sins) they had earned..." (V.3:155)

Allâh has absolutely forbidden any dispute on any matter concerning the fighting (battle) and to be always in complete agreement (about it), and informed them that the dispute is the reason for failure and the losing of the strength and kingdom:

"... And do not dispute (with one another) lest you lose courage and your strength departs, and be patient. Surely Allâh is with those who are patient."(V.8:46)

And to beware of fleeing from the enemy during the fight (battle), and it is one of the biggest sins and those who commit it are threatened with grave punishments:

"O you who believe! When you meet those who disbelieve in a battlefield, never turn your backs to them." (V.8:15)

"And whosoever turns his back to them on such a day, — unless it be a stratagem of war, or to retreat to a troop (of his own) — he indeed has drawn upon himself the wrath form Allâh. And his abode is Hell, worst indeed is that destination!" (V.8:16)

Allâh تعالى forbade *Al-Ghulul* (stealing from the war booty before its distribution) i.e. the taking (a part) of war booty illegally, and warned the Muslims with an extreme warning. And a person who takes it, shall bring it forth (on the Day of Resurrection) carrying it over his back and neck, being tortured by its heavy burden and weight, terrified with its voice, rebuked for his dishonesty in front of all the witnesses.

"It is not for any Prophet to take illegally a part of booty (*Ghulul*), and whosoever deceives his companions as regards the booty, he shall bring forth on the Day of Resurrection that which he took (illegally). Then every person shall be paid in full what he has earned, and they shall not be dealt with unjustly." (V.3:161)

Similarly, one should be cautious, not to fight (with the intention) to show off, or for good reputation or for dignity, or for pride and haughtiness, or for the clamour (noise) of nationalism and for false-forged slogans. Whenever the Messenger صلى الله عليه وسلم appointed a Commander-in-Chief for an army unit, he used to advise him specially to be afraid and dutiful to Allâh, and to be good to those Muslims who were accompanying him. He then used to say (to that Commander):

"Invade in the Name of Allâh تعالى and in the Cause of Allâh تعالى and kill those who disbelieve in Allâh تعالى. Invade and do not press heavily by exceeding the limits, and do not betray, and do not kill children...."

And he (the Prophet صلى الله عليه وسلم) used to say to his companions when they intended invasion:

"Proceed in the Name of Allâh تعالى and for Allâh تعالى and upon the religion of Allâh's Messenger صلى الله عليه وسلم : Do not kill the very old or a child or a woman and do not press heavily by exceeding the limits. Collect the (war) booty, reconcile, and do good as Allâh loves the good-doers."

For that, the Messenger صلى الله عليه وسلم and those who believed in him were tried with fair trials (martyrdom or mighty reward) to make victorious this religion (Islâm) and to invite others to it (Islâm). So Allâh assisted them with victory and sent down upon them tranquility and helped them with angels and united their hearts and cast terror into the hearts of their enemies.

So they fought in the Cause of Allâh تعالى (for) Islâmic Faith (worshipping none but Allâh Alone) and sincerely (for Allâh's sake) and to make victorious Allâh's religion till it becomes superior over all religions, and mankind is brought out — (1) from darkness into the light, (2) from the worshipping of men to the worshipping of Allâh Alone (the only true God), (3) from the narrowness of the world to its wideness (ease) and (4) from the injustices of the religions to the justice of Islâm. They knew well that Allâh has guaranteed them victory and promised them that they will be the conquerors. So they were sure of Allâh's Support, and of his Messenger's promise and considered the matter easy with a small or great (number) and thought little of the fears and dangers. They remembered the Statement of Allâh تعالى:

"If Allâh helps you, none can overcome you ..." (V.3:160)

And that they are troops of Allâh تعالى, and that they are fighting in Allâh's Cause, and surely Allâh تعالى will help and support them and will defeat their enemies, as their enemies fight for the cause of Satan.

Here is the example of 'Umar bin Al-Khattab رضي الله عنه , as he consulted his companions regarding sending troops to 'Irâq (for participating in the battle of Nahâwand). 'Ali bin Abi Tâlib رضي الله عنه said to him ('Umar): "O Chief of the believers! This matter cannot be 'victory or defeat' because of a great number, or a small number but it is His (Allâh's) religion which He has made superior and His troops which he has honoured and supported (them) with the angels till it reached far as it has reached. We have been promised (victory) by Allâh, and Allâh fulfills His Promise and supports His troops."

And here is the example of Khâlid bin Walîd رضي الله عنه, as he came from 'Irâq, a man from the Arab Christians said to Khâlid: "How great is the number of Romans and how small is the number of Muslims?" Khâlid replied: "Woe to you! Do you make me afraid of the Romans?... But the greatness of the troops is with victory and the smallness of the troops is with defeat, not with the number of men, by Allâh I wish if the red ones (i.e. the camels and the horses) are cured from their journey hurts, I will proceed to attack them (Romans) even if their number is doubled. (The hoofs of his horse had chafed and received injuries during its return form 'Irâq to Al-Madinah)."

They used to endanger their lives, used to do wonders and extraordinary deeds being sure of Allâh's Help, depending upon His Promise as it happened in the Islâmic army under the command of Sa'd bin Abî Waqqâs. He stood in front of the town of Al-Madyan المدائن and could not find any ship or boat (it became completely impossible for him to find anything of that sort) and the water of the river Tigris increased tremendously with overflooding and it overthrew its foam from excessive water in it. Sa'd addressed the troops on their bank (saying): "I have resolved to cross this sea (great river) in order to assault them (the enemy)." They (the people) replied: "May Allâh direct us and you to follow the right path. So please do it." Then he (Sa'd) rushed heedlessly into the (river) Tigris with his horse and all his troops too rushed heedlessly into it (Tigris) and not a single man was left behind; so they marched over it as if they were marching over the surface of the earth, till they filled it (the space) between its two banks and one could not see the water surface from the cavalry and the foot-soldiers. The people spoke to one another over the surface of water as they used to speak to one another over the land surface. So when the Persians saw them they said: Diwana... Diwana, (i.e. mad people... mad people). By Allâh! You are not fighting against human beings, but against jinn." On that Sa'd رضى الله عنه started saying: "Allâh is Sufficient for us and He is the Best Disposer (for our affairs); by Allâh! Surely Allâh تعالى will give victory to His friends; verily, Allâh will make superior His religion, and verily Allâh will defeat His enemy, as long as there are neither adulterers nor thôse who commit (similar) sins in the army (Sa'd's troops), then the good deeds will overcome the evil."

Yes! they (the Muslims) used to be afraid of: (1) their sins and (2) disobedience of Allâh تعالى , more than they used to be afraid of their enemy or their enemy's great number and mighty weapons, as we find 'Umar bin Al-Khattab رضى الله عنه saying: (in his letter to the Commander a'd bin Abi Waqqâs when he sent him for the conquest of Persia):

"... Then after, I order you and all the troops that are along with you to be obedient to Allâh in all circumstances as this (being obedient to Allâh تعالى) is better than the weapons against the enemy and a strong stratagem (device) in the war. I order you and the soldiers who are with you to be more cautious and afraid of your own crimes and sins (and not to commit them) than your enemy, as the crimes and sins of the soldiers are more dangerous to them than their enemy. The Muslims are victorious only because their enemies are disobedient to Allâh تعالى and had it not been so, we have no power over them, because neither our number is equal to their number, nor our weapons are like theirs. If we commit crimes and sins as they do, then they (our enemies) will have superiority over us in power. And if we will not gain victory over them by our merits, we do not overpower them by our strength. And you should also know that in this marching of yours (in Allâh's Cause) there are guards (angels) upon you from Allâh تعالى (to watch you); and they know all that you do. So be shy of them and do not commit Allâh's disobedience (crimes and sins) while you are going in Allâh's Cause and do not say: 'Our enemy is worse than us, so they will not overpower us.' Perhaps some people who are worse than the others may overpower the others as the (disbelievers) Magians overpowered the Children of Israel when they (the latter) involved themselves with Allâh's disobedience (crimes and sins). So they (disbelievers, Magians) entered the very innermost parts of their homes and it was a promise (completely) fulfilled. And ask Allâh تعالى the assistance over your ownselves (to save you from crimes and sins), just as you ask Allâh for the victory over your enemies... I ask of Allâh تعالى that, both for you and for us."

So the Muslim warriors (Al-Mujâhidîn) strictly followed what this rightly guided caliph 'Umar had mentioned (as above): And they (Mujâhidîn) were as they were described by a Roman to a Roman Chief, (he said): "I have come to you from men, very precise in their manners; they ride swift race-horses, during the night they worship (Allâh Alone) in seclusion, during the day they are cavaliers, if you speak to your companions something, your friend will not understand anything from you because of the high tone of their voices while reciting the Qur'ân and the mentioning of Allâh much." So he (the Roman Chief) looked at his companions and said: "It has come to you from that over which you have no power."

And here is the story of 'Uqbah bin Nâfi': He ('Uqbah) intended to take a place (town) in Africa, so as to be a place for the Muslim army and to protect their families and properties from revolt against them by the natives of the country. So he betook himself to the place of Al-Qairawan, and it was a muddy place, full of every kind of beasts of prey (lions, tigers, leopards, etc.) and snakes..., etc. So he ('Uqbah) invoked Allâh تعالى, and Allâh answered his invocation, he then said: "O snakes and wild beasts of prey! We are the Companions of Allâh's Messenger (Muhammad صلى الله عليه وسلم), go away from us as we are landing here, and afterwards if we find any (of you wild beasts and snakes) we will kill you." So the people saw that day, the (wild) animals and snakes carrying their young ones, shifting from that place... And a great number of natives (Al-Barbar) saw (all) that and embraced Islâm.

And when the term (time limit) was prolonged for the Muslims and their hearts were hardened and they forgot their religion and became ignorant of the fact (that for what purpose) Allâh تعالى has sent and chosen them from among the great number of mankind and from the great number of nations of the earth... Allâh تعالى said:

"You [true believers in Islâmic Monotheism, and real followers of Prophet Muhammad صلى الله عليه وسلم, and his Sunnah (legal ways)] are the best of peoples ever raised up for mankind, you enjoin Al-Ma'rûf (i.e. Islâmic Monotheism and all that Islâm has ordained) and forbid what is Al-Munkar (polytheism, disbelief and all that Islâm has forbidden), and you believe in Allâh..." (V.3:110)

So (today) they (Muslims) are leading a life of the one who knows not any Prophet, nor believes in any Divine Message or Divine Inspiration, nor expects any reckoning nor is afraid of the Hereafter. They (Muslims) resemble the pre-Islâmic ignorant nations, against whom they used to fight in the past. They have turned on their heels (back) as apostates from Islâm, they have imitated them (ignorant nations) in their civilization, in their social affairs, in their political affairs, in their character and in the pleasures of their lives. They (Muslims) also imitated them in many other things because of which Allâh تعالى hated and forsook them. He (Allâh) put them (Muslims) into trials under the effects of (1) Western civilization (2) and the Eastern Communist propaganda. So their land became "a free wealth" with no protector, their kingdom became a victim for every beast of prey and a food (nourishment) for every eater and the meaning of the statement of the Prophet (Muhammad صلى الله عليه وسلم) became apparent:

"It is expected that all other nations will call other nations to share them against you (Muslims) as the eaters call each other to eat from the food in front of them in a large wooden plate." A person asked the Prophet صلى الله عليه وسلم: "Will that happen because of our small number on that day?" The Prophet said: "Nay! Your number (will be) great, but you will be rubbish like the rubbish of flood-water. And certainly Allâh will remove from the hearts of enemies 'the fear from you' and surely He (Allâh) will throw Wahn in your hearts." A person asked: "What is Wahn, O Allâh's Messenger?" The Prophet صلى الله عليه وسلم said, "Wahn is to love (this) world and to hate death."

The Prophet صلى الله عليه وسلم also said:

"If you: (1) practiced Bai'a Al-'Înah (i.e. selling goods to a person for a certain price and then buying them back from him for a far less price), (2) and followed the tails of the cows (i.e. indulged in agriculture and became contented with it) (3) and deserted the *Jihâd* (holy fighting) in Allâh's Cause, Allâh will cover you with humiliation and it will not be removed till you return back to your religion." (*Abû Dâwûd*)

And now they (Muslims) have deserted the *Jihâd* and asked help from (their) enemies and protection from the disbelievers, begging them; turning towards them, expecting good from them. So they (Muslims) have become mean, despised before Allâh in spite of their Islâmic names and in spite of the presence of righteous pious persons amongst them and in spite of the fact that some of the religious laws, signs and ceremonies are practiced in their countries.

One of the orientalists said: "When the Muslims turned away from their religious teachings and became ignorant of its wisdom and its laws, and deviated towards the contradictory (man-made) laws taken from the opinions of men, there spread in them immorality of character, falsehood, hypocrisy, ill-will and hatefulness increased in them. Their unity disintegrated and they became ignorant of their present and future state and became unaware of what will harm them or will benefit them. They have become contented with the life in which they eat, drink, sleep and compete not with others, in superiority." All this is a visible fact, which every true believer feels, and which every enthusiastic person (about his religion) observes in every community (nation) that gives up *Al-Jihâd* and is engrossed: (1) in a luxurious life, (2) in the worshipping of wealth and (3) in the love of this world.

History informs us: What the most wretched (*Al-Maghool* and *At-Tâtâr*) did to the Muslims? That which will sadden the hearts and will make the eyes shed tears...

Ibn Al-Athîr said: "I remained for many years, avoiding the mentioning of this accident because of its great magnitude, disliking to speak about it, so that I put a foot forward and another backward and thought deeply, who is there who can write the wailing and crying of the Muslims and who is there on whom it is easy to mention that ... would that my mother had not begotten me... would that I had been dead before this, and had been forgotten and out of sight... This job (work) includes the mentioning of the great event and the severe calamity which made the days and the nights extremely hard and bitter that no similar calamity will happen and that did befall (cover) the mankind and particularly the Muslims." Ibn Al-Athîr then mentioned the weaknesses of the Muslims and the victory of their enemies over them...he said: "A woman from the *Tâtârs* entered a house and killed a group of its dwellers and they thought her to be a man... one of them (the *Tâtârs*) entered a street in which there were one hundred men and he went on killing them one by one, till he killed them all, and not even a single man (out of the hundred) raised his hand against him (the *Tâtâr*) to harm him... and humiliation was put over the men... so they did not defend themselves neither little nor more. We take refuge with Allâh تعالى from being defeated (by the enemy)." Ibn Al-Athîr further said: "One of the *Tâtârs* got hold of a man and he (the *Tâtâr*) could not find any (weapon) to kill him, so he told the man: "Put your head over this stone and do not move (keep it on)"... and so the man put his head over the stone and remained there till the same man came with a sword and killed him... and there were many similar incidents"...

So it is absolutely obligatory upon the Islâmic nation, and particularly upon the religious scholars and the rulers from them to be obedient to Allâh تعالى , fear Him and to be dutiful to Him and to settle the matters of differences amongst themselves and to propagate "The invitation to this religion (Islâm) to others, publish its good aspects, and instruct (teach) the people its (Islâm's) laws and wisdom as did the Muslim nobles of early days." They (Muslim nobles of early days) strove hard in Allâh's Cause as they ought to have striven with sincerity and with all their efforts that His (Allâh's) Name should be superior... They stood... inviting people to Allâh's religion (Islâm), explained to them the good aspects and the excellence of Islâm... and that was the reason their kingdom was extended and their countries expanded, and they subjected others to its (Islâm's) teachings. But before long their descendants deviated from the Right Path, tore themselves into pieces after they were one united entity, they doubted the Truth, so, for them the path was separated and they became as groups (and sects) having different (views and) opinions opposing each other in their aims... So how can they be elevated?... How can there be any progress or priority possible for them while they are following the disbelieving nations, they drag along behind them, pursue their ways and footsteps and imitate their actions, small or great.

They judge their people with the contradictory (man-made) laws which conflict and clash with the Islâmic laws, which were the origin of their honour and pride and in which was their peace and steadfastness. Allâh تعالى says:

"Do they then seek the judgment of (the Days of) Ignorance. And who is better in judgement than Allâh for a people who have firm Faith?" (V.5:50)

We beseech Allâh to make victorious His religion (Islâm) and to make superior His Words and to lead all the Muslims to that in which His Pleasure is — *Amîn*.

Sheikh 'Abdullah bin Muhammad bin Humaid
Chief Justice of Saudi Arabia